APPEAL

COUNTER THE COUNTERFEIT & BUILD A STRONG FOUNDATION FOR SUCCESS

Books are our best friends, is the adage we have grown up with. However, the pirates of piracy are continuously forging 'our best friends'. Our books and their supplementary online resources are copyrighted, and we don't lend any right-to-copy. Piracy is synonymous to stealing books.

Knowledge comes real, let's not encourage its counterfeit. Therefore, we appeal all our readers to discourage pirated books and **choose authentic ones**.

HOW TO IDENTIFY THE PIRATED BOOKS?

1 Cover and Spine

- Look and feel (new or used book)
- Blurred images on the cover
- Hologram pasted on front
- Defective spine (wrinkles) or air pocket at its bottom
- Unclear ISBN/bar codes
- Missing/non-operational Unique Coupon Code for exclusive access to **McGraw Hill** Edge

2 Text/Printing/Binding

- Uneven inking of pages
- Poor quality or blurred photographs/images/ charts
- Substandard paper quality and opacity
- Misaligned pages
- Missing pages
- Inferior binding quality

You can further watch this video on How to identify a pirated book

For more information about identifying piracy, visit **https://www.mheducation.co.in/piracy**

To report a pirated book, send 'Hi' on WhatsApp code given on the back cover or write to us at **support.india@mheducation.com**.

Reported pirated books are examined to combat their piracy.

Let's fight the Pirates of Piracy and resolve to go for original!

About the Authors

The authors, Snehil Tripathi and Sonali Bansal, are educational writers, researchers, and consultants imparting training to aspirants of UPSC Civil Services and other competitive examinations. They are associated with several institutes at various places across the country. While Snehil Tripathi worked with Unacademy as Educator and Academic Head in UPSC CSE Category, Sonali Bansal was educated at Lady Shri Ram College, New Delhi.

The authors also have several other book titles published by McGraw Hill Education to their credit including *An Introduction to Madhya Pradesh General Knowledge* (2017), *General Studies Manual Paper I* (Physics), *Post Independence India* (2018), *Swatantra Bharat* (2019), and *Adhunik Bharat* (2019).

THIRD EDITION

MODERN INDIAN HISTORY

For CIVIL SERVICES PRELIMINARY AND MAIN EXAMINATIONS

Sonali Bansal

Snehil Tripathi

Mc Graw Hill

McGraw Hill Education (India) Private Limited

Published by McGraw Hill Education (India) Private Limited
Registered Office: Anjana Complex No: 5/90 A, Butt Road, St. Thomas Mount, Chennai 600 016

Modern Indian History, 3e

Print Edition:
ISBN (13): 978-93-5532-571-6
ISBN (10): 93-5532-571-1

E-Book Edition:
ISBN (13): 978-93-5532-570-9
ISBN (10): 93-5532-570-3

1 2 3 4 5 6 7 8 9 7091297 28 27 26 25 24

Printed and bound in India.

Typeset at Pee-Gee Graphics, A-6/95, Sector 15, Rohini, Delhi-110089 and printed
at Rajkamal Electric Press, Kundli, Haryana.

Cover Designer: Vipin Kumar Raghav

Cover Image Source: Vipin Kumar Raghav

Visit us at: www.mheducation.co.in
Write to us at: support.india@mheducation.com
CIN: U80302TN2010PTC111532
Toll Free Number: 1800 103 5875

In Memory of

Shri Akshayvarnath Tiwari

Shri Ramgopal Bansal

Shri Chandra Prakash Goel

Foreword

After securing rank 5 in UPSC CSE 2022, I received a number of questions regarding the sources that I was using. For Modern Indian History I was using a book written by Snehil Tripathi sir and Sonali Bansal ma'am. Instead of relying on multiple sources, I relied on multiple revisions of the same book.

Why did I choose this book? I think there are three reasons for this. Firstly, the book is very comprehensive and detailed. It's almost like a story. Secondly, it's very systematic and well organized. It helped me in building the timeline in a more vivid manner. And thirdly, it has Prelim Capsules at the end of chapters, which help in quick revision.

Dr Mayur Hazarika (IFS)

AIR-5 (2022 Batch), Anthropology Optional

The Civil Services Exam conducted by Union Public Service Commission is a much coveted exam which attracts lakhs of candidates from all over the country every year to compete for various services and posts under the Government of India. There is no doubt that good quality course material is an absolute necessing for cracking this tough exam. More so now, as UPSC is continuously changing the exam pattern and diversifying its sources.

True that there is no dearth of good books on Modern Indian History meant for various purposes including academic, research or even general purpose reading. However, for cracking the IAS exam, a student needs material developed for the IAS exam and not for any other purpose. Needless to explain, such books come with decisive advantage and one such book on Modern India was much awaited.

I am pleased to announce that an impressive effort in this direction has been made in the form of *Modern Indian History* by authors Sonali Bansal and Snehil Tripathi. The book covers the **complete exam syllabus** (for both prelim and main), broken down into well organised chapters- as is evident from the neatly organised Table of Contents. Language is simple, lucid and thought provoking that acts as an aid to memory. Highlighted facts and events give the students an idea about how the material should be read and processed. The most outstanding feature of the book which I appreciate as a history optional student is that for general studies, the book strikes a perfect balance between facts (needed for prelim) and views/ analysis (for main).

With such features and many more, I am fully confident that the book will be of immense value for UPSC as well as State PSC candidates, not only for General Studies paper but also for optional studies.

Nitish Kumar Singh (IAS)

AIR-23 (2016 Batch), History Optional

PREFACE

Over the years, the change in pattern of civil services examination and the increasing level of difficulty have posed many problems for the candidates. Even a 'static' subject like history can no longer be prepared from a single source as the UPSC itself is fast to catch-up and is keeping pace with the new trends and perspectives in history.

As a result, while teaching for the examination, we often found the candidates struggling for exam-relevant material from a range of sources. However, the fact remains that candidates have to manage a vast syllabus in a limited span of time and it is only natural that they end up restricting their sources to two or three books for each subject. Clearly, the examiners have no such limitation and they freely make use of the widest pool of knowledge.

Keeping in view such and other difficulties faced by the candidates, we have developed this book as an exam-aid, with all the qualities of a standard test-prep material. After nearly two-years of exhaustive research work, we are reasonably confident that the book provides the most comprehensive and reliable coverage of the Modern Indian History portion of the syllabus.

Special attention has been paid to the requirements of new aspirants. Content has been built from scratch without making any assumptions regarding previous knowledge. To guide the readers throughout the book, pedagogical tools such as bolding, highlighting, Flashbacks and Flashforwards have been liberally used. Backgrounders, evaluations and criticisms of historical events have been provided, keeping in view the increasing tendency to ask concept-based questions. 'Prelim Capsule' is another novel and outstanding feature of the book. It is meant to act as a ready reference list of important events and will address the challenge of revision for the candidates.

In this Third Edition, we proudly present to you the testimonial of one of our readers, **Dr Mayur Hazarika** (rank#5 in CSE 2022), who relied upon this book as his standard resource material for Modern Indian History.

As authors, we hold the firm belief that this book will continue to prove to be a **single point solution** for Modern Indian History needs of the candidates and will play a key role in their success in UPSC and other competitive examinations. We are also open to any constructive feedback from the readers for further improvements. Please feel free to reach out to us on: sonalibansal1@yahoo.com

Sonali Bansal
Snehil Tripathi

Contents

Syllabus for Civil Services Examination

(Modern Indian History Portion)

Exam	Description
Preliminary	❑ History of India and Indian National Movement.

Exam	Description
Main	❑ Modern Indian history from about the middle of the eighteenth century until the present significant events, personalities, issues. ❑ The Freedom Struggle — its various stages and important contributors/ contributions from different parts of the country.

Appendices

Find at the End of Every Chapter

Previous Years' Questions – Preliminary Exam
Previous Years' Questions – Main Exam

Unit 1
Mid-Eighteenth Century India (India on the Eve of British Conquest)

1 Decline of Mughal Empire (1707–1857)

Sandwiched between the two empires, the Mughal and the British, the mid-18th century India is often depicted as 'a dark age' or 'an age of chaos'. But was it really so?

Let us try to see this period through the eyes of someone living in mid-18th century India. The Mughal Empire was now weak but not yet dead. The regional powers were rapidly gaining strength and autonomy. India was open to trade and had emerged as an attractive destination for European Trading Companies, but none of these companies were perceived as destined to rule India. In the world context, India was not yet an economically backward region. Neither were Europe and North America as rich as they became in the 19th and 20th centuries. All these potentialities still lay in the womb of the future. Perhaps this depiction as 'a dark age' suited a certain way of looking at Indian history which highlighted the British achievements of re-unification of India under the British and the inauguration of a new age of enlightenment in India with the spread of western knowledge and culture. Not many historians would agree today with this kind of depiction.

Hence, it is only appropriate that we refrain from such view and rather look at the mid-18th century Indian polity as a chronological whole, comprising the following three broad themes:

Theme 1: Decline of Mughal Empire (First half of the 18th century)
The early decades of 18th century saw the decline of the Mughal Empire—a long-drawn-out process effected by many factors. The reign of Aurangzeb (1658-1707) marked the beginning of this process of decline which was further hastened by the invasion of Nadir Shah in 1739. Though the Mughal Empire did not survive, its institutions and traditions continued in the regional states as well as in British provinces, especially in respect of land revenue administration.

Theme 2: Rise of Autonomous States (Middle decades of the 18th century)
The middle decades of the 18th century saw the rise of autonomous states or regional powers that can be categorised into three groups—the successor states (Hyderabad, Awadh and Bengal), the new states (Marathas, the Sikhs, the Jats and the Afghans) and the independent kingdoms (Mysore, Kerala and the Rajputs). How come all these powers failed to keep the British out? Answers to such questions and more shall be discussed under this theme.

Theme 3: Rise of British Supremacy (Second half of the 18th century)
The weakening of the Mughal Empire also provided an opportunity to the East India Company and the last decades of the 18th century saw the transformation of this Company from a trading company to a political power. We shall trace this transition from where it first began, i.e. in south India and Bengal.

Unit-1 covers the above political themes comprehensively and also gives you a glimpse of 18th-century Indian society and economy. In this chapter, you will learn about the first theme, i.e. the decline of the Mughal Empire.

Decline of the Mughal Empire

The first half of the 18th century witnessed the decline of the Mughal Empire that had dazzled the world since many years with its extensive territories, military might and cultural achievements. The era of the Great Mughals that had begun in 1526 with Babur's accession to the throne, ended with the death of Aurangzeb in 1707 which also marked the end of an era in Indian history.

The process of decline had set in during Aurangzeb's reign itself (1658–1707) and could not be arrested by his weak successors. When Aurangzeb died, the empire of the Mughals was the largest in India; yet it only represented an inflated balloon. The empire had expanded beyond manageable limits and its vastness only tended to weaken the centre. Aurangzeb's socio-religious policies and fundamentalism, in sharp contrast to his ancestors, provoked the subject population into rebellion, including the great Marathas against whom he waged fruitless wars in the Deccan for 20 years! It had been aptly said, "The Deccan ulcer proved to be as fatal to the Mughal Empire as the 'Spanish ulcer' was to prove later on to the Napoleonic Empire."

A combination of factors further ensured that within 50 years of Aurangzeb's death, the Mughal Empire disintegrated—nine Mughal emperors followed one another in quick succession and many adventurers, Indian and foreign, carved out independent principalities for themselves in India. By 1739 Delhi had been invaded by Nadir Shah, by 1761 (when Abdali invaded) the Mughals had been replaced by the Marathas as the defenders of India, and by 1765 the Mughal emperor had been reduced to a pensioner of the British.

The British carefully kept alive the fiction of the Mughal Empire till 1858. In the 150 years' period between 1707 and 1857 (when the last of the Mughals Bahadur Shah Zafar was deposed by the British) there emerged as many as 12 Mughal emperors, known as the Later Mughals. Two of the longest surviving of these, Muhammad Shah (1719–48) and Shah Alam II (1759–1806), witnessed devastating attacks by Nadir Shah (1739) and Ahmad Shah Abdali, who attacked India seven times during 1748–67.

Thus, internal weaknesses of the Mughal Empire combined with external aggressions left the foundations of the Mughal Empire completely shaken, tempting regional powers to assert independence and European trading companies to dabble in Indian politics.

Later Mughals (1707–1857)

Aurangzeb's death in 1707 (at the age of 89) signalled a war of succession among his three sons. The eldest brother, Prince Muazzam, defeated and killed the other two (Muhammad Azam at Jajau in June 1707, and Kam Bakhsh near Hyderabad in January 1709), emerged victorious and ascended to the throne of Delhi assuming the title of Bahadur Shah I.

Bahadur Shah I or Muazzam Shah Alam I (1707–12)

Bahadur Shah I (1707–12), was also known as Shah Alam I. He was an elderly man of 65, was learned and reversed some of the narrow-minded policies of Aurangzeb. He adopted a more tolerant attitude towards the Hindus and there was also no destruction of temples during his reign. Whether out of statesmanship or weakness, he adopted a **pacific policy** in general with respect to various regional powers:

Bahadur Shah I

- **Marathas** Bahadur Shah allowed the Maratha prince **Shahu**, held as Mughal captive since 1689, to go back to Maharashtra.
- **Rajputs** He made peace with the Rajput chiefs and confirmed them in their states.
- **Jats and Bundelas** He made peace with the Jat chief Churaman and Bundela chief Chhatrasal who had joined him in the campaign against Banda Bahadur.
- **Sikhs** Bahadur Shah tried to make peace with the rebellious Sikhs by giving Guru Gobind Singh a high mansab. But after the death of the Guru, the Sikhs once again raised a revolt under the leadership of Banda Bahadur. This time the emperor decided to be strict and he himself led a campaign against the rebels. He defeated **Banda Bahadur** at **Lohgarh**, a fort built by Guru Govind Singh in the foothills of the Himalayas. Yet, the Sikhs could not be crushed and they later recovered the fort in 1712.

However, Bahadur Shah lavishly granted jagirs and promotions which led to a deterioration in the field of administration during his reign. Called **Shah-i-Bekhabar** (Headless King) by Khafi Khan, he died in 1712.

Parties at Mughal Court and Kingmakers After Bahadur Shah's death, a new element entered Mughal politics and war of succession—while previously the contest for power was between the royal princes and the nobles had merely backed them, now the nobles became direct aspirants to the throne and began using the princes as pawns to capture positions of authority. In other words, powerful nobles emerged as 'kingmakers'. For instance, at the time of Emperor Jahandar Shah, Zulfiqar Khan emerged as the kingmaker. Similarly, during emperor Farrukhsiyar, it were the Sayyid Brothers who raised Farrukhsiyar to throne in 1713 and pulled him down in 1719 when he ceased to serve their interests.

Worst of all, these nobles belonged to different parties like Irani and Turani, which represented merely interest groups or factions looking for their own self-advancement, even if at the cost of the welfare of the 'nation', the Mughal empire. Though there emerged various parties at the Mughal Court, there were 4 prominent ones—**the Turanis, the Iranis, the Afghans** and **the Hindustanis**. The first three were descendants of foreigners from Central Asia, Iran and Afghanistan and formed the backbone of the 'army of occupation'. They held important civil and military offices in India. The Turanis and Afghans were mostly Sunnis, while Iranis were mostly Shias. In opposition to this Mughal or Foreign party was the Hindustani party which mostly comprised of Muslims born in India and got the support of the Rajputs and the Jats. However, it must be noted that the slogans of race and religion were raised by the nobles only to suit their interests, and given up when it was no longer profitable.

Jahandar Shah (1712–13)

In 1712, a war of succession broke out among the four sons of Bahadur Shah. They were in such indecent haste of grabbing the throne that they plunged themselves into the war of succession, leaving Bahadur Shah's dead body unburied for about a month. In the struggle for succession, one of the less able sons, Jahandar Shah, emerged victorious, supported by the most powerful noble of the time—**Zulfiqar Khan** (Irani Party).

Jahandar Shah was a degenerate prince wholly devoted to pleasure. His administration was virtually in the hands of the extremely capable Zulfiqar Khan, who had become his wazir or prime minister.

Zulfiqar believed that it was important to establish friendly relations with the Rajput rajas and the Maratha sardars. Therefore, he rapidly reversed the policies of Aurangzeb.

- **Marathas** Zulfiqar Khan confirmed the agreement reached between his deputy of Deccan, Daud Khan Panni, and Shahu in 1711, whereby the Marathas were granted the chauth and sardeshmukhi of the Deccan on the condition that these collections would be made by Mughal officials and then handed over to the Marathas.
- **Rajputs** Jai Singh II of Amber was appointed Governor of Malwa while Maharaja Ajit Singh of Marwar was appointed Governor of Gujarat.
- **Jats, Bundelas, Sikhs** Zulfiqar Khan continued to pacify Churaman Jat and Chhatrasal Bundela. He also continued to suppress the Sikhs.
- He also abolished the hated jeziah.

Jizya (or Jizyah) It was a per capita yearly tax historically levied by Islamic states on non-Muslim subjects.

Zulfiqar Khan tried to improve the finances of the empire by checking the reckless growth of jagirs and offices. But he gave up Todar Mal's land revenue settlement and introduced the evil practice of revenue farming or **Ijarah** whereby the government established contact with the revenue farmers and middlemen who paid the government a fixed amount while they were free to extract whatever they could from the peasant, leading to increased oppression of the peasantry.

Jahandar Shah was soon defeated by his nephew Farrukhsiyar at Agra, thus bringing an end to the reign of Jahandar Shah. Zulfiqar Khan was also executed.

Farrukhsiyar (1713–19)

Farrukhsiyar came to power with the help of **Sayyid brothers**—Abdullah Khan and Hussain Ali Khan Barahow—who came to be known as the kingmakers. As a token of gratitude, Farrukhsiyar appointed Abdullah Khan as his wazir and Hussain Ali Khan as the Mir Bakshi. Farrukhsiyar was incapable, coward and he allowed himself to be influenced by worthless flatterers. Taking advantage, the two brothers soon acquired dominant control over the affairs of the state (1713–20).

Traditional Mughal emperor riding elephant caravan

The Sayyid brothers adopted the policy of religious tolerance. They believed that India could be ruled harmoniously only by associating Hindu chiefs and nobles with the Muslim nobles in governance. They **abolished the jeziah** and pilgrimage tax. They continued to conciliate the Marathas, the Rajputs and the Jats while suppressing the Sikhs. Farrukhsiyar's reign saw the victory of the Mughals over the Sikhs as the Sikh leader **Banda Bahadur** was taken prisoner at Gurdaspur and later executed at Delhi (19 June 1716).

In 1714, William Hamilton, a surgeon in the British East Indian Company successfully cured Farrukhsiyar of a disease (swelling in the groin). After successful treatment, Farrukhsiyar finally arranged his marriage to the daughter of Raja Ajit Singh of Jodhpur, which had been delayed by the illness. As a reward to the Company, the emperor issued a farman (royal order), known as the **Farman of 1717**, heedlessly granting the British East India Company many trading privileges including the exemption from custom duties for its trade through Bengal. The provisions of the farman became a source of perpetual conflict between the Bengal Nawabs and the English Company.

Soon, Farrukhsiyar wanted to exercise his own authority and conspired to get rid of the Sayyid brothers. However, the Sayyids proved to be too clever for him and with the help of **Peshwa Balaji Vishwanath**, they dethroned the emperor and blinded and killed him. It was the first time in the Mughal history that an emperor was killed by his nobles.

After the execution of Farrukhsiyar, the Sayyid Brothers raised to the throne in quick succession two young princes, Rafi-ud-Darajat and Rafi-ud-Daula, both of whom died of **consumption** (old name for tuberculosis).

- **Rafi-ud-Darajat (April 1719–June 19)** He ruled for the shortest period.
- **Rafi-ud-Daula or Shah Jahan II (June 1719–September 19)** He took the title of Shah Jahan II. He was an opium addict and suffered from dysentery.

The kingmakers now made the 18-year-old Roshan Akhtar, better known as Muhammad Shah the emperor of India. All the three successors of Farrukhsiyar were mere puppets in the hands of the Sayyids. Even their personal liberty to move around and meet people was restricted.

Muhammad Shah or Roshan Akhtar Bahadur (1719–48)

Even though Sayyid brothers had tried hard to befriend all sections of the nobility, a powerful group of nobles headed by Nizam-ul-Mulk and Muhammad Amin Khan began to conspire against them. These nobles were jealous of the growing power of the brothers. Moreover, the murder of Farrukhsiyar also frightened many of them. For, if the emperor could be killed, what safety was there for mere nobles? Muhammad Shah too desired to free himself from the control of the Sayyid brothers and succeeded in killing them in 1720 with the help of a powerful noble, **Nizam-ul-Mulk** (full name-Qamar-ud-din Siddiqi Nizam-ul-Mulk Asaf Jah).

After the fall of the Sayyid brothers, Muhammad Shah ruled for a long period of nearly 30 years (1719–48). This was probably the last chance to save the empire—the Mughal rule was still held in high esteem, the Mughal army was still a force to reckon with, the Maratha sardars were still confined to the south and the Rajputs were still loyal to the Mughals. A strong and farsighted ruler might have still saved the situation. But Muhammad was not the man of the moment. He was weak minded and frivolous, and came to be known in Indian history as **Muhammad Shah 'Rangeela'** because of his fondness for wine and women. After the fall of Sayyid brothers he fell into the clutches of a dancing girl Koki Jiu and the eunuch Hafiz Khidmatgar Khan.

In this way, Muhammad Shah's reign initiated an irreversible decline of the Mughal Empire and the **physical breakup** of the Empire now began:

- Powerful nobles now began to carve out semi-independent states. For example, Nizam-ul-Mulk in Hyderabad (1724), Murshid Quli Khan in Bengal (1717) and Saadat Khan in Awadh (1722) carved out their autonomous states.
- The Marathas began their northern expansion and in 1737 **Baji Rao I** raided Delhi and terrorised the emperor.
- In 1739 **Nadir Shah invaded India**, defeated the Mughals in the **Battle of Karnal** and annexed strategically important areas west of the Indus (including Kabul) to the Persian Empire. And India once again became vulnerable to the attacks from the north-west. Soon after the assassination of Nadir Shah (1747), **Ahmad Shah Abdali** was chosen as the King of Afghanistan. Between 1748 and 1767, Abdali invaded and plundered the Mughal Empire seven times, beginning his first invasion in 1748 during the reign of Muhammad Shah.

Nadir Shah's Invasion Mughal Empire received a fatal blow when the King of Persia Nadir Shah invaded India in 1738–39. Nadir Shah was attracted to India by its well-known fabulous wealth and the bankrupt Persian Empire found an easy prey in the weak Mughal rule. Earlier, Aurangzeb had kept a vigilant eye over the north-west frontier. However, after this death, the frontier had been neglected for years. The danger was recognised only after Nadir Shah occupied Lahore. Hurried preparations were made for the defence of Delhi but the nobles could not agree on a plan for defence. The emperor Muhammad Shah accompanied by Nizam-ul-Mulk marched from the capital to confront the invader.

On 13 February 1739, the two armies met at **Karnal (Battle of Karnal)** and Nadir Shah inflicted a crushing defeat on the Mughal army. While Khan-i-Dauran (Mir Bakshi) fell in the battlefield, Saadat Khan (governor of Awadh) and emperor Mohammad Shah were taken prisoner. Nadir Shah now marched to Delhi and ordered a terrible massacre in imperial capital to revenge the killing of a handful of his soldiers. The devastation of Delhi has been famously lamented by the poets **Mir and Sauda.**

Nadir Shah took possession of the royal treasury; the **Peacock throne** and the **Kohinoor diamond** were the two most priced items of his loot. His total plunder, estimated at 70 crore, enabled him to exempt his own kingdom from taxation for 3 years! Nadir Shah also annexed territory to the west of the River Indus.

Nadir Shah's invasion inflicted a heavy damage on the Mughal Empire and its dwindling image suffered a severe blow. It exposed the hidden weakness of the empire to the Maratha sardars and the foreign trading companies. The invasion ruined central finances; the impoverished nobles began to oppress the peasantry even more in an effort to recover their lost fortunes. The loss of areas west to the Indus once again exposed the empire to dangers from the North-West.

Ahmad Shah Abdali's Invasions After the assassination of Nadir Shah in 1747, **Ahmad Shah Abdali** (or Ahmad Shah Durrani) was chosen as the King of Afghanistan and assumed the title 'Durr-i-Durrani' or Pearl of pearls. He also began invading India during Muhammad Shah's reign in 1748, his first invasion being a fiasco. Between 1748 and 1767, he invaded and plundered Mughal Empire seven times.

Third Battle of Panipat

In early 1749, he again crossed the frontier and defeated the Punjab Governor Muin-ul-Mulk. However, Muin-ul-Mulk promised him an annual remittance of ₹14,000 and Abdali returned.

In 1752, Abdali invaded India a third time as he stopped receiving the promised remittance regularly. The emperor Ahmad Shah, with a view to saving Delhi from devastation, appeased Abdali by surrendering **Punjab and Multan**. But when the Punjab Governor Muin-ul-Mulk passed away, wazir Imad-ul-Mulk appointed Adina Beg as Punjab Governor to restore order (in November 1753). This was seen as interference in Punjab affairs by Abdali.

Hence, in November 1756, Abdali invaded India for the fourth time. In January 1757, he entered Delhi and plundered as far as Mathura and Agra. Before returning, Abdali recognised **Alamgir II** as the emperor, **Imad-ul-Mulk** as the wazir, the Rohilla chief **Najib-ud-Daulah** as Mir Bakshi of the empire and his son **Timur Shah Durrani** (wedded to the daughter of Alamgir II) as his 'supreme agent' to safeguard his interests in India. In this way, Abdali returned to Afghanistan without displacing Mughal dynasty so long it accepted Abdali's suzerainty.

However, in 1758 Najib was expelled from Delhi by the Maratha chief Raghunath Rao who also captured Punjab, forcing Abdali to invade India for the fifth time in 1759 to take revenge on the Marathas. In 1761, he defeated the Marathas in the third **Battle of Panipat**, giving a fatal blow to their ambition of controlling the Emperor and dominating the country. True, the Marathas escorted the Mughal Emperor to the throne of Delhi in 1772 and again in 1789, they never again made an attempt to capture Punjab and Multan or play the defenders of the North-West frontier of India.

A cumulative effect of the Irani and Durrani invasions as well as the internal feuds of the Indian nobility was that by 1761, the Mughal Empire had ceased to exist in practice as an all India Empire.

Najib-ud-Daulah He was a Rohilla chief (Afghani) who had joined Ahmad Shah Abdali in 1757 during his attack on Delhi. For a certain period of time, Najib-ud-Daulah and later his son Zabita Khan and grand-son Ghulam Qadir exercised undisputed power at Delhi. Najib was the founder of the city of Najibabad in Bijnor district.

Ahmad Shah (1748–54)

Mohammad Shah's successor Ahmad Shah was born of **Udham Bai**, a public dancing girl. He was weak and left the state affairs in the hands of his mother. Udham Bai, the Queen Mother (title of Qibla-i-Alam) was of poor intellect and ruled with the help of her paramour, Javid Khan a notorious eunuch.

During Ahmad Shah's reign, Ahmad Shah Abdali invaded India twice: in 1749 and again in 1752 when he marched upto Delhi. Emperor Ahmad Shah, with a view to saving Delhi from devastation, appeased Abdali by surrendering **Punjab and Multan**. Thus, Punjab and Multan were lost to the Afghans.

In 1752, **Ghazi ud-Din Khan Feroz Jung III** (or **Imad-ul-Mulk**, grandson of Nizam-ul-Mulk Asaf Jah), upon the recommendation of Nawab Wazir Safdar Jung, was appointed as Mir Bakshi (Pay Master General) and received the titles of Amir ul-Umara (Noble of Nobles) and Imad-ul-Mulk by the Mughal Emperor Ahmad Shah. Feroz Jung III soon emerged powerful and began to intimidate the emperor himself who now wished to have him removed from the court. Before this could be done, Feroz Jung III sought an alliance with the Maratha chief Sadashiv Rao Bhau; together they blinded and deposed Ahmad Shah in 1754 and raised a puppet ruler (Alamgir II) to the throne. Imad-ul-Mulk now became the new wazir and kingmaker.

Note: In this way, Mohammad Shah was succeeded by a number of weak and inefficient rulers - Ahmad Shah (1748–54), Alamgir II (1754–59), Shah Alam II (1759–1806), Akbar II (1806–37) and Bahadur Shah II (1837–57).

Alamgir II or Aziz-ud-din (1754–59)

After dethroning Ahmad Shah, **Imad-ul-Mulk** now raised Aziz-ud-din (Jahandar Shah's son) to the throne who began his reign as Alamgir II. It was during his reign that the **Battle of Plassey** was fought (23 June 1757).

During his reign, Ahmad Shah Abdali invaded India and plundered Delhi in 1757. The same year **Imad invited the Marathas** to invade Delhi in order to drive out the Afghans and the Rohillas. Accordingly, in March 1758 a massive force of Marathas led by Raghunath Rao appeared at Delhi, defeated the Afghan garrison at Delhi, expelled Najib and overran Punjab, occupying Lahore. They deposed Timur Shah (who had been appointed a year earlier as viceroy by his father, Ahmad Shah Abdali) and instead appointed Adina Beg as Governor of Punjab on behalf of the Peshwa Balaji Baji Rao. In August 1759, the Afghan monarch Ahmad Shah Abdali returned to India to avenge the Marathas. (It took him almost two years to deal a fatal blow to Marathas in the Third Battle of Panipat, fought on 14 January 1761, resulting in a crushing defeat of the Marathas).

In November 1759, Wazir Imad-ul-Mulk got the emperor murdered and raised to throne his puppet Mughal emperor, Shah Jahan III.

Shah Jahan III or Muhi-ul-Millat (1759–60)

He reigned as Mughal emperor for a very brief period. He was the son of the eldest son of Muhammad Kam Bakhsh (who was the youngest son of Aurangzeb). He was placed on the Mughal throne in December 1759 as a puppet ruler by wazir Imad-ul-Mulk. He was later deposed by Maratha chiefs.

Shah Alam II or Ali Gauhar (1760–1806)

During 1759–60, Northern India was swept by the Marathas, led by **Sadashivrao Bhau**, who deposed Shah Jahan III and installed Ali Gauhar, the son of Alamgir II as the rightful emperor under the Maratha suzerainty. Ali Gauhar took the title of Shah Alam II. He was a man of some ability and courage, but the Empire was now beyond redemption. His reign saw two decisive battles: the **Third Battle of Panipat (1761)** and **the Battle of Buxar (1764)**.

In 1761, after the battle of Panipat and before leaving Delhi (20th March 1761), Ahmed Shah Abdali named Shah Alam II as emperor and Najib-ud-Daulah as Mir Bakshi. Abdali last invaded India in 1767. His invasions hastened the downfall of the Mughal Empire, creating anarchy and confusion all around. The Emperor Shah Alam II was not allowed to enter Delhi for 12 years (1760–72, until he was escorted to his throne by the Marathas in 1772). Thus, he remained in exile for 12 years and came to be known as the **'fugitive Mughal Emperor'**. During his absence, the Rohilla leaders Najib-ud-Daulah and later his son Zabita Khan and grandson Ghulam Qadir exercised undisputed power at Delhi.

In 1764, Shah Alam II joined hands with Mir Qasim of Bengal and Shuja-ud-Daulah of Awadh in the Battle of Buxar against the English East India Company. Defeated at Buxar, the Mughal Emperor signed the **Treaty of Allahabad (1765)** with the British. According to the treaty, he was forced to grant the Diwani (right to collect revenue) of Bengal, Bihar and Orissa to the British. In return, the emperor was given a subsidy of ₹26 lakh and the districts of Kora and Allahabad. The Emperor resided in the fort of Allahabad for the next six years as a virtual **prisoner of the English**.

In 1771, the Marathas under **Mahadji Shinde** (or Scindia) returned to northern India, captured Delhi and reinstated Shah Alam II at the Delhi throne (January 1772) under Maratha suzerainty. Shah Alam II appointed Scindia in charge of Delhi administration (Henceforth, the Scindias remained the overlords of Delhi until Daulat Rao Scindia was defeated by Lord Lake in 1803).

During 1772–73, the Mughal Emperor supported by the Marathas led an expedition against Rohilla leader Zabita Khan who was earlier appointed as Mir Bakshi by Shah Alam II. Zabita Khan was taken prisoner along with his family and other Rohilla leaders and severely humiliated. Zabita's son Ghulam Qadir Rohilla was castrated and made to serve as a page in the palace. Several years later, in September 1787, Ghulam Qadir was able to force the emperor to appoint him as Mir Bakshi and Regent. But soon he had to leave Delhi due to differences with the emperor and re-entered Delhi the next year to take revenge. On 30 July 1788, he took possession of the royal palace, deposed Shah Alam II and later ruthlessly blinded him (10 August 1788). Shah Alam II was also referred to as the **'blind Mughal Emperor'**. Mahadji Scindia, however, hunted Ghulam Qadir down and the blind Shah Alam was restored as the king (October 1788).

In 1803, Delhi was recaptured by the English after defeating Daulat Rao Scindia and the blind Mughal emperor once again accepted the protection of the British. From 1803 till 1857, the Mughal dynasty merely served as a political front for the English (the Company's coins continued to carry the stamp of Emperor Shah Alam till 1835).

Shah Alam's power was so depleted during his reign that it led to a saying in Persian, **'Sultanat-e-Shah Alam, Az Dilli ta Palam'**, meaning, 'The kingdom of Shah Alam is from Delhi to Palam', Palam being a suburb of Delhi. Shah Alam II also authored his own **Diwan of poems** and was known by the pen-name **'Aftab'**.

In this way, Shah Alam II and his successors were emperors only in name, being puppets in the hands of their own nobles or the Marathas or the British. In fact, the British kept alive the fiction of the Mughal Empire until 1858 when the last of the Mughal Emperors Bahadur Shah Zafar was exiled to Rangoon.

Akbar Shah II (1806–37)

After the death of Shah Alam II, his son succeeded as Akbar Shah II. Akbar, the penultimate Mughal Emperor of India, gave the title of **'Raja' to Ram Mohan Roy** and sent him to England to seek a raise in pension. In 1835, the East India Company stopped calling itself a subject of the Mughal Emperor and discontinued issuing coins in his name by deleting Persian lines on Company's coins to this effect.

Bahadur Shah II or Bahadur Shah Zafar (1837–57)

After the death of Akbar II, Bahadur Shah II became the Mughal Emperor. He was fond of poetry and was known by the title of **'Zafar'**. During the **Revolt of 1857**, Bahadur Shah Zafar was proclaimed as the Emperor of India by the rebels. After the Revolt of 1857, he was captured and deported to **Rangoon** where he died in November 1862.

Bahadur Shah Zafar

In legal terms, the Mughal Empire came to an end on 1 November 1858, with the declaration of Queen Victoria. The most important consequence of the decline of the Mughal Empire was that it enabled the British to conquer India and push it into the very vortex of colonial exploitation for nearly 200 years.

Causes of Decline of the Mughal Empire

Various internal as well as external factors that contributed to the decline of the Mughal Empire are as follows:

Internal Weaknesses

The Mughal Empire was a 'war state' in its core. Its vitality depended ultimately on its military power. The emperor stood at the apex of this structure followed by the military aristocracy followed by the Mughal army. Multiple issues emerged at all three levels of this broad military structure. These may be understood under the following heads:

Aurangzeb's Misguided Policies Historians BL Grover and Alka Mehta have rightly stated that the expansion of Mughal Empire under Aurangzeb only resembled an inflated balloon. The Mughal Empire had expanded beyond the point of effective control and its vastness only tended to weaken the centre. Aurangzeb failed to realise that the vast Mughal Empire depended on the willing support of the people. His policy of religious intolerance antagonised the Rajputs, Sikhs, Jats and Marathas and pushed them into open rebellion. Aurangzeb's mistaken policy of continuous war in the Deccan against the Marathas drained the resources of the empire, breaking Aurangzeb's back and ensuring that his reign marked the beginning of the end of the Mughal Empire.

Weak Successors The government of the Mughals was a personal despotism and its success depended on the character of the reigning monarch. The later Mughals proved to be weak and incapable. They became victims of intrigues and conspiracies of the faction-ridden nobles. They proved to be inefficient generals and administrators who were incapable of suppressing revolts.

Bahadur Shah I (1707–12) was too old to maintain the prestige of the empire and he liked to appease all parties by profusing grants of titles and rewards. Due to such attitude, he was nicknamed 'Shah-i-Bekhabar'. Jahandar Shah (1712–13), the next in succession, was wildly extravagant; Farrukhsiyar was a coward, while Muhammad Shah spent more of his time in watching animal fights. Due to his addiction of wine and women, Muhammad Shah got the title of 'Rangeela'. Ahmad Shah extended the harem (a separate place for concubines/wives of emperor) to a very large area where he spent weeks or months. The later Mughals were evidently weak and incapable, which hastened the process of disintegration.

Wars of Succession and Role of Kingmakers In the absence of a definite law of succession (like the law of primogeniture), there usually occurred a war of succession among the Mughal princes. After the death of Bahadur Shah I in 1712, the rival claimants to the throne began to be used as tools by the leaders of rival factions to promote their own personal interests. For instance, Zulfiqar Khan acted as the kingmaker in the war of succession which followed after 1712. From 1713 to 1720 the Sayyid Brothers acted as kingmakers and were instrumental in appointing four kings to the throne. After them, Mir Mohammad Amin and Asaf Jah Nizam-ul-Mulk acted as kingmakers. This weakened the stability of the Mughal government and fostered partisanship at the cost of patriotism.

Nature of Mughal State The Mughal state was essentially a police state that confined itself chiefly to maintenance of law and order and collection of revenue. The Mughals failed to foster a feeling of harmony between Hindus and Muslims and create a composite nation. Some efforts in this direction were made by Akbar but these were undone by the bigotry of Aurangzeb and his weak successors. As a result, many Indian chiefs looked at the Mughals as foreigners and as enemies of Hindus and aspired for freedom from Mughal rule.

Degeneration of Mughal Nobility (or Military Aristocracy) In the late 16th century, Akbar had organised this aristocracy or ruling class through the mansabdari system. The mansabdars were appointed by the emperor himself on the basis of personal loyalty to the Emperor. They were required to maintain a given number of savars or horsemen, and were often paid in the form of a **jagir (landed estate)**. With time, the mansabdari system became hereditary and the offices of the state became a close preserve of selected few. It also became a closed corporation of nobles belonging to certain ethno–religious groups (the most powerful being the Irani and the Turani groups) and gave no opportunity of promotion to capable men belonging to other classes, as had been the case earlier.

The degeneration of the Mughal rulers further added to the degeneration of the nobility. Many nobles discarded the discipline of military life and took to luxurious living. They spent huge sums on keeping large harems, maintaining a big staff of servants, etc., and indulged in other forms of pomp and show. Such habits of extravagant living drained their limited financial resources and weakened their morality; they now rivalled each other not in gallantry but in flamboyance and flattery. Such degeneration that gripped the later Mughal nobility ensured that the state was now deprived of able administrators and military leaders.

Shifting Loyalty of Zamindars The zamindars and the nobles were the two classes that shared State power with the emperor. The zamindars or landlords were the hereditary owners of lands and were variously known as Rais, Rajas, Khuts, Thakurs or Deshmukhs. They played an important role in the collection of revenue and local administration. These zamindars also helped the nobility to take advantage of the weakness of the empire and to establish autonomous states for themselves.

Jagirdari Crisis and resulting Court Factions In the 18th century there emerged an economic crisis, also known as jagirdari crisis. It is defined by Satish Chandra in the following words: 'The available social surplus was insufficient to defray the cost of administration and give the ruling class a standard of life in keeping with its expectations". This happened because of the unusual increase in the number of mansabdars at a time when the area to be distributed as jagir remained stagnant or even declined.

The jagirdari crisis increased during the last years of Aurangzeb, mainly because of the Deccan wars. The jagir crisis is believed to have led to an unhealthy competition among the nobles in order to have control over good jagirs. Group politics in the Mughal Court became an order of the day, each group wanting to have influence over the emperor to get access to good jagirs. Proximity of any particular group to the emperor naturally alienated the others and this gradually affected the personal bonds of loyalty between the emperor and his nobility. Such a nobility no longer espoused the cause of the empire, they stopped maintaining the required number of soldiers and horses and became more interested in carving out their own autonomous states.

Politicking at the imperial court reached its height after the death of Bahadur Shah in 1712. The reigns of Jahandar Shah (1712–13), Farrukhsiyar (1713–19) and Muhammad Shah (1719–48) were most intrigue ridden. The Irani group was led by Asad Khan and his son Zulfiqar Khan, the Turani group was led by Ghazi-ud-Din Khan Feroz Jung and his son Chin Qilich Khan (Nizam-ul Mulk) and the Hindustani group was led by the Sayyid brothers. Each faction tried to win the emperor to its view point and poisoned his ears against the other faction. Though these factions were formed based on family relations, yet personal interests played a dominating role. The personal interest of Nizam-ul-Mulk (Qilich Khan) and Burhan-ul-Mulk (Saadat Khan) led them to intrigue with Iranian ruler Nadir Shah.

Military Weakness The Mughal military was also infested with some inherent weaknesses. It was organised in a kind of feudal style, where the soldiers owed greater allegiance to the mansabdari rather than the Emperor and fostered conditions of indiscipline and revolt.

The degeneration of the military aristocracy led to weakening of the Mughal army as well. There was a lamentable dearth of able commanders, effective supervision, military reform and new technology. Further, the Mughal army usually moved with a huge tail of camps which looked like a city with markets and stores. Women and children, cattle and other non-combatants accompanied the army, making it unwieldy and reduced it to the likes of an armed rabble.

The weakness of the military invited both internal as well as external challenges. For instance, the Marathas under Shivaji repeatedly challenged Aurangzeb's rule. After his death, the Maratha depredations increased and in March 1737, they even plundered the suburbs of Delhi. This was followed by the Persian invasion under Nadir Shah (1739) and the sack of Delhi, which was an enormous blow to the prestige of the empire.

Empty Treasury Shah Jahan's zeal for construction had already depleted the treasury which was further drained by Aurangzeb's long wars in the Deccan. The military marches also destroyed standing crops in the Deccan; whatever little was left was destroyed by Maratha raiders. The peasants began to give up agriculture and took to life of plunder and robbery. Under the later Mughals, the financial condition further deteriorated; even as autonomous states gradually stopped the payment of revenue to the centre, political upheavals and lavish living of the emperors and nobles continued.

Size of Empire and Rise of Regional Powers The Mughal Empire had become too large and unwieldy to be controlled by any ruler from one centre specially under medieval conditions of transport and communication. During Aurangzeb's rule itself, powerful regional groups like Sikhs, Jats, Rajputs and Marathas defied the Mughal authority in a bid to carve out their own kingdoms. Continuous struggle between the Mughals and these regional powers weakened the empire considerably and contributed to its decline.

External Challenges and Causes

Rise of Marathas Perhaps the most significant external factor that contributed to the collapse of the mighty Mughals was the rising power of the Marathas under the Peshwas. They emerged as the strongest regional power and propounded the ideal of Hindu Rashtra that could be built only at the cost of the Muslim empire. After the death of Aurangzeb, the tide soon changed in favour of the Marathas who now emerged on the offensive, reached upto northern India and even began playing the kingmakers at Delhi court. They acted as the defenders of the country against foreign invaders like Ahmad Shah Abdali. Though the Marathas did not succeed in taking the place of the Mughals, their conquests in Northern India in the 18th century certainly gave a death-blow to the Mughal Empire.

Invasions of Irani (Persian) and Durrani (Afghan) Kingdoms The Iranian monarch, Nadir Shah attacked India in 1738–39 and defeated the Mughal army in the Battle of Karnal. Nadir Shah's successor Ahmad Shah Abdali invaded India seven times between 1748 and 1767. These invasions, besides depleting the Mughal treasury of its wealth, also exposed to the world the military weakness of the empire and its prestige suffered a severe blow.

Advent of European Powers The European trading companies also took advantage of the prevailing conditions in India and saw themselves as contenders for power. They participated in court intrigues and hastened the process of disintegration of the Mughal Empire.

Continuity of Mughal Traditions

Contrary to the physical disintegration of the Mughal Empire, the Mughal form of government continued to survive stubbornly for many years. The prestige associated with the Mughal Emperor was so considerable that his sanction was sought by all rebel chiefs and kings. They also continued with Mughal administrative practices. Even the Maratha state which had risen as a reaction to Mughal rule, adopted Mughal methods of administration. However, it must be remembered that these adaptations were only regional and not all India in scale. Thus, several Mughal traditions and institutions were reintegrated into Indian polity by the regional chiefs and also by the British.

Causes of Decline of Mughal Empire (Views of Prominent Historians)

- **Personal Failings of Emperors and Nobles** (William Irvine, Jadunath Sarkar): Irvine and Sarkar highlighted the personal failings of the emperors and the nobles. Mughal rule was portrayed as Muslim rule and Maratha, Sikh and Bundela uprising were portrayed as Hindu reaction to Islamic onslaught. According to Sarkar, Aurangzeb was a religious fanatic. He discriminated against sections of the nobles and officials on the basis of religion which led to wide scale resentment among the nobility.
- **Jagirdari Crisis** (Satish Chandra, Athar Ali): In the opinion of Satish Chandra, it was the economic crisis which played a key role in the fall of the Mughal Empire. According to him, towards the end of Aurangzeb's rule, the mansabdari-jagirdari system went into disarray. This happened because of a shortage of jagirs and overabundance of jagirdars.
- **Agrarian Crisis** (Irfan Habib): Habib also stressed the role of economic crisis. He showed that the agrarian system had become exploitative which sparked off peasant revolts and ruined imperial stability. The Mughal government and the nobles tried to extract as much revenue as possible. This subjected the peasantry to a crushing burden which ultimately destroyed the peasants' capacity to pay the revenue. Moreover, the jagirdars were frequently transferred and had little interests in any long-term agricultural development.
- **Deccan Crisis** (M.N. Pearson, J.F. Richards and P. Hardy): According to them, the leading cause of Mughal decline was the Mughal involvement in the Deccan and fight with the Marathas.
- **Rise of Regional Powers** (Muzaffar Alam and Chetan Singh): In their opinion, the main cause for the Mughal decline was the impressive economic progress in Awadh and Punjab regions as opposed to the economic stagnation in Delhi and Agra. Many social and political elements in these regions got rich quickly and began to assert their independence.

Evaluation The generally accepted view remains one of economic crisis. Yet, we may conclude that there was no one single common cause applicable to the whole of India that led to the decline of the Mughal Empire, but there was a combination of factors that brought about a disequilibrium in the fragile political edifice of the Mughal state and encouraged the revival of the regional identities as reflected in the emergence of regional powers.

Prelim Capsule

Later Mughals (1707–1857)

Bahadur Shah I or Muazzam Shah Alam I (1707–1712)

Allowed the Maratha prince **Shahu**, held as Mughal captive since 1689, to go back to Maharashtra.

Gave Guru Gobind Singh a high mansab.

Defeated Banda Bahadur at Lohgarh, a fort built by Guru Govind Singh.

Was called **Shah-i-Bekhabar** (Headless King) by Khafi Khan.

Jahandar Shah (1712–1713)

Sat on the Mughal throne with the support of Zulfiquar Khan, a powerful noble.

Zulfiquar Khan introduced the evil practice of revenue farming or **Ijarah**.

Various parties at the Mughal court emerged, e.g. the Turanis, Iranis, Afghans and Hindustanis.

Farrukhsiyar (1713–1719)

Came to power with the help of **Sayyid brothers**- Abdullah Khan and Hussain Ali Khan Barahow.

Sayyid brothers abolished the jeziah and pilgrimage tax.

Sikh leader Banda Bahadur was executed.

Farrukhsiyar issued the **farman of 1717**, granting the East India Company many trading privileges.

Sayyids killed Farrukhsiyar with the help of Peshwa Balaji Vishwanath- the first time in the Mughal history that an emperor was killed by his nobles.

Rafi-ud-Darajat (1719)

Ruled for the shortest period and died of tuberculosis.

Rafi-ud-Daula or Shah Jahan II (1719)

Was an opium addict, suffered from dysentery, died of tuberculosis.

Muhammad Shah or Roshan Akhtar Bahadur (1719–1748)

Killed the Sayyid brothers in 1720 with the help of a powerful noble, **Nizam-ul-Mulk**.

Known in history as **Muhammad Shah 'Rangeela'**.

Fell into the clutches of a dancing girl Koki Jiu and the eunuch Hafiz Khidmatgar Khan.

Physical breakup of the Empire began.

Powerful nobles now began to carve out semi independent states, eg- Nizam-ul-Mulk in Hyderabad (1724), Murshid Quli Khan in Bengal (1717) and Saadat Khan in Awadh (1722) carved out their autonomous states.

In 1737, Baji Rao I raided Delhi.

In 1739, **Nadir Shah** invaded India, defeated the Mughals in the battle of Karnal and took possession of the Peacock throne and the Kohinoor diamond.

In 1748, **Ahmad Shah Abdali** first invaded India.

Ahmad Shah (1748–1754)

State control fell in the hands of **Udham Bai**, his mother (earlier a public dancing girl).

Abdali invaded India twice (1749 & 1752).

To save Delhi from devastation, Ahmad Shah surrendered Punjab and Multan to Abdali.

In 1754, he was deposed by Imad-ul-Mulk with the help of Maratha chief Sadashiv Rao Bhau.

Alamgir II or Aziz-ud-din (1754–1759)

Was raised to the throne by **Imad-ul-Mulk**, the new vazir and kingmaker.

In June 1757, **Battle of Plassey** was fought.

In 1757, Abdali invaded India and plundered Delhi. Before returning, he recognised Alamgir II as the emperor, Imad-ul-Mulk as the vazir, the Rohilla chief **Najib-ud-Daulah** as Mir Bakshi of the empire and his son **Timur Shah Durrani** (wedded to the daughter of Alamgir II) as his 'supreme agent'.

In 1757, Imad invited the Marathas to drive out the Afghans and the Rohillas.

In March 1758, the Marathas led by **Raghunath Rao** appeared at Delhi, defeated the Afghan garrison at Delhi, expelled Najib and overran Punjab, occupying Lahore. They deposed Timur Shah and instead appointed **Adina Beg** as Governor of Punjab on behalf of the Peshwa Balaji Baji Rao.

In August 1759, the Afghan monarch Ahmad Shah Abdali returned to India to avenge the Marathas (and later defeated them in the battle of Panipat).

In November 1759, Alamgir II was killed by wazir Imad-ul-Mulk.

Shah Jahan III or Muhi-ul-millat (1759–1760)

Was placed on the Mughal throne as a puppet ruler by Wazir Imad-ul-Mulk.

Was later deposed by Maratha chiefs.

Shah Alam II or Ali Gauhar (1760–1806)

Was raised to the throne as the rightful emperor by the Marathas led by Sadashivrao Bhau.

In 1761, Abdali defeated the Marathas in the **Battle of Panipat**. Before returning, Abdali named Shah Alam II as emperor and Najib-ud-Daulah as Mir Bakshi.

Shah Alam II was not allowed to enter Delhi for 12 years; remained in exile and came to be known as the **'fugitive Mughal Emperor'**.

During his absence, the Rohilla leaders Najib-ud-Daulah and later his son Zabita Khan and grandson Ghulam Qadir exercised undisputed power at Delhi.

In 1764, Shah Alam II joined hands with Mir Qasim of Bengal and Shuja-ud-Daulah of Awadh in the **Battle of Buxar** against the English Company.

In 1765, he signed the **Treaty of Allahabad** with the British; was forced to grant the Diwani of Bengal, Bihar and Orissa to the British and himself resided in the fort of Allahabad for the next six years as a virtual **prisoner of the English**.

In 1772, he was reinstated to the Mughal throne by the Marathas under Mahadji Shinde.

During 1772–73, Shah Alam supported by the Marathas led an expedition against Rohilla leader Zabita Khan.

In 1788, Zabita's son Ghulam Quadir deposed Shah Alam and blinded him. The emperor was henceforth known as the **'blind Mughal Emperor'**.

In 1803, Delhi was recaptured by the English after defeating Daulat Rao Scindia.

Shah Alam's depleted power led to a saying in Persian, **'Sultanat-e-Shah Alam, Az Dilli ta Palam'**.

He authored his own Diwan of poems and was known by the pen-name **'Aftab'**.

Akbar Shah II (1806–1837)

Was the penultimate Mughal Emperor.

Gave the title of **'Raja' to Ram Mohan Roy** and sent him to England.

In 1835, the English Company stopped calling itself a subject of the Mughal Emperor, discontinued issuing coins in his name by deleting Persian lines on Company's coins to this effect.

Bahadur Shah II or Bahadur Shah Zafar (1837–1857)

Was fond of poetry and was known by the title of **"Zafar"**.

During the **Revolt of 1857**, Bahadur Shah Zafar was proclaimed as the Emperor of India by the rebels. After the Revolt, he was captured and deported to **Rangoon** where he died in November 1862.

Previous Years' Questions – Preliminary Exam

1. Assertion (A): Shah Alam II spent the initial years as an emperor outside Delhi.
   Reason (R): There was always a lurking danger of foreign invasion from the North-West Frontier. **[UPSC 2003]**

   Select the answer for the options given below:
   (a) Both A and R are true, and R is the correct explanation of A.
   (b) Both A and R are true, but R is the not the correct explanation of A.
   (c) A is true, but R is false.
   (d) A is false, but R is true.
2. How did the Mughal emperor Jahandar Shah's reign come to an early end? **[UPSC 2003]**
   (a) He was deposed by his Wazir.
   (b) He died due to slip while climbing down steps.
   (c) He was defeated by his nephew in a battle.
   (d) He died of sickness due to too much consumption of wine.

Answers

Previous Years' Questions – Preliminary Exam

1. (c) 2. (c)

2 RISE OF AUTONOMOUS STATES

After the decline of the Mughal Empire, the second major theme of the 18th-century Indian polity was the rise of autonomous states. From the debris of the Mughal Empire arose a large number of autonomous and semi-autonomous states which the British had to overcome before emerging supreme in India. Thus, in this chapter, you will learn about the Indian States and Society on the eve of British conquest.

By 1761, the Mughal Empire was an empire only in name. Its weaknesses had enabled regional powers to assert their independence. Yet the new states did not directly challenge the authority of the Mughal emperor, as he continued to be seen as the source of political legitimacy. These states also continued the Mughal institutions in many areas of governance. Thus, the emergence of these states in the 18th century, therefore, represented a transformation rather than collapse of the polity. It signified a **decentralisation of power** and **not a power vacuum** or political chaos.

Broadly, three kinds of states arose:

1. **Successor States** They were the erstwhile provinces of Mughal Empire that broke away and arose as a result of assertion of autonomy by governors of Mughal provinces. These were Hyderabad, Carnatic, Bengal and Awadh.
2. **New States** They were the creations of rebellious local chiefs and arose as a result of rebellion against Mughal authority. These were the states set up by the Marathas, Sikhs, Jats and Afghans.
3. **Independent States** They were neither the result of a breakaway from or rebellion against Delhi. They had been only nominally a part of Mughal Empire, had already enjoyed considerable amount of autonomy in the past and now in the 18th century became completely independent. These were the regions on the south-west and south-east coast of India, i.e. Mysore, Kerala and the Rajputs (sometimes wrongly called the Hindu States).

These states were strong enough to destroy Mughal power but none was able to replace it. Though some states were very prosperous and some gained considerable military power, none could achieve resources and power to maintain an all-India polity. One of the major weaknesses of these states was their backwardness in science and technology. This became one of the major reasons for the total subjugation of India by the most modern country of the time—the Great Britain.

Successor States-Hyderabad, Carnatic, Bengal and Awadh

These states started exercising full autonomy, without formally renouncing their allegiance to the Mughal Emperor, thus giving rise to a new political order within the Mughal institutional framework. The fiction of Mughal sovereignty was kept alive through the following:

- Annual revenues were sent to the imperial treasury.
- Emperor's formal confirmation was taken for the appointment to high offices.
- Orders, titles, etc., were given in the name of the Mughal Emperor.

Hyderabad and the Nizams

Nizam-ul-Mulk Asaf Jah (1724–48)

The state of Hyderabad was founded in 1724 by a powerful noble of the Turani group at the imperial court, Qamar-ud-din Siddiqi. He is also known by his titles **Chin Qilich Khan** (awarded by Emperor Aurangzeb in 1690–91), Nizam-ul-Mulk (awarded by Farrukhsiyar in 1713) and Asaf Jah (awarded by Muhammad Shah in 1725).

As Viceroy of Deccan (1713–22) During the Mughal days, the Subahdar of Deccan was appointed at Hyderabad. The idea of an independent state in Deccan was first conceived by Zulfiqar Khan, who had obtained the viceroyalty of the Deccan in 1708. After his death in 1713, Qilich Khan became the Deccan Viceroy upon insistence of Farrukhsiyar who conferred upon him the title of **Nizam-ul-Mulk**. As Viceroy of Deccan, he reorganised the administration and streamlined the revenue system.

Later, Farrukhsiyar called upon Nizam-ul-Mulk to fight off the Sayyid Brothers (leaders of Hindustani group). However, the Sayyids proved to be too clever for Emperor Farrukhsiyar who was soon blinded and killed by the brothers with the help of Peshwa Balaji Vishwanath. However, in 1720 Nizam-ul-Mulk successfully assisted Mohammed Shah in killing the Sayyid brothers. He was then rewarded with the post of wazir in the court of Mohammad Shah.

As Wazir of Mughal Empire (1722–24) As wazir, he tried to reform the corrupt Mughal administration and earned many enemies for himself, who successfully poisoned the mind of the Emperor against him.

Establishment of Hyderabad State (1724) Disgusted with the suspicious nature of the emperor, Nizam-ul-Mulk decided to pursue his own ambition. He decided to leave the emperor and his empire to their fate and marched south to found the state of Hyderabad in the Deccan. His departure was symbolic of the 'flight of loyalty and virtue from the empire' and marked the beginning of the physical breakup of the Mughal Empire.

In 1724, Nizam-ul-Mulk resigned from his post and set off to Deccan only to find that Mubariz Khan, the then Viceroy of Deccan, refused to vacate his post. Nizam-ul-Mulk defeated and killed Mubariz in the **Battle of Shakar Kheda** (October 1724). The Emperor then bestowed upon him the title of Asaf Jah.

Asaf Jah never openly declared his independence, but in practice he acted like an independent ruler and founded the **Asaf Jah Dynasty**. His successors came to be known as the **Nizams of Hyderabad**. He conducted wars, signed treaties, conferred mansabs and made important appointments without any reference to the emperor. At the same time, the Nizam posed as the defender of Mughal Empire on several occasions. For instance, in the **Battle of Karnal (1739)**, the Nizam accompanied the emperor to fight against Nadir Shah.

The Nizam was a wise statesman and a benevolent ruler. He reformed the revenue system, subdued the power of the zamindars and followed a tolerant policy towards the Hindus (a Hindu, **Puran Chand,** was his Diwan). He also cleverly diverted Maratha energy by suggesting to the Peshwa the possibility of Maratha expansion in the north, a suggestion readily accepted by Baji Rao I.

War of Succession (1748) After his death in 1748, a bloody war of succession followed between his son Nasir Jung and grandson, Muzaffar Jung. Taking advantage of the political crisis, the Marathas, Mysore and the Carnatic, all settled their scores against Hyderabad. The Marathas invaded the state at will and collected chauth. The French under Dupleix also used this opportunity to play off one group against the other and supported Muzaffar Jung in return for handsome monetary and territorial rewards.

The Carnatic

Nawab Saadatullah Khan (1710–32) and Dost Ali (1732–40)

In the 18th century, the Mughal subah (province) of Carnatic came under the authority of Governor of Deccan (Nizam of Hyderabad). But just as in practice the Governor of Deccan had freed himself from the control of the Mughal Emperor, the Deputy Governor or the Nawab of Carnatic, had also established his independent authority. Accordingly, the Nawab Saadatullah Khan of Carnatic, headquartered at Arcot, appointed his nephew Dost Ali as his successor, without the prior approval of his superior, the Nizam. However, in 1740, the Marathas invaded the Carnatic, killed Nawab Dost Ali and took his son-in-law **Chanda Sahib** as prisoner to Satara.

Thereafter, the affairs of the Carnatic deteriorated and this provided an opportunity to the European trading companies to directly interfere in Indian politics. For nearly 20 years from 1744 to 1763, the English and the French remained embroiled in a bitter war in South India, a series of conflicts popularly known as the **Carnatic Wars** (1746–63).[1]

> **Carnatic Region** Carnatic region is the name given to the Coromandel Coast and its hinterland. Though no longer a political or administrative division, it is of great historical significance.

Bengal and the Nawab Nazims

The province or subah of Bengal emerged as an independent autonomous state in the first half of the 18th century and though the sovereignty of the Mughal emperor was not challenged, practically independent and hereditary authority of the governor was established by two men of exceptional ability—Murshid Quli Khan and Alivardi Khan.

Bengal in 18th Century: Under the Mughals

Bengal Provincial Administration

- Bengal in the 18th century comprised of **Bengal, Bihar and Orissa**. It was an integral part of the Mughal imperial system. Officials like Nazim and Diwan were directly recruited by Mughal emperors. The Diwan was separately appointed in order to keep control over the Nazim. The main officials in the subah or province were-
  - **Diwan**-Head of revenue administration

[1]Read about the Carnatic Wars and the British Conquest of South India in greater detail in the upcoming chapters.

- **Nazim**-Executive head of other matters of civil and military administration
- **Bakshi**-Military pay master of the subah
- **Kotwal**-Head of police department (law and order)
- **Qazi**-Dispensed justice
- **Waqai navis**-Collection of news bearing political significance

- A subah was divided into **Sarkars** (headed by Faujdars), Sarkars were further divided into **Parganas**. At local level, zamindars had maximum control over local people and administration. This system acted well till 17th century. In 18th century, gradually the relationship of the central authority with the provincial administration became loose and distanced. It merely received a tribute, and gradually even the tribute became irregular.

Nizamat and Diwani The Mughal provincial administration had two main branches: **Nizamat and Diwani**. Broadly speaking, Nizamat meant civil administration and Diwani, revenue administration. The provincial subahdar was in charge of Nizamat (He was also called Nazim, the Governor or Viceroy of the province). The Diwan was in charge of revenue administration of the province. To ensure checks and balances in subah administration, the two key officers were appointed by the Mughal emperor and were directly responsible to him. Thus the Diwan worked independent of the Nazim.

Bengal in 18th Century: Towards Autonomy (Nawab Nazims)

Murshid Quli Khan (1717–27)

The independent state of Bengal was founded in 1717 by Murshid Quli Khan, also known as **Mohammad Hadi**. Murshid Quli's tryst with Bengal began in 1700, when Aurangzeb sent him to Bengal as Diwan where he proved to be a successful revenue administrator.

As Diwan and Subahdar of Bengal In 1717, Farrukhsiyar appointed him as Subahdar or governor (Nizam or Nazim) of Bengal, thus holding the post of **Subahdar and Diwan** at the same time. He was given the unprecedented privilege of holding the two offices of Nazim (executive and military head) and Diwan (collector of revenue) simultaneously. The division of power, which was maintained throughout the Mughal period to keep both the imperial officers under control through a system of checks and balances, was thus done away with. This helped Murshid Quli, who was already known for his efficient revenue administration, to consolidate his position further. He now declared himself as the Nawab of Bengal.

As Nawab of Bengal Murshid Quli became the first independent Nawab of Bengal. He shifted the capital from **Dhaka to Murshidabad**, proved to be a capable ruler and made Bengal a prosperous state.

Rationalisation of Land Revenue System In the field of revenue collection, the main challenge faced by Murshid Quli Khan was that the whole province had been allotted to the officers as jagirs in lieu of their salary. To rationalise revenue collection, he adopted two measures. Firstly, he resumed all the jagirs and converted them into **khalisa lands** (state lands) and gave the dispossessed officers fresh jagirs in the wild province of Orissa. Secondly, he replaced the Mughal jagirdari system with the system of **revenue farming** or **ijara** or **malzamini system**. This was a contract system under which ijaradars, i.e. contractors were granted contracts for collection of land revenue by taking security bonds from them. In choosing the ijaradars, Quli Khan is known to have preferred the Hindus. The second or third generation of these contractors came to be known as 'the zamindars'.

Rise of new powerful elite classes under Murshid Quli Thus, under Murshid Quli, the old hereditary zamindars were largely extinguished and a new official capitalist class emerged. In this way, he created a **new class of landed aristocracy** in Bengal whose position was later confirmed by Permanent Settlement in 1793. Further, Quli Khan was able to raise revenue collection by paying attention to details. But at the same time, in matters of revenue collection, he was uncompromising to the extent of being ruthless. The system of revenue farming also increased pressure on zamindars and peasants, leading to the growing importance of monied and commercial elements. The relentless pressure on zamindars to pay their obligations in full opened up opportunities for financiers. This period saw the emergence of the **House of the Jagat Seths** who not only acted as guarantor of the larger zamindars but also assumed full responsibility of the remittance of the Bengal revenue to Delhi, thus enjoying unstinted patronage of the Nawab.

After 1717, Bengal's link with Delhi remained limited to sending tribute. Indeed, the Bengal revenue was often the only regular income for the beleaguered Mughal emperors during periods of financial uncertainty. Behind the veneer of formal allegiance to the Mughal ruler, Murshid Quli began to enjoy considerable autonomy and **established a dynastic rule**, ensuring that the Nizamat of the province would pass on to a member of his family and not to an outsider. He was indeed the last governor of Bengal appointed by the Mughal emperor.

Shuja-ud-Din Muhammad Khan (1727–39)

Murshid Quli named his daughter's son Sarfaraz Khan his successor. But Sarfaraz was ousted by his father **Shuja-ud-Din Muhammad Khan**, who took control of the two provinces of Bengal and Orissa in 1727. In this way, Murshid Quli's son-in-law Shuja-ud-Din ruled Bengal from 1727 till 1739.

Sarfaraz Khan or Ala-ud-Din Haidar Jung (1739–40)

After Shujauddin's death in 1739, his son Sarfaraz Khan became the Nawab. But Sarfaraz was soon deposed and killed by Alivardi Khan, the Deputy governor of Bihar, in the **Battle of Gheria** (10 April 1740).

Alivardi Khan (1740–56)

After emerging victorious in the Battle of Gheria, Alivardi Khan made himself the Nawab with the help of the banking family of Jagat Seth and a few powerful zamindars. His reign showed a virtual break with the Mughals, two important forms of imperial control over province, i.e. payment of annual tribute to the emperor and appointment of higher provincial officials by the emperor—were not visible during Alivardi's reign. However, like the Nizam of Hyderabad and Nawab Wazirs of Awadh, Alivardi Khan also kept alive the fiction of Mughal sovereignty.

External Threats faced by Alivardi Khan Alivardi faced two strong external threats during his regime—one from the Marathas and the other from the Afghan rebels. In fact, Alivardi's rule of 15 years was spent in fighting the Maratha menace which had assumed alarming proportions during this period. Driven by the dream of a Maratha Empire and the desire for wealth, the Marathas attacked Bengal three to four times during 1742 to 1751. In 1751, Alivardi finally signed peace with the Marathas; he agreed to pay annual **chauth** and parted with **Orissa** on the condition that the Marathas will not enter Alivardi's territory in future. Alivardi faced another formidable challenge from the Afghan General, **Mustafa khan**. These prolonged wars that Alivardi had to fight against the Marathas and the Afghans put severe strain on the Bengal government.

In 1756, Alivardi died, nominating his grandson Siraj-ud-Daulah as his successor.

Murshid Quli Khan and Alivardi Khan

- **Strengths** Both were men of exceptional quality and were fiercely independent. They gave Bengal a long period of peace and orderly administration. The Bengal rulers established regular thanas and chowkies and did not discriminate on religious grounds in making public appointments. They promoted its trade and industry and at the same time maintained strict control over foreign companies trading in their realm. They checked private trade by officials and prevented abuses in customs administration. Alivardi Khan rightly did not allow fortifications of French and English factories at Chandernagore and Calcutta.
- **Weakness** However, the Bengal Nawabs proved to be short sighted and ignorant in one aspect. They failed to see that the English Company was not merely a company of traders, but representative of the most aggressive colonial force of the time. Their lack of contact with the rest of the world was to prove them dear, or else they would have known how these European trading companies devoured Africa, South-East Asia and Latin America.

Bengal in 18th Century: Towards Political Subjection

Siraj ud-Daulah (1756–57)

Siraj's succession was challenged by two other contenders for the throne, Shaukat Jung (Faujdar of Purnea) and Ghaseti Begum (Alivardi's daughter). This resulted in intense court factionalism and support was offered to different warring groups by a dominant group in the Nawab's court comprising of **Jagat Seth, Umichand (or Amir Chand), Raj Ballabh, Rai Durlabh, Mir Jafar**, zamindars and others who were also opposed to Siraj. This seriously destabilised the administration of Bengal and the advantage was taken by English East India Company.

Conflict with East India Company Though the Farman of 1717 had become a perpetual source of conflict between the Company and the Bengal Nawabs, the breaking point came when the English Company, anticipating another round of Anglo–French struggle, began to strengthen the **fortifications of Fort William** and mounted guns on its walls. The Bengal Nawabs had objected to these fortifications time and again, but the conflict became particularly acrimonious during Siraj's reign and led to a military conflict.

The disaffected nobles of Siraj's court, particularly the Jagat Seths, Rai Durlabh, Amir Chand (or Umichand) joined hands with the English to oust Siraj and install their protégé, leading to the **Plassey Conspiracy of 1757**. More than the might of the English, it was the treachery of the Nawab's confidants that decided the fate of the battle of Plassey where the British victory ended the rule of Siraj and inaugurated a new phase of Company's rule and British relations with India.[2]

Awadh

The subah of Awadh was strategically situated between the north bank of the Ganges and the Himalayas. It extended **from Kannauj district in the west to the river Karmnasa in the East**. It comprised Benaras and some districts near Allahabad.

[2] Read about the British conquest of Bengal in detail in the upcoming chapters.

Its proximity to Delhi added to its importance. Awadh was also economically prosperous in the 18th century and enjoyed flourishing agriculture and trade. The rise of Awadh as an autonomous state was the result of political pursuit by the Irani and Shiite family of Burhan-ul-Mulk Saadat Khan.

Saadat Khan (1722–39)

Saadat Khan was the founder of independent kingdom of Awadh. He was a very bold and intelligent person. In 1722, he was appointed Governor of Awadh by the Mughal Emperor. He was given the difficult charge of subduing rebellious zamindars who had sprung up everywhere in the province. They had refused to pay land tax and behaved like autonomous chiefs with their forts and armies. He was successful in this task within a year and in appreciation, the Emperor Muhammad Shah conferred on him the title of **Burhan-ul-Mulk**.

Illustration of an elephant in the state of Awadh

Soon afterwards, he returned to Delhi but ended up in a quarrel with one of the emperor's favourites and was forced to return to Awadh. Frustrated with court politics, he decided to build up a power base in Awadh. As a first step, he got his nephew and **son-in-law Safdar Jung** recognised by the emperor as his deputy governor. In this way, he made the province a hereditary possession and gradually secured the independence of Awadh.

In 1723, Saadat Khan introduced a new land revenue settlement and improved the lot of the peasants by levying equitable land revenue. Like the Bengal Nawabs, he too did not discriminate between the Hindus and the Muslims. His troops were well trained and well paid. His administration was efficient.

By 1735, Saadat Khan extended his influence to the adjoining regions of **Kora, Jahanabad, Banaras, Jaunpur, Ghazipur and Chunargarh**. During this entire period, he kept the communication channels open with the imperial court.

In 1739, Saadat Khan was called to Delhi to assist the Mughal Empire in fighting against the invader, Nadir Shah. However, he was taken prisoner in the **Battle of Karnal**. He felt further frustrated when the position of Mir Bakshi went to the Nizam despite his support during the invasion. He considered this a betrayal and in vengeance changed sides and joined Nadir Shah. His dirty game recoiled on him when the invader demanded a sum of ₹20 crore promised to him. In sheer frustration, Saadat Khan poisoned himself to death, thus committing **suicide** the day after the occupation of Delhi.

Safdar Jung or Abul Mansur Khan (1739–54)

Nadir Shah remained the emperor of India for just two months. He recognised Safdar Jung as the successor of Awadh by accepting ₹2 crore as peshkash. Jung's opportunity really came when both Muhammad Shah and Nizam-ul-Mulk died in 1748 and he was appointed **wazir** by the new emperor Ahmad Shah. He and his successors popularly came to be known as **Nawab Wazirs**. He was also granted the **province of Allahabad**.

He gave a long period of peace and stability to the people of Awadh and Allahabad before his death in 1754. He also suppressed rebellious zamindars and made an alliance with the Maratha sardars to save his province form Maratha incursions. He set up an equitable justice system. He too did not discriminate on religious grounds. The highest post in his government was held by a Hindu-Maharaja **Nawab Rai**.

Safdar Jung maintained a very high standard of personal morality. In fact, all the founders of the three autonomous states—Hyderabad, Bengal and Awadh—were men of high personal morality. They led austere and simple lives.

Shuja-ud-Daula (1754–75)

After Safdar Jung's Death in 1754, his son Shuja-ud-Daula (not to be confused with Shuja-ud-din of Bengal) was appointed the governor of Awadh.

Role in Third Battle of Panipat (1761) When Afghan invader Ahmad Shah Abdali arrived again in India in 1761 and fought the Third **Battle of Panipat** against the Marathas, Shuja joined the Afghan invader to see his opponents, the Marathas, humbled and weakened. Within his own domain of Awadh and Allahabad his autonomy and power remained unchallenged till his encounter with the English East India Company in the Battle of Buxar.

Role in Battle of Buxar (1764) In the Battle of Buxar, the combined forces of the Nawab of Bengal, Shuja-ud-Daula (Nawab of Awadh) and the Mughal Emperor were defeated by the English Company and Awadh was brought into the British dragnet by the **Treaty of Allahabad** (16 August 1765). As per the Treaty, among other things, Shuja was required to pay war indemnity of ₹50 lakh and enter into a reciprocal arrangement with the Company for defence of each other's territory. In the following years, seeing the prosperity of Awadh, the company gradually stepped up its fiscal demands by yet another treaty in 1773; the Nawab agreed to pay ₹2,10,000 monthly for each brigade of company troops that would remain present in Awadh. This led to Awadh's chronic indebtedness to the Company. The military presence of English troops in Awadh also seriously undermined the Nawabi regime.

Asaf-ud-Daula (1775–97)

After the death of Shuja-ud-Daulah in 1775, his son Asaf-ud-Daula became the Nawab. In 1775 itself, he shifted the capital from **Faizabad to Lucknow**. Despite English threat, he concentrated his energies in cultural pursuits and built up around Lucknow court a vibrant cultural arena, giving rise to a distinct **Lucknow culture**. Lucknow soon rivalled Delhi in its patronage of arts and literature. It became a second home for sensitive men of letters who had left Delhi and lamented for the world they had lost. These luminaries and poets included **Mirza Rafi Sauda** and **Mir Ghulam Hasan**. He also built the famous monument **Bara Imambara**. The Nawab also earned a lot of fame for his generosity and gave rise to a well-known saying in Lucknow, 'he who does not receive from the Lord, will receive it from Asaf-ud-Daula' (Jisko na de Moula, usko de Asaf-ud-Daula).

Till 1801, the English saw Awadh as a buffer state protecting Bengal against the western powers notably the Marathas and they did not contemplate annexation. Soon afterwards, Awadh became an obstacle to further British expansion and was finally taken over in 1856.[3]

[3]Read about the British Conquest of Awadh in greater detail in the upcoming chapters.

Prelim Capsule

Hyderabad, Carnatic, Bengal and Awadh

Regional Power	Nawabs	Important Events
Hyderabad (1724)	**Nizam-ul-Mulk Asaf Jah (1724–48)**	In 1713, Chin Qilich Khan was made Viceroy of the Deccan by Emperor Farrukhsiyar and given the title of **Nizam-ul-Mulk**. In 1720, he assisted Mohammed Shah in killing the Sayyid brothers. In 1722, he was appointed wazir in the court of Mohammad Shah. In 1724, he founded the independent state of Hyderabad in the Deccan. He founded the **Asaf Jah dynasty**. His successors came to be known as the **Nizams of Hyderabad.**
Carnatic (Early 18th century)	**Nawab Saadatullah Khan (1710–32)**	He appointed his nephew **Dost Ali** as his successor. In 1740, the Marathas invaded the Carnatic, killed Nawab Dost Ali and took his son-in-law **Chanda Sahib** as prisoner to Satara.
Bengal (1717)	**Murshid Quli Khan (1717–27)**	In 1717, he became the first to hold the two offices of Nizam and Diwan of Bengal simultaneously. Using this opportunity, he now declared himself as the Nawab of Bengal. He shifted the capital from **Dhaka to Murshidabad.** He replaced the Mughal jagirdari system with the system of **revenue farming** or **ijara** or **malzamini system**. His reign saw the rise of new elite classes (zamindars and the bankers) in Bengal. For e.g., The **House of the Jagat Seths.**
	Alivardi Khan (1740–56)	He killed Sarfaraz Khan in the **Battle of Gheria** and became the Nawab. During his reign, payment of annual tribute to the emperor stopped. He agreed to pay chauth and ceded Orissa to the Marathas. He faced challenge from the Afghan General, **Mustafa khan**.
	Siraj ud-Daulah (1756–57)	He was defeated by the EIC in the **Battle of Plassey** (1757).
Awadh (1722)	**Saadat Khan (1722–39)**	He subdued the rebellious zamindars of Awadh and was given the title of Burhan-ul-Mulk by the emperor. He got his nephew and son-in-law **Safdar Jung** recognised by the emperor as his deputy governor and made the province a hereditary possession. He was taken prisoner by Nadir Shah in the **Battle of Karnal** (1739).
	Safdar Jung (1739–54)	He and his successors popularly came to be known as **Nawab Wazirs**.

	Shuja-ud-Daula (1754–75)	He joined Abdali against the Marathas in the **Third Battle of Panipat** (1761). He was defeated by the EIC in the **Battle of Buxar** (1764).
	Asaf-ud-Daula (1775–97)	He shifted the capital from **Faizabad to Lucknow**. He concentrated his energies in cultural pursuits, giving rise to a distinct **Lucknow culture**. He also built the famous monument **Bara Imambara**.

New States – The Marathas, Sikhs, Jats and Afghans

The Marathas

Flag of the Maratha Empire

Historical Context The Maratha kingdom was constituted in the 17th century in western Deccan. In the 18th century, it became the nucleus of the much wider Maratha swarajya (sovereign state). The Marathas were the most significant of all the regional powers. The first part of the 18th century saw the decline of the Mughals, the last part saw the rise of the British and the middle part saw the swaying political fortunes of the Marathas, the lone Indian power that was strong enough to offer an alternative to the Mughal rule.

After the Mughals retreated from the Deccan, the Marathas grew as a confederacy of military leaders called Maratha sardars. Originally, the Maratha sardars only held temporary assignments of land revenue. But in practice, they tended to become hereditary once they established themselves. But the Maratha sardars lacked unity and vision for founding an all India empire. However, they successfully waged continuous struggle against the Mughals till they were destroyed.

Chhatrapati Shivaji Maharaj, the founder of the Maratha Empire

Relationship with Mughals Marathas had a long history of suppression by the Mughals, particularly during the **27-year war** started by Aurangzeb in 1681. The Marathas believed in Hinduism and the religious intolerance practiced by the Mughal emperors further provoked the Maratha resentment.

In 1689 Aurangzeb defeated and killed Shivaji's son and successor Sambhaji and captured Sambhaji's son Shahu. Aurangzeb had treated Shahu and his mother with great dignity hoping to arrive at a political agreement with Shahu. However, the whole Maratha nation rose in arms against the Mughals in what was to become a people's war. The younger son of Shivaji, Raja Ram carried on the struggle till his death in 1700 and thereafter the struggle was carried on further by his wife Tarabai, acting as a regent for his minor son Shivaji II. In 1707 after Aurangzeb's death, his successors released Shivaji's grandson Shahu in the hope of throwing an apple of discord in Maharashtra.

As expected by the Mughals, Shahu's release divided the Marathas into two rival camps—one led by Tarabai at Kolhapur and the other led by Shahu at Satara. Tarabai, Shahu's aunt, declared Shahu as an imposter and refused to recognise Shahu's right to succession. The consequence was **a long civil war** in which Shahu ultimately emerged victorious mainly with the help of a group of new independent sardars and an able Chitpavan Brahmin from Konkan, Balaji Vishwanath.

In this way, the civil war between Shahu and Tarabai gave rise to a new system of Maratha government under the leadership of Balaji Vishwanath, the Peshwa (Prime Minister) of King Shahu. This change marked the beginning of the second period in Maratha history—**the period of Peshwa domination**. It was in this period that the Maratha state transformed into an empire. The Marathas mainly relied on the political mechanism of '**fitna**' (using existing political grievances to cause civil strife as opposed to using pure military operations) to penetrate the Mughal Empire.

Peshwa Balaji Vishwanath (1713–20)

In recognition of the services rendered by Balaji Vishwanath, King Shahu appointed him as the Peshwa or Prime Minister in November 1713. By virtue of his diplomacy and statesmanship, Balaji Vishwanath turned the office of the Peshwa as the functional head of the Maratha Empire while Raja Shahu became a mere figurehead.

Help to Sayyid Brothers In 1719, Balaji helped the Sayyid brothers remove Farrukhsiyar from the Mughal throne and place a puppet emperor in Delhi. He had himself gone to Delhi with a Maratha contingent of 15,000 troops. This gave him the opportunity to witness firsthand the weakness of the Empire and filled him with ambition of expansion in the North. Moreover, as a reward, he secured for the Maratha king a Mughal sanad (imperial order).

Mughal Sanad of 1719 As per the Sanad, the Marathas were allowed to collect chauth (literally: one-fourth of revenues) and sardeshmukhi (an additional 10% of revenues) from the entire Deccan (Aurangabad, Berar, Bidar, Bijapur, Hyderabad and Khandesh) and Karnataka. In return for the above privileges, the Marathas were to place at the Emperor's disposal a contingent of 15,000 troops, maintain peace and order in the Deccan and pay an annual tribute of ₹10 lakh to the emperor. In this way, the Maratha king became the **sardeshmukh of the entire Deccan** and Karnataka. The sanad is also known in history as 'the **Magna Carta** of the Maratha dominion'.

Foundation of Maratha Confederacy For the efficient collection of chauth and sardeshmukhi of the Deccan, Balaji Vishwanath assigned separate areas to Maratha sardars, thus laying the foundation of the Maratha Confederacy. This system of **watans** and **saranjams** (grants of land) was just another form of Jagir system which Balaji found as best suited to bring peace from anarchy at that time. However, it later turned into a major Maratha weakness as it made the King largely dependent on the sardars for his finances. The sardars now began to establish their control in distant lands of Mughal Empire where they gradually settled down as more or less autonomous chiefs. In this way, the conquests of the Marathas outside their original kingdom were not made directly by the Maratha king or the Peshwa, but by the sardars with their own private parties. During these conquests, they often clashed with one another and did not hesitate to join hands with the enemies, be they the Nizams, the Mughals or the English.

Balaji Vishwanath has been rightly called '**the second founder of the Maratha State'.** He emerged as first of a series of hereditary Peshwas who now gained effective control of the Maratha Empire. After his death in April 1720, he was succeeded by his 19-year-old son Baji Rao I.

Peshwa Baji Rao I (1720–40)

Balaji Vishwanath was succeeded by his eldest son, Baji Rao I as the Peshwa in April 1720. In spite of his youth, he was a bold commander and a wise statesman and has been called '**the greatest exponent of guerilla tactics after Shivaji**'.

Maratha Expansion under Baji Rao I

- He formulated a new policy of Maratha imperialism which aimed at expanding the Maratha kingdom beyond the Narmada. He proposed his policy of conquest of the north in the following words: 'Let us strike at the trunk of the withering tree (Mughal Empire) and the branches will fall off themselves. Thus, should the Maratha flag fly from the Krishna to the Indus'. He preached the ideal of '**Hindu Pad Padshahi',** i.e. 'Hindu Empire' to secure the support of Hindu chiefs against the Mughals.
- All the 20 years of his Peshwaship, Baji Rao kept marching and winning battles. Under his leadership, the Marathas won control over Malwa, Gujarat and parts of Bundelkhand. He is remembered in Maharashtra as the **fighting Peshwa**. It was he who picked up war leaders like the Scindias and the Holkars who rose into prominence during this time.
- Baji Rao faced severe challenge from the Nizam-ul-Mulk in the Deccan. Twice the two met in the battlefield and both times the Nizam was defeated and compelled to grant the Marathas the chauth and sardeshmukhi of the **six Mughal provinces in the Deccan**.
- In 1733, Baji Rao launched a campaign against **the Sidis of Janjira Island** and in the end expelled them from the mainland. Simultaneously, he also started a campaign against the Portuguese. In the end, Salsette and Bassein were captured.
- Baji Rao also transformed the kingdom of Maharashtra into an empire expanding in the north. It was his forward policy which brought the provinces from **Punjab to Bengal** under Maratha influence by 1760.

However, strong foundation for the empire could not be laid and little attention was paid to the administration of new territories. This was because the interest of the new sardars remained limited to revenue collection. Baji Rao made no attempt to check the dangerous feudal tendency which in the end proved ruinous to the Maratha Kingdom. In 1740, Baji Rao met a premature death at the age of 40.

Peshwa Balaji Bajirao (1740–61)

Bajirao's 19-year-old son Balaji Bajirao also known as **Nana Sahib**, was the Peshwa from 1740 to 1761. After the death of Chhatrapati Shahu in 1749, Nana Sahib became the supreme authority in Maratha polity. Shahu's successor Raja Ram executed a document known as the **Sangola Agreement** (also known as constitutional revolution of 1750) which transferred the supreme power from the Chhatrapati to the Peshwa. Henceforth, the Peshwa became the de facto ruler of the Maratha State, and as a symbol of this fact, shifted the government to Poona, his headquarters.

Balaji Bajirao's rule also witnessed the appearance of new powers in the political scene, namely the Afghans, the Sikhs, the French and the English.

Maratha Expansion under Balaji Bajirao

- The Maratha power achieved its **territorial zenith** during the rule of Peshwa Balaji Baji Rao, extending from **Cuttack to Attock**. The Maratha armies now overran the whole of India.
- In the east, Marathas under Raghuji Bhonsle regularly raided Bengal, Bihar and Orissa (then ruled by Alivardi Khan). The raids were stopped after a treaty in 1751, under which Alivardi surrendered Orissa and agreed to pay ₹1,20,000 as annual chauth for the three provinces.

- In the south, states including the state of Mysore were forced to pay tribute.
- In the north, the Maratha bands regularly raided the Rajput kingdoms of Jaipur, Udaipur, Bundi, Kotah, etc. Soon they also became the power behind the Mughal throne. In the face of Afghan invasion, a treaty in 1752 brought the Mughal emperor under Maratha protection. In 1752, the Marathas helped Imad-ul-Mulk to become the new wazir and in 1753, they installed their chosen candidate on the Mughal throne.

Conflict with Abdali The Marathas were not content with their victories in the north and looked greedily at Punjab, which was ruled by an agent of Abdali. This was a blunder. Abdali had retreated from India taking away whatever he could. But now he decided to return and challenge the ever-growing ambitions of the Marathas.

Abdali formed an alliance with Najib-ud-Daulah of Rohilkhand and Shuja-ud-Daulah of Awadh, both of whom had suffered in the face of Maratha depredations. Seeing the importance of the coming struggle, the Peshwa dispatched an army to the north under the nominal command of his minor son Vishwas Rao. But the actual command was in the hands of Peshwa's cousin **Sadashiv Rao Bhau** (son of Chimaji Appa, younger brother of Peshwa Baji Rao I). Thus Bhau was the commander-in-chief of the Maratha forces. The army also had a contingent of European style infantry and artillery commanded by **Ibrahim Khan Gardi**.

The Marathas now also tried to find support from northern powers. But their earlier behaviour had antagonised all such powers. For instance, they had imposed heavy fines and tributes upon the Rajputana, Punjab and Awadh. Therefore they had to fight their enemy all alone, except for the weak support of Imad-ul-Mulk.

Third Battle of Panipat (14 January 1761) The forces of Abdali and the Marathas met at Panipat on 14 January 1761. The Maratha army was completely routed, causing over 40,000 casualties. This marked the beginning of the decline of the Maratha glory. Both Vishwas Rao and Sadashiv Rao Bhau perished along with many other Maratha commanders and 28,000 soldiers. Those who fled were chased by the Afghan cavalry and robbed by the Jats, Ahirs and Gujars of Panipat region. The Peshwa got the news while he was on his way to the north to help his cousin. Shocked by the tragic news, he met with an early death in June 1761. In this way, Ahmad Shah gave a death blow to the Maratha glory.

Neither the Marathas nor the Afghans benefitted from this battle. The beneficiaries were the British who grasped this opportunity to expand influence in Bengal. In reality, the Third Battle of Panipat did not decide who would rule India, but rather who would not. It, therefore, cleared the way for the rise of British power in India... 'If Plassey had sown the seeds of British supremacy in India, Panipat afforded time for their maturing and striking roots'.

After this there was no looking back. In 1772, Peshwa Madhav Rao I died and followed a factional struggle for power. This exposed the Marathas to defeat at the hands of the British in the first Anglo-Maratha war.[4]

Causes of Maratha Defeat in Third Battle of Panipat

- Abdali's forces enjoyed both numeric and qualitative superiority.
- While Abdali's army was estimated at 60,000; the Maratha army was estimated at 45,000. The Marathas were also accompanied by several non-combatants (around 2 lakh as per an estimate) that virtually turned the Maratha forces into a slow moving caravan, hampering swift movement of the forces. The Marathas had to play the dual role of fighting the war and protecting these

[4]Read about the Anglo-Maratha Wars in detail in the upcoming chapters.

civilians who were like sitting ducks before the Afghans. When these civilians were slaughtered in cold blood, it further pulled down Maratha morale.

- Abdali's forces were better organised and better equipped. While Abdali's men fought with muskets (light gun with a long barrel) and swivel guns (small cannon mounted on a swivelling stand), the Maratha forces mostly fought with their swords and lances.
- The Marathas fought alone without any support. Their overbearing attitude and policy of indiscriminate plunder had estranged the Muslims and the Hindu chiefs alike, such as the Jats, the Rajputs and the Sikhs. On the other hand, the Muslim powers of North India rallied behind Abdali.
- Near famine conditions prevailed in the Maratha camp as the road to Delhi was cut-off by the Afghan war. The Maratha camp turned into a virtual hell owing to the stench of carcasses lying around unburied.
- Mutual jealousies infested the Maratha leadership which also considerably weakened their position. Bhau took pride in his Brahmin birth and looked down upon Malhar Rao Holkar.

Significance of Third Battle of Panipat

- Neither side benefitted from this battle.
- It produced disastrous consequences for the Marathas and seriously deflected the course of Maratha imperialism.
- The Marathas suffered immense losses in terms of men, money and prestige. The Marathas lost the cream of their army and their political prestige suffered a big blow.
- The Marathas could never recover their pre-1761 position or status. Their defeat gave an opportunity to the British East India Company to consolidate its power in Bengal and south India.
- Afghans too did not benefit from their victory. They could not even hold the Punjab.

Peshwa Madhav Rao I (1761–72)

The 17-year-old Madhav Rao became the Peshwa in 1761. He was a talented statesman and within a short period of 11 years, he restored the lost fortunes of the Maratha Empire, a phenomenon known as **Maratha Resurrection**, with the help of his able minister, **Nana Phadnavis** (abbreviated as Nana Phadnis). Nana Phadnis played a pivotal role in holding the Maratha Confederacy together in the midst of internal dissension and the growing power of the English Company.

Madhav Rao successfully subdued the old enemies, the Rohillas, the Rajputs and the Jat Chiefs in the north and Mysore and Hyderabad in the south. In 1771, the Marathas brought back Emperor Shah Alam II to Delhi, who now became their pensioner. Thus it appeared as if Maratha ascendency in the north had been recovered. However, Madhav Rao died of tuberculosis in 1772.

Peshwa Narayan Rao (1772–73)

After the death of Madhav Rao, the Maratha Empire was thrown into a state of confusion. At Poona there was a struggle for power between Raghunath Rao (younger brother of Balaji Bajirao) and Narayan Rao (younger brother of Madhav Rao). Narayan Rao succumbed to the intrigues of his uncle Raghunath Rao in 1773.

Peshwa Raghunath Rao (1773–74)

He became the Peshwa of the Maratha Empire for a brief period from 1773 to 1774. He was deposed by Nana Phadnis and 11 other administrators (Baarbhai) in what is known as **'the Baarbhai Conspiracy'**. The Baarbhai included influential Maratha sardars like **Mahadji Shinde** (or Scindia) and Tukojirao Holkar.

Mahadji Shinde (or Scindia, 1768–94) Mahadji was a Maratha Sardar who ruled over the Gwalior state in central India. He was instrumental in resurrecting Maratha power in north India after the Third Battle of Panipat in 1761. Along with Madhav Rao I and Nana Phadnavis, he was one of the three pillars of Maratha Resurrection.

Mahadji Shinde

During his reign, Gwalior became the leading state in the Maratha Empire and one of the foremost military powers in India. He started recruiting some Rajputs and even Muslims in the army. He reorganised his army along European and scientific lines. For this reason, he also appointed a Savoy resident, Count **Benoit de Boigne** (from the Duchy of Savoy in Italy, but under French occupation during 1792–1814) and later on **Monsieur Perron**, as specialists.

The Marathas under Mahadji returned to northern India, overrunning the Rajputana, defeating the Jats and expelling the Rohillas from the Doab and captured Delhi (February 1771) and reinstated Shah Alam II at Delhi throne under Maratha suzerainty. During 1772–73, he along with the Mughal Emperor, led expeditions against the Rohillas and even destroyed the power of the Jats of Mathura.

During the First Anglo-Maratha War (1775–82), Mahadji played the most important role from the Maratha side since he humbled the British in Central India single-handedly, which resulted in the Treaty of Salbai in 1782. In the Treaty of Salbai, British government accepted him as an independent king. After his death, he was succeeded by Daulat Rao Scindia.

Peshwa Sawai Madhav Rao or Madhav Rao II (1774–95)

The Baarbhai installed Narayan Rao's posthumous son, Madhav Rao II, as the Peshwa with themselves, led by Nana Phadnavis, as the Regents (known as Baarbhai Council). Madhav Rao II was made Peshwa when he was barely 40 days old; his time in power was dominated by the political intrigues of Nana Phadnis. The succession of Sawai Madhav Rao (Sawai means 'One and a Quarter') gravely frustrated Raghunath Rao's ambitions and he turned to the British and tried to capture power with their help, resulting in the **First Anglo–Maratha war.**

The Peshwa's power now gradually waned. Poona became the seat of constant intrigues between the supporters of Sawai Madhav Rao, headed by Nana Phadnis and the supporters of Raghunath Rao. Taking advantage of the weakening of central authority, the big Maratha sardars or chiefs carved out semi-independent states in the north. These were the-**Holkar (Indore), Scindia (Gwalior), Gaekwad (Baroda) and Bhonsle (Nagpur).** They possessed their own armies and their allegiance to the Peshwas became more and more nominal. Among the Maratha sardars in the north, **Mahadji Shinde** was the most important. He organised a powerful European style army with the help of French and Portuguese officers, consisting equally of Hindu and Muslim soldiers.

Sawai Madhav Rao committed suicide in 1795 probably because of the high-handedness of Nana Phadnis. A power struggle ensued among the Maratha nobles for control of the Confederacy. The powerful chief, Daulat Rao Scindia, and minister, Nana Phadnis, installed Baji Rao II, son of Raghunath Rao, as a puppet Peshwa.

Peshwa Baji Rao II (1796–1818)

Baji Rao II was the last Peshwa of the Maratha Empire. By now, the British had decided to put an end to the Maratha challenge. The British divided the warring sardars through clever diplomacy and then defeated them in separate battles in the Second Maratha War (1803–05) and Third Maratha War (1817–18). The **seat of the Peshwa was extinguished** while the Maratha states were allowed to exist as subsidiary states.

First Reign (1796–1802) First reign of Baji Rao II saw the Second Anglo–Maratha War (1803–05). After the death of Nana Phadnavis (March 1800), the Poona court once again fell victim to various court conspiracies. In the struggle for power in Maratha polity, Peshwa Baji Rao II, Daulat Rao Scindia and Yashwant Rao Holkar emerged as the main Maratha leaders. Peshwa and Scindia formed an alliance against Holkar and tried to insult him. In 1801, Peshwa brutally killed Holkar's brother **Vithoji Rao Holkar** (also known as Vithoba). This made Holkar attack Poona (battle of Poona), who then defeated the combined armies of Peshwa and Scindia near Hadapsar and captured Poona. Peshwa fled, took refuge in Bassein and approached Wellesley for help. This provided the British an ideal opportunity to intervene in the Maratha affairs. Baji Rao II accepted subsidiary alliance and signed the Treaty of Bassein in 1802. This affected the patriotic feelings of other Maratha chiefs and provoked the Second Anglo–Maratha War that began the breakup of the Maratha confederacy.

Second Reign (1803–18) During his second reign began the Third Anglo–Maratha War. On 3 June 1818, Peshwa surrendered before the British. He was dethroned and pensioned off and ordered to spend his last days in **Bithoor** near Kanpur.

> **Nana Sahib (Peshwa)** He was a leader during the Revolt of 1857. As the adopted son of the exiled Maratha Peshwa Baji Rao II, he sought to restore the Maratha confederacy and the Peshwa tradition.

In this way, the Maratha dream of establishing their own empire could not be realised. This was mainly because the Maratha Empire represented the same decadent social order as the Mughal Empire did and suffered from the same weaknesses. Their revenue system and administration were quite similar. The Marathas did not try to develop a new economy, nor did they encourage science and technology or trade and industry. Like the Mughals, their dominion depended on force and force alone. They failed to establish a bond with the common people and their interest remained limited to squeezing out revenue from the helpless peasantry. Nearly half of the agricultural produce was collected as tax. Thus, the Marathas failed to transform themselves into a modern state, and made way for the rise of the British.[5]

Prelim Capsule

The Marathas

Peshwas	Important Events
Peshwa Balaji Vishwanath (1713–20)	He supported Shahu against Tara Bai in the Maratha civil war; in return, Shahu appointed him as his Peshwa (Prime Minister). He launched the **period of Peshwa domination** during which the Maratha state transformed into an empire. In 1719, Balaji helped the Sayyid brothers remove Farrukhsiyar. As reward, he secured the **Mughal sanad of 1719**, known in history as 'the Magna Carta of the Maratha dominion'. The Maratha king became the sardeshmukh of the entire Deccan and Karnataka. He laid the foundation of the Maratha Confederacy. He is known as '**the second founder of the Maratha State**'.

[5]Read about the British Conquest of the Maratha state in greater detail in the upcoming chapters.

Peshwa Baji Rao I (1720–40)	He preached the ideal of '**Hindu pad-padshahi**'. He is remembered in Maharashtra as the **fighting Peshwa**. In 1733, he defeated **the Sidis of Janjira Island**.
Peshwa Balaji Bajirao (1740–61)	He was also known as **Nana Sahib.** It was during his reign that Raja Ram executed the **Sangola Agreement** (also known as constitutional revolution of 1750) which transferred the supreme power from the Chhatrapati to the Peshwa. Maratha power reached its **territorial zenith.** Marathas were defeated by Abdali in the **Third Battle of Panipat** (1761). The Marathas fought under the nominal command of his minor son Vishwas Rao, but the actual command was in the hands of Peshwa's cousin **Sadashiv Rao Bhau.** Maratha army had a contingent of European style infantry and artillery commanded by **Ibrahim Khan Gardi**.
Peshwa Madhav Rao I (1761–72)	He restored the lost fortunes of the Maratha Empire, a phenomenon known as Maratha Resurrection, with the help of his able minister, **Nana Phadnavis.** In 1771, the Marathas re-installed Emperor Shah Alam II to Delhi.
Peshwa Narayan Rao (1772–73)	He succumbed to the intrigues of his uncle, Raghunath Rao.
Peshwa Raghunath Rao (1773–74)	He was deposed by Nana Phadnis and 11 other administrators (Baarbhai) in what is known as '**the Baarbhai Conspiracy**'. Baarbhai included influential sardars like **Mahadji Shinde** and Tukojirao Holkar.
Peshwa Sawai Madhav Rao (1774–95)	His succession frustrated Raghunath Rao who now went over to the British and tried to capture power with their help, resulting in the **First Anglo-Maratha war.** Taking advantage of the weakening of central authority, the big Maratha sardars carved out semi-independent states: **Holkar (Indore), Scindia (Gwalior), Gaekwad (Baroda) and Bhonsle (Nagpur).** In 1795 Sawai Madhav Rao committed suicide.
Peshwa Baji Rao II (1796–18)	The British divided the warring sardars and then defeated them in separate battles in the Second Maratha War (1803–05) and Third Maratha War (1817–18). The **seat of the Peshwa was extinguished**. In 1818 Peshwa was dethroned by the EIC and pensioned off and ordered to spend his last days in **Bithoor** near Kanpur.

The Sikhs

Guru Nanak Dev

The development in the Punjab, former **Mughal province of Lahore**, was somewhat different as compared to other Mughal provinces. In other Mughal provinces, it was some Mughal provincial governor who established an autonomous state. But in the case of Punjab, it was a group of local people, the Sikhs.

Sikhism Sikhism was founded by **Guru Nanak** in the Punjab region in the 15th century. The Sikh Panth was as old as the Mughal Empire. When Guru Nanak began to preach his message of devotion and equality in Punjab in the 15th century, Babur was founding the Mughal Empire. 'Sikh' literally means **learner or disciple**. In the course of time, the new cult took the form of a religious movement and spread quickly among the Jat peasantry and other lower castes in Punjab. Guru Nanak's religious movement was peaceful and secular. Nanak was succeeded by nine Gurus; all the ten Sikh Gurus emphasised on simplicity of religion and freedom from bigotry.

1. **Guru Nanak**- founder of Sikhism.
2. **Guru Angad**- developed the Gurumukhi script, introduced the **langar** (free kitchen) and tradition of mall akhara for the youth.
3. **Guru Amar Das**- composed the Anand Sahib, introduced the simple **Anand Karaj** marriage and abolished sati among the Sikhs.
4. **Guru Ram Das**- laid the foundation of the holy city of **Amritsar** (earlier known as Ramdaspur and Guru-ka-Chak) and initiated the construction of the Golden Temple.
5. **Guru Arjan Dev**- compiled the Adi Granth and completed the construction of the Golden Temple (It was during Ranjit Singh's reign that the shrine of the temple was richly decorated with marble and gold plates and came to be known as the Golden Temple).
6. **Guru Hargobind**- created the **Sikh marital art** called Gatka, trained the Sikhs in military art and war tactics, built the Akal Takhat, and was known as the 'soldier saint'.
7. **Guru Har Rai**- he maintained the large army of Sikh soldiers that the sixth Sikh Guru had amassed, yet avoided military conflict, and was known as the 'tender-hearted guru'.
8. **Guru Har Krishan**- was the youngest of all gurus, installed as guru at the age of five.
9. **Guru Teg Bahadur**- he refused to convert to Islam and was beheaded in Delhi on the orders of Mughal Emperor Aurangzeb.
10. **Guru Gobind Singh**- transformed the Sikhs into a military force by establishing the body of the **Khalsa** in 1699.

Relationship with Mughals

The last four gurus were persecuted by the Mughals, Guru Arjan and Guru Teg Bahadur were tortured and brutally killed for refusing to convert to Islam. Subsequently, Sikhism militarised to oppose Mughal dominance. Aurangzeb was initially not very hostile to the Sikhs; but as the community grew in size and challenged the central authority of the Mughals, the emperor turned against them. Guru Tegh Bahadur was executed in Delhi in 1675 (however, the emergence of Sikh empire under Ranjit Singh was characterised by religious tolerance and pluralism).

Guru Gobind Singh (1666–1708)

He was installed as the Sikh guru at age nine, after his father, Guru Teg Bahadur, was beheaded by the Mughals for refusing to convert to Islam. Four of his sons were also killed during his lifetime, falling victim to Mughal–Sikh conflict.

Guru Gobind Singh, the tenth and last guru of the Sikhs transformed the Sikhs into a military force by establishing the body of **Khalsa in 1699**. Members were initiated into the body by the guru himself, who were obliged to show their allegiance by five signs including kesh (uncut hair) and kirpan (short sword). Perhaps the guru was now convinced about the need of armed resistance for the defence of the panth. It might have also been due to the rise of Jat peasantry among the Sikhs as carrying arms was already a part of Jat cultural tradition. The Khatri traders were another component of the Sikh community. Their aspiration for equality with the Jats was fulfilled when Guru Gobind Singh decided to end the guruship, the power of guru was henceforth to be vested in the panth and the granth.

Guru Gobind Singh's conflict with Aurangzeb is well known. From about 1696, Guru Gobind had tried to carve out an autonomous domain in and around **Anandpur**. In 1704, Anandpur was captured by the Mughals and the guru was compelled to leave. Guru Gobind was murdered in a conspiracy in 1708 and the leadership of Sikhs passed to his disciple, Banda Bahadur.

Banda Bahadur (1708–16)

Banda Singh or Banda Bairagi, more widely known as Banda Bahadur, waged a relentless though unequal struggle against Aurangzeb's successors for eight years. The Mughals tried to suppress the rebellion ruthlessly as Punjab was strategically crucial. In the course of time, the position of Banda Bahadur had weakened due to dissension within the Sikh community. Some of the Jat zamindars and Khatri revenue farmers went to the Mughal side (for instance, Churaman Jat of Agra). Banda Bahadur was captured and was put to death in 1716. Even this could not suppress the Sikhs who finally succeeded in establishing their political power in the Punjab.

Factors that contributed to the political supremacy of the Sikhs in the Punjab were as follows

- **The weakening of the Mughal imperial authority** in the early decades of the 18th century contributed to the rise of the Sikhs.
- **The series of Persian and Afghan invasions** from 1739 onwards seriously undermined the Mughal authority in the Punjab.
- **The Maratha incursions took place** in the wake of foreign invasions and added to political turmoil in the province. The Marathas also tried to establish control over the Punjab.
- **The ensuing internal struggle within provincial administration was another reason.** Zakariya Khan was the Mughal governor of Lahore during 1726–45. His death resulted in a fratricidal struggle among his three sons over the governorship of the Punjab.

All the above factors created a very fluid situation in Punjab in the 18th century, allowing the Sikhs to emerge supreme. The adversity of the Mughal Empire proved to be a beneficial opportunity for the Sikhs. The invasion of Nadir Shah and Abdali seriously undermined Mughal authority in the Punjab. The Afghans under the leadership of Abdali also crushed the Marathas in the **Third Battle of Panipat in 1761**. In this way, the defeat of the Mughals and the Marathas at the hands of the Afghans allowed Sikhs to consolidate their position in the Punjab.

With the withdrawal of Abdali from the Punjab, the Sikh confederacies began to fill the political vacuum. Between 1765 and 1800, they brought the Punjab and Jammu under their control. In this way, the period from 1765 onwards saw steady development of Sikh political power which culminated in the establishment of an autonomous state in the early 19th century.

Misls During the second half of the 18th century, power in the Sikh polity became more horizontally structured, as misls (brotherhood or confederacies based on kinship ties) now held territories as units.

Period of Sovereign Sikh Rule in Former Mughal Province of Lahore (1765–1845)

Sikh Confederacies In the face of severe Mughal repression, the Sikhs had organised themselves into several small mobile bands called **Jathas**, each headed by a **Jathedar**. After 1765, numerous small Jathas regrouped themselves into 12 larger regional confederacies or Misls led by local chiefs. These included the Bhangis, the Ramgarhias, the Kanhayias, the Singhpurias, the Ahluwalias and the Sukerchakias. The misls did occasionally unite, but largely the political authority in Punjab remained decentralised and more horizontally dispersed during this whole period until Ranjit Singh, the chief of the **Sukerchakia misl**, tried to raise a more centralised Sikh state at the end of the 18th century. Thus, Punjab's rise to prominence had to wait till the end of the century for Ranjit Singh.

Punjab under Ranjit Singh (1792–1839)

Maharaja Ranjit Singh statue in Amritsar

At the end of the 18th century, Punjab rose to prominence under Ranjit Singh, who was the son of Mahan Singh, the leader of Sukerchakia misl. Ranjit Singh was a courageous soldier, an efficient administrator and a skilful diplomat. He brought under his control the area extending from Sutlej to Jhelum. He conquered **Lahore in 1799** and **Amritsar in 1802**.

Conflict with the English When the Sikhs were trying to establish themselves as a political power in the north, simultaneously, the English Company was trying to establish itself in eastern India. Having emerged supreme in the east, the English turned their attention to the north, thus making their conflict with the Sikhs inevitable. In 1809, Ranjit Singh signed the **Treaty of Amritsar** with the British East India Company. As per the terms of the treaty, the English recognised him as the sole sovereign ruler of Punjab, permitting him complete freedom of action to the north of the Sutlej, but the British established their control over cis-Sutlej Sikh States, thus preventing Ranjit Singh from any further expansion to the south of the Sutlej.

Expansion north of the Sutlej Later Ranjit Singh also conquered **Kashmir, Peshawar and Multan**. In this way, he established his own kingdom. He made no changes in the land revenue system and allowed the Mughal system to continue. Land revenue was charged at the rate of 50 per cent of the gross produce. Ranjit Singh, popularly known as '**Sher-e-Punjab**', was an efficient administrator. He greatly modernised his army along European lines with the help of European instructors. His army was not confined to the Sikhs. He recruited Gorkhas, Biharis, Oriyas, Pathans, Dogras and even Punjabi Muslims.

As a person, Ranjit Singh was tolerant and liberal in religious matters. He was a devout Sikh, but he also patronised Hindu and Muslim holy men. He is known to 'step down from his throne to wipe the dust off the feet of Muslim mendicants with his long grey beard'. **Fakir Azizuddin** and **Diwan Dina Nath** were some of his most trusted Ministers. The Punjab under Ranjit Singh was in no sense a Sikh State.

Tripartite Treaty of 1838 With his diplomatic realism, Ranjit Singh was temporarily able to save his kingdom from British encroachment. But towards the close of his reign, the British forced him to sign a Tripartite Treaty (1838) with Afghan Shah Shuja and the English Company whereby he agreed to provide passage to British troops through Punjab, enabling them to place Shah Shuja on the throne of Kabul.

After 1809 till 1839, when Ranjit Singh died, there was no major tension between the Sikhs and the English. Ranjit Singh's eldest son Kharak Singh proved to be an unworthy successor and suddenly died in 1839. Kharak Singh's son Naunihal also accidently died while returning from his father's funeral, leading to an anarchic situation in the Punjab. An intense internal struggle for power followed and the British moved quickly to conquer the Punjab. The First Anglo–Sikh war began in 1845 and the British finally annexed the Punjab in 1849. In this way, within a decade after the death of Ranjit Singh, the mighty Sikh State was absorbed into the arms of British imperialism.[6]

Cis-Sutlej States The term, now obsolete, first came into use in 1809, when the Sikh chiefs south of the Sutlej passed under British protection. The term was generally applied to the country south of the Sutlej and north of the Delhi territory.

The Jats

Taking advantage of the weakness of the Mughal Empire in the 18th century, a few smaller states also emerged in north India. These were the Jats and the Afghans. The Jats were an agriculturist caste that inhabited the **Delhi–Agra belt**. They revolted against the oppressive policies of Aurangzeb under the leadership of the Jat zamindars in the latter half of the 17th century. Even though the revolt was suppressed, the region remained disturbed. Despite its origin as a peasant rebellion, the Jat state remained feudal, with zamindars holding the main power (the revenue demand under Suraj Mal were higher than under the Mughals).

The foundation for the **Jat state of Bharatpur** in Rajasthan was laid by Churaman and Badan Singh-

Churaman (1695–1721) Churaman built a strong fort at **Thoon** and challenged Mughal authority in the region. When, in 1721, the Mughal army led by Jai Singh II (governor of Agra) attacked and captured his fort, Churaman committed suicide.

Badan Singh (1721–56) Badan Singh, Churaman's nephew, now assumed leadership of the Jats. He considerably strengthened his position and built four forts at Deeg, Kumher, Weir and Bharatpur, consolidating the Bharatpur kingdom.

Suraj Mal (or Sujan Singh, 1756–63) The Jat power reached its glory under Suraj Mal. He was a brave soldier and an able administrator. His state extended from Delhi in the north to Chambal in the south, Agra in the west to Ganga in the east; including the subahs of **Agra, Mathura, Meerut and Aligarh**.

Suraj Mal's Role in Third Battle of Panipat The struggle against the Afghan invader Abdali was given the appearance of a great religious battle by the Marathas. Agents of the Peshwa visited the court of every Hindu prince to gather support, including that of Suraj Mal. Following a meeting with Sadashiv Rao Bhau, Suraj Mal decided to join the Marathas against Abdali. Soon differences emerged between them on the plan of campaign against Abdali and Bhau made an enemy of the only powerful Hindu Raja who had come to serve him with all his resources. Abdali at once seized this opportunity

[6]Read about the British conquest of Punjab in greater detail in the upcoming chapters.

and tried to secure Suraj Mal's neutrality, if not active assistance. Raja Suraj Mal agreed to maintain neutrality, but his sympathies continued to be with the Marathas.

The neutrality of Raja Suraj Mal is considered to be a major contributory factor in the defeat of the Marathas. Vast areas around Delhi had been completely ruined due to constant ravages; and during the struggle, while Abdali depended on supplies from Rohilkhand, the Marathas depended on the Jat kingdom. With his arrogant attitude, Bhau had lost this resource and the Marathas had to fight on empty stomach at Panipat.

However, when the Maratha survivors fled form Panipat and entered the Jat kingdom, the Jats provided them with food, medicine and clothes for relief. Had it not been for Suraj Mal's generosity, few of them would have been able to cross the Narmada to tell the woeful tale of Panipat to the Peshwa. Hence it is clear that the Jats under Suraj Mal did not participate in the Battle of Panipat. They, however, provided considerable assistance to the Maratha soldiers and civilians who escaped the fighting.

Suraj Mal has been called as the **'Plato of the Jat tribe'** and as **'the Jat Ulysses'** for his steady intellect and clear vision. However, his rule was short-lived and he died on 25 December 1763 fighting the Rohillas under Najib-ud-Daulah. His death marked the end of the Jat state.

The Afghans (at Farrukhabad and Rohilkhand)

The states of Farrukhabad and Rohilkhand were a fallout of the Afghan migration in the mid-18th century because of political disruption in Afghanistan.

Farrukhabad **Muhammad Khan Bangash** (also known as Ahmad Khan Bangash), an Afghan adventurer, established his control over Farrukhabad (territory between present day Aligarh and Kanpur), during the reigns of Farrukhsiyar and Mohammad Shah.

Rohilkhand Similarly, an Afghan (Pathan or Pashtun) soldier Daud and his son **Ali Muhammad Khan** carved out an independent principality for themselves. Ali Muhammad Khan took advantage of the collapse of authority in north India following Nadir Shah's invasion to set up a petty kingdom—Rohilkhand. It was located at the Himalayan foothills (north-west of present state of UP, between Kumaon in the north and the Ganga in the south) with its capital at **Aonla** in Bareilly and later at **Rampur**.

The Afghani use of artillery, particularly the flint-gun, ended the domination of cavalry since the discovery of the stirrup in the early medieval times. Politically, the role of the Afghans was negative. Both the Rohillas and the Bangash helped Ahmad Shah Abdali during the Third Battle of Panipat and accentuated the decline of the Mughals. The Rohillas themselves suffered heavily at the hands of other powers in the area—the Jats and the Awadh rulers, and later the Marathas and the British.

Independent Kingdoms—Mysore, Kerala and The Rajputs

Mysore

Mysore was located south of Hyderabad at the junction of Eastern and Western Ghats. It was originally a viceroyalty under the **Vijayanagara Empire** in the 16th century. The Kingdom of Mysore had preserved its fragile independence ever since the end of Vijayanagara Empire and had been only nominally a part of the Mughal Empire.

In the early 18th century, Mysore was ruled by Wadiyar (or Wodeyar) King **Chikka Krishnaraja**. Two of his ministers, Nanjaraja (the Sarvadhikari or prime minister) and Devaraja (the Dulwai or commander in chief) seized power and reduced the king to a mere puppet. The mid-18th century saw the emergence of Mysore as the second most significant power in south India, after Hyderabad. The foundation of Mysore power was laid by Hyder Ali, which was later consolidated by his able son, Tipu Sultan.

From Wadiyars to Tipu Sultan, Mysore was sought after by various powers (Marathas, Hyderabad, Carnatic and the English) who turned it into a **constant battlefield**.

Map of Mysore (1704)

Hyder Ali (1761–82)

In 1721, Hyder Ali was born in an obscure family and started his career as a petty officer in the Mysore army (hostile English contemporaries often termed him as a usurper). Though uneducated, he was a man of great energy and intellect. He gradually rose in the Mysore army to be a brilliant commander. In 1761, Hyder **overthrew Nanjaraja** and established his authority over Mysore state.

Expansion under Hyder Ali

- Hyder Ali established control over rebellious poligars (zamindars) and conquered Bidnur, Sunda, Sera, Canara and Malabar. Major reason for occupation of Malabar was to have access to the Indian Ocean.
- Hyder was an expansionist at heart and naturally clashed with other regional powers—the Marathas, the Nizam and the English.
- He faced Maratha raids in 1764, 1766 and again in 1771 as the Marathas recovered fast under Peshwa Madhav Rao. However, after the death of Peshwa in 1772, Hyder Ali not only quickly recovered the territories earlier lost to the Marathas, but also acquired several territories in the Krishna-Tungabhadra Doab.
- He also inflicted a heavy defeat on the English near Madras in 1769.

Hyder Ali

Hyder's most remarkable achievement was his realisation that only a modern army could be the basis for a powerful state. Thus, he inducted **French experts** and established a modern **arsenal at Dindigul** (est. 1755) with their help. He made an attempt to induce organisational discipline along European lines. He organised his army through the system of risalas, with a clear chain of command going upto the ruler. He practiced religious toleration and many of his ministers were Hindus.

Hyder died during the course of the second Anglo-Mysore war (1782) and was succeeded by his son, Tipu Sultan.

Tipu Sultan (1782–99)

Tipu Sultan

Tipu Sultan strongly asserted his autonomy, unlike other 18th-century states. In 1787, he assumed the title of Padshah, issued coins in his name without any reference to the Mughal emperor, and instead of Emperor Shah Alam's name he inserted his own name in the **khutba (Friday sermons at the mosque)** and even issued a new calendar. He also sought a **sanad (royal order)** from the Ottoman Khalif to legitimise his rule. At the same time, he did not completely sewer the links with the Mughal monarch. Being a realist, he recognised Mughal authority when it suited him and defied it when it did not.

As ruler and administrator, Tipu Sultan was successful and earned the praise of his contemporaries. In spite of the absence of any checks on his authority, he did not behave like an irresponsible despot and took great care to work for the welfare and **happiness of his people**. More than any other 18th-century Indian ruler, Tipu thoroughly recognised the threat that the English posed to South India. Accordingly, Tipu raised an efficient military force. He employed French officers to train his troops and even raised **a French corps**. He also made an effort to build a modern navy after 1796.

Economically, Mysore flourished under Tipu, though not free from contemporary economic backwardness. He understood the importance of modern trade and industry. He was the lone Indian ruler who recognised economic strength as the foundation of military strength. Hence he promoted both inland as well as foreign trade, but also imposed tight government control over it. He set up a number of factories in Mysore state which manufactured a wide range of articles such as paper sugar, silk fabrics, tools and implements, etc. He sent **emissaries** to France, Turkey, Iran and Pegu Myanmar to develop foreign trade. He also tried to set up **trading companies** on the lines of European companies. He worked for modernisation of agriculture and introduced sericulture in Mysore.

Tipu, almost a folk hero, was an innovator and a modernist in many ways. He was an avid learner and had a library with books on diverse subjects. He showed proper appreciation for western thought and sciences which had freed his mind of 'eastern conservatism and apathy'. Tipu showed a keen interest in French Revolution. He is believed to have planted a '**Tree of liberty**' at Seringapatam, became a member of the **Jacobin Club** and allowed himself to be addressed as **Citizen Tipu**.

The imperialist writers depict Tipu as a 'monster pure and simple' and a 'bigoted monarch'. These views are obviously biased. The **Sringeri Letters** reveal that he issued funds for repair and other temple works and never interfered with worship in temples situated within the Seringapatam fort. In personal life, he remained free from vices. He would fondly say that it was "better to live a day as a lion than a lifetime as a sheep".

Tipu Sultan ruled Mysore till his death at the hands of the British in 1799—he died defending his capital Seringapatam (or Srirangapatnam) during the course of the **Fourth Anglo-Mysore war**. Hyder Ali and Tipu Sultan fought four wars against the British before the final surrender of Mysore in 1799. The Marathas, the Nawab of Carnatic and the Nizam of Hyderabad aligned with the British from time to time to subdue the Mysore ruler.[7]

[7]Read about the British conquest of Mysore in greater detail in the upcoming chapters.

Tipu Sultan's Administration Tipu Sultan's government, like all other governments of the time, was a despotic one. The Sultan himself was the highest civil, political and military authority of the state. There was no office of the wazir in his administration. However, there were 7 principle departments, each under a Mir Asif including:

- **Mir Asaf Cutchehri** Revenue and Finance department
- **Mir Miran Cutchehri** Military department
- **Malik-ut-Tujjar Cutchehri** Commerce department
- **Mir Yam Cutchehri** Marine department
- **Mir Khazain Cutchehri** Treasury and mint department
- **Mir Sadar Cutcheheri** Ordnance and garrison department

Kerala

At the beginning of 18th century, Kerala was divided among a large number of chiefs and rajas. The four most important states were Calicut (under Zamorin), Chirakkal, Cochin and Travancore. Travancore, the southernmost state, had always maintained its independence from Mughal rule. It also withstood the shock of Mysorean expansion in 1766 when Hyder Ali invaded Kerala and annexed Malabar and Calicut; Travancore was spared. The kingdom of Travancore had its initial capital at **Padmanabahapuram** (1729–95), later shifted to **Thiruvananthapuram** (1795–49).

Rise of Travancore (After 1729)

- **Marthanda Varma** Travancore had risen into prominence after 1729 under **King Marthanda Varma**. He expanded his kingdom from Kanyakumari to Cochin with the help of **modern army** trained on Western lines. He defeated the Dutch and ended their political power in Kerala.
- **Rama Varma** Successor of Marthanda Varma, Rama Varma was a man of great creativity and learning, including western knowledge. He conversed fluently in English and regularly read newspapers published in London, Calcutta and Madras. He was responsible for making **Trivandrum**, the capital centre of scholarship and art. After his death, the state lost its glory and soon succumbed to British pressure, accepting a resident in 1800.

The Rajputs

Rajputs were warrior clans that ruled in overwhelming majority in Rajasthan and Saurashtra. Since the time of Akbar, Rajput chiefs were patronised by Mughal emperors following a policy of indirect rule. They paid an annual tribute (peshkash) to the emperor as a mark of subordination and enjoyed autonomy in matters of internal administration. Many of them were given high military ranks in the Mughal army. In this way, they contributed to the strength of the empire and in return they were given help to consolidate their own hold over their kingdoms.

Relationship with Mughals Eighteenth century was marked by a **love-hate relationship** between the Mughals and the Rajputs. Rajput rulers did not lag behind in taking advantage of the declining Mughal Empire to consolidate their position and tried to re-establish their independence.

According to Bipan Chandra, the desire for independence partially arose from the harsh treatment of the Rajputs dating back to Aurangzeb's reign. Aurangzeb had led many ruthless campaigns in

Rajasthan. He practiced religious intolerance and revived jeziah. Such harsh treatment aroused the anger of many Rajputs and left a sore which never healed. Thus, a race which had been the right arm of the Mughal Empire at the beginning of the Mughal period, was gradually alienated and never again served the throne without distrust.

Shekhar Bandopadhyaya writes that Aurangzeb did not discriminate against the Rajput sardars, but he could not tolerate the continuous territorial expansion of Mewar. The situation took an ugly turn when Aurangzeb interfered in the succession of Marwar. He refused to recognise Ajit Singh (the posthumous son of Rana Jaswant Singh of Marwar) as Rana. Instead he appointed Inder Singh Rathore, a nephew of Jaswant Singh, as Rana there. Consequently, Ajit Singh of Marwar rose in revolt and was ably helped by Mewar.

Anti-Mughal League (1708) In 1708, Emperor Bahadur Shah I marched towards Jodhpur and forced Ajit Singh into submission. It led to the formation of an anti-Mughal League led by **Ajit Singh, Jai Singh II** and **Durgadas Rathore** (a senior officer of Jaswant Singh). They adopted the method of slowly loosening their ties with Delhi and function as independent states in practice. They participated in the struggle for power in the Delhi court and gained lucrative governorships.

For instance, in the Farrukhsiyar–Sayyid brothers' tussle in Delhi, the Rajput chiefs of Jodhpur and Jaipur followed the policy of "opportune adherence or aloofness". In order to win Ajit Singh to their side, the Sayyids appointed Ajit Singh with the governorship of Ajmer and Gujarat, a position he held till 1721. On the other hand, the anti-Sayyid party appointed Jai Singh II of Jaipur as the governor of Agra in 1721. In this way, at one point, the Rajputs controlled the entire territory from 600 miles south of Delhi to Surat on the western coast.

However, the Rajputs rulers remained divided among themselves and none proved powerful enough to compete with the Marathas or the English for the position of paramount power.

Jai Singh II or Raja Sawai Jai Singh (1699–1743) The most powerful Rajput chief of this time was Raja Sawai Jai Singh of Amber who ruled in Jaipur from 1699 to 1743. He was a distinguished statesman and reformer. His interest in science was the most remarkable aspect of his personality, especially at a time when Indians were in oblivion of scientific progress.

Jai Singh founded the city of **Jaipur** and made it a seat of science and art. Jaipur was scientifically built based on a city plan, having broad streets which intersected at right angles. Jai Singh was also a great **astronomer**. He erected observatories at Delhi, Jaipur, Ujjain, Varanasi and Mathura; some of them had instruments which were his own invention. He drew up a set of tables called **Zij Muhammadshahi**, to enable people to make astronomical observations. He got several important texts on geometry and trigonometry translated into Sanskrit including Euclid's 'Elements of Geometry'.

Jai Singh was also a **social reformer**. He tried to reduce lavish expenditure by Rajputs on their daughters' weddings which had given rise to the practice of female infanticide.

Conclusion

Thus, we see that the regional powers were unable to take the place of the Mughals; none had the resources to provide an all India polity. The regional powers could not reverse the general economic stagnation that had plagued the Mughal economy. The jagirdari crisis intensified as income from agriculture declined while the number of contenders for a share of the surplus multiplied. Consequently, many regional powers made desperate attempts to preserve internal and external trade.

Satish Chandra argues that it is wrong to talk of generalised socio-economic stagnation in the 18th century. He points out that there were considerable economic variations. There was creation of new wealth and social power in the provinces, which resulted in the decline of the centralised Mughal power. Those regions with considerable amounts of resources actually attracted the English and other European traders and triggered off a competition among them for supremacy in the subcontinent.

The biggest weakness of the regional states lay in their **scientific backwardness**; limited attempts were made to modernise industry and commerce. These backward regional states easily succumbed to the superior British system.

18th-Century India—Economic and Social Conditions (Indian Economy and Society on the Eve of British Conquest)

Socially and economically, 18th-century India failed to progress at an adequate pace. India was a land of contrasts as extreme poverty and extreme luxury existed side by side. While the common people remained impoverished, backward and oppressed, the rich and the powerful enjoyed a life of luxury and abundance. Yet, the life of the masses in general was better than what it became after 100 years of British rule. The socio-economic life of the people in the 18th century may be understood under the following heads:

Economic Conditions

Village Economy

- **Self-sufficient, self-governing village community** In the beginning of 18th century, the basic unit of Indian economy was the self-sufficient, self-governing village community which produced almost everything for its local needs (except perhaps a few items like salt and iron) and had very little to do with the outside world.
- **Agriculture and handicraft industry** The two industries worked in close union; while the peasant grew crops, his family carried out spinning and weaving and other secondary activities to produce goods needed for the family. Various other services were provided by craftsmen like carpenter, potter, goldsmith, blacksmith and others who received a share in the village crops in return. Handicrafts had reached a high level of development and were in much demand. Some of the famous handicrafts of the time included cotton, silk and woollen fabrics and metal works.
- **Agrarian structure** The concept of private property in land had not yet developed. Land in the village was plentiful and belonged collectively to the cultivating community, each family having its share of arable land. **Karl Marx** had described this kind of collective ownership of land as the Indian form of communism. Different classes connected with land possessed certain rights. The actual cultivators enjoyed the right to cultivate and had security of tenure provided a fixed share of produce was paid to the overlord. The land revenue was collected by the village headman or **Patil** and passed onto the ruler or Nawab. The state demand of revenue generally varied from one-sixth **to one-third**. Other land related issues and disputes were settled by the Patil in consultation with the village Panchayat.

- **Self-governance** The villages were also self-governing. The Village Panchayat administered the village affairs and settled disputes. The local chief or the subahdar did not interfere in the day-to-day village affairs and limited himself to claiming a share in the village crops. In this way, the main link of the village with the state was the payment of land revenue. Even as rulers and dynasties changed continuously, the life in the villages carried on as usual, phenomena referred to as the "unchangeableness of Asiatic communities" by Karl Marx. It has been aptly said that the village communities in India 'lasted **when nothing else seemed to last'**.
- **Stagnation** The unchanging character of village communities was responsible for socio-economic stability on one hand and stagnation on the other. Agriculture was technically backward and stagnant. Though the farmer's produce supported the rest of society, yet his own reward was miserably inadequate. The farmers had to pay exorbitant amounts to the state, the zamindars and the revenue farmers. The isolation of village communities obstructed the creation of a wider market for Indian handicrafts. The caste-bound socio-economic structure permitted little mobility of individual and labour. Political indifference acted as a barrier to growth of national consciousness. As a result, Indian villages represented a picture of stagnation, untouched from all modern scientific developments taking place in other parts of the world.

Urban Economy

- Even as economic stagnation continued, India remained a land of extensive manufacturers and Indian manufactures enjoyed a worldwide renown. Though urban economy presented a better picture, there was no sharp division between urban centres where industries were concentrated and rural centres which supplied raw materials. Industrial production in India continued to be largely a rural-based activity.

Condition of Indian Industry

- **Textiles** Cotton textiles which were produced virtually all over India constituted the most important manufacture. The cotton manufactures of Bengal (Dacca, Murshidabad), Gujarat (Ahmedabad, Surat, Bharuch) and Andhra (Masulipatam, Aurangabad, Vishakhapatnam) the silk fabrics of Murshidabad, Lahore and Agra, woollen shawls and carpets of Agra, Lahore and Kashmir were in demand both in India and abroad.
- **Other agro-based industries** In addition to cotton and silk, dye stuffs (particularly indigo) and sugar were the next most important commercial industrial products. Significant agro-based industries included oils, tobacco, opium and alcoholic beverages.
- **Mining and ship-building** Though mining was inadequately developed, India was self-sufficient in iron. Ship-building was another important and developing industry.
- **Luxury goods** High-class luxury goods were also produced and largely consumed by the rich nobility.
- **Manufacturing centres** Some other important manufacturing centres included Patna (Bihar), Chanderi and Burhanpur (MP), Jaunpur, Varanasi, Lucknow (UP), Multan, Lahore (Punjab), Bangalore, Coimbatore and Madurai (south India). The emerging Indian cities had also developed their own banking system comprising Shroffs, Mahajans, Chetties and others.
- **Stagnation** Though India was, on the whole, self-sufficient in agriculture and craft industries, some observers feel that the pre-British industrial sector was stagnant and technically backward and there was an overall declining trend in agriculture and craft industry production. However, this decline was far greater in the post-British 18th and 19th centuries.

Condition of Indian Trade

- **Favourable balance of trade** As India was self-sufficient in food grain production and handicrafts, it did not import goods on a large scale. On the contrary, its agricultural and industrial produce was in great demand in the foreign market. The 17th century saw Indian cotton textiles emerge as the most important Asian import to the West, displacing spices (the marked expansion of cotton textile exports provided employment to a sizeable section of Indian population). Hence India exported more than it imported and its trade was heavily balanced in India's favour.
- **Inflow of bullion** The remarkable rise in Indian textile exports ensured a steady flow of bullion into India from buyer nations and India came to be known as the **sink of precious metals**. Indian trade with Europe then was essentially based upon the price differential between Asia and the rest of the world. The European merchants bought Indian goods at a low price and sold them at a much higher price in Europe, Africa and other New World markets. Since there was no demand for European goods in India, the purchases of Indian goods had to be financed by bullion payments. This comprised the main problem faced by European companies in Indian trade.
- **Rise of merchants and bankers** Flourishing trade brought into existence the merchant capitalists and bankers who further promoted trade and commerce. In fact, in the beginning of 18th century, India was one of the **main centres of world trade and industry**.
- **Major items of export** These included cotton textiles (most important export item), silk, indigo, saltpeter, rice, wheat, sugar, spices, precious stones and drugs.
- **Major items of import were**
  - (From) **Persian Gulf**-pearls, silk, wool, dates, dry fruits, rose water
  - **Arabia**-coffee, gold, drugs, honey
  - **China**-tea, sugar, porcelain and silk
  - **Tibet**-gold, musk, woollen sloth
  - **Indonesian islands**-spices, perfume, sugar
  - **Africa**-ivory, drugs
  - **Europe**-woollen cloth, metals, paper
- **Disruption** However, political disintegration of the Mughal Empire in the 18th century inevitably brought economic fragmentation as well. Economic activities were disrupted by continuous wars and conflict between the regional powers. New agencies of pillage and plunder sprang up. Every small or large ruler tried to increase his income by imposing heavy duties on goods passing through his territories. Many trading centres were looted by foreign invaders (like Nadir Shah and Abdali) and European trading companies began to dabble in Indian politics.

Examples of Trading Centres Looted by Foreign Invaders were

- Delhi was plundered by Nadir Shah
- Lahore, Delhi, Mathura was plundered by Abdali
- Agra was plundered by Jats
- Gujarat and Deccan were plundered by Marathas
- Sarhind was plundered by Sikhs

Main Industrial Products of India in the 18th Century India was a large-scale manufacturer of cotton and silk textiles, dyes, sugar, oils, tobacco, opium, alcoholic beverages, jute, ivory, ships, iron and other mineral and metallic products (like gold and silver jewellery, arms and shields, etc.) and high-class luxury goods.

Social Conditions

Despite political upheavals of the 18th century, the social life of the masses remained traditional, marked by stagnation and dependence.

Social Stratification At the apex of the social order was the emperor, followed by the nobility. During peace time, they led a life of luxury with a taste for wine, women and music. The middle classes comprised of the merchants, shopkeepers, etc. The lowest rung of the society comprised of vast numbers of the poor peasants and artisans. Society was divided on the lines of religion, region, tribe, language and caste. In fact, caste was a central feature of the social life of the Hindus. Caste rules prevailed in matters of inter-dining and inter-marriage. Even though Islam preached social equality to the Muslims, they too were divided along class and caste lines. These considerations kept not only Shia and Sunni apart but also Irani, Afghani, Turani and Hindustani Muslims apart from each other.

Status of Women Family system was primarily patriarchal (Kerala Nairs were an exception) and the will of the male head of the family usually prevailed. Though examples can be sighted of women who played significant roles in polity or arts, the status of women was certainly **not of equality**. Evils of child marriage, dowry and purdah system prevailed. Polygamy was common among the rich classes. In fact, the caste system, the custom of sati and the conditions of widows were the greatest social evils of 18th-century India.

Slavery Prevalence of slavery was yet another social evil of the time. European travellers and administrators have reported widespread practice of slavery in India. Extreme poverty or natural calamities compelled some to sell off their children. However, slaves in India were treated better than their counterparts in America or Europe. They were usually seen as hereditary servants rather than as menials. They were allowed to marry among themselves and their children were considered free citizens. Slave trade in India touched new dimensions with the coming of Europeans. The European companies bought slaves from the markets of Bengal, Assam and Bihar and sold them in the American and European markets. In 1789, trafficking of slaves was abolished by a proclamation, yet it continued to survive in various forms until recent times.

State of Education The education system prevalent in India in 18th century was traditional, decadent and out of touch with modern developments in the West. The idea of Indian education (both Hindu and Muslim systems) was culture and not literacy; learning was linked with religion. Vocational education was imparted according to one's varna or family tradition.

- **Elementary education** was fairly widespread, though mainly confined to males of higher castes. Elementary schools were called **pathshalas** and **maktabs** and were often attached to temples or mosques. School's curriculum included instruction in reading, writing and arithmetic as well as moral and religious instruction. The study of science and technology was excluded. Original thought and innovation was discouraged.

- **Higher education** centres were called chatuspathis or tols (for Sanskrit) and madrasas (for Persian and Arabic). **Persian was the court language** and was learnt by Muslims as well as the Hindus. The French traveller Bernier described Kashi or Banaras as '**the Athens of India**'.
- **Literacy** Interestingly, literacy was not less than what it was under the British later. In 1813, Warren Hastings wrote that Indians had in general 'superior endowments in reading, writing and arithmetic than the common people of any nation in Europe'. A good feature was that the teachers enjoyed high prestige in society.

Hindu–Muslim Relations In 18th-century India, Hindus and Muslims enjoyed friendly relations with one another. They respected each other's religion and practiced religious tolerance. This was particularly true among common people in villages and towns, where Hindus and Muslims cooperated with one another in socio-cultural affairs. This resulted in the emergence of composite Hindu–Muslim culture, accelerated by the development of Urdu language.

Art and Culture Culturally too, there were some signs of exhaustion. It remained wholly traditionalist. The most rapid decline was seen in those arts which depended on patronage of kings and nobles (for example,- Mughal architecture and painting). Yet the 18th century cannot be called a dark age. With the decline of Delhi, talent fled to newly established state capitals like **Hyderabad, Lucknow, Murshidabad and Jaipur**. Cultural continuity with preceding centuries was maintained and local traditions continued to evolve.

- **In the field of architecture**
  - **Jaipur** Sawai Jai Singh built the famous pink city of Jaipur. He also built five astronomical observatories at Jaipur, Delhi, Banaras, Mathura and Ujjain.
  - **Lucknow** Asaf-ud-Daula built the Bara Imambara (building for celebration of the Muharram festival) in 1784.
  - **Amritsar** Maharaja Ranjit Singh renovated the Sikh shrine, decorating the entire upper portion with a thin layer of gold, giving it the modern name of Golden Temple.
  - **Kerala** The famous **Padmanabhapuram Palace** was built with its remarkable architecture and mural paintings.

Bara Imambara, Lucknow

- **In the field of literature**
  - The spread of Urdu language and poetry was a distinct feature of 18th century and saw the emergence of famous Urdu poets like Mir, Sauda, Nazir and Mirza Ghalib.
  - Vernacular languages also greatly developed during this period including languages such as Hindi, Punjabi, Marathi, Bengali, Assamese and Telugu. In South India, Malayalam literature was revived under Travancore rulers Marthanda Varma and Rama Varma. Kunchan Nambiar arose as one of the great poets of Kerala. Katahakali literature, dance and drama saw its full development during this period. Some famous Sindhi poets of the 18th century were Shah Abdul Latif, Sachal and Sami. Latif composed the famous collection of poems called Risalo. Warris Shah wrote the famous romantic epic in Punjabi-Heer Ranjha. In Assam, literature developed under the patronage of Ahom Kings. Dayaram was a great lyricist from Gujarat.

Thus, we see that, 18th-century India was characterised by traditional outlook and stagnation. It was totally ignorant of the scientific, cultural, political and economic achievements of the West. Though some preconditions for development along modern lines did exist, such a development was severely hampered due to political instability, feudal society and presence of European companies with deep politico-economic interests. The greatest weakness of Indian life and society lay in the field of science. This weakness became the most significant reason for the total subjugation of India by the most advanced country of the time.

Previous Years' Questions – Preliminary Exam

1. Who among the following streamlined the last Maratha administration after Sambhaji? **[UPSC 2000]**
   (a) Raja Ram
   (b) Balaji Vishwanath
   (c) Ganga bai
   (d) Nanaji Deshmukh
2. Who among the following Indian rulers established embassies in foreign countries on modern lines? **[UPSC 2001]**
   (a) Hyder Ali
   (b) Mir Qasim
   (c) Shah Alam II
   (d) Tipu Sultan
3. What was the immediate reason for Ahmad Shah Abdali to invade India and fight the third Battle of Panipat? **[UPSC 2010]**
   (a) He wanted to avenge the expulsion of his viceroy Taimur Shah from Lahore by the Marathas
   (b) The frustrated governor of Jullundhar Adina Beg Khan invited him to invade Punjab
   (c) He wanted to punish Mughal administration for non-payment of the revenues of the Chahar Mahal (Gujarat, Aurangabad, Sialkot and Pasrur)
   (d) He wanted to annex all the fertile plains of Punjab up to the borders of Delhi to his Kingdom
4. The staple commodities of export by the English East India Company from Bengal in the middle of the 18th century were **[UPSC 2018]**
   (a) Raw cotton, oil-seeds and opium
   (b) Sugar, salt, zinc and lead
   (c) Copper, silver, gold, spices and tea
   (d) Cotton, silk, saltpetre and opium
5. With reference to Indian History, which of the following statements is/are correct? **[UPSC 2021]**
   1. The Nizamat of Arcot emerged out of Hyderabad State
   2. The Mysore Kingdom emerged out of Vijayanagara Empire
   3. Rohilkhand Kingdom was formed out of the territories occupied by Ahmad Shah Durani

   Select the correct answer using the code given below
   (a) 1 and 2
   (b) 2 only
   (c) 2 and 3
   (d) 3 only

Previous Years' Questions – Main Exam

1. Clarify how mid-eighteenth century India was beset with the spectre of a fragmented polity. **[UPSC 2017]**

Answers

Previous Years' Questions – Preliminary Exam

1. (b) 2. (d) 3. (a) 4. (d) 5. (a)

3 RISE OF BRITISH SUPREMACY: A BACKGROUNDER (EMERGENCE OF IMPERIALISM IN EUROPE AND ARRIVAL OF EUROPEANS IN INDIA)

The third theme of 18th-century Indian polity was the rise of the British supremacy in India. It inaugurated a new phase in the history of India. For the purpose of your convenience, this theme has been dealt with in two chapters. In this chapter, you will learn about why and how the British came to India. In the subsequent chapter, you will become familiar with how the British subsequently expanded their influence.

The British came to India in the context of the emergence of capitalism and modern imperialism in Europe. Both these systems had deep roots in the past patterns of European socio-economic evolution. Thus, the first half of the chapter provides you a brief survey of socio-economic developments in Europe from the 14th to the 19th century leading to the emergence of capitalism and imperialism in Europe. It introduces you to the decline of feudalism in Europe and the emergence of new ideas which prompted the geographical discoveries, overseas trade and colonisation, thus helping you understand the nature of British imperialism in India.

In the 14th century, significant changes occurred in Europe. Capitalism began replacing the feudal economy and society. This opened a new chapter in the history of the world. This is because capitalism as a system is based on profit making. It is always looking for new markets and more profits. Capital accumulates and seeks outlets for reinvestment for future profits. Expansion of capitalist system, therefore, was worldwide, engulfing many other economies, societies and cultures.

Thus, the second half of the chapter explains to you in greater detail the 15th century, when the Europeans went out in the world. Henceforth world history got closely related to developments in Europe. Industrial Revolution and capital formation in Europe led to the search for new markets. Asia and Africa were the ideal grounds for colonial powers to make their fortune. Different trading companies were formed in Europe to carry out external trade. Soon there was clash of interests and struggles started among the colonial powers—the Portuguese, the Dutch, the French and the English. From this struggle, the English East India Company emerged victorious and established its monopoly over Indian trade.

Emergence of Capitalism and Imperialism in Europe

Socio-Economic Changes in Europe (14th Century Onwards)

One of the significant landmarks of the 18th century was the competition among various European colonial powers to establish their hegemony over the Indian subcontinent. Why did the various

European countries jump into fierce competition to establish a colonial empire? This can be understood in the context of socio-economic developments of Europe from the 14th century onwards which led to expansion of European nations for trade and markets, finally giving rise to European capitalism and imperialism.

The prominent socio-economic changes may be understood as follows:

- The European feudal crisis (14th century)
- Renaissance and Reformation (14th to 16th century)
- Geographical Exploration and Colonisation (15th century)
- Merchant Capitalism (16th and 17th centuries)
- Emergence of Organised Trade: Joint Stock Companies and Chartered Companies (17th century)
- Mercantilism (17th century)
- Scientific Ideas and Industrial Revolution (18th century)

Together the above changes accounted for commercial revolution in Europe (16th and 17th centuries) and culminated in the transformation of Europe from merchant capitalism to industrial capitalism.

European Feudal Crisis (14th Century) Feudalism had been in existence for about a thousand years and was the dominant social system in medieval Europe. Under this system, the nobility held lands from the Crown in exchange for military service, and vassals were in turn tenants of the nobles, while the peasants (serfs) had to live on their lord's land and give him homage, labour, and a share of the produce, notionally in exchange for military protection.

Hence, the whole of feudal society was based on ties of dependence. The strong needed the weak as dependents to serve them. The economy and society was primarily land-based. The bottom of the social hierarchy consisted of peasants or serfs who were bound to serve their masters or lords. These lords in turn served their overlords. The Christian church with its clergy was extremely powerful in the feudal society.

By the 14th century, limits to growth of feudal society had been reached and the feudal society of Europe was in a crisis. Technology and resources could not keep pace with the rise in population. Accordingly, when Black Death (plague) spread from 1348 onwards, it wiped out people in large numbers, resulting in abandoning of cultivable land and decline in agricultural production. Consequently, the income of the feudal lords also declined and they reacted by attempting a tightening of their feudal control over the peasants. The peasants resisted and the 14th and 15th centuries were marked by a series of peasant rebellions all over Europe.

The crisis was particularly intense in Western Europe (broadly the area west of River Elbe consisting of countries like England, France, Holland, Spain and parts of Germany and Scandinavia). Here the hold of feudal lords weakened and serfdom declined after the feudal crisis, leading to the emergence of nation-states under **strong monarchs**. On the contrary, in Eastern Europe (the region of present day Poland, Romania, Bulgaria, Hungary, former USSR, etc.) the landlords succeeded in subjugating the serfs and serfdom consolidated after the crisis. As a result of this, Eastern Europe lagged behind Western Europe in trade, industry and urbanisation.

As a result of the feudal crisis, agriculture became less profitable, whereas gains in **trade and commerce** increased substantially. For instance, in Italy (also the birthplace of Renaissance) the merchants had been prospering immensely since the 11th to 12th century by supplying various artisanal goods and luxury items to Europe. **Marco Polo** (1254-1324) emerged as a legendary Italian merchant who travelled to China and fascinated Europeans with his travel tales. Italy also enjoyed a geographical advantage in the Mediterranean as it was connected by both land and sea routes to the East. By 1500 AD Italy had emerged as the most prosperous state in Europe with flourishing trade centres, including Venice, Milan, Florence, Geneva and others.

Renaissance and Reformation (14th–16th Century) Renaissance was a period (14th– 16th century) of great social and cultural change that spread across Europe from its birthplace in Italy. Some historians consider the European Renaissance as the dawn of the Early Modern Era. The term 'Renaissance' is derived from the French word meaning **'rebirth'**. It was a period characterised by **innovation, imagination and creativity**. The Renaissance was also a time during which Europe's classical past was revisited and reinvigorated. The most notable changes were experienced in the fields of art and architecture, literature, philosophy and science. Naturally, renaissance led to the questioning of orthodox beliefs and decline in the influence of the Catholic Church.

The Reformation was a 16th-century movement for the reform of abuses in the Roman Church ending in the establishment of the Reformed and Protestant Churches. Such a development had widespread impact and Reformation emerged as a religious, political, intellectual and cultural upheaval that splintered Catholic Europe, setting in place the structures and beliefs that would define the continent in the modern era.

In the 14th century, Europe simultaneously entered the period of Renaissance even as its feudal society was being questioned and transformed in many ways. Europeans, particularly the rising class of traders and bankers (who constituted the new middle class of Europe), began to question the subordination of the individual to the hierarchies of the feudal age.

Geographical Exploration and Colonisation (15th Century) Several factors contributed in the discovery of new routes and lands.

- **Italian and Arab monopoly over old trade routes** Soon the other countries of Europe had become eager to break the Italian monopoly over trade. But in 1453, Constantinople was captured by the Ottoman Turks and the old Red Sea Trade route now became a state monopoly of the Islamic rulers. Other known routes were also controlled either by the Arabs or the Italians who refused to share them with emerging European nations. In such circumstances, the Western European states, particularly Portugal and Spain, were keen to search for new routes to India and the Spice Islands in Indonesia (then known as East Indies).
- **Rise of nation-states** The rise of nation-states under strong monarchs in the 15th century also promoted geographical explorations and most of the early European explorers were state sponsored.
- **Renaissance** Renaissance had generated a great spirit of adventure and enquiry among the people of Western Europe. Technological advancements in the form of availability of compass, gunpowder and maps also fostered the spirit of travel and exploration.
- **Spirit of 'God, Glory and Gold'** The explorers were also driven by the zeal to spread Christianity in new lands, return home with fabulous riches and achieve glory, popularly known as the spirit of 'God, Glory and Gold'.

- In 1487, **Bartholomew Diaz** of Portugal reached the southernmost tip of Africa (named Cape of Good Hope).
- In 1492, **Christopher Columbus** of Spain set out to reach India but discovered America instead.
- In 1498, **Vasco da Gama** of Portugal discovered a new sea route from Europe to India and became the first European to reach India by sea. From Africa, he sailed via the Cape of Good Hope and continued to India, reaching Calicut. He returned with a cargo which sold for 60 times the cost of his voyage! (Read Ahead: The Arrival of Europeans)

Merchant Capitalism (16th–17th Century) This was clearly an age of the merchant. The geographical explorations and new colonies had opened vast opportunities for profits. The capital accumulated by the merchant class from trade profit was termed as merchant capital, hence this earliest phase in the development of capitalism is termed as merchant capitalism.

Capitalism now began to replace feudal economy and society, giving rise to **commercial revolution** in Europe. The term is used to denote a series of changes which brought about tremendous expansion of market and money economy. For instance, use of currency became widespread and began replacing the age-old barter system. By 1600, almost all major cities of Europe got connected with postal service. Urbanisation picked up and cities like London, Paris and Amsterdam grew at a very fast pace.

In addition to the merchants, capital was also being accumulated by craftsmen who showed enterprise and profited from the expanding market. In fact, Industrial growth and manufacturing in the era of merchant capitalism has also been termed as **proto-industrialisation** as it created conditions for the emergence of full-fledged factory-based Industrial Revolution in the late 18th century.

Emergence of Organised Trade: Joint Stock Companies and Chartered Companies (17th Century) The 17th century saw the emergence of more sophisticated business organisations such as the Joint Stock Companies and Chartered Companies. A major advantage of a Joint Stock Company was that a much larger amount of capital could be raised and the high risks and costs could be shared by the shareholders. The Chartered companies were authorised by the government which often granted them monopoly of trade with a particular country. Several such companies were established such as the **English East India Company (1600)** and the French East India Company (1664). As a result of these developments, the 17th and 18th centuries witnessed an enormous increase in world trade.

Mercantilism (17th Century) In the 17th century, Europe was swayed by a set of economic ideas and practice known as mercantilism. It is an economic theory which states that trade generates wealth and is further stimulated by the accumulation of profitable balances, which a government should encourage by means of protectionism. In fact, mercantilism can be understood as the economic counterpart of the spirit of aggressive nationalism.

Its ideas and policy prescription are summarised as follows:

- That the volume of world trade is more or less fixed and the state should endeavour to gain as large a share of this trade as possible.

- That gold and silver were the most desirable forms of national wealth and if a state did not possess them naturally then the chief way of obtaining them was trade.
- That for accumulation of wealth or precious metals, the state should ensure a favourable balance of trade.
- That the state should impose high tariffs to reduce imports of manufactured goods and lower tariffs to encourage import of cheap raw materials.
- That the state should promote exports, especially of manufactured goods through measures like granting monopolies and regulating the guilds.
- Acquisition of colonies was desirable both as a market for exports and as source of supply of raw material. For acquisition or protection of colonies, wars could be waged if required.

Naturally, mercantilist period was a period of **accumulation of capital** in Europe which proved to be a vital requirement for the forthcoming Industrial Revolution in the 18th century (Much of this capital was extracted from the colonial trade carried out in America, Africa and India. Hence, much of the commercial supremacy of the English and the French was based upon their colonial trade during the mercantile era).

Scientific Ideas and Industrial Revolution (18th Century)

The Industrial Revolution (1760-1840) which began in **Britain** was marked by the transition to new manufacturing processes. This transition included shifting from hand-production methods to machine-based production, the development of machine tools, new chemical manufacturing and iron production processes, the increasing use of steam power and the rise of the factory system. Textiles were the dominant industry of the Industrial Revolution in terms of employment, value of output and capital invested; the textile industry was also the first to use modern production methods. Britain was the first to undergo industrialisation and most of the important technological innovations were British.

Industrial Revolution
(steam hammer at work)

Factors that contributed to Industrial development in Britain:

- **Britain's expanding trade** Britain's overseas trade had been expanding rapidly in the past decades thanks to its growing influence and the acquisition of new colonies all over the world including Africa, West Indies, Latin America, Canada, Australia, China and India, providing unlimited opportunities for export. This raised the demand for production which necessitated new inventions.
- **Role of British government** The government in Britain, at the time, was under the influence of commercial and manufacturing interests and extended determined support for markets and colonies.
- **Scientific discoveries and inventions** The desire of British manufacturers to increase production for the expanding markets pushed them to utilise the existing technology and even to seek new inventions. Thus, it is noteworthy that it was not the scientific inventions that brought about Industrial Revolution, but the need of British manufacturers to increase production.

- **Role of scientific ideas** At the same time, scientific ideas contributed to the Industrial Revolution by making the society more receptive to new inventions and discoveries. Scientific outlook was immensely enriched by thinkers such as Nicholas Copernicus, Isaac Newton, Galileo, James Watt and others. The Spinning Jenny was developed by **James Hargreaves** (1765) which increased the artisans spinning capacity by a hundred times. Now one person could do the work of eight persons. Richard **Arkwright's** water frame turned the jenny into a commercial proposition. **Crompton's** mule was a further improvement. The use of power looms developed in the 1780s and this led to a rapid increase in Britain's cotton exports which served as the main vehicle of the Industrial Revolution in Britain (and had significant impact on the industry and society of a colony like India). The invention of steam engine by **James Watt** (1790s) proved a boon for many industries. Use of steam power in shipping revolutionised maritime transport. Finally, the railways ushered in an altogether new era in land transport.
- **Role of increasing population** Population in Britain increased rapidly after 1740 and began to meet the need for the growing industries for more and cheap labour (Industrial Revolution in turn also aided population growth and it doubled in the 50 years after 1780).
- **Role of accumulated capital** By now, sufficient capital had accumulated in Britain for investment in the factory system. Further, this capital was now concentrated not in the hands of feudal elements who would waste it in luxurious living, but in the hands of the merchants who were keen in investment in trade and industry. Here again, the wealth drawn from colonies, including from the plunder of Bengal (1757) aided immensely in the Industrial Revolution in Britain (1760).

Earlier we saw how Britain's expanding overseas trade pushed Industrial Revolution. But that's not all; Industrial Revolution itself began to strengthen overseas trade and colonialism. As England's industrial manufactures developed, correspondingly the need to import manufactured goods from abroad was reduced. Soon the manufacturers fully supplied the internal market of England and now began to seek export markets. Such export markets initially exited in Europe, but later as industrialisation began to spread in the European continent, export markets could be found only in less-developed colonial countries which had not yet undergone modern industrialisation. These countries, including India, were converted into almost exclusively agricultural goods exporting and industrial goods importing countries. A classic example of this conversion was India—from being a major exporter of cotton textiles in 18th century to being a major importer from England in 19th century.

Thus, the industrial revolution transformed Europe **from merchant capitalism to industrial capitalism**. While the merchant capitalist interests lay in promoting trade in goods (goods which included industrial manufactures such as cotton textiles produced by Indian manufactures) from countries like India to Europe, the industrial capitalist interests lay in promoting Europe's exports of industrial goods.

> The merchant capitalists invested capital in industries and used wage labour and strove to make profits in the market. The mechanisation process brought about a rapid rate of capital accumulation. Between 1820 and 1845, the net output of cotton industry grew by about 40%, whereas its wage cost increased by only 5 per cent. This further accelerated accumulation of capital in the hands of the merchants who now began to look for opportunities of reinvestment.

Arrival of Europeans (15th Century Onwards)

We have already seen that the 14th century onwards, significant changes occurred in Europe. Italy, the birth place of renaissance, had been prospering since the 11th to 12th century by supplying various artisanal goods to Europe from the East. Other European countries soon became eager to break the Italian monopoly over trade and began their search for new routes to India and the Spice Islands in Indonesia, then known as East Indies. Asia and Africa were the ideal grounds for colonial powers to make their fortune. The Portuguese were the first ones to arrive, followed by the Dutch, the English, the Danes and the French.

Different trading companies were formed in Europe to carry out external trade. Industrial Revolution and capital formation in Europe led to the search for new markets and further strengthened the colonial pattern. Soon there was clash of interests and struggles started among these colonial powers. From this struggle, the English East India Company emerged victorious and established its monopoly over Indian trade.

The Portuguese

The Portuguese were the **first ones to arrive** on the Indian scene. The reasons for arrival of the Portuguese in India were both **economic** as well as **religious**. They had come to seek spices especially pepper as well as to destroy the monopoly of Arabs and Italians over trade with the East. They also wished to spread Christianity in Asia and Africa and restrict the increasing influence of Arabs and Turks. Prior to the Portuguese, trade in the Indian Ocean was a monopoly of Arab merchants. But within 15 years of their arrival, the Portuguese completely destroyed Arab trade and established their control over Eastern trade which lasted nearly a century.

Depiction of Armada

Early Efforts

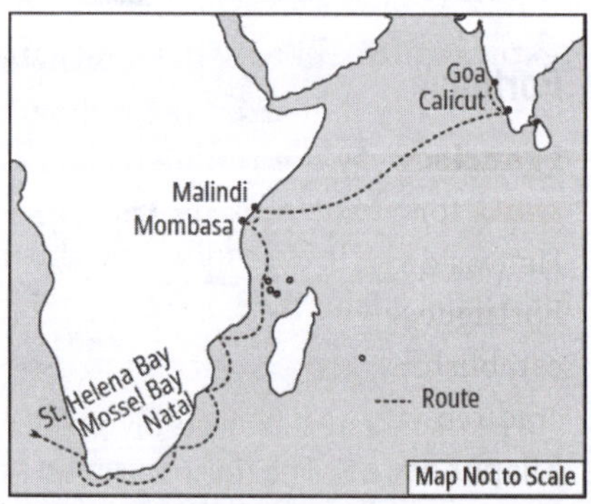

Route followed by Vasco Da Gama in 1498

- **Prince Henry the Navigator** Prince Henry of Portugal, nicknamed the **'Navigator'** had become obsessed with the idea of finding a sea route to India. He was keen to circumvent the Muslim-dominated route of the Red sea. However, Prince Henry died before his dream could be fulfilled. He is remembered as a great patron and sponsor of voyages than as a sailor.
- **Bartholomew Diaz (1487)** In 1487 Bartholomew Diaz reached the southernmost tip of Africa (which he named Cape of Storms) and became the **first known European to reach the Indian Ocean from the Atlantic**! The Portuguese later renamed the cape as 'Cape of Good Hope' as it represented the opening of a new route to the East! Diaz later used his experience in the construction of a ship which was later used by Vasco da Gama.

- **Vasco da Gama (First Portuguese India Armada, 1498)** Piloted by a Gujarati named Abdul Majid, Vasco da Gama sailed from the Cape of Good Hope and continued to India, reaching **Calicut (Kozhikode)** in 1498. He thus discovered a **new sea route** from Europe to India and became the first European to reach India by sea! This opened a new chapter in the history of India's trade relations with Europe. Vasco da Gama led two Portuguese India Armadas (or fleet of warships), the first and the fourth, sent under the patronage of **King Manuel I** of Portugal and was well received by the Zamorin (ruler) of Calicut, Manna Vikrama. Vasco da Gama returned with a cargo which sold for 60 times the cost of his voyage!
- **Pedro Alvarez Cabral (Second Portuguese India Armada, 1500)** In March 1500, Pedro Alvarez Cabral led the Second India Armada (also the First Brazil Armada as it marked the arrival of Europeans to Brazil on the way) with the aim of making a treaty with the Zamorin of Calicut and setting up a Portuguese factory. However, Cabral ran into a **conflict with the local Arab Merchants** who then attacked the Portuguese factory at Calicut, killing more than 50 Portuguese. Outraged, Cabral captured ten Arab merchants' ships anchored in the harbour, massacred nearly 600 Arabs on board and confiscated the cargo before putting the ships on fire.
- **Vasco da Gama (Fourth Portuguese India Armada, 1502)** In 1502, Vasco da Gama revisited India and set up the following:
    - In 1503, the 1st Portuguese factory was set up at **Cochin** (Kochi).
    - In 1505, the 2nd factory was set up at **Cannanore** (or Kannur).

Soon, Calicut, Cochin, Cannanore and Quilon (Kollam) became important trading centres of the Portuguese. The Portuguese trading points or factories on land were called **Feitorias**—these were unfortified trading outposts which also served as bases for naval fleet called armadas. The early spice trade comprised of mainly pepper and cinnamon.

Formation of Portuguese State of India (Estado da India, 1503–04) The Portuguese State of India was meant to be a governing body of the various Portuguese fortresses and colonies overseas and it was required to function under a Viceroy. In effect, the formation of this body indicated that the Portuguese would no longer be content with mere spice trade but would set out to establish a Christian Portuguese state in the East and launch a **holy war against Islam** there.

Portuguese Governors

Francisco De Almeida (1505–09) Almeida was appointed as the first **Portuguese Viceroy of India** for a term of three years and sent with sufficient armed ships to protect Portuguese interests. He was directed by the government to build such Portuguese fortresses that would aim to establish Portuguese control over trade of the Indian Ocean. He adopted the **'Blue Water Policy'** aimed at establishing naval supremacy of the Portuguese in the Indian Ocean, rather than over land. He is credited with the construction of **Fort Anjediva** on Anjediva Island lying at the border of Muslim Bijapur and Hindu Vijayanagar states.

In 1508, Portuguese fleet was attacked by joint Muslim naval force (Gujarat Sultanate and Mameluk Egyptian fleet) at **Chaul and Dabul**, with Almeida's son losing his life in the battle of Chaul. Almeida, however, defeated the joint force in the **Battle of Diu**, thus establishing Portuguese supremacy over Indian Ocean.

Alfonzo-De-Albuquerque (1509–15) He was the greatest Portuguese Viceroy in India and is also called as the real **founder of Portuguese power in India**. He set up his headquarter at **Cochin**.

In 1509, Albuquerque conquered **Diu** and in 1510 he conquered **Goa** from the Sultan of Bijapur, Yusuf Adil Shah. With the victory of Goa, regional kingdom of the Portuguese in India was established and Goa became 'the first bit of Indian territory to be under the Europeans since the time of Alexander the Great'. Under Albuquerque, the Portuguese established their domination over the entire Asian coast from Hormuz in Persian Gulf to Malacca in Malaya and the Spice Islands in Indonesia. They shied away neither from waging wars nor from piracy and plunder for expanding their influence. In Bengal, **Hooghly and Balasore** became the Portuguese trading centres.

Albuquerque thus made the Portuguese strong in India. He was an efficient administrator and integrated the locals into the administration. He wanted to establish permanent Portuguese settlements in India and with this aim in mind he encouraged his countrymen to marry Indian women and propagate **Christianity**. He also **abolished sati** in regions under his control.

Nino de Cunha (1529–38) He was the next major Portuguese Governor after Albuquerque. In 1530, he transferred the government head office from **Cochin to Goa**, thus making Goa the official capital of the Portuguese in India.

In this way, the Portuguese succeeded in establishing their foothold in India. They also erected ports at Colombo Kollam, Pondicherry, Maldives etc. One of the main reasons for the success of Portuguese on the sea was the inability of Mughals to develop a strong navy. Southern India was also outside the direct territorial influence of the Mughals, thus allowing the Portuguese to establish control.

Cartaze System This was a method used by Portuguese to extract money from Indian ships. Under this system, captains of all Indian ships sailing to a destination not reserved by the Portuguese were obliged to buy passes or license from the Viceroy of Goa. In the absence of a pass, their ships could be seized by the Portuguese.

Decline of the Portuguese Several factors contributed to the decline of the Portuguese. The Viceroys who came after Albuquerque were weak and inefficient. Also in 1661, Portugal was at war with Spain and needed support from England. This led to the marriage of Princess Catherine of Portugal to Charles II of England and as dowry the insular and less inhabited areas of southern Bombay were handed over to the English (the Portuguese managed to retain all the mainland territory north of Bandra up to Thane and Bassein). This marked the beginning of the strong English presence in India.

Reasons for Decline of the Portuguese

1. After Albuquerque, the Portuguese administration in India became inefficient because his successors were weak & inefficient.
2. The Portuguese society was dominated by the aristocracy and merchants did not enjoy the social influence necessary to mould state policy according to their interests, making it difficult for Portugal to maintain its maritime empire.
3. The Portuguese officials were neglected by the home government. Their salaries were low which encouraged them to indulge in corruption and malpractice.

4. The Portuguese proved to be intolerant and fanatic in matters of religion. They resorted to forcible conversions to the Christian faith which made the natives hostile.
5. The Portuguese drew a very thin line between trade and piracy, which also aroused the hostility of the natives.
6. In 1580 Portugal was merged with Spain which dragged Portugal into Spain's wars with England and Holland, badly neglecting the Portuguese interest in India.
7. Portuguese discovered Brazil which diverted their imperial interests away from India.
8. Lastly and most importantly, the Portuguese power declined in the face of stiff competition from other European powers who came behind them. The Dutch gained control over Indonesia and the British over India, Sri Lanka and Malaya.

By mid-17th century, the Portuguese finally left India. But three of their settlements, namely Goa, Diu and Daman remained in their hands till 1961. In this way, Portuguese were not only the first to come to India but also the last ones to leave India.

Impact of Portuguese Portuguese control of the Indian Ocean had significant socio-political, religious and economic consequences:

1. The Portuguese began to **propagate Christianity** in the Malabar and the Konkan coast. Missionaries like St. Francis Xavier, Father Rudolf and Father Monserette played a leading role in propagating the Christian faith. In 1540, all temples of Goa were destroyed.
2. The missionaries started schools and colleges along the west coast, where education was imparted in the native language.
3. The missionaries undertook research on Indian history and culture. Fa Heras has made a deep study on the Indus Valley Civilisation.
4. The Portuguese brought the **printing press** to India. The Bible came to be printed in the Kannada and Malayalam language.
5. The Portuguese introduced into India several types of **crops, fruits & vegetables** which they had obtained from different countries. These included—potato, sweet potato, tobacco, corn, lady's finger, chilly, pineapple, papaya, sapota, leechi, orange, black pepper, groundnuts, cashew, almonds, etc.
6. Portuguese influence also established the significance of navy in sea trade.

Prelim Capsule

The Portuguese

Year	Personality	Important Events
—	**Prince Henry the Navigator**	A key figure in the early days of the Portuguese Empire and in the 15th-century European maritime discoveries and expansion. Is remembered more as a great patron and sponsor of voyages than as a sailor. Nicknamed **'Navigator'**.

1487	**Bartholomew Diaz**	Reached the **southernmost tip of Africa** (which he named Cape of Storms) and became the first known European to reach the Indian Ocean from the Atlantic. The Portuguese later renamed the cape as **'Cape of Good Hope'**.
1498	**Vasco da Gama**	Headed the **First Portuguese India Armada**. Sailed from the Cape of Good Hope and continued to India, reaching **Calicut (Kozhikode)**. Discovered a **new sea route** from Europe to India and became the first European to reach India by sea. Was piloted by a Gujarati named **Abdul Majid**. Led two Portuguese India Armadas, the first and the fourth. Was sent under the patronage of **King Manuel I** of Portugal. Returned with a cargo which sold for 60 times the cost of his voyage.
1502	**Vasco da Gama**	In 1503, 1st Portuguese factory was set up at **Cochin** (Kochi). In 1505, 2nd factory was set up at **Cannanore** (or Kannur).
1505–1509	**Francisco De Almeida** (1st Portuguese Viceroy)	The **1st Portuguese Viceroy of India**. Adopted the **'Blue Water Policy'** aimed at establishing naval supremacy of the Portuguese in the Indian Ocean. Credited with the construction of **Fort Anjediva**. In 1508, Almeida defeated the joint Muslim naval force (Gujarat Sultanate and Mameluk Egyptian fleet) in the **Battle of Diu**.
1509–1515	**Alfonzo-De-Albuquerque**	Known as the **real founder** of Portuguese power in India. He set up his headquarter at **Cochin**. In 1509 he conquered **Diu**. In 1510 he conquered **Goa** from the Sultan of Bijapur. Encouraged his countrymen to marry Indian women and propagate **Christianity**. **Abolished sati** in regions under his control.
1529–1538	**Nino de Cunha**	In 1530 he transferred the government head office from **Cochin to Goa**.

The Dutch (From Netherland/Holland)

As Portuguese power wavered in the aftermath of the Spanish union, the Dutch took over from them. The Dutch came to India for trade. They were innovative people in business as well as in shipping techniques. They had designed the **fluitship** (the Fluyt) which was much lighter and required a smaller crew, thus reducing its operating costs. These ships eventually proved to be superior to the bulkier and slower Portuguese ships.

Cornelius de Houtman (1596) In 1596, Cornelius de Houtman was the **first Dutch traveler** to reach India.

Dutch East India Company (1602) In 1602, the Dutch East India Company was formed and the Dutch Parliament gave it a charter empowering it to make war and peace with other states, acquire territories and build fortresses. But the main interest of the Dutch was in the Indonesian archipelago and the Spice Islands and not India. They soon pushed out the Portuguese from the Malay Straits and the Indonesian Spice Islands of Java and Sumatra and even defeated English attempts there. However, they discovered that Indian trade was necessary to carry out trade with South-West Asia, as there was a good demand of Indian cloth there. In return, Indians demanded pepper and spices. Hence, the credit of first making 'Indian cloth' as an item of export goes to the Dutch.

Dutch Factories

- In 1605, the first Dutch factory was established at **Masulipatnam** in Andhra.
- The second factory was set up in 1606 at **Petapuli (Nizampatnam)**.
- In 1610, the Dutch signed a treaty with the king of Chandragiri (under the rule of Vijayanagar empire) and established their headquarters at **Pulicat**. Here they minted their gold coins called pagodas.
- They soon established trading depots at Surat, Broach, Cambay and Ahmedabad in Gujarat, Cochin in Kerala, Nagapatam (or Nagapattinam) in Madras, Masulipatnam in Andhra, Chinsura (Gustavus fort) and Peepli in Bengal, Mahe on the Malabar Coast, Agra in present-day Uttar Pradesh and Patna in Bihar.
- Dutch factories were also established at Kasimbazaar, Karaikal, Balasore, Baranagore and Golconda.
- In 1690, the Dutch headquarters were transferred from Pulicat to **Nagapattinam**.

The head of Dutch factories were called **factors** who were classified as traders and the Dutch Model of Trade was based on Cartel or Cooperative System. The Dutch struck many decisive blows to the Portuguese at Goa, Malabar, Ceylon, Malacca, Colombo and Cochin and virtually replaced the Portuguese. But meanwhile, an important rival, the English had emerged.

Anglo-Dutch Rivalry In 1623, **Amboyna massacre** took place in Indonesia where the Dutch killed 10 Englishmen and 9 Japanese. After this massacre, the Dutch began to restrict themselves to Malay Archipelago and the English to India. In 1759, the Dutch were defeated by the English in the decisive **Battle of Bedara** (Bengal), ending the Dutch power in India (the English, however, had to bitterly contest another European rival, the French, before emerging fully victorious by the end of the 18th century).

Cochin/Kochi (Ernakulum district, Kerala) – Known as the '**Queen of the Arabian Sea**', Cochin was the center of Indian spice trade for many centuries. The kingdom of Cochin came under foreign influence many times and witnessed the Portuguese period followed by the Dutch and the British. The Kingdom of Cochin became a princely state during the British rule. In 1947, Cochin became the **first** princely state to join the Indian Union willingly.

The English

Flag of English East India Company

English East India Company (1600) England too had become impatient to participate in the profitable Asian trade. In 1599, a company to trade with the East was formed under the auspices of a group of merchants known as the Merchant Adventurers. The Company popularly came to be known as the East India Company (or EIC, nickname- John Company).

In 1600, The East India Company was granted a **royal charter** by Queen Elizabeth giving it the exclusive privilege of trading east of the Cape of Good Hope for a period of 15 years. As compared to the Dutch Company, it was a much smaller concern. Its chief asset was its simple organisation—a court of 24 directors elected annually by the general court of shareholders. In the beginning, the English Company concentrated on **spice trade**. The initial voyages of the Company were made to the Spice Islands in Indonesia. Soon the English discovered the importance of Indian goods especially textiles as a barter commodity for spice trade. Thus, in 1608, Surat in Gujarat was established as the trade transit point and the company ships were docked there. The Company now planned to open a factory at Surat in Gujarat and Captain Hawkins was sent to negotiate consent with the Mughal Emperor.

Captain Hawkins (1608) In 1608, Captain William Hawkins was sent as a representative of the English Company to the Court of **Jahangir** to obtain permission to open a factory at Surat. Hawkins was the **first Englishman** to set foot on Indian soil (Surat, 24 August 1608). He could speak Turkish language and he came in a ship named **'Hector'**. He arrived at Surat and from there he went to the **court of Jahangir** at Agra in 1609. The English Company was given permission by a royal farman to open factories on the west coast. But the English were not satisfied with this concession as they wanted permission for the whole of the country. Moreover, Hawkins had to leave Agra owing to Portuguese intrigue and the English realised that they would first have to deal with the Portuguese before gaining favours from the Mughals.

English Factories A factory was merely a trading post within which were located the warehouses, offices and houses of the company's employees. It is noteworthy that no manufacturing activity was carried out in this factory.

Early Factories

- In 1611, the English opened their first factory in the south at **Masulipatnam** (Machilipatnam). In 1611 itself, the English defeated the Portuguese in the **Battle of Swally Hole** near Surat. This convinced Jahangir and, the English were allowed to set up a permanent factory at **Surat** in 1613.
- In 1615, taking the policy of expansion further, **Sir Thomas Roe** was sent by King James I as an **ambassador to the court of Jahangir**. Roe was successful in obtaining royal farman permitting the British to trade and establish factories in all parts of the Mughal Empire.

Soon the English began to feel insecure in the absence of fortified settlements and made an attempt to fortify Surat (in 1625) but the Mughals frustrated the attempt and imprisoned the English. The

English then decided to shift their focus to South India to avoid direct confrontation with the Mughals. Conditions in South India were more favourable to the English as they did not have to face a strong Indian government there. The great Vijayanagara kingdom had been overthrown in 1565 and its place taken up by relatively smaller and weaker states.

Madras

- In 1632, **Sultan of Golconda** issued a Golden Farman in favour of the English, permitting them to trade freely from the ports of Golconda on annual payment of 500 pagodas.
- In 1639, Francis Day was able to obtain **Madras** on lease from the Raja of Chandragiri and shifted the centre of English activity to Madras. The Raja allowed the English to fortify Madras, to administer it and to coin the money on the condition that they will pay him half the customs revenue of the port. Thus the English set up a factory and built a small fort around it called **Fort St. George**.
- In 1690, the British bought the Fort Devanampatnam, near Madras, and renamed it as **Fort St David**.

Bengal

- In 1651, at **Hugli**, the first English factory in Bengal was set up upon receiving permission from Sultan Shuja (second son of Emperor Shah Jahan), the Subahdar of Bengal. In 1658, all establishments of the Company in Bengal, Bihar, Orissa and Coromandel Coast were brought under the control of Fort St. George.
- In 1690 Job Charnock established a factory at **Sutanuti** which was fortified in 1696 and called **Fort William.**
- In 1698 the English Company obtained from Subahdar of Bengal Azim-us-Shan, the zamindari (i.e. right to collect revenue) of the villages of **Sutanuti, Kalikata and Gobindapur** on payment of ₹1,200 to the previous proprietors. In 1700, the Bengal factories were placed under Fort William. Soon the villages grew into a city known as Calcutta.

Bombay

In 1662, King Charles-II of England received Bombay as **dowry** on marrying a Portuguese princess. In 1668, the Crown transferred it to the Company on an annual rent of ten ponds and it was soon fortified in the wake of threats from the rising Maratha power. Bombay quickly replaced Surat as the principal depot of the Company on the West coast.

English and the Mughals

Internal Developments of the Company Between 1615 and 1686, the company grew from strength to strength. In 1625, the Governors and Directors of the company were given judicial powers. In 1661, the company was empowered to send ships of war with men and ammunition for the safety of its possessions overseas. In 1683, it got full powers to declare war and make peace, to raise and maintain an army. As early as the 1680s, the Company had plans to secure English dominion in India and was determined to make Indians pay for the conquest of their own country. On several occasions, the Court of Directors wrote to the Company authorities advising them to adopt such a civil and military policy that would secure a large revenue and enable the English to maintain their force and make English a nation in India.

Aurangzeb In 1680, Aurangzeb had issued a farman that the Company's trade was to be customs-free everywhere except Surat. In 1688, hostilities between the English and the Mughal authorities first broke out when the English captured Hugli and declared war on Emperor Aurangzeb. The English had seriously misjudged the situation and underestimated Mughal strength; they were soon defeated and driven out of the factories in Bengal. Realising that they were not yet strong enough to fight the Mughal power, they once again decided to rely on humble entreaties and flattery and get concessions from the Mughal emperor. Aurangzeb too readily pardoned the English for their mistake as he saw that foreign trade benefitted Indian artisans and merchants and enriched the state treasury. He therefore permitted them to resume trade on payment of ₹1.5 lakh as compensation. The farman of 1691 granted by Aurangzeb exempted the English Company from payment of customs duties in Bengal in return for an annual payment.

Farrukhsiyar In 1717, The East India Company succeeded in securing valuable privileges under a royal farman, **Farman of 1717**, by the Mughal Emperor Farrukhsiyar. Described as the Magna Carta of the Company, the farman was instrumental in increasing the Company's stronghold in Bengal. The Company later colonised Bengal followed by the rest of India.

Provisions of the Farman The farman confirmed the privileges granted in 1691 and extended them to Gujarat. It contained following provisions:

- The British were allowed duty-free trade in Bengal in lieu of an annual payment of ₹30,000.
- Exemption from payment of all dues at Surat in lieu of one-time settlement of ₹10,000.
- The Company retained its old privilege of exemption from payment of all dues at Hyderabad and for Madras was required to pay only the existing rent.
- The Company was allowed to rent more territory around Calcutta.
- The Company was allowed to use their own currency (minted at Bombay) throughout India.
- The Company was also granted the right to issue passes or dastaks (a permit exempting payment of transit duties) for the movement of such goods.
- The Company's servants were also permitted to trade but were not covered under this farman and were required to pay the same taxes as Indian merchants. (However, the dastaks were later misused by the Company's servants to carry out private trade. The Company's' servants were paid low salaries and their real income came from the permission the Company granted them to carry on private trade within the country, even as trade between India and Europe was reserved for the Company).

Farman as Source of Conflict The provisions of the farman became a source of perpetual conflict between the Company and the Nawabs of Bengal. The strong Nawabs of Bengal such as Murshid Quli Khan and Alivardi Khan objected to the English interpretation of the farman of 1717. They exercised strict control over the English traders and prevented them from misusing the dastaks.

Despite strong political control by native rulers, commercial affairs of the company flourished. Madras, Bombay and Calcutta became the nuclei of such activities. Large number of Indian merchants and bankers were attracted to these cities. As far as the company's servants were concerned, they were keen to take up service in India despite low salaries. This was because they were permitted to carry on private trade in India on payment of same taxes as Indian merchants.

Prelim Capsule

The English

Year	Personality	Important Events
1600	**The English Company**	The Company was granted a **royal charter** by Queen Elizabeth giving it the exclusive privilege of trading east of the Cape of Good Hope for a period of 15 years.
1608	**Captain Hawkins**	He was sent as a representative of the English Company to the Court of **Jahangir** to obtain permission to open a factory at Surat. He was the **first Englishman** to set foot on Indian soil. He could speak Turkish language and he came in a ship named **'Hector'**. He arrived at Surat and from there he went to the **court of Jahangir** at Agra in 1609. He obtained permission to open factories on the west coast but the Company was not satisfied as it wanted permission for the whole of the country.
1611	—	The English opened their 1st factory in the south at **Masulipatnam.** The English defeated the Portuguese in the **Battle of Swally Hole** near Surat.
1613	—	The English were allowed to set up a permanent factory at **Surat.**
1615	**Sir Thomas Roe**	He was sent by King James I as an **ambassador to the court of Jahangir**. Roe was successful in obtaining royal farman permitting the British to trade and establish factories in all parts of the Mughal Empire.
1632 (Madras)	—	**Sultan of Golconda** issued a Golden Farman in favour of the English, permitting them to trade freely from the ports of Golconda on annual payment of 500 pagodas.
1639	**Francis Day**	He was able to obtain **Madras** on lease from the Raja of Chandragiri. The English set up a factory and built a small fort around it called **Fort St. George**.
1651 (Bengal)	—	First English factory in Bengal was set up at **Hugli** upon receiving permission from Sultan Shuja, the Subahdar of Bengal.
1658	—	All establishments of the English Company in Bengal, Bihar, Orissa and Coromandel Coast were brought under the control of Fort St. George.
1690	**Job Charnock**	He established a factory at **Sutanuti** which was fortified in 1696 and called **Fort William**.
1696	—	**Sutanuti** factory was fortified and called **Fort William**.

1698	—	The English Company obtained from Subahdar of Bengal Azim-us-Shan, the zamindari of the villages of **Sutanuti, Kalikata and Gobindapur**.
1700	—	The Bengal factories were placed under Fort William. Soon the villages grew into a city known as **Calcutta**.
1662 (Bombay)	—	King Charles-II received Bombay as **dowry** on marrying a Portuguese princess. In 1668 the King transferred Bombay to the Company on an annual rent of ten ponds.
1717	—	Farrukhsiyar granted the English Company valuable trading privileges under the Farman **of 1717** described as the Magna Carta of the Company.

The Danes (From Denmark)

The Danes came from Denmark and they were a minor colonial power to set foot in Indian soil. The Danish East India Company was established in 1616 and they set up trading outposts in 1620 at Tranquebar near Tanjore (Tamil Nadu). In 1755, they founded a colony called **Fredericknagore** near Serampore in Bengal. Occupied twice by the English, the Danish colony failed as a commercial venture. In 1777, the Danish company went bankrupt and Serampore was transferred to the Danish Crown. However, Serampore became a safe haven for missionaries in India and earned immense fame for the cultural and educational activities of the missionaries. In 1845, Denmark ceded Serampore to Britain, thus ending nearly 150 years of Danish presence in Bengal.

The French

The French were the **last** of the European colonial powers to set foot in India. They were also keen on profiting from the Asian trade.

The French Trading Company (1664) In 1664, **Colbert** formed the Companie des Indes Orientales. The French trading company (under the governorship of Colbert) was granted a license by King Louis IV to trade with India and the East Indies.

French Factories

- In 1667, the first French factory was set up at **Surat** with Francis Caron as its Director General.
- In 1669, a factory was set up at **Masulipatnam**.
- In 1672, Caron was replaced by Francois Martin who, in 1673, received the village of Pondicherry (now renamed as Puducherry) as grant from the King of Bijapur Sher Khan Lodhi. Martin initiated the ambitious project to transform Pondicherry from a small fishing village into a flourishing port-town. Pondicherry later emerged as the French capital in India, and Martin came to be known as the Father of Puducherry.
- In 1674, the French also received a site near Calcutta from the ruler of Bengal where they built the town of **Chandernagore** (1690–92).

- In 1693, the Dutch snatched Pondicherry but it was restored to the French under the **Treaty of Reswick** (1697). In this way, the French East India Company established its firm base in Chandernagore and Pondicherry.
- The French also acquired control over Islands of **Mauritius** and **Reunion** in the Indian Ocean.
- Between 1697 and 1739, the French further consolidated their position by adding several bases including **Mahe, Karaikal, Balasore** and **Kasimbazar**.

The real trouble started when the French won control of Tanjore which the British considered vital for their trade security. (Read about the Anglo–French rivalry in the upcoming chapter). In the period of Anglo-French wars from 1746 to 1763, Pondicherry changed hands again and in 1761 the British East India Company captured Pondicherry from the French. The French Company's administration was restored by the Treaty of Paris in 1763.

Pattern of European Trade

In the 16th century, when European powers first started trading with India, they had few goods to offer (only wine and oil) in return for Indian commodities. For nearly three centuries, they struggled with the problem of financing an adverse balance of trade with Asia. In the beginning, they used **gold and silver** to pay for their imports from the East. However, the European companies were severely criticised for doing so as flow of bullion out of the country was considered bad under mercantilist beliefs. It was only in the 18th century that a final solution came when the English began receiving Bengal revenues and revenues from export of opium to China.

As far as items of trade were concerned, **Indian spices** were the most sought after commodity in Europe, especially pepper. Towards the end of the 17th century, cotton textiles, silk, indigo and saltpeter gradually rose in importance in place of spices. The increase of imports of Indian textiles alarmed indigenous Englishmen who began pressurising the government to prohibit such imports. This led to the passing of protectionist regulations in England from 1700 onwards. (Note- Saltpeter, KNO3 or Shora was an important ingredient in the manufacture of gunpowder. Being a heavy material, it was also used to stabilise the ships. Patna emerged as a major centre of saltpeter).

The change in European economy due to growth of **industrial capitalism** also affected its politico–economic relations with India. The industrial capitalists soon began resenting East India Company's monopoly over Indian trade. Ranging from Adam Smith (Wealth of Nations 1776) to various business lobbies, all attacked the Company's monopoly rights ultimately leading to the abolition of monopoly of the East India Company in Indian trade in 1813 and in China trade in 1833. Sometimes it was the English trade that followed their flag, sometimes the other way round, but together they ensured the rise of the British Empire in India.

To sum up, in this chapter, you read about the transformation which occurred in Europe since the 15th century. The growth in trade and commerce was accompanied by the European nations' search for potential colonies in Asia, Africa and America. Different trading companies were formed to carry out external trade. Various European East India Companies arrived in India as well. However, owing to clash of interests, many sided struggles started among the Portuguese, the Dutch, the English, the Danes and the French. Subsequently, English and the French East India Companies emerged as the main contenders in India. Read about this Anglo-French rivalry and the final victory of the English East India Company in the next chapter.

Previous Years' Questions – Preliminary Exam

1. Which one of the following pairs is not correctly matched? **[UPSC 1999]**
   (a) Jahangir : William Hawkins
   (b) Akbar : Sir Thomas Roe
   (c) Shahjahan : Travernier
   (d) Aurangzeb : Manucci
2. In India, among the following locations, the Dutch established their earliest Factory at **[UPSC 2003]**
   (a) Surat (b) Pulicat
   (c) Cochin (d) Kasimbazar
3. With reference to the entry of European powers into India, which one of the following statements is not correct? **[UPSC 2003]**
   (a) The Portuguese captured Goa in 1499.
   (b) The English opened their first factory in South India at Masulipatnam.
   (c) In Eastern India, the English company opened its first factory in Odisha in 1633.
   (d) Under the leadership of Dupleix, the French occupied Madras in 1746.
4. Which of the following is the correct statement? **[UPSC 2005]**
   (a) The modern Kochi was a Dutch Colony till India's Independence.
   (b) The Dutch defeated the Portuguese and built Fort Williams in the modern Kochi.
   (c) The modern Kochi was first a Dutch Colony before the Portuguese took over from them.
   (d) The modern Kochi never became a part of the British Colony.
5. In the year 1613, where was the English East India Company given permission to set up a factory (trading post)? **[UPSC 2006]**
   (a) Bangalore (b) Madras
   (c) Masulipatnam (d) Surat
6. Which one of the following was the first Fort constructed by the British in India? **[UPSC 2007]**
   (a) Fort William (b) Fort St. George
   (c) Fort St. David (d) Fort St. Angelo
7. Who among the following Europeans were the last to come to pre-independence India as traders? **[UPSC 2007]**
   (a) Dutch (b) English
   (c) French (d) Portuguese
8. With whose permission did the English set up their first factory in Surat? **[UPSC 2009]**
   (a) Akbar (b) Jahangir
   (c) Shahjahan (d) Aurangzeb
9. With reference to Pondicherry (now Puducherry), consider the following statements: **[UPSC 2010]**
   1. The first European power to occupy Pondicherry were the Portuguese.
   2. The second European power to occupy Pondicherry were the French.
   3. The English never occupied Pondicherry

   Which of the statements given above is/are correct?
   (a) 1 only (b) 2 and 3 only
   (c) 3 only (d) 1, 2 and 3
10. With reference to Indian history, consider the following statements: **[UPSC 2022]**
    1. The Dutch established their factories/warehouses on the east coast on lands granted to them by Gajapati rulers.
    2. Alfonso de Albuquerque captured Goa from the Bijapur Sultanate.
    3. The English East India Company established a factory at Madras on a plot of land leased from a representative of the Vijayanagara empire.

    Which of the statements given above are correct?
    (a) 1 and 2 only (b) 2 and 3 only
    (c) 1 and 3 only (d) 1, 2 and 3

Answers

Previous Years' Questions – Preliminary Exam

1. (b)	2. (b)	3. (a)	4. (d)	5. (d)
6. (b)	7. (c)	8. (b)	9. (a)	10. (b)

4 Rise of British Supremacy: Carnatic, Plassey, and Buxar

After the death of Aurangzeb, the Mughal Empire witnessed decline and decentralisation of power evident in the emergence of several autonomous states. The English and the French companies began to see political future in India. By the early 18th century, the English and the French companies had already settled down with a profitable trade. The two had already become rivals in Europe and North America. The stage was therefore set for Anglo–French rivalry in India which began in the 1740s and ended in an eventual victory of the English and then began the conquest of India beginning with Bengal from the Battle of Plassey in 1757. In the words of Rabindranath Tagore, 'darkness settled on the face of the land and the weighing scales in the merchant's hand changed into the imperial scepter'.

The struggle with the French for supremacy marked the first phase of the rise of the British power. The conquest of Bengal was the second and decisive step. Thus in this chapter, you will read about the Anglo–French rivalry, taking the form of the Carnatic Wars and leading to the elimination of the French as main contenders of power in India. You will also read about the British conquest of Bengal, through the gradual transfer of power from the Nawabs to the British in Bengal during the period 1757 to 1765 with the Battle of Plassey and Buxar emerging as major landmarks. The British initially ruled through indigenous institutions but introduced constitutional changes from 1773 onwards. British power in India was integrated into Britain's worldwide imperial system.

English East India Company: From Trading Company to Political Power

The mid-18th century saw the gradual transformation of the English East India Company from a trading company into a political power. During the period 1600 to 1744, the Company slowly expanded its trade network in India, simultaneously easing out the rivals through a strategy combining diplomacy and war. Though the rise of British supremacy in India is usually traced to 1757 with the British victory in the Battle of Plassey, the ground for the victory was laid in South India where the British might was successfully tested out against the French Company.

Anglo–French Struggle for Supremacy: The Carnatic Wars

When the declining Mughal authority and the weak regional powers proved incapable of safeguarding the interests of European Companies in India, they saw the necessity to empower themselves militarily. Further, they were commercial entities, seeking to maximise their profit margins, which necessitated the elimination of competition and establishment of monopoly. Nay, they not only wanted to monopolise their trade and sell dear, they also wanted to buy their commodities cheap, necessitating acquisition of some political control over the country they traded with.

In this context, emergence of hostilities between the English and the French was but natural. South India emerged as the arena of Anglo–French rivalry as it had become the main centre of French activities with Pondicherry as capital. The French had also begun to wield great influence in the neighbouring states of Hyderabad and Mysore. Besides, there was not much scope in western India because of the powerful Marathas, while Eastern India was under the strict control of Alivardi Khan. It was only in Southern India that conditions became favourable, especially after the death of Nizam-ul-Mulk in 1748.

Thus, for nearly 20 years from 1744 to 1763, the English and the French remained embroiled in a bitter war in south India, a series of conflicts popularly known as the Carnatic Wars (1746–63).

First Carnatic War (1746–48)

Immediate Context: Austrian War of Succession (1740) The immediate context for conflict between two European rivals in India was provided by the War of Austrian Succession in Europe which broke out in Europe in 1740 between Austria and Prussia. In this war, Britain and France joined opposite camps. Perhaps conscious of their relatively weaker position, the French tried hard to prevent the extension of war to India and Dupleix advised his English counterpart to maintain neutrality. But the English did not agree, instead deliberately adopted aggressive stand and seized some French ships off the south-eastern coast of India. The French had no fleet in India, hence Dupleix (the French Governor General) messaged **La Bourdonnais** (the French Governor of Mauritius) for reinforcements. La Bourdonnais immediately left with a squadron of 3,000 men towards the Coromandel Coast. As soon as the help arrived, the French attacked the English and captured the British possessions in Fort St George, Madras and other nearby areas (21 September 1746). Included among the prisoners of war was Robert Clive. The First Carnatic War had begun.

Dupleix, governor of French India from 1742 to 1754

The English Seek Protection from the Nawab of Carnatic, Nawab Anwaruddin Anwaruddin, the Nawab of Carnatic, disapproved of hostilities in his kingdom. Thus, when the English appealed to him for protection, the Nawab asked the French to quit Madras. But the French were now in no mood to retreat and neglected the advice just as the English had done earlier.

Battle of St. Thomas (or St. Thome, 1746) The Nawab now sent a large army to fight against the French. A large Indian army of 10,000 under Mahfuz Khan met a small French army consisting of 230 Europeans and 700 Indian soldiers under Capt. Paradise on the banks of **River Adyar** at Mylapore near St. Thomas in 1746. But to everyone's surprise, a handful of properly trained soldiers of the French army routed Anwaruddin's vast army. This amply demonstrated the superiority of the European troops and exposed the military weakness of the Indian rulers.

Dupleix learnt the lesson that in any quarrel between Indian princes, his disciplined army would be very useful. And in the 18th-century political chaos, there was no dearth of Indian princes who would invite Dupleix's assistance to turn the scales in their favour. At that time, Indian rulers were not guided by patriotism and did not hesitate in inviting foreigners in settling accounts with their rivals. In this way, it was Dupleix who first showed the way of intervening in disputes of the Indian rulers and thereby acquiring political control—a technique which was later perfected by the English Company.

Treaty of Aix-la-Chapelle (1748) Even as the French continued the siege, the War of Austrian Succession came to an end by the Treaty of Aix-la-Chapelle (1748) on the basis of mutual restitution of conquests. This brought an end to the first round of Anglo–French conflict in India as well. Madras was restored to the English and the French got Louisburg in North America. The first round of conflict had ended in a draw.

Second Carnatic War (1749–54)

Dynastic feuds in South India provided the context for the second round of Anglo–French conflict in the south. The succession disputes at both Carnatic and Hyderabad provided the French Governor General Dupleix an opportunity to intervene in Indian politics.

Immediate Context: Succession Disputes in Carnatic and Hyderabad Earlier we saw that in 1740, the Marathas had invaded the Carnatic, killed Nawab Dost Ali and took his son-in-law Chanda Sahib as prisoner to Satara. In 1743, the Nizam of Hyderabad felt prompted to come to the Carnatic and appoint Anwaruddin Khan as the Nawab of Carnatic. But in 1748, Chanda Sahib was set free by the Marathas and the same year, Nizam of Hyderabad Nizam-ul-Mulk Asaf Jah passed away. He was succeeded by his son Nasir Jung but his grandson, Muzaffar Jung laid claim to the throne. Muzaffar Jung now allied with Chanda Sahib to gain their respective seats in Hyderabad and the Carnatic.

Intervention by Dupleix In this way, Dupleix soon got his opportunity and astounding success awaited his plans. He was able to interfere in the wars of succession that started after the death of Asaf Jah (1748). He pledged French support to Muzaffar Jung and Chanda Sahib. Thus, a tripartite understanding was developed among the **French, Chanda Sahib** and **Muzaffar Jung**.

French Install their Protégé, Chanda Sahib, in Carnatic (1749) In August 1749, the three allies ambushed and killed Anwaruddin at the **Battle of Ambur**, near Vellore. His son Muhammad Ali fled to Trichinopoly and Chanda Sahib became Nawab of Carnatic. He rewarded the French with a grant of 80 villages near Pondicherry.

Feeling the extension of French influence, the British decided to support Nasir Jung for the throne of the Nizam and Muhammad Ali for the Nawabship of the Carnatic. Thus, began the second phase of the Anglo–French War, also known as the Second Carnatic War.

French Install their Protégé, Muzaffar Jung, in Hyderabad Soon the French and their allies marched to the Deccan. The French army surprised and killed Nasir Jung and installed French protégé Muzaffar Jung as the Nizam of Hyderabad. Muzaffar Jung amply rewarded Dupleix by appointing him **honorary governor** of all the Mughal Dominions south of the River Krishna. Territories near Pondicherry as well as the famous market town of Masulipatam in Orissa were also ceded to the French. In return, Dupleix placed at the disposal of Muzaffar Jung the services of his best officer—**Marquis de Bussy**, with a French army. This was also the best way of safeguarding French interests at the Hyderabad court.

Dupleix was now at the height of his political power and his dream of an empire now seemed likely to be realised. Soon afterwards, Muzaffar Jung was killed in an accidental skirmish (February 1751). However, Bussy maintained French influence in the Deccan by quickly placing his nominee Salabat Jung on the throne. In this way, Bussy went on to control the political fortunes of the Deccan for seven years and even induced the Nizam to grant him four rich districts on the Coromandel Coast known as the **Northern Circars** (or Northern Sarkars), comprising Mustafanagar, Ellore, Rajamundry and Chicacole. The French power in south India was now at its height but not far away from its fall.

Emergence of Robert Clive Meanwhile, Muhammad Ali (the son of the late Nawab Anwaruddin) had taken refuge in the fortress of Trichinopoly and the repeated attempts of Chanda Sahib and the French to capture the fortress had failed. The British, realising that the situation implied a serious threat to their position in Southern India, now decided to put their entire strength behind Muhammad Ali.

Robert Clive

At this crucial juncture, there appeared a man on the scene endowed with a daring genius, whose intelligence and bravery saved the fortunes of the English. He was a young clerk of the Company, Robert Clive. He suggested that French pressure on Muhammad Ali could be released by attacking Arcot, the capital of Carnatic. Thus, attack upon Arcot was to be used as a diversionary tactic. Chanda Sahib would have to divert an effective part of his army for the protection of Arcot.

Siege of Arcot (August 1751) Clive's plan seemed well conceived and once it was approved, Clive stormed Arcot with a small force of only 210 men and captured it (August 1751). The plan had the desired effect and Chanda Sahib, alarmed by the fall of his capital, sent a large portion of his force from Trichinopoly which comprised of 4,000 men to recapture Arcot. Clive successfully sustained the famous siege for 53 days (23 September to 14 November). In the meantime, Clive received help in the form of reinforcements from Madras and some Indian allies (rulers of Mysore, Tanjore and the Marathas). Clive then came out of the besieged town, attacked and defeated Chanda Sahib at several important battles including one fought at Kaveripak.

Meanwhile, encouraged by the capture of Arcot, a strong English force led by Stringer Lawrence relieved Trichinopoly following the surrender of French forces (June 1752). Chanda Sahib was **treacherously captured and beheaded** by the Raja of Travancore. Muhammad Ali then became the undisputed Nawab of the Carnatic. Dupleix's high hopes were thus dashed to the ground.

Recall of Dupleix, 1754 The French defeat at Trichinopoly sealed the fate of Dupleix. The Directors of the French Company did not appreciate his political ambitions and disproved of the expenses they involved and recalled him. On 1 August 1754, **Godeheu** succeeded Dupleix as French Governor General in India. Recall of Dupleix proved to be a big blow to the fortunes of the French Company in India.

Treaty of Pondicherry, 1755 In complete reversal to Dupleix's policy, Godeheu signed a peace treaty, the Treaty of Pondicherry, with the English in 1755. As per this treaty, both the companies agreed not to interfere in the quarrels of the Indian princes. The second round of conflict had also proved inconclusive.

Nevertheless, after this treaty, though the French continued to maintain their hold over Hyderabad for some time, they had lost much of their prestige and their predominant position in the Deccan had been definitely undermined. On the other hand, English influence had been established in Carnatic, with their candidate Muhammad Ali installed as the Nawab of Carnatic.

Third Carnatic War (1757–63 AD)

Immediate Context: Seven Years' War in Europe Like the first Carnatic war, even this war was an echo of the hostilities in Europe. In 1756 the Seven Years' War broke out in Europe. In this War, England and France joined opposite camps which ended the short peace between the European companies in India as well.

Arrival of Count de Lally (April 1758) This time the French Government made a determined effort to oust the English from India. For this purpose, the French sent an impressive French army headed by Count de Lally, who reached India after a long voyage of 12 months in April 1758. By this time, the English had already won the **Battle of Plassey** and they returned to India with fresh reinforcements of men and material.

Problems Faced by the French Army Lally started his work vigorously. He attacked **Fort St. David** and captured it and other small English possessions in this region. But the French victory was only short-lived as problems of varying nature began to surface on the horizon. Lally's attack on Madras ended in failure as he could not get naval support in time. The French Company also faced shortage of ammunition as well as lack of funds to pay the troops. Lally was rude and overbearing in his conduct with the subordinates, i.e. the Company's servants of Pondicherry. He held a very low opinion of them and looked down upon them as dishonest rogues to be set right with threats and punishment. In such circumstances, both Lally and his soldiers distrusted each other and the French troops felt badly demoralised.

At this critical juncture, rash and headstrong Lally committed another great blunder of prevailing upon Bussy and recalling him from the Nizam's court, leaving the French army under incompetent commanders. Having assessed the situation, the English sent an army from Bengal to the Northern Circars. They occupied Rajamundry and Masulipatam and also concluded a favourable treaty with Nizam Salabat Jung. French influence in Deccan was thus irrevocably lost.

Battle of Wandiwash (1760) The battle still continued and Lally was eventually defeated decisively at the Battle of Wandiwash or Vandvasi now in Tamil Nadu (22 January 1760). The English army led by General **Eyre Coot** totally routed the French army under Lally and Bussy was taken prisoner.

Defeated, the French retreated to Pondicherry. But, the English soon laid siege to Pondicherry as well, forcing Lally to ask for help from Nawab **Hyder Ali** of Mysore. However, due to lack of coordination, the contingent sent by Hyder returned to Mysore without fighting even a single battle.

The French capital of Pondicherry finally surrendered on 16 January 1761. The fall of Pondicherry sounded the death knell of French dominions in India. Shortly thereafter Jinje and Mahe on the Malabar Coast also surrendered to the English, leaving the French without even a toehold in India.

Peace of Paris, 1763 The Third Carnatic War ended officially in 1763 with the conclusion of the Peace of Paris, at the end of the Seven Years' War. As per the treaty, Pondicherry and some other French settlements were no doubt returned to France, but these were never to be fortified again and could only function as mere trading centres. The worst fate awaited Lally. He was detained as a prisoner of war for two years, after which he was allowed to return to his home country, where, far from receiving any kind treatment, he was first imprisoned and then executed.

Thus, the Third Carnatic War brought down the curtain to the Anglo–French rivalry in India and cleared the way for the establishment of the British Empire.

Reasons for Defeat of the French Against the English

Various factors are held responsible for the defeat of the French in India and the victory of the English, some of which are enumerated as follows:

Continental Ambitions of France Several historians, including BL Grover, have pointed out that France in the 18th century remained preoccupied with its continental ambitions, which considerably strained its resources. The French monarchs of the time were fighting for the 'natural frontiers' of their country, which meant acquisition of territory towards Rhine and towards Italy. Such an expansionist policy of France kept it perpetually trapped in the wars of Europe and diverted its energies away from colonial acquisitions. In the end, the French gained almost nothing on the continent and even lost its colonial possessions. On the other hand, England did not covet an inch of European territory but followed its single-minded objective of colonial expansion, an objective in which it achieved considerable success.

Different Systems of Government Several historians have attributed the failure of France to its inferior system of government as compared to England. While the French government of the time was autocratic and suffered from corruption and inefficiency, the English government was run by an enlightened oligarchy, under which it was making immense progress towards a constitutional set up. Emphasising on the rottenness of the French system of government, historian **Alfred Lyall** wrote, 'It was the short sighted, ill managed European policy of Louis XV, misguided by his mistresses and by incompetent ministers, that France lost her Indian settlements'.

Difference in Organisation of two Companies The French Company had been formed with a majority of capital contributed by the monarch with a guarantee of dividend to the shareholders. As a result, the directors of the Company, nominated by the king himself, took very little interest in the progress of the Company. Naturally, the financial position of the Company suffered badly and many times it was revived by government subsidy. Such a body was ill-equipped to support the ambitions of Dupleix and his expensive wars. On the contrary, the English Company was an independent commercial corporation with a court of Directors who were greatly interested in the welfare of the Company. The Company mostly maintained good financial health and was at one time seen as the milch-cow of the British government.

Responsibility of Dupleix Despite Dupleix's political capabilities, he could never escape the responsibility for French defeat. He was so gripped by his political ambitions that he put a blind eye to several other aspects of the struggle. For instance, in his zeal for political conquests, he failed to attend to the fast deteriorating financial and trading aspects of the Company. Hence, Dupleix is also held partly responsible for the French defeat at the hands of the English.

Impact of British Success in Bengal Some historians consider the British success in Bengal as the most significant factor for French defeat and English victory in India. According to them, what really turned the tide in Britain's favour was its recent access to the **rich resources of Bengal**. British had occupied Bengal and its resources were liberally used in the Third Carnatic War. It was rightly said by VA Smith that no General could have won the empire of India by starting from Pondicherry as a base and contending with a power which held Bengal and command of the sea.

Other Factors

- **Recall of Dupleix** Recall of Dupleix proved to be a mistake of the French.
- **Rashness and Arrogance of Lally** Count de Lally was rash and arrogant. His behaviour so greatly alienated his subordinates that they openly rejoiced when he was defeated by the English.
- **Absence of Permanent Naval Presence** The French had no permanent naval presence in India while the British had a formidable naval presence. The British Navy was also superior.

Marriot wrote, 'Dupleix made a cardinal blunder in looking for the key of India in Madras, Clive sought and found it in Bengal'.

In this way, the English Company proved to be the superior force in many ways. It was wealthier, had a vastly superior infrastructure with larger fleets. The English Company conducted more frequent voyages and had superior knowledge of commerce. The English Company was a great private corporation, not dependent on any way on the state. In fact the state was in its debt. While Pondicherry grew as strong and impressive as the English settlement in Madras, it could not match the latter in extent and variety of commerce. Chandernagore in the east proved no match for Calcutta. Such were the qualitative differences between the two companies that ultimately led to the defeat of the French at the hands of the English in India.

Prelim Capsule

The Carnatic Wars (1746–1763)

Wars	Period	Important Details
First Carnatic War Dupleix	**1746-48**	Immediate context- **War of Austrian Succession** in Europe in which England and France had joined opposite camps. Main battles fought- **Battle of St. Thomas**. Ended with the Treaty of **Aix-la-Chapelle** in Europe. Result- It was a drawn struggle.
Second Carnatic War Dupleix, Godeheu	**1749-54**	Immediate context- Succession disputes at Carnatic and Hyderabad. Main battles fought- **Battle of Ambur** and **Arcot**. Ended with the **Treaty of Pondicherry**. Result- Though inconclusive, the English had an edge over the French.
Third Carnatic War Count de Lally	**1757-63**	Immediate context- **Seven Years' War** in Europe. Once again, England and France joined opposite camps, ending the short peace between the European companies in India as well. Main battle fought- **Battle of Wandiwash**. The English army led by General **Eyre Coot** totally routed the French army under Lally. Ended with the **Treaty of Paris** signed at the end of Seven Years War. Result- The British decisively defeated the French in India.

British Conquest of Bengal–Plassey to Buxar (1757–65)

The beginning of British conquest in India may be traced back to the Battle of Plassey in 1757, in which the English Company's forces defeated the Nawab of Bengal Siraj-ud-Daulah. In fact, the history of British conquest of Bengal is the history of gradual transfer of power from the Nawabs to the British during the short period of eight years, from 1757 to 1764, the main cause of conflict being the commercial rivalry between the British and the Bengal Nawabs.

Francois Bernier, a traveller who visited India during the reign of Aurangzeb, wrote about Bengal- 'A popular proverb among the Europeans goes that the kingdom of Bengal has hundred gates open for entrance, but not one for departure'.

Backgrounder

- Since the 17th century, Bengal had emerged as a happy hunting ground of the Dutch, the English and the French Companies who were attracted to Bengal mainly owing to its rich resources.
- In 1651, at **Hugli**, the first English factory was set up upon receiving permission from **Sultan Shuja** (second son of Emperor Shah Jahan), the subahdar of Bengal.
- In 1651 itself, Shuja also granted the English East India Company the **privilege of free trade** in Bengal, Bihar and Orissa in return for lump sum payment of ₹3,000 (350 pounds) at a time when

the Company's exports from Bengal were worth more than 50,000 pounds a year. This was because Sultan Shuja was pleased by the services of one Mr. Boughton, who had successfully cured a royal lady of a disease. Thereafter, English factories sprang up at **Kasimbazar, Patna** and other places.

- In 1698, the English Company obtained the zamindari of the villages of **Sutanuti, Kalikata and Gobindapur** from Subahdar Azim-us-Shan, on payment of ₹1,200 to the previous proprietors. In 1700, the Bengal factories were placed under **Fort William**. Soon the villages grew into a city known as Calcutta.
- In 1717, Emperor **Farrukhsiyar** confirmed the **trade privileges** granted to the Company by earlier subahdars. By early 18th century, exports from Bengal consisted of nearly 60 per cent of the English Company's imports from Asia, comprising of products such as cotton and silk textiles, handicrafts and raw products such as saltpeter, rice, indigo and pepper.
- In 1717 itself, Farrukhsiyar appointed **Murshid Quli Khan**, the Diwan of Bengal, as Subahdar or Governor (Nizam or Nazim) of Bengal, thus holding the post of Subahdar and Diwan at the same time. Taking advantage of his position, Murshid Quli now declared himself as the Nawab of Bengal and became the first independent Nawab of Bengal.
- In 1740, **Alivardi Khan**, the Deputy Governor of Bihar, deposed and killed Nawab Sarfaraz Khan (grandson of Murshid Quli). Alivardi Khan rightly did not allow fortifications of French and English factories at Chandernagore and Calcutta. In 1756, Alivardi died, nominating his grandson Siraj-ud-Daulah as his successor.

Battle of Plassey (23 June 1757)

The English Company first acquired a foothold in Bengal politics through Plassey conspiracy of 1757 which ended the rule of Siraj-ud-Daulah and inaugurated a new phase of British relations with India. Several developments converged to culminate into the Battle of Plassey which marked the beginning of British conquest of India.

Siraj-ud-Daulah (April 1756–June 1757)

Siraj-ud-Daulah (Nawab of Bengal)

Siraj's succession was challenged by two other contenders for the throne, Shaukat Jung (Faujdar of Purnea) and Ghaseti Begum (Alivardi's daughter). This resulted in intense court factionalism and support was offered to different warring groups by a dominant group in the Nawab's court comprising **Jagat Seth, Umichand (or Amir Chand), Raj Ballabh, Rai Durlabh, Mir Jafar**, zamindars and others who were also opposed to Siraj. This seriously destabilised the administration of Bengal and the advantage was taken by English East India Company.

Main reasons for conflict between the Nawab of Bengal and the English Company were:

- **Farman of 1717** In 1717, the Mughal Emperor Farrukhsiyar issued a farman (royal order) granting the British East India Company many trading privileges. This farman became a perpetual source of conflict between the Bengal Nawabs and the English Company. For one, it meant loss of revenue to the Bengal government and second, dastaks were misused by the Company's servants to evade taxes on their private trade.
- **Shelter to Krishna Das** The English Company had given shelter to Krishna Das, son of Raj Ballabh, who had fled with immense treasures against the Nawab's will.

- **Support to Ghaseti Begum** The Company had also offended the Nawab by giving support to the claims of Ghaseti Begum.
- **Immediate Cause** The breaking point came when the English Company, anticipating another round of Anglo–French struggle, began to strengthen the **fortifications of Fort William** and mounted guns on its walls. Siraj pleaded repeatedly with the English to desist from further fortification, but to no avail. Seeing his own authority flouted in his own dominion, Siraj-ud-Daulah decided to launch an offensive.

Black Hole Tragedy On 15 June 1756, Siraj-ud-Daulah surrounded Fort William and the siege lasted for five days. During this while, Governor Roger Drake and some of his men escaped through the back door down the Hooghly River, took refuge at **Fulta** near the sea and waited for help from Madras. They left behind 146 persons, including some women and children, under the command of John Zepahnaih **Holwell**. After the fort fell on 20 June, the Nawab renamed **Calcutta as Alinagar**, placed it under the charge of Manik Chand, and himself returned to Murshidabad.

Subsequently, Holwell and others were imprisoned in a small room of the fort popularly known as Black Hole (18 feet long and 14 feet 10 inches wide) in conditions of excessive heat and crowding owing to summer solstice. It is believed that out of **146 persons** imprisoned in that room, only 26 survived the next morning, the rest were probably trampled down by the others for places near the window. The incident came to be known as the 'Black Hole Tragedy'.

The incident was held up as an example of British heroism and Nawab's callousness. Siraj-ud-Daulah was portrayed a cruel monster and held directly responsible for the deaths. The English Company used the episode to sway British public opinion and sympathy in favour of the wars of aggression it intended to wage.

Meanwhile, help came from Madras in the form of a strong naval force under the command of **Robert Clive**. Manik Chand, the Nawab's officer in charge of Fort William, was bribed and he surrendered after a brief pretence of resistance.

Treaty of Alinagar (9 February 1757) Consequently, in February 1757, the Nawab had to make peace with the English and sign the humiliating Treaty of Alinagar. As per the treaty, the Nawab had to restore to the English their former privileges of trade, grant permission to fortify Calcutta and even pay compensation amount for the losses suffered by the English.

In this way, Clive had regained Calcutta and even forced the Nawab to concede to all English demands. Still, the English were not satisfied. They had decided to replace the Nawab with Mir Jafar. With this in mind, they placed an impossible set of demands before the Nawab, thus making a war inevitable. Clive organised a web of intrigue with the leaders in the Nawab's court. Chief among these were:

- **Mir Jafar** the Mir Bakshi (Commander-in-Chief of the Nawab's army)
- **Manik Chand** the Officer incharge of Calcutta
- **Amir Chand** a rich merchant
- **Jagat Seth** the biggest banker of Bengal
- **Khadim Khan** commanded a large number of the Nawab's troops

These disaffected nobles of Siraj's court joined hands with the English to oust Siraj and install their protégé, leading to the **Plassey Conspiracy of 1757**.

The Battle (23 June 1757) On 23 June 1757, both armies met at **Plassey, 30 km south of Murshidabad**. The English force comprised of 950 European infantry and 2100 Indian sepoys, while that of the Nawab comprised of 50,000 commanded by the treacherous Mir Jafar. Only a small group of Nawab's soldiers fought bravely. They were led by **Mir Madan** and **Mohan Lal**. After Mir Madan was killed by a stray shot from the English side, Mir Jafar played upon the fears of the Nawab and advised him to retire from the battlefield, leaving the command in the hands of his generals. The trick was well played. Once the Nawab retired with 2,000 horsemen, a large part of the Nawab's army led by Mir Jafar and Rai Durlabh merely looked on, as Clive routed the rest of Nawab's forces. As a result, the Nawab had to flee but was captured and put to death by an assassin, Mohammad Ali Beg, on the orders of Mir Jafar's son, Miran.

KM Panikkar- 'Plassey was a transaction in which the rich bankers of Bengal and Mir Jafar sold out the Nawab to the English'.

Consequences of Battle of Plassey

- Mir Jafar was proclaimed as Nawab of Bengal (he was promised the Nawabship by Clive even before the Battle of Plassey).
- Robert Clive was confirmed as the Governor of Bengal (Clive's First Governorship: 1757–60).
- The Company was granted undisputed right to free trade in Bengal, Bihar and Orissa.
- It was also understood that British officials would no longer need to pay any taxes on their private trade.
- The Company received the **zamindari of 24-Parganas** near Calcutta.
- Mir Jafar paid out a sum of ₹50 lakh as gift or bribe to the Company's officials, besides a large amount as personal present to Clive and compensation for the Company's losses.
- All the French settlements in Bengal were surrendered to the English.

Significance of Battle of Plassey The battle was hardly significant from the military point of view as the English army showed no military superiority. It was a mere skirmish, resulting in 65 casualties on the English side and 500 on the Nawab's side. More than the might of the English, it was the treachery of the Nawab's confidants that decided the fate of the battle of Plassey.

However, the battle turned out to be of great historical significance because of the events that followed.

- **The British emerged as kingmakers in Bengal** The British now appointed their man, Mir Jafar, as the new Nawab. Jafar was completely dependent on the English for maintenance of his position in Bengal. Hence, an English force of 6,000 troops was stationed in Bengal for Nawab's protection with the natural consequence that all real power passed into the Company's hands and **Mr. Watts**, the British Resident at Murshidabad, began to wield considerable influence.
- **Transformation in position of the English Company** The victory in Plassey brought about a great transformation in the position of the English Company in Bengal. Until now the English Company was just one of the European companies trading in Bengal. After Plassey, the Company emerged supreme and established its monopoly over Bengal trade by marginalising the French and the Dutch Companies. The English also emerged as powerful contenders in Bengal politics.
- **Vast resources of Bengal placed at British disposal** The victory in the battle placed vast resources at the disposal of the British. The first instalment of wealth paid to the Company immediately after Plassey was paid in silver coins, carried in more than 100 boats. Bengal then was the most prosperous province of India—its manufactures were in huge demand not only in India but also in

world outside. Victory in Bengal played a decisive role in Anglo–French struggle. In fact, with the revenues of Bengal, the English were able to meet the cost of conquest of rest of the country.

Thus, the 'Plassey Revolution' as it is called, proved to be a battle with far-reaching consequences. The British victory in Plassey marked the beginning of British conquest of Bengal and later of India. It helped the Company and its servants to amass unimaginable wealth at the cost of the people of Bengal.

Col. Malleson 'There never was a battle in which the consequences were so vast, so immediate and so permanent'.

In the words of the Bengali poet **Nabin Chandra Sen**, the battle of Plassey was followed by, 'a night of eternal gloom for India'.

Mir Jafar (June 1757–October 1760)

Immediately after his succession, Mir Jafar began to face some serious problems-

- Some zamindars like Raja Ram Sinha of Midnapore and Hizir Ali Khan of Purnea refused to accept Mir Jafar as their ruler.
- Mir Jafar also suspected the loyalty of some of his soldiers, who had not been receiving their regular salary, as well as that of his officials like Rai Durlabh.
- There was also an attempt by the Mughal Emperor's son, who later on became Shah Alam, to capture the throne of Bengal.
- Mir Jafar's growing dependence on the Company for military support was used by the Company to demand more finances and other privileges from the Nawab. But the Nawab failed to meet the growing demands of the Company which brought about his ruin.

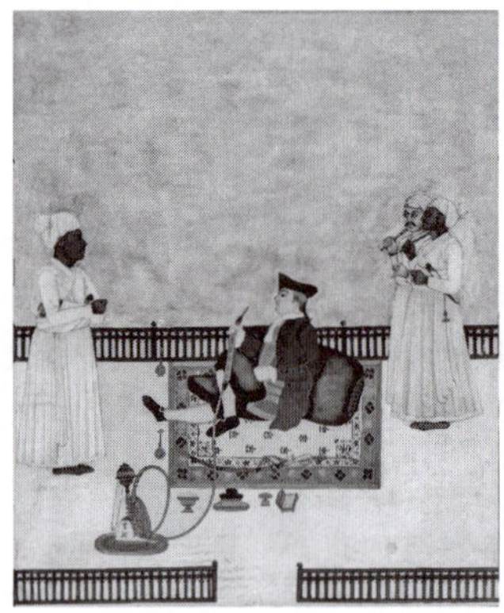

Portrait of an East India Company Official by artist Dip Chand (The pictures made by Indian artists for the British in India are called Company paintings.)

Mir Jafar, who had played the role of **'Clive's Jackal'**, soon began to repent the deal he had struck and in order to shed off the British yoke, Jafar began intriguing with the Dutch against the British. Clive, however, thwarted this design by defeating the Dutch in the decisive **Battle of Bedra** (November 1759). But by now the English Company had grown considerably suspicious of the Nawab and had begun to look for a suitable replacement. From the Company's perspective, its role had considerably changed since Plassey, and it now had to play the role of a commercial-cum military-cum political power. How was it going to fund its new responsibilities? The Nawab was unable to pay the stipulated payments and by 1760, he was in debt to the Company to the tune of ₹25 lakh. The Company had lost its confidence on Mir Jafar.

Meanwhile, Mir Jafar's son, Miran, died and once again conflict over succession followed. The conflict was between Miran's son and Mir Qasim, the son-in-law of Mir Jafar. Mir Qasim secretly promised **Vansittart** (who had succeeded Clive as the Governor of Bengal in 1760) the necessary funds if the English Company agreed to support his claims to the Nawabship. Accordingly, Vansittart decided to take the side of Mir Qasim and in October 1760, Mir Jafar was ultimately forced to abdicate in favour of his son-in-law, Mir Qasim. In this way, Mir Jafar reaped as he had sowed, got betrayal in return for betrayal.

Mir Qasim or Itmad-ud-Daulah (October 1760–63)

Mir Qasim rewarded his benefactors by granting the Company the zamindari of **Burdwan, Midnapore and Chittagong**. He promised to give the Company half the share in chunam trade of Sylhet. He also heavily bribed his kingmakers namely, Vansittart, Holwell and other English officials with handsome presents totalling 29 lakh rupees.

The first few months of Mir Qasim's reign went very well. But soon the relationship with the British embittered due to several reasons. But Mir Qasim belied English hopes. He was able and efficient ruler and wanted to free himself from foreign control.

- He shifted the capital from **Murshidabad to Monghyr** in Bihar, away from the influence of the Company at Calcutta and court intrigues of Murshidabad.
- He also majorly overhauled the bureaucracy by men of his choice and sought to improve the finances of the state.
- He sought to **modernise his army** along European lines and preparations were made for the manufacture of guns at Monghyr.
- **Ram Narayan**, the Deputy Governor of Bihar, had shown refractory behaviour since the days of Mir Jafar and continued to do so, banking on English support as he had received in the past. In spite of repeated reminders, he failed to submit the accounts of Bihar. In fact, this time he went on to proclaim himself as an independent ruler. Mir Qasim decided not to tolerate such open defiance of his authority and ordered his dismissal and execution.
- The **misuse of the Company's dastaks** for private trade was a perpetual cause of tension between the English Company and the Nawab. The Company's servants were not paying any duty on their goods, whereas the local merchants had to pay duty with the following consequences:
    - The Nawab lost tax revenue
    - The local merchants faced unequal competition
- Further, the Company's servants even sold the dastaks to Indian merchants for a commission.
- The Company's servants were not even content with duty free trade and used coercive methods to get things at cheaper rate. They ignored the officials of the Nawab and forcibly took away the goods and commodities of the peasants and merchants for a fourth part of their value. They also used violence and oppression to force the peasants into buying goods at prices many times higher their value.

In such conditions, though Mir Qasim did not seek independence from the British, he did seek to limit the fast expanding encroachments of the English on his jurisdiction, which were driving him to desperation. He wrote a letter to the Governor Vansittart and pleaded with him for justice and reason. Following the receipt of the desperate plea, **Vansittart and Warren Hastings**, another member of the Calcutta Council, met the Nawab at Monghyr and concluded a compromise. It was agreed that the Nawab would give the English traders a share in the inland trade provided they paid 9% duty. It was also agreed that the Nawab alone would be competent to grant dastaks and his authority would be ultimate in the resolution of disputes regarding trade.

Unfortunately, the agreement was disproved by the Calcutta Council. Most of the Council members themselves participated in inland trade and instead of the compromise they rather favoured the deposition of Mir Qasim, which would provide them with yet another opportunity for receiving bribes.

Out of desperation, Mir Qasim abolished all inland duties to bring the Indian merchants on the same footing as the English, provoking hostilities by an attack on Patna town. In this way, war between the Nawab and the English broke out in 1763 and the Nawab was defeated in a series of battles that year. Subsequently, he fled to Awadh and formed an alliance with **Shuja-ud-Daulah** (Nawab of Awadh) and **Shah Alam II** (the fugitive Mughal Emperor) in a final bid to overthrow the English.

Ghulam Hussain, a prominent contemporary writer and author of **'Siyar-ul-Mutakherin'** praised Mir Qasim profusely for his administrative achievements.

HH Dodwell had rightly remarked that the war between the Nawab and the Company was, 'a war of circumstances rather than intentions'.

Battle of Buxar (22 October 1764)

Immediate Cause The **abuse of dastaks** (duty free trade permits) by the Company's servants for their private trade became the immediate cause of the war of 1764.

The Battle The three allies clashed with the Company's army at the battlefield of Buxar on 22 October 1764. The allies' forces stood at nearly 40,000 to 60,000, whereas the English forces stood at nearly 7,000 commanded by **Major Munro**. It was a closely contested battle with heavy casualties on both sides and ended in the victory of the superior military power, the British.

This was one of the most decisive battles in Indian history. It firmly established the British as masters of Bengal, Bihar and Orissa. Awadh was placed at their mercy.

Consequences of Battle of Buxar

- Buxar sealed the fate of the Bengal Nawabs and, for all practical purposes, power was transferred into the hands of the English Company.
- Mir Jafar was brought back to the throne of Bengal, this time on much harsher terms. Mir Jafar agreed to hand over the districts of Midnapore, Burdwan and Chittagong to the English and permitted them duty free trade in Bengal (with the exception of 2% duty on salt). He and his successors had to pay ₹5 lakh per month to the English Company, allow Company's intervention in matters of appointments and reduce military establishments. Mir Jafar died shortly thereafter and his minor son, **Najim-ud-Daulah** was appointed as Nawab.
- Clive was resent as Governor and Commander-in-Chief of Bengal (Clive's Second governorship: 1765–67). First and foremost, he took up the tasks of defining relations with the defeated powers and showed considerable practical wisdom in his settlements with them.
- **Settlement with Nawab of Awadh** Clive went to Awadh, met Shuja-ud-Daula at Allahabad and concluded with him the **First Treaty of Allahabad** (16 August 1765). As per the treaty,
  - The Nawab of Awadh was made to pay a war indemnity of ₹50 lakh to the Company.
  - The Nawab was made to surrender Allahabad and Kora to Emperor Shah Alam II and confirm Balwant Singh, the zamindar of Banaras, to his estate.
  - The Nawab was made to enter an offensive and defensive treaty **(subsidiary alliance)** with the Company. The Company promised to support the Nawab against an outside attack, provided he paid for the services of the troops. In this way, the Nawab of Awadh became dependent on the Company. (In this way, Clive did not annex Awadh since annexing would have placed the Company under an obligation to protect extensive land frontier, which was vulnerable to attack by the Afghans under Ahmad Shah Abdali and the Marathas. Instead, Clive converted Awadh into a friendly **buffer state** between the British territories in Bengal and the Maratha possessions).
- **Settlement with Mughal Emperor, Shah Alam II** Clive concluded the **Second Treaty of Allahabad** (August 1765) with the Mughal Emperor Shah Alam II. As per the treaty:

- The Emperor was taken into Company's protection and given the districts of **Kora and Allahabad** ceded by Awadh (the Emperor resided in the fort of Allahabad for 6 years as a virtual prisoner of the English).
- In return, the Emperor issued a farman dated 12 August 1765 granting to the Company the **Diwani** (right to collect revenue) of Bengal, Bihar and Orissa in return for the Company making an annual payment of ₹26 lakh to him and providing for the expenses of the Nizamat of Bengal, Bihar and Orissa which was fixed at ₹53 lakh. (In this way, the farman legalised the Company's gain in Bengal; it established a 'dual system' in Bengal in theory and converted the Emperor into a useful 'rubber stamp' of the Company).

- **Settlement with Nawab of Bengal** After the death of Mir Jafar, **Najm-ud-Daulah** was allowed to succeed his father (February 1765) on the following conditions:
    - The Nawab would surrender Defence and Foreign Affairs (both were nizamat functions) into the hands of the Company and civil administration into the hands of a Naib-Subahdar nominated by the Company and not removable without their consent (Clearly, the Company gained Diwani from the emperor and nizamat functions from the Nawab of Bengal. In this way, the infamous dual system was 'dual' only in theory; while in practice the Company acquired all real power in Bengal. The Nawab lost all independent military or financial power and became a mere figurehead).
- **Dual System of Administration (Dual/double governance or Dyarchy) was established in Bengal** In theory, Dual System meant the system of governance where the Company exercised Diwani functions (revenue collection) while the Nawab of Bengal exercised the Nizamat functions (defence, law and order and administration of justice). However, Najm-ud-Daulah was allowed to succeed as Nawab of Bengal only on the condition that he surrendered the Nizamat functions. Hence, in reality, the 'dual system' was only a sham as it was the Company that exercised all political power and merely used the Nawab and his administration as an instrument for its purposes. Thus, in practice, the dual system referred to the system of government whereby the Company acquired all real power while the 'responsibility' for administration rested on the shoulders of the Nawab. A fatal divorce of power from responsibility was inherent in this dual system.
    - The advantage of this system was that the British had **power without responsibility**. This had adverse consequences for the people of Bengal, as neither the Company nor the Nawab cared for their welfare. In the words of Clive himself, 'Such a scene of anarchy, confusion, bribery, corruption and extortion was never seen or heard of in any country but Bengal'.
    - Thus, began the **drain of wealth from Bengal**. The Company stopped sending money from England to buy Indian goods. These goods were now purchased from the revenues of Bengal and sold abroad.
    - This drain of wealth greatly impoverished Bengal and was a major factor responsible for the terrible Bengal famine of 1770. Though the famine was caused by failure of rains, its devastating effects were accentuated by the Company's policies.
    - The Company had to pay a handsome sum per year to the British Government as its share of the rich prize.

Why did Clive go for Dual System?

- Clive wanted to maintain Nawab as a shadow authority which the Company should seem to venerate. Open assumption of authority would have shown the true colours of the Company and might have resulted in uniting Indian princes against it.
- The Company did not wish to generate England's interest regarding the functioning of the Company. It wanted to avoid interference of the British Parliament.

- It was also doubtful whether other European companies would acknowledge the Company's subahship and pay duties that they paid to Nawabs of Bengal.
- Open assumption of political power would have attracted the attention of other European powers.
- The Company did not have adequate personnel to run the administration of Bengal.
- Directors of the Company were more interested in financial and commercial gains rather than territorial acquisitions. A dual system would serve the Company's interests well.

As a result of the system of Dual Government, the English Company acquired real power without any responsibility while the position of Nawab was virtually reduced to a cipher.

Adverse Impact of Dual System

The dual system proved to be a total failure and had the following evil effects:

- It led to complete **breakdown of administration** and law and order in Bengal. While the Nawab had no real power to enforce law, the Company also shunned all responsibility in this regard.
- Bengal, once the granary of India, now faced the specter of famines. The Company appointed two Naib-Diwans, **Mohammad Reza Khan** and **Raja Sitab Roy** for Bengal and Bihar respectively, and directed them to collect as high revenue as possible (Reza Khan was also the Naib-Nazim). The Bengal peasant faced some of the worst exactions by the revenue officials and many of them ran away into the jungles or simply joined the ranks of the robbers. Clearly, the Company's policies in Bengal greatly contributed to the terrible Bengal famine of 1770.
- Dual government led to **disruption of trade and commerce** in Bengal. The Company's merchants exercised strict monopoly and would undersell the Indian merchants in Bengal, pushing many of them into destitution and beggary.
- It also **ruined indigenous industry and skill**. The Company used its political power to compel the cotton weavers of Bengal to buy raw material from and sell woven cloth to the Company exclusively at arbitrary prices. The Company also encouraged the industries selectively. For instance, as per an order of 1769, the Company was asked to encourage production of raw silk but discourage woven silk fabrics as they competed with silk fabrics manufactured in England. Even the Company's factories where raw silk was produced, the silk winders were compelled to work under oppressive conditions; many even cut-off their thumbs to escape the miseries of factory life.
- The Company's avaricious policies in Bengal vitiated the entire atmosphere and led to an overall **moral degradation** and decay of Bengal society. The Indian servants of the Company followed the example of their corrupt masters. The peasants and artisans, unsure of receiving fair price for their labour, lost incentive for good work.

> **KM Panikkar** aptly remarked, 'During 1765–72, the Company established a 'robber state' in Bengal and plundered and looted Bengal indiscriminately'.

Significance of Battle of Buxar Buxar confirmed the result of Plassey and the British had once again emerged as the supreme power. Now the Nawab of Bengal was their puppet, the Nawab of Awadh a pliant ally and the Mughal emperor their pensioner. Lands from Bengal up to Allahabad lay at their feet and the road to Delhi open. While Plassey had made the British a powerful factor in Bengal politics, Buxar made them a powerful factor in politics of north India. In fact, the British now emerged as strong contenders for the Indian Empire.

Evaluation of Political Events in Bengal (1757–65)

The political events in Bengal from 1757 to 1765 have been termed by many historians as a **'political revolution'**. Reasons behind this revolution go beyond the arrogance of Siraj, the treachery of Mir Jafar or individual limitations of Mir Qasim. The English Company and its officials played a significant role in shaping these events. An equally significant role was played by their Indian collaborators including the House of Jagat Seths, zamindars, merchants and local officials who felt alienated owing to civil and military reorganisation by Siraj, and conspired to replace him by their own man. The British were also in search of a more plaint Nawab for their own commercial ends and found allies in this Indian group. Thus their common objective was to replace the present Nawab by a man of their common choice.

To sum up, the economic interests of the Company and political interests of their Indian collaborators together lead to the Plassey Conspiracy of 1757. The political transformation of Bengal began with the British victory at Plassey and culminated with their victory at Buxar. The victory at Buxar was not merely a victory against the Nawab of Bengal but also against the Mughal Emperor and the Nawab of Awadh. Hence, the British victory at Buxar not only indicated the rise of the British power in Bengal but also indicated the impending rise of the British power in the rest of India.

Previous Years' Questions – Preliminary Exam

1. Which one of the following pairs is correctly matched? **[UPSC 1995]**
   (a) Battle of Buxar : Mir Jafar vs Clive
   (b) Battle of Wandiwash : French vs East India Company
   (c) Battle of Chillianwala : Dalhousie vs Marathas
   (d) Battle of Kharda : Nizam vs East India Company
2. Who among the following was the first European to initiate the policy of taking part in the quarrels of Indian princes with a view to acquire territories? **[UPSC 1996]**
   (a) Clive (b) Dupleix
   (c) Albuquerque (d) Warren Hastings
3. Consider the following statements: **[UPSC 2004]**
   1. In the third Battle of Panipat, Ahmad Shah Abdali defeated Ibrahim Lodi
   2. Tipu Sultan was killed in the Third Anglo Mysore war
   3. Mir Jafar entered in a conspiracy with the English for the defeat of Nawab Siraj-ud-Daulah in the Battle of Plassey

   Which of the statements given above is/are correct?
   (a) 1, 2 and 3 (b) 3 only
   (c) 2 and 3 (d) None
4. Which of the following is the correct chronological order of the battles fought in India in the 18th century? **[UPSC 2005]**
   (a) Battle of Wandiwash, Battle of Buxar, Battle of Ambur, Battle of Plassey
   (b) Battle of Ambur, Battle of Plassey, Battle of Wandiwash, Battle of Buxar
   (c) Battle of Wandiwash, Battle of Plassey, Battle of Ambur, Battle of Buxar
   (d) Battle of Ambur, Battle of Buxar, Battle of Wandiwash, Battle of Plassey

Answers

Previous Years' Questions – Preliminary Exam

1. (b) 2. (b) 3. (b) 4. (b)

Unit 2
British Expansion and Consolidation in India (1767–1857)

1 British Expansion in South India (Conquest of Mysore and the Marathas, 1767–1818)

After the conquest of Bengal, the process of British expansion and consolidation ensued through conquests and elimination of rivals in various parts of the subcontinent which has been discussed in this unit. This unit also gives an overview of the emerging imperial ideology and traditions that shaped the attempt to consolidate and systematise British rule in India.

After the conquest of Bengal, the British turned to South India, primarily driven by commercial interests. Thus, in this chapter, you will learn about the British expansion in South India, i.e. Mysore and the Maratha states.

The English East India Company had already eliminated the French from the region by 1761 through the Carnatic Wars—wars which had also brought to the forefront many weaknesses of the Indian regional powers. The existing rivalry among the southern rulers and the volatile political situation in the region provided a favourable ground for political intervention by the Company. It took many years to get political control over the region and the English Company fought several wars to subdue the local rulers. The internal weaknesses of these South Indian states decided the final outcome of this struggle for power, and the defeat of Mysore and the Marathas proved fatal for other Indian powers as well.

Tipu Sultan's failure was a tragedy for him and a tragedy for the subcontinent for his defeat meant the end of the first round of the struggle for Freedom.

Causes for Power Struggle in 18th Century

The 18th century was ridden with power struggle between various groups. There was the struggle for power among the Indian States, and there was also the struggle for power between the Indian States and the English Company.

What Brought the Country Powers in Conflict with One Another?

The main cause of conflict among the country powers was their desire for **territorial expansion**. The traditional approach of explaining this struggle in terms of personal desire of rulers, their insatiable search for territory or even their religious zeal seems an oversimplification. Territorial expansion was mainly a response to the need for further resources. For instance, the Marathas mostly relied on chauth and sardeshmukhi collected from their spheres of influence. In this way, the desire for territorial expansion driven by the need for more resources brought the neighbouring states into conflict with each other. This mutual enmity among the 'country powers' ultimately helped the British to intervene effectively in their internal polity. In the following section, we see how the English Company outwitted the country powers by playing one against the other.

What Brought the British in Conflict with Indian States?

The main reason for British intervention in Mysore and Maratha states was **commercial interest**. The conflict among country powers gave the British an opportunity to intervene in the internal political affairs of Indian states so that they could expand their area of control and increase their profits.

British Intervention in Mysore and the Maratha States

The reasons for British intervention in Mysore and the Maratha states were primarily commercial. These are given as follows:

- Hyder and Tipu's control over the rich trade of the Malabar Coast was seen as a threat to the English Company's trade in pepper and cardamom. In 1785, Tipu declared an embargo on export of pepper and cardamom through the ports within his kingdom. In 1788, he clearly forbade dealings with English traders.
- Mysore was also seen as a threat to English control over Madras.
- The French alliance with Mysore was seen as a threat to English dominance.

- The Marathas were seen as a threat to the English trade from Bombay (there had been a sudden rise in the Company's cotton trade after 1874 to China from Gujarat through Bombay).
- The development in infantry and gunnery in both these states caused great uneasiness in the Company.
- The British home government was in need of finances for growing expenditure in Napoleonic wars, and so it encouraged an aggressive expansionist policy of the Company's merchants.

The British colonialists put forward another argument in support of their military actions in India 'that most contemporary Indian rulers were usurpers of previous dynasties and therefore could be dispensed with and previous dynasties be resorted to the full enjoyment of their civil rights' (as in the case of Wadiyar dynasty). Such an argument was born more out of the willingness to legitimise their political intervention in India, rather than anything else.

Anglo-Mysore Wars (During 1767–99)

The rise of Mysore under Hyder Ali was viewed as a threat by the neighbouring states—the Marathas, the Nawab of Carnatic and the Nizam of Hyderabad. The Marathas and the Nizam formed an alliance against Mysore and also cooperated with the English Company to curb Mysore. But the Nizam was equally apprehensive of the Marathas and therefore cooperated with the English Company against the Marathas.

In all, there took place four Anglo–Mysore wars. Except the first war, the British emerged victorious in all of them. The English Company was mainly represented by the Madras Presidency. The basic cause of these wars was the Company's objective to undermine the independent authority of the Mysore rulers. The Marathas, the Nawab of Carnatic and the Nizam of Hyderabad aligned with the English from time to time to subdue the Mysore ruler.

After the victory in the fourth war, the British disintegrated the Mysore state and gave one part of the kingdom to the minor prince of Wadiyar dynasty.

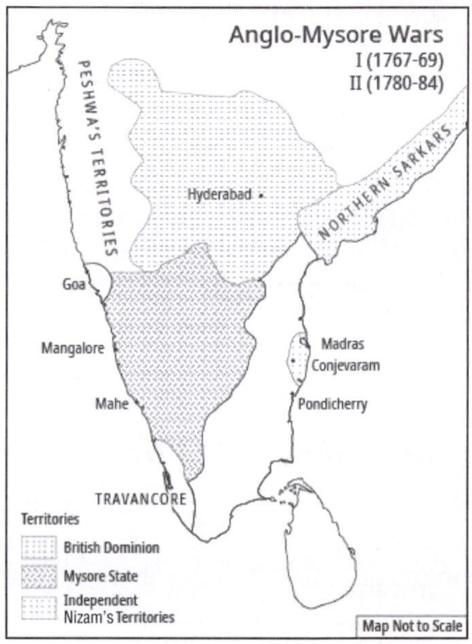

Anglo-Mysore Wars

First Anglo–Mysore War (1767–69)

Hyder Ali's friendship with the French is considered as one reason for the Anglo–Mysore war. Another important reason was the Mysore border dispute between the Madras government and the Nawab of Carnatic.

The immediate context for war was provided by the rivalry over control of **Northern Circars**. The English Company was seeking an overland connection between its territories in Madras and Bengal, and Northern Circars (held by the French until 1758) was a series of coastal territories that lay in between. **Robert Clive** demanded access to this area from the Nizam of Hyderabad (a French protégé), which the Nizam initially rejected.

However, in 1766, the English Company began expanding in the Northern Circars and the Nizam objected and considered going to war with the English, but later signed a treaty with the Company in view of his poor financial condition. As per this treaty, the Company got the Northern Circars and in return promised to give military support to the Nizam in his endeavours against Hyder Ali.

At the same time, the Nizam had formed an alliance with the Marathas as both felt threatened by the expansionist attitude of Hyder. Hyder himself was annoyed with the English as they had set up a fortified outpost at Vellore.

In this way, the Marathas, the Nizam and the English entered into **a tripartite treaty** against Hyder Ali and attacked Mysore in 1766. But Hyder successfully persuaded the Nizam and the Marathas to join hands with him against the English. He then launched an attack against the Company and reached up to the gates of Madras. He forced the Madras Council to sign peace on his terms in April 1769, known as the **Treaty of Madras**. As per the treaty, both the powers agreed to help each other in case of an attack by a third party.

Expansion under the Various Governor-Generals The Mysore and Maratha Wars:

- **Expansion under Warren Hastings (1772–85)**
  First Anglo–Maratha War (1775–82)
  Second Mysore War (1780–84)
- **Expansion under Cornwallis (1786–93)**
  Third Mysore War (1790–92)
- **Expansion under Lord Wellesley (1798–1805)**
  Fourth Mysore War (1799)
  Second Anglo-Maratha War 1803–05
- **Expansion under Lord Hastings (1813–23)**
  Third Anglo-Maratha War 1817–18

First Governor-General Warren Hastings (1772–85) Warren Hastings became the deputy ruler of Madras after the end of the First Anglo–Mysore War (1769). In 1772, he was appointed as the Governor of Calcutta Presidency, the most important of the three major British Presidencies—Calcutta, Madras and Bombay. In 1774, Hastings was considered as the natural choice to be the first Governor-General.

The task before Warren Hastings was enormous. He had to transform a company of traders into a force of administrators and develop a workable system of administration in Bengal. Most importantly, he had to rehabilitate the Company's finances.

Administrative Reforms In 1772, it was decided to end the dual system of administration set up by Clive. The Company now decided to collect land revenue itself and not through the Naib-Diwan who was earlier appointed by Clive for the purpose. Thus, the President was required to take over the charge of the entire management of revenues of Bengal, Bihar and Orissa. Accordingly, the Governor and the Council formed the **Board of Revenue** and the Company appointed its own European officers called **Collectors** to collect land revenue and manage revenue affairs. The treasury was also removed from Murshidabad to Calcutta.

Revenue Reforms In 1772, Hastings made a five-year settlement (quinquennial settlement or **panchshala bandobast**) of land revenue by the crude method of farming out estates to the highest bidder. The revenue farmers had no permanent interest in land and therefore tried to extort the maximum revenue from the cultivators. The officers of the Company themselves participated in the bidding under the name of their servants. Warren Hastings himself was accused of such forgery. Hence this system caused much hardship to the farmers and failed miserably.

After the expiry of the five-year settlement, Hastings reverted to the system of annual settlement (salana bandobast) in 1777, once again based on the method of farming out estates to the highest bidder.

Judicial Reforms Hastings made several successful reforms in the existing judicial system of Bengal. Before Hastings, civil and criminal cases were decided by zamindars. He then tried to build up a judicial framework based on the Mughal model and set up the **Diwani Adalat** (decided civil cases, appeals went to Sadr Diwani Adalat) and the **Faujdari Adalat** (decided criminal cases, appeals went to Sadr Nizamat Adalat, followed the Muslim law). These courts followed both Muslim and Hindu laws. However, as per the Regulating Act of 1773, a Supreme Court competent to try all 'British subjects' was set up at Calcutta, which followed the English law. This dualism in the legal system continued throughout the Company's rule in India. Hastings also attempted to codify Hindu and Muslim laws. In 1776, a translation of the Code in Sanskrit appeared under the title of **'Code of Gentoo laws'**.

Expansion under Warren Hastings comprised of First Anglo–Maratha War (1775–82) and Second Mysore War (1780–84).

Second Anglo–Mysore War (1780–84)

The British had no intention of sticking to the treaty of Madras. When Marathas invaded Hyder's territory in 1771, the English Company did not come to his help. So, it was now a question of time before a second round of war between the Company and the Mysore state started. On the other hand, the French proved more helpful to Hyder with his military demands as saltpeter, lead, guns and other military hardware naturally found their way into Mysore through **Mahe** (a French settlement on the Malabar coast within Hyder's jurisdiction). Further, the American War of Independence had broken out in 1775 and the French help to American colonists made Governor-General **Warren Hastings** extremely anxious of Hyder's relations with the French. Under these circumstances, the Company attempted to capture Mahe, which was a direct challenge to Hyder Ali. The English had also offended Hyder Ali when an English force trespassed on Hyder's territory in order to take over Guntur in the Northern Circars.

The English capture of Mahe provided the immediate pretext for the second Mysore war. The English won over the Marathas and the Nizam (Hastings bribed Nizam with the cession of Guntur district). In July 1781, the English army under **Sir Eyre Coote** defeated Hyder Ali at **Porto-Novo**. The French help under **Admiral Baillie de Suffren** reached India in 1782. Skirmishes continued but later in December 1782, Hyder died of cancer during the course of the second Mysore war.

Tipu, son and successor of Hyder, continued the war against the British. However, in 1783, the American War of Independence ended. Thereafter, Suffren sailed back for Europe leaving Tipu to fight his own battles. The Madras government also desired peace due to lack of resource and uncertainty of the Maratha attitude. Tipu also needed time to strengthen his own administration. Thus, the war ended with the **Treaty of Mangalore** (March 1784) signed on the basis of mutual restitution of each other's territories. This was the last British treaty with an Indian ruler on an equal footing.

Governor-General Lord Cornwallis (1786–93) Cornwallis was sent to India specially charged with the duty of finding out a satisfactory solution to the land revenue problem. The administrative superstructure built by Cornwallis remained substantially in force till 1858.

Lord Cornwallis

Revenue Reforms In 1790, Cornwallis decided to recognise the zamindars as the owners of land, subject to annual payment of land revenue to the state. A ten-year settlement was made with the zamindars on the basis of 89 per cent of the rental, leaving 11 per cent with the zamindars. In 1793, this decennial settlement was declared permanent (called **Permanent Settlement of Bengal**).

Cornwallis Code In 1793, Cornwallis compiled his judicial reforms in the form of the Famous Cornwallis Code based on the principle of separation of powers. The Code divested the Collector of all his judicial powers and left him with the duty of revenue administration alone. The judicial powers were given to a new class of officer—**the District Judge**.

Reform of Criminal Law Cornwallis brought about changes in the criminal law as well, even though the Muslims took their criminal law to be divinely ordained. For instance, in cases of murder, the law officers were now to be guided by the intention of the murder and not merely by the manner of perpetration. The usual punishment of amputation of body parts was to be replaced by imprisonment or fine. Further, non-Muslims were now allowed to give testimony against Muslims in criminal cases.

Undesirable effects- Though the judicial reforms of Cornwallis were based on the principle of equity, in its immediate context it produced many undesirable effects. The new code was unfamiliar and elaborate, beyond the comprehension of the common man. The traditional judicial functionaries were replaced by European judges who knew very little about Indian customs and habits.

Suppression of Bribery and Corruption Cornwallis himself was beyond the greed for money that had tarnished the names of Clive and Warren Hastings. Cornwallis forbade the Company's employees from indulging in private trade and required each officer to declare his property under oath before he left India. He also raised the salaries of the Company's officials in order to desist them from indulging in corruption.

Europeanisation of Administration Unfortunately, Cornwallis, like most of his countrymen, suffered from the evil infection of **racial discrimination**. He had very low opinion of Indians in general and regarded every Indian to be corrupt. He sought to reserve all higher services for Europeans and reduced the Indians to 'hewers of wood and drawers of water'. For instance, in the army, Indians could not rise above the position of Jemadar or Subedar and in civil services not above Deputy Collector. In this way, he put the official seal on the policy of racialism that infested Anglo–Indian relations till the very end.

Expansion under Cornwallis comprised of the Third Mysore War (1790–92).

Third Anglo-Mysore War (1790–92)

The above treaty was only a temporary respite before a final showdown. **Lord Cornwallis** had become the Governor-General in 1786 and through his diplomacy he brought the Marathas and the Nizam to the English side. Convinced of the inevitability of war, Tipu also sought help from the Turks and the French by sending embassies to Constantinople and France during 1784–87.

However, Tipu's attack on **Travancore** became the immediate cause of the Third Anglo–Mysore war. The Raja of Travancore had purchased Jaikottai and Cranganore from the Dutch in Cochin and since Cochin was a tributary state of Mysore, Tipu considered this as a violation of his sovereign rights. Thus, in April 1790, Tipu attacked Travancore. The English were already itching for a war and decided to side with the ruler of Travancore.

The war started in 1790. Supported by the Maratha and the Nizam's troops, Cornwallis himself headed a large army and approached Seringapatam. Tipu suffered a serious setback and showed initiative for peace. Thus, the **Treaty of Seringapatam** (or Srirangapatnam) was signed in March 1792 and Tipu had to surrender half of his territory to the Company and its allies. While the Company acquired Baramahal, Dindigul and Malabar, the Marathas gained territory on the Tungabhadra side and the Nizam acquired territories from the Krishna to beyond the Pennar. Tipu was also required to pay war indemnity of ₹3 crore, but as he was unable to pay this sum immediately, his two sons were kept as prisoners with Cornwallis.

Tipu lamented after losing Malabar, 'I can ruin their resources by land but I cannot dry up the sea'. On the other hand, Cornwallis declared, 'We have effectively crippled our enemy, without making our friends too formidable'.

After Cornwallis, **Sir John Shore** became the Governor-General but he adopted the **policy of non-intervention** towards Mysore. For this reason, John Shore is known as the father of the policy of non-intervention. Later, Sir John Lawrence also adopted the policy of non-interference towards Afghanistan.

Governor-General Lord Wellesley (1798–1805) Lord Richard Colley Wellesley came to India in 1798 at a time when the British were locked in a life and death struggle with France all over the world. He was an imperialist to the core and believed that the only way to safeguard India against French danger was by bringing as many Indian states as possible under British control. To achieve his political aims, Wellesley relied on three methods—the System of Subsidiary Alliance, outright war and the assumption of territories of previously subordinated rulers.

The Subsidiary Alliance System comprised of the following provisions:

- The Indian state had to surrender its foreign relations into the hands of the Company. It could not negotiate with any other Indian state without consulting the Governor-General.
- The Company assured the Indian state complete protection against foreign as well as internal threat.
- An English force was stationed within the territory of the Indian state for its protection in return for an annual subsidy in cash to the Company. The larger states had to cede a part of their territory for the purpose.

- A British Resident was posted in the capital.
- The Indian state could not employ any European in its service without the approval of the British.

Negative Impact on Indian States The system had several disadvantages for the Indian state. It also led to internal decay of the state in many ways. These are as follows:

- Politically, the ruler signing a Subsidiary Alliance virtually signed away his independence. He lost the right to self-defence as well as to maintain independent foreign relations.
- Economically, it was drained as the annual subsidy was arbitrarily fixed and was very high (usually one-third of the annual revenue of the state), much beyond the paying capacity of the state. The ruler transferred this burden onto the people by means of heavy taxes, impoverishing them. Its army was disbanded which also resulted in loss of livelihood to several thousand people.
- Morally, it made the rulers irresponsible and oppressive as they no longer feared their subjects. They were fully protected by the English Company from internal as well as external aggression.

Advantages for the British On the other hand, the Subsidiary Alliance System was very advantageous to the British in the following ways:

- The British could maintain a large army that too at the cost of the India states, and without arousing the suspicion of other European nations.
- It allowed the Company to counter the French threat, as the subsidiary ally was required to dismiss all Frenchmen from its service.
- The Company became the intermediary in interstate relations, thereby closing all possibility of states coming together in conspiracy against the British.
- It also allowed them to gradually increase their control over the signatory state by transforming the British Resident from political agent to virtual dictator.
- The state could then be overthrown easily with the help of the English army stationed in the very heart of the Indian state.
- Thus, the Subsidiary System proved to a **Trojan horse** tactic. It has been truly said, 'it was a system of fattening allies, like oxen, till they were worthy of being devoured'.

Subsidiary alliance treaty was signed with the following: Nizam of Hyderabad (1798 and 1800), Mysore (1799), Tanjore (1799), Awadh (1801), Peshwa (1802), Bhonsle Raja of Berar (1803), Scindia (1804), Holkar (1818, under Lord Hastings). The Rajput states of Jodhpur, Jaipur, Macheri, Bundi and Bharatpur were also annexed. Though the detailed provisions of the alliance varied from state to state, Wellesley was particularly severe with Mysore, Carnatic, Tanjore and Surat.

Karl Marx said that "the native states virtually ceased to exist from the moment they became subsidiary to the Company. If you divide the revenue of a country between two governments, you are sue to cripple the resources of one or the administration of both".

Sir Thomas Munro said that "a state purchased security by the sacrifice of independence, of national character- and of whatever renders a people respectable".

Note: Do not confuse GG RC Wellesley with his younger brother Arthur Wellesley. Arthur began his career as a soldier and later rose to become the Prime Minister of the United Kingdom (1828). He arrived in India in 1797 (the same year he learnt that his brother was being appointed as GG of India) and participated in the Fourth Anglo-Mysore War and the Second Anglo-Maratha War under the supreme command of his older brother GG Lord Wellesley. Both brothers returned to England together in 1805.

Fourth Anglo–Mysore War (1799)

Lord Wellesley sailed for India in 1797, probably the toughest year in English history when England was struggling for its survival against France all over the world. Napoleon Bonaparte had conquered Egypt and Syria and he now turned towards India. In 1801, he made an alliance with Czar Paul of Russia and drew up a serious plan to invade India via Herat and Kandahar. The English well realised the consequences of a defeat at the hands of Napoleon; it would mean an end to its commerce that had brought it immense financial and political gains. To us, Napoleon's plans may appear fanciful today but the contemporaries did not regard them as such. To them they posed a very real danger and Wellesley could ill afford to take any risks.

In Napoleon's plans, Tipu Sultan of Mysore saw the right opportunity to oust the English from India. He entered into negotiations with the French and started making elaborate preparations for war with the Company. He planted a **'flag of Liberty' at Seringapatam**, styled himself 'Citizen Tipu'. He employed the French Commandant **Monsieur Raymond** and raised a corps of 14,000 men with his help.

Wellesley concluded that it was urgently needed to bring the Indian states under the English sphere of influence and tame not only the actual allies but even the potential allies of France. For this purpose, he tried to convert as many Indian states into the subsidiary allies of the Company, either by persuasion or by force.

After he successfully forced the treaty of subsidiary alliance upon the Nizam, he turned his attention to Tipu Sultan. Wellesley estimated that a French invasion via the Red Sea could only be possible after mid-1799 and he decided to deal with Tipu before that time. After Tipu refused all offers of the Governor-General for acceptance of the subsidiary alliance, war began in February 1799 and was over by May the same year. The English Company won a decisive victory at the **Battle of Seringapatam** (1799). Tipu was killed during the defence of the city, before French help could reach him. He died a hero's death defending his capital.

Much of the remaining Mysorean territory was annexed by the Company, the Nizam and the Marathas, giving the Company the command over the sea coast of the Lower Peninsula. Any French mischief from the Malabar Coast was now rendered impossible. The remaining core, around Mysore and Seringapatam, was restored to the minor Indian prince, two-year-old Krishnaraja of the Wadiyar Dynasty, whose forefathers had been the actual rulers before Hyder Ali became the de facto ruler. A special **Treaty of Subsidiary Alliance** was imposed on the Wadiyar King and Mysore virtually became a dependency of the British. The Wadiyars ruled the remnant state of Mysore until 1947, when it joined the Union of India. Tipu's family members were imprisoned in Vellore and his two sons pensioned.

After the success in the fourth Anglo–Mysore war, Wellesley arrogantly pronounced, 'Now the kingdom of the east is under our feet'.

After Mysore, Wellesley turned his attention to Awadh, forcing the Nawab to accept subsidiary alliance (1801). Next Wellesley turned his attention to the Marathas, the only power of importance and French nest outside British protection. The French officers in Scindia's army were beyond Wellesley's toleration and the Maratha influence over the western coast also left open the possibility of French infiltration from that corner. Even though the Governor General's offer of subsidiary alliance was turned down, internal dissensions in the Maratha camp drove the Peshwa into the Company's trap in 1802.

Prelim Capsule

Anglo-Mysore Wars (during 1767–99)

Wars	Period	Important Details
First Mysore War	**1767–69**	Immediate context—provided by the rivalry over control of **Northern Circars**. The rivalry ultimately led to a tripartite treaty between the Marathas, the Nizam and the English against Hyder Ali. Began with the attack on Mysore by the allies in 1766. Soon, Hyder persuaded the Nizam and the Marathas to join hands with him against the English and finally forced the Madras Council to sign peace on his terms. Thus, the war ended with the **Treaty of Madras** in 1769. Result—Hyder Ali had an edge over the English.
Second Mysore War Warren Hastings	**1780–84**	Immediate context—capture of **Mahe** by the English. In this war, the Marathas and the Nizam sided with the English. Main battle fought—**Battle of Port-Novo**. Ended with the **Treaty of Mangalore**. Result—It was a drawn struggle.
Third Mysore War Lord Cornwallis	**1790–92**	Immediate context—provided by Tipu's attack on **Travancore**. In this war too, the Marathas and the Nizam sided with the English. Ended with the **Treaty of Seringapatam**. Result—Tipu Sultan lost. He surrendered half of his territory to the Company and its allies. The Company acquired Baramahal, Dindigul and Malabar. 2 sons of Tipu were kept as prisoners with Cornwallis.
Fourth Mysore War Lord Wellesley	**1799**	Immediate context—provided by **Napoleon's plans** to invade India and Tipu's consequent negotiations with the French. Main battle fought- **Battle of Seringapatam**. Result—Tipu was killed during the defence of the city. Mysore lost its independence.

Anglo-Maratha Wars (During 1775–1818)

From the ashes of the Mughal empire had emerged the Marathas as well as the English East India Company. Both had emerged victorious in their own spheres—the Marathas among other Indian states, the English among other European contenders in India. But now, towards the last quarter of the 18th century, the two came face to face and indulged in direct clash and conflict.

The first, second, and third Anglo-Maratha wars were fought between the army of the English East India Company, which after 1757 was de facto ruler of Bengal, and the Maratha Empire in the south of India. The Maratha Empire comprised of five major chiefs—the Peshwa at Poona, Bhonsle at Nagpur, Scindia at Gwalior, Holkar at Indore and Gaekwad at Baroda. Peshwa was the nominal head of this Maratha confederacy and there existed bitter mutual rivalry among all of them, particularly **Scindia and Holkar**. The wars started in 1775 and ended with British victory in 1818. This left the British in control, directly or indirectly via treaties with Princely states, of a vast proportion of India, making India the jewel in the crown of the British Empire.

First Anglo–Maratha War (1775–82)

The first Maratha war was a result of the excessive ambition of the English, accentuated by the internal strife of the Marathas. While the Bengal and Madras governments had increased their influence over Awadh and Carnatic respectively, the Bombay government had no such political achievement to its credit due to the presence of the powerful Maratha confederacy in the area and it had begun to feel somewhat belittled. It now cast its longing eyes upon the Maratha territories, particularly the ports of Salsette and Bassein and hoped to gain political influence at the Poona Court. The dispute over succession to the Peshwaship after the death of the Peshwa Madhav Rao gave the English the much-needed opportunity to intervene in the Maratha affairs.

> **Flashback** The Baarbhai installed Narayan Rao's posthumous son, Madhav Rao II, as the Peshwa with themselves, led by Nana Phadnavis, as the Regents. The succession of Sawai Madhav Rao gravely frustrated Raghunath Rao's ambitions and he now went over to the British and tried to capture power with their help, resulting in the **first Anglo–Maratha war**.

Thus, out of frustration, Raghunath Rao went over to the British and tried to capture power with their help. This was the immediate background of the first Anglo-Maratha war. The war began with the Treaty of Surat and ended with the Treaty of Salbai. In Raghunath Rao, the Bombay government saw a plaint and a tool and hoped to set up in Maharashtra the type of dual government as Clive had done in Bengal.

Treaty of Surat (7 March 1775) This treaty was signed between Raghunath Rao (Raghoba) and the British Government at Bombay on 7 March 1775. There were 16 conditions in all in the treaty. As per the treaty it was decided that the British would help Raghunath Rao in becoming the Peshwa by sending 2500 soldiers. In return, Raghoba would cede territories of Salsette and Bassein and revenues from Surat and Bharoch to the British.

In accordance with the Treaty of Surat, a British army reached Surat led by Colonel Keating. On 18 May 1775, at Adas (**Battle of Adas**) there took place a terrible battle between the English and the Maratha armies. In this battle, though the Marathas were defeated, they retained control over Poona.

Treaty of Purandar (1 March 1776) When a copy of the Treaty of Surat reached the superior British Government in Bengal, i.e. the Calcutta Council, it condemned the treaty as unjust and unauthorised. Further, Warren Hastings sent Colonel Upton to Poona Darbar and signed the treaty of Purandar. Thus, the Treaty of Purandar was signed between the British Government at Calcutta and Poona Court (Poona Darbar) and it stated the following:

1. The Treaty of Surat was annulled.
2. The British left the side of Raghoba and it was decided that Raghoba will be given a monthly pension of ₹25,000 by Peshwa government and he will go to Gujarat and reside there in Kopar village.

However, the Treaty of Purandar was not implemented due to a sudden turn of events. The American War of Independence had broken out in 1775 and in 1778 France joined on the American side against England. At the same time, a French adventurer, Chevalier de St. Lubin, reached Poona. This greatly alarmed Warren Hastings, who immediately scrapped the Treaty of Purandar, sent a large force to reinforce the Bombay government and sanctioned operations against the Marathas. Thus, the Bombay Government resumed the war and sent an army towards Poona under Colonel Egerton (who was later replaced by Colonel Cockburn).

The English and the Maratha armies met on the outskirts of Poona. The Maratha army was led by the brilliant General **Mahadji Shinde**. He lured the English army into valleys of the Western Ghats near Talegaon (**Battle of Talegaon**, 9 January 1779) and trapped them from all sides. The Marathas also used the **'scorched earth policy'**, burning farmlands and poisoning wells. The English were forced to retreat to a village named Wadgaon. Finally, by mid-January 1779, the English surrendered and the Bombay Government was forced to sign a humiliating treaty with Poona Darbar called the Treaty of Wadgaon.

Treaty of Wadgaon (1779) As per this treaty, it was decided that the Bombay Government would return all territory conquered by it after 1773 and the Scindias will get a part of the revenue from Bharoch.

Hastings refused to accept this humiliating Treaty of Wadgaon. He quickly sent an army from Bengal led by Colonel Goddard which soon captured Ahmedabad and Vasai. But this British army got defeated by the Marathas in Poona. Meanwhile, Hastings sent another detachment from Bengal led by **Colonel Popham** which captured Gwalior on 3 August 1781. **General Camac** also defeated Scindia in the **Battle of Sipri** (modern day Shivpur).

Mahadji Scindia aspired to become the leader of the Maratha confederacy, and he therefore tried to strike a treaty with the British. Subsequently, an understanding was struck between Scindia and the English Company as the latter promised to allow him to carry out his designs in and around Delhi. Finally, the Treaty of Salbai was signed between the British and the Poona Government.

Treaty of Salbai (Gwalior District, 1782)

This treaty was signed between the British and the Poona Government with the mediation of Mahadji Scindia. The treaty of Salbai was signed on the basis of mutual restitution of each other's territories or 'status quo ante bellum'. The main provisions of this treaty were:

1. Madhav Narayan Rao will be accepted as Peshwa.
2. British will give up the cause of Raghoba and he be given yearly pension of ₹3.5 lacs.
3. The Company gave up Bassein and other territories captured since the Treaty of Purandar, but retained Salsette and the Elephanta Island.
4. Scindia got back the entire territory on the west of Yamuna.

In this way, the British attempt to gain supremacy in the Maratha state proved premature. The First Anglo-Maratha War was drawn. Both sides had a taste of each other's strengths which ensured mutual respect and peace for the next **20 years**. It also gave the British the needed time to concentrate on other fronts specially Mysore.

Among the Marathas, Ahilyabai Holkar, Mahadji Scindia and Nana Phadnavis are remembered as able leaders of this period. But in general, the Maratha state was in a bad shape during these years. There was disagreement regarding the succession to the Peshwaship and Nana Phadnavis was in complete control of the Maratha affairs. Fed up by the dictatorial rule of Nana, the young Peshwa Madhav Rao Narayan committed **suicide** on 25 October 1795. Raghoba's son Baji Rao II became the next Peshwa. On 13 March 1800, Nana Phadnavis died in Poona. And once again Poona Darbar became a centre of conspiracies.

Second Anglo-Maratha War (1803–05)

Lord Wellesley came to India in 1798 and aggressively followed his policy of subsidiary alliance. The Marathas earlier refused all offers to accept subsidiary alliance; however, their internal differences ultimately drove them into Wellesley's trap.

Flashback: Peshwa- Baji Rao II, 1st Reign (1796–1802)
His first reign saw the Second Anglo–Maratha War (1803–05). After the death of Nana Phadnavis (March 1800), the Poona court once again fell victim to various court conspiracies. Peshwa fled, took refuge in Bassein and approached Wellesley for help. This gave the British an ideal opportunity to intervene in the Maratha affairs. Baji Rao II accepted subsidiary alliance and signed the Treaty of Bassein in 1802.

Treaty of Bassein (Subsidiary Alliance, 31 December 1802) This treaty of 'perpetual and general alliance' was signed between Peshwa Bajirao II and the English Company. It was a treaty of **Subsidiary Alliance**. The main provisions of the treaty were as follows:

1. Peshwa accepted the Company's protection and had to pay a large annual subsidy.
2. Peshwa accepted that an English army will be stationed at Poona and no European enemy of the English will be kept in the Maratha army.
3. Peshwa accepted that his foreign relations with other states will go under British control.

In this way, the Peshwa, i.e. the head of the Maratha confederacy, lost his independent authority and eventually the other Maratha chiefs were also reduced to a similar position of subordination to the Company. This affected the **patriotic feelings** of other Maratha chiefs and provoked the Second Anglo–Maratha War that began the breakup of the Maratha confederacy. Daulat Rao Scindia and Raghuji Bhonsle immediately formed an alliance against the English. They tried to include Yashwant Rao Holkar but could not succeed. Gaekwad remained neutral. Thus even in time of national danger, the Maratha chiefs did not unite.

The English decided to attack all Maratha regions. The war was fought in two main centres—in Deccan under Arthur Wellesley and in North India under General Lake. It was also fought in three sub-centres namely—Gujarat, Bundelkhand and Orissa.

- In the Deccan, Wellesley defeated the combined armies of Scindia and Bhonsle in the **Battle of Assaye** (near Aurangabad, September 1803) and the **Battle of Argaon** (near Burhanpur, November 1803).
- In the north, Lord Lake defeated Daulat Rao Scindia in the **Battle of Delhi** (September 1803) and the combined armies of Scindia and Bhonsle in the **Battle of Laswari** (near Alwar, November

1803). General Lake captured Aligarh, Delhi and Agra. It is noteworthy that now the control of Delhi passed from the Marathas into British hands and once again the blind Mughal ruler, Shah Alam II, became a pensioner of the Company (He had first become a pensioner of the Company after his defeat in the Battle of Buxar in 1764).

In this way, Scindia and Bhonsle faced total defeat within five months and had to sign two separate treaties with the English Company.

Treaty of Deogaon (17 December 1803) This treaty of subsidiary alliance was signed between **Raghuji Bhonsle and the Company**. As per this treaty, Bhonsle lost to the English Company the territories of Balasore, Cuttack and entire kingdom west to the Wardha River. Bhonsle agreed to keep a British Resident in Nagpur. **M Elphinstone** was sent for this post.

Treaty of Surji-Arjangaon (30 December 1803) This treaty was signed between **Scindia and the Company**. As per this treaty, he gave the Company a large part of his kingdom including the territory between the Ganga and the Yamuna. He agreed to keep a British Resident **Sir John Malcolm** is his court. As per another treaty (**Treaty of Burhanpur**, 27 February 1804), Scindia entered subsidiary alliance with the Company.

War with Yashwant Rao Holkar Until now Holkar had kept himself away from the war, but in April 1804, war between him and the British began. Holkar defeated Colonel Monson near Kota and advanced towards Delhi. But Delhi was successfully defended by local resident there, **Lt. Colonel Octor Loni**. One detachment of Holkar's army was defeated in the **Battle of Ding**, while another detachment which was being led by Holkar himself was defeated by **General Lake**. Holkar fled to Amritsar and asked the Sikhs for help. But the Sikhs refused. Now he began considering peace with the British. At the same time, the shareholders of the EIC felt that continuous wars were proving costly. Company's directors felt that it was time to stop expansion. Similarly, the home government in Britain was facing financial crunch at a time when Napoleon was reemerging as a threat in Europe. Thus **Wellesley was recalled** and Sir George Barlow was sent to India who made peace with Holkar. In this way, expansion under Wellesley was checked just before the end, yet the Company had now emerged as the supreme power in India.

Treaty of Rajpurghat (24 December 1805) This treaty was signed between **Yashwant Rao Holkar and the English Company**. As per this treaty, Holkar agreed to renounce all claims to the north of the River Chambal and the Bundi hills (Bundelkhand) but at the same time, he got back the major part of his lost kingdom. The English also promised not to disturb Holkar's possessions in Mewar and Malwa. The Treaty of Rajpurghat marked the end of the Second Anglo-Maratha War.

The result of Second Anglo-Maratha War was that it tore apart the Maratha confederacy.

Governor-General Lord Hastings (1813–23) If Lord Wellesley had succeeded in expelling the French and establishing the Company's military ascendancy in India, Lord Hastings succeeded in unmistakable terms, in establishing the British Paramountcy in India. In fact, Hastings completed the fabric of British supremacy in India, almost exactly the way his predecessor had planned it.

Lord Hastings

Prior to becoming the Governor General of India, Lord Hastings had served the British forces in the American War of Independence. In India, he adopted an **aggressive forward policy** and waged extensive wars, thus completing and even consolidating Wellesley's policy.

Expansion under Lord Hastings His governorship saw the Anglo–Nepal war, the suppression of the Pindaris and the Third Anglo–Maratha War. Lord Hastings' era marks a milestone in the expansion and consolidation of British power in India.

Administrative Reforms Though Hastings' genius was more suited for war, yet his era saw some significant administrative reforms thanks to his capable band of administrators that included—Sir John Malcolm, Sir Thomas Munro, Mountstuart Elphinstone, Jenkins and Charles Metcalfe.

- Munro, governor of Madras in 1820, established the **Ryotwari system** of land settlement in Malabar, Canara, Coimbatore, Madura and Dindigul. Under it, the settlement was made directly with the ryots, i.e. the actual tiller of soil.
- In the north-west provinces, the **Mahalwari system** was introduced in 1822. Under it, the settlement was made with a village community or mahal.
- Hastings modified Cornwallis' laudable system of separating the judiciary from the executive and henceforth the **Collector could hold the office of the Magistrate also.**

Suppression of Pindaris, the Robber Bands It is popularly believed that the term 'Pindari' is of Marathi origin, meaning 'consumer of pinda' a fermented drink. The Pindaris were first heard of in 1689 during the Mughal invasion of Maharashtra and were referred to as irregular horsemen attached to the Maratha army, serving without pay but instead receiving the license to plunder. The declining Mughal authority, the weak regional states and repeated Maratha raids created conditions in India for the rise of the Pindaris like 'masses of putrefaction in animal matter'. The Pindaris often described as 'scavengers of the Marathas', greatly swelled in ranks during Wellesley when native armies were disbanded in large numbers. In fact, the Pindaris were a heterogeneous mix of elements drawn from disbanded soldiers, hardy peasants, idle and unscrupulous men.

The chief characteristic of Pindari plunders was their speed and secrecy. Even before it was possible to gain any information of their movement, their operation was over. They came like swarms of locusts, destroying and plundering whatever came in their way.

In the early 19th century, the chief Pindari leaders who emerged were: **Chitu, Wasil Muhammad** and **Karim Khan**. The Pindaris gradually extended their area of operation and in 1812, plundered the English districts of Mirzapur and Shahabad and later the Northern Circars (in 1816), instigating Lord Hastings to take stern action against them. He planned to suppress the Pindaris and defeat the Marathas in one sweep. Hastings collected a large army, himself took the command of the North Force and delegated the charge of the Deccan to **Sir Thomas Hislop**.

By January 1818, the Pindaris were effectively crushed. Karim Khan surrendered, Wasil Muhammad committed suicide in British custody while Chitu escaped into the forests where he was devoured by a tiger.

Third Anglo–Maratha War (1817–18)

The third and final phase of Anglo–Maratha war started with the arrival of British Governor-General Lord Hastings. He tried to establish the supremacy of English East India Company in India and resumed the threads of aggressive policy abandoned in 1805 with the recall of Wellesley. The breathing space that the Marathas had got since 1805 was not utilised by consolidating their power but wasted in mutual conflicts. Hastings' main objective now was to destroy the independence of the three Maratha rulers—the Bhonsle, the Scindia and the Holkar.

The Bhonsle Raja of Berar proved to be the weakest link of the three Maratha chiefs. After the death of Raghuji Bhonsle on 22 March 1816, his son Parsoji's succession to the gaddi was challenged by Parsoji's cousin, Appa Sahib also known as Mudhoji II Bhonsle.. The British **Resident Jenkins** saw in this the right opportunity to impose a subsidiary alliance on the state. Appa Sahib, in his keenness to gain the Company's support, offered very favourable terms to the Company.

Treaty of Nagpur (Subsidiary Alliance, 27 May 1816) Accordingly, on 27 May 1816, the treaty of Nagpur was signed between Appa Sahib and the English Company and subsidiary force was stationed at Nagpur.

Peshwa Baji Rao II had earlier signed the Treaty of Bassein (December 1802) but with time, he had begun to feel strangulated and began to show signs of independence. He began to reassert his authority over the Gaekwad of Baroda, a feudatory of the English, and laid claim over the tribute of Kathiawar and Baroda. The Baroda sent its Chief Minister **Gangadhar Shastri** to negotiate with the Peshwa but the negotiations failed and Shastri was killed on his way back at Nasik at the instance of Trimbakji, the Chief Minister of Peshwa. The British Resident Elphinstone demanded the surrender of Trimbakji. While the Peshwa vacillated, the English Company prepared for war and its troops surrounded Poona. The Peshwa reluctantly surrendered and accepted the new treaty of Poona.

Treaty of Poona (Subsidiary Alliance, 13 June 1817) As per this treaty, among other things, the Peshwa accepted the **dissolution of the Maratha Confederacy**, a milestone in the establishment of British Paramountcy in India. He also gave up some important forts to the Company including Konkan and ceded Bundelkhand, Malwa and Hindustan.

Daulat Rao Scindia was asked by Lord Hastings, who had arrived with a big force in September 1817, to either surrender or face war. Scindia surrendered and accepted subsidiary alliance, yet it was a treaty of 'amity and friendship' and Scindia continued to remain independent in many ways.

Treaty of Gwalior (Subsidiary Alliance, 5 November 1817) Daulat Rao Scindia was also forced by the English to sign the Treaty of Gwalior. As per this treaty, he pledged to help the Company in suppressing the **Pindaris**, the irregular forces of the Marathas. Thus the Third Maratha War began as a campaign against the Pindaris. The British troops were led by Lord Hastings supported by a force under General Thomas Hislop.

Though the Maratha chiefs had been humbled, they had not yet reconciled with the loss of their independence, and they rose once again under the leadership of the Peshwa. Peshwa's forces supported by those of Bhonsle (Mudhoji II Bhonsle, also known as Appa Sahib of Nagpur) and Holkar (Malhar Rao Holkar II of Indore) rose against the EIC. On 5 November 1817, the Peshwa set ablaze the British residency of Poona and attacked the British camp at Khadki. But the Peshwa was defeated at **Khadki** (also known as Kirkee or Ganesh Khind, 5 November), Bhonsle was defeated at **Sitabaldi hills** (26 November) and Holkar was defeated at **Mehidpur** (21 December 1817).

Holkar and the Treaty of Mandsaur (Subsidiary Alliance, 6 January 1818) Malhar Rao Holkar II of Indore was forced to sign the Treaty of Mandsaur and now a British Resident was placed in Indore. Holkar had to surrender all his territories south of the Narmada including Khandesh. He also renounced his claim over the Rajput states (later Scindia also ceded Ajmer and the Rajputana states which were under the control of Scindia and Holkar for last several decades now came under British control). Since the Holkar was only 11 years old, Tantia Jog was appointed as the Chief Minister. In this way, Holkar became the **last Maratha chief** to sign a subsidiary alliance with the British.

After the defeat at Khadki, Peshwa fought two more battles with the British—**Battle of Koregaon** (1 January 1818) and **the Battle of Ashti** (20 February 1818). He was defeated in both the battles and finally surrendered in front of Sir John Malcolm. In this way, the entire Maratha force was routed by superior military power of the EIC.

Hastings decided to get rid of both—the Peshwa and the Peshwaship. Hence, the Peshwa was dethroned, pensioned off and ordered to spend his last days in **Bithoor near Kanpur**. His kingdom was brought under British control and enlarged Presidency of Bombay was brought into existence. To satisfy Maratha pride, a small kingdom of **Satara** was carved out of Peshwa's kingdom and given to **Pratap Singh**, a direct descendant of Shivaji.

Thus by 1818, the entire Indian subcontinent except Sind (now spelled Sindh) and Punjab had been brought under British control, directly or indirectly.

Prelim Capsule

Anglo-Maratha Wars (during 1775–1818)

Wars	Period	Important Details
First Maratha War Warren Hastings	**1775–82**	Immediate context—Sawai Madhav Rao succeeded as Peshwa, which gravely frustrated Raghunath Rao and he now tried to capture power with British help. Began with the **Treaty of Surat** and ended with the **Treaty of Salbai**. Main battles fought—Battles of **Adas, Talegaon** and **Sipri.** Result—It ended in a draw. Treaty of Salbai gave the Marathas 20 years of peace.
Second Maratha War Lord Wellesley	**1803–05**	Immediate context—In 1801, Peshwa Baji Rao II killed Holkar's brother Vithoji Rao Holkar. When Holkar launched a counter attack, Peshwa fled, took refuge in Bassein and approached Wellesley for help. Began with the **Treaty of Bassein** and ended with the **Treaty of Rajpurghat**. Main battles fought- Battles of **Assaye, Argaon, Delhi, Laswari** and **Ding**. Result—the English had an edge over the Marathas. Separate treaties were signed with Scindia, Bhonsle and Holkar by the Company which tore apart the Maratha confederacy.
Third Maratha War Lord Hastings	**1817–18**	Immediate Context—The War began as a campaign against the **Pindaris**, the irregular Maratha forces. Began with the **Treaty of Gwalior** and ended with the **Treaty of Mandsaur**. Main battles fought—Battles of **Khadki, Sitabaldi, Mehidpur, Koregaon** and **Ashti**. Result—Maratha forces were decisively defeated. Peshwa's territories were annexed by the British. The House of the Peshwa was extinguished.

Reasons for the Defeat of Mysore and the Marathas

We find that there were some common weaknesses in both the states of Mysore and Marathas that were also characteristic of 18th century Indian polity. These weaknesses contributed to their defeat at the hands of the English Company. The static eastern people could not successfully contend with the dynamic English nation rejuvenated by the forces of renaissance, industrial revolution and Machiavellian methods of statecraft. The main reasons are as follows:

1. **Mutual rivalry among Indian states** Constant rivalry among the 'country powers' made them an easy prey to the imperialist powers. We have seen in this chapter that there were disputes between the states of Mysore and Maratha. The English took this as an opportunity and used one against the other to establish their control over both of them.
2. **Presence of factions and interest groups in the administration** In both the states, there were different interest groups that opposed each other and weakened the central authority. In the case of the Marathas, there were the Maratha chiefs like the Scindias and the Holkars. They constantly competed with one another for power and tried to establish independent authority. This certainly weakened the central Maratha authority and caused political instability which the English fully exploited in their favour.
3. **Lack of resources** Lack of resources with the Indian states was a major constraint while fighting the British, especially when we see that the British were already in control of Bengal, the most productive part of the country, and had the backing of their home government. The Marathas were primarily dependent on resources from outside, such as chauth and sardeshmukhi. Mysore was comparatively better off under Hyder Ali and Tipu, yet lacked resource mobilisation from the countryside.

Some historians also mention causes such as incapacity of individual rulers, weak military organisation and religious or caste differences of the rulers and the ruled, etc. Such arguments are only myths and misrepresent the true situation. For instance, in the case of Mysore we find that the Mysore rulers were able leaders who also tried to organise the army along European lines. Their great misfortune was that they were pitted against imperial giants who had both the will and capacity to bulldoze the whole of India.

To sum up, in this chapter we saw the process of British expansion in South India in the form of conquest of Mysore and Maratha states. The British first came in the region for commercial gains. The existing rivalry among the states gave the British an opportunity to interfere in their political matters. The administrative weakness of the states finally led to their defeat at the hands of the British. The defeat of Mysore and the Marathas proved fatal for Indian states and laid the foundation of British rule in India.

Previous Years' Questions – Preliminary Exam

1. Who among the following Indian rulers established embassies in foreign countries on modern lines? **[UPSC 2001]**
   (a) Hyder Ali (b) Mir Qasim
   (c) Shah Alam II (d) Tipu Sultan
2. Assertion (A): Marathas emerged as the strongest native power in India after the decline of Mughal Empire.
   Reason (R): Marathas were first to have a clear concept of united nation. **[UPSC 2003]**

Select the answer for the options given below:
(a) Both A and R is true and R is the correct explanation of A
(b) Both A and R is true but R is not a correct explanation of A
(c) A is true but R is false.
(d) A is false but R is true.

3. Consider the following Princely states of the British rule in India: **[UPSC 2003]**
   1. Jhansi
   2. Sambalpur
   3. Satara

   The correct chronological order in which they were annexed by the British is:
   (a) 1-2-3 (b) 1-3-2
   (c) 3-2-1 (d) 3-1-2

4. Which one of the following statements does not apply to the system of Subsidiary Alliance introduced by Lord Wellesley? **[UPSC 2018]**
   (a) To maintain a large standing army at other's expense
   (b) To keep India safe from Napoleonic danger
   (c) To secure a fixed income for the Company
   (d) To establish British paramountcy over the Indian States

Previous Years' Questions – Main Exam

1. 'Dalhousie's predecessors had acted on the general principles of avoiding annexations, if these could be avoided. Dalhousie acted on the principles of annexation if he could do so legitimately. His annexations were both of War and Peace'. Analyse. **[UPSC 2010]**
2. In many ways, Lord Dalhousie was the founder of modern India. Elaborate. **[UPSC 2013]**
3. Why did the armies of the British East India company – mostly comprising of Indian soldiers – win consistently against the more numerous and better equipped armies of then Indian rulers? Give reasons. **[UPSC 2022]**

Answers

Previous Years' Questions – Preliminary Exam

1. (d) 2. (a) 3. (c) 4. (c)

2 British Expansion Beyond Indian Frontiers (Nepal, Burma and Afghanistan, 1814–42)

In this chapter, you will read about the British colonial expansion beyond Indian frontiers. By 1818, with the defeat of the Marathas and the pensioning of the Peshwa, the British supremacy in India was complete. The British had conquered almost the whole of India except Sind and Punjab and their annexation now was only a matter of time. The British followed a two-fold policy for the consolidation of the Raj—the introduction of a suitable administrative system and securing the newly conquered territories. In the process of securing British frontiers in India, several states were brought under direct or indirect control to serve as outposts against external threat.

Further, the East India Company also used India as a base to expand its control over lands of South and South-East Asia. During the period 1757 to 1857, English control was established from Nepal in the north to Sri Lanka in the south, Afghanistan in the north-west, Mauritius in the south-west to Andaman and Nicobar, Burma, Malaya and Philippines in the south-east. Only mainland Asia—China, Siam, Laos, Cambodia and Vietnam—was left relatively untouched.

Reasons for Expansion Beyond Indian Frontiers

Shifting Financial Base of East India Company (from Trade to Land Revenue)

The province of Bengal was the first substantial area in the Asian mainland to pass under direct control of the English Company. Until now, the Company's primary source of income was trade, which soon began to face multifarious challenges.

By 1770s, Bengal had been milked dry and its economy was in shambles. This not only affected Company's profits but also jeopardised its extremely lucrative trade with China, as the Chinese at that time sold their goods only in exchange for silver which had been mostly provided from Bengal treasury. Further, the industrial revolution in England had gained strength and the industrial interests were demanding an end to the Company's trade monopoly in the East. The Company itself was getting involved in costly military conflicts in India with the country powers. In this context, with declining income from trade and increasing expenditure on armed conflict, the Company's financial base began to shift from trade and commerce to land revenue, **from business of trade to business of government**. This naturally pushed the Company to go ahead with continuous territorial expansion.

Need to Obtain Spices from South-East Asia for Trade

For several years, the Company had been carrying out profitable trade with China, especially in silks, nankeens (yellowish cotton cloth) and tea. But the Chinese traded mostly in exchange for silver, which had been provided by the Bengal treasury since 1757. With the depletion of Bengal's wealth, the Company sought to pay for China's trade, first, by replacing the silver with opium from Malwa region of Central India, and second, by obtaining costly spices (like clove and nutmeg) from South-East Asia for sale in China and Europe. This impelled the Company to expand itself into South-East Asia.

Need for New Markets and Supplies

The English Company's interest in expansion outside India was also fuelled by the need to find new markets for goods procured in India and also to procure supplies either for cross trade or for use by the Company's military forces.

Need to Safeguard Indian Empire

The Company also needed to safeguard its Indian empire and the trade routes to China and India. Hence, the Company's expansion outside India was also strategically driven.

Note: The first English conquests outside India were in the Straits of Malacca, later known as the **Straits Settlements** and comprised the ports of Penang (1791), Malacca and Singapore (1824). However, some of the major conquests are mentioned in detail below.

Major Conquests

Nepal

Anglo–Nepal War (1814–16)

Historical Context In 1768, the Gorkhas (hardy people belonging to the hill town of 'Gorkha') wrested the control of Kathmandu from the successors of Ranjit Malla of Bhatgaon. In their attempt to expand beyond the mountains, they were checked by the Chinese in the north. Hence, they pushed towards the frontiers of Bengal and Awadh, coming in contact and clash with the English in India.

In 1801, Governor-General Wellesley, in pursuance of his scheme of Subsidiary Alliance to consolidate Company's territories in India and create outposts against Tibet or China, forced the **Hindu Gorkha Kingdom of Nepal** to sign the treaty and accept a British Resident at Kathmandu. However, in 1803, the Resident left owing to Nepalese hostility. The following decade saw numerous problems all along the 1,100-km long border shared between Nepal and India.

Causes

- Pursuance of British foreign and frontier policy- British did not want to solely depend on the Himalayas to provide India protection from the North. They looked at Nepal as a stable **buffer state** between India and Tibet or China.
- The ensuing border disputes.
- Expansionist policy followed by both the English and the Gorkhas.

The War In May 1814, the Gorkhas attacked three police stations of **Butwal**, then under the English East India Company's authority. **Governor-General Hastings** took it as a challenge to Company's authority and decided to launch an offensive along the whole frontier, from the Sutlej to the Kosi.

In October 1814, Governor-General Hastings launched the Nepal War. The hill people put up a strong resistance and engaged the British in military conflict for over a year. Battles of **Butwal, Almora, Malaon** and **Makwanpur** were the important battles fought; all went in favour of the English.

The Nepalese were finally defeated and forced to sign the **Treaty of Sugauli (March 1816)**. As per the treaty, the British gained the districts of Garhwal and Kumaon (comprising a great portion of the **rich Terai forests**) and a resident was placed at Kathmandu. The north-west frontier of the Company was pushed up to the mountains as English also gained the entire area of the Sutlej hills comprising **hill stations of Simla, Mussoorie, Ranikhet, Landour** and **Nainital**.

After the Treaty of Sugauli, the British used a great deal of tact in their dealings with the rulers of Nepal. They treated Nepalese ruler as sovereign and in return, even they allowed no diplomatic mission, other than that of Britain into Nepal. **Nepal also maintained neutrality during the Revolt of 1857**, while the British enlisted a large number of Gorkhas as mercenaries in their army. About 5,000 Nepali men entered British service in 1815, most of whom were not 'real' Gorkhas but Kumaonis, Garhwalis and other Himalayan hill men. These groups, eventually lumped together under the term Gurkha, and became the backbone of British Indian forces.

Burma

First Anglo–Burmese War (1824–26)

Immediate Cause In 1823–24, the Burmese military, in its pursuit for rebels, entered and occupied Assam and Manipur and prepared to attack Chittagong. These territories were, however, claimed by the English in India. The British Indian army attacked Burma in retaliation, which came to be known as the First Anglo-Burmese War.

In 1824, the British Indian army attacked Burma. The main attack on Arakan region of Burma was launched from the sea. The Burmese forces led by Maha Bandula were easily defeated and the King was forced to sign a peace treaty, Treaty of Yandabo.

Treaty of Yandabo (24 February 1826) As per the treaty,

- The English regained control over Assam, Manipur and occupied **Arakan** and **Tenasserim** region (Tavoy and Mergui). Thus, the King lost most of his coast.
- The King was forced to accept a **British Resident** at his capital and pay war indemnity.

Arakan region, Burma

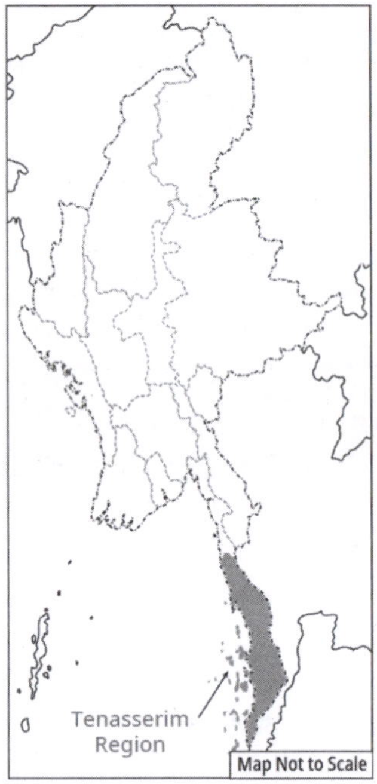

Tenasserim region, Burma

Second Anglo–Burmese War (1852–53)

In 1839, the British Resident claimed that the Burmese did not treat him well and left. Meanwhile, Burma had emerged as a major supplier of timber (needed for ship-building and repair industry of the English Company based in Calcutta) and other costly items like tin, pepper and ivory. The deltas of the Irrawaddy River had also emerged as important suppliers of rice to Bengal and to the growing settlements in South-East Asia. These developments tempted the British to look for opportunity to annex Burma.

Immediate Cause After the Treaty of Yandabo, several British merchants had settled on the southern coast of Burma and Rangoon. They often complained of ill-treatment at the hands of the Burmese. Two British captains were heavily fined by the Burmese government on certain charges brought against them. Following this incident, the British merchants sent a petition to the then Governor-General Lord Dalhousie, providing the desired opportunity. Thus, in 1852, Dalhousie decided to attack Burma on the pretext of restoring the dignity of the English.

The war started in 1852 and by 1853, the English had annexed Rangoon, Pegu (or Lower Burma) and the region upto Toungoo, thus gaining control of the entire coast of the Bay of Bengal. The Burmese King, Mindon Min, was forced to shift his capital to **Mandalay**.

The annexation of Pegu faced much criticism in Britain itself and was variously described as 'a very serious evil' and as motivated by 'exaggerated ambition to extend India to its illusory natural frontiers'.

The London Times commented, 'the maintenance of British prestige in India did not require fresh annexations'.

Note: Third Anglo-Burmese War (1885) The Third Burmese War took place in 1885 when the English attacked Burma on the pretext that the king Thibaw Min was intriguing with the French in Vietnam to weaken English control over Asia. The war ended in English victory and annexation of Upper Burma. Thus, Burma was turned into a province of British India (1937 onwards, Burma was governed as a separate colony).

Afghanistan

Context of Russian Threat The idea of 'Russian peril' was propagated by **Lord Palmerston**, British Foreign Secretary in the mid-19th century and was first mentioned by William Bentinck.

The 19th century was a period of diplomatic competition between the British and Russian empires for spheres of influence in Asia known as **'the Great Game'** to the British and the 'Tournament of Shadows' to the Russians. Thus, for most of the 19th century, Russia was viewed as 'the enemy' in Britain, and any Russian advance into Central Asia was always assumed in London to be directed towards the conquest of India. In 1832, Britain had expanded its franchise which was condemned by Emperor Nicholas I of Russia. This set the stage for 'cold war between autocratic Russia and democratic Britain. Consequently, the 19th-century Russia's 'Special mission in the East' (more directed against the alleged 'Yellow Peril' of China rather than India) was misinterpreted. In 1837, Lord Palmerston, fearing the instability of Afghanistan, the Sind, and the increasing power of the Sikh kingdom in the northwest, raised the spectre of a possible Russian invasion of British India through Afghanistan, the only entrance to India from Central Asia.

British Reaction to Russian Threat

The British reaction to the Russian threat was two-fold.

- **Forward Policy** One reaction was to secure commanding influence in Afghanistan, either by annexation or by creating it as a buffer state. This view was generally held by the members of the Conservative Party.
- **Policy of Masterly Inactivity (also known as the 'Stationary School')** Another reaction was to reach a diplomatic understanding with Russia and follow a policy of watchful non-intervention as far as Afghanistan was concerned. This view was held by the Liberals.

In the 1830s, the British became over-anxious to protect Afghanistan leading to the First Anglo–Afghan War which proved to be a great disaster for the British. A direct consequence of this was the annexation of Sind (1843) and Punjab (1849) in an attempt to recover the lost British prestige and made the British India's frontier directly co-terminus with that of Afghanistan.

First Afghan War (1839–42)

The concern for imperial defence and search for a scientific border in the north-west brought the English in contact with the Afghans. Afghanistan was considered by the British as a **buffer state** against the Napoleonic France and Czarist Russia. It was felt that Afghanistan should be under the control of a friendly prince.

Dost Mohammad, the Amir (ruler) of Afghanistan was initially anxious for English friendship and sent a congratulatory letter to Auckland, on the latter's appointment as Governor-General. Dost, however, made his friendship conditional on the receipt of English help in recovering Peshawar from Ranjit Singh. Auckland decided to maintain neutrality and wrote, 'It was not the practice of British Government to interfere in the affairs of independent states'. In desperation, Dost Mohammad began showing signs of friendship with Russia.

Burnes Mission In September 1837, Auckland sent Capt. Alexander Burnes to Kabul outwardly on a commercial mission, but in reality to judge the political situation there. Burnes reported from Kabul that the Amir was entirely 'English in views' but insisted that British pressure must be exerted on Ranjit Singh to restore Peshawar to the Afghans. But Auckland was adamant that Dost Mohammad must give up all hopes of obtaining Peshawar and that the Government of India was already rendering him a great service in keeping peace between Lahore and Kabul; hence Dost Mohammad must not conclude any alliance with British enemies. At this, Dost Mohammad felt despaired and received the Russian ambassador with much warmth. Having failed in his mission, Burnes left for India in April 1838.

The causes of the First Afghan War were as follows:

- The concern for imperial defence
- Search for a scientific border
- **Immediate cause** Failure of Burnes' Mission

After the failure of Burnes' mission, Governor-General Auckland decided to follow a 'Forward Policy'; he planned to depose Dost Mohammad and entrust the country in the hands of some friendly prince.

Tripartite Treaty (26 June 1838)

As per the plan, a Tripartite Treaty was signed between the English, Shah Shuja (ex-ruler of Afghanistan) and Ranjit Singh. Following the treaty, combined forces of the three parties, known as the **'Army of the Indus'** launched an attack on Kabul.

By July 1839, the army had captured Kandahar and Ghazni. Dost Mohammad felt so disheartened by these defeats that he gave up the fight and fled to Bemian, a town north-west of Kabul. Shah Shuja was placed on the Afghan throne.

However, the glitches in the plan became evident soon after. Shah Shuja was unacceptable to the people of Afghanistan and his position could be maintained only with the help of the British army. Thus, a small garrison was placed at Kabul under the command of **General Elphinstone**. But the English continued to face retaliations.

- In September 1840, Dost Mohammad, upon getting military help from the Wali of Kholoom, attacked the English but failed. Subsequently, he was arrested and sent to Calcutta as a prisoner.
- Again, in 1841, the **Afghans rose in rebellion** against the English. Several Englishmen in Kabul, Jalalabad, Kandahar and Ghazni were killed, and their cantonments were seized. Burnes was also killed. Macnaghten, the British official was forced to sign a humiliating treaty with Akbar Khan (son of Dost Mohammad), agreeing to evacuate Afghanistan within three days. However, Macnaghten was murdered.

- In January 1842, the **disastrous retreat** began from Kabul. Elphinstone, along with his 4,500 army men and 12,000 camp followers were substantially annihilated in the snow covered passes. Shah Shuja was also murdered in April.

Auckland Replaced by Ellenborough Auckland's grandiose plan had exploded like a balloon and he was soon replaced by Lord Ellenborough. Ellenborough ordered the forces to retreat after inflicting reprisals and securing the release of prisoners. Consequently, by September 1842, the combined British forces were able to re-establish control over Jalalabad, Kandahar and Kabul. The forces rescued the prisoners, demolished Kabul's' main bazaar and then retreated through the Khyber Pass. Dost Mohammad was released and he re-established his authority in Kabul.

Evaluation of Auckland's Afghan Policy The Afghan War came to be known as **'Disaster in Afghanistan'** and is described as **'a compound of folly, ignorance and arrogance'**. It had proved to be too costly, and it was also a massive blow to the prestige of British Indian Army.

Auckland Afghan policy was subjected to universal condemnation. Morally, it was not justified as Auckland had contradicted his own previous stand of not interfering in internal affairs of independent states. Afghanistan was an independent state and Dost Mohammad was its acknowledged ruler. Politically again, it was not justified as Auckland took an exaggerated view of the Russian danger when in reality the enemy was several thousand miles away. The main aim of installing a friendly prince on the throne of Afghanistan could not be realised and Dost Mohammad returned to the throne after the war was over.

Further, one political crime leads to another. The passage of British troops through Sind and occupation of regions like Shikarpur, Bukkar and Karachi were in gross violation of the 'Treaty of Perpetual Friendship' concluded with the Amirs of Sind, and ultimately led to war and annexation of Sind (Read about the annexation of Sind in the next chapter).

Note: The Second Afghan War (1878–80) occurred at the time of Governor-General Lytton and ended with the **Treaty of Gandamak**. As per the treaty, the Amir Yakub Khan agreed to station a permanent British Resident at Kabul and conduct his foreign policy on advice of the Government of India. Afghanistan was created as a buffer state between British Indian and Russian Empire.

To sum up, in this chapter we learnt about the British efforts to colonise outside India. The English Company got interested in territories outside India mainly to protect and promote their trade and colonial interests. Indulging in diplomacy and war, the Company established its control over Sri Lanka, Mauritius, Andaman and Nicobar, Burma, Malaya, Philippines, Nepal and Burma. The areas it did not directly capture, it still wielded considerable influence. The high cost of such expansionist activities were borne by the Indian treasury (filled by the land revenue exacted by the Indian peasant), while the Indian sepoy provided the necessary cannon fodder. Thus, it was mainly at the cost of India and the Indian peasant and soldiers that England emerged as a dominant power in the whole of South Asia.

Prelim Capsule

British Expansion beyond Indian Frontiers (Nepal, Burma and Afghanistan)

Wars	Period	Important Details
Nepal War Lord Hastings	**1814–16**	Immediate context—Gorkha attack on three police stations of **Butwal** (1814), then under the English East India Company's authority. Main battles fought—Battles of **Butwal, Almora, Malaon** and **Makwanpur**; all went in favour of the English. Ended with the **Treaty of Sugauli (March 1816)**. Result—The British gained the districts of Garhwal and Kumaon (comprising a great portion of the **rich Terai forests**) and the entire area of the Sutlej hills comprising of **hill stations of Simla, Mussorie, Ranikhet, Landour** and **Nainital**.
First Burma War Lord Amherst	**1824–26**	Immediate context—The Burmese military, in its pursuit for rebels, entered and occupied Assam and Manipur and prepared to attack Chittagong. These territories were however claimed by the English in India. Ended with the **Treaty of Yandabo**. Result—The English regained control over Assam, Manipur and occupied **Arakan** and **Tenasserim** region (Tavoy and Mergui). Thus, the King lost most of his coast.
Second Burma War Lord Dalhousie	**1852–53**	Immediate context—Two British captains were heavily fined by the Burmese government. Dalhousie decided to attack Burma on the pretext of restoring the dignity of the English. Result—The English annexed **Rangoon** and **Pegu** (or Lower Burma).
Third Burma War Lord Dufferin	**1885**	The British annexed **Upper Burma**. Burma lost its independence.
First Afghan War Lord Auckland	**1839–42**	Immediate context—Failure of **Burnes Mission**. Result—Afghan invasion was a failure. The English who were forced to retreat, Shah Shuja was killed and Dost Mohammad re-establish his authority in Kabul.
Second Afghan War Lord Lytton	**1878–80**	Ended with the **Treaty of Gandamak**. Result—Amir Yakub Khan agreed to station a permanent British Resident at Kabul and conduct his foreign policy with advice of the Government of India. Afghanistan was created as a buffer state between British Indian and Russian Empire.

3 British Expansion in North India (Conquest of Sind, Punjab and Awadh, 1843–57)

In north India, Rohilkhand and Etawah had been annexed by Shuja-ud-Daula in 1774, and later incorporated into Company's territory in 1801. Thus, only Punjab and Awadh were left as major powers in north India. Sind (now spelled Sindh) in the west was conquered in 1843, which has also been mentioned here. In this way, from 1818 to 1857, the British completed the task of conquering the whole of India.

Conquest of Sindh (1843)

In 1780s, Sindh was captured by the Talpuras, a Baluch tribe, led by **Mir Fatah Ali Khan**. After his death, it came to be shared by his four brothers, known as **'Char Yar'** who called themselves the Amirs or Lords of Sindh. Soon these Amirs extended their kingdom on all sides, capturing Amarkot from the Raja of Jodhpur, Karachi from the chief of Luz, Shikarpur and Bukkar from the Afghans.

Context of Anglo–French Rivalry

From 1740 to 1800, Anglo–French rivalry was primarily confined to south India and ended with the defeat of Tipu Sultan and his French connection (1799). After 1807, the Anglo–French conflict shifted to the North-west. After the French defeat in naval conflict, Napoleon planned to invade India via land route. Alarmed by the prospect, Lord Minto I immediately sent **four diplomatic missions—** Malcolm to Tehran, Elphinstone to Kabul, Charles Metcalfe to Lahore and Seton to Sindh. With the efforts of these diplomatic missions, friendly treaties were concluded with the respective governments to counter the French challenge.

Thus, in 1809, the **Treaty of Eternal Friendship** was signed with the Amirs, who promised not to allow the French to settle in Sindh. In 1820, the treaty was renewed to further exclude the Americans from Sindh. But soon, the commercial and navigational value of the Indus began to attract the attention of the Company's authorities. Consequently, in 1832, William Bentinck sent **Colonel Pottinger** to Sindh to sign a new commercial treaty with the Amirs. As per the treaty, the Amirs allowed a free passage to English travellers and merchants through Sindh and also allowed the use of Indus for commercial pursuits. Later, Pottinger was stationed as the Company's political agent in Sindh.

Context of Anglo–Russian Rivalry

However, Lord Auckland began to see Sindh from a larger perspective of defence for India from the Russian threat (mentioned in the previous chapter). To him, Sindh was a necessary prelude to the annexation of Afghanistan. Thus, Sindh was conquered to counter Russia. The commercial benefits from the Sindh River were also an attraction.

Soon Ranjit Singh captured Rojhan, a town on the Sindh frontier, giving the Company a chance to offer protection to the Amirs. The Amirs had neither desired nor asked for foreign help, yet they were forced to sign a **Subsidiary Treaty in 1839** and accept a British Resident at Hyderabad. The Amirs had virtually passed under British protection.

During the Afghan war (1839–42), the Amirs of Sindh found themselves saddled with the responsibility of helping the British forces. Parts of their territory like Shikarpur, Bukkar and Karachi were taken away in gross violation of the Treaty of Perpetual Friendship and they also had to contribute a large amount of money in order to maintain troops in their midst whom they did not want. The independent position of the Amirs was gone forever.

In 1842, Lord Ellenborough succeeded Auckland as Governor-General and proved to be equally unscrupulous in his dealings with the Amirs. He was eager to find a pretext for the annexation of Sindh and in doing so, regain the English prestige which had suffered during the First Afghan war.

In September 1842, Major Outram was replaced by Sir Charles Napier as British Resident in Sindh. Napier was equally eager to annex the province and followed a bullying policy. He charged the Amirs of hostility and disaffection towards the British government.

> **Sir Charles Napier** said, 'We have no right to seize Sindh, wet we shall do so and a very advantageous, useful, humane, piece of rascality it will be'.

Causes of Annexation of Sindh

- To counter Russian threat, Sindh was seen as a necessary prelude to the annexation of Afghanistan;
- To gain commercial benefits from the Sindh river; and
- To regain the English prestige which had suffered during the First Afghan war

Statue of Charles James Napier, Trafalgar Square, London, England

Sindh was finally annexed in 1843 after a brief campaign (**Battles of Miani and Dabo**) led by **Sir Charles Napier**. Napier called the Sindh war as 'the tail of the Afghan storm'. In 1847, Sindh was made part of British India's Bombay Presidency.

Conquest of Punjab (1849)

Punjab after Ranjit Singh

Maharaja Ranjit Singh had died in June 1839. Despite his great personal achievements, he had failed to establish a stable Sikh state in Punjab and his death was followed by political instability. He was a despot and had established a military rule. He left behind a standing army of 40,000 soldiers. The strength of the army increased three-fold within five years of his death which proved to be a great burden on the shrinking resources of the state. When the soldiers could not be paid salaries, they went out of control and interfered in politics. A war of succession ensued amongst the many sons of Ranjit Singh, the legitimacy of many of whom was doubtful. These incompetent heirs were unable to check the forces of disorder.

Ranjit Singh's sons Khadak Singh and Naunihal Singh sat on the throne in quick succession. In 1843, **Dalip Singh**, a minor son of Maharaja, was proclaimed king under the guardianship of **Rani Jindan**.

The English Cast Their Eye

The English were closely watching the happenings in Punjab and cast longing eyes on the fertile plains on the other side of the Sutlej. The disastrous defeat in the Afghan war had lowered British prestige, which they wanted to regain at the cost of the Sindh and Punjab. In 1843 itself, they annexed Sindh, to the south of Punjab, which did not gain the British any respect in Punjab but only increased suspicions of British motives.

In 1843, **Major Broadfoot** was appointed as Company's political agent in Punjab. He stressed on the disorder in Punjab and recounted every tale of corrupt behaviour at the court, affecting British attitudes.

In 1844, Lord Ellenborough was succeeded by Lord Hardinge as Governor-General. Hardinge undertook vigorous measures to strengthen the Company's military position. The Company's troops in Punjab and Sindh were trained and fortified. The Company took a hypocritical stand and contended that the preparations were only defensive in nature and calculated to meet a possible attack from the Sikhs. In an attempt to shift the responsibility of war on the shoulders of the Sikhs, the English variously wrote:

- 'If the army could not be controlled it must be disbanded or its energies diverted in war. No one dreaded to do the former and so the latter was the only recourse'.
- 'Rani Jindan dreaded the absolute power of the Khalsa army and found her only hope of security in urging it on to challenge British supremacy'.

In 1845, **Lal Singh**, a lover of Rani Jindan, had won over the army on his side and become the wazir. Teja Singh had become the new commander of the Sikh forces.

To the Sikhs, the British moves appeared more as an act of aggression rather than defence. Consequently, on 11 December 1845, the Sikh troops, led by Lal Singh, crossed the Sutlej and took offensive action against the English troops commanded by **Sir Hugh Gough**. On 13 December, Hardinge made his declaration of war and thus the war began.

Causes of Anglo–Sikh War

- British desire to expand their influence and control over Punjab, as it was the only remaining formidable force that could threaten the British hold in India and the last remaining independent kingdom not under British influence.
- Glorious wealth of the kingdom of Punjab-the Kohinoor was but one of its treasures.
- Political instability after the death of Maharaja Ranjit Singh.
- Indiscipline of the Khalsa army.
- Instigating role of Major Braodfoot.
- English attempt to regain the prestige which had suffered during the First Afghan war.

First Anglo–Sikh War (1845–46)

Four successive battles were fought between the British and the Sikh army. These were the **battles of Mudki, Ferozeshah, Baddoval and Aliwal**. But the fifth and decisive battle was the **Battle of Sabbraon** (10 February 1846). Due to the treachery of **Lal Singh and Teja Singh**, who gave all critical information to the English, the battle resulted in a bloody slaughter of Sikh troops. After the defeat of the Sikhs, the British occupied Lahore and forced the Sikhs to sign the Treaty of Lahore.

A high relief marble carving showing soldiers and a coffin on the side of the Sutlej Campaign, or 1st Sikh War (memorial in Lichfield Cathedral, Staffordshire, UK)

Treaty of Lahore (9 March 1846) The main provisions of the treaty were as follows:

1. Maharaja gave up all his territories lying to the south of the River Satluj.
2. Sikhs had to pay ₹1.5 crore as war indemnity. Unable to pay the entire sum, they had to give up certain additional territories including Kashmir and Hazara. The British sold **Kashmir to Gulab Singh** for ₹1 crore.
3. Minor Dalip Singh was accepted as King with Queen Jindan as his guardian (Queen Regent) and Lal Singh as the wazir.
4. **Sir Henry Lawrence** became the British Resident at Lahore.

The Sikhs disliked the British move of selling away Kashmir to Gulab Singh. Consequently, the Sikhs revolted under Lal Singh. The revolt was suppressed and yet another treaty, Treaty of Bhairoval, was signed with Dalip Singh.

Treaty of Bhairoval (22 December 1846) Main provisions of the treaty were as follows:

1. Rani Jindan's guardianship was ended and she was pensioned.
2. A Council of eight Sikh chiefs under the Chairmanship of British Resident was appointed for governance works.
3. It was decided that a permanent British army will be placed at Lahore until Dalip Singh becomes a major.

Evaluation Punjab was not annexed after the First Anglo–Sikh war. The argument that this was done in deference to the memory of Ranjit Singh, a friend of the Company, may be dismissed as childish. A closer study of the events suggests that the annexation of Punjab would have created some serious problems for the British. The Khalsa army had been defeated but not annihilated. Further, every Sikh peasant knew the use of arms and the possibility of guerrilla warfare could not be ruled out. The British government also did not have the resources to keep control over the vast territory of Punjab. It was clear that Punjab had to be territorially reduced, militarily enfeebled and financially crippled before it could be absorbed into the British Empire.

Second Anglo–Sikh War (1848–49)

After the Treaty of Bhairoval, the British Resident became the virtual ruler of Punjab with unlimited civil and military powers. When Rani Jindan showed her resentment towards such usurpation of powers, her jewellery was seized and she was sent to Sheikhpura under spies. Her pension was also arbitrarily reduced from ₹1.5 lakh to mere ₹48,000 per annum.

Governor-General Lord Dalhousie and the Policy of Annexation (1848–56) In 1848, Lord Dalhousie succeeded Lord Hardinge. He was young (36 years old), aristocratic and despotic when he came to India as Governor-General. He was an imperialist and an avowed annexationist. Dalhousie firmly believed that the British government should not neglect any opportunity of acquiring a territory and was determined to extend direct British rule over as large an area as possible. Thus, while his predecessors avoided annexation if it could be avoided, Dalhousie annexed if he could do so legitimately.

The underlying motive behind Dalhousie's annexation policy was the expansion of British exports to India. Like other imperialists, he also believed that British exports to Princely States were suffering due to maladministration in these states. He also thought that the policy of subsidiary alliance had served its purpose of facilitating the British conquest of India and the allied states could now be got rid of to the benefit of the empire.

Dalhousie's annexations were of both 'war' and 'peace'. Annexations of war were based on right of conquest (Punjab and Pegu) and of peace came by application of Doctrine of Lapse.

Doctrine of Lapse This was the chief instrument of Dalhousie's annexation policy. It was based on Dalhousie's declared conviction that the system of ruling through 'sham royalties' resulted in misery of the people. Accordingly, he wanted to dispossess Indian princes who pretended to be descendants of the Mughals.

According to the doctrine, any princely state or territory under the British subsidiary system, would automatically be annexed if the ruler was either 'manifestly incompetent or died without a male heir'. The latter supplanted the long-established right of an Indian sovereign without an heir to choose a successor. Applying this doctrine, many states were annexed including Satara (1848), Jaitpur and Sambalpur (1849), Baghat (1850), Udaipur (Chhattisgarh, 1852), Jhansi (1853), Nagpur (1854), Tanjore and Arcot (1855).

Dalhousie also refused to recognise the titles of many former rulers or to pay their pensions. These included the rulers of Carnatic, Surat, Tanjore and Bithoor. Awadh was annexed on pretext of misgovernance. It must be noted that **Dalhousie did not invent the doctrine**. In fact, as early as 1834, the Court of Directors had laid down that in case of failure of lineal successors, the permission to adopt was an indulgence and annexed Maandavi (1839), Kolaba and Jalaun (1840). In 1841, the British authorities also decided in favour of a uniform policy and directed the Governor-General not to abandon any just and honourable accession of territory or revenue.

Dalhousie's Reforms Dalhousie's chief aim was the consolidation of British rule in India. He introduced various social and public reforms to consolidate the gains of the English East India Company. However, they also laid the foundation on which modern India has been built up, earning Dalhousie the title of **'Maker of Modern India'**.

Administrative Reforms Dalhousie introduced reforms in almost every department of administration. For the newly acquired territories, he introduced the system of centralised control as per which he appointed a Commissioner for every such territory and he was made directly responsible to the Governor-General.

Military Reforms Dalhousie's annexations had extended the British Empire upto Punjab and Sind in the west. Thus, for better control over these areas, the headquarters of Bengal Artillery were shifted from

Calcutta to Meerut. The permanent headquarters of the army were gradually shifted to Simla, which emerged as the seat of the Government of India for a major part of the year.

Educational Reforms During Dalhousie's rule came **Wood's Dispatch** (July 1854), the famous education dispatch of Charles Wood, the President of the Board of Control. It abandoned the 'infiltration theory' and provided for a properly articulated scheme of education from primary to university level. It recommended Anglo-Vernacular schools in each of the three presidencies of India and laid the foundation on which the modern education system of India has been built. Based on the reforms, the first three universities in India were later established in 1857.

Railway Department It was Dalhousie who first introduced Railways in India. The **first railway line was laid down in 1853**, connecting Bombay with Thane. Dalhousie's famous Railway Minute of 1853 formed the basis for the future railway extension in India. Dalhousie encouraged private enterprise to develop railways in India to reduce absolute dependence on the government and to give English capital and enterprise a chance for investment. Establishment of railways in India was not completed with the intention of benefiting local citizens, especially Indians. It was done to transport large amounts of natural resources such as coal and metal from inland mined areas to the coast to be exported to Britain. Nevertheless, besides encouraging trade and commerce and binding India by iron lines, the railways went a long way in uniting the country into one nation.

Public Works Department Before Dalhousie, the construction of Public works had been part of the Military Board. Dalhousie set up a separate Public Works Department for the first time and large amount of funds began to be spent on works of public utility such as irrigational works, construction of canals, bridges and roads. Dalhousie also laid down the basis of **modern postal system** and **electric telegraph** (known as the 'Father of Electric Telegraph in India').

Evaluation of Dalhousie Eight years of Dalhousie's rule were full of important developments in every field, and he is regarded as one of the greatest Governor-Generals of India. However, Dalhousie also proved to be a ruthless imperialist. His annexations are considered to generally represent an uneconomic drain on the financial resources of the Company in India and his policies were greatly responsible for stirring unrest and ultimately leading to the Revolt of 1857.

Immediate Cause (Revolt of Mulraj)

The new Governor-General Dalhousie soon got his opportunity for annexation when two British officers, Vans Agnew and Lieutenant Anderson, were sent for taking charge of Multan from its Governor, Mulraj. The officers were murdered there and within a short period of time, other Sikh chiefs joined in with their armies in open rebellion under the banner of Mulraj. The rebellion soon developed into a national uprising in Punjab.

Taking this as an excuse, **Dalhousie** declared war, saying: 'the Sikh nation has called for war and on my word, sirs, they shall have it with a vengeance'. Three battles were fought in the Second Anglo–Sikh War, namely:

1. **Battle of Ramnagar** (22 November 1848)
2. **Battle of Chillianwala** (13 January 1849): The first two battles were indecisive. In these battles, the British army was led by **General Gough**.
3. **Battle of Gujarat** (21 February 1849): The Sikh army was defeated and it surrendered before the English led by **Charles Napier**.

Once the Sikh army collapsed, Dalhousie decided in favour of annexation declaring that, 'There never can be now any guarantee for the tranquility of India, until we shall have affected the entire subjugation of the Sikh people and destroyed its power as an independent nation'. Hence, on 29 March 1849, Dalhousie annexed Punjab. Maharaja Dalip Singh was pensioned and sent to England for education (There he adopted Christianity but later returned to Punjab and re-embraced Sikhism). Punjab administration was entrusted to a Board of Commissioners. **Kohinoor diamond** was taken away from Dalip Singh and placed in the British royal crown. In this way, Punjab was made part of the British Empire.

Evaluation

Politically, Punjab annexation was beneficial for the British as it extended the British frontiers to its natural boundaries and placed the famous passes of the North-West under the British protection. However, Dalhousie had no moral or legal justification to annex Punjab and as such, the annexation has often been described as 'avoidable' and as 'violent breach of trust'. Ever since the Treaty of Bhairoval, the British Resident was the virtual ruler in Punjab. It was his duty to crush the rebellion of Mulraj or the Sikh army that joined in. Since the Maharaja could not be held responsible for the rebellion, it was clearly unjust to deprive him of his kingdom on this pretext. The English Company, through the Resident, was acting as the guardian of the minor Maharaja. In such circumstances, annexing the kingdom of its ward was a horrific breach of trust.

Annexation of Awadh (1856)

The state of Awadh first came into contact with the British as early as 1764 when the English East India Company defeated the combined army of Mir Qasim, Shuja-ud-Daula (Nawab of Awadh) and Shah Alam II (the fugitive Mughal emperor) in the Battle of Buxar. Awadh then lay at the mercy of the British but Clive decided not to annex it. As a part of post-war settlement with Awadh, the state was restored to the Nawab but he had to sign the Treaty of Subsidiary Alliance and made to part with the districts of Kora and Allahabad. Hence, **Awadh was created as a buffer state** between the Company's territories and the turbulent western India.

Despite the subordinate status of Awadh within the subsidiary alliance system, the Awadh Nawab asserted his independence in many ways. Despite Company's protests, Shuja-ud-Daula raised an army of one lakh soldiers on European lines and even retained 150 French officers. In 1774, he also annexed **Rohilkhand** and **Etawah**.

Awadh after Shuja-ud-Daula

Awadh's position significantly weakened after the death of Shuja-ud-Daula in 1775. His son Asaf-ud-Daula tried to gain control but since Mughal practice did not allow dynastic continuity at provincial level, he faced challenge from other aspirants. Frustrated, he struck a compromise with the Company. The Company secured the Nawabi for him but at the same time seized this opportunity to consolidate its position in Awadh.

Treaty of 1801 (Subsidiary Alliance)

When Governor-General **Lord Wellesley** came to India, he forced the Nawab, **Saadat Ali Khan**, to sign a new treaty in 1801. As per the Treaty, the Nawab had to cede half of his territory including the Lower Doab, Gorakhpur and Rohilkhand to the Company (called the Ceded Districts).

He was also required to act as per the advice of the Council of officers of the Company. Henceforth, the Nawab became increasingly dependent upon the Company for external and internal defence and shut his eyes to the welfare of the people, who groaned under the misrule of the state officers (In part, though, the British were also responsible for the bad state of affairs in Awadh since it were the British who indirectly governed Awadh since 1801). The Treaty of 1801 formed the primary basis for annexation of Awadh in 1856.

By mid-19th century, British opinion was ripe in favour of annexation of Awadh. In fact, the British imperialists during this time had come to believe that Britain alone had the capacity for good governance. However, Dalhousie's greed had chiefly been aroused by the immense potential of Awadh as a market for Manchester goods (similarly, to satisfy Britain's growing demand for raw cotton, Dalhousie annexed the cotton producing province of Berar from the Nizam in 1853).

Accordingly, in 1848, when **Lord Dalhousie** became Governor-General, he skilfully planned the annexation of Awadh. The same year itself, he sent **Colonel Sleeman** as Resident to Lucknow. Sleeman wrote lengthy reports about the prevailing misgovernance in Awadh. He, however, did not recommend annexation but favoured increasing British control over administration. In 1854, Sleeman was replaced by **Outram** who again reported on the ailing governance in the state causing suffering to millions.

Annexation of Awadh (1856) Finally, in 1856, Awadh was annexed by Lord Dalhousie on the pretext of maladministration based on Outram's report. The Nawab, Wajid Ali Shah, was kept under house arrest in Calcutta.

Thus, we see that the Company kept on encroaching on the material and moral domains of Awadh rulers and the annexation of 1856 became a logical conclusion. Yet, this final move of annexation severely hurt the self-respect of the Awadh people, particularly the sepoys of the British army since most of them came from Awadh itself. The dismissal of the court also meant unemployment for the many courtiers, the artisans and the army men. The talukdars were dispossessed of their estates and their forts demolished. The land revenue settlement introduced in Awadh after the annexation further intensified the people's discontent with the cumulative result that nearly 3/4th of the adult population of Awadh, including landholders, peasants and sepoys, participated in the Revolt of 1857.

To sum up, in this chapter we learnt about the annexation of Sindh in the north-west and the subjugation of the remaining two major regional powers in north India, namely Punjab and Awadh. As far as Awadh was concerned, use of force in the battlefield remained minimal after Battle of Buxar and no major confrontation took place until Awadh was fully annexed in 1856. While the rulers of Awadh capitulated easily to British pressures, it was not so easy to pacify the people who soon rose in revolt in large numbers in 1857.

What was the North Western Provinces? (Not to be confused with North-West Frontier Province) Between 1801 and 1806, the British conquered large territories in North India (roughly modern UP) under the aggressive policies of Lord Wellesley. In 1836, the North Western Provinces was established by merging all the administrative divisions of the Ceded and Conquered Provinces. In 1856, the kingdom of Awadh was annexed and merged with North Western Provinces to form the larger and renamed North Western Provinces and Awadh. Allahabad served as its capital in 1858 when it also became the capital of India for a day. After the Revolt of 1857, the province was reorganised and downsized- e.g. Delhi and Gurgaon territories were transferred to Punjab, the Saugor and Nerbudda territories were transferred to Central Provinces. In 1902, the province was further reorganised and renamed as United Provinces of Agra and Awadh— commonly referred to as the United Provinces and abbreviated to UP.

Prelim Capsule

British Expansion in North India (Conquest of Sindh, Punjab and Awadh, 1843-1857)

Wars	Period	Important Details
Conquest of Sindh Lord Ellenborough	**1843**	Main battles fought—**Battles of Miani** and **Dabo**. Result—English led by Sir **Charles Napier** emerged victorious. Sindh was annexed and was later made part of British India's Bombay Presidency in 1847.
First Sikh War Lord Hardinge	**1845–46**	Main battles fought—**Battles of Mudki, Ferozeshah, Baddoval** and **Aliwal**. But the fifth and decisive battle was the Battle of **Sabbraon**. Ended with the **Treaty of Lahore**. Result—Sikh lost territories to the south of the River Satluj. Sir **Henry Lawrence** became the British Resident at Lahore.
Second Sikh War Lord Dalhousie	**1848–49**	Immediate context—Revolt of Multan Governor Mulraj. Main battles fought—**Battles of Ramnagar, Chillianwala** and **Gujrat**. Battle of Gujrat was decisive. Sikh army was defeated and it surrendered before the English led by **Charles Napier**. Result—Dalhousie annexed Punjab. Maharaja Dalip Singh was pensioned and sent to England for education. **Kohinoor diamond** was taken away from Dalip Singh and placed in the British royal crown.
Annexation of Awadh Lord Dalhousie	**1856**	Awadh annexed on the pretext of maladministration based on **Outram's report**.

Previous Years' Questions – Preliminary Exam

1. Which of the following pairs are correctly matched? **[UPSC 2004]**

	List-I	List-II
1.	1767–69	First Anglo–Maratha War
2.	1790–92	Third Anglo–Mysore War
3.	1824–26	First Anglo–Burmese war
4.	1845–46	Second Anglo–Sikh war

Select the correct answer using the codes given below:

(a) 2 and 4 (b) 3 and 4
(c) 1 and 2 (d) 2 and 3

2. The ruler of which one of the following states was removed from power by the British on the pretext of misgovernance? **[UPSC 2007]**

(a) Awadh (b) Jhansi
(c) Nagpur (d) Satara

Answers

Previous Years' Questions – Preliminary Exam

1. (d) 2. (a)

Unit 3
Changes and Impact
(Mid-18th to Mid-19th Century)
(Changes Introduced by the British and their Impact on Indian Economy, Polity, Administration and Society)

1 Changes and Impact: Indian Economy

We have already read about the circumstances in which the East India Company came to India, i.e. during the evolution of merchant capitalism in Europe. The East India Company was originally a trading company and its main aim was to establish profitable trade with India. It was driven by economic interests throughout. Even the political gains were inspired by economic interests. Consequently, when the company gained political supremacy in India, governance degenerated into a tool for maximising company's profits, instead of being a vehicle for public welfare. The most visible impact of the British rule in India was therefore the impoverishment of the common man and exploitation of peasants and artisans.

Hence, in this chapter, we shall begin by understanding the nature and aim of the East India Company. This will in turn explain its economic impact on India.

Flashback: Indian Economy on the Eve of British Conquest (Chapter 1.2)

Economic Model of British East India Company

East India Company: A Joint Stock Company

The East India Companies of Europe, including the English Company, were the earliest joint stock companies of the world. Today we see that business in India is dominated by companies which sell stocks and shares to raise capital, as compared to single proprietorship or even partnership. This is because the joint stock structure allows these companies to raise a much larger quantity of capital and also ensures continuity of business over a longer period of time.

Grant of Monopoly by Government of England

This means that the Company was granted exclusive control of trade with India and other countries in the Indian Ocean. This was done because, firstly, it was felt that the state must promote foreign trade to bring home wealth. The risky trade with distant countries was particularly in need of such government protection. Secondly, the merchants of the East India Company were also relatively more wealthy and influential in the monarch's court and were able to secure monopoly rights for the company.

What was a 'Charter'? A charter is a written grant issued by a government by which a body such as a company or a university is created or its rights and privileges defined. Thus, the instrument by which monopoly rights were conferred was known as the **'Charter Act'** which was passed by the English Parliament and renewed from time to time.

However, legal monopoly is one thing, and to make it effective in practice is quite another. From mid-18th century onwards, the Company's management had to struggle very hard to make its monopoly rights effective and exclude others form Indian trade.

Policy of 'Buy Cheap and Sell Dear'

The business model of the company was simply, 'buying cheap and selling dear'. If you wish to buy cheap, you will find it helpful to have fewer buyers in the market. Thus, reduction of competition was an important aim. For this, the Company resorted to all sorts of means including legislation, force and even warfare. The East India Company capitalised on the weakness of successor states and bribed and bullied them into granting the Company special trade privileges. From the last decades of the 18th century, peasants and artisans (particularly the indigo cultivators and weavers) were subjected to coercive practices such that the Company could procure goods at cheap prices; they were even forced into producing goods only for the Company.

Need for New Markets

With the ongoing industrial revolution in England, it now sought new markets for its manufactures, particularly cotton manufactures. Also, it now needed more raw material than before to feed its rapidly growing industries. Thus, the whole basis of economic relationship between India and England was steadily changing. As England rapidly transformed into the world's first industrial capitalist country, the merchant company that had acquired the Indian Empire was now required to fulfil a different role.

Territorial Expansion for More Secure and Profitable Business

Initially, the English made only voyages to India for trade by a ship or two. But no large-scale trade was possible in this manner as it was not possible to procure large quantities of goods at a short notice when a merchant ship arrived. Therefore, it became necessary to set up 'factories', meaning trading stations for storing goods for export. No production activity was carried out in these factories and the officials posted here were called 'factors'. Naturally, the East India Company, like other Companies, wanted to protect these factories and **began building 'forts' around them**. This may have become all the more necessary in the view of declining Mughal power.

However, gradually the Companies began to cross the reasonable limits of fortification and militarised their trading stations into centres of armed power, challenging the local governments. These forts began to provide the nucleus around which the Company spread its control over surrounding territory.

Such an evolution of the East India Company, from voyage system to territorial power, helped it immensely in increasing its business and profits in many ways. It was useful to have military power to bully and coerce the peasants and artisans to produce goods on dictated terms, to eliminate rivals and even to extract special trade privileges form local powers. Lastly and most importantly, the control over territories brought in land revenue. Let us understand this from the classic example of Bengal—after its victory in the Battle of Buxar, the East India Company acquired the Diwani of Bengal in 1765. Now the Company began using the land revenue collected from Bengal to pay for exports from India, greatly reducing bullion export from England that was required earlier.

In short, the territorial ambitions of the East India Company made a lot of economic sense. Consequently, the East India Company emerged as the most powerful territorial power in India by the beginning of 19th century.

Shifting Financial Base of the Company (from Trade to Land Revenue)

From the mid-18th century till 1813, the Company's directors had to struggle very hard to retain Company's effective monopoly for many reasons:

- There were always merchants and adventurers who somehow managed to make their way into Indian trade.
- The Company's own employees were not above temptation to set up their own private trade.
- The company's monopoly also came under severe attack in England owing to the emergence of the doctrine of **Free Trade or laissez faire** promoted by economists like **Adam Smith** (Wealth of Nations, 1776).

- The capital accumulating in England also wanted freedom of investment.
- With the ongoing industrial revolution, the importance of purely merchandising activities of the Company (i.e. importing goods from India) diminished in comparison with industrial manufacturing. There emerged strong lobbies in England that began pressurising for the abolition of the Company's monopoly.

Owing to the above factors, the Company's monopoly was gradually ended by the Charter Acts of 1813 and 1833. With the prospect of declining income from trade, the Company's financial base began to shift from trade and commerce to land revenue, **from business of trade to business of government**. This naturally pushed the Company to go ahead with continuous territorial expansion.

> **Adam Smith wrote in the Wealth of Nations (1776),** 'The government of an exclusive company of merchants is perhaps the worst of all governments for any country whatever'.

Changing Phases of Colonialism and Impact on Indian Economy and Industry

Pre-Colonial Stage (1600–1757)

During this period, the role of East India Company in India was like any other trading company- it brought goods or precious metals into India and exchanged them for Indian goods which it sold abroad. The company's profits mainly came from sale of Indian goods abroad and so, naturally, it was interested in production of Indian goods and creation of new markets for them. This is why Indian rulers encouraged Company's factories in India. With its goods in high demand, India's balance of trade was highly favourable and the various European trading companies, including the East India Company competed with one another for their share of Indian trade.

However, soon the British manufacturers grew jealous of the popularity of Indian textiles as the fine cotton cloth from India began to replace the coarse woollens there. They began to put pressure on the English government to restrict or prohibit the sale of Indian goods in England. By 1720s, laws had been passed prohibiting the wear or use of printed or dyed cotton cloth (there was a case in 1760 when a lady was fined for possessing an imported handkerchief!) Additionally, the English government also imposed heavy duties on the import of plain cloth and Indian silks. Other European countries such as Holland also followed in the British footsteps. Despite this, Indian cotton and silk textiles continued to retain their stronghold in certain foreign markets until mid-18th century, when the English textile industry itself began to develop along modern lines, thanks to industrial development.

> **Daniel Dafoe,** author of Robinson Crusoe, complained that Indian cloth had 'crept into our houses, our closets and bed chambers; curtains, cushions, chairs and at last beds themselves were nothing but calicos or Indian stuffs'.

Colonial Stage (After 1757)

According to **Rajani Palme Dutt**, a Marxist dialectician and a theoretician in the Communist Party of Great Britain, there were three phases in the history of colonial rule in India-

- Era of Merchant Capitalism or Mercantilism (1757 to 1813)
- Era of Industrial Capitalism (1813 to 1858)
- Era of Fiscal Capitalism (1858–1947)

Era of Merchant Capitalism or Mercantilism (Period of Monopoly of Trade and Plunder, 1757 to 1813)

This 'mercantilist' phase was marked by direct plunder, exercise of monopoly trade and investment of surplus revenues in the purchase of Indian finished goods for export to England and Europe.

As mentioned earlier, mercantilism is an economic theory which states that trade generates wealth and is further stimulated by the accumulation of profitable balances, which a government should encourage by means of protectionism. Mercantilism emerged as the dominant economic doctrine of the times and its policy prescription included the following ideas-

- **Buy cheap, sell dear** The essence of merchant capitalist operation is to 'buy cheap and sell dear'. It refers to purchase of goods at cheap rates and sale of goods at very high rates.
- **Monopoly control** It refers to monopoly control over trade and elimination of all possible rivals. It is desirable to have a monopoly in order to achieve the above objective.
- **Political control** It is even more desirable to be able to achieve the above objectives with the use of coercion backed by state power. Hence, the merchants should seek to establish political control over the countries they traded with.

Thus, the activities of the English East India Company during 1757-1813 were driven by the above objectives. Determined to buy cheap and sell dear (which is the essence of mercantilism), the East India Company eliminated rival European companies, dabbled in Indian politics and waged wars to establish its political supremacy, which in turn was used to control the economy of India.

The changes in Company's role and its **corresponding impact** on Indian economy and industry may be understood under the following heads-

Use of State Power for Monopolistic Control (After 1757) The Company's victory in the Battle of Plassey (1757) brought about a drastic change in the role of the Company in India and its economic relationship with the country. After Plassey, the East India Company began to use its political power and position to exercise monopolistic control over Indian trade and production; to buy cheap and sell dear. An era of **trade-cum plunder** was launched.

Use of Gomasta System (1753) Up to 1753, the European Companies and 'free traders' depended on the Indian merchants to procure cloth: these merchants were called Dadni merchants since it was through them that **dadan or advance** was given by the Company to the artisans or weavers. From 1753, the Company began to replace the independent dadni merchants with Gomastas (agents of the East India Company) who were paid commission on the cloth collected by them. After Plassey, the Company used its political power to switch to the Gomasta system, which reduced the Indian merchants to commissioned brokers, leading to **subordination of native traders and their capital**.

Use of 'Direct Agency' System (1789) In 1789, the system of 'direct agency' was introduced, with which the Company dispensed with the Indian middleman altogether. Similarly, after the Company became Diwan of Bengal, the banking house of Jagat Seth ceased to be the state banker, its minting rights were gradually taken away and it also lost its European clients to English banks. In this way, step by step the **Indian businessmen were reduced to a subordinate position or excluded altogether**.

Transfer of Diwani to the British (1765) A period of 'open and unashamed plunder of Bengal' began, when, after the Battle of Buxar, the East India Company acquired Diwani rights of Bengal. It was as if the Company had discovered a new mine of gold (i.e. India) and something like 'gold rush' gripped the English mind. RC Dutt, an Indian Marxist and economist estimated that during 1757-65, the Company's servants exacted an amount which was more than four times the total land revenue collection of the Nawab of Bengal in 1765, which severely **impoverished the peasants**. The peasants were also often compelled to perform forced labour or begar and to pay illegal dues which pushed them into the hands of the money lenders; indebtedness and evictions became common. Vast stretches of land began to fall out of cultivation and what followed was the deadly **Bengal famine** in which nearly one-third of the population was wiped out.

Transfer of Funds Thus, the Company's accounts now showed 'Territorial Revenue' (i.e. land revenue collected) alongside 'Commercial Revenue' (i.e. profits of business). The Company began using its territorial revenue from one region to pay for conquests of other regions. In fact, it was the **Bengal peasant who bore the main burden of British conquest of India**. It was also used to finance Company's exports to Europe and its investment in China to buy tea and silk. Thus, the Company now ran a perfectly self-contained system, needing no funds from England. This system continued in full swing from 1765 till 1813 when the Company's monopoly was abolished. The native Indian courts were the biggest patrons of fancy arts and handicrafts and often employed the best craftsmen. Their destruction spelled **doom upon court artisans as well**.

As mentioned above, the territorial revenue thus extracted was also used to buy Indian goods (purchases known as 'Investments') and export them to Britain in the form of **'Indian tribute'** to Britain. This is how there began the **'drain of wealth'** or the unilateral transfer of funds from India. Such exports remitted resources out of India, while India received no imports in return. Other forms of transfer of funds from Indian to England included business profits of private traders, earnings of Englishmen from plunder and bribery, payments made to shipping companies, banks and insurance companies in England as well as Company's remittance to England. The remittance was to pay for the salary of Company's employees in England, interest on loans taken by the Company in England, dividends to the stockholders of the Company, etc. This became known as **Home Charges** and was the sum total of money transferred to England by the Company's government after it stopped trading in 1833. Such a transfer of funds naturally **impoverished India**.

Use of Coercion Even though exports to Britain (in the form of tribute) increased, the Indian artisans did not gain anything as the company used its political power to bully the weavers and artisans of Bengal into selling their products at low and dictated prices, even if they incurred a loss. In fact, the Company's servants coerced the Bengal weavers to restrict their buying and selling activities to the Company alone (they were forced to buy raw cotton from and sell cloth to the Company alone). In this way, the **Indian weaver lost both ways**, as buyer as well as seller, and a large number of them felt compelled to **abandon their ancestral professions**.

Khatbandi System The weavers were even bullied and harassed by the factors, through the agency of the Gomastas (agents of the East India Company), to accept advance to produce cloth and then sell their products below market price to the Company. In the 1780s, this practice became systematised and came to be known as the 'khatbandi system': the artisans were indentured to sell exclusively to the Company under Regulations passed by the Bengal government. By the regulation of 1789, they were even forced to pay a penalty of 35% on the advance taken if they defaulted in supplying the goods. In this way, the Company virtually reduced the weavers to the status of **indentured or bonded labourers**, by the denial of free access to the market, by the use of coercion and by discriminatory laws passed by the Company's government. Similar coercion was used in the production of indigo under the ryoti system, and to a lesser degree in the production of opium.

Ryoti System or Asamiwar Unlike in the case of tea, where crops were produced by hired labour, in the case of indigo the preferred system was one in which the ryot or peasant could be coerced into supplying the required product at a very low price, known as the ryoti system. The peasant had to use his own plough, bullocks, etc., to raise the crop. But he was not paid enough for this by the planters. The Company found it more profitable to use state power to coerce the small peasant into **unprofitable cultivation** rather than engage in direct production with hired labour. In this way, the Company's commercial production fastened itself on the existing structure of small peasant production and impoverished it. Such unprofitable cultivation owing to the exacting regime of the tax collector and the planter **checked the growth of a market in land** as well, since no one wanted to buy it. Vast stretches of land fell out of cultivation and **famines** stared the people of India on their face.

Domination of Markets and Producers By 1770s and 1780s, through the use of coercion and state power, the Company and its servants who were engaged in private trade had developed a 'collective monopoly' in respect of certain commodities, particularly cotton cloth in Bengal. The company also established its monopoly by eliminating rivals; Indian as well as foreign merchants were prohibited from offering higher prices to the Bengal handicraftsmen or buying commodities directly from the producers.

A result of this system of monopoly and coercion was the **creation of a buyers' market,** i.e. a market where the buyer can dictate the price, (the buyer here being the English Company and its servants) at the cost of the seller (the seller being the India peasant and artisan). Such short-sighted policies of the Company to make quick and large profits **severely affected the textile industry and the economy on the whole**.

Use of Import Restrictions Further, Indian textiles were also subjected to heavy import duties on entering England, since the British government wished to protect its indigenous manufactures. The Company's own short-sighted policy together with sanctions against Indian import into Britain resulted in a progressive **decline in the export** of Indian cotton goods. The **income of weavers and spinners was drastically reduced** and thereby **restricted any possibility of capital accumulation and technological innovations** in this sector of Indian industry (However, the real blow to Indian manufactures came in 1813, as now they began to lose in their home market itself).

While the system of taking funds out of India was being gradually perfected and India's traditional manufacturing sector was being steadily weakened under the Company, in the same period Britain had begun its Industrial Revolution and was rapidly expanding its own industries. Wealth from India (Plunder of Bengal 1757) played a significant role in the accumulation of capital in England needed for industrialisation (1760).

Britain's Industrial Revolution (1760–1840) completely transformed Britain's economy and it now sought new markets for its manufactures, particularly cotton manufactures, which served as the main vehicle of Industrial Revolution in Britain. Also, it now needed more raw material than before to feed its rapidly growing industries. Thus, the whole basis of economic relationship between India and England was steadily changing. As England rapidly transformed into the world's first industrial capitalist country, the merchant company that had acquired the Indian Empire was now required to fulfil a different role. Thus, the East India Company used its power and position to transform India into a market for its industrial goods and a supplier of raw material.

Industrial Revolution in Britain further strengthened this colonial pattern when British manufacturers launched a powerful campaign against the company (1793–1813) and succeeded in abolishing its monopoly. Now the policy of free trade was introduced, allowing unrestricted entry of British goods into India that **wreaked havoc on Indian indigenous industry**.

Let Us Know
- **Lancashire, Paisley and Manchester** were some of the prominent centres of textile manufacture in England in contemporary times.
- **Sarrafs** were bankers chiefly involved in money-changing.

Era of Industrial Capitalism 1813 to 1858 (Period of Free Trade)

India Thrown Open to Machine Made Foreign Goods (1813) This period saw the classic age of free trade industrial capitalist exploitation. The year 1813 was an important landmark in the history of colonial exploitation of India as this year marked the end of company's monopoly on Indian trade. The commercial policy of the East India Company after 1813 was guided by the needs of British industry and its main aim was to transform India into a consumer of British industrial products and a supplier of raw materials for British industries. The government of India now followed the policy of free trade and allowed unrestricted entry of British goods. Indian handicrafts faced **unequal competition** from machine made goods and faced extinction. The Indian manufacturers had already lost out in the foreign market owing to import restrictions, now they began to lose out in their home market itself.

One-sided Free Trade But this free-trade was only one-sided. While India was thrown open for foreign goods, Indian products were subjected to heavy import duties in Britain (e.g. in 1824, 67.5 per cent duty was levied on Indian calicos and 37.5% duty on Indian muslin. Duty on Indian sugar was three times its cost price while that on certain items reached as high as 400%). Accordingly, Indian exports to England rapidly declined. This changed the character of Indo-British trade. Now onwards, **India became chiefly an importer of goods**. The value of cotton cloth exported from India to England declined from pound 1.3 million to only 0.1 million during 1815-1832. While the import of cotton cloth increased more than 5 times during the same period. Now the balance of trade tilted heavily in favour of Britain.

Indian Economy Turned into Colonial Economy Gradually, Indian economy was turned into colonial economy—a **supplier for raw materials and a market for finished goods**. There was a marked change in the composition of Indian exports from manufactured goods to primary products. The **local handicraft industry was destroyed** and India was converted into a predominant agrarian economy. This general change in the composition of India's foreign trade and the resultant impact it had on the country's domestic industry has led many historians (like RC Dutt, Madan Mohan Malviya and Bipan Chandra) to describe this phenomena as **de-industrialisation** or the destruction of Indian industry.

Other Changes To further transform India into a colonial economy, the Company's government brought about various other changes.
- It went ahead with **fresh conquests** to increase the number of buyers of British goods (e.g. Annexation of Awadh 1856).

- It **advocated westernisation** of India to enable the Indians to develop a taste for British goods.
- Many British officials and leaders recommended a reduction in land revenue, to leave Indian peasants in a better position to buy British goods.
- Big farmers were encouraged to increase production of **cash crops**, resulting in rise in food grain prices. (Read ahead- Commercialisation of Agriculture and its Impact)
- For sale of British goods in the remote corners of India, transport facilities were developed, particularly the railways.

Era of Fiscal Capitalism (1858–1947)

With industrial development and exploitation of colonies, huge capital got accumulated in Britain. Seeing the increasing property of industrialists, the labour class felt motivation to unite. On the other hand, the increasing strength of labour class made the industrialists feel uneasy and suspicious. They began to feel that the increasing strength of labour class will decrease their negotiating power and reduce their profits. More industrialisation in England meant further increase in the negotiating power of the labourers. This was also the time when 'the Communist Manifesto' by Marx and Engels had been published in English language. Thus, it was felt appropriate to invest capital in India, and thus began the new era of capitalism in India.

In modern times, developing countries welcome inflow of capital to supplement domestic resources for economic development. Unfortunately, the capital inflow in colonial era was used by the colonial government not for development of Indian economy but for **fuller exploitation of Indian resources**. Further, the British did not invest capital in industries of cotton and iron because they did not want their capital to compete with industries in Britain. Instead they invested in activities that were complementary to British industries and the investment was in **no way planned to bring about industrial development of India**.

British Capitalists Investment in India British capitalists felt attracted to invest in **tea plantations (from 1839), jute, coal, mining and railways (early 1850s)** and by the turn of the century, major investments were also made in the ports. The British made heaviest capital investment in railways in India as development of railways was considered necessary for commercial and administrative needs of the British. After railways, next highest capital investment was done for the development of plantation crops. Capital was also invested in Indian industries to capture Indian market. Availability of cheap labour was an added advantage. Capital investment in India was done by means of public debt.

'Opening Up' India (After 1813) Each age has its favourite catchwords and in 19th-century Europe it was 'opening up' India or China or some other African or Asian country awaiting the wonders to be brought by European capital and commerce. Opening up meant preparing the country for receiving British capital and industrial goods and in Indian context it chiefly meant **railway development**.

Various interest groups began to pressurise the British and Indian government to take up railway construction in India. The British manufacturers hoped to open a vast and untapped market in the interior of India and simultaneously facilitate collection of raw materials from the interiors to feed their hungry machines in England. The investors and bankers looked at railways in India as means for safe investment of their surplus capital. The British steel manufacturers regarded it as a big outlet for their steel products. The Government of India soon fell in line with these views and saw additional merit of imperial defence. They intended to use the railways for better control and administration of their vast territories and for speedy movement of army in times of internal rebellion or external aggression.

Clearly, the primary consideration behind the construction of railways in India was to serve the economic, political and military interests of British imperialism and may be enumerated as under-

- Railways would facilitate the distribution of British industrial goods in interiors of India.
- It would facilitate the collection of raw materials from Indian interiors for export to Britain.
- It would allow an opportunity for investment of British capital in railway companies operating in India.
- Lord Dalhousie was of the view that the railways would help the government to control distant parts of the country and allow movement of army to quell internal disturbances.

All Indian railway companies were set up in England as joint stock companies. In order to encourage the English investors to buy their shares, the Government of India offered a guarantee of at least 5% interest on their investments. In this way, all Indian railway companies were in reality English companies protected by a **'guaranteed interest contract'**.

The impact of railway development in India was negative in many ways—A government guarantee of interest meant that irrespective of profit or loss, interest had to be paid out to the English investors out of Indian tax payers' money (for the first 50 years, they were financially losing concerns). This also encouraged over-expenditure and mismanagement in railway construction. Besides, the railway companies imported almost all they needed, thus **increasing India's foreign exchange expenditure**. The railway freight rates were also so fixed as to favour export-import and discriminate against movement of India-made goods.

Despite the above adverse consequences, the railways had some positive impact as well—It brought modern technology and skills to India and served to unify the country into one common market. Railways were laid through the length and breadth of the country, bringing the people from different parts of India into closer contact with one another. People from different classes had to buy the same ticket and travel in the same compartment which gave them the opportunity to interact, unite and finally emerge as one nation.

- **DH Buchanan** had remarked, 'the armour of the isolated self-sufficient village was pierced by the steel rail and its life-blood ebbed away'.
- **Edwin Arnold** had written in 1865, 'Railways may do for India what dynasties have never done-what the genius of Akbar could not effect by government, nor the cruelty of Tip Saheb by violence, they have made India a nation'.
- **Karl Marx** had correctly projected the railways as '**Forerunners of Modern Industry** (in India)'.

Changes in Indian Agrarian Structure and Impact on Economy

Collection of taxes is a business of all governments and the taxes collected are normally spent for the welfare of the taxpayers. However, the East India Company needed to collect taxes from people of India to pay for its purchase of goods for export, to meet costs of further conquests and consolidation of British rule as well as to meet the costs of administration.

Since the olden times, kings and rulers have drawn a large part of their taxes from agriculture, it being the chief economic activity of a majority of Indian people. With the rise of British supremacy in India, it was the Company's government which became increasingly involved with the collection of

land revenue. Thus, it is clear from the very outset that the land revenue collected from the Indian 'ryot' or peasant was spent, not for his welfare, but for meeting the colonial needs of the Company.

Moreover, the Company's land revenue policies were vastly different from the previous eras. They put in place new types of land revenue settlements to assess and collect these taxes (these were broadly of three types—Permanent Settlement, Ryotwari System and Mahalwari System), new concepts of land ownership and heavier state demand for land revenue (generally raised to half of produce from earlier one-sixth or one-third) which triggered far-reaching changes in Indian agrarian structure, rural economy and social relationships.

New Land Revenue Settlements and their Impact

The British conquerors were driven by the zeal to derive maximum economic advantage from their rule in India. After the British industrial and mercantile interests restricted the Company's capacity to raise revenue from trade, the company's government diverted its attention to land revenue as principle means of income and as such land revenue matters began to receive the maximum care and attention of the British rulers.

The early British administrators considered India as a vast estate and felt that the Company was entitled to the entire economic rent, leaving to the cultivators merely the wages of their labour and expenses of cultivation. Such excessive land revenue demands soon proved counter-productive. Agriculture became increasingly economically non-viable, large areas of land fell out of cultivation and famines began to stare people in their face.

First Experiments in Land Revenue Management

After the victory of Battle of Plassey (1757), the Company acquired zamindari of 24 parganas from Bengal Nawab Mir Jafar. In 1760, the East India Company was given rights to collect land revenue from Burdwan, Midnapur and Chatgaon by Bengal Nawab Mir Qasim. After the victory Battle of Buxar (1764), the Company acquired the Diwani of Bengal, Bihar and Orissa.

During 1765–72, Clive introduced dual governance in Bengal. The British decided to continue with the administration established by the Nawabs of Bengal and use it to collect more and more land revenue. The Company appointed two Naib-Diwans, **Mohammad Reza Khan** and **Raja Sitab Roy** for Bengal and Bihar respectively, and directed them to collect as high revenue as possible (Reza Khan was also the Naib-Nazim). The Bengal peasant faced some of the worst exactions by the revenue officials and many of them ran away into the jungles or simply joined the ranks of the robbers. The avarice and corruption of the Company's employees and their continuous interference in the administration led to complete disorganisation and worsened the effects of the terrible Bengal famine of 1769–70. Harsh measures of revenue collection were adopted so much so that even in the year 1770, when one-third of Bengal population was wiped out in the famine, the land revenue was collected satisfactorily.

In 1772, it was decided to end the dual system of administration set up by Clive. The Company now decided to collect land revenue itself and not through the Naib-Diwan. The President was required to take over the charge of entire management of revenues of Bengal, Bihar and Orissa. Accordingly, the Governor and the Council formed the **Board of Revenue** and the Company appointed its own European officers called **Collectors** to manage revenue affairs. The treasury was also removed from Murshidabad to Calcutta.

Hence, in 1772 Governor General Warren Hastings introduced a new system, known as the **'farming system'** under which he auctioned the right to collect revenue to the highest bidder. He made a 5-year settlement (quinquennial settlement or **panchshala bandobast**) of land revenue with the contractor (known as 'farmer' or 'revenue farmer' in those days) who offered to pay the largest amount from a certain land area and was given full powers for a period of years.

Obviously, these contractors had no permanent interest in land and tried to **extort as much revenue as possible** during the period of their contract. They were not concerned if the people were ruined or the production declined in later years. After all, they would have made their share of profit. Clearly, malpractices such as extortion and oppression were a result of such a system.

Another significant result of this system was corruption. As with many government contracts even today, profitable contracts were given away to friends and favourites and 'benamidars' of men in power, bringing loss to the government. The officers of the Company themselves participated in the bidding under the name of their servants. Warren Hastings himself was accused of such forgery. Hence, this system caused much hardship to the farmers and failed miserably. After the expiry of the 5-year settlement, Hastings reverted to the system of annual settlement (salana bandobast) in 1777 which was again based on the basis of farming out estates to the highest bidder.

Under both these systems, though the amount of land revenue was pushed high, the actual collection varied for year to year and seldom matched the official expectations. This brought instability in the Company's revenues at a time when the Company was in a continuous mode of expansion. The system was also killing the ryot's or the contractor's motive to do anything to improve cultivation.

It was at this stage the idea of fixing the land revenue at a permanent amount first emerged and in 1784, under the Pitts India Act, the Company was advised to introduce permanent land settlement in Bengal. Accordingly, in 1786, Lord Cornwallis was sent to India specially charged with the duty of cleaning up the system and finding out a satisfactory solution to the land revenue problem.

In 1790, Cornwallis decided to recognise the zamindars as the owners of land, subject to annual payment of land revenue to the state. A ten-year settlement was made with the zamindars on the basis of 89 per cent of the rental, leaving 11 per cent with the zamindars. In 1793, this decennial settlement was declared permanent (called **Permanent Settlement of Bengal**).

John Shore and James Grant differed in their views on whether zamindars be regarded as owners of land or tax collectors. John Shore regarded them as owners of land while Grant felt that all land belonged to the government and the zamindars were mere tax collectors. Here, **Cornwallis agreed with Shore's views**.

Permanent Settlement (by Cornwallis, Bengal, 1793)

(Permanent Zamindari Settlement or Jagirdari/ Malguzari/ Biswedari/ Istemrari Bandobast)

The London authorities as well as Cornwallis could see that the existing system was not sustainable. It was impoverishing people and destroying agriculture. It was therefore decided that land revenue should be permanently fixed. The government promised never to increase it in future. Several positive effects were expected from this system—it would reduce oppression and corruption activities, it would ensure regular tax collection. It was also expected that now the landholders will feel motivated to invest in the land since the government will not charge any extra tax on excess production and the whole benefit will remain with them.

Permanent Settlement was a Settlement with whom and why? After fixing the revenue, the next question was, from whom was it to be collected? The Nawabs of Bengal had collected it from the zamindars; the big ones were known as Rajas and had their own armies. The zamindars collected the revenues directly from the peasants. At times, extra charges or **'abwabs'** were also collected.

Permanent Settlement too was made with the Zamindars (though, by now, some of the zamindars had been replaced by contractors). A special feature of this system was that the zamindars and the revenue farmers were now converted into landlords; they were now the **owners of the entire land of their zamindari**. Their right of ownership was also made **hereditary and transferable**.

The new Governor General Cornwallis himself belonged to landed aristocracy in Britain and was in favour of ownership rights to the zamindars. He hoped that the zamindars would improve the land as English landlords had done, since the entire benefit of increase in productivity will accrue to them alone. Moreover, there must have been 4–5 million cultivating families in Bengal, Bihar and Orissa at that time and collecting tax from them would have been a tedious task for the British. It was much simpler option to collect tax from a small number of big zamindars.

Why were Zamindars recognised as owners of land? Some historians think that it was by mistake; the British mistook the zamindar to be the Indian counterpart of the English landlord (However, it is noteworthy that while the English landlord was the absolute owner of land, the Indian zamindar was owner of land only in relation to the tenant and not in relation to the state).

Other historians attribute the decision to political, financial and administrative reasons-

- Politically, the British needed to create political allies in India, particularly in view of the rising popular revolts in Bengal during the last quarter of the 18th century. Later, developments fully justified this view as the wealthy class of zamindars, who owed their existence to the British, stood with the British during the rising tide of the national movement.
- Financially, the newly created property of the zamindars acted as a security against financial crisis at a time when the Company was constantly engaged in wars of expansion. Further, the revenue fixed was higher than ever before, at an absolute maximum, allowing the company to maximise its income.
- Administratively, it was a much simpler option to collect tax from a small number of big zamindars. It was also hoped that the zamindars would improve the land, since the entire benefit of increase in agricultural productivity will accrue to them alone.

What was Permanent Settlement? Permanent Settlement was introduced in Bengal and Bihar in 1793. The land revenue was fixed at a very high level of ₹2 crore and 68 lakh. Every bit of land in these provinces now became a part of some zamindari. The zamindar had to pay a fixed tax (10/11) upon it. So, long as he paid the tax, he remained the owner of his land. He could sell, transfer or mortgage it. After his death, his land would be inherited by his heirs. But if he failed to pay the tax, the government could take away his zamindari and sell it by auction (Sunset Rule). In this way, the position of zamindars was kept quite precarious.

Negative Impact of Permanent Settlement on Zamindars Under this system, 10/11 part of the land tax went to the state while **1/11 belonged to the zamindar**. The zamindars found it very difficult to pay the high tax demanded by the British. As a result, many zamindars **lost their zamindari**. Between 1794 and 1819, 68 percent of zamindari land was sold in Bengal. Many zamindars further divided their land into smaller estates and permanently rented them to sub-holders who promised to pay a fixed rent. This gave birth to **subinfeudation** and furthered oppression of the cultivators.

Negative Impact of Permanent Settlement on Cultivators The hereditary rights of the peasants on land was taken away and given to the zamindars. The cultivators were reduced to the status of simple tenants of the zamindars. They were also deprived of other customary rights including right to use pasture and forest lands, irrigation canals, fisheries, protection against rent enhancement, etc.

The land revenue fixed at ₹2 crore and 68 lakh was the largest sum that could be got from the land. It was a heavy assessment that could be collected only by oppressive means. Further, while the state's demand was fixed, the rent to be realised from the cultivator was left unsettled. This worsened the position of the actual cultivators of soil, who were now left wholly at the mercy of the zamindars. **Rack-renting, indebtedness and ejections** became common. In fact, as per regulations issued in 1793 and 1799, zamindars could even seize the property of the tenants who failed to pay the rent, thus legalising harassment. This also encouraged the zamindars to resort to illegal methods like beating and flogging the tenants for non-payment of the required amount. In this way, the peasantry was crushed under the triple burden of the government, the zamindar and the moneylender. The Permanent Settlement ultimately broke down due to excessive state demand and harshness in its working and collection of revenue.

Note: It was only in 1859 that the Government of India passed a legislation providing limited protection to old tenants, who were now termed as 'occupancy tenants'.

Areas Covered Permanent Settlement was introduced in **Bengal, Bihar, Orissa, Varanasi and Ghazipur regions of UP and northern Karnataka**. It covered **19%** area of British India.

British Disillusionment with Permanent Settlement As early as 1811, the British had begun to feel that permanent settlement left no scope for increase in land revenue, even as the expenditure of the Company's government continued to rise, particularly in view of constant wars. Some officials had also begun to feel that, back in 1793, the zamindars had got off very easily and that the mistake should not be repeated.

Ryotwari System (by Sir Thomas Munro and Captain Alexander Read, Madras, 1820)

The defects of Permanent Settlement became more prominent with time and the British began to devise other ways of collecting land-tax. Moreover, new challenges emerged when the British conquered South and South Western India.

What was Ryotwari System? In 1792, two officers **Munro and Read** were sent to administer the newly conquered regions of Madras. They found that there were no large zamindars with large estates in these regions with whom land revenue settlement could be made. They therefore recommended that settlement should be made directly with the **actual cultivators or 'ryots'** based on their field assessment, thus giving rise to the 'Ryotwari System'. Under this system, the cultivator was to be recognised as the owner of his land so long as he paid the land tax. The tax payable on each field was fixed by a government officer and then the cultivator had the choice of cultivating the field and paying the amount, or not cultivating it. The Settlement under this system was not made permanent but was revised after **every 20 or 30 years** and the revenue demand was usually raised.

Land Survey and Assessment under Ryotwari In fixing the assessment, the revenue officers surveyed each field, considered the **soil quality** as well as the **field area** and then fixed the assessment on it based on their survey. Thus, land revenue assessment under Ryotwari was a difficult task—thousands of fields had to be surveyed and care had to be taken to fix the assessment such that burden on each field was approximately equal. If the burden was not equally distributed, then the cultivators would not occupy the heavily assessed ones and the field would lie fallow.

However, in practice, the Ryotwari System was extended in the Madras Presidency in forms different from the one originally envisaged by Munro. No survey was carried out in many districts and assessment was done based on tax paid in previous years, known as **'putcut assessment'**. The government officers also began to compel the ryots to cultivate land against their wishes and employ oppressive methods of collection, leading to the setting up of **Madras Torture Commission** in 1854.

Adoption of Ryotwari in Madras (1820) After some initial experiments, the Ryotwari System was adopted in Madras presidency in 1820 and Munro himself was appointed as Governor of Madras to ensure its smooth implantation. Munro advanced many arguments in its favour. He claimed that this was a system which had always prevailed in India and it was best suited for Indian conditions. He also pointed out that in Permanent Settlement the Company was a financial loser as it could not claim a share of the growing income from increased agricultural productivity. However, the system was mainly adopted because it yielded **larger revenue than any other system** as all revenue went to the state and there were no zamindars or other intermediaries who received any part of the agricultural surplus. The Madras government was always short of funds and readily introduced the temporary Ryotwari System.

Negative Impact of Ryotwari System However, Ryotwari System did not bring about a system of peasant ownership of land. The government later also declared that the land revenue was **rent and not tax**. Also, the revenue was fixed at a very high rate (45–50%), the government could raise it at will and the ryot had to pay the revenue even when his crop was wholly destroyed. Use of harsh collection practices was common and included vile practices of torture such as preventing the defaulters from taking meals or answering nature's calls, tying a man in a bent position or tying by the hair to the tail of a donkey or a buffalo. On non-payment of land-tax (lagan), land could be confiscated.

The system caused widespread oppression; the peasantry sank deep in poverty and fell into the clutches of the **chetty** (moneylender) whose power and position had greatly risen under the British. In pre-British times, the moneylender was subordinated to village community—he was not allowed to charge usurious interest rates or confiscate land. But now such malpractices by moneylenders became common. They were also greatly helped by the new revenue policies, the judicial system and the police. The impoverishment of peasantry and the ruin of traditional agrarian structure under the Ryotwari System significantly contributed to the terrible Madras famine of 1867–78.

Areas Covered

- In 1792, Ryotwari System was first implemented in **Baramahal** district of Madras Presidency by **Capt. Read**.
- After 1820, this system was extended to most of **Madras Presidency**. To ensure smooth implementation, Munro was appointed Governor of Madras.
- In 1825, this system was introduced in **Bombay** and by 1858 it was being implemented in entire **Deccan**.

Thus, Ryotwari System was implemented in Madras, Bombay, East Bengal, Assam and Coorg. It covered **51 per cent** area of British India. In this way, this system was implemented on maximum land area.

Mahalwari System (Northern India, 1822)

What was Mahalwari System? Between 1801 and 1806, the British conquered large territories in North India (roughly modern UP) under the aggressive policies of Lord Wellesley. In 1836, the North-Western Provinces was established by administrative divisions of the region (It was renamed as North Western Provinces and Awadh after the annexation of Awadh in 1858, with Allahabad as capital. The province was further reorganised in 1902 and renamed as United Provinces of Agra and Awadh).

Initially, Wellesley ordered his officials to make the settlement with zamindars wherever possible, provided they agreed to pay the high land revenue. But if the zamindars were not present or they did not agree to pay the high revenue, then settlement could be made village by village, giving preference to the village headman or any other respectable ryot of the village. Ultimately, the settlement was to be made permanent, like in Bengal.

Accordingly, heavy land revenue was imposed. It was also substantially increased overtime- from ₹188 lakh in 1803–04 to ₹297 lakh by 1817–18. Such heavy increases provoked resistance from many zamindars and many of them were driven away by the new administration. Those who could not pay, their estates were sold away. In such a situation, it became necessary to collect tax directly from the village through its headman (pradhan, muqaddam or lambardar). In the revenue records, the term used for one such fiscal unit was 'mahal' and this village-wise settlement therefore came to be known as the Mahalwari settlement. The term **'mahal' thus meant a village or a jagir** (estate). Under this system, revenue settlement was fixed with each mahal, and not the cultivator.

Negative Impact of Mahalwari System Like in other settlements, even under this system the land tax demanded was very heavy, creating opportunities for the local officials to practice coercion and corruption; large areas of land were illegally acquired by them in the early years, bringing about ruin of the village zamindars. Many zamindars also fell into the clutches of money lenders and merchants who often ousted them or reduced them to tenants at will upon non-payment of debt. In this way, the Mahalwari System brought about ruin in the form of impoverishment and dispossession of the cultivating communities in North India during the 1830s and 1840s. Their simmering resentment soon found expression during the Revolt of 1857, when several villagers and zamindars all over North India attacked the government officials and money lenders; burnt down their records and accounts.

Regulation of 1822 In his Minute of 1819, **Holt Mackenzie**, Secretary of Board of Directors, first developed the theory of Mahalwari System, emphasising the existence of village communities in Northern India. He recommended a land survey, preparation of land records, village-wise settlement of land revenue and collection of revenue through the village headman.

The above recommendations got legal sanction by the Regulation of 1822. Revenue was fixed at 80% of the rental value when settlement was made with the zamindar; and at 95% of the rental value when settlement was made with the cultivators in common tenancy. The heavy state demand caused widespread misery and the system failed under the weight of its harshness.

Regulation of 1833 The above scheme of 1822 was thoroughly reviewed under William Bentinck who sought to improve upon it and after prolonged consultations, passed the Regulation of 1833. The new scheme fixed the state demand at 66% of the rental value, the mahal was empowered to make internal adjustments and the settlement was made for 30 years. It also prescribed the system of using average rents for different classes of soil and prescribed for the first time the use of **field maps** (drawings) and **field registers** (records) for assessments.

The Settlement work began under the supervision of **Robert Martins Bird**, known as the **'Father of Land Settlements in Northern India'**, and was completed under the administration of **James Thomson** (Lt. Governor 1843–53).

Even the 66 per cent rental demand was oppressive and was further reduced in 1855 by Dalhousie to 50 per cent, however, the corrupt Settlement Officers of the Company evaded its implementation. Thus, the system caused widespread oppression of the cultivating classes and the resentment found its vent during the popular uprising of 1857–58.

Areas Covered This system was introduced in North West Province (Awadh, Ganga Valley or UP), Punjab Province and Central Provinces. It covered **30 per cent** area of British India.

Economic Impact of Various Land Revenue Settlements

The various land revenue settlements introduced by the British meant loss of land for the landholders (owing to changes in concept of land ownership) and heavy taxation for zamindars and cultivators. The land revenue assessments under all the systems were heavy and oppressive, reaching upto 50 per cent or more of the produce and tax was extracted even when the crop was fully damaged. In such cases, the cultivators had no option but to take loans from the local money lenders who charged them exorbitant interest rates. This made the cultivators heavily indebted. To make matters worse, harsh methods of revenue collection were deployed that included coercion, violence and abuse; with the effect that the land revenue policy of the British resulted in oppression, frequent evictions, indebtedness, impoverishment and extreme misery for the agricultural classes. Many of them later participated in the Revolt of 1857, driving away government officials and burning money lenders' records.

A direct result of the oppression of the peasantry was the stagnation and deterioration of agriculture and yield per hectare steadily declined. The government also shunned responsibility and hardly spent any amount on agricultural improvement, agricultural education or public works.

The heavy burden of tax also distorted the land market. The British made land a commodity which could be freely bought and sold; a change that had been effected to secure government income. If land had not been made saleable or mortgageable, the government would have found it very difficult to raise revenue from a defaulter. Now, such defaulting cultivators could pay revenue by borrowing money on the security of his land or even by selling off part of it. The government could also auction the land and realise the amount. This was a critical change in the existing land system of India, and it shook up the entire structure of village society and economy. With the passage of time, land also lost its value as no one wanted to buy it, since the new owner would have to pay the heavy land revenue.

In fact, the East India Company's new land revenue systems coupled with the new and corrupt judicial and administrative set up broke down the entire socio-political and economic framework of the old village communities. Socially, new classes were created; the landlord, the trader, the moneylender and the new landed gentry emerged. The numbers of the rural poor comprising the small peasant, the sub-tenant and the agricultural labourer multiplied. The climate of cooperation was gradually replaced by competition and individualism. Politically, the Village Panchayats were deprived of their main functions, viz. land settlement and judicial and executive functions. Economically, agriculture began to emerge as an unviable economic activity, and famines stared the people of India in their face. Undoubtedly, rural underdevelopment and backwardness in India is a legacy of the British colonial rule.

Prelim Capsule

New Land Revenue Settlements and Impact on Economy

Changes Introduced	Important Details	Impact on Indian Economy
Permanent Settlement (by Cornwallis, Bengal, 1793)	It was a settlement with the zamindars. Zamindars were now considered the owners of the entire land of their zamindari.	The zamindars found it very difficult to pay the high tax & many **lost their zamindari.** High tax encouraged **subinfeudation** and furthered oppression of the cultivators.

	Land revenue was fixed at a very high level-of ₹2 crore and 68 lakh. The zamindar had to pay a fixed tax **(10/11)** upon it. So, long as he paid the tax, he remained the owner of his land. It was introduced in Bengal, Bihar, Orissa, Varanasi and Gazipur regions of UP and northern Karnataka. It covered **19%** area of British India.	The hereditary rights of the peasants on land was taken away and given to the zamindars. The cultivators were reduced to tenants of the zamindars. Cultivators were also deprived of other customary rights, e.g. right to use pasture and forest lands. Zamindars resorted to **rack-renting** as well as oppression and **ejection** of tenants for non-payment of rent.
Ryotwari System (by Sir Thomas Munro and Captain Alexander Read, Madras, 1820)	It was a settlement with the ryots or actual cultivators. Assessment was done after **field survey** based on soil quality and farm area. It was revised after every 20 or 30 years. In 1792 Ryotwari System was first implemented in **Baramahal** district by **Capt. Read**. After 1820, this system was extended to most of Madras Presidency. It was implemented in Madras, Bombay, entire Deccan, East Bengal, Assam and Coorg. It covered **51%** area of British India.	Revenue was fixed at a very high rate (45-50%). Ryot had to pay the revenue even when his crop was wholly destroyed. It caused widespread oppression. The peasantry sank deep in **poverty** and fell into the clutches of the chetty (moneylender). The system resulted in **indebtedness** and frequent **evictions**. It significantly contributed to the terrible **Madras famine** of 1867–78.
Mahalwari System (Northern India, 1822)	It was a settlement with the 'mahal' or village. Tax was collected through the headman or **lambardar**. It was introduced in North West Province (Awadh, Ganga Valley or UP), Punjab Province and Central Provinces.	Land tax demanded was very heavy. It led to impoverishment and **dispossession** of the cultivating communities. The simmering resentment soon found expression during the **Revolt of 1857**.

Economic Impact of British Rule in India

The economic impact of British rule under the East India Company (1757–1857), also known as the process of **colonisation of Indian economy**, may be understood under the following heads:

1. Disruption of Traditional Economy
2. Ruin of Peasantry and Agriculture

3. Ruin of Old Zamindars and Rise of New Landed Classes
4. Ruin of Artisans and Craftsmen, De-Industrialisation and Ruralisation of Indian Economy
5. Commercialisation of Agriculture
6. Drain of Wealth
7. Poverty and Famines
8. Rise of Modern Industries under the British
9. Rise of New Indian Bourgeoisie

Disruption of Traditional Economy

The rise of British supremacy led to the subordination of Indian economy as per the needs and interests of the British rulers whose main interests lay in exploitation of Indian resources and enrichment of their own people at the cost of Indian people. British economic policies such as new land revenue policies, discriminatory trade restrictions, domination of markets and continuous conquests had an adverse impact on almost all classes of Indian people from peasants and artisans upto the ruling class. The British policies brought about a ruin of Indian agriculture, trade and industry and resulted in a complete breakdown of the traditional economic structure. The self-sufficiency of the villages was destroyed and Indian economy was rapidly transformed into colonial economy.

Ruin of Peasantry and Agriculture

Mentioned under the economic impact of various land revenue settlements.

Ruin of Old Zamindars and Rise of New Landed Classes

The old zamindars were replaced by a new class of landlords, particularly under the land revenue settlements of Warren Hastings. By 1815, nearly all great zamindars of Bengal were ruined and replaced by merchants and moneyed classes who lived in towns (absentee landlordism), had no permanent interest in land and tried to **extort as much revenue as possible** during the period of their contract. Clearly such a system further accelerated the impoverishment of the peasantry, impoverishment of land and stagnation and deterioration of agriculture.

Ruin of Artisans and Craftsmen, De-Industrialisation and Ruralisation of Indian Economy

De-industrialisation refers to the process of continued and marked industrial decline. With reference to India, it refers to the destruction of traditional Indian craft industries as one of the earliest consequences of British rule in India. The **cotton-weaving** and **cotton-spinning** industries were the worst hit. Strangely, while India's traditional manufacturing sector was being steadily weakened under the Company; in the same period Britain had begun its Industrial Revolution and was rapidly expanding its own industries. Wealth from India (Plunder of Bengal 1757) played a significant role in the accumulation of capital in England needed for industrialisation (1760).

Various causes of de-industrialisation under the British rule are listed as follows:

- **Misuse of political power** The British used political power to bully the weavers and artisans of Bengal into selling their products at low and dictated prices, even if they incurred a loss. This forced many of them to leave their profession. The Khatbandi System virtually reduced the weavers to the status of indentured or bonded labourers.
- **Creation of a buyers' market** The British created a buyers' market where the buyer can dictate the price, (the buyer here being the English Company and its servants) at the cost of the seller (the seller being the India peasant and artisan).
- **Destruction of regional powers and their courts** The princely states were the biggest buyers of handicraft, luxury commodities and military weapons. Their decline gave a big blow to these industries.
- **Westernisation of Indian educated middle class** This class imitated European standards and scorned on everything Indian.
- **Import restrictions** This ruined the foreign market of Indian artisans.
- **Forced policy of British Free Trade with India** Far from providing protection to Indian industries, the British opened Indian market to British manufactured goods, thus ruining the home market of Indian artisans. Many indigenous industries faced unequal competition with imported machine-made goods and perished.
- **Development of railways** Besides other things, the railway policy of the government discriminated against Indian goods such that transportation of Indian goods was costlier than that of British goods.
- **Lack of government support** The British government extended no support, financial or otherwise to heavy or capital goods industry (First steel in India was produced as late as in 1913!) and to technical education.
- Import of cheap synthetic dyes destroyed dying industry of Indian villages.
- Export of raw materials from India.
- Grant of special privileges to British manufacturers in India.

The ruin of Indian industries was reflected in the ruin of once famous industrial centres like Dhaka, Surat and Murshidabad. Destruction of handicraft industry ruined the independence of villages, forced artisans to leave their profession and become labourers and made the economy predominantly agrarian.

This increasing dependence of the population on agriculture for subsistence and increasing tendency to produce agricultural goods and raw materials, to the neglect of industrial development, has been described by historians as trend towards **ruralisation or peasantisation of Indian economy**. The change was the most glaring in the cotton textile industry—India that had been for centuries the largest exporter of cotton goods in the world, was now transformed into an importer of cotton goods and exporter of raw cotton! This was a direct result of de-industrialisation and comprised yet another impact of British rule on Indian economy.

During the National Movement, Britain's role in de-industrialisation of India and its callous indifference towards development of modern industry became a rallying point against the colonial rule. Several efforts were made to revive indigenous industries, particularly by Congress and Mahatma Gandhi (Gandhi had formed All India Spinners Association and All India Village Industry Association).

- **The government of William Bentinck noted in 1834,** 'The misery hardly finds a parallel in the history of commerce. The bones of the cotton weavers are bleaching the plains of India'.
- **Karl Marx** had noted, 'It was the British intrude who broke up the India handloom and destroyed the spinning wheel. England began with depriving the Indian cottons from European market; it then introduced twist into Hindustan and in the end inundated the very mother country of cottons with cottons'.

Commercialisation of Agriculture

Commercialisation simply means production of agricultural crops for sale in market, rather than for family consumption. In the process of commercialisation, markets for certain products may develop before others. Commercialisation of agriculture existed even under the Indian rulers, for instance the cultivators were selling their products for money in order to pay land tax. But the commercialisation under the East India Company was different in many ways:

- **Forced commercialisation** For the Indian peasant, commercialisation under the Company's rule was a forced process. Often the cultivator had to hurriedly sell off a part of his produce at whatever price it fetched in order to meet the high land revenue demand of the state and interest of the moneylender.
- **Selective commercialisation** Initially the company also exported Indian manufactures, particularly textiles. But after the Industrial revolution, the cotton mill industry grew in Britain. Soon the mill owners agitated against the East India Company claiming that the Indian fabrics injured their business. The company was now forced to promote other safe lines of export and agriculture products was one such line. These products would not compete with British products and could also serve as **raw materials for British industry**. Thus, the East India Company being a trading company, it brought about commercialisation of those crops and agri-products which would not compete with British products and had a demand in the European market at the same time (such as indigo, cotton, raw silk, opium, pepper, tea, sugar, etc.). These were sown **at the cost of food grains** in India.

  Further, the British bought tea from China and paid for it in silver as the Chinese did not want Western goods. But the Chinese did buy Indian products like ivory, raw cotton and opium. So, the British East India Company gradually brought about commercialisation of these commodities in India—the tea could be got in exchange for Indian products. This trade came to be known as **'triangular trade'** with main trading points at Calcutta, Canton and London with wealth accumulating at London.
- **At the cost of drain of wealth** Earlier there was little demand for British goods in India. So, the company purchased Indian goods in gold and silver bullion. After the conquest of Bengal, it made these purchases from revenue collected from Indian subjects. This resulted in **drain of wealth** from India.

What Crops were Commercialised and why? The commercialised crops included indigo, cotton, raw silk, opium, pepper, tea and sugar. Those crops were commercialised which were in demand in European market and did not compete with British products. Raw silk and raw cotton could not be produced in Britain. Indigo, a textile dye, was needed in British market. British commercialised tea cultivation in Assam as they did not want to rely on China for tea. None of these commodities competed with any British products.

Effects of Commercialisation of Agriculture

Some of the common effects of commercialisation of agriculture by the British were as follows:

- **Exploitation of Indian peasants** Except in the case of tea, the crops were not produced by hired labour. Say in the case of indigo, the preferred system was to coerce the small peasants into supplying the required product at very low price (called the **Ryoti System**). The European businessmen found it profitable to squeeze the small peasant household than to engage in direct production with hired labour, thus preventing the appearance of developed labour market. Further, the Indian cultivators were often forced to grow these crops against their wishes. They were also forced to sell them to the British at as low cost as possible. This often drove them into the clutches of local moneylenders and created heavy indebtedness.
- **Market instability** Agriculture in India was already exposed to many hazards such as droughts and floods, but commercialisation of agriculture added another hazard—the instability associated with widely fluctuating world markets. For instance, Bundelkhand grew a lot of cotton for the China market after 1816. Claiming that the region had become very prosperous, the British officials raised the land revenue. But when the export declined in the 1830s and prices fell, the taxes were not reduced. Both landlords and peasants were pushed into deep poverty and vast stretches of land went out of cultivation, culminating in the **Bundela Rebellion of 1842**. Thus, while product market was commercialised, land and labour could not develop.
- **Famines** Commercialisation of agriculture contributed to famines by substituting food grains for commercial crops as well as by increasing instances of land falling out of cultivation because it was no longer profitable to cultivate it.
- **Impoverishment of India** You have seen that the crops were produced for exports to Britain. These were bought from land revenue collected from British territories in India and transferred in the form of 'tribute' to Britain. In this way, such exports remitted resources out of India, while India received no imports in return. Such a transfer naturally impoverished India.

Drain of Wealth

The continuous transfer of wealth from India to England for which India did not receive any adequate economic or material return has been termed by Indian economists and national leaders as 'drain of wealth from India'. It refers to all those payments which were made by India to Britain without any adequate returns or responsibility (one-sided transfer of funds). It has also been interpreted as Indian 'tribute' sent to Britain by the Company's government. The focal point of Drain theory was that a portion of the national product of India was not available for consumption for its people or for capital formation, but was being drained away to England owing to political subordination of India.

Peculiar to British Rule

This drain of wealth happened only during the British rule. All previous Indian rulers, including foreign conquerors such as the Mughals finally settled in India and made India their home. They spent on roads and canals, temples and mosques and even on personal luxuries, but the wealth remained in India, encouraged Indian trade and industry and gave employment to Indians. But this was never the case with the British. Nearly all Englishmen working in India planned to go back to Britain, taking as much wealth with them as possible; the British remained perpetual foreigners in India.

Comparing the British methods of plunder with the plunder of medieval invaders and rulers, historians have pointed out that while the old-time plunder was restricted to rich men's houses, the colonial plunder reached the most lowly, the most humble and the most remote. Like the blood sucking leeches, the British methods were less painful but more thorough.

Forms of Drain of Wealth

Drain of wealth from India began in 1757 when the Company's servants carried home bribes and extortions from Indian rulers as well as the common people. Henceforth, the drain continued to occur in the following ways:

1. Land revenue collected from Bengal began to be used to buy goods in India for export. In other words, the company used its **'Territorial Revenue'** to provide funds for business and generate 'Commercial Revenue'. In this way, the East India Company developed a self-sufficient system needing no funds from England.
2. Drain of wealth also occurred in the form of Company's remittance to England to pay for salaries and pensions of Company's employees, **interest on loans** (public debt) taken by the Company in England, dividends to stockholders of the Company, etc. This was also known as **'Home Charges'**.
3. Drain of wealth also occurred in the form of bribes, payments to shipping companies, insurance companies and banks.
4. Wealth was also drained out of India in the form of **Interest on Foreign Capital Investments**. For example, in the case of railway companies, interest had to be paid out to the English investors out of Indian tax payers' money.

Economic Impact of Drain of Wealth

- The drain adversely affected income and employment potential in India.
- It checked capital accumulation in India, thereby retarding industrialisation of India.
- Drain of wealth from India led to accumulation of capital in England and contributed to Industrial Revolution there.
- Part of that capital reentered India as finance capital on which India had to pay interest and further drained India of its wealth.

Some Important Facts

- Marx referred to the drain of wealth as the **'bleeding process'**.
- The newspaper **'Amrit Bazaar Patrika'** particularly opposed the drain of wealth from India.
- Newspapers Hindustan Review and Kayastha Samachar described the use of foreign capital as 'a system of international degradation'.

> **John Sullivan, President, board of Revenue, Madras,** had remarked, 'Our system acts very much like a sponge, drawing up all the good things from the banks of the Ganges, and squeezing them down on the banks of the Thames'.

Poverty and Famines

The Indian economy reached a new low under the British with the net effect that there was widespread poverty and starvation among the masses. Though famines in India occurred due to a number of factors such as failure of rains and frequent wars between the British and regional powers, the British economic policies added to these factors and culminated in a series of famines that struck India in the second half of the 18th century (and later the 19th century as well).

A notable characteristic of India's poverty was that it was man-made and not due to any deficiency in natural or human resources. In the pre-British period, India was no more backward than the West. It was not a coincident that Plunder of Bengal (1757) was succeeded by Industrial Revolution in Britain (1760). And while the next hundred years witnessed the rapid industrialisation and modernisation of Europe, India was subjected to some of the worst forms of colonialism. Far from modernisation, India was sapped of its wealth and vitality, its masses veered on the fringes of poverty and starvation.

Rise of Modern Industries under the British

The British did not plan to bring about any industrial or economic development in India. However, the need for better **imperial control** and **fuller exploitation of Indian resources** led them to construct roads, railways, post and telegraph lines, develop ports, irrigation works, banking and insurance facilities, etc.—developments that later provided the material basis for emergence of modern industry in India.

An important social consequence of this limited industrial development was the emergence of the **industrial capitalist class** and the **working class**. Even as these classes formed a minuscule part of the Indian population, they represented new technology, new social relations and new outlook with the consequence that their economic and political contribution in 19th and 20th centuries far outweighed their numbers.

Roads and Indian Railways

Upto the 1850s, the means of transport in India were confined to animal driven carts. Driven by the need for imperial defence from both external and internal threats and fuller exploitation of Indian resources, the British began development of roadways, railways and waterways.

- In 1839, work on the **Grand Trunk Road** from **Calcutta to Delhi** was started and completed in 1850s. However, real change came with the introduction of Indian Railways.
- The First railway engine was designed by **George Stephenson**. In 1814, it was first put on the rails.
- In 1848, **Lord Dalhousie** became Governor-General of India and advocated rapid railway construction.
- In 1853, first railway line in India was laid in **between Bombay and Thane** by Great Indian Peninsula Railway.
- In 1854, 120-mile railway line was laid between Calcutta and Raniganj by East India Railway.

Postal System and Telegraph

- For Communication, the British set up an efficient Postal system. Dalhousie introduced the first postage stamps in India.
- The telegraph was also introduced.
- In **1853, first telegraph line** was opened from **Calcutta to Agra**. Until 1857, Dr. O'Shaughnessey's (a professor of chemistry in Calcutta Medical College) instrument was used all over India. Later, it was replaced by the Morse instrument.

Press

- In 16th century, Press was first introduced in India by the Portuguese.
- Early attempts to publish newspapers were made by the disgruntled East India Employees.
- In 1780, the first newspaper in India was published by **James Augustus Hickey** titled **The Bengal Gazette**.

Rise of New Indian Bourgeoisie

Some Indian traders, money lenders and bankers got to amass some wealth as junior partners of English traders and businessmen and emerged as the new Indian middle class. The Indian traders helped in the distribution of British manufactures in the remotest corners of India and collection of raw materials for export to Britain. The money lenders lent money to the agriculturalists in distress and ensured collection of land revenue by the government. The bankers helped both in carrying out their businesses and other financial transactions.

It was this very class that initially formed the Westernised loyalists but later evolved into the educated Indian intelligentsia and raised the banner of the national movement in the second half of the 19th century. One such cotton trader was Dadabhai Naoroji (1825–1917), who devoted his entire life to the creation of a national movement in India.

To sum up, in this chapter we have learnt that the main motive of the English Company in India was to maximise its profits. All other purposes were subordinated to this aim and all its activities were guided by it, including acquisition of political hegemony and territorial expansion. After Plassey, the Company emerged supreme in Bengal and began using its political power for its own commercial gains. The more powerful the Company grew, the more tightly it gripped the Indian economy and sucked away its vitality. One by one it wreaked havoc on Indian peasants, artisans, traders and businessmen, ate into their share of profits and rendered their industry financially unviable. Plunder of Bengal, drain of wealth, de-industrialisation, commercialisation of agriculture and ruralisation of Indian economy were some of the major impacts of the Company's policies in India. We may conclude that the British Rule had a far-reaching impact on India life, particularly the economy which was gradually transformed into a fully developed colonial economy by the end of the 19th century.

Flashforward:

Railways

- By 1869, more than 6,000 kms of railways had been built by the guaranteed companies but this system proved to be too expensive and in 1869 the government decided to build new railways as state enterprises. After 1880, they began to be built through private enterprise as well.
- By 1905, nearly 45,000 kms of railways had been built.

MNCs

- Many Multinational Companies began to operate their subsidiary companies in India and penetrated deep into almost every sector of Indian economy.
- These included MNCs like Hindustan Lever Ltd., Dunlop, ITC, Union Carbide, Ashok Leyland, Imperial Chemicals and others. Even after independence, these MNCs continued to maintain their stronghold in Indian market.

Flashforward:

Growth of Indian Capitalist Class The industrialisation in India which began in the latter half of the 19th century, began as a reaction to British de-industrialisation policies. The nationalist leaders felt that industrialisation of India was the first condition for economic progress of the country. **Swadeshi movement** (1905) with its impetus on India-made goods is rightly considered as the foundation of indigenous modern industry. Henceforth, the Indian capitalist class got bound up with the national movement, supporting Congress leadership and financing some of its programmes and policies.

- **Mahadev Govind Ranade** was one of the first leaders who called upon his countrymen to set up industries.
- In 1870, KT Telang and Ferozeshah Mehta opened soap factory in Mumbai and set an example before others.
- **Lala Lajpat Rai**, as director of Punjab National Bank, helped people in establishment of industries.

Cotton Cloth Industry The foundation for this industry was laid in the 1850s with the help of local capital. The textile industry first attracted the attention of Parsi and Gujarati entrepreneurs. Bombay had the necessary climate for raw material, availability of cheap labour and even ready market for textiles.

- In 1818, a mill was set up in Calcutta. But this was an exception and the industry remained centred around Bombay.
- In 1853, first factory was set up in **Bombay** by Parsi Kavsaji Nanabhai Davar. With this began the history of this industry.
- In 1874, JN Tata set up a cloth manufacturing company; renamed Empress Mill Nagpur in 1877.
- During 1853–80, thirty factories were set up, out of which thirteen were set up by Parsis.

Jute or Putson Industry

- In 1855, first Jute factory (Acland Mill) in India was set up at **Risra** near Serampur, Bengal.
- Towards the end of 19th century, the Birlas went to Calcutta and entered raw jute trade with the help of Seth Tarachand Ghanshyam Das Birla.
- In 1919, Birla Jute Company was established.
- 1940 onwards Ghanshyam Das Birla bought several companies from the English and expanded his business, thus establishing the predominance of Indians in jute industry.

Iron-Steel Industry

- In 1907, JN Tata (son of Jamshedji Tata) first set up TISCO in **Jamshedpur**, Bihar. It produced pig iron in 1911 and steel by 1913.
- Later, steel companies were also set up at Mysore (Bhadravati) and Bengal.

Flashforward:

Economic Critique by Early Nationalists After 1857, economic exploitation of India continued and even intensified in many ways. The rising Indian intelligentsia threw up the early national leaders (the Moderates) who were the first to develop an economic critique of the colonial rule. Soon the critique, along with the themes built around it, emerged as the single most significant factor that contributed to the rise of the Indian National Movement in the second half of the 19th century.

Dadabhai Naoroji

In the beginning, the educated middle class supported British rule in India as they felt that British rule was needed to modernise India. But after 1860, the disillusionment set in gradually in the wake of glaring economic disparity between India and England. Many of them went to England for work or for higher education and were shocked to see the hypocrisy of British rulers. While they themselves enjoyed all comforts of a modern lifestyle and based their social relations upon the modern values of equality and democracy, Indian masses were subjected to political, psychological and economic subjugation.

One among such Indian intellectuals was **Dadabhai Naoroji** (1825–1917), also known as the Grand Old Man of India. He was also the first economic thinker of India and was the first to give the theory of Drain of Wealth in his book 'The Poverty and Unbritish Rule in India' (1901). Another stalwart economic thinker of this time was **RC Dutt**. He gave a detailed economic record of British rule since 1757 in his work 'The Economic History of India' (1902). Justice **Mahadev Govind Ranade** was another hero who taught the Indians of his generation the value of modern industrial development. He remarked that factories could, 'far more effectively than Schools and Colleges give a new birth to the activities of a nation'.

GV Joshi, DE Wacha, G. Subramaniyam Iyer, GK Gokhale, Prithwis Chandra Ray and several other political activists gave their own analysis of the economic impact of colonial rule and subjected the entire range of colonial policies to minute scrutiny. Eventually all their efforts converged at one point and found the British rule at the vortex of India's underdevelopment. They were able to see that India's poverty was not inherent or natural but very much man-made (or rather British-made) and removable and made this economic critique as the main plank of their nationalist economic agitation.

The early nationalists showed trade, industry and finance as the three pillars of economic domination. They highlighted that economic exploitation of India was no longer carried out by the crude tools of plunder and tribute but through more sophisticated modern phenomenon of 'free trade'. Of particular concern to them was the decline of Indian traditional handicraft industry. They looked upon foreign capital as disguised evil and were unanimous on the view that India's future economic development should be based on Indian capital and not foreign capital.

On the expenditure side, GV Joshi denounced investment on railways as 'Indian subsidy to British industries' and Tilak equated it to 'decorating another's wife'. The early economists highlighted that developmental and welfare departments were starved at the cost of those departments that fulfilled British needs such as defence. However, the drain theory remained the backbone of the economic critique of British rule.

Drain of wealth Dadabhai Naoroji first explained drain of wealth from India in his article **'England's Debt to India'** which he read out in the conference of East India Association (2 May 1867). He was also the first to give the theory of Drain of Wealth in his book **The Poverty and Unbritish Rule in India** (1901). Naoroji declared this drain of wealth as the chief cause of all diseases and destitution in India. In 1896 Calcutta Session of the Congress, his Drain of Wealth theory was first accepted and it was in 1906 Calcutta Session that Naoroji demanded swaraj or self-rule based on this theory. He also referred to the **'moral drain'**, consisting of the exclusion of Indians from positions of trust and responsibility in their own land.

Following in his footsteps, RC Dutt made the drain a major theme of his Economic History of India (1902). He remarked, 'Taxation raised by a King , says the Indian poet, is like the moisture sucked up by the sun, to be returned to the earth as fertilising rain, but the moisture raised from the Indian soil now descends as fertilising rain largely on other lands, not on India... So great an Economic Drain out of the resources of a land would impoverish the most prosperous countries on earth; it has reduced India to a land of famines more frequent, more widespread, and more fatal than any known before in the history of India or of the world'.

With the strong imagery that it evoked and by the virtue of it being almost self-explanatory, the drain theory found ready acceptability among the Indian masses, specially the peasants. It eroded the moral basis of British rule in India and went a long way in sowing the seeds of disaffection and disloyalty towards the British rule. It ensured that the early nationalists did not base their nationalism on shallow sentiments but on scientific study of the complex phenomenon of modern colonialism.

Romesh Chunder Dutt (1848–1909) He was a member of the ICS, a writer and a prominent economic historian of India of the 19th century. Post-retirement, he served as the President of INC in 1899. He translated the Ramayana and the Mahabharata into English and famously authored **Open Letters to Curzon on Famines and Land Assessments in India** (1900) and **The Economic History of India** (1902).

Previous Years' Questions – Preliminary Exam

1. Which among the following was the reason for the lack of independent development of industries in India during British rule? **[UPSC 1999]**
   (a) Absence of heavy industries
   (b) Scarcity of foreign capital
   (c) Scarcity of natural resources
   (d) Preference of the rich to invest in land
2. The term 'Imperial Preference' was applied to which one of the following? **[UPSC 1999]**
   (a) Special privileges on British imports in India
   (b) Racial discrimination by the Britishers
   (c) Subordination of Indian interests to that of the British
   (d) Preference given to British political agents over Indian Princes
3. Match List-I with List-II. **[UPSC 2000]**

List-I	List-II
A. Land allotted to big feudal landlords	1. Jagirdari System
B. Land allotted to revenue farmers or rent collectors	2. Ryotwari System
C. Land allotted to each peasant with the right to sublet, mortgage, transfer, gift or sell	3. Mahalwari System
D. Revenue settlements made at village level	4. Zamindari System

Select the correct answer from the following options.

	A	B	C	D
(a)	1	3	2	4
(b)	1	4	2	3
(c)	3	4	1	2
(d)	2	1	3	4

4. Under the Permanent Settlement of 1793, the Zamindars were required to issue pattas to the farmers which were not issued by many of the Zamindars. Which among them was the reason for this? **[UPSC 2001]**
   (a) The Zamindars were trusted by the farmers
   (b) There was no official check upon the Zamindars
   (c) It was the responsibility of the British government
   (d) The farmers were not interested in getting pattas
5. With reference to the period of Colonial rule in India, 'Home Charges' formed an important part of drain of wealth from India. Which of the following funds constituted 'Home Charges'? **[UPSC 2011]**
   1. Funds used to support the Indian office in London
   2. Funds used to pay salaries and pensions of British personnel engaged in India
   3. Funds used for waging wars outside India by the British.

Select the correct answer from the following options.

(a) 1 only (b) 1 and 2 only
(c) 2 and 3 only (d) 1, 2 and 3

6. Karl Marx explained the process of class struggle with the help of which one of the following theories? **[UPSC 2011]**
   (a) Empirical liberalism
   (b) Existentialism
   (c) Darwin's theory of evolution
   (d) Dialectical materialism
7. The tendency for increased litigation was visible after the introduction of the land settlement system of Lord Cornwallis in 1793. The reason for this is normally traced to which of the following provisions? **[UPSC 2011]**
   (a) Making Zamindars position stronger vis-a-vis the Ryot
   (b) Making East India company an overlord of Zamindars
   (c) Making judicial system more efficient
   (d) None of the (a), (b) and (c) above
8. With reference to Ryotwari settlement, consider the following statements. **[UPSC 2012]**
   1. The rent was paid directly by the peasants to the government
   2. The government gave Pattas to the Ryots
   3. The land was surveyed and assessed before being taxed.

   Which of the statements given above is/are correct? Select the correct answer from the following options.
   (a) 1 only
   (b) 1 and 2 only
   (c) 1, 2 and 3
   (d) none
9. Consider the following statements. **[UPSC 2012]**
   1. Assessment of land revenue on the basis of nature of the soil and the quality of crops
   2. Use of mobile cannons in warfare
   3. Cultivation of tobacco and red chillies

   Which of the above was/were introduced into India by the English? Select the correct answer from the following options.
   (a) 1 only (b) 1 and 2
   (c) 2 and 3 (d) none
10. Who of the following was/were economic critic/critics of colonialism in India? **[UPSC 2015]**
    1. Dadabhai Naoroji
    2. G Subramanyam Iyer
    3. RC Dutt

    Select the correct answer from the following options.
    (a) Only 1 (b) 1 and 2
    (c) 2 and 3 (d) 1, 2 and 3
11. Who among the following was/were associated with the introduction of Ryotwari Settlement in India during the British rule? **[UPSC 2017]**
    1. Lord Cornwallis
    2. Alexander Read
    3. Thomas Munro

    Select the correct answer from the following options.
    (a) Only 1 (b) 1 and 3
    (c) 2 and 3 (d) 1, 2 and 3
12. Economically, one of the results of the British rule in India in the 19th century was the **[UPSC 2018]**
    (a) increase in the export of Indian handicrafts
    (b) growth in the number of Indian owned factories
    (c) commercialization of Indian agriculture
    (d) rapid increase in the urban population
13. Which of the following statements correctly explain the impact of Industrial Revolution on India during the first half of the nineteenth century? **[UPSC 2020]**
    (a) Indian handicrafts were ruined.
    (b) Machines were introduced in the Indian textile industry in large number.
    (c) Railway lines were laid in many parts of the country.
    (d) Heavy duties were imposed on the imports of British manufactures.

Previous Years' Questions – Main Exam

1. The economic policies followed by the British led to the transformation of India's economy into a colonial economy. They disrupted the traditional structure of the Indian economy. Explain how this happened with special reference to agricultural rural employment and development of our industries. **[UPSC 1983]**
2. The Railways did in India what they did elsewhere; they hastened the transition from handicraft to mechanical industry by transforming the transport situation. Discuss. **[UPSC 1992]**
3. What is meant by 'Un-British' rule in India? How did the Indian Nationalists react against it? Evaluate the role of Dadabhai Naoroji in exposing the evils of British rule in India. **[UPSC 1994]**
4. What do you understand about 'Drain of Wealth' during British rule? Examine its effects on Indian economy. **[UPSC 1997]**
5. How did the policy of free trade hurt Indian textile industry and crafts in the latter half of 19th century? **[UPSC 1998]**
6. How did economic nationalism mirror the work of the early Nationalist leadership in India? **[UPSC 1998]**
7. The emergence of new social classes in British India was the direct consequence of the establishment of new social economy, new state system, administrative machinery and western education. Discuss. **[UPSC 2008]**
8. 'British vision of India had no single coherent set of ideas. On the contrary, the ideas were shot through with contradictions and inconsistencies'. Discuss. **[UPSC 2008]**
9. 'Many Englishmen honestly consider themselves the trustees for India and yet to what a condition they have reduced our country'. Critically analyse. **[UPSC 2009]**
10. Examine critically the various facets of economic policies of the British in India from mid-18th century till independence. **[UPSC 2014]**
11. Examine how the decline of traditional artisanal industry in colonial India crippled the rural economy. **[UPSC 2017]**

Answers

Previous Years' Questions – Preliminary Exam

1.	(a)	2.	(a)	3.	(b)	4.	(b)	5.	(a)
6.	(d)	7.	(d)	8.	(c)	9.	(d)	10.	(d)
11.	(c)	12.	(c)	13.	(a)				

2 Changes and Impact: Indian Polity (Constitutional Development-Part 1, 1757–1858)

So far, we have learnt how and why the British East India Company came to India, essentially as a trading company. Additionally, we learnt that driven by economic motives, how it gradually acquired political power and revenue-yielding territories and became an empire in itself. The British government soon realised that the Company could no longer be allowed to remain outside the ambit of the state. Accordingly, the British Parliament subjected the Company to control through various constitutional laws and acts.

Regulating Act 1773

Factors Leading to the Act

Administrative Chaos in Bengal After the East India Company came to power in Bengal, the Company showed unwillingness to recognise itself as the new ruler, hence refusing to take up any responsibility towards the subject population. How could the Company take responsibility for the welfare of a people when its main interest lay in looting and plundering them? It was with this interest in mind that Clive established a dual government (1765–72) in theory, with the Company as Diwan and the Nawab as Nazim. The Deputy Subahdar (appointed by the Company) was to function in the interest of the Company, while maintaining a fiction of Mughal sovereignty. A fatal divorce of power from responsibility was inherent in this dual system. It led to complete **breakdown of administration** and law and order in Bengal. The Company's demand for high land revenues led to gross oppression of the peasantry. The abuses of private trade reached a greater height than ever before. Clive himself returned to England at the age of 34, with wealth and property in India yielding 40,000 pounds a year!

Even in England, what attracted the chief attention was the wealth the Company was expected to derive from the revenues of Bengal. Some in the government suggested even then that the Crown should take over the Company. However, with King George III as its patron and powerful friends in the Parliament, the Company fought back. In the absence of wide support, the first intervention of the British Parliament in the Company's affairs in 1767 merely took the form of a demand for a share of Bengal's plunder to the tune of 400,000 pound per annum.

As recorded in **Siyar-ul-Mutakherin,** a contemporary Muslim text, 'the new rulers paid no attention to the concerns of the people and suffered them to be mercilessly oppressed and tormented by officers of their own appointing'.

Spread of Socio-political Corruption in Britain The Company's employees began using their newly amassed wealth to spread social and political corruption in Britain; the Company even bought seats in the House of Commons for its agents! Many thinkers and statesmen in Britain now began to fear that the Company may grab dangerous supremacy in the British government.

Jealousy among Englishmen in Britain The fabulous wealth brought home by the Company's officials began to give rise to jealousy in Britain. The newly rising 'free enterprisers' also aspired for a share in the profits from Indian trade. Why should the East India Company alone enjoy all the profits? They wished to end the monopoly of the EIC and with this aim in mind they heartily criticised the administration of the Company in Bengal. The Company's officials began to be looked down upon in England and were given the derisive title of **'Nabobs'**; it symbolised the corrupt form of Nawab and was used for exploiters of India.

Financial Crisis in East India Company By 1770, the continuous wars and expansionist policy of the Company had pushed it on the brinks of bankruptcy. By now the Company was in debt to the tune of 6 million pound and it felt incapable of paying even the salaries of its employees. What an irony it was! Even as the Company's servants amassed huge wealth, the Company itself faced bankruptcy! Subsequently, in 1772 the Company approached Lord North and requested him for a loan. Lord North, too, grasped this opportunity and moved the British Parliament for appointment of a select committee to look into the affairs of the Company and submit a report.

Lord North, Prime Minister of Great Britain from 1770–1782.

Based on the committee's report, **Lord North** (Prime Minister of Great Britain from 1770–1782) presented his famous Bill on 18 May 1773, which later came to be known as the Regulating Act. Naturally, the bill was not passed unopposed and faced fierce opposition from the Company and its supporters. Once passed, the Regulating Act became the first significant step towards Parliamentary regulation of Indian administration. (By a separate act, the Company was granted a loan of 1,400,000 pounds at 4% interest).

Main Provisions of Regulating Act

The main aim of Regulating Act was to regulate the activities of the Company in both India as well as England and remove the deficiencies.

Provisions related to Company's government in Britain:

- The Company's administration was looked after by two institutions in England—Court of Proprietors (CoP) and Court of Directors (CoD). The CoD was the Company's executive in England and comprised of 24 Directors who were elected by a body of share-holders knows as the CoP. Any shareholder holding shares worth 500 pounds was entitled to vote in the CoP, while one holding shares worth 100 pounds was eligible to be elected to the CoD. The post of Director was highly sought as it gave ample opportunity for nepotism-Directors could easily find jobs for their relations in India. Many servants of the Company aimed to return home and get into the CoD using their ill-gotten wealth from India.

- The Regulating Act addressed this issue by **raising the qualification** for both CoP (raised to 1000pounds) and CoD (raised to 2000 pounds).
- The Act also provided for direct Parliamentary control over the CoD for the **first time**. Under the Act, the Directors were required to 'lay before the Treasury all correspondence from India dealing with the revenues and before a Secretary of State everything dealing with civil and military administration'.

Provisions related to Company's government in India:

- The most serious concern in Bengal administration was the Company's inability to check corruption by its servants.
  - The Act addressed this by providing a new executive for the Bengal Presidency. It would comprise of a Governor-General (GG) and four Councillors (known as **Governor-General-in-Council**) and vested in them the civil and military powers of Bengal, Bihar and Orissa. Through this, the Parliament aimed to control the Governor, who was now required to function in Council, the decision of the Council was binding upon him.
  - The Council comprised of men specially sent from England and who were not servants of the Company.
  - The Council was to take all decisions by majority, though the GG had the casting vote in case of equality of votes. The Council was given a term of 5 years. 3 members formed a quorum.
  - The First Governor-General **(Warren Hastings)** and Councillors **(Philip Francis, Clavering, Monson and Barwell)** were named in the Act. Of them, only Barwell was a supporter of Hastings. Francis was a staunch opponent.
- The Company's servants also indulged in corruption because of their low salaries.
  - The Act provided for payment of **liberal salaries** and **prohibited immoral activities** such as-private trade, receiving or giving bribes, money lending, etc.
- Another deficiency in Indian administration was that the Bengal, Madras and Bombay Presidencies were separate and independent of each other. Each Presidency had direct relations with the Court of Directors in England. There was no supreme authority in India that could bring about synergy among them. Regulating Act tried to do away with this deficiency and tried to establish an empowered central authority.
  - Accordingly, **Bengal Presidency was made supreme** with exclusive powers to deal with matters of war and peace, and other Presidencies were made subordinate to it.
  - Governor of Bengal was now called the Governor-General of all British territories in India.
  - The Governors of Madras and Bombay were required to send regularly, to the Governor-General, information connected with government, revenues, etc. In this way, the Act laid the **foundation for central administration** in India.
  - The Governor-General in turn was kept under direct control of the Court of Directors.
- Another defect in the system was that there was no independent judicial body to keep check over the executive.
  - The Act addressed this by providing for a **Supreme Court** of Justice at Calcutta (established in 1774). Its jurisdiction included civil, criminal, admiralty and ecclesiastical matters.
  - It comprised of a Chief Justice and three puisne Judges. **Sir Elijah Imphey** was appointed as the Chief Justice.
  - All the public servants of the Company were made amenable to its jurisdiction. All British subjects, both European and Indian, could seek redressal in the Supreme Court against oppression.
  - Appeal against the Court's decision could be made to the King in Council in England.

Weaknesses of Regulating Act

Many weaknesses or defects of this Act were exposed when it was put to working:

- The Act was based on the principle of checks and balances and was intentionally vague in many of its provisions. It had 'neither given the state a definite control over the Company, nor the Directors a definite control over their servants, nor the Governor-general a definite control over his council, nor the Calcutta Presidency a definite control over Madras and Bombay'. When put to practice, it broke down under the weight of its own defects.
- The working of the Governor-General in Council proved most inefficient. The Governor-General faced continuous opposition of his Councillors; he had no power to override them, though in case of equal division, he had the casting vote. Such obstructionism made the Council dysfunctional.
- The Act was especially vague regarding the extent to which the Bengal Presidency was to exercise control over other presidencies. As a result, the Maratha and the Mysore wars were initiated by the Bombay and the Madras Presidencies, even as Hastings was opposed to both.
- The Act also did not define the relationship between the Supreme Court and the Company courts as well as the various country courts in Bengal over which the GG-in-Council had appellate powers. This naturally resulted in conflict between the Court and the GG-in-Council and seriously hampered the law-making process, proving to be the worst defect of the Act.
- Further, the Supreme Court administering English law also claimed jurisdiction over the entire native population (and not just the British subjects) and proved quite unpopular with them.

Significance of Regulating Act

In its working, the Regulating Act was a disaster. Yet, it was significant in many ways. It was the first main step towards Parliamentary control over Company's administration in India. It fixed the administrative centre at Calcutta. It was also a praiseworthy effort to secure a corruption-free administration. Overall, it was a well-meant attempt to introduce a better system of governance but only ended up 'adding to Hastings' difficulties instead of strengthening his hands'.

Pitt's India Act 1784

William Pitt (he became the youngest British Prime Minister in 1783.)

On assumption of office of the Prime Minister, **William Pitt** (in office, 1783-1801) introduced an India Bill which later came to be known as Pitt's India Act. The aim of Pitt's India Act was to remove the weaknesses of the Regulating Act and bring Company's administration in India under the **supreme control of British Parliament**.

As a measure of caution, Pitt had taken care not to antagonise the Court of Directors and they were allowed to manage the commercial affairs of the Company as they liked. They retained their patronage, i.e. the power of appointment and dismissal of Company's servants. The right of the Company on its territorial possessions was also not touched. (It may be noted that a previous bill on similar lines was introduced by Fox-North coalition but the Bill was defeated and the Ministry had to resign. This was the **first and the last time** a British Ministry was wrecked on an Indian issue).

Main Provisions

- This Act allowed the Court of Directors to manage the commercial affairs of the Company. But for political affairs, the Act appointed a Board of six Commissioners, known as the **Board of Control**. The Board included the Chancellor of the Exchequer, a Secretary of State and 4 Privy Councillors. They were all appointed by the King. In this way, a form of **Double Government** was introduced. The aim was to allow the Company to rule, and the Board to control. The power of the Board was veiled; the Board's approval was necessary for all dispatches that were not purely commercial. The Act thus placed the civil and military government of the Company in due subordination to the Government in England. This continued until 1858. (The President of the board of Control was ultimately responsible for the government of British India until he was succeeded in 1858 by the Secretary of State for India).
- Changes with respect to Company's governance in India were few.
  - The number of members in the Governor-General's Council was **reduced to 3**, so that even if one member of the Council supported the GG, he could have his way.
  - The power of GG-in-Council over subordinate presidencies was extended to include all matters of war, diplomatic relations and revenue.
  - The GG and Council were made subordinate to British Government. They were forbidden to declare war without prior sanction of the directors.
  - The Act also introduced the principle of non-intervention in the affairs of **Indian Princely** states to end further wars and conquests. (This provision was honoured more in breach than in observance in the subsequent years).

Significance of Pitt's India Act

Pitt's India Act was an effective instrument of control and worked with slight alterations till 1858. The Act gave the British government supreme control over the Company's affairs and its administration in India. With this Act, began a new phase in the history of British conquest of India; while the East India Company became an instrument of British imperialism, India was to serve as a colony meeting the interests of all sections of ruling classes in Britain.

Act of 1786

In 1786, Pitt moved this Bill in order to make **Cornwallis** accept the Governor-Generalship of India. Cornwallis wanted to assume the powers of both-the GG and the Commander-in-Chief (CnC). This Act conceded his demand and the office of the **GG and the CnC** were united in the same person. The GG was further empowered and allowed to override the majority of his Council in matters of war and peace on his own responsibility (this power was extended to all future Governor-Generals and Governors by the Act of 1793).

Charter Act of 1793

- It extended the Company's exclusive privileges of trade for a further period of 20 years.
- A code was framed for all regulations that could be enacted in Bengal.
- The Act also required that all laws relating to rights of persons and property be printed with translation in Indian languages so that people could know about their rights and immunities. In this way, this Act laid the foundation of governance based on **written laws** in British India in place of personal rule of past rulers.
- All members of the Home government were in future to be paid salaries not out of the State Exchequer but **out of the Indian revenues**.

Charter Act of 1813

Factors Leading to the Act

Before the passage of this Act, there took place elaborate discussion on the continuation of the commercial privileges enjoyed by the Company. By 1813, the Company's territories in India had greatly expanded and it was considered nearly impossible for the Company to function both as a commercial and as a political entity. Moreover, Englishmen had begun to demand a share for themselves in the Indian trade in view of the laissez faire theories as well as the imposition of the continental system of Napoleon which had closed the European ports for British trade. In the above context, the demand for ending the Company's trade monopoly had grown much louder.

Main Provisions

- Thus, the Charter Act of 1813 renewed the Company's Charter for next 20 years but ended the **Company's monopoly of trade with India.** It, however, retained its monopoly in tea trade and trade with China. In this way, Indian trade was thrown open to all British merchants.
- The Act explicitly declared the **sovereignty of the Crown** over the territories acquired by the Company. The constitutional position of the British territories in India was thus explicitly defined for the first time.
- It relaxed controls on Christian missionaries by giving them license to enter India and propagate English language and Christian religion. This marked the beginning of ecclesiastical settlement in India.
- It provided a yearly **fund of ₹1 lakh** for promotion of literature and sciences among Indian subjects (As a declaration of the principle of state responsibility for education, this provision may be taken as one of the most significant British pronouncements with respect to India).

Charter Act of 1833

Factors Leading to the Act

The last 20 years witnessed great changes in England. Industrial Revolution had turned Britain into a manufacturer of cotton textiles and other factory-made goods. The Englishmen were looking for new export markets. Laissez faire had become the basic philosophy of the new industrial policy in Britain and there was popular desire for trade free from monopolies and restrictions.

In 1830, the Whigs (later known as the Liberal Party) came into power. The first Parliamentary Reform Act , also known as the great **Reform Act of 1832** had been passed (it was the Representation of People Act of 1832 that introduced widespread changes in the electoral system of England and Wales) and had brought in a reformed House of Commons where liberalism was in the ascendency. Two liberals in fact, **Macaulay** and **James Mill**, had a visible impact on the Charter of 1833. While Macaulay was Secretary to the Board of Control, Mill the renowned historian worked as Examiner of Indian Correspondence at India House. Slavery had been abolished all over Britain (1833) and dignity of mankind was being recognised (the Factory Act 1833). It was in this atmosphere of reform that the Charter Act of 1833 was passed.

The Act of 1833 provided for comprehensive provisions for regulating the affairs of the East India Company. Both Wellesley and Hastings had followed the policy of territorial expansion. Leaving the administration of such a vast empire in the hands of a joint stock company, without any association with the native population was no longer felt to be desirable.

Main Provisions

- Accordingly, the last traces of Company's exclusive **trade privileges were ended** and the Company was asked to **wind up its commercial business** as soon as possible. Thus, the union of the trader and sovereign was finally resolved. The President of the Board of control became the Minister of Indian Affairs. The Act declared the complete power of the British Parliament over the GG-in-Council.
- All restrictions to immigration of Europeans into India and acquisition of land and property by them were removed. Hence, the act lifted the legal barrier on the **colonisation of India** by Europeans. This also necessitated the reform of Indian law.
- Accordingly, an **Indian Law Commission** was appointed for the **codification of existing laws**. The Indian Penal Code and the Codes of Civil and Criminal Procedure were enacted by its efforts.
- The Act enlarged the Executive Council of the GG by addition of the fourth member. **A law member** (a British barrister) was added to the GG's Council and his work was fully legislative. He had no vote in the Council and he could attend meetings only on invitation. **Macaulay** became the first Law Member and the President of the Law Commission.
- A notable provision of the Act was that, under section 87, it provided for the education and employment of Indians in **public services**. The Act stated-'fitness is henceforth to be the criteria of eligibility. No native shall by reason only of his religion, place of birth, descent or colour be disabled from holding any employment under the Company'. Provision was made for the training of civil servants at the Company's College at **Haileybury** (in actual practice, very little was done to give effect to this provision).
- Another commendable provision was that the Act also directed the GG to work towards **abolition of slavery** in India. (This policy did reflect the liberal humanitarian attitude of the British Parliament and slavery was later abolished in India by Act V of 1843).
- The Act further centralised the Indian administration and the **GG of Bengal was made the GG of India**. The powers of the GG-in-Council were further extended and Bombay, Madras and all other territories were placed under the complete control of GG-in-Council.

- The Act also brought about **legislative centralisation**. The GG-in-Council was given the powers to legislate for the whole of British territories in India while the legislative powers of other presidencies were simultaneously ended. These laws were applicable to all persons British or Indian, including the servants of the Company.
- The Act created the **new Presidency of Agra**.

Significance of the Act of 1833

- This Act marked the culmination of the centralisation process which first began with the Regulating Act. Now the GG-in-Council held complete authority over the entire Indian administration.
- Provision under section 87 was noteworthy for ending the ill-conceived policy introduced by Cornwallis of Europeanisation of administration in India. It was a well-meant measure intending to remove any governing caste in British India as well as distinctions of race or religion for occupying any place or office under the Company.
- With the prospect of declining income from trade, the Company's financial base began to shift from trade and commerce to land revenue, **from business of trade to business of government**. This naturally pushed the Company to go ahead with continuous territorial expansion.

Charter Act of 1853

- It did not renew the Company's Charter for **any specified period**. Instead, it said that Indian territories would remain 'in trust for the Crown, until Parliament should otherwise direct'. Thus, it was clear that the Crown could take over the Company's administration any time now. Now the Company disappeared as a commercial agency, remaining as a political agent for the Crown.
- The **separation of executive and legislative functions** was carried a step further and additional members of the Council were appointed for legislative work. The Law Member was made a full member of the GG's Executive Council and this Council while sitting in its legislative capacity was enlarged by the addition of six members namely—the Chief Justice and a puisne judge of the Calcutta Supreme Court and four representatives, one each from Bengal, Madras, Bombay and the North-Western Provinces. The provincial representatives were to be civil servants of the Company with not less than a standing of 10 years.
- In this way, the **central legislature** was formed, though no Indian element was associated with the Legislative Council. A clear distinction was made between Legislative Councillors and Executive Councillors; legislation was for the first time treated as a special function of the government. The business of the Council was to be conducted on the lines of the British Parliament. Questions could be asked, policy of the Executive Council could be discussed, government could be criticised for its lapses, Bills were referred to Select Committees and legislative business was conducted in public. The Executive Council retained power to veto a bill of the Legislative Council.
- The number of Directors was reduced from 24 to 18 of which 6 were to be appointed by the Crown.
- The **Court of Directors was divested of its patronage** and power of appointments as the services were thrown open to **competitive examinations**, in which no discrimination of any kind was to be made. A Committee headed by Macaulay was appointed in 1854 to enforce this scheme.
- The Court of Directors was empowered to create new Presidency or alter the boundaries of the existing ones to accommodate new territories. Using this power, a separate Lieutenant Governorship was created for **Punjab** in 1859.

Significance of the Act of 1853

Contrary to the framers of the Act (which included Sir Charles Wood, President of the Board of Control), the newly formed Legislative Council displayed a spirit of independence from its very inception and soon developed into an Anglo-Indian House of Commons, questioning every act of the Executive. This forced Charles Wood to later clarify, 'I do not look upon the Legislative Council as some of the young Indians do as the nucleus and beginning of constitutional parliament in India'. Whatever be the clarification, it was aptly clear that the authors of the Act had failed to limit the consequences of the Act to its intentions and the Legislative Council of 1853 proved to be the most significant constitutional provision of the 19th century.

Government of India Act 1858

Factors Leading to the Act

The Act of 1853 had clearly left the door open for the Crown to step in any time and take over the Company's Indian possessions. The Revolt of 1857 gave a death blow to the existing system of governance, gave an immediate push to the demand for the transfer of power form the Company to the Crown. The Bill for the transfer of control of Government of India from the East India Company to the Crown was first introduced by **Lord Palmerston**, the then Prime Minister of the United Kingdom. However, Palmerston had to resign on another issue even before the Bill could be passed. Later, Edward Henry Stanley (who became the first Secretary of State for India) introduced another bill originally titled as 'An Act for the Better Government of India', and it was passed on **2 August 1858**.

Main Provisions

- The Act **ended the Company's rule in India** and power was transferred from the Company to the Crown.
- The Court of Directors and the Board of Control were abolished and their powers transferred to the **Principal Secretary of State for India** and **India Council** (a 15-member Council to aid and advice the Secretary of State. Of the 15 members, 8 were to be appointed by the Crown and 7 by the Court of Directors). They were to govern India in the name of the Crown. The Secretary of State was a member of the British Cabinet and as such responsible to the Parliament. He was required to submit a periodic report on the moral and material progress of India.
- The Governor-General received the title of **Viceroy**, as he was now the direct representative of the Crown.
- The Act **divided the patronage** between the Crown, the Secretary of State in Council and the authorities in India.
- The Act also declared the Secretary of State for India as a **corporate body** who could sue and be sued in England and in India.

Significance of the Act

The Act ushered in a new era in Indian history, bringing an end to the Company's rule in India. At the same time, the transfer of power was more 'formal' than 'substantial'. It was intended that the change of name will immediately condone the past and give a fresh starting point to the empire. In reality, the Act did not change anything in India and only brought about some cosmetic changes in England. Starting from the Regulating Act of 1773, the British Parliament had progressively curtailed the powers of the Court of Directors through a series of statutes and, by 1858, main rules governing India were already those passed by the British Parliament. The Company, in other words, had been a dead political entity long before 1858; only its skin remained, which too was done away with in 1858.

A few months later, the Act was followed by Queen Victoria's proclamation. The royal proclamation was announced on **1 November 1858** at a grand Darbar held at **Allahabad**. The document is also known as the 'Magna Carta of the people of India' and it declared the future policy of the British rule in India.

The Queens' Proclamation of 1858 said among other things:

1. We have taken upon ourselves the said government.
2. We appoint Viscount Canning, to be our first Viceroy and Governor-General in India...to act on our behalf subject to... orders received through one of our Principal Secretaries of State.
3. We announce to the native Princes of India that all treaties made with them by the Company will be accepted.
4. We desire no extension of our territorial possessions.
5. We shall respect the rights, dignity and honour of native Princes as our own.
6. We disclaim alike the desire to impose our convictions (religious) on any of our subjects.
7. It is our further will that our subjects, of whatever race or creed, be freely and impartially admitted to office in our service.
8. We will that generally, in framing the law, due regard be paid to the ancient rights and customs of India.
9. It is our earnest desire to stimulate the peaceful industry of India, to promote works of public utility and to administer the government for the benefit of all subjects' resident therein.
10. Our clemency will be extended to all offenders except those who have been convicted of directly taken part in murder of British subjects.

Previous Years' Questions – Preliminary Exam

1. Match List-I (Acts of Colonial Government of India) with List-II (Provisions) and select the correct answer from the options that follow the list. **[UPSC 2002]**

List-I (Acts of Colonial Government of India)	List-II (Provisions)
A. Charter Act, 1813	1. Set up a Board of Control in Britain to fully regulate the East India Company.
B. Regulating Act 1773	2. Company's trade Monopoly in India was ended.
C. Act of 1858	3. The power to govern was transferred from the East India Company to the British Crown.
D. Pitt's India Act	4. The Company's Directors were asked to present to the British Government all correspondence and documents pertaining to the administration of the Company.

Codes

	A	B	C	D
(a)	2	4	3	1
(b)	1	3	4	2
(c)	2	3	4	1
(d)	1	4	3	2

2. Which one of the following Acts of British India strengthened the Viceroy's authority over his executive Council by substituting 'Portfolio' or departmental system for corporate functioning? **[UPSC 2002]**
   (a) Indian Councils Act, 1861
   (b) Government of India Act, 1858
   (c) Indian councils Act, 1892
   (d) Indian councils Act, 1909
3. Which one of the following provisions was **NOT** made in the Charter act of 1833? **[UPSC 2003]**
   (a) The trading activities of the East India Company were to be abolished.
   (b) The designation of the supreme authority was to be changed as the Governor-General of India-in-Council
   (c) All law-making powers to be conferred on Governor-General-in-Council
   (d) An Indian was to be appointed as a law member in the Governor-General's Council
4. Consider the following statements: **[UPSC 2005]**
   1. Warren Hastings was the first Governor-General who established the regular police force in India on the British pattern.
   2. Supreme Court was established at Calcutta by the Regulating Act 1773.
   3. The Indian Penal Code came into effect in the year 1860.

   Which of the statements given above are correct?
   (a) 1 and 2 (b) 2 and 3
   (c) 1 and 3 (d) 1, 2 and 3
5. Consider the following statements: **[UPSC 2006]**
   1. The Charter Act of 1853 abolished East India Company's monopoly of Indian trade.
   2. Under the Government of India Act 1858, the British Parliament abolished the East India Company all together and undertook the responsibility of ruling India directly.

   Which of the statements given above is/are correct?
   (a) 1 only (b) 2 only
   (c) Both 1 and 2 (d) Neither 1 or 2
6. What was/were the object/objects of Queen Victoria's Proclamation (1858)? **[UPSC 2014]**
   1. To disclaim any intention to annex Indian states.
   2. To place the Indian Administration under the British Crown.
   3. To regulate East India Company's trade with India.

   Select the correct answer from the following options.
   (a) 1 and 2 only (b) 2 only
   (c) 1 and 3 only (d) 1, 2 and 3
7. Consider the following statements about 'the Charter Act of 1813': **[UPSC 2019]**
   1. It ended the trade monopoly of the East India Company in India except for trade in tea and trade with China.
   2. It asserted the sovereignty of the British Crown over the Indian territories held by the Company.
   3. The revenues of India were now controlled by the British Parliament.

   Which of the statements given above are correct?
   (a) 1 and 2 only (b) 2 and 3 only
   (c) 1 and 3 only (d) 1, 2 and 3
8. By which one of the following Acts was the Governor General of Bengal designated as the Governor General of India? **[UPSC 2023]**
   (a) The Regulating Act
   (b) The Pitt's India Act
   (c) The Charter Act of 1793
   (d) The Charter Act of 1833

Answers

Previous Years' Questions – Preliminary Exam

1. (a)	2. (a)	3. (d)	4. (b)	5. (b)
6. (a)	7. (a)	8. (d)		

3 CHANGES AND IMPACT: INDIAN ADMINISTRATION AND SOCIETY

After Plassey and Buxar, the East India Company emerged as a supreme commercial military power and gradually transformed itself from trader conquerors to rulers. This shift necessitated the establishment of a new legislative and institutional framework for governing the subject population. This process was marked by an initial dependence on existing framework but gradual establishment of new systems and institutions, thus bringing changes to different aspects of Indian life. In this task of formulating state policies, the British were guided by economic and intellectual developments in England, the requirements of the time as well as by the limits of newly established colonial government.

Indian Administration Under the British

The early administration of East India Company was that of a trading corporation. **'Factories'** or trading establishments were run by Company's servants. Less important factories were headed by a senior merchant or a 'factor' while each main factory was headed by a **President,** later called Governor. The main factories later came to be known as Presidencies like Calcutta, Madras and Bombay Presidencies.

The jurisdiction of the Company steadily grew through various processes, and so did its administration.

- In 1698, the Company bought the zamindari rights of villages of **Sutanuti, Calcutta and Govindpur**.
- In 1757, the Company received the zamindari of **24 parganas** near Calcutta.
- In 1760, Mir Qasim rewarded the Company with zamindari rights of **Burdwan, Midnapore and Chittagong.**

After 1764, the Company emerged as the supreme power in Bengal. However, the Company had little intention of making any innovations in Bengal administration and only desired to carry on their profitable trade, collect taxes and maintain British hold over Bengal. Further, direct annexation of Bengal would have created unnecessary complications. Hence, the Company opted for **Dual Government (1765–72)** in theory, with the Company as Diwan and the Nawab as Nazim. The Deputy Subahdar (appointed by the Company) was to function in the interest of the Company, while maintaining a fiction of Mughal sovereignty. Indian officials were allowed to function as before, but under overall supervision of British officials. Even in exercise of Diwani rights, revenue collection was initially carried out by Nawab's deputees. The main stress was on maintenance of law and order so that Company's trade and exploitation of resources could be carried out without disturbance. However, both British as well as Indian officials were corrupt men and only busied themselves in grasping their share in Bengal's plunder, resulting in total administrative breakdown in Bengal.

By 1772, administrative breakdown in Bengal (along with other factors, such as financial crisis faced by the East India Company) led to the passing of **Regulating Act of 1773** to control Company's administration. The Act remodelled the Company's constitution at home as well as in India. Gradually, as the Company transformed from a commercial body to a commercial-cum political body, it realised that it could hold its empire together only by evolving a suitable system of administration. Such a system evolved from time to time with economic developments in Britain and with changing imperial interests.

Until 1813, the British interests were restricted to the following-

- Controlling financial resources through taxation
- Sustaining British superiority in terms of monopoly of trade

Both these interests could be fulfilled without disturbing the existing administrative system. Hence, Warren Hastings (1772–85) and Cornwallis (1786–93) only modified the administration from the top, thus initiating the process of change, leaving the rest of the system untouched.

After 1813, the British society began to face drastic changes as a consequence of the Industrial Revolution. Now, the British interests mainly lay in converting India into-

- A market for British manufactures
- A source of raw materials for their industries

This required greater penetration into Indian economy and society and the existing legal system had to be overhauled to promote modern business and regulate various economic transactions with the help of modern laws, giving rise to the need for new administrative and legal systems. Broadly speaking, the entire administrative structure of the East India Company composed the following-

1. Home Government in London
2. Government of India
3. Financial and Revenue administration
4. Organisation of Civil Services, Army and Police
5. Organisation of Judicial Services
6. Economic Policy
7. Social Policy
8. Educational Policy

Ideas Influencing Indian Administration

The intellectual current called **Utilitarianism** with James Mill, Jeremy Bentham, David Ricardo and John Stuart Mill as its exponents, was largely responsible for the kind of administration and judicial system that was put in place in India under the Company's rule. Their ideas on Indian problems and their prescriptions were as follows:

- **Problems**
  - Indian society was backward, decadent and despotic. The people were completely devoid of values of rationalism and individualism, which were seen as essential building blocks for a modern society.
  - There was absence of any security for individual rights.
  - There was degradation of the many by the few, resulting in servility, superstition, poverty and crime.
- **Prescriptions**
  - Such a society could be improved through proper legislation which would impart 'human justice' as opposed to 'divine justice'. Administration based on justice and uniformity could convert India

into a progressive society. In brief, Utilitarianism chiefly stood for an advocacy of the rule of law; the laws were to be scientifically defined and embodied in a written form in codes. These were to be implemented by a body of local courts accessible to every man.

Note: In 1819, James Mill was included as a member of the executive government of the East India Company.

Home Government in London

The Company's administration was looked after by two institutions in England—Court of Proprietors (CoP) and Court of Directors (CoD). The CoD was the Company's executive in England and comprised of 24 Directors who were elected by a body of share-holders knows as the CoP. Beginning from the Regulating Act of 1773, the powers and privileges of the CoD were progressively curtailed by successive acts of the British Parliament, until they were completely taken over by the Crown in 1858.

Government of India

The powers and privileges enjoyed by the Company in India were derived from two sources—partly from the British Crown and Parliament and partly from the Mughal emperors and regional kings. The Company's factories in Bengal and on the east and west coast were administered at each of its principle settlements at Calcutta (Fort William), Madras (Fort St. George) and Bombay by a President (or Governor) and a Council comprising of senior servants of the Company. Initially, the three 'Presidencies' were independent of one another and answerable directly to the Court of Directors in London. The administration of Government of India was first centralised (1773–1858) and then decentralised (Act of 1861 onwards) by successive acts of the British Parliament.

Financial and Revenue Administration

After the victories at Plassey and Buxar, the Company emerged as a commercial-cum-military-cum-political power in Bengal. Henceforth, land revenue emerged as its main source of income. Other sources included customs and excise duties, tribute received from Indian states, monopolies, opium and salt trade, etc. The Company's land revenue policy in India and its impact has been discussed in detail in the chapter 'Changes and Impact: Indian Economy'.

Organisation of Civil Services, Army and Police

The chief goal of British administration in India was the maintenance of law and order for the perpetuation of British rule in India. Keeping this goal in mind, the British administration was based upon three main pillars, namely the Civil Service, the Police and the Army.

Civil Service The term 'civil service' was used by the Company to differentiate them from their military and ecclesiastical employees. The main function of civil service was to implement laws and collect revenue. The civil service worked according to a set of rules as opposed to the personal whims of a monarch and formed a distinct feature of the Company's administration.

In the beginning, the Court of Directors exercised the patronage of nominating the civil servants. The Directors nominated their favourites, often their sons and relatives, as posting in India gave them ample opportunity to make quick money by indulging in private trade and bribery.

Governor General Lord Cornwallis tried to address this issue of corruption by banning private trade and raising salaries (e.g. the salary of the Collector of a district was raised to ₹1500 a month and 1 per cent commission on the revenue collected from his district). At this time, the Company's civil service became one of the highest paid services in the world. Simultaneously, Cornwallis also adopted the short-sighted policy of Europeanisation of services and no Indian could enter the Civil Service. In fact, it was officially laid down in 1793 that all higher posts in administration worth more than 500 pounds a year in salary could be held by Englishmen only. In view of his efforts to reform, modernise and rationalise the civil service, Cornwallis is also known as the **'Father of Civil Service in India'**.

To further deal with the problem of corruption, Lord Wellesley introduced **training** for civil servants in 1798. Accordingly, in 1800, **Fort William College** at Calcutta was founded which also trained civil servants in Indian languages, literature and sciences. However, the College did not find favour with the Directors of the Company and in 1806 they replaced it with the East India College founded at **Haileybury** in England which ran a training course of two years for young officers appointed for services in the East. For the next 50 years, the Company's civil servants were a product of the Haileybury College.

The Charter of 1833 carried Section 87 which introduced **limited competition** for civil service. The Court of Directors were now required to nominate four times the vacancy. Only one-fourth of them were selected on the basis of a competitive exam.

The Charter of 1853 took away the privilege of the Directors to appoint the civil servants and introduced **open public competition**. A committee headed by Macaulay was set up to make recommendations regarding age, qualification, etc. Subsequently, the Haileybury College was abolished (1858) and the competitive examinations became the sole responsibility of Civil Service Commission. This competitive exam was to be held every year in London in English language, thus making it virtually impossible for an Indian to compete in it. Thus, these provisions did not materially change the policy of keeping the Civil Service of the Company a close preserve of the British nationals.

Though, in 1863, **Satyendranath Tagore** (brother of Rabindranath Tagore) became the first Indian to enter the Civil Services, the number of Indians in the service remained negligible. As a sop to Indians, the Company later created the uncovenanted posts of Deputy Collector, placed between the Collector and the Tehsildar, to which experienced Indian could hope to rise.

The collector (a civil servant) was the senior most officer in the district who was chiefly responsible for collection of revenue. In this task, he was assisted by a Tehsildar who was an Indian.

The Indian Civil Service developed into one of the most powerful services in the world, known as the **steel frame** which sustained the British rule. Given their enormous power, the Civil Servants came to believe that they had a divine right to rule India, opposed everything that was progressive in Indian life and became a target of Indian nationalists during the freedom movement. After 1947, independent India continued with this system of civil service which is retained almost in its original form till date.

Army The bulk of the Company's army comprised of Indian soldiers (in 1857, Indians comprised 86 per cent of the total strength of the Company's army). This was mainly because maintaining an exclusive British army would have been very expensive. However, all the officers in the army, as in other branches of administration, were British and the highest an Indian could reach was at the level of a Subedar. Yet, it is surprising that a handful of British officers could control a predominantly Indian army. This is mainly attributed to the absence of modern nationalism in India at that time. Moreover, the Company was a good paymaster to Indians who already had the tradition of loyalty to the salt! The main task of the army was to keep India under subjugation. A secondary task was to fight England's wars with the Russians and the French and other enemies.

Police The Police as the third pillar of administration was again a creation of **Cornwallis**. Prior to this, policing was done by Zamindars with the help of armed retainers. Cornwallis disbanded these armed retainers and replaced them with an organised police force directly under the command of the Company. The police force was divided into **thanas (circles) headed by a Daroga** who was an Indian. In the beginning, this force was headed by a District Judge but later handed over to the civil service. The main task of the police was to keep crimes under check and prevent conspiracy against the British rule. In the 20th century, the police was deployed on a large scale mainly to contain the rising tide of national movement.

Organisation of Judicial Services

The pre-British judicial setup in India was a diverse mix of Hindu law of the Shastras, the Muslim Koranic law as well as the customary law backed by the ruling authority. Once the Europeans began to settle in India they could not accept the Muslim law that talked about amputation of limbs or stoning of criminals as penalties, nor could they accept special privileges for the Brahmins.

Rudimentary Judicial Framework It was Warren Hastings who first tried to build up the initial judicial framework based on Mughal model and set up the Diwani Adalat (decided civil cases, appeals went to Sadr Diwani Adalat) and the Faujdari Adalat (decided criminal cases, appeals went to Sadr Nizamat Adalat, followed Muslim law). These courts followed both Muslim and Hindu laws.

Europeanisation of Judiciary Lord Cornwallis brought further changes in this framework and gave a stable structure to Indian Judiciary. He abolished the District Faujdari Adalats presided over by Indian judges and replaced them with four circuit courts presided over by European covenanted servants who decided the cases with the help of Qazis and Muftis. Similarly, he also abolished the Sadr Nizamat Adalat at Murshidabad and replaced it with a similar court set up at Calcutta comprising of the Governor General and members of the Supreme Council assisted by the Chief Qazi and two Muftis.

Separation of Judicial from Executive Functions In 1793, Cornwallis compiled his judicial reforms in the form of the famous **Cornwallis Code** based on the principle of separation of powers. The Code divested the Collector of all his judicial powers and left him with the duty of revenue administration alone. The judicial powers were given to a new class of officer-the District Judge. In this way, the separation of judicial from executive functions was first made under Cornwallis.

Reform of Criminal Law An important feature of the new judicial setup under the British was that enough tolerance was shown towards existing civil and criminal laws. Only the most important modifications were introduced here and there as a complete overhaul of the system was neither needed nor desirable at that time.

Cornwallis went ahead with reforms in criminal law, which the Mohammedans took to be divinely ordained, and set up a judicial system based on **principle of equity** and western notion of justice. He replaced religious or personal law of the ruler or his local agent with written (and later codified) **secular law** and the sovereignty of law was proclaimed. Punishments such as amputation of limbs and other body parts were replaced by imprisonment or fines. Non-Muslims were allowed to testify against Muslims in criminal cases, not permitted so far by Muslim law of evidence.

However, the reforms by Cornwallis produced many undesirable effects as well. The secular code was complicated and unfamiliar to the common man. Lawyers, therefore, had to be employed that added to the litigation costs; people could no longer hope to get affordable justice. Indian judicial functionaries like panchayats, zamindars and qazis were replaced by European judges ignorant of the habits and customs of the Indian people. People now had to come to the district towns which made the process quite lengthy and cases dragged on for years; the common man was thus denied speedy and affordable justice. For instance, a zamindari in Madras went into litigation in 1832 on account of dispute regarding inheritance and debt. The judgement was finally delivered only in 1896, after 64 years! Lastly, like other branches of administration, even the judiciary ultimately served the interests of the Company, often at the cost of true justice to the common people.

The Charter Act of 1793 also required that all laws relating to rights of persons and property be printed with translation in Indian languages so that people can know about their rights and immunities. In this way, this Act laid the foundation of governance based on **written laws** in British India in place of personal rules of past rulers.

Recognition of Personal Civil Law The British, however, allowed personal civil laws of various Indian communities to continue in civil matters such as those concerning marriage, divorce, adoption, succession, inheritance, etc.

Codification of Laws Notably, the British also systematised the entire process of law making and law keeping. Under the Charter Act of 1833, all law-making authority was vested in the Governor-General-in-Council. An **Indian Law Commission** headed by Lord Macaulay was appointed for the **codification of existing laws**. The Indian Penal Code and the Codes of Civil and Criminal Procedure were enacted by its efforts. These codes were applicable throughout the country and for the **first time**, all Indians came under the ambit of a single system of laws. Further, the laws were now open to judicial interpretations and subsequent amendments.

Rule of Law and Equality before Law The British deserve the credit for introducing in India the modern concept of rule of law, which meant that administration was to be carried out as per the formulated laws and not according to the whims and fancies of any ruler (yet, the police and the civil servants continued to exercise a great deal of extra-legal powers!). Equality before law meant that all persons were equal in the eyes of law irrespective of their religion, caste or class. For instance, a Brahmin and a shudra, a zamindar and a peasant, shall all be equal before law.

Though the Europeans were kept out of their fold and there were different laws and different courts for them, both these modern concepts of justice significantly contributed to a sense of equality among Indians. The new judicial system set in motion a process of **unification of India**; India was now one unit, at least in judicial terms.

Extent of Indian Participation in Administration and Judiciary In the new judicial and administrative system introduced by the British, **Indians were excluded from higher offices** as a matter of policy since the task of British consolidation could not be left to Indians. Though Indianisation of covenanted services (services held by Englishmen only) was done eventually, it was mainly done in order to cut down state expenditure even as the British government provided justification for the same in terms of justice, moral obligation and local needs.

Economic Policy

This area has been extensively covered in the chapter 'Changes and Impact: Indian Economy'.

Social Policy

The idea of British responsibility towards welfare of Indian people did not emerge immediately after Plassey and Buxar, but only during the period of dual government (1765–72) when the Company's servants carried out open and unashamed plunder of Bengal. A servant of the Company wrote in 1769, 'It must give pain to an Englishman to have reason to think that since the accession of the Company to the Diwani the condition of the people of this country has been worse than it was before...this fine country which flourished under the most despotic and arbitrary government, is verging towards its ruin'. Adam Smith preferred to call the Court of Proprietors as the court 'for appointment of plunderers of India'.

The corruption and plunder carried out by the Company in Bengal attracted severe criticism and increased the pressure on the British Parliament to regulate the affairs of the Company, leading to the passing of the Regulating Act of 1773. It was through this Act that the British government accepted for the first time the power and responsibility (though partial) for Company's administration. Henceforth, the process continued through subsequent Acts.

Social Policy During 1773-1813 (Blend of Orientalism and Political Pragmatism)

Warren Hastings, the First Governor-General, was in favour of an administration which was well versed in Indian languages and responsible to Indian traditions. He personally encouraged study and translation of Indian texts. Under his patronage, Bengali became the first vernacular to be studied systematically by the Englishmen. Hastings encouraged a close associate **Nathaniel Halhed** to compile a set of Hindu customary and religious laws and translate them into English - the translation was published in 1776 as 'A Code of Gentoo Laws'. In 1778, Halhed also published a **Grammar of the Bengali Language**. In 1784, the first English translation of the Bhagavad Gita by Charles Wilkins appeared in Banaras. In 1784 itself, Hastings supported the establishment of the **Asiatic Society by Willaim Jones** which helped in the 'rediscovery' of early traditions of Indians. In 1781, Hastings had set up the **Calcutta Madrasa** for the study of Persian and Arabic languages. In this way, the early social policy during the days of Warren Hastings reflected a happy combination of British Orientalism and political pragmatism.

Social Policy After 1813 (Cautious Intervention)

Until 1813, the British broadly followed a policy of non-interference in socio-cultural and religious life of the Indians. However, after 1813, there was a change in British attitude towards Indian problems in the aftermath of industrial and intellectual Revolutions in Britain and Europe, which filled the Englishmen with the modern liberal ideas of humanism, liberty, equality and fraternity. Several officers who came to India after 1813 were deeply influenced by these ideals and wished to change the socio-cultural life of the Indians along modern lines. However, the existing officials were ready to modernise Indians only to the extent it made them better customers of British goods and reconciled them to the British rule. The challenge therefore was to maintain a workable balance between the two forces and what emerged was a policy of 'cautious intervention' in Indian social institutions.

The term social policy covers a wide range of policies pertaining to law, social customs, family, criminality, education, status ranking, etc. Given the wide range of social issues, and that some of these have been dealt with earlier, we shall concentrate here on spread of Christianity, social customs of infanticide, sati, widow-remarriage, slavery and education. It is also noteworthy that Bengal, being the headquarters of the Company's government, emerged as the **social laboratory** where the British developed some of their early state policies with the view to regulating the collective life of subject population.

Religion

Spread of Christianity Christian missionaries and religious persons such as Charles Grunt (Chairman of Court of Directors) and William Wilberforce asserted that Hinduism was based on superstition, idolatry and domination of the priestly classes. They encouraged the spread of Christianity which, in their view, was the only true religion while all others were false. They also extended enthusiastic support to the policy of modernising and Westernising India in the hope that this would eventually lead to conversions to Christianity and encouraged the establishment of several modern schools, colleges and hospitals. Subsequently, under the pressure of missionary lobby, the British Parliament inserted a provision in the **Charter of 1813** allowing **missionaries** to go to India and even settle there under a license. But after the revolt of 1857, this attitude was reversed and the British began to support orthodox elements in society including promotion of casteism and communalism.

Social Customs

Female infanticide The evil custom of female infanticide was the first social custom to be suppressed by the British. It was prevalent in many parts of India, especially among the Rajputs, Mewatis and the Jats. Girls in these communities were seen as an economic burden, leading to the practice of killing female infants by various dubious practices including starvation and poisoning.

- **Jonathan Duncan**, the Resident of Banaras, was the first official to suppress infanticide.
- Infanticide was later banned by Bengal Regulations of 1795 and 1802 **(Regulation VI of 1802)**, only once the British were convinced that such a law will not evoke any major public outrage.

Sati and Widow Remarriage

Sati was the next social evil to be suppressed by the British. Sati was practiced in almost all parts of India with maximum cases being reported from Bengal.

- In 1789, **Colebrooke**, the Collector of Shahabad, stopped an act of sati and tried to prove that sati was against Vedic culture.
- In 1813, the government fixed the minimum age for a sati at 16 years. It also declared that a widow whose child was less than three years could not become sati unless the child was entrusted in someone else's care.

- Even as the government shied away from immediately suppressing this custom, a group of Bengali intelligentsia led by **Ram Mohan Roy** actively agitated for the abolition of sati. Moved by the loss of his sister-in-law to sati, Ram Mohan wrote a series of articles to build a strong public opinion against the custom and his journal **'Sambad Kaumudi'** became the main organ of the agitation. Ram Mohan's efforts were opposed by a group of orthodox Hindus led by **Kasinath Tarkavagish** and **'Samachar Chandrika'** emerged as their main mouthpiece.
- In 1829 sati was finally abolished in Bengal Presidency by means of a legislation passed by Governor General **Bentinck**. In fact, Bentinck made it a crime to associate with the act of sati in any form. The legislation was later extended to Bombay and Madras presidencies in 1830.
- In 1856, the **Hindu Widow Remarriage Act** was passed which legalised remarriage of widows and declared issues from such marriages as legitimate.

It is noteworthy that the initiative for abolishing infanticide as well as sati chiefly came from individual administrators, Christian missionaries and Indian intelligentsia even as the Company's government delayed total suppression of these customs for the extreme fear of inciting a violent Indian reaction.

Slavery

Slavery was a system of labour exploitation prevalent in India. Once again, British attitude towards slavery was marked by procrastination.

- Evangelical propaganda against slavery was led by **William Wilberforce**.
- The **Charter Act of 1833** directed the Government of India to take measures for the abolition of slavery.
- Slavery was finally abolished by the **Indian Slavery Act of 1843** (also known as Act V of 1843).

Both European and Indian social reformers believed that no amount of social legislation alone could eradicate social evils, until people were themselves convinced about the desirability of a law. And for such an attitudinal change, education was a key intervention. Yet, social and religious institutions were an area in which the British intervened with great caution. The interventions came after much procrastination and adequate pragmatic political consideration. It was also seen that the impact of most of these legislations was limited and did not evoke any violent Indian response. All the same, even this policy of limited social intervention was abandoned by the colonial government in the wake of the Revolt of 1857 and replaced by support to orthodox elements of society.

Educational Policy

Education in Pre-British Era In the pre-colonial times, the indigenous system of education comprised of Madrasas and Maktabs for Muslims and Tols and Pathshalas for Hindus. Schools were funded by rich zamindars and the state played little role in school education. Curriculum mainly comprised of study of religious scriptures and philosophical texts which were rather crammed than understood; as such the spirit of enquiry and rationalism hardly developed in India. Languages like Sanskrit, Persian and subjects like grammar, law, medicine, etc., were also taught. The system mostly followed oral tradition in the absence of printing press and in general, women were denied formal education. The main merit of this system was that it provided basic literacy to meet the needs of day today life; a major drawback was the lack of scientific and secular learning.

During the 18th century, the numerous political convulsions created situations that were hardly conducive for any intellectual pursuits. Both Hindu and Muslim seats of learning were in a state of decay.

Early European Efforts in the Field of Education The Western Christian Missionaries deserve the credit for introducing Modern System of Education in India. They were the first to set up modern schools and publish literary works. In 1556, at Goa, the first modern printing press in India was established by the Portuguese Missionaries. The Danish missionaries published a Tamil dictionary. However, their intention behind these efforts was not to educate people as an end in itself but as a means to evangelisation.

Similarly, the English Company, as per its charter, was initially obliged to bring Christian missionaries on their ships and protect them. These missionaries too started their proselytizing activities, opened schools for the converted and taught them the Bible.

Education under the Company Orientalist policy Situation changed once the Company began occupying territories and ruling over the native population. Missionary activities were criticised by the Indian upper castes whose support was needed by the Company to consolidate its position in India. Hence, immediately after the Company came to power, it preferred not to interfere in social and religious life (including the educational sphere) of the subject population. It even restricted the entry of missionaries in India. Yet, the politico-economic compulsions forced the Company to adopt a pro-native education policy.

With time the Company faced increasing pressure from different quarters such as the Missionaries (particularly the Serampore Missionaries) and a section of British statesmen (the Liberals) to take responsibility for promotion of learning. Accordingly, the Company made some half-hearted efforts to foster oriental learning. These were as follows:

Work of the Orientalists

- In 1781, Calcutta Madrasa was set up by **Warren Hastings** for the study of Persian and Arabic.
- In 1791, Banaras Sanskrit College was set up by **Jonathan Duncan** for the cultivation of the laws, literature and religion of the Hindus. The aim of both these institutions was to provide a regular supply of qualified Indians to help in Company's administration.
- In 1784, Asiatic Society of Bengal was set up by **William Jones**.
- In 1800, Fort William College was founded by **Lord Wellesley** to train British administrators equipped with oriental knowledge.

Apart from starting a few Persian and Sanskrit higher learning centers as mentioned above, the Company did not spend any money on school education. This educational policy of the Company to support centers of oriental higher learning is termed as orientalist policy.

The Company's charter was renewed every 20 years. The **Charter Act of 1813** granted license to missionaries to enter India and carry out their activities. Further, under the pressure of missionary lobby, the British Parliament inserted a provision in the Charter providing for a yearly fund of **₹1 lakh** for promotion of literature and sciences among Indian subjects. The Charter is historically significant as the first formal educational policy of the East India Company. It was for the first time that the Court of Directors accepted state responsibility for promotion of learning in India. But even this small sum was not released by the Company until 1823.

Anglicist Policy 1813 onwards, the Company's mercantile interests were replaced by industrial interests who saw India as a market for their manufactures. An influential politician Charles Grant (later became chairman of Board of Directors of the Company) and his lobby particularly advocated English eduction and came to be known as the Anglicists. Moreover, as the British Empire in India expanded, the administrative needs of the Company increased and an all European staff was proving to be too expensive. Hence, the need arose for affordable local staff to serve at the clerical and middle level, particularly in Revenue and Judicial departments. Naturally, this staff was required to have a working knowledge of English language, apart from the knowledge of Persian and vernaculars; and gave rise to the Orientalists vs. Anglicists debate.

The Liberals They were the followers of Liberalism, i.e., the belief in individual freedom, gender and racial equality, democracy and human rights. John Locke, an English philosopher and a political theorist, one of the most influential of Enlightenment thinkers, is widely regarded as the **'father of Liberalism'**.

Serampore Missionaries They were the pioneering English missionaries, namely William Carey, William Ward and Joshua Marshman (known as the Serampore Trio). Since the English Company's government discouraged missionary work in its territories, they chose Serampore (then known as Fredericknagore) near Calcutta but in Danish India, to carry out their activities. Subsequently, a Mission and a Press were established at Serampore in 1799.

During 1800–34, the press printed the Bible in several Indian vernaculars. In 1802-03, Bengali translations of Ramayana and Mahabharata were published, marking the first ever appearance of the two great epics in printed form. The press also printed vernacular textbooks, grammars, dictionaries, Hindu mythological tales, newspapers etc.

Orientalists-Anglicists Controversy It referred to the prolonged debate on whether the Company should promote Indian (Oriental) or Western (Anglicist) learning. Till 1823 the educational fund allocated by the Charter of 1813 remained unutilised. Even in 1823, when **the General Committee of Public Instruction** was set up, the 10 members of the committee remained divided in two equal groups namely the Orientalists (led by **HT Prinsep**) and the Anglicists (who advocated that the funds be utilised for promotion of Western subjects through English medium).

The Stalemate was broken only when Governor General Bentinck appointed GB Macaulay as the Chairman of the Committee (both of them were Anglicists). Macaulay showed great contempt for Indian customs and literature and had once stated, 'a single shelf of a good European library was worth the whole native literature of India and Arabia'. According to him, the immediate aim of education was to prepare a class of persons who could occupy subordinate positions in colonial government and help in administering the natives; while the long term aim was to westernize the Indians with a taste for western products, facilitating the conversion of India into a market for British goods.

The debate was finally settled in favour of the Anglicists with the presentation of the famous **Macaulay's Minute** on 2 February 1835, formally accepted by the government of Bentinck in a resolution passed on 7 March 1835. Bentink's landmark decision paved the way for emergence of 'English as the most important and powerful language'; and origin of education in Modern India can be traced back to Macaulay's Minute.

As per the Minute it was decided to devote the limited resources to the teaching of Western learning in English medium to the upper classes only. Education of masses could not be attempted in the limited resources and thus Macaulay instilled an implicit faith in the **'downward filtration theory'** (that education would gradually filter down from the elites to the masses). He believed that the English educated Indians would in turn enrich the vernacular, enabling western knowledge to reach the masses. Hence, the development of vernacular was seen ancillary to the spread of western education.

Accordingly, the government soon opened a few English schools and colleges at the cost of a large number of elementary schools. In higher courts, Persian was replaced by English as the court language by **Bentinck** in 1835. By a further notification of 1838, all state funds for oriental learning were declared closed. In 1844, it was further announced that applicant for government employment should possess knowledge of English. In this way, the traditional Indian system of education gradually withered away in the absence of official support.

Note: In the North-West Provinces, James Thomason (Lieutenant Governor during 1843–53) tried to develop a comprehensive scheme of village education through vernacular, known as **Thomason's Plan**.

Role of Bengali Intellectuals It is widely believed that the main factor which tipped the scale in favour of the Anglicists was the economic factor, duly highlighted by a group of Indians who wanted an education system that would help them earn their livelihood. Even without discounting the value of oriental learning, they believed that it was generally more beneficial for Indians to receive English education. A notable role in this regard was played by **Raja Ram Mohan Roy**. Protesting against the government proposal to strengthen the Sanskrit College, he wrote to Lord Amherst in 1823 that Sanskrit education could, 'only be expected to load the minds of youth with grammatical niceties and metaphysical distinctions of life which are of little or no practical use to their possessors or to the society'. Clearly, Ram Mohan's protests did not go unheeded.

The Orientalists The Orientalists were in favor of vernacular education embedded in indigenous culture and civilization.

The Anglicists The Anglicists were in favour of Western education in English language only and included various groups in England, such as the Evangelicals, the Liberals and the Utilitarians. The Evangelicals were convinced about the superiority of Christian ideas and hoped that modern education would destroy the existing faith of Indians and help them in converting people to Christianity. As for the Utilitarians, they were convinced about the superiority of modern Western knowledge and were highly critical of Indian religion and culture.

The Anglicists included persons like Charles Grunt, Thomas Babington Macaulay and James Mill. Western educated Indians, led by **Ram Mohan Roy** also advocated study of Western knowledge and considered it as 'key to the treasures of scientific and democratic thought of modern West'. He joined hands with David Hare and founded the **Hindu College at Calcutta** (later known as Presidency College) in March 1817 for promotion of secular education (it was one of the pioneering institutions to have no religious connection). It imparted instruction mainly in English language and emphasised the study of Western humanities and sciences.

We may now conclude that education policy in India under the British was guided by the following considerations:

- **Political** To serve as an instrument for consolidation of British rule in India, Macaulay aimed of creating a class of persons who would be 'Indians in blood and colour, but English in taste, opinion, morals and intellect'. In the beginning, the class of English educated Indians like lawyers, doctors and engineers did support the British rule in India as their interests were linked with the continuation of the British rule. Thus, initially, Macaulay's dream did materialise.

- **Evangelical** To propagate the Christian religion. Macaulay had written to his father stating, 'No Hindu who has received English education ever remains attached to his religion. It is my firm belief that if plans of education are followed up, there will not be a single idolator among the respectable classes of Bengal thirty years hence'. (Macaulay clearly failed to realise the profundity of Hinduism and his hopes here did not materialise!).
- **Administrative** To obtain a cheap supply of clerks (educated Indians on subordinate posts in Company's administration).
- **Commercial** To raise the demand for British manufactures and create new markets for British goods as modern educated Indians were expected to be British in their taste.
- **Moral** To inculcate a new set of values that justified the colonial rule and glorified the British ways.

Wood's Education Despatch (1854) Sir Charles Wood, the President of the Board of Control (1852–55) and later the Secretary of State for India (1859–66), sincerely believed in the superiority of the English race and that the English institutions could serve as a useful model for the world. In 1854, he sent a comprehensive dispatch on the scheme of future education to the Government of India, famously known as the Wood's Despatch. The document was the first comprehensive plan for the spread of education and came to be considered as the **Magna Carta of English education** in India. It recommended a properly articulated scheme of education from the primary school to the University for the whole of British India. Its main features may be summarised as follows:

- At least on paper, the Wood's Despatch repudiated the 'downward filtration theory' and ordered the state to take up responsibility for education of the masses.
- It declared that the aim of government's education policy was the teaching of Western education. Wood had clearly stated, 'the education we desire to extend in India is ...European knowledge' and reiterated that the aim of education in India was the diffusion of European knowledge through the use of both English and vernacular.
- It further clarified that Indian languages shall be the **medium of instruction** in primary schools, followed by Anglo-vernacular schools in middle and high school levels and education in English medium at College and University level.
- It also recommended the following:
  - Creation of a Department of Public Instruction in each province.
  - Establishment of a network of graded schools-elementary, middle and high schools.
  - Establishment of **University at Calcutta, Bombay and Madras** on the model of the London University.
  - Setting up a system of **grants-in-aid** for financial help to foster private enterprise in education.
  - Setting up of Technical Schools and Colleges (vocational instruction was emphasised).
  - Setting up Teachers' Training Institutions and vernacular schools.
  - The Despatch also made recommendations in support of education for women.

Almost all the above recommendations were implemented.

- In 1857, Universities were set up in Calcutta, Bombay and Madras. These universities merely functioned as examining bodies and there was no direct teaching. **Bankim Chandra Chatterjee**, the novelist, was one of the first two graduates of Calcutta University.

- Girls' Schools set up mostly by Bethune's efforts were brought under the grant-in-aid system.
- Similarly, in Bombay and Madras also, several missionary schools were established.

In this way, by 1850s, the foundation for English education was laid by the British. The next fifty years witnessed rapid westernisation of education system in India and the indigenous system was replaced by the English system.

Education of Women

In the first half of 19th century, female education owed its spread to missionary activities and initiatives of some zealous philanthropic individuals.

- The first step in the field was taken by Christian missionaries and in 1819, the Calcutta Female Juvenile Society was set up by them.
- In 1849, Hindu Balika Vidyalaya (a Girls' School in Calcutta; later renamed as Bethune School) was founded by JED Bethune, President of the Council of Education.
- Lord Dalhousie (1848–56) is credited to be the first Governor General to give official support to female education and supported Bethune's experiment.
- Wood's Dispatch of 1854 also emphasised the need for female education.

However, after the Revolt of 1857, the British slashed educational expenditures and henceforth women's education was fostered almost entirely by some individuals and associations.

In a final analysis, the spread of English education in India came with its own **merits and demerits**. On one hand, western education broadened the horizon of knowledge and infused a new spirit of rationalism among younger generation. Modern ideas spread through the educated Indians, political parties, press etc. and included the ideas of democracy and nationalism.

On the other hand, the reality was that neither the Company nor the Crown was really interested in promoting any kind of learning in India. Changes in education system were made to promote British interests such as supply of clerks, creation of market for British goods and justify the colonial rule. A meagre sum was allocated for promotion of learning activities. This sum was spent in the establishment of a handful of English schools and colleges at the cost of mass education with the net effect that literacy was hardly better in 1921 than in 1821. The filtration theory did not work in practice and instead created a linguistic and cultural divide between the educated few and the illiterate masses. Scientific and technical education and women's education was also neglected as it lacked usefulness in the eyes of the British. By 1857, there were only 3 medical colleges in the country in Calcutta, Bombay and Madras (1835). And the only good engineering college at Roorkee (1847) was open only for Europeans and Eurasians. Emphasis on English and high fees for schools and colleges made education a virtual monopoly of the rich. For the next 100 years, education was so very limited that it even failed to compensate for the destruction of the traditional education system!

To sum up, it was in the 19th century that the British put in place new systems of administration and judiciary. While they benefitted the British by providing greater control and penetration into India, they benefitted the Indians by uniting them under uniform administrative and judicial framework and provided ground for the first stirrings of national consciousness.

Note: To read about Development of Education Post 1857, refer to Appendix.

Previous Years' Questions – Preliminary Exam

1. What is the correct chronological sequence of the following? **[UPSC 1997]**
   1. Wood's Education despatch
   2. Macaulay's minute on education
   3. The Sargent Education Report
   4. Indian Education (Hunter Commission)

   Choose the correct answer from the following options.

   (a) 2 1 4 3 (b) 2 1 3 4
   (c) 1 2 4 3 (d) 4 3 1 2
2. Which of the following was the aim of education as stated by the Wood's despatch of 1854? **[UPSC 2002]**
   (a) The creation of employment opportunities for native Indians.
   (b) The spread of western culture in India.
   (c) The promotion of literacy among the people using English medium of language.
   (d) The introduction of scientific research and rationalism in the traditional Indian education.
3. By a regulation in 1793, the District Collector was deprived of his judicial powers and made the collecting agent only. What was the reason for such regulation? **[UPSC 2010]**
   (a) Lord Cornwallis felt that the District Collector's efficiency of revenue collection would enormously increase without the burden of other work.
   (b) Lord Cornwallis felt that judicial power should compulsorily be in the hands of Europeans while Indians can be given the job of revenue collection in the district.
   (c) Lord Cornwallis was alarmed at the extent of power concentrated in the District Collector and felt that such absolute power was undesirable in one person.
   (d) The judicial work demanded a deep knowledge of India and a good training in law and Lord Cornwallis felt that District Collector should be only a revenue collector.
4. Regarding: Wood's Dispatch, which of the following statements are true? **[UPSC 2018]**
   1. Grants-in-Aid system was introduced.
   2. Establishment of universities was recommended.
   3. English as a medium of instruction at all levels of education was recommended.

   Select the correct answer using the code given below:

   (a) 1 and 2 only (b) 2 and 3 only
   (c) 1 and 3 only (d) 1, 2 and 3
5. Which of the following led to the introduction of English Education in India? **[UPSC 2018]**
   1. Charter Act of 1813
   2. General Committee of Public Instruction, 1823
   3. Orientalist and Anglicist Controversy

   Select the correct answer using the code given below:

   (a) 1 and 2 only (b) 2 only
   (c) 1 and 3 only (d) 1, 2 and 3
6. With reference to educational institutions during colonial rule in India, consider the following pairs: **[UPSC 2018]**
   1. Sanskrit College at Benaras- William Jones
   2. Calcutta Madarsa- Warren Hastings
   3. Fort William College- Arthur Wellesley

   Which of the pairs given above is/are correct?

   (a) 1 and 2 (b) 2 only
   (c) 1 and 3 (d) 3 only

Answers

Previous Years' Questions – Preliminary Exam

1. (a) 2. (d) 3. (c) 4. (a) 5. (d)
6. (b)

4 Rise and Growth of National Consciousness

The rise of national consciousness in the 19th century India was partly a result of the British rule and partly occasioned by it. The British rule brought about political, economic and social changes resulting in the oppression of almost all classes of Indian people. All the same, it also brought about uniform system of administration, development of railways, education, post and telegraph and printing press. Though the primary objective of the new administrative framework was to run an effective administration, it also ended up providing favourable conditions for the rise and growth of Indian nationalism. Hence, Indian nationalism grew partly as a result of British colonial rule and partly as a reaction to it.

Factors Responsible for Rise and Growth of Indian Nationalism

The British Rule, along with its various direct and indirect consequences, provided the material, moral and intellectual conditions for the rise and growth of national consciousness in India.

Impact of British Rule

The British had set foot in India to serve their own interests and consequently, the rule they established in India was a colonial one. Thus, **clash of interests** with the subject population was inherent to the British rule in India.

Most classes of Indian society gradually discovered that their interests were suffering at the hands of the British rulers. The peasants realised that the government took away a large part of their produce as tax. It supported the zamindars and the money lenders who exploited them in various ways. The artisans could see that the government had ruined their industry by encouraging foreign competition and had done nothing to compensate them. The workers in industries, mines and plantations saw that their living conditions were pitiable and their labour was thoroughly exploited.

Even the educated middle class and the Indian capitalist class, which had earlier shown faith in British rule, was gradually disillusioned. They were able to see the true nature of British colonial rule in India and how it served the British in keeping India educationally and economically backward.

Thus, the British rule in India evoked a strong reaction from various sections of Indian people (with the only exception of the zamindars, landlords and the princes who remained loyal to the British rule till the end). This united the Indians against their common enemy-the British Raj- in an anti-imperialist movement which gradually took the form of a full-fledged national movement.

The colonial policies of the British rule and their consequences are discussed below-

Direct Consequences of British Rule

- **Economic Exploitation of India** The British rule in India led to the ruin of Indian agriculture and handicraft industries, badly impoverishing the Indian peasants and artisans in the process. The peasants were impoverished owing to heavy land revenue and commercialisation of agriculture. A large number of peasants were reduced to landless labourers (20 per cent of population in 1901).

  Indian artisans and industrialists also suffered as restrictions were imposed on import of Indian manufactured goods in Britain while British manufactured goods were allowed to enter Indian markets freely. The Indian handicrafts could not face competition from machine made goods from Britain and suffered a severe blow. The Indian artisans and industrialists could see that the British tried to use India as source of cheap raw materials for their own industries and as market for their finished goods.

  Thus, various classes of Indian people suffered economic hardships under the British rule. Yet, this discontent could not automatically lead to the rise of national consciousness due to factors such as vastness of the country, lack of means of communication, lack of education, absence of a common language, common system of administration, etc. But these factors were also annoying the British as they were coming in the way of effective British control over the country. Hence, British took several measures with the aim of bringing about ease of governance which simultaneously contributed to the rise of national consciousness among Indians.
- **Unified System of Administration** During British rule, large parts of India were brought under uniform system of administration for ease of governance and better exploitation of resources. Important measures adopted for bringing about this uniformity were related to land revenue administration, police, law and order machinery and judicial system.
- **New Means of Transport and Communication** Driven by administrative convenience, fool-proof defence and economic penetration, the British carried out a planned development of modern means of transport in India. A network of roads was built to link all metropolitan with mofussil areas. 1853 onwards, the British planned to link all presidencies with each other and the hinterland with major ports via the railways.

  The British intention was to develop a cheap means of transport for carrying goods but far more than anything else, the development of railways unified the country. Railways were laid through the length and breadth of the country, bringing the people from different parts of India into closer contact with one another. People from different classes had to buy the same ticket and travel in the same compartment which gave them the opportunity to interact, unite and finally emerge as one nation.

  Post and Telegraph were given impetus. All major towns were linked with telegraph. Letters and newspapers could be sent anywhere in India at the cheap rate of ½ anna or even less, bringing about a transformation in the socio-political life of the people. National literature could now be circulated in every nook and corner of the country. In fact, pan India organisations like the Indian National Congress could not have been conceived in the absence of modern transport and communication facilities.
- **Introduction of Printing Press** Modern press, both English and vernacular, was also an offshoot of the British rule in India. With the introduction of the printing press, a large number

of newspapers and other inexpensive literature emerged, accelerating the pace at which news and views could be exchanged. The literate nationalists used this medium to expose British excesses and spread nationalist ideas across the country.

Some of the prominent nationalist writers of the period included Bankim Chandra Chatterjee and Rabindranath Tagore (in Bengali), Lakshminath Bezbarua in Assamese, Vishnu Shastri Chiplunkar in Marathi, Subramanya Bharati in Tamil, Bharatendu Harishchandra in Hindi and Altaf Hussain Hali in Urdu. Many of their novels, essays, plays and poetry had magically touched the hearts and minds of the people.

Despite numerous restrictions imposed on the press from time to time, Indian journalism continued to make rapid strides. Soon the press emerged as the primary medium of public education and the mirror of Indian nationalism.

- **New Education System** In 1835, the British inaugurated the system of English education in India with the intention of creating a loyal class of English educated Indians who could carry out clerical tasks. According to Macaulay, the idea was to form 'a class of persons, Indian in blood and colour, but English in taste, in opinions, in morals and in intellect'.

  However, the English system of education opened to the Indians the floodgates of European liberal thought. It familiarised the Indians with the modern European ideas of equality, liberty, nationalism and democracy. The English educated Indians became aware of nationalist movements in Europe. They were exposed to the works of western liberal thinkers like **John Milton, Bentham, John Stuart Mill, Herbert Spencer, Rousseau, Voltaire, Mazzini and Garibaldi**. Some of them visited England for higher education. There they saw firsthand the life of people in a free country. Thus, realising the hypocrisy of the British in India, this educated Indian middle class itself took on the leadership of the Indian national movement.

  Moreover, English itself became the lingua franca of the Indian nationalists. In the absence of such a common language, it would have been very difficult for the nationalists to organise a movement of all India character.

Sir Charles Trevelyan famously stated in 1835 that the British Raj in India could not last forever and was bound to die one day either at the hands of those who subscribed to the indigenous model of political change or at the hands of those who subscribed to the British model of political change. If it was to die at the hands of the latter, i.e., the English educated, 'it would take a long time and the severance of the British connection with India would be neither violent nor harmful to Britain, for cultural and commercial bonds would continue'.

- **Policy of Continuous Expansion** The British followed the policy of continuous expansion in India, annexing even those states which were not at war with the British. Important among these were the **annexations of Sind (1843), Punjab (1849), Rangoon and Pegu (1852), and Awadh (1856)**. Jhansi, Satara and Nagpur were also annexed. This made the Indian rulers highly apprehensive of the British.
- **Racial Discrimination** The British in India adopted an attitude of racial superiority and discriminated against Indians in all matters including social and judicial. Trevelyan pointed out in 1864- 'the testimony of a single one of our countrymen has more weight with the court than that of any number of Hindus, a circumstance which puts a terrible instrument of power into the hands of an unscrupulous Englishman'.

Irrespective of class or caste, all Indians were looked down upon as inferior people. Extreme racial humiliation was inflicted upon them by reserving clubs, railway compartments and other public places exclusively for the Europeans. Thus, racial domination and discrimination infuriated every self-respecting Indian, to whichever class he belonged. It began to be seen as a form of 'national humiliation' and united the Indians as 'one people' against the British.

- **Foreign Character of British Rule** A foreign rule invariably unites the subject population against their common oppressor and arouses patriotic feelings in them. This was true even in case of British Rule in India.

Indirect Consequences of British Rule

The above mentioned colonial policies further gave rise to the following factors:

- **Political unity of India** It was under the British that political unity of India was achieved for the first time in modern era. The British conquered the whole of India from the Himalayas in the north to Cape Comorin in the south and from Assam in the east to Khyber Pass in the west. They created **a political entity larger than that under the Mauryas or the great Mughals**. Moreover, common laws and common institutions began to shape India in a common mould.
- **Economic and administrative unity of India** The unified system of government introduced by the British throughout the country also welded India into one nation. The destruction of local self-sufficient economy and introduction of colonial economy at an all India scale also brought about economic unity. The economic fate of the people all over the country got interlinked and scarcity in one part began to affect prices in other parts of the country too.
- **Psychological unity of India** The harmful effects of the British colonial rule on the lives of all sections of Indian people, united them against one common enemy—the British rule. In the course of time, the feeling of solidarity among the oppressed people brought them together in an **anti-imperialist struggle** which gradually grew into a full-fledged national movement.

  Later, the British tried hard to keep India divided through the policy of divide-and rule. They sowed the seeds of communalism and regionalism. Yet, in the end, the forces uniting India into one nation proved more powerful than the divisionary forces.
- **Establishment of peace and orderly Government in India** The British rule brought about peace and orderly government in India in contrast to the chaotic conditions that prevailed in the 18th century. The British set up an administration that was highly centralised and impersonal, which did not change with the change in top administrators. Further, the district administration was kept in the firm hands of the highly trained and professional Indian Civil Servants. A unified civil as well as judicial administration further consolidated the political unity achieved.

Edwyn Bevan said, 'the British Raj was like a steel frame which held the injured body of India together till the gradual process of internal growth had joined the dislocated bones, knit up torn fibers and enabled the patient to regain inner coherence and unity'.

- **Rise of middle-class intelligentsia** The English system of education and administration gave rise to a new urban middle class in towns. It emerged as a well-integrated all-India class with a common foreground of knowledge and ideas. The class also gained a prominent status in society because of its knowledge of English and close links with the ruling class. Men such as **Surendrenath Bannerjee** and

Aurobindo Ghose formed the nucleus of newly arising political unrest. Gradually this class emerged as the new soul of modern India and provided leadership to the Indian National Congress in all stages of its growth.

- **Intellectual awakening among Indians** In the backdrop of new education system, 19th-century India was marked by process of socio-cultural ferment. Among those who benefitted from modern education and emerged as the leading intellectuals of 19th-century India were—**Raja Ram Mohan Roy, Keshub Chandra Sen, Ishwar Chandra Vidyasagar, MG Ranade and Sir Syed Ahmed Khan**. They threw light on the achievements of Indians in the field of art, architecture, literature, philosophy and science and contributed to the growth of national consciousness.

  Here it must be remembered that it was not the English education system that gave rise to the national movement. It only facilitated such a development. In reality, the British authorities tried to inculcate docility and servility among the children studying in Indian schools and colleges. Though English became the lingua franca of early nationalists, it soon became a hindrance in the spread of mass nationalism. Leaders such as Gandhi and Tilak were conscious of the bigger role of regional languages in the national movement.

- **Progressive character of socio-cultural reform movements** In the 19th century, the educated Indians began to re-examine their socio-cultural beliefs in the light of the new western scientific knowledge they had acquired. This process led to the rise of various socio-religious reform movements among the Hindus such as the **Brahmo Samaj, the Prarthana Samaj, the Arya Samaj and the Ramkrishna Mission,** etc. Similar movements arose among the Muslims, the Sikhs and the Parsis.

  In the sphere of religion, these movements attacked religious superstition, idolatry, polytheism and hereditary priesthood. In the social sphere, they attacked social evils such as the caste system, untouchability, sati, child marriage, purdah system, etc. These movements sought to reorganise the society along progressive lines guided by the ideals of democracy, equality, liberty and reason. Since many of them drew inspiration from India's rich cultural past, they enthused their followers with a sense of self-respect and patriotism.

  Thus, even without having any political agenda, the 19th-century reform movements inspired numerous people with a spirit of nationalism.

- **Impact of rediscovery of India's past** A consequence of foreign rule was that many Indians lost self-confidence. The foreign rulers also constantly forwarded the thesis that Indians had always been unable to rule themselves. Their backward religion and society made them unfit for democracy. Many nationalists tried to counter this propaganda by turning to the achievements of ancient Indian rulers such as Ashoka and Akbar. In this task, they also took the help of new researches on ancient Indian past.

  European scholars such as **Max Muller** conducted researches on ancient Indian past and rediscovered India's rich cultural heritage. Archeologists like **Marshall** and **Cunningham** presented a new picture of India's ancient past, a past as great and glorious as the ancient civilisations of Greece and Rome. The scholars praised the wisdom and philosophy of the **Vedas and the Upanishads**. Further, the theory of **Aryan origin of Indians as well as Europeans** also boosted the morale of the Indian people. These factors together also inspired the Indians with a sense of national pride and patriotism.

  However, certain negative consequence also emerged when some nationalists went to the extreme and began glorifying India's past uncritically. Gripped in a false sense of pride, it prevented some Indians from benefitting from the fresh and healthy ideas emerging in other parts of the contemporary world. This tendency also weakened India's struggle against its socio-cultural backwardness. Yet another negative tendency was to glorify India's ancient past at the cost of the medieval period. This encouraged Muslims to look upto Arabs and Turks for cultural past and encouraged communal feelings.

Additional Factors

In addition to the above, the following factors also contributed to the rise of national consciousness in India:

Impact of Contemporary European Movements

In Europe, the national liberation movements of **Ireland, Italy and Greece** also stirred great national emotions in India. Leaders like Surendranath Banerjee and Lala Lajpat Rai often referred to national heroes like Mazzini and Garibaldi in their speeches. There is no doubt that nationalist movement in other countries greatly inspired the national leaders in India and strengthened Indian nationalism.

Lord Lytton's Reactionary Policies

Lord Lytton's short-sighted policies acted like a catalyst and accelerated the national movement against the British. During his Viceroyalty, the **upper age limit for ICS exam was reduced to 19 years from 21 years**, thus making it practically impossible for Indians to compete for it. The holding of the **grand Delhi Durbar in 1877**, even as the country was in severe grip of famine, solicited severe criticism. He introduced two highly unpopular legislations—the **Vernacular Press Act** and the **Indian Arms Act**, stirring a great storm of opposition in the country.

Ilbert Bill Controversy (or White Mutiny, 1883)

During **Lord Ripon**, the Ilbert Bill (written by Sir Ilbert, the law member of the Viceroy's Council) sought to give Indian members of the ICS the same judicial powers as their European colleagues enjoyed and accordingly, Indian judges could try European accused. This raised a lot of hue and cry among the Europeans who stood united to oppose the bill in what came to be known as the **White Mutiny** of 1883.

The most vocal opposition to the Bill came from British tea and indigo plantations owners in Bengal. English women also opposed the bill and argued that 'ignorant' Bengali women are neglected by their men, and hence the Bengali men should therefore not be given the right to judge cases involving English women. On the other hand, the Bengali women supported the bill and pointed out that more Indian women had academic degrees than British women did at the time, alluding to the fact that the University of Calcutta became one of the first universities to admit female graduates to its degree programmes in 1878, before any of the British universities had done the same. In face of opposition by a majority of English women, Ripon had to modify the Bill in favour of the Europeans and an amendment was introduced whereby a jury of 50% Europeans was required if an Indian judge was to face a European on the dock.

This controversy proved to be an eye-opener to the Indian intelligentsia. It proved to them that justice and equality could not be expected where the interests of European community were involved.

It also demonstrated to them the value of organised protest. The bitter controversy ended up deepening antagonism between the British and the Indians and emerged as a prelude to the formation of the Indian National Congress in 1885.

Indian Response and Rise of a National Movement

Different classes of the Indian people responded to the British exploitation which gradually took the form of a national movement. The Indian response can be broadly divided into two forms:

1. Opposition by the peasants and tribals (in the form of peasant and tribal movements) and,
2. Opposition by the middle classes (in the form of a new consciousness among the middle classes leading to an organised national movement).

Thus, Indian response to British exploitation first emerged in the form of popular uprisings, which first united the Indians against the British and embraced the people in a rudimentary wave of national consciousness. This national sentiment was further strengthened and channelised by the educated middle classes in the form of an organised national movement.

Peasant and Tribal Movements

Throughout the 19th century, Indian masses struggled against the British rule. It is noteworthy that the early uprisings were **not consciously nationalist uprisings**, but, over a period of time, they helped in the emergence of national consciousness. In the beginning, these uprisings were directed against oppressive British policies. Sometimes they were also triggered due to oppression by a zamindar, money lender or a state official.

It was in the **Revolt of 1857** that we saw, for the first time, some sort of national sentiments inspiring the people. Even though the revolt was brutally crushed, popular uprisings in India continued unabated. Tribal movements were the most militant and the tribals revolted more often and more violently than any other community in India. Even though all these revolts ended in failure, they contributed immensely in uniting the Indians against the British and fostering a national consciousness among them.

Middle Class Consciousness

In the context of British rule in India, the 19th century saw the emergence of new consciousness among the educated Indian middle class. The educated Indians, which included lawyers, teachers, journalists, doctors, merchants, traders, etc., began to critically examine the Indian society and started making efforts in the direction of socio-culture reforms. **Ram Mohan Roy** emerged as a pioneer reformer in this field. Other prominent reforms included the likes of Dayanand Saraswati and Swami Vivekananda. The prominent social evils targeted were untouchability, sati, rituals, etc.

More than any other class, it was this class that was able to analyse the true nature of the colonial rule. In the beginning they supported the changes brought about by the British in the fields of administration, education, means of communication etc., thinking that they would benefit the masses. But gradually they understood that the real motive was to assist in the consolidation of the British Raj.

While other Indian classes (peasant, workers and tribals) voiced their protest in the form of popular uprisings and revolts, the educated middle classes voiced their protest chiefly in two forms: 1) literary activities, and 2) associations and organisations.

Literary Activities

Again, Ram Mohan Roy was a pioneer in this field. He wrote several books and published several articles on various themes. Prominent literary activities in the 19th century included the following:

- Ram Mohan Roy started a journal named **Sambad Kaumudi** (in Bengali, in 1821).
- Din Bandhu Mitra wrote the play **Nil Darpan** (1859) depicting the plight of indigo cultivators.
- Bankim Chandra wrote **Anand Math** (1882), full of nationalist aspirations.

A large number of periodicals and newspapers were also published in different languages. By 1877, there were as many as 169 newspapers in the vernacular.

Associations and Organisations

This was the second method adopted by the middle classes for joint action against the British policies harming their interests. Some of the early organisations were the Landholders' Society (1838) and the Bengal British India Society (1843). They chiefly adopted the method of petitioning against the Company with the aim of bringing about reforms in the Company's Charter.

In 1858, when the British Crown tookover the Indian administration, it was hoped that exploitation would end and the British government would work for the welfare of the Indian people. But such was not the case and the organisational activities of the Indians further intensified. London India Association was formed in England, Indian Association (1876) in Maharashtra and the Indian National Conference (1883) in Bengal. As opposed to earlier organisations, the ones formed now were political in character. Their agenda included protesting against British policies through resolutions and petitions, garnering support for their cause through public meetings and statements, exchange of views on national issues, etc. These organisations prepared the ground for the formation of an all India organisation-the **Indian National Congress in 1885**.

Growth of National Consciousness in Second Half of 19th Century

The full flowering of the national consciousness had to wait until the second half of the 19th century. It was during this period that the Indian National Congress was formed in 1885.

At its root, modern Indian nationalism arose to meet the challenge of the foreign rule. The British Raj itself, along with its direct and indirect consequence provided the material, moral and intellectual ground for the development of an anti-imperialist movement in India which subsequently grew into a full-fledged national movement.

With the passage of time, more and more sections of people realised that their interests clashed with the British interests in India and that the welfare of the Indian people would never gain priority over and above British imperial interests. Even those who had earlier supported the British rule in the hope that it would modernise India, were gradually disenchanted.

It was during the latter half of the 19th century that even the British shed all pretensions of benevolence and of guiding India towards self-governance. They adopted a hostile attitude towards higher education, particularly scientific and technical. Instead of helping give freedom to people and press, they simply strangulated it. The British officials and leaders adopted a hostile attitude towards higher education, particularly scientific and technical education.

British Response

The growth of Indian nationalism in the latter half of 19th century was certainly not liked by the British. Their first response was of denial and they denied the very idea of India as a nation.

- In 1883, JR Steeley described India as mere '**geographical expression**' with no sense whatsoever of national unity.
- In 1884, John Strachey stated while addressing the alumni of Cambridge University, 'this is **the first and most essential thing to learn about India-that there is not, and never was, an India**'.

In the beginning of the 20th century, when Indian nationalism began to demonstrate visible strength, the British modified their response.

- The authors of Montford Report claimed credit that the British rule was the harbinger of nationalist upsurge in India. It stated, '**the politically minded Indians...are intellectually our children**. The present intellectual and moral stir in India...is rather a tribute to our work'.
- R. Coupland wrote, '**Indian nationalism was the child of the British Raj**'.

What Coupland failed to mention was that Indian nationalism, in reality, was an unwanted child of the British Raj whom it refused to acknowledge at first and tried to strangulate it subsequently.

In the final analysis, it would be correct to say that a number of factors contributed to the rise of Indian nationalism in the 19th century. It was partly a product of the worldwide upsurge of the ideas of nationalism and self-determination initiated by the French Revolution, partly the result of modernisation initiated by the British in India, partly a result of the popular uprisings and Indian Renaissance and partly a reaction to the British Raj.

Note: Read in detail about the Popular Uprisings and Revolts, 19th-Century Socio-Cultural Reform Movements and the Indian National Movement, in the upcoming chapters.

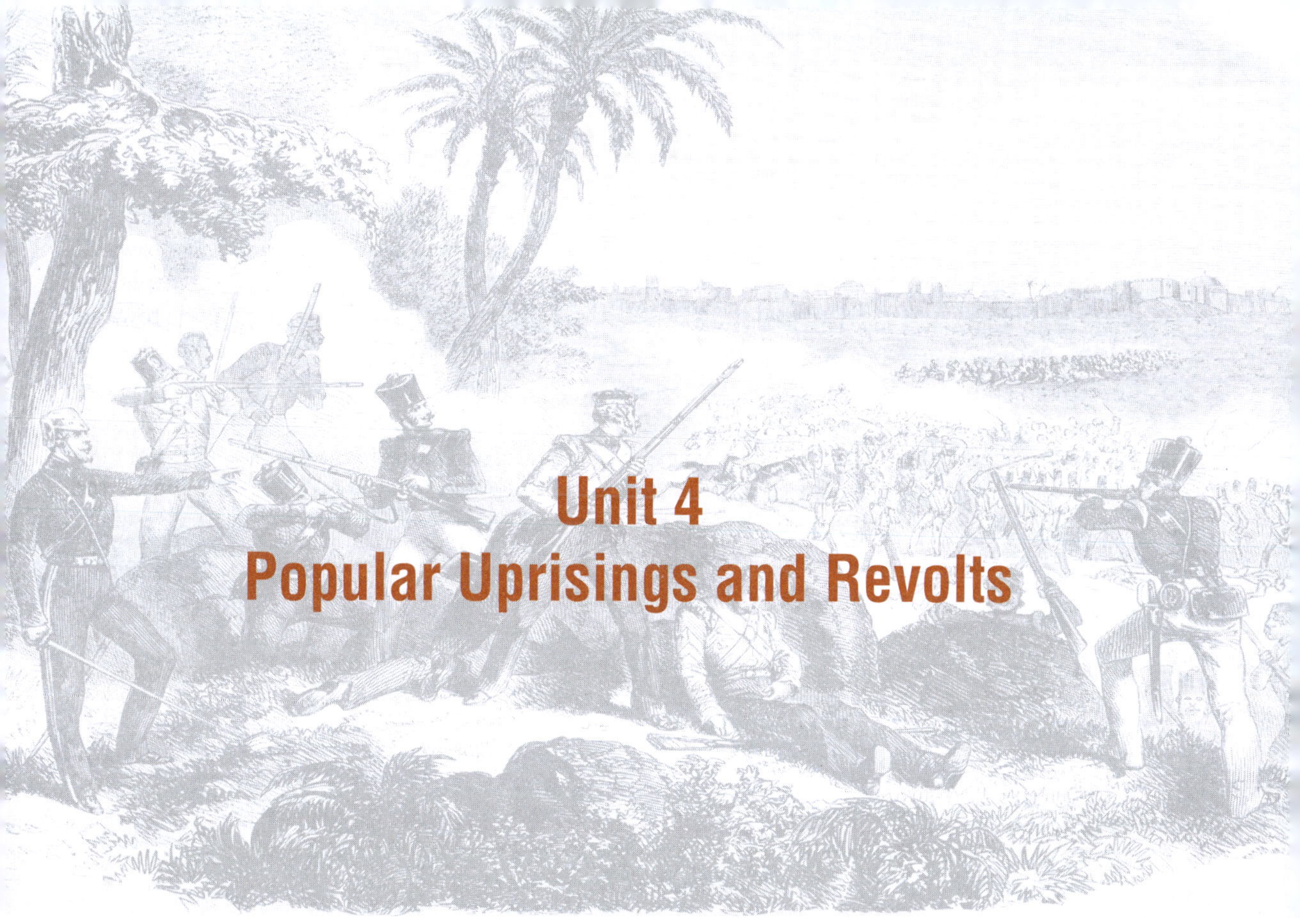

Unit 4
Popular Uprisings and Revolts

1 Popular Uprisings up to 1857

In previous units, you learnt about the establishment of British rule in India and its impact on different spheres of Indian life. A question that assumes importance now is, how did the people react to this new rule and the changes that it brought about?

The establishment of British rule in India was not a sudden event but a slow and gradual process comprising many wars and conquests, resulting in forceful subjugation of the Indian people. Naturally it was a process resented and resisted at every stage. The British introduced rapid changes, which had adverse impact on various aspects of Indian life. Consequently, people reacted to this new rule in two broad ways-

1. In the form of popular uprisings (i.e. revolts, rebellions, peasant and tribal movements) (Covered in this Unit)
2. In the form of socio-cultural reform movements (Covered in Unit 5)

This unit attempts to examine the various popular uprisings that emerged in different parts of the country till 1900. In this chapter, uprisings during the first 100 years of colonial rule, i.e. from 1757 till 1857, have been covered.

A series of popular resistance run like a thread throughout the first 100 years of colonial rule. During this period, the simmering discontent of the people broke out in three broad forms— civil rebellions, tribal uprisings and peasant movements. Whatever may be their immediate cause, these uprisings were directed against the common experience of oppression brought about by the colonialists and their indigenous supporters. Though these uprisings were localised in varying degrees, they emerged as the first expression of protest against the foreign rule and formed a significant prelude to the Revolt of 1857, also referred to as the 'First War of Independence'.

Civil Rebellions Civil Rebellions were generally led by the rulers or their descendants, officials and retainers of the conquered Indian states as well as by impoverished landlords and poligars (landed military magnates in South India). The mass base of these rebellions was provided by ruined peasants, artisans and soldiers.

Indian peasant

Who were they?

The Peasants The term 'peasant' refers to a small farmer or a farm labourer. The peasants were the sons of soil, i.e. all those who were directly engaged in agricultural production.

The Tribals The term 'tribal' or 'adivasi' refers to the earliest inhabitant of a region. The tribals generally lived in deep forests or hilly areas and shared a close bond with their land, forest and forest resources. The tribal peasants combined agriculture with hunting and food gathering and even manufacturing from forest-based products. Their relative isolation and closer ethnic bonds differentiated them from peasants.

The Artisans Artisans are workers involved in manufacture of goods by hands, like cotton, wood and iron products. Mostly, these skilled professions were pursued as caste professions. Historical evidence about them is extremely limited. They are often clubbed with peasants and tribals.

Causes of the Pre-1857 Uprisings

Even during the Mughal times, popular protests against the rulers and their officials were not uncommon and various factors including high land revenue, harsh practices of tax collectors and other corrupt practices prevailing at the time forced the people to rise in revolt.

However, the establishment of British rule had a far more devastating impact on the lives of various sections of Indian people, forcing them to rise in revolt against the colonial rule:

- **Devastating impact on rulers and zamindars**
    - Several Rajas and Nawabs lost their principalities owing to the Company's policy of expansion. Thousands of zamindars and poligars were **uprooted**; their rights taken over by the colonial state. Often, they were forced to sell their rights due to inability to pay higher revenues.

- **Devastating impact on peasants**
  - The Company introduced rapid changes in administration and land revenue system, disrupting agrarian society.
  - The new land settlements (Permanent, Ryotwari and Mahalwari) created new types of land ownerships. The new landlords were bereft of traditional paternalism towards their tenants and raised rents to unbearable heights. For instance, in Bengal in less than 30 years of British rule, land revenue collection was raised to nearly double the amount collected under the Mughals.
  - Further, the colonial rulers insisted payment of revenue in cash, encouraging money lending practices which often resulted in heavy peasant **indebtedness** and **landlessness**.
  - To make matters worse, not even a part of the collected revenue was spent on the welfare of the cultivators or development of agriculture.
  - The new land settlements also did away with certain customary rights like forest and pasturage rights.
  - Though class differences were not a new feature, the colonial policies **accentuated the class differences** between those who owned land and wealth and those who did not. Further, class differences also accentuated polarisation along the lines of caste and religion. For instance, if in an area, the landowner belonged to a particular caste or religion, and peasants to another, their **caste/communal differences got strained**.
  - As per colonial policy, India was to be a supplier of raw materials for British industries. Hence agriculture was forcibly commercialised. Peasants were forced to grow cash crops like indigo and cotton instead of food grains, even in years of food grain scarcity, resulting in increased peasant exploitation and even **famines**. In fact, the period during 1770 and 1857 witnessed 12 major and several minor famines, endorsing the decline of Indian peasantry.
  - The new judicial and administrative systems further encouraged the rich to oppress the poor. Cultivators were **flogged, tortured** and **jailed** for non-payment of rent, taxes and interests.
  - Corruption in lower levels of judiciary and administration made the life of the common man miserable.
- **Devastating impact on artisans**
  - Colonialism also spelt doom for Indian artisans. As per the colonial policy, India was to be a market for British goods. These machine-made British goods were cheaper and finer than those made by Indian artisans. Without demand for their handmade goods, the Indian artisans were thrown into **unemployment**.
  - Further, while India was flooded with British manufactures, discriminatory tariffs were levied against Indian goods in Britain, ruining Indian handloom and handicraft industry both ways.
  - Misery of the artisans was further compounded by the disappearance of their traditional patrons and buyers—the princes, chieftains and landlords.
  - Destruction of indigenous industry led to large scale migrations from industry to agriculture (a process called **peasantisation**) with no simultaneous improvement in agriculture. This further increased pressure on land.
- **Devastating impact on tribals**
  - The colonial administration **ended the relative isolation** of tribals and brought them within the ambit of colonial economy and exploitation.

  - It intruded into tribal polity, **encroached upon tribal lands** and transformed tribal relationship with land and forests.
  - It recognised the tribals as zamindars and introduced new land revenue system, **taxed tribal products**.
  - The tribals had traditionally practiced shifting cultivation or jhum. The colonial administration disallowed this practice by restricting tribal access to new forest lands and forest products.
  - The colonial administration introduced a large number of **outsiders** among the tribals. These included middlemen such as the traders, revenue farmers and money lenders who pulled the tribals into the very centre of colonial exploitation.
  - The money lenders gradually pushed the tribals into **indebtedness** and **landlessness**. As a result, the tribals were reduced to the position of farm labourers and tenants on land that had traditionally belonged to them. It also intensified the process of **peasantisation**.
  - The revenue farmers intensified the system of **begar**. The policemen and petty officers were notoriously corrupt and apathetic towards everyone including the tribals.
  - The colonial administration also encouraged influx of **Christian missionaries** into tribal regions.
- **Devastating impact on scholarly and priestly classes**
  - The traditional rulers had provided generous patronage to pandits and maulvis as well as to men of art and literature in their courts. With the conquest of Indian states by the British, this **patronage came to an end** resulting in wide scale displacement and consequent impoverishment of the scholarly and priestly classes. These uprooted men also played an active role in inciting feelings of hatred and rebellion against the foreign rulers.
- **Colonial nature of the Company's rule**
  - Another major cause of the uprisings was the very foreign character of the Company's rule. The Company's officials remained **perpetual foreigners** in India, whose only aim was to amass as much wealth as possible and return to England.
  - Indians had begun to feel that they were being ruled by foreigners from a distant land who were draining India of its wealth with the effect that the English enjoyed the fruits of production while Indian masses faced worst forms of poverty.

Thus it is clear that the Company's rule had an adverse impact on the lives of almost all sections of Indian people. The exploitative colonial practices lead to massive impoverishment of Indian peasants and discontentment amongst tribes, forcing them to rise in revolt against British administration.

Important Popular Uprisings

Naturally, the rebellions occurred in one area after another as it was incorporated under the Company's rule, beginning from Bengal. During the 100 years from 1757 to 1857, there occurred more than 40 major rebellions apart from several minor ones. These uprisings were in the nature of protests, revolts and rebellions and were known differently as **fituris, melis, hools** and **ulgulan**.

Revolts in Bengal and Eastern India

Sanyasi-Fakir Rebellion (Bengal-Bihar, 1763–1800) The establishment of British rule in Bengal in 1757 was followed by widespread plunder by the East India Company, ruining peasants, artisans and zamindars alike. The Bengal famine of 1770 was seen as a direct result of foreign rule and its callousness.

The Sanyasis and Fakirs (Hindu and Muslim holy men), with the tradition of fighting against oppression, took up the popular cause and organised raids on the Company's factories and treasuries. Sometimes they would distribute the looted wealth among the poor. They even established independent government in Bogra and Mymensingh. Another noteworthy feature of the movement was equal participation of the Hindus and the Muslims.

After the Bengal famine, the Sanyasis were joined by a large number of uprooted zamindars, disbanded soldiers, dispossessed peasants and rural poor. They moved around in parts of Bengal and Bihar in bands of five to seven thousand and adopted guerrilla techniques of attack.

As per the official records of the East India Company, 'A set of lawless banditti under the name of Sanyasis and Fakirs have long infested these countries and under the pretence of religious pilgrimage, have been accustomed to traverse the chief parts of Bengal, begging, stealing and plundering wherever they go.'

Main leader(s): **Musa Shah, Majnu Shah, Chirag Ali Shah, Bhawani Pathak** and **Debi Chaudharani**.
Suppression: The Sanyasi and the British forces regularly clashed with each other in Bengal and Bihar until 1800. The British finally succeeded in containing the Sanyasi raids after prolonged military action under **Warren Hastings**.
The Sanyasi Rebellion was made famous by Bankim Chandra Chatterjee in his novel Anand Math.

Chuar Rebellion (Midnapur, 1766–72, 1795–1816) Chuar tribesmen of Midnapur district rose in rebellion several times in the context of famine and increasing land revenue demands.

Peasant Uprising of Rangpur and Dinajpur (Bengal, 1783) Rangpur and Dinajpur were two districts of northern Bengal which faced all kinds of oppression by the East India Company and its revenue contractors. One such contractor was Debi Singh, who along with his agents exercised a reign of terror in the two districts of Rangpur and Dinajpur. In order to extract taxes, they often resorted to beating and flogging the peasants and even burnt down their houses.

When the peasants' appeals to the Company officials for help fell on deaf ears, they decided to take the law in their own hands. They elected Dirjinarain as their leader, armed themselves with their swords, sickles, bows and arrows, attacked the contractor's agents and looted their granaries. They even formed a government of their own, stopped payment of all revenues to the government and even levied insurrection charges or **dhing kharcha** to meet rebellion expenses. Hindus and Muslims participated in equal numbers in this uprising as well.

Main leader: **Dirjinarain**
Suppression: The uprising was finally suppressed by the British by use of military force.

Ho and Munda Rising (Chota Nagpur and Singhbhum, 1820–37) Ho and Munda tribesmen challenged the Company's forces several times during 1820 and 1837.

Kol Uprising (Chota Nagpur Plateau, 1831–37) The Kol tribesmen of Singhbhum had long enjoyed independent existence under their tribal chiefs. Following British occupation of Singhbhum, the British began to intrude into the life of the Kols and tried to impose their own jurisdiction. Even outsiders (including Sikh and Muslim farmers) began to settle in this area, resulting in occupation of tribal lands by outsiders.

Such activities were much resented by the Kols and their discontentment broke out in the form of an uprising in 1831 directed against the outsiders. The rebels killed around 1000 outsiders, burnt down their houses and looted their property. The rebellion quickly spread to adjoining Ranchi, Hazaribagh, Palamu and Manbhum and was finally suppressed only after large-scale military operations of the British forces. Thousands of Kols were massacred before British authority could be restored.

Pagal Panthis Revolt (Bengal, 1825) Pagal Panthis belonged to a semi-religious sect founded by Karam Shah of north Bengal. His son and successor **Tipu Shah** was driven by both religious as well as political motives and took up the cause of the tenants against the oppressive zamindars. In 1825, Tipu captured Sherpur and assumed royal power. The insurgency soon spread to adjoining areas and the region remained disturbed in until 1830s and 1840s.

Ahoms' Revolt (Assam, 1828) After the end of Anglo Burma war (1824–26), the Ahom nobility of Assam accused the British Company of breaking its promise and not withdrawing from their territory. Feeling threatened that the Company intended to include Ahom territory in its dominion, the Ahoms rose in revolt. In 1828, they declared Gomdhar Konwar as their king and planned a march to Rangpur.

Main leader: **Gomdhar Konwar**
Suppression: The revolt was suppressed in the face of superior military might of the Company. But later the Company followed a pacific policy, and in 1833 handed over upper Assam to Maharaj Purander Singh Narendra restoring part of kingdom to the Assamese King.

Khasi Revolt (Khasi Hills, 1829) The East India Company occupied Khasi hills, lying between Jaintia and Garo hills. They also planned to build a military road linking Brahmaputra valley with Sylhet and stationed a large number of outsiders including Englishmen, Bengalis and labourers to complete the project. Tirat Singh, the Khasi king and the ruler of Nunklow, resented this intrusion by the British and launched an attack on a British garrison, which soon developed into a full-blown revolt against the British rule in the region.

Main leader: **Tirat Singh**
Suppression: The British successfully suppressed the revolt in 1833.

Faraizi Disturbances (Eastern Bengal, 1838–57) The Faraizi sect was founded by **Haji Shariatullah of Faridpur** in eastern Bengal. The Faraizi movement originally began as a peasant movement directed against the landlords and the British oppressors. However, under the leadership of Dudu Mian (founder's son), the Faraizis turned into a religious sect, advocating radical religious and socio-political changes. Dudu Mian propagated an egalitarian ideology that all men are equal and that all land belongs to God and no one has the right to levy tax on it. He took upon himself the task of driving away the British intruders from Bengal. The Faraizis opposed the right of the zamindars to collect tax, set up parallel government in some parts of Bengal and even established village courts.

Main leader: **Dudu Mian**
Suppression: The movement was finally crushed by the government forces and ended in the arrest of Dudu Mian. The Faraizi disturbances continued till 1857 and most of the Faraizis later joined the ranks of the Wahabis.

Khond Uprising (Orissa, 1837–56) The British tried to put an end to the Khond practice of human sacrifice (mariah), first through persuasion and later through force. This was resented by the Khonds who retaliated under **Chakra Bisoi**. The uprising covered the regions of Kalahandi, Patana, Ghumsar and China-ki-Medi. Bisoi could never be arrested.

Savara Rebellion (Orissa, 1856–57) The Savara tribesmen of Parliakhemedi rebelled under the leadership of **Radhakrishna Dandasena**. The colonial administration saw links between Chakra Bisoi and the Savara rebellion which was crushed with the hanging of Dandasena in 1857.

Santhal Rebellion (Rajmahal Hills, 1855–56) The Santhal **hool** or 'uprising' was the most massive of all tribal revolts. The people of the Santhal tribe inhabited the region between Bhagalpur and Rajmahal, known as **'Daman-i-koh'**, covering the districts of Birbhum, Bankura, Singhbhum, Hazaribagh, Murshidabad, Pakur, Purnea, Dumka, Bhagalpur and Monghyr.

In 1793, Permanent Settlement was introduced in Bengal. Under this system, the land of the tribals which they had cultivated for centuries was handed over to the zamindars. These zamindars raised the rent to excessive heights. The moneylenders, who were mostly from Bengal and upper India, started their usurious practices. In this way, outsiders (called **Dikus** by the Santhals) began to intrude into the Santhal territory and disturbed their traditional way of life, forcing the Santhals to retreat to the Rajmahal Hills.

The Santhal's main resentment was against the usurious people from Bengal, but they turned against the government when they saw that the government officials were hand in gloves with their oppressors. The landlords, money lenders, merchants together with revenue officials and police subjected the Santhals to all sorts of exploitation including illegal extortions, dispossession from property and even personal violence.

The timid and yielding Santhals severely resented the treatment meted out to them by the dikus (outsiders). Their growing discontent broke out in open insurrections under the leadership of brothers Sidhu and Kanhu. The leaders claimed that Thakur (God) had communicated with them and asked them to take up arms against the outsiders and usher in Satyug (the rule of truth). Soon the leaders were able to mobilise nearly 60,000 Santhals and the revolt spread quickly in the adjoining areas. In popular tribal perception, it was the fight of the 'good' against the 'evil'.

The Santhals cut off postal and rail communications between Bhagalpur and Rajmahal. They proclaimed the end of Company's rule.

Once the government realised the scale of the rebellion, it organised a massive military campaign and the rebellion was suppressed with immense brutality. Violent suppression of the Santhal rebels made them even more aggressive. They declared the end of the Company's rule and declared themselves independent.

Main leaders: **Sidhu** and **Kanhu**

Suppression: The heroic struggle of the Santhals against British oppression was brought under control only after extensive military operations in 1856. More than 15,000 Santhals were killed, several villages were destroyed. Sidhu was betrayed, captured and killed while Kanhu was also arrested at the tail end of the rebellion. Afterwards, the government adopted pacific policy towards the Santhals and created a separate district of '**Santhal Parganas**'.

Revolts in Western India

Bhil Uprisings (Khandesh; 1818, 1825, 1831 and 1846) The Bhils were an aboriginal tribe that inhabited the **Western Ghats**, with their stronghold in Khandesh. During 1817–19, the English Company occupied Khandesh, enraging the tribal Bhils who revolted against the intruders. The Company authorities alleged that the Bhils had been instigated against the British by Peshwa Baji Rao II and his minister Trimbakji Danglia and ruthlessly crushed the revolt.

In 1825, the Bhils revolted again under the leadership of **Sewram**. Subsequently the Bhils ravaged the plains in several small groups and clashed with the British forces for several years, signifying the popular character of the discontent, before being finally suppressed.

Waghera Rising (Okha Mandal, 1818–19) The Wagheras of Okha Mandal also resented the imposition of Company's rule. The Company also supported the exactions by the Gaekwad of Baroda, forcing the Waghera chiefs to rise in revolt. The Wagheras invaded British territory, culminating in a peace treaty in November 1820.

Kutch Rebellion (Kutch and Kathiawar or Saurashtra, 1819 and 1831) In 1819, the Company's forces defeated the Kutch ruler, Rao Bharmal, in favour of his infant son, while actual administration of Kutch went into the hands of a British Resident. Such administrative innovations as well as steep land revenue assessment by the Company generated much resentment. The Kutch chiefs rose in rebellion and demanded restoration of Bharmal. The disturbances erupted again in 1831, forcing the Company to follow conciliatory policy.

Ramosi Risings (Western Ghats, 1822) The Ramosis were also the hill tribes of Western Ghats and resented British invasion. In 1822, the Ramos tribesmen, led by **Chittur Singh**, revolted against the outsiders and plundered the region around Satara. The area remained disturbed till 1829.

Again in 1839, the British deposed Raja Pratap Singh of Satara, causing widespread resentment. The move triggered a chain of disturbances, compelling the British to use force and restore order.

Koli Risings (Gujarat; 1824–29, 1839 and 1844–48) The Kolis lived in the neighbourhood of the Bhils and equally resented the imposition of British rule. The foreigners had destroyed their forts and introduced new order of administration, causing widespread unemployment. They rose in revolt against the outsiders several times between 1824 and 1848.

Surat Salt Agitation (1844–48) In 1844, the Company's government raised the salt duty from fifty paise to one rupee, causing great discontent among the people of Surat. Surat, with its long tradition of opposition to unpopular measures, rose in revolt. Anti-British sentiments raged high, and some Europeans were attacked. Seeing the popular nature of the revolt, the government was compelled to roll back the raise in salt duty. In 1848 again, the government's decision to introduce Bengal Standard of Weights and Measures had to be withdrawn owing to popular protest.

Kolhapur and Savantvadi Revolts (1844) Maharashtra was in a perpetual state of revolt after the final defeat of the Peshwa. Prominent revolts included Bhil uprisings 1818, Kittur uprising led by Chinnava 1824, the Satara uprising 1841 and the revolt of the Gadkaris 1844.

After 1844, administrative reorganisation in Kolhapur had been carried out, causing widespread dissatisfaction. The **Gadkaris**, a hereditary military class which garrisoned Maratha forts, had been disbanded. Faced with unemployment, the Gadkaris were compelled to rise in revolt. A similar issue caused a revolt in Savantvadi as well.

Revolts in Southern India

Revolt of the Raja of Vizianagaram (1794) In 1765, the English Company had acquired Northern Circars and adopted an overbearing attitude. Raja's troops were disbanded and an unreasonable demand of ₹3 lakhs was raised. Upon Raja's refusal, his estate was annexed. The Raja retaliated in the form of a revolt with the full support of his people and his troops. Even though the Raja lost his life in a battle in 1794, the Company was compelled to follow a conciliatory policy. It restored the estate to the dead Raja's son and even reduced the demand for money and gifts.

Revolt of Diwan Velu Thampi (Travancore, 1808) In 1805, subsidiary alliance was imposed on the ruler of Travancore by Wellesley. Unable to pay the subsidy, the ruler fell in arrears. The high-handed attitude of the British Resident also evoked resentment and Diwan Velu Thampi organised a heroic revolt with the support of Nair battalion. A superior British force later restored peace in the area. Velu Thampi was hanged publicly after death to instil fear among the people.

Rebellion at Mysore (1830–31) After the British victory in the Fourth Anglo–Mysore War, the British restored Mysore to the Wadiyar ruler and imposed on him a special Treaty of Subsidiary Alliance. The financial demand from the Company forced the Mysore ruler to shift the burden to the zamindars and ultimately to the cultivators. The simmering discontent of the peasants finally broke out in the open in the province of Nagar, one of the four divisions of Mysore. The rebel peasants defied the authority of the Mysore ruler.

Main leader: **Sardar Malla**
Suppression: The revolt was finally suppressed by the British forces and the administration of the region finally passed into British hands.

Mappila (Moplah) Uprisings (Malabar, 1836–54) The **Muslim cultivators of South Malabar** were popularly known as Mappilas (or Moplahs). They were mainly converts to Islam from the lower caste Hindus, some of them were also the descendants of the Arab settlers in the Malabar Coast. The Moplahs mostly took to agriculture and worked as **jemis or janmi** (bonded labour) of mostly upper caste (Namboodri or Nair) Hindu landlords.

The Moplahs were adversely affected by the British occupation of Malabar in the last decade of the 18th century. Subsequently, Moplah agrarian grievances such as harsh attitude of government officials, high land revenue demand, insecurity of land tenure and landlord exactions compelled the Moplahs to rise in protest against the British and the Hindu landlords.

The religious leaders made significant contribution in mobilising the Moplahs and infusing them with anti-British sentiments. Between 1836 and 1854, there took place more than **22 Mappila uprisings** in Malabar, posing a serious challenge to the British rule. The rebels killed numerous government officials and Hindu landlords.

Since the landlords were mostly upper caste Hindus and the Moplahs were Muslim converts from Hindu lower castes, the uprisings assumed dimensions of a class conflict with religious overtones. Many Moplahs believed that it was a religious virtue to kill oppressive landlords who were also kafirs (non-believers) even at the cost of martyrdom or shahadat.

The British rulers always branded the uprisings as communal outbursts and suppressed the rebels. Similarly, the **poligars of South India** (Dindigul, Malabar and North Arcot) first began revolting against the Company's land revenue system during the 1790s. The sporadic poligar uprisings continued in Madras Presidency up to 1856.

Revolts in Northern India

Northern India was no less rebellious and some of the prominent revolts were- Bilaspur revolt (1805), revolt of Aligarh taluqdars (1814–17), rebellions in present-day states of western UP and Haryana (1824) and the revolt of the Jabalpur Bundellas (1842). The Second Punjab War (1848–49) was also in the nature of a popular revolt.

Kuka or Namdhari Movement (Western Punjab, 1840) The Namdhari Movement was started in 1840 by **Bhagat Jawahar Mal** (Sian Saheb) and **Baba Balak Singh** in western Punjab. It was popularly called Kuka because its followers resorted to shrieks (kukan) while in ecstasy. It emerged as a powerful instrument of socio-religious reform among the Sikhs under **Baba Ram Singh** who preached worship of one God and attacked social evils like caste system, female infanticide, early marriage and barter of daughters in marriage. He also popularised simple and inexpensive Anand marriages.

However, some of the followers of Baba Ram Singh got out of control and began committing religious excesses. For instance, some fanatics got angry over the killing of cows and murdered the butchers in places like Amritsar and Rajkot. This resulted in clash with the government and several of them were violently repressed. Later, in 1872 Ram Singh was deported to Rangoon.

Though there is difference of opinion among the historians whether the movement was religious or political, violent repression of the Kukas definitely created much hatred against the British rule in the minds of the people in Punjab.

Nature of Pre-1857 Uprisings

The nature of pre-1857 uprisings is interpreted differently by different historians. The British historians tended to regard them as mere law and order problems and to project the rebels as primitive savages resisting 'civilization', while neglecting the problems faced by peasants and tribals as possible causes. Thus, the nature of these uprisings may be understood by studying the following features-

- **Aim to overthrow immediate oppressors** The rebels aimed at overthrowing their immediate oppressors—whether it was the oppressive zamindars, money lenders or even the colonial British. For instance, the tribals did not attack all outsiders as enemies. The non-tribal rural poor were not only spared, they even allied with the tribals in their fight against oppression.
- **Keenness to restore past conditions** The rebel peasants and the tribals sought to restore the good old past, before the outsiders acquired control and 'bad times fell upon them'. This does not necessarily mean they were backward looking; it merely represents an attempt to regain a 'condition' perceived as ideal by them.
- **Socio-political consciousness** The peasant and tribal movements of this period also demonstrated a certain level of socio-political consciousness. The rebels' targets were the political sources of their oppression such as the landlords, revenue contractors or even the British rule itself. They also simultaneously tried to bring about social reform (for instance, the Mappila and the Faraizi leaders simultaneously gave a call for socio-religious reform).
- **Popular character** Despite British efforts to term these rebellions as criminal actions, they were rather political actions of a popular character. The rebellions drew their legitimacy from the people, allowing public meetings, planning and attack. The tribal uprisings were especially broad based and often involved the entire tribal population of a region.

  True, in the early stages the insurgencies were often preceded by acts of crime, ranging from theft to killings emerging from extremely difficult conditions of rural life, yet the crime to rebellion transition has been conveniently neglected by the government of the time. For instance, the Santhal uprising began with a series of dacoities against the moneylenders, later justified by the Santhal leaders as arising from the failure of the government officials to address the genuine grievances of the tribals against the moneylenders.
- **Local leadership** These movements threw up leaders who themselves belonged to the immediate context of the movements. They were local leaders who had themselves been affected by foreign intrusion, whereas leaders of the national movement were often outsiders who intervened into the peasant and tribal movements as and when necessary.
- **Regional extent** The extent of the uprisings was limited to the region inhabited by the affected community. For instance, the Santhals fought for their ancestral land which had been grabbed by the outsiders.

- **Drew strength from ethnic ties** In various degrees, the rebels drew their strength for ethnic ties, religious sentiments and messianic leadership.
- **Unequal nature of war** The warfare between the rebels and the British forces was grossly unequal. While the peasants and tribals fought with their primitive weapons such as stones, axes, spears, bows and arrows, the British forces were armed with most modern weapons of the time. As a result, the rebels died in lakhs in this unequal war.

Limitations of Pre-1857 Uprisings

- **Localised and isolated** Even though the uprisings were continuous and massive in totality, they were isolated from one another and were wholly local in nature. They not only arose out of local grievances, they were also local in extent and effect, which limited their impact on national level.
- **Traditional outlook** The leaders of these uprisings were backward looking and traditional in outlook, with total disconnect from the modern scientific world. Their basic objective was to re-establish previous forms of socio-political order and offered no modern alternative. The tribal leaders often projected themselves as messengers of God, who had ordered them to take up arms against their oppressors.
- **Failed to achieve their goal of overthrowing foreign rule** Such local, disunited, backward looking uprisings were bound to fail in overthrowing the foreign oppressors.

As a result of the above weakness, the uprisings failed to contain British march over Indian land. On the other hand, the British succeeded in containing the rebellions one by one. The less fiery rebel chiefs were given concessions in the form of land reinstatement, reduction in revenue assessment, etc., while the fierier ones were physically wiped out. The ruthless suppression of these uprisings was the major reason why the Revolt of 1857 did not spread to the east, west and south of India.

Significance of Pre-1857 Uprisings

- They were the first expressions of protest against colonial rule.
- The uprisings established a strong tradition of resistance to British rule. Later Indian leaders drew their inspiration from these traditions during the national movement.
- They marked a valuable prelude to the watershed Revolt of 1857.

To sum up, in this chapter we saw that the century after 1757 witnessed a large number of popular upsurges and uprisings against the colonial rule and its accompanying evils. The loss of independence, excessive land revenue demands, administrative innovations, foreign intrusion into local autonomy and destruction of village economy were experienced in different regions of India at different points of time, emerging in the form of various peasant and tribal uprisings.

Even though these uprisings suffered from various shortcomings and were finally suppressed in the face of superior British might, they were significant in as much as they were the first expressions of protest against oppression in the colonial period, established a tradition of resistance to the British rule and formed a valuable prelude to the watershed Revolt of 1857.

Prelim Capsule

Popular Uprisings Upto 1857
Bengal and Eastern India

Revolts	Period	Important Details
Sanyasi-Fakir Rebellion	**1763–1800**	Causes—Plunder by EIC, famine of 1770. Led by—**Musa Shah, Majnu Shah, Chirag Ali Shah, Bhawani Pathak** and **Debi Chaudharani**. Suppressed by—**Warren Hastings**. It was made famous by Bankim Chandra Chatterjee in is novel **'Anand Math'**.
Chuar Rebellion (Midnapur)	**1766–1772, 1795–1816**	Causes—Chuar tribesmen rose against famine and increasing land revenue demands.
Peasant Uprising of Rangpur & Dinajpur	**1783**	Causes—Oppression by the East India Company and its revenue contractors. Led by—**Dirjinarain.**
Ho and Munda Rising	**1820–37**	Challenged Company's forces several times in Chota Nagpur & Singhbhum region.
Kol Uprising (Chota Nagpur Plateau)	**1831–37**	Causes—Kol tribesmen rose against British occupation of Singhbhum & intrusion into the life of the Kols.
Pagal Panthis Revolt	**1825**	Causes—Oppression of tenants by zamindars. Led by—**Tipu Shah**.
Ahoms' Revolt (Assam)	**1828**	Causes—Ahom tribesmen opposed continued occupation of Assam by the British. Led by—**Gomdhar Konwar**. Consequences—Part of kingdom was restored to the Assamese King.
Khasi Revolt (Khasi Hills)	**1829**	Causes—Occupation of Khasi Hills by the British. Led by—**Tirat Singh**.
Faraizi Disturbances	**1838–57**	Causes—Oppression of peasants by the landlords and the British. Led by—**Dudu Mian**. In 1857, most of the Faraizis later joined the ranks of the Wahabis.

Khond Uprising (Orissa)	**1837–56**	Causes—British attempt to put an end to the Khond practice of human sacrifice (mariah). Led by—**Chakra Bisoi**.
Savara Rebellion	**1856–57**	Led by—**Radhakrishna Dandasena**.
Santhal Rebellion (Rajmahal Hills)	**1855–56**	Causes—The Santhal tribesmen rose against land alienation under Permanent Settlement, excessive rent, usury by moneylenders & intrusion by **Dikus**. The people of the Santhal tribe inhabited the region between Bhagalpur and Rajmahal, known as **'Daman-i-koh'**. It is also known as Santhal **'hool'** or uprising. Led by—**Sidhu** and **Kanhu**. Consequence—Government created a separate district of **'Santhal Parganas'**

Western India

Revolts	Period	Important Details
Bhil Uprisings (Khandesh, Western Ghats)	**1818, 1825, 1831 and 1846**	Causes—British occupation of Khandesh and intrusion by outsiders. Led by—**Sewram.**
Waghera Rising (Okha Mandal)	**1818–19**	Causes- Imposition of Company's rule & Company's support to exactions by the Gaekwad of Baroda.
Kutch Rebellion (Kutch and Kathiawar)	**1819 & 1831**	Causes—Company's forces defeated the Kutch ruler Rao Bharmal in favor of his infant son, while actual administration of Kutch went into the hands of a British Resident. Kutch chiefs rose in rebellion and demanded restoration of Bharmal.
Ramosi Risings (Western Ghats)	**1822, 1839**	Causes—British invasion into Western Ghats, deposition of Raja Pratap Singh of Satara in 1839. Led by—**Chittur Singh**.
Koli Risings (Gujarat)	**1824–29, 1839 & 1844–48**	Causes—Koli tribesmen rose against the imposition of British rule. The British had destroyed their forts and introduced new order of administration, causing widespread unemployment.

Surat Salt Agitation	**1844–48**	Causes—Salt duty was raised from fifty paise to one rupee by the British government. Consequences—Government was compelled to roll back the raise in salt duty.
Kolhapur and Savantvadi Revolts	**1844**	Causes—Administrative reorganisation in Kolhapur and disbanding of the **Gadkaris**, a hereditary military class which garrisoned Maratha forts.

Southern India

Revolts	Period	Important Details
Revolt of the Raja of Vizianagaram	**1794**	Cause—Annexation of Raja's estate by the British. Consequences—The Company restored the estate to the dead Raja's son and even reduced the demand for money and gifts.
Revolt of Diwan Velu Thampi (Travancore)	**1808**	Causes—Heavy demand for subsidy, high handed attitude of the British Resident. Consequences—Velu Thampi was hanged publicly after death to instill fear among the people.
Rebellion at Mysore	**1830–31**	Causes—Peasants rose against heavy revenue demand. Led by—**Sardar Malla.**
Mappila Uprisings (Malabar)	**1836–54**	Causes—Moplah peasants rose against agrarian grievances such as harsh attitude of government officials, high land revenue demand, insecurity of land tenure and landlord exactions.

Northern India

Kuka or Namdhari Movement (Western Punjab)	**1840**	Led by **Bhagat Jawahar Mal** and **Baba Balak Singh.** Later by **Baba Ram Singh.** In 1872, Ram Singh was deported to Rangoon.

Previous Years' Questions – Preliminary Exam

1. Which one of the following mountain tribes did the British first came into contact with after the grant of Diwani in the year 1765? **[UPSC 2002]**
   (a) Garos (b) Khasis
   (c) Kukis (d) Tipperahs
2. Which one of the following revolts was made famous by Bankim Chandra Chatterjee in his novel Anand Math? **[UPSC 2006]**
   (a) Bhil uprising
   (b) Rangpur and Dinapur Uprising
   (c) Bishnupur and Birbhum rebellion
   (d) Sannyasi rebellion
3. Which of the following provided a common factor for tribal insurrection in India in the 19th century? **[UPSC 2011]**
   (a) Introduction of a new system of land revenue and taxation of tribal products
   (b) Influence of foreign religious missionaries in tribal areas.
   (c) Rise of a large number of money lenders, traders and revenue farmers as middlemen in tribal areas.
   (d) The complete disruption of the old agrarian order of the tribal communities.
4. After the Santhal Uprising subsided, what was/were the measure/measures taken by the colonial government? **[UPSC 2018]**
   1. The territories called 'Santhal Paraganas' were created.
   2. It became illegal for a Santhal to transfer land to a non-Santhal.

   Select the correct answer using the code given below:
   (a) 1 only
   (b) 2 only
   (c) Both 1 and 2
   (d) Neither 1 nor 2

Previous Years' Questions – Main Exam

1. Discuss the character of major Tribal Uprisings in British India in the 19th century. **[UPSC 1994, 2003]**
2. Why was there a sudden spurt in famines in colonial India since the mid-18th century? Give reasons. **[UPSC 2022]**

Answers

Previous Years' Questions – Preliminary Exam

1. (b) 2. (d) 3. (c) 4. (c)

2

Revolt of 1857

The Revolt of 1857 was not a sudden occurrence but the culmination of a century long tradition of popular resistance to the Company's rule. Neither was it merely a result of sepoy discontent but a result of accumulated grievances of people against the foreign rule and its administration.

For the last 100 years, the East India Company had been conquering the country bit by bit and then plundered and exploited it, till it was milked dry. The impact of British Rule was felt on all spheres of Indian life whether polity, economy, administration, culture and religion; and had adversely affected the position of all including rulers of Indian states, sepoys, landlords, peasants, traders, pundits and maulvis and others. The only exception was the English educated middle class which owed its origin to the British. As a result, resistance was offered against the colonial rule at various times from the mid-18th to the mid-19th century. But the Revolt of 1857, also termed as the First War of Independence, posed the most serious challenge to the British supremacy in India and shook the Empire to its very foundations.

The Revolt first started as a sepoy mutiny but soon it was joined by thousands of peasants and civilian population and spread widely in northern and central India. This linkage of the army with the masses naturally proved to be dangerous for the colonial rulers.

Causes of the Revolt

The British historians tend to emphasise the issue of the greased cartridges as the most important cause of the Revolt of 1857. But the modern Indian historians are of the view that the causes lay deeper and are to be found in the 100 years of British Rule from Plassey in 1757 to the rebellion of Mangal Pandey in 1857. The issue of greased cartridge ignited the simmering discontent accumulated overtime on account of socio-political and economic grievances.

Political Causes

Annexations of Princely States The Company made several annexations under **Wellesley's subsidiary alliance** and **Dalhousie's Doctrine of Lapse** (Satara 1848, Jaitpur 1849, Sambalpur 1849, Baghat 1850, Udaipur 1852, Jhansi 1853, Nagpur 1854). The Indians shared a common fear that the absorption of all states was now merely a matter of time. It was also believed that the annexations were not because of Doctrine of Lapse but because of 'lapse of morals' on the part of the East India Company. Thus, the expansionist policy followed by the Company gravely embittered the rulers of the Indian States, forcing them to rise in revolt, as is clear from the following examples.

Rani Laxmi Bai

Jhansi: Jhansi was a Maratha-ruled princely state in the Bundelkhand region. In 1853, the Raja of Jhansi, Gangadhar Rao, had died without leaving a biological male heir. The same year Dalhousie applied the **Doctrine of Lapse** and annexed Jhansi, rejecting the claim of Damodar Rao (adopted son of Rani and her late husband Gangadhar Rao) to the throne. Further, in March 1854, Rani was given an annual pension of ₹60,000 and ordered to leave the palace and the fort. Aggrieved, the Rani decided to raise the banner of revolt and joined the great uprising of 1857 against the British rule.

Nawab Wajid Ali Shah

Awadh: In 1856, Awadh was annexed on the pretext of **misgovernance**, dethroning Nawab Wajid Ali Shah who was later deported to Calcutta. The reason stated by Dalhousie was that he wanted to free the people from the Nawab's mismanagement and taluqdar's oppression! The British had already been draining the Awadh economy since 1765, thus draining its administrative viability. This final move of annexation severely hurt the self-respect of the Awadh people, particularly the sepoys of the British army since most of them came from Awadh itself. The dismissal of the court also meant unemployment for the many courtiers, the artisans and the army men. The taluqdars were dispossessed of their estates and their forts demolished. The land revenue settlement introduced in Awadh after annexation further intensified the people's discontent with the cumulative result that nearly three-fourth of the adult population of Awadh participated in the Revolt of 1857.

Nana Sahib: Nana, the **adopted son of the last Peshwa Baj Rao II**, was refused pension by the British that was being paid to Baji Rao. Nana was also forced to vacate Pune, his family seat, and live far away at Kanpur. Thus, when the rebellion broke out in 1857, it was Nana Sahib who raised the banner of revolt at Kanpur.

As stated by **Malleson,** 'The policy of Dalhousie had created bad faith and Indians got the feeling that the British were 'playing the wolf in the garb of the lamb'.

Abolition of Regal Titles The Mughal emperor, Bahadur Shah II, had grown old and weak. Lord Dalhousie recognised the succession of Mughal Prince Faqir-ud-Din, but he was not in favour of retaining an **imperium in imperio** (empire within an empire) and imposed strict conditions on him. In 1856, Faqir-ud-Din died and Lord Canning (who was also the Governor-General during the Revolt of 1857) declared that the prince next in succession would have to renounce the regal title and the ancestral Mughal palaces. This grievously hurt the feelings of Muslim subjects who felt that the British wanted to humble the House of Timur. In addition to the Mughal Emperor, the British also abolished the regal titles of the Nawabs of Carnatic and Tanjore.

Alien Rule of the British India has had a long history of foreign invasions and even before the British, several foreigners had ruled over different parts of the country, for instance, the Afghans and the Mughals had conquered India but in course of time they had settled here and made India their home. Whatever revenue they collected from the people, it was spent in India itself. But this was not so in the case of the British. The British never intended to settle down in India and make it their home. The officials of the Company wanted to make as much money as possible here and then quickly go back to England. As a result, the British remained perpetual foreigners in India.

Further, the practice of **'absentee sovreigntyship'**, i.e., rule by foreigners from a distant land, also embittered the Indians against the British. They had begun to feel that they were being ruled by officials from England, who were draining their own land of its wealth.

Economic and Administrative Causes

Exploitative Land Revenue Settlements Introduced by the British The various land revenue settlements (Permanent, Ryotwari and Mahalwari settlements) introduced by the British meant loss of land for the landholders and heavy taxation for zamindars and cultivators. The land revenue assessments under all the systems were heavy and oppressive, reaching upto 50 per cent or more of the produce and tax was extracted even when the crop was fully damaged. In such cases, the cultivators had no option but to take loans from the local money lenders who charged them exorbitant interest. This made the cultivators heavily indebted. Many of them later participated in the Revolt of 1857, driving away government officials and burning money lenders' records.

The economic decline of the peasantry also found expression in **12 major and several minor famines** from 1770 to 1857. The **complex judicial system** also aided the rich in oppressing the poor. Flogging and jailing of cultivators for arrears was common. The miserable condition of the peasants made them desperate to join a revolt against their oppressors.

Destruction of Indian Trade, Handicraft and Industry The economic policies of the British in India also destroyed the Indian traders, artisans and industrialists. The Company's traders enjoyed various privileges such as duty-free trade, which made their goods comparatively cheaper than those of the Indian traders, who had to pay full duties and made their goods uncompetitive. Similarly, the Company destroyed Indian handicrafts and industry in an attempt to convert India into a market for British manufactures.

In this way, driven by self-interest, the British destroyed the two major sources of employment, i.e. agriculture and handicrafts, for the vast population of the country.

Alienation of Upper and Middle Classes Under the administration of local princes and chieftains, Indians served at all levels—both lower and upper. But under British administration, all higher posts were reserved for the Europeans. **Indians could serve only as subordinates** and occupied all petty posts. The dissolution of princely courts also meant **loss of job for cultural persons** such as the poets, dramatists, writers, and musicians, who were patronised by the princes.

Further, in some provinces, the British had made land revenue settlements directly with the cultivators. This dispossessed many landlords and taluqdars (i.e. the landed aristocracy) of their lands and position. As if this was not enough, a British official **Coverly Jackson** demanded strict enquiry into the titles of the taluqdars of Awadh, who were the hardest hit, and drove Awadh into the vortex of the rebellion. In 1852, the **Inam Commission** was appointed in Bombay to inquire into the titles of Inamdars (holders of land grants/gifts) and nearly 20,000 estates were confiscated. In this way the land revenue settlements introduced by the British had an adverse impact even on Indian aristocracy, driving them into poverty without even benefitting the cultivators. 'Peasants visiting their previous landlords with tears in their eyes' had become a common sight.

Social and Religious Causes

Arrogant Attitude of the British and Racial Discrimination Like all conquerors, even the British were arrogant and rude towards their subject population. They felt racially superior and treated the Indians with contempt, often describing them as **'barbarians'** or 'uncivilised'. The behaviour of English officers was particularly contemptuous, who commonly spoke of Indians as **'nigger'** and abused them. Criminal assaults on Indians by Englishmen were also common, but the Whites were seldom punished as they were tried by European judges who acquitted them with light or no punishment. Such repeated insults had begun to simmer in the hearts of the subjects like a burning sore.

British Interference in Religion and Culture It may still be easy to withstand political and economic exploitation but religious persecution embitters the very soul of a subject population. That **conversion of Indians into Christianity** was a clear aim of the British is certain from the speech of Mangles, the Chairman of the Directors of East India Company, who declared in the house of Commons, 'Providence has entrusted the extensive empire of Hindustan to England in order that the banner of Christ should wave triumphant from one end of India to the other'.

The **Charter of 1813** allowed missionaries to go to India and also allowed them to settle there under a licence. Christian missionaries and religious persons such as Charles Grunt, Chairman of Court of Directors, felt that westernization would help in the spread of Christianity, and in this opened several modern schools, colleges and hospitals. According to Vir Savarkar, the military officials abused the very name of Ram and Mohammad in front of the sepoys and tempted them into embracing Christianity by promises of promotion.

The British had also begun to interfere in the socio-cultural affairs of the country. For instance, legislations were passed regarding prohibition of female infanticide, sati and slavery and passing of legislation regarding widow remarriage. In 1850, the **Religious Disabilities Act** was passed which modified certain Hindu customs; for example, it stated that a change of religion would not debar a son from inheriting the property of his heathen father.

Thus, Indians had begun to feel that their religion and culture was in danger. The atmosphere had become so charged with suspicion that even railways and telegraph began to be looked upon as instruments of conversion. The rebels referred to the telegraph as 'the accursed string that strangled them' and the education offices set up by the British as 'shaitani daftars'. In such a context, the greased cartridge incident proved a trigger and convinced both the Hindus and the Muslims that the British were deliberately trying to destroy their religion.

Military Causes

Grievances of Sepoys Over the years, several grievances of the sepoys in the British army had got accumulated. But first we need to understand who were these sepoys and where did they come from.

The sepoys in the British army were in reality, **'peasants in uniform'**. Owing to the impoverishment caused by the new land revenue settlements, many of them had joined military service to supplement their agricultural income (only to realise that life was equally tough and exploitative for an Indian sepoy!). Further, in the Bengal Army, service was hereditary and nearly three-fifth of the sepoys came from peasant population of **Awadh** and the **high caste Brahmin and Rajput families** of North-West Provinces. Naturally, these sepoys reflected all the grievances of the civil population of Awadh as well as the grievances of the high caste and royal families.

Thus, annexations of princely states did not go down well with these sepoys. Particularly when Awadh was annexed, they suddenly realized that the Company had used their services to liquidate their own King.

Maulana Azad stated that, 'Annexation of Awadhmarked the beginning of a rebellious mood in the army generally and in the Bengal army in particular...it gave a rude shock to the people'.

Other causes of growing resentment among the sepoys may be understood under the following heads:

Professional Grievances

- An Indian sepoy was paid one-third the salary of a European sepoy (₹7–9 monthly).
- There was racial discrimination in matters of promotion and pension.
- Indian sepoys were treated roughly, abused and humiliated.
- They were forced to serve in far-away regions without payment of any extra batta (allowance).
- They were no longer gifted with jagirs and other prizes for their meritorious deeds, as was the case under Indian rulers.
- In 1854, the **Post Office Act** (Lord Dalhousie) was passed which withdrew the free-postage privilege of the sepoys.

Religious Grievances

In addition to the above, the upper caste sepoys found that their service conditions frequently came in conflict with their religious beliefs.

- The high caste sepoys resented the part of army discipline that treated them at par with the low caste recruits.
- In **1806, at Vellore**, the turban was replaced by a leather cockade. This caused the sepoys to rise in mutiny.
- In 1824, the sepoys at Barrackpore refused to go to Burma as crossing the sea meant loss of caste. The regiment was disbanded and some leaders put to death.
- In 1844, the sepoys of Bengal Army refused to go to Sind as crossing Indus again meant loss of caste.
- In **1856, General Service Enlistment Act** was passed by the Canning government—it stated that all future recruits of the Bengal army would have to give an undertaking to serve anywhere their service might be required by the government. This aroused wide-scale hostility since the sepoys who had gone to Afghanistan during 1839–42 Afghan invasion, had not been readmitted into the folds of their castes.
- Closer to 1857, there were reports of bone dust in flour ration.

Invincibility of British Rule Shattered In the years immediately preceding the Revolt, the British army suffered major reverses in wars such as the First Afghan War (1838–42), Punjab Wars (1845–49) and the Crimean War (1854–56). In 1855–56, the powerful Santhal uprising took place and temporarily swept away the British from their area. These events had lowered the general morale of the British soldiers but had added immensely to the confidence of the Indian masses, particularly the sepoys who had begun to feel that if they struck at that hour, they had reasonable chances of success against their foreign perpetrators. Thus, the sepoys were only waiting for the right occasion and the occasion was supplied by the greased cartridges incident.

Immediate Cause

In 1857, the old-fashioned musket 'Brown Bess' was replaced by the **new Enfield Rifle**. Its cartridges were covered with a greased paper which had to be bitten off before the cartridge was loaded into the rifle. A rumour gained currency in the Bengal Army that this grease was made of **beef and pig fat**. This completely outraged the religious sentiments of both Hindu and Muslim sepoys and they were now convinced that the British were deliberately trying to destroy their religion. This issue of Enfield Rifles became the immediate cause of the Revolt of 1857.

Beginning of the Mutiny and the Revolt

Revolt of the Army

Initial Stages Even before the Meerut incident of 10 May, there were rumblings of resentment at various cantonments. On 25 February 1857, the 19th Bengal Native Infantry at Berhampore (also spelled Berhampur or Baharampur; about 200 km north of Calcutta; presently in Murshidabad district of West Bengal) refused to use the newly introduced rifle and was disbanded in March the same year. Again, on 29 March 1857, in Barrackpore near Calcutta, the sepoys of 34th Native Infantry refused to use the greased cartridges. One young Brahmin sepoy, **Mangal Pandey**, went a step further and killed one of his European officers. Pandey was overpowered, hanged and his regiment disbanded.

Revolt Begins (Meerut, 10 May 1857) In May 1857 at Meerut, 85 sepoys of the 3rd Cavalry regiment were court-martialled and sentenced to long terms of imprisonment on their refusal to use the greased cartridges. Thereafter, on 10 May 1857 sepoys stationed at Meerut broke out in open rebellion, killed some of their European officers, released some of their fellow sepoys and marched to Delhi to appeal to Bahadur Shah II, the Mughal Emperor and a pensioner of the British, to lead the revolt and give legitimacy to their cause; though at this time Bahadur Shah possessed nothing but the name of the mighty Mughals.

Bahadur Shah Zafar

On 12 May 1857, Delhi was seized by the rebels after they overcame **Lieutenant Willoughby**, the commanding officer at Delhi. Some European inhabitants of Delhi were shot at and killed, the palace occupied and Bahadur Shah was proclaimed Emperor. The loss of Delhi was a serious blow of prestige for the British.

Revolt of the People

In the next 24 hours, what began as a sepoy mutiny swelled into a **full-scale political rebellion**. As soon as the gunshots fired at the British officers were heard, people from surrounding areas joined in including the peasants, artisans, shop keepers, traders, labourers, zamindars, pundits, maulvis and others. They burnt the bungalows of the British, looted the military bazaars, cut the telephone wires and stopped horsemen carrying messages to Delhi. Once the sepoys reached Delhi, they proclaimed the old Bahadur Shah II as the Emperor of India.

In the next one month (from 11 to 30 May), the entire Bengal army rose in rebellion. The Revolt was joined by almost half of the sepoys of the Company, the bulk of whom were upper caste Hindus and nearly one-third came from Awadh. Soon the rebellion spread throughout **Northern and Central India** at Lucknow, Allahabad, Kanpur, Bareilly, Banaras, in parts of Bihar, Jhansi and other places. The worst affected areas were Western Bihar, Awadh, Rohilkhand, Delhi and the region between the Chambal and the Narmada. Luckily for the British, bulk of Indian rulers remained loyal and extended valuable support in suppression of the rebellion. In fact, India **south of Narmada remained practically undisturbed**.

Between Delhi and Calcutta, wherever there were Indian troops, they revolted. The people in the city and countryside quickly joined in. The Indian troops burned barracks and court houses, flung open the prison gates, plundered government treasury. In the city, the people attacked British establishments such as revenue offices, courts and thanas. In the countryside, people surrounded the zamindars and the moneylenders; destroyed their account books and government records. In this way, the **rebels tried to destroy every symbol of British power**.

Even in places where the people did not directly participate in the revolt, they offered their help and sympathy. They offered food and shelter to the rebels and misled the British troops by giving wrong information. Both Hindu and Muslim sepoys demonstrated solid unity.

Hindu–Muslim Unity During the Revolt Much of the strength of the revolt came from Hindu–Muslim unity which was seen reaching a new peak in 1857. The rebels had unanimously proclaimed Bahadur Shah Zafar, a Muslim, as their leader. The Hindus and Muslim sepoys respected each other's religious sentiments. For instance, cow slaughter was immediately banned in several affected areas, as a symbol of solidarity. A British officer Aitcheson bitterly complained-'In this instance, we could not play off the Mohammedans against the Hindus'. The events of 1857 clearly bring out that the people and politics of India were not really communal before 1858.

Storm Centres and Leaders

Several storm centres emerged in north India, covering present-day Uttar Pradesh and Bihar. These included Delhi, Kanpur, Lucknow, Bareilly, Jhansi and Arrah. These centres threw up their own leaders who accepted Bahadur Shah as the Emperor of India but remained independent for all practical purposes. In the absence of any leaders from their own ranks, the rebels had turned to traditional leaders—the princes and landed aristocrats who had suffered at the hands of the British.

Delhi (12 May 1857, Led by Bahadur Shah II and Bakht Khan)

On 12 May 1857, Delhi was seized by the rebels after they overcame **Lieutenant Willoughby**, the commanding officer at Delhi. Some European inhabitants of Delhi were shot at and killed, the palace was occupied and Bahadur Shah II was proclaimed Emperor. However, the real command lay in the hands of a Court of soldiers (consisting of 10 members, 6 of them from the army) led by Bakht Khan. Bakht Khan had earlier served as a Subedar of artillery in the British army. Leading the revolt of the sepoys in Bareilly, he brought them to Delhi where he now emerged as a popular leader.

Lucknow (4 June 1857, Led by Begum Hazrat Mahal, Begum of Awadh)

At Lucknow, the revolt was led by the Begum Hazrat Mahal who declared her son Birjis Kadr as the Nawab of Awadh. The Begum gained the support of the sepoys, peasants and zamindars of Awadh and drove away the British (including British **Resident Henry Lawrence**) who took refuge in the Residency building. The rebels soon attacked the residency, killing Sir Henry. British officers Havelock and Outrum tried in vain to relieve Lucknow. It was only in November 1857 that **Sir Colin Campbell**, sent from England, recaptured Lucknow with the help of Gorkha regiments and evacuated the residency.

Kanpur (5 June 1857, Led by Nana Sahib and Tatya Tope)

On 5 June, the sepoys at Kanpur rose in rebellion and declared Nana Sahib, the adopted son of Peshwa Baji Rao II, as the Peshwa. General Sir **Hugh Wheeler** commanding the station finally surrendered on 27 June. Most of the fighting, however, was carried out by Tatya Tope, Nana's able and experienced Lieutenant, on his behalf; and it was Tatya who rose to immortality with his patriotism and skilful guerrilla fighting. Azimullah was another loyalist of Nana Sahib who had an expertise in political propaganda.

The counter operations for recovering Kanpur were closely associated with the recovery of Lucknow. On 6 December, Sir Campbell recovered Kanpur following which Tatya Tope escaped and joined Rani Laxmi Bai at Jhansi.

Jhansi (June 1857, Led by Rani Laxmi Bai)

In 1853, Dalhousie had applied the **Doctrine of Lapse** and annexed Jhansi, rejecting the claim of Damodar Rao (adopted son of Rani and her late husband Gangadhar Rao) to the throne. When the Rebellion broke out in 1857, Jhansi quickly emerged as a storm centre. The troops of Jhansi raised the banner of revolt under the leadership of Rani Laxmi Bai, and proclaimed her as the ruler of the state.

Though the Rani showed some hesitation in the beginning, she fought valiantly once she joined the ranks of the rebels. In fact, she is considered as the most outstanding leader of the revolt who later emerged for Indian nationalists as a symbol of resistance to the British Raj.

Deciding to fight for independence from the British rule, the Rani assumed control over Jhansi administration. She bravely defended Jhansi against British troops when **Sir Hugh Rose** besieged

Jhansi on 23 March 1858. Rani raised the battle cry, **'Mera Jhansi, deugi nahin'** and the struggle went on for two weeks. Meanwhile, Kanpur fell and Tatya Tope escaped and joined the Rani of Jhansi. Soon Jhansi also fell but Rani managed to escape in the guise of a man with Damodar Rao on her back, joining Tatya's forces at Gwalior. The Scindia ruler of Gwalior decided to remain loyal to the English and took shelter at Agra.

Bareilly (Led by Khan Bahadur Khan)

Khan Bahadur Khan was the descendant of the former ruler of Rohilkhand. He was dissatisfied with the pension being granted to him by the British and joined the revolt. He raised an army of 40,000 soldiers and proclaimed himself the Nawab Nazim of his new government.

Arrah (25 July 1857, Bihar, Led by Kunwar Singh)

Kunwar Singh was a ruined zamindar of **Jagdishpur**. He was an old man in his seventies and nursed a grudge against the British who had dispossessed him of his estates. He unhesitating joined the sepoys and emerged as one of the most outstanding military leaders of the revolt as the British dreaded him the most.

In addition to the above, there were several unsung heroes and martyrs of the Revolt. These were the sepoys, the peasants and the small zamindars who had come together forgetting their differences of class, caste and religion, and raised their voice against the British rule.

These included-

- **Maulavi Ahmadullah of Faizabad-** He was an important leader of the Revolt in Awadh region; was originally from Madras and had moved to Faizabad where he preached armed rebellion.
- **Surendra Sai of Sambalpur-** In 1827 when the Maharaja Sai of Sambalpur died without leaving an heir, the British placed a puppet ruler, ignoring Surendra Sai's claim for succession. In 1849 Sambalpur was finally annexed by Lord Dalhousie under Doctrine of Lapse. When the revolt broke out in 1857, Sai raised the banner of revolt and fought valiantly against the British.

Defeat of the Rebels

Delhi Recaptured (20 September 1857, Led by John Nicholson)

The recapture of Delhi was of great psychological importance for the British and they directed all their energies towards it. Hence, Delhi was the first to fall, though after a prolonged battle. On 20 September 1857, the British finally recaptured Delhi with the help of forces rushed from Punjab. However, John Nicholson, the leading British officer was grievously injured and he later died. Terrible vengeance was wrecked on the inhabitants of Delhi. The Emperor Bahadur Shah Zafar, who had been hiding in Humayun's Tomb, was taken prisoner and exiled to **Rangoon** where he later died in 1862. Two minor sons and a grandson of the Emperor were

British soldiers defending near Delhi

also captured and publicly shot by **Lieutenant Hudson** himself. In this way, the last of the Mughals were finally extinguished and with the capture of Delhi, the focal point of the Revolt was lost.

With the fall of Delhi, the back of the revolt was broken and one after the other, all the other main leaders of the revolt also fell.

Kanpur Recaptured (6 December 1857, Led by Sir Colin Campbell)

On 6 December 1857, Kanpur was occupied by Sir Colin Campbell. Nana Sahib was defeated and he later escaped to Nepal. Tatya Tope also escaped and joined Rani Laxmi Bai at Jhansi.

Lucknow Recaptured (March 1858, Led by Sir Colin Campbell)

After Lucknow was recaptured, Begum Hazrat Mahal escaped to Nepal.

Jhansi Recaptured (3 April 1858, Led by Sir Hugh Rose)

After Jhansi fell, Rani managed to escape in the guise of a man with Damodar Rao on her back, joining Tatya's forces at Gwalior. The Rani died fighting the British clad in a soldier's uniform on the ramparts of the fort on 17 June 1858. General Hugh Rose, who had defeated her, said in her praise and memory, 'here lay the woman who was the only man among the rebels'.

Tatya Tope fled into the jungles of central India and fought bitter guerrilla warfare. In April 1859, he was later betrayed by a friend and caught by the British while asleep. He was tried and hurriedly put to death the same year.

In May 1858, the English recaptured Bareilly and Jagdishpur. By 1859, Kunwar Singh of Jagdishpur, Khan Bahadur Khan of Bareilly, Bakht Khan of Delhi and Maulvi Ahamadullah of Faizabad were all dead. A rebellion at Banaras was mercilessly suppressed by **Colonel Neil** who put to death all rebels and even suspected persons.

In this way, by July 1858, the revolt had been almost completely suppressed and by the end of 1859, the British authority in India was firmly re-established. The British had poured in immense supplies of men and material into the country and the Indians had to repay this entire cost through their own suppression.

Prelim Capsule

Revolt of 1857

Date	Place	Main Event
25th Feb 1857	**Berhampur**	19th Bengal Native Infantry at Berhampur (Orissa) refused to use the newly introduced rifle.
29th Mar 1857	**Barrackpore**	34th Native Infantry refused to use the greased cartridges. **Mangal Pandey**, a Brahmin sepoy, killed one of his European officers. Pandey was hanged and his regiment disbanded.

10th May 1857	**Meerut**	Sepoys of 3rd Cavalry regiment broke out in open rebellion against the use of greased cartridges and marched to Delhi to appeal to Bahadur Shah II to lead the revolt.
12th May 1857	**Delhi**	The rebels occupied the palace and proclaimed **Bahadur Shah II** as Emperor. However, the real command lay in the hands of **Bakht Khan**.
4th Jun 1857	**Lucknow**	Begum Hazrat Mahal who declared her son Birjis Kadr as the Nawab of Awadh.
5th Jun 1857	**Kanpur**	The sepoys declared **Nana Sahib**, the adopted son of Peshwa Baji Rao II, as the Peshwa. Most of the fighting, however, was carried out by **Tatya Tope**.
June 1857	**Jhansi**	The troops of Jhansi raised the banner of revolt under the leadership of **Rani Laxmi Bai**, and proclaimed her as the ruler of the state.
—	**Bareilly**	**Khan Bahadur Khan** raised an army of 40,000 soldiers and proclaimed himself the Nawab Nazim of his new government.
25th Jul 1857	**Arrah**	The revolt was led by Kunwar Singh, a ruined zamindar of **Jagdishpur**.
Recapture		
20th Sep 1857	**Delhi**	Recaptured by John Nicholson with the help of forces rushed from Punjab. Bahadur Shah was captured and exiled to Rangoon. His two sons were publicly shot by **Lieutenant Hudson**.
6th Dec 1857	**Kanpur**	Recaptured by Sir **Colin Campbell**. Nana Sahib was defeated and he later escaped to Nepal. Tatya Tope also escaped and joined Rani Laxmi Bai at Jhansi.
March 1858	**Lucknow**	Recaptured by Sir **Colin Campbell**. Begum Hazrat Mahal escaped to Nepal.
3rd Apr 1858	**Jhansi**	Recaptured by Sir **Hugh Rose**. Rani managed to escape in the guise of a man with Damodar Rao on her back, joining Tatya's forces at Gwalior. The Rani died fighting the British clad in a soldier's uniform on the ramparts of the fort.
—	—	Tatya tope fled into the jungles of central India and fought bitter guerilla warfare. In April 1859, he was caught by the British, tried and hurriedly put to death the same year.
May 1858	**Bareilly & Jagdishpur**	Recaptured.

Causes of Failure of the Revolt

Revolt did not Embrace the Entire Country

Even though the revolt engulfed vast territory and received widespread sympathy, yet it could not embrace the entire country. India south of the Narmada remained largely unaffected. Punjab remained well controlled under John Lawrence. Rajasthan and Sind remained quiet. Afghanistan under Dost Mohammad remained friendly to the British who also received much needed help from Nepal.

Lack of Unity Among Indians

An even bigger cause of the failure was the appalling disunity among the Indians themselves. Almost half the Indian soldiers not only did not participate, but also fought against their own countrymen. The recapture of Delhi was effected by 1700 British troops and 3200 Indian troops.

While the sepoys in Bengal were revolting, those in Punjab and south India sided with the British in crushing the rebellion.

Lack of Support from Various Sections of People

The revolt did not receive the support of a vast section of Indian people including the Indian rulers, merchants, zamindars and educated intelligentsia.

There were various groups who chose to remain loyal to the British for their own reasons. The Sikhs, for example, feared the revival of the Mughals; the Rajput chiefs and the Nizam of Hyderabad feared the revival of the Marathas. The Bengal zamindars were a creation of the British. Big merchants and some sections of peasantry had also profited under the British. The taluqdars (big zamindars) of Awadh abandoned the revolt once the British reassured them that their estates would be returned.

Further, the revolt did not receive the support of educated Indian intelligentsia. The new educated middle classes were a product of the British system and they mistakenly believed that the British influence was needed to lead India to modernisation. They had little understanding of the evils of colonialism and could not foresee that the colonial rule was incapable of modernising India.

Then, just about 1 per cent of the Indian rulers joined the revolt. An overwhelming majority of Indian rulers actively supported the British in suppression of the revolt and included **the Scindias, the Holkars, the Nizam of Hyderabad, Nawab of Bhopal, the Maharaja of Kashmir and the Ranas of Nepal**. States of **Rampur, Patiala, Jind** and **Baroda** also remained loyal to the British. How valuable their role was for the British during the Revolt is evident from the following remarks of Canning, the Governor General during the Revolt- 'If Scindia joins the Mutiny, I shall have to pack off tomorrow'. About the role of the Indian chiefs, he had remarked, 'They acted as the **breakwaters to the storm** which would have otherwise swept us in one great wave'.

Lack of a Unified Programme and Ideology

All those elements who rebelled against the British had their own reasons for doing so—the Rani of Jhansi fought for her Jhansi, Nana Sahib for his Peshwaship. Khan Bahadur Khan fought for Rohilkhand, the Begum of Awadh for the rights of her minor son. The sepoys were driven into the vortex of the struggle owing to their specific professional and religious grievances. Thus, it is clear that the rebels were driven by their own narrow and selfish motives which totally sapped the movement of its very strength and vitality.

Lack of a Forward-Looking Plan

The rebels revolted against the British authority, but did not know what to create in its place. They relied on leaders such as Bahadur Shah II and Nana Sahib who belonged to the old feudal system which had been defeated by the British. They could not see that the progress of the country lay not in going back to feudal monarchy but in going forward to modern society and polity.

Feelings of modern nationalism alone could have provided a viable alternative to the British rule, which were yet to emerge. The Hindus and the Muslims came together against a common enemy, but their differences were not yet dead. The soldiers from Bombay and Madras were mostly from lower castes and they remained loyal. Thus, we see that the rebels were united only in their hatred for the British but divided in their vision for future and had no common ideal before them.

Poor Leadership and Poor Organisation of the Revolt

On one hand, old Bahadur Shah was proclaimed as leader of the Revolt whose weak personality, old age and lack of leadership qualities created political weakness at the nerve centre of the revolt. On the other hand, the Company's army was led by men of exceptional abilities and experience: like Nicholson, Outram, Havelock, Edwards and Lawrence brothers.

The revolt was also poorly organised and lacked a plan of action. After the suppression of the revolt, various commissions were appointed to find any plan or scheme of the rebellion, but there was found to be none. Though the rebels were not lacking in courage, they were certainly lacking in experience and organising ability.

Superiority of British Resources

The British forces were decidedly superior to the rebel forces—the British had modern weapons of war while the Indians fought with spears and swords; the British were better organised while the rebels often behaved like a riotous mob. The British were empowered with a strong central command, a plan for military action and regular supply of men, money and material; while the rebels had no such support system. The strength of the British forces may be gauged from the fact that many rebels felt demoralised at the very sight of the British troops and fled back to their villages. Moreover, considering the vast resources of the British army, it may be safely stated that even if the English had been driven into the sea, it would have only been a matter of time before they had recaptured India.

> In context of the use of modern weaponry by the British troops, **Nana Saheb** had remarked, 'The blue cap kills before they fire'.

Significance of the Revolt

The Revolt of 1857, an unsuccessful but heroic effort to eliminate the foreign rule, stands out as a **major milestone in Modern Indian History**. It represented the crystallisation of resentment against the alien rule. It was the desperate last effort to save India under traditional leadership, and the first great popular effort to rid India of the foreign rule. The Revolt of 1857 shattered the invincibility of the British rule and paved the way for the rise of modern national struggle.

In fact, the significance of the revolt was not limited to its immediate achievements; even in failure it served a great purpose. The revolt, along with all the previous uprisings, created a valuable tradition of resistance to British rule and the leaders of the revolt emerged as the earliest nationalist leaders who continued to inspire feelings of nationalism for all ages to come.

Debate Regarding Nature of the Revolt

The nature of the Revolt of 1857 has been much debated. Different historians describe it variously—as a mutiny, as a religious war against the Christians, or even as a racial struggle for supremacy. Still others describe it as a struggle between Oriental and Occidental civilisations and cultures, or as a Hindu–Muslim conspiracy to overthrow the British. Some Indian nationalists have also called it the 'First War of Indian Independence'.

Revolt of 1857: A Sepoy Mutiny or a National Struggle?

Was it a Sepoy Mutiny? British historians such as Sir John Lawrence and Sir John Seeley tend to define the Revolt as nothing more than a sepoy mutiny. Their narration focuses more on the accounts of rebel sepoys and ignores the civil rebellion. There is a marked tendency to minimise the Indian grievances and overlook the colonial context in which the revolt occurred. Some contemporary Indians also agreed with this view. These included **Sir Sayed Ahmad Khan** (Sadr Amin at Bijnor in 1857), Munshi Jiwan Lal and Moinuddin (eyewitnesses at Delhi), and Durgadas Bandopadhyaya (eyewitness at Bareilly).

Later, British historians such as **Judith Brown** have admitted this imperial bias and stated that- 'Many British people preferred to see the events largely as a military mutiny, understandably, as any wider interpretation could have cast doubt on the nature of the Raj'.

VD Savarkar, author of *The Indian War of Independence of 1857.*

Was it a National Struggle? This view was first put forth in 1902 by **VD Savarkar** in his book The Indian War of Independence of 1857. By that time, nationalist agitations had emerged and the happenings of 1857 were viewed as part of that struggle. In this account, the focus now shifted from the sepoy mutiny to the colonial context.

However, the critics point out that the Revolt cannot be seen as a freedom struggle due to **absence of feelings of modern nationalism** in the rebels and lack of a common vision for future.

Other Opinions on Nature of the Revolt

- **L. E. R. Rees** The Revolt was 'a war of fanatic religionists against Christians'.
- **T. R. Holmes** The Revolt was 'a conflict between civilisation and barbarism'.

- **Sir James Outram and W. Tyler** The outbreak was 'a result of Hindu–Muslim conspiracy'.
- **Benjamin Disraeli (Former British Prime Minister, then a contemporary leader in England)** It was a 'national rising'.
- **Marxist Interpretation** It was 'the struggle of the soldier peasant democratic combine against foreign as well as feudal bondage'.
- **Pt. Jawaharlal Nehru** Essentially it was 'a feudal outburst headed by feudal chiefs and their followers and aided by the widespread anti-foreign sentiment'.
- **S. N. Sen** 'What began as a fight for religion, ended as a war of independence'.
- **Anonymous** '1857 was not the inauguration of a freedom movement but the dying groans of an absolute aristocracy'.

Recent scholarly researches support the view that while it began as a military mutiny, the uprising quickly assumed the character of a popular rebellion. Whatever may the nature of the Revolt, it did become a symbol of struggle against the British rule and during the freedom struggle our people drew inspiration from the heroic stories of 1857.

Revolt of 1857: Planned or Spontaneous?

It seems that there was some kind of organised plan but it did not mature sufficiently once the revolt broke out. It is believed that **red lotuses** and **chappatis** were used as symbols of freedom. Roaming sanyasis and fakirs delivered speeches and mobilised anti-colonial elements. All this helped in stirring up the rebellion.

Consequences or Impact of the Revolt

Even though the Revolt of 1857 was suppressed and British authority re-established, the revolt gave a severe jolt to the British government. It emerged as a milestone event, an eye-opener, full of lessons and warnings for the Raj.

The structure and policies of the re-established British Raj were, in many respects, drastically changed and inaugurated a new era of colonialism in India. Mid-19th century had witnessed the spread of Industrial Revolution in other countries. Countries of Europe, USA and Japan underwent industrialisation. With this began the race for new markets and colonies. Consequently, Britain began vigorous efforts to save its existing empire.

Thus, the changes introduced in the post-revolt years were guided by a **renewed imperialist ideology** evident in the reactionary policies of Viceroys such as Lytton, Dufferin and Curzon. The feudal and vested interests were protected, policy of divide and rule was more vigorously pursued and European control over key positions was tightened.

Change of Power

After the Revolt of 1857, the British government was forced to pass the Government of India Act of 1858 which called for the liquidation of British East India Company and the power to govern India was transferred from the Company to the Crown.

Note: Act of 1858 and its significance has been discussed in detail in Chapter 3.2.

Changes in Military Policy

The Indian Army had been chiefly responsible for the crisis of 1857 and it was thoroughly reorganised. Measures were taken to prevent future revolts:

- The number of **European soldiers was increased**. In the Bengal army, ratio was fixed at one European soldier for two Indian soldiers (1:2). In Bombay and Madras armies, ratio was fixed at 1:3 or 2:5.
- European troops were strategically placed at key areas; all big positions in army and artillery were reserved for Europeans.
- European troops were given exclusive charge of critical branches like artillery.
- Soldiers from Awadh, Bihar and Central India were declared as **non-martial** while Punjabis, Gorkhas and Pathans (who had fought for the British) were declared as martial and recruited in large numbers. By 1875, half of the British Indian army was recruited from Punjab.
- Indian troops were organised on the policy of **'divide and rule'** or **'balance and counterpoise'**. Regiments were formed along the lines of caste, community and region to prevent development of feelings of solidarity and nationalism.

In 1861, **Charles Wood**, Secretary of State for India, communicated to Canning, 'If one regiment mutinies, I should like to have the next regiment so alien that it would be ready to fire into it'.

The British section of the Indian army served as an army of occupation and became the ultimate guarantee of Britain's hold over India. The British Indian army was also used to further the cause of British imperialism in Asia and Africa.

Change in Policy Towards Upper Classes (Princes and Landlords)

- **Policy of annexations abandoned** Prior to the Revolt, the British took up every opportunity to annex the princely states. Yet, no more than 1 per cent of the Indian princes participated in the revolt. They largely remained loyal to the British and actively participated in suppression of the revolt. Viceroy Canning later declared that they had acted as **'breakwaters in the storm'**.

  Realising their utility as significant allies, the British abandoned the policy of annexations. The Queen declared in her proclamation of 1858 that there shall be no more annexations, the states will be allowed to adopt their heirs. **Canning abandoned the Doctrine of Lapse** (that had aggrieved Rani of Jhansi, Nana Sahib and Begum Hazrat Mahal). The princes, zamindars and landlords were now to be utilised as counterweights against the nationalists.
- **Princes and landlords rewarded and befriended** Villages were restored to taluqdars, subject to loyalty and transmission of information. The princes who had remained loyal to the British during the Revolt were rewarded (these included **Gwalior, Rampur, Patiala and Jind**). They were organised into a Board of privileged dependents. In 1861, a special order of knighthood 'the star of India' was instituted and its recipients were the rulers of **Bhopal, Baroda, Gwalior, Patiala and Rampur**.
- **Britain as paramount power** At the same time, as a price, the Indian States were made to acknowledge Britain as the paramount power (Prior to 1857, at least in theory, the princely

states were considered subsidiary but sovereign). In 1876, Queen Victoria assumed the title of **'the Empress of India'**. Curzon also declared that the princely states were mere agents of the British Crown.

Thus, the British now aimed to befriend the strongest elements of Indian society, i.e. the princes and the landlords to consolidate their position.

Change in Attitude Towards Educated Indians

Hostility Towards Higher Education Even though the educated Indians did not participate in the revolt, some of them had begun to understand the real nature of the colonial rule. The British now became **hostile to higher education** in India and took active steps to curtail it particularly after the formation of Indian National Congress in 1885.

Indian Civil Service Act of 1861 One of the assurances contained in the Queen's Proclamation stated- 'our subjects, of whatever race or creed, be freely and impartially admitted to office in our service...'. In order to give expression to this pledge the Indian Civil Service Act of 1861 was passed, which provided for an annual competitive exam to be held in **London**. However, the detailed rules framed were such that they had the effect of keeping the civil services a close preserve of the Englishmen.

Indian Councils Act of 1861 The British realised that a major cause for the revolt was the miscommunication between the ruler and the ruled. Sir Bartle Frère, in his famous Minute of 1860, pushed for the representation of Indians in the Legislative Councils. It was felt that the association of Indians in legislation would familiarise the rulers with popular sentiments and avoid future misunderstandings. In this way, the Act of 1861 marked a humble beginning towards representative institutions in India.

Change in Policy Towards Common Masses

Socio-religious Reforms The Queen's proclamation declared that, 'We disclaim alike the desire to impose our convictions (religious) on any of our subjects'. Social and religious institutions were an area in which the British intervened with great caution. Yet, even this policy of limited **social intervention was abandoned** by the colonial government after the Revolt of 1857. It was now openly put forward that there were many social and cultural defects in Indian society which made Indians unfit to rule themselves! Hence, they must be governed by the British for an indefinite period of time!

According to **Percival Spear**, 'The Indian Government's honeymoon with progress was over'.

Divide and Rule Further, to prevent feelings of unity and nationhood among civilian population, the policy of **divide and rule** was introduced even among the masses. The unity showed by Hindus and Muslims during the revolt disturbed the colonial rulers and they got determined to break this unity.

Immediately after the revolt, the Muslims were repressed (Since Bahadur Shah II was appealed to head the revolt, the British believed the Revolt to be a Muslim conspiracy). Later, this policy was reversed and policy of appeasement of Muslims was introduced which sowed the **seeds of communalism** in India and disrupted the national movement.

Racial Discrimination Racial bitterness emerged as the worst legacy of the crisis. The British had always stayed aloof from Indians but the Revolt of 1857 widened this racial divide. The British began to assert vigorously the doctrine of **racial supremacy** to assert their authority and humiliate the Indians. The notices of 'Europeans only' came up across railway coaches, parks, restaurants, etc. In The Punch, a British weekly magazine of humour and satire, the Indian was cartooned as half gorilla-half negro who could be controlled only by a superior race, and henceforth, the British rule was justified by the philosophy of **'Whiteman's burden'**-the burden of civilising the non-whites.

In this way, the Revolt of 1857 marked the beginning of a new phase of British rule in India. For the British, the dangers from the feudal India ended and a new challenge emerged in the form of the English educated middle class.

Opinions of Various Historians

- **Tara Chand** 'Revolt of 1857 was the last attempt of an effete order to recover its departed glory'.
- **S. B. Chaudhuri** 'First War of Independence it certainly was, as in the whole canvas of recorded history of India it would be difficult to find a parallel to this gigantic anti-foreign combine of all classes of people and of many provinces of India. There was never a war in India lasting continuously for more than a year and simultaneously in all the regions which had for its objective the ejectment of the alien ruling power'. (Theories of the Indian Mutiny).
- **R. C. Majumdar** 'Apart from individual cases here and there, no evidence has yet been brought to light which would support the view that the patriotic motive of freeing the country formed the chief incentive to the general outbreak of the people...It is difficult to avoid the conclusion that the so-called First National War of independence of 1857 is neither First, nor National, nor War of Independence'. (British Paramountcy and Indian Renaissance, p. 624)
- **S. N. Sen** 'The mutiny was inevitable...No dependent nation can forever reconcile itself to foreign domination. A despotic government must ultimately rule by the sword though it might be sheathed in velvet. In India, the sword was apparently in the custody of the sepoy army. Between the sepoy and his foreign masters, there was no common tie of race, language and religion...the Mutiny was inherent in the constitution of the empire'.
- **Eric Strokes** '1857 stands firmly in a historical continuum...Like 1848 in Europe-despite obvious disparities-it was an uprising sans issue that could catch a society moving into the early stages of modernisation'. (The Peasant and the Raj, p. 39)

Previous Years' Questions – Preliminary Exam

1. Who among the following was the leader of some anti-British revolts in Sambalpur? **[UPSC 1994]**
   (a) Utirat Singh
   (b) Surendra Sai
   (c) Kattabomman
   (d) Syed Ahmad Barelvi

2. The educated middle class in India: **[UPSC 1998]**
   (a) Opposed the Revolt of 1857
   (b) Supported the Revolt of 1857
   (c) Remained neutral to the Revolt of 1857
   (d) Fought against native rulers

3. "In this instance, we could not play off the Mohammedans against the Hindus". To which of the following events did this remark of Aitchison relate? **[UPSC 2000]**
   (a) Revolt of 1857
   (b) Champaran Satyagraha (1917)
   (c) Khilafat and Non-Cooperation Movement (1919–22)
   (d) August Movement of 1942
4. Which one of the following places did Kunwar Singh, a prominent leader of the Revolt of 1857, belong to? **[UPSC 2005]**
   (a) Bihar
   (b) Madhya Pradesh
   (c) Rajasthan
   (d) Uttar Pradesh
5. Which one of the following territories was not affected by the Revolt of 1857? **[UPSC 2005]**
   (a) Jhansi
   (b) Chittor
   (c) Jagdishpur
   (d) Lucknow
6. With reference to the Revolt of the Year 1857, who among the following was betrayed by a friend; captured and put to death by the British? **[UPSC 2006]**
   (a) Nana Sahib (b) Kunwar Singh
   (c) Khan Bahadur Khan (d) Tatya Tope
7. Who was the Governor General of India during the sepoy mutiny? **[UPSC 2006]**
   (a) Lord Canning (b) Lord Dalhousie
   (c) Lord Hardinge (d) Lord Lytton
8. What was/were the object/objects of Queen Victoria's proclamation (1858)? **[UPSC 2014]**
   1. To disclaim any intention to annex the Indian states.
   2. To place the Indian administration under the British crown
   3. To regulate East India Company's trade with India.

   Select the correct answer from the following options.
   (a) 1 and 2 only (b) 2 only
   (c) 1 and 3 only (d) 1, 2 and 3

Previous Years' Questions – Main Exam

1. 'What began as a fight for religion ended as a war of independence, for there is not the slightest doubt that the rebels wanted to get rid of the alien government and restore the old order of which the king of Delhi was the rightful representative'. Do you support this viewpoint? **[UPSC 1999]**
2. What administrative changes were introduced in India after 1858? What were the objectives of these changes? **[UPSC 2001]**
3. Examine the policy of Subordinated Union towards Princely states. Account for the shift from the policy of Subordinate Isolation. **[UPSC 2005]**
4. What are the salient features of Government of India Act of 1858? **[UPSC 2007]**
5. Explain how the uprising of 1857 constitutes an important watershed in the evolution of British policies towards colonial India. **[UPSC 2016]**
6. The 1857 Uprising was the culmination of the recurrent big and small local rebellions that had occurred in the preceding hundred years of British rule. **[UPSC 2019]**

Answers

Previous Years' Questions – Preliminary Exam

1. (b)	2. (a)	3. (a)	4. (a)	5. (b)
6. (d)	7. (a)	8. (a)		

3 Popular Uprisings After 1857 (1857–1900)

Even though the Revolt of 1857 was suppressed, the anti-British sentiments continued to simmer in the hearts and minds of the people, particularly the peasants, the tribals and the artisans who faced the worst forms of colonial exploitation. They faced dual oppression, i.e. oppression by colonial state as well as by the feudal elements of Indian society such as the landlords and moneylenders.

Opposition to such exploitation continued to be expressed in the form of popular uprisings. In official language, these were often described as rebellions, dacoities, criminal activities and even as manifestations of communalism or casteism by the British. In reality, they were expressions of protest against oppression, struggle between the haves and the have-nots. Even though these uprisings failed in their attempt to overthrow their oppressors, they prepared the ground for the mass struggles of the upcoming era.

Another impact of the British rule in India was the creation of a new class—the working class. The British capitalists had invested their capital in India and set up a few modern industries, introduced railways and plantations, giving rise to the new working class. This class was also subjected to severe exploitation by their paymasters. Even though this class was not organised, isolated strikes had begun to emerge in the second half of the 19th century. Strikes took place in the factories owned by Indians as well. The main demands of the workers were better wages and work conditions. Thus, this phase laid the foundation for future working-class movements, which also played a significant role in the national movement.

Hence, in this unit, you will learn about the popular uprisings of the peasants, tribals, artisans and workers during the period 1857–1900 directed against colonialism as well as the indigenous exploiters of Indian society.

Popular Uprisings After 1857

Indigo Revolt (Bengal, 1859–60)

As early as 1770, Indigo plantations had been set up by the East India Company. Indigo planting became more and more profitable with the increasing demand for **blue dye** in Europe. Consequently, the Indigo planters, mostly Europeans, forced the peasants to grow indigo crop at a loss, in place of food grains necessary for their survival. The planters relied upon reign of terror by lathiyals (armed retainers) and even legal manipulation. In reality, the planters were even above law. In 1857, twenty-nine planters were appointed as honorary magistrates; giving rise to the saying- 'je rakhak se bhakak'. (one who protects us is the one who devours us). This generated a lot of resentment among the peasants.

In April 1860, the revolt first started from the villages of **Gobindpur** (Nadia district) under the leadership of Bishnucharan Biswas and Digambar Biswas. The indigo farmers refused to sow indigo, in what may be called as the **first general strike in the history of Indian peasantry**. The strike quickly spread to other places in Bengal, including Pabna, Khulna, Birbhum, Burdwan and Murshidabad.

Special Features of Indigo Revolt

Unity of indigo farmers A major reason for the success of the Indigo Revolt was the unity and organisation showed by the peasants. There was complete unity among Hindu and Muslim peasants as well.

Support of Bengali middle class The movement, also called **Nilbidroh**, received wholehearted support of the Bengali intelligentsia. It was duly covered in the contemporary newspaper **The Bengalee**. Special role was played by **Harish Chandra Mukherjee**, editor of the Hindoo Patriot, who published regular reports on the hardships of the peasants and their resistance. Dinbandhu Mitra depicted the plight of the peasants in his play in Bengali, **Nil Darpan**. The play evoked much controversy and was banned by the Company's government.

Impact on emerging nationalists The intelligentsia's support left a significant impact on young nationalists for whom the Indigo Revolt had laid down a valuable tradition of resistance against oppression by foreign rulers.

Main leaders: **Bishnucharan Biswas** and **Digambar Biswas**
Government response: Apprehending a great agrarian uprising, the government ordered an enquiry and appointed an Indigo Commission (1860). The enquiry exposed the corruption underlying the entire system of indigo cultivation. Subsequently, the government issued a notification to the effect that the peasants could not be forced to grow indigo. The recommendations were embodied in the Act of 1862. By then, the Bengal indigo planters had already developed cold feet and many moved out to regions such as present-day Bihar and Uttar Pradesh.

Mappila (Moplah) Uprising (Malabar, 1850–1900)

The period 1850–1900 also saw a series of Moplah Uprisings in Malabar. The Moplah peasants rose against the oppression of their **Jenmi** landlords who were backed by the British administration (police, law courts and revenue officials). Essentially a rich–poor conflict, the Moplah uprising was given a **communal colour** by the colonial state as the Moplahs were Muslims, while the landlords were Hindus.

The landlords resorted to ruthless repression including burning of rebel bodies to generate fear. However, this only made the peasants more aggressive who retaliated with looting property, burning houses of landlords and even defiling Hindu temples. By 1896, the Moplah uprising assumed an increasingly communal orientation.

Pabna Revolt (East Bengal, 1873–85)

At the root of Pabna revolt were the malpractices of zamindars to enhance rent beyond legal limits and to destroy the tenant's newly acquired occupancy right. The occupancy tenants were forced to give up their occupancy rights and convert into tenants-at-will through forcible written agreements.

Special Features of Pabna Revolt

Formation of agrarian leagues Soon the Pabna peasants became aware of the new laws and in 1873, and formed an agrarian league. The struggle spread to other districts of east Bengal and everywhere agrarian leagues were formed. The formation of the league was opposed by most pro-landlord newspapers, including **Amrit Bazaar Patrika**.

A legal resistance The movement was largely within the bounds of law and violence was rare. Forms of mobilisation included drum beats, blasts from conch-shells and night shouts. The leagues organised rent strikes and challenged the zamindars in courts. The peasants had developed a strong awareness of their legal rights and an ability to put up peaceful resistance.

Neither against zamindari system, nor anti-colonial A noteworthy feature of the revolt was that the aim of the peasants was limited to redressal of immediate grievances. It was neither anti-zamindari nor anti-colonial at any stage. Peasants did not defy British authority, rather declared that their aim was to become the '**ryots of the Queen of England and of Her only**'.

Support of Indian intellectuals Once again a number of young Indian intellectuals rose in the support of the peasants' cause. These included men such as Bankim Chandra Chatterjee and RC Dutt. The Indian Association led by Surendranath Banerjee, Anand Mohan Bose and Dwarkanath Ganguli also campaigned for the rights of the tenants.

Hindu-Muslim unity Once again, the Bengal peasants demonstrated complete Hindu–Muslim solidarity as shown previously in case of indigo riots. The landlords tried to paint it as a communal movement, since more than two-third of the peasants and nearly 70 per cent of Pabna's population was Muslim. However, it is noteworthy that two prominent leaders of the Pabna peasants, namely Keshab Chandra Sen and Sambhunath Pal, were Hindus.

Main leader: **Keshab Chandra Sen, Ishan Chandra Roy** and **Sambhunath Pal**.
Government response: In the beginning of the revolt, there are references of sympathetic attitude adopted by the colonial administration towards the peasants. The government defended the zamindars, whenever violence took place. But it became neutral as far as legal battles or peaceful agitations were concerned. In **1885, the Bengal Tenancy Act** was passed, in an attempt to protect the tenants from zamindari oppression.

For nearly a decade, the Pabna peasants successfully resisted the landlords' efforts to fleece them. Many zamindars developed cold feet with the prospect of long and costly litigation. Many peasants were able to acquire occupancy rights and resist enhanced rents.

Deccan Riots (1875)

The Deccan uprising was an uprising of the Deccan peasants chiefly directed against the exploitation of the Marwari and Gujarati moneylenders. It occurred in the context of a combination of factors such as introduction of Ryotwari system in the Deccan (1858), slump in world cotton prices at the end of the American Civil War (1864), and raise in land revenue by government by nearly 50 per cent in 1867. This situation was worsened by successive bad harvests.

Under the Ryotwari system, the land revenue was settled directly with the peasant who was also recognised as the owner of his land. Like other peasants under the ryotwari system, the Deccan peasants also found it difficult to pay the high revenues without getting into the clutches of the moneylenders. This led to growing resentment between the peasants and the moneylenders, most of whom were outsiders–Marwaris or Gujaratis.

The moneylenders who came from outside were greedy and often fooled the illiterate Deccan peasants into signing unfavourable bonds. The civil courts also always favoured the usurious moneylenders, awarding them with decrees of eviction against the peasants. This naturally resulted in increased transfer of land holdings from peasants to moneylenders and further accentuated the differences between the **Vanis** (moneylenders) and the **Kunbis** (cultivator caste).

In December 1874, the riots first started in village Kardah (Sirur taluka) when a Marwari moneylender obtained a decree of eviction against Baba Saheb Deshmukh, a cultivator who owed ₹150 to him. Deshmukh's house was callously pulled down, arousing the wrath of the villagers who then organised complete social boycott of the 'outsider' moneylenders and even imposed social sanctions on the 'balutedars' (village servants and peasants who would not join the boycott).

When the social boycott did not prove very effective, the peasants resorted to agrarian riots. By June 1875, the **Poona** and **Ahmednagar** districts were set ablaze, with peasants attacking the shops and houses of moneylenders and burning them down. The chief targets were the mortgage bonds, which the peasants perceived as the instruments of oppression. This class conflict was also given the colour of caste conflict.

Special Features of Deccan Riots

Absence of anti-colonial consciousness As in the case of Pabna, the Deccan uprising also lacked anti-colonial consciousness.

Support of nationalist intelligentsia Here again, the modern intelligentsia of Maharashtra supported the cause of the peasants. A notable role was played by the Poona Sarvajanik Sabha, led by Justice Ranade as well as by the nationalist newspapers.

Government Response- The police assisted by the military was swung into action. Thousands of peasants were arrested and the uprising completely suppressed. However, the government could not find any evidence against the peasants, demonstrating the popular base of the movement. The government was compelled to appoint the **Deccan Riots Commission**, to enquire into the causes of the uprising. Subsequently, the **Deccan Agriculturalists' Relief Act of 1879** was passed, which put restrictions on alienation of the lands of peasants and arrest for failure to pay debts.

Koya Rebellion (Eastern Godavari Region, 1879–80)

The rebellion occurred in the eastern Godavari tract of present-day Andhra Pradesh and also affected some regions of Malkangiri (Koraput district, Orissa). At the root of the Koya rebellion were the tribal grievances such as erosion of forest rights, exploitation by moneylenders, etc.

The rebels rose under the leadership of Koya leader, Tomma Dora, hailed as the 'King of Malkangiri'. It is believed that the rebels took over a police station, soon after which Dora was shot dead, bringing the movement to an end.

Main leader: **Tomma Dora**

Munda Rebellion (Chota Nagpur, 1874–1901)

This was a tribal movement that developed between 1874 and 1901 and was led by Birsa Munda from 1895. It affected an area of about 400 square miles in the Chota Nagpur region of South Bihar. The movement was born out of basic problems that affected the tribals in the colonial period. The Munda system of common land holdings had been destroyed by the intrusion of jagirdars, revenue farmers and merchant moneylenders.

Statue of Birsa Munda in Pune, Maharashtra

It is noteworthy that the movement had a **distinct connection with Christianity** in its early phase. The Mundas accepted Christianity with the belief that the German missionaries would help them against the exploitation of the zamindars. However, dissatisfaction with the German missionaries made them turn to the Catholic mission. But seeing the colonial ties between the colonial officers and the zamindars, the Munda sardars turned against all outsiders and finally rose in a rebellion **'ulgulan'**, led by Birsa Munda. Previously, Birsa Munda had declared himself as messenger of God with miraculous healing powers. But under the influence of sardars, his religious movement began to acquire agrarian and political content.

In 1899, Birsa Munda declared a rebellion to establish the Munda rule and encouraged the killing of 'jagirdars and rajas and hakims (rulers) and Christians'. Birsa succeeded in mobilising nearly 6000 Mundas armed with swords and spears, bows and arrows. There was active participation of women in this movement. Economically weaker non-tribal people were not attacked.

Main leader: **Birsa Munda**
Suppression: The rebellion was ruthlessly suppressed by the British forces. Birsa was arrested in 1900 and he died in prison the same year.

Rampa Rebellion (Andhra, 1879 and 1922)

The Rampa Rebellion of 1879 was an uprising of the hill tribes of the Rampa region in coastal Andhra against British administration, particularly forest regulations and oppression by the government supported mansabdars. The rebellion was suppressed only after large scale military operations; several Rampa revolutionaries were arrested and deported to Andamans.

The Rampa Rebellion of 1922 (also known as the Second Rampa Rebellion) was a tribal uprising led by **Alluri Sitaram Raju** in Godavari Agency of Madras Presidency. The Rampas rose against the Raj laws, erosion of their forest rights, restrictions on their **'podu'** system (slash and burn system) and forced labour in road construction. The rebellion took the form of guerilla struggle and ended with the shooting of Raju in May 1924.

Other Peasant Uprisings included:

- **Kuka Uprising (Punjab, 1872)** It was a messianic movement led by **Baba Ram Singh**.
- **Ramosi Uprising (Maharashtra, 1879)** The uprising was led by **Vasudev Balwant Phadke** who organised social banditry on a large scale.
- **Assam (1893–93)** A series of peasant riots inflicted Assam on account of high land revenue.

Most of these uprisings were brutally suppressed.

Prelim Capsule

Revolts after 1857

Revolt	Period	Important Details
Indigo Revolt (Bengal)	**1859–1860**	Causes—European planters forced the peasants to grow indigo crop at a loss, in place of food grains necessary for their survival. The revolt first started from the villages of **Gobindpur** (Nadia district). The indigo farmers refused to sow indigo, in what may be called as the **first general strike** in the history of Indian peasantry. The movement was also known as **Nilbidroh.** It was duly covered in the contemporary newspaper—**the Bengalee**. Dinbandhu Mitra depicted the plight of the peasants in his play in Bengali, **Nil Darpan**. Led by—**Bishnucharan Biswas** and **Digambar Biswas**. Consequences—Indigo Commission 1860 was appointed.
The Mappila Uprising (Malabar)	**1850–1900**	Causes—The Moplah peasants rose against the oppression of the **Jenmi** landlords who were backed by the British administration. It was given a **communal color** by the colonial state as the Moplahs were Muslims, while the landlords were Hindus.
Pabna Revolt (East Bengal)	**1873–1885**	Causes—Pabna peasants rose against the malpractices of zamindars to enhance rent beyond legal limits and to destroy the tenant's newly acquired occupancy right. The revolt was opposed by pro-landlord newspaper—**Amrit Bazaar Patrika**. Peasants declared that their aim was to become the 'ryots of the Queen of England and of Her only'. Supported by—Bankim Chandra Chatterjee, RC Dutt & the Indian Association (led by Surendranath Banerjee, Anand Mohan Bose and Dwarkanath Ganguli). Led by—**Keshab Chandra Sen, Ishan Chandra Roy** and **Sambhunath Pal**. Consequences—**The Bengal Tenancy Act 1885** was passed.

Deccan Riots	**1875**	Causes—Deccan peasants revolted against the exploitation of the Marwari and Gujarati moneylenders. Other causes included introduction of ryotwari system in the Deccan (1858), slump in world cotton prices at the end of the American Civil War (1864) and raise in land revenue by government by nearly 50% in 1867. Supported by—**Poona Sarvajanik Sabha**, led by Justice Ranade. Consequences—The **Deccan Riots Commission** was appointed to enquire into the causes of the uprising. Subsequently, the **Deccan Agriculturalists' Relief Act of 1879** was passed.
Koya Rebellion (eastern Godavari region)	**1879–1880**	Causes—Tribal grievances such as erosion of forest rights, exploitation by money lenders etc. Led by—**Tomma Dora**.
Munda Rebellion (Chota Nagpur)	**1874–1901**	Causes—The Munda system of common land holdings had been destroyed by the intrusion of jagirdars, revenue farmers and merchant money lenders. Uprising was known as **'ulgulan'**. Led by—**Birsa Munda**.
Rampa Rebellion (Andhra)	**1879 & 1922**	Causes—The Rampa tribesmen rose against British administration and forest regulations. Led by—**Alluri Sitaram Raju** (Second Rampa Rebellion).

Nature and Characteristics of Popular Uprisings After 1857

A major shift occurred in the nature and characteristics of popular uprisings after 1857 which may be understood under the following heads:

Peasants Emerged as the Main Force

Since most of the princes, chiefs and landlords had either been crushed or co-opted, the peasants now emerged as the main force behind these uprisings. The peasants now fought directly for their demands and also showed remarkable spirit of sacrifice and solidarity which cut across lines of caste and religion.

Limited in Aim, Region and Organisation

The peasants and tribals rose in revolt with the limited aim of solving their immediate grievances, which were almost wholly economic in nature. They did not aim to fight against colonialism or even against landlordism but merely objected to vile practices like unreasonable evictions and rent enhancements. These movements were directed against the immediate oppressors such as the indigo planters, zamindars and moneylenders (sahukars) and not against the imperialist rulers as such. Conversely, in some cases like the Munda rebellion, we see an association with imperialism in a struggle against the landlords and the moneylenders.

The movements were also limited in terms of the region affected. They were localised and isolated from one another. They also lacked continuity or any long-term organisation. The leaders rose and fell with the movement, and left behind no successors.

Envisaged Fair and Just Order

The uprisings were moved by strong notions of justice and fair play. The peasants and tribals envisaged a just order, free from exploitation where everyone lived a happy and dignified life. They had also demonstrated a strong awareness of their legal rights and asserted them inside and outside the courts.

Role of Indian Intelligentsia

Unlike the revolt of 1857, these movements saw the beginnings of the support of Indian intelligentsia, whose pro-peasant sympathies were expressed in certain newspapers and contemporary literary works like Nil Darpan.

Association with Religion and Caste

This was another notable feature of these uprisings. Given the multiplicity of caste and religion in India, these class conflicts were given a communal or caste angle on several occasions, as in the case of Mappila and Pabna peasant struggles.

Lack of Adequate Understanding of Colonialism

This was a major weakness of the 19th-century peasant movements. Unlike the previous tribal uprisings and the Revolt of 1857, the post-1857 peasant uprisings did not directly challenge the colonial state. As a result, the British government's treatment of these rebels was also qualitatively different and the state was willing to walk a certain distance to mitigate their concerns.

Tendency to 'Look Back'

Like the previous uprisings, even these uprisings attempted to look back into the past when 'life was much better'. Thus they were 'restorative in character' and sought to establish a previous order. They did not put forth any new ideology or an alternative socio-economic political system. In the absence of a fresh vision of society and modern outlook, it was easy for the British to reconcile and then suppress these movement one after the other. An alternative, forward looking view of society could only be formed by a modern intelligentsia, which was itself in the process of emerging (Read about the 19th-century socio-cultural awakening in the upcoming unit (Unit 5).

In the 20th century, most of these limitations were overcome and the peasant movements merged with the larger anti-imperialist struggle (Read about the peasant movements of the 1920s and 1930s in Unit 6).

Working Class Movements (1850–1900)

The period after 1850 saw the emergence of the earliest working class movements in India. The working class at that time mainly comprised of the peasants and artisans, who had been thrown out of their occupations under the impact of the colonial rule and had become associated with the emerging 'modern' industrial sector. This sector, which had been growing in India since the 1840s, was a result of investment of British capital in India, and was originally an exclusive preserve of the British capitalists.

The British capitalists felt attracted to invest in tea plantations (from 1839), jute, coal, mining and railways (early 1850s) and by the turn of the century, major investments were also made in the ports. The only industry with which the Indian business class was associated was the textile industry, born around 1850s and was located chiefly in Bombay and Ahmedabad.

It needs to be emphasised here that this so-called 'modern' sector was born in a colonial economy and as such was not meant to foster development of India or its people. Consequently, the work conditions were miserable and the workers (including women and children) were treated almost like slaves. They worked for long hours (15 to 16 hours) with no weekly holiday, were paid extremely low wages and were even beaten up or tortured. Such oppressive conditions gave little scope for workers to organise themselves and what emerged were mostly instinctive and spontaneous outbursts of the workers in response to their work condition.

Early Efforts of Educated Class (1850–1900)

During this period, sections of educated gentry came forward to focus on the problems of the working class. They were attracted to the workers due to humanitarian notions triggered off by socio-religious reform movements and other contemporary workers' movements taking place in different parts of the world. Some of the early efforts of the intelligentsia were directed at organising the workers and are enumerated as follows:

- **Working Men's Club (1870)** It was founded by **Sasipada Banerjee**, a Brahmo Samajist.
- **Working Men's Mission (1878)** It was founded by Calcutta Brahmo Samaj, to propagate religious morality, etc., among the workers.
- **Memorandum of 1884** It was drafted by **Sorabjee Sapurjee Bengalee** and **Narayan Meghaji Lokhande** and signed by 5000 workers of the cotton mills in Bombay demanding for a rest day on every Sunday, a half-an-hour break at noon, a 6:30 am to sunset working day, full wages in case of injury and pension in case of disability. The memorandum was presented before the Commission of 1884 appointed by the Government of Bombay and left its imprint on the **First Indian Factories Act of 1891**.
- **On 10 June 1890** The request of workers for a weekly holiday was granted by the Bombay Mill Owners' Association, but without any legal sanction and could not be enforced.

Strikes

In addition to the above efforts directed at organising the workers, several spontaneous strikes also occurred. In many cases the workers were led by jobbers or 'Sardars' who recruited them. In 1862, the first big strike occurred when about 1200 labourers of Howrah Railway Station went on strike demanding an 8-hour working day. It is noteworthy that this action preceded the historic May Day Movement of the Chicago workers by about 24 hours.

It is clear that workers in these early struggles were mostly led by 'outsiders', i.e. either by the intelligentsia or the jobbers. These early efforts also failed to produce any serious impact on the workers' organisation or their consciousness. The degrading conditions of women and child labourers remained completely ignored given the dominant feudal mindset of the times. As a result, much like the peasant movements, even these early working-class movements remained limited to the immediate problems facing the community, such as their wages, rest and retrenchment.

To sum up, in this chapter we have read about the popular uprisings of peasants, tribals and workers during the period 1857–1900. These classes were subjected to dual oppression, i.e. oppression by the colonial state as well as by the indigenous exploiters like the zamindars and the sahukars. The peasants and workers usually broke out in an instinctive and spontaneous manner against their immediate oppressors. An important characteristic of these uprisings was that they were limited in their aim, spread and organisation. Though basically class struggles, they were often given a communal or casteist colour in this country of myriad castes and religions. In essence, these may be seen as struggles between the haves and the have-nots. Though limited in their impact, they prepared the ground for future mass movements of peasants and working classes at the national level and immensely added to the strength of the national movement.

Previous Years' Questions – Preliminary Exam

1. Which one of the following upheavals took place in Bengal immediately after the Revolt of 1857? **[UPSC 1994]**
   (a) Sanyasi Rebellion
   (b) Santhal Rebellion
   (c) Indigo disturbances
   (d) Pabna disturbances

2. Match List-I with List-II and select the correct answer using the code given below the lists **[UPSC 1997]**

List-I	List-II
A. Moplah revolt	1. Kerala
B. Pabna revolt	2. Bihar
C. Eka movement	3. Bengal
D. Birsa Munda revolt	4. Awadh

Code:

	A	B	C	D
(a)	1	3	4	2
(b)	2	3	4	1
(c)	1	2	3	4
(d)	3	4	1	2

3. Consider the following events: **[UPSC 1999]**
   1. Indigo Revolt
   2. Santhal Rebellion
   3. Deccan Riot
   4. Mutiny of sepoys

   The correct chronological sequence of these events is:
   (a) 4, 2, 1, 3
   (b) 4, 2, 3, 1
   (c) 2, 4, 3, 1
   (d) 2, 4, 1, 3

4. With reference to the history of India, "Ulgulan" or the Great Tumult is the description of which of the following events? **[UPSC 2020]**
   (a) The Revolt of 1857
   (b) The Mappila rebellion of 1921
   (c) The Indigo revolt of 1859–60
   (d) Birsa Munda's revolt of 1899–1900

Answers

Previous Years' Questions – Preliminary Exam

1. (c)
2. (a)
3. (d)
4. (d)

Unit 5
Socio-Religious Reform Movements

1 Socio-Religious Reform Movements-Part 1 (Awakening in Eastern, Western, Northern and Southern India)

The forces which were leading Indians to revolt against the British rule were also leading them towards reforming their social and religious life. The conquest of a vast country like India by a handful of British and the spread of western culture exposed serious drawbacks in the Indian society and occasioned a new awakening. While a large number of Indians refused to accept western ideas, others gradually came to hold that India had lagged behind in the race for civilisation and that western knowledge had to be imbibed for regeneration of Indian society. In this way, the British conquest evoked diverse reactions in Indian society which may be understood as under-

1. **Revulsion against Hindu religion and culture** The Derozians (English educated Bengali youth), for instance, gave up old religious ideas and traditions and took to practices considered offensive to Hindu sentiment such as drinking wine and eating beef.
2. **Accepting the best of the East and the West** Individuals led by Ram Mohan Roy, for instance, showed a more mature reaction. They were certainly attracted by western ideas and values but at the same time they refused to break away from their own religion. Rather they wanted to reform their religion and society just as the Europeans had done.
3. **Rise of Neo-Hinduism** Yet another reaction was the denial of western superiority and insistence on India's spiritual past from which the West had much to learn.

Consequently, several individuals and groups tried to bring about reform and revitalise the society along modern lines. These efforts collectively came to be known as **'Indian Renaissance'**.

Hence, 19th century India witnessed a series of socio-cultural reform movements in different parts of the country. Many intellectual currents emerged in almost all aspects of Indian life—social, cultural, religious, economic and political. However, socio-cultural reform remained the major plank of the 19th century reform movements.

Socio-Cultural Reform in India: An Impact of the West?

Though western impact on Indian renaissance cannot be denied, yet attributing the entire phenomenon wholly to western influence alone would be a misjudgment.

The reform movement should rather be seen as a response to the challenge posed by the British domination and should be seen as integral to the emerging anti-colonial consciousness. Yet another perspective is to look at these reforms as an expression of the social aspirations of the newly emerging educated middle class in colonial India. Some historians are of the view that the British were bound to be a hindrance rather than a help to subject people's regeneration.

A negative aspect of the reforms was the tendency of revivalism, a tendency to look back upon India's glorious past and defend Indian culture. Even though this tendency imparted a regressive character to these movements, it played an important role in fostering a **sense of pride** and **confidence** among the Indian people.

> **Bipan Chandra** - 'The socio-cultural regeneration in 19th century India was occasioned by the colonial presence, but not created by it'.

Indian Society in 19th Century

Religious Conditions

Indian society in the 19th century was a dark web of religious and social malpractices. Faith had been replaced by superstition and abominable rites and sacrifices had replaced the worship of God. Religion had become a monopoly of the Brahmins, who exercised an unhealthy influence on the minds of the people. They encouraged idolatry and polytheism to reinforce their own position. Even the scriptures were misinterpreted to suit their own class interests. The common Indian lived in complete submission to the whims and fancies of the priests. Religion, in fact was the dominant ideology of the times and Indians could be persuaded to do nearly anything under the name of religion.

Social Conditions

Social conditions were equally despicable. The most distressing was the condition of girls and women. The birth of a girl child was hardly a cause for celebration. If she escaped the threat of female infanticide, she faced discrimination in food and nutrition, health and education. Her marriage was a burden, widowhood inauspicious. Many girls were married off at an early age, often without their consent, to men many times their own age. Polygamy was prevalent both among Hindus as well as Muslims.

Equally distressing was the condition of the lower caste people, especially the untouchables. Strict rules of purity and pollution were followed. There were rules regarding who could dine with whom, who could marry whom, etc. Anyone who tried to defy caste laws faced the spectre of social boycott. The caste system thus created multiple divisions in society, relegating the lower castes to a life of utter humiliation and indignity.

Factors Contributing to the Rise of 19th Century Reform Movements

British Conquest of India

The conquest of a vast country like India at the hands of a handful of British exposed serious drawbacks in the Indian society and occasioned a new awakening. While a large number of Indians refused to accept western ideas, others gradually came to hold that India lagged behind in the race for civilisation and that western knowledge had to be imbibed for the regeneration of Indian society.

Spread of Colonial Culture

The establishment of colonial rule in India was followed by an attempt to spread British culture and ideology as the dominant cultural current. Faced with the challenge of foreign intrusion an attempt was made to preserve and re-energise indigenous culture.

Religious and Social Conditions Ripe for Reform

On one hand, 18th century Europe had seen the Age of Enlightenment which had impacted every aspect of European life—political, economic, social and religious. Modern ideas of democracy, nationalism, rationality and scientific outlook had propelled Europe as a civilisation par excellence.

On the other hand, India presented a picture of decadent society and stagnant civilisation with the result that the British rulers in India considered themselves culturally advanced and racially superior. In this context, thoughtful Indians felt the urgency to re-instill pride and confidence in their own civilization.

Role of Enlightened Indians

The British conquest of India also gave rise to factors such as spread of education, spread of modern western ideas and culture, increased awareness of world affairs, emergence of new economic forces and growth of nationalist sentiments. These factors also significantly contributed to the rise of 19th century reform movements.

Aim of the Reform Movements

The ultimate aim of the reform movements was the attainment of **well-being of the individual and the society** as well as national progress. Truth, equity and justice emerged as the governing values for the emergence of the new India.

Classification of Reform Movements

The Educated Indians were particularly attracted to the blend of rationalism and humanism. They began to scrutinise all religious and social practices on the principal of reason and discarded everything that did not stand this test of modern knowledge. They discovered that practices such as pollution and purity, image worship, pilgrimages, elaborate rituals, etc., were no longer of any use. They also discovered that the knowledge in the Geeta and the Vedanta was still as relevant as ever before. The result was the birth of several socio-religious reform movements, which are also sometimes classified into two groups.

1. **The reformist movements** The reformist movements such as the Brahmo Samaj, the Prarthana Samaj and the Aligarh movement were aimed at changing the fundamental system and structures of society through gradual reforms within the existing system.
2. **The revivalist movements** The revivalist movements such as the Arya Samaj, the Ramkrishna Mission and the Deoband Movement were aimed at going back to the societal system that once existed in the past which was considered as superior to the present degenerate form.

Both types of movements sought to purge religion of the impurities that had crept into it. The classification is done solely on the basis of the degree to which a movement relied on tradition or on reason and conscience.

Social and Ideological Bases of Reform

Social Base The social base of the Indian Renaissance was provided by the newly emerging **middle class** as well as the intellectuals educated in Indian and Western thought.

Ideological Base Two important ideas which influenced the 19th century reform movements and their leaders were **rationalism** and **religious universalism**.

Methods of Reform

Reform from Within

The intellectuals believed that for any reform to be effective, the urge for change had to come from within the individuals themselves. As a result, their main thrust was to create awareness among the people which they tried to achieve by publishing illuminating literary works, organising debates and discussions on various social problems, etc.

Reform through Legislation

Several intellectuals believed that reforms cannot be effective unless supported by the state. Therefore, they strived to secure legislative sanction for reforms like widow remarriage and increase in the age of consent.

Reform through Symbols of Change

Some reformers also tried to create symbols of change through non-conformist individual or group activities. For instance, they would eat food cooked by lower caste people or defy other caste rules.

Reform through Intellectual Work

1. **Spread of education** Ignorance and illiteracy were seen as the root cause of Indian backwardness. Thus, nearly all intellectuals considered education as the **main agent of reform**. Great stress was laid on the spread of education to all sections of Indian society, including non-Brahmins and women. The knowledge of science and technology, neglected in the colonial education system, was also emphasised.
2. **Role of Indian languages** The intellectuals emphasised the role of Indian vernaculars in the spread of education. They believed that if the goal of mass education was to be realised, the medium of instruction had to be Indian languages. English could be an aid but not the instrument of social change.
3. **Use of rationality** The reformers developed a rationalist critique of socio-religious reality. Faith was sought to be replaced by rationality and socio-religious practices were evaluated from the standpoint of social utility. For instance, the Brahmo Samaj rejected the infallibility of the Vedas. The Aligarh movement advocated the teaching of Islam as per the needs and requirements of modern age. Scientific and medical reasons were cited against malpractices such as child marriage.
4. **Use of scriptures** The intellectuals of the 19th century also sought scriptural sanction and often quoted lines from them to support their arguments in favour of reform. The priestly classes were blamed for distorting scriptural knowledge to suit their own ends.
5. **Appeal to universalism** A large number of reformers appealed to the universality of religion, that all religions were essentially the same. (However, under colonial policy, later developments would reveal how universalism, instead of providing the basis for a broader secular ethos, retreated into religious particularism).

Reform through Social Work

There was a clear recognition among several reformers about the limitation of purely intellectual work without supportive social work. For instance, Vidyasagar did not stop himself at writing columns or giving lectures in advocacy of widow remarriage. Instead, he spent his entire life, energy and money for improving the condition of Indian widows. Similarly, Arya Samaj and Ramakrishna Mission also undertook substantial social work.

Major Social and Religious Issues

Social Issues

Ignorance and Illiteracy Ignorance and illiteracy were widespread social evils and thus nearly all intellectuals laid great emphasis on mass education in Indian languages. Special emphasis was laid on the knowledge of science and technology as the gateway to material development.

Brahmin Bigotry The reformers bitterly criticised Brahmin bigotry. They blamed the Brahmins for keeping the people in ignorance and perpetuating social degradation. Denouncing Brahmin domination, reformers like Phule and Chandavarkar advocated upliftment of the lower castes and depressed classes. This attack on Brahmins was, however, not confrontationist and effort was made to avoid any caste hostility.

Caste System The intellectuals severely attacked the caste system and discriminations based on caste including untouchability. It was seen as an inhuman practice, degrading Indian society. It was also held responsible for keeping the Indian society divided, depriving it of feelings of patriotism. Hence, the caste system was understood as a major deterrent to socio-political progress of India.

Condition of Women The deplorable condition of women in Indian society was viewed as a pressing social problem. The reformers sought to end the subjugation of women and bitterly criticised degrading practices such as female infanticide, child marriage, purdah, sati, enforced widowhood, polygamy and prostitution.

Both Hindu and Muslim women were denied education and kept socially and economically dependent. While the Hindu women had no right to inherit property, the Muslim women could inherit but only half as much as men could. In matters of divorce in both communities, there was no equality between men and women. Nearly all reformers saw education as a necessary prerequisite for women's emancipation. Lokahitwadi and Jambhekar also demanded equal rights for women at par with men, representing one of the most striking aspects of 19th century thought.

Further, the question of women's emancipation was seen from a humanistic perspective. Their upliftment was not a question of upliftment of women alone, but of the entire humanity. There was a clear understanding that no society could ever hope to progress, so long as one half of its members were subjected to a life of ignorance, indignity and disrespect. Clearly, a changed society would emerge from changed men, and changed men would emerge from changed homes, where initial socialisation of individuals takes place and where a crucial role is played by women.

Religious Issues

Idol Worship and Polytheism The 19th century thinkers denounced idolatry and polytheism. However, their attack on Hinduism was different from the attack by Christian missionaries. Giving reasons against religious conversion, Ram Mohan Roy argued that if Hinduism was lacking in rationality, so was Christianity. He also upheld the knowledge of Upanishads and Vedanta as way superior. He based his teachings on the worship of one God, who was omnipresent, omnipotent and omniscient.

Rituals and Ceremonies The reformers denounced the meaningless rituals and religious practices based on superstition as well as intermediation of priestly classes as a deterrent to the development of a healthy individual and society.

A Survey of Reform Movements and Their Leaders

Eastern India

The impact of western ideas was felt much earlier in Bengal than in any other part of India.

Raja Ram Mohan Roy (1774–1833) and the Brahmo Samaj (1828)

Ram Mohan Roy (1774–1833), the **Morning Star** of reform movement in the country, was the first great leader of modern India, who contributed to nearly every aspect of Indian life. He was a very learned scholar of his times and was proficient in many languages, both Oriental and European, like Sanskrit, Arabic, Persian, English, French, Latin, Greek, etc. His extensive learning had opened his mind to new knowledge and freed him of bigotry. At a time when other English-educated Bengali youth were getting attracted to Christianity, he stood for a healthy synthesis of the East and the West.

Raja Ram Mohan Roy, the father of Indian Renaissance (also known as Herald of New Age)

Synthesis of the East and the West Ram Mohan Roy possessed great love and respect for the traditional philosophical systems of the East, particularly the knowledge of the Vedas and the Upanishads. At the same time, he believed that modern ideas alone can regenerate Indian society. He therefore, wanted his countrymen to imbibe western ideas particularly reason and humanism.

Critique of Hinduism Ram Mohan Roy vigorously opposed the evil practices in Hinduism such as idolatry, casteism and meaningless religious rituals. He condemned the Brahmin priests for encouraging such malpractices and for keeping people ignorant about the true teachings in the scriptures.

He held that all principal texts of the Hindus such as the **Vedas and Upanishads** preached monotheism or worship of one God. He himself published the Bengali translation of some of them to support his point. His translations and writings in vernacular also promoted the growth of Bengali literature.

In 1805, he published in Persian his first philosophical work, **Tuhfat-ul-Muwahiddin** (Gift to Monotheists), in which he analysed the major religions of the world in the light of 'reason' and put forward arguments for the worship of a single God. In 1820, he published the **Precepts of Jesus** in which he tried to apply rationalism to Christianity as well. Though he remained a rationalist throughout, in Tuhfat his rationalism was in full bloom.

However, in Ram Mohan's view, the power of human reason was the final authority on any doctrine. One should not hesitate to depart from holy books and scriptures if human reason so dictates and if traditions are proving harmful to individual and society.

Ram Mohan's daring religious outlook bore him much hostility. The orthodox elements condemned him as a heretic and outcast him by organising a social boycott, which was joined even by his mother.

Atmiya Sabha (1815) In 1814, he settled down in Calcutta and took up various reform activities. He formed the Atmiya Sabha in 1815 in Calcutta and thereafter carried on a persistent struggle against various socio-religious malpractices prevalent among Hindus in Bengal.

Brahmo Samaj (The Society of God, 20 August 1828, Calcutta) In **1828,** Roy founded the **Brahmo Sabha**, later renamed as Brahmo Samaj. The Brahmo Samaj forms the starting point for all the various reform movements in Hindu society, religion and politics of the time. It was the **first reform movement of India** based on modern western ideas.

Emancipation of women Ram Mohan's contribution in the field of woman emancipation is particularly noteworthy. He condemned the subjugation of women and their inferior status. He condemned the evil practices of polygamy, early marriage and sati (the burning of a widow on her husband's funeral pyre). As a child, Ram Mohan had witnessed his 17 year old sister-in-law being dragged into the flames of his brother's funeral pyre. The heart-wrenching sight made a deep impact on Ram Mohan's mind. He later launched a historic struggle against the evil practice of sati leading to the abolition of **sati** in 1829 through a legislation passed by William Bentinck. However, the alternative put forward by Ram Mohan for widows was ascetic widowhood and **not widow remarriage**. To raise the status of women, he advocated property rights for women and women's education.

Education Ram Mohan Roy was in favour of modern education in Indian society. He wanted the Indians to benefit from western scientific knowledge and progress. His aim was the fusion of the best in the East and the West. He extended enthusiastic support to David Hare for the establishment of Hindu College in Calcutta in 1817. Hare had come to India as a watchmaker but spent his entire life in the promotion of modern education. Ram Mohan himself opened an English school in Calcutta the same year which he maintained at his own cost. In 1825, he founded the **Vedanta College** that imparted Indian as well as western learning.

Economy and Polity Ram Mohan took up not only socio-cultural problems, but also economic and political ones. He condemned the oppressive practices of the Bengal zamindars, demanded abolition of Company's trading rights and removal of heavy export duties on Indian goods. He stood for Indianisation of services, freedom of press, separation of the executive from the judiciary, trial by jury and equality between Indian and European judges.

> **Ram Mohan Roy** had stated, 'I regret to say that the present system of religion adhered to by the Hindus is not well calculated to promote their political interest. The distinctions of caste introducing innumerable divisions and sub-divisions among them has entirely deprived them of patriotic feeling, and the multitude of religious rites and ceremonies and the laws of purification have totally disqualified them from undertaking any difficult enterprise. It is, I think, necessary that some change should take place in their religion at least for the sake of their **political advantage** and **social comfort**'.

Nationalism Ram Mohan Roy represented the **first sparkle of nationalist consciousness** in India. His every effort was aimed at nation building. He blamed the caste system in particular for creating inequality and keeping the Indians disunited and deprived of patriotic feelings.

Ram Mohan Roy was also the pioneer of Indian journalism as well as public agitation. He brought out several journals to spread his message among the people, to build public opinion on matters of current interest and to put forward popular demands and grievances before the government.

Internationalism Ram Mohan Roy was an ardent internationalist who took keen interest in world affairs and wanted amity and cooperation among nations. He supported the cause of liberty, democracy and nationalism everywhere in the world.

Ram Mohan Roy was undoubtedly the first luminous star on the on the socio-cultural ferment of 19th century and a great path-finder of his century. He is aptly known as the **father of Indian Renaissance and of Modern India**. In 1833, this great Indian passed away, leaving behind his ideas and message of modernisation for others to pursue.

Dr. Macnicol said, 'Ram Mohan Roy was the herald of new age and the fire he kindled in India has burnt ever since'.

Brahmo Samaj (Society of God)

Originally founded as the **Brahmo Sabha** by Ram Mohan Roy in 1828, the Brahmo Samaj was the first reform movement of India based on modern western ideas. Its primary purpose was to **teach monotheism** and **rid Hinduism of its evils**. Incorporating the best teaching of other religions, the Samaj emerged as a powerful platform for the promotion of humanism and social regeneration.

Teachings and Activities of Brahmo Samaj

Religious reforms Brahmo Samaj played a notable effort in cleansing Hinduism of evil practices.

- The Samaj was opposed to the entire Brahmanical system based on superstitious practices and rituals.
- It discarded the infallibility of religious scriptures, idol worship, polytheism and concept of avatars.
- It also criticised the need for a priestly class, but took no definite stand on karma and transmigration of soul.
- The Brahmo Samaj based itself on the worship of one God, without the mediation of priests, and the teachings of Vedas and Upanishads (but did not say that they were infallible).
- It also tried to incorporate the best practices of modern western thought, basing itself on human reason to decide what was to be kept and what was to be discarded in socio-religious practices. Thus, every individual had the right and capacity to decide what was right or what was wrong in a religious book or principle.

Social reforms The Brahmos were also great social reformers and attacked various social evils present in Hindu society.

- They condemned caste system, untouchability and supported the general upliftment of women.
- They actively opposed sati and purdah, child marriage and polygamy.
- They made tireless efforts in the field of widow remarriage and modern education for women.

Brahmo Samaj after Ram Mohan Roy After the death of Ram Mohan Roy in 1833, the Brahmo tradition was carried forward by Debendranath Tagore.

Debendranath Tagore (1817–1905) and Brahmo Samaj Debendranath Tagore, father of Rabindranath Tagore, was a product of the best in Indian and western knowledge. In 1839, he established the **Tattvabodhini Sabha** with the aim of propagating Ram Mohan's ideas and finding the spiritual truth. It aimed at countering the rapid influence of Christianity in India by enthusiastic advocacy of Vedantism and indigenous culture.

The Sabha also established a Tattvabodhini Press and started publishing the **Tattvabodhini Patrika** (1843) for the propagation of its ideas. It promoted study of India's past in Bengali language and also published texts on various subjects in Bengali.

In 1843, Debendranath Tagore became a Brahmo and he reorganised the Brahmo Samaj the same year, putting new life into it. Under his leadership, the influence of the Samaj widened, many new branches were established and the message of the Samaj spread even to the countryside of Bengal.

Keshub Chandra Sen (1838–84) and Brahmo Samaj In 1858, Keshub Chandra Sen joined the Brahmo Samaj. Soon he was appointed as Acharya of the Samaj by Debendranath Tagore. Keshub's entry brought new energy and vigour and the influence of the Samaj expanded even outside Bengal. Branches were opened up in UP, Punjab, Bombay, Madras and other towns. Keshub laid stress on women education. He also laid stress on universalism as opposed to Debendranath's stress on national Hindu identity.

Split in Brahmo Samaj Consequently, under Keshub, the Samaj began to drift away from its Hindu moorings and religious texts of Christians, Muslims, Parsis, etc., began to be read in the Brahmo Samaj meetings. This liberal and cosmopolitan outlook of Keshub was seen as too radical by Tagore and he dismissed Keshub from the office of the Acharya in 1865. This led to a split in Brahmo Samaj-Keshub had his followers left the parent body and formed the **Brahmo Samaj of India** in 1865. Tagore's Samaj henceforth came to be known as **Adi Brahmo Samaj**.

Despite their differences, the Brahmos collectively contributed to the dissemination of Ram Mohan's views and changing Bengal's society.

Keshub's Samaj was to see yet another split when dissatisfaction grew within his body. Keshub began to be accused of authoritarianism. Moreover, some followers had begun to worship Keshub as an incarnation, which was also disliked by some of his other followers. Discontent reached its peak when Keshub, who had always advocated a minimum age for marriage among the Brahmos, married his own 13-year-old daughter with the Maharaja of Kooch-Bihar with all elaborate Hindu ceremonies. Many of Keshub's followers felt disgusted and set up a new organisation called the **Sadharan Brahmo Samaj** (1878).

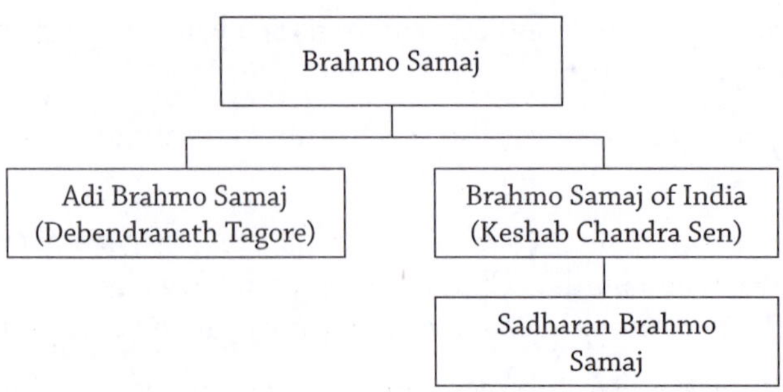

Keshub Chandra Sen - 'What we see around us today is a fallen nation, a nation whose primitive greatness today lied buried in ruins...As we survey the mournful scene of desolation-spiritual, social and intellectual-which spreads around us, we in vain try to recognise therein the land of Kalidas—the land of poetry, of science and of civilisation'.

Reasons for decline of Brahmo Samaj were as follows:

- The influence of the Brahmo Samaj remained confined mostly to the educated Bengalis.
- Samaj was also weakened by internal dissensions in the latter half of the 19th century.
- The activities of Brahmo Samaj were opposed by the **Dharma Sabha** (1830), founded by orthodox Hindus led by **Raja Radhakant Deb**.
- The early death of Ram Mohan in 1833 left the Brahmo Samaj without a guiding soul and a steady decline set in.

Despite the above, Brahmo Samaj cast adequate influence on the socio-religious and political life of Bengal and the rest of India.

Derozio (1809–31) and Young Bengal Movement (1820s–30s)

Henry Vivian Derozio

Henry Vivian Derozio was an Anglo-Indian teacher of the Hindu College. Drawing inspiration from the French Revolution, he followed the most radical views of his time. He was a free thinker and a rationalist. A charismatic teacher, he taught his students to develop a critical outlook, question all authority, love liberty, equality and freedom. Derozio was perhaps also the first nationalist poet of modern India.

His followers, known as **Derozians or Young Bengal**, attacked the old and decadent customs and traditions of Hindu society and religion. They stood for women's rights and laid great stress on female education. Together, they represented a radical trend in the 1820s and the 1830s, known as the Young Bengal Movement. They carried on agitations in support of numerous public issues including revision of Company's Charter, better treatment of Indian labour in British colonies, freedom of press, protection of rights and Indianisation of services.

The movement, however, saw limited success due to lack of support for their advanced ideas as well as their impractical radicalism. In 1831 Derozio was dismissed from the Hindu College owing to his radicalism and he died of cholera soon after at the young age of 22. Even so, Derozians will always be remembered as one of the pioneer reformers and harbingers of modern civilisation of Bengal.

Ishwar Chandra Vidyasagar (1820–91)

Ishwar Chandra Vidyasagar, a key figure of the Bengal Renaissance.

Pandit Ishwar Chandra Vidyasagar was a great scholar and reformer. Born on 26 September 1820 in a poor family, he struggled hard to educate himself and managed to get a scholarship to Sanskrit College, Calcutta. Upon his graduation from the College, he received the title 'Vidyasagar' and in 1851 rose to the position of the **Principal of the Sanskrit College**. Though he was a Sanskrit scholar, he was also a happy blend of eastern and western thought. He thus opened the gates of the college to western thought as well as non-Brahmin students.

Vidyasagar was a great humanist and possessed immense sympathy for the poor and the oppressed. He was fearless in mind and practiced what he believed in. He also evolved a new methodology of teaching Sanskrit. In general, reformers chose Indian languages as vehicles of reform. To enable the vernacular to perform this role successfully, they even prepared language primers. Both Vidyasagar and Rabindranath Tagore wrote **Bengali primers.**

However, his most significant contribution lay in the field of female emancipation. In fact, he devoted his entire life to the specific cause of widow remarriage, a great advance from Ram Mohan's idea of ascetic widowhood. He took the help of old Sanskrit texts and scriptures to prove that Vedic texts sanctioned widow remarriage. He sent a petition signed by 987 persons to the government, pleading it for legislative action. His agitation in support of legalising the re-marriage of widows bore fruit when the **Hindu Widows Remarriage Act 1856** was passed. Hence it was in 1856, under the supervision of Vidyasagar, the first legal Hindu widow remarriage among the upper caste in India took place.

Vidyasagar also promoted higher education for women. As Secretary of the **Bethune School** (founded in Calcutta in 1849) he led the movement for women's education. He also struggled against child marriage and polygamy. His prominent literary works include books such as **Bahubibaha** and **Bidhaba Bibaha**. He also started the Bengali newspaper **Shome Prakash** (1858).

Ramkrishna Paramhansa (1834–86)

Ramakrishna Paramhansa was a poor priest at the Kali temple in Dakshineswar near Calcutta. He was a saintly person and in his search for God, he lived with saints of other faiths including Muslims and Christians. His main teachings were as follows:

- Ramakrishna denounced religious particularism and stressed on religious universalism. Even as his own thinking was rooted in Indian thought and culture, he recognised the truth in all religions. He preached that Hinduism, Islam and Christianity were different paths that lead to the same God.
- He also recognised the utility of idol worship in evoking spiritual feelings and fervour in the devotees. Yet he put his emphasis on the intention and spirit and not symbols and rituals.
- He had great compassion for human suffering, and taught his disciples- **'yatra jiv, tatra shiv'** (wherever there is a living being, there is Shiva). He also taught 'not just kindness to living beings but serving the living beings as Shiva himself'.
- However, Ramakrishna's main stress remained on religious salvation rather than social salvation.

Ramakrishna's most famous disciple was Swami Vivekananda, who took his gurus message to different parts of the country and the world.

Swami Vivekananda (1863–1902) and Ramakrishna Mission (1897)

Swami Vivekananda

The last of the great thinkers of 19th century Bengal who created a stir in Hindu society was Narendranath Datta, known as Swami Vivekananda. His spiritual guru was Ramakrishna Paramhansa.

In 1893, Swami Vivekananda leapt into fame at the **Parliament of Religions** held at Chicago in which he represented Hinduism. In his keynote address, he stressed on the need for a **healthy balance between spiritualism and materialism.** His vast knowledge of Eastern and Western cultures, his eloquence, human sympathy and learned interpretations left a deep impression in the minds of many among his international audience.

Teachings of Vivekananda

- Vivekananda emerged as a preacher of **Neo-Hinduism**. He envisaged a new culture for the whole world where the materialism of the West and the spiritualism of the East would be harmoniously blended to produce happiness for mankind.
- He denounced the socials evils prevalent in Hindu society of the time including caste system, rituals and superstition. He attacked the tacit approval to the oppression of the poor by the rich.
- Though Vivekananda never gave any political message, through his speeches and writings he infused the youth with a sense of pride in India's past and faith in India's future. In this way, he immensely contributed to the concept of **nationalism** in colonial India.
- He criticised Indians for having lost touch with the world. He said that, 'motion is the sign of life', that stagnation results in degeneration.
- He was most influenced by his guru's teaching that all living beings are an embodiment of the divine self; therefore, the best way to serve God was to **serve mankind**. In this way, he gave a new social purpose to Hinduism.
- His famous literary works include:
  - Bartaman Bharat
  - Lectures from Colombo to Almora
  - The East and the West

Ramakrishna Mission, 1897 In 1897, Vivekananda founded the Ramakrishna Mission, 11 years after the death of his spiritual guru Ramakrishna Paramhansa, to carry out humanitarian and social work. To achieve its objective, the Mission opened various charitable schools, hospitals, orphanages, libraries, etc., in different parts of the country.

Subhas Chandra Bose said, 'So far as Bengal is concerned, Vivekananda may be regarded as the **spiritual father of the modern nationalist movement**'.

Special Note on Rabindranath Tagore (1861–1941) Also known as **'Gurudev'**, Rabindranath Tagore, was a polymath, a nationalist and a key exponent of Bengali Renaissance. He was a writer and an artist par excellence who in 1913 became the first non-European to receive the **Nobel Prize** in literature. Two of his compositions, Jana Gana Mana and Amar Shonar Bangla form the national anthems of India and Bangladesh, respectively.

Rabindranath Tagore

Tagore extended significant support to India's freedom struggle through his **nationalist compositions**; many of them were adopted as slogans of various agitations during the national movement. 'Where the mind is without fear' and 'Ekla Chalo Re' became particularly popular, with the latter favoured by Gandhi. Though somewhat critical of Gandhian activism, specially burning of foreign cloth and advocacy of charkha, he played a key role in resolving Gandhi–Ambedkar dispute over the issue of separate electorates for Dalits. For attainment of freedom, Tagore stood for self-help and steady purposeful education rather than any blind revolution. He had also **renounced his knighthood** to register his protest against the Jallianwala Massacre.

In 1918, he established a school named **Visva-Bharati** which emphasised on holistic learning rather than rote learning. His brother Satyendranath Tagore was the first Indian to be appointed to the Indian Civil Service (June 1863).

Prelim Capsule

Reform Movements (Eastern India)

Leaders and Movements	Important Events
Raja Ram Mohan Roy (1774–1833) and the Brahmo Samaj (1828)	Ram Mohan Roy is known as the **Morning Star** of reform movement. He believed in the synthesis of the East and the West. He held that all principal texts of the Hindus preached monotheism or worship of one God. In 1805, he published in Persian his first philosophical work, **Tuhfat-ul-Muwahiddin** (Gift to Monotheists). In 1820, he published the **Precepts of Jesus**. In 1814, he formed the **Atmiya Sabha** in Calcutta to carry on a socio-religious reform. In 1825, he founded the **Vedanta College** that imparted Indian as well as western learning. In 1828, he founded the **Brahmo Sabha**, later renamed as Brahmo Samaj. His struggle led to the abolition of **Sati** in 1829 through a legislation passed by William Bentinck. He represented the first sparkle of nationalist consciousness in India. He is aptly known as the **Father of Indian Renaissance** and of Modern India.
The Brahmo Samaj	Its primary purpose was to teach monotheism and rid Hinduism of its evils. The activities of Brahmo Samaj were opposed by the **Dharma Sabha**, founded by Radhakant Deb.
Debendranath Tagore (1817–1905)	He was the father of Rabindranath Tagore. In 1839, he established the **Tattvabodhini Sabha** to propagate Ram Mohan's ideas. The Sabha also published the **Tattvabodhini Patrika** (1843). In 1843, Debendranath Tagore joined Brahmo Samaj and began putting new life into it.
Keshub Chandra Sen (1838–84)	He joined the Brahmo Samaj in 1858. He was appointed as Acharya of the Samaj by Debendranath Tagore. Under him, branches of the Samaj were opened up in UP, Punjab, Bombay, Madras, etc. He laid stress on universalism as opposed to Debendranath's stress on national Hindu identity, leading to a split in Brahmo Samaj. Keshub had his followers left the parent body and formed the **Brahmo Samaj of India** in 1865. Tagore's Samaj henceforth came to be known as **Adi Brahmo Samaj**. Keshub married his own 13-year-old daughter with the Maharaja of Kooch-Bihar. Feeling disgusted, many of Keshub's followers set up a new organisation called the **Sadharan Brahmo Samaj** (1878).

Derozio (1809–31) and Young Bengal Movement (1820s–30s)	Henry Vivian Derozio was an Anglo-Indian teacher of the Hindu College. He was inspired by French Revolution and followed the most radical views of his time. His followers, known as **Derozians or Young Bengal**, attacked the old and decadent customs of Hindu society and religion. In 1831, Derozio was dismissed from the Hindu College owing to his radicalism.
Ishwar Chandra Vidyasagar (1820–91)	He was a Sanskrit scholar and rose to the position of the Principal of the **Sanskrit College, Calcutta**. He opened the gates of the college to western thought as well as non-Brahmin students. Both Vidyasagar and Rabindranath Tagore wrote **Bengali primers.** He devoted his entire life to the specific cause of widow remarriage. His efforts culminated in the passing of the **Hindu Widows Remarriage Act 1856**. As Secretary of the Bethune School he led the movement for women's education. He also struggled against child marriage and polygamy. His prominent literary works include books such as **Bahubibaha** and **Bidhaba Bibaha**. He also started the Bengali newspaper **Shome Prakash** (1858).
Ramkrishna Paramhansa (1834–86)	He was a poor priest at the Kali temple in Dakshineswar near Calcutta. He had great compassion for human suffering, and taught his disciples- 'yatra jiv, tatra shiv'. Ramakrishna's main stress remained on religious salvation rather than social salvation.
Swami Vivekananda (1863–1902)	He was the greatest disciple of Ramkrishna Paramhansa. In 1893, Swami Vivekananda leapt into fame at the **Parliament of Religions** held at Chicago. He stressed on the need for a healthy balance between spiritualism and materialism. His teachings are termed as **Neo-Hinduism.** He immensely contributed to the concept of **Nationalism** in colonial India. Like his guru, he too believed that the best way to serve God was to **serve mankind**. In this way, he gave a new social purpose to Hinduism. In 1897, he founded the Ramakrishna Mission to carry out humanitarian and social work. His famous literary works include **Bartaman Bharat, Lectures from Colombo to Almora, The East and the West**.

Western India

In terms of the social conditions the 19th century Maharashtrian society was divided as per Varnashrama dharma into an unequal hierarchical order comprising Brahmans, Kshatriyas, Vaishyas and Shudras. Social interactions between different castes were maintained by strict rules of purity and pollution. The Shudras were deprived of all rights including education. The Brahmins, on the other hand, exercised considerable domination over the other castes due to their monopoly in matters of religion and learning. During the British years, the Brahmins successfully took to English education and came to dominate the colonial administration. They occupied strategic positions as officials, lawyers, teachers, writers, editors, etc., thus creating fear in the minds of the non-Brahmins. Such a state of affairs was bitterly criticised by the Christian missionaries as well as the national intelligentsia.

Consequently, in Western India, the main focus of reform movements was social reform, unlike Bengal, where the focus was religious reform. Hence, the early intellectuals of Maharashtra had a rather practical approach and were not much concerned with religious or philosophical aspects.

The reformers in Maharashtra can be divided into two distinct strands:

1. The early radical reformers like Jyotiba Phule who sought a revolutionary reorganisation of traditional society on the basis of principles of equality and rationality. (Their efforts led to the emergence of a general awareness among the lower castes regarding the various forms of discrimination they were subjected to and gave birth to non-Brahmin movement in Maharashtra. This has been dealt with in the next chapter).
2. The later moderate reformers like MG Ranade, who sought a return to past society with some modifications.

Early Phase of Reform Movement in Western India

Balshastri Jambhekar (1812–46) Jambhekar was the pioneer of the intellectual movement in Maharashtra. He attacked Brahmanical orthodoxy. In 1832, he started a weekly, the **'Darpan'**, and initiated the reform movement through his numerous writings in the early 1830s.

Dadoba Pandurang Tarkhadkar (1814–82) and Paramhansa Mandali (1849) The intellectual movement further developed with the efforts of Dadoba. In 1849, he assumed leadership of **Paramhansa Mandali**, the first reform organisation of 19th century Maharashtra. The chief objective of this Mandali was the demolition of all caste distinctions. Each member had to pledge that he would not observe any such distinctions based on caste or religion. In its meetings, members would eat food cooked by low-caste people. The Mandali, however, had to function as a **secret society**, for fear of facing the wrath of the orthodox sections.

Bhaskar Pandurang Tarkhadkar (1816–47) Bhaskar Pandurang emerged as a militant critic of the colonial rule in India. In 1841, he wrote a series of letters in the Bombay Gazette, exposing nearly every aspect of colonial domination.

Jyotiba Phule (1827–90) Phule was born in a low-caste Mali family and was acutely aware of the degraded position of non-Brahmins in Maharashtra. All his life he passionately campaigned against upper-caste domination and in 1854, he became the **first Indian to start a school for the untouchables**.

Phule also championed the cause of the liberation of Indian women. He was a pioneer of the widow remarriage movement in Maharashtra. In 1851, Jyotiba and his wife started a **girl's school** in Poona.

Students' Literary and Scientific Society (1848) It was established in 1848 by several educated young men and had two branches known as the Marathi and the Gujarati **Gyan Prakashak Mandalis**. The society organised questions on popular science and social questions. It also aimed to start schools for female education.

Karsondas Mulji He was another activist in the field of widow remarriage. In 1852, he started Gujarati weekly **'Satyaprakash'** to promote the cause.

'Lokahitwadi' Gopal Hari Deshmukh (1823–82) During 1848–50, Deshmukh (better known by his pen-name **'Lokahitwadi'**) wrote his famous 100 letters **'Shatapatren'** in the Prabhakar, a Marathi weekly. This formed the magnum opus of the early intellectual work in Maharashtra. These letters are all encompassing in dimension and touch upon nearly every aspect of the contemporary society. He advocated the restructuring of Indian society along modern humanistic lines.

To him, whether social reforms had the sanction of religion was immaterial. If religion did not sanction them, he advocated that religion itself be changed, as what was laid down in the scriptures need not necessarily be of contemporary relevance.

Lokahitwadi wrote, 'Enforced widowhood is a murder of a living human being. It involves the killing of human passions, feelings and emotions. You are butchering your own daughters in cold blood. Should not your blood boil with rage?'

Vishnu Bhikaji Gokhale (1825–71) Vishnu Bhikaji Gokhale was also known as **Vishnubawa Brahmachari**, for he remained a Brahmachari for life. He denounced caste system and stood for oneness in society. Though he was a Brahmin, he had employed a Muslim cook and ate food served by anyone. Thus, he openly defied caste rules and worked for an equitable and just society.

Later Phase of Reform Movement in Western India

Vishnu Parshuram Shastri Pandit (1827–76) Pandit was a leading figure in the sphere of the agitation for female emancipation. He began his public career with the advocacy of widow-remarriage. He founded the **Widow Remarriage Association** in the 1850s and the **Vidhava Vivaha Uttejaka Mandal** (Society for Encouragement for Widow Marriage) in 1865. He set an example by marrying a widow himself in 1875.

Brahmos in Maharashtra (Prarthana Samaj, Bombay, 1867) In 1867, under the guidance of Keshab Chandra Sen, the Prarthana Samaj (Prayer Congregation) was set up in Bombay. The members of the Samaj looked upon themselves as a body within the general Hindu body. You have already read how in Western India, the main focus of reform movements was social reform, unlike Bengal, where the focus was religious reform. Hence, they believed that true love of God lay in serving God's children.

The members of the Samaj worked in the field of widow remarriage, women's education, raising the age of marriage for both men and women and denunciation of caste system. The Samaj also preached monotheism and attacked priestly domination.

The prominent leaders of the Prarthana Samaj included RG Bhandarkar (1837–1925), Justice Mahadev Govind Ranade (1842–1901) and NG Chandavarkar (1855–1923). **Depressed Classes Mission, Social Service League** and **Deccan Education Society** led by the Samaj leaders also made significant contribution in the field of social reform. The Brahmo activities spread to South India through the efforts of the Telugu reformer, Kandukari Veeresalingam.

Ramkrishna Gopal Bhandarkar (1837–1925) Bhandarkar earned the title of **'Maharishi'**, owing to his profound scholarship. In 1891, he arranged the marriage of his widow-daughter, in the face of great opposition. He was a strong advocate of Hindu–Muslim unity.

Narayan Mahadev Parmanand (1838–93) Parmanand was also a great social reformer and a constructive critic of the British administration. He wrote under the pen name of **'Political recluse'**.

Mahadev Govind Ranade (1842–1901) Ranade was a product of the Elphinstone College, Bombay and rose to be a Judge of the Bombay High Court during 1891–1901. He held that the caste system was the main blot on Indian society and that religious reform was a prerequisite for social reform. In 1867, he helped in the setting up of the Prarthana Samaj, a Brahmo movement in Maharashtra, by reorganising the Paramhansa Mandali. He guided this movement in Maharashtra till the end of his life. In 1870, he helped in the establishment of Poona Sarvajanik Sabha and even edited the Bombay daily Induprakash founded on his ideology. In 1887, he founded the **Indian National Social Conference** along with Raghunath Rao. It functioned as the social reform cell of the Indian National Congress. It launched the famous **'Pledge Movement'** to inspire people to take oath to prohibit child marriage. Upon the death of his first wife, his reformer friends expected him to marry a widow, instead he married a child bride, Ramabai Ranade, who also emerged as a prominent social reformer.

Vishnu Shastri Chiplunkar (1850–82) and Deccan Education Society (Pune, 1884) In 1874, Chiplunkar started his famous **Nibandhamala**, a monthly Marathi magazine, devoted to the cause of social reform. In 1880, Vishnushastri Chiplunkar and Bal Gangadhar Tilak founded the New English School in Pune, one of the first schools by Indians offering western education. In 1884, they created the **Deccan Education Society** with Gopal Ganesh Agarkar, Mahadev Ballal Namjoshi and others. Soon afterwards, they established **Fergusson College** with Tilak and Agarkar as early lecturers. Chiplunkar died at the young age of 32.

Justice Mahadev Govind Ranade (1842–1901)- He was a scholar, social reformer and a founding member of the Indian National Congress.

KT Telang (1850–93) Telang played a prominent role in introducing **compulsory primary education** in Bombay. He was the **first Indian Vice-Chancellor**.

Ganesh Vyankatesh Joshi (1851–1911) Joshi provided a brilliant critique of the economic policy of the British government. He was a great intellectual of his times and emphasised on education as the most effective agent of social change.

Narayan Ganesh Chandavarkar (1855–1923) Chandavarkar was primarily a philosopher and emerged as a great leader of the Prarthana Samaj. He presided over the INC session in 1900.

Gopal Ganesh Agarkar (1856–95) Agarkar was an iconoclast and an uncompromising rationalist. He bitterly denounced blind dependence on traditions and false glorification of India's past.

Prof. D. K. Karve (1858–1962) Prof. Dhondo Keshav Karve made his name as a social reformer in the field of women's welfare. He started his career as a teacher in a Girls' school in Bombay and later became a professor in Fergusson College (Poona). After he lost his wife, he remarried a Brahmin widow in 1893 and spent the rest of his life for the uplift of Hindu widows. In 1896, he established a **Widow's Home in Poona** where high caste widows were encouraged to take up careers in teaching, nursing and medicine. He culminated his work by opening an **Indian Women's University at Bombay in 1916**.

Sakharam Ganesh Deuskar (1869–1912) Though born in a Marathi family, Deuskar was brought up in Bengal; he thus emerged as a bridge between the reform movements of Bengal and Maharashtra. He was a teacher, writer and an activist of the freedom movement activist. Most of his writings are in Bengali. In politics he considered BG Tilak as his guru; and a section of people call him the **'Tilak of Bengal'**. His book **'Desher Katha'**, in which he recounted the miserly of an enslaved nation, was banned by the British administration.

Behramji M. Malabari (1853–1912) and Seva Sadan (1885) Behramji Malabari was a Parsi social reformer who is best known for his ardent advocacy of women's rights and his campaign against child marriage and enforced widowhood. In 1885, he founded Seva Sadan, an organisation which took care of those women who were exploited and then neglected by society. His efforts were crowned by the enactment of the **Age of Consent Act 1891** which forbade the marriage of girls below the age of 12.

Rukhmabai Case and the Age of Consent Act The UPSC asked a question on Rukhmabai in the **CSE-2020** after Google doodle commemorated her 153rd birth anniversary in 2017. Rukhmabai was one of the first women doctors in British India. She was married off at age 11 to Dadaji Bhikaji, aged 19. Her refusal to live with Bhikaji led to the Bhikaji vs. Rukmabai case of 1884, in which Bhikaji asked for restitution of conjugal rights. In the final judgment, Rukhmabai was asked to live with her husband or face imprisonment for six months—to which she responded by declaring that she rather face imprisonment than obey the verdict. The case created immense social and political uproar. BG Tilak wrote in the Kesari that her defiance was a result of English education. Her marriage was finally dissolved upon the Queen's intervention and the case became an important precursor to the Age of Consent Act of 1891.

Gopal Krishna Gokhale (1866–1915) and Servants of India Society (Pune, 1905) Gokhale was a prominent social and political leader of India during the Indian national movement. In 1889, he joined the Indian National Congress as a protégé of MG Ranade and emerged as a leader of the moderates, advocating reforms by constitutional means. In 1905, Gokhale was elected president of the Indian National Congress and reached the height of his political power.

In 1905 itself, he left the Deccan Education Society and founded the Servants of India Society to further the expansion of Indian education, a cause very dear to his heart. The aim of the Society was **to train national missionaries for service of India**. The Society worked for the promotion of education and health and organised many campaigns to fight the social evils of poverty, untouchability, alcoholism, oppression of women and domestic abuse. In 1911, the Society began the publication of its organ, **the Hitavada** in English from Nagpur.

Vitthal Ramji Shinde (1873–1944) and Depressed Class Mission (Bombay, 1906) Shinde was a prominent social reformer of Maharashtra. He was selected by Prarthana Samaj in 1901 to go to England and study comparative religion. He returned in 1903 and devoted his life to socio-religious reform. In 1906, he established the Depressed Classes Mission to provide education to the Dalits, remove untouchability and solve their social problems.

Narayan Malhar Joshi (1879–1955) and Social Service League (Bombay, 1911) N. M. Joshi was a follower of Gokhale and a leader of the Indian trade union. In 1911, N.M. Joshi established the Social Service League in Bombay with an aim to secure for the masses better and reasonable conditions of life and work. The League trained volunteers to carry out relief work during disasters such as famines, epidemics and floods, and also to carry out welfare work among the poor. On 31 October 1920, Joshi started the **All India Trade Union Congress (AITUC)** along with Lala Lajpat Rai and served as the general secretary of AITUC from 1925 to 1929 and again from 1940 to 1948. In 1931, he left AITUC and started the All India Trade Union Federation.

Prelim Capsule

Reform Movements (Western India)

Leaders and Movements	Important Events
Balshastri Jambhekar	He was the pioneer of the intellectual movement in Maharashtra. In 1832, he started a weekly, the **Darpan.**
Dadoba Pandurang Tarkhadkar	In 1849, he assumed leadership of **Paramhansa Mandali**, the first reform organisation of 19th century Maharashtra. It functioned as a secret society. The chief objective of this Mandali was the demolition of all caste distinctions.
Jyotiba Phule	Phule was born in a low-caste Mali family. In 1854, he became the first Indian to start a school for the untouchables. He was a pioneer of the widow remarriage movement in Maharashtra. In 1851, Jyotiba and his wife started a girl's school in Poona.
Students' Literary and Scientific Society	These were also known as **Gyan Prakashak Mandalis**.
Karsondas Mulji	In 1852, he started the **'Satya Prakash'** in Gujarati to promote the cause of widow remarriage.
'Lokahitwadi' Gopal Hari Deshmukh	He was better known by his pen-name 'Lokahitwadi'. He wrote his famous 100 letters '**Shatapatren**' in the Prabhakar, a Marathi weekly.
Vishnu Parshuram Shastri Pandit	In 1850s, he founded the **Widow Remarriage Association.** In 1865, he founded the Vidhava Vivaha Uttejaka Mandal.

The Brahmos in Maharashtra	In 1867, under the guidance of Keshab Chandra Sen, the **Prarthana Samaj** was set up in Bombay. Prominent leaders of the Samaj were- RG Bhandarkar, Justice MG Ranade and NG Chandavarkar.
Narayan Mahadev Parmanand	He was a great social reformer and he wrote under the pen name of **'Political recluse'**.
Mahadev Govind Ranade	In 1867, he helped in the setting up of the Prarthana Samaj by reorganising the Paramhansa Mandali. In 1870, he helped in the establishment of **Poona Sarvajanik Sabha**. He edited the Bombay daily **'Induprakash'** founded on his ideology. In 1887, he founded the **Indian National Social Conference** (social reform cell of the Congress). It launched the famous 'Pledge Movement' to inspire people to take oath to prohibit child marriage.
Vishnu Shastri Chiplunkar	In 1874, he started a monthly magazine **'Nibandhamala'**, devoted to the cause of social reform. In 1880, Vishnushastri Chiplunkar and BG Tilak founded the New English School in Pune. In 1884, they created the **Deccan Education Society** with GG Agarkar, MB Namjoshi and others. Soon afterwards, they established Fergusson College with Tilak and Agarkar as early lecturers.
KT Telang	He played a prominent role in introducing compulsory primary education in Bombay. He was the **first Indian Vice-Chancellor**.
Prof. DK Karve	Prof. Dhondo Keshav Karve started his career as a teacher in a Girls' school in Bombay. In 1896, he established a **Widow's Home in Poona.** He culminated his work by opening an **Indian Women's University at Bombay in 1916**.
Behramji M. Malabari	Behramji Malabari was a Parsi social reformer, best known for his advocacy of women's rights. In 1885, he founded **Seva Sadan**, an organisation which took care of exploited women. His efforts led to the passing of the **Age of Consent Act 1891** which forbade the marriage of girls below the age of 12.

Gopal Krishna Gokhale	In 1905, he left the Deccan Education Society and founded the **Servants of India Society**. The main aim of the Society was to train national missionaries for service of India. In 1911, the Society began the publication of **the Hitavada** in English from Nagpur.
Vitthal Ramji Shinde	In 1906, he established the **Depressed Classes Mission**.
Narayan Malhar Joshi	In 1911, he established the **Social Service League** in Bombay to carry out relief and welfare work. On 31 October 1920, he started the All India Trade Union Congress **(AITUC)** along with Lala Lajpat Rai and served as its general secretary. In 1931, he left AITUC and started the All India Trade Union Federation.

Northern India

Swami Dayanand Saraswati (1824–83) and Arya Samaj (1875)

The Arya Samaj movement emerged as a **reaction** to western influences. The founder, Swami Dayanand, denounced western ideas and sought to revive the ancient religion of the Aryans. His slogan was **'Go back to the Vedas'** which meant revival of Vedic learning and Vedic purity of religion and not revival of Vedic times. Hence, his movement is called **revivalist in form**, not in content. He displayed modernity in many aspects and held patriotic views on national problems.

Swami Dayanand (1824–83) was born as **Mulshankar** in a Brahmin family in the old Morvi state in **Gujarat**. He acquired a good insight into Vedic literature, philosophy and ethics from his father who was a great Vedic scholar himself. In 1845, Dayanand left home and for the next 15 years wandered as an ascetic in the country studying Yoga.

In 1875, Swami Dayanand founded the **first Arya Samaj unit** in **Bombay**. A few years later, the headquarters of the Arya Samaj were established at **Lahore**. Henceforth, Dayanand extensively toured India for the purpose of propagating his ideas.

Ideas and Teachings of Dayanand Saraswati

- Dayanand's aim was to **unite India religiously, socially and nationally**: Aryan religion to be the common religion, society to be classless and casteless, and India to be a nation free from any foreign domination.
- He gave the slogan **'Go back to the Vedas'** as he considered the Vedas as the original seed of Hinduism. However, his belief in the Vedas as infallible gave his teachings an orthodox hue.
- He disregarded the authority of the Puranas (the later Hindu scriptures) and blamed them for spreading evil practices like idol worship and superstitions in Hindu religion.
- He gave his own interpretation of the Vedas and published his views in his famous work **Satyartha Prakash** (The True Exposition).

- Dayanand attacked various evils that had crept into Hindu religion in the 19th century, including idolatry, polytheism, superstitions and sacrifices. He believed in the unity of Godhead.
- He rejected the philosophy of 'maya', which stated that man's soul is merely a part of God and that man's objective is to escape the world where evil existed and seek union with God. Instead he held that God, soul and matter were distinct and eternal entities.
- He also rejected the theory of 'niyati' (destiny) and upheld the doctrine of 'karma'. According to him, the world was a battlefield where every individual had to work out his own salvation by right deeds.
- Dayanand rejected the domination of Brahmin priestly class over the religious and social life of the Hindus. He asserted **every Hindu's right to read and interpret the Vedas**.
- He also rejected the caste system based on birth though **he subscribed to the Vedic notion of four-Varna system based on occupation**.
- He condemned child marriage and was a passionate advocate of widow remarriage as well as equal status for both men and women.

Contributions

- The most phenomenal contribution of Arya Samaj has been in the field of social reform and spread of education. The Samaj laid great emphasis on brotherhood of man, equality of sexes, and values of justice, love and charity towards all. It established the **Dayanand Anglo-Vedic Institutions (DAV)** all over the country with the aim of providing the best of Eastern and Western learning. The nucleus for the DAV movement was provided by the Anglo-Vedic School established at Lahore in 1886. The orthodox elements of the Samaj set up the Gurukul Pathshala at Hardwar in 1902.
- As a disciplined Hindu organisation, the Samaj succeeded in protecting Hindu society from the onslaught of Christianity and Islam.
- The Samaj started the **'Shudhi' movement** to convert non-Hindus to Hinduism.
- On the political front, it raised the slogan of **'India for Indians'** and infused a spirit of intense patriotism. The Samaj produced several eminent national leaders like Lala Hans Raj, Pandit Guru Dutt and Lala Lajpat Rai.
- The Arya Samaj movement succeeded in undermining the superiority of the White Race and re-instilling a sense of pride among the Hindus.

While the appeal of Brahmo Samaj and the Theosophical Society was limited to the English educated elite only, Dayanand's message was for the Indian masses and his movement spread far and wide in several parts of the country specially Punjab, Haryana, UP, Bihar and Rajasthan.

Shiv Narain Agnihotri (1850–1929) and Deva Samaj (Lahore, 1887)

Agnihotri was an active member of Brahmo Samaj in 1875 and worked tirelessly for various reform movements started by it. In 1887, he resigned from the Brahmo Samaj to form a new society, the Deva Samaj. The Deva Samaj was originally established as a theistic society, but later it emerged as an atheistic society, denying the existence of gods and emphasising ethical conduct. It called for an ideal social behaviour such as not accepting bribes, avoiding intoxicants and non-vegetarian food and observing non-violence. Its teachings were compiled in a book, **Deva Shastra**.

Prelim Capsule

Reform Movements (Northern India)

Leaders and Movements	Important Events
Swami Dayanand Saraswati (1824-83) and the Arya Samaj (1875)	He was born as **Mulshankar** in a Brahmin family in the old Morvi state in Gujarat. He denounced western ideas and sought to revive the ancient religion of the Aryans. His slogan was '**Go back to the Vedas**' which meant revival of Vedic learning. Hence his movement is called revivalist in form, not in content. He displayed modernity in many aspects and held patriotic views on national problems. He asserted every Hindu's right to read and interpret the Vedas. He rejected the caste system though he subscribed to the Varna system based on occupation. He gave his own interpretation of the Vedas and published it in his work '**Satyartha Prakash**'. In 1875, Swami Dayanand founded the first Arya Samaj unit in Bombay. Later, the headquarters of the Arya Samaj were established at Lahore.
Arya Samaj (1875)	Arya Samaj movement emerged as a **reaction** to western influences. The Samaj established the **D.A.V.** (Dayanand Anglo-Vedic) Institutions all over the country. It started the '**Shudhi' movement** to convert non-Hindus to Hinduism. On the political front, it raised the slogan of '**India for Indians**'. It produced several national leaders like Lala Hans Raj, Pandit Guru Dutt and Lala Lajpat Rai.
Shiv Narain Agnihotri (1850–1929)	In 1887, he resigned from the Brahmo Samaj to form a new society, the **Deva Samaj**. Deva Samaj was originally established as a theistic society, but later it emerged as an atheistic society and emphasised on ethical conduct. Its teachings were compiled in a book, **Deva Shastra**.

Southern India

In South India, a leading light in the field of social reform was Kandukari Veersalingam.

Kandukari Veersalingam (1848–1919)

The Brahmos activities spread to South India through the efforts of the Telugu reformer, Kandukari Veeresalingam. Veersalingam was born in a poor family and worked as a school teacher for the major part of his life. He was a prolific writer and produced a large number of tracts and pamphlets on social reform in Telugu language. His writings contributed significantly to the development of Telugu prose literature, and hence he is also known as the **Father of Modern Telugu Prose Literature**. He worked with a missionary zeal for the removal of social evils, particularly on issues like widow-remarriage, female education and general upliftment of women. He thus emerged as a father figure for the later generation of social reformers of Andhra region.

Caste Associations in Madras Presidency

The all-India wave of socio-cultural awakening acquired a distinct colour in the Madras Presidency and saw the emergence of caste associations of various kinds. These associations stressed on a common heritage of caste members and simultaneously pushed forward reforms in socio-religious practices. Some of the prominent caste associations were as follows:

- Kongu Vella Sangam of Gounder Caste in Tamil Nadu
- Vokkaliga and Lingayat Associations in Mysore
- Sri Narayan Guru Dharma Paripalana Yogam of the Ezhavas of Kerala (SNDP Yogam, 1902)

Another notable feature of the caste associations is their gradual transformation into political forces in the 20th century. (Read more about the non-Brahmin movements in South India in the next chapter).

Theosophical Movement (1875)

The Theosophical Society was started by westerners who were inspired by Indian traditional thought and philosophy. The foundation of the movement was laid in 1875 in USA by a lady of Russo-German birth, **Madame Helena Blavatsky** (1831–91), who was later joined by **Col. Henry Steel Olcott** (1832–1907) of the US Army. In 1882, they shifted their headquarters to India at **Adyar**, near Madras.

Views and Teachings of Theosophical Society

- It accepts the Hindu beliefs of karma and reincarnation.
- It draws inspiration from the philosophy of Upanishads, Sankhya, Yoga and Vedanta.
- It believed that a relationship could be established between a person's soul and God by meditation, prayer, etc.
- It stood for universal brotherhood of humanity without distinction of race, creed, caste, sex, colour, etc.
- It also sought to investigate the unexplained laws of nature and the powers latent in man.

In 1889, Mrs. Annie Besant (1847–1933) joined the Theosophical Society and became the most brilliant exponent of Theosophy, both as orator and as author. In 1893, Besant represented the Theosophical Society at the **World Parliament of Religions in Chicago**. The same year she landed in India as she had begun to feel lonely following the death of Madame Blavatsky (1891).

Gradually, Besant turned a Hindu, not only in her views but also in her dress and social manners. She was well acquainted with Indian thought and culture as is evident from her remarkable translation of the Bhagwat Gita.

In 1898, Besant laid the foundation of the **Central Hindu College in Benaras** (now Varanasi) where both Hindu religion and western scientific subjects were taught. (The College was later developed into Benaras Hindu University in 1916 by Madan Mohan Malaviya. The same year, Besant also formed the Home Rule League on the lines of the Irish Home Rule movement.) Besant was also a passionate advocate of female education in India.

In 1907, following the death of Olcott, Mrs. Annie Besant was elected **President of the Theosophical Society**. Under her guidance, the Theosophical movement in India gained popularity and became a movement of Hindu revival.

Miscellaneous Movements

Radhakanta Deb (1784–1867) Radhakanta Deb was a scholar and a leader of the Calcutta conservative Hindu society. He was the adopted son and heir of Maharaja of Shovabazar Raj. He published Shabda-Kalpadruma, a Sanskrit dictionary with the help of Hara Kumar Tagore. He defended the custom of sati when government contemplated its abolition.

Radhakanta Deb (1784–1867) and Dharma Sabha (1830)

Radhakanta Deb founded Dharma Sabha in 1830. It was an orthodox society which stood for preservation of status quo in socio-religious matters, and opposed even the abolition of sati. However, it favoured the promotion of western education, even for girls.

Ved Samaj (Madras, 1864)

Veda Samaj was established by **Keshub Chandra Sen** and **K. Sridharalu Naidu** when the former visited Madras in 1864. K. Sridharalu Naidu later visited Calcutta to study the Brahmo Samaj movement and when he returned, he renamed the Veda Samaj as **Brahmo Samaj of Southern India (1871)**. He translated the books of Brahmo Dharma into Tamil and Telugu and undertook missionary tours to propagate the faith. However, Naidu's untimely death in 1874 in an accident led to several schisms in the organisation.

Pandit Madan Mohan Malaviya (1861–1946) and Bharat Dharma Mahamandala (Varanasi, 1887)

Pandit Madan Mohan Malaviya

Mahamana Pt. Madan Mohan Malaviya emerged as a notable leader of the Indian National Movement. He is best known as the **founder of Banaras Hindu University** (BHU) which he founded at Banaras in 1916.

In 1887, he established **Bharata Dharma Mahamandal**, to propagate Sanatan Dharma and Hindu culture. The offshoots of the Mahamandala were the Sanatan Dharma Sabhas, founded for the defence of Hinduism from critics both within the community and outside it. In 1918, he presided over the Delhi Congress Session and said that the slogan **'Satyameva Jayate'** (Truth alone triumphs) from the Mundaka Upanishad should be the slogan for the nation.

Pt. Malaviya condemned untouchability and emerged as a key leader of the Harijan movement. In 1933, he presided at a meeting in which the **Harijan Sevak Sangh** was founded. He worked for the eradication of various religious and caste barriers and made massive efforts for the entry of untouchables in Hindu temples. Pandit ji was posthumously conferred with Bharat Ratna (2015), India's highest civilian award, in December 2014.

Radhaswami Movement (Agra, 1861)

The Radhaswami movement was founded by **Tulsi Ram**, a banker from Agra, also known as **Shiv Dayal Saheb**. The movement first started in Agra and still has its contemporary headquarters in Beas, with parallel branches found in India and outside India. The Radhaswamis reject the concept of sacred scripture, rituals and pilgrimages. They believe in one supreme being, supremacy of the guru, company of pious people (satsang) and a simple social life. They believe that spiritual attainment does not come from renunciation of worldly life. They consider all religions to be true and emphasise on works of faith, charity, service and prayer.

Pandita Ramabai (1858–1922) and Sharda Sadan (1889)

Pandita Ramabai Sarasvati was a social reformer who worked for the education of women and their emancipation. In 1889, she established Sharda Sadan at Bombay which functioned as a shelter home for widows. It was shifted to Poona the following year.

Pandita Ramabai

The 19th century socio-cultural awakening emerged in the wake of British conquest of India and the spread of colonial culture. Defeat at the hands of a foreign power set Indians thinking about the strengths and weaknesses of their society and culture. Consequently, the 19th century witnessed a series of intellectual stirrings led by individuals and groups. By and large, the goals of the reformers were to end polytheism, idol worship, unnecessary rituals, superstitions, child marriage, purdah, polygamy, enforced widowhood, sati and caste distinctions. The common concern of all reform attempts was to bring about an overall regeneration of Indian society.

Prelim Capsule

Reform Movements (Southern India)

Leaders and Movements	Important Events
Kandukari Veersalingam (1848–1919)	He was a Telugu reformer who contributed in the spread of Brahmo activities in South India. He is also known as the father of modern Telugu prose literature.
The Theosophical Movement (1875)	The Theosophical Society was started by westerners inspired by Indian philosophy.

	It was started in the USA by a lady of Russo-German birth, **Madame Helena Blavatsky** who was later joined by **Col. Henry Steel Olcott** of the US Army. In 1882, they shifted their headquarters to India at **Adyar**, near Madras. In 1889, Mrs. Annie Besant joined the Theosophical Society. In 1893, Besant represented the Society at the World Parliament of Religions in **Chicago**. In 1907, Besant was elected President of the Theosophical Society.

Prelim Capsule

Reform Movements (Miscellaneous)

Leaders and Movements	Important Events
Radhakanta Deb	He founded **Dharma Sabha** in 1830, an orthodox society which stood for preservation of status quo in socio-religious matters, and opposed even the abolition of sati. However, it favoured the promotion of western education, even for girls.
Ved Samaj (1864)	It was established by **Keshub Chandra Sen** and **K. Sridharalu Naidu** when the former visited Madras in 1864. Naidu later renamed the Veda Samaj as **Brahmo Samaj of Southern India (1871)**.
Pandit Madan Mohan Malaviya	In 1887, he established **Bharata Dharma Mahamandal** to propagate Sanatan Dharma & Hindu culture. In 1916, he founded the **Banaras Hindu University** (BHU). In 1933 he presided at a meeting in which the **Harijan Sevak Sangh** was founded. Pandit ji was posthumously conferred with Bharat Ratna (2015).
Radhaswami Movement (1861)	The movement was founded by **Tulsi Ram** from Agra, also known as **Shiv Dayal Saheb**. It first started in Agra and has its contemporary headquarters in Beas. The Radhaswamis believe in one supreme being, supremacy of the guru, company of pious people (satsang) and a simple social life.
Pandita Ramabai	In 1889, she established **Sharda Sadan** at Bombay (later shifted to Poona) which functioned as a shelter home for widows.

Previous Years' Questions – Preliminary Exam

1. Consider the following statements: **[UPSC 2001]**
   1. Arya Samaj was founded in 1835.
   2. Lala Lajpat Rai opposed the appeal of Arya Samaj to the authority of Vedas in support of its social reform programmes.
   3. Under Keshab Chandra Sen, the Brahmo Samaj campaigned for women's education.
   4. Vinoba Bhave founded the Sarvodaya Samaj to work among refugees.

   Which of these statements is/are correct? Select the correct answer from the following options.

   (a) 1 and 2 (b) 2 and 3
   (c) 2 and 4 (d) 3 and 4

2. Consider the following statements: **[UPSC 2001]**
   1. Ishwar Chandra Vidyasagar founded the Bethune School at Calcutta with the main aim of encouraging education for women
   2. Bankim Chandra Chattopadhyay was the first graduate of the Calcutta University.
   3. Keshav Chandra Sen's campaign against Sati led to the enactment of a law to ban Sati by the then Governor General.

   Which of the following given above is/are correct? Select the correct answer from the following options.

   (a) 1 only (b) 1 and 2
   (c) 2 and 3 (d) 1, 2 and 3

3. Lectures from Colombo to Almora is based on the experiences of which of the following? **[UPSC 2006]**

   (a) Veer Savarkar
   (b) Annie Besant
   (c) Ramakrishna Paramhans
   (d) Swami Vivekananda

4. Who among the following wrote the book Bahubivah? **[UPSC 2007]**

   (a) Raja Ram Mohan Roy
   (b) Ishwar Chandra Vidyasagar
   (c) Pandita Ramabai
   (d) Rabindranath Tagore

5. Who among the following started the newspaper Shome Prakash? **[UPSC 2007]**

   (a) Dayanand Saraswati
   (b) Ishwar Chandra Vidyasagar
   (c) Raja Ram Mohan Roy
   (d) Surendra Nath Banerjee

6. In collaboration with David Hare and Alexander Duff, who out of the following established Hindu College at Calcutta? **[UPSC 2009]**

   (a) Henry Louis Vivian Derozio
   (b) Ishwar Chandra Vidyasagar
   (c) Keshab Chandra Sen
   (d) Raja Ram Mohan Roy

7. Which of the following statements is/are correct regarding Brahmo Samaj? **[UPSC 2012]**
   1. It opposed idolatry.
   2. It denied the need for a priestly class for interpreting the religious texts.
   3. It popularised the doctrine that the Vedas are infallible.

   Select the correct answer from the following options.

   (a) 1 only (b) 1 and 2 only
   (c) 3 only (d) 1, 2 and 3

8. Annie Besant was **[UPSC 2013]**
   1. responsible for starting the Home Rule movement.
   2. the founder of the Theosophical Society
   3. once the president of the Indian National Congress

   Select the correct answer from the following options.

   (a) 1 only (b) 2 and 3 only
   (c) 1 and 3 only (d) 1, 2 and 3

9. In the context of Indian history, the Rakhmabai case of 1884 revolved around: **[UPSC 2020]**
   1. women's right to gain education
   2. age of consent
   3. restitution of conjugal rights

   Select the correct answer using the code given below:

   (a) 1 and 2 only (b) 2 and 3 only
   (c) 1 and 3 only (d) 1, 2 and 3

10. With reference to the book "Desher Katha" written by Sakharam Ganesh Deuskar during the freedom struggle, consider the following statements: **[UPSC 2020]**
    1. It warned against the Colonial State hypnotic conquest of the mind.
    2. It inspired the performance of swadeshi street plays and folk songs.
    3. The use of 'desh' by Deuskar was in the specific context of the region of Bengal.

    Which of the statements given above are correct?
    (a) 1 and 2 only (b) 2 and 3 only
    (c) 1 and 3 only (d) 1, 2 and 3
11. Who among the following was associated as Secretary with Hindu Female School which later came to be known as Bethune Female School? **[UPSC 2021]**
    (a) Annie Besant
    (b) Debendranath Tagore
    (c) Ishwar Chandra Vidyasagar
    (d) Sarojini Naidu

Previous Years' Questions – Main Exam

1. In the second half of the 19th century India witnessed a strong wave of reformation in the spheres of religion and society. What part was played in this directly or indirectly by Raja Ram Mohan Roy, Keshab Chandra Sen and Justice M G Ranade? **[UPSC 1980]**
2. The 19th century is generally called a period of Indian Renaissance. Which were the major social reform movements of this period and what changes did they bring about? **[UPSC 1984]**
3. Discuss the major social reform movements of the second half of the 19th century. In what ways did they contribute to the rise and growth of Indian National Movement? **[UPSC 1984]**
4. Give a critical account of the Ramakrishna Mission with special reference to the role played by Swami Vivekananda. **[UPSC 1990]**
5. Discuss the role of the Theosophical Society in the history of religious movements in India. **[UPSC 1991]**
6. What were the contributions of the Arya Samaj to the social and religious movements of India? **[UPSC 1992]**
7. 'Swami Vivekananda might well be called the father of Indian Nationalism'. Elucidate. **[UPSC 1995]**
8. The name of Raja Ram Mohan Roy stands foremost in the field of religious and social reforms. Elucidate **[UPSC 1997]**
9. Assess the contributions of Ishwar Chandra Vidyasagar to the making of modern India. **[UPSC 1999]**
10. In what ways did Ramakrishna infuse a new vigour and dynamism into Hinduism? **[UPSC 1999]**
11. Write a short note on Theosophical Society **[UPSC 2004]**
12. Who established the Arya Samaj? What was its goal? **[UPSC 2004]**
13. Characterise the main features of Indian Renaissance. **[UPSC 2006]**
14. What was the character of socio-religious reforms in the 19th century and how did they contribute to the national awakening in India? **[UPSC 2007]**
15. Trace the rise and growth of socio-religious reform movements with special reference to Young Bengal and Brahmo Samaj. **[UPSC 2021]**

Answers

Previous Years' Questions – Preliminary Exam

1.	(d)	2.	(b)	3.	(d)	4.	(b)	5.	(b)
6.	(d)	7.	(b)	8.	(c)	9.	(b)	10.	(a)
11.	(c)								

2 Socio-Religious Reform Movements-Part 2 (Awakening among the Muslims, Sikhs, Parsis and Non-Brahmins)

In this chapter, you will learn more about the reform movements of the 19th and the 20th centuries, particularly the reform movements among Muslims, Sikhs, Parsis and the Depressed Classes.

Muslim Reform Movements

While the Hindu community responded to western influences with a desire to learn, the first reaction of Muslim community was to shut itself in a shell and resist all forces of change. Hence, Muslim reform movements arose relatively later, i.e. only after 1860s.

Wahabi/Waliullah Movement (1830s–60s)

The Wahabi Movement was the first Muslim movement to emerge in response to western influences. It was a revivalist movement which tried to purify Islam of all the un-Islamic practices that had crept into Muslim society through the ages. The movement was led by Abdul Wahab of Arabia and Delhi's Saint Shah Waliullah Dehlawi (1702–62). In India, their teachings were popularised by **Syed Ahmad Barelvi** (also known as Syed Ahmed of Rae Bareli) and **Shah Abdul Aziz**.

Views and activities of the movement were:

- Barelvi condemned all innovations in Islam and advocated a return to original religion of Islam and Islamic society of Arabia as it was during the Prophet's times.
- Barelvi and Aziz gave the movement a political colour and aimed at creating a Muslim homeland (Dar-ul-Islam).
- Aziz set out a fatwa (ruling) declaring that India was **Dar-ul-harb** (land of the kafirs) and the need was to make it Dar-ul-Islam. Jihad was initially declared against the Sikhs of Punjab then ruled by Ranjit Singh.
- After the British annexation of Punjab in 1849, jihad was directed against the British.
- During the **Revolt of 1857**, the Wahabis played a significant role in spreading anti-British sentiments.

By 1860s, the movement was suppressed by the British in the presence of superior military might. In 1870, the term 'sedition' was added in the Indian Penal Code to outlaw speech that attempted to 'excite disaffection towards the government established by law in India'; thus, this movement marked the beginning of **sedition law** in India.

Titumir's Movement Mir Nisar Ali, popularly known as Titu Mir, was an Islamic preacher and a disciple of Sayed Ahmad Barelvi. Titu organised a peasant agitation of the Muslim peasants of Bengal against the Hindu landlords and the British indigo planters. Mir was killed in a confrontation with the British in 1831.

Faraizi Movement (Eastern Bengal, 1838–57)

Note: given in detail in Unit 4.1

Nawab Abdul Lateef and Mohammedan Literary Society (Calcutta, 1863)

The Society promoted western education among the Muslims and also encouraged discussions on religious, social and political issues.

Sir Syed Ahmad Khan (1817–98) and the Aligarh Movement (Aligarh, 1875)

After the Revolt of 1857, the official impression was that the Muslims were main conspirators and they were immediately repressed. Since Bahadur Shah II was appealed to head the revolt, the British believed the revolt to be a Muslim plot. This was also confirmed by the activities of the Wahabis.

However, during the 1870s, winds of change were perceptible. WW Hunter's book, The Indian Musalman, made a vigorous plea for reconciling and 'rallying the Muslims' round the British government through thoughtful concessions. Syed Ahmad Khan wrote the booklet **'Asbab-e-Baghawat-e-Hind'** (Causes of the Indian Revolt), in which he rejected the notion of the revolt as Muslim conspiracy and instead blamed the East Indian Company's policy of aggressive expansion as the cause of the Revolt. Sir Syed advised the British to appoint Muslims to assist in administration, to prevent such revolts in the future.

Sir Syed Ahmad Khan (1817–98) was born in Delhi in a respectable Muslim family and received education in traditional Muslim style. In 1838, he entered the service of East Indian Company and during the Revolt of 1857 he remained loyal to the British. He went on to become a judge at a Small Causes Court in 1867 and later retired from the service in 1876. In 1878, he became a member of the Imperial Legislative Council and earned a knighthood for his loyalty in 1888.

Portraits (left to right): Sir Syed Ahmad Khan, Mohtarma Fatima Jinnah, Quaid-e-Azam Muhammad Ali Jinnah, and Allama Sir Muhammad Iqbal. 75 Rupees 2022 Banknotes.

Role of Syed Ahmed

Sir Syed's name stands out among the Muslim reformers of the 19th century. The Revolt of 1857 was a turning point in his life. During the Revolt, he remained loyal to the British, blamed the British policies for the revolt, and saw the urgent need to restore the previous respect and status enjoyed by the Muslims in India. This, he felt, could be done if the Muslims could safeguard their share in the administrative services by coming out of their shell, ending resistance to modern ideas and opening themselves to western style modern education. He clearly saw that proficiency in English language and modern sciences were a prerequisite for maintaining the socio-political identity of the Muslims in British India.

Thus, he started a movement in order to give respectable position to Muslims in society as they had in the past and this movement came to be known as the **Aligarh Movement**. The nucleus for the movement was provided by the **Muhammadan Anglo Oriental Collegiate School** founded at **Aligarh in 1875** (renamed as Muhammadan Anglo-Oriental College after two years). The city of Aligarh along with the institute and the accompanying educational reforms provided a firm base for the wider Aligarh Movement: a movement of Muslim Renaissance with widespread implications for religion, politics, culture and society of the Indian subcontinent. Syed Ahmed became the leading light of the wider Aligarh Movement.

The main focus of the Aligarh movement was:

- **Loyalty to the British:** Syed Ahmed tried to reconcile the Muslims to the British rule and urged them to loyally serve the British Empire by accepting services under the government.
- **Modern western education for the Muslims to compete with the Hindus:** In the field of education, Syed Ahmed believed that the future of the Muslim community was threatened by their orthodox outlook and began promoting western style scientific education by founding modern schools and journals.

Syed Ahmad took concrete steps to attain the objectives of the movement and initiated the following reforms-

Educational Reform

- In 1875, Sir Syed opened the Muhammadan Anglo Oriental College at Aligarh, where instruction was imparted both in western arts and sciences and Muslim religion. Hindus, Parsis and Christians had freely contributed to the funds of this college and its doors were also open to all Indians.
- Soon Aligarh emerged as the centre of religious and cultural revival of the Muslim community.
- The School provided the nucleus for the formation of **Aligarh Muslim University** (AMU) in 1920, known more as a movement than as an academic institution.

Social Reform

- Syed Ahmad condemned the customs of polygamy and purdah and advocated the spread of education among women.
- He taught tolerance and urged the people to develop rational outlook and freedom of thought.
- He attacked the system of **'piri and muridi'** in which the pirs claimed to be followers of the Sufi school and passed on mystic words to their murids (disciples).
- He also denounced the institution of slavery, calling it un-Islamic.
- He propagated his progressive social ideas through his magazine **Tahzib-ul-Akhlaq** (Improvement of Manners and Morals).
- His other literary works included Tuhafa-i-Hasan and the Loyal Muhammadans of India.

Religious Reform

- Syed Ahmad respected all religions and spoke against religious fanaticism and bigotry.

- In his work **'Commentaries on the Quran'** Sir Syed criticised the narrow outlook of traditional interpreters and gave his own broader interpretation of the Quran in the light of contemporary rationalism and scientific knowledge.

However, towards the end of his life, Syed Ahmad had begun to talk of Hindu domination to prevent his followers to join the rising tide of nationalism. This was unfortunate, though basically he was not a communalist. He also did not believe in the drain theory of Dadabhai Naoroji. He was a loyalist who opposed the Congress idea of self-rule and end of British Raj.

The Deoband School or Darul-Uloom Deoband (Saharanpur, UP, 1866)

The Deoband School, also known as 'Darul-Uloom Deoband', was organised by the orthodox section among the Muslim ulema who stressed on the traditional Islamic learning. It was a **revivalist movement** which focused mainly on the attainment of two objectives:

- Propagating the pure teachings of the **Quran** and the Hadis among the Muslims.
- Keeping alive the spirit of **Jihad** against the British rulers.

The Deoband School was founded in 1866 at Deoband town in the Saharanpur district of UP by the ulema under the leadership of **Muhammad Qasim Nanotvi** (1832–80) and **Rashid Ahmad Gangohi** (1828–1905). The school curricula included original Islamic religion and it totally shut out English education and western culture. The aim was to bring about religious and moral regeneration of the Muslim community and to train religious leaders for the community. Thus, while the Aligarh Movement aimed to reform the Muslim community through western education and prepare them for government jobs, the Deoband School aimed to revive pure Islamic religion of the past and prepare them for preaching Islamic faith.

In 1885, the Deoband School welcomed the formation of the Indian National Congress. In 1888, the Deoband ulema issued a fatwa (religious decree) **against Syed Ahmad Khan's organisations** 'the Patriotic Association' and 'The Muhammadan Anglo-Oriental Association'. The critics often pointed out that the main aim of Deoband school was to oppose the activities of Syed Ahmad, more than anything else.

Mahmud-ul-Hasan (1851–1920), the new Deoband leader, tried to work out a balance between the religious and political aspirations of the Muslims in the overall context of national unity. He thus added a political and intellectual content to the religious ideas of the school. The Jamat-ul-Ulema later gave a concrete shape to Hasan's ideas.

Shibli Nomani, a supporter of the Deoband School, favoured the introduction of English language and western sciences in the education system. He founded the Darul-Uloom in Lucknow in 1894-96. He had faith in the idealism of Congress and advocated peaceful co-existence between the Hindus and the Muslims.

Ahmadiyya Movement (Punjab, 1889)

The Ahmadiyya Movement was an Islamic religious movement founded in Punjab towards the end of the 19th century. The movement takes its name from its founder **Mirza Ghulam Ahmad** (1835–1908) born in the town of Qadian in Punjab, who claimed that he was the awaited Messiah and Mahdi prophesised by Prophet Muhammad and foretold by the Holy Quran. He proclaimed that Muslim religion and society has deteriorated to the point requiring divine intervention and that Allah has chosen him as the renewer (Mujaddid) of Islam.

Mirza Ghulam Ahmad stated that all the major world religions were propounded by God himself and were part of God's plan towards the establishment of Islam as the most complete and final religion. The message of all religions was, therefore, essentially the same as that of Islam, albeit incomplete. Thus, the movement laid stress on **non-violence** and **tolerance of other faiths** (though he also believed that other religions had drifted away from their original form and had been corrupted).

Thus, it may be said that the Ahmadiyya Movement was based on liberal principles and believed in universality of religion, much like the Brahmo Samaj. It opposed jihad and stood for modern education among the Muslims.

Prelim Capsule

Reform Movements (Muslims)

Leaders and Movements	Important Events
The Wahabi/Waliullah Movement (1830s-60s)	It was the first Muslim movement to emerge in response to western influences. It was a revivalist movement which tried to purify Islam of all the un-Islamic practices. The movement was led by Abdul Wahab of Arabia as well as Delhi saint Shah Waliullah Dehlawi. In India, their teachings were popularised by **Syed Ahmad Barelvi** and **Shah Abdul Aziz**. Aziz declared that India was **Dar-ul-harb** and the need was to make it Dar-ul-Islam. During the Revolt of 1857, the Wahabis played a significant role in spreading anti-British sentiments. The movement marked the beginning of **sedition law** in India.
Titumir's Movement (1831)	Titu Mir, a disciple of Sayed Ahmad Barelvi, organised a peasant agitation of the Muslim peasants of Bengal against the Hindu landlords and the British indigo planters.
The Faraizi Movement (eastern Bengal, 1838-57)	The Faraizi sect was founded by **Haji Shariatullah of Faridpur** in eastern Bengal. The movement originally began as a peasant movement. Under the leadership of **Dudu Mian** (founder's son), the Faraizis turned into a religious sect, advocating radical religious and socio-political changes. Dudu Mian propagated an **egalitarian ideology**- that all men are equal and that all land belongs to God and no one has the right to levy tax on it.

Nawab Abdul Lateef and Mohammedan Literary Society (Calcutta, 1863)	It promoted western education among the Muslims and also encouraged discussions on religious, social and political issues.
Sir Syed Ahmad Khan (1817–98) and the Aligarh Movement (1875)	During the **Revolt of 1857**, he remained loyal to the British and blamed the British policies for the revolt, and saw the urgent need to restore the previous respect and status enjoyed by the Muslims in India. Thus, he started a movement in order to give respectable position to Muslims is society as they had in the past and this movement came to be known as the **Aligarh Movement**. The nucleus for the movement was provided by the **Muhammadan Anglo Oriental Collegiate School** founded at Aligarh in 1875. The School provided the basis for the formation of **Aligarh Muslim University** (AMU) in 1920 Soon Aligarh emerged as the centre of religious and cultural revival of the Muslim community. He propagated his progressive social ideas through his magazine **Tahzib-ul-Akhlaq**. Syed Ahmad wrote the booklet **Asbab-e-Baghawat-e-Hind** in which he rejected the notion of the revolt of 1857 as Muslim conspiracy.
The Deoband School or Darul-Uloom Deoband (Saharanpur, 1866)	The Deoband School was organised by the orthodox section among the Muslim ulema who stressed on the traditional Islamic learning. It was a **revivalist movement** which focused mainly on the attainment of two objectives- • Propagating the pure teachings of the **Quran** and the Hadis among the Muslims. • Keeping alive the spirit of **Jihad** against the British rulers. The School was founded under the leadership of Muhammad Qasim Nanotvi and Rashid Ahmad Gangohi. The School welcomed the formation of the Congress and opposed Syed Ahmad Khan's organisations 'the Patriotic Association' and 'The Muhammadan Anglo-Oriental Association'. **Shibli Nomani**, a supporter of the Deoband School, favoured the introduction of English language and western sciences in the education system.
Ahmadiyya Movement (Punjab, 1889)	It was founded by **Mirza Ghulam Ahmad** who proclaimed that Muslim religion and society has deteriorated to the point requiring divine intervention and that Allah has chosen him as the renewer (Mujaddid) of Islam. He stated that all the major world religions were propounded by God himself, though Islam as the most complete of them all. Thus, the movement stressed **non-violence** and **tolerance of other faiths.**

Sikh Reform Movements

The Sikh community did not remain untouched by the intellectual currents of the 19th century. The Sikh community had also, in some ways, got deviated from the path shown by the Sikh gurus and stood in need of socio-religious reform.

Historical Background

Sikhism was founded by Guru Nanak Dev as a movement of social protest against social evils such as caste based discrimination, meaningless rituals that had replaced true spirit of religion and the domination of priests in society and religion. Instead, Nanak preached the unity of Godhead and the brotherhood of mankind. Like other saints of medieval India, he emphasised on good actions and honest living. He also advocated equality for women and a just social order.

However, in due course of time, the Sikh religion firmly established its own rituals and institutions. The Sikh rule established by Ranjit Singh saw the introduction of pomp and show in religious places, giving rise to the very evils that the Sikh gurus had condemned. Thus, there arose the need for reform once again.

Nirankari Movement (Rawalpindi, Punjab)

Baba Dayal Das (1783–1855), a contemporary of Maharaja Ranjit Singh, emerged as the first among the reformers of Sikh community.

- Baba Dayal taught his followers to believe in one formless God (hence the name Nirankari).
- He preached against idol worship of human gurus and worship of tombs and graves.
- He introduced a simple version of marriage named 'Anand Karaj' (a joyous deed). Under this system, marriage is performed in the presence of the Guru Granth, the holy book of the Sikhs with the priest singing four relevant hymns from this book. No other rituals are performed such as marriage procession, dancing and drinking, dowry, etc. Later, this version marriage got formal recognition through the **Anand Marriage Act of 1909**.

After the death of Baba Dayal in 1855, he was succeeded by his son **Baba Darbara Singh** and after him, by Ratan Chand or **Baba Ratta ji**.

Namdhari or Kuka Movement (Western Punjab, 1840)

Note: Given in detail in chapter 4.1

Singh Sabha Movement, 1873

The year following the suppression of the Kukas saw the emergence of the Singh Sabha Movement (1873, Amritsar). The movement was founded in an era when Sikh Empire had been dissolved and annexed by the British (in 1849), Khalsa had lost its prestige, and mainstream Sikhs were rapidly converting to other religions. Its leaders believed that social evils in the Sikh community were chiefly due to lack of education. It was thus founded with two-fold objectives:

- To bring to the Sikh community the benefits of **western enlightenment** through modern education.
- To **oppose the proselytising activities** of Christian missionaries, Brahmo Samaj, Arya Samaj, the Aligarh and Ahmadiyya Movements.

The Singh Sabha leadership, either because of their own vested interests as landlords or because of the perceived 'interest of the Sikhs', did not want to incur displeasure of the British rulers. They, therefore, did not hold the British directly responsible for the manifold ills prevalent in Sikh society.

To achieve its objectives, the Sabha opened a number of **Khalsa schools and colleges** throughout Punjab. The educational activities of the Sabha received ready support and patronage of the government and the rulers of Sikh princely states, leading to the foundation of **Khalsa College at Amritsar in 1892**.

Though the College was opened for purely educational aims, its students and teachers could not remain untouched from the prevailing political unrest and growing movement of **nationalism** in the country. The CID officials reported that by 1907, the Khalsa College had 'become an important centre for inculcating national feelings among the students'.

The above movements of socio-religious reform among the Sikhs indirectly inculcated in them a desire for overall reform and prepared ground for the Akali struggle directed against the Mahants and other vested interests in Sikh shrines on the one hand and against the British imperialism in Punjab on the other.

Akali Movement or the Gurdwara Reform Movement (1920–25)

The Akali Movement was an off-shoot of the Singh Sabha Movement and was launched with the aim of liberating the Sikh gurdwaras (temples) from the control of corrupt Mahants (priests) who enjoyed the support of the government.

Historical Context The establishment of the Sikh kingdom by Maharaja Ranjit Singh in 1799 brought about significant changes in Sikh religion. The Maharaja gave generous endowments in terms of property and privileges to almost all well-known Gurdwaras. The sudden rise in income brought about a change in the style of living of the hereditary Mahants, who gradually began to live a life of luxury.

Following the annexation of Punjab by the British in 1849, the British government took over the control of the Golden Temple and Akal Takht and appointed a committee of ten members headed by a '**Sarbarah**' to manage their day-to-day affairs.

Corruption in Gurdwaras The appointment of the Sarbarah by the government created several problems. The control of the Sikh community over management declined before the increasing hold of the officialdom. The Sarbarah did not feel responsible to the people but was only interested in pleasing his appointing authority. The priests indulged in all sorts of evil practices such as misappropriation of offerings, misusing shrine properties for immoral activities and even abusing women visitors. Further, while Sikh religion did not recognise any caste distinctions, the priests of the Golden Temple did not allow the so-called low-caste Mazhabi Sikhs to offer their prayers in the temple directly.

The British authorities in Punjab resisted any attempt to change the existing state of affairs. Subsequently, the **Akali Jathas (band of volunteers)** of Sikhs of Amritsar thought of creating public awareness on the subject and defy the authority of the corrupt priests. They took control of the Golden Temple and the Akal Takht in their own hands and formed a committee (named as Shiromani Gurdwara Parbandhak Committee, SGPC) for the management of these two shrines, while the priests ran away from the scene.

Toshakhana Keys Affair The Committee of the reform group asked the government appointed manager of the Golden Temple to hand over the keys of the Toshakhana (treasury). But before the manager could do so, the keys were taken away by the British Deputy Commissioner.

This action of the British official created great resentment in the Sikh community. To get the keys, the Akali reformers launched a powerful agitation which came to be known as the 'Keys Affair'. During this time, Mahatma Gandhi's Non-Cooperation movement was going on and the Sikh reformers were joined by the Congress volunteers in Punjab. Feeling threatened, the Punjab government decided to step back and handed over the keys to the then President of the SGPC, **Baba Kharak Singh**. The Punjab government also passed the **Sikh Gurdwaras and Shrines Act, 1922**, which provided for a committee nominated by the government to take over control of the gurdwaras. This, however, was not acceptable to the Akali leaders and remained for this reason a dead letter.

However, after the suspension of the non-cooperation movement in February 1922, Punjab government got its chance of teaching a lesson to the Akali reformers which led to another agitation known as Guru-ka-Bagh Morcha.

Guru-ka-Bagh Morcha, 1922 The return of the keys had undermined the prestige of the Punjab government and its officials were waiting to retrieve their lost prestige. They arrested the Akali volunteers who were cutting wood from the dry kikar trees attached to the Gurdwara Guru-ka-Bagh, on the pretext that the dry wood was the private property of the Mahant and the Akali reformers were committing 'a theft' by taking this wood for community kitchen.

To assert their right and register protest, the Akali Jathas started marching to Guru-ka-Bagh and the police started arresting them. Over 5000 reformers were arrested, until finally there was no more space in the jail. The police then started beating them mercilessly till they fell unconscious and then released them. In this peaceful suffering, the Akalis won wide sympathy of the press and the national leaders.

Rev. CF Andrews, a British missionary sympathetic to Indian political aspirations, visited the scene of Akali beatings and described the police actions as, 'inhuman, brutal, foul and cowardly which was incredible to an Englishman and a moral defeat of England.'

In the face of widespread criticism, the Punjab Governor ordered the police to stop beating the Akali Jathas. Those arrested were released and the volunteers were allowed to collect wood for use in the community kitchen.

Passage of Gurdwara Bill and End of Akali Movement, 1925 The Akali agitation was fast becoming the main vehicle for the spread of Congress ideology and programme among the Sikh peasantry in Punjab and was also likely to affect the Sikh soldiers in the British army. Due to these factors, the Punjab government felt compelled to find a solution to the Akali problem.

Consequently, the Punjab government passed the **Sikh Gurdwaras Act 1925**, giving the Sikh community a legal right to elect functionaries to manage their gurdwaras. This legislation ended the hereditary control of the Mahants and introduced democratic control in the Gurdwara management. Any Sikh, irrespective of caste, can be elected to any position including that of the President of the SGPC. Women also got the right to vote at par with men. With this ended the five-year long Akali agitation in Punjab.

Significance The movement created immense social, religious and political awakening among the people. Of special significance is the awareness created among the people of the Sikh princely states of Patiala, Nabha, Jind and Faridkot. The movement gave these people the much-needed moral support to organise themselves and fight against oppression in these princely states. Even after the Akali Movement was over, the people in these states continued their fight under the leadership of **Sardar Seva Singh Thikriwala** till independence.

Further, the Akali Movement was regional but not communal in nature. In general, the Akali leaders played a notable role in the national freedom struggle.

Prelim Capsule

Reform Movements (Sikhs)

Leaders and Movements	Important Events
The Nirankari Movement (Rawalpindi, Punjab)	It was started by **Baba Dayal Das** (1783–1855), one of the first reformers of Sikh community & a contemporary of Maharaja Ranjit Singh. He taught his followers to believe in one formless God (hence the name Nirankari). He popularised a simple version of marriage named 'Anand Karaj'.
Namdhari or Kuka Movement (Western Punjab, 1840)	It was started by **Bhagat Jawahar Mal** (Sian Saheb) and **Baba Balak Singh**. It was popularly called 'Kuka' as its followers resorted to shrieks (kukan) while in ecstasy. It emerged as a socio-religious reform movement under **Baba Ram Singh**. In 1872, a group of 62 Namdhari Sikhs were blown up by cannon for protesting against the British, while Ram Singh was deported to Rangoon.
Singh Sabha Movement, 1873	It was founded with two fold objectives- **promote western education** and **oppose the proselytising activities** of the Christians, Muslims, the Brahmos and the Arya Samajists. The Sabha opened a number of **Khalsa schools and colleges** throughout Punjab, including Khalsa College at Amritsar (1892).
Akali Movement or the Gurdwara Reform Movement (1920–25)	It was launched to liberate the Sikh gurdwaras from the control of corrupt Mahants (priests) who enjoyed the support of the government. It led to the passing of the **Sikh Gurdwaras Act 1925**. This legislation ended the hereditary control of the Mahants and introduced democratic control in the Gurdwara management.

Parsi Reform Movements

Rahnumai Mazdayasan Sabha (Bombay, 1851)

The rationalist and progressive ideas of the 19th century influenced the Parsi community as well. In 1851, in Bombay, the Rahnumai Mazdayasan Sabha (Religious Reform Association) was formed by a group of English educated Parsis with the following dual objectives:

- Regeneration of the social condition of the Parsis
- Restoration of the Zoroastrian religion to its pristine purity

Dadabhai Naoroji

Main Leaders and Reforms

- Prominent leaders of the Sabha included **Naoroji Furdunji** (President), **Sorabji Shapurji Bengali** (Secretary), **KN Kama** and **Dadabhai Naoroji**.
- The Anglo-Gujarati newspaper **Rast-Goftar** (Truth-Teller) started by Naoroji and Kama in 1851 was the main organ of the association; it championed social reform among the Parsis.
- The Sabha severely criticised the elaborate ceremonies at marriages and funerals and stood for uniform laws of inheritance and marriage for the Parsi community.
- Special attention was paid on improving the condition of Parsi women. Purdah system was attacked and efforts were made to increase the age of marriage and to endure education for women.

Gradually, the Parsis emerged as the most westernised section of Indian society.

Prelim Capsule

Reform Movements (Parsis)

Leaders and Movements	Important Events
Rahnumai Mazdayasan Sabha (Bombay, 1851)	This Religious Reform Association was formed by a group of English educated Parsis. Prominent leaders of the Sabha included Naoroji Furdunji (President), Sorabji Shapurji Bengali (Secretary), KN Kama and **Dadabhai Naoroji**. It published the Anglo-Gujarati newspaper **Rast-Goftar** (Truth-Teller) started by Naoroji and Kama in 1851.

Non-Brahmin Movements in Western and Southern India

A number of factors in the 19th and 20th centuries gave rise to the non-Brahmin movements in western and southern India. These were as follows:

- The 19th century reform movements (though mostly pioneered by upper-caste Hindus, condemned the caste system and untouchability)

- Spread of western education
- Enactment of common Indian Penal Code (1860) and Code of Criminal Procedure (1861)
- Extension of the railway network (where every Indian could buy a ticket of any class and occupy any seat available)
- Growth of national consciousness and modern political ideas of equality and democracy

The above factors created an environment in which the caste system could no longer be defended. They created a class consciousness among lower castes and they themselves took upon the task of struggling for caste equality.

Non-Brahmin Movements in Western India

Jyotirao Govindrao Phule (1827–90) and Satya Shodhak Samaj (1873)

Mahatma Jyotirao Govindrao Phule

Jyotiba Phule was born in a low-caste Mali family and was acutely aware of the degraded position of non-Brahmins in Maharashtra. His family members supplied flowers to the Peshwa house and came to be called Phule. He received initial education in a mission school but had to discontinue it in 1833. In 1848, as Phule attended a Brahmin friend's wedding, some orthodox Brahmins insulted him by calling him a shudra and asked him to leave. This incident turned him into a social revolutionary. The incident made Jyotiba search for the roots of caste discrimination and the inhuman practice of untouchability.

In his search for truth, Phule read the holy books and scriptures of almost all the major religions including Christianity, Islam, Buddhism and Jainism. He judged them in the light of equality and rationality. The caste system reserved a lifelong slavery for the shudras. They were not allowed to walk on the streets during sunrise and sunset, as their long shadows would fall upon the Brahmins' houses and pollute them. In fact, the principle of equality called for a complete rejection of caste system, authoritarian family system and subordination of women. Similarly, the principle of rationality called for the rejection of rituals and superstitions. Thus, Phule turned into a social rebel and called for a complete rejection of the existing system which was sustained by the irrational and inequitable institutions.

Phule argued that as per the Vedas, the Aryans had imposed the unequal caste system upon the Dravidians, after conquering them and Brahmins continue to hide the Vedas from the Shudras as they contain this truth. Naturally, he looked upon education as the most important liberating factor. He also believed that illiterate people are incapable of rebelling against their mental and physical slavery. Similarly, he held the Brahmins responsible for keeping women uneducated and slaves to men. Jyotiba was ever critical of the Indian National Congress leaders for their neglect of the lower castes and the downtrodden.

Activities of Phule

All his life Phule passionately campaigned for the cause of education and for equality between classes as also between men and women.

- He urged the government to impart compulsory primary education to the masses through teachers drawn from the cultivating classes.

- In 1851, Jyotiba and his wife started a **girl's school** in Poona.
- In 1854, he became the **first Indian to start a school for the untouchables**.
- He was also a pioneer of the widow remarriage movement in Maharashtra. He offered widows protection and shelter.
- In September 1873, Phule started the **Satya Shodhak Samaj** (Society for Finding Truth) as a social reform society to attain equal rights for the people of lower castes.
- Phule made generous use of the print media to propagate his ideas and wrote extensively in Marathi language-
  - **Deen Bandhu (1877, Pune)** It was a Marathi journal, published and edited by Phule for exposing the oppressive character of the Aryan–Vedic tradition.
  - **Gulamgin (slavery, 1873)** It was a book by Phule, where he elaborated upon his views on the historical roots of Shudras' slavery and compared it with the slavery of the Blacks in America.
  - **Setakaryancha Asuda (the whip-cord of the peasantry, 1881)** Here he discussed upon the solutions to peasant problems.
  - **Isara (a warning, 1885)** A pamphlet that published Phule's main ideas on economic concerns of the agrarian classes. Aware of the problems of Indian peasants, he extended his whole-hearted support to the peasants in their struggle. He was **one of the first to introduce the peasantry class in Indian politics**. He opposed the Indian National Congress for failing to take up the peasant cause.

Thus, throughout his life, Phule struggled for the downtrodden classes. However, he failed to perceive the colonial character of the British rule and believed in its progressive role. He failed to perceive that the type of revolution envisaged by him could not be achieved in the presence of exploitative colonial rule. With the death of Phule in 1890, the Satya Shodhak Movement saw a steady decline.

Satya Shodhak Samaj in Kolhapur

In 1913, Chhatrapati Shahu Maharaj of Kolhapur (1874–1922, also known as Rajarshi Shahu of the Bhonsle dynasty) established the Samaj in Kolhapur. This revived the activities of the Samaj, albeit temporarily, with a narrow complexion. No doubt, during 1913 and 1922 Shahu Maharaj was associated with several non-Brahmin activities and started several educational institutions, hostels and scholarships for the depressed classes. However, under him, the movement passed into the hands of feudal upper-caste non-Brahmins and business groups who began to use it for their political gains.

Shahu Maharaj waged a major battle for gaining Kshatriya status for his community. After 1919, post Montagu-Chelmsford Reforms, he demanded special political representation for backward classes in the Councils. This was nothing but a betrayal of Phule's ideology and only perpetuated caste inequalities.

Non-Brahmin Movements in Southern India

Like in western India, in south India as well, the Brahmins dominated the social hierarchy. Traditionally the literate class, the Brahmins quickly took to English education and monopolised opportunities in professions during British times. This aroused the envy and hostility of the non-Brahmin communities, giving rise to a tide of non-Brahmin movements.

Self-Respect Movement in Tamil Nadu

Context

During 1887 and 1904, several Tamil texts were published such as Pathupattu, Manimekalai and Silappatikaram, which had presented the picture of classical Dravidian civilisation, distinct from the Aryan and Sanskrit culture. Some Tamil scholars also propagated that the Dravidians were the original inhabitants of India while the Aryans were the outsiders who brought the evil caste system with them. It was this rediscovered sense of distinct identity which expressed itself in the form of non-Brahmin movements after 1916.

Justice Party (Victoria Memorial Hall, Madras, 1916)

In November 1916 in Madras, the non-Brahmin resentment took a political form with the formation of the South Indian Liberal Federation (SILF), known as the Justice Party by **TM Nair, P. Theagaraya Chetti** and **C. Natesa Mudaliar**. The party claimed to represent the interests of all non-Brahmins in the Madras Presidency including Muslims, Christians and Untouchables. The initial demand of the Justice leaders was to secure reserved seats in the provincial councils and was slowly extended to concessions in education institutions, public appointments, etc.

However, during the 1920s, a conflict arose within the party as some members began to feel that the party should not restrict itself to the narrow quest for reservations and jobs but should also be working for the reform and regeneration of non-Brahmin society and culture. Thus, leaders such as EV Ramasamy Naicker launched a separate Self-Respect Movement, giving a new lease of life to the non-Brahmin movement in Madras.

EV Ramasamy Naicker (1879–1973) and Self-Respect Movement

Ramasamy Naicker rebelled against the caste system early in life. In 1919, he joined the Indian National Congress and in 1924, emerged as the hero of the **Vaikom Satyagraha**. Soon he abandoned Hindu mythology and went to the extent of advocating the burning of Manusmriti (a dharmashastra) and the Ramayana. In 1925, he resigned from the INC as he felt that the party was serving only upper caste interests. Henceforth, he emerged as a **radical social reformer** and in 1927, even broke off with Gandhi on the issue of varnashrama dharma. His followers called him **Thanthai** (father) and **Periyar** (great soul).

A commemorative postal stamp depicting E. V. Ramasamy

Ideas and Works of Ramasamy

- Like Phule in Maharashtra, he also attacked the caste system and Brahmin domination.
- He stood for equality and basic dignity for all human beings.
- He held religion as mainly responsible for the low social status of non-Brahmins as well as women.
- He rejected religion and scriptures as guiding principles of social organisation. He rejected Hinduism as an instrument of Brahmanical control, the laws of Manu as inhuman and the puranas as fairy tales.
- He opposed the imposition of Hindi on Dravidians.
- An iconoclast, he tarred caste name boards on hotels, cut-off holy thread of the Brahmins, beat the deities with chappals, broke idols and advocated burning of scriptures.
- He encouraged non-Brahmins to do away with the services of the priests in various ceremonies and popularised **'self-respect marriages'**. Such marriages were solemnised without the Brahmin

priest, the groom and the bride took a simple vow that they accept each other as equal partners in life, exchanged garlands and took the blessings of the elders. Interestingly, several such marriages were also inter-caste.

- In the field of women's emancipation, he advocated their freedom and autonomy in every field of life. He passionately advocated women's' rights in the field of marriage, re-marriage, divorce and birth control. He attacked the patriarchal notion of women's chastity or 'karpu'.
- In 1925, Ramasamy started his paper **'Kudi Arasu'** to propagate his ideas.
- In 1939, he was elected the President of the Justice party.

The main limitation of Ramasamy's movement lay in its social base which remained limited to the upper non-Brahmin castes. In an attempt to expand his influence, Periyar merged the Self-Respect League with the Justice party in 1944 to form the **Dravida Kazhagam** (Dravidian Federation). This changed the character of Periyar's earlier social reform movement. Henceforth, the non-Brahmin movement got increasingly engaged in narrow electoral politics.

Ramasamy Naicker There are certain things which cannot be mended but only ended. Brahmanical Hinduism is one such.

Self-Respect Movement in Andhra

In Andhra, the non-Brahmin movement was basically for socio-cultural reform of the non-Brahmin groups like Kammas, Reddis, Balijas and Velamas. These were peasant groups with substantial landownership and though they were relatively well off, economically they were relegated to a low social status in society as they lacked knowledge of scriptures and even modern English education.

Hence, the movement in Andhra was a response of the non-Brahmin section belonging to the landowning, rich upper class. Naturally, it addressed only the problems of the upper caste non-Brahmins and left out the Harijans. It aimed at restructuring the caste system, with the upper-caste non-Brahmins at the top, rather than fighting for its complete abolition.

Tripuraneni Ramaswami Chowdary (1887–1943)

A prominent non-Brahmin leader of the movement in Andhra was Tripuraneni, who had himself faced caste-based discrimination.

Views and Works

Tripuraneni grew up to be an eminent scholar and spent his entire life propagating the Self-Respect Movement in Coastal Andhra. His ideas were very similar to the basic ideas put forward by Phule and Periyar.

- He challenged the authority of the sacred texts and argued that the caste system, sustained by religion, was a handiwork of the Aryans.
- He stood for emancipation of the women and the Shudras from the **'Slavery of Shastras'**. He demanded the non-Brahminisation of the services and tried to propagate his ideas through his literature:
  - In **Kurukshetra Sangraman**, he argued that the Kauravas were more upright than the Pandavas and that the latter had no right to rule.

- In **Sambuka Vadha**, he exposed how king Rama, encouraged by Vasistha and in the name of preserving the Varnashrama dharma, killed the shudra sage Sambuka for spreading the sacred knowledge, denied to Sudras by the Brahmins.
- In **Vivah Vidhi**, he explains marriage rites in Telugu as the Shudras could not understand most of the Sanskrit mantras. In fact, his most successful reform was in the system of traditional marriages. The Kammas started performing marriages in the presence of their own community priests.

The Self-Respect movement in Andhra played a significant role in introducing modern education and increasing inter-caste interaction in terms of inter-dining and inter-marriages.

Non-Brahmin Movement in Karnataka

Vokkaligas and Lingayats Associations

Around 1918, the non-Brahmin movement emerged in Karnataka and was spearheaded by the **Vokkaligas** and **Lingayats**. A delegation of the non-Brahmin leaders met the Maharaja of Mysore to register their protest against caste-based discrimination. This resulted in the appointment of a committee headed by **Sir Lesle Miller**. On the committee's recommendation, the government passed an order for an equitable communal representation in the public service.

Gradually, the non-Brahmin movement was drawn towards the national movement and it finally merged with the Congress in 1938. After the 1930s, secular politics in India began recognising caste-based demands, with the result that the non-Brahmin groups began to lose their cohesion and each caste began to demand separate representation for itself in the government. Thus, the non-Brahmin movement transformed into a Backward classes movement from the 1940s.

Non-Brahmin Movement in Kerala

Shri Narayan Guru (1856–1928) and SNDP Yogam (1903)

In Kerala, a leader of the Ezhava Caste (untouchable caste), Shri Narayan Guru, established the SNDP (Shri Narayan Dharma Paripalana) Yogam in 1903 with the aim of-

1. giving up the practice of untouchability; and
2. building temples which would be open to all castes.

Views and Works

- Narayan Guru openly criticised the Congress for its lip-service towards lower castes. He opposed Gandhi for his faith in chaturvarnas, which he considered as the originator of caste system and untouchability.
- He gave the slogan, **'one religion, one caste and one God for mankind'**.
- He simplified rituals regarding birth, death and marriage.
- He achieved notable success in transforming the untouchables into backward class.

Role of Bhim Rao Ambedkar (1891–1956)

Bhim Rao Ambedkar, popularly known as Baba Saheb, was a stalwart social reformer who initiated the Dalit Buddhist movement and championed the cause of the Dalits, women and labour.

He was born in 1891 in a Mahar (untouchable) caste at **Mhow**. Although he and other Dalit children attended school, they were not allowed to sit inside the class. He graduated from Elphinstone College,

Bombay and went on to do his MA and PhD from Columbia University. Next, he went to London and earned another PhD from London School of Economics and a degree in Law from Grey's Inn.

Activities of Ambedkar

- **Bahishkrit Hitkarni Sabha (Bombay, 1924)** this organisation was started by Ambedkar for the moral and material progress of the untouchables.
- He resorted to satyagraha agitation to secure civic rights for Dalits such as right to enter Hindu temples and to draw water from wells.
- In 1930, he founded the **Depressed Classes Federation**, entered national politics and demanded separate electorates for the untouchables.
- He represented the Dalit community in the three Round Table Conferences (1930-32).
- In 1936, he founded the **Independent Labour Party**.
- The Communal Award of 1932 provided for separate electorates for the Depressed Classes.
- In 1942, one of his earlier political parties transformed into the **All India Scheduled Caste Federation**, as an all India party. It later evolved into the Republican Party of India.
- In 1956, he converted to Buddhism and initiated mass conversions of Dalits.
- His famous literary works include the following.
  - The Annihilation of Castes
  - The Buddha and his Dhamma
  - Who were the Shudras?

BR Ambedkar, the emancipator of the lower castes, was the principal architect of the Constitution of independent India which accepted the principle of equality for all Indian citizens and **abolished untouchability** by law. He became independent India's First Law Minister. In 1990, the **Bharat Ratna**, India's highest civilian award, was posthumously conferred upon him.

BR Ambedkar

Miscellaneous Movements

Aravippuram Movement (Kerala, 1888)

In 1888, on the occasion of Shivrathri, **Shri Narayan Guru**, despite belonging to the lower caste, installed an idol of Shiv at Aravippuram in Kerala in an attempt to show that the consecration of a God's idol was not a monopoly of the Brahmins. On the wall of the temple he got the following words inscribed, 'Devoid of dividing walls of caste or race, or hatred or rival faith, we all live here in brotherhood'. The event had a far-reaching impact in South India and inspired several socio-religious reform movements, including the famous Temple Entry Movement.

Temple Entry Movement (Kerala, 1920s–30s)

The Temple Entry agitation of Kerala emerged as a landmark in the history of religious and social reform in India. Since the end of the 19th century, the struggle against the disabilities imposed on the avaranas or members of depressed classes was being waged in South India. In Kerala, the struggle was being led by intellectuals such as **Shri Narayan Guru, N Kumaran Asan and TK Madhavan**.

Vaikom Satyagraha, 1924 In 1924, a new beginning was made when the struggle became a part of the Gandhian constructive programme and a Satyagraha led by **KP Kesava** was launched at Vaikom in Kerala demanding the throwing open of Hindu temples and roads to the untouchables. Though this struggle did not succeed in securing the entry of avarnas or lower castes inside the Mahadeva Temple in the town, it managed to open the roads around the temple for their use. In this way, the Vaikom Satyagraha proved to be a big push for the Temple Entry Movement in the rest of the country.

Guruvayur Satyagraha, 1931 The Guruvayur Satyagraha took place on 1 November 1931 demanding the entry for the untouchables inside the Guruvayur Temple in Thrissur district of Kerala. The ten-month long satyagraha protest was led by K. Kelappan, popularly known as **'Kerala Gandhi'**. Kelappan's 12-day long hunger strike during the protest attracted country-wide attention to the Temple Entry Movement. He later broke the fast only on the advice of Mahatma Gandhi on 2 October 1932. With the Guruvayur Satyagraha, the call to open temples for the avarnas grew louder.

Temple Entry Proclamation, 1936 As a result of the agitation, a Gazette Extraordinary was published in which the Maharaja of Travancore historically proclaimed that the temples under his administration would be opened to all Hindus, without any discrimination on caste basis. The Proclamation was a big step in establishing the rights of the lower castes in Kerala, and the nation as a whole. The Proclamation had a far-reaching effect and not only state temples but even private temples were thrown open to the lower castes. Outside of Travancore, temples in Malabar and the rest of the Madras Presidency felt the cascading effects.

Prelim Capsule

Reform Movements (Non-Brahmins)

Leaders and Movements	Important Events
Jyotirao Govindrao Phule (1827–90) and Satya Shodhak Samaj (1873)	Phule campaigned for the cause of education and for equality between classes as also between men and women. In 1851, Jyotiba and his wife started a girl's school in Poona. In 1854, he became the **first Indian** to start a school for the untouchables. In 1873, Phule started the **Satya Shodhak Samaj** (Society for Finding Truth) to attain equal rights for the people of lower castes. His prominent literary works included- Deen Bandhu, Gulamgin, Setakaryancha Asuda and Isara.
Justice Party (Madras, 1916)	The Justice Party was formed by **TM Nair, P. Theagaraya Chetti** and **C. Natesa Mudaliar**. The party claimed to represent the interests of all non-Brahmins in the Madras Presidency including Muslims, Christians and Untouchables.

EV Ramasamy Naicker (1879–1973) and Self-Respect Movement	In 1924, Naicker emerged as the hero of the **Vaikom Satyagraha**. In 1925, he resigned from the INC as he felt that the party was serving only upper caste interests. Later, he even broke off with Gandhi on the issue of Varnashrama dharma. He emerged as a leader of Self-Respect Movement in Tamil Nadu. He popularised **'Self-Respect marriages'**. In 1925, Ramasamy started is paper '**Kudi Arasu**' to propagate his ideas. In 1939, he became elected the President of the Justice party. He was popularly known as **Thanthai** (father) and **Periyar** (great soul).
Tripuraneni Ramaswami Chowdary (1887–1943)	He was a non-Brahmin leader of the Self-Respect Movement in Coastal Andhra. He tried to propagate his ideas through his literary works such as Kurukshetra Sangraman, Sambuka Vadha, and Vivah Vidhi.
Shri Narayan Guru (1856–1928) and SNDP Yogam (1903)	Narayan guru emerged as the leader of the Ezhava Caste (untouchable caste) in Kerala. He established the SNDP (Shri Narayan Dharma Paripalana) Yogam in 1903 with the aim of: • Giving up the practice of untouchability. • Building temples which would be open to all castes. He gave the slogan, 'one religion, one caste and one God for mankind'.
Bhim Rao Ambedkar (1891–1956)	Popularly known as Baba Saheb, he initiated the Dalit Buddhist movement and championed the cause of the Dalits as well as women and labour. He founded the **Bahishkrit Hitkarni Sabha** (Bombay, 1924) for the moral and material progress of the untouchables. In 1930, he founded the **Depressed Classes Federation**, entered national politics and demanded separate electorates for the untouchables. In 1936, he founded the **Independent Labour Party.** In 1942, one of his earlier political parties transformed into the **All India Scheduled Caste Federation**, as an all-India party. It later evolved into the Republican Party of India. In 1956, he converted to Buddhism and initiated mass conversions of Dalits. His famous literary works include- The Annihilation of Castes, The Buddha and his Dhamma, Who were the Shudras? In 1990, he was posthumously awarded the **Bharat Ratna**.
Aravippuram Movement (Kerala, 1888)	It began when **Shri Narayan Guru**, despite belonging to lower caste, installed an idol of Shiv at Aravippuram in Kerala. The event inspired several reform movements, including the Temple Entry Movement.

Temple Entry Movement (Kerala, 1920s–30s)	In Kerala, the struggle for the rights of the avarnas was being led by intellectuals such as **Shri Narayan Guru, N Kumaran Asan and TK Madhavan**. In 1924, **Vaikom Satyagraha** was launched by KP Kesava at Vaikom. in Kerala demanding the throwing open of Hindu temples and roads to the untouchables. On 1 November 1931, the **Guruvayur Satyagraha** took place demanding the entry for the untouchables inside the Guruvayur Temple in Thrissur district of Kerala. The above efforts culminated in the **Temple Entry Proclamation of 1936** in which Maharaja of Travancore proclaimed that the temples under his administration would be opened to all Hindus, without any discrimination on caste basis.

Reform Movements-An Analysis

Nature of Reform Movements

Reformation, not Revolution The nature of the movement was reformative and not revolutionary. Reforms were sought in the existing socio-cultural order and the reforms did not envisage any abrupt departure from it. The transformation of society was to be evolutionary and not revolutionary.

Revivalist Tendencies Another tendency of the thinkers was to view the existing socio-religious practices as distortions that had crept in Indian society overtime. For them, the Vedic period of Indian history represented an ideal type of society free from the evils of the present times.

Removal of Socio-Religious Evils The scope of reform movements was socio-religious and they targeted the elimination of various socio-religious evils and malpractices that were prevalent in India at the time.

Urban Phenomenon The 19th-century reform movement was majorly an urban phenomenon, originating and operating in urban areas only. The movement relied heavily on urban communication channels (such as press and lectures) for the spread of its messages. Even so, the movement was not localised in its inspiration as their messages of equity and justice had universal appeal and applicability.

Limitations of Reform Movements

Limited Impact The impact of 19th-century reforms remained limited in extent and achievement. In practice, the reforms affected a very small minority of people. The masses remained largely untouched from the intellectual currents of the time. Although the reformers attempted to reach the masses through writings in vernacular, their appeal remained confined to the educated urban middle classes alone. Moreover, religious malpractices continued. Caste distinctions remained strong and tradition of child marriage did not die away.

Several factors were responsible for the limited impact of the reform movements. These included widespread illiteracy, presence of hostile colonial state as well as the stubborn nature and deep rootedness of traditions and prejudices.

Localised and Isolated Each of the reform movements was confined, by and large, to one region, caste or religion. For instance, Brahmo Samaj and Arya Samaj did have branches in other parts of the country, yet they were more popular in Bengal and Punjab, respectively. While Brahmo Samaj was concerned with the problems of the 'bhadralok', the Aligarh Movement was concerned with those of the Muslim upper classes. They were also isolated from one another as they all emerged at different points of time in different parts of the country.

Overemphasis on Religion The reform movements tended to overemphasise religious and philosophical aspects at the cost of other aspects of culture such as art, architecture, literature, music, science and technology. Further, any over-emphasis on religion in a multi-religion country was bound to give rise to **religious chauvinism** and have a divisive effect.

Tendency to Look Back Some reformers and movements tended to look backward and appeal to the greatness of ancient past or ancient scriptures. This not only created a sense of false pride and smugness, it also acted as a check on full acceptance of modern ideas. Further, Hindu reformers generally tended to praise India's ancient past at the cost of the medieval period or the so called 'Muslim period'. This not only alienated the Muslims but also the lower castes as the oppressive caste system traced its roots back to the ancient period. Thus, due to the looking back tendency, what we see is a simultaneous rise of national as well as **communal consciousness**. The colonial rulers were quick to take advantage of this communal divide and used it to weaken the Indian national movement.

Inability to Perceive Exploitative Nature of British Rule Some intellectuals erroneously perceived the British rule as God-sent, that would lead Indians to the path of modernity. Since their model of desirable Indian society was like that of the 19th-century Britain, they felt that British rule was necessary in order to make India British-like and openly preached loyalty to the British. Although the socio-religious aspects of Indian society were accurately perceived, the reformers tended to miss the political aspect of basically exploitative British rule.

Achievements of Reform Movements

Historic Legislations Limitations apart, the reform movements do have certain concrete achievements to their credit, including the historic legislations abolishing sati and legalising widow remarriage. Enlightened British and Indian opinion was unanimous in condemning certain practices such as infanticide. Even the prolonged debate over the age of consent bill and other activities of the intellectuals generated much intellectual fervour and raised the level of consciousness of the people. The following pathbreaking legislations were enacted.

The Regulation of 1829

The Regulation of 1829 declared the practice of sati, or burning or burying alive of widows illegal and punishable by criminal courts as culpable homicide. The regulation of 1829 was initially applicable to Bengal Presidency alone, and was later extended to Madras and Bombay Presidencies in 1830 in slightly modified forms.

Bengal Regulations of 1795 and 1804

These regulations declared infanticide illegal and equivalent to committing a murder. To further support these legislations, the Government of India passed an Act in 1870 making it compulsory for parents to register the birth of all babies and providing for verification of female children for some years after birth.

Hindu Widows' Remarriage Act of 1856

Hindu Widows' Remarriage Act of 1856 legalised marriage of widows and declared issues from such marriages as legitimate. However, in Bengal, this legislation achieved very limited success.

Native Marriage Act (known as Civil Marriage Act) 1872

Native Marriage Act prohibited marriage of girls below the age of 14 and boys below 18 years. However, this Act was not applicable to major recognised faiths including Hindus and Muslims and as such had very limited impact on Indian society.

Age of Consent Act 1891

Age of Consent Act 1891 forbade the marriage of girls below the age of 12.

Sharda Act 1929 (in effect from April 1930)

Sharda Act 1929 further pushed up marriageable age and provided for penal action in case of marriages of boys under 18 and girls under 14 years of age. (The Child Marriage Restraint Act of 1978 raised the marriageable age for girls to 18 and boys to 21 years).

Female Education Another significant achievement of the intellectuals lay in the field of female education. An increasing number of people no longer viewed female education as dangerous and the number of girls joining school increased at a consistent pace. Vidyasagar himself was associated with no less than 35 girls' schools in Bengal. It was this groundwork prepared by the early intellectuals that later enabled Mahatma Gandhi to bring the Indian women into the very vortex of national political life. The women themselves began to set up organisations for the uplift of women, the most outstanding among them was the **All India Women's Conference** founded in 1927. Thus, undoubtedly, the reform movements did set in motion the winds of change, however slow their pace might have been.

Realisation of Interconnection between Religion and Society An important achievement of the 19th-century thought was the realisation of the interconnection between religion and society—how healthy beliefs were a gateway to healthy society, and a healthy society a stepping stone to politico-economic progress. Religious reform was therefore understood as the precondition for socio-political and economic progress of India.

This does not, however, imply that social reform was seen as secondary to religious concerns. It was their primary concern for social and material progress of society that made them take up the religious concerns. It was this understanding that distinguished the 19th century reforms (driven mainly by social and material concerns) from the earlier Bhakti Movement (driven mainly by religious concerns).

Significance of Reform Movements

Cleansing of Religion and Society The reform atmosphere helped Indians to discard many malpractices that had crept in their religion and society. Those that had not been immediately discarded were thrown open to debate and discussion. The socio-religious practices were no longer held unquestionable, but reviewed through the newly acquired lenses of rationality and humanism.

Regained Confidence and Pride The various reform movements gave the much-needed confidence to Indians who had come under their influence. The movements reminded the Indians about the greatness of their ancient religions and rich cultural heritage. They developed a new self-concept, an identity they could be proud of.

New Values of Secularism and Democracy The reform movements infused the Indian mind with novel values of secularism and democracy.

Prelude to Rise of Indian Nationalism Finally, the 19th century reform movements were a prelude to the rise of Indian nationalism. They were directly or indirectly related to the task of national reconstruction and nation building. The socio-religious ideas and activities of the intellectuals were loaded with wider national political and economic considerations. Bhaskar Pandurang was the first to provide a critique of colonial rule. Lokahitwadi was the first to seek Swaraj. His national and political farsightedness is noticeable in the lines below in which he chalked out the future course of the national movement, even as it still lay in the womb of the future.

> **Lokahitwadi Gopal Hari Deshmukh wrote,** 'In order to remove our discontent, the British might part with some power. The more power they give, the more will it whet our appetite for it and the British may begin to oppose our demands. If they do so we may perhaps have to do what the Americans did when they drove away the English from their land'.

In this way, even as the 19th century reformers did not directly take up political issues, they created space for them in the hearts and minds of the Indian people. In the 20th century, it was the national movement that carried forward the torch of social reform, with Mahatma Gandhi at its forefront.

Previous Years' Questions – Preliminary Exam

1. Who among the following leaders did not believe in the drain theory of Dadabhai Naoroji? **[UPSC 1996]**
   (a) B G Tilak
   (b) R C Dutt
   (c) M G Ranade
   (d) Sir Syed Ahmed Khan
2. BR Ambedkar was elected to the constituent assembly from which of the following? **[UPSC 1996]**
   (a) West Bengal
   (b) The Bombay Presidency
   (c) the then Madhya Bharat
   (d) Punjab
3. Which of the following parties were established by Dr B R Ambedkar? **[UPSC 2012]**
   1. The Peasants and Workers Party of India.
   2. All India Scheduled Castes Federation
   3. The Independent Labour Party

Select the correct answer from the following options.

(a) 1 and 2 only
(b) 2 and 3 only
(c) 1 and 3 only
(d) 1, 2 and 3

4. Satya Shodhak Samaj organised which of the following? **[UPSC 2016]**
(a) a movement for upliftment of tribal's in Bihar
(b) a temple entry movement in Gujarat
(c) an anti-caste movement in Maharashtra
(d) a peasant movement in Punjab

Previous Years' Questions – Main Exam

1. Explain the significance of the following in socio-religious context. **[UPSC 1986]**
(a) Faraizi Movement
(b) Shuddhi Movement
(c) Self-respect Movement
(d) Rehnumai Mazdayasan
(e) The Wahabi Movement
2. 'Dr. Bhimrao Ambedkar's versatile career went through various phases.' State briefly the various facets of his life. **[UPSC 1991]**
3. Write a short note on Temple Entry Programme. **[UPSC 1993]**
4. Write about: Vaikom Satyagraha. **[UPSC 2008]**
5. Write about: Gurdwara Reform movement **[UPSC 2009]**

Answers

Previous Years' Questions – Preliminary Exam

1. (d) 2. (a) 3. (b) 4. (c)

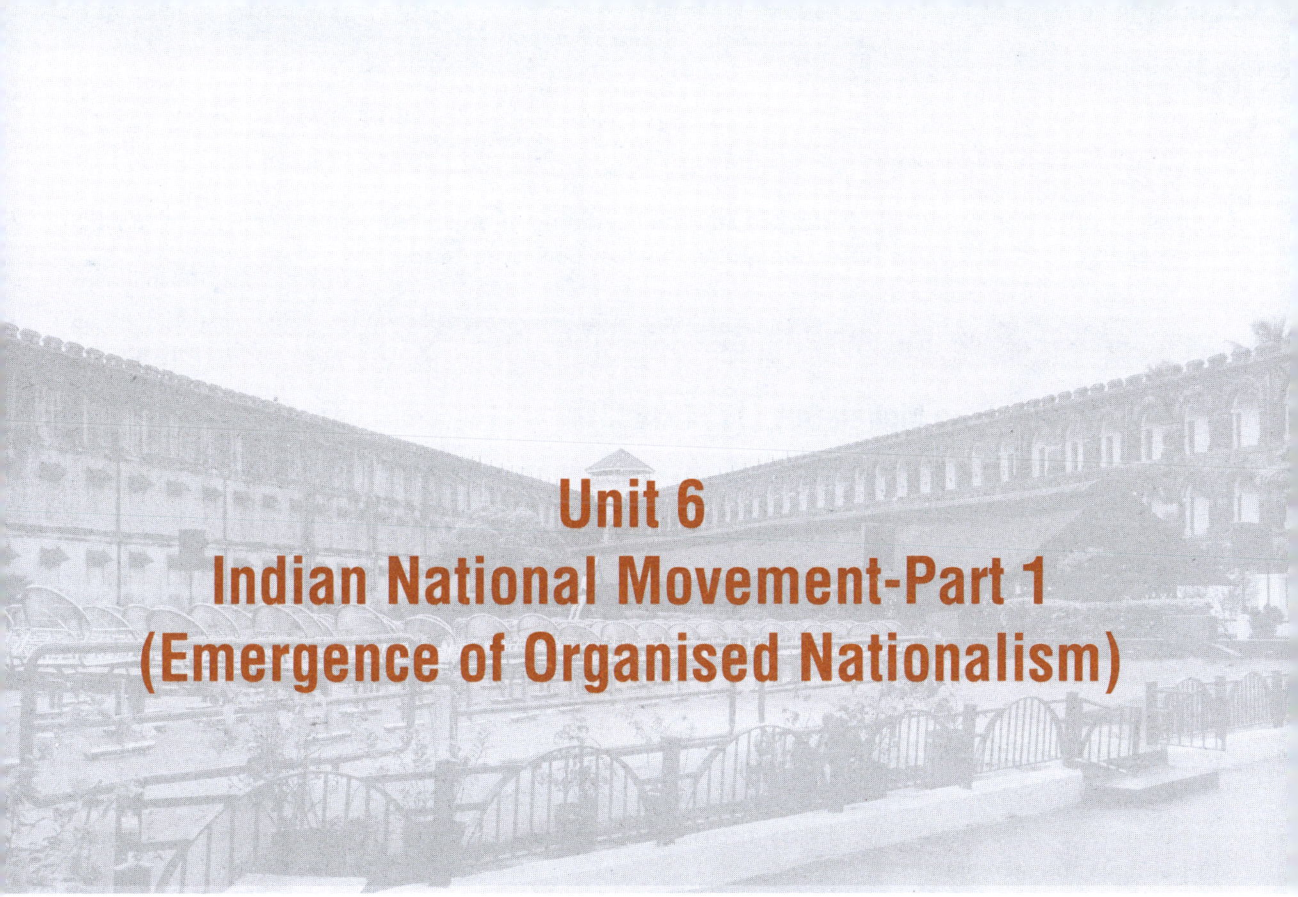

Unit 6
Indian National Movement-Part 1
(Emergence of Organised Nationalism)

1 Political Associations Before Indian National Congress

Earlier we have seen that the educated middle class responded to the British rule in two important ways— in the form of literary activities and in the form of organisations and associations. One of the consequences of the spread of Western culture in India was the growth of modern political concepts like nationalism and political rights. The 19th-century India witnessed the growth of political ideas and political organisations hitherto unknown to the Indians. And it was these political organisations which ushered India into the era of modern politics. Moreover, while the earlier organisations were formed along religion or caste lines, the new organisations were formed along secular lines for promoting secular interests of the Indian people.

It does not matter to what extent the early political associations directly contributed to the national movement, they definitely contributed to political awakening and formed the substratum for political evolution much needed for national movement. Even though they were localised in their approach, their significance cannot be overlooked and the beginning of organised political activity in India is generally traced back to the formation of Landholders' Society in 1838.

Political Associations in Bengal Presidency

Role of Raja Ram Mohan Roy (1774–1833)

Ram Mohan Roy, the Morning Star of reform movement in the country, was the first great leader of modern India, who contributed to nearly every aspect of Indian life. He was also the **pioneer of the political movement in India**. He was a well-read man and was deeply influenced by Western ideas. He is considered to be the first to focus the attention of the Englishmen on the grievances of the Indian people. He demanded liberty of press and appointment of Indians to higher posts. It is believed that some of the beneficent provisions of the **Charter of 1833** were due to his efforts in England. He acted as a catalyst in political awakening not only in Bengal but in the entire country as well.

Bangbhasha Prakashika Sabha (Calcutta, 1836)

The Bangbhasha Prakashika Sabha was a political association formed by the associates of Raja Ram Mohan Roy in 1836 with the aim of discussing government policy and seeking redressal through petitions and memorandums.

Landholders' Society (1838)

In July 1838, the Zamindari Association or the Landholders' Society (Calcutta) was founded by Dwarkanath Tagore, Radhakanta Deb and others to safeguard the interests of the landlords of Bengal, Bihar and Orissa. This organisation is credited with the **launching of organised political activity in India** and the use of constitutional methods for grievance redressal. In July 1839, the Landholders' Society cooperated with the British India Society founded by William Adam in London.

> **Dwarkanath Tagore** (1794–1846) He was one of the first Indian industrialists and was the founder of the Jorasanko branch of the Tagore family. He founded the Landholders' Society (1838) with his old time rival Radhakanta Deb, with whom he had earlier founded the Gaudiya Sabha.

Bengal British India Society (1843)

In April 1843, the Bengal British India Society was founded with the wider objective of protecting and promoting general public interests. It aimed at disseminating information related to the actual condition of the people in British India and advancing the interests of all classes of Indian subjects by lawful and peaceful means.

British Indian Association (1851)

On 29th October 1851, Landholders' Society (representing aristocracy of wealth) and Bengal British India Society (representing aristocracy of intelligence) were merged into one and named the British

Indian Association as the two did not flourish well individually. In 1852, its branches were also established in Bombay and Madras and were known as the **Bombay Association** and the **Madras Native Association**, respectively.

When the time came for the renewal of the East India Company's Charter, the three Presidency associations sent petitions suggesting changes in the Company's Charter. In general, the petitions prayed for a separate popular legislature, bigger share for Indians in administration of their country, separation of judicial from executive functions, reduction in the salaries of higher officials, abolition of taxes such as salt, stamp and abkari (excise) duties and aid to indigenous industry. Even as a desire was expressed for preserving existing interests in land, the petitions also prayed for the need of improving the condition of peasants. Many of these demands were later taken up by the Congress.

British Indian Association Stated in one of its petitions, 'while Indians acknowledged the blessings of an improved form of government, they could not but feel that they had not profited from their connection with Great Britain to the extent which they had a right to look for'.

The prayers of the Association were partially met and the **Charter of 1853** provided for the addition of six members in the Governor General's Council for legislative purpose. The British Indian Association continued to function even after the formation of the Indian National Congress (INC).

Associations before 1858 The chain of political activity was first triggered in 1838 with the formation of **Landholder's Society** in Bengal. One by one, several political associations emerged in different parts of the country. They did a good job in stirring political momentum but soon people became dissatisfied with many of them for various reasons. For instance, all these associations were dominated by wealthy landed gentry. The annual subscription fee for British India Association was ₹50 per annum which was too high for the middle class. Another drawback was that such associations tended to promote their class interests. They were also found to be active in their own provinces and had little influence over the rest of the country.

Associations after 1858 However, those formed after 1858 were dominated by the educated middle class and had a larger agenda. The period after 1858 saw a gradual widening of the gulf between the educated Indians and the British government. By 1870s, a new elite had emerged in the Presidency towns, sharing a similar educational background and aspirations. Ideas of nationalism moved in the air and individuals belonging to this class now began to form popular, mass-based associations to promote political consciousness among various sections of Indian people. Thus, during the period 1875–85, political thrust came from younger, more radical nationalist intellectuals.

India League (1875)

In September 1875, **Sisir Kumar Ghosh** founded the India League with the objective of stimulating nationalism among the people and of promoting political education. Ghosh himself was a noted journalist and founder of Amrita Bazaar Patrika (1868, a noted Bengali newspaper).

Indian Association (1876)

Indian Association was the most important of the pre-Congress organisations and was founded in July 1876 by **Ananda Mohan Bose** and **Surendranath Banerjee**. The people of Bengal were getting discontented with the narrow class interests of the British India Association and wanted a sustained political agitation on wider issues. They found a leader in Banerjee who had been ejected from the ICS on 'insufficient grounds' and was embittered with the British in India. He had declared that the new association was based on the concept of **United India derived from the inspiration of Mazzini**.

Surendranath Banerjee (1848-1925) He was one of the earliest Indian political leaders. He founded the Indian National Association and later emerged as a senior leader of the INC. He was known by the sobriquet 'rashtraguru'.

Surendranath Banerjee

With the hope of attracting the masses, the Indian Association kept its annual subscription low at **₹5** as opposed to ₹50 charged by British Indian Association (It is noteworthy that according to Lord Curzon's estimate, per capita income in British India in 1898 was ₹30 per annum). Its aims included establishing contact with the masses, spreading awareness among them, developing a strong public opinion on political questions, promoting Hindu–Muslim unity and uniting the Indian people on a common political programme. The Indian Association certainly showed all signs of a broad-based nationalist movement.

Soon the Indian Association became the leading representative of the educated community of Bengal as well as a major force in Indian politics. When in 1876, Lytton reduced the maximum age for appearing in the ICS to 19 years from 21 years, the Indian Association took up this issue and organised a pan-India agitation, also known as the **Indian Civil Service Agitation**.

Political Associations in Bombay Presidency

Bombay Association (1852)

Bombay Association was founded on the lines of British Indian Association of Calcutta and its objective was sending prayers and petitions to the government to advance Indian interests. This association did not survive for long.

Poona Sarvajanik Sabha (1870)

Poona Sarvajanik Sabha was formed in Poona by MG Ranade, Ganesh Vasudeo Joshi and SH Chiplunkar with the aim of serving as a bridge between the government and the people. It worked in close association with the Bombay Presidency Association and played an important role in arousing political consciousness. This body is considered as a **precursor to the Indian National Congress** which was also formed in Maharashtra. The Sabha produced many of the early leaders of the national movement including Bal Gangadhar Tilak.

Bombay Presidency Association (1885)

Bombay presidency association was formed by popularly called brothers-in-law—Pherozeshah Mehta, KT Telang and Badruddin Tyabji, representing the three communities of Bombay.

Pherozeshah Mehta (a leading lawyer of Bombay and a political activist)

Political Associations in Madras Presidency

Madras (Native) Association (1852)

A branch of the British Indian Association of Calcutta was set up at Madras under the name of the Madras Native Association. This body faded into obscurity after 1857.

Madras Mahajan Sabha (1884)

Madras Mahajan Sabha was formed by a group of younger nationalists of Madras such as M Viraraghavachariar, G Subramaniya Iyer, P Ananda Charlu and others to coordinate the activities of local associations. It also demanded reforms in legislative councils, viz. expansion of councils and greater representation for Indians.

Political Associations in England

East India Association (1866)

East India Association was formed in **London** by some Indian students like Pherozeshah Mehta, Badruddin Tayabji, Dadabhai Naoroji and Manmohan Ghose to carry on political propaganda in England, discuss the Indian question and work for the interest and welfare of the Indians.

Dadabhai Naoroji (1825–1917) Born in 1825, he devoted his entire life to the creation of a national movement in India and soon came to be known as the 'Grand Old Man of India'. He was a Parsi intellectual, cotton trader and early nationalist leader and also the first economic thinker of India. He is credited with the founding of the INC along with AO Hume and DE Wacha. He served as the President of the INC three times. He was the **first Indian to become a British MP** in the British House of Commons during 1892–95. He was also the first to give the theory of Drain of Wealth in his book The Poverty and Unbritish Rule in India, and showed that India's poverty was due to British exploitation and drain of wealth.

Dadabhai Naoroji

In this way, many political bodies were established in different parts of India with branches in mofussil towns, thus setting the stage for the emergence of a national body. After the formation of Indian National Congress in 1885, these local bodies became the regional arms of the Congress.

Trends Towards an All-India Political Organisation

With nationalism in the air, the need was thus felt for an all-India association. By 1885, the formation of a national level body had become a political necessity. Nationalists all over the country had begun to feel the need to unite politically against the common enemy—the British rule.

Pre-Congress Political Work (1875–1885)

Indians gained tremendous experience and confidence through the political work carried on during this decade. For instance:

- The Indian Mirror of Calcutta was carrying out a continuous campaign on the need for an all-India association.
- There were protests all over India over imposition of **License Tax** (1878) and abolition of **Cotton Import Duties** (1879).
- A massive campaign had been organised during 1877–88 around the demand for Indianisation of government services.
- Indians also opposed the Afghan war (1878–80) of Lord Lytton.
- Major campaigns were waged against the **Vernacular Press Act** and the **Indian Arms Act** (aimed at disarming the Indians) of 1878, and the **Plantation Labour and the Inland Emigration Act** (during 1881–82) which condemned plantation labourers to serfdom) were also opposed.
- During 1883, a major agitation was organised in favour of the **Ilbert Bill** which aimed at bringing the Indian magistrates at par with the European magistrates.
- In 1885, a massive all India campaign was organised to raise a National Fund to promote political agitation in India as well as in England.
- Indians also appealed to the British voters to elect candidates who were friendly towards India.
- In December 1883, the Indian Association organised an **All India National Conference** and gave a call for another one in December 1885. Surendranath Banerjee and Anand Mohan Bose were the main architects of the All India National Conference (this was the reason why SN Banerjee could not attend the founding session of the INC in December 1885).
- Two other conferences were held during the same time: one by Eurasians at Jabalpur and the other by Prayag Central Hindu Samaj at Allahabad.

Now, it was only a matter of time before a national body was created and the stage was set for the birth of the Indian National Congress. The stage was set for some basic objectives to be struggled for and the founders of the INC were inspired by these basic objectives. India had begun to enter the process of becoming a nation, and the first major objective of the founders of INC was to weld India into one nation. The INC, founded in 1885, thus emerged as the first organised expression of the Indian national movement on an all-India scale.

In 1878, the Commissioner of Berar wrote, 'within the 20 years of my own recollection, a feeling of nationality, which formerly had no existence...has grown up. Now we are beginning to find ourselves face to face, not with the population of individual provinces, but with 200 millions of people united by sympathies... which we have ourselves fostered. This seems to me the great political fact of the day'.

Previous Years' Questions – Preliminary Exam

1. His principal forte was social and religious reform. He relied upon legislation to do away with social ills and worked unceasingly for the eradication of child marriage, the purdah system.... To encourage consideration of social problems on a national scale, he inaugurated the Indian National Social Conference, which for many years met for its annual sessions alongside the Indian National Congress.

   Who is being referred to in this passage? Select the correct answer from the following options. **[UPSC 1996]**

   (a) Ishwar Chandra Vidyasagar
   (b) Behramji Merwanji Malabari
   (c) Mahadev Govind Ranade
   (d) B. R. Ambedkar

2. Consider the following pairs: **[UPSC 2017]**

   1. Radhakanta Deb -First President of the British Indian Association
   2. Gazulu Lakshminarasu Chetty-Founder of the Madras Mahajan Sabha
   3. Surendra Nath Banerjee- Founder of the Indian Association

   Which of the above pairs is/are correctly matched? Select the correct answer from the following options.

   (a) Only 1 (b) 1 and 3
   (c) 2 and 3 (d) 1, 2 and 3

Answers

Previous Years' Questions – Preliminary Exam

1. (c) 2. (b)

2

Formation of Indian National Congress

The 19th-century reform movements had led to an intellectual awakening in India. A major consequence of this was the emergence of various political organisations in different parts of the country. But their influence remained limited to their provinces or certain classes of people. The need was felt for a common political organisation for the whole country and it was finally met in 1885 with the formation of the Indian National Congress (INC). With the foundation of INC, India's struggle for freedom from British rule was also launched. Henceforth, the national movement was to grow and it was to no rest till the freedom was won.

It will not be an exaggeration to say that the formation of INC marked the beginning of a movement, not just a body. INC opened a new chapter in Modern Indian History. Its development was closely linked with the development of the National Movement and consisted of three broad phases:

1. 1885–1905: This phase is also known as the Moderate Phase. During this period, the vision and activities of the Congress were dim and vague.
2. 1905–18: This phase is also known as the Extremist Phase. Swaraj or self-government was adopted as the political goal.
3. 1919–47: This period is known as the Phase of Mass Mobilisation under Mahatma Gandhi. Purna Swaraj or complete independence was the goal.

Background to the Birth of Indian National Congress

Accumulated Dissatisfaction Against British Rule

With the spread of foreign rule in India, people had begun to feel the unpleasantness of the British Raj. They felt that they were being insulted and subordinated in their own country, their religion and way of life threatened. The opportunities available for their progress were limited in all facets of life and this had begun to suffocate them. People belonging to the lowest rung of society, the peasants and the tribals, started to rebel in the form of uprisings in various parts of the country. The great Revolt of 1857 was also an outburst of the accumulated grievances of the masses.

Emergence of Educated Indians as New Leaders

The failure of the Revolt of 1857 had exposed the inadequacy of traditional leadership. The raja-maharajas and the landlords had all been defeated by the British. The new English educated middle class now emerged as the new leaders. They are also described by the historians as the **'professional**

classes' or the **'English educated elite'** or the **'intelligentsia'**. Their struggle against the British rule was of a completely new character. With their minds, full of modernity and their hearts full of pride for their glorious past, they had begun to understand the evils of imperialism. In the beginning, these early leaders adopted moderate ways of agitation, which became more radical with time.

What was meant by educated Indians? Broadly speaking, it referred to Indians who had the knowledge of English language and were professionals such as lawyers, journalists, teachers and government servants. They first emerged in the presidencies of Calcutta, Bombay and Madras and gradually spread out thinly over the whole country. This section formed the middle class, i.e. above the toilers but below the landlords and they normally belonged to the higher castes. This section was also called elite in the sense that it was the select group which knew the English language.

During the 19th century, the educated middle class in India played the same role that was played by the middle class in the West—that of spearheading the Renaissance and Reformation.

Role of Nationalist Art and Literature

This was the period when nationalist ideas had begun to emerge in people's songs, poems and plays.

Dinbandhu Mitra's Bengali play **Neel Darpan** (1860) based on Indigo Revolt reflected the plight of indigo farmers and gained immense popularity. Bankim Chandra Chatterjee, the most outstanding among writers, also described British oppression in his historical novels. His most celebrated work **Anandamath** (1882), was written in the backdrop of Sanyasi Rebellion and contained the immortal song 'Vande Matram'(earlier composed in 1875, also pronounced 'Bande Mataram'). Bhartendu Harsihchandra, the father of modern Hindi, also urged his countrymen in his plays and poems to buy Swadeshi goods. Some Bengali leaders also organised the **Hindu Mela** for some years (1867 onwards) to promote indigenous art and craft (During this time, British policies were blamed for Indian poverty and need for Swadeshi goods was emphasized).

Many newspapers and journals of this period also played a significant role in building up public opinion against the excesses of the British rule. These included English language newspapers such as Amrit Bazaar Patrika, Som Bazaar and The Hindu. Some important Hindi language newspapers were Bharat Mitra and Jagat Mitra.

Role of Political Associations Prior to INC

The chain of political activity was first triggered in 1838 with the formation of **Landholder's Society** in Bengal. One by one, several political associations emerged in different parts of the country. They did a good job in stirring political momentum and set the stage for the birth of an all India body, the INC.

Formation of Indian National Congress

The first meeting of the Congress was organised by **AO Hume**. He was a retired civil servant who did not go back after retirement. Hume and Lord Ripon were of the view that the educated middle class in India is here to stay, its legitimate aspirations should be met and grievances addressed. For this purpose, Hume worked hard and revived his network of contacts to discuss the political agenda of educated Indians. It was decided that a conference of **'Indian National Union'** (the name earlier decided upon) would be convened at Poona in March 1885. But there was an outbreak of **cholera in Poona** and the venue had to be shifted to Bombay.

First Meeting

Date and venue On **28 December 1885, at Bombay**, the first meeting of the INC was held in the hall of a College called **Gokuldas Tejpal Sanskrit College**.

First President **W. C. Banerjee** of Bengal was the first Congress President. He was one of the first four Indian Barristers. His election established a convention that the President should be chosen from a province other than the one where the Congress Session was being held.

> **W. C. Banerjee (1844–1906)** Womesh Chandra Banerjee was a lawyer and the first president of the INC. He was also the first Indian to contest the election for the British House of Commons, although he lost the election.

Speech of W. C. Banerjee In his speech, WC Banerjee clarified the aims, objectives and intentions of the Congress. The **aims and objectives** of the Congress as put forth were as follows:

- Promotion of friendship among the countrymen
- Eradication of all possible prejudices relating to race, creed or province
- Consolidation of sentiments of national unity
- Recording of the opinions of educated classes on pressing problems of the day
- Representation of popular demands before the government
- Laying down lines for future course of action in public interest

In his speech, the President further clarified that the Congress members had immense faith in the British sense of justice. They were loyal well-wishers of the government. Banerjee enumerated the numerous blessings bestowed upon Indians by the British. And that the Congress should not be mistaken as a nest of conspirators.

The President reassured that the purpose of the formation of the Congress was simply to represent the views of the educated Indians to the ruling authorities. All they wanted was that the government should run for the welfare of the Indians. This was possible only when Indians themselves got representation in the government. In this way, the basis of government should be widened. For this, **they demanded greater representation of Indians in government and higher posts**.

Participation

The first meeting was attended by **72 delegates, of whom 39 were lawyers**. This trend continued and in every session of the Congress, more than one–third of the delegates came from legal profession. The old aristocratic class like rajas, maharajas and big zamindars did not participate. At this stage, the Congress relied on **petitions** and discussions and made no attempt to associate with the masses.

Resolutions passed

The proceedings were conducted in **strict parliamentary fashion**. In their speeches, the members expressed moderation and loyalty to the Crown. In all, **nine resolutions** were adopted, for instance,

- One resolution demanded appointment of a Royal Commission to enquire into Indian affairs on which Indians would be adequately represented.
- Another resolution demanded abolition of the Indian Council of the Secretary of State for India.
- Yet another resolution condemned annexation of **Upper Burma**.

The Congress also decided that attempt should be made to get resolutions passed by the Congress ratified by all other political associations in India. Thus, it is clear that the members did not conceive of Congress as an isolated body but intended it to become the voice of political aspirations of all Indians.

Controversies regarding the origin of Indian National Congress

The origin of the Congress has been a matter of controversy and various theories have emerged surrounding its origin. This is particularly because of the role played by A. O. Hume. Had there been an Indian in place of Hume, it would have been considered normal. But Hume was an Englishman and that too a former civil servant. Why should such a person take the initiative for forming an all-India body?

Safety-Valve Theory (or Official Conspiracy Theory)

Hume had himself stated that his aim was to provide a 'safety valve' to control the 'great and growing forces generated by the British themselves'. W. C. Banerjee had also stated that the idea of INC was first suggested to Hume by Governor-General **Lord Dufferin**. These two facts together gave rise to the argument that the Congress was an official conspiracy, idea being to provide a peace and constitutional outlet to the growing discontent among educated Indians, thus securing the British Raj.

Lord Dufferin (Governor-General of India during 1884–88. Major events— Third Anglo Burmese War and Formation of INC)

Criticism The critics have given several arguments against this theory. They point out that the aim of Hume was nobler than mere creation of a safety valve. He was an 'enlightened imperialist' and aimed at the genuine regeneration of the Indian people. He had genuine sympathy for Indians and served the Congress tirelessly for many years **(1885 to 1906, Hume was the General Secretary of the Congress)**.

The historians further point out that the credit for survival of a national body cannot be given to one person alone. The early nationalists accepted Hume as their leader because first, he was an Englishman, and thus capable of providing unbiased leadership, free from regional bias. Second, his leadership was less likely to arouse state suspicion. Finally, historian Bipan Chandra writes that, 'if Hume wanted to use the Congress as a safety valve, the early Congress leaders hoped to use him as a **"lightening conductor"**'.

Ambitions of Indian Elite

Historian Anil Seal has put forth the view that the Congress was a body of self-interested individuals driven by parochial factors and not national interest.

Criticism Though it is true that desire to serve one's self interest and lust for power cannot be totally ignored, such a view belittles the nationalist vision that enthused the founders of the Congress. The memories of 1857 were still fresh, the British rule was firmly established and these leaders were conscious that any attempt for a complete break may result in the premature death of the political movement they envisioned.

Need for an All-India Body

Most historians feel that the need for an all-India body was very much in the air, and the formation of the Congress was nothing but the culmination of a process which had started way back in the 1838 (Landholder's Society).

Most noteworthy fact about the formation of the INC was that both the participants and the observers were conscious of two things—that they were making history and that the Congress was a symbol of feeling of nationhood. And this has been confirmed by the verdict of history.

Previous Years' Questions – Preliminary Exam

1. Where was the first session of the INC held in December 1885? **[UPSC 2008]**
   (a) Ahmedabad (b) Bombay
   (c) Calcutta (d) Delhi

Previous Years' Questions – Main Exam

1. Discuss briefly the basic aims with which the INC was founded. When and under what circumstances did it decide to have complete Independence (Purna Swaraj) from the British rule as its goal? **[UPSC 1985]**
2. Trace the emergence of Indian nationalism till the foundation of the INC. **[UPSC 1995]**

Answers

Previous Years' Questions – Preliminary Exam

1. (b)

3 MODERATE PHASE (1885–1905)

The period from 1885 to 1905 constituted the early phase of the Congress and is also referred to as the **Moderate Phase** or the **Period of Tea-Party Politics** or **Political Mendicancy**. This is because the early Congress leaders were firm followers of 'moderate' politics. They believed in a happy combination of liberalism and moderation. They were termed as moderates (or Sudharaks or soft faction or naram dal) to distinguish them from the 'extremists' (or hot faction or garam dal) of the early 20th century. The extremists were the neo-nationalists who believed in more radical methods of opposing the colonial rule. The differences between the moderates and the extremists later led to a split in the Congress in 1907.

Early Composition of the Congress

From 72 delegates in Bombay, the Congress swelled to **434 delegates in Calcutta session (1886)**. These delegates were elected from various local bodies from different parts of the country. Henceforth, they decided to meet every year in a different part of the country each time. The number of delegates soon increased to thousands.

In this way, the composition of the Congress was **all-India in character** with delegates belonging to different races, castes, professions, trades and provinces. Despite this, the Congress was largely a **middle-class affair** with the largest number of delegates coming from the affluent middle class intelligentsia, i.e. the lawyers, doctors, engineers, writers, journalists and teachers. The legal profession was most heavily represented among various professions, the Brahmins among various castes. The presidencies of Bombay, Calcutta and Madras were the most heavily represented among various provinces.

These educated middle-class leaders loved their titles and government jobs, they were mainly drawn from the cities and had no real contact with the masses.

There were a handful of women delegates as well. In **1890, Kadambini Ganguly**, the first woman graduate of Bethune College, Calcutta University, addressed the Congress session. The participation of women in India's Freedom struggle later became the single most significant factor in elevating the role and status of women in Indian society.

Kadambini Ganguly (1861–1923) Kadambini Ganguly and Chandramukhi Basu were the first two female graduates from India. Ganguly was also the first South Asian female physician, trained in Western medicine. She was the daughter of a Brahmo reformer and wife of Dwarkanath Ganguly.

Moderate Leaders and Their Ideology

The moderates were the early leaders of the Congress, the prominent among them and those who also served as Presidents of the Congress were **Womesh Chandra Banerjee, Dadabhai Naoroji, Badruddin Tayabji, Sir Pherozeshah Mehta, Gopal Krishna Gokhale, Surendranath Banerjee, P Ananda Charlu, Romesh Chandra Dutt** and **Ananda Mohan Bose**.

Gopal Krishna Gokhale

Other important leaders of the Congress and of the national movement during this time were-**Sir Dinshaw Edulji Wacha, Mahadev Govind Ranade, the brothers Sisir Kumar and Motilal Ghosh, Madan Mohan Malviya, Bal Gangadhar Tilak, G Subramaniya Iyer** and **C Vijayaraghava Chariyar.**

These early leaders were of the following views:

- India was still a nation-in-making, and its nationhood needed to be carefully nurtured.
- They were powerfully attracted to democracy and modern civil rights. They believed that India should gradually move towards democratic self-governance.
- They felt that the time was not yet ripe for direct struggle for freedom and the British connect should be looked upon as a political necessity of the time.
- The Moderates were full of admiration for British culture; they had faith in the justice and goodness of the British people.
- In 1886, Calcutta session, Congress President Dadabhai Naoroji talked about the many 'Blessings of British Rule'. In 1898, Congress President Anand Mohan Bose declared, 'the educated classes were the friends and not the foes of England'. Hence, **loyalty to the British Empire was their political faith**.
- They believed that the British rule was much needed in India as it was the reason behind the peace and order in the country.
- They believed that the progress of the country was being hindered not because of the British rule but because of the socio-economic backwardness of the country and the oppressive bureaucracy.
- The Indians had certain grievances, but they would be addressed only if the British were made aware of them and justice would be done.

Statue of Dinshaw Edulji Wacha

Note: The readers may get confused when they read about the loyalty of the Moderates to the British rule. Please remember that the Moderates merely felt that the British connection of India was a **necessary evil** of that time. Their immediate plan was therefore to make the British rule as close to national rule. Later, when the British failed to accept nationalist demands, many of them abandoned British loyalty and started demanding self-rule.

Method of Work of the Moderates

The moderates relied on **peaceful, constitutional agitation**, within the four walls of law. They relied mainly on **prayers and petitions, meetings, speeches and resolutions**. They voiced their opinions through the press and through the Congress sessions. Many Congress leaders were editors of important newspapers and used the platform of press throughout the year to criticise government policy. At the Congress sessions, the members expressed opinions on all important measures of the government, protested against unpopular ones and passed resolutions. But the Congress sessions were held for only three days in a year and the Congress had no machinery to carry on its work throughout the year.

The intention of the moderates was to **reach out to the people and government**, in India as well as in Britain, and educate them about the concerns of the Indian people. For this, the following measures were taken:

- The memorials of the Congress were nominally addressed to the government, but their real aim was to educate the people. In the words of **Justice Ranade**, 'In reality, they (memorials) are addressed to the people, so that they may learn how to think in these matters. This work must be done for many years, without expecting any other results, because politics of this kind is all together new to this land'.
- The Congress sent deputations of Indian leaders to Britain to present the Indian view point.
- **Dadabhai Naoroji** spent a major part of his life and income in Britain for this work. He became a member of the British House of Commons and set up a strong Indian lobby there.
- In 1889, a **British Committee of Indian National Congress** was set up.
- In 1890, the **weekly journal 'India'** was started by this Committee to educate the British people about Indian issues.
- In 1892, a session of the INC was scheduled to be held in London to spread awareness about Indian grievances but the idea was postponed due to British elections and was never taken up again.

The outlook and the methods of the moderates may be summed up in the words of Dadabhai Naoroji- 'Nothing is more dear to the heart of England, than India's welfare; and if we only speak out loud enough and persistently enough, to reach that busy heart, we shall not speak in vain'.

The Demands of the Moderates (Congress Program during 1885–1905)

The demands of the moderates (or the Congress program) during 1885–1905 were very modest. They believed that a direct struggle for freedom was not yet on the agenda of history. What was on the agenda was the arousal of national feeling, consolidation of this feeling, stirring up a large number of Indian people out of political dormancy and training them in political agitation.

For this, they needed to arouse public interest on political questions, formulate demands on a pan-India basis and create national unity. The early Congress leaders were aware of the fact that India was a nation-in-making and its nationhood had to be carefully nurtured. Thus, the demands of the early nationalists were formulated with the aim of uniting the Indian people around a common political, social and economic program.

They mainly demanded increased representation of Indians in government and government services, constitutional-economic-military reforms and civil rights. For instance, some of the important demands were:

Political Demands

- Expansion of Legislative Councils with more powers and more representation of Indians in them
- Representation of Indians in the Secretary of State Council, Viceroy's Executive Council and Governor's Executive Councils
- Separation of judiciary from the executive work to protect people from arbitrary acts of bureaucracy and the police
- Formation of provincial councils
- Abolition of Indian Council
- More opportunities for Indians in Civil Service and simultaneous examinations for ICS in London and in India
- End of aggressive foreign policy against India's neighbours
- The agenda of the Congress during this time also included arousal and consolidation of national sentiment, educating and uniting Indians on political questions

Economic Demands

- End of economic drain
- Enquiry into the economic and industrial condition of the country
- Reduction of land revenue
- Abolition of salt tax
- Encouragement to modern industry through direct government aid
- Development of agricultural banks to end the atrocities of moneylenders
- Extension of irrigation facilities to save the people from famines
- Introduction of Permanent Settlement in other parts of the country

Military Demands

- Repeal of Arms Act
- Appointment of Indians to commissioned ranks in the army
- Reduction of military expenditure

Social Demands

- More expenditure on welfare activities—education, health, sanitation
- Civil rights like freedom of speech, thought, association and press
- Basic Human rights for Indian workers in South Africa and elsewhere in the Empire
- Improvement in the condition of plantation labourers
- Timely justice and reduction in litigation costs
- Sympathetic behaviour of the police and other government officers towards the common people

The early leaders demanded Indianisation of bureaucracy on the following grounds:

- Europeans were paid hefty salaries which made Indian administration very costly.
- Their pensions were paid in England which added to the drain of wealth from India.
- It was hoped that Indian bureaucrats would be more responsive to Indian needs.

Note on Economic Demands You may note that even though the political demands were moderate, the **economic demands were quite radical**. The demands were such that they required changes in the basic imperialist economic policies. The Moderates strongly opposed the attempts of the British to convert India into a market for raw materials and a supplier of British goods.

All the above mentioned demands were always carefully worded in prayerful and apologetic language. The Moderates only demanded some concessions and not freedom from British rule. This Congress program remained the same for the next 20 years (1885–1905). The same demands were repeated year after year with hardly any response from the government. The moderates adopted a very patient, cautious approach for fear of attracting government hostility.

At the same time, it is true that the demands were quite comprehensive and the Congress Program was truly national in nature. The program was broad enough to accommodate interests of all classes and communities.

In 1895 Poona Congress, President Surendranath Banerjee stated that the Congress had never asked for representative institutions for the masses, but such institutions for the educated community, 'who by reason of their assimilation of English ideas and their familiarity with English methods of government might be presumed to be qualified for such a boon'.

British Reaction to Congress Demands

Initially, the British adopted a neutral attitude to the Congress demands. After 1887, their attitude stiffened. The British began to brand the nationalists as 'disloyal babus', 'seditious Brahmins' and 'violent villains'. The Congress was described as 'a factory of sedition' and Congressmen as 'disappointed candidates for office and discontented lawyers who represent no one but themselves'.

Challenging the national character of the Congress, Lord Dufferin stated that the Congress represented only **"a microscopic minority"** and its demands as 'big jump into the unknown'.

George Hamilton, Secretary of State, ridiculed the Congress leaders and accused them of possessing 'seditious and double sided character'.

The government adopted a hostile stance against some Congress literature, particularly pamphlets condemning government despotism such as 'A conversation between Maulvi Farukhuddin and one Ram Buksh of Kambakhtpur'.

Henceforth, the British began encouraging pro-British elements like Sir Sayed Ahmed Khan and Raja Shiv Prasad of Banaras. The **Aligarh Movement** and the **United India Patriotic Association** were formed to counter the Congress.

Seeing the growing unity of the Indian people, the British pushed further the policy of **'divide and rule'** to increase the divide between Hindus and Muslims.

In 1890, government employees were forbidden to attend Congress meetings. As the century drew to a close, the British attitude became even more hostile to the Congress under Lord Curzon.

In 1900 Lord Curzon openly declared, 'The Congress is tottering to its fall, and one of my greatest ambitions while in India is **to assist it to a peaceful demise**'. Writing to the Madras Governor in 1903, he further stated, 'My policy ever since I came to India has been to reduce the Congress to impotence'.

Evaluation of the Moderates

Criticisms

The moderates were thoroughly criticised by the radical or extremist leaders. Their methodology of 3Ps-Prayer, Petition and Protest was decried as political mendicancy. According to the Extremists, the only political religion of the Moderates was their loyalty to the Crown and their only political aim was to improve their chances of getting seats in the central/provincial legislatures or judicial services or acquiring titles. Their only political activity included excessive speeches and attending Congress sessions as 'annual recreation' every year. The Moderates were also accused of limiting Congress to a narrow social base, i.e. the middle class, for fear of losing their leadership if the masses joined the movement. In fact, **narrow social base** emerged as a major weakness of the early Moderate phase. The leaders lacked political faith in the masses and in the absence of mass support a strong political stand could not be adopted.

In the words of **Lala Lajpat Rai**, 'it was at best an opportunist movement. It opened opportunities for hypocrites and enabled some people to trade in the name of patriotism'.

Tilak described the Congress as 'a Congress of flatterers', the Congress session as 'a holiday recreation' and the Moderates as 'frogs' who croaked once a year.

Achievements of the Moderates

Despite their shortcomings and criticisms, the role of the moderates cannot be completely ignored and even within the four walls of constitutional laws by their soft yet proactive nationalist approach led to some fruitful results-

Political Achievements

- **Indian Councils Act of 1892** As a result of the sustained agitation of the Moderates, the British government was forced to pass the Indian Councils Act of 1892. But this act did not fully satisfy the Congress leaders. They were demanding that public purse be controlled by Indian representatives and had raised the slogan, 'No taxation without representation', which was earlier raised by the Americans during their War of Independence.
- **ICS Examination in India** In 1893, the House of Commons passed a resolution for simultaneous examination for ICS in London and in India.
- **Demand for Swaraj** Later, in 1905 Banaras Session, the Congress first demanded **Swaraj** or self-rule for Indians within the British Empire **on the model of self-governing colonies like Australia or Canada (equivalent of Dominion Status)**. This demand was first referred to by GK Gokhale. In 1906 at Calcutta session, swaraj was explicitly demanded by Dadabhai Naoroji.
- **Birth of Democratic Ideas** The early nationalists put up a strong defence of civil rights wherever the government tried to curtail them. This political work of the early nationalists contributed in germination of democratic ideas among Indian people.
- **Training of Indians in Political Work** The early nationalists also contributed in training the people in political work, popularising among them modern ideas and in exposing the evils of British rule.

Economic Achievements

- **Economic Critique of British Rule** Another great work of the moderates was their economic critique of British rule in India. Early economists like Dadabhai Naoroji, RC Dutt, DE Wacha and others put forth the theory of 'Drain of Wealth' which explained how Indian poverty was a result of colonial exploitation. Naoroji first mentioned the drain theory in his book **Poverty and Un-British Rule in India**. RC Dutt mentioned it in his book **Economic History in India**. Later, this theory was used as a burning argument by the extremists to denounce the British rule.
- **Welby Commission on Indian Expenditure** In 1895, the Welby Commission on Indian Expenditure was appointed to enquire into Indian Expenditure.

Social Achievements

- **Spread of Awareness for Civil Rights** It was due to their incessant campaign that the defence of civil rights became an integral part of the freedom struggle. Consequently, there was a great public outrage at the arrest of Tilak in 1897 and at the arrest and deportation of Poona leaders, the Natu brothers (also known as Chapekar brothers) without a trial.

Evaluation

It is true that the INC could not achieve much success in its early phase. But at the same time, the Moderate Phase cannot be called a failure. Moderates like Naoroji, DE Wacha, GK Gokhale, SN Banerjee were some of the most progressive Indians of their times and true patriots. They sincerely wished the progress of Indian society. They succeeded in creating a wide national awakening and the feeling among the people that they belonged to one nation-Bharat. History stands verdict that in later years, the weaknesses of the Moderate Phase were to be removed and achievements were to serve as a platform for more vigorous national movement.

Opinions

Bipan Chandra

The period from 1858 to 1905 was the seed time of Indian nationalism, and the early nationalists sowed the seeds well and deep. Instead of basing their nationalism on obscurantist appeal to the past, they rooted it in a hard-headed and penetrating analysis of the complex mechanisms of modern imperialism and chief contradictions between the interests of the Indian people and British rule. The result was that they evolved a common political and economic program which united rather than divided the different sections of the people. In spite of their many failures the early nationalists laid strong foundations for the national movement to grow upon and that they deserve a high place among the makers of modern India.

Pattabhi Sitaramayya

We cannot blame them for the attitude they adopted as pioneers of Indian political reform any more than we can blame the brick and mortar that is buried six feet deep in the foundation and plinth of a modern edifice. They have made possible the superstructure, story by story, by colonial self-government, Home Rule within the empire, and on top of all, complete independence.

Previous Years' Questions – Preliminary Exam

1. Which one of the following Indian leaders was dismissed by the British from the Indian Civil Service? **[UPSC 1999]**
   (a) Satyendranath Tagore
   (b) Surendranath Banerjee
   (c) R C Dutt
   (d) Subhash Chandra Bose
2. That the per capita income in India was ₹20 in 1867–68, was ascertained for the first time by **[UPSC 2000]**
   (a) MG Ranade (b) Sir W Hunter
   (c) RC Dutta (d) Dadabhai Naoroji
3. Who among the following used the phrase 'Un-British' to criticise the English colonial control of India? **[UPSC 2008]**
   (a) Anand Mohan Bose
   (b) Badruddin Tyabji
   (c) Dadabhai Naoroji
   (d) Pherozeshah Mehta
4. Who among the following rejected the title of knighthood and refused to accept a position in the Council of the Secretary of State for India? **[UPSC 2008]**
   (a) Motilal Nehru (b) M G Ranade
   (c) G K Gokhale (d) B G Tilak
5. Consider the following statements: **[UPSC 2012]**
   The most effective contribution made by Dadabhai Naoroji to the cause of Indian National Movement was that he
   1. Exposed the economic exploitation of India by the British
   2. Interpreted the ancient Indian texts and restored the self confidence of Indians
   3. Stressed the need for eradication of all the social evils before anything else

   Which of the statements given above is/are correct? Select the correct answer from the following options.
   (a) 1 only (b) 2 and 3 only
   (c) 1 and 3 only (d) 1, 2 and 3
6. Who out of the following was/were economic critic/critics of colonialism in India? **[UPSC 2015]**
   1. Dadabhai Naoroji
   2. G Subramaniam Iyer
   3. R C Dutt

   Select the correct answer from the following options.
   (a) Only 1 (b) 1 and 2
   (c) 2 and 3 (d) 1, 2 and 3

Previous Years' Questions – Main Exam

1. What were the contributions of the Moderates in the formative stage of the Indian National Congress? **[UPSC 1994]**
2. What do you understand about 'Drain of Wealth' during British rule? Examine its effects on Indian economy. **[UPSC 1997]**
3. Why did the moderates lose appeal with the Indians and failed to elicit a desired response from the British? **[UPSC 1998]**
4. How did economic nationalism mirror the work of the early Nationalist leadership in India? **[UPSC 1998]**
5. Discuss the main objectives of the Indian National Movement upto 1905. What were its basic weaknesses during this period? **[UPSC 2001]**
6. Why did the 'Moderates' fail to carry conviction with the nation about their proclaimed ideology and political goals by the end of the 19th century? **[UPSC 2017]**
7. To what extent did the role of moderates prepare a base for the wider freedom movement? Comment. **[UPSC 2021]**

Answers

Previous Years' Questions – Preliminary Exam

1. (b)	2. (d)	3. (c)	4. (c)	5. (a)
6. (d)				

4 Rise of the Extremists (Phase of Militant Nationalism or Radical Politics)

The Extremists did not emerge all of a sudden in the first decade of the 20th century. The extremist ideology had been simmering ever since the Revolt of 1857 and finally surfaced in 1905 during the Bengal partition. The Moderate politics had already trained the educated Indians in political agitation. Some of them had now begun to get disillusioned with the methods of the Moderates which had achieved little and evoked a cold and contemptuous response from the British. Consequently, there emerged a strong demand for a more vigorous political action than mere prayers, petitions and protests.

The Moderate ideology based on the adoration of western culture did not find appeal among the masses and the Congress remained limited to a narrow social base. There was an awkward void which got created between the common people and the first all-India representative body. In due course of time, this gap was filled by the Extremists—the English educated Indians who took pride in their glorious past.

Let us recall that during the Revolt of 1857, the educated middle class remained aloof and did not participate in the Revolt. With time, there emerged a section of educated Indians who began to see the evils of colonialism, and simultaneously took pride in their cultural past. These educated Indians were particularly influenced by the teachings of Ramkrishna Paramhansa, his English educated disciple Swami Vivekananda, Swami Dayanand Saraswati and Bankim Chandra Chatterjee.

Within the Indian National Congress, this change was reflected in the emergence of a new and younger group that demanded Swaraj as the goal to be achieved not by passive petitions but by more active, militant and self-reliant methods, through self-help, determination and sacrifice. This new group came to be known as the New Party or the Extremists within Congress.

Note: The term militant in 'militant nationalism' means vigorously active, combative and aggressive, in support of a cause. As per the dictionary, the word 'militancy' may or may not include physical violence or armed combat.

Causes for Rise of the Extremists

Recognition of True Nature of British Rule

The early nationalist leaders made painstaking effort in exposing the evils of the British rule in India. **Ranade's Essays in Indian Economics** (1898), Dadabhai Naoroji's Indian Poverty and un-British Rule in India (1901) and RC Dutt's Economic History of India had been published. These works demolished the moral basis of British rule in India and formed the arsenals from which the new leaders shot their arrows.

The politically conscious Indians were now able to see the true nature of British rule and were convinced that its main purpose was to exploit India economically and to enrich England at the cost of India. They were now able to see that the Indian economy and industry could progress only under an Indian government which would protect and promote it.

Increasing Miseries of Indian Life

The evil consequences of British rule emerged in the form of destitution, famines and diseases. The plight of the Indians in their own country moved many Indian leaders into extremism or radical politics. **Terrible famines** took place during 1896–97 and 1899–1900 while **bubonic plague** broke out in Maharashtra killing thousands of Indians. Tilak criticised the government's relief efforts and the arrogant attitude of the Government Plague Commissioners. When riots broke out, the government tried to stifle public opinion. In 1903, Congress President Lal Mohan Ghose referred to the **Delhi Durbar of 1903** and stated, 'Nothing could seem more heartless than the spectacle of a great government imposing the heaviest taxation upon the poorest population in the world, and then lavishly spending the money so obtained over fire-works and pompous pageants, while millions of the poor were dying of starvation'.

Even on the socio-cultural front, no progress was being made under the British rule. Primary and technical education was already neglected; the British had now also become suspicious of higher education. In 1904, the Indian Universities Act was passed which was seen as an attempt to tighten British control over higher education.

Thus, increasing number of Indians were now getting convinced that self-rule was an absolute prerequisite if India was to make any kind of progress.

Rise in Number of Educated Indians and Unemployment

The number of educated Indians had perceptibly increased by the close of the 19th century. Many of them worked in the administration at very low salaries while many others faced unemployment. The lack of opportunities available to them turned them against the British government and attracted them powerfully towards radical politics. These Indians were thoroughly influenced by the western ideas of democracy, nationalism and radicalism and were convinced that European revolutionary methods need to be adopted to meet European imperialism.

Socio-Cultural Reforms After 1858

The writings of Vivekananda, Dayanand and Bankim had begun to grasp the imagination of the educated Indians. Vivekananda was a great Vedantist who urged his countrymen to conquer the West with India's spirituality. Dayanand referred to India's rich civilisation during Vedic times when Europe was steeped in ignorance. Bankim Chandra dreamt of a united India under the leadership of Lord Krishna, who fought evil and stood for righteousness.

This kind of literature filled the Indians with 'new confidence' and a common vision for a New India. They had now acquired faith in their capacity to govern themselves and to create the India of their dreams.

Dayanand Saraswati He was the first man to give a call for Swaraj as **'India for Indians'** in 1876, which was later pursued by Lokmanya Tilak. Some historians also call him 'the grandfather of the Indian Nation'.

Bankim Chandra Chatterjee (1838–94) He was a Bengali writer and poet associated with the Bengal Renaissance. While serving as a civil servant under the British Indian Government, he noted that the British were trying to promote 'God Save the Queen' as the national anthem for Indian subjects. It is believed that he wrote the poem Vande Mataram to counter the British attempt, and was later published in Bengali script in his novel Anandamath (1882), set in the backdrop of Sanyasi Rebellion. During the Congress Session of 1896, the poem was first sung as a song by Rabindranath Tagore. In October 1937, the Congress adopted the first two verses of the song as the National Song of India.

International Influences

Contemporary international events exercised a powerful influence on the minds of younger generation in India-

- They despised the humiliating treatment meted out to Indians in other British colonies, particularly in South Africa.
- **Boer War** (1899–1902) in South Africa showed the Indians that united people willing to make sacrifices could challenge even the most despotic governments.
- They felt inspired by the nationalist movements in **Turkey, Egypt, Persia, Ireland, China and Russia**.
- The rise of modern Japan after 1868 showed that a backward Asian country could develop on its own. Within a few decades, Japan had emerged as a top industrial and military power and introduced universal primary education.
- The confidence of Indians immensely increased upon seeing the **defeat of Italian army** at the hands of the Abyssinians (1896) and the **defeat of Russia by Japan** (1905). It showed that even a small Asian country (Japan) could defeat the biggest military power of Europe.

Such events pricked the balloon of British superiority and gave the Indians new hopes and aspirations.

Disillusionment with Methods of the Moderates

The Congress had achieved little in its first 20 years of existence and the younger elements within the Congress had begun to turn desperate. They had begun to lose faith in the British sense of justice and fair play and decried Moderate methods as political mendicancy. Instead of giving Indians wider political rights, even their existing rights were being taken away:

- The Indian Councils Act of 1892 was a complete disappointment.
- In 1897, the Natu brothers were deported without trial.

- In 1897, Tilak and some other editors were sentenced to long terms of imprisonment for arousing the people against the government.
- In 1898, exciting 'feelings of disaffection towards the British government' was made an offence.
- In 1899, in the Calcutta Corporation, the number of Indian members was reduced.
- In 1904, the Indian Official Secrets Act was passed restricting the freedom of the Press.

In 1905, Lala Lajpat Rai returned from England and told his countrymen that the British were too busy with their own affairs to do anything worthwhile for India. Further, if the people really cared for their country, 'they would have to strike a blow for freedom themselves, and they should be prepared to give unmistakable proof of their earnestness'.

Tilak decried the Congress as 'a Congress of flatterers' and the Congress session as 'a holiday recreation'. He asserted that, 'We will not achieve any success in our labors if we croak once a year like a frog'.

Rise of Bal Gangadhar Tilak and Other Militant Nationalists

Militant nationalism in India found exemplary personification in the form of Bal Gangadhar Tilak, also known as Lokmanya Tilak. Born on 23 July 1856, he graduated from Bombay University and dedicated the rest of his life in the service of his country. In 1880, he founded the New English School which later became the Fergusson College. Tilak did not believe in an armed struggle, rather he felt that the Indians should **withdraw all cooperation** with the foreign government and attain Swaraj through self-help, determination and sacrifice. He gave the slogan, **'Swaraj is my birthright and I will have it'**. Tilak was militant and was ready to make sacrifices to get wrongs redressed. He was the first Congress leader to serve several terms of imprisonment for speaking his mind against the government.

Apart from Tilak, other outstanding leaders of militant nationalism were Bipin Chandra Pal, Aurobindo Ghose and Lala Lajpat Rai.

Reactionary Policies of Lord Curzon

Curzon held a very low opinion of Indian Intelligentsia, refused to recognise India as a nation and condemned nationalist activities as 'letting off of gas'. Several acts passed during his tenure such as the Official Secrets Act (1904) and the Indian Universities Act (1904) created great resentment in India. The Delhi Darbar held in 1903 during his tenure (at a time when India had not fully recovered from the devastating famine of 1899–1900) attracted loud criticism and was dubbed as 'a pompous pageant to a starving population'.

Partition of Bengal

The Partition of Bengal into two provinces was the most hated act of Curzon administration. The partition was forced upon the people in the face of immense opposition. It was a clear attempt to divide Indians on the basis of religion. Now, it was abundantly clear that the British administration was deaf to popular Indian demands and opinions.

Extremist Leaders

Bipin Chandra Pal

The Extremist leaders emerged in three geographical groups-the Maharashtra group led by Bal Gangadhar Tilak, the Bengal group led by Bipin Chandra Pal and Aurobindo Ghose, and the Punjab group led by Lala Lajpat Rai (also known as **Lal-Bal-Pal triumvirate**). Most of the extremists belonged to the urban lower middle class and aimed at spreading the Congress message to the masses.

Lala Lajpat Rai (1865–1928) Popularly known as **Punjab Kesari**, he was a veteran leader of the Congress and one of the **Lal-Bal-Pal triumvirate**. He was born in a Hindu **Agrawal family in Punjab**, as son of a Urdu and Persian government school teacher. While studying law in Government College at Lahore, he came in contact with other freedom fighters such as Lala Hansraj and Pandit Guru Dutt. At Lahore, he came under the influence of Arya Samaj movement of Swami Dayanand that shaped his views on Hinduism and nationality and he fought against many social evils, especially untouchability. He was also deeply influenced by the nationalism of Italian revolutionary Giuseppe Mazzini. In 1886, he helped setting up of **Dayanand Anglo-Vedic School at Lahore**. The same year he moved to Hissar (where his father was transferred) and founded the Hissar district branch of Indian National Congress. In May 1907, he was deported to **Mandalay** without trial for taking part in political agitation in Punjab. In November the same year, however, he was allowed to return once Lord Minto decided that there was insufficient evidence to indict him for subversion.

Travel to Britain and America In 1914, Lalaji quit his law practice and joined the freedom struggle full time. Believing that it was important to explain India's position to the world, he left for Britain in April 1914. At this time, WW1 broke out and he was unable to return to India. He then left for the USA to gather support for the Indian cause. In the USA, he founded the **India Home Rule League of America** (1917) and wrote a book called **Young India**. He was able to return to India only in 1920 after the war ended.

After his return, Lalaji led the Punjab protests against the Jallianwala Bagh Massacre and the Rowlatt Act. He was given the title of 'Punjab Kesari' for fiercely opposing the Rowlatt Act.

In 1921 at Lahore, he founded Quami Vidyapeeth and also the **Servants of the People Society**, a social welfare organisation. Disappointed with the suspension of the Non-Cooperation Movement, he went on to form the **Congress Independence Party**, with a Hindu ideology. In 1926, he joined Swaraj Party briefly and was elected its Deputy Leader in the Central Legislative Assembly.

In 1928, when the Simon Commission visited Lahore, Rai led a peaceful march in protest. However, the Superintendent of Police, James Scott, ordered **lathi charge** and struck blows on Rai himself. Despite being grievously injured, Rai addressed the crowd and famously said, 'The blows struck at me today will be the last nails in the coffin of British rule in India'. Later, when Rai succumbed to his injuries, Bhagat Singh vowed to avenge his death and decided to kill Scott. He plotted the revenge along with other revolutionaries Rajguru, Sukhdev and Chandrasekhar Azad, but mistakenly killed another police official John Saunders.

Lala Lajpat Rai was a prolific writer- he wrote many books and edited many journals. He launched three English weeklies, The Regenerator of Aryavarta (1883); The Panjabee (1904) and The people (1925); an Urdu weekly Deshopkarak(1883) and an Urdu daily Bande Mataram (1920). Other prominent works written by him include- 'The Story of My Deportation' (1908), 'The United States of America: A Hindu's Impression' (1916) and 'England's Debt to India' (1917). He founded many organisations and institutions. He founded **Punjab National Bank** (Lahore, 1894) with Lala Harkishan Lal and **Lakshmi Insurance Company** to support exports by Indian traders. He was also closely associated with the **Hindu Mahasabha.**

Aurobindo Ghose (1872–1950) He was an influential nationalist leader who later became a spiritual reformer. In 1926, he founded Sri Aurobindo Ashram (Auroville) in **Pondicherry** with the help of his spiritual collaborator Mirra Alfassa. He was **nominated for the Nobel Prize** in Literature in 1943 and for the Nobel Peace Prize in 1950.

Extremist Ideology

The extremist ideology did not spring up all of a sudden on the Indian political scene but had been brewing invisibly since the revolt of 1857, which the extremists believed was inspired by the ideas of Swadharma and Swaraj. They felt that western ideas and high rationalism had alienated the moderates from the masses, which was urging to look up to its ancient past.

The historic task of bridging this gulf between the masses and the educated few was accomplished by Ramkrishna Paramhansa along with his English educated disciple, Swami Vivekananda (1863–1902). Swami Vivekananda had carried his message of nationalism to the West and generated immense self-confidence among the educated Indians. The Bengal extremists were also greatly influenced by Bankim Chandra (a liberal conservative like Edmund Burke) who believed that reforms should wait on moral and religious regeneration since an abrupt break from the past would only create more problems than it would solve; that change should come from within rather than being precipitated from outside forces. Aurobindo was also very much attracted by the teachings of Dayanand Saraswati and credited him with more definite work than any other Indian reformer.

In this way, Vivekananda, Dayanand and Bankim Chandra prepared the ideological ground on which the Extremists based their ideology and political program outlined below-

- They firmly believed that the remedy to Indian problems lay in the hands of Indian themselves and that they should now become fearless and strong.
- They had no faith in British benevolence and declared in a clear-cut manner **Swaraj** or self-rule as the goal of the national movement.
- They firmly believed that swaraj could be obtained only through direct political action based on **self-reliance**, **self-sacrifice** and **strong will**.
- They had deep faith in the capacity of the masses and worked to make both the Congress as well as the national movement **mass movements**.
- They were inspired by **India's glorious past**, but at the same time they had no desire to eternally dwell upon the past, but wanted to manfully build the future.
- They were inspired by the ideology of **Swami Vivekananda**, **Dayanand Saraswati** and **Bankim Chandra Chatterjee**.
- The hallmark of extremist ideology was **emotionally charged nationalism**. All their socio-economic and political ideals revolved around this central vortex.
- The Extremists were attached to their native culture, religion and polity.
- They were inspired by their traditional cultural values, had tremendous sense of self-respect and wanted to keep their heads high.

- They are also sometimes termed as political radicals who wanted to have relations with other countries along lines of equality and self-respect.
- They wanted to build a new India of their dreams in which the British had no contribution to make.
- The Extremist thoroughly criticised the Moderates and called them servile and political mendicants.

Swami Vivekananda Anything that makes you weak physically, intellectually and spiritually, reject as poison, there so no life in it, it cannot be true.

Tilak 'Swaraj or self-government is essential for the exercise of Swadharma. Without Swaraj, there could be no social reform, no industrial progress, no useful education, no fulfilment of the national life'.

Bipin Chandra Pal the demand of the New Party is 'the abdication of the right of England to determine the policy of the Indian Government, the relinquishment of the right of the present foreign despotism to enact whatever law they please to govern the people of the country, the abandonment of their right to tax the people according to their own sweet will and pleasure, and to spend the revenues of the country in any way they like'.

Aurobindo Ghose 'Swaraj is the fulfilment of the ancient life of India under modern conditions, the return of satyug of national greatness, the resumption by her of her great role of the teacher and guide, self-liberation of the people for final fulfilment of the Vedantic ideal in politics, this is the true Swaraj for India'.

Lajpat Rai 'A subject people has no soul, just as a slave can have none..A man without a soul is a mere animal. A nation without a soul is only a dumb driven cattle. Swaraj is the first requisite for a nation and reforms or good government could be no substitute for it'.

Work of the Extremists

- In 1891, Tilak opposed the **Age of Consent Bill** (introduced after the death of a child bride from sexual injuries and which aimed to raise the age of consent for sexual intercourse for all girls, married or unmarried, from 10 to 12 years, its violation subject to criminal prosecution as rape) and insisted that the British should not interfere in the private life of Indians.
- In 1893, Tilak started using the traditional **Ganapati festival** to propagate nationalism.
- During 1893-94, Aurobindo published a series of articles entitled **'New Lamps for the Old'** in the Indu Prakash wherein he described the Congress as being out of contact with the 'proletariat' and as 'dying of consumption'.
- In 1895, Tilak introduced the **Shivaji festival** to further stimulate nationalism among young Maharashtrians, holding up Shivaji as a patriotic hero figure to be emulated (The first Shivaji festival was held on 15 April 1896).
- In 1895, Tilak ousted Gokhale and Ranade from the **Poona Sarvajanik Sabha** and now the control of the Sabha came into the hands of the Extremists.
- Later, on 4 November 1896, Gokhale organised a separate political association called the **Deccan Sabha**. This completed the division between the Extremists and the Moderates in Maharashtra.

- In 1897, when Tilak was arrested on charge of spreading hatred and disaffection against the government, he set an example of boldness and sacrifice.
- Tilak started newspapers **the Mahratta** (in English) and **the Kesari** (in Marathi) in 1881, and encouraged his countrymen to become self-reliant and selfless fighters.
- He urged the peasants of Maharashtra to stop payment of land revenue if their crops had failed due to famine.
- Between 1893 and 1900, Lala Lajpat Rai did not attend the Congress sessions.
- Till 1902, BC Pal remained in the Moderate camp and it was only in 1902 that he first wrote-'The Congress and its British Committee in London are both begging institutions'.

With time, what we see is a gradual weakening of the Moderates while Extremists moved from strength to strength. International events such as the defeat of the Italian army by the Ethiopians (1896) and the defeat of Russia at the hands of the Japanese (1904–05) finally pricked the bubble of European superiority and gave new self-confidence to the Extremists in India.

Extremist Programme

The Extremist programme comprised of boycott of foreign goods, use of Swadeshi goods, National Education and Non-Cooperation or Passive Resistance.

- **Boycott and Swadeshi** The Extremists promoted boycott of British-made goods and use of swadeshi or goods made in India to encourage Indian industries and provide employment to Indian people. Boycott proved to be one of the most effective weapons to injure British interests in India. Besides, it was also hoped that the newly rising Indian manufacturing class will provide liberal funds to the Congress and strengthen it.
- **National Education** National Scheme of Education was set up for students who boycotted the government schools and colleges:
  - The Bengal Council of National Education was led by **Gurudas Banerjee** (Earlier in 1890 Gurudas had become the first Indian Vice-Chancellor of Calcutta University).
  - A large number of national schools were opened in East Bengal and a Bengal National Education College was established at Calcutta.
  - In Madras, Pachaiappa National College was established.
  - In Punjab, the DAV schools were set up.
- **Non-Cooperation or Passive Resistance** Tilak was the most ardent preacher of non-cooperation. He asserted, 'You must realise that you are a great factor in the power with which the administration of India is controlled. You are yourselves the great lubricants which enable the gigantic machinery to work smoothly...You must be conscious of your power of making the administration impossible if you choose to make it'.
- **Co-operative Organisations** The extremists also encouraged cooperative bodies. Organisations were formed on voluntary basis for rural sanitation, organising fairs and pilgrimages and relief work during calamities.

Bipin Chandra Pal explained the objective of co-operative movement in the following manner-'To create in the first place a strong civic sentiment in the people with the help of co-operative organisations for the furtherance of the common good, and thus to train them gradually for heavier responsibilities of free citizenship'.

Difference between the Moderates and the Extremists

Though there was much in common, yet there were marked differences between the Moderates and the Extremists which finally culminated in the Surat split in 1907. The differences may be understood as follows:

- **Difference in the understanding of Swaraj** The extremist's demand for Swaraj was a demand for complete freedom from British rule and full independence to manage national affairs without any foreign interference. While the Swaraj of the Moderates was merely a demand for self-government within the colonial rule.
- **Difference in attitude towards British benevolence** While Moderates had infinite faith in the British sense of justice and fair play, the Extremists had no such faith.
- **Difference in methodology** While the Moderates relied on 3Ps—Prayer, Petition and Protest to press their demands, the Extremists emphasised on 3S—self-reliance, self-sacrifice and strong will. The new leadership sought to create passionate love for the country and willingness to suffer for the cause for the country.
- **Difference in the personalities of BG Tilak and GK Gokhale** The Moderate vs. Extremist controversy in Congress also revolved around the personalities of BG Tilak and GK Gokhale. In many ways, their early careers were quite similar, both were Chitpavan Brahmins from Pune, both attended Elphinstone College, both became mathematics professors and both were important members of the Deccan Education Society, yet when they joined the Congress, their divergent views began to surface.
- While Gokhale was gentle and soft-spoken, Tilak was militant (though he did not believe in an armed struggle) and felt that the Indians should withdraw all cooperation with the foreign government and attain Swaraj through self-help, determination and sacrifice. He was the first Congress leader to serve several terms of imprisonment for speaking his mind against the government and was charged of sedition three times (1897, 1909 and 1916) as mentioned below-
    - In 1882, Tilak was first sentenced to four months' imprisonment for criticising the government over treatment meted out to the Maharaja of Kolhapur.
    - During the summers of 1897, bubonic plague raged in Poona in severe epidemic form. British troops were deployed to deal with the emergency and harsh measures were used such as forced entry into houses and examination of occupants. Though well meant, these acts were widely seen as acts of oppression. Tilak wrote inflammatory articles in his papers Kesari and Maratha quoting the Gita that no blame could be attached to anyone who killed an oppressor without any thought of reward. Following this, when **Commissioner Rand** and Lt. Ayerst were killed by Chapekar brothers, Tilak was charged with incitement to murder and for preaching disaffection against the Raj and sentenced to 18 months' imprisonment.
    - In April 1908, Prafulla Chaki and Khudiram Bose threw a bomb at a carriage in Muzzafarpur to kill a British Magistrate Douglas Kingsford, but erroneously killed two women travelling in it. Bose was hanged while Chaki committed suicide when caught. Tilak, in his paper Kesari, defended the revolutionaries and gave a call for immediate Swaraj. The government quickly charged him with sedition and sentenced him to 6 years' imprisonment in **Mandalay**, Burma (1908-14). In this case, he was unsuccessfully defended by lawyer Muhammad Ali Jinnah. After the sentence, **Max Muller** had pleaded for mercy and had said 'My interest in Tilak is that of a Sanskrit scholar'. While in prison, he wrote Gita Rahasya.

- While Gokhale set up the **Servants of India Society** to train a band of Indians in the service of motherland, Tilak wielded a powerful pen and greatly influenced public opinion through his papers the **Maratha** and the **Kesari**.
- During Bengal partition, Tilak extended support to the extremists led by Bipin Chandra Pal and this Tilak-Pal alliance became a cause of distress to many in the government as well as in the Congress. It was because of these differences that the Moderates tried to keep Tilak and his group members out of positions of power within the Congress and never allowed him to become the Congress President. The tussle for presidentship that ensued for the 1906 and 1907 Congress sessions culminated in the Surat Split of 1907 (Read about the Surat Split in the next chapter).

Bal Gangadhar Tilak (1856–1920) Tilak was a nationalist and a social reformer who is considered as the first leader of the Indian national movement, and conferred with the title of 'Lokmanya' meaning 'accepted by the people (as their leader)'. He was called the **'Father of the Indian Unrest'** by the British journalist and writer **Valentine Chirol** in his book 'Indian Unrest'. Objecting to the comment, Tilak brought up a civil suit against Chirol in London which was later dismissed by the King's Bench. Tilak was the first to advocate Swaraj and gave the slogan 'Swaraj is my birthright and I shall have it'. He was a radical nationalist but a social conservative. Though he was personally opposed to early marriage, **Tilak was against the 1891 Age of Consent Bill** (which raised the marriageable age for girls from 10 to 12 years), seeing it as an interference with Hindu religion. In his view, self-rule took precedence over any social reform.

Tilak started two weeklies, **Kesari** in Marathi and **Mahratta** in English. He popularised the **Ganapati** and **Shivaji Festivals** in 1893 and 1895 respectively and dispersed the values of Swaraj in the air of Maharashtra. Tilak opposed the moderate views of his contemporary, Gopal Krishna Gokhale.

Assessment of the Extremists

Criticisms

Extremists are mainly criticised for being backward looking in matters of social reform. For instance, Tilak opposed the Age of Consent Bill (which proposed to raise the age of consummation of marriage for girls from 10 to 12 years), encouraged anti-cow killing societies and organised Ganesh festival. All these project him as Hindu orthodox leader. Similarly, Lala Lajpat Rai and BC Pal spoke of a Hindu nation and protection of Hindu interests at all political levels. Though these revivalist measures were directed against the British government, they also encouraged communalism.

Achievements

- The Extremists saw clearly the clash between the British interest and Indian national interests. They realised that their goals could not be achieved without pressure tactics and some sort of direct action. Their pressure tactics included 3S—self-reliance, sacrifice and strong will.
- Their agenda included boycott and swadeshi, non-cooperation, national education and setting up cooperative organisations. In this way, the Extremists successfully transformed patriotism from 'an academic pass time' to 'service and suffering for the nation'.

- The Extremists were successful in getting **annulled the partition of Bengal in 1911** which gave a new sense of self-confidence to Indian nationalists.
- The aim of Swaraj, though denied by Morley, was no longer seen as a revolutionary demand and the British government (still under shock of the First World War, 1914–18) was compelled to declare self-government institutions as the goal of constitutional development in India.

Opinions

Daniel Argov

Both the Moderates and the Extremists came from the middle class, both were reacting to British rule and both voiced Indian grievances. The Moderates claimed social equality and a share in the British government of India on the grounds that they were British subjects; the **Extremists demanded social equality and political emancipation as their birth right**. The Moderates appealed to Englishmen in England and placed their reliance on English history and English political ideas; the extremists drew sustenance from India's heritage and appealed to Indians by invoking religious patriotism. The Extremists disparaged the constitutional agitation of the moderates as 'mendicancy'. Instead they called for self-reliance through Swadeshi, Boycott and Passive Resistance. In contrast, the moderates stressed that their constitutional agitation was practical statesmanship that emotional idealism was fraught with peril, that rashness was not courage, that British rule would not come to an end because of Boycott and above all, the removal of British rule would result in chaos and anarchy.

BG Tilak

The new words have recently come into existence with regard to our policies, and they are Moderates and Extremists. These words have a specific relation to time and they, therefore, will change with time. The **Extremists of today will be Moderates of tomorrow**, just as the Moderates of today were Extremists of yesterday.

Lal-Bal-Pal

Previous Years' Questions – Preliminary Exam

1. Which one of the following defines the extremist ideology during the early phase of Indian freedom movement? **[UPSC 1998]**
   (a) Stimulating the production of indigenous articles by giving them preference over imported commodities
   (b) Obtaining self-government by aggressive means in place of petitions and constitutional ways
   (c) Providing national education according to the requirements of the country
   (d) Organising coups against the British Empire through military revolt

2. The Indian Muslims in general, were not attracted to the extremist movement because of the **[UPSC 1998]**
   (a) Influence of Sir Syed Ahmed Khan
   (b) Anti-Muslim attitude of Extremist leaders
   (c) Indifference shown to Muslim aspirations
   (d) Extremists policy of harping on Hindu past

3. Who organised the 'Abhinav Bharat' a secret society of revolutionaries? **[UPSC 1999]**
   (a) Khudiram Bose (b) VD Savarkar
   (c) Prafulla Chaki (d) Bhagat Singh

4. Who among the following gave a systematic critique of the moderate politics of the Indian National Congress in a series of articles entitled 'New Lamps for Old? **[UPSC 2008]**
   (a) Aurobindo Ghosh
   (b) RC Dutt
   (c) Syed Ahmed Khan
   (d) Viraghavachariar
5. He wrote biographies of Mazzini, Garibaldi, Shivaji and Shrikrishna; stayed in America for some time; and was also elected to the Central Assembly. He was **[UPSC 2018]**
   (a) Aurobindo Ghosh
   (b) Bipin Chandra Pal
   (c) Lala Lajpat Rai
   (d) Motilal Nehru
6. Which among the following events happened earliest? **[UPSC 2018]**
   (a) Swami Dayanand established Arya Samaj.
   (b) Dinabandhu Mitra wrote Neeldarpan.
   (c) Bankim Chandra Chattopadhyay wrote Anandmath.
   (d) Satyendranath Tagore became the first Indian to succeed in the Indian Civil Services Examination.

Previous Years' Questions – Main Exam

1. What were the attitudes of the Moderates and the Extremists toward the freedom movement in India? What led to their showdown in Surat (1907)? **[UPSC 1986]**
2. How did Lala Lajpat Rai and Bal Gangadhar Tilak champion the cause of militant Nationalism in India? **[UPSC 1990]**
3. Analyse the main differences between the approaches of Tilak and Gokhale on social and political issues. **[UPSC 1993]**
4. What was Tilak's contribution towards shaping the course of the nationalist movement in India? **[UPSC 1996]**
5. Bring out the ideological basis of the moderate–extremist divide in the Indian National Congress. **[UPSC 2003]**
6. Evaluate the contribution of revolutionary terrorism represented by Bhagat Singh to the cause of India's struggle for independence. **[UPSC 2007]**

Answers

Previous Years' Questions – Preliminary Exam

1. (b)	2. (d)	3. (b)	4. (a)	5. (c)
6. (b)				

5 EXTREMIST PHASE, PART 1 (1905–18) (PARTITION OF BENGAL AND THE SWADESHI MOVEMENT)

In 1905, the Bengal Partition was announced at a time when conditions were ripe for the emergence of radical politics. The partition was firmly opposed by Indian National Congress as well as the Bengal nationalists and with this the Indian national movement entered its second stage. The Anti-Partition Movement gave birth to the Swadeshi movement (sometimes used synonymously with Anti-Partition Movement) and brought about distinct changes in the content and form of Indian struggle for freedom.

By 1900, many of the early nationalists had realised the futility of praying and petitioning to the government. Their appeals for a just British rule in place for the prevailing 'unBritish' misrule had fallen on deaf ears. The imperialist policies of Lord Curzon, the Viceroy, had ruffled the nationalists, and they were no longer willing to swallow every humiliation. They had gained self-respect and confidence from the social reformers and were now willing to ask for their rights on an equal footing. A confrontation between Curzon and the nationalists was now impending and the occasion finally came with the decision of Curzon administration to partition Bengal.

Curzonian Attack in Bengal

Curzon began his attack in Bengal by passing the **Calcutta Corporation Act 1899** which reduced the number of elected members in Calcutta Corporation and dealt a major blow to the advancement of local self-government initiated by Lord Ripon. The move was carried out in an undemocratic manner and its primary intention was to serve the European Business interests who often complained about delays in the grant of licenses. The Calcutta intelligentsia was deeply offended.

Even before this wrong could be digested, Curzon passed the **Indian Universities Act 1904** which attacked the autonomous character of Calcutta University. The Act was passed despite strong opposition by the only Indian member of Indian Universities Commission, Gurudas Banerjee. The Act transferred the power of affiliating schools and colleges to the government officials under the pretext that this would 'raise the standard of education all round'. This act of Curzon convinced the educated Indians that the Viceroy was determined to humiliate Indians in every conceivable way. When Curzon announced the **partition of Bengal in 1905**, a decision forced in the teeth of fierce opposition, the people broke out in open rebellion in the form of anti-partition movement.

Governor General Lord Curzon

Governor-General Lord Curzon (In office 1899–1905) The appointment of Lord Curzon as the Viceroy of India was the fulfilment of his long-cherished dream. It is believed that he knew more about India and Indian problems than any other Viceroy before him. However, Curzon came to India in the backdrop of famine and plague of 1896–97; the revenues were declining, the administration was in need of an overhaul. Far more importantly, the Indian voices questioning the very right of the British to rule India were growing louder and louder.

Administrative Reforms Curzon was convinced about the urgency of a thorough reform of the entire administrative machinery. There was hardly a department which escaped the Curzonian storm of reform. 'Efficiency' and 'centralisation' were the key guiding forces. His method of work was to first appoint an expert commission and then enact the required legislations.

Police Reforms Curzon appointed a Police Commission in 1902 headed by **Sir Andrew Frazer**. The commission reported, among other things, that the police was corrupt, oppressive and had failed to secure the trust and cooperation of the people. It recommended increase in salaries of police officials, setting up training schools, provincial police service and Central Department of Criminal Intelligence. Curzon accepted most of its recommendations.

Educational Reforms Curzon also appointed a Universities Commission in 1902 in view of falling standards and rising indiscipline. He believed that the Universities had become factories for the production of political revolutionaries. Based on its recommendations, he passed the **Indian Universities Act of 1904** which sought to increase official control over the universities and exercise stricter control over affiliation of private colleges. Criticising the act, a historian had remarked, 'The Act left the Indian University to be an institution meant not for the fostering of love of learning but for providing efficient hurdles in a race for job'.

Railway Reforms Curzon built more mileage of railway lines than any other Viceroy so far. He formed the Robertson Railway Commission (1901), headed by railway expert Thomas Robertson from England, which recommended the setting up of a Railway Board.

Army Reforms These were carried out under **Lord Kitchener**, the Commander-in-chief in India (1902-08). The Indian Army was grouped in two commands, the Northern Command (headquartered at Murree and striking point at Peshawar) and the Southern Command (headquartered at Poona and striking point at Quetta). Every army battalion was subjected to a severe test, **'the Kitchener Test'**.

Foreign Policy Tibet- Curzon sent a special mission to Tibet (1903) headed by **Colonel Younghusband** to counter the Russian influence there.

Persian Gulf- a mission was sent under Sir Henry McMahon.

Other Works and Reforms included

Famine Commission: headed by Sir Anthony MacDonnell
Irrigation Commission: headed by Sir Colin Scott Moncrieff
Calcutta Corporation Act, 1899
Co-operative Credit Societies Act, 1904 (to provide loans to cultivators at cheap interest rates)
Ancient Monuments Act, 1904 (to protect and preserve the historical monument in the country)
Formation of Imperial Agriculture Department (to improve Indian agriculture and livestock and encourage scientific methods)
The Partition of Bengal, 1905

Estimate of Curzon According to historian BL Grover, Curzon was a great imperialist. His domestic and foreign policies were guided by the urge to make the British position in India impregnable. Possessing great administrative talent, he tried to bring about a 'root and branch reform' of administration, took up painstaking study of Indian problems and appointed several commissions to guide his policy reforms. However, his obsession for efficiency did him more harm than good as it ensured that all his reforms were directed towards enhancing efficiency rather than the lot of the people. The wisdom of his reforms was further undermined by his attitude of superiority and his contempt for Indian opinion. He refused to meet the President of the Congress and termed Congress activities as 'letting off of gas'. He soon emerged as the most hated person in India, whose insults pushed the political unrest in India to a breaking point. If bad rulers could be seen in a positive light, Curzon's policies provoked India into a new dawn of nationhood.

Partition of Bengal

Reasons for Partition of Bengal

The British authorities said that Bengal had grown too big to be efficiently administered by a single provincial government. Bengal was a province with a population of 78 million, which formed about a quarter of the population of British India. However, the plan they worked out showed other motives in mind.

Bengal originally comprised of Bengal, Bihar, Orissa and Assam. It was a vast province with diverse population speaking various languages and also diverse in terms of regional development. The British authorities had been making piecemeal efforts for reducing the size of Bengal since 1874 mainly for reasons of administrative convenience, the other reason being providing equal developmental opportunities for all the regions concerned. Accordingly,

- In 1874, Assam was separated from Bengal and made into a Chief Commissioner's province.
- Later, the South Lushai hills of Bengal were also added to Assam.
- In 1904, when Curzon talked about reorganisation of Bengal province, he did not appear to be altogether unreasonable.
- The nationalists had themselves supported the separation of linguistically divergent Orissa and Bihar. They felt that administrative efficiency could be better achieved by partition along linguistic lines. Instead, Curzon and his advisers (Sir Andrew Fraser, the Lieutenant governor of Bengal, and HH Risley, Home Secretary to the Government of India) mischievously decided to partition Bengal proper, i.e. Bengali speaking people along religious lines, chiefly to hurt the Bengali speaking educated middle class that was spearheading the national movement in eastern India.

The Motive

Whatever may be the justification for the administrative viewpoint; Curzon's main motive was political and Machiavellian. Bengal had emerged as the centre of nationalistic activities and the British were keen in its partition in a manner that would throttle the voice of nationalism. According to official assessment by **Risley**, 'Bengal united is a power, Bengal divided will pull in several different ways' and the British found their answer in partition of Bengal along the already existing **Hindu-Muslim fault line**.

The Hindus in Bengal were relatively better off—socially and economically than their Muslim brethren and were able to take better educational advantage of the British rule. On the other hand, the Muslims were mainly agriculturalists and were unable to take a similar advantage. With the aim of creating mutual suspicion and jealousy between the two communities, Curzon declared that the British government wished to stand by the Muslims and allow them equal opportunity for advancement with the Hindus. He cleverly suggested that the only way of securing the Muslims from Hindu domination would be to carve out a Muslim-majority Bengal and join it with Assam, thus forming a new province with Dacca as its capital. Thus, Curzon and his advisers aimed to create Dacca, chiefly representing Mohammedan interests, as a counterweight against Calcutta, chiefly representing nationalistic interests.

The Plan

The final plan was to create out of Bengal a Muslim-majority province, where 15 million Muslims would live with 12 million Hindus while simultaneously reducing the Bengali speaking people into a minority in what would remain as Bengal, where 19 million Bengali speaking people would be outnumbered by 35 million speakers of Hindi, Oriya and other languages! Clearly, Curzon's plan for the partition of Bengal was a plan to make the Bengalis suffer both physical and mental division.

The Partition

- The scheme for partition first began with Curzon's Minute on Territorial Redistribution on 1st June 1903.
- On 20th July 1905, Curzon issued the order dividing Bengal into two parts:
  1. 'Eastern Bengal and Assam' with a population of 31 million (comprising of Chittagong, Dacca, Rajashahi divisions, Hill Tippera (Tripura), Malda and Assam) and
  2. The rest of Bengal with a population of 54 million (18 million Bengalis and 36 million Biharis and Oriyas).
- On 16th October 1905, the new province came into existence by breaking up Bengal and its 41.5 million Bengali speaking people.

Curzonian Miscalculation

Curzon and his advisers had made their own calculation of the kind of resistance they may have to face. They had expected the regular petitions and protests, which could be easily tolerated and ignored. They had anticipated the worries such as:

- The worries of the Bengal nationalists who feared unnecessary Hindu-Muslim discord.
- The worries of the Calcutta High Court lawyers who feared the loss of practice due to the establishment of a separate High Court in the new province.

- The worries of the jute and rice traders of Calcutta who feared the loss of business with the emergence of Chittagong as an alternative port.
- The worries of the educated Indians (babus) who feared the loss of clerical jobs and also the worries of the Bengali zamindars.

But as it emerged, the government had gravely miscalculated and underestimated the threat perception from above quarters. Unlike the prayerful petitions and protests they had expected, the partition evoked a stormy response including unprecedented spike in militancy and the radical demand for swaraj. The British authorities had grossly miscalculated the Bengali dislike for authoritarianism owing to their long history of virtual independence from the central authority. They had also underestimated the Bengali feeling of unity and pride in their achievements arising out of the intense socio-cultural and educational activities of the 19th century.

With their nerve centre at Calcutta, the Bengalis were spearheading Indian Renaissance and inspiring their countrymen in other parts of the country. Led by prominent leaders like Swami Vivekananda (religion), Rabindranath Tagore (literature), Jagdish Chandra Bose and Prafulla Chandra Roy (science), Surendranath Banerjee, Aurobindo Ghosh and Bipin Chandra Pal (politics), the Bengalis were in no mood to swallow the humiliation ignominiously. They had now grown in stature in the eyes of their own people, in self-confidence and self-respect.

Anti Partition Movement-Boycott and Swadeshi (1905–08)

Anti-Partition Movement Under the Moderates

- In December 1903, the partition proposals of the government first became public. This was followed by immediate protests. During 1903 to mid-1905, the leadership of the anti-partition movement was provided by the Moderates. The prominent Moderates during this time were Surendranath Banerjee, Krishnakumar Mitra, Narendra Kumar Sen and Prithwishchandra Ray. They adopted methods like prayers, petitions to the government, memoranda, speeches and public meetings. They started a strong press campaign through pamphlets and newspapers like **Hitabdi, Sanjibani** and **Bengalee**. Their objective was to form a strong public opinion in India and England against the partition so that it could pressurise the government to reverse its decision.
- The Moderates still had faith in British sense of justice and fair play and were not in favour of stretching the agitation too far. They were hoping that the Liberal John Morley will be appointed as Secretary of state for India soon and their prayers will be heard. However, such was not to be the case.
- On 20th July 1905, Curzon announced the partition of Bengal, ignoring all the loud noises created by the Moderates. It was now clear to the nationalists that the Moderate prayers were falling on deaf ears and they needed to find other methods to make their voice heard. Within days of the announcement, a large number of protest meetings were held in towns such as Barisal, Pabna, Dacca, Birbhum, Faridpur, Tangail and Jessore. It was in these meetings that the pledge to boycott foreign goods was first taken. The students in Calcutta organised numerous meetings against partition and for Swadeshi.

- On 7th August 1905, the **Swadeshi Movement was formally announced** in a massive demonstration held in the Calcutta Town Hall. The demonstration was carried out by all the national leaders of Bengal and the movement, hitherto sporadic, was now getting definite leadership. It was in this meeting itself that the famous **Boycott Resolution** was passed. The leaders began touring the country urging people to boycott Manchester cloth and Liverpool salt. 7th August is now celebrated as the National Handloom Day. The first National Handloom Day was inaugurated on 7 August 2015 by Prime Minister Narendra Modi in Chennai.
- In September 1905, it was announced that the partition will be given effect on 16 October. Then onwards protest meetings were held almost every day all over Bengal, some of these meetings drew crowds of ten to twelve thousand-a huge number given the level of politicisation in those days. Even the boycott resolution was a huge success given the fact that the value of British cloth fell sharply during the year from September 1904 and 1905.
- On 16th October 1905, the partition took effect. The day was declared as a day of national mourning throughout Bengal. People fasted and lit no fire in their kitchens. They took out processions walking barefoot, bathed in the Ganga in the morning and took to the streets singing **'Vande Mataram'** which soon became the theme song of the national movement. Rabindranath Tagore composed the song **'Amar Sonar Bangla'** for the occasion (the song was later adopted as **national anthem by Bangladesh** in 1971).
- On the day of partition, Tagore also gave a call for the observance of **raksha-bandhan** or tying of rakhi as a symbol of unbreakable unity of the Bengalis. Ramendra Sunder Trivedi urged for the observance of **arandhan,** i.e. keeping the hearth unlit as a sign of mourning in all homes. Later in the day, Surendranath Banerjee and Anand Mohan Bose addressed massive gatherings. Within a few hours ₹50,000 were raised for the movement.
- It was evident that the social base of the movement was expanding rapidly. The Swadeshi Movement began to spread outside Bengal to different part of the country with Lokmanya Tilak playing the key role in this process. It spread to:
    - Poona and Bombay under Tilak
    - Punjab and northern India under Ajit Singh and Lala Lajpat Rai
    - Delhi under Syed Haidar Raza
    - Madras under Chidambaram Pillai
    - Rawalpindi, Kangra, Jammu. Multan and Hardwar also witnessed active participation in the movement.

Role of Indian National Congress

- In 1905 Banaras Session of the Congress (presided by GK Gokhale), the INC took up the issue of Bengal partition and **both Moderates and the Extremists** supported the cause of Swadeshi and Boycott for Bengal.
- However, differences arose between the Moderates and the Extremists regarding the manner in which the partition was to be opposed. The Extremists (led by Lal-Bal-Pal and Aurobindo Ghosh) wanted to **extend the Boycott** and Swadeshi Movement even to regions outside Bengal. They also wanted to extend it from foreign goods to all other spheres of association with the British government like the provincial councils, municipalities, government services, law courts, etc., (or introduce 'Passive Resistance') thus turning the anti-partition movement into a nation-wide mass movement. Whereas, the moderates wanted to confine the boycott to Bengal and to foreign goods.

- A split in the INC was averted for the time being when a compromise was struck, the INC condemned the partition of Bengal and the reactionary policies of Curzon and supported the Boycott and Swadeshi movement in Bengal.
- In 1906 Calcutta Session of the INC (presided by Dadabhai Naoroji), four resolutions on **Swaraj**, **Swadeshi**, **Boycott** and **National Education** were passed. This was a major leap forward for the INC as, for the first time, swaraj or self-government (like that of the United Kingdom or the Colonies), was declared as the political goal of the Congress.
- Even though the four resolutions were passed, the meaning of the four resolutions was not clearly spelt out. Consequently, throughout 1907, the moderates and the extremists kept arguing over their differing interpretations. Matters came to a head in 1907 Surat Session where the party split with disastrous consequences for the Swadeshi Movement.

Anti-Partition Movement Under the Extremists

The Extremists had no faith in British benevolence and firmly believed that the remedy to Indian problems lay in the hands of Indians themselves. They demanded in clear-cut manner **swaraj** or self-rule free from all British influences and not under British Paramountcy, as the Moderates wished.

After 1905, in Bengal, the leadership of the anti-partition movement soon passed into the hands of the extremists like BG Tilak, Bipin Chandra Pal, Aurobindo Ghosh and Brahmabandhav Upadyaya. This was due to several reasons. The Moderate methods had yielded no results, the government of East Bengal was actively supporting communalism and even tried to crush the nationalist movement and most importantly, the government had adopted aggressive measures to contain the movement. These factors pushed the people into militant nationalism and even revolutionary terrorism.

As the leadership of the movement came into the hands of the extremists, they gave a call for extending the boycott movement from foreign goods and educational institutions to other areas such as legislative councils and municipalities, government services and law courts that would shake the foundation of British hegemony in India. This was called **Non-Cooperation** and termed as '**Passive Resistance** or refusal to render any voluntary service to the government' by Bipin Chandra Pal.

The Extremists raised the question, 'how could the British rule in India continue, if the chowkidar, the constable, the deputy, the munsiff and the clerk, not to speak of the sepoy, all resign their respective functions. No powder and shot will be needed, no sepoys will have to be trained...'. Thus, in general, the extremists saw great potential in a large scale peaceful resistance in winning swaraj from the British.

In April 1904, Aurobindo Ghosh further extended the idea in a series of articles in 'Vande Mataram' and propounded the theory of 'organised and relentless boycott' including **civil disobedience** of unjust laws. He openly declared 'political freedom is the life breath of a nation and was also prepared for an armed struggle against the British rule, if the need be'.

Among all forms of struggle introduced by the extremists, boycott of foreign goods met with the greatest success. Public burning of foreign cloth and picketing of shops selling foreign goods became common sight even in the remote areas of Bengal. Women refused to wear foreign bangles and use foreign utensils and washer men refused to wash foreign clothes, even priests declined to accept foreign goods as offerings.

The Extremist call for swaraj relegated all other matters to the background, including the demand for unification of Bengal. Now the central question of Indian politics was independence from foreign rule while the partition of Bengal became the secondary one. Clearly, it was the partition of Bengal that occasioned the emergence of swaraj as the national goal.

The extremist ideas found expression in periodicals like:

- New India (edited by Bipin Chandra Pal)
- Vande Mataram (edited by Aurobindo Ghosh)
- Sandhya (edited by Brahmabandhav Upadyaya)
- Yugantar (edited by Bhupendranath Dutta)

Extremist Program

Boycott The agitation against the partition of Bengal began along the regular moderate lines. There were angry protests, numerous public meetings, sharp press campaigns and big conferences. All this was impressive but yielded no results. The search now began for new methods and led to the discovery of **boycott of British goods** as the new weapon. At many places, foreign cloth was publicly burnt and shops selling foreign goods were picketed.

Note: Boycott was first suggested in Krishna Kumar Mitra's journal, **Sanjibani** (3rd July 1905).

Swadeshi The Boycott of British goods forced the leaders to think in terms of simultaneously advocating swadeshi goods (indigenously produced) as a patriotic duty. Swadeshi melas held for popularising handicrafts and charkha (the spinning wheel) emerged as a symbol of country's concern for economic self-sufficiency.

Swadeshi as self-reliance, self-help An important element of swadeshi was the emphasis on **self-reliance** or **'Atmashakti'**. In many fields it meant assertion of self-confidence and national dignity. Economically, it meant reliance on indigenous products and encouragement to indigenous industries. Socially, it meant pride in one's cultural past. Another important element of swadeshi was **self-help** or **constructive work** which was carried out for socio-economic regeneration of the villages and mobilising the masses. It involved many social reform activities and campaigns against social evils like caste oppression, untouchability, child marriage, etc.

Swadeshi in the realm of economy During the Swadeshi Movement, a number of exclusively Indian enterprises were established such as-Bange Laxmi Cotton Mills (1906), Mohini Mills (1908), Calcutta Potteries, National Tannery, etc. Many other textile mills, soap and match-making factories, swadeshi banks and insurance companies were opened. **Acharya PC Ray** set up the famous Bengal Chemicals Factory.

Swadeshi in the realm of culture In the realm of culture, the Swadeshi Movement saw the flowering of nationalist literature, plays, poetry and prose. It saw the creative use of traditional popular festivals and fairs (melas) to reach out to the masses. Traditional folk theatre forms such as **Jatras** were also widely used for spreading the message of swadeshi. Swadeshi also evoked the rise of Bengali folk music such as Palligeet and Jarigan and fairy tales such as **Thakurmar Jhuli** (grandmother's tales written by Dakshinaranjan Mitra Majumdar).

This was the period when **Abanindranath Tagore** took his inspiration from indigenous Mughal, Rajput and Ajanta paintings. Tilak popularised the **Ganapati** and **Shivaji festivals**. The outstanding poets of this time were Rabindranath Tagore, Rajni Kant Sen, Dwijendralal Ray, Sayed Abu Mohammed and Mukund Das. These nationalists made intelligent use of local culture to reach out to the masses who were being introduced to modern political ideas for the first time.

National Education Boycott also spread in the student community who boycotted officially controlled schools and colleges. In fact, the students of Bengal played a prominent role in the swadeshi agitation. They regarded the existing system of education as de-nationalising and inadequate and took the lead in promoting Swadeshi.

The government adopted a stern attitude, making every attempt to suppress the students. On 22nd October 1905, Carlyle, the Chief Secretary of Bengal government, issued the infamous **Carlyle circular** threatening the student activists with disciplinary action. Schools and colleges whose students took active part in Swadeshi agitation were to be penalised, they were to be disaffiliated, their grants-in-aid withdrawn and their students were to be barred from all appointments under the government.

This further pushed more and more students in leaving the educational institutions of 'slavery'. Consequently, the leaders of the Swadeshi Movement were moved to think in terms of a parallel educational system in Bengal and soon the program for National Education was formulated. The chief medium of instruction was **vernacular** for widest reach.

Distinguished intellectuals took the responsibility of National Education in their own hands and a large number of primary and secondary schools sprang up.

- On 25th July 1906, the Bengal Technical Institute was established (which later turned into the College of Engineering and Technology, Jadhavpur).
- On 15th August 1906, **National Council of Education** was set up with the aim 'to organise a system of education-Literary, Scientific and Technical-on national lines and under National control' from primary to university level.
- Taking inspiration from Tagore's Shantiniketan, the Bengal National School and College was established in Calcutta led by Aurobindo Ghosh as Principal.

Abanindranath Tagore (1871–1951) A distinguished member of the Tagore family, he was a painter and writer who established the **'Indian Society of Oriental Art'**. In an attempt to counter the western influence on art as taught in art schools under the British Raj, he tried to modernise the Mughal and Rajput styles, giving rise to Bengal School of Art. His paintings were classified as **revivalist** in nature and he himself emerged as the first major exponent of **Swadeshi values in India art**. The British art institutions eventually accepted his work as a national Indian style and promoted it under the label of 'Indian Society of Oriental Art'.

Krishan Kumar Mitra (1852–1936) He was a writer and a leader of the Brahmo Samaj. He significantly contributed to the Swadeshi Movement through his journal, Sanjibani. The idea of Boycott was first suggested in Mitra's Sanjibani.

Stamp shows drawing of *Abhisarika* by Abanindranath Tagore

Formation of Samitis (Volunteer Corps)

For spreading the message of Boycott and Swadeshi movement to the villages, several volunteer bodies sprang up in Calcutta. These were the Dawn Society, the Anti-Circular Society (originally formed to protest against the Carlyle Circular), the Anushilan Samiti, the Brati, the Suhrid and the Sadhena Samitis. The most famous of them all was the **Swadeshbandhav Samiti** set up by **Ashwini Kumar Dutta** who was a school teacher in Barisal. With the help of its 159 branches, Dutta was able to reach the remotest of regions and mobilise the people, particularly Muslim peasants. Barisal itself emerged as the most significant centre for samiti activities.

The Samitis spread the message of Swadeshi to villages through **magic lantern lectures** and swadeshi songs. They also imparted physical and moral training and took up social work during epidemics and famines. They also encouraged folk singers and artists to perform on swadeshi themes in local dialects. The prominent among them were **Mukunda Das, Bhushan Das and Mufizuddin Bayati**. In terms of their ideology, these samitis ranged from religious reform to secularism, from moderate politics to political extremism.

Ashwini Kumar Dutta (1856–1923) He was a Bengali educationist, social reformer and a nationalist. He is remembered for his contribution to the Swadeshi Movement through the formation of the Swadeshbandhav Samiti.

Mukunda Das (1878–1934) He was a Bengali poet, ballad singer and a nationalist. He contributed to the spread of the Swadeshi movement in rural Bengal.

Political Trends during Swadeshi Movement

During the Swadeshi Movement, what we see is the emergence of various political trends which competed with one another for popularity. These were mainly:

The Moderates

The Moderates still had faith in British sense of justice and fair play and were not in favour of stretching the agitation too far. They were hoping that the Liberal John Morley will be appointed as Secretary of state for India soon and their prayers will be heard. The prominent Moderates during this time were Surendranath Banerjee, Krishnakumar Mitra and Narendra Kumar Sen. This lukewarm Moderate outlook rapidly and conclusively fell out of popularity in the midst of the prevailing militant atmosphere.

The Constructive Swadeshis

These were also known as the Social Reformists and they aimed at strengthening national sentiment through continuous self-help (or Atmashakti according to Rabindranath Tagore). Their main emphasis was on constructive swadeshi program like establishing indigenous industry and enterprise, national education and village upliftment. The prominent swadeshis were Rabindranath Tagore, Ashwini Kumar Dutt, Prafulla Chandra Roy, Nilratan Sircar and Satishchandra Mukherji.

The Extremists or Militant Nationalists

The Extremists had no faith in British benevolence and firmly believed that the remedy to Indian problems lay in the hands of Indians themselves. They demanded in clear cut manner **swaraj** or self-rule free from all British influences, and not under British Paramountcy, as the Moderates wished. (For more details, refer to anti-partition movement under the extremists.)

Extent of Participation

The Extremists tried to make the anti-partition movement a mass movement. Swaraj had now emerged as the national goal which was to be achieved through boycott in all spheres. This was possible only by means of mass participation of all sections of Indian society. With their tireless efforts and multi-pronged strategies, the swadeshis were able to rope in certain sections of society into active politics for the first time. These were a section of the zamindari, urban lower middle classes, women and a massive participation of school and college students.

Thus, different sections of the Bengali population such as the zamindars, merchants, lawyers, students and even women rose up in opposition against the partition. The participation of women was the most remarkable development. The traditional women of urban middle class were seen joining the processions and picketing. Their participation broke several old barriers and marked the beginning of women's participation in the national movement.

However, the militant nationalists failed to mobilise the real masses of the country—the workers and particularly the peasants. The movement remained confined to urban lower and middle classes and a certain section of the zamindars. As for the Muslims, the Hindu revivalist propaganda of the swadeshis only aired more suspicion and widened the gulf between the two communities.

Participation of Workers

Some swadeshi activists made an effort to organise Bengal workers and politicise their economic grievances. Such activists included Ashwini Coomar Banerji, Prabhat Kusum Roychoudhary, Althanasius Apurba Kumar Ghosh and others.

- In September 1905, first instance of boycott by the workers emerged when 247 clerks of Burn Company in Howrah struck work against a humiliating work regulation.
- Next came the strikes in the tramways, printing press and jute mills in Calcutta.
- In October 1905, first real labor union namely the Printers' Union was formed as a result of bitter strikes in government owned presses.
- In July 1906, the Railwaymen's Union was formed.
- August 1906, Indian Millhands' Union, Budge-Budge was formed when the jute mill workers were organised by Ashwini Coomar Banerji (The participation of workers however declined after 1907 in face of government repression).

Participation of Peasants

The movement was unable to make much headway in mobilising the peasantry. The only exception was the district of **Barisal**. Historians consider this as a valuable achievement given the fact that peasants were being exposed to modern political ideas for the first time; and that even at the peak of national movement, peasant participation remained limited to specific pockets alone.

In general, the participation of peasants remained negligible as the nationalist leaders of the time did not take much interest in mobilising the peasants for various reasons:

- First, there was a conflict of interest between the Bengali middle class and the peasantry. The middle class in Bengal depended heavily on the rental income from their ancestral lands for economic stability. Accordingly, the swadeshi activists did not raise any voice to protest against peasant grievances such as heavy land revenue and rent, debts, begar and even eviction from land. In other words, no effort was made to organise the peasantry around peasant demands.
- Second, a majority of agriculturalists in Bengal were Muslims and the Swadeshi Movement, which had acquired a predominant Hindu overtone, failed to capture their imagination.

Participation of Muslims

The Swadeshi Movement was unable to gain support of the mass of Muslims as well, which proved to be its main weakness, and which may be chiefly attributed to the British policy of communalism. As we have seen earlier, Curzon and his men had played the communal card in partition of Bengal and tried to divide the Hindus and the Muslims along class lines (the Hindus being the zamindars and the Muslims being the peasantry). They wanted to use the Muslims as counterweights against the rising nationalist powers, and planned the partition such that it created a new Muslim majority province. Here they encouraged the educated Muslims to think in terms of a Muslim Political Power.

Accordingly, in October 1906, their efforts culminated in the formation of the **All India Muslim League** under the leadership of **Nawab Salimullah of Dacca** and with government patronage as a political organisation dedicated to advance Muslim political interests. Salimullah was also given a loan of ₹14 lakh by the government to support the creation of a Muslim Majority province. Thus, a majority of the Muslims followed Salimullah's lead. The League soon became the main weapon of the British to fight the national movement; they also used it to keep the Muslim intelligentsia from joining the national movement. Moreover, the mullahs and the maulvis also communalised the grievances of the Muslim agriculturalists against the Hindu zamindars.

Despite all this, appeals were made for Hindu-Muslim harmony during the Swadeshi Movement and some great scenes of brotherhood were also witnessed. Some outstanding Muslim leaders played a lead role in the agitation such as Liakat Hussain, Abdul Rasul (the barrister), Abdul Hakim Ghaznavi (the businessman), Ismail Hussain Siraji, Din Mahammed and Maniruzzaan. Maulana Abdul Kalam Azad joined a revolutionary terrorist group.

Yet, these achievements were neutralised when some forms of protest adopted by the swadeshi leaders resulted in unintended negative consequences and gave a predominant **Hindu overtone** to the movement. These militant nationalists emphasised ancient Indian culture while excluded the medieval Indian culture. They identified Indian culture with Hindu religion and Indian nation with the Hindus. Muslims could hardly be attracted by the dips in Ganga, the Shivaji and Ganpati festivals (as propagated by Tilak) or the concept of India as mother and nationalism as a religion (ideas of Aurobindo Ghosh), such actions being against the spirit of Islam. Muslims could not be expected to respond when Pratap or Shivaji were hailed as 'national heroes' who fought against 'foreigners' Akbar or Aurangzeb.

In this way, the militant nationalists utilised the images and myths of Hindu orthodoxy to mobilise their people. Practices such as uncritical glorification of Hindu past, nostalgia for the lost Hindu rashtra, references to the Gita and vow of sacrifice before goddess Kali further increased the gulf between the two communities and harmed the movement considerably.

It must be noted that the above does not mean that the militant nationalists were anti-Muslim in any way. Most of them, including Tilak, were in favour of Hindu–Muslim unity and the Swadeshi Movement largely remained secular. But the unintended Hindu-tinge was picked up by the British to poison the minds of the Muslims.

Such Hindu revivalist propaganda gave enough reason to Salimullah's men to spread communal hatred, much to the pleasure of the British authorities. At the peak of the Swadeshi Movement (1906–07), eastern Bengal saw a series of **communal riots** in Mymensingh, Comilla, Jamalpur, Dewangunj and Bakshigunj. The nationalists also did not make an effort to understand the depth of the matter correctly and continued with their religious propaganda.

Thus, it is clear that a large-scale participation of the masses was not realised during the Swadeshi Movement. The nationalists were able to make some sort of beginning in worker participation but they showed no interest in rallying the peasants. They also failed to manage the communal card played by the British authorities and only ended up alienating the Muslims further with their Hindu revivalist propaganda. Failing to become a true mass movement, the Swadeshi Movement was unable to rise to its full potential after 1907. Consequently, the government succeeded in suppressing the movement to a large extent.

All India Spread of the Movement

The movement was not restricted to Bengal alone and it spread to other provinces as well. The most significant contribution in making the anti-partition movement and all India one was made by BG Tilak. He quickly gauged that the partition was the right opportunity to spread the cry of Swadeshi and Swaraj to the rest of the country and foster the feelings of unity and brotherhood.

Sir Khwaja Salimullah Bahadur, fourth Nawab of Dacca (1871–1915) He was a prominent Muslim leader during the British Raj and a staunch supporter of partition of Bengal. While the Congress opposed it, Salimullah organised meetings all over East Bengal to build a movement in favour of Bengal partition. In 1906, the All Indian Muslim League was formed at the All India Muhammadan Educational Conference held at Dacca and it appointed Salimullah as its Vice-President.

Government Repression

The British unleashed powerful repressive measures to deal with the movement:

- Meetings and processions were banned, the government prohibited shouting of the slogan 'Vande Mataram' in public places
- Laws regulating the press were enacted
- Those participating in the movement in any form were disqualified from government employment
- Student participants were expelled, fined and even beaten up by the police
- Police were given a free hand to launch physical assaults-delegates attending conferences were lathi-charged, picketers were caned, innumerable arrests and convictions were made.
- In April 1906, in Barisal, the police infamously attacked the peaceful delegates of Bengal Provincial Conference
- In 1907 in Punjab, Lala Lajpat Rai and Ajit Singh were deported
- In December 1908, nine major leaders in Bengal including Krishna Kumar Mitra and Ashwini Kumar Dutt were also deported
- In 1908, **Tilak** was again arrested and sentenced to 6 years' imprisonment in Mandalay
- Bipin Chandra Pal and Liakat Husain were also arrested
- Chidambaram Pillai in Madras and Harisarvotta Rao in Andhra were put behind bars

The movement could not survive this government repression, particularly the arrest of Tilak. Henceforth, Bipin Chandra Pal and Aurobindo Ghosh also retired from active politics (an event not connected with government repression). Consequently, the Swadeshi Movement was rendered leaderless and completely declined by mid-1908.

Reasons for Decline of Swadeshi Movement

The following causes contributed to the movements' decline:

- No support of the Muslim masses
- Only the first major attempt at mass mobilisation—the movement was only partially successful in mobilising the vast sections of Indian masses
- Its methods were new and unfamiliar, both for the leaders as well as the led
- The movement was unable to convert several forms of struggle like passive resistance and constructive work into real political practice
- Predominant Hindu overtone of the Swadeshi Movement
- Bitter government repression
- Split in the Congress, the apex all-India organisation, in 1907 (known as Surat Split)
- Nature of mass movement-mass movements cannot be sustained endlessly at the same height of struggle and self-sacrifice, but need pause to regain energy for the next round of struggle.

Consequence: Rise of Revolutionary Terrorism

With the failure of moderate methods, inability of the extremists to give a positive lead to the people and violent repression of constructive swadeshis and extremists, the desire to meet force with force and violence with violence naturally came to the forefront. Finding all avenues of peaceful protest blocked, patience of the Bengali youth had run out as far as mass movements and open politics was concerned. There was a group of nationalists, who, having been aroused into the nationalist struggle, were unable to tame themselves into oblivion and were now ready to take up arms against the hated British officials.

Even though some sporadic activities were visible even earlier, revolutionary terrorism emerged as a major trend only after 1907–08. During the period 1908-1918, 186 revolutionaries were killed or convicted. Despite periodical setbacks, revolutionary terrorism continued to operate and even spread in India and abroad as a secret child of the Swadeshi Movement.

But even terrorism was bound to fail as a political weapon. It did not aim at mobilising the masses and remained limited to a very narrow social base. Yet the terrorist acts of heroism made valuable contribution to the growth of national feelings in India. In the words of a historian, 'they gave us back the pride of our manhood'.

Yugantar wrote after the Barisal repression (22nd April 1906), 'The remedy lies with the people themselves. The thirty crores of people inhabiting India must raise their sixty crores of hands to stop this curse of oppression. Force must be stopped by force'.

Significance of Swadeshi Movement

Even though the Swadeshi Movement declined by mid-1908, without achieving its aim of swaraj, it cannot be termed as a failure.

- The Swadeshi Movement inaugurated a new phase in Indian politics, marking a total reversal from the earlier moderate approach of praying and petitioning.
- The leadership of the national movement came into the hands of the militant nationalists who gave the Indian people the new goal of swaraj or complete independence from the British rule on the lines of United Kingdom or other colonies.
- For the attainment of swaraj, it introduced new and innovative techniques of political struggle, far in advance of its time. The techniques of boycott, passive resistance and constructive swadeshi relegated constitutionalism to the background and hugely resembled Gandhian techniques of mass-mobilisation like non-cooperation, civil disobedience and constructive programme to be practiced 15 years hence.
- For the first time, the social base of the national movement was now extended to include a certain section of the zamindari, urban lower middle classes, women and a massive participation of school and college students.
- In the economic realm, it contributed to the revival of indigenous artisan crafts and industries.
- In the cultural and intellectual realm of Bengal, the movement left deep imprints, eroding further the ideas of European hegemony and inspiring the rest of the nation. These included the following:
    - A rich collection of patriotic compositions and dramatic performances
    - The formation of Bengal School of Painting under the leadership of Rabindranath Tagore

- Scientific progress led by Jagdish Chandra Bose and Prafulla Chandra Roy
- Historical research kindled by the findings of Rakhaldas Bannerjee, Hariprasad Shastri and Akshay Kumar Maitra

Even though the movement was finally suppressed, it had already stirred the Indian Nationalism to a revolutionary new height. People had been aroused of their political slumber and trained in new forms of struggle. As a result of the Swadeshi Movement, the **partition of Bengal was finally annulled in 1911**. The government declared its intention of uniting the Bengalis while carving a new province out of Bihar and Orissa. The seat of the British government in India was also shifted from **Calcutta to Delhi** with a view to providing the empire with a stronger base. However, the chief success of the movement lay in the rise of swaraj as the new national goal. The national movement that followed was to draw heavily from the achievements of the Swadeshi Movement.

Bipan Chandra The Swadeshi Movement may be imagined as an important 'battle' in the long drawn out and complex war of position for Indian independence.

Impact of Swadeshi Movement on the Congress and Surat Split

The anti-partition movement left a deep impact on the INC. The INC took up the issue of Bengal partition and both Moderates (led by Gokhale) and the Extremists (led by Tilak) supported the cause of Swadeshi and Boycott for Bengal. Yet, there emerged significant differences regarding the manner in which the agitation should be carried out, culminating in the split in the Congress at Surat Session (1907). After the split, the Moderates and the Extremists remained divided from 1907 till 1916, until the reunion under the Lucknow Pact (1916). The split came with serious consequences for the Swadeshi Movement, the Extremists, the INC as well as the Indian National Movement on the whole. The Swadeshi Movement petered out by the end of 1907, the Extremists faced bitter government repression, the INC lost its popular appeal and remained defunct while the National movement itself came to a temporary halt.

Run-up to Surat Split

- The December **1905 Banaras Session** of the INC, was presided over by GK Gokhale.
- The differences between the Moderates and the Extremists intensified- The Extremists wanted to extend the Boycott and Swadeshi Movement even to regions outside Bengal. They also wanted to extend it from foreign goods to all other spheres of association with the British government like the provincial councils, municipalities, government services, law courts, etc. (or introduce **'Passive Resistance'**) thus turning the anti-partition movement into a nation-wide mass movement. Whereas, the moderates wanted to confine the boycott to Bengal and to foreign goods.
- A split in the INC was averted for the time being when a compromise was struck, the INC condemned the partition of Bengal and the reactionary policies of Curzon and supported the Boycott and Swadeshi Movements in Bengal.
- Gokhale said, 'the goal of the Congress is that India should be governed in the interests of the Indians themselves'.

BG Tilak was the main extremist leader who wanted to make the anti-partition movement an all India one. He had quickly gauged that the partition was the right opportunity to spread the cry of Swadeshi and Swaraj to the rest of the country and foster the feelings of unity and brotherhood. During the partition, Tilak extended support to the extremists led by Bipin Chandra Pal and this Tilak-Pal alliance became a cause of distress to many in the Congress. It was because of these differences that the Moderates tried to keep Tilak and his group members out of positions of power within the Congress and never allowed him to become the Congress President.

Tussle for Presidentship

Tussle for Presidentship for 1906 Calcutta Congress At the Calcutta session, the extremists had gained popularity owing to various reasons, including the rise of revolutionary terrorism. Here the extremists wanted Tilak or Lala Lajpat Rai to be the President for the Calcutta session but the Moderates secretly wired Dadabhai Naoroji to accept the Presidentship, which he did. As a concession to the extremists, four compromise resolutions on Swaraj, Swadeshi, Boycott and National Education were passed. This was a major leap forward for the Congress as, for the first time, swaraj or self-government (like that of the United Kingdom or the Colonies), was declared as the political goal of the Congress. Even though the four resolutions were passed, the meaning of the four resolutions was not clearly spelt out. Consequently, throughout 1907, the moderates and the extremists kept arguing over their differing interpretations.

1906, Calcutta Congress Session, President Dadabhai Naoroji
- Four compromise resolutions on **Swaraj**, **Swadeshi**, **Boycott** and **National Education** were passed.
- Naoroji, in his presidential address, declared swaraj as the goal of the Indian National Congress.

Tussle for Presidentship for 1907 Congress Session The Extremists were encouraged by the proceedings at Calcutta session and wanted a strong resolution to be passed extending boycott to the councils, municipalities, government services, etc. They felt that the battle for swaraj had begun and the Moderates were acting as drag. They were now prepared to part with the moderates, not realising that the moderates could have acted as the outer line of defence in case of government repression.

On the other hand, in 1906, Viceroy Minto and Secretary of State Morley began discussing fresh council reforms with the moderate leadership. Encouraged by the news of the upcoming Council Reforms, the Moderates decided to tone down the Calcutta session. They also felt that further association with the Extremists could be dangerous as their struggle for swaraj would invite bitter government repression. Thus, the Moderates were equally willing now to part company with the Extremists, not realising that the British were negotiating with them because of the fear of the Extremists.

Both sides did not realise that in a vast country like India, only a broad-based movement had any chance of success against the imperialist power and that the imperialist government would only capitalise further on the growing division within the Congress. At the same time, historian Bipan Chandra writes that both Tilak and Gokhale were mature leaders who were well aware of the dangers of disunity among nationalists. However, when matters came to a head, both knuckled under pressure of their own extremists, such as more extreme Aurobindo Ghosh and autocratic Pherozeshah Mehta.

Once again, the election of the Congress President became an occasion for show of strength between the Congress and the Moderates. Once again, the extremists wanted BG Tilak or Lala Lajpat Rai to be the President and reiterate the boycott, swadeshi and national education resolutions. On the other hand, the moderates wanted Rash Bihari Ghosh to the President and wanted the resolutions, viz. swadeshi, boycott and national education to be dropped.

Consequently, the Moderate leader Pherozeshah Mehta changed the venue from **Nagpur (Central provinces) to Surat (Bombay Province)** at the last moment. Surat being the hometown of Tilak and in his home province of Bombay, he could not be the President, as per Congress convention. Hence, it was decided that Rash Bihari Ghosh (Gokhale's choice) will be the Congress President.

Gokhale in 1907 'You (the Extremists) do not realise the enormous reserve of power behind the government. If the Congress were to do anything such as you suggest, the government would have no difficulty throttling it in five minutes'.

HA Wadya 'the union of these men (the Extremists) with the Congress is the union of a diseased limb to a healthy body, and the only remedy is surgical severance, if the Congress is to be saved from death by blood poisoning'.

Surat Split

On 26th December 1907 Congress Session was held at Surat, on the bank of the **River Tapti**. The Congress was now dominated by the Moderates. The delegates met in an atmosphere surcharged with anger. The Extremists wanted a guarantee that the four resolutions would be passed. To pressurise the Moderates, they began by objecting to the election of Rash Bihari Ghosh as the President. What followed was a pandemonium among 1600 delegates. There were shouts and counter shouts, breaking of chairs and unrolling of Turbans. Someone threw a shoe which hit Pherozeshah Mehta and Surendranath Banerjee. The police was called and the session was suspended. The British rejoiced and Minto immediately sent a letter to Morley saying- 'the Congress collapse was a great triumph for us'.

Tilak, who had not anticipated the Surat fiasco, tried to do some damage control. He wrote a letter of apology and offered his future cooperation. But Pherozeshah Mehta and his men did not relent. They excluded the Extremists from the party. They continued to indulge in their obsolete ideas and quickly rolled back all the radical ideas adopted at Banaras and Calcutta sessions. The Moderates quickly reiterated the Congress commitment to the goal of swaraj within the British Empire through constitutional means alone.

The Extremists led by Tilak announced the formation of the **Extremist Party**. However, they decided to work as part of the INC.

December 1907, Surat Congress Session, President Rash Bihari Ghosh

- Held at the bank of the **River Tapti.**
- The Extremists were led by Lal-Bal-Pal.
- The Moderates were led by Gopal Krishna Gokhale.

Lala Lajpat Rai, who had witnessed the fiasco wrote- 'Instead of leading his party, he (Tilak) allowed himself to be led by some of its wild spirits..he found himself helpless before the volume of opinion that surrounded him'.

This split was further cemented in 1908 Madras Session of the INC where a change was made in the party's constitution. It provided that the Congress delegates were now to be elected only by the Congress Committee and associations affiliated to the Congress. The net result was that members of the Extremist Party could not attend Congress sessions. Consequently, Tilak and his followers remained outside the Congress Party until 1915 when a compromise was struck.

Impact of Surat Split on Extremists

Attack on Extremists After the split, the government launched a massive attack on the Extremists. During 1907 and 1911, several new laws were passed to check anti-government activity. These included:

- The Seditious Meetings Act 1907
- The Indian Newspapers (Incitement to Offences Act) 1908
- Criminal Law Amendment Act 1908
- The Indian Press Act 1910

Tilak, the leader of the extremist camp was sent to **Mandalay** (Burma) jail for 6 years on the charge of sedition. Lala Lajpat Rai left for Britain and then USA. Bipin Chandra Pal also retired from active politics. Aurobindo Ghosh, who was tried in a revolutionary conspiracy case, was judged innocent, immediately gave up politics and retired to Pondicherry to take up religious work. Even though the youth rallied behind the extremists, they were unable to organise any effective body. Without the extremists, the moderates were left with no popular base. They had lost the respect and support of their own people.

During 1908–1914, there was a temporary halt in nationalist activities. It was only when Tilak was released in 1914 that he picked up the threads gradually.

Tilak's imprisonment in Mandalay In April 1908, Prafulla Chaki and Khudiram Bose threw a bomb at a carriage in Muzaffarpur to kill a British Magistrate Douglas Kingsford, but erroneously killed two women travelling in it. Bose was hanged while Chaki committed suicide when caught. Tilak, in his paper Kesari, defended the revolutionaries and gave a call for immediate swaraj. The government quickly charged him with sedition and sentenced him to 6 years' imprisonment in Mandalay, Burma (1908–14). In this case, he was unsuccessfully defended by lawyer **Muhammad Ali Jinnah**. While in prison, he wrote **Gita Rahasya**.

Impact of Surat Split on Government Strategy

The attitude of the government towards the Congress had been hostile. After the Swadeshi Movement, the government came up with a novel strategy, that of 'rallying' the nationalists or the policy of **'carrot and stick'**. It may also be seen as a three-pronged approach of repression, conciliation and suppression. In the first step, the extremists were to be repressed mildly, chiefly to frighten the moderates. In the second step, the moderates were to be conciliated with some carrots or concessions to ensure that they maintained distance from the extremists. Now with the moderates on their side, the third step was to suppress the extremists with full might. This policy of carrot and stick brought rich dividends to the government and the nationalist activities were temporarily contained.

Taking advantage of the split, the British played the game of **divide and rule**. In 1909, they announced the constitutional reforms, known as the Morley-Minto Reforms with the aim of appeasing the Moderates as well as the Muslims. The **so-called 'Reforms' of 1909** were merely designed to confuse the moderates. They increased the number of elected members in the Councils. This, in no way, democratised the Indian polity. The reformed Councils enjoyed no real power as they were merely advisory bodies. Morley had himself declared in British Parliament- 'If it could be said that this chapter of reforms led directly or necessarily up to the establishment of a Parliamentary system in India, I, for one, would have nothing at all to do with it'.

Further, the reforms also introduced the system of **separate electorates** to please the Muslims under which all Muslims were grouped in separate constituencies from which Muslims alone could be elected. This measure was based on the notion that the interests of Muslims were different from that of the Hindus and could be best protected under a Muslim leader. Such a decision furthered mutual suspicion between the Hindus and the Muslims and proved very harmful for national unity. It ensured ghettoisation of Muslims in India, encouraged separatism and politics of religion rather than one based on common socio-economic problems.

Even though the Moderates were not fully satisfied with the reforms, they continued to support the government and oppose the extremists at the cost of their own popularity among the people.

Impact of Surat Split on National Movement

The Surat Split is often termed as a **national calamity** as it did immense harm to the Congress as well as the national movement. The moderates and the extremists were like the brain and the heart of the nation—one was the law, the other the impulse. Their unified function was a prerequisite for the growth of the national movement. The exit of the Extremists left the Congress paralysed for more than a decade as the Moderates could achieve little. It was only in 1916 after re-entry of the Extremists and exit of the Moderates (1918) that the Congress was re-activated. But by then it was a different story all together. Mohandas Karamchand Gandhi had entered the political scene and associated himself with the programme of the Extremists. He represented a new synthesis of faith and reason, law and impulse and inaugurated a new era in Modern Indian History.

Previous Years' Questions – Preliminary Exam

1. "The Congress is tottering to its fall and one of my great ambitions while in India, is to assist it to a peaceful demise'. The statement is attributed to **[UPSC 1998]**
   (a) Lord Dufferin (b) Lord Curzon
   (c) Lord Lytton (d) None of these
2. Assertion (A): Partition of Bengal in 1905 brought an end to the Moderates' role in the Indian freedom movement.
   Reason (R): The Surat session of Indian National Congress separated the Extremists from the Moderates. **[UPSC 1998]**
   Select the answer for the options given below:
   (a) if both A and R are true and R is the correct explanation of A
   (b) if both A and R are true but R is not the correct explanation of A
   (c) if A is true but R is false

(d) if A is false but R is true

3. The paintings of Abanindranath Tagore are classified as **[UPSC 1999]**
   (a) realistic (b) socialistic
   (c) revivalistic (d) impressionistic

4. A London branch of the All India Muslim League was established in 1908 under the presidency of **[UPSC 2001]**
   (a) Aga Khan (b) Ameer Ali
   (c) Liaqat Ali Khan (d) M A Jinnah

5. With reference to the period of extremist nationalist movement in India with its spirit of swadeshi, which one of the following statements is not correct? **[UPSC 2002]**
   (a) Liaqat Hossain led the Muslim peasants of Barisal in their agitations.
   (b) In 1898, the scheme of national education was formulated by Satish Chandra Mukherjee.
   (c) The Bengal National College was founded in 1906 with Aurobindo as the principal.
   (d) Tagore preached the cult of Atmashakti, the main plan of which was social and economic regeneration of the villages.

6. The song 'Amar Sonar Bangla' written during the Swadeshi Movement of India inspired the liberation struggle of Bangladesh and was adopted as the National Anthem of Bangladesh. Who wrote this song? **[UPSC 2007]**
   (a) Rajni Kanta Sen
   (b) Dwijendralal Ray
   (c) Mukunda Das
   (d) RabindranathTagore

7. In the context of the Indian freedom struggle, 16 October 1905 is well known for which of the following reasons? **[UPSC 2009]**
   (a) The formal proclamation of Swadeshi Movement was made in Calcutta Town Hall.
   (b) Partition of Bengal took effect.
   (c) Dadabhai Naoroji declared that the goal of Indian National Congress was Swaraj.
   (d) Lokmanya Tilak started Swadeshi Movement in Poona.

8. Four resolutions were passed at the famous Calcutta session of Indian National Congress in 1906. The question of either retention or of rejection of these four resolutions became the cause of split in Congress at the next congress session held in Surat in 1907. **[UPSC 2010]**
   Which of the following was not one of those resolutions?
   (a) Annulment of partition of Bengal
   (b) Boycott
   (c) National education
   (d) Swadeshi

9. What was the immediate cause for the launch of the Swadeshi Movement? **[UPSC 2010]**
   (a) The partition of Bengal done by Lord Curzon.
   (b) A sentence of 18 months rigorous imprisonment imposed on Lokmanya Tilak.
   (c) The arrest and deportation of Lala Lajpat Rai and Ajit Singh; and passing of the Punjab colonisation bill.
   (d) Death sentence pronounced on the Chaplekar brothers.

10. The partition of Bengal made by Lord Curzon in 1905 lasted until **[UPSC 2014]**
    (a) The First World War when Indian troops were needed by the British and the partition was ended.
    (b) King George V abrogates Curzon's Act at the Royal Darbar in Delhi in 1911.
    (c) Gandhiji launched his Civil Disobedience Movement.
    (d) The partition of India in 1947 when East Bengal became East Pakistan.

11. Which one of the following movements has contributed to a split in the Indian National Congress resulting in the emergence of 'Moderates' and 'Extremists'? **[UPSC 2015]**
    (a) Swadeshi Movement
    (b) Quit India Movement
    (c) Non-Cooperation Movement
    (d) Civil Disobedience Movement

12. What was the main reason for the split in the Indian National Congress at Surat in 1907? **[UPSC 2016]**
    (a) Introduction of communalism into Indian politics by Lord Minto

(b) Extremists lack of faith in the capacity of the Moderates to negotiate with the British government
(c) Foundation of Muslim League
(d) Aurobindo Ghosh's inability to be elected as the President of Indian National Congress

13. The 'Swadeshi' and 'Boycott' were adopted as methods of struggle for the first time during the...? **[UPSC 2016]**
(a) Agitation against the partition of Bengal
(b) Home Rule Movement
(c) Non-Cooperation Movement
(d) Visit of the Simon Commission to India

14. With reference to Swadeshi Movement, consider the following statements: **[UPSC 2019]**
1. It contributed to the revival of the indigenous artisan crafts and industries.
2. The National Council of Education was established as a part of Swadeshi Movement.

Which of the statements given above is/are correct?
(a) 1 only (b) 2 only
(c) Both 1 and 2 (d) Neither 1 nor 2

15. Consider the following statements **[UPSC 2023]**
Statement-I: 7th August is declared as the National Handloom Day.
Statement-II: It was in 1905 that the Swadeshi Movement was launched on the same day. Which one of the following is correct in respect of the above statements?
(a) Both Statement-I and Statement-II are correct and Statement-II is the correct explanation for Statement-I.
(b) Both Statement-I and Statement-II are correct and Statement-II is not the correct explanation for Statement-I.
(c) Statement-I is correct but Statement-II is incorrect.
(d) Statement-I is incorrect but Statement-II is correct.

Previous Years' Questions – Main Exam

1. What were the motives which led to the partition of Bengal? What were its consequences? Why was it annulled? **[UPSC 1988]**
2. 'If Aurobindo was the high priest, Rabindranath was the great poet of the Swadeshi Movement'. Elucidate. **[UPSC 1990]**
3. How far was the Swadeshi Movement linked with Boycott? Analyse the nature of mass participation in the movement. **[UPSC 1992]**
4. Why was Bengal partitioned in 1905? How did it lead to the growth of extremist and terrorist schools of nationalism? Why was it annulled and with what consequences? **[UPSC 1993]**
5. How did the Swadeshi Movement in Bengal influence the national politics? **[UPSC 1998]**
6. Trace the origin of Swadeshi Movement. How did it evolve the masses? **[UPSC 2000]**
7. What led to the partition of Bengal in 1905? **[UPSC 2004]**
8. Evaluate the policies of Lord Curzon and their long-term implications on the national movement. **[UPSC 2020]**

Answers

Previous Years' Questions – Preliminary Exam

1.	(b)	2.	(d)	3.	(c)	4.	(b)	5.	(a)
6.	(d)	7.	(b)	8.	(a)	9.	(a)	10.	(b)
11.	(a)	12.	(b)	13.	(a)	14.	(c)	15.	(a)

6 Extremist Phase, Part 2 (1905–18) (Revolutionary Terrorist Movement, Ghadar Movement, Home Rule Movement)

By mid-1908, the Swadeshi Movement had died down and the next major attempt for a nationwide mass movement came only after the First World War. The intervening years saw the emergence of three major political trends—Revolutionary Terrorist Movement, the Ghadar Movement and the Home Rule Movement. All of these contributed in their own way to the furthering of feelings of nationalism. The beginning of the first trend, i.e. revolutionary terrorism, got merged with the end of the mass phase of Swadeshi movement. The other two, the Ghadar and the Home Rule Movements, synchronised with the years of the First World War (1914–18).

Revolutionary Terrorist Movement

The reasons for the rise of revolutionary terrorism in India are largely similar to the ones that gave rise to Extremist nationalism. As a movement, it emerged with real force only after 1908 and may be aptly called a secret child of the Swadeshi Movement. It was adopted by a generation of highly motivated nationalist youth who found all other avenues of political expression blocked or frustrated; the common political aim of all revolutionaries everywhere in the country being—Freedom from the British rule.

Reasons for the Rise of Revolutionary Terrorist Movement

The following factors mainly contributed to the rise of revolutionary terrorism:

1. Failure of Moderate Methods The 1905 Bengal partition was forced in the teeth of moderate protest. A group of nationalists had now realised the futility of praying and petitioning to the government. They were convinced with the Extremists' critique of moderate politics and sneered at the political mendicancy of Congress moderates.

2. Failure of Extremists to give a Positive Lead to Youth The Extremists had rightly emphasised the need to go beyond praying and petitioning and advocated the need for a more militant program. They had put forward the ideas of boycott and passive resistance. They had aroused the youth for direct action and self-sacrifice.

Yet, the extremists were unable to give a practical expression to these ideas. They had also failed to organise any effective body that could direct the revolutionary energies of the youth in a positive direction. Unsurprising, such youth found recourse in the 'politics of the bomb'.

Once again, even as the extremist leadership praised the heroic activities of the revolutionaries, they failed to educate them, that in a vast country like India only a peaceful mass movement could be successful against the imperialist power and not violent individual actions, however heroic. They not only failed to oppose the notion of revolutionary terrorism, some like Aurobindo Ghose even encouraged it.

Moreover, the youth had participated actively in the Swadeshi Movement in the hope that the Extremist methods of boycott, swadeshi and passive resistance would lead the country to Swaraj. Instead, the Swadeshi Movement not only failed in achieving the goal of Swaraj, it could not even immediately reverse the partition of Bengal (Partition was later reversed in 1911).

3. Violent Repression of Swadeshis Another factor that contributed to the rise of revolutionary terrorism was the brutal repression of the Swadeshis by the government. The Congress split in 1907 facilitated this further and the government launched an all-out attack on the extremists.

Methods of the Revolutionaries

The Revolutionaries believed that Western Imperialism could be countered be western methods of violence alone. Hence, they took to the cult of the revolver and the bomb. They formed secret societies, recruited young persons and trained them in values of **Action** and **Sacrifice** for the freedom of the country.

These revolutionary terrorists based their style on the lines of Irish terrorists and the Russian Nihilists and resorted to assassinations of unpopular officials, heroic individual acts, secret societies and political robberies (popularly called Swadeshi dacoities). Though they did believe in the final necessity of an armed mass revolt to overthrow the imperialist forces, they were aware of the enormity of the task. Subverting the loyalty of the army was equally daunting and they were left with only one choice for immediate action—individual heroic action. With this, they aimed to terrorise the British into submission, remove the fear and inertia of the people and consolidate the feelings of nationalism.

A General Survey of Revolutionary Activities in India

Revolutionary Activities Prior to 1908 Even though revolutionary terrorism emerged as a major trend only after 1907–08, some sporadic activities were visible even earlier-

- In 1897, first act of revolutionary terrorism was carried out when the **Chapekar brothers** (Damodar and Balkrishna) assassinated two unpopular British officials at Poona.
- In 1904, **Abhinav Bharat** and **Mitra Mela**, secret societies of revolutionaries, were formed by VD Savarkar and his brother Ganesh.
- Other prominent revolutionary groups were **Yugantar group** in Calcutta and **Anushilan Samiti** in Dacca.
- During the Swadeshi movement (1905), many prominent newspapers advocated revolutionary terrorism like **the Sandhya** and **the Yugantar** in Bengal and **the Kal** in Maharashtra.
- During the Swadeshi movement, a political pamphlet **Bhavani Mandir** was published and was penned anonymously by Aurobindo Ghosh. It carried an article by Barindra Kumar Ghose,

containing a detailed plan for organising a centre for revolutionary activities. Barin also published **Vartaman Rananiti**.

- Pamphlet **Mukti Kon Pathe** (Which way lies salvation) urged the Indian soldiers to supply arms to the revolutionaries.
- In 1907, unsuccessful attempts were made on the life of Lt. Governors of Bengal and Eastern Bengal.

Revolutionary Activities After 1908 The launch of the revolutionary movement with real force is said to have begun only when, in **April 1908, Prafulla Chaki and Khudiram Bose** threw a bomb at a carriage, which they believed was occupied by the unpopular British Magistrate Douglas Kingsford, district judge of Muzaffarpur (now in Bihar) and ended up killing two English women travelling in it. On seeing the impending arrest, Chaki shot himself dead. Khudiram was arrested and later hanged, in what came to be known as the Muzaffarpur Conspiracy Case.

The violent repression of the Swadeshis triggered a spate of assassinations, secret societies and political robberies. Soon Bengal emerged as the main centre of revolutionary activities spearheaded by Anushilan and Jugantar societies. Maharashtra, Bengal and Punjab and United Provinces emerged as the main provinces of revolutionary activity. During 1908–18, an estimated 186 revolutionaries were either killed or convicted.

Revolutionary Activities in Maharashtra

- Chapekar Brothers and Rand Murder Case (Poona, 1897)
- Savarkar Brothers (Vinayak Damodar Savarkar and Ganesh Damodar Savarkar)
  - Mitra Mela (1899) and Abhinav Bharata Mandal (1904)
  - Veer Savarkar and activities at Indian House, London (1906)
  - Nasik Conspiracy Case (December 1909)

In 1879, early revolutionary activities were organised by the **Ramosi Peasant Force** led by Vasudev Balwant Phadke which aimed to overthrow the British Rule by instigating an armed revolt.

As per the Sedition Committee Report 1918, the first instances of revolutionary movement were observed in Maharashtra, particularly among the Chitpavan Brahmins of Poona district. The forefathers of these Brahmins had served as the Peshwas (Ministers) of the rulers of Maharashtra. The Peshwa rule, or Chitpavan government, was overthrown by the East India Company at the time of Lord Hastings. They had retained their love for Swaraj and yearned to return to power someday.

Bal Gangadhar Tilak, a Chitpavan Brahmin, popularised the Ganapati and Shivaji Festivals in 1893 and 1895 respectively, and dispersed the values of Swaraj in the air of Maharashtra. He also supported revolutionary activities through his papers Mahratta and Kesari. Bombay, Poona and Nasik emerged as the main revolutionary centres in Maharashtra.

Chapekar Brothers and Rand Murder Case (Poona, 1897)

The Rand murder case is also known in Indian history as **the first political murder** of Europeans. During the summers of 1897, bubonic plague raged in Poona in severe epidemic form. To deal with the situation, a Special Plague Committee was formed under the Chairmanship of WC Rand, an Indian Civil Services Officer, and British troops were deployed comprising mainly of British officers. The troops employed harsh measures including forced entry into houses, forced examination and stripping of persons including women by officers in public, evacuation to segregation camps, destruction of personal possessions, etc., which were considered tyrannical by the local populace and complaints were ignored by Rand.

Tilak wrote inflammatory articles in his papers Kesari and Maratha, 'Plague is more merciful to us than its human prototypes now reigning in the city'. Quoting the Gita he wrote that no blame could be attached to anyone who killed an oppressor without any thought of reward.

Following this, on 22 June 1897, Rand and his young military escort Lt. Ayerst were shot dead by the Chapekar brothers, Damodar, Balkrishna and Vasudev Hari (Chitpavan Brahmins). The brothers were caught, tried and hanged. Tilak, on his part, was charged with incitement to murder and for preaching disaffection against the Raj and sentenced to 18-months imprisonment.

Savarkar Brothers (Vinayak Damodar Savarkar and Ganesh Damodar Savarkar)

Mitra Mela (1899) and Abhinav Bharata Mandal (1904) In 1899, at Nasik, the Savarkar brothers—Vinayak and Ganesh, had set up a revolutionary secret society called Mitra Mela while Vinayak Savarkar was still a student at Fergusson College Pune. It was one of several such societies that had emerged in Maharashtra during that time with the aim of overthrowing the British rule through an armed revolution. In 1904, in a meeting attended by several political activists, Vinayak Savarkar renamed Mitra Mela as Abhinav Bharata, on the lines of Mazzini's Young Italy. Vinayak Savarkar was greatly impressed by the Italian revolutionary Mazzini and his techniques of secret societies and guerrilla warfare. In 1906, Savarkar also wrote **Mazzini Charitra** which was a translation of Mazzini's writings. Savarkar's revolutionary propaganda led to a few assassinations, including that of William Wyllie in London and AMT Jackson at Nasik.

Veer Savarkar and activities at Indian House, London (1906) In 1906, VD Savarkar upon graduating from Fergusson College, availed of Shyamji Krishna Varma's fellowship and left for London to study law, taking accommodation in India House. India House was a thriving centre for student political activities in London and was organised by an expatriate, Pandit Shyamji.

Savarkar soon founded the **'Free India Society'** to help fellow Indian students to work for India's freedom through a revolution (by any means), a guerrilla war along the lines of the Revolt of 1857. Savarkar's views on the revolt were published in a book, **The Indian War of Independence, 1857**, and he became one of the first writers to interpret the events of 1857 as 'First War of Independence', what the British preferred to call a 'Sepoy Mutiny'.

In the book, he condemned British rule in India as unjust and oppressive. The book was banned throughout British India; however, it was widely smuggled and circulated, and gained immense popularity among young Indians. Madame Bhikaji Cama, another expatriate Indian revolutionary circulated the book in France, Germany and Netherlands.

Meanwhile, Savarkar continued to study revolutionary methods and even learnt the art of bomb-making from a Russian revolutionary and circulated a pamphlet on bomb-making and guerrilla warfare.

On 1st July 1909, London, **Madan Lal Dhingra** (a protégé of Savarkar) shot dead **Col. William Curzon Wyllie**, political aide-de-camp to the Secretary of State for India. Following the assassination, the British authorities were swung into action. Madan Lal was caught and hanged. Savarkar was arrested and deported to India and sentenced to transportation for life in the Nasik Conspiracy case. Shyamji left London and settled in Paris and the activities of Indian House in London had to be wound up.

Note: 'Grave Warning' was a pamphlet that was widely distributed in London.

Nasik Conspiracy Case (December 1909) On 21st December 1909, **AMT Jackson**, the District Magistrate of Nasik was shot dead by a 17-year-old young boy, **Anant Kanhere**. It is believed that Kanhere was upset with Jackson for insulting Ganesh Savarkar (elder brother of VD Savarkar) by committing him to trial. Subsequent investigation into the Nasik conspiracy revealed the existence of Abhinav Bharat Mandal and the role of Savarkar brothers. Apparently, the Browning pistol used in the assassination of Jackson had been dispatched by Savarkar from London. Charged of murder, Vinayak Savarkar was sentenced to life imprisonment and deported to Andamans (1910).

Note: Jackson was an Indologist and widely read on Indian history and culture, which had earned him his nickname, Pandit Jackson.

Vinayak Damodar Savarkar (1883–1966) VD Savarkar, popularly known as Veer Savarkar was a lawyer, freedom fighter and an atheist who denounced religious orthodox beliefs of all kinds. Born as a Chitpavan Brahmin in a village near Nasik, he earned the epithet 'Veer' after he heroically led the defence of his village from a Muslim mob attack. As a young student, he was greatly inspired by the Swadeshi movement and the militant nationalism of Lal-Bal-Pal.

While serving prison term in Nasik conspiracy case, Savarkar began focusing his energies to writing and wrote the book 'Hindutva: who is a Hindu?', becoming the first person to coin the term **'Hindutva'** and described a Hindu as a patriotic inhabitant of Bharatavarsha (thus going beyond religious identity). In this sense, his vision of India was that of **'Hindu Rashtra'** and **'Akhand Bharat'**. His critics point out that to Savarkar, Hindu was a cultural and political identity to the exclusion of Muslims and Christians. He also wrote— 'Transportation for life', 'Kale Pani' and 'Gandhi Gondhal' (Gandhi's confusion), a political critique of Gandhi's policies. Denied pen and paper, Savarkar wrote on prison walls with thorns and pebbles and even memorised thousands of lines of his literary work.

In 1937, with the grant of provincial autonomy, Savarkar was finally released from jail and the same year got elected as President of the Hindu Mahasabha (1937–43). During the Second World War, he opposed Quit India Movement, supported British war efforts with the aim of providing military training to the Hindus and gave the slogan, 'Hinduise all politics and Militarise Hindudom.'

Madan Lal Dhingra (1883–1909) Dhingra was a revolutionary independence activist. Dhingra left for England in 1905 for studies and came in contact with independence activists like Shyamji Krishna Varma and VD Savarkar, who were all deeply enraged over partition of Bengal. While studying in England, he **shot dead Col. William Wyllie**, considered as one of the first acts of revolutionary terrorism in the 20th century. After the assassination, he was tried and hanged. Earlier, he had been disowned for his political activities by his father, who had even published his decision in the newspaper in this regard. Today, he is widely remembered as a heroic revolutionary who laid down his life for the freedom of his motherland.

Revolutionary Activities in Bengal

- Anushilan Samiti (1902)
    1. Dhaka Anushilan Samiti (1905–06)
        - Barisal Conspiracy Case (1913)

2. Jugantar or Yugantar (April 1906)
   - Muzaffarpur Conspiracy and the Alipore Bomb Conspiracy Case (1908)
   - Indo-German Plot

Pramathanath Mitra (1853–1910) He was a Bengali lawyer, nationalist and founding member of Anushilan Samiti.

Anushilan Samiti (1902)

Anushilan Samiti was the main revolutionary organisation in Bengal which propagated revolutionary violence as means of ending British rule in India.

By 1900, Calcutta had emerged as the nerve centre of organised political activity and many young students and nationalists had begun to meet in secret societies which promoted a culture of physical and moral strength. In 1902, Anushilan Samiti (literally meaning 'body-building society') gradually emerged from a conglomeration of local gyms or akharas. During this time, there were three societies in Calcutta working under the umbrella of the Samiti—one founded by a Bengali student Satish Chandra Basu and promoted by the Calcutta Lawyer P. Mitra, second led by Sarla Devi and a third one led by Jatindranath Banerjee (Niralamba Swami) and Aurobindo Ghosh. Ghosh was one of the strongest proponents of militant nationalism at that time. With the efforts of Aurobindo and his younger brother Barindranath Ghose (Barin), Anushilan Samiti spread like wildfire throughout Bengal. The **journal Jugantar**, founded by Barin along with **Bhupendranath Datta** and others, emerged as a major mouthpiece of the Samiti leaders (and later lent its name to the Calcutta chapter of the Anushilan Samiti).

The partition of Bengal in 1905 further stimulated the radical nationalist sentiments and the Samiti now came to comprise of two independent arms.

1. Dhaka Anushilan Samiti in East Bengal (centred at Dhaka)
2. Jugantar group in west Bengal (centred at Calcutta)

1. Dhaka Anushilan Samiti (1905–06) A branch of Anushilan Samiti, it was initially set up as a group of 80 under the leadership of **Pulin Behari Das**. It spread rapidly throughout East Bengal and emerged as a highly organised secret society with over 500 branches in Dhaka. It broke up with the Jugantar group owing to differences with Aurobindo's approach. The activities of the Samiti came to a temporary halt after the Barisal Conspiracy Case.

Barisal Conspiracy Case (1913) It was a trial of 44 Bengalis accused of inciting rebellion against the Raj. The police authorities of Barisal, a district in the south-eastern corner of Bengal, had reported that they had seized documents that carried a proposal of the Anushilan Samiti to incite the Indian troops and kill the British in large numbers. Five of the accused including Pulin, were transported to the Cellular Jail in Andamans to serve long terms of imprisonment and the Anushilan Samiti was banned.

During the First World War, the Dhaka Anushilan Samiti decided not to participate in the Indo-German plot. Pulin was released in 1918 and refusing to accept the leadership of Mohandas Gandhi, he founded the **Bharat Sevak Sangha** in 1920 and resumed revolutionary activities. In this way, the Samiti continued to exist in an underground manner.

Pulin Behari Das (1877–1949) He was the founder President of the Dhaka Anushilan Samiti. In 1906, Pramathanath Mitra along with Bipin Chandra Pal toured the newly created province of East Bengal and Assam. In a speech, Mitra asked those to step forward who were willing to lay down their lives for the freedom of their motherland, and Pulin stepped forward. Later, he was chosen to organise the Dhaka branch of the Anushilan Samiti. In 1908, the Samiti led by Pulin organised the sensational **Barrah dacoity**, which was carried out in broad daylight at the residence of the zamindar of Barrah.

Cellular Jail in Andamans

Rash Behari Bose (1886–1945) He was a revolutionary leader, chief organiser of the Ghadar Revolution and later the INA. During the Alipore Bomb Case trials (1908), he fled to Dehradun. Following the Delhi conspiracy Case (1912), he was again forced to go into hiding. During the First World War, he became extensively involved with the Ghadarites who planned a mutiny in India during the war years. But the government came to know of the plan and suppressed the efforts. Rash Behari escaped and reached Japan in 1915. There he survived with the help of Pan-Asian supporters; married a Japanese lady, acquired Japanese citizenship in 1923 and even introduced Indian-style curry in Japan! During the Second World War, Bose persuaded the Japanese authorities to support the Indian cause for freedom. In March 1942, Rash Behari convened a conference in Tokyo and established the **Indian Independence League.** He was awarded by the Japanese government with the 'Order of the Rising Sun'.

Bhupendranath Datta (1880–1961) He was a revolutionary and the hot-blooded younger brother of Narendranath Datta (Swami Vivekananda). He was a member of the revolutionary society founded by P. Mitra, became the editor of the Jugantar Patrika (1906) and became a close associate of the Ghosh brothers.

2. Jugantar or Yugantar (April 1906) Jugantar or Yugantar was a revolutionary group formed by the inner circle of Anushilan Samiti and was headquartered at Calcutta. **Barin Ghosh** (younger brother of Aurobindo Ghose) and **Bagha Jatin** were the main leaders. Others included **Bhupendranath Datta** and **Rash Behari Bose**. Barin and Bagha also formed a Maniktala group which collected arms and manufactured bombs at a garden house in Maniktala suburb of Calcutta (Maniktala bomb factory).

The Jugantar group also sent some members abroad for political and military training. One of the first batches, comprising **Surendra Mohan Bose**, **Guran Ditt Kumar** and **Tarak Nath Das**, was sent to North America. The batch became extremely active among the Hindu and Sikh communities in the USA who provided the nucleus for the future Ghadar Party.

Hemchandra Kanungo (or Hem Das), a senior member of Jugantar, was sent to Paris for military training under a Russian Revolutionary in exile there. After returning to Calcutta, he joined the Maniktala group.

Muzaffarpur Conspiracy and the Alipore Bomb Conspiracy Case (1908) Muzaffarpur Conspiracy-On 30 April 1908, **Prafulla Chaki** and **Khudiram Bose** threw a bomb at a carriage, which they believed was occupied by the unpopular British Magistrate Douglas Kingsford, district judge of Muzaffarpur (now in Bihar) and ended up killing two English women travelling in it (Muzaffarpur Murders). On seeing the impending arrest, Chaki shot himself dead while Bose was tried and hanged in what came to be known as the Muzaffarpur Conspiracy Case.

Khudiram Bose (1889–1908) One of India's youngest revolutionaries, Khudiram was inspired by Aurobindo's lectures, and had joined the Anushilan Samiti.

Alipore Bomb Conspiracy Case (or the Maniktala bomb Conspiracy Case)- The Muzaffarpur Conspiracy Case led to a series of government searches. The Maniktala bomb factory was also discovered and several revolutionaries were arrested including the **Ghosh brothers—Barindra and Aurobindo**. The trial came to be known as the Alipore Bomb Conspiracy Case (or Alipore Bomb Case).

During the trial, Bagha Jatin took over the leadership of the Jugantar group, which now turned against persons who were helping the authorities in conducting the trial. When the revolutionary **Narendra Gosain** turned approver, he was shot dead in jail. In February 1909, the Public Prosecutor who was conducting the prosecution of assassins of Gosain, was shot dead in the Calcutta High Court premises. And in January 1910, a Deputy Superintendent of Police Samsul Aslam, who was conducting the Alipore Case, was shot dead while leaving the Calcutta High Court. Several including Bagha were arrested in connection with the **Samsul Aslam case**.

Though released in this case, he was immediately re-arrested with regard to the **Howrah-Sibpur conspiracy case (1910–11).** Bagha and other were charged of conspiring to wage war against the King and tampering with the loyalty of Indian soldiers (mainly the Jat regiment posted in Fort William). While lodged in Howrah jail awaiting trial, Bagha counted on the outbreak of First World War to start an uprising with the help of native soldiers. In 1911, Bagha was released in the absence of proper evidence.

In verdict of the Alipore case though, Barin Ghosh was sentenced to death. The sentence was later reduced to life imprisonment and he was deported to Cellular Jail in Andaman in 1909. Aurobindo was initially put under solitary confinement in the Alipore jail but was later acquitted, having been successfully defended by **Chittaranjan Das**.

Indo-German Plot During the First World War, Jugantar group (led by Bagha Jatin along with **Rashbehari Bose**) also planned a revolt against the British with the help of Germans known as the **Indo-German plot**. Importation of German arms and ammunition was arranged via some Indian revolutionaries residing in Germany (particularly **Virendranath Chattopadhyaya alias Chatto**) and an all-India insurrection backed by a mutiny in the Indian Armed Forces was planned. Fund raising for this Indo-German conspiracy was done by Jugantar by carrying out a series of dacoities, known as **'taxicab dacoities** and **boat dacoities'**. However, the plot leaked out and the police surrounded Bagha as he was waiting for a German arms delivery at Balasore. A gunfight ensued; Bagha was wounded and caught and later succumbed to his injures. In this way, the German Plot was foiled.

During the period 1906–17, in Bengal alone, the number of dacoities stood at 110 and over 60 cases of attempts at murder as per the Rowlatt Committee Report.

Flashforward: Refer to Unit 6.12- Second Phase of Revolutionary Terrorist Movement.

Barindra Kumar Ghosh (1880–1959) Barindranath Ghose, popularly known as Barin Ghosh was a journalist and a revolutionary, fonder member of Jugantar (a Bengali revolutionary outfit) and was the younger brother of Aurobindo Ghosh. Born in London, he returned to Calcutta in 1902 and began organising revolutionary groups in Bengal with the help of Jatindranath Mukherjee (Bagha Jatin). Soon he began publishing a Bengali weekly **Jugantar (1906)** and the **Jugantar group** followed. Barin and Bagha also formed a **Maniktala group** which collected arms and manufactured bombs at a garden house in Maniktala, near Calcutta. Barin was tried in the Alipore/Maniktala Bomb Case and deported to Cellular Jail, Andamans (1909–20). Released in 1920 during a general amnesty, he returned to Calcutta and started a career in journalism.

Bagha Jatin (1879–1915) Born as Jatindranath Mukherjee, he was a Bengali revolutionary, founder member of Anushilan Samiti (1902) and Jugantar party of Bengal. In 1906 in his native village, Jatin found himself face to face with a **royal Bengal tiger**. Though he himself got painfully injured, he managed to kill the tiger with a khukuri. Impressed by his heroism, the Bengal Government honoured him with a silver shield with the scene of him killing the tiger engraved on it. Since then, the epithet 'Bagha' has stuck with him. In 1908 in Darjeeling, he helped establish a branch of Anushilan Samiti, called the **Bandhab Samiti**. Shortly before the outbreak of First World War, he met the German crown prince in Calcutta who promised him help against the British. Thus, Jatin emerged as the brain behind the German plot. However, the plot leaked out and Jatin was surrounded and caught; grievously injured, he died in Balasore hospital (1915).

Revolutionary Activities in Other Provinces

Punjab

In the Punjab, revolutionary activities are traced back to **1907 Punjab Unrest**, a period also known as the beginning of the Freedom moment in Punjab. The unrest was built up mainly around the Punjab Colonisation Act of 1906.

Context to the Punjab Colonisation Act of 1906—Since 1885, the British government took up the task of constructing canals to draw water from the Punjab Rivers and irrigate the arid land of western Punjab and colonise it. This was expected to boost commercial production in canal colonies and remove demographic pressure. The Chenab Colony was the largest of the nine colonisation projects and one of the worst affected by the Act; water from Chenab was to be taken to Lyallpur (now in Pakistan). The government had earlier promised to allot free land and persuaded several ex-servicemen and peasants to settle in the new canal colonies. But once they did, it passed the new Colonisation Act (Amendment) 1906 which provided that the property of a person shall be transferred to the government incase the person died without leaving any heirs, evoking severe public reaction in Punjab.

The affected people first approached the well-known Congress leader and lawyer, Lala Lajpat Rai for help but later accepted the leadership of Sardar Ajit Singh (uncle of Bhagat Singh).

Sardar Ajit Singh and Bharat Mata Society (Anjuman-e-Muhibban-e-Watan, 1906) In 1906, Ajit Singh had already organised a secret society named Bharat Mata Society called Anjuman-e-Muhibban-e-Watan in Urdu to organise patriots who wished to go beyond the moderate methods of the Congress. With members like Mahashay Ghasita Ram and Sufi Ambaprasad, it was already preparing to re-enact 1857 on its 50th anniversary in 1907.

Sardar Ajit Singh and Pagdi Sambhal Jatta Movement (1907) Assuming leadership of the movement to oppose the Colonisation Act, Ajit Singh organised mass rallies and gave fiery speeches. In March 1907, at a rally in Lyallpur, Banke Dayal introduced the song 'Pagdi sambhal Jatta Pagdi sambhal oye', henceforth the movement came to be known after it.

However, the government acted promptly, arresting and deporting Lala Lajpat Rai and Ajit Singh to Mandalay in May 1907. Nonetheless, both men were released under immense public pressure in November the same year. After their release, Ajit Singh fled to Persia while Lala Lajpat Rai left for USA (Ajit Singh remained in exile for the next 38 years and returned to India only in March 1947, breathing his last on 15 August 1947, the day India got independence!) Other leaders such as **Lal Chand Falak** and **Bhai Parmananda** were also arrested and imprisoned. Consequent to government repression, Ajit Singh and other associates like Lal Chand, Bhai Parmanand, Lala Har Dayal (also spelled Hardayal), Sufi Ambaprasad grew into full-scale revolutionary terrorists.

Delhi

Delhi Conspiracy Case (1912) On 23rd December 1912, Rash Behari Bose and Sachin Sanyal organised a daring attempt and a bomb was thrown on **Viceroy Lord Hardinge** in Chandni Chowk, Delhi, killing his attendants. 13 people were arrested and tried in what is known as the Delhi Conspiracy Case (1912). Dina Nath became government approver under pressure. Four persons were hanged, these were-Master Amir Chand, Awadh Bihari, Bal Mukund and **Basant Kumar Biswas**. Rash Behari Bose fled to Japan.

Madras

Vanchinathan Iyer (or Vanchi, 1886–1911) was a Tamil revolutionary who assassinated British officer **Ashe** (the district collector of Tirunelveli) responsible for firing at a crowd that was protesting the arrest of the Extremist leader VO Chidambaram Pillai. Vanchi shot Ashe at point blank range when Ashe's train had stopped at Maniyachi station. After the assassination, Vanchi took cover in the station toilet and committed suicide by shooting himself. Vanchi was a close associate of VVS Aiyar who led the Pondicherry Branch of VD Savarkar's Abhinav Bharat Society. Both Vanchi and VVS were members of **Bharatha Matha Association**.

Revolutionary Activities Outside India

Shyamji Krishna Varma (1857–1930) He was a lawyer, journalist and a revolutionary leader. An admirer of Dayananda Saraswati and Herbert Spencer, he believed in Spencer's dictum, 'Resistance to aggression is not simply justified, it is imperative'.

Kranti Teerth (Mandvi, Kutch) is a Varma Memorial

London, Shyamji Krishna Varma and India House Shyamji was a native of Kathiawar (Gujarat) and a disciple of Dayanand Saraswati. He later went to Cambridge University and also qualified for the Bar. After his return from London, he pursued a brief legal career in India and even served as a Diwan of some Indian princely states, but soon decided to return to England and work for India's liberation from British rule.

In February 1905, Shyamji founded the **Indian Home Rule Society** in London, also known as the **India House**, to serve as a residence for Indian students and promote nationalist views. The establishment of India House was supported by Dadabhai Naoroji (the then President of British Committee of INC) and Bhikaiji Cama (then the private secretary of Naoroji).

He also started six scholarships of ₹1000 each for qualified Indians to visit foreign countries. Soon, India House became a centre of Indian activities in London and rapidly developed into one of the most prominent centres for revolutionary Indian nationalism outside India. Revolutionaries such as **VD Savarkar**, **Har Dayal** and **Madanlal Dhingra** also became members of India House. Shyamji also published a monthly journal **'The Indian Sociologist'** which was a noted platform for anti-colonial views and was banned in India as 'seditious literature'.

In 1909 in London, Madanlal Dhingra assassinated Col. William Curzon Wyllie and the London police was swung into action. Dhingra was hanged, Har Dayal moved to USA and VD Savarkar was arrested and deported to India. Shyamji himself escaped to Paris and thus India House had to be wound up.

USA, the Ghadar Movement In November 1913, the Ghadar Party was founded at San Francisco in USA by the firebrand revolutionary from Punjab, **Lala Har Dayal** (1884–1939). His active supporters were **Ram Chandra** and **Barakatullah**. The party published a weekly paper, the Ghadar (Rebellion), named after the Revolt of 1857. The paper propagated pro-independence and anti-British ideas. Soon the British complained and the US authorities launched proceedings against Har Dayal, leaving him with no option but to leave the United States. (Read in detail about the Ghadar Movement later in this chapter).

Germany, Berlin Committee During World War-I, other Indians abroad united in Germany and set up the **'Indian Independence Committee' at Berlin** in 1915, also known as the 'Berlin Committee for Indian Independence' with the full backing of German Foreign Office. The lead role was played by Virendranath Chattopadhyaya (alias Chatto) and also included Lala Har Dayal and Bhupendranath Datta. The objectives of the Committee included inciting rebellion among the troops, supplying explosives to Indian revolutionaries and even organising invasion of British India.

Paris and Berlin, Madame Bhikaiji Cama In 1905, Bhikaiji Cama relocated From London to Paris and together with Singh Rewabhai Rana and Munchershah Burjorji Godrej, she co-founded the **Paris Indian Society** (1905). Cama also wrote and distributed revolutionary literature **Bande Mataram** (in response to the Crown ban on the poem Vande Mataram) and later **Madan's Talwar** (in response to the execution of Madan Lal Dhingra). These weeklies were smuggled into India through the French colony of Pondicherry.

Madame Bhikaiji Cama (1861–1936) Cama was born in a well-off Parsi family in Bombay and later emerged as a prominent figure of the national movement. She was married to Rustom Cama, a pro-British lawyer but the alliance was not a happy one and she diverted her energies towards social work. During the 1897 Bubonic Plague, she assisted in the relief and contracted the disease herself and left for Britain for medical care. In 1907, she participated in the Second Socialist Congress at **Stuttgart, Germany**, and unfurled what she described as the **'Flag of Indian Independence'**. The flag later served as a template from which the current flag of India has been created.

In 1908, as she was preparing to return, she came in contact with Shyamji Krishna Varma and through him, met Dadabhai Naoroji (then the President of the British Committee of the INC). She worked for Naoroji as his private secretary for some time and later moved to Paris. In 1909, when Madan Lal Dhingra assassinated Col. William Curzon Wyllie, the British authorities asked for Cama's extradition but the French refused.

Other prominent revolutionaries active outside India included Raja Mahendra Pratap, Abdul Rahim, Maulana Obaidullah Sindhi, Champakaraman Pillai and Sardar Singh Rana.

Government Response

In order to meet revolutionary activities, the government of India passed several repressive legislations including:

- The Prevention of Seditious Meetings Act 1907
- The Explosives Substances Act 1908
- The Indian Criminal Law Amendment Act 1908
- The Newspaper (Incitement to Offences Act) 1908
- The Press Act 1910
- The Defence of India Rules 1915

Decline of the Revolutionary Trend

After 1918, the revolutionary activities came to a temporary halt due to several reasons.

- Stern government repression along with a series of draconian laws
- Lack of popular response
- World War-I ended and the government released all political prisoners arrested under the Defence of India Act
- Discussions began on the new Constitutional Reforms (Government of India Act 1919) which generated an atmosphere of compromise
- Gandhiji arrived on the national scene and emphasised on non-violent means which also halted the pace of revolutionary activities

On account of the very nature of revolutionary terrorism, it could be taken up by only a handful of individuals while the masses still awaited a form of political action that could accommodate their weaknesses while utilising their strengths simultaneously.

Second Phase of Revolutionary Terrorism The second phase of Revolutionary Terrorism in India began after the failure of Non-Cooperation Movement. Old and new revolutionary organisations erupted in in two broad strands- one in northern India and the other in Bengal (refer to chapter 6.12).

Ghadar Movement

In June 1914, the First World War broke out between Great Britain, France, Russia and Japan on one side (joined later by Italy and USA), and Germany, Austria-Hungary and Turkey on the other side. The years of the war gave a new lease of life to the national movement in India.

Britain's difficulty was seen as India's opportunity by many nationalists. They felt that Britain would be preoccupied with war issues in Europe and would not be able to attend fully to the nationalist challenge in India. Two groups that tried to take advantage of Britain's difficulty during this time were—the Ghadar revolutionaries based in USA and the Home Rule Leagues of Tilak and Annie Besant in India.

Who were Ghadar Revolutionaries?

The Ghadar revolutionaries were mainly Punjabi immigrants settled in the West Coast of North America since 1904, particularly USA and Canada. Many of them were landless, debt-ridden peasants mainly from Jalandhar and Hoshiarpur. Many of them were also ex-soldiers who had also served in the British Indian Army and had acquired the confidence for emigration. Pushed out of their homeland by economic crisis and lured by promise of better life, they had set out to these foreign lands.

However, when they reached Canada or USA, the welcome was not what they had expected. Many of them were refused entry; others had to face the hostility of white labour force who resented the competition they offered. The Secretary of State for India also supported restrictive immigration laws here as he considered close interaction between Indians and Whites quite undesirable and damaging to British prestige.

By 1908, effective restriction on Indian immigration into Canada had been put in place. Another disabling legislation was the **Alien Land Law** which prohibited Indians from owning land in the US. Such discriminatory policies of host countries moved the Indian emigrants into a flurry of political activity. They were convinced that they were relegated to an inferior status in America as they were citizens of an enslaved country. Hence, they decided to organise themselves with the aim of securing India's freedom from the British rule.

Tarak Nath Das (1884–1958), an Indian student, emerged as one of the first leaders of Indian community in North America and understood quite well that while the British encouraged emigration of Indian labourers to places such as Fiji (where they were needed by British planters), they discouraged their emigration to North America where they ran chances of coming in contact with modern ideas of freedom and liberty.

Early Activities of the Ghadarites

- In 1907, **Circular-e-Azad** (Circular of Liberty) was published by Ramnath Puri, a political exile, which extended support to the Swadeshi Movement.
- **Free Hindustan** (1908), a paper, was started by Tarak Nath Das.
- **Swadesh Sevak Home** in Vancouver was set up by GD Kumar on the lines of India House in London. Kumar also started a paper in Gurumukhi by the name of Swadesh Sevak, asking the Indian troops to rise in revolt. Consequently, Tarak Nath and GD Kumar were soon driven out of Vancouver and in 1910, they together founded the **United India House in Seattle** (USA) where weekly meeting of Indian labourers were organised.
- In 1913, Bhagwan Singh, a Sikh priest, visited Vancouver in Canada and fired the imagination of his audience by openly preaching violent overthrow of British rule.

Such early activities aroused national consciousness and created feeling of solidarity among immigrant Indians in North America. And when they failed to arouse any sympathetic response from the host government, the simmering discontent grew into a revolutionary movement.

Formation of Ghadar Party

Lala Har Dayal (1884–1939) Lala was a revolutionary leader, a key leader in the formation of the Ghadar Party, an intellectual who had turned down a career in the Indian Civil Service. He was born in Delhi in a Punjabi family and graduated in Sanskrit from St. Stephen's College, Delhi. In 1907, he wrote a letter to 'The Indian Sociologist' in which he explored anarchist ideas. The letter and other harsh articles he wrote in leading newspapers criticising the British rule brought him under police surveillance. In 1909, he moved to Paris on the advice of Lala Lajpat Rai and worked as editor of Vande Mataram. However, not finding happiness there, he wandered and started leading an ascetic life, eating boiled food, sleeping on floor and meditating in seclusion. Bhai Parmanand, a missionary of the Arya Samaj, persuaded him to go to the USA.

In California in the USA, Har Dayal came in contact with the emigrated Sikh farmers and learnt about their mistreatment at the hands of the Canadians and the British governments. The first decades of the 20th century saw large scale emigration from Punjab to Pacific Coast of North America owing to economic depression and agrarian unrest in Punjab. To meet this influx, the native governments had passed a series of legislations, giving rise to anti-colonial sentiments in the emigrant community.

Subsequently, Har Dayal set up Guru Gobind Singh Sahib Educational Scholarship for Indian students with the help of Tarak Nath Das and others and even set up a residence for these students in USA, on the lines of India House of Shyamji Krishna Varma. When Basant Kumar Biswas threw a bomb on Viceroy Lord Hardinge (Delhi, 1912), it convinced him that revolutionary sprit was still alive in India; he visited the **Nalanda Club comprising nationalist students** and thoroughly rejoiced.

Pacific Coast Hindustan Association (Portland, May 1913) The Indian community in North America had begun to feel the acute need for a central body and a leader. Consequently, in May 1913, **Lala Har Dayal**, a political exile from India, assumed the leadership and founded the Hindi Association in Portland, also known as the Pacific Coast Hindustan Association. At the first meeting of the association, **Baba Sohan Singh Bhakna** (Ghadari Baba) was elected the President, Lala Har Dayal the General Secretary and Pandit Kanshi Ram Maroli the Treasurer. Har Dayal's active supporters were **Ram Chandra** and **Barakatullah**. Other prominent persons attending the meeting included Bhai Parmanand and Harnam Singh Tundilat.

At the meeting, Har Dayal stated-'Do not fight the Americans, but use the freedom that is available in the US to fight the British, you will never be treated as equals by the Americans until you are free in your own land; the root cause of Indian poverty and degradation is British rule and it must be overthrown, not by petitions, but by armed revolt; carry this message to the masses and to the soldiers in the Indian army; go to India in large numbers and enlist their support'. Har Dayal's ideas were immediately applauded.

Further, at the meeting, a sum of $10,000 was collected and decision was taken to set up a headquarter by the name of **Yugantar Ashram at San Francisco**, and to start a free weekly paper, **the Ghadar** (Rebellion) named after the Revolt of 1857. The paper propagated pro-independence and anti-British ideas.

A commemorative postal stamp depicting Bhai Parmanand, 1876-1947

Hindustan Ghadar Party (November 1913) Later, in November 1913 at San Francisco, the name of the Hindi Association was changed to the Hindustan Ghadar Party. The party was said to have active members in other countries as well, such as Japan, China, Philippines, Malay, Singapore, Thailand, South Africa and Mexico.

Other prominent Ghadarites included Baba Gurmukh Singh, Kartar Singh Sarabha, Rahamat Ali Shah, **Bhai Parmanand**.

Sohan Singh Bhakna (1870–1968) He was a revolutionary and founding President of the Ghadar Party. He was born in a village north of Amritsar and was proficient in Urdu and Persian. After a brief stint in nationalist activity and agrarian unrest in Punjab, he sailed for the US, reached Seattle in 1909 and found work as a labourer in a timber mill near the city.

Abdul Hafiz Mohamed Barakatullah (1854–1927) Born in Itwara Mohalla Bhopal, Maulana Barakatullah was a revolutionary who fought for the freedom of India from foreign land. He came in contact with Lala Har Dayal and Raja Mahendra Pratap (son of Raja of Hathras) in England and became a founder member of the Ghadar party in San Francisco. On 1st December 1915, he became the **first Prime Minister of the Provisional Government of India** established in Kabul with Raja Mahendra

Pratap as its President. With the aim of seeking support for freedom of India, Maulana travelled to several countries and met several contemporary leaders including Kaiser Wilhelm II, Lenin and Hitler.

Kartar Singh Sarabha (1896–1915) A Sikh revolutionary and one of the youngest members of the Ghadar Party (at age 17), he was executed at Lahore in 1915 for his role in the Ghadar Movement when he was only 19.

Ghadar Ideology

- The Ghadar party pledged to wage **revolutionary war against the British** in India. The Ghadarities firmly believed that the British rule could be overthrown only by means of an armed revolt. They felt that Indians could never be accepted as equals abroad so long as they were enslaved in their own country. They believed that the Indian migrants must carry this message to India and spread it among the masses, particularly the Indian troops. Driven by this ideology, the Ghadarities launched a massive campaign in North America visiting farms and factories where Indian immigrants worked.
- The ideology of the party was also **strongly secular**. Sohan Singh Bhakna had declared, 'We were not Sikhs or Punjabis. Our religion was patriotism'.

Ghadar Paper

The Ghadar paper was launched on 1 November 1913 from San Francisco. Its first issue was in **Urdu**, and its **Gurumukhi** version came a month later.

The aim of the Ghadar paper was loud and clear, 'Ghadar' meant revolt. The caption on its masthead read **'Angrezi Raj ka Dushman'** (meaning an enemy of British Rule).

The Ghadar paper declared, 'Wanted brave soldiers to stir up Rebellion in India. Pay-death, Price-martyrdom; Pension-liberty, Field of Battle-India'.

Further, the front page of each issue carried **'Angrezi Raj ka Kacha Chittha'**, i.e. an expose of British rule, consisting of 14 points enumerating the negative effects of British rule. In this way, the chittha was a critique of British rule and included issues such as-high land revenue, drain of wealth, increasing poverty, recurring famines, heavy expenditure on army, low expenditure on education and health, policy of divide and rule, etc. Lastly, it also pointed out the solution in the form of another Revolt.

The Ghadar was widely circulated in North America. It also reached the Indian immigrant community as well as Indian regiments stationed in Hong Kong, Philippines, China, Malay states, Singapore, Trinidad and the Honduras. It was sent to India as well. The paper generated tremendous response and contributions were raised. Most popular were the poems published in the Ghadar which were put together in the form of a collection called **Ghadar di Goonj**, often recited and sung in Indian gatherings. The poems gave the message of revolution and unity of Indians, particularly Hindus and Muslims.

'No pundits or mullahs do we need

No prayers or litanies do we need recite

These will only scuttle our boat
Draw the sword; it is time to fight'.

Addressing the Punjabis and Sikhs, the Ghadar also urged them to make up for their pro-British role during 1857, shed the image of a loyal soldier (carefully cultivated by the British) and instead rise up to their earlier image of 'Lions' who fought ferociously against oppression. They were urged to become a rebel with the only aim of gaining freedom for India.

'Why do you disgrace the name of Singhs?
How come! You have forgotten the majesty of 'Lions'
People say that the Singhs are no good
Why did you turn the tides during Delhi mutiny?
Cry aloud. 'Let us kill the Whites'
Why do you sit quiet shamelessly?
Let the earth give way so that we may drown
To what good were these thirty-crore born?'

Main Events during Ghadar Movement

The movement was influenced by three major events that took place in 1914—the escape to Switzerland of Lala Har Dayal, the Komagata Maru case and the outbreak of First World War.

1. Har Dayal's Escape to Switzerland In March 1914, Har Dayal was arrested by the US authorities on pretext of spreading anarchy though it is widely believed that the measure was instigated by the British. He was released on bail and decided to jump bail and escape to Switzerland.

2. Komagata Maru Case For some years now, Canada had imposed strict restrictions on Indian immigration. Its law forbade entry to all except those who made a continuous journey from India to Canada—'direct passage in their own ship' (this law was formulated keeping in mind that there were no shipping lines that offered such a route).

However, in November 1913 the Supreme Court of Canada had allowed entry to 35 Indians who had made a continuous journey. Encouraged by this judgment, Gurdit Singh, an Indian contractor living in Singapore, decided to charter a ship and carry to Vancouver, Indians living in East and South East Asia.

Thus, a Japanese ship named Komagata Maru, carrying 376 Indians (351 Sikhs and 21 Punjabi Muslims) began its journey to Vancouver. At Yokohama, in Japan, Ghadarites visited the ship, gave lectures and distributed Ghadar literature. On the other hand, the press in Vancouver warned of the 'Mounting Oriental Invasion' and the Canadian government prepared itself to meet the challenge.

On its arrival, the ship was not allowed to land in Vancouver. To fight for the rights of the passengers, a **'Shore Committee'** was formed in Vancouver led by **Hussain Rahim**, **Sohan Lal Pathak** and **Balwant Singh**. Protest meetings were organised, funds were raised and revolt against the British in India was threatened. A powerful campaign was carried out in the USA led by Barkatullah, Bhagwan Singh, Ram Chandra and Sohan Singh Bhakna. Yet, Komagata Maru was forced out of Canadian waters.

On its way back, First World War broke out and before the ship could reach Yokohama, the British government passed orders that no passenger be allowed to disembark anywhere on the way, but only at Calcutta. This triggered immediate resentment among Indian community.

On 27th Sep 1914, the ship reached Budge, Calcutta. The harassed passengers resisted the hostile attitude of the police which escalated into a clash resulting in the death of 18 passengers. Two hundred and two were arrested and the rest ran away. This created widespread discontentment in Punjab and political dacoities erupted in the districts of Jalandhar, Amritsar and Ludhiana.

3. Outbreak of the First World War The outbreak of the First World War was the most significant event that affected the Ghadar movement. The Ghadarites saw it as once in a life time opportunity to make use of Britain's difficulties. A special meeting of the Ghadar leaders was called and the party issued its **Ailan-e-Jung** (or Proclamation of War) which was circulated among Indians living abroad. The Ghadar activists urged people to return to India in large numbers and foment a revolt. The biggest weakness, the lack of arms, was to be met by winning over the Indian soldiers. Prominent leaders toured Japan, Philippines, China, Hong Kong, the Malay States, Singapore and Burma and tried to persuade Indians living there.

These efforts met with tremendous success and hundreds of emigrant Indians offered themselves and their belongings to the cause of the nation. With this began the exodus to India and several revolutionaries arrived in India by mid of 1914.

Last Attempts to Rise in Revolt

The government of India received the returning immigrants with the new ordinance—Ingress into India. The immigrants were thoroughly scrutinised and of the estimated 8000 who returned, nearly 3000 were detained. Yet many activists succeeded in reaching Punjab.

One among the first to reach Punjab safely was **Kartar Singh Sarabha**, a young student who had joined the Ghadar Movement in USA. He, along with other Ghadar mobilisers toured villages, distributed party literature and worked hard to urge the people to rise in revolt. They also tried to spread the message of Ghadar among the soldiers and engineer a mutiny. But their efforts met with lukewarm response. The mood in Punjab in 1914 was very different. The Chief Khalsa Diwan called the Ghadarites 'apostates or fallen Sikhs' and fully supported the British in crushing them. Lack of a central leadership also frustrated Ghadar efforts. In all, Punjab was not prepared to embark upon the Ghadar adventure.

One last attempt to rise in revolt was made in 1915, when Sachin Sanyal and Vishnu Ganesh Pingley roped in Rash Behari Bose, the Bengali revolutionary who had shot into fame after his daring attack on Viceroy Hardinge. Rash Behari arrived in Punjab in January 1915 and assumed the leadership. The date for an armed revolt in Punjab was fixed as 21 February 1915. But once again the government came to know of the plan and succeeding in suppressing the efforts.

Government Repression

First Lahore Conspiracy Case (1915) In the aftermath of the failed Ghadar conspiracy, the trials were held at Lahore by a special tribunal set up under the Defence of Indian Act 1915. The government came down heavily upon the Ghadarites—42 of them were put to death and 200 sent to long terms in prison. Thus, the government succeeded in beheading an entire generation of nationalists in Punjab and the Ghadar Movement was effectively crushed in India. Many of them after their release founded the **Kirti and Communist Movements in Punjab**.

Note: The Second Lahore Conspiracy Case was the trial of Bhagat Singh, Sukhdev and Rajguru in 1931.

Kirti Kisan Sabha Meaning Sabha (party) of the kirtis (workers) and kisans (peasants), the Kirti Kisan Sabha was established on 12 April 1928 with a view to organising small agriculturists and industrial workers and other low-paid urban labour, for revolutionary activity. The Sabha owed its origin to the Kirti movement started by **Bhai Santokh Singh**, a Ghadar leader who had spent two years in Moscow studying Soviet methods of village propaganda. The Sabha was fostered and, to some extent, funded by the Ghadar Party.

Other Indian revolutionaries abroad including Hardayal, united in Germany and set up the **Indian Independence Committee at Berlin**. The objectives of the Committee included inciting rebellion among Indian troops, supplying explosives to Indian revolutionaries and even organising invasion of British India. Raja Mahendra Pratap and Barkatullah tried to enlist the aid of Amir of Afghanistan. Both these attempts proved abortive. It seems, violent rebellion to overthrow the British rule was not fated to see much success.

Revolt at Singapore Inspired by the Ghadar activities, 700 men of the 5th Infantry at Singapore revolted under the leadership of Jamadar Chishti Khan and Subedar Dundey Khan. The revolt was also bitterly crushed.

Evaluation of Ghadar Movement

Success or failure of a movement depends on the yardstick we choose. If the yardstick of success is the achievement of the immediate stated goal of a movement, then all major national struggles such as the Swadeshi (1905–07), the Non-Cooperation (1920–22), the Civil Disobedience (1930–34) and the Quit India (1942) would have to be termed as failures. But if the yardstick for the success of the movement was whether it led to the growth of nationalist ideology, arousal of the people and their training in political action, emergence of new methods of struggle, and spread of modern values of liberty, equality and democracy, then the Ghadar Movement was definitely a success and has many achievements to its credit.

Achievements

- The Ghadar activists were successful in popularising nationalist feelings among a large number of Indians in India as well as abroad.
- They raised a cadre of highly motivated individuals who were willing to give up all for the cause of their nation. Individuals like Hardayal and Sohan Singh Bhakna became folk heroes whose stories of courage continued to inspire generations afterwards.
- Ghadar ideology was deeply secular and democratic in content. So much so that, some historians consider the secular outlook as the most important achievement of the Ghadarites. Despite the fact that most of them were Punjabi Sikhs, they never betrayed any communal tendencies. In fact, any concern to religion was seen as narrow-minded and unworthy of revolutionaries. Several non-Sikhs and non-Punjabis were readily accepted as leaders-Hardayal was a Hindu, Barakatullah a Muslim and Rash Behari Bose a Bengali Hindu. They were able to see that the labelling of Sikhs as a martial race was a creation of the British and they tried hard to counter it.
- The Ghadar mobilisers adopted Bande Mataram as their slogan rather than any religious greeting such as Sat Sri Akal.

Sohan Singh Bhakna (the Ghadari Baba) 'We were not Sikhs or Punjabis, our religion was patriotism'.

Weaknesses

- The biggest weakness of the Ghadar Movement was their miscalculation regarding the readiness of the people. They went ahead with Ailan-e-Jung without examining the readiness of their own army. They had received tremendous response from the immigrant community which misled them into believing that the vast masses in India were in a similar state of readiness.
- They also underestimated the might of the British rulers. With the result that they faced brutal government repression; an entire cadre of nationalist leadership of Punjab was eliminated. Had it not been so, the Ghadarites, with their deeply nationalist and secular tendencies, would have played an important role in checking the rise of communalism that was to divide India in later years.

Opinions

Madanlal Dhingra (1883–1909) 'Neither rich nor able, a poor son like myself can offer nothing but his blood on the altar of mother's deliverance. May I be reborn of the same mother and may I die in the same sacred cause, till my mission is done and she stands free for the good of humanity and to the glory of God'.

Tilak (the Kesari, 1897) 'Srimat Krishna's advice in the Gita is to kill even our own teachers and our kinsmen. No blame attaches to any person if he is doing deeds without being actuated by a desire to reap the fruits of his deeds...God has not confined upon the foreigners the grant inscribed on a copper plate of the kingdom of Hindustan...Do not subscribe your vision like a frog in a well; get out of the Penal Code and enter the extremely high atmosphere of the Srimad Bhagavad Gita and consider the actions of great men'.

Subhas Chandra Bose 'The ultimate object of the revolutionaries is not terrorism but revolution and the purpose of the revolution is to install a national government'.

Home Rule Movement (1916–18)

In 1914, when the First World War broke out, the Indian National Congress decided to support the British in their war efforts as a matter of duty as well as a bargaining tactic to get concessions later.

However, as stated earlier, Britain's difficulty was seen as India's opportunity by many nationalists. Two groups that tried to take advantage of Britain's difficulty during this time were-the Ghadar revolutionaries based in USA and the Home Rule Leagues of Lokmanya Tilak and Annie Besant in India. We have just seen the rise and fall of the Ghadar Movement and its historic contribution in the freedom struggle. A less dramatic but more effective role was played by the Home Rule Leagues.

Factors Leading to the Rise of the Home Rule Movement

A number of factors began to stir the political scene in India and set the stage for the rise of the Home Rule Movement. These included:

Outbreak of First World War The Home Rule Movement began in the background of the First World War when a section of nationalists believed that 'Britain's difficulty is India's opportunity'.

Moreover, the war left a deep impact on Indian economy and society. It affected different classes differently. For the poor, it meant increased poverty—war time demands created a heavy shortage of agricultural products and other products of daily use. This meant inflation and heavy taxation. The war time miseries made the people desperate to join any movement against the government.

For the rich industrialist, the war was an opportunity to make fortunes. The war created economic crisis and shortage of industrial goods in Britain, for which it had to depend on Indian industries. In this way, the war promoted the advance of Indian industries, the momentum of which the industrialists wanted to preserve even after the war. Thus they were eager to organise themselves and support any nationalist movement. In this way, the war created a **wave of nationalism** among different sections of Indian society and consequently the war years became the years of intense political activity in India.

Further, the war, involving struggle among imperialist powers over new colonies, also destroyed the myth of racial superiority and exposed their lust for trade and territories. The American President **Woodrow Wilson** had said that the war was being fought **'to make the world safer for democracy'**. In Europe, in one country after another, democratic institutions were set up. Thus, the war provided **impetus to democratic forces and urge for self-government all over the world**, including the colonies of European empires.

Disillusionment with Reforms of 1909 The Moderates felt disillusioned with constitutional reforms of 1909 that thoroughly failed to satisfy the nationalist leaders. Many of them were now convinced that the government was unlikely to yield any real concessions unless popular pressure was brought to bear upon it.

Repression of Ghadar Movement The bitter repression of the Ghadar Movement had also aroused the feeling of resentment against the British rule.

Tilak's Release from Mandalay and Efforts for Re-entry into Congress On 16th June 1914 Tilak was released from Mandalay jail in Burma where he had been imprisoned for six years, and he returned to an India that had changed much. Aurobindo Ghosh, the firebrand swadeshi, had taken sanyas; Lala Lajpat Rai had left for USA and the Congress was yet to recover from the Surat Split and repression of the swadeshis.

Tilak's first priority now was to get himself and other extremists readmitted into the Congress, from which they had been thrown out in 1907. Tilak had never been happy about the Congress split and he was well aware of the significance of a united Congress. The disunity in Congress was thoroughly used by the British, the Extremists were bitterly repressed and the Moderates were conveniently fooled with the bait of 1909 constitutional reforms. The national movement itself had come to a halt since the split in 1907 and many in Congress now were favourably inclined towards the return of the Extremists. Moreover, the Congress had become a symbol of national movement in the minds of the people and its sanction was desirable for any political activity.

Tilak declared, with the aim of convincing the Moderates as well as the government of his good intentions-'I may state once for all that we are trying in India, as the Irish Home Rulers have been doing in Ireland, for a reform of the state of administration and not for the overthrow of the government; and I have no hesitation in saying that the acts of violence which had been committed in different parts of India are not only repugnant to me, but have, in my opinion, only unfortunately retarded to a great extent, the pace of our political progress'.

Tilak also pledged loyalty to the Crown and urged all Indians to assist Britain in its hour of difficulty.

Annie Besant's Entry into Indian Politics At the same time, **Mrs. Annie Besant**, then President of Theosophical Society, decided to expand her activities and build up Home Rule Movement on the lines of Irish Home Rule League. For this, she too realised that the sanction of the Congress was a pre-requisite. Also needed was the active cooperation of the Extremists as well as the Muslim League. Consequently, she joined the Congress, began urging the Moderates to accept Tilak and his Extremist men back, and worked to build consensus between the Congress and the Muslim League to support a home rule movement in India.

Annie Besant (1847–1933) was a British theosophist, women's rights activist, supporter of Irish and Indian self-rule. She was married to a clergyman, but her anti-religious views led to separation and she joined the National Secular Society. However, in 1890 she met Helena Blavatsky and subsequently joined the Theosophical society.

She had come to India from England in 1893 as part of her theosophy related work. In 1898, she played a key role in the establishment of **Central Hindu College, Banaras** which later became the nucleus of Banaras Hindu University (1916). In 1907, she became the **President of the Theosophical Society**, whose international headquarters were in Adyar, near Madras. She increasingly became involved in Indian politics and joined the INC. In 1914, during the First World War, she build up **Home Rule Movement** on the lines of Irish Home Rule League, leading to her election as **President of the Calcutta Congress Session in 1917**.

Formation of the Two Leagues

In December 1914 Madras Congress Session, the efforts for re-entry of Extremists failed.

However, Tilak and Annie Besant decided to revive nationalist activity on their own and simultaneously exert pressure on the Congress to re-admit the Extremists. Both began their political activities but Tilak was careful not to alarm the Moderates in any way. Their efforts paid off and finally in December 1915 Bombay Congress session, it was decided that the Extremists be allowed to join the Congress. This was also made possible partly with the passing away of Moderate leaders Gopal Krishna Gokhale and Pherozeshah Mehta in 1915 who were most strongly opposed to the Extremists' return.

Annie Besant also succeeded in taking a commitment from the Congress that it will start a program of educative propaganda and reviving local level Congress Committees by September 1916. Failing which, Besant will feel free to set up her own League.

Tilak's Home Rule League Post Congress decision of readmitting the Extremists, Tilak took the lead in setting up the Home Rule League in **April 1916** at **Belgaum** during the Bombay Provincial Conference. **GS Khaparde** was a founding member of Tilak's League. Joseph "Kaka" Baptista was another prominent activist of the Home Rule Movement from Bombay.

To spread the message of home rule, the league was organised into six branches—one each in Central Maharashtra, Bombay city, Karnataka and Central Provinces and two in Berar. It published pamphlets in Marathi, Gujarati, Kannada and also in English. But the most important role in gathering the support of the people was played by Tilak's lectures during his tour of Maharashtra.

Explaining the demand for home rule, he said, 'India was like a son who had grown up and attained maturity. It was right now that the trustee or the father should give him what was his due'.

It was during this agitation that Tilak gave the slogan, **'Swaraj is my birthright and I will have it'**. It is widely believed that the slogan was first coined by Joseph Baptista and later popularised by Tilak.

Readers may note that there was a positive change in Tilak's speeches now—there was **no trace of any religious appeal**. He stated, 'Alienness is not connected with religion, trade or profession; it is a question of interests. He who does what is beneficial to the people of this country, be he a Mohammedan or an Englishman, is not alien'.

Further, his ideas were free of any linguistic chauvinism or even caste bias. He argued in favour of formation of states on linguistic basis and education in vernacular. Do the English educate their people in French language? He asked.

He frontally opposed untouchability and urged Brahmins to be tolerant to the non-Brahmin demands. Tilak declared- 'If a God were to tolerate untouchability, I would not recognise him as God at all'.

Soon the government tried to suppress Tilak's movement and he was served a show-cause notice. Tilak was defended by a group of lawyers led by **Mohammad Ali Jinnah**. He lost the case in lower court but the High Court exonerated him in November 1916. Encouraged by the court's decision, Tilak went on to declare that Home Rule now had legal sanction. He further intensified his propaganda and by April 1917, his league had registered 14,000 members.

Annie Besant's Home Rule League The Congress failed to keep its promise of starting a program of educative propaganda by September 1916 and reviving local level Congress Committees. Thus, Annie Besant announced the formation of her **All India Home Rule League in September 1916 in Madras**, with George Arundale as the Organising Secretary. Sir S. Subramania Aiyar agreed to serve as the honorary President.

Sir S. Subramania Iyer (1842–1924) Also known as the **'Grand Old Man of South India'**, he was a lawyer, jurist and founding member of the Indian National Congress who had led the Madras delegation to its first session at Bombay. He became the first Indian to serve as the Chief Justice of Madras High Court (in 1899, 1903 and 1906). Deeply interested in religion and spirituality, he founded the Dharma Rakhana Sabha (1908), the Suddha Dharma Mandala and joined the Theosophical Society. In September 1916, he became a founding member of the All India Home Rule League set up by Annie Besant in Madras. When, in June 1917, Besant was arrested, he gave up his knighthood in protest.

Even earlier than this, some of Besant's impatient followers could not wait till September and had already setup Home Rule groups. **Jamnadas Dwarkadas, Shankerlal Banker** and **Indulal Yagnik** had started the Bombay paper **Young India** and also set up an All India Propaganda Fund to publish pamphlets.

The League published pamphlets in English and Indian languages to explain the demand for self-rule. From her headquarters at Adyar, Annie Besant along with her lieutenants—**Arundale, CP Ramaswamy Aiyar** and **BP Wadia**, brought out the newspapers **'New India'** and **'Commonweal'**. Arundale wrote a column on 'Home Rule' in New India, urging the members to promote political discussions and debates and persuade people to join the movement. New members who joined the league included: **Jawaharlal Nehru** in Allahabad, B Chakravarti and J Bannerjee in Calcutta.

Two hundred branches of Besant's League were established. But the strength of the League could not be judged by the mere number of branches as many of them were inactive. Besant's league was more loosely organised than Tilak's as three members could form a branch. The membership to Besant's League also increased at a slower pace.

Program of the Leagues

Both the leagues worked with the aim of achieving home rule or self-government for India. For achieving this aim, both the leagues carried out intense propaganda all over the country in favour of the demand for the grant of Home rule. This aim was to be achieved by promoting political education and discussion through propaganda including public meetings and lectures, holding conferences, organising classes for students on politics, circulation of pamphlets, press campaign, collection of funds and organisation of social work, setting up libraries containing books on national politics and discussing with friends about the need for self-rule and persuading them to join the movement.

Their objective was to educate the people and unite the country under one common aim. The leagues functioned independently as the Congress was not in a position to adopt such a radical program.

Since the Leagues were only implementing more vigorously the long advocated Moderate program of political education, they enlisted the support of many Moderates. Members of Gokhale's Servants of India Society, though not permitted to become members of the leagues, extended their support in large numbers and toured the country propagating the demand for home rule.

In Annie Besant's words, the reason why the two leagues did not merge was that, 'some of his (Tilak's) followers disliked me and some of mine disliked him. We, however, had no quarrel with each other'. The two Leagues avoided any friction by demarcating their areas of operation-

- Tilak's League- in **Maharashtra (excluding Bombay city), Karnataka, Central Provinces** and **Berar**
- Annie Besant's League- in the **rest of India, including Bombay city**.

1916, Lucknow Congress Session

The Lucknow session of the Congress was an opportunity for the Home Rule Leaguers to present their strength. The Leaguers were urged to get themselves elected as Congress delegates and flood the Lucknow session. Tilak's League started **a special train** known as the 'Congress Special' or the 'Home Rule Special' to carry delegates from Western India to Lucknow, thus establishing a new Congress tradition.

- **Re-union of Moderates and Extremists** The Lucknow session marked the re-union of the Moderate and the Extremist parties after the Surat Split in 1907. Congress President Ambika Charan Mazumdar extended a warm welcome to the Extremists. In his address, he stated, 'Both the wings of the Indian National Party have come to realise the fact that united they stand, but divided they fall, and brothers have at last met brothers...'
- **Congress-League Pact** It is also known as the **Lucknow Pact**, it was a pact signed between the Congress and the Muslim League. It was made possible with the joint efforts of Tilak and Annie Besant, much against the wishes of important leaders like Madan Mohan Malviya.

  Under the Pact, the Congress accepted the controversial provision of separate electorates for the Muslims. The parties also jointly came up with the Congress-League Scheme and the 'Nineteen Memorandum'. When Tilak was accused of yielding too much to the Muslim demands, he answered,

'When we have to fight against a third party, it is very important that we stand on this platform united, united in race, united in religion, united as regards all different shades of political creed'. Considering that such a response came from an orthodox Hindu leader and writer of ancient religious texts, the opposition gradually faded away. (Refer to Special Note on Lucknow Pact at the end of the chapter).

- **Tilak's demand for Congress Working Committee turned down** At the Lucknow Congress, Tilak had made a significant demand for the formation of Congress Working Committee, to be responsible for carrying out day-to-day work and for implementing Congress resolutions with the objective of giving Congress the machinery to carry out continuous political activity for sustained agitations. This demand was turned down by the Moderates.
- **Joint Meeting of the Home Rule Leagues** After the Congress session ended, a joint meeting of the two leagues was held under the same canopy. Tilak and Annie Besant addressed a gathering of more than 1000 delegates.

Government Repression Fires Back

Soon the government decided to take action against the movement. The Madras government came up with the harshest measures and banned students from attending political meetings. In June 1917, Besant, Arundale and BP Wadia were arrested, attracting nation-wide protests.

Angered by the arrests, Sir S. Subramania Aiyar renounced his knighthood. Some of those also joined the home rule movement, who had until now maintained distance. Most prominent among them were- **Jinnah, Surendranath Bannerjee** and **Madan Mohan Malviya**. Thus, once again, government efforts to silence the nationalist efforts gave further fillip to the movement as people's participation intensified.

In July 1917 at the AICC meeting, Tilak advocated passive resistance if the government refused to release the leaders arrested. As directed by Gandhiji, Shankarlal Banker and Jamnadas Dwarkadas carried out a signature campaign of 1000 men willing to defy the internment orders and march to Besant's place of detention.

Montagu, the Secretary of State for India, wrote- 'Shiva cut his wife into fifty-two pieces only to discover that he had fifty-two wives. This is what happens to the government of India when it interns Mrs. Besant'.

Government Adopts a Soft Line and Montagu Declaration

On seeing the intensification of the movement, the unity of the Moderates and the Extremists and the coming together of the Congress and the Muslim League and the psychology created by the War, the government decided to adopt a soft line as indicated by the historic declaration of Montagu in the British House of Commons on **20 August 1917**.

The Montagu Declaration stated 'the policy of His Majesty's government...is that of increasing association of Indians in every branch of administration and the gradual development of self-governing institutions with a view to the progressive realisation of responsible government in India as an integral part of the British Empire'.

Now compare this statement by Montagu with that of Morley given in 1909 when he had categorically stated that the constitutional reforms of 1909 were not meant to lead to self-government in India.

Montagu declaration was a definite advance over the stand taken in 1909 with the net effect that now the **demand for self-government or home rule could no longer be treated as seditious**.

However, this does not mean that the British were going to grant self-government anytime soon. An accompanying part of the statement also mentioned that the nature and timing of reforms would be decided by the government alone. Thus, Montagu kept enough room for continuous postponement of home rule in any true sense for the Indians.

In September 1917, Annie Besant, now at the height of her popularity, was released as a consequence to the change in attitude of the government.

In December 1917 Congress Session, **Besant was elected President** on Tilak's insistence.

Decline of Home Rule Movement

During 1918, the Home Rule movement gradually petered out. Several factors were responsible for the decline.

- The Moderates lost interest in the movement as they had again been distracted with the bait of fresh reforms.
- They also felt intimidated by the increasing talk of civil disobedience among the League leaders.
- In July 1918, the Reforms Scheme was published which further divided the nationalists-whole some wanted to reject them, others wanted to give them a try.
- Annie Besant herself could not take a definite stand and remained inconsistent on both the issues- the issue of reforms as well as the issue of civil disobedience. Tilak was consistent in his stand and considered the reforms unworthy, but there was little he could do given the change in attitude of the Moderates and Besant's indecisiveness.
- Tilak himself left for England at the end of 1918 in matter of a libel case he had filed against **Valentine Chirol**, the author of **'Indian Unrest'**. In this way, the movement was essentially left leaderless.
- In 1920, All India Home Rule League elected Mahatma Gandhi as its President (last President of the League). Within a year, it was merged with the INC. In 1921, the League changed its name to **Swarajya Sabha**.

Significance of Home Rule Movement

- The most remarkable achievement of Home Rule Movement was the change in British attitude and acceptance of the demand for Home Rule as a legitimate demand which could no longer be treated as seditious. This change in policy was reflected in the Montagu Declaration, which marked a distinct advance over the position taken in 1909.
- Another significant achievement of the Home Rule Movement was the creation of a rich cadre of nationalist workers including the likes of Jawaharlal Nehru, who were now ready and trained to take up leadership role in future struggles.
- The Home Rule activists had also extensively toured Indian towns and villages, narrowing the urban-rural divide in national politics.
- The movement succeeded in popularising the idea of Home Rule, which had now become a commonplace thing.

- The movement played a significant role in arousal of people in political action and furthered national sentiment.
- The movement also saw the reunion of Moderates and Extremists with the efforts of Tilak and Annie Besant and revived the Congress as an effective instrument of national movement.

Yes, it is true that the leaders of the Home Rule Movement were unable to translate this agitation into a real mass movement, yet their achievements were tremendous and the movement prepared a ready ground over which the next and final stage of the struggle could be built-a stage of mass movements shaped by the unique character and personality of Mohandas Karamchand Gandhi.

Special Note on Congress-League Pact

The Congress-League Pact, also known as the Lucknow Pact was signed between the Indian National Congress and the Muslim League during the joint session of both the parties held in 1916 at Lucknow. Mohammad Ali Jinnah, then a member of both, the Congress as well as the Muslim League, was himself the mastermind and architect of this pact. Due to this role of Jinnah, he was called 'the Ambassador of Hindu-Muslim Unity' by Sarojini Naidu.

Earlier, in December 1915, the annual session of both the parties were held at Bombay. This was for the first time, that their annual sessions coincided at the same place and time.

The Muslim League had been witnessing gradual changes and its younger members were now inclined to bolder politics. Despite government efforts to appease the Muslims (Morley-Minto reforms), the gulf between the two was steadily growing wider. The League was also shedding its previous limited Aligarh school of thought and growing closer to the Congress tone and thought due to several factors.

- In 1911, the British annulled the partition of Bengal, annoying those Muslims who had been shown the dream of a separate political state.
- In 1912, Lord Hardinge's government refused the setting up a University at Aligarh with powers of affiliating colleges all over India.
- Outside India, Britain had refused to help Turkey (then ruled by the Khalifa who claimed politico-religious leadership of all Muslims) in the Italian and the Balkan Wars (1911–13).
- In 1912, at the Calcutta Session of the Muslim League, it agreed 'to work with other groups for a system of self-government suited to India, provided it did not come in conflict with its basic objective of protection of interests of the Indian Muslims'.
- Muslims were also angered by wartime repression by the government. In 1914, the government had suppressed the publication of **the Al-Hilal** (of Abul Kalam Azad) and **the Comrade** (of Maulana Mohammad Ali).
- The government had also interned the Ali brothers-Mohammad Ali and Shaukat Ali. Hasrat Mohani and Abul Kalaam Azaad were also arrested.
- Further, Muslims could not have remained untouched with the aspirations generated by the World War.

Understanding reached It was agreed that Muslim League and Congress together will present joint scheme of constitutional reforms before the government while the Congress will accept Muslim League's demand for separate electorates.

Joint demands of the Congress and the League

1. The government will provide for self-government in India at an early date.
2. Muslims should be given one-third representation in the central government.
3. There should be separate electorates for all the communities until a community demanded joint electorates.

4. A system of weightage to minority political representation (giving minorities more representation in the government than is proportional to their share of the population) should be adopted.
5. No bill concerning a community should be passed if the bill is opposed by three-fourth of the members of that community in the Legislative Council.
6. The Executive should be separated from the Judiciary.
7. The salaries of the Secretary of State for Indian Affairs should be paid by the British government and not from Indian funds.
8. Of the two Under Secretaries, one should be Indian.
9. Half of the members of Imperial Legislative Council should be Indians.
10. The number of the members of Central Legislative Council should be increased to 150.
11. At the provincial level, four-fifth of the members of the Legislative Councils should be elected and one-fifth should be nominated.
12. The size of provincial legislatures should not be less than 125 in the major provinces and from 50 to 75 in the minor provinces.
13. The term of the Legislative Council should be five years.
14. Members of Legislative Council should themselves elect their president.
15. All members, except those nominated, should be elected directly on the basis of adult franchise.

Positive Outcomes of the Pact

- Immediate impact of the unity achieved at Lucknow was tremendous and evoked great political enthusiasm.
- The British felt intimidated and adopted a soft line of appeasement, culminating in Montagu declaration with the net result that the demand for self-rule could no longer be treated as seditious.
- It was a major effort from the Congress to ally minority fears regarding Hindu-domination.

Negative Outcomes of the Pact

- The Pact did not involve the Hindu and Muslim masses.
- It accepted the controversial principle of separate electorates, thus giving recognition to the Leagues' communal politics—the notion that Hindus and Muslims were separate political entities with separate political interests. This was a major landmark in the development of the two-nation theory.
- It undermined the role of secular, nationalist Muslims.
- Concessions to one community soon prompted other communities to seek similar concessions.
- The demand of giving minorities more representation in the government than is proportional to their share of the population-not only recognised communal representation but also recognised communal privileges.
- The demand stating-No bill concerning a community should be passed if the bill is opposed by three-fourth of the members of that community in the Legislative Council-introduced communal-veto.

The INC leaders thought that they were sacrificing their seats in the legislature for the greater cause of the nation. In their zeal, they did not realise that the Pact ensured the resurgence of communal politics in India in future years and the unity achieved at Lucknow proved short lived.

Previous Years' Questions – Preliminary Exam

1. Who was the leader of the Ghadar Party? **[UPSC 1998]**
   (a) Bhagat Singh (b) Lala Hardayal
   (c) Bal Gangadhar Tilak (d) VD Savarkar
2. Where were the Ghadar revolutionaries, who became active during the outbreak of the World War I, based? **[UPSC 2005]**
   (a) Central America (b) North America
   (c) West America (d) South America
3. Annie Besant was **[UPSC 2013]**
   1. responsible for starting the Home Rule movement
   2. the founder of the Theosophical Society
   3. the President of the Indian National Congress

   Select the correct answer from the following options.
   (a) Only 1 (b) 2 and 3
   (c) 1 and 3 (d) All of these
4. The Ghadr (Ghadar) was a **[UPSC 2014]**
   (a) revolutionary association of Indians with headquarters at San Francisco
   (b) nationalist organisation operating from Singapore
   (c) militant organisation with headquarters at Berlin
   (d) communist movement for India's freedom with headquarters at Tashkent
5. In 1920, which of the following changed its name to "Swarajya Sabha"? **[UPSC 2018]**
   (a) All India Home Rule League
   (b) Hindu Mahasabha
   (c) South Indian Liberal Federation
   (d) The Servants of India Society
6. Consider the following freedom fighters: **[UPSC 2022]**
   1 Barindra Kumar Ghosh
   2. Jogesh Chandra Chatterjee
   3. Rash Behari Bose

   Who of the above was/were actively associated with the Ghadar Party?
   (a) 1 and 2 (b) 2 only
   (c) 1 and 3 (d) 3 only

Previous Years' Questions – Main Exam

1. Discuss the growth of revolutionary terrorism with special reference to its ramifications in Maharashtra, Bengal and Punjab till the first decade of the 20th century. **[UPSC 1991]**
2. 'The Lucknow Pact of 1916 was signed without regard for its consequences'. Elucidate **[UPSC 1993]**
3. Explain the part played by Annie Besant in the Home Rule movement. **[UPSC 1994]**
4. Examine the causes and nature of extremism in Indian politics in the early part of the present century. **[UPSC 1997]**
5. How did the terrorist movement gather strength in countries other than India? **[UPSC 2000]**
6. Write short notes: Ghadar Party **[UPSC 2001]**
7. Trace the growth of the Indian Home Rule Movement in Britain **[UPSC 2002]**
8. Write about: Bhavani Mandir. **[UPSC 2005]**
9. Several foreigners made India their homeland and participated in various movements. Analyse their role in the Indian struggle for freedom. **[UPSC 2013]**

Answers

Previous Years' Questions – Preliminary Exam

1. (b) 2. (b) 3. (c) 4. (a) 5. (a)
6. (d)

7 MAHATMA GANDHI: EMERGENCE AND IDEOLOGY

Mohandas Karamchand Gandhi, better known as Mahatma Gandhi, emerged on the Indian political scene during the period 1917-18 and significantly transformed the ideology and range of the National Movement. With his entry, the national movement entered its third and final phase of struggle, also known as the era of Mass Mobilisation under Mahatma Gandhi (1919–47). Purna Swaraj or complete Independence emerged as the goal of the national movement during this phase.

The period of Gandhian activities before 1920 is described as the formative stage of Gandhi. It includes his struggle in South Africa and early Satyagraha agitations in India (Champaran, Ahmedabad, Kheda and Rowlatt Satyagraha). This was also the period during which he mainly tried to understand the socio-political and economic reality of India.

Thus, in the first half of this chapter, we shall learn about the early life and political career of Gandhi. In the second half, we shall also cover some of the most significant aspects of Gandhian ideology to enable the reader, better appreciate Gandhian techniques and methods.

Gandhi's Early Life and Career

Childhood Mohandas Karamchand Gandhi was born at Porbandar, also known as Sudamapuri, in Kathiawar Gujarat on 2nd October 1869. The Gandhi's belonged to the Bania caste, traditionally grocers but for the past three generations they had been Prime Ministers in several Kathiawad States. The Gandhi's were **Vaishnavites** who laid emphasis on ahimsa and vegetarianism. They were also deeply influenced by Jainism which had a strong presence in Gujarat. Such was the culture in which Gandhi was born and bred. **Shravana Pitribhakti Nataka** (a play about Sharavana's devotion to his parents) and **Harishchandra** (a play on Harishchandra's truthfulness) left an indelible impression on Gandhi's young heart and mind. When Gandhi was about age 7, his father left Porbandar for Rajkot to become a member of the Rajasthanik Court (a body for settling disputes between the chiefs and their fellow clansmen). At age 13, he had a **child marriage** to Kasturbai.

Travel to England On 4 September 1888 Gandhi sailed for England to study law. Vegetarianism was then a new cult in England. Gandhi read the book 'A Plea for Vegetarianism' by HS Salts, following which he claimed to have become a **vegetarian by choice**. Gandhi joined the Vegetarian Society in England and got elected to its Executive Committee. He even started a vegetarian club in his locality, which according to him, gave him training in organising and training institutions.

In his second year in England, Gandhi met two Theosophist brothers, under whose influence he read the **Gita** and Sir Edwin Arnold's translation – 'The Song Celestial' for the first time. The brothers also introduced Gandhi to Madame Blavatsky and **Mrs. Besant**. When asked to join the Theosophical Society, Gandhi politely declined saying, 'With my meagre knowledge of my own religion I do not want to belong to any religious body'. At the brothers' instance, Gandhi also read 'The Light of Asia' by Sir Edwin Arnold and 'Key to Theosophy' by Madame Blavatsky. Blavatsky's book stimulated in Gandhi the desire to read books on Hinduism.

On the insistence of a vegetarian Christian, Gandhi read the New Testament and especially liked the Sermon on the Mount and compared it with the Gita. The verses, 'But I say unto you, that ye resist not evil: but whosoever shall smite thee on thy right cheek, turn to him the other also. And if any man take away thy coat let him have thy cloke too,' touched his heart in particular and he began to see **renunciation** as the highest form of religion.

In England, Gandhi also met **Narayan Hemchandra**, the Gujarati writer and translator, credited for introducing Debendranath Tagore's works to Gujarat.

Return from England In 1891, Gandhi returned to India as a young barrister, and landed at Bombay from SS Assam. There he was introduced to the poet **Raychand** (or Rajchandra), also known as 'Shatavadhani' (one having the faculty of remembering or attending to a hundred things simultaneously). Raychand impressed Gandhi with his knowledge of the scriptures, his spotless character, and his burning passion for self-realization.

Trouble had been brewing in Gandhi's caste over his foreign voyage. Thus Gandhi's life in India began by seeking **readmission into his caste**. From Bombay, Gandhi was taken to Nasik by his elder brother for a bath in the sacred river, followed by a caste dinner at Rajkot. This pacified one section of the caste, while another section continued to regard him as ex-communicated.

Though Gandhi passed his examinations in London, he had not learnt how to practice law and learnt nothing at all of Indian law. To save himself from ridicule at Rajkot, he decided to go to Bombay and gain experience at Bombay High Court. Gandhi was unable to establish a successful practice there. He even tried to get a job as an English teacher in a High School but was rejected since he was not a graduate. Within six months he shifted back to Rajkot and took up the work of petition-writing for earning his livelihood. In April 1893, Gandhi sailed to **Durban (Natal province, capital Pietermartizburg)** in connection with a legal case of Dada Abdulla and Co., an Indian firm doing business in South Africa.

Gandhi's Experiences in South Africa

In 1893, at age 24, Gandhi was the first Indian barrister to have arrived in South Africa. Gandhi's experiences in South Africa had a profound impact on his life and career that followed. He had gone there on a year's contract with Dada Abdulla and Co., but ended up staying for the next 20 years, i.e. up to 1914 with brief spells in India and England, having picked up struggle against racial discrimination (apartheid) in South Africa and fought for the rights of the Indian community.

Apartheid: It refers to discrimination against a community based on the colour of the skin.

Condition of Indians in South Africa

At Durban (also known as Port Natal), Gandhi was received by Abdulla Sheth. Gandhi immediately noticed that Indians were not held in much respect there. In the next two to three days, he observed that Indian community in South Africa (of nearly 2 lakh Indians) comprised of different groups. One group was that of Muslim merchants. Another was that of Hindu, and yet another of Parsi, clerks.

But the largest group comprised of Tamil, Telugu and North Indian indentured and freed labourers. Indentured labourers were those who had emigrated from India to labour under an indenture for five years or less and came to be known there as **girmitiyas** (from girmit, corrupt form of the word 'agreement').

There was a fearful amount of color prejudice in South Africa and Indians were subjected to various forms of **racial discrimination** by the Englishmen. For instance,

- All Indians were addressed as 'coolies' (meaning labourer). Hence Gandhi was known as 'coolie barrister; merchants as 'coolie merchants'.
- The indentured labourers were treated as semi-slaves.
- Indians could reside only in prescribed locations and were not allowed to use the public footpath or move out at night without a permit.
- They were prohibited from travelling in first and second class railway compartments.
- There were hotels and restaurants that were exclusively reserved for Europeans and Indians were prohibited to enter.
- There existed racial discrimination with respect to citizenship rights, freedom of trade and right to property, etc.
- According to a Transvaal legislation of 1885 (amended in 1886), all Indians were required to pay a poll tax of £3 as fee for entry into the Transvaal.

The ex-indentured labourers who had continued to live in South Africa with their children were not educated, knew little English and accepted racial discrimination as part of their daily existence. However, with Gandhi, things were different. He was the son of a Diwan of an Indian state and belonged to a highly-respected family of Kathiawar. He had spent three years in London studying for the bar and had not contacted overt racialism either in India or in England, but which he now contacted within days of his arrival in South Africa. Naturally, he found it hard to swallow and decided to protest.

Gandhi's First Racial Humiliation

Gandhi first faced racial humiliation while travelling from **Durban to Pretoria** (capital of neighboring province, the Transvaal) in the context of the legal case. In fact, this journey which he undertook within a week of his arrival comprised of a series of racial humiliations. Abdulla Sheth had booked a first class train ticket for Gandhi. But on seeing that Gandhi was 'colored', a white passenger objected to travelling with him in the same compartment. He complained to railway officials who then asked Gandhi to shift to the van compartment. When he resisted, he was roughed up, pushed out of the train onto the platform and left to spend the night shivering in the waiting room. Next, while traveling from Charlestown to Johannesburg, despite possessing a ticket for the stage coach, Gandhi was not allowed to sit with the white passengers but made to sit on a seat on the side of the coach box. Though it was sheer injustice and an insult, Gandhi decided to pocket it. After some time, the white leader incharge of the coach wanted to smoke and he asked Gandhi to vacate his seat and sit on the footboard instead. When Gandhi resisted, he was boxed in the ears, seized by the arm and dragged down. On reaching Johannesburg, was denied a room at the Grand National hotel. Again, while travelling from Johannesburg to Pretoria he was subjected to considerable humiliation.

Subsequently, Gandhi called a meeting of all Indians in Pretoria and presented before them the condition of Indians in the Transvaal. Gandhi regarded his speech at this meeting as his **first public speech** ever. He encouraged the Indians to be truthful in business, acquire sanitary habits, learn English and form an association that could voice the hardships of Indian settlers and represent them before the authorities. However, it was the proposed bill of Natal government to disfranchise Indians, which finally compelled Gandhi to launch his struggle in South Africa.

In conclusion, Gandhi's year long stay in Pretoria proved to be a most valuable experience. It was during this period that Gandhi got the opportunity to **learn public work**. As regards Sheth Abdulla case, Gandhi was able to persuade the parties for arbitration and the case was successfully settled out of court to the pleasure and benefit of both parties. It was while dealing with this case that Gandhi acquired the **true practice of law**. In Gandhi's words, "I had learnt to find out the better side of human nature and to enter men's hearts. I realised that the true function of a lawyer was to unite parties riven asunder."

This was also a year of **religious ferment in Gandhi**. While Sheth Abdulla tried to pull him to Islam, his Christian friends tried to convert him to Christianity. Gandhi now took to wide reading of religious books. He could not accept either Christianity or Islam as perfect religions, nor did he believe Hinduism as one. At the same time, he saw no reason to change his religion, to believe that he could attain salvation only by becoming a Christian. Though Gandhi did not take the path his Christian and Muslim friends had intended for him, such proselytizing activities awakened in him a religious quest, which was to stay with him for the rest of his life.

Gandhi's Political Career in South Africa (1893–1914)

First Phase—The Moderate Phase (1894–1906)

Gandhi's struggle against Disfranchisement Bill and Formation of Natal Indian Congress (NIC) Gandhi had settled the legal case of Abdulla and Co. and was preparing to return to India when, in a farewell party, he read the news regarding the proposed legislature of the Natal government. Known as the Natal Legislative Assembly Bill of 1894 (Disfranchisement Bill or Franchise Bill), it sought to deprive the Indians of their right to elect members of the Natal Legislative Assembly.

Genesis of the disfranchising bill and a tax levied on indentured Indians- Around 1860, Europeans found scope for sugar-cane cultivation in South Africa, but the native Zulus were not used to hard work. The white planters then sought permission from Indian Government to recruit Indian labour to work in Natal under an indenture of five years, upon the expiry of which they would be free to settle there and enjoy full rights of ownership of land. The permission was granted and the first batch of indentured labourers from India reached Natal in November 1860. The Indians soon outgrew the expectations. They proved to be rather enterprising, introduced mango, entered trade and became owners of land and houses, antagonizing the Europeans. The antagonism found expression in the disfranchising bill and the bill to impose a tax on the indentured Indians.

The Indian merchants present at the party pleaded with Gandhi to stay on a little longer and help them organise the protest as they did not know enough English to draft petitions and so on. Infuriated as he was, Gandhi decided to postpone his return and the farewell party immediately turned into a planning committee, formulating a plan of action against the bill. Thus, **Gandhi's first struggle in South Africa** was launched against the disfranchising bill of the Natal government.

It is also noteworthy that before Gandhi, Indians did not demand equal treatment because they felt that they were discriminated against due to their 'backwardness' or 'lack of civilisation'. However, discrimination against Gandhi, the first westernised Indian in South Africa, demonstrated to all that the root cause of discrimination lay, above all else, in the colour of their skin. Further, the responsibility of waging a struggle against racial discrimination lay heavily on the shoulders of Gandhi as he could speak the White Man's language, understand their law and confront them as an equal.

Led by Gandhi, several Indians living in Natal submitted a petition against the Bill. When the Bill was passed despite Indian opposition, Gandhi sent a monster petition signed by 10,000 Indians to the Secretary of State for the Colonies in England (then Lord Ripon) with the appeal that the unjust Bill should not be assented to by the Queen. A thousand copies of the petition were circulated, acquainting the Indian public **for the first time** with conditions in Natal. Several newspapers, including The Times of India and The London Times supported Indian demands. Hopeful of the bill being vetoed, Gandhi felt that sustained agitation would be needed to impress the Colonial Secretary. Thus, feeling the need for a permanent organisation to unite the Indians for a continuous struggle, Gandhi founded the **Natal Indian Congress (NIC)** on 22 May 1894.

The formation of NIC is seen as the beginning of the **'moderate phase'** of Gandhi's struggle in South Africa. In this period, Gandhi sent petitions and memorials to the South African legislatures, to the Colonial Secretary in London and to the British Parliament to voice the demands of the Indian people and arouse the British sense of justice and fair play. He also made efforts to unite the Indians and give wide publicity to their demands. He tried to secure the support of people and governments in South Africa, India as well as in Britain for the Indian cause. In India, the Indian National Congress even passed a resolution condemning the disfranchising bill.

Colonial-born Indian Educational Association was also founded under the aegis of the Congress. It was a kind of debating society with a mini library for the members. It thus served to stimulate thought and ventilate the needs and grievances of educated youth. For the purpose of propaganda, Gandhi wrote two pamphlets namely, 'An Appeal to Every Briton in South Africa' and the other entitled 'Indian Franchise – An Appeal'.

Taking note of the strong opposition against the Franchise Bill, the Colonial office in London vetoed it on the ground that it discriminated against the inhabitants of another part of the British Empire and that the empire could not agree to the establishment of a color bar in legislation. Despite this, the Natal government achieved its objective by passing the Bill in an amended form.

Campaign against £25 tax on the indentured Indians The white planters and the Natal government were not likely to stop at the disfranchising bill. Nipping the political rights of Indians was only the first step. The real point of attack was free Indian immigration and flourishing Indian trade.

Thus in 1894, the Natal Government proposed to impose an annual tax of £25 on every freed indentured Indian, who refused to go back to India or wished to renew his indenture. The proposal came as a shock and the NIC resolved to take up the cause. Subsequently, when Natal Government sought approval from Indian Government, Viceroy Lord Elgin disapproved of the £25 tax, but agreed to a poll tax of £3. Even this was atrocious given the fact that average income of a labourer was merely

14 shillings a month. Thus NIC was able to safeguard the interests of the labourers only partially and had to wait for twenty years before the tax could be abolished (by the Indian Relief Act 1914).

Gandhi visits India (1896) In the middle of 1896, Gandhi sailed for India to fetch his wife and children. He intended to utilise his India visit by mobilising public support for his work in South Africa. Upon reaching Rajkot, he wrote a pamphlet on the situation in South Africa which came to be known as the **Green Pamphlet** because of its green cover (Around the same time, plague broke out in Bombay and threatened to spread in adjoining regions such as Rajkot. Gandhi volunteered his services to the state, offering to work in the sanitation department). Gandhi travelled to Bombay, Poona, Madras, Calcutta and Allahabad seeking help from people of all parties and shades of opinion. "Sir Pherozeshah had seemed to me like the Himalaya, the Lokamanya like the ocean. But **Gokhale was as the Ganges**. One could have a refreshing bath in the holy river. The Himalaya was unscaleable, and one could not easily launch forth on the sea, but the Ganges invited one to its bosom", Gandhi wrote in his autobiography. He called at the offices of the Pioneer, Amrit Bazaar Patrika, the Bangabasi, The Statesman, The Englishman and others, requesting them to endorse Indian demands in South Africa. Suddenly Gandhi received a cable from Durban: 'Parliament opens January. Return soon'. In December 1896, Gandhi sailed a second time for South Africa, this time with his wife and two sons. Another steamship Naderi sailed at the same time.

Young Gandhi on postage stamp of Nevis

Gandhi gets lynched in Natal In his Green Pamphlet, Gandhi had drawn a purposely subdued picture of the conditions of Indians in South Africa. Yet, an exaggerated version reached Natal trough the newspapers, evoking the wrath of many Europeans there. Consequently, when Gandhi reached the Port of Durban on 18th December, his ship was quarantined on the pretext of Bombay plague. But the real reasons lay elsewhere. Gandhi was the real target and his entry was being opposed based on two charges (1) that whilst in India he had indulged in unmerited condemnation of the Natal whites; (2) that with a view to swamping Natal with Indians, he had specially brought the two shiploads of passengers to settle there.

Gandhi was absolutely innocent and maintained his right to land at Port Natal. When finally the ships were permitted to enter harbor, Gandhi was caught and lynched by a European mob while he was walking his way home. He was saved in time by the efforts of the wife of a senior police official. Gandhi however refused to prosecute his assailants producing a profound impression, and the whites felt ashamed of their conduct.

Gandhi volunteers during Boer War (1899–1902) The Boers were South Africans of Dutch origin. They were fighting the British. Though neither of the two parties had treated the Indians well, and though Gandhi's personal sympathies lay with the Boers, yet his loyalty to the British and his conviction that India could achieve emancipation only within and through the British Empire drove him to participate with the British in the Boer War. Gandhi raised a group of stretcher–bearers as the Natal Indian Ambulance Corps comprising of 1100 volunteers with 40 leaders. Soon the British won the war and Gandhi's war efforts were liberally praised by English newspapers.

Gandhi attends 1901 Calcutta Congress Session (President, WE Wacha) In 1901, Gandhi felt that his future activity lay not in South Africa but in India and he decided to return. On his arrival, he set off for a tour of the country to understand India and the problems of its people. He also attended the Calcutta Congress Session that year; **his first contact with the INC**. Gandhi came face to face with the functioning of the Congress. It would meet for three days in a year, then go to sleep. English occupied a prominent place, there was fair amount of untouchability, sanitation was nearly absent, latrines exuded oppressive stench and conditions were ripe for outbreak of an epidemic. While reading his resolution on the grievances of settlers in South Africa, Gandhi was quite nervous and he read it trembling. The resolution was later passed by the Congress.

Gandhi had just begun to settle down in Bombay, when once again a cable reached him requesting his presence in South Africa on an urgent matter.

Indian Opinion (1903) and Phoenix Settlement (1904) Thus in 1902, Gandhi again returned to South Africa and resumed his struggle against racial discrimination. He opened an office in Johannesburg, which had the largest population of Indians in the Transvaal. He started the journal **Indian Opinion** (1903), which became a mouthpiece of Gandhi's struggle. The journal was published from Durban every week in English and Gujarati and was edited by **Mansukhlal Nazar**.

Statue of M. K. Gandhi as a young attorney at law on Gandhi Square in the business district of Johannesburg, South Africa

Inspired by **John Ruskin's** book on economics, Unto the Last, Gandhi hit upon the idea of starting a farm and leading a simple community life. In 1904, he and his associates shifted to Phoenix near Durban; Indian Opinion was also shifted to the farm, complete with press and office. Families at the farm lived simple lives, cultivating the soil or working at the press. It was the inhabitants of Phoenix who later became the chief participants of Gandhi's Satyagraha protest.

- Gandhi wrote a series of articles on dietetics for Indian Opinion, which were later published in the form of a book named as **'A Guide to Health'**.
- Gandhi translated Ruskin's 'Unto this Last' into Gujarati under the title **'Sarvodaya'**. Gandhi summarized the most significant teachings of this book into three points:
    1. The good of the individual is contained in the good of all.
    2. A lawyer's work has the same value as the barber's, in as much as all have the same right of earning their livelihood from their work.
    3. A life of labour, i.e., the life of the tiller of the soil and the handicraftsman, is the life worth living.
- Gandhi wrote his autobiography not as a separate book, but as a weekly article for the Gujarati weekly Navajivan, under the title **'The Story of My Experiments with Truth'**. Most of these articles were written from Yerawada jail during 1925–29, covering his life till 1921.

Gandhi volunteers in the Zulu Rebellion (1906) In 1906 the Zulu Rebellion (also known as Bambatha Rebellion) broke out in Natal. Though Gandhi bore no grudge against the Zulus, yet owing to his loyalty to the British Empire, he once again participated with the British and raised an Indian Ambulance Corps. To Gandhi's delight, the main work was to nurse the wounded Zulus who were either friendlies or flogged suspects.

Second Phase—Phase of Civil Disobedience/Satyagraha (1906–14)

The second phase began with the first use of passive resistance or civil disobedience or rather 'Satyagraha'. Gandhi had deep faith in the British sense of justice until, in 1906, the Transvaal government proposed a bill to further humiliate the Indians and scare them out of the country. In the course of his struggle against the discriminatory law, he realised that his petitions and memorials fell on deaf ears and it became clear to him that the British were not interested in addressing the grievances of the Indian people. Once disenchanted, he now turned to **civil disobedience**, which he called Satyagraha.

Gandhi's struggle against Asiatic Registration Act and Advent of Satyagraha (1906–14) In 1906, a draft Asiatic Law Amendment Ordinance (later known as Black Ordinance or **Black Act**) to be introduced into the Legislative Council was published in the Transvaal Government Gazette. The ordinance proposed compulsory registration of Indians above the age of eight years with the Registrar of Asiatics. Whoever failed to register within the window period given would be guilty of an offence and liable to be suitably punished. Further, an Indian could be asked to produce his registration certificate any time. The police officers were also permitted to enter into private houses and check for the papers. Such a legislation directed against free men was unknown anywhere in the world and shocked the Indian community violently.

- **Advent of Satyagraha** On 11 September 1906, a meeting of Indians in the Transvaal was called. Gandhi invited each attendee to take a pledge 'to die but not to submit' to the proposed legislation; not to demonstrate to any outsider but only if the inner voice assures him that he has the requisite strength to carry him through. Initially Gandhi used the term passive resistance to denote the struggle but soon realised that passive resistance could not explain the real nature of the movement he had authored. (Thus, Gandhi first used Satyagraha against the Asiatic Registration Act).

  Among the English people, whenever a small minority did not approve of some legislation, instead of rising in rebellion they took to 'passive or milder form of resistance' that involved not submitting to the law and inviting the penalties of such non-submission upon their heads. But unlike in passive resistance or civil disobedience, in Gandhi's new movement there was no scope for violence whatsoever. Instead there was immense scope for love. Hence Gandhi wanted a new word be coined by Indians to denote their struggle. He therefore invited suggestions through Indian Opinion and Maganlal Gandhi's 'Sadagraha' won the prize. Gandhi later changed it to 'Satyagraha' that is to say, the Force which is born of **Truth and Love** or non-violence, and gave up the use of the phrase 'passive resistance'. 'Satyagraha' has since then emerged as a byword for Gandhian struggle.
- **Delegation to England** Despite vehement opposition by Indians, the ordinance was passed practically in the shape in which it was first drafted (only the clause affecting women was deleted). Gandhi now led a delegation to England to personally request the British Crown to withhold royal assent. Gandhi's efforts, however, did not bear fruit. Meanwhile, responsible government was established in the Transvaal and its new Parliament hurriedly passed the Asiatic Registration Act in March 1907.
- **Formation of Passive Resistance Association** Owing to several reasons it was decided that Satyagraha struggle should not be carried on through any of the existing organisations. Thus a new body named **'Passive Resistance Association'** (later called Satyagraha Association once the term 'Satyagraha' was coined) was formed with the aim of uniting Indians to boycott the permit offices. The boycott proved to be a huge success and the Transvaal authorities failed to exhort Indians to get themselves registered. When the last date for registration was over, many passive resisters including Gandhi, were sent to jail. Many others offered to go to jail and the numbers swelled to 155.
- **Compromise** **General Smuts**, Secretary for colonies, proposed to meet Gandhi for talks and offered to withdraw the legislation if Indians voluntarily registered themselves. Gandhi accepted this proposition and called a meeting to discuss views on the agreement reached. Gandhi was, however, severely criticised by fellow Indians who expected no justice from General Smuts. The

next day, on his way to the registration office, Gandhi was even **attacked by a Pathan Mir Air Alam** for his alleged betrayal.

- **Resumption of Satyagraha** Soon the Indian fears proved true when Smuts backed out from his words and did not withdraw the legislation. Gandhi restarted the satyagraha agitation and exhorted Indians to burn their certificates and face the consequences. It was during this agitation that Gandhi decided to **give up his legal practice**. He felt that he could no longer practice law when he was himself defying it! Even as this agitation was going on, the Transvaal government enacted the Transvaal Immigrants Restriction Bill 1907 preventing new immigrants from India and the satyagraha movement was extended against this law as well. Several satyagrahis were imprisoned and even deported to India. When Satyagraha funds began to run out, Gandhi received a generous donation of ₹25,000 from Sir **Ratanji Jamshedji Tata** from England, just in the nick of time.
- **Setting up the Tolstoy Farm (May, 1910)** As the satyagrahis continued to court arrest with no end to the struggle visible in near future, the question of maintaining satyagrahis' families emerged supreme. Gandhi felt that if the families be kept at one place and live in a sort of cooperative commonwealth, public funds could be saved and the families too could be trained in simple community life and satyagraha agitation. Phoenix was inconvenient as it was three hundred miles from Johannesburg. At this juncture, **Hermann Kallenbach** (Gandhi's German architect friend) bought a farm of about 1,100 acres near Johannesburg and offered it to Satyagrahis free of any charge. Thus was founded the Tolstoy Farm to house the families of the satyagrahis. Financial support for this task was also provided by the **Nizam of Hyderabad**, the **Congress** and the **Muslim League**. This farm became a precursor of later Gandhian ashrams in India.

According to Gandhi, an ideal satyagrahi was to be truthful and perfectly peaceful, but at the same time, he would refuse to submit to what he considered wrong. During his insistence on truth, he would accept suffering willingly; but even while resisting evil, he would not hate the evil doer. Hatred would be alien to the nature of a true satyagrahi.

With their principles and conduct, the satyagrahis placed themselves on a high moral ground forcing a British army officer to once remark, 'I do not like your people (satyagrahis), and do not care to assist them at all. But what am I to do? You help us in our days of need. How can we lay hands upon you? I often wish you took to violence like the English strikers, and then we would know at once how to dispose of you. But you will not injure even the enemy. You desire victory by selfsuffering alone and never transgress your self-imposed limits of courtesy and chivalry. And that is what reduces us to sheer helplessness'.

- **Continuation of Satyagraha** During 1911–12, coinciding with the coronation of King George V, a brief agreement was reached between the government and the Indians. During this period, **Gopal Krishna Gokhale** visited South Africa (Oct–Nov 1912). He was treated as a state guest and was promised that all discriminatory laws against Indians will be removed. The promise, however, was not kept and the satyagrahis resumed their protest in 1913. This time, the satyagraha was widened and included protest against the following:
  1. Asiatic Registration Act
  2. Three pound poll tax
  3. Immigration Law
  4. A Supreme Court judgment invalidating all marriages except those celebrated according to Christian rites and registered by the Registrar of Marriages (known as the Searle judgment):

In 1913, this judgement came as yet another blow to Indians in South Africa. It implied that all Hindu, Muslim and Parsi marriages were illegal and the children born out of such marriages were illegitimate. The act was seen as particularly offensive to Indian women, who now joined the satyagraha movement in large numbers (including Kasturba, Gandhi's wife).

As the protest continued, the satyagrahis were imprisoned en masse. They were treated badly in jail and forced to undergo hard labour. They were starved and whipped and forced to work in mines. Even Gandhi was kept in a dark cell, he had to dig stones and sweep the compound.

- **Smuts-Gandhi Settlement (1914)** In India, GK Gokhale toured the country to garner support for Gandhi's movement and arouse public opinion against such atrocities inflicted upon peaceful satyagrahis. Gokhale also initiated the policy of sending out able men from India (for instance, CF Andrews was sent). Even Viceroy Hardinge condemned the repression and demanded an enquiry into the charges of atrocities levelled against the South African government. Subsequently a series of negotiations were held involving Gandhi, Hardinge, General Smuts and CF Andrews. A compromise was finally reached and the government of South Africa conceded to major Indian demands. General Smuts passed the **Indian Relief Act 1914** abolishing the three pound poll tax on freed labourers, marriages performed as per Indian rites were declared legal and the domicile certificate was now required only to enter the Union of South Africa.

  In this way, Gandhi's eight-year long satyagraha movement (1906–14) was finally called off.

Significance of Gandhi's Experiences in South Africa

Gandhi's experiences in South Africa had a deep impact on his life, thoughts, ethics and politics. It was in South Africa that Gandhi's abilities as an organiser, fund-raiser and journalist first came to the forefront. It was in South Africa that Gandhi evolved the blueprint of his methods that prepared him for the leadership of India's freedom struggle.

Gandhi was able to build faith in the capacity of the masses and their ability to sacrifice. It was in South Africa that Gandhi learnt to unite diverse sections of society-Hindus, Muslims, Christians, Parsis, Tamilians, Gujaratis, the poor labourers and the rich merchants, men and women in a struggle against a common oppressor. Gandhi learnt that leadership involved facing the anger of the enemy as well as the followers. When he reached a compromise, or withdrew a protest, there were instances when he faced the ire of his own people. Thus, South Africa was a huge learning experience for Gandhi where he evolved his skills as a leader and politician, tried new techniques and perfected them.

Though historian Judith Brown is of the view that satyagraha was merely a clever technique designed by Gandhi in South Africa, a wider look at Gandhi's struggle shows that Gandhi had developed an abiding faith in this method and it was not merely a convenient tool applied in a given situation.

Finally, Gandhi's struggle in South Africa made him something of an international celebrity. While leaders like Tilak, Lala Lajpat Rai and Bipin Chandra Pal mostly had a regional base, Gandhi emerged as a leader of the Indian people and not of any region or community, giving Gandhi a definite edge in Indian politics.

Charles Freer Andrews (1871–1940) He was a Christian priest who became a close friend of Gandhi and played a key role in convincing Gandhi to return to India from South Africa. He emerged as a Christian missionary and educator in India who identified with the cause of India's independence. For his contribution to India's freedom struggle, his students at St. Stephen's College Delhi and Gandhi named him **Deenbandhu** (friend of the poor).

Gandhi Arrives in India (9th January 1915)

Gandhi had begun to feel that his mission in South Africa was over and he should now return to India. At that time Gokhale was in London and he wanted that Gandhi should meet him first before he returned to India. Accordingly, in July 1914 Gandhi, Kasturbai and Kallenbach sailed for England. By the time they reached London (6th August 1914), First World War had been declared.

Gandhi's Part in the War On reaching London, Gandhi discovered that Gokhale was stranded in Paris, where he had gone for health reasons, and all communication between Paris and London had been cut off. Gandhi did not want to leave without meeting Gokhale. But what could Gandhi do in the meanwhile? English students were volunteering to serve in the army and Gandhi felt that the Indians should do no less. Thus a meeting of Indians was called and Gandhi expressed the view that Indians residing in England ought to help Britain in war effort and that England's difficulty should not be turned into India's opportunity. He insisted on rendering all possible help and organised an **Ambulance Corps** which, in spite of all difficulties, helped the British in their time of need (the British authorities later thanked Gandhi by honouring him with **Kaiser-e-Hind** Gold Medal in 1915). While in London, Gandhi met Sarojini Naidu for the first time. She was also involved in war effort through a ladies' club, the Lyceum, that had taken up the cause of manufacturing clothes for the soldiers. Soon Gandhi had an attack of pleurisy and due to its persistence, he decided to return home to India.

Little Satyagraha On 9th January 1915, Gandhi finally reached Bombay, returning to India after an exile of ten years, at the age of 46. The receptions organised at Bombay gave Gandhi the opportunity to offer what he called 'little satyagraha'. In addition to Gokhale's reception, one was also thrown by the Gujarati party where everyone spoke in English including Jinnah (who was also a Gujarati). However, Gandhi registered his protest by replying in Gujarati!

Gokhale, the political guru From Bombay, Gandhi went to Poona where Gokhale had arranged Gandhi's meeting with members of Servants of India Society. Though Gokhale eagerly wanted Gandhi to join the Society, he could not join on account of opposition by certain members owing to difference in Gandhi's methods of work and theirs. The moderate leader Gokhale was also Gandhi's **political guru** in India. He took from Gandhi a promise that he should travel the country for gaining experience and should not express any opinion on public question for the first one year. This was also in keeping with Gandhi's own style of never intervening in a situation without first studying it meticulously.

Advent of Satyagraha in India From Poona, Gandhi left for Rajkot to meet his relatives. On his way, he came to terms with the Viramgam customs line, a tariff cordon between the Kathiawar states and British India, and the hardships faced by railway passengers on account of it. The passengers were routinely harassed by the officials. Gandhi took up the cause and started preparing people to offer satyagraha. The CID informed the government regarding imminent satyagraha and a meeting was called between Lord Chelmsford and Gandhi after which the cordon was removed. Gandhi regarded this event as one that **marked the advent of Satyagraha in India**.

Visit to Shantineketan From Rajkot, Gandhi proceeded to Shantineketan where the Phoenix family, that had followed him from South Africa, was currently lodged. It had hardly been a week when Gandhi received a telegram concerning Gokhale's death. Immersed in grief, he left for Poona the same day and upon reaching, attended the shraddha ceremonies there.

Kumbha Mela Next, Gandhi left for Rangoon to meet a friend, Dr. PJ Mehta. This year, 1915, was the year of the Kumbha Mela, the fair which is held at Haridwar every 12 years. Gokhale's Society was volunteering there and Phoenix party was also invited to assist them. Thus, on his return, Gandhi joined the band at Haridwar, where masses flocked to him for his 'darshan'.

Founding the Ashram On 25th May 1915, with the objective of settling down in Gujarat with his Phoenix family, Gandhi set up his India ashram at Kochrab bungalow of barrister Jivanlal Desai in Ahmedabad and named it as **Satyagraha Ashram**. It was later shifted to a place on the banks of River Sabarmati and came to be known as the **Sabarmati Ashram** (June 1917). Gandhi chose to settle down in Ahmedabad on account of many reasons. Being a Gujarati himself, he felt that he was best fitted to serve the country by serving Gujarat. Ahmedabad, being an ancient center of handloom weaving, was also a favorable choice for revival of hand-spinning cottage industry. Being the capital of Gujarat, Gandhi also hoped that monetary help from wealthy citizens would be more readily available there. Gandhi lived in his ashram for nearly 12 years with his friends and followers, learning and practicing the ideas of truth and non-violence. The doors of the ashram were open to people from all sections of society, including the untouchables/harijans.

Abolition of Indentured Emigration (1917) Although the three pound tax in respect of indentured immigrants to Natal had been abolished in 1914, indentured emigration from India still needed treatment. In March 1916 Pandit Madan Mohan Malaviya moved a resolution in the Imperial Legislative Council for the abolition of the indenture system. Lord Hardinge responded by promising the abolition 'in due course' of time. However Gandhi felt that Indians had tolerated the system long enough and it ought to be abolished immediately. When in February 1917, Pandit Malaviya asked for leave to introduce a bill for the immediate abolition of the system, Lord Chelmsford refused permission. Gandhi now decided to tour the country for an all-India satyagraha agitation. In a meeting in Bombay, 31st July was decided as the latest date by which the abolition should be announced. Gandhi visited Karachi, Calcutta and various other places where he was continually followed by CID men. Feeling the pressure, the government soon announced the abolition of indentured emigration from India. Thus, an agitation that Gandhi had first launched in 1894 against this system of 'semi-slavery', ended successfully. After Viramgam customs issue, this was the second instance when success came merely through preparedness of satyagraha (Satyagraha was actually offered for the first time during Champaran struggle).

Gandhi maintained distance from the Home Rule Movement of 1916. When Annie Besant approached him to join her in starting a Home Rule League, he refused on the ground that he did not wish to embarrass the British government during their time of difficulty (First World War was going on). Similarly, though Gandhi attended the October 1916 Lucknow Session of the Congress, he took care not to associate himself with either the moderates or the extremists.

Gandhi's Entry into Indian Politics: Champaran, Ahmedabad and Kheda (1917–18)

Gandhi's first political agitations in India involved Champaran, Ahmedabad and Kheda struggles. All these were local-level agitations and gave Gandhi the reputation of a man who works at the grass root level. These agitations also successfully tested his techniques on Indian soil.

> Gandhi in his autobiograhy wrote, "I must confess that I did not then know even the name, much less the geographical position, of Champaran, and I had hardly any notion of indigo plantations. I had seen packets of indigo, but little dreamed that it was grown and manufactured in Champaran at great hardship to thousands of agriculturists."

Champaran Satyagraha (Bihar, 1917) Gandhi's first intervention was for the indigo farmers of Champaran, the ancient land of King Janak. Champaran in the Tirhut division of north Bihar had been seething with agrarian discontent for some time. In the beginning of the 19th century European planters had established indigo farms and factories in Champaran. Indigo was cultivated under the **Tinkathia** system, under which the Indian tenant cultivators were usually pressurised into contracts to cultivate indigo on 3/20th of their land holdings in return for an advance at the beginning of the cultivation season. The cultivators were then forced to sell their crop for a fixed and usually uneconomic price.

But now synthetic dyes began to be produced in Germany which were cheaper than indigo. The European planters in Champaran began to face losses and tried to transfer the burden of this loss to the tenants. They offered to release the tenants from growing indigo, if the latter paid some compensation. They also increased the rent and imposed illegal dues.

Rajkumar Shukla was one of the affected agriculturists who wanted the Congress and particularly Gandhi to help the indigo farmers of Champaran. He caught hold of Gandhi at Lucknow during the **Congress of 1916**. 'I can give no opinion without seeing the condition with my own eyes', replied Gandhi and urged that a resolution be moved in the Congress first. Advocate Brajkishore Prasad moved the resolution, expressing sympathy for the people of Champaran, and it was unanimously passed. Rajkumar Shukla was glad, but far from satisfied as he wanted Gandhi to personally visit Champaran and witness the miseries of the ryots there.

Champaran was located in the Himalayan foothills, cut off from the rest of India. The peasants were all ignorant, Congress and Gandhi were unknown to them and no political work had yet been done amongst them. When Gandhi reached Champaran, the Bihar government felt threatened and served him with a notice to leave on the pretext that he was 'a danger to public peace'. Gandhi decided to disobey the notice which constituted **Gandhi's first act of civil disobedience in India**. During his trial before the Magistrate, Gandhi had stated, "I have disregarded the order served upon me not for want of respect for lawful authority, but in obedience to the higher law of our being, the voice of conscience." Taken aback, the Magistrate postponed judgment and later Gandhi was allowed to conduct his inquiry.

Thus, Gandhi continued with his investigation along with his co-workers that included **Brajkishore Prasad, Rajendra Prasad, Gorakh Prasad, Mahadev Desai, Narhari Parekh, Mazhar-ul-Haq, and JB Kripalani**. Together they toured the villages and mobilised the peasants. Whilst on one hand, they carried out the work of recording statements of the ryots' grievances; on the other hand, they also carried out constructive work in the villages including primary education, medical relief and sanitation. Congress being the bête noire of the government, Gandhi decided that nothing should be done in the name of the Congress.

Finally, Lieutenant Governor Edward Gait felt compelled to appoint the **Champaran Agrarian Committee**, with **Frank Sly** as Chairman and Gandhi as one of its members, to enquire into the matter. Gandhi convinced the committee to recommend abolition of Tinkathia system as well as various illegal exactions. The committee also recommended that the planters should refund 25% of the exactions made by them which the Committee had found to be unlawful. All major recommendations of the committee were included in the Champaran Agrarian Bill which was thoroughly opposed by the powerful lobby of planters. But Sir Edwin Gait remained firm on fully carrying out the recommendations of the Committee and the **Champaran Agrarian Act of 1917** was finally passed. In this way, the tinkathia system which had been in existence for about a century was thus abolished, the planters' raj came to an end, the notion that the stain of indigo could never be washed out was exploded and Gandhi won his first battle of civil disobedience in India.

Though the chief supporters of Gandhi came from the educated middle class, the real massive support came from the Champaran peasantry who rallied behind him impressed by his unassuming conduct. Gandhi had walked on foot or bullock-cart and talked to them in a language they understood, with the effect that the psychological impact of Champaran struggle was greater than anything else. It was a stepping stone towards emergence of Gandhi as a leader of the downtrodden. With its success, it not only gave the peasants their initial taste of empowerment but also dented the notion of invincibility of the British rulers.

Rajendra Prasad (1884–1963) Born in Bihar, Babu Rajendra Prasad began his career as a teacher and in 1916 joined the High Court of Bihar and Orissa as a lawyer. Having joined the Congress in 1911, he met Gandhi for the first time during the 1916 Lucknow Session and emerged as an active leader of the 1917 **Champaran Satyagraha**. Greatly impressed by Gandhi's courage and conviction, he gave up his legal practice and joined the freedom movement full time (1920 onwards). In the Interim Government formed on 2nd September 1946, Prasad headed the **Food and Agriculture Department**. On 11th December 1946, he was elected as the President of the Constituent Assembly and on 26th January 1950 when Indian became a republic, he rose to become the **first elected President of Indian Republic** and was subsequently awarded the **Bharat Ratna**.

Rajendra Prasad

Ahmedabad Mill Strike (Gujarat, 1918) Even as Gandhi was winding up his work at Champaran, he received a letter from Mohanlal Pandya and Shankarlal Parikh informing him about the failure of crops in Kheda and asking him to guide the peasants who were unable to pay the asesssment. At the same time, he received another letter from **Anasuya Sarabhai** about the condition of labour in Ahmedabad. Wages were low and they had long been agitating for an increment. Even as Kheda peasants' question was still being discussed, Gandhi took up the question of mill-hands at Ahmedabad.

Thus Gandhi's second agitation was for Ahmedabad Mill workers and it was **not against the British**. It was an intervention in the internal dispute between the Gujarati mill owners and their workers. Gandhi was in a delicate situation. Anasuyabai was battling against her own brother and mill owner Ambalal Sarabhai who was leading the fray on behalf of mill-owners and had previously financially helped Gandhi's ashram. Gandhi had good relations with the brother-sister duo which made fighting the case all the more difficult.

Ahmedabad was fast emerging as a leading industrial town in Gujarat. However, the mill owners often faced scarcity of labour. The shortage of labour was further accentuated by the outbreak of plague in 1917, which drove many workers away from Ahmedabad (a plague epidemic had struck Ahmedabad in 1917–18, killing more than 20,000 people). To hold back the workers in Ahmedabad, the mill owners decided to pay 'Plague Bonus' which was sometimes as high as 75 per cent of the regular wages of the workers. The dispute started when the mill owners tried to end the 'plague bonus' once the epidemic had ended. The workers wanted the bonus to stay on the ground that it was helping them offset the war time rise in prices. The mill owners were ready to pay 25 per cent increase but the workers were demanding 50 per cent raise in wages in view war-time inflation.

Gandhi kept himself informed of the workers' conditions in Ahmedabad through the Gujarat Sabha as well as through Ambalal Sarabhai. Following a discussion with Sarabhai, Gandhi decided to intervene in the matter. Initially, both the mill-owners and the workers agreed for arbitration by a board chaired by the Collector; Gandhi was on the board representing the workers. But suddenly the mill owners withdrew stating that Gandhi had no real mandate from the workers and there was no guarantee that the workers would accept the arbitration award.

Following this episode, Gandhi took up a detailed study of the case. He went through a mass of data concerning the financial state of the mills and made a comparative study of workers' wages with the wages given in Bombay. He concluded that the workers can justly demand upto 35 per cent wage hike and no more. He advised the labourers to go on strike and not to resume work unless 35 per cent wage raise was conceded. Gandhi also urged the workers to follow the conditions of a successful strike i.e. 1) never to resort to violence 2) never to molest blacklegs (strike breakers) 3) never to depend upon alms, and 4) to remain firm, no matter how long the strike continued, and to earn bread, during the trike, by any other honest means. The labourers pledged themselves at a general meeting not to resume work until either their terms were accepted or the mill-owners agreed to refer the dispute to arbitration.

In this struggle, Gandhi was assisted by Anasuya Sarabhai, even as her brother Ambalal Sarabhai was one of the main adversaries. Gandhi organised daily mass meetings of workers under the shade of a tree on the banks of Sabarmati River and reminded them of their pledge. The tree later came to be known as 'Ek Tek' (keep the pledge) tree! After a few days, when workers began to show signs of fatigue, Gandhi decided to go on hunger strike from 15th March 1918 to encourage workers to continue with their struggle. This was the **first time, Gandhi used the weapon of hunger strike**. Gandhi's fast stirred high passions in Ahmedabad and the mill owners agreed to submit the whole issue to a tribunal.

Finally, the tribunal award went in favour of a 35 per cent wage raise for the workers, earning Gandhi tremendous popularity among the Ahmedabad workers.

Kheda Satyagraha (Gujarat, 1918) Hardly was the Ahmedabad mill-hands' strike over, that Gandhi had to plunge himself into the Kheda Satyagraha struggle. Thus, Gandhi organised his third agitation for the peasants of Kheda (called Kaira by the British) in Gujarat, a fertile region producing ample food grains, tobacco and cotton.

In 1917, Kheda faced large scale failure of kharif crops and emergence of famine like situation. This coincided with the war time rise in prices which further disturbed the shoe-string budget of the peasants. The Patidars (rich peasant proprietors) of Kheda began considering the question of getting the revenue assessment for the year suspended. The revenue code too stated that there should be a total remission of land revenue if crops were less than 25 per cent of normal production. Two Bombay barristers, VJ Patel and JK Parekh had already conducted an enquiry and concluded that a major portion of crop had been damaged and there was a case for remission. However, the government did not agree with this view and after an independent enquiry, the collector decided that there was no case for remission.

Gandhi, who was the president of the Gujarat Sabha then, maintained that crops had been significantly damaged and that the cultivators were entitled to revenue suspension as a legal right and not as any concession by grace. On 22nd March 1918, at a meeting at Nadiad, Gandhi decided to launch a satyagraha. He toured the villages and urged the peasants not to pay land revenue and to expel their fear of government authority. He tried to make them realise that the officials were not the masters but the servants of the people, in as much as they received their salaries from the tax-payer.

In this struggle, Gandhi was supported by Vallabhbhai Patel, Shankarlal Banker, Shrimati Anasuyabehn, Indulal Yajnik, Mahadev Desai and others. Vallabhbhai, in joining the struggle, had to suspend his splendid practice at the bar, which for all practical purposes he was never able to resume. The satyagrahis fixed up their headquarters at the Nadiad Anathashram. Bombay merchants sent liberal finances for the campaign to Gandhi. Within a month, the satyagraha reached its peak with more than 2000 peasants taking an oath for non-payment of revenue. Most of the Patidars also participated. Unlike Champaran, Kheda developments were reported in the press from day to day. Soon Kheda saw a good rabi crop which weakened the case for remission.

The satyagrahis had also begun to show signs of exhaustion. Moreover, the government had also issued an undertaking to the effect that if well-to-do Patidars paid up, the poorer ones would be granted suspension. In view of these developments, Gandhi decided to call off the agitation. However, Gandhi was far from satisfied with such as end. The poor hardly got any relief. It was the people's right to determine who was poor, but they could not exercise it. Gandhi also felt that neither Kheda nor Ahmedabad mill-hands had fully grasped the lesson of non-violence.

In Gandhi's words, "Kheda Satyagraha marks the beginning of an awakening among the peasants of Gujarat, the beginning of their true political education...Dr. Besant's brilliant Home Rule agitation had certainly touched the peasants, but it was the Kheda campaign that compelled the educated public workers to establish contact with the actual life of the peasants...through the Kheda campaign Satyagraha took firm root in the soil of Gujarat." True, the Kheda Satyagraha did not involve the entire Kheda region and only 70 out of 559 villages actually participated. True, it was called off after a mere token concession. Yet, it helped Gandhi in broadening his social base in rural Gujarat.

Sardar Vallabhbhai Patel (1875–1950) A young Gujarati lawyer during the Kheda satyagraha, Vallabhbhai rose to be the first Deputy Prime Minister and Home Minister of free India. Patel was ushered into Indian Freedom Movement following a meeting with Gandhi in October 1917. Henceforth, he emerged as an avid supporter of Gandhi and played a prominent role in Gujarat satyagrahas of Kheda and Bardoli. It was during the Bardoli Satyagraha that the women of Bardoli bestowed upon him the title of **'Sardar'** meaning chief or leader.

Vallabhbhai Jhaverbhai Patel

As Home Minister, he led the task of integrating into India nearly 565 princely states that had become independent following the lapse of British paramountcy in 1947, earning him the title of **'Iron Man of India'** or the 'Unifier of India'. His birthday, 31st October, is celebrated every year as **'Rashtriya Ekta Divas'** since 2014. Having played a key role in establishment of modern all-India services system, he is also remembered as **'Patron saint of India's civil servants'**.

Significance of Local Agitations These local agitations served as a demonstration of Gandhian politics and techniques. They helped Gandhi find his feet among Indians and study their problems first hand. During these agitations, Gandhi earned respect and commitment of an entire generation of political workers. They were especially impressed by his willingness to take up the cause of ordinary Indians. Gandhi was the first Indian nationalist leader who identified his life with the life of the common people. Finally, the success of these agitations gave Gandhi the confidence to later launch an all-India satyagraha against Rowlatt Act in February 1919.

According to **Judith Brown** (a historian and a biographer of Gandhi), the significance of these early agitations lay in the recruitment of 'sub-contractors' who would serve as Gandhi's lifelong lieutenants and included Rajendra Prasad, Anugraha Narayana Sinha and JB Kirpalani in Chamaparan; Vallabhbhai Patel, Mahadev Desai, Indulal Yajnik and Shankarlal Banker in Ahmedabad and Kheda. But this view is criticised as too simplistic as these agitations ultimately paved the way for Gandhi's emergence as an all-India leader.

Gandhi's Recruiting Campaign

Even as Kheda Satyagraha was going on, the Viceroy **Lord Chelmsford** invited various leaders including Gandhi to a war conference in Delhi (WW1 was still going on). Gandhi hesitated on account of several reasons, the principal one being the exclusion from it of leaders like Lokmanya Tilak, Annie Besant and the Ali Brothers (who were in jail then) whom Gandhi regarded as representatives of large masses of people. At the same time, Gandhi was seeking friendship of patriotic Muslims and he felt that the task would become much easier if he could secure the release of the Brothers, and a just settlement of the Khilafat question. He therefore went to Delhi and planned to submit the Muslim case to the Viceroy, despite much criticism from his friends and critics for his attitude towards the Khilafat question which had not then assumed the shape it did subsequently.

But on reaching Delhi, another difficulty arose when Dinabandhu Andrews questioned the morality of Gandhi's participation in the war conference. However, the Viceroy (with whom Gandhi shared cordial relations) made an emotional appeal 'if you believe that India has, on the whole, benefited by the British connection, would you not admit that it is the duty of every Indian citizen to help the Empire in the hour of its need?'. Gandhi finally decided to attend the conference out of his regard for the Viceroy, if nothing else.

The Viceroy was very keen on Gandhi supporting the resolution about recruiting. Gandhi spoke but one sentence to this effect in Hindustani: **'With a full sense of my responsibility I beg to support the resolution'.** That was the first instance within living memory of anyone having spoken in Hindustani at such a meeting. The Viceroy left for Simla immediately after the conference. Thus Gandhi dispatched his letter on Muslim demands to the Viceroy (the letter was simultaneously published). In a separate letter to the Viceroy, Gandhi clarified that in supporting Britain in its hour of need, India expects to be rewarded with Home Rule. Gandhi **declined any financial assistance** to Britain stating that India had already donated to the Empire beyond her capacity. He ended the letter by reiterating his faith in the British sense of justice and his love and loyalty towards the English nation.

After dispatching his letter, Gandhi left for Kheda and started his recruitment work, but he was in for a rude shock. 'You are a votary of Ahimsa, how can you ask us to take up arms?' 'What good has Government done for India to deserve our co-operation?' These and similar questions were raised and people hardly offered themselves as recruits. However, Gandhi persisted and argued that, 'If the middle classes render voluntary help to Government in the hour of its trial, distrust will disappear, and the ban on possessing arms will be withdrawn (i.e. Arms Act shall be repealed)'. Soon the war ended with the complete defeat of Germany, ending Gandhi's recruiting campaign.

Excerpt from Gandhi's letter to the Viceroy I would make India offer all her able-bodied sons as a sacrifice to the Empire at its critical moment... We must perceive that, if we serve to save the Empire, we have in that very act secured Home Rule'.

Rowlatt Satyagraha (1919)

During the period 1917–1918, Gandhi busied himself in local issues and did not take active interest in the Reform proposals. However, it was the government decision to pass the Rowlatt Bills which plunged him forcefully into national politics and it was to protest against the 'Rowlatt' Act that Gandhi launched an **all-India satyagraha for the first time**.

Rowlatt Act (the Anarchical and Revolutionary Crimes Act of 1919)

In 1917, the Government of India had appointed a committee under the chairmanship of **Justice Sydney Rowlatt** to investigate 'revolutionary crime' in the country and recommend measures to suppress it. The publication of this report coincided with the Montagu-Chelmsford Report.

The committee produced evidence of detailed subversive activities and proposed to strengthen anti-revolutionary law. On the basis of Rowlatt's recommendations, the government drafted two bills and presented them before the Imperial Legislative Council in 1919. The new bills provided for:

- Continuation of war time restrictions.
- Trial of offences by a special court comprising of three high court judges. The court could meet in camera and take into consideration evidence not permissible under Indian Evidence Act. Further, no appeal could be made against the decision of this court.
- Proposed authorisation of the government to search and arrest without warrant.
- Detention without trial for up to two years.

Indian Response

These proposals were considered by the nationalists as a grave insult and as an attempt to conciliate a section of white opinion that had been offended by the Montagu reform proposals.

Gandhi severely criticised the bills stating that the proposed powers were out of all proportion to the danger, especially when the Viceroy possessed emergency powers of legislation by ordinance. He condemned the bills as instruments of repression and distrust, nullifying the advance achieved by Montagu proposals. He also condemned the manner in which the bills were formulated, with complete disregard to public opinion. Gandhi now prepared to launch his struggle.

The Movement

Expecting no existing body to adopt the novel weapon of satyagraha, Gandhi formed a **Satyagraha Sabha** (on 24 February 1919, headquartered at Bombay) with himself as President to protest against the Rowlatt Bills. The members signed a pledge proclaiming their determination 'to refuse civilly to obey these laws and such other laws as a committee hitherto appointed may think fit and we further affirm that in this struggle, we will faithfully follow truth and refrain from violence to life, person or property'. While launching the satyagraha agitation, Gandhi declared, 'It is my firm belief that we shall obtain salvation only through suffering and not by reforms dropping on us by the English- they use brute force, we soul force'.

Gandhi began holding public meetings and contemplating on how to offer civil disobedience against the Rowlatt Bill if it was finally passed into law. At this juncture, Vijayaraghavachari had suggested to Gandhi to draw up a detailed manual on the science of Satyagraha.

Who opposed Gandhi's Rowlatt Satyagraha? A group of **Liberals** led by Surendranath Banerjee, DE Wacha, TB Sapru, Srinivas Sastri opposed the satyagraha on the ground that it would hamper the upcoming constitutional reforms. Some of them also felt unsure about the capacity of the ordinary citizens to follow the discipline of satyagraha. **Annie Besant** opposed the satyagraha on the ground that there was nothing in the Act to resist civilly. Tilak's main followers **NC Kelkar** and **GS Khaparde** also opposed the satyagraha.

Who supported Gandhi's Rowlatt Satyagraha? However, **the younger elements of Besant's Home Rule League** supported Gandhi and formed his main cadre in different parts of the country! These included Jamnadas Dwarkadas, Shankarlal Banker, Umar Sobhani and BG Horniman. Mahadev Desai, Rajagopalachari, Vijayaraghavachari and Kasturi Ranga Iyengar also supported Gandhi.

Simultaneously, the issue of Khilafat in Turkey had emerged. Ottoman Turkey was defeated in the First World War and Indian Muslims began to worry about the future of Khilafat in Turkey. As a result, Gandhi was also supported by certain Pan-Islamic leaders, particularly **Abdul Bari** of Firangi Mahal Ulema group at Lucknow (the religious preceptor of the Ali brothers who were still interned) and some radical members of the Muslim League such as **Dr. M.A. Ansari** (Jinnah had also condemned the Rowlatt Bills). Ansari hailed Gandhi as 'the intrepid leader of India, who has endeared himself as much to the Muslims as to the Hindus'.

Despite strong opposition all over the country, one of the Rowlatt Bills was rushed through the Council between 6th February and 18th March 1919. Gandhi attended the proceedings of India's legislative chamber **only once in his lifetime**, and that was on the occasion of the debate on this Bill. Lal Bahadur Shastri gave an impassioned speech and warned the government of adverse consequences. Even though all the non-official members had voted against the Bill, it was passed and became an Act after receiving Viceroy's assent on 21st March 1919.

Gandhi inaugurated his satyagraha by calling upon the countrymen to observe a day of 'hartal' by striking work and fasting and praying at home in protest against the Rowlatt Act. The date for the hartal was initially fixed for 30th March but later changed to 6th April. The success of the hartal varied considerably throughout the country. In Delhi, a hartal was observed on 30th March and witnessed remarkable Hindu-Muslim unity. Swami Shraddhanand was invited to deliver a speech in the Jumma Masjid, which he did. All this was more than the authorities could bear and a reign of repression was unleashed. The police opened fire at the hartal procession causing a number of casualties. In all other major towns, the hartal was observed on 6th April.

Gandhi described the hartal in Bombay as a magnificent success and intensified the agitation by starting civil disobedience. Only such laws were selected that could be easily disobeyed by the masses. Thus Gandhi urged people to prepare salt from sea water in their own houses in disregard of the salt laws. The volunteers also sold copies of prohibited literature and two of

Gandhi's proscribed books, **Hind Swaraj** (1909) and **Sarvodaya** (1908, Sarvodaya was Gujarati adaptation of Ruskin's Unto This Last), were used for the purpose.

On 7th April, Gandhi left Bombay to promote the agitation in Delhi and Punjab. He had been invited to Amritsar by Drs. Satyapal and Kitchlu whom he had never met earlier. However, the Punjab Lieutenant Governor **Michael O'Dwyer** apprehended a disturbance of peace if Gandhi entered the region. On 8th April and Gandhi was thus removed from train at Palwal near Delhi and taken back to Bombay. The news of Gandhi's arrest precipitated the situation and violence broke out at several places. Martial law was enforced in Ahmedabad. The Punjab region as a whole and Amritsar, in particular, witnessed the worst scenes of violence.

Punjab and Amritsar Punjab was already seething due to unpopularity of the Punjab administration under Lieutenant Governor Sir Michael O'Dwyer (1912–19). It witnessed forced war recruitments, war exactions, severe repression of the Ghadar outbreak (1915) and rise in food grain prices. The remarkable Hindu-Muslim-Sikh unity of early 1919 in Punjab also frightened the British. The hartals of 30th March and 6th April in Punjab were peaceful but massive.

On 9th April, on Ram Navami, two local Congress leaders of Amritsar—**Dr. Saifuddin Kitchlew** and **Dr. Satyapal** were arrested. These arrests coincided with Gandhi's arrest and precipitated the crisis, leading to widespread violence and arson. The town hall and the post office were attacked, telegraph wires were cut and five Europeans were killed. The army was called in and the city was handed over to **Brigadier-General Reginald Dyer** who issued an order prohibiting public meetings and assemblies.

Jallianwala Bagh Massacre

Jallianwala Bagh Tragedy (Amritsar, 13th April 1919) On 13th April, on **Baisakhi day**, a large crowd had assembled at Jallianwala Bagh to protest against the arrests. Most of them were not aware of the ban on meetings as they were visitors from neighbouring villages who were there to attend Baisakhi celebrations. Enraged on seeing the orders flouted, Brigadier General Reginald Dyer ordered his Gurkha troops to open fire on the peaceful unarmed crowd, without the slightest warning. The Bagh was enclosed on three sides and had only on exit. The troops fired at the trapped crowd until their ammunition was exhausted. At the end of the shooting, which had continued for 10 minutes, 379 were left dead as per official estimates. As per unofficial estimates, this number was nearly three times higher.

The entire nation was shaken by the brutality at Jallianwala Bagh. Yet, repression was intensified and Punjab was placed under martial law the same day (13th night). Acts of repression included indiscriminate arrests, torture, public flogging, aerial bombing, fancy punishments such as crawling on their bellies before Europeans, removal of fans from Indian houses and giving them for use by Europeans, etc.

On 18th April, Gandhi called off the satyagraha in view of the widespread violence and confessed it to be a **'Himalayan blunder'** or **'Himalayan Miscalculation'** to have called upon people to launch civil disobedience prematurely and to have allowed insufficiently trained people to offer satyagraha. Henceforth he decided to raise a corps of satyagrahi volunteers through the Satyagraha Sabha. On 30th May 1919 **Rabindranath Tagore renounced his knighthood** to register his protest against the Jallianwala Bagh massacre.

'The time has come when badges of honour make our shame glaring in their incongruous context of humiliation, and I for my part wish to stand shorn of all special distinction, by the side of my countrymen who, for their so-called insignificance, are liable to suffer degradation not fit for human beings'

-Rabindranath Tagore

Evaluation of Rowlatt Satyagraha

The Rowlatt Satyagraha was the first all-India satyagraha agitation called by Gandhi and it suffered from several weaknesses and organisational defects. The main focus of Satyagraha Sabha was mainly on publication of propaganda literature and collecting pledge signatures, the Congress was hardly in the picture and people participated mainly owing to their own socio-economic grievances against the British rule. The Congress played a very limited role as it lacked the machinery for agitational politics in most parts of India then. Gandhi himself called it a **'Himalayan Blunder'** to have asked people to join in this agitation even as they were not sufficiently trained for a non-violent struggle.

Despite very limited preparation, the April 1919 agitation turned out to be the biggest and the most violent upsurge India had seen since 1857. Rowlatt disturbances included sporadic attacks on government buildings, on telegraph lines and occasionally on the Whites. But the repression was far more violent, brutal and ruthless. The movement was more intense in cities than in rural areas.

However, the main significance of Rowlatt satyagraha lay in the forceful emergence of Gandhi on the national political scene. That the people rallied behind Gandhi was quite evident from the massive participation of people in Punjab, a region Gandhi had not even visited before the movement. From this point onwards, Gandhi emerged as the new Messiah of the Indian masses and dominated Indian politics down to 1947.

Saifuddin Kitchlew (1888–1963) He was a lawyer and a Muslim nationalist leader. He is most remembered for leading a protest in Punjab against the Rowlatt Act after which he along with Dr.Satyapal were arrested and secretly sent to Dharmashala. A public meeting organised in protest of these arrests led to the most unfortunate Jallianwala Bagh massacre (April 1919). Kitchlew was a founder member of the **Naujawan Bharat Sabha** (Indian Youth Congress) as well as **Jamia Milia Islamia**. He founded the Urdu daily **Tanzim** as well as the **Swaraj Ashram** (Amritsar, 1921). Kitchlew strongly opposed the demand for Pakistan, shifted to Delhi after his house was burnt down during the partition riots. Sometime after independence, he left the Congress party, moved closer to the Communist party of India was recipient of the Stalin Peace Prize in 1952.

Young India and Navajivan

Even as Gandhi was training his cadres in satyagraha, repression in Punjab continued. Martial law was proclaimed, leaders were arrested, innocent men and women were made to crawl like worms on their bellies. Gandhi had become desperate to bring justice to the people of Punjab.

Meanwhile, BG Horniman, the editor of The Bombay Chronicle (first started in 1910 by Pherozeshah Mehta), was suddenly deported by the authorities and the Chronicle was suspended. Gandhi's friends Umar Sobani and Shankarlal Banker who were directing the management of the Chronicle were also controlling Young India. They now urged Gandhi to take up the editorship of Young India. Gandhi too readily accepted the suggestion, seeing in it the dual opportunity of voicing his opinion on the Punjab wrongs and carrying out his training in satyagraha. But how could the masses be trained through an English language newspaper? Thus Sobani and Banker also placed the Guajarati monthly Navajivan at Gandhi's disposal. It was now converted into a weekly and Indulal Yajnik offered to work on it. Soon the journals started enjoying wide circulation that reached upto forty thousand each.

At a time when other political activity was not possible, these journals enabled Gandhi to freely ventilate his views.

Hunter Committee (or Disorders Enquiry Committee, October 1919)

In October 1919, the Government of India announced the formation of Hunter Committee (also known as Hunter Commission) to hold an inquiry in connection with the Punjab Government's doings under the martial law. The committee was named after its Chairman William Hunter, a member of the ICS.

Subsequently, Gandhi travelled to Punjab for the first time and reached Lahore. The Congress along with Gandhi decided to boycott the Hunter Committee and instead appointed a non-official Inquiry Committee, to hold almost a parallel inquiry on behalf of the Congress. Gandhi, Pandit Motilal Nehru, Deshabandhu CR Das, Abbas Tyabji and MR Jayakar were appointed to this Committee, virtually by Pandit Malaviya. The responsibility for organising the work of the Committee and drafting its report fell on Gandhi who now got an opportunity to observe at close quarters the people of the Punjab. The tales of Government's tyranny filled Gandhi with deep anguish particularly in view of the fact that the province had furnished the largest number of soldiers to the British Government.

Dyer was initially lauded for his actions in Britain but as the inquiry progressed and full extent of the massacre and Dyer's statements became widely known, the British press and several British officials turned increasingly hostile towards Dyer. The final report (released on 8 March 1920) unanimously condemned Dyer's actions.

All India Khilafat Conference, Delhi (November 1919)

Even as the Congress inquiry into Dyerism was in progress, Gandhi received an invitation to be present at a Hindu-Muslim joint conference at Delhi to deliberate on the **Khilafat question** and whether or not to boycott the post war peace celebrations. The invite went on to say that the conference would afford a golden opportunity for a settlement of the **cow question** as well. Gandhi felt that it would neither be appropriate on the part of the Hindus to ask for stoppage of cow slaughter as a price for their support on the Khilafat question. Nor would it be appropriate on the part of the Muslims to offer cow protection as a bargain. On Gandhi's appeal, therefore the question of cow protection was not discussed at this conference.

Maulana Hasrat Mohani called for a boycott of British goods as a vengeance against British Empire in case justice was denied in the matter of the Khilafat. However, Gandhi felt that something new, over and above boycott of foreign goods, would be necessary. For nearly every individual in that assembly was carrying some article of British manufacture on his person. Moreover, it was useless to talk about effective resistance to a government with which one was co-operating in more than one way. The only true resistance to the government, it therefore seemed to Gandhi, was to cease to cooperate with it. Thus Gandhi arrived at the word **'Non-Cooperation'** and it was here that Gandhi used the term for the first time. It was at this conference that Gandhi felt convinced that Hindi-Urdu alone could become the **lingua franca** of India.

Amritsar Congress (26 December 1919, presided by Motilal Nehru): Gandhi's Real Entry into Congress Politics

Upto this time, Gandhi's participation in the Congress had been confined to the advocacy of Hindi by making a speech in the national language and presenting the case of Indians overseas. However, Gandhi regarded his participation in Amritsar Congress as his **real entrance into the Congress politics**.

Under the martial law regime, the Punjab Government had clapped into jail hundreds of Punjabis and could keep them in confinement no longer. Many were released before the Congress opened (the Ali Brothers arrived straight from jail!) The King's announcement on the 1919 reforms had just been issued and Gandhi felt that the reforms, though not fully satisfactory, should be accepted rather than rejected. And he led an amendment to Congress resolution in this regard. Secondly, Gandhi also undertook the responsibility of **framing a new constitution for the Congress** (The exiting constitution comprising of a few rules had been framed by Gokhale and it was felt that these rules were no longer adequate to deal with the ever increasing size and business of the Congress. There was no limit set to the number of delegates that each province could return. There was hardly any machinery functioning during the interval between sessions). And with the assumption of this responsibility, it may be said, that Gandhi made his real initiation into the Congress.

Gandhi and his Ideology

Gandhi's ideology evolved out of several influences. In his autobiography, **The Story of My Experiments with Truth** (1927), he states that his parents and his family's socio-religious milieu left a deep impact on him, particularly the values of Vaishnavism and Jainism. Teachings of the Bhagwat Geeta and Jainism influenced his early thought. The writings of Tolstoy, Thoreau and Ruskin were significant influences in his later life. Finally, his own experiences played a key role in giving final shape to his ideology.

Mahatma Gandhi

The fundamental principles of Gandhian ideology were satya (truth), ahinsa (non-violence), asteya (non-stealing), aparigraha (non-possession) and brahmacharya (self-control). Gandhi advocated that the weapons of satya and ahimsa be used to gain freedom for India. From satya, he derived the technique of satyagraha (literally, persistence in truth) which sought to convert the adversary to one's own side. From the principle of ahinsa, he derived the technique of non-violent struggle. Gandhi maintained that non-violence is the law of our species as violence is the law of the brute.

The very nature of Gandhian thought was spiritualistic as Gandhi believed that the spiritual side is the permanent side of human nature. That by following the path of truth, love and non-violence, one will get true freedom i.e. spiritual freedom. Gandhi had remarked, 'the mundane affairs of life should be so governed, the material side of life should be so led, the bodily requirements should be so met that the man is enabled to secure the development of his spiritual side, and thus achieve the spiritual freedom which alone is his goal'.

'As the microcosm, so the macrocosm'- this idea prevailed throughout his thought and action. He believed in leading by example and insisted that principles should be practiced by oneself first, before one can motivate others to follow them.

As far as Gandhian method was concerned, it was highly empirical and pragmatic. A man of action, Gandhi believed in trial and error and learning by committing mistakes. US Mohan Rao states that, 'while Gandhi's belief in fundamental principles like truth and non-violence was unshakable, his application of these principles was governed by a continuous process of experimentation and developed by practice; and that his methods of conflict-resolution had no finality about them and could be improved by further experimentations'.

Gandhi has often been criticised for living in a world of ideas that had no relevance in the real world. Contrary to this, Gandhi preached only what he practiced. He developed his philosophy based on his own experiences in life and aptly named his autobiography 'The Story of My Experiments with Truth'. The chief aspects of Gandhian ideology may be discussed under the following heads.

Satyagraha

Satyagraha was the chief aspect of Gandhian ideology. Literally it means persistence of truth or 'true force'. Satyagraha was evolved by Gandhi in South Africa and later used as a dominant tool in India's freedom struggle from 1919 onwards. In satyagraha, the aim was to insist on truth and make the enemy see one's own point of view by 'self-suffering' and not by violence. This may be done variously by showing passive resistance or civil disobedience to authority, by non-cooperation with evil, by fasting, striking, marching, etc. As a result, a satyagrahi would not seek to vindicate the truth by violent means, rather he would wean the opponent from error by patience and sympathy.

For Gandhi, satyagraha was not merely a political tool but an integral part of his philosophy of life and action. Gandhi worshiped God as Truth only. This truth was not only truthfulness in word, but also in thought, and was not only the relative truth of our conception, but the Absolute Truth, the Eternal Principle, that is God. He believed that the search for truth was the goal of human life and that since no one could know the ultimate Truth, one should never attack another's integrity or prevent another's search for truth. While distinguishing between satyagraha and passive resistance, Gandhi had clarified that satyagraha excluded the use of violence in any shape, whereas passive resistance did not.

The superiority of satyagraha over violent means lies in the fact that it leaves no bitterness as its aftermath. Instead, it only leaves goodwill between the oppressor and the oppressed. Though the principle of returning good for evil is not new and has been practiced by many thinkers and preachers including Buddha and Christ, Gandhi's contribution lies in the fact that he brought satyagraha out from merely personal life to larger public life. He made satyagraha a tool for social, political and economic problems which was a truly original and novel contribution. The critics of Gandhi have also pointed out that Gandhi used satyagraha techniques to control the mass movements from above. Nonetheless, it was satyagraha that succeeded in bringing almost all sections of Indian society together, like never before, to join the freedom struggle.

- **P. Sitaramayya,** 'Satyagraha involves self-chosen suffering and humiliation for the resisters. It is effective, it is so by working on the conscience of those against whom it is being used, sapping their confidence in the exclusive rightness of their cause making their physical strength important, and weakening their resolution by insinuating a sense of guilt for the suffering they have part in causing'.
- **Stanley Jones,** 'the satyagrahi bears no ill-will or hatred against the evil-doer, he tries to overcome hatred and anger by love, evil by good, untruth by truth and hinsa by ahinsa. Possessing faith in the existence of the soul behind the physical exterior and striking directly at it, the satyagrahi thus values soul force as the most important component in his arsenal'.

Ahinsa

Non-violence formed the basis of satyagraha. According to Gandhi, 'when a person claims to be non-violent, he is expected not to be angry with one who has injured him. He will not wish him harm... He will put up with all the injury to which he is subjected by the wrong doer. Thus, non-violence is complete innocence. Complete non-violence is complete absence of ill will against all that lives'.

Further, Gandhi would say that 'non-violence is the law of human species as violence is the law of the brute. The history of mankind shows that man has been steadily progressing towards ahinsa. Had it been otherwise, the human species would have been extinct by now even as many lower species have disappeared'. He added, 'Non-violence is infinitely superior to violence, forgiveness is more manly than punishment. But abstinence is forgiveness only when there is the power to punish, it is meaningless when it pretends to proceed from a helpless creature'.

Gandhi also gave reasons why non-violence should be preferred over violence. First, the non-violent struggle is always conducted gracefully and with a minimum of bitterness; it does not lead to brutalisation of humanity as a violent war does. Second, the non-violent warrior is always prepared for negotiation and compromise. Third, non-violence renders useless the weapons of violent warfare which the enemy has and makes his position difficult. Fourth, the use of moral weapon of non-violence ennobles both the sides. Finally, in a non-violent struggle, the victory of the satyagrahi is certain as he fights on the side of God.

Gandhi also insisted that his was the non-violence of the brave and not the coward. However, sometimes he took a stand which fell short of complete non-violence. For instance, Gandhi is also quoted to have said that violence was preferable to cowardly surrender to injustice. That violence offered in self-defence or the defence of the defenceless is an act of bravery. Such statements often created delicate problems of interpretation. During the First World War, Gandhi also campaigned for military recruitments in the hope of gaining concessions from the British government after the war which again cannot be easily reconciled with the doctrine of non-violence.

Swaraj

Swaraj comes from 'swa-raj', meaning self-rule. In other words, it refers to popular sovereignty where people govern themselves. Gandhi believed in this concept of popular sovereignty and was of the view that as people get the government they deserve, self-government can come only through self-effort. He used to say, 'people are the roots, the state is the fruit. If the roots are sweet, the fruits are bound to be sweet'.

For Gandhi, Swaraj of his dreams was the poor man's Swaraj. A true democrat, he wanted to bridge the gap between the rich and the poor, the weak and the strong. He was of the view that basic amenities should be similarly available to all in society.

Hind Swaraj It comprised a body of ideas which Gandhi illustrated in his book 'Hind Swaraj' or 'Indian Home Rule' (1909). The book was banned in 1910 in British India as seditious literature. In this work, Gandhi pointed out that the real enemy was not the British rule but the modern western civilisation which was luring India into its stranglehold. He criticised the railways for contributing to plague and famine (by export of food grains). Though criticised as obscurantist, these ideas reflected the adverse effects of 'modernisation' on the masses in the countryside. Gandhi saw Swaraj or self-rule as a state of life which could only exist where Indians followed their traditional life uncorrupted by modern ways.

Later on, Gandhi's ideas of Hind Swaraj evolved to include his programme of village reconstruction, promotion of Khadi and Harijan welfare, bringing the need for socio-economic reconstruction to the very vortex of nation's attention.

Swadeshi

Gandhi also stood for Swadeshi, meaning the use of things made in ones' own country. This was particularly aimed at replacing the machine made foreign cloth with handmade cloth as a solution to poverty of peasants who could spin at home to supplement their income and as a solution to drain of wealth from India in payments for imported cloth.

It may be noted that despite Gandhi's opposition to western influences, he was not particularly opposed to the emerging modern industries in India. In fact, he had good relations with industrialists like Ambalal Sarabhai and GD Birla. He believed in the interdependence of capital and labour and advocated that the capitalists should consider themselves as **'trustees'** of the workers (Gandhi's trusteeship theory). He was not in favour of politicisation of workers along class lines and denounced militant economic struggles.

Sarvodaya

Literally, sarvodaya means the upliftment of all. According to Gandhi, it refers to the welfare of all secured by the conscious effort of everyone in the community. He stated that a believer of sarvodaya will strive for the greatest good for all and die in the attempt to achieve this ideal.

Views on Ideal State and Ideal Society-Ram Rajya & Sarvodaya Society Gandhi envisioned Ram Rajya as an ideal society. For him, it implied a system of 'cooperative commonwealth and statelessness'. He rejected the state because it is rooted in violence in so far as it is highly centralised system and such a system cannot be sustained without some measure of force and violence. He said, 'I look upon an increase in the power of the state with the greatest fear, because although while apparently doing good by minimising exploitation, it does the greatest harm to mankind by destroying individuality which lies at the root of all progress'.

Gandhi agreed with **Henry David Thoreau** (1817–62) that government is the best which governs the least. To Gandhi, the prime function of the state was the regulation of social behaviour. In an ideal society or Ram Raj, there would be no need for an external authority to regulate the behaviour of individuals. They would be self-disciplined and would never act against the interest of another member. Here it may be remembered that Gandhi's rejection of the state was on moral grounds and not on the communist ground that the state promotes capitalism.

Gandhi envisioned that an ideal stateless society would consist of villages that would function on the basis of voluntary cooperation. Every village would be a republic or panchayat with full powers. Such a society would represent perfect democracy. They would be organised into a loose federation on the basis of morality and not force. Being a practical idealist, Gandhi realised that an ideal stateless society was not viable due to human weaknesses, so the next best alternative had to suffice, that is, not a wholly non-violent society but a predominantly non-violent one.

Like Kant, Gandhi also felt that individual is the end, state is the means. But individual freedom cannot exist at the cost of similar freedom of others. Thus, an individual must enjoy his freedom within limits. He must exercise restraint on his freedom in order to allow others to enjoy their own freedom. Clearly for him, duties were more important than rights and inner development of individual was possible only through discharging of social obligation.

Thus, Gandhi idealised **stateless and classless** society of self-sufficient villages based on non-violence instead of force, on service instead of exploitation and renunciation instead of acquisitiveness. Gandhi named the ideal society as sarvodaya society—a stateless society where social life would become so perfect as to be self-regulated. Being a practical idealist, Gandhi also realised that Sarvodaya Society could not come into existence immediately, so practically it was best to continue with the existing model and continuously improve it with the noble ideas of sarvodaya.

Other Ideas of Gandhi

On Religion For Gandhi, religion was the struggle for truth. According to him, religion could not be confined to the realm of private opinion alone but must influence and **permeate all activities** of men. A devout Hindu himself, Gandhi's religious outlook was not narrow but universalist. He wanted Indians to be deeply rooted in their own culture but at the same time acquire the good things from other cultures.

He would say, 'I want the culture of all lands to be blown about my house as freely as possible. But I refuse to be blown off my feet by any'.

On Decentralisation Gandhi idealised the end of centralisation since it was incompatible with individual freedom. Also, it could not be sustained without force. So, for a predominantly non-violent society, there must be decentralisation. The villages should have the largest measure of autonomy in managing their affairs. Every individual should be able to participate in the governance process.

On Economic Decentralisation It refers to replacing centralised large-scale industries with cottage industries. Gandhi felt that modern centralised industrialisation has led to division of society into haves and have-nots, and makes people insensitive to sufferings of others. It has led to the rise of colonialism and the mad rush for accumulation of more and more wealth. So, man's pursuit for higher values is possible only in a system of cottage industries in which workers own the means of production. In brief, introducing cottage industries was the best method to end exploitation of man by man and infuse principle of satya and ahinsa in the economic field.

On Varna System and Non-possession Gandhi took a **favourable view of the varna system**. To him, it implied equality of all professions as well as equal earning of all professions. He felt that every person should follow his hereditary profession as a duty to society and not as a way of amassing wealth. This would end unworthy competition and remove distinction of high and low. This would also enable the person to improve his skills and increase the income of society.

Gandhi, like Buddha believed that miseries of life were due to multiplication of wants and hence recommended reduction of wants. Non-possession or aparigraha is an ancient principle for leading a contented life and attaining liberation. Gandhi's originality lies in extending its meaning and application.

On Democracy Gandhi defined democracy as, 'the art and science of mobilising the entire physical, economic and spiritual resources of all the various sections of the people in the service of the common good of all'. Thus, democracy was not just a political value for Gandhi, it was also a social and economic value. For him, it was not just about representative democracy, majority rule or greatest good of the greatest number. Instead, he idealised true individual democracy and greatest good of all. In his view, certain conditions were necessary for the success of democracy, such as-discipline, obedience to laws, selflessness, tolerance, citizen empowerment and alert citizen opinion or participation.

On Education Gandhi defined education as an all-round development of an individual's **body, mind** and **spirit**. By development of spirit, he meant teaching the heart to feel. At the same time, he stressed that the main aim of education should be employability. He was of the view that education which does not equip a person with the skills to earn, is a sheer waste. Gandhi also supported state funding of education. The state should provide free and compulsory primary education and should educate all those whose services it needs.

The Wardha Scheme: The Wardha Scheme was a scheme of indigenous education **proposed by Gandhi** in 1937 and published in the Harijan. It was a scheme for **Basic Education**. The main principle of the scheme was 'learning by activity'. It was a seven-year course to be taught in the pupils' mother tongue. The details of Wardha Scheme were further worked out by Zakir Hussain Committee but the scheme had to be postponed due to the resignation of Congress Ministries in 1939. He rejected colonial education and felt that it blocked channels of creative energy and destroyed 'cultural common sense' in India.

On Status of Women Gandhi severely criticised all forms of discrimination against women. He rejected views of Manu that 'for woman there can be no freedom'. He stood for **perfect equality** between men and women. He would say that a woman is a companion of man, equal in all aspects. A woman has an equal right to life and liberty as a man. He rejected the notion of women as 'weaker sex'. He declared that, 'to call women the weaker sex is a libel. If by strength is meant brute strength, then indeed a woman is less brute than a man. If by strength is meant moral power, then woman is immeasurably man's superior'.

He also severely criticised all sorts of social disabilities imposed on women such as child marriage, dowry, purdah, enforced widowhood and devdasi system (temple prostitution). He advocated full protection of women in social, political and economic spheres. He demanded equal pay for equal work for both men and women. Time and again, he urged women to join the Indian National Movement. In fact, he felt that women were better suited for a non-violent struggle and the satyagraha protest. As a result of Gandhi's efforts, the period witnessed a massive participation of women in India's freedom struggle and became the single most significant factor in changing the role and status of women in Indian society. Some important women leaders who emerged during this time were-Kasturba Gandhi, Kamala Nehru, Sarojini Naidu, Kamla Devi Chattopadhaya and Raj Kumari Amrit Kaur.

On Untouchability Gandhi denounced untouchability as 'crime against humanity'. 'None can be born untouchable as all are sparks of one and the same divine fire'. He therefore named the untouchables as the Harijans, i.e. the people of God. He felt that untouchability is a disease that has struck Hinduism through the ages. If untouchability lived, Hinduism and India would die. Gandhi's efforts against untouchability, along with that of others, ultimately resulted in abolition of untouchability in Indian Constitution under Article 17.

To sum up, Gandhian ideology have been a subject of much debate and controversy, particularly with regard to its relevance in today's world, and has evoked different reactions from different people. All the same, his ideas deeply influenced the course of our freedom struggle and laid down its major thrust and direction.

Special Note– Mass Mobilisation under Gandhi

The entry of Mohandas Karamchand Gandhi into the freedom struggle of India proved to be a turning point. The national movement acquired a distinct ideological orientation under his leadership. In a short span of time, he became the undisputed leader of the Congress as well as the masses. Under Gandhi's leadership, the Indian National Movement became a movement of the masses for the first time. This was because Gandhi had a huge mass appeal. His life, personality and ideology influenced almost all sections of Indian society.

Gandhi was of the view that freedom for India could come only with the active participation of the masses. He based the freedom struggle on the basic premise that the masses are the subjects and not objects of politics. Hence, Gandhi tried to bridge the gap between the leaders and the led. He chose the middle path between the Moderates and the Extremists and was able to strike the right balance between organisation and spontaneity. He was responsible for making the Congress Party more democratic and brought it closer to the masses. This attitude of Gandhi also fostered healthy and democratic relations among leaders themselves. Finally, the bedrock of his politics was his immense faith in the capacity of the masses, their courage and moral strength.

Gandhi's Methods of Mass Mobilisation The Gandhian methods proved quite effective as methods of mass mobilisation. He first experimented with them in South Africa and later applied them successfully to India's freedom struggle. He incorporated the following methods of mass mobilisation:

1. **Careful training of disciplined cadres** Gandhi undertook careful training of his cadres at Sabarmati Ashram.
2. **Use of Satyagraha** It involved peaceful violation of unjust laws, passive resistance or civil disobedience, peaceful marches, courting arrest, etc.
3. **Social reform or constructive program** Gandhi stressed on social reform to strengthen the Indian society. He would point to five fingers of his hand and ask people to observe five virtues—spinning, ending untouchability, non-consumption of alcohol, Hindu–Muslim amity and gender equality.

Through these methods, Gandhi transformed the Congress Movement into a mass movement.

According to Sumit Sarkar, Gandhi's methods included a combination of quixotic ways with meticulous planning, negotiation skills, willingness to compromise and cultivation of Gandhian 'Fads' (vegetarianism, nature cure, sexual restraint, etc.). Through this, he was able to involve the masses during movements and at the same time keep their energies directed towards predetermined, peaceful ways in other times.

What made Gandhi a Mass Leader? A combination of factors contributed to the rise of Gandhi as a mass leader and may be discussed as under:

1. **Role of 'rumour'** According to Sumit Sarkar, rumour played its role in the backdrop of largely illiterate, poor and miserable society. Gandhi came to be known as a Mahatma, a holy man, a sage with miracle powers. A CID report on the kisan movement in Allahabad in 1921 states that, 'The currency which Mr. Gandhi's name has acquired even in the remotest villages is astonishing. No one seems to know who or what he is, but it is an accepted fact that what he says is so, and what he orders must be done'. In this way, peasants could imagine that Gandhi could end zamindari exploitation and labourers could imagine that he could provide land holdings to them.
2. **Historical necessity for a 'saviour from above'** Scholars argue that popular perceptions about Gandhi were also shaped by a historical necessity. That the masses needed to be represented by a saviour from above and Gandhi filled this need. In the 1920s, many local leaders emerged but they needed a national level guiding force. This is explained by what happened at Pratapgarh—Baba Ramchandra gave leadership to the masses at the local level and got bedakhali (forced eviction) stopped. Gandhi or the Congress leadership had little to do with it directly. Yet, he attributed his success to Gandhi.
3. **Gandhi's political strategy** Bipan Chandra attributes Gandhi's popularity to his political strategy. He writes that Gandhi was a political leader and it was through his political practice that he was able to move the masses into political action. Further, he writes that Gandhi's political strategy was guided by a deep understanding of the nature of British rule and the nature of Indian masses. He realised that the British had consciously nurtured political passivity in the masses for a stable colonial rule. So, Gandhi aimed to win the hearts and minds of the masses and instil in them a national consciousness. He declared: 'people can have Swaraj for the asking when they have attained the power to take it'. He aimed to bring the masses from remote corners of India onto the vortex of national politics.

   The British had also nurtured twin notions of 'benevolence' and 'invincibility' of the British rule. Gandhi attacked both these notions. He attacked 'benevolence' by exposing the exploitative nature of the colonial rule. He attacked 'invincibility' by introducing law-breaking mass movements. In this way, Gandhi's political strategy contributed to his popularity, according to Chandra.
4. **Long drawn nature of Gandhian struggle** Bipan Chandra adds that the long-drawn nature of Gandhi's struggle also contributed to his popularity. During the 'passive phases', he carried out intense ideological work. This involved training the masses for nationalist struggle, inculcating national consciousness and capacity building of the masses in general. As a result, he was able to produce thousands of full-time workers who devoted their entire lives to the freedom struggle.
5. **Gandhi's Constructive Programme** Gandhi's constructive program was built around spinning and khadi, village industries, boycott of foreign goods and liquor. It was also centred on social reform such as upliftment of the poor, women and Harijans, Hindu–Muslim unity, etc. This constructive program helped in sustaining his mass movements in many ways. During the passive phase of a movement, constructive work helped in diverting the energies of the masses into productive work. It also gave them a sense of continued activism. Further, the constructive program of Gandhi could involve the masses as opposed to parliamentary efforts which could be carried out by only a few.

6. **Role of Ahinsa and participation of Women** Gandhi's struggle was essentially a non-violent struggle. He had adopted ahinsa as a matter of principle. This was another reason for his popularity as the masses could join a non-violent struggle while the same was not possible for a violent-armed struggle. This was particularly true in the case of women.

Previous Years' Questions – Preliminary Exam

1. Where did Mahatma Gandhi start his Civil Disobedience Movement from in 1930? **[UPSC 1995]**
   (a) Sevagram (b) Dandi
   (c) Sabarmati (d) Wardha
2. What was The Anarchical and Revolutionary Crime Act 1919 popular known as? **[UPSC 1996]**
   (a) Rowlatt Act (b) Pitt's India Act
   (c) Indian Arms Act (d) Ilbert Bill
3. What was the first venture by Gandhi in all India politics? **[UPSC 1999]**
   (a) Non-Cooperation Movement
   (b) Rowlatt Satyagraha
   (c) Champaran Movement
   (d) Dandi March
4. Where did Gandhiji launch his first successful Satyagraha after returning from South Africa? **[UPSC 2000]**
   (a) Chauri Chaura (b) Dandi
   (c) Champaran (d) Bardoli
5. What was the name of the famous person of India who returned the Knighthood conferred on him by the British government as a token of protest against atrocities in Punjab in 1919? **[UPSC 2004]**
   (a) Tej Bahadur Sapru
   (b) Ashutosh Mukherjee
   (c) Rabindranath Tagore
   (d) Syed Ahmed Khan
6. Which of the following pairs are correctly matched? **[UPSC 2005]**

	Movement/ Satyagraha	Person actively associated with
1.	Champaran	Rajendra Prasad
2.	Ahmedabad mill workers	Morarji Desai
3.	Kheda	Vallabhbhai Patel

   Choose the correct answer from the following options.
   (a) 1 and 2 (b) 2 and 3
   (c) 1 and 3 (d) 1, 2 and 3
7. Which one of the following aroused a wave of popular indignation that led to the massacre by the British at Jallianwala Bagh? **[UPSC 2007]**
   (a) The Arms Act
   (b) The Public Safety Act
   (c) The Rowlatt Act
   (d) The Vernacular Press Act
8. At which one of the following places did Mahatma Gandhi first start his Satyagraha in India? **[UPSC 2007]**
   (a) Ahmedabad (b) Bardoli
   (c) Champaran (d) Kheda
9. Who among the following Gandhian followers was a teacher by profession? **[UPSC 2008]**
   (a) A N Sinha
   (b) Braj Kishore Prasad
   (c) J.B. Kriplani
   (d) Rajendra Prasad
10. Who was the Viceroy of India when the Rowlatt Act was passed? **[UPSC 2008]**
   (a) Lord Irwin
   (b) Lord Reading
   (c) Lord Chelmsford
   (d) Lord Wavell
11. During the Indian freedom struggle, why did Rowlatt Act arouse popular indignation? **[UPSC 2009]**
   (a) It curtailed the freedom of religion.
   (b) It suppressed the Indian traditional education.
   (c) It authorised the government to imprison people without trial.
   (d) It curbed the trade union activities.

12. Who among the following founded the Ahmedabad Textile Labour Association? **[UPSC 2009]**
    (a) Mahatma Gandhi
    (b) Sardar Vallabhbhai Patel
    (c) N.M. Joshi
    (d) J.B. Kriplani
13. Consider the following statements: **[UPSC 2010]**
    1. Dr Rajendra Prasad persuaded Mahatma Gandhi to come to Champaran to investigate the problem of peasants.
    2. Acharya J.B. Kriplani was one of Mahatma Gandhi's colleagues in his Champaran investigation.

    Which of the statements given above is/are correct?

    Choose the correct answer from the following options.

    (a) 1 only (b) 2 only
    (c) Both 1 and 2 (d) Neither 1 nor 2
14. Mahatma Gandhi said that some of his deepest convictions were reflected in a book titled, 'Unto the Last' and the book transformed his life. What was the message from the book that transformed Mahatma Gandhi? **[UPSC 2011]**
    (a) Uplifting the oppressed and poor is the moral responsibility of an educated man.
    (b) The good of individual is contained in the good of all.
    (c) The life of celibacy and spiritual pursuit are essential for a noble life.
    (d) All the statements (a), (b) and (c) are correct in this context.
15. What was the reason for Mahatma Gandhi to organise a Satyagraha on behalf of the peasants of Kheda? **[UPSC 2011]**
    1. The administration did not suspend the land revenue collection in spite of a drought.
    2. The administration proposed to introduce Permanent Settlement in Gujarat.

    Which of the statements given above is/are correct?

    (a) 1 only (b) 2 only
    (c) Both 1 and 2 (d) Neither 1 nor 2
16. What was the aim of the Rowlatt Act? **[UPSC 2012]**
    (a) Compulsory economic support to war efforts
    (b) Imprisonment without trial and summary procedures for trial
    (c) Suppression of the Khilafat movement
    (d) Imposition of restrictions on freedom of the press
17. With reference to Rowlatt Satyagraha, which of the following statements is/are correct? **[UPSC 2015]**
    1. The Rowlatt Act was based on the recommendations of the Sedition Committee.
    2. In Rowlatt Satyagraha, Gandhiji tried to utilise the Home Rule League
    3. Demonstrations against the arrival of Simon Commission coincided with Rowlatt Satyagraha.

    Choose the correct answer from the following options.

    (a) 1 only
    (b) 1 and 2
    (c) 2 and 3
    (d) 1, 2 and 3
18. Which one of the following is a very significant aspect of the Champaran Satyagraha? **[UPSC 2018]**
    (a) Active all-India participation of lawyers, students and women in the National Movement
    (b) Active involvement of Dalit and Tribal communities of India in the National Movement
    (c) Joining of peasant unrest to India's National Movement
    (d) Drastic decrease in the cultivation of plantation crops and commercial crops
19. Indigo cultivation in India declined by the beginning of the 20th century because of **[UPSC 2020]**
    (a) Peasant resistance to the oppressive conduct of planters
    (b) Its unprofitability in the world market because of new inventions

(c) National leaders' opposition to the cultivation of indigo
(d) Government control over the planters

20. One common agreement between Gandhism and Marxism is **[UPSC 2020]**
(a) The final goal of a stateless society
(b) Class struggle
(c) Abolition of private property
(d) Economic determinism

Previous Years' Questions – Main Exam

1. Point out clearly the contributions of Mahatma Gandhi and Rabindranath Tagore to the social and cultural life of India. **[UPSC 1984]**
2. 'Mahatma Gandhi's succession during 1916-20, in getting the technique of non violent Satyagraha accepted by the nation as a weapon of struggle against the British was phenomenal'. Elucidate. **[UPSC 1993]**
3. Trace the emergence of Gandhiji in Indian political scene till the Champaran Satyagraha of 1917. What was the basic philosophy of Satyagraha enunciated by him? **[UPSC 1994]**
4. Discuss Mahatma Gandhi's concept of 'Basic Education'. How far is it a departure from conventional system of education? **[UPSC 1997]**
5. What do you know about Rowlatt Act? **[UPSC 1997]**
6. Write a short note on Satyagraha. **[UPSC 2002]**
7. 'The mainstay of Mahatma Gandhi's movements was the rural India'. Elucidate. **[UPSC 2003]**
8. Mahatma Gandhi and Dr BR Ambedkar, despite having divergent approaches and strategies, had a common goal of amelioration of the downtrodden. Elucidate. **[UPSC 2015]**
9. How different would have been the achievement of Indian Independence without Mahatma Gandhi? Discuss. **[UPSC 2015]**
10. Discuss the role of women in the freedom struggle especially during the Gandhian phase. **[UPSC 2016]**
11. Highlight the differences in the approach of Subhash Chandra Bose and Mahatma Gandhi in the struggle for freedom. **[UPSC 2016]**
12. Throw light on the significance of the thoughts of Mahatma Gandhi in the present times. **[UPSC 2018]**

Answers

Previous Years' Questions – Preliminary Exam

1.	(b)	2.	(a)	3.	(b)	4.	(c)	5.	(c)
6.	(c)	7.	(c)	8.	(c)	9.	(c)	10.	(c)
11.	(c)	12.	(a)	13.	(b)	14.	(d)	15.	(a)
16.	(b)	17.	(b)	18.	(c)	19.	(b)	20.	(a)

8 CONSTITUTIONAL DEVELOPMENT-PART 2 (1861–1920)

This chapter introduces you to the main stages in the development of legislative bodies in India during the period 1892 and 1919. These are also termed as Constitutional Reforms or Council reforms and were brought about by various Acts of the British Parliament. The chapter also deals with the factors responsible for these council reforms, main provisions of the Acts and their impact in India. We will also analyse their weaknesses and achievements and understand the link between the growth of legislative bodies in India and the freedom struggle.

Flash Back:

Under the Charter Act of 1833, the Executive Council of the Governor-General (GG) was enlarged by adding a fourth member, known as the Law Member, to it. He was expected to give professional advice on law making and therefore could sit and vote in the GG's Council only when it met for legislative purposes. Thus, for the first time, a separation was introduced between **the executive and legislative functions** of the Central Government. Another change introduced by this Act was that of legislative centralisation, owing to which the Presidency Governments lost their rights to make their own laws.

Under the Charter Act of 1853, The separation of executive and legislative functions was carried a step further as **six 'Additional Members'** of the Council were appointed for legislative work- Law member was given full rank as a Member of the GG's Council, the Chief Justice of Supreme Court of Calcutta was to be the ex-officio member of the Council, one representative from each province (Calcutta, Bombay, Madras and the North-Western province, i.e., western half of undivided UP) and two more civilians could be nominated by the GG, but this authority was never exercised. In this way, the central legislature was completed, though no Indian element was associated with the Legislative Council. A clear distinction was made between Legislative Councillors and Executive Councillors. In this way, legislation was for the first time treated as a special function of the government.

Under the Government of Indian Act of 1858, the English East India Company was liquidated. The Act did not change anything in India, and only brought about some cosmetic changes in England. Ever since the Act of 1784, the Crown had exercised considerable influence over India affairs through the Board of Control. Now it was to do this directly. Further, no new policy was inaugurated by the Act.

Indian Councils Act of 1861

Factors Leading to the Act

- Act of 1833 had introduced centralisation of legislation and the central legislature was empowered to make laws for all the territories. Bombay and Madras having lost their right to make their own laws. Such centralisation of law-making power was resented by the provincial governments. The central legislature was also ill-fitted for the job as first, it was ignorant of the local conditions and second, it neither had the time nor the will to establish legislative standards applicable for the whole of the country.

- Act of 1853 had set up a Legislative Council which had grown into a sort of a debating society or a petty Parliament. With the passage of time, it adopted all the formalities of parliamentary procedure and laid down an elaborate procedure for transaction of business, such as three readings and references to committees which all caused great delay. Further, in an attempt to act as independent legislature, it sometimes even stopped supplies, much to the embarrassment of the Home Government.
- Act of 1858 had brought about changes only in the Home Government and did not touch the administration set-up in India. After the Revolt of 1857, it was felt that sweeping changes in the constitution were called for. It was also felt that there was a lack of contact and understanding between the government and the governed. The government now understood the dangers of excluding the Indians from the legislation of the country. The question of giving representation to Indians in the legislative councils was mooted even in 1858, but was put off for fear that the reform may be ascribed to the fear the rebellion had produced.

To address the above issues, further changes were made in the next Act in 1861.

Sir Bartle Frere, Governor of Bombay had remarked, 'Unless you have some barometer or **safety valve** in the shape of a deliberative council, I believe you will always be liable to very unlooked for and dangerous explosions'.

Main Provisions of the Act of 1861

The Regulating Act had begun the process of centralisation, culminating in the Act of 1833 which took away legislative powers from the provinces. The Indian Councils Act of 1861 started an opposite process-a process of **decentralisation**. Lord Canning (the then GG) and **Sir Charles Wood** (Secretary of State) were responsible for the passing of the Act of 1861.

Note: Main provisions of the Act are discussed below. These provisions introduced changes in the size, composition and functions of the Central Legislature. The figures denoting the size do not include the Governor-General and the Commander-in chief who were ex-officio members.

Change in Size and Composition of Central Legislature

- The Executive Council of the GG was enlarged by the addition of a **fifth member** who was to be a jurist. The Secretary of State retained the power to appoint the Commander in Chief as an extraordinary member. A Governor could also be co-opted as a member if the Council meeting was held in a province.
- For the purpose of legislation, it enlarged the Central Council by addition of **not less than six and not more than twelve** additional members. These were to be nominated by the GG for a period of two years and it was provided that at least half of them were to be non-officials (i.e. persons not in the civil or military service of the Crown). Under this provision, three Indians were usually nominated, though no statutory provision was made for the admission of Indians. In this way, in the absence of representative bodies, the Executive Council of the GG was enlarged by addition of these non-officials. Further, the function of the Council for legislative purposes was confined

strictly to legislation only. It was an answer to the attempt made by the Legislature created under the Act of 1853 to transform itself into and sort of a debating society.

In those days, it was not easy to find qualified Indians familiar with Western methods of governance. The kind of non-officials the Act had in view were probably the Indian rajas or diwans or big zamindars or even retired officials of high rank. For the first 20 years, this power to nominate non-officials was used to expand official patronage. Even among the princes, only those who had helped the British during 1857 were nominated. Yet, it was a subtle acceptance of the fact that **Indian opinion** was worth listening to and that the British were not the best judge of Indian wishes. No one could have imagined then that this very same body, in the course of time, would evolve into a strong representative body of the Indian people.

Changes in Functions of Central Legislature

- The Act **restored the legislative powers of Councils of Bombay and Madras**. However, rigid restrictions were placed on legislative powers of these provinces and no laws passed by the provincial councils were to be valid until they received the assent of the GG. In certain matters such as Defence and Communication, prior approval of the GG was needed.
- The Act allowed establishment of **new Councils** in other Provinces. Accordingly, Councils of Bengal (1862), North-Western Provinces (1886) and Burma and Punjab (1897) were established.
- The GG was empowered to issue **ordinances** in case of emergency and without the concurrence of the Legislative Council, which could remain in force for a maximum period of six months.
- The Act also empowered the GG to create new provinces for legislative purposes and appoint Lieutenant Governors for them. It also empowered him to make territorial adjustment between different provinces.
- **Provision regarding decentralisation of business** The Act empowered the GG to make rules for more convenient transaction of business in the Council. Using this authority, Lord Canning introduced the **portfolio system** in India for the first time. Prior to this, the Government of India was considered a government by the entire body of the Executive Council; and so, all business and matters had to be brought before the Council. This was quite cumbersome and caused unnecessary delays. Canning now divided the various departments among the Council members, thus laying the **foundation of Cabinet System** in India. Now routine matters of administration were discharged by the member-in-charge and more important ones were decided in consultation with the GG. Only matters of general policy were placed before the Council as a whole.

Significance of the Act of 1861

From the constitutional perspective, the Act was important on account of the following reasons:

- It introduced the process of legislative devolution which gradually gave more and more legislative functions to the provinces and culminated in the grant of autonomy to provinces by the Act 1935.
- It initiated a process of Indian association in legislation.
- It initiated recognition of local needs and local knowledge by means of local councils.
- The local councils also ensured publicity and discussion throughout the law-making process.

However, it is noteworthy that no attempt was made to demarcate the legislative powers of Central and Local Legislatures and the GG could legislate for the whole of India. The local councils created were mere committees for assisting and advising in legislative work. Charles Wood, the author of the Act, had clarified that the proposed local councils were to function more like the Darbar of an Indian ruler, where the nobles could express their opinion, but the ruler was not bound by their advice.

Indian Councils Act of 1892

The Act of 1892 was merely an amending Act and its main objective as explained by Curzon (the then Under-Secretary of State) was to further expand the functions of the government in India and to give further opportunities to the non-officials and native elements in Indian society to take part in the work of government.

Question Why did an autocratic government think about adding more Indians in the Councils and making government representative even in the absence of any mass movement?

Answer lead In context of growing nationalism, the motive of the British was to confine the nationalist demands within a narrow constitutional framework. It was with this motive that the Act of 1892 was passed.

Factors Leading to the Act

The development of Indian Constitution after the Act of 1861 was broadly the result of political agitation for more reforms. Constitutional concessions given by the government were always found to be inadequate, evoking further disaffection and demand for fresh reforms. The same story was repeated Act after Act until, finally, the demand for complete independence was conceded by the Act of 1947.

- **Dissatisfaction with the Act of 1861** Naturally, the Act of 1861 failed to satisfy the aspirations of the Indian people. Official majority in the Central Legislature was maintained. Non-official element, negligible as it was, did not even represent the people. It comprised of the 'natives of high rank' who could not claim to understand the needs of the Indian people.
- **Famine of 1876–78** In 1877 a terrible famine, perhaps the worst till then, afflicted the country and covered the regions of Madras, Mysore, Hyderabad, Maharashtra, western UP and the Punjab. There was acute shortage of food grains in several parts of the country and the economic condition in India was fast deteriorating, causing acute resentment against the State.
- **Growth of national consciousnesses** The second half of the 19th century saw the flowering of national consciousness in India. A number of factors were responsible for this growth.
  - The brutal repression of the Revolt of 1857 had caused widespread resentment against the government.
  - The arrogant and racist behaviour of the ruling class, particularly the civil servants, also embittered the Indians against the British.
  - In 1878, the twin Acts of Repression were passed namely the Vernacular Press Act and the Indian Arms Act which further antagonised the people of India.
  - Reactionary policies of Lord Lytton, the controversy regarding abolition of 5% cotton duties in favour of Lancashire manufacturers, and the controversy over the Ilbert Bill, well demonstrated the hollowness of British sense of justice and fair play and proved that justice could not be expected from the British when their own interests were involved.

- In 1857, Universities of Calcutta, Madras and Bombay had been established that had led to the spread of English education, western ideas and political awakening in India. Year after year, they produced an increasing number of qualified Indians who were now demanding a greater share in governance and administration.
- By now, certain Englishmen like AO Hume believed that masses were seething with discontent and some educated young men were likely to lead them to a national revolt. Thus in 1885, the Indian National Congress had been formed with the support of Hume to vent such aspirations through moderate channels. However, within three years of the formation of the INC, the party evoked antipathy of the government. In its very first session, the Congress had passed resolution demanding council reforms. Its program included furthering of national consciousness, demanding increased representation of Indians in the government, expansion of the councils and enlargement of their functions. These demands were continuously reiterated. In this way, under the aegis of the Congress, the number of nationalists grew rapidly, forcing the British to consider enlarging their support base in India. And the British began to think in terms of satisfying the aspirations of the nationalists within a narrow constitutional framework.
- Other cumulative factors that furthered the growth of national consciousness included socio-cultural awakening and faith in India's glorious past; the influence of Indian press and nationalist literature; development of means of communication and holding of imperial darbars.

All these factors were cumulatively responsible for the passing of the Act of 1892. Realising the importance of the movement launched by the Congress, Lord Dufferin secretly sent a proposal to England to further liberalise the Councils. All the same, he declared that he was not contemplating setting up a Parliamentary system in India.

Main Provisions of the Act of 1892

The Indian Councils Act of 1892 was an amending Act and so its basic provisions remained the same as those of the Act of 1861. It mainly introduced changes in the size and functions of the councils.

- **The Act increased the number of 'additional' members** In the Central Executive Council the number of additional members was increased to not less than 10 and **not more than 16** and at least half were to be non-officials. With regard to Provincial Legislatures, minimum 8 and maximum 20 members were fixed in case of Councils of Bombay and Madras. The maximum for Bengal was fixed at 20 and that for North-West Province and Oudh at 15. However, in Centre as well as in provinces, **official majority** was maintained (the official members together with ex-officio members constituted official majority).
- **The Act empowered the GG to introduce a system of limited election** The Act empowered the GG-in-Council to make regulations for nomination of additional members and to prescribe the manner in which such regulations should be put into effect. Under this provision, the GG could introduce a half-hearted system of election (limited or indirect election), even as the provision itself very carefully **avoided the use of the word 'election'**. This meant that where corporations had been established (for example, Municipalities and District Boards) and where Associations had been formed (professional such as Universities, commercial such as Chambers of Commerce, or territorial such as land-holders), the GG and the local Governors might consult such bodies from time to time. In practice, these bodies elected their representatives and forwarded their names. These names were always accepted by the government. In this way, these members were in fact elected members. However, it is noteworthy that these members occupied their seats in the

council not as representatives of the various bodies but as nominees of the GG. This underlines the cautious approach of the government towards introducing any 'elective principle'.

- **The Act enlarged the functions of the Councils** The members of the Central Legislature were now allowed to hold a **discussion on the annual financial statement**. Please note that the statement was unalterable. The members could only discuss their views that could be incorporated in the subsequent statements. They could also ask questions to the government on matters of public interest (internal matters) after six days' notice. In the case of provinces, the discussion was limited to only those branches of revenue and expenditure which were under the control of provincial governments. The members were also permitted to ask questions to the government on matters of public interest. They could also discuss the policy of the government and ask questions (however, only after six days' prior notice in the case of the centre). Supplementary questions were not allowed.

Significance of the Act of 1892

The Act proved significant in many ways:

- The size of the legislatures, both at the Centre and in the Provinces, was enlarged.
- The provisions of the Act proved liberal enough to enable many Indians to enter the councils. These included Pherozeshah Mehta, Gopal Krishna Gokhale, WC Banerjee, Surendranath Banerjee, Asutosh Mookerjee, Rash Behari Ghosh and Lalmohan Ghosh.
- The non-official members aptly demonstrated the patriotism of educated Indians, gave a good account of their debating skills and took up every opportunity to advance the Indian point of view.
- The Legislature was given some control over the Executive.
- The introduction of the 'elective principle', though veiled, was a significant constitutional measure and paved the way for introduction of representative government in the future.

However, the Act had several shortcomings and failed to satisfy the aspirations of the Indian nationalists and was criticised by the INC during its sessions in 1892 and 1893 particularly because the principle of direct election had not been introduced. The functions of the legislatures were also severely restricted. The members could not ask supplementary questions, any question could be disallowed and the members had no substantial control over the budget. However, the leadership of the national movement was now passing into the hands of the extremists, who soon began to demand another dose of legislative reforms.

Morley–Minto Reforms 1909

Factors Leading to Morley–Minto Reforms

- **Tremendous rise in national consciousness** During 1885–1906, the number of students passing the matriculation in India increased from 1286 to 8211 amounting to a sevenfold increase. A similar rise was seen in the number of newspapers and journals published, indicating that the number of Indians who were likely to be conscious of their rights as citizens and of the duties of the government, had substantially increased. Yet, far from getting their due share, the educated Indian were not given any share in government services or administration.

- **Economic critique of colonial rule** Economic thinkers Dadabhai Naoroji and RC Dutt had published in 1902 their energetic economic critiques 'The Poverty and Unbritish Rule in India' and 'The Economic History of India' respectively. Naoroji put forward the theory of drain of wealth and claimed that the British were draining and bleeding India. A raging campaign was launched against the drain through every possible form of public communication. The agitation succeeded in undermining the moral basis of British rule in Indian and gained tremendous popularity with the masses.
- **Role of Curzon's reactionary policies** Lord Curzon, who was the GG from 1898–1905, was a proud imperialist. He promoted the policy of centralisation, nurtured contempt for aspirations of educated Indians and the Indian National Congress. His unpopular measures included Calcutta Corporation Act of 1899, the Indian Universities Act and the Official Secrets Act of 1904. However, it was his plan for partition of Bengal that provoked unprecedented resentment; it was seen as an attack on growing Bengali nationalism and pushed the people into open rebellion. During the anti-partition movement, the leadership of the Congress slipped into the hands of the Extremists who had now raised the slogan of swaraj, swadeshi, boycott and national education.
- **Rise of the extremists and the revolutionaries** The last decade closer to reforms (1899–1909) was also the period of turmoil that saw the rise of militant nationalism and revolutionary terrorism. Condemning the moderate policy of the Congress, Tilak had remarked, 'Political rights will have to be fought for. The Moderates think that these can be won by persuasion. We think that these can be won by pressure'.
- **Other significant factors** In addition to the above, various other factors also contributed to the passing of the Act. In 1904–05, the Oriental Japan defeated the Occidental giant Russia and gave rise to a new hope across colonies in Asia. The mistreatment of Indians overseas in South Africa and other British colonies also embittered the Indian people who had now begun to feel that unless they were free in their own country, they could not hope to receive any respect or justice outside India. In the closing years of the 19th century, India was also afflicted by the horrors of famine and bubonic plague, seen largely as a result of government neglect and misadministration. All these events had been carefully covered by the Indian press, free since 1882, and had ignited national outrage against the foreign rule.
- **Rise of Liberal Party to power in Britain** At the end of 1905, Liberal Party came to power in Britain and two Liberals-John Morley (Secretary of State) and Lord Minto (GG) assumed office. Both Morley and Minto had similar views as regards policy in India. Both believed that the partition of Bengal was a great blunder that had furthered anti-government feelings in India. They feared that this feeling of animosity was fast filtering down to the masses and an English officer no longer held the commanding position that he once did. At the same time, they were aware that the Congress demand of 'governing India in the interests of the Indians themselves' could not be accommodated within an imperialist framework. Thus, they concluded that the British policy in India was badly in need of a "new departure", the contents of which were clear in their mind—they had to appease the Moderates, suppress the Extremists, raise new pillars of support for the British rule (the Indian princes and the Zamindars) and weaken the nationalist movement by counterpoising Muslims against the Hindus.
- **Simla Deputation, 1st October 1906** Meanwhile, a deputation headed by Aga Khan met Viceroy Lord Minto at Simla on 1st October 1906. The deputationists expressed loyalty to the British Crown but also expressed apprehension that if the principle of 'election' was introduced without conceding reservation for Muslims it would prove detrimental to their interests. Thus, the deputationists demanded reservation of seats for Muslim Community not only on the basis of their population

but also on the basis of their **political importance** and their 'services in the defence of the British Empire'.

The British saw in these demands a promising counterpoise to the increasing demands of the Congress. Grasping the opportunity, Lord Minto readily accepted these demands and promised not only separate communal representation but also representation much in excess of their population on account of their 'services to the Empire'. Minto's response to the deputation may be seen as the first official manifestation of the policy of divide and rule.

Under the policy of conciliation, another demand of the Indian leaders was fulfilled even before the act was passed and without introducing any statutory change. This was the appointment of two Indians to the Council of the Secretary of State for India and of the Governor General and Provincial Governors. Hence in August 1907, **KG Gupta** and **Syed Hussain Bilgrami** were appointed to the Secretary of State's India Council. Under this provision, comparatively unimportant portfolios like education and law were given to the Indians.

Main Provisions of the Act of 1909

Like the Act of 1892, the Act of 1909 was also an amending Act and introduced changes in the size and functions of the councils of the GG and the Governors. Both size and functions of the councils were enlarged.

Changes in Composition of Councils

The changes in councils were brought in three respects—numbers, proportion of official and non-official members and methods of appointment or selection.

- **Change in numbers** Under the Act of 1909, the number of additional members were doubled or more than doubled. For instance, under the Act of 1892, the maximum number of additional members in GG's Council was only 16. The Act of 1909 raised this to 60. The Central Legislature, was thus composed of 69 members (37 officials, 32 non-officials). Of the officials, 9 were ex-officio and 28 were to be nominated by GG. Of the non-officials, 5 were to be nominated by the GG, 27 were to be elected. Similarly, for presidencies of Madras, Bombay and Bengal, it was raised from 20 to 50.
- **Change in the proportion of official and non-official members** Under the Act of 1892, official majority was maintained both in the Centre and in the provinces. But under the Act of 1909, even though official majority was maintained in the centre, the proportion of non-official members increased substantially. In the provinces, for the first time, a **non-official majority** was introduced. Readers please note that this unofficial majority was in practice impotent in translating its will into action because of the overriding powers of the central majority.
- **Methods of appointment** Under the Act of 1892, nomination was the practice. The Act of 1909 became a landmark because of the manner in which non-official seats were to be filled. Of the 32 non-official seats, 5 were to be nominated by GG while the remaining 27 were to be elected. It was further declared that territorial representation did not suit India and that, 'representation by classes and interests is the only practicable method of embodying the elective principle in the constitution of the Indian Legislative Councils'. Thus, the remaining 27 seats were distributed as follows:
    - By non-official members of the Provincial Legislative Councils (general electorates): 13
    - By landholders of six provinces (Landholders' constituencies): 6
    - By Muslims of five provinces (separate Muslim constituencies): 5
    - Alternately by Muslim landholders of UP or of Bombay: 1
    - Chambers of Commerce of Calcutta and Bombay (special electorates): 2

For the 13 'open seats', doubly indirect system of elections was introduced. The tax payers in a town or village elected representatives for municipal committees who in turn elected representatives for provincial councils. These non-official members of the provincial councils, in their turn, elected representatives to the central council. On the other hand, the representatives of Muslims and landholders were elected directly. This distinction was unjust and it hurt.

Further, Muslims were elected by **separate electorates**, i.e., electorates comprising Muslims only. Separate registers were prepared containing the names of solely Muslim voters. In addition to this, Muslims were also given **weightage**, i.e., more seats were given to them than the number warranted by their proportion in the local population. They were also allowed to compete for seats to be elected by general electorates. These provisions were severely criticised as they were brought about not with the aim of correcting any imbalance in Indian society but to appease some Muslim leaders and bind them to the government in 'silken chains of gratitude'.

Sir Charles Aitcheson A member of the Executive Council in 1892 had stated, 'the division of the people into creeds and castes and sects with varying and conflicting interests rendered representation in the European sense an obvious impossibility'.

Changes in Functions of Councils

Under the Act of 1861, the functions of the councils were strictly limited to the field of legislation. Under the Act of 1892, the members were allowed to hold discussion on the annual financial statement but were not allowed to move resolutions or divide the House in respect of any financial question. Under the Act of 1909, the functions of the Councils were enlarged in three ways:

1. The members were allowed to discuss the financial statement at length and move resolutions on it, before it was presented in its final form.
2. The members were given the right to move resolutions on matters of general public interest. But these resolutions were to be in the form of recommendations only and may or may not be accepted by the government. However, there were certain subjects on which questions could not be asked. These included foreign relations of the government of India and its relations with Indian princes, expenditure on railways, interest on debt, etc.
3. The right to ask questions was also extended and the member asking an original question was given the right to ask **supplementary questions** as well.

Critical Analysis of the Act of 1909

- The Morley–Minto Reforms were a great improvement upon the Act of 1892. The provisions under the Act proved liberal enough to enable several Indian leaders to enter the legislative bodies. Some of the prominent members of the Central Legislative Council were: GK Gokhale, DE Wacha, Surendranath Banerjee, Madan Mohan Malaviya, Tej Bahadur Sapru, Srinivas Shastri, Mohammad Ali Jinnah, Nawab Saiyid Mohammad Bahadur, Raja of Mahmudabad and Mazharul Haque. The members used the debates on bills to manifest their debating skills and often placed the official members in an embarrassing situation. Their arguments found wide coverage in the press and helped in eroding the moral foundations of the Raj.
- Though the British had hoped that an assortment of classes in the councils would act as counterweights against one another. However, their legislative behaviour mostly belied British expectations and they tended to unite, rather than divide, on issues of national significance.

- Nevertheless, the Act failed to satisfy the aspirations of the people in several ways. The Act gave no answer to the demand for responsible government. Narrow franchise and indirect elections failed to instil in the members a sense of responsibility. The Councils had no real power and were merely debating bodies that could air certain criticisms.
- In its actual working, the reforms created much confusion. Since no responsibility was conceded, it led to thoughtless and irresponsible criticism of the government by Indian leaders, throwing the British government and the Indian community into two antagonistic camps.
- The Act was passed to appease the Moderates, the Muslims and the elite sections (the landholders) with the aim of raising them as new pillars of support for the British rule.
- Initially it seemed that the British were successful in rallying the above classes but soon they realised that it was not so. The Moderates were soon disillusioned with the Morley–Minto Reforms and many of them extended support to the Home Rule Movement from outside. After the Lucknow Pact of 1916, the leadership of the Congress went onto the hands of the Extremists decisively. Though the historians are divided in their view regarding the extent to which the British succeeded in keeping apart the politically active Hindus and the Muslims, it cannot be denied that the strategy of weightage and separate electorates was an imperialist master stroke. It ensured that **politics in India was communalised** for years to come.
- Separate electorates for Muslims led the other communities to fight for their rights and even claim that they had rendered 'better services to the empire'. In view of such claims, special representation was conceded to the Sikhs in the Act of 1919. The Harijans, the Indian Christians, the Anglo Indians and the Europeans got separate representation by the Act of 1935.

Thus, the Act of 1909 created a hotchpotch of representative government and gave the people of India 'the shadow rather than the substance'.

- **Morley declared in British Parliament** 'If it could be said that this chapter of reforms led directly or necessarily up to the establishment of a Parliamentary system in India, I, for one, would have nothing at all to do with it'.
- **Prof M.V. Pylee** 'Based on the principle of benevolent despotism, the Reforms may be seen as an attempt to graft constitutionalism upon existing autocracy of the British rule'.
- **Report on Indian Constitutional Reform (1918)** 'It (the system of communal electorates) was opposed to the teachings of history. It perpetuated divisions of creeds and classes which meant the creating of camps organised against each other and taught them to think as partisans and not as citizens. It stereotyped existing relations and was a very serious hindrance to the development of self-governing principle'.

Montagu–Chelmsford Reforms 1919

Factors Leading to Reforms of 1919

- **Disillusionment with the Act of 1909** The Act of 1909 greatly disappointed the people and reinforced the demand for self-government. So, great was the disillusionment with Morley–Minto Reforms that it aggravated the political atmosphere in India and led to the passing of several repressive legislations like the Indian Press Act of 1910, the Seditious Meetings Act of 1911 and the Criminal Law (Amendment) Act of 1913. The Defence of India Act of 1915 which provided for the trial of revolutionaries by a strong bench without appeal and the internment of suspects was particularly repressive.

- **Congress-League Pact 1916** Gradually, Muslims too grew discontented with the British. The disagreement over the foundation of a Muslim University at Aligarh as well as annulment of the partition of Bengal in 1911 greatly upset the Muslims. Certain international factors too had an adverse impact on Anglo-Muslim relations. These included the hostile attitude of England towards Turkey in the Turco-Italian War (1911–12) and in the Balkan Wars (1912–13), often represented as a struggle between the Cross and the Crescent. This alienation of the Muslims with the British brought the Congress and the League closer together and they finally joined hands in 1916 in what is known as the Lucknow Pact.
- **Outbreak of First World War** When the war broke out in August 1914 in Europe, India automatically got involved in it. Indians helped Britain with men, money and material during a crucial time and this gesture naturally increased their expectations. Not because they were loyal servants who deserved to be rewarded by their masters, but because they had helped the British at an equal footing which had destroyed the myth of racial superiority and raised the confidence of the Indian people. They now wanted recognition for their ability to rule themselves. The war which began as a struggle among imperialist powers over new colonies had also exposed their lust for trade and territories. As the war went on, American President Woodrow Wilson declared that the war was being fought 'to make the world safer for democracy'. In Europe in one country after another, democratic institutions were being set up. Thus, the war provided enormous impetus to democratic forces and urge for self-government all over the world.
- **Emergence of various schemes of constitutional reform** So charged was the atmosphere that many Indian political theorists themselves began formulating new schemes for the Indian political problem:
    - **Gokhale's scheme** It was one of the first but published posthumously in 1917 and advocated substantial measure of self-government.
    - **The Round Table scheme** The Round Table was a group formed to study imperial problems of British Empire. Its members such as **Lionel Curits** and **Williams Duke** felt that any further extension of elected majorities without giving them any responsibility would only create permanent opposition in the councils. Thus, they forwarded the idea of 'dyarchy' in the provinces (the Greek term 'dyarchy' refers to a form of government in which any two persons or bodies are jointly vested with supreme powers).
    - **Joint scheme of the Congress and Muslim League** After the Lucknow Pact in December 1916, Congress and Muslim League also came up with a Joint Scheme for constitutional reforms.
- **War time politics in India** The war created a wave of nationalism among different sections of Indian society and consequently the war years emerged as the years of intense political activity in India. The people had realised that swaraj would not descend upon them as a gift of the British. Thus, many nationalists saw Britain's difficulty as India's opportunity. The Home Rule Movement and the Ghadar Movement emerged and heated up the politics of India during the war years.
- **British demand for one million pounds towards War Fund** The government of India was asked to contribute one million pounds to the war fund and it was felt that some concessions would have to be given in return.
- **Change in government attitude and Montagu Declaration** The above factors and the intensification of the Home Rule Movement made political atmosphere tense and forced the government to adopt a soft line as indicated by the historic declaration of Montagu (the new Secretary of State) in the British House of Commons regarding the goal of British Government in India. He announced:

The Montagu Declaration (20th August 1917) 'the policy of His Majesty's government, with which the Government of India are in complete accord, is that of increasing association of Indians in every branch of administration and the gradual development of self-governing institutions with a view to the progressive realisation of responsible government in India as an integral part of the British Empire'.

In his declaration, Montagu also stated that certain substantial steps in the realisation of the above goal will be taken immediately while progressive steps in the above direction will be decided by the British Parliament as per the performance of Indians. Montagu decided to visit India and prepare a scheme of constitutional reforms himself. Accordingly, in November 1917, Lord Montagu arrived in India and held deliberations with Viceroy Chelmsford, government officials and Indian leaders. Based on these deliberations, he prepared a **Report on Indian Constitutional Reforms**, also known as Montagu–Chelmsford Report or simply Montford Report (published in July 1918).

Indian Response

While the Montagu declaration was welcomed, the scheme of reform fell far short of expectations and was denounced by most Indian leaders with the exception of some Moderates.

August 1918, Bombay, Special Congress Session (President Hasan Imam) In August 1918, a Special Session of the Congress was held at Bombay to discuss the report. The Congress passed a resolution condemning the scheme as 'inadequate, unsatisfactory and disappointing'.

However, some moderates, led by Surendranath Banerjee were in favour of accepting the reform proposals and left the Congress at this juncture. They met in a separate All India Conference in Bombay, formed a new party—**Indian Liberal Federation** (November 1918) and came to be known as Liberals. The President Surendranath Banerjee defined his party as 'the friends of reform and enemies of revolution'. Banerjee also led a deputation of moderates to England to give evidence before the Joint Parliamentary Committee, in support of the scheme (May 1919). In this way, on the basis of the Montford Report, the new Government of India bill was drafted and passed in December 1919 as 'The Government of India Act 1919'.

Government of India Act 1919

Preamble The Act carried a preamble which laid down the basic principles on which reforms were to be carried out. It was based on the Montagu Declaration of 20th August 1917 and embodied the following general principles:

- British India is to remain an integral part of the British Empire.
- Responsible government in British India is the objective of the declared policy of Parliament.
- Responsible government is possible through progressive reforms only.
- For this, it is necessary to provide for two things: (1) increasing association of Indians in every branch of administration, and (2) gradual development of self-governing institutions.
- Complete popular control, as far as possible, in the field of local government.
- The provincial governments to be in a large measure independent of the Government of India and to be responsible in some measure to popular representatives.

Main Provisions of the Act of 1919

Changes in 'Home' Government

The Secretary of State for India was now to be **paid by the British Exchequer** and not out of the Indian revenues as had been the case since 1793, thus undoing a long-drawn injustice. Some of his functions were also taken away and given to the High Commissioner for India who was to be appointed and paid by the Government of India and was to act as an agent of GG-in-Council. It is commonly held that the powers of the Secretary of State were curtailed in the wake of Congress resolution passed in 1916, demanding the governance of India from Delhi and not from Downing Street.

Changes in Government of India

Changes in Central Government

The Central Executive Under the Act of 1919, the Central government did not undergo any change in its basic principle. The chief-executive authority remained vested in the Governor-General who was responsible to the British Parliament through the Secretary of State and not to the Indian Legislature. Thus, it continued to remain unrepresentative government. To implement the policy of increasing association of Indians, of the eight members of the GG's Executive Council, **three would be Indians**. However, these members were always allotted portfolios of lesser significance, like Law, Education, Labour, Health or Industry.

The Central Legislature Under the Act, a **bicameral legislature** was established. The two Houses were the Indian Legislative Assembly and the Council of State.

The Indian Legislative Assembly (Lower House):

- It was to consist of 145 members of whom 41 were to be nominated and 104 were to be elected members. Of the 104 elected members, 52 were to be returned by General constituencies, 32 by the Communal constituencies (30 by the Muslims, 2 by the Sikhs) and 20 by Special constituencies (7 by landlords, 9 by Europeans and 4 by the Indian Commercial community).
- The method of indirect election as prevalent under the Act of 1909 was abolished and, for the first time, **direct election** was introduced.
- The system of communal electorate continued and was extended to **Sikhs** also. The seats were distributed among the provinces not on the basis of their population but on the basis of their so-called importance. For example, both Bombay and Madras were granted 12 seats each though the population of Bombay was only half of that of Madras, the reason being the commercial importance of Bombay.
- The term of the Assembly was fixed at three years but it could be extended by the GG (It is noteworthy that the last Assembly elected in 1936 was dissolved only after 10 years).

The Council of State (Upper House):

- It was to consist of 60 members, 26 of whom were to be nominated by the GG and 34 were to be elected, thus introducing an elected majority. Of the 34 elected members, 20 were to be elected by general constituencies, 10 by Muslims, 3 by Europeans and 1 by Sikh constituencies.
- Each member held his seat for five years, though the Council itself was partially renewed every year.
- The members were called 'Honorable'. **Women were not allowed** to become a member of the House.
- Franchise was highly restricted to secure the representation of hereditary aristocracy or mercantile aristocracy.

Other Changes:

- The right to ask **supplementary questions was extended to all members** of the legislature (Under the Act of 1909, member asking original question alone could ask supplementary questions). Short notice questions could also be asked. The members enjoyed the right to freedom of speech.
- Since partial responsible government was introduced in the provinces, it became necessary to demarcate the spheres of central and provincial governments. Accordingly, **two lists** were drawn—the Central list and the Provincial list (mentioned in detail below).
- Under the Act, complete separation of sources of revenue between the centre and the provinces was made, to give meaning to the partial transfer of power to Indians.

Special powers of the GG In addition to the veto power, he was given the **power of certification.** Meaning, once the Bill was refused by the legislature, he could certify that a Bill was essential for safety, tranquility or interests of British India and secure its enactment. The GG could refuse his assent to Bills passed by the Legislature. In practice, the GG made liberal use of his overriding powers and the reforms proved totally inadequate in establishing a responsible government at the centre.

Significance of the changes introduced at the Centre The Act of 1919 introduced a **responsive if not responsible** government at the Centre. Though the GG and his Executive Council were irremovable, this did not mean they could neglect the wishes of the Legislature. The members became part of the standing committees such as Public Accounts Committee and got ample opportunity to exercise control on government policy. They also exercised control by asking questions and moving motions of adjournment. They could also reject the budget and pass resolutions against the government. The large elected majority in the Assembly made it virtually impossible for the Executive Councillors to remain unresponsive to the wishes of the members of the Legislature.

Changes in Provincial Government

In order to give effect to the aim of decentralisation and devolution of powers, **provincial autonomy** was introduced for the **first time**. It means freedom of a provincial government from control by the central government. The independent powers of the provinces were defined in the **'Devolution Rules'**. Devolution was brought about in areas of finance, legislation and administration. Let us now consider the extent of decentralisation brought about by the Act.

Financial Devolution:

- The first step towards devolution was taken by providing for a **complete separation of sources of revenue** between the centre and the provinces. Accordingly, land revenue, excise, irrigation and stamps were made exclusively provincial items.
- The loss of income was compensated by introduction of the system of provincial contribution to the central government.
- The provinces were given near complete freedom in preparation of provincial budgets.
- Taxation powers of the provinces were enlarged by doing away with the requirement of previous sanction of the GG.

Legislative Devolution:

- This was brought about by separating the items of legislation by the Centre and the provinces. Accordingly, two lists were drawn-Central list and Provincial list.
- **Central List** included subjects of national importance or which related to more than one province like Foreign Affairs, Political Relations, Defence, Communications, Post and Telegraph, Public Debt, Tariff and Customs, Patents, Currency, etc.

- **Provincial List** included subjects which were only of provincial importance like Local Self Government, Public Health and Sanitation, Education, Public Works, Agriculture, Land Revenue Administration, Forests, Water Supply, Famine Relief, Law and Order, etc.
- **Residual powers** were vested in the GG-in-Council.
- The provincial government could also make laws for the 'peace and good government' of the provinces.
- Central control over provincial legislation still remained and was carried out in two ways. First, a copy of every provincial act had to be sent to the GG, who might or might not give his assent to it. Second, if the GG gave his assent, then its copy was sent to the Secretary of State, who again might or might not give his assent.

Administrative Devolution:

- It was a natural by-product of the financial and legislative devolution.

The Provincial Executive

Dyarchy (or diarchy) The most significant change brought about by the Act of 1919 was in the field of provincial administration. Dyarchy was introduced in the provinces to meet two main aims—first, to give responsibility to popular representatives, and second, to meet the condition of political backwardness and administrative inexperience of the Indian people. Thus, responsibility for certain subjects of the government was transferred to the Indian hands (Transferred list) while control over others was reserved in British hands (Reserved list). In this way, the provincial government was divided into two halves—the Governor and his Executive Council administered the reserved list while the Governor and his Ministers administered the transferred list. This novel distribution of executive powers in the provinces was called 'dyarchy'. On matters of common concerns, there was provision for joint consultation, with the Governor presiding and having the last word.

Transferred list It included the so-called nation-building subjects which were mainly four, i.e., Local Self Government, Health, Education (other than European and Anglo-Indian Education) and some departments relating to Agriculture. Other subjects were Public Works, Libraries, Museums, Co-operatives, Veterinary Departments, Fisheries, Industries, Weights and Measures, Public Entertainments, Religious and Charitable Endowments, etc.

These subjects were administered by the Governor acting with Ministers appointed by him from among the elected members of the legislature and who were **responsible** to the Legislature. As per letter of the law, the ministers held office during the pleasure of the governor. In practice, they were allowed to remain in power so long as they enjoyed the confidence of the legislature.

Reserved list It included all remaining subjects like Land Revenue, Police, Justice, Printing Presses, Pensions, Irrigation and Waterways, Electricity, Mines, Factories, etc.

These were administered by the Governor with the help of members of the Executive Council who were nominated by him and who were **not responsible** to the Legislature. The Governor and his Executive Councillors were appointed by the Crown for a period of five years and were jointly responsible to the GG and the Secretary of State. The number of executive councillors was fixed at maximum four.

Role of the Governor He acted as the link between two halves of the Executive and played a complex role. **Instrument of Instructions** was a document issued to the Governor and it laid down the basis of relations between the provincial governors and ministers. It also defined special responsibilities of the Governor which gave him wide powers to override his ministers. The special powers of the Governor, for that matter, emerged as the biggest weakness of the Councils and prevented the principle of responsible government from being put into practice.

Originally, the Act of 1919 applied to only **eight provinces**—Bengal, Madras, Bombay, United Provinces, Punjab, Bihar and Orissa, Central Provinces, and Assam. In 1923, the Act was extended to Burma, and sometime later to North Western Frontier Province.

The Provincial Legislature (or the Provincial Council) The Montford Reforms envisaged the introduction of a new principle called **'responsible government'**. The provincial councils were modified as per this principle in the following ways-

- **Composition**
  - In each province, **unicameral legislature** was created which was called the Legislative Council.
  - It was to comprise a Governor's Executive Council, elected members and nominated members.
- **Numbers**
  - The size of the provincial councils was considerably increased and it varied from province to province. The maximum number was 140 for Bengal and minimum was 53 for Assam (as against the maximum of 50 under the Act of 1909). Thus, while the Act of 1909 laid down the maximum number, the Act of 1919 specified the minimum.
- **Proportion of officials and non-officials**
  - In the new Councils, minimum 70 per cent of the members were to be elected and maximum 20 per cent could be officials.
- **Method of appointment**
  - The elected members were to be elected by **direct election**, i.e., the primary voters electing the members.
  - Though the authors of the Montford report criticised **separate electorates**, they decided to continue with the system. In fact, these were extended to the **Sikhs in Punjab**. Later, seats were also reserved for the non-Brahmins on demand of the Justice Party.
  - Constituencies were designed to represent particular communities or special interests such as Universities, Landlords and Chambers of Commerce.
- **Qualification for voters**
  - Even in general constituency, the right to vote depended on a number of qualifications such as-residence in that constituency for a minimum period of time, ownership or occupation of a house with minimum rental value, payment of a minimum municipal tax or income tax, receipt of a military pension, etc. As a result, the **franchise was extremely narrow**.
  - In 1920, less than 5 per cent people got the right to vote. **Women could not vote or contest elections**. In Britain itself, women got the right to vote only in 1918.
- **Duration of the council**
  - The term of the Council was fixed at three years. But it could be dissolved earlier by the Governor and in such a case a new Council was to be elected within six months after the dissolution.
- **Functions of the councils**
  - The functions were also enlarged. The members enjoyed the right to freedom of speech. They could ask questions and supplementaries, move resolutions and initiate legislations concerning any provincial subject and could even reject the budget (though the Governor could restore it).

Criticisms of the Act of 1919 The Act of 1919 had the following major defects:

1. The absence of even partial responsible government at the Centre.
2. The continuation and even extension of separate electorates, even as the Montford Report had declared the separate electorates as a very serious hindrance to the development of the self-governing principle.
3. The special powers of the Governor. Given these powers, the principle of responsible government could not be put into practice.
4. The introduction of dyarchy.

Failure of Dyarchy The Dyarchy was put into operation during the period April 1921 to April 1937, though it ceased to function for some time in two provinces—in Bengal (1924–27) and the Central Provinces (1924–26). In its operation, dyarchy was a complete failure. This was reiterated by the official committee formed to examine the working of Dyarchy, led by **Sir Alexander Muddiman**. It reported the following defects:

1. **Interference of the 'reserved half' of the government on the 'transferred half' and vice versa** This problem arose due to lack of division of subjects along scientific lines. First, such a division of administration into two halves is opposed to political theory and it was not possible to divide the functions of the state into water tight compartments. This difficulty was further compounded by illogical and irrational division. For instance, while education was transferred subject, European and Anglo-Indian education were reserved subjects. While agriculture was a transferred subject, land revenue and irrigation were reserved subjects, though the two cannot be separated for obvious reasons. Further, whenever conflicts arose, the Governor was to act as arbitrator and he generally sided with the reserved half.
2. **Excessive control exercised by the Finance Department (a reserved subject) over the transferred departments** The finance department did not restrict itself to furnishing financial advice but constantly tried to control the policy of the Ministers by withholding funds. While reserved departments got all the money they wanted, the ministers kept requesting for funds.
3. **Failure of the Indian Civil Service to cooperate with the Ministers** This was perhaps the most unwholesome feature of dyarchy. The ministers had to implement their policies through the services. But they had no control over civil servants even in transferred departments. The members of the Indian Civil Service were recruited by the Secretary of State and were responsible only to him. They did not owe any great responsibility to the ministers. Further, the departmental secretaries had direct access to the Governor which further undermined the Minister's position. This privilege made the services insubordinate and defiant in attitude.
4. **Failure to encourage joint deliberation between two halves of the government** Joint deliberation was not made a necessary part of the system. Initiative on this rested with the Governor and only a few Governors encouraged this practice.
5. **Weak position of the Ministers** The position of the ministers was greatly weakened by the overriding powers of the Governor, the Governor General and the Secretary of State. Further, the governor looked upon the ministers as mere advisors and dismissed them as and when he liked. This struck at the very root of ministerial responsibility. The position of ministers was also made very complex as they were made to serve two masters—while they were appointed by the governor and could be dismissed by him, they were made responsible to the legislature.

6. **The absence of joint responsibility of the Ministers** The principle of joint responsibility of ministers was not secured and was not possible either since the ministers were not selected on the basis of any organised political parties but on individual basis.

Dyarchy was further confounded when it was rejected by the Congress. Congress was against dyarchy and its representatives refused to accept Ministership. As a result, most of the ministers came from smaller parties or were independents and had no majority to back them in the legislature. The sword of successful no-confidence motion hung above their heads. In such circumstances, they could not be expected to do any useful work for the people. Hence ministership under dyarchy only trained Indians in flattery rather than in science of responsible government. In fact, dyarchy became so unpopular that it became fashionable to deride it.

Significance Despite above criticisms, the Act of 1919 marked a major milestone in the history of constitutional development in India for several reasons:

- The government had made a declaration of its intentions regarding increasing association with Indians and development of self-governing institutions in India. Going back on this declaration would amount to breach of commitment. Thus, the declaration **guaranteed future reforms**.
- The Act created legislative bodies both in the centre and the provinces. Indian opinion was voiced in these legislatures and reverberated via press throughout the length and breadth of the country. The articulate and often logically incontrovertible debates played a significant **role in demolishing the moral basis of the British Raj in India**.
- The holding of elections and appointment of Indian ministers also **familiarised Indians with the parliamentary system**.
- Despite all the criticism, dyarchy itself was probably the best transitional mechanism that emerged after prolonged study of the Indian problem.

Indian Response The Reforms came at a time when conditions in India were not conducive to a favourable reception of the reforms. The year 1918–19 saw a bad monsoon and trade depression. The Rowlatt Bills were being bitterly opposed. On 13th April 1919, the Jallianwala tragedy occurred and relations between the government and the people reached a new low. Owing to all these factors, the objections to the new reforms hardened into rejection.

Muslims were unhappy with the hostile attitude of the British towards the Khalifa, the ruler of Turkey and the years during 1920–22 saw the launching of the twin movements of Khilafat and Non-Cooperation under the leadership of Mahatma Gandhi and the Congress. Accordingly, the Congress boycotted the elections of November 1920 and once boycotted by the Congress, the new constitution suffered a severe blow. In this way, failure of dyarchy and widespread disappointment with the new Act gave rise to a new unity and a new movement led by Mahatma Gandhi, which soon gathered momentum and grew into a full-fledged agitation demanding complete transfer of power into Indian hands.

> **Sir Courtney Ilbert observed about the Act** 'It was like one of those caravan serais which could be run up rapidly for an Indian prince to meet a temporary need'.
>
> **Lord Oliver, Secretary of State,** compared the Act to a sea-worthy vessel and observed that it should carry Indians across if only they would get into it and row.

Prelim Capsule

Constitutional Development (1861–1920)

Acts	Important Provisions
The Indian Councils Act 1861	The Executive Council of the GG was enlarged by the addition of a **fifth member** who was to be a jurist. For the purpose of legislation, it enlarged the Central Council by addition of **not less than six and not more than twelve** Additional Members. These were to be nominated by the GG and that at least half of them were to be non-officials. Under this provision, three Indians were usually nominated. Thus, it initiated a process of Indian association in legislation. The Act restored the legislative powers of Councils of **Bombay and Madras**. The Act allowed establishment of **new Councils** in other Provinces. Accordingly, Councils of Bengal (1862), North-Western Provinces (1886) and Burma and Punjab (1897) were established. Thus, it initiated recognition of local needs and local knowledge by means of local councils. The GG was empowered to issue **ordinances** in case of emergency. The Act provided for decentralisation of business. Using this authority, Lord Canning introduced the **portfolio system** in India for the first time, thus laying the **foundation of Cabinet System** in India.
The Indian Councils Act of 1892	In the Central Executive Council, the number of additional members was increased to not less than 10 and **not more than 16.** However, in Centre as well as in provinces, **official majority** was maintained. The Act empowered the GG-in-Council to make regulations for nomination of additional members. Under this provision, the GG could introduce a half-hearted system of election (limited or indirect election), even as the provision itself very carefully avoided the use of the word 'election'. The **introduction of the 'elective principle'**, though veiled, was a significant constitutional measure. The members of the Central Legislature were allowed to hold a discussion on the **annual financial statement**. Under the Act, many Indians entered the councils. These included Pherozeshah Mehta, Gopal Krishna Gokhale, WC Banerjee, Surendranath Banerjee, Ashutosh Mookerjee, Rash Behari Ghosh and Lalmohan Ghosh.
Morley–Minto Reforms 1909	The number of additional members were doubled or more than doubled and the maximum number of additional members in GG's Council was raised to 60. The Central Legislature was thus to comprise of 69 members. In the provinces, for the first time, a **non-official majority** was introduced. Of the 32 non-official seats, 5 were to be nominated by GG while the remaining 27 were to be elected by the system of **indirect election**.

	It introduced the system of **separate electorates** for Muslims who were also given **weightage**, i.e., more seats were given to them than the number warranted by their proportion in the local population. They were also allowed to compete for seats to be elected by general electorates. The member asking original question was given the right to ask **supplementary questions** as well.
Montagu–Chelmsford Reforms 1919	The Act began with a Preamble based on the **Montagu Declaration** of 20 August 1917. The Secretary of State for India was now to be paid by the British Exchequer. Some of his functions were also taken away and given to the **High Commissioner for India**. In the GG's Executive Council, three **Indians** would be included. **Bicameral legislature** was established at the Centre namely, the Indian Legislative Assembly and the Council of State. The Indian Legislative Assembly (Lower House): • It was to consist of 145 members. • The Act introduced the system of **direct election** for the first time. • The system of communal electorate continued and was extended to **Sikhs** also. The Council of State (Upper House): • It was to consist of 60 members. • The members were called 'Honorable'. **Women were not allowed** to become a member of the House. The right to ask **supplementary questions was extended** to all members of the legislature. The GG was given the **power of certification**. Under the Act, **Provincial Autonomy** was introduced for the first time. The independent powers of the provinces were defined in the **'Devolution Rules'**. Accordingly, two lists were drawn-Central list and Provincial list. **Residual powers** were vested in the GG-in-Council. The system of **Dyarchy** was introduced in the provinces and the responsibility for certain subjects of the government was transferred to the Indian hands (Transferred list) while control over others was reserved in British hands (Reserved list). Governor acted as the link between two halves of the Executive. **Instrument of Instructions** was the document which laid down the basis of relations between the provincial governors and ministers.

Previous Years' Questions – Preliminary Exam

1. Which among the following was the most short-lived of all the Britain's constitutional experiments in India? **[UPSC 1999]**
   (a) Indian Council Act of 1861
   (b) Indian Council Act of 1892
   (c) Indian Council Act of 1909
   (d) Government of India Act of 1919
2. Which one of the following Act of British India strengthened the Viceroy's authority over his executive Council by substituting 'portfolio' or departmental system for corporate functioning? **[UPSC 2002]**
   (a) Indian Council Act, 1861
   (b) Government of India Act, 1858
   (c) Indian Council Act, 1892
   (d) Indian Council Act, 1909
3. When Congress leaders condemned the Montagu–Chelmsford Report, many moderates left the party to form which of the following? **[UPSC 2003]**
   (a) Swaraj Party
   (b) Indian Freedom Party
   (c) Independence Federation of India
   (d) Indian Liberal Federation
4. The Montagu–Chelmsford Report formed the basis of which of the following? **[UPSC 2004]**
   (a) The Indian Councils Act, 1909
   (b) The Government of India Act, 1919
   (c) The Government of India Act, 1935
   (d) The Indian Independence Act, 1947
5. Which of the following is/are the principal feature(s) of the Government of India Act, 1919? **[UPSC 2012]**
   1. Introduction of dyarchy in the executive government of the provinces.
   2. Introduction of separate communal electorates for Muslims.
   3. Devolution of Legislative authority by the centre to the provinces.

   Choose the correct answer from the following options.
   (a) 1 only (b) 2 and 3 only
   (c) 1 and 3 only (d) 1, 2 and 3
6. The Montague-Chelmsford proposals were related to which of the following? **[UPSC 2016]**
   (a) Social reforms
   (b) Educational reforms
   (c) Reforms in public administration
   (d) Constitutional reforms
7. In the context of Indian history, the principle of 'Dyarchy (diarchy)' refers to which of the following? **[UPSC 2017]**
   (a) Division of the central legislature into two houses.
   (b) Introduction of double government that is central and state governments.
   (c) Having two sets of rulers: one in London and another in Delhi
   (d) Division of the subjects delegated to the provinces into two categories.
8. In the Government of India Act 1919, the functions of Provincial Government were divided into "Reserved" and "Transferred" subjects. Which of the following were treated as "Reserved" subjects? **[UPSC 2022]**
   1. Administration of Justice
   2. Local Self-Government
   3. Land Revenue
   4. Police

   Select the correct answer using the code given below:
   (a) 1, 2 and 3
   (b) 2, 3 and 4
   (c) 1, 3 and 4
   (d) 1, 2 and 4

Previous Years' Questions – Main Exam

1. 'The Morley–Minto Reforms did not and could not provide an answer to Indian problems'. Explain. **[UPSC 1993]**
2. 'In the Montague-Chelmsford report, communal representation and reservations were not only retained but considerably extended'. Comment **[UPSC 1993]**
3. 'The reforms of 1909 introduced a Cardinal problem and ground of controversy at every revision of the Indian electoral system'. Comment. **[UPSC 2003]**
4. What are the salient features of the Government of India Act of 1858 and 1909? **[UPSC 2007]**

Answers

Previous Years' Questions – Preliminary Exam

1. (c)	2. (a)	3. (d)	4. (b)	5. (c)
6. (d)	7. (d)	8. (c)		

9 Khilafat and Non-Cooperation Movement (1919–22)

The national movement in India entered its third and final stage during 1920–21 with the launch of two mass movements—Khilafat and Non-Cooperation under the leadership of Mahatma Gandhi. Though emerging out of separate issues, both the movements adopted a common program of action against the British, i.e. use of non-violent mass struggle. The movements were launched in the backdrop of disappointment with Montagu–Chelmsford Reforms, Post-War miseries, the Rowlatt Act, the Jallianwala Bagh massacre, and the Khilafat wrongs. These events greatly disillusioned Gandhi and turned him from a cooperator, into a non-cooperator.

Background

Disillusionment with Montagu–Chelmsford Reforms

The constitutional reforms of 1919 fell far short of Indian aspirations and failed to bring about a responsible government in any real sense. Failure of diarchy and failure of the government to establish self-governing institutions evoked widespread disappointment with the new Act and gave rise to a new unity and a new movement led by Congress and Mahatma Gandhi in the form of 'non-violent non-cooperation movement'. It soon gathered momentum and grew into a full-fledged agitation demanding complete transfer of power into Indian hands.

Post-War Miseries

Post-World War, the economic situation in India became alarming. There was a sharp rise in prices of daily commodities, heavy taxes and rents were imposed on the peasantry and volume of imports had risen sharply affecting Indian industries and their production. Thus, all sections of Indian people were facing post-war miseries that strengthened anti-British sentiment.

Rowlatt Act

The Rowlatt Act, passed in March 1919, also evoked wide-scale resentment of the Indian people. As per the Act, the government could imprison any person without trial in a court of law. The real motive behind the act was to enable government to imprison the nationalists without giving them any opportunity to defend themselves. To oppose the Act, a non-violent mass agitation known as the Rowlatt Satyagraha was launched under the leadership of Gandhi. The new form of protest created a new political awakening and stirred large masses of Indian people.

Jallianwala Bagh Massacre

It was an incident of naked brutality on the Indians. On 13th April 1919, in Amritsar, a large but unarmed crowd had gathered in the Jallianwala Bagh to protest against the arrest of their two leaders—Dr. Saifuddin Kitchlew and Dr. Satyapal. The British commander of Amritsar Brigadier-General Reginald Dyer, ordered his troops to open fire on the crowd without warning, killing thousands of peaceful protestors including women and children. The heartless massacre sent a shock wave across the world.

Clearly, in 1919 India stood highly discontented and the nationalists felt outraged with one insult after another. They were no longer ready to swallow these insults which made them feel dishonoured and cowardly. The above developments prepared a ready ground for the next anti-British movement to build on. The Khilafat issue, which provided the immediate background, also gave the added advantage of Muslim support.

In fact, this period saw the emergence of unprecedented Hindu–Muslim unity in the backdrop of Lucknow Pact, Rowlatt agitation and emergence of nationalist leadership among Muslims. The Hindu–Muslim unity was also a byproduct of government repression in Amritsar as Hindus and Muslims were handcuffed together, made to crawl together and made to drink and eat together.

First World War (1914–18) The First World War was a global war originating in Europe, engaging all the world's great powers that assembled in two opposing groups—the Allies (France, Britain, Russia) and the Central Powers (Germany and Austria-Hungary). The groups expanded as more nations joined the war gradually. The war ended with the victory of the Allies and territorial readjustments followed. As per the **Treaty of Versailles (1919)** which was the most important of all the peace treaties, the territorial extent of the Ottoman Empire was reduced.

First World War

Khilafat Movement (1919–22)

The Khilafat Issue (or the Khilafat Wrongs)

During the First World War, Turkey was an ally of Germany and Austria against the British. After the War, victorious British dethroned the Sultan of Turkey who was also regarded as the Khalifa or Caliph (religious head of entire Muslim world). Although this act of the British angered Muslims throughout the world, the most prominent activities were organised in India.

To voice their opposition, the Indian Muslims built up a movement known as the Khilafat Movement and put forth the following demands:

1. The Khalifa's position should be restored.
2. The Khalifa's control over the Muslim sacred places should be retained.
3. In territorial adjustments after the war, Khalifa should be left with sufficient territories.

Formation of Khilafat Committee (Bombay, 1919)

In early 1919 in Bombay, a Khilafat Committee was formed on the initiative of Muslim merchants. Some of its prominent leaders were **Ali Brothers (Muhammad Ali and Shaukat Ali), Maulana**

Abul Kalam Azad, Hakim Ajmal Khan, Hasrat Mohani, Dr. Mukhtaar Ahmed Ansari and others. The activity of the committee remained confined to moderate measures like meetings and petitions in favour of the Khalifa. However, some Muslim leaders were not satisfied with this moderate approach and they advocated a more militant attitude.

All India Khilafat Conference (Delhi, 22–23 November 1919)

During 22–23 November 1919, the All India Khilafat Conference was held in Delhi and the militant Muslim leadership gave a call for non-cooperation with the British government in India. In the conference, Dr. Hasrat Mohani made a call for boycott of British goods.

Alliance with Congress and Role of Gandhi (1920)

In April 1920, Shaukat Ali threatened the British with a joint Hindu–Muslim movement of non-cooperation if the British failed to pacify the Muslims. He further declared that the movement would start 'under the guidance of Mahatma Gandhi, a man who commands the respect of both Hindus and Muslims'. It was clear that the Muslims were eager to gain the support of Hindus in India to pressurise the British. Seeing in this an excellent opportunity to forge Hindu–Muslim unity in India, Gandhi extended full support to the Khilafat movement and was also appointed as the **President of the All India Khilafat Committee**. Yet, till May 1920, Gandhi had adopted a moderate approach.

Gandhi's attitude hardened with the publication of the terms of treaty with Turkey and the Hunter Committee Report on Punjab disturbances in May 1920. The reports infuriated the Indians who felt both hurt and humiliated. The House of Lords had voted in favour of General Dyer's action and even the British public had supported him by making generous donations in his name. The **Treaty of Sevres** (1920) signed with Turkey had slapped harsh peace terms and completed the dismemberment of Turkey. The government also refused to annul the Rowlatt Act or satisfy the nationalist urge for self-government. All excuses in favour of any leniency towards the British government had now run out.

From 1–3 June 1920, the Central Khilafat Committee **met at Allahabad** and was attended by both Congress and Khilafat leaders. It was from this platform that Gandhi declared the program of non-cooperation with the government which was to include:

- Boycott of all government jobs, i.e. the civil services, army and the police
- Boycott of titles conferred by the British
- Non-payment of taxes

In the meeting, it was also suggested that unless the Khilafat and Punjab wrongs were undone, the movement shall be launched from 1st August 1920. The Khilafat Committee unanimously accepted the suggestion of non-cooperation and asked Gandhi to lead it. On 22nd June 1920, Gandhi wrote a letter to the Viceroy referring to the 'right from time immemorial of the subject to refuse to assist a ruler who misrules'. Gandhi knew that for the success of the movement in India, cooperation of the Indian National Congress was needed. He thus began efforts to make the Congress adopt the program of non-cooperation.

Maulana Mohammad Ali Jauhar (1878–1931) He was a journalist, activist, founder member of the Muslim League and a key leader of the Khilafat Movement. In 1923, he was also elected as the President of the Indian National Congress for a few months. A product of the Aligarh Muslim University, he went onto study modern history at **Oxford**. After his return to India, he took to writing in major British and Indian newspapers; and subsequently launched his own journals-**the Comrade** (an English weekly, launched from Calcutta in 1911, shifted to Delhi, the newly announced capital, in 1912) and **Hamdard** (an Urdu daily, Delhi, 1912).

In 1919, he took the initiative of bringing together the Muslim nationalist leaders as well as Gandhi (who then enlisted the support of the Congress) in a show of Hindu–Muslim unity against the British government. In 1920, Mohammad Ali along with other Khilafat leaders such as Maulana Azad, Hakim Ajmal Khan and Dr. Ansari founded **Jamia Milia Islamia** to promote independent education and social regeneration of Muslims. Disappointed with the sudden withdrawal of the Non-Cooperation Movement, he left the Congress party; he later opposed the Nehru Report (1928) and grew into a Gandhi critic.

Hasrat Mohani

Hasrat Mohani (1875–1951) Syed Fazl-ul-Hasan, known by his pen name Hasrat Mohani, was an Indian independence activist and a noted Urdu poet who wrote under the pen name 'takhallus'. He was one of the founders of Communist Party of India, is credited with the coining of the term **'Inquilab Zindabad'** (1921) and was also the **first person to demand complete independence** (Poorna Swaraj) for India in 1921 at the Ahmedabad Congress Session, despite opposition by Gandhi. In 1921, he simultaneously presided over the Ahmedabad Session of the Muslim League and demanded complete independence (Azadi-e-Kaamil).

Non-Cooperation Movement (1920–22)

Gandhi's Efforts within Congress to Adopt the Program of Non-Cooperation

The task of building consensus within the Congress for adopting non-cooperation program was not easy. According to some historians, Gandhi made an ardent effort to convince Tilak about the need for a Hindu–Muslim alliance over Khilafat Issue. But **Tilak was not in favour of any Hindu–Muslim alliance over a religious question**. He argued that the basis of alliance between the two communities should be a secular one such as the Lucknow Pact. Lala Lajpat Rai and CR Das also strongly opposed Gandhi's proposal of boycotting council elections. In fact, almost the entire old Guard of the Congress opposed Gandhi's proposal of non-cooperation.

As a next step, the program of non-cooperation was placed before the Provincial Congress Committees (PCC). The PCCs of United Province, Bengal, Madras and Bombay were largely unanimous in their view—they approved the principle of non-cooperation but rejected the idea of council boycott. While such was the attitude of traditional bases of Indian politics towards Gandhi's program, the non-traditional areas in Indian politics like Gujarat and Bihar fully backed Gandhi's program.

Launching of the Non-Cooperation Movement (1st August 1920)

On 1st August 1920, even as the discussions were on way, the Non-Cooperation Movement was formally launched on the expiry of the notice period. That very day, in the early hours, **Tilak passed away**. 'My strongest bulwark is gone', Gandhi had exclaimed on hearing the news. The launching of the movement got merged with the mourning—people kept fast, offered prayers, observed strikes and took out processions.

September 1920, Calcutta, Special Congress Session (President Lala Lajpat Rai)

In September 1920 in Calcutta, a special session of All India Congress Committee was called. Congress and Khilafat specials were run to Calcutta from Bombay and Calcutta saw a mammoth gathering of delegates and visitors. It was during this session that the Congress accepted non-cooperation as its own.

The Session was presided over by Lala Lajpat Rai and it was also in the air that there will be strong opposition to Gandhi's program. On the contrary, Gandhi's proposals were passed by the Congress by a majority of 1,000 votes! This success of Gandhi is mainly attributed to the support of the Muslims and the business class.

Supporters of Gandhi included- Motilal Nehru, Jitendralal Banerjee, Saifuddin Kitchlew, Shaukat Ali, Dr. Ansari and Yakub Hassan.

Opponents of Gandhi included- CR Das, Pt. Madan Mohan Malviya and Annie Besant.

The Calcutta Congress approved a program of:

- Boycott of titles conferred by the British
- Boycott of foreign goods, schools, courts and councils
- Encourage khadi, national schools and arbitration courts

The Congress also approved Gandhi's program till the Punjab and Khilafat wrongs were undone and swaraj granted. The decision was to be finalised in the annual session to be held in December 1920.

In the meantime, in November 1920, the council elections were held as per the Government of India Act 1919. Gandhi's program of council boycott saw a massive response and the elections were boycotted by all the Congress candidates. Even those who disagreed with the council boycott accepted the party discipline and withdrew. The voters too largely stayed away.

20th December 1920, Nagpur Congress Session (President C. Vijayaraghavachariar)

On 20th December 1920, when the Congress session began at Nagpur, there was change in the air. The opposition had melted away. The elections were over and so the boycott of councils had become a non-issue. Most surprising was the transition of CR Das from a critic of Gandhi to his ardent supporter and he himself moved the main resolution on non-cooperation.

Following were the main achievements of the Nagpur Congress:

- The Congress **endorsed the non-violent non-cooperation resolution** with the triple purpose of Non-Cooperation as a satisfactory solution to the Khilafat question, redressal of the Punjab wrongs and attainment of swaraj.
- Detailed aspects of the programme of non-cooperation were suggested which were to be put into force at a time decided by the Congress (refer to the **Programme of Non-Cooperation Movement**).
- To enable Congress to fulfil this new commitment, important changes were introduced in its aim and organisational structure. **A new constitution of the Congress party** (handiwork of Gandhi himself) was adopted and the party was reorganised on modern, democratic lines. This was the first

major effort in transforming the Congress into a real mass based political party and the changes included the following:

- Formation of Congress Committees starting from mohalla and village level up to provincial level.
- Formation of an **All India Committee** of 350 members at the apex level.
- Formation of a **Working Committee** of 15 members to act as chief executive (this proposal was first made by Tilak in 1916, but was turned down by the Moderates). This body would enable the Congress to work round the year and carry out sustained agitations.
- Formation of Provincial Congress Committees on **linguistic basis** to enable mass contact.
- The Congress was to use Hindi as far as possible.
- Opening of Congress membership to all men and women of **age 21 years** and above on payment of a reduced fee of **4 annas (25 paise) as annual subscription** to enable the poor to become members.

- The goal of the Congress was changed from 'attainment of self-government by constitutional and legal means to attainment of swaraj by peaceful and legitimate means'.
- The Congress aim of swaraj was reaffirmed but now it was explained to mean-**'self-government within the empire if possible and outside if necessary'**.
- Resolutions about Hindu-Muslim unity, the removal of untouchability and promotion of Khadi too were passed in this Congress.

It is noteworthy that henceforth, the Congress began to transform in both body and mind as reflected in its social base and policies. The Nagpur Session committed the Congress to program of extra-constitutional mass action. Gandhi, with his charismatic personality and novel methods, emerged as the new leader of the Congress party. He gave the **slogan, 'Swaraj in one year'** assuring that, if the program of non-cooperation was fully implemented, swaraj shall be attained within a year.

Leaders who left Congress

However, there were some older leaders who now left the Congress. Mohammad Ali Jinnah, GS Khaparde, Bipin Chandra Pal and Annie Besant were some prominent leaders who left the Congress during this time. They still believed in the traditional methods of agitation which were strictly confined within the four walls of law.

Program of Non-Cooperation Movement

The program of non-cooperation comprised of both destructive as well as constructive aspects.

The Destructive aspects (or the aspects of non-cooperation) included the following seven points:

1. Surrender of titles and honorary offices
2. Refusal to attend government darbars and official functions
3. Boycott of government–aided schools and colleges
4. Boycott of British courts
5. Refusal of all classes to offer themselves for service in Mesopotamia
6. Boycott of elections to provincial and central assembly
7. Boycott of foreign goods

The program of non-cooperation could be extended to include resignation from government service and mass civil disobedience including the non-payment of taxes.

The Constructive aspects included the following points:

1. Urging people to develop the spirit of discipline and self-sacrifice
2. Setting up national education institutions and organising workers for national service
3. Deciding disputes through mutual arbitration
4. Promoting indigenous goods, charkha and khadi
5. Maintaining Hindu-Muslim unity
6. Giving up untouchability
7. Observing strict non-violence and **raising of a national fund**

Various Phases of Non-Cooperation Movement

The Non-Cooperation Movement (also known as Gandhi's first Civil Disobedience Movement) was first initiated by the Khilafat Conference and later adopted by the Congress Committee. Once adopted by the Congress, the movement acquired a new energy from early January 1921 and rapidly gained momentum. Gandhi, along with Ali brothers (main Khilafat leaders) toured the whole country to gather support for the movement, addressing hundreds of people and meeting a large number of political workers.

During the period between 1920 and 1922, different aspects/items of the Non-Cooperation program assumed central emphasis at different times-

In the First Phase (January to March 1921), the main emphasis was on boycott of schools, colleges, law courts and the promotion of Charkha. Student community boycotted educational institutions in large numbers and nearly 90,000 students left government schools and colleges. Educational boycott was particularly successful in Bengal where CR Das played a key role in encouraging the boycott while **Subhas Chandra Bose** became the principal of the National College in Calcutta. Punjab too responded well to educational boycott with Lala Lajpat Rai playing a leading role despite his initial reservations about this part of the program.

The boycott of law courts was less successful but more dramatic as many leading lawyers like **Deshbandhu CR Das, Motilal Nehru, MR Jayakar, Saifuddin Kitchlew Sardar Vallabh Bhai Patel, C. Rajagopalachari, T. Prakasam and Asaf Ali** gave up their lucrative legal practice, becoming a source of inspiration for others.

In the Second Phase (April to June 1921), the main focus was on raising One Crore Rupees for **Tilak Swaraj Fund** by August 1921, enrolling one crore Congress members and installing 20 lakh charkhas by June 30. The Congress membership reached a figure of ₹50 lakh while the Tilak fund got oversubscribed, exceeding its target of ₹1 crore.

In the Third Phase (July 1921 onwards), again the main emphasis was on boycott of foreign cloth, boycott of the **visit of Prince of Wales** in November, popularisation of charkha, khadi and jail bharo by Congress volunteers.

Most successful of all items was the boycott of foreign cloth. Volunteers went door to door collecting clothes made of foreign cloth and were later burnt in a community bonfire. Picketing of toddy shops (drinking establishments), though not part of the original plan, also became very popular in many parts of the country. So much so that, to push sales in the face of boycott, the government of Bihar and Orissa had to publish a list of great men in history (like Alexander, Napoleon, Julius Caesar, Shakespeare and Bismarck) who enjoyed their drink!

Promotion of khadi was highly successful and it soon became the uniform of the national movement. While addressing a meeting at Madurai, a student complained to Gandhi that khadi was expensive. Gandhi answered that the solution then lay in wearing less clothes and hence forth gave up his dhoti and kurta and wore only a langot for the rest of his life, acquiring the nickname of **'half-naked fakir'**.

In July 1921, the Khilafat Committee passed a resolution that no Muslim should serve in the British Indian Army as it was religiously unlawful for the Muslims to do so. In September, the Ali brothers were arrested for sedition. In protest, the resolution was repeated in several meetings across the country, giving a severe blow to government prestige. Gandhi himself issued a manifesto repeating the resolution and asking Indians to severe all connections with the repressive government.

Next dramatic event was the visit of the Prince of Wales (King Edward VIII) which began on 17th November 1921. He had come to India to encourage loyalty towards the British Crown. The day was observed as a day of hartaal all over India. The same day, Gandhi himself lighted a huge bonfire of foreign cloth in the Elphinstone Mill owned by nationalist Umar Shobhani. However, the crowd returning from Gandhi's meeting clashed with the crowd returning from the Prince's welcome function. In the riots that followed over the next three days, identifiable loyalists (like Christians, Anglo-Indians and Parsis) became special targets and resulted in 59 deaths. Gandhi was profoundly disturbed and fasted for three days.

The Prince was greeted with empty streets and downed shutters wherever he went. Such successful gestures of protest gradually emboldened the non-cooperators and they began to grow more and more aggressive. The **Congress Volunteer Corps** grew powerful and acted as parallel police. By mid of November 1921, the country was on the verge of a revolt.

Government Response

The government closely observed the developments of the movement and obtained secret reports from the provinces. In September 1920, in the beginning of the movement, it tried to ignore the events thinking that repression only makes martyrs of nationalists and fans the spirit of revolt.

In May 1921, the government tried to create a rift between the Khilafat leaders and Gandhi through **Gandhi-Reading talks** (in which Viceroy Reading tried to persuade Gandhi to ask Ali brothers to withdraw their speeches suggesting violence), but the talks failed.

By December 1921, government changed its policy and launched repression measures:

- Congress and Khilafat Volunteer Corps were declared unlawful
- Public meetings and processions were banned
- Newspapers were gagged, offices of Congress and Khilafat raided at midnight
- At many places, police lathi charged and even fired at the satyagrahis
- A large number of activists were arrested and by end of 1921, all prominent leaders except Gandhi were imprisoned

Simultaneously, in mid-December, Viceroy Reading made a futile attempt to negotiate with the Congress through **Madan Mohan Malviya** and repression continued.

Developments Leading upto Chauri Chaura (1922)

- The government showed no signs of relenting and Gandhi came under tremendous pressure to start the civil disobedience movement as laid down under the Program of Non-Cooperation Movement.

- **In December 1921, at Ahmedabad Congress Session (presided by CR Das while still in jail, with Hakim Ajmal Khan as the acting president)**, the party appointed Gandhi as the sole authority on the issue.
- In January 1922, an All Parties Conference was held where Gandhi shared his assessment of the Non-Cooperation Movement and built a consensus on his views.
- On 1st February, Gandhi sent an ultimatum to the Viceroy threatening him with mass civil disobedience unless government repression was abandoned and political prisoners were released.
- The Viceroy was unmoved and left Gandhi with no choice.
- Gandhi decided to begin mass civil disobedience and no-tax campaign from **Bardoli taluqua of Surat district** and **5th February 1922 was fixed as the date** of the launch (the Congress had, by now, granted permission to the PCCs to start mass civil disobedience wherever the people were ready. No-tax movements were already sanctioned in **Midnapur** in Bengal and **Chirala-Pirala** and **Pedanandipadu** in Andhra). However, it seems Bardoli was fated to wait another 6 years to play its role in the national movement.
- On 5th February 1922, the day when civil disobedience was to be launched, the Chauri Chaura incident took place and changed the whole situation. At Chauri Chaura, in Gorakhpur district of UP, a mob of angry peasants attacked a local police station and set it on fire, killing 22 policemen. Shocked by this incident of violence, Gandhi withdrew the movement (Read ahead in detail about the decline of the movement).

Extent of Participation

The Non-Cooperation Movement was the first attempt at an all India mass struggle and it commanded the support and sympathy of vast sections Indian people including peasants, workers, artisans, shopkeepers, traders, professionals and white collar employees.

Middle Class

The middle class provided initial leadership to the movement but they had a lot of reservations regarding Gandhi's program. In traditional centres of elite politicians like Calcutta, Bombay and Madras, the response was very limited and there was lukewarm response towards boycott of titles and government jobs.

Indian business group-the big businessmen kept away from the movement as they were afraid of labour unrest in the factories. But the regular businessmen extended support to economic boycott, particularly the textile industry which had benefitted from the promotion of swadeshi.

Comparative newcomers in Indian politics like **Rajendra Prasad in Bihar** and **Vallabh Bhai Patel in Gujarat** found expression of their aspirations in Gandhian movement and extended solid support to Gandhi.

Women and Students

The response from women and students was very encouraging. Women joined the movement in large numbers and participated in various forms- they picketed shops selling foreign cloth and liquor; they gave up purdah and offered jewellery for Tilak Fund. Students participated in massive numbers—thousands of them left government schools and colleges and joined national schools and colleges like Kashi Vidyapeeth, Gujarat Vidyapeeth and Jamia Milia Islamia of Aligarh (Jamia was established in

October 1920 at Aligarh as the new National Muslim University on the demand of some students of AMU who felt that AMU had a pro-British stance) that came into existence during this time. Dr. Zakir Hussain, Acharya Narendra Dev and Lala Lajpat Rai were among many distinguished teachers at these national institutions. The students actively took up voluntary work in the movement.

Peasants and Workers

The massive participation of peasants and workers was the most remarkable aspect of the Non-Cooperation movement that turned it into a real mass movement.

> **Dr. Zakir Husain (1897–1969)** A product of Aligarh Muslim University and founder member of **Jamia Milia Islamia**, Dr. Zakir Husain was a great educationist of his time. He served as the third President of independent India (1967–69), was the **first Muslim President** and was awarded the **Bharat Ratna** in 1963.

Spread of the Movement and Local Variations

The year 1921 was marked by numerous protests against the British Raj in India and the Non-Cooperation Movement undoubtedly saw a huge response from different parts of the country. The spatial spread of the movement was nearly nationwide. Areas that were particularly active were UP, Bihar, Orissa, Assam and even Bombay. However, the response to the movement remained relatively weak in traditional areas of Indian politics such as Bengal, Maharashtra and Madras. There was also significant local variation in terms of expression of the movement due to **linkup with local grievances**. Instructions of the Congress were not also always followed.

United Provinces (UP)

The response from United Provinces was very effective. The programme of non-cooperation was well organised in cities and towns. In the countryside of UP, it got entangled with the **kisan movement**. The peasants there repeatedly burst in violent protest against the talukdars and merchants despite Congress appeals for maintaining non-violence at all times. Widespread peasant riots under the leadership of **Baba Ram Chandra** were also witnessed in districts of Rae Bareilly, Pratapgarh, Faizabad and Sultanpur. Their major demands included-no begar (forced labor) and rasad (forced supplies), no nazarana (extra premium on rent) and no eviction from holdings. In late 1921, the **'Eka movement'**, another strong peasant outburst, took place under the leadership of radical leader **Madari Pasi.**

Bihar

In Bihar, several local grievances got linked with the non-cooperation movement. These issues included right to graze cattle on government wasteland, right to wear sacred thread, issues of cow protection and kisan rights. As a result, several districts of Bihar like **Champaran, Saran** and **Purnia**, emerged as storm centres of the movement.

Assam

The movement received enthusiastic support in the distant province of Assam where the local grievances of the labourers working in Assam tea gardens found expression in the movement. They hailed **'Gandhi Maharaj ki Jai'** for higher wages and better conditions of work.

Orissa

In Orissa, the tenants of Kanika Raj refused payment of abwabs.

Rajasthan

In Rajasthan, once again peasant movements provided impetus to Non-cooperation as the peasants raised voice against cesses and begar. **Bijolia Movement in Mewar** (a peasant movement against excessive land revenue exactions, that originated in the Bijolia jagir of Mewar and gradually spread to neighboring jagirs) and the **Bhil Movement led by Motilal Tejawat** (an adivasi peasant movement against oppressive jagirdars exacting begar and unfair taxes) also gained strength from the Non-Cooperation Movement.

Andhra

In Andhra, the issues of peasants and tribals found expression in the Non-Cooperation Movement. They protested against forest laws and forcibly sent their cattle into forests to break grazing laws. **Alluri Sitram Raju** played a prominent role in organising the tribals and linking their demands with those of the Non-Cooperation Movement.

Punjab

In Punjab, the response to non-cooperation per se was not very remarkable but the movement got linked with the local Akali Movement (1920–25) for reform and control of the Gurudwaras. The Akalis freely used the non-cooperation tactics of Gandhi and remained non-violent even in the face of severe repression. The period manifested tremendous communal unity amongst the Sikhs, the Hindus and the Muslims.

Bengal

In Bengal, response to Gandhian methods was less encouraging. The elites of Calcutta were critical of Gandhian ways. Rabindranath Tagore **appreciated Gandhi's efforts but attacked his 'narrowness' and charkha**. Nevertheless, the movement brought about immense political awakening in urban and rural masses.

Maharashtra

In Maharashtra, the response to Non-Cooperation Movement was not very encouraging since the followers of Tilak did not show much enthusiasm about Gandhi. However, there were some radical outbursts, for instance at Malegaon (Nasik), a few policemen were burnt to death following the arrest of some local leaders.

Karnataka

In Karnataka, the response was lukewarm and the Madras presidency saw little participation of people. Not much enthusiasm was seen in surrender of titles and renunciation of legal practice.

Abwabs refer to miscellaneous kinds of fines, cesses or taxes levied by native chiefs upon the subjects like the house tax, grazing tax, irrigation tax, etc.

Chauri Chaura (5th February 1922) and Decline of Movement

On 5th February 1922, the day when Civil Disobedience was to be launched, the Chauri Chaura incident took place and changed the whole situation. At Chauri Chaura, in Gorakhpur district of UP, police tried to stop a procession of Congress and Khilafat activists. Irritated by this behaviour, some activists attacked the policemen, who in turn opened fire. Infuriated, the entire procession attacked the police and when the police took shelter inside the police station, the station itself was set on fire, killing all of its occupants. In all, 22 policemen were killed.

Shocked by this incident of violence, Gandhi withdrew the movement. The civil disobedience at Bardoli was also postponed. Gandhi now advised people to direct their energies in constructive work.

Response to Withdrawal of Movement

Gandhi's decision to withdraw the movement came as a shock to many Congressmen who even protested against the withdrawal. Motilal Nehru, CR Das, Subhas Chandra Bose, Jawaharlal Nehru and others expressed their bewilderment. They could not understand why the entire country has to pay the price for erroneous behaviour of some people in a remote village!

- Subhas Chandra Bose, in his autobiography The Indian Struggle, called it a **'national calamity'**.
- Jawaharlal Nehru also expressed his 'amazement and consternation' at the withdrawal.

To the above criticism, Gandhi replied- 'The movement had unconsciously drifted from the right path. We have to come back to our moorings, and we can again go straight ahead'. According to Gandhi, the incident proved that the countrymen were not yet properly trained in the lesson of non-violence.

On 12th February 1922, Movement came to an end

On 12th February, at Bardoli, a meeting of the Congress Working committee was held. The committee condemned Chauri Chaura violence and endorsed the withdrawal of the civil disobedience movement, known as **Bardoli Resolution**. It also asked the peasants to pay taxes and tenants to pay rents. On that day itself, Gandhi started his five day fast as penance. This marked the formal end of the movement. On 10th March 1922 Gandhi was arrested in his ashram and sentenced to six years of imprisonment.

Trial of Gandhi Trial was held before **Mr. Broomfield,** District and Sessions Judge of Ahmedabad. The Judge behaved with great consideration and Gandhi also made his task easy by pleading guilty. The trial was made historic by the statement that Gandhi made before the court while pleading guilty. He invited the court to award him 'the highest penalty that can be inflicted upon me for what in law is a deliberate crime and what appears to me to be the highest duty of a citizen'. The trial was also remarkable due to the personality of the accused and due to absence of any acrimony on either part. Gandhi as well as the judge presented themselves as models of moderation and mutual respect. While passing the sentence, the judge followed the precedent of the case decided 12 years ago, i.e. the case of **Bal Gangadhar Tilak**, under the same section. Gandhi was sentenced to six years' simple imprisonment for the crime of spreading disaffection against the government and was lodged in **Yerawada jail, Poona**. He was released early on 5 February 1924 itself on account of ill health.

End of Khilafat Issue

The Khilafat issue also ended when people of Turkey rose under the leadership of Mustafa Kamal Pasha (or Kemal Ataturk) in November 1922. He deprived the Sultan of his political power and took many steps to modernise Turkey and declared Turkey as a secular state. Pasha eliminated Islam from Turkish Constitution, granted women extensive rights, introduced legal codes based on European lines and introduced modern industries. All these developments broke the back of the Khilafat movement. **Pasha abolished the Caliphate itself in 1924** and thus ended the issue of the Khilafat the world over.

Reasons for Withdrawal of Non-Cooperation Movement (An Analysis)

1. The Chauri Chaura violence proved that the countrymen were not yet properly trained in the lesson of non-violence. It was clear that revolution was in the air and yet, no revolutionary leadership existed. In such a situation, it was feared that further continuation of the movement would only lead to chaos.
2. It was also felt that the movement was gradually deflecting from its original path and turning into a no-rent movement against the zamindars. The original aim was a mass movement involving various classes and not a class revolution.
3. Despite Gandhi's repeated requests to remain non-violent at all times, random incidents of violence continued. It was feared that such incidents could be cited as examples by the government to launch a massive round of repression. This could upset the entire strategy of non-violent non-cooperation which relied on the principle that repressive forces will invariably lose for raising arms against peaceful protestors.
4. Had the movement not been withdrawn, it was likely to have been brutally crushed leading to mass demoralisation and questioning of the very principle of non-cooperation.
5. Gandhi's decision was also partly influenced by the fact that, by the end of 1921, the movement had begun to show signs of ebbing. Students had begun to drift back to schools and colleges, lawyers and litigants back to courts, the businessmen had become weary of mounting stocks of foreign cloth and attendance had dwindled in meetings and rallies.

Critics of Gandhi fail to recognise that mass movement are inherently cyclic in character and have a tendency to ebb after reaching a certain height since the capacity of the masses to sacrifice and withstand repression is not unlimited. The ebb comes as a breathing space to regain energy for the next round of struggle. Thus, withdrawal should not be taken as betrayal but as an inherent part of the strategy itself.

Mind Map for Chapters 6.10 to 6.15

Following the withdrawal of Non-Cooperation Movement, various national as well as anti-national forces emerged. The prominent among them were (covered in the upcoming chapters):

- The Swarajists and their program of council entry (1922–29)
- The No-changers and their Constructive work (after 1922)
- Communalism and revival of Muslim League and Hindu Mahasabha (1922–37)
- Revolutionary Movement with a turn towards Socialism (after 1922)
- Growth of the Left Movement and spread of Socialist and Communist ideas (1920s–30s)
- Peasants' and Workers' Movements (1920s–30s)
- States' People's Movement (1920s–30s)
- Caste Movements like Self-Respect movement (1920s–30s)

Thus, we see that the **third decade of the 20th century was a watershed in modern Indian history** in more ways than one. It not only marked the entry of the Indian masses into the national movement, it also saw the emergence of a variety of political currents on the Indian scene. All these diverse currents owed their origin to Gandhian philosophy of non-violence, as they embodied positive or negative reaction to it.

Note: For the purpose of organisation, one chapter per theme has been developed, covering all developments upto 1947. Readers may like to refer to Chapters 6.16 to 6.19 from time to time to keep track of mainstream national movement.

Significance of Non-Cooperation Movement

True, the movement failed to achieve its main aims of restitution of Khilafat and attainment of swaraj. Yet, the Non-Cooperation Movement was a landmark in India's Struggle for Independence in many ways—social, economic and political:

In the social field, the impact of the movement was immense. Gandhi emphasised on the need for unity among Indians and removal of barriers of caste, class, religion and gender. Consequently, in meetings and processions, people of all castes and communities worked and ate together. For the first time, the lower classes raised their head and worked shoulder to shoulder with all others, accelerating social mobility and reform. The Hindu-Muslim unity reached its peak and many-a-times it was difficult to distinguish between Non-Cooperation and Khilafat gatherings. Swami Shraddhanand, an Arya Samajist, was asked by Muslims to preach from the pulpit of Jama Masjid at Delhi, while Dr. Saifuddin Kitchlew, a Muslim, was given the keys to the Golden Temple (the Hindu–Muslim unity seen during the days of non-cooperation was never to be seen again and henceforth communalism began to take its toll).

In the economic field, the economic boycott proved to be more successful than the one during Swadeshi Movement of 1905–08. While this created panic among British industries, the Indian industries immensely benefitted due to promotion of swadeshi. The Indian textile industry particularly benefitted from the popularisation of charkha and khadi. Emphasis on village reconstruction and self-help through panchayats brought about overall economic revival.

In the political field, the movement emerged as the first true mass movement involving all classes and communities in India. The national awakening, for the first time, reached the remotest corners of the country with the commoners participating in the mainstream national movement. The INC emerged as a true mass party and the charge of it representing 'a microscopic minority' could never be hurled at Congress again (as earlier remarked by Lord Dufferin). The movement also demonstrated the capacity of 'poor dumb millions' of Indians to participate in a national movement on modern lines. The movement demonstrated that the urge for freedom was not merely a preserve of the educated elite but the cry of the nation.

The above positive gains in the social, economic and political fields immensely increased the self-confidence and self-esteem of the Indian people. It replaced the feelings of bondage and suppression with those of freedom and national dignity. Gandhi had rightly said that the movement had achieved in one year what could not be done in 30 years by earlier methods. Admittedly, the two years between 1920–22 constituted a stormy period of national movement when the whole of India, for the first time, stood up against the British Raj.

With the withdrawal of the Non-Cooperation Movement on 12th February 1922, a battle was over, not the war. On 23rd February, in an article in Young India, Gandhi wrote, 'It is high time that the British people were made to realise that the fight that was commenced in 1920 is a fight to the finish, whether it lasts one month or one year or many months or many years'.

Prelim Capsule

Prelim Capsule- Khilafat and Non-Cooperation Movement

Date	Event	Important Details
1919–22	Khilafat Movement	The First World War ended with the **Treaty of Versailles.** Victorious British dethroned the Sultan of Turkey who was also regarded as the Khalifa or Caliph. Indian Muslims organise the Khilafat Movement. Aim of Khilafat Movement: 1. The Khalifa's position should be restored 2. The Khalifa's control over the Muslim sacred places should be retained 3. In territorial adjustments after the war, Khalifa should be left with sufficient territories.
1919 (Bombay)	Khilafat Committee	Leaders—**Ali brothers**, Maulana Azad, Hakim Ajmal Khan, Hasrat Mohani, Dr. MA Ansari.
November 1919 (Delhi)	All India Khilafat Conference	Dr. Hasrat Mohani made a call for boycott of British goods and non-cooperation with the British government.
1920	Alliance with Congress	**Gandhi appointed as the President of the All India Khilafat Committee.** Till May 1920, Gandhi was still a moderate but afterwards his attitude hardened with the publication of the terms of treaty with Turkey and the Hunter Committee Report on Punjab disturbances.
June 1920 (Allahabad)	Central Khilafat Committee Meet	**Attended by both Congress and Khilafat leaders.** Ultimatum given to government unless the Khilafat and Punjab wrongs were undone, the movement shall be launched from 1st August 1920. **Tilak opposed** Hindu–Muslim alliance over a religious question.
1st August 1920	Non-Cooperation Movement	Non-Cooperation movement launched. Tilak passes away.
20th December 1920 (Nagpur)	Nagpur Congress Session	President C.Vijayraghavachariar. **CR Das turns from a critic to Gandhi's supporter** and moves the main resolution on Non-Cooperation Resolution of non-violent non-cooperation endorsed with the triple purpose of Non-Cooperation as the follows: 1. Satisfactory solution to the Khilafat question, 2. Redressal of the Punjab wrongs and 3. Attainment of swaraj.

		Detailed program of non-cooperation was suggested, to be put into force at a time decided by the Congress. **A new constitution of the Congress party** (handwork of Gandhi himself) was adopted. Gandhi gave the slogan, 'Swaraj in one year'. **Mohammad Ali Jinnah, GS Khaparde, Bipin Chandra Pal and Annie Besant left the Congress**, they still believed in the lawful methods of agitation.
January to March 1921	First Phase of Non-Cooperation Movement	Emphasis was on boycott of schools, colleges, law courts and promotion of Charkha. CR Das played a key role in encouraging boycott. **Subhas Chandra Bose** became the principal of the National College in Calcutta. Many leading lawyers like CR Das, Motilal Nehru, MR Jayakar, Saifuddin Kitchlew, Sardar Vallabhbhai Patel, C. Rajagopalachari, T. Prakasam and Asaf Ali gave up their lucrative legal practice.
April to June 1921	Second Phase	Main focus was on raising **One Crore Rupees for Tilak Swaraj Fund**.
July 1921 onwards	Third Phase	Main emphasis was on **boycott of the visit of Prince of Wales** in November and boycott of foreign cloth. **Congress Volunteer Corps** acted as parallel police.
May 1921	Gandhi-Reading talks	Viceroy Reading tried to persuade Gandhi to ask Ali brothers to withdraw their speeches suggesting violence, but the talks failed.
December 1921	Government Repression	Congress and Khilafat Volunteer Corps were declared unlawful.
	Ahmedabad Congress Session	Presided over by CR Das while still in jail, **Hakim Ajmal Khan was the acting President**.
1st February 1922	Gandhi sends ultimatum to Viceroy	Gandhi threatens with mass civil disobedience unless government repression was abandoned and political prisoners were released. The Viceroy was unmoved. Gandhi decided to begin mass civil disobedience and no-tax campaign from Bardoli taluqua of Surat district. 5th February 1922 was fixed as the date of the launch.
5th February 1922	Chauri Chaura violence	At Chauri Chaura (Gorakhpur district, UP), a mob of angry peasants attacked a local police station and set it on fire, killing 22 policemen. Shocked by this incident of violence, Gandhi withdrew the movement calling it a **'Himalayan blunder'**. Subhas Chandra Bose, in his autobiography 'the Indian Struggle', called it a **'national calamity'**.
12th February 1922 (Bardoli)	CWC Meeting, Bardoli	CWC endorses the withdrawal of the civil disobedience movement, known as **Bardoli Resolution**.

10th March 1922	Gandhi arrested	Trial was held before **Mr. Broomfield**. While passing the sentence the judge followed the precedent of the case of **Bal Gangadhar Tilak, under the same section**. Gandhi sentenced to 6 years' imprisonment and was lodged in Yerawada jail, Poona.
November 1922	End of Khilafat Issue	Mustafa Kamal Pasha declared Turkey as a secular state and later abolished the Caliphate itself (1924). Thus, ended the issue of the Khilafat the world over.

Previous Years' Questions – Preliminary Exam

1. Which of the following were the main objectives of the Khilafat Movement? **[UPSC 1993]**
   1. To raise anti British feelings among the Muslims of India.
   2. To reform the Muslim society.
   3. To demand separate electorate and preserve the Khilafat.
   4. To save the Ottoman Empire and preserve the Khilafat.

   Choose the correct answer from the following options.
   (a) 1 and 2 (b) 2 and 3
   (c) 3 and 4 (d) 1 and 4
2. The title given by the British government to Mahatma Gandhi which he surrendered during the Non-Cooperation Movement was: **[UPSC 1993]**
   (a) Hind Kesari (b) Kaiser - i - Hind
   (c) Rai Bahadur (d) Rt. Honorable
3. Consider the following statements: **[UPSC 1996]**
   The Non-Cooperation movement led to the:
   1. Congress becoming a mass movement for the first time
   2. Growth of Hindu–Muslim Unity
   3. Removal of fear of the British might from the minds of the people
   4. British government willingness to grant political concessions to Indians

   Which of these statement/s is are correct? Select the correct answer from the following options.
   (a) 1, 2, 3 and 4 are correct
   (b) 2 and 3 are correct
   (c) 1 and 3 are correct
   (d) 3 and 4 are correct
4. Which one of the following events was characterised by Montague as 'Preventive Murder'? **[UPSC 1998]**
   (a) Killing of INA activists
   (b) Massacre of Jallianwala Bagh
   (c) Shooting of the Mahatma
   (d) Shooting of Curzon Willy
5. Assertion (A): Gandhi stopped the Non-Cooperation Movement in 1922.
   Reason (R): Violence at Chauri Chaura led him to stop the movement **[UPSC 1998]**
   Select the answer for the options given below:
   (a) if both A and R are true and R is the correct explanation of A
   (b) if both A and R are true but R is not the correct explanation of A
   (c) if A is true but R is false
   (d) if A is false but R is true
6. Assertion (A): The Khilafat movement did bring the urban Muslims into the fold of the National Movement.
   Reason (R): There was a predominant element of anti-imperialism in both the National and Khilafat Movements. **[UPSC 1998]**
   Select the answer for the options given below:
   (a) if both A and R are true and R is the correct explanation of A
   (b) if both A and R are true but R is not the correct explanation of A
   (c) if A is true but R is false
   (d) if A is false but R is true

7. Who among the following leaders proposed to adopt Complete Independence as the goal of the Congress in the Ahmedabad session of 1920? **[UPSC 2001]**
   (a) Abul Kalam Azad
   (b) Jawaharlal Nehru
   (c) Hasrat Mohani
   (d) Mohandas Karamchand Gandhi
8. The Hunter Commission was appointed after the **[UPSC 2001]**
   (a) Black hole incident
   (b) Jallianwala Bagh massacre
   (c) Uprising of 1857
   (d) Partition of Bengal
9. Consider the following events during India's freedom struggle: **[UPSC 2004]**
   1. Chauri–Chaura Outrage
   2. Minto–Morley Reforms
   3. Dandi March
   4. Montagu–Chelmsford Reforms

   Which one of the following is the correct chronological order of the events given above?
   (a) 1-3-2-4
   (b) 2-4-1-3
   (c) 1-4-2-3
   (d) 2-3-1-4
10. Who among the following was not associated with the formation of UP Kisan Sabha in February 1918? **[UPSC 2005]**
    (a) Indra Narayan Dwivedi
    (b) Gauri Shankar Misra
    (c) Jawaharlal Nehru
    (d) Madan Mohan Malviya

Previous Years' Questions – Main Exam

1. What were the effects of the Non-Violent Non-Cooperation Movement in India? When was the movement suspended and why? **[UPSC 1986]**
2. Why did Gandhiji launch the Non-Violent Non-Cooperation movement on the Khilafat question? How were other issues joined to it later on? Discuss the constructive programme of the Non-Cooperation movement. **[UPSC 1989]**
3. What were the reasons that changed Gandhiji's attitude of responsive cooperation to Non-Cooperation in 1920? What were its consequences? **[UPSC 1996]**
4. Discuss the aims and objectives of the Khilafat Movement. To what extent was it successful? **[UPSC 2001]**
5. Form a critical assessment of the Non-Cooperation movement. **[UPSC 2004]**
6. Do you think Mahatma Gandhi's support to Khilafat Movement had diluted his secular credentials? Give your arguments based on the assessment of events. **[UPSC 2007]**
7. 'Non-Cooperation Movement gave new direction and energy to the National Movement'. Explain. **[UPSC 2008]**
8. Since the decade of the 1920s, the national movement acquired various ideological strands and thereby expanded its social base. Discuss. **[UPSC 2020]**

Answers

Previous Years' Questions – Preliminary Exam

1. (d)	2. (b)	3. (b)	4. (b)	5. (a)
6. (a)	7. (c)	8. (b)	9. (b)	10. (c)

10

Swarajists and Constructive Work (1922–29)

The period between 1922 and 1929 saw the emergence of the Swarajists as a new trend in Indian politics. The Swaraj Party was formed under the leadership of Motilal Nehru and Chittaranjan Das with the twin aims of council entry and constructive work. The era of the Swarajists witnessed new problems and new dilemmas; it enriched the national movement with new leaders and their new forms of political action.

Backdrop

When Gandhi launched the Non-Cooperation Movement, he had given the slogan of 'Swaraj in one year'. This new hope had stirred the imagination of the masses who had been aroused into vigorous action. The sudden withdrawal of the movement had created widespread disappointment and consternation. Taking advantage of people's demoralisation, government resorted to the policy of repression; and the British Prime Minister Lloyd George (1916–22), delivered his famous 'steel frame speech' (praising the efforts of the ICS officers) upholding British aristocracy.

Feeling betrayed, a section of leaders had begun to question the very efficacy of Gandhian methods of struggle. The Civil Disobedience Enquiry Committee concluded that the country was not ready for mass civil disobedience, and the constructive program found only a limited response. The upper middle class intellectuals were never really attracted by the idea of constructive work which was essentially a program for socio-economic amelioration. Gandhi was in prison now and there was little he could do from behind bars. In his absence, the unity he had assiduously created began to dwindle away and there emerged an open division within Congress. Two intellectuals—Motilal Nehru and Chittaranjan Das now took the lead and put forward their new agenda of council entry.

Chittaranjan Das (1870–1925) Popularly known as **Deshbandhu** (Friend of the Nation), Das was a lawyer and a freedom fighter. In 1894, in a stunning move, Das gave up his lucrative practice and joined the **Anushilan Samiti** with Pramathanath Mitra. In 1909, he successfully defended **Aurobindo Ghosh** in the Alipore Conspiracy Case (1909). During the Non-Cooperation Movement, he emerged as a key leader and initiated boycott of British clothes by burning his own western clothes (while at one point of time, he maintained a laundry in Paris and got his clothes stitched and washed there!). As a means to fight the British rule, he started the newspaper **'Forward'** and later changed its name to **'Liberty'**. He became the **first Mayor** of Calcutta Municipal Corporation.

Chittaranjan Das

His wife Basanti Devi was the first woman to court arrested along with her sister-in-law Urmila Devi in 1921 during the Non-Cooperation Movement. In 1922, he co-founded the Swaraj Party along with Motilal Nehru and HS Suhrawardy. His legacy was carried forward by his protégé Subhas Chandra Bose.

Motilal Nehru (1861–1931) He was a lawyer and a veteran leader of the INC. Born in a Kashmiri Brahmin family, he graduated in law from University of Cambridge and set up a lucrative practice at Allahabad. He started the daily The Independent (1919) and emerged as one of the few wealthy leaders of the Congress. Under the influence of Gandhi, he gave up Western lifestyle and participated actively in the Non-Cooperation Movement. He, however, criticised Gandhi's decision to withdraw the movement after Chauri-Chaura and helped found the Swaraj Party. His declining health kept him out of the historic events of 1929-31 when Congress adopted purna swaraj as goal. During this time, he was succeeded by his son Jawaharlal, who later rose to become the first Prime Minister of free India.

Motilal Nehru

Formation of Swaraj Party (1st January 1923)

Chittaranjan Das and Motilal Nehru now proposed that Non-Cooperation should be taken inside the councils and they be transformed into arenas of political struggle. They suggested that the nationalists should not boycott the councils, but enter them, obstruct their working, expose them as 'sham parliaments' and wreck them from within.

In December 1922 at Gaya Session of the INC, CR Das (as the President of the Congress) and Motilal (as its Secretary) put forward their program of 'either mending or ending' the councils. The opposition led by Rajgopalachari opposed the new proposal which was finally defeated. Das and Motilal resigned from their respective offices.

On 1st January 1923, CR Das announced the formation of the Congress- Khilafat Swarajya Party (better known as Swaraj Party), with himself as President and Motilal as Secretary. It accepted the Congress program except in one respect, it would take part in council elections. In this way, the proposal of Nehru–Das combine divided the Congress into Pro-Changers (later called the Swarajists) and No-Changers (or orthodox Gandhians).

The Pro Changers they wanted the constructive program to be coupled with council entry. They were led by **CR Das** and **Motilal Nehru** and included other prominent Congressmen like Ajmal Khan, NC Kelkar, Subhas Chandra Bose, Vithalbhai Patel, Hussain Shaheed Suhrawardy.

The No-Changers they denounced the idea of council entry and wanted the Congress to focus on constructive program alone. They were effectively led by Gandhi (in jail now) and included C. Rajgopalachari, Rajendra Prasad, Vallabhbhai Patel, **Jawaharlal Nehru** and MA Ansari.

In September 1923, Delhi, Special Session of the Congress was held under the presidentship of Maulana Azad and Congressmen were allowed to contest forthcoming elections in the month of November. The Swarajists got only a few weeks to prepare, yet they managed to do quite well and swept the polls in some provinces despite extremely narrow franchise (only about 3 per cent).

In the annual session of the Congress at Cocanada (or Kakinada), it was further stated that Non-Cooperation could be practiced inside the councils. Efforts on constructive program were also stressed, thus avoiding another split in the Congress.

CR Das and Motilal Nehru CR Das and Motilal Nehru were highly successful lawyers, had once been moderates but had accepted the politics of boycott and non-cooperation in 1920. They had given up their legal practice and joined the Non-Cooperation movement as full-time workers and donated to the nation their magnificent houses in Calcutta and Allahabad, respectively.

Note: It is noteworthy that during 1923–24, Congressmen, both Swarajists and No-changers participated in large numbers in elections to municipalities and local bodies. The No-changers wished to use the local bodies to promote their constructive work. Consequently, they held the following offices:

- CR Das became the Mayor of Calcutta
- Subhas Chandra Bose became the Chief Executive Officer of Calcutta
- Vithalbhai Patel became the President of Bombay Corporation
- Vallabhbhai Patel became the President of Ahmedabad Municipality
- Rajendra Prasad became the President of Patna Municipality
- Jawaharlal Nehru became the President of Allahabad Municipality

Gandhi and the Swarajists

Gandhi Adopts a Harsh Stand

On 5th February 1924, Gandhi was released from jail and took a hard stand against the Swarajists. In June 1924, AICC meeting was held at Ahmedabad where Gandhi's resolutions were virtually aimed at eliminating the Swarajists.

- One was the **Hand Spinning Resolution** which made it compulsory for every office bearer of the Congress to spin 2000 yards of yarn every month and the defaulters were to be penalised.
- Those who did not accept the council boycott were asked to resign.

Gandhi Dilutes his Stand

Das–Nehru combine were amply disturbed as their popularity with the electorates was to a great extent due to the name and resources of Congress, and they offered stiff resistance. Eventually, Gandhi decided to dilute his stand due to a combination of reasons:

- When Gandhi was released in February 1924 the Bombay government was quite hopeful for another split in the Congress. They banked on the hope that Gandhi would denounce the Swarajists which would lead them to defect. Gandhi was in no mood to oblige them, even though he continued to believe in the futility of the Swarajist program.
- Gandhi shared warm personal relations with both Das and Motilal Nehru and he had full trust in their bonafides. He saw them as the most valued and respected leaders who had made great sacrifices for the cause of the country.
- In any case, council entry had already occurred. He felt that public opposition to the 'settled fact' of council entry would be counterproductive and could be misunderstood or even seen as a weakness.
- The Swarajists had attained formidable success in 1923 elections, had grown in stature and conducted themselves in the most uncompromising manner in the councils. They were certainly not becoming a limb of imperial administration.
- Finally, towards the end of 1924 the government launched a brutal attack on the civil liberties of the Swarajists in Bengal on the pretext of fighting terrorism. Several Congressmen were arrested

including Subhas Chandra Bose and two Swarajists, Anil Baran Roy and SC Mitra. Gandhi decided to show his solidarity and surrendered before the Swarajists.

On 6th November 1924, Gandhi brought the struggle between the Swarajists and the No-changers to an end by signing a **joint statement** with Das and Motilal Nehru that the Swaraj Party would carry on work in the legislatures on behalf of the Congress and as an integral part of the Congress (a decision later endorsed by the Belgaum Congress). In this way, Gandhi decided to accommodate them, avoiding another split in the Congress. He allowed the Swarajists, as agents of the Congress, to deal with the government. The Swarajists in turn expressed their willingness to carry on the constructive work of Gandhi.

In the Belgaum Congress presided by Gandhi, mutual trust between the Swarajists and No-Changers was furthered.

- The Congress endorsed Gandhi's decision to allow the Swaraj Party to carry on work in the legislatures **on behalf of the Congress and as an integral part of the Congress**.
- Gandhi gave the Swarajists a majority of seats on his Working Committee.
- Gandhi also stressed on the boycott of foreign cloth and prescribed constructive program (mainly spinning khadi, Hindu–Muslim unity and removal of untouchability) as the chief means for attainment of Swaraj.

Aims and Objectives of Swaraj Party

The aims and objectives of the Swaraj Party were specified in its constitution first published in February 1923. Henceforth, it underwent many changes until December 1924 (Belgaum Congress), when its relationship was finally defined vis-a-vis the Congress. The constitution of 1924 laid down the party's aim as 'attainment of Swaraj by the people of India by all legitimate and peaceful means', though the exact nature of Swaraj was left undefined. The manifesto of the party stated that inside the legislatures, the Swarajists would demand 'the right of the people of India to control the existing machinery and system of government', and will 'resort to a policy of **uniform, continuous and consistent obstruction**' in case the government refused to entertain such a demand.

Program of Swaraj Party

The Swaraj Party was an integral part of the Congress and functioned as one of its departments and as such, its program could not have been much different from that of the Congress. The Swaraj Party proclaimed to carry the non-violent non-cooperation inside the councils with a view to wrecking the councils (or the Constitution of 1919) from within. With this aim, it resolved to adopt the following program:

Inside the Council The party decided that whenever possible it would:

- Refuse supplies and throw out budget to force recognition of their rights.
- Throw out all proposals by which the bureaucracy proposed to consolidate its powers.
- Move resolutions and support bills necessary for healthy growth of the national life.
- Help the constructive program of the Congress.
- Follow a definite economic policy to prevent the drain of public wealth from India.
- Project the rights of labor and adjust the relations between landlords and tenants, capitalists and workmen.

Outside the Council The party resolved to work for:

- Inter-communal unity
- Removal of untouchability
- Organisation of labor in the country-agricultural and industrial
- Acquisition of economic control of the country
- Establishment of control of nationalists over municipal affairs
- Carrying out the constructive program of the Congress
- Formation of federation of Asiatic countries to secure mutual solidarity
- Enlisting support of foreign countries in the struggle for Swaraj

It is clear that the program of the Swaraj Party was quite comprehensive and formulated to please all sections of society with an eye on the elections.

Methods of the Swarajists

The Swarajist policy of 'uniform, continuous and consistent obstruction to wreck the reforms from within' is comparable to the **method of sabotage** which the British felt was more difficult to deal with than open rebellion.

The methods of the Swarajists included blocking the passage of government bills, creating deadlocks, resorting to adjournment motions and asking inconvenient questions to expose the alienness of the British government. Later, the Swarajists also adopted the method of frequently walking in and walking out. This method became popular as **'patriotism in locomotion'** and earned the Swarajists the nickname of **'peripatetic patriots'**.

The destructive methods of the Swarajists included rejection of the votable parts of the budget and rejection of proposals emanating from the bureaucracy. Their constructive methods included moving resolutions calculated to promote a healthy national life and displacement of the bureaucracy. The Swaraj Party had also laid down rules of conduct for its members in the legislative bodies. They were not to serve as members on committees by official nomination.

The methods of the party for work inside the councils were summed up by **CR Das** in the following manner-'I want you to enter the councils and to secure a majority and to put forward national demand. If it is not accepted, I want to oppose the government in every measure, good, bad and indifferent, and make the work of council impossible. If the government conducted its work through certification, the Swarjist members would resign making it a political issue..In spite of it all, if the government did not yield, then the voters would be advised to stop the payment of taxes and resort to civil disobedience'.

In this way, civil disobedience was to be their method of last resort.

Elections and the Swarajists

Under the provisions of the Act of 1919, altogether three elections were held in 1920, 1923 and 1926.

Elections of 1920 were boycotted by the Congress owing to Non-Cooperation Movement.

Elections of 1923 were fought by the Swarajists. Liberals constituted their main opposition. The Liberals had participated in the previous election as well and a stigma of association with the government was attached to them. On the other hand, the Swarajists were hailed as heroes and 'men of Gandhi' who had faced the wrath of the government during Non-Cooperation Movement. Their open agenda of taking non-cooperation inside the councils had a wide appeal among the electorates.

As a result, the Swarajists earned wide success. They won absolute majority in Central Provinces and emerged as the single largest party in the Central Assembly, Bombay and Bengal Councils. With this victory, they now came to be known as the **'Parliamentary wing of the Congress'**. The following table shows the number of seats won by the Swarajists in the councils.

S.No.	Legislative Body	Total Number of Seats	Seats won by Swarajists
1	Legislative Assembly	105	42
2	Madras Council	98	..
3	Bombay Council	86	32
4	Bengal Council	111	36
5	United Provinces (UP) Council	101	31
6	Punjab Council	71	9
7	Bihar and Orissa Council	73	13
8	Central Provinces (CP) Council	54	40
9	Assam Council	39	13
	Total	633	174

A majority of the candidates elected were lawyers. Landlords and businessmen were also elected in significant numbers.

Elections of 1926 came as a rude shock to the Swarajists. They suffered heavy losses everywhere. They were routed in CP, UP and Punjab securing 1, 19 and 35 seats, respectively. Thus, by the eve of 1926, the Swarajists had effectively lost ground. **On 16th June 1925, CR Das passed away** leaving a great void in the Swaraj Party. The party soon became a house divided and mutual bickering eroded even the remnants of credibility.

Work of Swarajists in the Legislatures

In the year 1924–25, the Swarajists led by Motilal Nehru, registered many victories in the central legislature. Early in February 1924, the Swarajists (not being in majority), formed a coalition of 70 members and came to be known as **Nationalist Party,** which included individuals such as Madan Mohan Malviya and Independents led by Jinnah. In 1924, it was this coalition that dominated the proceedings of the legislature.

The Swarajists intervened on several issues and often outvoted the government. Three issues remained at the centre of their demands. These were-constitutional advancement leading to self-government, grant of civil liberties, release of political prisoners and repeal of repressive laws, and third issue was the development of indigenous industries. Though the legislatures formed under the provision of 1919 Act had only a 'semblance' of power without any real authority, and the Viceroy or governor could certify any legislation if it was rejected in the legislature, yet the Swarajists registered many victories:

- In 1924, the Nationalist Party led by the Swarajists rejected the first four demands of the budget and did not allow the Finance Bill to be introduced in the legislature.
- **C. Vijayaraghavachariar** moved a resolution demanding provincial autonomy and Dominion status for India.
- In 1924, Swarajists led by Motilal Nehru introduced an amendment demanding the framing of an **Indian Constitution** by an Indian Constituent Assembly. Motilal also moved a resolution in favour of a **Round Table Conference** of all Indian, European and Anglo Indian interests to recommend a scheme of full responsible government.
  - This forced the government of India to appoint a **Reforms Enquiry Committee** under **Sir Alexander Muddiman** to enquire into the working of the Act of 1919 and suggest remedies.
  - The government also requested eminent Indians (like Motilal Nehru, MA Jinnah, TB Sapru, RP Paranjpaya and Sir Sivaswamy Iyer) to serve on the Committee, a request which was turned down as per the principles of the Swarajists.
- The Swarajists also refused to attend the parties of the Viceroy as a mark of protest.
- When the recommendations of the Lee Commission (constituted to enquire into the organisation and condition of Public Services) were introduced in the Assembly for approval, Motilal moved an amendment which was carried by a majority vote.
- The success of the Swaraj Party in Central Provinces and Bengal was also impressive. In the CP, it secured absolute majority while it emerged as the largest party in Bengal. It succeeded in creating deadlocks and forcing the government to rely on their special powers. It virtually **blew up the Dyarchy** in these provinces with its method of obstruction.
  - In March 1925, the Swarajists succeeded in electing **Vithalbhai Patel** as the President of the Central Legislative Assembly.
  - The Swarajists succeeded in defeating the government on a number of bills. For instance, in 1928, the government was defeated on the **Public Safety Bill** by which the government proposed to deport 'undesirable' and 'subversive' foreigners (as the government feared that British and other foreign agitators were being sent to into India by the Communist International).

In this way, the Swarajists achieved significant success inside the legislative bodies and achieved whatever could be achieved by constitutional methods. Their tactics stirred the otherwise dull political atmosphere of the country. They embarrassed the government with their questions and debating skills, eroding moral foundations of British Raj in India. In fact, the parliamentary duels of this period constitute a brilliant page in the annals of parliamentary politics of Modern India. These were fully reported in press and read avidly every morning by the readers.

Constructive Work by the No-Changers and the Swarajists

Introduction to Gandhian Constructive Work

As per Gandhi, the chariot of freedom struggle had two wheels—mass movements and constructive work. Of the 18 items enumerated by Gandhi under constructive program, the most important were Hindu-Muslim unity, removal untouchability, prohibition (of alcohol and other intoxicants), Swadeshi and boycott. According to Gandhi, when a mass movement was at its ebb, the energies of the people were to be diverted to constructive work. That is why, once the Non-Cooperation Movement was suspended, he had advised constructive work to the people.

Thus, the No-Changers quietly carried on the grass-root constructive work, they established hundreds of ashrams all over the country where young men and women promoted charkha and khadi, worked for the elevation of the lower castes and tribal people. They set up hundreds of National Schools and Colleges where young Indians were trained in a non-colonial ideological framework.

In reality, the Gandhian constructive work was multi-faceted in aim and content. It diverted the energies of the masses in positive direction, it made the elite classes familiar with conditions of villages and lower castes and brought much needed financial help to the poor. In this way, it silently promoted the process of nation building. Further, it gave continuous engagement to the Congress political workers during passive phases of the national movement, helped build their bonds with the masses and honed their organising skills. In this way, constructive work was a significant means of preparing freedom fighters and also of testing their leaders. It were these constructive workers who served as the steel frame during the active phase of the national movement.

Constructive Work by Swarajists

The Swaraj Party had put forth the twin aims of council entry and constructive work. Though the Swaraj party was founded by nationalists who did not see eye to eye with Gandhi in his approach to non-cooperation, they could ill afford to neglect Gandhi's constructive program which alone linked them with Congress and Gandhi. After all, the Swarajists owed their political power and prestige to the Congress and to Gandhi. They also knew that there will come one day in future when they will have to leave the councils and join mass civil disobedience along with the No-Changers. Thus, the **constructive work provided a common platform to both the factions of the Congress**-the Swarajists and the No-Changers. However, being busy with council work, the Swarajists could not implement this program as zealously as the No-Changers did.

Hindu-Muslim Unity and Political Education of Masses

These were regarded as pre-requisites for the attainment of Swaraj by the top Swarajists. The rise of Swarajists coincided with the worst period of Hindu-Muslim tension in Indian polity. But, like other groups, the Swarajists could not achieve much in halting the downward trend except talking about the desirability of Hindu–Muslim unity. In 1926, the Congress made a resolution on the establishment of Permanent Publicity Bureau for educating the masses on communal harmony and healthy national life. **Sarojini Naidu, Motilal Nehru and Maulana Azad** were made incharge of this work.

Swadeshi

Gandhi's definition of Swadeshi not only included charkha and khadi (or khaddar, coarse cloth) but also all other forms of indigenous industries. The Swarajists also espoused the cause of khadi but not as passionately as the orthodox Gandhians. Though the Swarajists were required to attend the council meetings dressed in khadi (as per their instruction manual), they opposed tooth and nail when Gandhians proposed to make khadi and charkha a basis for Congress membership. They also opposed Gandhi's Hand Spinning Resolution for making spinning mandatory for Congress members, forcing Gandhi to remove the penalty clause.

From the above, the stand of the Swarajists becomes amply clear—they were always ready to contribute to the cause of khadi but at the same time, they made no fetish of khadi and strongly resented anything being forced upon them.

Untouchability

The removal of untouchability from Indian society and elevation of depressed classes received unfailing attention of the Congress as well as of the Swarajists. In 1924, the Belgaum Congress passed a resolution on untouchability with full agreement of the Swarajists. The Swarajists fully supported the opening of temple doors to the depressed classes. They also fully supported and stood by the rights of the depressed classes in legislative bodies.

Prohibition (of alcohol and other intoxicants)

The government received a significant part of its revenue from the sale of alcohol and other intoxicants in India. As a result, the British were unwilling to impose prohibition on the sale and consumption of such substances. Realising how the alien government was willing to forego the long-term interests of Indian society for the sake of some immediate revenue, the Swarajists stood for prohibition.

True, the Swarajists were an integral part of the Constructive Program of the Congress during 1922–29. At the same time, it is also true that, though they lent support to the constructive program, they did not share Gandhi's idealism in this regard.

Decline of the Swarajists

In 1923, the Swarajists with their program of council entry appeared very promising. But the success of 1924–25 was short-lived and the years 1925–27 saw the decline of the Swarajists. The various factors that lead to their decline included-

Lure of Office

Having entered the councils, the Swarajists were not averse to enjoying the privileges. The Swarajists began to accept offices and now sat on various committees:

- Motilal, who had earlier declined to sit on the Muddiman Committee, now sat on the **Skeen Committee** (also known as 'Indian Sandhurst Committee' on Indianization of Army).
- **Vithalbhai Patel** became President (Speaker) of the Legislative Assembly.
- Ramaswamy Iyenger sat on the Public Accounts Committee.

Rise of Spirit of Responsive Cooperation

The policy of continuous obstruction began to give way to the spirit of responsive cooperation. Many of the Swarajists had no real faith in non-cooperation. The government also succeeded in persuading the Swarajists into some kind of cooperation. Soon the party split into two wings—**Responsivists and Non-Cooperators**.

The Responsivists wanted to work for reform and hold offices wherever possible. Some of the prominent responsivists were **Madan Mohan Malviya, Lajpat Rai, NC Kelkar, MR Jayakar** (all of them became members of the Hindu Mahasabha). The responsivists openly voiced the demand to reconsider party program. When Motilal rebuked them saying **'the diseased limb of the Swaraj party must be amputated'**, the responsivists were ready to break out in open revolt against the central leadership. The Bombay Swarajists forcefully advocated the path of responsive cooperation and the Swaraj Party was now ridden with defections and dissensions.

Elitist Outlook of Swarajists

The Swarajists represented the upper-class elements of the Congress who had not much faith in direct mass action and had been drawn into the Non-Cooperation Movement quite unwillingly. On the failure of the moment, they immediately took to parliamentary politics and later became content with playing the role of the opposition. Lack of any sound ideological basis, preoccupation with party politics and lukewarm support to the constructive work further distanced the Swarajists from the masses.

Rising Communalism

After 1923, communalism raised its ugly head and the country was repeatedly plunged into communal riots. The Muslim League (1906) and the Hindu Mahasabha (1915) became active again.

In the years 1926–27 there developed an ideological gap between the Sawarjists and the Hindu Mahasabha. The Responsivists Madan Mohan Malviya and Lajpat Rai organised a new party of Congress Independents, rallied the Hindus under their banner and offered cooperation to the government to safeguard the so-called Hindu interests. They felt that continuous opposition to the government harmed the interests of the Hindus. They even accused Motilal Nehru of being anti-Hindu and of favouring cow-slaughter and of eating beef.

As the crisis deepened, Gandhi tried to intervene and improve the situation. In September 1924, he went on a 21-day fast in the house of Maulana Mohammad Ali in Delhi to do penance for the inhumanity inflicted during the riots, but to no avail.

Later, Motilal tried to make peace between the two factions of the Congress at Sabarmati. The **Sabarmati Compromise** proved abortive and failed to keep the party united. By 1927, the diarchy that was destroyed in CP and Bengal was restored. It was now amply clear that the Swaraj Party had only succeeded in wrecking itself rather than the constitution of 1919.

Their tactics proved unavailing in ending or mending the constitution of 1919, forcing the Swarajists to walk out of the central Assembly twice—first in 1926 and then in January 1930 due to the launch of Civil Disobedience Movement.

Disintegration of Nationalist Party

The unity of the coalition formed under the banner of the Nationalist Party proved to be short-lived. The non-Swarajist members of the party felt that the Swaraj Party gave precedence to its interests over their cost. This led to rift and defections and the party broke down. Before the elections of 1926, the Nationalist Party had broken into three clear groups:

- The Swaraj Party (or the Congress Party)
- The Nationalist Party led by Madan Mohan Malaviya and Lala Lajpat Rai
  - It included Responsive Cooperators like Hindu Mahasabha and Independent Congressmen
- The Independent Party led by MA Jinnah

Swaraj Party Remerges with Congress

In May 1927, the situation in the country appeared grim, the Swarajists were declining, communalism was raising its ugly head and Gandhi wrote, 'My only hope lies in prayer and answer to prayer'. But it seems the forces of national upsurge were silently growing behind the scenes and the country united once again against the Simon Commission.

In 1927, **Simon Commission** (an all-white commission to frame a constitution for India) was announced which was unanimously boycotted by all nationalists. **Lord Birkenhead** justified the exclusion of Indians from Simon Commission on the plea that there were vital differences among various Indian political parties and then threw a challenge to Indians to produce a constitution acceptable to all sections of Indian society.

The Indians accepted the challenge and an All Parties Conference (1928) was called which appointed a sub-committee headed by Motilal Nehru to draft a constitution. The committee drafted a constitution, famously known as **Nehru Report**. In 1928 Calcutta Congress, the Swarajists and the No-Changers resolved in one voice that in case the government did not accept the Nehru Report **by 31st December 1929**, the Congress would declare **complete independence as its goal** and would also launch a civil disobedience movement to achieve that goal.

Preparations now began for a second round of mass action to achieve complete independence. With this, the council entry program of the Swaraj Party faded into irrelevance and it now merged with the Congress.

Evaluation of the Swarajists

The sudden withdrawal of the Non-Cooperation Movement had led to the demoralisation of the nationalist ranks. To prevent the movement from lapsing into inactivity, the Swarajists advocated a new line of activity under the changed conditions. They placed before the nation the twin programs of council entry and constructive work. The Swarajists filled the political void at a time when the national movement was recouping its strength. They exposed the hollowness of the reforms of 1919. Though, the years 1925–27 saw the demoralisation and decline of the Swaraj Party itself, and the announcement of the Simon Commission and the subsequent changes in political scenario led to the merger of the party with the Congress; yet, it cannot be denied that during 1922–29, the Swarajists played a significant role and kept the political atmosphere alive during this period.

Prelim Capsule

Prelim Capsule- The Swarajists and Constructive Work

Date	Events	Important Details
December 1922 (Gaya)	Gaya Congress Session	CR Das (President), Motilal Nehru (Secretary). Council entry proposal of Das and Nehru defeated, on account of opposition of majority of delegates led by **Rajgopalachari**. Das and Motilal resign from office.
1st January 1923	Formation of Congress-Khilafat Swarajya Party	**CR Das (President), Motilal Nehru (Secretary)**. Twin aims-**council entry & constructive work**. Congress gets divided into Pro-Changers (later called the Swarajists) and No-Changers (or orthodox Gandhians).
September 1923 (Delhi)	Delhi, Special Congress Session	Maulana Azad (President). Swarajists allowed to contest elections due in November.
November 1923	1923 Council Elections	Swarajists sweep the polls despite narrow franchise.
December 1924 (Belgam)	Belgam Congress Session	**Gandhi (President).** Congress endorsed Gandhi's decision to allow the Swaraj Party to carry on work in the legislatures on behalf of the Congress.
16th June 1925	CR Das passes away	Swaraj Party becomes a house divided and loses credibility. The Nationalist Party also breaks into three groups- • The Swaraj Party (or the Congress Party) • The Nationalist Party led by Madan Mohan Malaviya and Lala Lajpat Rai (It included Responsive Cooperators like Hindu Mahasabha and Independent Congressmen) • The Independent Party led by MA Jinnah
1926	1926 Council Elections	Swaraj Party suffers heavy losses.
1927	Simon Commission announced	Boycotted by all nationalists. **Lord Birkenhead** challenges Indians to frame their own constitution.
1928	All Parties Conference	Appoints a sub-committee headed by Motilal Nehru to draft a constitution. Nehru Committee drafted a constitution-known as **Nehru Report**.

1928 (Calcutta)	Calcutta Congress Session	Swarajists and No-changers unanimously give ultimatum-if demand of complete independence not accepted by 31st December 1929, Civil Disobedience will be launched. Congress prepares for next round of mass action. Council entry program becomes irrelevant. Swaraj Party remerges with Congress.

Previous Years' Questions – Main Exam

1. Trace the origin of the Swaraj Party. What was the manifesto of the Swaraj Party? What were the Swarajists demands and the reactions of the British? **[UPSC 1990]**
2. Trace the formation of the Swaraj Party. What were its demands? **[UPSC 1999]**

11 Rise and Growth of Communalism up to the Second World War

Maintaining unity of its people is a prerequisite for any nation, particularly so when it is fighting against imperialist forces. This unity of the Indian people was put to a severe test by the growth of communalism that divided India along religious lines. In fact, 19th century India saw the emergence of nationalism and communalism simultaneously. Communalism in India was born due to the presence of a number of factors such as peculiar socio-economic factors, role played by British policies and activities of communal organisations such as the All India Muslim League and the All India Hindu Mahasabha.

Meaning of Communalism

Communalism means different things to different people. It may be seen as a belief, an ideology or even an instrument of politics. It is therefore important to understand the meaning of communalism first.

In general, communalism or communal ideology refers to **allegiance to one's own ethnic group or religious community rather than to society as a whole**. In the Indian context, it refers to the belief that Hindus, Muslims, Sikhs and Christians form different religious communities and that India comprises not one nation but many nations—Hindu nation, Muslim nation and so on. India can therefore, only be a mere confederation of religious communities. In other words, it refers to the advocacy of religious identity and attempts to incite strife between people belonging to different religious communities, particularly Hindus and Muslims. Accordingly, for a communalist, a person's religious identity is the most important and he will emphasise it out of proportions. At its base, the communal problem in India was more politically driven rather than religiously driven. The communal problem or rather the **communal triangle** had the British as the base and Hindus and Muslims as the other two arms, the strongest arm being the base.

Levels of Communalism

Broadly, three levels of communalism have been defined. These are as follows:

1. Belief that interests of people belonging to one religious community are the same. In other words, all those who belong to a common religion also have common political, socio-economic and cultural interests.
2. **Liberal Communalism (upto 1937)** Belief that the interests of different religious communities are different. In other words, the interests of Hindus are different from that of Muslims and vice versa. Most of the communalist forces before 1937 belonged to this stage and included the Muslim League, the Hindu Mahasabha, Ali Brothers, MA Jinnah and NC Kelkar.

3. **Extreme Communalism (after 1937)** Belief that not only these interests are different but also **incompatible** or even **hostile** to one another. In other words, it implies that Hindus and Muslims cannot co-exist peacefully due to conflicting interests. Extreme communalism is based on fear and hatred and has a tendency to use violent language or behaviour. After 1937, the Muslim League and the Hindu Mahasabha increasingly tilted towards extreme communalism.

It is noteworthy that the above beliefs are not rooted in reality and are based on wrong understanding of interests. Indian society was not always communal. Throughout the medieval period, Hindus and Muslims lived harmoniously and religious identity was seen as merely one among different identities of an individual (identity based on gender, caste, occupation, region, etc). Communalism in India is a product of peculiar circumstances and it intensified along with the intensification of the freedom struggle.

Myths Regarding Communalism

There are many myths surrounding communalism, it being a widely misunderstood phenomenon. To have a clear understanding of communalism, it is important to know what communalism is not:

- Communalism is **not** merely the entry of religion into politics. For instance, even Mahatma Gandhi and Abul Kalam Azad defined their politics in religious terms yet this did not communalise politics.
- Communalism is **not** caused by religious differences. This is clear from the fact that religious differences between Hindus and Muslims had always existed and yet medieval Indian society was not communalised.
- Communalism did **not** always exist in Indian society. It is a product of a combination of forces in modern India.

Factors Responsible for the Rise and Growth of Communalism in India

Most historians are of the view that communalism was not a remnant of the medieval period. Though religion did constitute a significant part of peoples' lives, and they did fight over religion at times, there was hardly any communal ideology before 1857, when Hindus and Muslims fought shoulder to shoulder against the British Raj. Communalism is really a **modern phenomenon** and its roots can be found in the modern colonial socio-economic and political structure of colonial India.

The rise of communalism, as per most historians, should be traced from the British conquest of India which had a tremendous impact on every aspect of Indian life—its polity, society and economy. It led to the emergence of a combination of factors favourable for the rise and growth of communalism. These factors included the following:

Role of Socio-Economic Factors in 19th-Century India

The rise of the British power in 18th-century India was accompanied with the decline of the later Mughals and the upper-class Muslims in general. The upper-class Muslims were deprived of their land holdings and employment in upper posts of army, administration and judiciary. As a result, for the first seven decades of the 19th century, the upper-class Muslims remained very anti-British and hostile to modern education, while the Hindus responded more positively to the modernising forces that came along with the British. The Hindus adapted faster than Muslims, to English education, new posts in administration, and culture, giving rise to the Hindu Middle class.

Consequently, the socio-cultural awakening among Hindus came earlier than Muslims. Thus, there emerged a **time 'lag'** between Ram Mohan Roy and Syed Ahmad Khan that gave birth to the feelings of insecurity among the Muslims. This explains, to a large extent, the alienation of Muslims from the national mainstream and the early phase of the national movement, the foundations of which were laid by the Hindu Middle Class.

About a generation later, the Muslims also took to English education (with the efforts of Syed Ahmad Khan, Abdul Latif, Badruddin Tayabji and others) and sought employment in state services. According to Jawaharlal Nehru, **a conflict arose between the Hindu and Muslim middle classes for state services** and this was the beginning of communal problem in modern phase. Yet, a large number of middle class individuals remained free from this tendency even in the 1930s and 40s, and tended to be both secular and broadly left-wing.

Bipan Chandra "Communalism was an expression of the interests and aspirations of the middle classes in a social situation in which opportunities for them were grossly inadequate. The communal question was, therefore a middle-class question par excellence".

Role of British Policy

The British policy of **'divide and rule'** played a very significant role in the growth of communalism in India. At the same time, it must be remembered that the British did not create communalism. They only took advantage of the conditions ripe for the use and growth of communalism in India.

The genesis of the policy of divide and rule can be traced back to the Revolt of 1857. The unity showed by Hindus and Muslims during the revolt disturbed the colonial rulers and they got determined to break this unity and the policy of divide and rule was introduced among the masses. The policy of divide and rule is also understood as the policy of concession, counterpoise and coercion because what was conceded was always counterpoised by utilising the rivalries of various classes and interests.

For instance, immediately after the revolt, the Muslims were repressed and 27,000 Muslims were hanged in Delhi alone (Since Bahadur Shah II was appealed to head the revolt, the British believed the Revolt to be a Muslim plot). Later, in the 1870s, this policy was reversed in the wake of rise of the national movement and policy of appeasement of Muslims was introduced. Muslims were given concessions at the cost of Hindus, thus counterpoising one sectional interest against the other. In other words, communal and separatist tendencies in Indian politics were encouraged.

In this way, communal ideology was used by the British to serve their political ends in several ways:

- To gain support base in Indian society by making some friends.
- To prevent the Indian people from uniting as one nation. If all sections of Indian society united against the British, they could threaten the British Empire. Thus, the British made all attempts to keep the Muslims away from the Congress and then dismissed all claims of the Congress on the pretext that it did not represent all sections of Indian society (first encouraging communalism and then using it to further their own political ends).

- Communal deadlock thus created was used as a justification for the continuation of the colonial rule. The British stressed on the lack of consensus among the major political parties, i.e., the Congress, the Muslim League and the Hindu Mahasabha and argued that the Indian people were deeply divided among themselves and were thus incapable of governing themselves.

Here it may be stated that religion was not the only division that was used under the policy of divide and rule. In fact, every existing division of Indian society was encouraged to prevent the emerging unity of Indian people. It was of course the communal division that proved to be most profitable.

In addition to the above, other ways in which British encouraged communalism were as follows:

- By treating Hindus, Muslims and Sikhs as separate communities.
- By extending official patronage to communalists and readily accepting communal leaders as the real spokespersons for their communities, while the nationalist leaders were treated as representing only a 'microscopic minority'.
- By showing extraordinary tolerance towards communal press and agitations.
- By readily conceding to communal demands, for e.g., while none of the Congress demands were accepted during the period 1885–1905, the communal demands of Muslim League were readily accepted almost as soon as they were put up i.e., in 1906 itself.
- By giving the communalists a complete veto on any political advance.

Unscientific View of Indian History

British writers on Indian history also presented a communal and distorted view of Indian history to spread communal consciousness. A beginning was made in the early 19th century by the **British historian James Mill** (1773–1836) who described the ancient period of Indian history as the Hindu period and the medieval period as the Muslim period. The Hindu communalists readily adopted this distorted view and glorified India's ancient past at the cost of the medieval period which was projected as an age of barbaric invaders. Similarly, the Muslims looked to the history of Arabs for pride and glory.

This added a historical angle to the already existing socio-cultural and economic differences between the Hindus and the Muslims. So much so that, Mohammad Ai Jinnah, while propounding his two-nation theory asserted that Hindus and Muslims were two nations also because each had a separate historical past and often **the hero of one was the villain of the other**.

Communal Side-Effects of 19th-Century Revivalism

The world over revivalism was a common phenomenon in societies under colonial rule. It was an attempt at restoration of self-respect deeply injured by political subjugation. Even in India, socio-cultural reform and revivalism helped in restoring pride in India's glorious past but at the same time, it created certain unintended negative consequences as well. The Wahabis crusaded against all non-Muslims with the aim of establishing Dar-ul-Islam (the world of Islam). Dayanand aimed at 'shuddhi' (reconversion of non-Hindus to Hinduism) and Aryanisation of India. Even Vivekanand's references to ancient Indian achievements as constituting the real glorious Indian past created a reaction in the Muslim mind who turned to Western Asian history for pride and glory.

Role of Change in Outlook of Sir Syed Ahmad Khan

The early activities of Sir Syed Ahmad Khan were free from any communal bias. He took the lead in introducing reforms among the Muslims. In 1875, he founded the Aligarh College or the Muhammadan Anglo-Oriental College at Aligarh (which received financial support from many Hindus and later grew into Aligarh Muslim University) with the aim of introducing modern education among Muslims and securing for them British patronage, thus laying the **foundation of the Aligarh Movement** (the Pakistan Movement is believed to be an indirect consequence of the Aligarh Movement). He also preached harmony between the Hindus and the Muslims and described them as 'two eyes of a beautiful bride, i.e. India'.

However, his outlook changed after the formation of the Indian National Congress in 1885. He found the anti-imperialist and nationalist program of the Congress to be in complete contrast with his own loyalty to the British government and his aim of securing more and more government jobs for the Muslims. He further voiced his disapproval by terming **Congress as a Hindu body** that would promote Hindu interests at the cost of the Muslim interests. He also stressed that India was a Hindu majority state where the Hindus would dominate the Muslims once transfer of power takes place. He therefore opposed the establishment of modern democracy or democratic institutions in India.

Syed Ahmad Khan decided to oppose the Congress by organising a movement of loyalty to the British rule along with **Raja Shiv Prasad of Banaras**. In 1888, he set up the **United Indian Patriotic Association** with the avowed objective of countering the Congress and keep people away from joining the Congress. In this way, Sir Syed Ahmad Khan's ideology provided the three main themes of communalism:

- Opposition to unifying, nationalist forces
- Opposition to democratic processes
- Loyalty to the British government

Please note that the above ideology was entirely faulty. Even though there were several Hindus in the Congress, it could certainly not be termed as a Hindu organisation, by any stretch of imagination. Several prominent members of the Congress were Muslims such as **Badruddin Tayabji, Mir Hussain, A. Bhimji and Hamid Ali Khan** and there was nothing Hindu about its demands and program. In 1887, the Congress session was presided over by Badruddin Tayabji, a Muslim. Moreover, democratic institutions posed no threat to the Muslims; they only posed a threat to feudal elements in society, to which Syed Ahmad himself belonged.

Hindu Overtone of National Movement

In the 20th century, the nationalist movement acquired a Hindu overtone which also contributed to the growth of communalism. For instance, many of the extremists introduced strong Hindu elements in nationalist propaganda. They identified Indian nation and culture with Hindus. Tilak used the Ganesh and Shivaji festivals to ignite national sentiments. Aurobindo put forth the concept of India as a mother and nationalism as a religion. The revolutionary terrorists took oath before goddess Kali. The Anti-partition movement began with dips in the Ganga. Such actions could hardly appeal to the Muslims and they could not be expected to respond with full enthusiasm to the national movement. Even Gandhi's slogan of Ram Rajya had a religious tinge and was unpalatable to the Muslims.

The above does not mean that the militant nationalists were anti-Muslim or wholly communal. The unintended Hindu overtone was taken advantage of and misused by clever British elements to poison the minds of the Muslims. Thus, the Hindu overtone to the national movement not only alienated the Muslims from the national movement but also provided ideological openings for Hindu communalism. It also helped the spread of a Muslim tinge among Muslim nationalists.

Role of Communal Organisations

Communal organisations played an important role in further development of communalism. Two such leading organisations were **All India Muslim League** (formed in 1906) and **All India Hindu Mahasabha** (formed in 1915). They resorted to communal propaganda and aired the feelings of mistrust between Hindus and Muslims. Communal organisations, in addition to promoting the interests of a particular community, also indirectly promoted British imperial interests and the personal ambitions of opportunistic leaders.

Jawaharlal Nehru 'One communalism does not end the other, each feeds on the other and both fatten'.

Weakness of Nationalist Forces

The growth of communalism in the 19th century could have been checked by strong nationalist forces and ideology. But the nationalist forces, including the Congress, failed in this regard. Even though fully committed to secularism and nationalism, the Congress ultimately lost the battle against communal forces due to certain weaknesses.

The Congress failed to fully comprehend the nature of communalism. It also failed to shed off the Hindu revivalist tendencies that had crept in and that had no appeal to the Muslim masses (such as use of Hindu symbols and festivals as in the case of Swadeshi movement). The Congress also stands guilty of making some wrong choices—while dealing with the Muslim League it offered concessions and made compromises which only added to the strength of communal ideology.

The nationalist leaders failed to see that it was not possible to conciliate the communalists. During 1937–39, several efforts were made to appease Jinnah who would agree to negotiate only if the Congress accepted itself as a Hindu party. This was an impossible demand for the Congress, as it meant giving up its nationalist and secular character. Hence, what was required was not appeasement but a frontal attack on communalism.

However, it cannot be denied that the communal problem in India had become extremely complicated, particularly so with the attitude of the British government. No matter what the Congress offered to the League, the government always offered more, rendering all attempts at unification, futile.

Growth of Communalism in the 20th Century

Partition of Bengal and Anti-Partition Movement (1905)

Viceroy Curzon and his men had played the communal card during the partition of Bengal and had tried to divide the Hindus and the Muslims along class lines (the Hindus being the zamindars and the Muslims being the peasantry). They wanted to use the Muslims as counterweights against the rising nationalist powers, and planned the partition such that it created a new Muslim majority province. Here they encouraged the educated Muslims to think in terms of a Muslim Political Power.

Muslim separatist tendencies, during this period, were also encouraged by the Hindu overtone acquired by the Anti-partition movement which began with dips in the Ganga. Hindu symbols and myths were readily used. Writers like Bankim Chandra Chatterjee and others also referred to the Muslims as foreigners in their writings which produced resentment among the Muslims and alienated them from the national movement.

Simla Deputation (1st October 1906)

A deputation headed by Aga Khan III (Sultan Mohammed Shah, 1877–1957) met Lord Minto at Simla on 1st October 1906. The deputationists expressed loyalty to the British Crown but also expressed apprehension that if the principle of 'election' was introduced without conceding reservation for Muslims, it would prove detrimental to their interests. Thus, the deputationists demanded reservation of seats for Muslim Community not only on the basis of their population but also on the basis of their **political importance** and their services in the defence of the British Empire. The British saw in these demands a promising counterpoise to the increasing demands of the Congress. Hence, these demands were readily accepted by Lord Minto and separate electorates and weightage for Muslims was introduced under the Act of 1909.

The nationalist leaders criticised the deputation as stage managed by the British (Maulana Ali called it **'a command performance'**). However, the followers of the Muslim League asserted that the demand for nomination of Muslims for safeguarding Muslim interests had been made since 1880s ever since the time of Sir Syed Ahmad Khan and when the prospect of elections emerged, a demand for separate electorates fell in the logic of events. However, it cannot be denied that the British encouraged communalism to foster their imperial interests in India. This explains why the League achieved its aims as soon as it was formed, while the Congress was unable to do so despite being much older and despite adopting the same methods of prayer and petition.

Formation of the Muslim League (30th December 1906)

Following the Simla Deputation, the Muslim leaders put forth the idea of a central Muhammadan association. Accordingly, on 30th December 1906, their efforts culminated in the formation of the **All India Muslim League,** under the leadership of **Nawab Salimullah of Dacca** and with government patronage, as a political organisation dedicated to advance Muslim political interests. Salimullah was also given a loan of ₹14 lakh by the government and he supported the creation of a Muslim Majority province in Bengal. The League comprised of upper class Muslims like Nawab Salimullah, Aga Khan and Nawab Mohsin-ul-Mulk (also known as Syed Mehdi Ali, 1837–1907).

The main aims and objectives of the League were as follows:

- To promote among Indian Muslims feelings of loyalty towards the British government and to remove any misconceptions that may arise, as to the intentions of the government with regard to any of its measures.
- To protect the political and other rights of Indian Muslims, and to place their needs and aspirations before the government in temperate language.

- So far as possible, without prejudice to the objectives mentioned above, to promote friendly relations between Muslims and other communities of India.

In this way, the Muslim League was a communal body from its very inception, formed to safeguard the interests of Muslim community alone. Its main motive was to keep the Muslim intelligentsia from joining the Congress and the national movement. The League was formed as purely a loyalist body which constantly looked upto the government for favour and patronage, and it was never disappointed.

The League under the nationalists (1913-1923) From 1913 to 1923, the League came under the influence of progressive Muslim leaders who overshadowed the loyalists. There was a section of patriotic Muslims who recognised the weakness of the League and founded the militantly nationalist **Ahrar movement** (1910) which included leaders like **Maulana Mohammad Ali, Maulana Mazhr ul Haq, Hussain Imam** and **Hakim Ajmal Khan**. These patriotic Muslims disliked the loyalist politics of the Aligarh School and the nawabs and zamindars. They were driven by the modern ideas of self-government and actively participated in the militant national movement.

Similarly, there was a section of the traditional Muslim scholars led by the **Deoband School** (1866) who were moved by the nationalist sentiments. The most well-known among these scholars was the young **Maulana Abdul Kalam Azad**. He propagated his nationalist ideas in his newspaper **Al Hilal** (1912).

In 1911, war broke out between Ottoman Empire (Turkey) and Italy and during 1912–13, Turkey fought the Balkan Wars (the British policy during the Balkan Wars was not sympathetic to Turkey). The Turkish ruler at this time was also the Caliph (or religious head of all Muslims). Also, nearly all Muslim holy places were located within Turkey. Naturally, the sympathy of Indian Muslims went with Turkey and their stand became pro-Turkey/Caliph and anti-imperialist. A medical mission, headed by Dr. M.A. Ansari, was sent to help Turkey. Further, during 1920–23, the League's activities remained suspended on account of Khilafat and Non-Cooperation Movement. In this way, during the period 1913–23, the League was completely overshadowed by the nationalists.

Following the withdrawal of the Non-Cooperation Movement, the communal elements in the League resurfaced. In 1927, the appointment of Simon Commission again brought the League into action and by 1934, MA Jinnah (once a progressive Muslim leader, now a communalist) emerged as its undisputed leader.

Introduction of Separate Electorates (1909)

The introduction of separate electorates under the Morley-Minto Reforms was a major landmark in the development of communalism in India. Separate Electorates meant electorates comprising of Muslims only (separate electorates were later extended for Sikhs and others as well). In practical terms, it meant introducing Muslim constituencies, Muslim voters and Muslim candidates. Thus, this system turned elections and legislatures into arenas of communal tussles.

In addition to this, non-Muslim voters could vote for a Muslim candidate. Muslims were also given **weightage**, i.e., more seats were given to them than the number warranted by their proportion in the local population. Under the principle of weightage, Muslims were assured representation in the councils, not merely according to their 'numerical strength' but also according to their 'political importance' and 'their service in defence of the empire'. They were also allowed to compete for seats to be elected by general electorates.

These provisions were severely criticised as they were brought about not with the aim of correcting any imbalance in Indian society but to appease some Muslim leaders, win them over as allies and at the same time bind them to the government in 'silken chains of gratitude'. They also created institutional structures containing separatism and ensured the impossibility of consensus among Indian political groups.

Formation of the Hindu Mahasabha (1915)

The formation of All India Muslim League (1906) and introduction of separate electorates (1909) made the Hindu leaders think in terms of a Hindu organisation to safeguard Hindu interests.

- In 1909, Arya Samaj leaders Lala Lajpat Rai, Lal Chand and Shadi Lal established the **Punjab Hindu Sabha** and its first session at Lahore was presided by Pt. Madan Mohan Malaviya (who founded the Banaras Hindu University). Over the next few years, several Hindu sabhas were established outside Punjab.
- In 1910, some prominent Hindus of Allahabad took steps in organising themselves into an All India Hindu Mahasabha.
- In April 1915, the first session of the All India Hindu Mahasabha was held during the Kumbh Mela at Hardwar under the presidentship of the **Maharaj of Kasim Bazar**.

Explaining the rationale of the Mahasabha, Pt. Madan Mohan Malaviya stated that the Muslims and Christians have been proselytising in India for centuries, with the effect that the majority of Indian Muslims were converts from Hindu religion. Further, the Muslim League has been putting forward exaggerated claims for representation in elected bodies. To check these processes, he explained, it was necessary for Hindus to organise themselves. Thus, **Shuddhi** and **Sangathan** became the objectives of the Sabha in the initial years. It also gave the slogan of **Akhand Hindustan**, against the League's demand for Pakistan.

In 1938, **VD Savarkar** became the President of the Hindu Mahasabha and was re-elected again and again. Under him, the sabha developed a political program. Savarkar popularised the concept of **Hindu Rashtra** maintaining that India comprised of one nation, i.e., only the Hindu nation and the Muslims must accept their position as a minority. After the death of Savarkar, the Mahasabha was led by **Dr. SP Mookerji** who had a more nationalist outlook.

The Hindu Mahasabha's propaganda of a Hindu Rashtra only hardened the League's attitude further. True, Muslim League was the first communal organisation, but the communal poison proved infectious and the Hindu Mahasabha, Akali Dal and others came into existence as counterpoises to one another.

Lucknow Pact (1916)

The Congress-League Pact, also known as the Lucknow Pact, was signed between the Indian National Congress and the Muslim League during the joint session of both the parties held in 1916 at Lucknow. While a step forward in many ways, it was also a step back. The **Congress accepted separate electorates in order to obtain League's support**, thus formally recognising communal politics. The following facts must also be remembered:

- The Pact was an arrangement between leaders and not the people.
- The pact was wrongly equated with Hindu-Muslim settlement, based on the assumption that the Muslim League was the sole representative of all classes of Muslims.
- Soon the Lucknow Pact became redundant as the Government of India Act 1919 granted much more to the Muslims than the Lucknow Pact.

Khilafat and Non-Cooperation Movement (1920–23)

During the Khilafat Movement, Muslims were eager to gain the support of Hindus in India to pressurise the British to adopt liberal attitude towards Turkey. Seeing in this an excellent opportunity to forge Hindu–Muslim unity in India, Gandhi extended full support to the Khilafat movement. The Non-Cooperation program of Gandhi was soon adopted first by the Khilafat Committee and then by the Congress. Consequently, the period 1920-22 witnessed unprecedented participation of Muslims in the national movement.

Unfortunately, with the exception of a few Muslims like Azad, the outlook of most Muslim leaders was not fully secular or even free from communal bias. This is clear from the fact that the most important issue they took up was not national freedom but protection of holy places and the rights of Caliph. Religious sentiments formed the vortex of their political appeal. This encouraged the wrong habit of looking at political questions from the religious point of view.

Revival of Communalism after the Withdrawal of Non-Cooperation Movement (1922–1927)

Once the Non-cooperation Movement was withdrawn, the Hindu–Muslim unity soon petered out and communalism began to raise its ugly head. The period between 1922 and 1927 saw the following symptoms of communalism:

- **Communal riots** occurred at unprecedented scale. UP alone saw as many as 91 incidents of riots. Issues of cow slaughter and music before mosques were raised.
- The period saw the revival of main communal organisations- the Muslim League and the Hindu Mahasabha (formed in 1915 but lying dormant since then), as they found favourable climate for revival.
- Swarajist got divided along communal lines and some responsivists joined the Hindu Mahasabha. The Congress failed to evolve a suitable strategy to deal with communalism.
- **Tabligh** (propaganda) and **Tanzim** (organisation) movements arose among the Muslims, partly as response to Shuddhi and Sangathan among the Hindus. These were again partly in response to forced conversions made during Moplah rebellion. Such developments embittered the whole atmosphere.
- **RSS** (Rashtriya Swayamsevak Sangh) was founded in 1925 by KB Hedgewar.

Various factors contributed to the above. Firstly, the Khilafat movement had brought Muslim religious heads into politics and they never went back even after the movement was withdrawn. This brought certain religious elements into politics. Secondly, system of separate electorates inherently contained seeds of communalism. This system was further enlarged by the Act of 1919 and provided space for political alignments along communal lines. Finally, lack of employment opportunities forced the youth to look upto religion for favours and jobs. In this way, the political situation in 1927 looked grim and the nationalist forces were divided and communal feelings soared high. At this point, an opportunity for unity was presented in the form of the **Simon Commission**.

Simon Commission (1927), Delhi Proposals, Nehru Report and Jinnah's Fourteen Points

Note: These topics have been covered in detail in Chapter 6.16.

In 1927, Simon Commission (an all-white commission to frame a constitution for India) was announced which was unanimously boycotted by all nationalists and once again provided an opportunity for unity.

With the aim of bridging the gulf between the Congress and the Muslim League and to enable them to present a common set of demands before the British, a group of prominent Muslim leaders met at Delhi in December 1927 with MA Jinnah presiding over the session. In a dramatic move, the leaders agreed to forego separate electorates, the first and the last time the League agreed to do so, if their four proposals were met. The proposals came to be known as Delhi proposals.

In December 1927, Madras Congress Session, the Congress passed a resolution accepting most of the demands of Delhi Proposals. However, the Muslim League split over the issue and a separate annual session of the League was held at Lahore under the presidentship of **Sir Mian Muhammad Shafi**, worsening the communal situation in India. The demands were also rejected by the Hindu Mahasabha at All Parties Conference (December 1928, at Calcutta). The incompatibility between the League and the Mahasabha complicated matters and frustrated all attempts at unity.

Further, the Nehru Report (prepared by Motilal Nehru and Tej Bhadur Sapru) was rejected by the Muslim League as it did not incorporate all their demands and had the following consequences:

- Jinnah rejected the Nehru Report calling it **'Parting of the Ways'** with the Congress and once the 'Ambassador of Hindu-Muslim Unity' was now convinced that the Hindu mindset in India was bent upon pushing the Muslim minority to the wall.
- He went back to separate electorates, formulated his **Fourteen Points** which became the text of communal demands and included-separate electorates, reservation for Muslims in legislatures, reservation of Jobs for Muslims, creation of new Muslim majority provinces, etc.
- It led to the estrangement of Jinnah and pushed him towards communalism.
- It led to the hostility of most Muslim leaders towards Civil Disobedience Movement.

Communalism Transforms into a Mass Force

The events of 1928–29 triggered an irreversible drifting apart of communal forces and marked the starting point of communalism transforming into a mass force. By 1940, all communal demands faded into insignificance in front of the ultimate communal demand-the demand for Pakistan, as a separate nation for Muslims.

Estrangement of Muslims from Civil Disobedience Movement (1930–34)

With the exception of Muslim groups (**Jamaat-e-ulema-i-Hind**, **Khudai Khidmatgars** and the **State of Kashmir**), Muslims in general remained aloof from the movement. While the Congress boycotted two out of three Round Table Conferences held in London, the communalists attended all three.

Communal Award (or MacDonald Award, 1932)

The Communal Award was a proposal on minority representation made by the British Prime Minister Ramsay MacDonald on 16 August 1932. The Award granted separate electorates for the Muslims, Sikhs, Depressed Classes, Indian Christians, Anglo-Indians, Europeans, Buddhists and even Marathas (some seats in Bombay were given to the Marathas). The principle of weightage was also applied.

Extreme Communalism (after 1937)

The Muslim League performed badly in the 1937 provincial elections and decided to resort to extreme communalism. Demand for a separate state for Muslims now gained rapid momentum.

The Government of India Act 1935 provided for provincial autonomy and a wider franchise. When elections were held in early 1937 under separate electorates, results were quite revealing:

- In general constituencies, the Congress swept the polls. But in the Muslim constituencies, its performance was disappointing.
- Even the Muslim League, that claimed to be a representative of the Muslims, performed very badly—it did not get a single seat in North-West Frontier Provinces, got only 2 out of 84 in Punjab and 3 out of 33 in Sind. It was not in a position to form a ministry anywhere.
- The landlord and money lender parties too fared badly in the elections.

Thus, the message was loud and clear:

- The Congress needed to reach out to the Muslim masses and bring them into its fold. It could also ignore the Muslim League completely as the election results had manifested its unrepresentative character.
- Muslim League needed to shed its elite character (dominated by princes and zamindars) and create a base among the Muslim masses.
- The landlords and money lenders now decided to shift their support to the communal parties since Congress had adopted a radical agrarian programme and was mobilising the peasants. Henceforth, the communal parties began to gather unprecedented strength.

In order to achieve its aim, the League led by Jinnah launched a massive campaign for popularisation of the League and hoped to form coalition ministries with the Congress in provinces like Bengal, Assam and Punjab. The Congress advised the League members to sign the Congress pledge and become its members, if they wished to accept responsibilities of office. Angered, Jinnah dubbed the Congress a Hindu organisation out to crush all minorities. The League now began to spread the cry that Muslim minority was in danger of being engulfed by the Hindu majority. It also put forth the unhistorical theory that Hindus and Muslims were two separate nations which could never hope to live together.

In 1938, the League appointed a committee under the chairmanship of the Raja of Pirpur (Raja Syed Mohammed Mehdi), to report on the oppression of the Muslims under Congress Ministries. **The Pirpur Report** fabricated cases of alleged horrible atrocities on Muslims by the Hindus. In October 1939, when the Congress ministries resigned over the Second World War issue, the League observed it as a **'Day of Deliverance and Thanks giving'**.

Finally, in **1940, at the Lahore Session of the Muslim League**, Jinnah propounded his two-nation theory that India comprised of two nations—a Hindu nation and a Muslim nation, who were different economically, politically, socially, culturally and historically. That Muslims were not a minority but a nation, and therefore they were rightfully entitled to a nation of their own. The League then passed a resolution (**Lahore Resolution**) demanding the partition of India. The press was quick to describe the resolution as demand for Pakistan, some also began to call it the **Pakistan Resolution**. The Muslim communal ideas were echoed by the Hindu communalists who declared that Hindus too were a distinct nation and that India was the land of the Hindus, thus reinforcing the two-nation theory.

Thus, 1940 onwards, the above activities of the Muslim League headed by Jinnah transformed communalism into a mass force ultimately leading to the partition of India and formation of the separate state of Pakistan.

The Pakistan Movement

- In 1930, at the Allahabad Session of the Muslim League, **Mohammad Iqbal**, poet and political thinker, first put forth the idea of a separate Muslim state.
- In 1933, the idea was further consolidated and the word Pakistan was coined by a young undergraduate at Cambridge, **Rahamat Ali** (1897–1951). He visualised Punjab, Afghan Province (or NWFP), Kashmir, Sind and Baluchistan as the national home of Indian Muslims and coined the term Pakistan taking the initials of the first four and last of the fifth.
- In March 1940, at the Lahore Session of the League, MA Jinnah made the most unequivocal declaration of the Hindus and Muslims as separate nationalities. The League then passed a resolution (**Lahore Resolution**, popularly called Pakistan Resolution) demanding the partition of India. The Lahore Resolution was written and prepared by Muhammad Zafarullah Khan and was presented by AK Fazlul Huq, the Prime Minister of Bengal. Henceforth, the demand for Pakistan became as much an article of faith for the Indian Muslims as their holy book Quran.

- **Maulana Mohammad Ali** 'We divide and they rule'.
- **Mahatma Gandhi** 'The Question of majority and minority community is a creation of the British Government and would disappear with their withdrawal'.

Previous Years' Questions – Main Exam

1. How did Communalism manifest in the Indian political scene? Explain the background of the passing of the momentous Pakistan Resolution. **[UPSC 1999]**

12 Second Phase of Revolutionary Terrorist Movement (After 1922)

During the First World War, the Revolutionaries were severely repressed and their movement temporarily declined after 1918. However, in late 1919 and early 1920, most of them were released under general amnesty as the government wanted to create an atmosphere of compromise for reception of Montagu-Chelmsford Reforms. The Reforms were rejected by the Congress and the Non-Cooperation Movement was launched under Gandhi. At this juncture, Gandhi, along with CR Das, met many revolutionary terrorist leaders and requested them to join the non-violent struggle or at least to suspend violent terrorist movement for some time. Consequently, many of these leaders attended the Nagpur session of the INC and joined the Congress. (Jugantar party also supported Gandhi in the Non-Cooperation Movement. However, one section under Sachindranath Sanyal remained active and later founded the HRA in north India.)

But this union was only short-lived. The sudden withdrawal of the Non-Cooperation Movement caused much disappointment with Gandhi's leadership and his non-violent struggle. Attracted neither by the parliamentary politics of the Swarajists, nor by the patient constructive work, once again the revolutionaries turned to the cult of the bomb. Old revolutionary leaders revived their organisations; the old Anushilan and Yugantar Samitis reappeared. New ones emerged from the ranks of enthusiastic non-cooperators such as Sukhdev, Bhagwati Charan Vohra and Jogesh Chandra Chatterjee. (During this phase, the Jugantar group got involved with the Chittagong armoury raid. It was only in September 1938 that the Jugantar group finally merged with the Congress.)

The Revolutionary movement that emerged in India after 1922 developed in two broad strands—one in Northern India (Punjab, UP, Bihar and MP, i.e. old Central Provinces) and the other in Bengal. In both the regions, the revolutionary terrorist movement moved away from individual heroism and religious nationalism to mass based, secular movement. Both the strands came under the influence of three new social forces:

1. One was the influence of militant trade unionism that had emerged after the war. The revolutionaries saw immense potential of the new class of workers and wished to harness it.
2. They were also inspired by the revolutionary movements in Russia, China, Ireland, Turkey and Egypt, particularly the Russian Revolution (1917) and the rise of the young Soviet Union. As a result, nearly all revolutionary groups of the time came under the influence of Socialist ideas all over the world. Nearly all of them tried to establish contact with the leaders of the Soviet Union and sought their assistance in terms of ideas and materials.
3. The third influence was that of the newly emerging communist groups with their stress on Marxism, Socialism and the proletariat.

Revolutionaries in Northern India

Context Ramprasad Bismil attended the 1922 Gaya Congress Session, and opposed Gandhi's decision of withdrawal of Non-Cooperation. When Gandhi refused to change his decision, INC got divided into two groups—the Swarajist Party and the Revolutionary Party. Subsequently, Bismil drafted the constitution of the new party known as **Yellow Paper Constitution** with the help of his associates and it was later adopted at the first constitutional committee meeting at Kanpur (1924).

Hindustan Republican Association or Army (HRA, Kanpur, October 1924)

In northern India, revolutionaries were reorganised by veterans like **Sachindranath Sanyal**, **Ramprasad Bismil** and Jogesh Chandra Chatterjee. These revolutionaries were of the view that better results could be achieved only through an all-India organisation and close coordination. Accordingly, in October 1924, at **Kanpur**, a meeting of revolutionaries from all parts of India was called with the aim of organising an all-India body. The meeting was attended by senior revolutionaries such as Ramprasad Bismil, Sachin Sanyal, Jogesh Chandra Chatterjee and young revolutionaries like Bhagat Singh, Sukhdev, Chandra Shekhar Azad, Bhagvati Charan Vohra and Shiv Varma. The deliberations resulted in the formation of Hindustan Republican Army or Association (HRA) with the following objectives:

- To overthrow the British rule through an armed revolution, and
- To establish a Federal Republic of the United States of India with a government elected on the basis of adult franchise.

HRA Ideology

HRA based itself on social revolutionary and communistic principles. Its manifesto, **the Revolutionary** (authored by Sachin Sanyal), declared that it stood for 'abolition of all systems which make the exploitation of man by man possible'. It proposed the nationalisation of the railways and large-scale industries on lines of the Soviet Union. The HRA had also planned to start peasant and labour organisations and work towards an organised armed revolution.

- **Sachindranath Sanyal (1893–1942)** wrote **'Bandi Jivan'**, which became the textbook of the revolutionaries. He was also the author of HRA manifesto, the Revolutionary. **Sanyal vs. Gandhi debate** was published in Young Indian during 1920–24. Sachin Sanyal was the mentor of revolutionaries like Chandrashekhar Azad and Bhagat Singh.
- **Sarathachandra Chatterjee** wrote the novel **Pather Dabi (1926)** meaning 'the Demands of the Road'. The book is about a secret society named Pather Dabi.

Kakori Robbery (9th August 1925)

The HRA leaders decided to organise government dacoities (dacoities against the government) to finance their activities as well as for propaganda and collection of arms. One such robbery was the Kakori robbery.

On 9th August 1925, ten revolutionaries of the HRA stopped the 8-Down train from Saharanpur to Lucknow at Kakori (a small village station near Lucknow) and looted its official railway cash. However, a large number of them were arrested and tried in the Kakori robbery case. During the trial, the accused were subjected to torture in jail, forcing them to resort to hunger strikes to register their protest. In his message from prison, Ramprasad Bismil had urged the youth to give up the desire for revolvers and pistols, not to get involved in secret conspiracies but to work in open movement. He had also urged them to establish communal harmony and work together in unison under the leadership of the Congress to overthrow the British rule.

At the end of the trial, **Ashfaqullah Khan, Ramprasad Bismil, Roshan Singh and Rajendra Lahiri** were sentenced to death and hanged. All the four showed enormous courage in their last hours. Khan and Bismil chanted verses from Gita and Koran as they were taken to the gallows. Four others were sent to Andamans (Kala Pani) for life. **Chandrashekhar Azad** was the only HRA leader who succeeded in escaping arrest, and henceforth lived the life of an absconder.

Hindustan Socialist Republican Association or Army (HSRA, Delhi, September 1928)

Chandrashekhar Azad reorganised HRA with the support of a new cadre of young revolutionaries that included **Bhagat Singh, Sukhdev and Bhagwati Charan Vohra** in Punjab and **Bejoy Kumar Sinha, Shiv Verma, Yashpal** and **Jaidev Kumar** in UP. All these men were intellectuals of the first order. The famous book on revolutionary thinking **'The Philosophy of the Bomb'**, was written by Bhagwati Charan Vohra with the help of Chandrashekhar Azad and Yashpal. It redefined revolution as 'Independence, social, political and economic...aimed at establishing a new order of society in which political and economic exploitation will be an impossibility'.

On 9th and 10th September 1928, these revolutionaries met at **Ferozeshah Kotla Ground** in Delhi and **renamed HRA into HSRA** or Hindustan Socialist Republican Association/Army, accepting socialism as their goal. Henceforth, the members also decided to finance their activities only by looting government treasuries and not by targeting private individuals.

Chandrashekhar Azad (1906–31) Azad was born as Chandrashekhar Tiwari in Bhavra village of the present day Alirajpur district of Madhya Pradesh. When he joined the Non-Cooperation Movement in 1921, he was only 15. Upon being arrested and produced before the magistrate, he gave his name as 'Azad', father's name as 'Swatantrata' and address as 'jail'. From that day onwards, he came to be known as Azad! The sudden withdrawal of the Non-Cooperation Movement severely disappointed Azad, who then joined the newly formed HRA under Ramprasad Bisimil. As a revolutionary, he lived under cover for a long period under the pseudonym of **Pandit Harishankar Brahmachari**.

Chandrashekhar Azad

Saunders Murder Case or Second Lahore Conspiracy Case

HSRA was fast moving away from individual heroic action and was planning a mass armed struggle when, on 30th October 1928 Lala Lajpat Rai died as a result of a brutal lathi-charge while leading an anti-Simon Commission at Lahore. The death of the great Punjabi leader, the **Sher-e-Punjab**, was seen as a national insult by the young romantic revolutionaries and they decided to avenge this killing by once again taking recourse to individual heroic action.

On 17th December 1928 at Lahore, **Bhagat Singh, Chandra Shekhar Azad, Sukhdev** and **Rajguru** assassinated a police officer Saunders, instead of James Scott who had ordered the police to lathi-charge the protesters. The revolutionaries escaped arrest and were given shelter by Durgawati Devi (also known as Durga Bhabhi), wife of Bhagwati Charan Vohra.

While the revolutionaries escaped after the assassination, the authorities unleashed a reign of terror in Lahore. Seeing the people suffer the consequences of their doing, the Punjab unit of HSRA decided to send two volunteers to commit a nominal crime and court arrest. It was following this decision that Bhagat Singh and Batukeshwar Dutt threw harmless bombs in the Central Assembly on 8th April 1929 in what came to be known as the Assembly Bomb Case.

Assembly Bomb Case

HSRA had decided to send two volunteers to court arrest in order to accomplish the following aims:

- To erase the impression that the people of Lahore had to suffer because of their doings.
- To use the case trail as a forum for propagating the new ideology and program of HSRA.
- To spread awareness regarding the need for a revolution by the masses.
- To protest against two government Bills (**Public Safety Bill** and the **Trade Disputes Bill**) which would reduce the civil liberties of the people and workers.

In pursuance of the above aims, HSRA leaders deputed Bhagat Singh and Batukeshwar Dutt to throw bombs in the Central Legislative Assembly, not to kill anybody but to demonstrate along the line of the French anarchist–martyr Valliant that, 'it takes a loud noise to make the deaf hear' (Hence the leaflet they threw in the Assembly along with the bomb read **'to make the deaf hear'**).

On 8th April 1929, Bhagat Singh and BK Dutt threw relatively harmless bombs in the Assembly and made no attempts to escape. During the trial of the Assembly Bomb Case, the police uncovered details of the Saunders assassination as well, and **Bhagat Singh, Sukh Dev, Rajguru** along with several others were tried in the Second Lahore Conspiracy case.

Second Lahore Conspiracy Case Trials

(Not to be confused with the First Lahore Conspiracy Case that occurred in the aftermath of failed Ghadar Conspiracy in 1915)

The three turned their trial into a forum for propaganda. They made courageous statements in the court which were covered by the press and read with great admiration by the people. Every day they entered the court-room shouting slogans of 'Inqlab Zindabad' (Long Live the Revolution), 'Down with imperialism' and 'Long live the proletariat' and singing songs such as 'sarfaroshi ki tamanna ab hamare dil Mei hai' and 'mera rang de basanti chola'. Unsurprisingly, their courageous and defiant attitude won the hearts of even those who believed in non-violence.

Jatindra Nath Das
(Jatin Das, HSRA)

Prison Hunger Strike- They stirred the country with their long hunger strike in protest against the horrible conditions in jail and demanded equality for Indian political prisoners with European prisoners. When, on the 64th day of the epic hunger strike, **Jatin Das (Jatindra Nath Das) died fasting**, the whole country was thrown into a fit of mourning, leading to one of the biggest demonstrations the country had so far witnessed.

Several revolutionaries were convicted in the Lahore Conspiracy Case. While many of them were sent to Cellular Jail in Andamans to serve long sentences, Bhagat Singh, Sukh Dev and Rajguru were hanged on **23rd March 1931** (observed as a Martyr's Day/Shaheed Diwas), sending shock waves across the country. Thousands of people were moved to tears, they refused to eat and work that day. For many years to come, Bhagat Singh's story of bravery and courage was told and retold; his songs were sung and he became a household hero, a martyr and a legend. At its height, Bhagat Singh's popularity briefly rivalled that of Gandhiji in northern India.

Contribution of Bhagat Singh A major shift in the ideology of revolutionary terrorism occurred when the likes of Bhagat Singh, Sukhdev, Bhagwati Charan Vohra, Bejoy Kumar Sinha and Shiv Verma turned to socialist and Marxist thought.

Bust of Bhagat Singh (1907–31), HSRA

Bhagat Singh, also referred to as **Shaheed** Bhagat Singh, was born in Lyallpur district of Punjab in a renowned patriotic family. His father was a Congressman and his uncle was the famous revolutionary Ajit Singh. His grandfather was a follower of Arya Samaj while his father and uncles were members of the Ghadar Party led by Kartar Singh Sarabha and Har Dayal. Young Bhagat was influenced by both these movements. With his shirt pockets always swelling with books, he was one of the most well-read political leaders of his times; he had read extensive literature on socialism, spending hours in the Dwarkadas Library at Lahore. Disappointed by the suspension of the Non-Cooperation Movement (1922), Bhagat Singh joined the ranks of the revolutionaries.

Ideological Rethinking Even before his arrest in 1929, Bhagat Singh abandoned his faith in terrorism and individual heroic action. He was convinced that there was nothing to gain through those methods and that popular mass-based methods alone could liberate India. This is why Bhagat Singh founded a socialist youth organisation, **Naujawan Bharat Sabha** (with himself as its founding secretary in 1926), on the lines of Mazzini's Young Italy Movement. The Sabha was formed as an open wing of the revolutionaries and to carry out political work among the students, peasants and workers. Later, in Sabha's meetings, Bhagat Singh used **magic lantern** to show slides and enliven his political lectures. Bhagat Singh and Sukhdev also organised the **Lahore Student's Union** for political education of the students.

Redefining Revolution Bhagat Singh did not declare openly his opposition to terrorism as he did not want to hurt the sense of heroic sacrifice associated with the terrorist leaders who had laid down their lives. In fact, Bhagat Singh and his comrades redefined the meaning of Revolution as independent from mere use of militancy or violence. During their trial, they clarified the meaning of revolution as a 'radical change that would reorganise society on socialistic line and end the exploitation of man by man and of nation by nation'.

Views on Religion and Communalism Bhagat Singh was one of the few contemporary leaders of the time who understood fully the dangers of communalism. He also sharply criticised Lala Lajpat Rai when he turned to communal politics after 1924. Since he could not openly criticise him, he launched a politico-ideological campaign against him. He printed a pamphlet named **'The Lost Leader'** based on Robert Browning's famous poem in which Browning criticises Wordsworth for turning against liberty. The poem begins with the line, 'just for a handful of silver, he left us'. Further, two rules of the Naujawan Bharat Sabha, drafted by Bhagat Singh, read—'to have nothing to do with communal bodies which disseminate communal ideas' and 'to create the spirit of general toleration among the people considering religion as a matter of personal belief of man'. He also wanted people to free themselves from the bondage of religion and superstition and develop faculty of critical and independent thinking. Just before his martyrdom, he wrote an article, **'Why I am an atheist'** which was a critique on religion and proclaimed his own faith on atheism and materialism.

Accordingly, the HSRA manifesto in 1929 declared, 'the hope of the proletariat is now centred in socialism which alone can lead to the establishment of complete independence and the removal of all social distinctions and privileges'.

Revolutionaries in Bengal

The second strand of revolutionaries that emerged after 1922 sprang up in Bengal. In Bengal, revolutionaries preferred to work underground while simultaneously working for the Congress from village to provincial levels. This enabled them to get access to the mass base of the Congress, while themselves serving as an organisational base to the Congress in small towns and villages. In fact, they cooperated with CR Das in his Swarajist work and for many years Das acted as an emotional link between the revolutionaries and the Congress. After his death, the Congress got divided into two wings—one lead by Subhas Chandra Bose and the other by JM Sengupta. The revolutionaries too got divided into Yugantar vs. Anushilan. The Yugantar supported the Bose wing while Anushilan supported the Sengupta wing.

By now, the Bengal revolutionaries too had got disillusioned with the method of individual heroic action, and yet in practice they still relied on such acts here and there. One such act was an attempt on the life of **Charles Tegart**, the hated Police Commissioner of Calcutta, in January 1924. The revolutionary **Gopinath Saha** was arrested and hanged in the midst of massive popular protests. The government got alarmed and unleashed massive round of repression and arrested a large number of Congressmen, including **Subhas Chandra Bose**, suspected of being sympathetic to the revolutionaries.

With all major leaders in jail, the revolutionary activities saw a decline. The decline was also due to frequent dissensions in the revolutionary cadres, particularly Yugantar and Anushilan.

After 1926, many of the revolutionaries were released and once again they began to reorganise themselves in the form of 'Revolt Groups', the most famous among them being the Chittagong group led by Surya Sen. These groups were also influenced by the **Russian and Irish Revolutionaries**.

The Chittagong Armoury Raid (18th April 1930)

Surya Sen had been a non-cooperator and had later joined as a teacher in a national school in a village in Chittagong. This is why he was also popularly known as **'Masterda'**. He was arrested in 1926 for revolutionary activities and released in 1928. After his release, even as he continued to work for the Congress, he gathered a large group of young revolutionaries including **Ganesh Ghosh, Ambika Chakravarty, Anant Singh and Loknath Paul**. Together they planned to organise an armed rebellion, however small, against the British rule. To equip themselves with arms, they decided to raid armouries, starting with Chittagong Armoury.

Statue of Masterda Surya Sen (1894–1934)

Their plan was to raid two main armouries in Chitttagong, carrying out the raid in the name of **Indian Republican Army**, Chittagong Branch. On the night of 18 April 1930, the Chittagong armoury raid was carried out by 65 revolutionaries. A smaller group of six young men led by Ganesh Ghosh, captured the Police armoury. All the revolutionaries gathered outside the police armoury where Surya Sen hoisted the national flag and was declared as the President of the Provisional Revolutionary Government.

Expecting police action, the revolutionaries left the town and took refuge on the Chittagong Hill ranges. On 22nd April, they got surrounded by British troops on the **Jalalabad Hill**. A fierce battle took place between the two forces, resulting in the death of 12 revolutionaries and 80 British troops. Surya Sen now decided to disperse into the neighbouring villages and carry on guerrilla warfare. Despite several combing operations by the police, he managed to survive for three years with the help of the villagers, most of whom were Muslims. Surya Sen was finally arrested, tried and hanged on 12th January 1934.

The Chittagong Armoury Raid left an immense impact in Bengal, affecting nearly every section of Bengali population including the bureaucracy, the police as well as the army. It led to a massive revival of revolutionary activity in Bengal and the three years—1930, 1931 and 1932 saw the killing of 22 officials and 20 non-officials. In Midnapore alone three British Magistrates and two Inspector Generals of Police were killed.

Government Repression

The government responded with bitter repression and unleashed a reign of terror, arming itself with 20 repressive acts. In Chittagong, several villages were burnt and several other villages were fined. Nationalists were arrested indiscriminately. In 1933, **Jawaharlal Nehru was arrested** and sentenced to two years of imprisonment on charge of sedition for praising the heroism of revolutionaries and condemning government repression.

Novel Aspects of Second Phase of Revolutionary Terrorism in Bengal

The new phase of revolutionary movement in Bengal made an advance in three ways—in terms of participation of women, trend towards group action and support from the Muslim community:

- **Participation of women** Participation of women in large numbers was a remarkable aspect of the revolutionary movement in Bengal. The women provided shelter, acted as messengers and custodians of arms and even fought with guns in hands:
  - **Kalpana Dutta** (later Joshi) was arrested and tried along with Surya Sen and given a life sentence.
  - In December 1931, two school girls of Comilla, **Santi Ghosh** and **Suniti Chaudhary**, shot dead the District Magistrate.
  - In February 1932, **Bina Das** shot at the Governor Stanley Jackson while receiving her degree at the convocation.
  - In September 1932, Pritilala Waddedar died following a raid on the Paharatali European Club in Chittagong.
- **Trend towards group action** Another important advance of the Bengali revolutionaries was that they made an effort to move away from individual heroic action and assassination towards group action and armed uprising.
- **Support from Muslim community** In yet another advance, the Bengal revolutionaries now also shed the slight Hindu tinge that their predecessors had acquired. Many of the Revolt Groups also included Muslims.
  - The Chittagong Group included Muslims such as Mir Ahmed, Sattar, Fakir Ahmed Mian and Tunu Mian.
  - Surya Sen and his men were given active support by Muslim villagers.
  - One of the Revolt Groups was founded by Abdul Razzaque Khan of Calcutta.
  - Sirajul Haq and Hamidul Haq were sentenced to Andamans for their revolutionary activities.
  - Dr. Fazlul Kader Chaudhary of Bogra participated in the Hijli Robbery and was sent to Andamans.
  - Rezia Khatun was also associated with Yugantar and Anushilan Samitis.

Decline of Revolutionary Terrorist Movement

In the 1930s, the revolutionary terrorist movement gradually declined due to various reasons:

- Government repression decimated the revolutionary cadres, several of them were now in jail, some languishing in Cellular Jail in Andamans. In fact, the trade union and communist movements were dealt with the same ferocity.
- On 27th February 1931, Chandrashekhar Azad was killed in an encounter with the police in Alfred Park at Allahabad (later named **Azad Park**), marking the virtual end of the revolutionary movement in Northern India.
- Surya Sen's martyrdom marked the end of revolutionary movement in Bengal.
- The revolutionaries, many of them languishing in jails, had already begun introspecting about their form of struggle. Like Bhagat Singh, many of them turned to Marxism and socialism, joining political parties, like the Communist Party, the Congress Socialist Party, the Revolutionary Socialist Party and others. Some of them also joined the Gandhian wing of the Congress.
- Above all, the mainstream national movement had come under the Gandhian fold, fully committed to non-violent struggle, relegating all other political methods to the fringes of freedom movement.

Significance of Revolutionary Terrorist Movement

Undoubtedly, the second phase of revolutionary terrorist movement failed in its objective of violent overthrow of the British rule or even in organising a mass-based armed struggle, yet they made a significant contribution to the national movement in many ways. They succeeded in stirring the Indian people with their patriotism and sacrifice. They inspired the Indian youth with their courage and heroic actions and restored in them a sense of pride and self-confidence.

The second phase of revolutionaries were not mere romanticists or revivalists. They were intellectuals of a high order who succeeded in giving a socialist orientation to the movement. The slogan of **Inqlab Zindabad**, which later became the chief slogan of the freedom movement, was first popularised by the revolutionaries. Many of the nationalist leaders, including Gandhi, admired their patriotism, courage and deep love for the Indian people. Gandhi had observed, 'Our heads bend before Bhagat Singh's bravery and sacrifice'. The All India Congress Committee observed 18th August 1929 as **'Political Sufferers' Day'** all over India.

Previous Years' Questions – Preliminary Exam

1. Who among the following organised the famous Chittagong armoury raid? **[UPSC 2001]**

   (a) Laxmi Sehgal (b) Surya Sen
   (c) Batukeshwar Datta (d) JM Sengupta

Previous Years' Questions – Main Exam

1. Evaluate the contribution of revolutionary terrorism represented by Bhagat Singh to the cause of India's struggle for independence. **[UPSC 2007]**

Answers

Previous Years' Questions – Preliminary Exam

1. (b)

13

Growth of Left Movement in India

Backgrounder

In 1917, the Russian Revolution had resulted in the overthrow of the despotic Czarist regime and formation of the first socialist state. Russia had further electrified the world by renouncing its claims in China and other parts of Asia. Socialist ideas became suddenly attractive, especially for the people of Asia. In India, they attracted the non-cooperators, the revolutionaries and the unemployed youth.

Socialist ideas began to take shape in the Indian minds and found chief embodiment in Jawaharlal Nehru and Subhas Chandra Bose. Worker and peasant movements grew rapidly in the 1920s. Socialist ideas gained further popularity during the economic depression of 1930s.

It was against this backdrop that the left parties emerged in India in the late 1920s and 30s, bringing closer together the struggle for independence and the struggle for socio-economic emancipation. Two main parties that arose were the CPI (Communist Party of India) and CSP (Congress Socialist Party).

Within the Congress, left-wing tendency found reflection in the election of Jawaharlal Nehru as president for 1929, and 1936 and of Subhas Chandra Bose for 1938 and 1939 Congress Sessions, as well as in the emergence of the Congress Socialist Party.

Meaning of Term 'Left'

There is a history as well as an ideology behind the term "Left". During the period of the French Revolution, in the National Assembly of France, there were three groups—a conservative group (which supported the monarch and nobility and did not want to reduce their powers), a liberal group (which wanted limited reforms of the government) and a radical group (which wanted drastic changes in the system of government, such as the adoption of a constitution and limitation of the powers of monarch).

Seating in French Assembly

Within the French Assembly, the conservatives sat on the right side of the speaker, the radicals sat to his left and the liberals sat in the centre. Since then, the term 'Left' has been added to the political dictionary.

Leftists Leftists are such groups (movements and ideology) which stand for radical reforms in socio-economic structure keeping in mind the interests of the oppressed sections of society.

Rightists Rightists are such groups which are opposed to any change in the existing socio-economic order because of their own stakes.

Centrists Centrists are those who stand for limited change in the socio-economic order.

Left is generally considered to be synonymous with socialism, as socialism is an ideology which aims at the upliftment of the toiling workers and protecting them from the exploitation by their employers, i.e. the capitalists.

Meaning of Socialism

Socialism is an ideology which aims at ending the exploitation of a vast majority of hapless humanity by a handful of powerful minority. It thus aims to establish complete social and economic equality in society. It is a form of society which results from the overthrow of capitalist system by means of a proletariat revolution. Since it is capitalism which creates conditions for the growth of socialist movements, no society can be socialist without having gone through the stage of capitalism.

Socialism destroys private ownership of means of production and replaces it with public ownership of means of production. This means that all resources that can be created out of wealth - e.g. land, factories, mines and banks- no longer remain property of one person or a group of persons. They become the property of the whole people. However, this does not mean that people cannot own anything individually. In socialist societies, people can own personal belongings like house, vehicle, household things, etc. Only, they cannot use those things (such as means of production) which may be used to deprive other people of the fruits of their labour. In fact, as production increases, through planned production, in a socialist society everyone owns more and more personal belongings, and not just a few people.

In this way, socialism ends the exploitation of one class by another and is based on the equality of all men. This equality is not only political or legal (as in capitalist societies) but also social and economic. Socialism abolishes private property, the root of all inequality and establishes socio-political justice.

Socialism also promises complete separation of religion and politics. It does not mean that people cannot hold personal beliefs. Only, they cannot bring it into public realm, use it in politics or propagate in schools. Socialist societies ensure basic social rights to all people—right to employment, rest and leisure, health protection, security in old age, housing, free and equal education and the right to participate in state administration.

Socialism also grants complete equality to women. It creates the material bases for this equality through shorter hours of work for women with small children, crèches at place of work, public kitchens, etc. Advanced capitalist societies also provide these facilities, but they are heavily charged. On the contrary, a socialist state guarantees these benefits to all women, at minimum cost, as children are considered the responsibility of the entire society. Socialist states also support all national liberation movements and the movements of working people against oppression.

In this way, socialist thought looks at man's life experience not from the view point of kings and rulers but form the viewpoint of the downtrodden. It emphasises the role of the working people in transforming society and seeks to organise the working people for the creation of an equal, human and just society.

Circumstances Leading to Rise and Growth of Left Ideologies in India

The rise of the Left in India was due to special politico-economic circumstances prevailing in India towards the end of the First World War and the left ideologies got intertwined with the nationalist movement.

1. Post First World War Economic Recession After the end of First World War, there was a sharp rise in prices of commodities in India, but the employers were unwilling to raise the wages. This led to large scale worker unrest and in the process the workers became conscious of their political role as well. For instance, in Bombay, the workers organised strikes to oppose the Rowlatt Act. Gradually the nationalist leaders also picked up the cause of the workers—in 1920, All India Trade Union Congress was held at Bombay under the presidentship of **Lala Lajpat Rai**.

2. Ideas of Marx and Russian Revolution of 1917 Worldwide, the leftist movement was an outcome of the Industrial Revolution in Europe. The most important leftist/socialist thinker was Karl Marx. And the first socialist revolution was the Russian Revolution of 1917 (led by the Bolshevik Party headed by Lenin) resulting in the emergence of Soviet Russia as the first socialist country in the world.

3. Formation of the Third Communist International (or Comintern) In 1919, the government of Soviet Union helped in the formation of an international organisation of the communist parties of different countries, known as the Third Communist International (as two similar bodies had already been formed earlier). Its aim was to assist communist revolutions all over the world.

4. Rise of Trade Unions in India In India, leftist movement owes its origin to the impact of socialist movements in other countries like Great Britain and Russia. Industrial development in certain places like Bombay, Calcutta and Madras led to large scale concentration of working population. Gradually, the workers began to organise themselves to demand better working conditions and higher wages. This led to the rise of trade unions which in turn prepared the ground for the formation of Leftist political parties.

5. Gandhi and Mass Mobilisation Gandhi's slogan of Swaraj and Swadeshi gave a new orientation to the national movement. Gandhi set out from the beginning to turn the national movement into a mass movement. Under his leadership, the country saw its first true mass national movement in the form of Non-Cooperation Movement. For the first time, the country woke upto the strength of its masses—its peasants, tribals, workers and women. This provided a fertile ground for the inauguration of socialist movement.

6. Disenchanted Non-Cooperators, Revolutionaries and Unemployed Youth In India, leftist ideology also attracted the non-cooperators, as well as those who were unhappy with the Gandhian approach and the Swarajist program. A section of radicals felt unhappy with the 'weak and watery reformism' of Gandhi and saw his cult of non-violence as an obstruction in the development of a real revolutionary mass struggle against British imperialism. Revolutionaries like Chandra Shekhar Azad and Bhagat Singh also turned to socialism. A section of educated middle class also felt disenchanted with 19th-century liberalism in the face of growing unemployment.

7. Economic Depression of 1929 In the year 1929, the USA experienced a severe economic slump which spread to the rest of the world in the early 1930s. All the capitalist countries saw a steep decline in production and foreign trade resulting in economic distress and large scale unemployment. On the other hand, the economic situation in USSR was just the opposite. There was no economic crisis, the first two five year plans had been successfully completed and industrial production had increased by more than four times. In this way, the world depression of 1929 brought capitalism into disrepute and drew attention towards socialism and Marxism.

What is Communism?

Communism is the philosophical, social, political and economic ideology and movement whose ultimate goal is the establishment of the communist society, which is a socio-economic order structured upon the commonownership ofthe meansofproduction andtheabsenceof socialclasses,capitalandthe state. It is based on the 1848 publication of **'Communist Manifesto'** by two German political philosophers,

Karl Marx (1818–1883) and his close associate Friedrich Engels (1820–1895). Communism as a political system never was fully implemented anywhere.

What is Marxism?
It refers to the political and economic theories of Karl Marx and Friedrich Engels, later developed by their followers to form the basis of communism.

Difference between Socialism and Communism Communism and socialism are economic and political structures that promote equality and seek to eliminate social classes. The two are interchangeable in some ways, but different in others. While Socialism is primarily an economic system that can exist in various forms under a wide range of political systems, Communism is primarily a political system which tends to centre on a one-party state that bans most forms of political dissent. Communism is therefore regarded as a more extreme form of socialism or 'hard left'.

Two Streams of Left Movement in India (Communism and Socialism)

The Left Movement in India developed in two main streams:

1. Communism- It functioned as a branch of the International Communist Movement and was by and large controlled by the Comintern.
2. Socialism- It functioned as left wing of the INC, mainly in the form of Congress Socialist Party which aimed to establish democratic socialism.

Both these movements thrived on the anti-imperialist movement going on in India.

Formation of the Communist Party of India

Historical Background

The Communist Party of India was first formed by MN Roy (Manabendra Nath Roy) in Tashkent (Uzbekistan) under the auspices of the Comintern.

MN Roy (1887–1954)

The original name of MN Roy was **Narendranath Bhattacharya**. Following his expulsion from high school for participating in the anti-partition movement (1905), Naren joined the Anushilan Samiti. While pursuing his goal as a revolutionary, he travelled to many countries and landed in the USA in the summer of 1916. It was here that he changed his name and also studied Marxist literature. Troubled by British spies, he fled to Mexico where he met the Russian Communist emissary, **Michael Borodin**. Roy helped Borodin organise the Communist Party of Mexico. From here, Roy went to Russia on the invitation of the Russian Communist Leader-Lenin.

Roy-Lenin Debate

In July–August 1920, at Mexico, Roy attended the Second Congress of the Communist International. Lenin was of the view that in colonial countries, the communists should extend active support to the revolutionary movements carried by the bourgeois (i.e. middle class including the propertied classes and the intelligentsia) nationalists. On the other hand, Roy was of the view that the bourgeois nationalists were opposed to progress and that the communists should carry on their struggle against imperialism independently by forming parties of workers and peasants. It was finally decided that even as the communists would extend support to the bourgeois nationalists in the struggle against imperialism, they would also work independently by allying directly with workers and peasants.

MN Roy forms Communist Party of India at Tashkent (October 1920)

Commissioned by Lenin to prepare the East, specially India for Revolution, Roy left for Tashkent in Russia (now the capital of Uzbekistan) and not very far from Afghanistan in October 1920. Here, he established a military school for training the Indian border tribes for an armed revolt against the British rule and also formed the **Communist Party of India (CPI)**. In 1921, the CPI got affiliated with the Communist International (also called Comintern). In 1922, Roy began publishing his own journal, the Vanguard, which became the mouthpiece of the CPI.

Peshawar Conspiracy Case (1922–23)

Another significant event at Tashkent was that thousands of Muslim Mujahirs (pilgrims), disappointed with British government's attitude towards the Sultan of Turkey, joined Roy's military school. During their return to India, they were caught by the police and tried at Peshawar. The case came to be known as the Peshawar Conspiracy Case in which several Mujahirs including—Mian Mohammad Akbar Shah and Gawhar Rahman Khan, were sentenced to rigorous imprisonment.

Early Communist Groups

- **Virendranath Chattopadhyaya, Bhupendranath Dutt** and **Barkatullah** These revolutionaries working outside India also converted to Marxism.
- **Shripad Amrit Dange** Some Non-Cooperators also turned to communism after the suspension of Non-Cooperation Movement by Gandhi. One such non-cooperator was Shripad Amrit Dange, who organised an early communist group in Bombay. In 1921, Dange published a book named **Gandhi vs. Lenin**, in which he showed his preference for Lenin. In 1922, he founded the **'Socialist'**, the first socialist weekly in India. Through this journal, on 16th September 1924, Dange announced the formation of the **Indian Socialist Labour Party** of the Indian National Congress.
- **Singaravelu Chettier** Singaravelu Chettier, an old communist lawyer announced the formation of the **Labour Kisan Party of Hindustan** (May 1923, Madras) and founded the **Labour-Kisan Gazette**.

Kanpur (Cawnpore) Bolshevik Conspiracy Case (1924)

The British government in India was hostile towards the Indian communists. In 1924, the government initiated a conspiracy case against four leading communists—**Muzaffar Ahmad, SA Dange, Shaukat Usmani and Nalini Gupta** alleging that they had started a revolutionary organisation with the aim of overthrowing the British rule in India. This case came to be known as the Kanpur Conspiracy Case as the trial was held at Kanpur. In May 1924, all four accused were sentenced to four years' rigorous imprisonment.

Flag of CPI (Marxist)

Formation of Communist Party of India (Kanpur, 26th December 1925)

On 1st September 1924, at Kanpur, **Satyabhakta** announced the formation of the Indian Communist Party, with himself as Secretary. Its provisional constitution declared attainment of complete independence and reorganisation of Indian society along communist lines as goals.

On 26th December 1925, Satyabhakta organised an All India Conference of the Communists at Kanpur. It met under the presidentship of Singarvelu Chettier. The Kanpur Conference is regarded as the formal beginning of the Communist Party of India. The conference constituted a Central Committee of the Party with SV Ghate and JP Bergarhatta as Joint Secretaries. The CPI asked all its members to enrol themselves as members of the Congress and form a strong left-wing within the Congress. 1925 onwards, the British communists started coming to India for organising the Indian Communist Movement. The CPI was formally affiliated to the Communist International in 1930.

Formation of Workers' and Peasants' Parties (WPP)

The main political work of early communists was to organise several parties of peasants and workers within the Congress to function as front organisation of the CPI. Hence, WPPs were formed in Bengal, Bombay, Punjab and Meerut.

- **Labour-Swaraj Party (Bengal, 1925–26)** It was the first organisation of the INC comprising peasants and workers and was later renamed as Peasants' and Workers' Party of Bengal. It was organised by **Muzaffar Ahmed** with the help of **Kazi Nazrul Islam** (then a havildar in the 49th Bengal Regiment, later gained popularity as a Bengali poet). Ahmed also brought out a magazine, **Navayug**.
- **Congress Labour Party (Bombay, 1926)** It propagated its program and ideology through the use of press and published its main organ **'Kranti'** in Marathi.
- **Kirti Kisan Party (Punjab, 1926)** The party was headed by Sohan Singh Josh and included many Ghadar members of 1914. Its main journal was **'Kirti'** (worker) earlier founded by Bhai Santokh Singh. **'Mihnatkash'** (worker) in Urdu was another important journal.
- **WPP (Meerut, October 1928)** Formation of this party was attended by British communist **Philip Spratt**.
- By 1928, all these provincial organisations were renamed as Workers' and Peasants' Party (WPP) and transformed into an all India party. All communists were members of this party. Its main aim was to work within the Congress, radicalise its program and make it a true 'people's party'.

Along with Jawaharlal and Subhas Chandra Bose, the WPPs played an important role in creating a strong left-wing within the Congress and giving a leftist touch to the national movement. The Communists also increased their influence rapidly over trade unions. During 1927, in Kharagpur, the communists led Railway Workshop Workers' strike. During 1928, the Bombay WPP led a general strike culminating in the formation of **Girni Kamgar Union**.

Government Repression of Communists (1929)

In the year 1928, worker strikes reached alarming proportions and government decided to behead the trade union movement and remove communist influence from the national movement. Consequently, the communists were severely repressed in the year 1929:

- **Public Safety Ordinance** On 13th April 1929, Viceroy Lord Irwin passed the Public Safety Ordinance for the purpose of deporting subversive elements (the Bill was introduced in the Legislative Assembly but was defeated and therefore had to be passed in the form of an ordinance).

- **Trade Disputes Act** At the same time, the Trade Disputes Act was passed. This legislation provided for compulsory appointment of tribunals (Courts of Enquiry and Conciliation Boards) for settling industrial disputes, made strikes illegal in public utility services (like Postal Service, Railways, Water and Electricity Departments) unless each individual worker planning to go on strike gave an advance notice of one month to the Administration, and above all, forbade trade union activities of coercive or purely political nature and even sympathetic strikes.
- **Meerut Conspiracy Case, 1929–33** On 14th March 1929, the government of Lord Irwin carried out the most severe anti-communist measure in the form of arrest of 31 communists (later one more was arrested). The communists were tried at Meerut allegedly for acting under the direction of Communist International to deprive the British Monarch of his sovereignty over British India by means of general strikes and armed uprising.

  The 32 accused included three Englishmen-two communists **Phillip Spratt** and **BF Bradley**, one journalist named **Lester Hutchinson**. Others were Indian communists including **Radharaman Mitra**. The trial went on for four years and was universally criticised. Far from being a setback for the communists, the Meerut case soon became a cause célèbre. It made heroes and martyrs out of the communists. Their speeches in court widely appealed to the anti-British sentiments, familiarised the people with communist ideas and further raised the popularity of the communist movement.

  The Congress set up a Central Defence Committee and the defence case was pleaded by eminent nationalists like **Jawaharlal Nehru, KN Katju and FH Ansari**. Gandhi visited the prisoners in jail and expressed sympathy with the communist leaders. In such an atmosphere, the Congress members of the Central Legislative Assembly successfully opposed the Public Safety Bill (directed against the communists). The trial lasted for 3.5 years and ended in the conviction of Muzaffar Ahmed, Dange, Joglekar, Spratt, Bradley, Usmani and others. The trial dealt a heavy immediate blow to the left movement.

Suicidal Sectarian politics of Communists (1929)

As if this blow was not enough, the communists inflicted an even deadly blow on themselves by suddenly taking turn towards sectarian politics. The Sixth Congress of the Comintern (1928) revised its **policy of United Front in the colonial world,** i.e. forming alliances with national bourgeoisie in colonial countries. Consequently, the Communists broke their connection with the INC, declaring the Congress as class party of the bourgeoisie. They alleged that the bourgeoisie was aiming to strike a compromise with the government to gain control over the masses. Congress left leaders, such as Nehru and Bose were described as 'agents of the bourgeoisie within the national movement'. The communists condemned the non-violent struggle of the Congress as a sham and advocated armed struggle against imperialism. The Gandhi Irwin Pact of 1931 was described as proof of Congress betrayal.

The communists also dissolved the WPPs and instead gave a call for the formation of an independent and illegal communist party. Taking advantage of this situation, the government **banned the CPI** on 23rd July 1934, forcing the communists to function underground or under the guise of the Congress and the newly formed Congress Socialist Party. Thus, the CPI was saved from the disaster and communist ideas continued to spread in the country.

Dutt-Bradley Thesis

In August 1935, in Moscow, the Seventh Congress of the Comintern took place and once again the communists radically changed their earlier position, deciding to take part in bourgeois led nationalist movement in colonial countries. It planned to organise a **'Front Populaire'** (Popular Front) with all parties that opposed fascism and not limit themselves to forming a United Front with those parties based in the working class.

Thus, the Indian communists once again decided to participate in the national movement led by the INC. The theoretical basis for this change in India was laid down by a document entitled "The Anti-Imperialist People's Front in India", known as Dutt-Bradley Thesis (Rajani Palme Dutt- Benjamin Francis Bradley Thesis, 1936). The document stated that "the National Congress could play a great part in the work of realising the anti-imperialist people's front". Once again, the communists called upon its members to join the Congress, utilise its solid organisation, strengthen the left wing within the Congress (CSP) and oust the right wing. Once again, the communists recovered their image as the most militant anti-imperialists.

> **PC Joshi** leader of the CPI (1939), wrote in the party weekly, **National Front**, "the greatest class struggle today is our national struggle, of which Congress was the main organ".

Difficulties faced by Early Communists in India

The infant communists faced hostility of the British government as well as the upper strata of Indian society; they also faced paucity of funds and cadres.

Formation of the Congress Socialist Party (Bombay, October 1934)

During 1930–34, the initial moves towards formation of a socialist party were made in jails by a group of young Congressmen disenchanted with the politics of Gandhi as well as the communists. Consequently, in 1931, the Bihar Socialist Party was formed by JP Narayan and Phulan Prasad Varma. In September 1933, the Punjab Socialist Party was formed.

In 1934, after the suspension of the Civil Disobedience Movement, a section of Congressmen took to council politics. At this point, the Congress socialists wanted to form a socialist party within the Congress to prevent the loss of revolutionary character of the Congress due to council entry. Thus, in May 1934, at Patna, the First All India Congress Socialists' Conference was convened by Jayaprakash Narayan and was presided by Acharya Narendra Dev. The Conference passed a resolution asking the Congress to adopt a socialist program. Henceforth, the Congress socialists made great efforts in organising an All India Congress Socialist Party.

Ultimately the Congress socialists came together and formed the Congress Socialist Party (CSP) in October 1934, at Bombay, under the leadership of **Jayaprakash Narayan**, **Acharya Narendra Dev** and **Minoo Masani**. The first annual session of the All India Congress Socialist Party was held under the presidentship of **Sampurnananda**. Congress socialists Nehru and Bose did not join the CSP.

From the very beginning, the Congress Socialists agreed upon four basic propositions. These were as follows:

1. The primary struggle in India was the national struggle for freedom.
2. The socialists must work inside the Indian National Congress.
3. They must give the Congress and the national movement a socialist direction (They wanted the Congress to incorporate radial socio-economic program for upliftment of the toiling masses. They stood for abolition of capitalism, zamindari and princely states).
4. To achieve this, they must organise the workers and peasants and make them the social base of the national movement.

Independence and socialism emerged as the twin objectives of the Party. The session adopted a comprehensive blueprint of a socialist society in India, including-

- Transfer of all power to the masses.
- Economic life of the county to be planned and controlled by the state.
- Abolition with compensation of princes and landlords and other classes of exploiters.
- Liquidation of debts owed by peasants and workers.
- "To everyone according to his needs" is to be the basis of distribution of economic goods.
- The state shall not discriminate between religions, castes or sexes.

The Congress socialists were inspired by Marxism and Democratic Socialism. They worked hard to secure acceptance of their programme by the Congress.

Jayaprakash Narayan Srivastava (1902–1979) Popularly known as JP or **Lok Nayak**, he rose to be a key leader of the national movement. Born in Chapra Bihar (at present Balia district, UP), JP went to the USA for higher studies, returned in 1929 as a Marxist, joined the INC the same year under the mentorship of Gandhi and won special fame during the Quit India Movement. He wrote the book- **'Why Socialism?'**. He was the recipient of the Magsaysay Award for social service (1965) and the **Bharat Ratna** (posthumously, 1999).

A stamp shows Jayaprakash Narayan

Meerut Thesis of Congress Socialist Party (1935)

The thesis laid down that the task of the CSP was to 'wean the anti-imperialist elements in the Congress away from its present bourgeois leadership and to bring them under the leadership of revolutionary socialism'. However, this notion was soon found to be unrealistic and the socialists instead agreed on composite leadership or alternate Left leadership of the Congress. It was later realised at Congress Sessions at Tripuri (in 1939) and at Ramgarh (in 1940).

Minor Leftist Parties

In the 1930s, particularly in 1939, several other left currents emerged. Most of these centered around personalities and became near defunct once the central figure disappeared.

The Forward Bloc (1939)

Subhas Chandra Bose and his followers founded the Forward Bloc after Bose was forced to resign from the presidentship of the Congress owing to differences with Gandhi. Bose opposed the Congress attitude of cooperation with the British war effort and went abroad to seek military help to fight the British in India.

Revolutionary Socialist Party (1940)

The party stood for violent overthrow of British imperialism and establishment of socialism in India. In the Gandhi–Bose tussle, RSP supported Bose.

Other Left Parties

The Bolshevik Party of India (1939) was founded by N Dutt Mazumdar, the Revolutionary Communist Party (1942) was launched by **Saumyendranath Tagore** and the Bolshevik-Leninist Party was announced in 1941 by Indra Sen and Ajit Roy. Each of them was a dissident communist group.

MN Roy, the pioneer of communist movement in India had come back to India in 1930 and had organised a strong group of 'Royists'. However, in 1940, he organised the Radical Democratic Party after his complete disillusionment with Marxism. He now upheld the idea that Indian Revolution could be brought about not by proletariats alone but by the leadership of a multi class party.

Weaknesses of the Left Movement

Despite the fact that the leftists were among the most militant and sacrificing of freedom fighters, they failed on several fronts, like:

- They failed in their basic goal of establishing the hegemony of socialist ideas and parties over the national movement.
- They also failed to make a deep study of the Indian reality. With the exception of Jawaharlal Nehru, the leftists saw the Congress leadership as bourgeois and compromising with the imperial forces to retain control over the masses.
- They also failed to understand the Gandhian strategy of struggle.
- They invariably fought with the Congress leadership over the wrong issues.
- They constantly overestimated their support among the people.
- The different left factions failed to work unitedly over long periods. Even Nehru and Bose could not work together for long and went their separate ways in 1939.

Congress Reaction to the Formation of Congress Socialist Party

The Congress gave a mixed reaction to the formation of the Congress Socialist Party. The Right Wing Congressmen criticised the socialist talk about confiscation of property and class war. Even Mahatma Gandhi rejected the idea of class war. He did not believe in the need for abolition of capitalism, zamindari or princely states. What he advocated was the need for a change of heart in the capitalist, zamindars and the princes so that they considered themselves not as owners but as trustees for their workers, tenants and subjects.

However, with the intervention of young leaders like Jawaharlal Nehru and Subhas Chandra Bose, socialist ideas received impetus and gradually influenced the political behaviour of the Congress.

Growth of Socialist Ideas in Indian National Congress: Role of Nehru and Bose

Socialist ideas acquired considerable following by the beginning of 20th century in many parts of the world. Yet, these ideas did not acquire prominence within the Congress for many years. However, socialist ideas first received impetus with the efforts of young leaders like Jawaharlal Nehru and Subhas Chandra Bose and gradually came to influence the programme and political activities of the Congress.

Growth of Socialism in Indian National Congress

In INC, seeds of socialism first came through Indian intellectuals and militants living in Europe and other Western countries. These included, **Madame Cama, Shyamji Krishna Verma, Shapurji Sakhlatvala, Virendra Nath Chattopadhyaya, Bhupendra Nath Dutta, Lal Hardayal, MN Roy** and a host of others. But none of these functioned within the framework of the main political organisation of India—the Indian National Congress. In fact, socialism had no influence over the INC till the end of the First World War. However, after this, the socialist ideas began influencing Congress policies.

In the beginning, socialism seemed to intimidate the early Congress leaders. This is quite understandable as most of them belonged to the upper strata of Indian society—the English educated middle class which included the rentiers, professionals and entrepreneurs. Such elements, at most, sympathised with the misfortunes of the common man from a distance; that too to the extent that their own interests were not threatened. Consequently, the INC largely remained a preserve of the elite, and made hardly any attempts to reach out to the Indian masses, with the sole exception of the Swadeshi Movement (1905–08).

The first stirrings of change were witnessed only after the emergence of Gandhi who set out from the beginning to turn the national movement into a mass movement. Under his leadership, the country saw its first true mass national movement in the form of Non-Cooperation Movement. For the first time, the country woke upto the strength of its masses—its peasants, tribals, workers and women. The disunity in the years following the withdrawal of the movement raised some significant questions-

- What could be done to ensure maximum possible participation of the people in the freedom struggle?
- How could the various classes and communities of people be united politically?
- What precisely are the goals that the national movement should strive to attain?

It was this intense intellectual and political exercise that gave rise to Socialist ideas within the Congress.

Jawaharlal Nehru (1889–1964) Born in Allahabad as the son of Motilal Nehru (of Kashmiri Pandit community), he studied law at Trinity College Cambridge. Upon his return, he practiced law at Allahabad High Court and emerged as a key leader of the Left Wing faction of the INC in the 1920s and eventually of the INC itself under the mentorship of Gandhi. He finally rose to be the **first Prime Minister** of free India.

Jawaharlal Nehru

Role of Jawaharlal Nehru

The young Jawaharlal was one among those who brainstormed over the future of India. He has actively participated in the Non-Cooperation Movement and had also worked closely with the peasants of Pratapgarh and Rae Bareilly in UP during the movement. Though committed to Gandhi's leadership and his non-violent struggle, he was gravely disappointed at the withdrawal of the Non-Cooperation Movement and was attracted neither by the no-Changers or the pro-changers.

In 1926, he went to Europe, mainly for medical treatment of his wife, Kamala, in Switzerland. During his year and a half long sojourn in Europe, Jawaharlal came in contact with political thinkers and socialist ideas. In February 1927, he represented the INC at the International **Congress Against Colonial Oppression and Imperialism** held at Brussels. There he met delegates from Africa, Latin America, Mexico, China and other Asian countries. The Brussels Conference had set up an organisation named **'The League Against Imperialism and for National Independence'**. Jawaharlal was appointed member of the executive committee of the League. He now came to understand how development in Europe was led by industrial development which in turn needed continuous supply of raw materials and new markets. This had led to imperialism and race for colonies and intensified exploitation in Asia, Africa and Latin America. He could now see how India's freedom struggle was in reality a part of an international fight against imperialism.

In November 1927, Jawaharlal was invited to visit Soviet Union. Here he was greatly impressed to see the novel experiments in governance and social reconstruction. By the time he returned to India in December 1927, Jawaharlal had for all practical purposes, turned a socialist.

In 1927, when Jawaharlal returned, India was witnessing a noisy debate over the character of Swaraj. The Simon Commission, an all white commission to recommend further reforms in the constitutional development in India, was rejected by all groups and parties. The Simon Boycott Movement brought to the forefront the issue of the type of constitution or kind of independence that India should obtain for itself.

So far, by Swaraj, the Congress had meant Dominion Status for India within the ambit of British Empire (similar to the status of self governing Australia, New Zealand and South Africa). To Jawaharlal, on the other hand, Dominion status only meant perpetuation of British exploitation of India from the back door.

Matters came to a head at the All Parties Conference (Feb 1928), at the Conference it was agreed that in framing the constitution for India, the principle of Dominion Status should be kept in mind. Now Jawaharlal had no alternative but to build up an opposition and gain support for the demand of purna swaraj or complete independence. The young Subhas Chandra Bose (one of the General Secretaries of the Congress in 1928, like Jawaharlal), was one among those who helped him in this task.

After 1929, Jawaharlal became a symbol of socialism in India. He became the president of the historic Lahore Congress where he declared in his presidential speech, **'I am a socialist and a republican and no believer in kings and princes'**. He also championed the cause of **Praja Mandal Movement** in Indian states against the tyranny of the princes. Nehru was reelected to the post in 1936 and 1937.

Praja Mandal Movement (also known as States' Peoples' Conference Movement) It refers to the **national movement in princely states** which started only after 1920 after the Non-Cooperation Movement. During this time, subjects of princely states had formed peoples' organisations called 'Praja Mandals'. The movement brought together representatives from hundreds of Indian princely states including Bhopal, Baroda, Travancore and Hyderabad. The movement was directed against both-feudalism and colonialism. The people fought against the feudal princes as well as the British administration simultaneously for their rights. Activities of the movement included implementation of constructive program of the Congress in princely states. The INC also joined hands with the Peoples' Conference and brought it under the fold of the national movement.

Jawaharlal emerged as the most popular leader of the National movement after Mahatma Gandhi. He popularised the ideas of socialism through his countrywide tours, through his books (**'Glimpses of World History'** 1934 and **'An Autobiography'** 1936) articles and speeches. He popularised the notion that **political freedom was meaningless without economic freedom**.

Nehru vs. Gandhi It was during these years that J Nehru developed a complex relationship with Gandhi. He criticised Gandhi for refusing to recognise class conflict and for putting forward the theory of trusteeship. In fact, he devoted an entire chapter in his Autobiography, arguing against some aspects of Gandhian ideology. Yet he defended Gandhi against other left-wing critics and appreciated his ability to reach out to the hearts of the masses.

Nehru and Gandhi

Nehru's approach towards Gandhi has been well worded by **Mohit Sen**, 'Nehru believed that the overwhelming bulk of the Congress was composed of amorphous centrists, that Gandhi not only represented them but was also essential for any genuinely widespread mass movement, that on no account should the Left be at loggerheads with him or the centrists, but their strategy should rather be to pull the centre to the left'.

At the same time, Nehru recognised the primacy of anti-imperialist struggle led by the Congress and Gandhi and was therefore not in favour of any separate organisations independent of the Congress. He thought it best to propagate socialism while remaining under the banner of the Congress.

Note: Here it may be noted that it was Gandhi who founded the **Ahmedabad Textile Labour Association (TLA)** in 1918 with 14,000 workers on its roll, making it perhaps the largest single trade union of its time. Clearly, Gandhi's philosophy on labour reflected the need of the time, i.e. giving primacy to the anti-imperialist movement which could ill-afford an all out class war among the different classes of an emerging nation.

Role of Subhas Chandra Bose

Subhas Chandra Bose had certain apparent similarities with Jawaharlal Nehru. Both came from upper middle class background and received education abroad. Both were intellectuals who had committed themselves to the cause of the nation.

Subhas Chandra Bose

Subhas Bose had been a political activist since student days and rose to fame when he rejected to join the esteemed Indian Civil Service to which he was selected on the basis of merit (1921). His political mentor was not Gandhi but **Deshbandhu Chittaranjan Das** who had declared in 1922 that India should secure "swaraj of the masses and not of the classes".

Subhas was also disappointed at the withdrawal of the Non-Cooperation Movement and briefly joined the pro-changers because of his loyalty. His main focus during this time were the civic affairs of Calcutta, of which he was the Chief Administrative Officer (July to October 1924) as was the case with Jawaharlal at Allahabad (Chairman April 1923 to April 1925).

Though Subhas was not as clear and sure about socialist ideas as Jawaharlal, he had no difficulty in endorsing Jawaharlal's anti-imperialist views and extended full support to him in favour of purna swaraj, even as he did not share Jawaharlal's commitment to Gandhi's leadership or his belief in non-violence as a technique in anti-imperialist struggle.

Congress March Towards Socialism

Formation of Independence of India League within the Congress (August 1928)

In August 1928, the **'Independence of India League'** was launched by J. Nehru with the support of Subhas Chandra Bose (Nehru and Bose as secretaries and S. Srinivas Iyengar as President), as **a pressure group within the Congress** with the aim of-

- Countering the concept of Dominion Status
- Pleading for complete independence of India from the British, and
- Working for establishment of an Indian Republic on Socialist lines.

Congress Adopts 'Complete Independence' as Goal (1928–29)

At Calcutta Session of Congress, December 1928, Jawaharlal and Subhas jointly moved a resolution to replace Congress goal of 'Dominion Status' by 'Complete Independence'. This year they achieved only limited success and they certainly succeeded creating awareness about the goal. Their real success came a year later at the Lahore Congress (1929), when the Congress adopted 'complete independence' as goal.

Emergence of Leftist Camp within Congress

Nehru and Bose along with their followers soon emerged as the leftist camp within the Congress. In the years that followed, on several occasions, Nehru and Bose expressed their concern for the toiling people and condemned the exploitative nature of imperialisms. Their talks on socio-economic justice stirred the imagination of the youth (through the Youth League, the Hindustani Seva Dal, the Naujavan Bharat Sabha and the Volunteers' Movement), the students and the workers (through the All India Trade Union Congress whose presidentship was taken over by Nehru in 1929 and by Bose in 1931).

Congress Resolution on Fundamental Rights and National Economic Program (March 1931)

In March 1931, at the Karachi Session of the Congress, a declaration on Fundamental Rights and the National Economic Program was adopted. The resolution declared: 'In order to end the exploitation of the masses, political freedom must include real economic freedom of the starving millions'. It was originally drafted by Jawaharlal and became the basic document of Congress' socio-economic programme for later years. The resolution was indeed a significant step in the Congress march towards socialism.

Formation of Congress Socialist Party (October 1934)

Both Jawaharlal and Subhas were unhappy about the withdrawal of the Civil Disobedience Movement. In the years following the withdrawal, Jawaharlal reoccupied himself with the agitation of the UP peasantry while Subhas associated himself with the working-class movement. Both continued to arouse the imagination of the youth, the students and the working class and infused them with a radical militant temper. This eventually facilitated the formation of the Congress Socialist Party (May 1934) within the framework of the Congress organisation. Though neither Jawahar nor Subhas joined the party, they welcomed its formation and drew its support whenever necessary.

Lucknow and Faizpur Sessions of Congress (1936, presided by Jawaharlal Nehru)

At Lucknow Session of Congress (April 1936), Jawaharlal espoused the cause of socialism in his presidential speech- 'I see no way of ending the poverty, vast unemployment, degradation and subjection of the Indian people except through socialism'.

At Faizpur Session of Congress (December 1936), also held under the presidentship of Jawaharlal, the **Congress adopted an agrarian program**, including items such as reduction of rent and revenue, abolition of feudal dues and levies, provision of cheap credit, security of tenure for tenants, introduction of cooperative farming, living wages for agrarian labourers and the right to form peasant unions.

In 1936 itself, Jawaharlal inducted three Congress Socialists-Jaya Prakash Narayan, Narendra Dev and Achyut Patwardhan into the Congress Working Committee.

The Congress Socialists played an important role in Kisan movement. For instance, **Prof. NG Ranga, Indulal Yagnik and Swami Sahajananda Saraswati** played a key role in the organisation of **All-India Kisan Sabha** and the first All India Kisan Congress met at Lucknow (1936), under the presidentship of Sahajananda Saraswati. The Congress Socialists also took part in the democratic movements in princely states.

The Election Manifesto of the Congress in 1936 (which declared that the Congress would take steps for the settlement of labour disputes and take effective measures for securing the rights to form unions and go on strike), convening of First All India States' Peoples' Conference (1936), formation of All India Students' Federation and the Progressive Writers' Association were some other achievement of the Left.

The impact of socialist ideas on Congress was also seen in the increasing shift of Gandhi towards radical positions on economic and class issues. Gandhi, along with Nehru, argued in favour of public sector in large scale industries in order to prevent concentration of wealth in a few hands. He accepted the principle of land to the tiller and declared in 1942 that "the land belongs to those who work on it and to no one else". In 1945, the Congress adopted a resolution on abolition of landlordism.

Jawaharlal and Subhas Chandra Bose continue to work for Socialism Jawaharlal continued to advocate that in order to attain independence from foreign rule, it was necessary for Congress to mobilise all sections of Indian people, particularly the downtrodden. The British exploiters had their native allies everywhere in India, and therefore the freedom struggle had to be combined with freedom of the poor from their immediate internal oppressors. For this, he insisted that the Congress must have a blueprint of the future of a free India which would include the following:

- Elections on the basis of adult franchise
- A Constituent Assembly for drawing up a constitution to guarantee the rights and privileges of all individuals
- Eradication of long-standing socio-economic injustices
- Achievement of economic independence on modern industrial lines

Jawaharlal persistently pleaded for Democratic Socialism in India and eventually succeeded in influencing the Congress in taking a pro-socialist turn.

Subhas left his Socialist mark on the Congress by laying emphasis on industrialisation and planned economic growth for India. In 1938, when Bose was president, the Congress committed itself to economic planning and set up a **National Planning Committee** under the chairmanship of Jawaharlal. In 1938, Bose was elected president of the Congress and re-elected in 1939, despite Gandhi's opposition. Gandhi and his followers later compelled Bose to resign from the presidentship, following which Bose and his followers founded the Forward Bloc. By then, socialism had emerged as the accepted creed of most of the youth of India, both within and outside the Congress.

To sum up, we see that socialist ideas within the Congress did not always find favour and some prominent Congressmen were even opposed to them. Yet the importance of the role of Jawaharlal and Subhas Chandra Bose should not be judged by their ultimate success or failure but by the sincerity and commitment with which they pursued their convictions.

Previous Years' Questions – Preliminary Exam

1. In October 1920, who among the following headed a group of Indians gathered at Tashkent to set up a Communist Party of India? **[UPSC 2005]**
   (a) H.K. Sarkar (b) P.C. Joshi
   (c) M.C. Chagla (d) M.N. Roy
2. Consider the following statements: **[UPSC 2010]**
   1. The 'Bombay Manifesto' signed in 1936 openly opposed the preaching of socialist ideas.
   2. It evoked support from a large section of business community from all across India.

   Which of the statements given above is/are correct? Choose the correct answer from the following options.
   (a) 1 only (b) 2 only
   (c) Both 1 and 2 (d) Neither 1 nor 2

Answers

Previous Years' Questions – Preliminary Exam

1. (d) 2. (a)

14 Growth of Peasants' and Workers' Movements 1920s–30s

In the previous chapters, you have read about the peasant and working class movements during the second half of the 19th century. You saw how these movements were directed against the oppression of the colonial government as well as that of the landlords and the mill owners. In this chapter, you will learn about the workers' and peasants' movements in the 1920s and 1930s and how they were different from their predecessors.

Several novel factors had emerged on the Indian scene (such as the emergence of mass politics, socio-economic consequences of the First World War and the rise of communism and socialism) and they ensured that the working class and peasant movements of the 1920s and 30s were radically different from what we had seen in the previous era. The rise of communist movement in the 1920s lent a militant and revolutionary content to these movements in India. They were now organised into Trade Unions or Kisan Sabhas all over the country.

The two national mass movements of 1920–22 and 1930–34 further politicised the workers and peasants on a large scale. The World Economic Depression of 1929 had worsened the condition of the workers and peasants all over the country and they began to demand relief and justice.

Workers' Movements of the 1920s and 1930s

Why did Trade Unions Emerge in India?

Problems of the Workers The miserable living and working conditions of the workers were the main reason for the rise of trade unions in India. These included long hours of work, low wages, dismissal from work, unhygienic conditions in factories, employment of child labour, bad housing and absence of all other amenities.

The working-class population was concentrated in Bombay (main centre for cotton textile industry) and Bengal (main centre for jute and tea industry). The workers worked here from 12 to 18 hours a day. There was no provision for weekly off. They lived in slums with no provision for water supply, electricity or sanitation.

In the coal mines of Jharia and Giridih, even women and children worked underground, fines were imposed for late attendance and under production and wages paid were low and exploitative. The workers often turned to local 'Kabuli' money lenders and got trapped in vicious cycle of debt. Pension or provident fund were also non-existent.

Thus, labour in India suffered from all forms of exploitation that existed in the early stages of industrialisation in England and the West, plus the evils of a rapacious colonial rule. The colonial situation gave a distinctive touch to Indian working class movement. The Indian working class had to face two basic antagonistic forces—an imperialist political rule and economic exploitation at the hands of both imperialist and native elements. It was under these circumstances that the Indian working class movement got inevitably intertwined with the political struggle for national freedom.

Such exploitative conditions urged the workers to come together and form trade unions in order to increase their bargaining power vis à vis the employers.

Meaning of Trade Unions Trade Unions are worker associations formed with the aim of improving their work conditions in factories and mills. These factories and mills emerged in India in large numbers in the 19th century and hundreds of workers began to interact with one another on daily basis. They shared their problems and developed an urge to unite. Even though most of the workers were uneducated, there were always some intellectuals (or 'outsiders' such as nationalists or socialists) among them who tried to educate them, organise them into trade unions and improve their lot.

Early Associations

Trade unionism slowly grew through the following efforts:

- In 1870s, in Bengal, **Sasipada Banerjee** (a Brahmo), founded the working men's club. In 1874, he published a journal **Bharat Sramjibi** and also organised night schools to educate the jute mill workers.
- In 1880, in Bombay, **NM Lokhande** started the weekly **Dinabandhu** and founded the Bombay Mill-Hands Association in 1890.
- In April 1918, in Madras, the **first Trade Union in India** was founded by **BP Wadia** (an associate of Annie Besant) known as the Madras Labour Union.
- In 1918, in Ahmedabad, Mohandas Karamchand Gandhi had led a strike of textile mill workers. The strike went on for 21 days, Gandhi sat on hunger strike and finally a compromise was reached.
- In 1920, Gandhi founded the **Majdur Mahajan** for arbitration between workers and employers and also advocated harmonious relations between them.

Gandhi's Philosophy on Labour

Mahatma Gandhi rejected the idea of class war and instead put forward the **theory of trusteeship** (the capitalist being the trustee of the workers' interest). He did not believe in the need for abolition of capitalism, zamindari or princely states. What he advocated was the need for a change of heart in the capitalists, zamindars and the princes so that they considered themselves not as owners but as trustees for their workers, tenants and subjects.

Gandhi's philosophy on labour reflected the need of the time, i.e., giving primacy to the anti-imperialist movement which could ill-afford an all-out class war among the different classes of an emerging nation. Often, Gandhi's principle of trusteeship and arbitration had been dismissed as class collaborationist, and mistakenly so. In the words of **Acharya JB Kripalani**, one of the staunchest followers of Mahatma Gandhi, 'trustee' by the very term meant that he was not the owner. The owner is one whose interest he is called upon to protect.

In 1918, Gandhi founded the **Ahmedabad Textile Labour Association (TLA)** with 14,000 workers on roll, making it perhaps the largest single trade union of its time.

Note: The period 1919–22 saw a resurgence of working class activity, both to protect their own rights and also to gain freedom from the colonial rule.

- In April 1919, following the Punjab wrongs and Gandhi's arrest, the working class in Gujarat resorted to strikes and demonstrations.
- During 1919–21, railway workers struck in support of the Rowlatt agitation and the Non-Cooperation and Khilafat movement.
- In November 1921, during the visit of the Prince of Wales, the workers responded to the Congress call of a country-wide general strike.

Formation of All India Trade Union Congress (AITUC, Bombay, 31st October 1920)

The year 1919–20 saw a wave of strikes in many industrial centres such as Bombay, Calcutta, Madras, Ahmedabad, Jamshedpur and Kanpur. This helped mobilise thousands of workers and it was against this backdrop that on 31st October 1920, in Bombay, the All India Trade Union Congress (AITUC) was formed. Lokmanya Tilak, who had developed a close association with Bombay workers, was one of the moving spirits in the formation of AITUC.

The inaugural session was presided over by **Lala Lajpat Rai** (also INC President of the year) and **Diwan Chaman Lal**, who later emerged as a prominent name in Indian labour movement, was the general secretary. The session was attended by several prominent leaders like Motilal Nehru, Annie Besant, CF Andrews, BP Wadia and NM Joshi.

The AITUC was formed as the central organisation of the Indian workers. Chaman Lal, while moving a resolution on Swaraj, declared- 'It was to be a Swaraj, not for the capitalists but for the workers'.

Congress Response

The Congress at its Gaya Session in 1922 (presided by CR Das) welcomed the formation of the AITUC and also formed a committee of prominent Congressmen to assist its work. In addition to Lajpat Rai, many other Congressmen became closely associated with the AITUC, these included CR Das (who presided over its third and fourth sessions), CF Andrews, JM Sengupta, Subhas Chandra Bose, Jawaharlal Nehru and Satyamurti.

Throughout the 1920s, workers' awareness grew and there were several strikes. Yet by 1929, majority of workers were not yet organised into trade unions. Differences of language and community as well as opposition by jobbers (sirdars) and employers were the main reasons that kept the workers away from trade unions.

Period of Growth of Trade Unionism (1920–29)

After 1922, there was a lull in the working class movement and a reversion to purely economic struggles. The next wave of working class activity came during 1927–29, spurred by the emergence of a clearly defined Left-block on the national scene.

Trade Union Act of 1926 It recognised trade unions as legal associations, laid down conditions for regulation and registration of trade union activities, secured their immunity from prosecution for legitimate activities but put some restrictions on their political activities.

The Geneva-Amsterdam group and the Moscovite group of AITUC During 1926–27, the AITUC got divided into groups called the Geneva-Amsterdam group (the reforming group) and the Moscovite group (revolutionary group). The former wanted AITUC to be affiliated to the International Federation of Trade Unions (IFTU) with its headquarters at Amsterdam while the latter group wanted affiliation with the Red Labour Union (RILU), based at Moscow. The communist thinking ultimately carried greater influence.

By 1927, various communist groups had organised themselves into **Workers' and Peasants' Parties** (WPP) under the leadership of activists like SA Dange, Muzaffar Ahmed, PC Joshi and Sohan Singh Josh. The WPPs functioned as left wing within the Congress and rapidly gained strength at provincial and all India level.

In November 1927, **AITUC decided to boycott the Simon Commission** and many workers participated in the massive anti-boycott demonstrations.

By 1928, communist influence on trade union movement became very strong and the year witnessed unprecedented industrial unrest. The communist led **Girni Kamgar Union (GKU)** shot to prominence after the historic six-month long strike by textile workers in Bombay (April to September 1928). Communist influence also spread to workers in railways, jute mills, municipalities, paper mills etc.

Bombay

In 1924, more than one lakh textile workers struck work against refusal of bonus. In 1926, Textile Labour Union was formed with NM Joshi as President. The strike forced the government to intervene. Again in 1928, there was a historic six month long general strike by textile workers.

Bengal

In 1928, the workers of Fort Gloster Mills in Bauria in Howrah district struck work. The strike was remarkable in the sense that it was carried out by some 15 thousand jute workers for more than six months. This strike also forced the government to intervene.

Jamshedpur

In 1928, the workers of Tata Steel Factory struck work for nearly six months against the dismissal of a large number of workers (The Tata Steel Factory was the first modern steel factory in India in Jamshedpur founded by Jamshedji Tata. Some 20 thousand workers worked here and had formed their Labour Association). Even though the strike was not fully successful, it forced the employers to recognise the Labour Association.

Ahmedabad and Madras were also important centres of trade union movement.

Thus, during 1927–29, several strikes occurred in mills and factories in Bengal, Bombay and Madras. By 1929, the government anxiously reported, 'there was hardly a single public utility service or industry which had not been affected in whole or part, by the wave of communism which swept the country'.

In 1923, in Madras, the **first May Day** (a day celebrated in honour of workers) was celebrated by Singaravelu.

Period of Decline of Trade Unionism (1929–35)

Government Repression of the Communists (1929)

By now, the government had grown nervous about the militancy and political involvement of the working class, particularly the coming together of the nationalists and the leftists. The government now launched a two-pronged attack on the labour movement of repression and concession. It passed repressive laws like Public Safety Act and Trade Disputes Act, and arrested in one swoop the entire radical leadership of labour movement (Meerut Conspiracy Case). On the other hand, concession was offered in the form of appointment of Royal Commission on Labour in 1929 (chairman- John Henry Whitley), to wean away as many labour activists and commit them to constitutional and corporatist mould.

Sectarian Politics of the Communists (1929)

As if this was not enough, the labour movement in India suffered a further setback when, in 1929, the communists reversed their policy of working within the mainstream national movement. This not only isolated the communists from the national movement, but also greatly reduced their hold over the working class. The membership of GKU fell from 54,000 in 1928 to 800 in 1929. They also got isolated within the AITUC and were thrown out in 1931.

Split in AITUC

There occurred two splits in the AITUC in the aftermath of the Great Economic Depression that started in 1929 in the USA and spread throughout the world. It lasted in India until 1936. During this period, hundreds of factories closed down, thousands of workers lost their job and trade unions also declined. The splits further weakened the trade union movement.

First Split

It took place in 1929, when Jawaharlal Nehru was the President of AITUC. It occurred over the issue whether the AITUC should boycott the Royal Commission on Labour or not. While the extremists wanted to boycott it, the moderates wanted to join it. Finally, the moderates led by NM Joshi and VV Giri left the AITUC and formed the **All India Trade Union Federation** with VV Giri as President.

Second Split

It took place in 1931, when the communists left the AITUC and formed the **Red Trade Union Congress**.

The communists withdrew from the Civil Disobedience Movement, leaving the field entirely to the Congress. The workers now followed the lead of the Congress and participated in large numbers in the first Civil Disobedience Movement. In Bombay, the Congress slogan during the civil disobedience was that the 'workers and peasants are the hands and feet of the Congress'. But a dip in the working class activity was seen during 1931 and 1935 and they did not actively participate in the second Civil Disobedience Movement (1932–34).

Period of Expansion of Trade Unionism (1935 onwards)

A period of expansion of trade unionism in India began 1935 onwards. The communists abandoned their suicidal sectarian politics and joined the mainstream national movement. They also joined the AITUC in 1935 and unity in the AITUC was restored.

The impact of economic depression ended and economy began to improve 1936 onwards. When the campaign for 1937 elections began, the AITUC in general, extended its support to Congress candidates. The Congress manifesto also declared several measures for securing the rights of the labour class.

Formation of Congress Ministries and Growth of Trade Unionism

In 1937, Congress Ministries were formed in the provinces and in the period 1937–39, the trade union movement showed a phenomenal rise; the number of trade unions doubled. Number of strikes also went up considerably with most of them ending in full or partial victory. The most successful strike during this period was the Kanpur workers' strike which continued for 55 days and involved 10,000 workers. The government appointed Kanpur labour enquiry Committee under the chairmanship of **Babu Rajendra Prasad**.

The Congress ministries showed a sympathetic attitude towards workers' demands. Some beneficial legislations like the Bombay Industrial Disputes Act (1938), the Bombay Shop Assistants Act (1939), the C.P. Maternity Act (1939) and the Bengal Maternity Act (1939) were enacted.

In 1939, when the Second World War broke out, the workers of Bombay were amongst the first in the world to hold an anti-war strike on 2nd October 1939.

Flashforward:
Impact of Second World War After the Nazi attack on Soviet Union in 1941, the communists insisted that now it was the duty of the working class to support the Allied powers to defeat fascism that threatened the socialist birthplace (the Allied Powers composed of France, Britain, Russia, Japan, Italy, and in the later years, the U.S.; and the Central Powers composed of Germany, Austria-Hungary, Bulgaria and Turkey).

Thus, the communist party distanced itself from the Quit India Movement of 1942. They also followed a policy of industrial peace with employers so that production and war effort would not be hampered. However, the working class did not remain totally aloof from the Quit India Movement and they struck work and observed hartals in many parts of the country.

During this entire period, the communists and the socialists made efforts to unite the workers and the peasants of the country under a single movement.

Peasants' Movements of the 1920s and 1930s

Earlier in this book, you have learnt about the peasant uprisings in the second half of the 19th century. You have read how the peasants were exploited both by the colonial government the landlords and how they rose in arms against this exploitation. In this chapter, you will learn about the peasant uprisings during the 1920s and 1930s and see how these were different from their predecessors. By now, the peasants had learnt to organise themselves and put up a united front against the oppressive forces.

Problems of the Peasantry

The peasants in India suffered great hardships and were always relegated to the lowest rungs of Indian society. Some of the common peasant grievances included:

- The peasants were crushed under the heavy burden of land revenue. This not only impoverished them but also made them indebted to local money lenders who charged high rates of interest. The peasants often found themselves trapped in a vicious cycle of debt that got transferred from one generation to the next.
- As if the burden of land revenue was not enough, the landlords compelled the tenants to pay **'abwabs'**, **'nazaranas'** and other forms of gifts on various pretexts.
- The peasants often did not have occupancy rights over the land they tilled, with the effect that they lived under constant threat of eviction.
- The outbreak of the First World War added to the miseries of the peasants as they were made to contribute to war fund, military service, etc.

In such circumstances, it was the duty of the government to protect the peasants. But the government itself was hand in gloves with the landlords and this forced the peasants to stand up in revolt for their own emancipation.

> **Abwabs** refer to miscellaneous kinds of fines, cesses or taxes levied by native chiefs upon the subjects like the house tax, grazing tax, irrigation tax, etc.

Peasants' Movements during 1920s

United Provinces (UP)

UP emerged as a main centre of peasant activity during this period. Here **Baba Ram Chandra** took the initiative to organise the peasants of Oudh against the zamindars and taluqdars. He would tell the peasants that they were kept in bondage by the government and the zamindars and that they could break free only by unifying themselves against their oppressors.

> Baba Ram Chandra was a Maharashtrian Brahmin by birth. In 1905, he went to Fiji as an indentured labourer and came to Oudh countryside in 1917–18. There he worked among the peasants, dressed like a sanyasi and quoting the Ramcharitmanas, and mobilised them for struggle against the oppressors.

In 1920, this peasant movement got associated with the Non-Cooperation Movement. In 1921, the movement became militant and spread to Rae Bareli, Faizabad and Sultanpur, forcing the government to amend the Oudh Rent Act of 1921.

Eka Movement–In early 1922, **Eka Movement led by Madari Pasi** was started by peasants in districts like Hardoi, Barabanki and Sitapur. The initial thrust was given by the leaders of Congress and Khilafat and the movement grew under the name Eka or unity movement. The main reason of movement was higher rent, which was generally higher than 50 per cent of recorded rent in some areas. Madari Pasi was a radical peasant leader and posed serious challenge to the landlords and the administration. By March 1922, due to severe repression of British, the Eka Movement came to an end.

Bihar

In north Bihar, the peasant movement was led by **Swami Vidyanand** and was chiefly directed against the Raja of Darbhanga who owned large estates and oppressed the peasantry. This movement against Darbhanga Raj was not as militant as that in UP.

Bengal

Peasants joined the no-tax agitation and refused to pay the **Union Board taxes**. Midnapore district emerged as the main centre of agitation which ended in victory with the government deciding not to process with the Union Boards.

Malabar

In 1921, the Muslim Moplah peasants revolted against continued landlord oppression as well as British government's anti-Khilafat policies. The Moplah peasants' movement of 1921 got inextricably merged with the Khilafat movement (a worldwide protest of the Muslims against the harsh treatment meted out to the Sultan of Turkey by the victorious Allied powers). While the Indian Muslims united under the leadership of Ali brothers, the Moplahs rose under the leadership of **Ali Musaliar**, a respected priest and local Khilafat leader. The Moplah rebels blocked roads, cut off telegraph lines, uprooted railway lines and even killed some Europeans.

In October 1921, the government sent a strong contingent to suppress the rebellion. Surrounded on all sides and suspecting a Hindu complicity, the desperate Moplahs resorted to brutal killings of Hindus including women and children. The government retaliated with heavy round of suppression, killing thousands of Moplahs (unofficial figure puts the number at 10,000). About 3,000 Moplahs were sentenced to life and sent off to Andaman Jail.

The ruthless crushing of the Moplah rebellion greatly demoralised the community and thereafter it remained aloof from any peasant or national political activity so long as the British remained in India.

Gujarat (Bardoli Satyagraha, 1928)

The Bardoli taluqa in Surat district had witnessed intense politicisation after the emergence of Gandhi on the political scene. The movement was triggered in 1927 when the government raised land revenue in Bardoli by 30 percent despite fall in prices of cotton. Congress leaders quickly protested and formed the **Bardoli Enquiry Committee** to enquire into the issue. The committee found the revenue hike to be unjustified. This prepared the context for Bardoli Satyagraha in 1928. Leaders like Vallabhbhai Patel and Kunwarji Mehta mobilised the peasants who refused to pay revenue to the government. **Bardoli Satyagraha Patrika** was brought out to mobilise public opinion. **An intelligence wing** was set up to ensure that all tenants follow the movement resolutions. Those who opposed the movement faced social boycott. Special emphasis was paid on the mobilisation of women. KM Munshi and Lalji Naranji resigned from the Bombay Legislative Council in support of the movement.

Despite severe repression by the government and seizure of lands, the agitation succeeded as the government was forced to reassess revenue at reduced rates. It was during the agitation that the women of Bardoli gave Vallabhbhai Patel the title of **'sardar'**.

In addition to above regions, peasants also revolted against exploitation in Malabar, Rajasthan, Orissa and Assam.

Peasants' Movements During the 1930s

The 1930s saw a nationwide awakening of Indian peasants in the context of Great Depression (beginning 1929) and the Civil Disobedience Movement (1930). Even during the Depression, the government did not scale down its own taxes, nor did it care to ask the zamindars to scale down their rents. Consequently, the Civil Disobedience saw mass participation of peasants and in many parts of the country it took the form of no-tax no-rent movement. The Civil Disobedience Movement also contributed to the peasant movement in yet another way—it prepared a whole new cadre of young, militant political activists who were first born from the womb of civil disobedience and later nurtured under the influence of leftist ideology. Once the civil disobedience was suspended, these men and women found their calling in organising the peasants. Formation of the Congress Socialist Party (CSP) in 1934 further consolidated the left and acted as a spur to the kisan movement.

UP

As in the 1920s, even in the 1930s UP emerged as the main centre of peasant revolt. While Congress gave a call for no-revenue movement, some leaders also began no-rent agitation. Leaders like **Kalka Prasad of Rae Bareli** asked the peasants to stop all kinds of payments. But the government resorted to severe repression and the movement was effectively crushed.

> **What is the difference between no-revenue and no-rent movement?** No revenue (or No-tax) movement is directed against the government while the no-rent movement affects the landlords (as rent is paid by tenants to landlords).

Bengal and Bihar

Here the movement confined itself to no-tax agitation. The tribal peasants of Manbhum, Singbhum and Dinajpur joined the salt satyagraha and went to jail. The region also saw the launch of powerful agitation against the hated **chowkidar tax** by which the villagers were made to pay for the upkeep of their own oppressors.

Madras Presidency

In 1928, the **Andhra Ryots' Association** was formed under the leadership of Professor NG Ranga that launched a powerful anti-zamindari struggle. Its first target was the **Venkatgiri zamindari in Nellore** district. The Association voiced demands of the peasantry including reduction of rent affecting the landlords. The agitation grew vigorously during the Civil disobedience movement and became particularly strong in Tanjore, Madura and Salem. Another feature of the movement in Andhra was the organisation of **Summer Schools of Economics and Politics** for peasant activists. These training camps were addressed by major Leftist leaders of the time.

In **Kerala**, a powerful peasant movement developed as a result of the efforts of CSP activists and led to the setting up of **karshak Sanghams** (peasant associations). The main demands of the peasants included abolition of feudal levies (akramapirivukal such as vasi, nuri, etc.), renewal fees (the practice of policceluthu) and advance rent. The Karshak Sanghams also organised a powerful campaign around the demand for amending the Malabar Tenancy Act of 1929. The campaign successfully created an awareness on the tenancy question that ensured that in later years their demands would inevitably have to be accepted.

Punjab

Earlier, peasant mobilisation had been organised by the Punjab Naujawan Sabha, the Kirti Kisan Party, the Congress and the Akalis. A new vigour was given by the Punjab Kisan Committee in 1937.

The immediate issues taken up were resettlement of land revenue in Amritsar and Lahore and increase in water rates in canal colonies of Multan and Montgomery. Here the peasants went on strike and were finally able to win concessions.

In Maharashtra, Bihar and Central Provinces, peasants and tribals resorted to **forest satyagrahas** and defied forest laws that prohibited them from using forest resources.

Formation of All India Kisan Sabha (AIKS, Lucknow, 1936)

During the 1920s, provincial kisan sabhas (or ryotu) had already been formed by the efforts of communists and socialists. But the need was felt for a central organisation of peasants and therefore, in 1936 in Lucknow, the All India Kisan Congress was formed (which later changed its name to All India Kisan Sabha).

Swami Sahajanand, the militant kisan leader and founder of the Bihar Provincial Kisan Sabha (1929) was elected the President, and **NG Ranga**, the pioneer of the kisan movement in Andhra, the General Secretary. Participants of the first session included Jawaharlal Nehru, Ram Manohar Lohia, Indulal Yagnik, Jayaprakash Narayan, Sohan Singh Josh, Ahmed Din and Kamal Sarkar. The Conference decided to bring out a kisan manifesto and a periodical edited by Indulal Yagnik. The kisan manifesto considerably influenced the agrarian program adopted by the Congress at its **Faizpur session**.

At Faizpur Session of Congress, held under the presidentship of Jawaharlal Nehru in December 1936, the **Congress adopted an agrarian program**, including items such as reduction of rent and revenue, abolition of feudal dues and levies, provision of cheap credit, security of tenure for tenants, introduction of cooperative farming, living wages for agrarian labourers and the right to form peasant unions.

Objectives Kisan Sabha explained its objective as, 'securing complete freedom from economic exploitation and achievement of full economic and political power for peasants and workers and all other exploited classes'. It also demanded the following:

- Protection of peasants from economic exploitation
- Abolition of landlordism, such as zamindari and taluqdari systems and vesting of land in the tiller of the soil
- Reduction of revenue and rent
- Licensing of moneylenders
- Moratorium on debts
- Minimum wages for agricultural labourers
- Fair price for commercial crops
- Irrigation facilities etc.

All these objectives were to be achieved by proper organisation and active participation in the national struggle for independence.

The AIKS proclaimed that the emancipation of the peasants lay in 'their own organisation' and decided to work independently of the Congress.

AIKS urged 'all anti-imperialist forces in the country, specially the kisans and the workers to develop their day to day struggles against the exploiters, as represented by the British government, the zamindars, the landlords, the industrialists and the moneylenders'.

Second Session of the AIKS was held at **Faizpur** in Maharashtra, along with the Congress session. It was presided by NG Ranga and attended by over 500 kisans who were welcomed by Jawaharlal Nehru, MN Roy, Narendra Dev, SA Dange, MR Masani, Yusuf Meherally, Bankim Mukherji and many others. In his presidential address, Ranga declared, 'We are organising ourselves for the final inauguration of a Socialist state and society'.

Congress Ministries in the Provinces and Growth of Peasants' Movements

1937–39: Years of high-watermark of Peasants' Movements

With the formation of Congress Ministries in the provinces, a new phase in peasants' movements began. The whole atmosphere of the country got enthused with new expectations, freedom and power born out of the feeling that 'our own people are in power'. The peasants were chiefly mobilised through kisan conferences and meetings where peasant demands were raised. Several pro-peasant legislations were also introduced by different ministries.

Bakasht Movement (Bihar, 1937–38)

It was a peasant movement directed against landlords to fight forceful eviction of peasants from bakasht lands. Bakasht lands were those which the occupancy tenants had lost to zamindars, mostly during the Depression years, due to non-payment of rent, and which they often continued to cultivate as share-croppers. The landlords often evicted the tenants from Bakasht land. In 1937, when the Congress Ministry was formed, the Kisan Sabha thought that it was an appropriate time to raise the issue of bakasht and demand for restoration of bakasht lands. The passing of the **Restoration of Bakasht Land Act** and the **Bihar Tenancy Act** in 1938 brought much relief to the peasants.

Hat Tola Movement (Bengal, 1939)

This was a peasant movement launched in the northern districts of Bengal against the landlords to fight a levy collected from peasants who sold their produce in 'hats' (weekly markets).

Burdwan Satyagraha (Bengal)

Burdwan Satyagraha was launched under the leadership of Bankim Mukherji in the Burdwan district of Bengal to protest against the **Canal Tax** imposed on the peasants after the construction of the Damodar Canal. The movement was withdrawn after the government partly accepted the demand of the Kisan Sabha.

Movement of the Share Croppers (Bengal)

Movement of the share croppers began in Bengal in 1939. Share croppers were very poor peasants who tilled the land of the landlords and gave a portion of the produce to them but they had no security of tenure and could be evicted anytime. The movement gained vigour in Dinajpur district in north Bengal and the government came to a compromise with the peasants.

In Gujarat, the main demand was for the abolition of the system of **hali (bonded labour)** and a significant success was registered.

In this way, through the above movements the peasants learnt the power of organisation.

Congress Response to the Peasants' Movements

Congress leaders were well aware of the strength of the peasantry and their importance in the anti-imperialist struggle. They were also concerned about peasant issues and their grievances. In 1937, Nehru had observed, 'the outstanding problem of India is the peasant problem. All else is secondary'.

Yet, the right wing within the Congress that belonged to the landed aristocracy, felt uneasy about the rise of class consciousness among Indian peasantry and their demands, particularly the demand for abolition of landlordism. They wanted the peasants to participate in the anti-British struggle but tried to overlook their grievances against the landlords. As a result, whenever the peasants revolted against the landlords, the Congress tried to restrain them. The Congress also hesitated much in sanctioning no-rent movements directed against the landlords.

Consequently, the kisan leaders chose to work independently from the very beginning. Though they had full faith in the Congress leadership in securing freedom from the British rule and at no stage the kisan leaders worked against the Congress, they preferred to rely on themselves in their struggle against the zamindars and the capitalists.

Sahajanand 'We all cling to the Congress not for its magic or mystery, but because it represents the nation, it has not taken any false step at critical junctures. All our attempts are simply to strengthen its hands in taking opportune decisions at this most critical juncture of our national struggle for deliverance'.

In 1939, the rising tide of peasant movement was checked with the outbreak of the Second World War which not only brought about the resignation of the Congress Ministries but also saw severe repression of the left wing due to their anti-war stand.

Previous Years' Questions – Preliminary Exam

1. Assertion (A): The effect of labour participation in the Indian Nationalist upsurge of the early 1930's was weak.

   Reason (R): The labour leaders considered the ideology of Indian National Congress as bourgeois and reactionary. **[UPSC 2002]**

   Select the answer for the options given below:

   (a) if both A and R are true and R is the correct explanation of A

   (b) if both A and R are true but R is not the correct explanation of A

   (c) if A is true but R is false

   (d) if A is false but R is true

2. Who was the leader of the Bardoli Satyagraha (1928)? **[UPSC 2003]**

   (a) Sardar Vallabhbhai Patel

   (b) Mahatma Gandhi

   (c) Vitthalbhai J Patel

   (d) Mahadev Desai

Answers

Previous Years' Questions – Preliminary Exam

1. (c) 2. (a)

15 THE STATES' PEOPLE'S MOVEMENT

British supremacy in India had been established through a long and complex process comprising direct conquest, intimidation or even accommodation of the pre-colonial Indian political entities. The result was direct British rule over three-fifths of the sub-continent, and indirect rule or 'Paramountcy' over the remaining two-fifths. The areas coming under the latter arrangement continued to be nominally ruled by Indian princes and comprised what was known as the Princely States or simply Indian States.

In this chapter, you will learn about the popular struggles in Princely States that took place during the period 1920 to 1947. You will also learn about the policy of the Indian National Congress on the issue as well as the role of the communists in spearheading these struggles.

British Relations with the Princely States

On the eve of British Conquest, there existed 562 Princely States, some as big as Hyderabad (as large as Italy) and some as tiny as Bilbari (with a population of 27). Like the East India Company, many Indian States too came into prominence in the later Mughal period, profiting from the decline of the central Mughal authority. States like Hyderabad and some Rajput states were not conquered by the English but accepted the Company's supremacy. Some states like the Rajput states of Central India had maintained their independence from the Mughals as well as the Marathas and were even saved from extinction by British intervention. Some states were created by the British in the process of overthrow of Maratha Confederacy.

The British relations with the Princely States were not constant and went through the following broad phases:

- 1740 to 1765 – Struggle for Equality
- 1765 to 1813 – Policy of Ring Fence
- 1813 to 1857 – Policy of Subordinate Isolation
- 1857 to 1935 – Policy of Subordinate Union
- 1935 to 1947 – Policy of Equal Federation

1740 to 1765 – Struggle for Equality

Prior to 1740, the English East India Company was merely a commercial body. The political ambitions of the Europeans are traced back to 1740, with the beginning of the Carnatic War, when Dupleix first started dabbling in Indian politics. In 1757, the English Company won the Battle of Plassey and emerged as the political force behind the Nawab of Bengal. In 1764, the Company won the Battle of

Buxar and gained the Diwani of Bengal, Bihar and Orissa (treaty of Allahabad 1765). Thus, during the period 1740–65, the Company was still subordinate to Indian States and was striving for a status of equality with them.

1765 to 1813 – Policy of Ring Fence

During this time, the Company followed the policy of creating buffer states around the Company's territory of Bengal and the defence of Awadh constituted the defence of Bengal at that time. Thus, Warren Hastings' wars against Mysore and the Marathas and Wellesley's formation of subsidiary alliances with the princely states were carried out under the policy of ring fence.

Under the **Subsidiary Alliance System**, also known as the **'Trojan Horse'** tactic in empire building, princely rulers were not allowed to have their independent armed force. They were to be protected by the East India Company but had to pay for the subsidiary forces that the Company maintained for such protection. If Indian rulers failed to make the payment, part of their territory was taken away as penalty. Though the Nawab of Awadh was the first to enter into such an alliance after the Battle of Buxar in 1764, the first victim of the policy of subsidiary alliance of Wellesley was the Nizam of Hyderabad in 1798.

1813 to 1857 – Policy of Subordinate Isolation

Under **Lord Hastings** (1813–23), the subsidiary alliances formed were no longer on the basis of reciprocity and mutual amity, but impelled the Indian states to act in subordinate cooperation with the British government. Under Lord Hastings to 1857, the Resident officers of the Company were slowly transformed from diplomatic agents of a foreign power to controlling officers of a superior government. Instead of functioning as an ambassador, he often assumed the functions of a 'dictator'.

The policy of subordinate isolation gained further push after the **Charter Act of 1833**, which ordered the Company to wind up its commercial business as soon as possible. With the prospect of declining income from trade, the Company's financial base began to shift from trade and commerce to land revenue, **from business of trade to business of government**. This naturally pushed the Company to go ahead with continuous territorial expansion. The Court of Directors ordered the Governor General to grasp every opportunity of just and honourable annexation. From this time onwards and until 1857, the Company's Governor Generals were frankly annexationists. Annexations were made on the plea of failure of heirs or misgovernance (Doctrine of Lapse).

Accordingly, William Bentinck annexed Mysore (1831), Cachar (1832), Coorg (1834) and Jaintia (1835). Lord Auckland annexed Karnal, Mandavi (1839), Kolaba and Jalaun (1840). And Lord Dalhousie annexed several Indian states including big states like Nagpur, Satara and Awadh.

1857 to 1935 – Policy of Subordinate Union

The Queen's Proclamation of 1858 announced the abandonment of the policy of annexations. The Doctrine of Lapse was buried deep and the Indian states were given the assurance that the Crown desired 'no extension of present territorial possessions'. This change in policy was due to the loyal attitude shown by the ruling princes during the Revolt of 1857 which had amply demonstrated that the princes could be used as 'breakwaters of future possible storms in India'.

However, the immunity from annexations came at a great cost and lowering of status of the Indian princes. For under the Company, the sanction of the Governor General was necessary only in case of failure of 'natural heirs'. But after 1858, the fiction of Mughal authority ended and the Crown emerged as the unquestioned **paramount power** in India. The Royal Titles Act of 1876 put the seal on this new relationship by proclaiming the Queen as Kaiser-i-Hind, i.e. the Queen Empress of India.

As such, all successions had to regularly seek the sanction of the Crown. The ruler now inherited the 'gaddi' not as a right, but as a gift from the Crown. Normally every ruler was installed on the gaddi by a British Agent and was granted possession of the state but not sovereignty. The continuation of his rule was conditional on his loyalty to the British Crown.

The Government of India retained the right to interfere in the internal matters of the Indian states and exercised this right on various occasions. For instance, in 1867, the Nawab of Tonk was asked to resign in favour of his son on charges of complicity in an attack on Thakur of Lawa. In 1875, the Gaekwad of Baroda was removed from the gaddi on charges of maladministration. Again in 1884, a British Resident was forced on the Maharaja of Kashmir and in 1891 the Maharaja was forced to resign in favour of a Council of Regency.

After 1905, the growth of political unrest in British India put the government on the defensive and it was eager to join hands with the Indian Princes to put up a common front against the nationalists and revolutionaries. Thus, the policy of subordinate isolation effectively gave way to the Policy of Subordinate Union.

The Chamber of Princes (or Narendra Mandal, February 1921)

Cordial cooperation between the government and the Princely states was further consolidated with the formation of Chamber of Princes. The creation of the chamber marked the culmination of the abandonment of the British policy of isolating the Indian rulers from each other and also from the rest of the world. It must be noted that the Chamber was merely an advisory and consultative body. For the purpose of representation in the Chamber, the Indian States were divided into three categories:

- 109 states which enjoyed full legislative and jurisdictional powers.
- 127 states which enjoyed limited powers.
- 326 states which could be better classified as jagirs or estates.

Indian States Committee (or Butler Committee, 1927)

Soon the princes were worried about the uninterrupted growth of political interference and raised the question of the extent of sovereignty or Paramount Power. In 1927, with fresh constitutional reforms on the anvil, they urged the government to properly examine and clearly define the nature and extent of British Paramountcy. This led to the appointment of the Indian States Committee, popularly known as the Butler Committee after its chairman Sir Harcourt Butler, set up with the aim of investigating the relationship between the Paramount Power and the Indian States.

The Indian Princes engaged Sir Leslie Scott as their legal counsel to advance their viewpoint before the Committee. Scott pleaded that the states were originally independent and should remain so except to the extent to which a part of its sovereignty was transferred to the Crown. Or simply that the residuary powers should rest with the Princes. The Butler Committee, however, reported that:

- Paramountcy must remain paramount. It must fulfil its obligations by defining and adopting itself according to the shifting necessities (thus leaving the concept of Paramountcy undefined).
- The Viceroy, and not the Governor-General in Council, was to be the Crown agent in dealing with the states.

1935 to 1947 – Policy of Equal Federation

The Indian Princes were invited to participate in the Round Table Conferences held during 1930–32. The Government of India Act of 1935 proposed an All India Federation. The federation of India was to come into existence only when:

- States entitled to at least half of the seats (i.e. 52 seats) allotted to the states in the proposed Council of States should agree to join the federation.
- The aggregate population of states in the above category should be at least 50 per cent of the total population of all Indian states.

Since the above conditions were not met, the proposed federation never came up. On the other hand, Congress successes in the Elections of 1937 gave a new push to the slowly but steadily growing national movement in the Princely states.

Princely States and the National Movement

Misgovernance in Princely States

The Princely States acknowledged the British as Paramount Power, and in return, the British guaranteed the rulers security against all threats—external and internal. Throughout history, internal revolt or external aggression had worked as checks on corrupt rulers. The British rule freed the Indian princes of both these checks, leaving ample scope for misgovernance.

Consequently, a majority of the rulers felt no responsibility towards ensuring welfare of their subjects. They were autocratic and squandered state revenues on living luxurious lives. They organised lavish 'shikar parties' and added several women to their harem. The burden naturally fell upon the subjects, who were impelled to pay very high taxes, sometimes even higher than the neighbouring British India. Serfdom, slavery and forced labour also flourished in many states.

There was also a small minority of enlightened rulers who tried to introduce socio-political reforms and promote industrial development. They tried to spread modern education and introduce some measure of popular participation in governance. However, such moves were often resisted by the British, who wanted to keep the Princely States away from any measure of Responsible Government as well as from national movement. And the British representatives in the States or the Residents exercised strict supervision or control in this regard.

Ideas of Democracy and Civil Liberties

The national movement, after it had taken roots in British India, began to exercise a growing influence upon the people of the States. The ideas of democracy and civil liberties that drove the national movement had equal relevance for them as well. In the beginning, these ideas were brought to them by individual nationalists, including 'terrorists' from British India seeking shelter in the states. But gradually the national movement assumed a mass character and its influence became more generalised. In fact, the first ever popular associations in the states were formed during the Non-Cooperation Movement.

Praja Mandals or State Peoples' Conferences

The first political organisations in the states emerged in the form of Praja Mandals or State People's Conferences. Initially, these were set up in states like Hyderabad, Mysore, Baroda, the Kathiawad States, the Deccan States, Jamnagar, Indore and Nawanagar. These bodies threw up some prominent leaders such as **Balwantrai Mehta, Maniklal Kothari and CR Abhyankar**. In 1927, they organised the first All-India gathering of the people of states that culminated in the formation of the **All India States People's Conference** (AISPC).

Congress and the Princely States

The Congress policy towards the Indian States was first enunciated in 1920 at Nagpur, when the INC passed a resolution calling upon the rulers of princely states to establish a full **responsible government**. However, Congress policy was more complex on the question of organising political movements in Indian States. Though people of the states were free to become members of the Congress and participate in the struggles led by it, they were not to carry any political activity in the states in the name of the Congress. This they could do only either on their own or as members of other organisations such as Praja Mandals.

Clearly, the reason behind this stand of the Congress was the immense difference between the political conditions prevailing in British India and in the Princely States. Since Congress framed its policies on the basis of conditions prevailing in British India, it could not afford to directly associate itself with political movements in the states in the initial stage. Further, the states were legally independent entities and political conditions within the states themselves varied a great deal. The people of the Indian states were also required to build their own strength and advance their own political consciousness to further their specific demands before participating in the more advanced types of movements in British India.

Despite above limitations, the Congress and its members continued to extend support to the struggles in the states in a variety of ways.

In 1929, **Jawaharlal Nehru** declared, 'the Indian states cannot live apart from the rest of India... the only people who have the right to determine the future of the States must be people of these states'.

During the 1920s and early 30s, the process of political awakening went ahead in many states. However, the real spurt in the state peoples' movement came after 1935 following two significant developments:

1. The Government of India (GOI) Act 1935 (proposing formation of an All India Federation).
2. The formation of Congress Ministries in 1937 in a majority of British India provinces.

Government of India Act 1935 and the Federal Scheme

As per the Federal Scheme of the Act of 1935, the Indian States were to be brought into a direct constitutional relationship with British India, as distinct from the existing position in which they were in a direct relationship with the British Crown. This was to be achieved by the establishment of a Federal Indian Legislature with representatives from both British India as well from the Indian States.

However, a peculiar feature of the federal scheme was that, while the representatives from British India were to be elected by the people, those of the States were to be nominated by the rulers. The States were also given disproportionate weightage. In short, the proposed federal structure was planned so as to check the **forces of nationalism**.

The Federal Scheme was therefore opposed by all nationalists and it was demanded that the representatives of states should also be elected instead of being nominated. Naturally, this brought to the forefront, the demand for responsible government in the states.

(The proposed federation never came into existence for the requisite number of states did not agree to join it. The Central government was carried on upto 1946 as per the provisions of the GOI Act 1919).

Congress Ministries (1937–39)

The formation of Congress Ministries in many provinces of British India also aroused the confidence and aspirations of the people of the states. This development exerted immense pressure on the rulers, with the state movements reaching a high watermark during the years 1938–39. Praja Mandals sprang up at many places and struggles started in Rajkot, Travancore, Mysore, Patiala, Jaipur, Kashmir and Orissa states. The Congress urged the princes to introduce democratic representative government and to grant fundamental civil rights to the people.

Tripuri Session of the Congress (March 1939) and change in Congress Policy Following the growth of popular movements in the states, the Congress lost no time in shedding its self-imposed restraint and henceforth increasingly identified itself with the state people's movements. A resolution to this effect was passed by the Congress at its Tripuri session in March 1939.

In 1939 itself, **Jawaharlal Nehru was elected as President of the AISPC** (Ludhiana Session) and became a symbol of fusion of the popular movements in British India and the Indian States.

Quit India in the States (1942)

In August 1942, the Quit India Movement was launched. For the first time the Congress gave a call to the people of the states to participate fully in the all-India struggle for independence. The people of the states now demanded not only responsible government, but also freedom for India and for states to become integral parts of the Indian nation. From now onwards, the struggle of the people of the states was formally integrated with the struggle of the people in British India.

The princes responded to these struggles with violent repression. The Nizam called the popular agitation anti-Muslim, the Maharaja of Kashmir branded it as anti-Hindu while the Maharaja of Travancore alleged that the agitation was instigated by Christians. Despite repression, the States' People's Movement succeeded in awakening national consciousness among the people of the states.

Question of Integration of Indian States (1945–47)

With the end of the Second World War, negotiations began regarding the transfer of power from British to Indian hands. The question of the future of Indian States became critical at this juncture.

Both, the Mountbatten Plan and the Indian Independence Act 1947 (refer to chapter 7.3 for details), did not make clear the position of the princely states regarding the option of independence, leaving them to luxuriate in wild dreams of independent power! Mountbatten later clarified that the Independence Act had released the States from all their obligations to the Crown, leaving them 'technically independent or to say, rudderless, on their own'. The old links were broken and if nothing was put in its place, chaos would result. He therefore advised them to forge links with the new nation closest to them.

In the National Provisional Government, **Sardar Patel headed the States Ministry** and urged the Indian princes to show their patriotism and join the Indian Union by surrendering the three subjects of Defence, Foreign Affairs and Communications. He played a vital role at this stage and succeeded in getting a vast majority of the states to accede to the Indian Union through a combination of diplomacy, popular movements and even some arm twisting. By 15th August 1947, 136 states had acceded to the Indian Union. Kashmir signed the Instrument of Accession on 26th October 1947, Junagarh and Hyderabad in 1948. Portuguese enclaves of Goa, Daman and Diu were annexed in December 1961.

Previous Years' Questions – Main Exam

1. What was the role of the States People's Movement in the integration of Indian states? **[UPSC 1996]**
2. What was the significance of the Prajamandal Movement in the Indian states in decade preceding India's Independence? **[UPSC 1998]**
3. Discuss the problem that impeded the integration of the Princely States in the Indian Union. How were these problems tackled? **[UPSC 2003]**
4. Examine the policy of Subordinate Union towards Princely States. Account for the shift from the policy of Subordinate Isolation. **[UPSC 2005]**

16 Simon Commission and Simon Boycott Movement (1927–29)

Flashback: Following the withdrawal of Non-Cooperation Movement, various national as well as anti-national forces emerged. The prominent among them were (covered in the previous chapters):

- The Swarajists and their program of council entry (1922–29)
- The No-changers and their Constructive work (after 1922)
- Communalism and revival of Muslim League and Hindu Mahasabha (1922–37)
- Revolutionary Movement with a turn towards Socialism (after 1922)
- Growth of the Left Movement and spread of Socialist and Communist ideas (1920s–1930s)
- Peasants' and Workers' Movements (1920s–1930s)
- States' People's Movement (1920s–30s)
- Caste Movements like Self-Respect movement (1920s–30s)

In May 1927, the situation in the country appeared grim, the Swarajists were declining, communalism was raising its ugly head and Gandhi wrote, 'My only hope lies in prayer and answer to prayer'. But it seems the forces of national upsurge were silently growing behind the scenes-and the country united once again against the Simon Commission.

Simon Commission (8th November 1927)

As per a provision of the Government of India Act 1919, an Indian Statutory Commission (or a Royal Commission) was to be appointed at the end of 10 years after the passing of the Act (i.e. in 1929), to enquire into the working of the Government of India under the Act of 1919 and suggest fresh reforms.

Thus, the Simon Commission was appointed to consider, under the terms of the Government of India Act of 1919, whether India was fit to receive a further instalment of constitutional government. The principal idea behind this was that the constitutional progress should be achieved gradually. However, this approach had certain drawbacks—a temporary constitution provided little incentive to people to make it successful. Moreover, ten years was too short a period to conclude about the workability of a constitution and those who were dissatisfied with it tried to prove that it was unworkable.

Why was Simon Commission appointed before time?

The Commission was appointed on 8th November 1927, two years in advance of the prescribed time. Why was it so? The British government had declared that it was doing so on account of its liberal attitude towards India. In reality, the reasons lay elsewhere:

1. Firstly, the political situation in Britain compelled the conservative Tory government to appoint the commission earlier. In 1927, the Tory Government of Britain was facing the prospect of electoral defeat at the hands of the Labor Party (as elections were due in 1929) and suddenly decided that it could not leave an important issue as the issue of India, Britain's most important colony, in the hands of an inexperienced Labor Party.
2. Secondly, the Tory government also wanted to send the delegation at a time when communal situation had deteriorated so that the Commission sees India unfit for fresh instalment of constitutional government.
3. Thirdly, the nationalist opinion in India also resented the method of periodic enquiry and had been demanding a complete revision of the constitutional system. The Indian nationalists had already declared the constitutional reforms of 1919 as inadequate and had been demanding an early reconsideration of the constitutional question. British government also wanted to divert the attention of nationalist Indians from a widespread agitation that was gathering momentum.
4. It is also believed that the early appointment of the commission was a result of the pressure created by the Swaraj Party and the youth activities led by Nehru and Bose. Yet another opinion is that the Commission was used as a bargaining counter to divide the Swaraj Party.

Thus, the British government appointed the statutory commission (better known as Simon Commission after the name of its Chairman) before time, virtually recognising the failure of the Act of 1919.

Composition of Simon Commission

On 8th November 1927, **Lord Birkenhead**, Secretary of State for India, announced the appointment of an Indian Statutory Commission comprising seven members (all British and all members of the British Parliament) under the chairmanship of Sir John Simon assisted by Clement Attlee. The Commission was appointed by **Prime Minister Stanley Baldwin**.

Mandate of the Commission

The Simon Commission was to enquire 'into the working of the system of government, the growth of education and the development of representative institutions in British India and matters connected therewith' and to report 'as to whether and to what extent it is desirable to establish the principle of responsible government or to extend, modify or restrict the degree of responsible government then existing, including the question whether the establishment of Second Chambers of the local legislatures is or is not desirable'. During the enquiry of the commission, the subject of relations between British India and Indian states was also added to the purview of the commission.

Members

Clement Attlee, Edward Cadogan, George Lane-Fox, Vernon Hartshorn, Donald Howard, Harry Levy-Lawson, Sir John Allsebrook Simon.

All the seven members of the Commission were Englishmen who were members of British Parliament. The British government gave two arguments for excluding the Indians from the Commission:

1. The British government argued that since the committee had to report to the British Parliament so it was justified to appoint British members only. This argument did not hold good as there were two Indian Members of British Parliament at the time—**Lord Satyendra Prasanna Sinha** and **Mr. Shapurji Dorabji Saklatwala**.

2. They also declared that it was not possible to appoint any Indian as member of the commission as there was no unanimity among Indians over the constitutional question. In reality, Birkenhead feared that in a mixed commission, Indians would ally with Labour Party representatives.

Further, Viceroy Irwin (1926–31) declared that the Indians had not been able to give an accurate picture of their capacity to govern themselves. However, taking cognizance of Baldwin's earlier statement, 'In the fullness of time we look forward to seeking India in equal partnership with the Dominions', Irwin made provisions for expression of Indian opinion. Joint committees comprising non-official members from centre and provinces were to express their opinion to the commission. Indian Legislature could also send delegations to discuss the Commission's Report with the Joint Parliamentary Committee in Britain.

Who Opposed Simon Commission?

The all-white commission, consisting solely of British Members of Parliament, was unanimously rejected by all nationalists. In the appointment of this Commission, the British government had not only marginalised the Indian opinion on a subject which concerned them the most, it was also guilty of insulting the Indians who were by implication viewed as unfit to make a constitution for themselves.

The Simon commission united different groups and parties in the country, at least temporarily. The call for boycott of the commission was endorsed by the following:

1. The Congress
2. A section of the Muslim League
3. Liberal Federation led by Tej Bahadur Sapru
4. The Indian Industrial and Commercial Congress
5. The Hindu Mahasabha

The Muslim League was divided on the issue but MA Jinnah succeeded in rallying the majority section in favour of the boycott. This section of the Muslim League, led by Jinnah, was even willing to forego separate electorates if certain conditions were met (Delhi proposals).

Thus, the Indian opinion was united on the issue of Indian representation. Congress tried to revive the Non-cooperation spirit through the boycott. Revolutionaries such as Bhagat Singh also opposed the Simon Commission and were of the view that only Indians should decide the kind of constitution they should have.

However, there were certain political groups who did not oppose the commission. These included, Muslim League led by Muhammad Shafi, Justice Party in Madras, Central Sikh Sangh and All India Achut Federation.

Simon Boycott Movement

The boycott was turned into a popular movement by the Indian National Congress. During the 1927 **Madras Congress Session** (presided by **Dr. Ansari**), the Congress decided to boycott the commission 'at every stage and in every form'. Jawaharlal Nehru even got a quick resolution passed, declaring complete independence as a goal of the Congress, instead of the mirage of Dominion Status. The Working Committee was authorised to prepare a constitution for India in consultation with other organisations.

On 3rd February 1928, the Simon Commission landed at Bombay and was greeted with the slogan of '**Go back, Simon**'. All the major cities and town remained closed, people took to the streets taking out mass rallies and processions carrying black flags. The scenes of Non-cooperation days were revived. The crowds could not be held back even by lathis and bullets.

In fact, everywhere the commission went-Poona, Vijaywada, Lucknow, Calcutta, Lahore-it was greeted with a sea of black flags. In Lucknow, where a reception was organised for the members of the commission, Khaliquzzaman floated black kites and balloons with the slogan 'Simon go Back' printed on them. In Madras, T. Prakasham (Andhra Kesari) bravely rose in protest.

The slogans 'Simon go Back' and Quit India' Both slogans were coined by Yusuf Meherally, a socialist and trade unionist who was also elected Mayor of Bombay in 1942.

Rise of Young Leaders

It was the Simon Commission that provided the first experience of political action to a new crop of nationalists. **Jawaharlal Nehru** and **Subhas Chandra Bose** were the two most prominent youth leaders who emerged during the Simon Boycott Movement. The movement also saw the formation of a large number of youth leagues and associations all over the country. As the youth and students of the country were being drawn into the national movement, they were also simultaneously being influenced by the ideas of socialism.

Subhas Chandra Bose

In 1927, Jawaharlal Nehru had represented INC at Brussels Congress organised by the League Against Imperialism. He had also visited the young Soviet Union, and returned deeply influenced by socialist ideas and played the most important role in popularisation of socialism in the country. In this regard, Subhas Chandra Bose, Naujawan Bharat Sabha and Workers' and Peasants' Parties organised by a group of communists had also played prominent role.

Jawaharlal Nehru

Police Repression and death of Lala Lajpat Rai

The police took to angry repression and lathi-charges became frequent. In Lucknow, Jawaharlal Nehru and Govind Ballabh Pant were lathi charged up by the police. The worst incident took place at Lahore where Lala Lajpat Rai, the veteran Extremist and Sher-e-Punjab, was fatally hit during a lathi-charge while leading an anti-Simon agitation. He succumbed to his injuries on 17th November 1928. (Bhagat Singh vowed to avenge his death and decided to kill James Scott, the police officer who had ordered the lathi charge. He plotted the revenge along with other revolutionaries Rajguru, Sukhdev and Chandrasekhar Azad, but mistakenly killed another police official, John Saunders.)

The commission visited India twice (February-March 1928 and October 1928-April 1929). It was boycotted each time. It toured the country extensively and prepared a report which was published in May 1930.

Lala Lajpat Rai (died during anti-Simon movement)

Lord Birkenhead Challenges the Indians

Lord Birkenhead, the then Secretary of State, justified the exclusion of Indians from Simon Commission on the plea that there were vital differences among various Indian political parties and then threw a challenge to Indians to produce a constitution acceptable to all sections of Indian society.

Delhi Proposals (December 1927)

With the aim of bridging the gulf between the Congress and the Muslim League and to enable them to present a common set of demands before the British, a group of prominent Muslim leaders met at Delhi in December 1927 with MA Jinnah presiding over the session. In a dramatic move, the leaders agreed to forego separate electorates, the first and the last time the League agreed to do so, if their four proposals were met. The proposals came to be known as Delhi proposals and included the following points:

1. Sind should be separated from Bombay presidency as a separate province (Muslim majority province).
2. In NWFP and Baluchistan, reforms were to be carried out on the same lines as in other provinces, i.e. they should be treated constitutionally on the same footing as other provinces.
3. Muslim representation in Central legislature should be either one-third of the total or more than that.
4. Representation in Punjab and Bengal should be made on the basis of population (to ensure Muslim majority in the legislature) and in other provinces, where Muslims were a minority, the existing reservation of seats for Muslims should continue.

During the Madras Congress Session of December 1927, the Congress passed a resolution accepting most of the demands of Delhi Proposals. However, the Muslim League split over the issue and a separate annual session of the League was held at Lahore under the presidentship of **Sir Mian Muhammad Shafi**, worsening the communal situation in India.

The Congress proposals came next in the form of Nehru Report.

All Parties Conference, Nehru Report and Jinnah's Fourteen Points

All Parties Conference (presided by Dr. MA Ansari, February 1928)

The Indians accepted the challenge and the representatives of the Congress as well as other organisations such as Muslim League, Hindu Mahasabha, etc., met at a conference in February 1928 which came to be known as the All Parties Conference. In the conference, it was decided that while framing the constitution, the principle of **full Dominion responsible government** should be kept in mind. The Madras Congress had earlier adopted the goal of complete independence, yet at the All Parties Conference 'fully responsible government based on the model of self-governing Dominions' was accepted as the desired aim. This was done to gain support of all those organisations which aimed at Dominion status and rally them behind a common plan.

Nehru Report (1928)

In May 1928, the All Parties Conference (Bombay, presided by Dr. MA Ansari) appointed a sub-committee headed by Motilal Nehru to draft a constitution. Thus, the Nehru Committee was the Indian response to the appointment of Simon Commission and to the challenge of Birkenhead.

Members of Nehru Committee

Motilal Nehru (Chairman), Jawaharlal Nehru (Secretary), Sir Tej Bahadur Sapru, Sir Ali Iman, MS Aney, Mangal Singh, Shuab Quereshi, GR Pradhan and Subhas Chandra Bose.

In August 1928, the committee's report, famously known as Nehru Report or Nehru Committee Report, was finalised and adopted. The Nehru Report firmly laid down that full responsible government was not to be considered as a remote step but as an immediate step, as opposed to the principle of gradual advancement envisaged by the Act of 1919.

Main Recommendations

The Nehru Report confined itself to British India, as it envisioned that in future there shall be a linkup between British India and Indian states on federal basis. The main recommendations of the Nehru Report were as follows:

- **Dominion Status** India should have the same constitutional status in the British Empire as other Dominions with Parliament having powers to make laws and should be known as the Commonwealth of India.
- **Safeguards and Guarantees for Minority**
  - It recommended that the proposed constitution should provide for **liberty of conscience and religion**.
  - **New provinces on linguistic basis** to be created.
  - On the principle of self-determination, the **Muslim majority provinces** should be given distinct politico-cultural identity, i.e. Sind was to be separated from Bombay Presidency and NWFP was to be given full provincial status.
  - It rejected separate communal electorates and recommended that elections should be held on the basis of **joint electorates subject to reservations of seats for Muslims** in centre and in those provinces where they were in a minority (and not where they were in a numerical majority), and for non-Muslims in NWFP.
  - Later the committee added two additional recommendations—communal representation was to be reconsidered after 10 years and Baluchistan was to be given full provincial status.
- **Fundamental Rights** The constitution should define citizenship and declare fundamental rights. The Report recommended 19 Fundamental Rights including universal adult suffrage, equal rights for women, freedom to form unions and dissociation of the state form religion in any form.
- **Responsible Government** It recommended responsible government at centre and in provinces.
- **Bicameral Parliament** The legislative powers should invest with the King and bicameral parliament, and executive powers with the King exercisable by the Governor General. Same provisions should be made for the establishment of responsible governments in provinces in respect of governors and executive councils. It suggested that Indian Parliament should consist of a) The Senate elected for 7 years, containing 200 members elected by the Provincial Councils, and b) the House of Representatives consisting of 500 members for 5 years through adult franchise. The Governor General (to be appointed by the British Government but paid out of Indian revenues) was to act on the advice of the Executive Council which was to be collectively responsible to the Parliament. Similarly, Provincial Councils were to be elected on the basis of adult franchise for 5 years and the Governor was to act on the advice of the Provincial Executive Council.
- **Hierarchy of Courts** Hierarchy of courts with Supreme Court at its apex should be established.

- **Federal Government** It recommended, **for the first time**, that India should be a federation on the basis of linguistic provinces and provincial autonomy but residual powers with the centre. That's why some scholars consider the Nehru Report proposal as unitary rather than federal.

The Nehru Report contained virtually no federal features. Though federal principle was introduced in the composition of the senate, the provinces were not equally represented in it. Decentralisation was carried to the same extent as in the Act of 1919. Residuary powers were vested in the centre. The position of princely states with relation to centre was also not made clear.

Status of Princely States

The Nehru Committee faced a complex problem with regard to the status of princely states. In 1927, the subjects of Princely states had formed the **States' Peoples' Conference** with the objective of introducing self-governing institutions. The Princes felt threatened and sought the help of the British who appointed a committee under the chairmanship of Sir Harcourt Butler to look into the issue. The **Butler Committee** laid stress on the preservation of Princely states through British Paramountcy.

The appointment of Butler Committee was criticised by the Nehru Committee which advocated that all rights and obligations of the Paramountcy should be transferred to the government of Commonwealth of India and that conflicts between the Commonwealth of India and Indian states should be resolved by the Supreme Court.

A number of leading princes now supported the formation of a federation. They detested the doctrine that 'Paramountcy was paramount'. They aimed to be completely free from every external influence so far as the internal affairs of the State were concerned. This they thought would be facilitated by an 'All India Federation'.

Concessions to Hindu Communalists in Nehru Report

These included the following features:

- Joint electorates everywhere but reservation of seats for Muslims only where in minority.
- Sind to be separated from Bombay presidency only after the grant of dominion status and subject to weightage to Hindu minority in Sind.
- Political structure proposed was broadly unitary as residual powers were vested with the centre.

Significance of Nehru Report

The committee drafted an admirable constitution. Its approach was truly national; it had considered the country as an organic whole and not as one composed of heterogeneous elements such as the Princes, linguistic or religious minorities and other vested interests. The Nehru Report was in fact one of the most constructive efforts made by any organisation in India. 'Its proposals were conceived in a sprit at once of idealism and accommodation, and there was width, warmth and largeness'.

Its most significant contribution was that it was the first and frankest attempt by Indians to face the problem of communalism and express an organised opinion of majority of Indian leadership on the communal problem. It clearly stated that the only way of giving a feeling of security to the minority was by providing for safeguards and guarantees (safeguards for Muslims have been mentioned above).

All Parties Conference Fails to Pass Nehru Report

In December 1928, All Parties Conference was held at Calcutta. The Conference failed to pass the Report as objections were raised by the Muslim League, the Hindu Mahasabha and the Sikh League. The incompatibility between the Muslim League and the Mahasabha complicated matters and frustrated all attempts at unity. A section of League and Khilafatists were willing to accept the Nehru Report provided three amendments, proposed by Jinnah, were accepted. Two of these were the same as the third and fourth demands in the Delhi proposals (as the first two demands had been accepted by the Nehru Report). The third and fresh demand was that the residuary powers be vested in the provinces-

Amendments Proposed by Jinnah (Calcutta Amendments)

- Muslim representation in Central legislature should be either one-third of the total or more than that.
- Representation in Punjab and Bengal should be made on the basis of population (to ensure Muslim majority in the legislature) and in other provinces, where Muslims were a minority, the existing reservation of seats for Muslims should continue.
- Residuary powers should be vested with the provinces.

Muslim League Rejects Nehru Report

Main objections of the Muslim League were:

- While the 1916 Congress-League agreement provided separate electorates and weightage to the Muslim community, they were rejected by the Nehru Report.
- The Muslims realised that while they would be a majority in the provinces of the North-East and North-West of India, and hence would control their provincial legislatures, they would always be a minority at the Centre. Thus, they demanded, in contrary to the Nehru Report, that residuary powers go to the provinces.

As the above-mentioned demands of Jinnah were not accepted at the All Parties Conference, he parted ways and joined the groups led by Aga Khan and Muhammed Shafi.

Thus, the Nehru Report was rejected by Jinnah, and had the following consequences:

1. Jinnah rejected the Nehru Report calling it **'Parting of the Ways'** with the Congress and once the 'Ambassador of Hindu-Muslim Unity' was now convinced that the Hindu mindset in India was bent upon pushing the Muslim minority to the wall.
2. On 1st January 1929, an All India Muslim Conference was held in Delhi and it passed a resolution emphasising two principles. Firstly, it said that since India was a vast country with substantial diversity, it required a federal system of government in which the states would have complete autonomy and residuary powers. Secondly, the system of separate electorates for Muslims should continue as long as their rights and interests were not safeguarded in the constitution.
3. In March 1929, Jinnah formulated his **Fourteen Points** which became the text of communal demands and included-federal government, separate electorates, reservation for Muslims in legislatures, reservation of Jobs for Muslims, creation of new Muslim majority provinces, etc.).
4. It led to the estrangement of Jinnah and pushed him towards communalism.
5. It led to the hostility of most Muslim leaders towards Civil Disobedience Movement.

Jinnah's Fourteen Points (March 1929)

Muhammad Ali Jinnah

Jinnah formulated the 'Fourteen Points' for safeguarding the rights and interests of the Muslims in any future constitution of the country. He further clarified that no constitution would be acceptable to the Muslims, unless it conformed to those fourteen points (which were basically a reiteration of Jinnah's objections to the Nehru Report). These were:

1. **Federal constitution** The form of the future constitution should be Federal, with the residuary power vested in the provinces.
2. **Provincial Autonomy** A Uniform measure of the autonomy shall be granted to all provinces.
3. **Effective representation of minorities** All legislatures in the country and other elected bodies shall be constituted on the definite principle of adequate and effective representation of minorities in every province without reducing the majority in any province to minority or even equality.
4. **Muslim Representation in Central legislature** In the Central legislature, Muslim representation shall not be less than one-third.
5. **Separate Electorates** Representation of the communal groups shall continue to be by separate electorates provided that it shall be open to any community at any time to abandon its separate electorate in favour of the joint electorates.
6. **Protection of Muslim majority in provinces** Any terrestrial redistribution that might at any time be necessary shall not in any way affect the Muslim majority in Punjab, Bengal and NWFP.
7. **Religious Liberty** Full religious liberty that is liberty of belief, worship and observance, propaganda, association and education shall be guaranteed to all communities.
8. **Communal Veto** No bill or resolution or any part thereof shall be passed in any legislature or any other elected body if three-fourth of the members of any community in that particular body oppose it as being injurious to the community.
9. **Separation of Sind from Bombay Presidency** Sind should be separated from the Bombay Presidency.
10. **Reforms in NWFP and Baluchistan** Reforms should be made in the NWFP and Baluchistan on the same footing as in other provinces.
11. **Representation of Muslims in the Services** Provision should be made in the Constitution giving Muslims an adequate share along with the other Indians in all the services of the State and Local self-governing bodies.
12. **Constitutional safeguards for Muslims** The Constitution should embody adequate safeguards for the protection of the Muslim Culture, education, language, religion, personal laws and Muslim charitable institutions. They should get their due share in grant-in-aid.
13. **Muslim representation in Cabinet** No cabinet, either central or provincial, should be formed without there being at least one-third of the Muslim Ministers.
14. No change shall be made in the constitution by the Central legislature except with the concurrence of the states constituting the Indian Federation.

Nehru and Bose also criticised the Nehru Report Within the Congress itself, young nationalists led by Jawaharlal Nehru and Subhas Chandra Bose also objected to the Nehru Report because of its acceptance of Dominion Status. Their slogan was 'Complete Independence or Purna Swaraj' and even the Congress had earlier (in Madras session 1927) adopted the goal of complete independence but later it made a compromise and accepted Dominion status as its goal in order to rally all parties behind a common plan.

In August 1928, the **'Independence of India League'** was launched by J. Nehru with the support of Subhas Chandra Bose (Nehru and Bose as secretaries and S. Srinivas Iyengar as President), as a pressure group within the Congress with the aim of-

- Countering the concept of Dominion Status
- Pleading for complete independence of India from the British, and
- Working for establishment of an Indian Republic on Socialist lines

Congress Gives Ultimatum to Government

Calcutta Congress Session (December 1928, presided by Motilal Nehru)

During the Congress Session at Calcutta, a large number of delegates led by **Jawaharal Nehru, Subhas Chandra Bose and Satyamurthy** pressed for Poorna Swaraj as the goal of the Congress. The older leaders such as Gandhiji and Motilal Nehru felt that unity over dominion status had been arrived at with great difficulty and could not be given away in haste and that the government should be given a grace period to accept the Nehru Report.

Finally, the Congress resolved in one voice that in case the government did not accept the Nehru Report **by 31st December 1929**, the Congress would declare **complete independence as its goal** and would also launch a civil disobedience movement to achieve that goal.

Preparations now began for a second round of mass action to achieve complete independence-

- With this, the council entry program of the Swaraj Party faded into irrelevance and it now merged with the Congress.
- Gandhi, now in his sixties, cancelled his Europe tour and instead decided to continue with his **mass contact tours** within India and prepare them for direct political action (Ever since his release from jail, Gandhi had been touring the country incessantly).
- At Gandhiji's insistence, the CWC formed a **Foreign Cloth Boycott Committee** to carry out an aggressive program of boycott of foreign cloth and its public burning.

Some other events also kept the political environment of the country stirred. Such as:

- On 20th March 1929, the government arrested 31 labour leaders and took them to Meerut for trial.
- On 8th April 1929, Bhagat Singh and BK Dutt of HSRA threw harmless bombs in the Central Legislative Assembly and were arrested. While in jail, Jatin Das, a member of HSRA died fasting, throwing the whole country into a fit of mourning and turmoil.

Labour Government Comes to Power in Britain (May 1929)

In May 1929, Labour Party headed by **Ramsay MacDonald** (1929–35) came to power in Britain. The effective boycott of the Simon Commission had opened many eyes and Viceroy Irwin was called to London for deliberations. Upon his return to India, Irwin famously declared on 31st October 1929 that as per the new government, natural progression to Dominion Status is implicit in Montagu Declaration of 1917. He also gave assurance of **Round Table Conference** to enlist the concurrence of all sections in India, as soon as the Simon Commission submitted its report.

Delhi Manifesto (2nd November 1929)

Two days later, major national leaders met and issued the Delhi manifesto, demanding that the **purpose of Round Table Conference** should not be to discuss when Dominion Status would be granted, but to draft a scheme for its implementation. Even though the Viceregal statement was welcomed all round, it soon became a subject of much controversy in the British Parliament. The trend of discussion in the House of Commons showed that the British were against giving Dominion Status to India.

On 23rd December 1929, Irwin, reversing his previous stand, himself told Gandhi and other leaders that he was unable to give any such assurance. With this, the grace period of one year for the government was over. The stage was now set for another round of confrontation and mass action.

Congress Adopts Purna Swaraj as Goal

Lahore Congress Session (31st December 1929, presided by J. Nehru)

On 31st December 1929, the annual session of the Congress was held at Lahore, the capital city of Punjab. It was presided over by Pandit Jawaharlal Nehru (son had now succeeded the father, marking a unique family triumph). Nehru gave a stirring speech, declaring **Purna Swaraj as the goal for India** and calling upon all his countrymen and countrywomen to join the non-violent mass struggle against the foreign rule. In this way, the session also announced the launching of a **civil disobedience** movement, though the program of struggle was not drawn and was left to Gandhi (later the Working Committee met at Sabarmati Ashram and invested Gandhi with all powers to launch the Civil Disobedience Movement at a time and place of his choice).

At midnight on 31st December 1929, on the banks of the **River Ravi**, Jawaharlal Nehru hoisted the newly adopted tricolour amidst mixed feelings of jubilation and grim resolve.

Note: Nehru became the president of the Lahore session on the insistence of Gandhi, despite only 3 of the 18 Provincial Congress Committees supporting him. Gandhi insisted that, 'the battle of the future has to be fought by younger men and women. Responsibility will sober and mellow the youth and prepare them for the burden they must discharge. Pandit Jawaharlal has everything to recommend him'.

Independence Pledge (26th January 1930)

The Congress decided to celebrate **26th January 1930** as the first Independence Day or Purna Swaraj Day, holding public meetings all over the country and taking Independence Pledge, drafted by Gandhi. This program of the Congress met with great success. In towns and villages, small and big, the pledge was read out in local language and national flag hoisted.

Excerpts from the Independence Pledge

'We believe that it is the inalienable right of the Indian people, as of any other people, to have freedom and to enjoy the fruits of their toil and have the necessities of life, so that they may have full opportunities of growth... The British government in India has not only deprived the Indian people of their freedom but has based itself on the exploitation of the masses, and has ruined India economically, politically, culturally and spiritually...

Village industries such as hand spinning have been destroyed, leaving the peasantry idle for at least four months in a year, and dulling their intellect for want of handicrafts, and nothing has been substituted, as in other countries, for the crafts thus destroyed... The British manufactured goods constitute the bulk of our imports...

Politically, India's status has never been so reduced, as under the British regime... All administrative talent is killed, and the masses have to satisfy with petty village offices and clerkships.

Culturally, the system of education has torn us from our moorings...

Spiritually, compulsory disarmament has made us unmanly, and the presence of an alien army of occupation has made us think that we cannot look after ourselves...

We hold it to be a crime against man and god to submit any longer to a rule that has caused this fourfold disaster to our country..We will prepare ourselves by withdrawing so far as we can, all voluntary association from the British Government, and will prepare for civil disobedience including non-payment of taxes. We hereby solemnly resolve to carry out the Congress instructions issued from time to time for the purpose of establishing Purna Swaraj'.

Report of the Simon Commission (7th June 1930)

The Report of the unrepresentative all white commission, made the following suggestions on constitutional reforms in India. It recommended the following:

- The establishment of responsible government at the centre was to wait indefinitely i.e. it was to be established sometime in the future.
- Retention of separate electorates.
- Reservation of seats for depressed classes.
- Federal government in India in order to cope with the diversity of the country. However, the all-India federation was not considered practical idea for immediate execution.
- Abolition of Dyarchy in the provinces and establishment of responsible unitary government in the provinces.
- Retention of the special powers of the Governors for the safety and tranquility of the provinces and for the protection of the minorities. They would also have full powers of intervention in the event of breakdown of the constitution.
- Extension of franchise and expansion of legislatures.
- Separation of Burma from British India.

In this way, the commission recommended provincial autonomy in India but rejected Parliamentary responsibility at the centre, ignoring the national demand for a responsible government at the Centre. Overall, it was not a constitutional scheme which deserved any detailed examination and was rejected by almost all Indian parties and the Indian people enthusiastically participated in the Civil Disobedience Movement.

Prelim Capsule

Event	Important Details
Simon Commission (1927)	It was an **Indian Statutory Commission** comprising seven members (all members were British and were members of the British Parliament). Appointed by- Prime Minister **Stanley Baldwin** on 8th Nov 1927. Chairman- Sir John Simon assisted by Clement Attlee. Aim- to enquire into the working of the Government of India under the Act of 1919 and suggest fresh reforms. The Congress decided to boycott the commission during the Madras Congress Session (presided by Dr. Ansari, December 1927). Unanimously rejected by all nationalists, since it consisted solely of British members; thus also called '**White Commission**'. Landed at Bombay on 3rd February 1928 and was greeted with the slogan **'Go back, Simon'**. **Lala Lajpat Rai** (Sher-e-Punjab) faced lathi-charge while leading an anti-Simon agitation at Lahore and later succumbed to his injuries (17th November 1928). The Commission toured the country extensively and prepared a report which was published on 7th Jun 1930. It recommended abolition of Diarchy in the provinces and establishment of responsible unitary government in the provinces, among other things.
Nehru Report (1928)	Lord Birkenhead had thrown a challenge to Indians to produce a constitution acceptable to all sections of Indian society. The Indians accepted the challenge and an **All Parties Conference (February 1928)** was called which was attended by the Congress, Muslim League, Hindu Mahasabha and others. Conference was presided over by **Dr. MA Ansari.** In May 1928, the All Parties Conference appointed a sub-committee headed by **Motilal Nehru** to draft a constitution. The Nehru Report confined itself to British India and recommended Dominion status as the desired form of government in India. It rejected separate communal electorates and recommended that elections should be held on the basis of **joint electorates.** It recommended 19 Fundamental Rights. It recommended, for the first time, a federation. It recommended responsible government at Centre and in provinces. In December 1928, **All Parties Conference was held at Calcutta** and the Conference failed to pass the Report as objections were raised by the Muslim League, the Hindu Mahasabha and the Sikh League. Jinnah rejected the Nehru Report calling it **'Parting of the Ways'** with the Congress. He went back to separate electorates, formulated his **Fourteen Points** which became the text of communal demands.

	Nehru and Bose opposed the Nehru Report, founded **Independence for India League** and demanded the adoption of complete independence as the immediate goal. Congress resolved in one voice that in case the government did not accept the Nehru Report by 31st December 1929, the Congress would declare **complete independence** as its goal and would also launch a Civil Disobedience Movement to achieve that goal.
Lahore Congress Session (1929)	On 31st December 1929, the annual session of the Congress was held at Lahore. At midnight on the banks of the **River Ravi**, President Jawaharlal Nehru hoisted the newly adopted tricolour and declared **Purna Swaraj** as the goal for India. Launching of a civil disobedience movement was announced. Congress decided to celebrate 26th January 1930 as the **first Independence Day**, holding public meetings all over the country and taking Independence Pledge collectively.

Previous Years' Questions – Preliminary Exam

1. The radical wing of the Congress party with Jawaharlal Nehru as one of its main leaders, founded the Independence for India League in opposition to which one of the following? **[UPSC 1995]**
   (a) The Gandhi Irwin Pact
   (b) The Home Rule movement
   (c) The Nehru Report
   (d) The Montford Reforms
2. Why was the Simon Commission of 1927 boycotted? **[UPSC 1998]**
   (a) There was no Indian member in the Commission.
   (b) It supported the Muslim League.
   (c) Congress felt that the people of India are entitled to Swaraj.
   (d) There were differences among the members.
3. Under whose Presidency was the Lahore Session of the Indian National Congress held in the year 1929 wherein a resolution was adopted to gain complete Independence from the British? **[UPSC 2006]**
   (a) Bal Gangadhar Tilak
   (b) Gopal Krishna Gokhale
   (c) Jawaharlal Nehru
   (d) Motilal Nehru
4. With reference to Simon Commission's recommendations, which one of the following statements is correct? **[UPSC 2010]**
   (a) It recommends the replacement of Dyarchy with responsible government in the provinces.
   (b) It proposed the setting up of inter provincial council under the Home Department.
   (c) It suggested the abolition of bicameral Legislature at the centre.
   (d) It recommended the creation of Indian Police Service with the provision for increased pay and allowances for British recruits as compared to Indian recruits.
5. With reference to the period of Indian freedom struggle, which of the following was/were recommended by the Nehru report? **[UPSC 2011]**
   1. Complete Independence for India.
   2. Joint electorates for reservation of seats for minorities.
   3. Provision of fundamental rights for the people of India in the constitution.

   Choose the correct answer from the following options.
   (a) 1 only (b) 2 and 3 only
   (c) 1 and 3 only (d) 1 , 2 and 3

6. The Lahore Session of the Indian National Congress (1929) is very important in history, because **[UPSC 2012]**
   1. The Congress passed a resolution demanding complete Independence.
   2. The rift between the extremists and moderates was resolved in that session.
   3. A resolution was passed rejecting the two-Nation theory in that session.

   Which of the statements given above is/are correct? Choose the correct answer from the following options.
   (a) 1 only
   (b) 2 and 3
   (c) 1 and 3
   (d) None of the above
7. The people of India agitated against the arrival of Simon Commission because **[UPSC 2013]**
   (a) Indians never wanted the review of the working of the Act of 1919.
   (b) Simon Commission recommended the abolition of Dyarchy in the province.
   (c) There was no Indian member in the Simon Commission.
   (d) The Simon Commission suggested the partition of the country.
8. Why is the 1929 session of Indian National Congress of significance in the history of the freedom movement? **[UPSC 2014]**
   (a) Attainment of Self-Government was declared as the objective of the Congress.
   (b) Attainment of Purna Swaraj was adopted as the goal of the Congress.
   (c) Non-Cooperation movement was launched.
   (d) Decision to participate in the Round Table Conference in London was taken.
9. The object of the Butler Committee of 1927 was to **[UPSC 2017]**
   (a) Define the jurisdiction of the Central and Provincial governments.
   (b) Define the powers of the Secretary of State for India.
   (c) Improve censorship on national press.
   (d) Improve the relationship between the Government of India and the Indian states.
10. With reference to Indian National Movement, consider the following pairs: **[UPSC 2019]**

    Persons : Position head
    1. Sir Tej Bahadur Sapru : President, All India Liberal Federation
    2. K.C. Neogy : Member, The Constituent Assembly
    3. P.C. Joshi : General Secretary, Communist Party of India

    Which of the pairs given above is/are correctly matched?
    (a) 1 only (b) 1 and 2 only
    (c) 3 only (d) 1, 2 and 3

Answers

Previous Years' Questions – Preliminary Exam

1.	(c)	2.	(a)	3.	(c)	4.	(a)	5.	(b)
6.	(a)	7.	(c)	8.	(b)	9.	(d)	10.	(d)

17

Civil Disobedience Movement 1930–34 (Civil Disobedience Movement, Round Table Conferences 1930–32 and Communal Award 1932)

The Civil Disobedience Movement (CDM) was the next mass movement launched by the Congress after a gap of 8 years. There were several factors that prepared the ground for the CDM, starting from the sudden withdrawal of the Non-Cooperation Movement in February 1922 to the non-acceptance of Nehru Report by the British government.

Run up to Civil Disobedience Movement (CDM)

Calcutta Session of Congress (December 1928, presided by Motilal Nehru)

You may recall that during the Congress Session at Calcutta in December 1928, the Congress had given an ultimatum to the British government and had resolved in one voice that in case the government did not accept the Nehru Report by 31st December 1929, the Congress would declare complete independence as its goal and would also launch a civil disobedience movement to achieve that goal.

Lahore Session of Congress (December 1929, presided by Jawaharlal Nehru)

On the expiry of this grace period, on 31st December 1929, during the annual session of the Congress held at Lahore, the Congress declared Purna Swaraj as its goal and announced the launching of a civil disobedience movement under Gandhi. In mid-February 1930, the Working Committee met at Sabarmati Ashram and invested Gandhi with all powers to launch the Civil Disobedience Movement, at a time and place of his choice.

Gandhi's Eleven Points (January 1930)

However, Gandhi was not sure about his plan of action and tried to negotiate with the government once again before launching the movement. He formulated 'Eleven Points' of administrative reforms and placed them before Lord Irwin in a letter dated 31st January 1930. He insisted that there would be no need for any agitation if his eleven points were accepted, which constituted for him the substance of purna swaraj. The Eleven Points included the following:

1. Abolition of Salt Tax and also the government's salt monopoly
2. Reduction of the Rupee Sterling ratio

3. Reduction of Land revenue by half and it be subjected to legislative control
4. Reduction of Salaries of highest grade services by half
5. Reduction of military and civil service expenditure by half
6. Protection for Indian textiles (protective tariff) and coastal shipping
7. Discharge of all political prisoners
8. Total prohibition of alcohol
9. Reforms in CID (Criminal Investigation Department)
10. Change in Arms Act, allowing popular control of issue of licenses and right of Indians to carry arms
11. Accept Postal Reservation Bill

Many national leaders looked at the Eleven Points as a climb down from the demand of purna swaraj. Jawaharlal Nehru in his Autobiography questioned whether Gandhi's purna swaraj was different from theirs? If not then what was the point for these eleven points when they were already talking in terms of complete independence? Further, **Government's response** was out rightly negative and Lord Irwin made no assurance for acceptance of Gandhi's Eleven Points.

Gandhi wrote, 'On bended knees I asked for bread and received a stone instead. The English nation responds only to force and I am not surprised by the viceregal reply'.

Civil Disobedience Movement (1930 to 1931)

Dandi March (12th March to 6th April 1930)

Seeing the uncompromising attitude of the government, Gandhi now decided to start the movement. On **12th March 1930**, Gandhi started his historic **'Dandi March'** from Sabarmati Ashram to Dandi Beach (nearly 385 km or 240 miles), accompanied with 78 followers. On 6th April 1930, Gandhi reached Dandi, picked up a handful of salt and broke the salt law as a symbol of defiance to British laws. Gandhi declared, 'The British rule in India has brought about moral, material, cultural and spiritual ruination of this great country. I regard this rule as a curse. I am out to destroy this system of government. Sedition has become my religion'. Subhas Chandra Bose had compared the Salt March to **Napoleon's March from Elba to Paris**.

Monuments of the Gyarah Murti depicting Mahatma Gandhi leading the Salt March in 1930

Programme of the Movement

This included the following in addition to the pledge of non-violence and truth.

- Disobedience of Salt law wherever possible
- Refusal to pay taxes to the government
- Boycott of law courts, colleges and government service
- Picketing of shops selling liquor and foreign cloth

Gandhi 'There is no article like salt outside water by taxing which the State can reach even the starving millions, the sick, the maimed and the utterly helpless. The salt tax constitutes therefore the most inhuman poll tax the ingenuity of man can devise'.

Why Gandhi Chose Salt to Register a Protest?

Representation of Gandhi during the historic Dandi March

The choice of salt initially puzzled many people. Later it appeared that Gandhi succeeded in spinning a fine strategy around the issue of salt. Salt tax was a universal grievance and affected all people of all classes, rich and poor. It was most ubiquitous of all taxes for the poor and carried with it implications of loyalty and mutual trust. In this sense, it had a far reaching emotional appeal. Salt manufacturing could also afford a paltry yet psychologically important income for the poor through self-help, much like khadi. Like khadi again, it offered to the urban adherents the opportunity of a symbolic identification with mass suffering.

Further, breaking of the salt law represented humble beginning of civil disobedience and its countrywide violation made an impressive demonstration of the power of non-violent struggle. Later, manufacture of salt became a part of Gandhi's constructive program as manufacture of khadi.

Salt Satyagraha

A commemorative postal stamp depicting Chakravarti Rajagopalachari

While Gandhi was marching to Dandi (Navsari district, Gujarat), the Congress leaders worked out the logistics of the salt satyagraha. They enrolled volunteers, formed grass root Congress Committees, collected funds and toured villages and towns to gain support. Once Gandhi gave the indication from Dandi, the salt laws were broken all over the country:

- In Tamil Nadu: **C Rajagopalachari** led a salt march from Trichinopoly to Vedaranniyam on the Tanjore coast and was arrested on 30th April.
- In Malabar: **K. Kelappan**, the leader of Vaikom Satyagraha, walked from Calicut to Payannur to break the salt law.
- In the North-East: A group of satyagrahis walked from Sylhet in Assam to Noakhali in Bengal to make salt and break the law.
- In Andhra: Several bands of satyagrahis marched from villages to coast to break the salt law. A number of **sibirums** (military style camps) were established to function as head offices of salt satygraha.

Government Repression and Popular Upsurge

Throughout 1930, the government's attitude remained ambivalent. The government found itself in a classic dilemma of 'damned if you do, damned if you don't'; a dilemma the Gandhian strategy of non-violent civil disobedience was designed to create. 'If we do too much, the Congress will cry "repression", if we do too little, the Congress will cry "victory"'—this was how the government dilemma was expressed. Either way it ensured erosion of British hegemony.

However, seeing the rapid spread of the movement, the government was left with little choice and it soon took to brutal repression. As reported by the American journalist **Webb Miller**- 'unresisting men were methodically bashed into bloody pulp'. The torture inflicted upon unresisting satyagrahis resulted in arousal of sympathy and respect which rapidly converted into participation.

Arrest of Jawaharlal Nehru

On 14th April 1930, Jawaharlal Nehru was arrested for breaking the salt law and his arrest was met with massive demonstrations and clashes with the police. The government tightened its repressive machinery and arrested most of the other Congress leaders as well. This resulted in the weakening of Gandhian confines of civil disobedience and there were several outbursts of violent forms. Some major outbursts were:

Chittagong Armory Raid: On 18th April 1930, the Bengal revolutionaries carried out the Chittagong armoury raid. In fact, in Bengal, the whole history of civil disobedience was accompanied by revolutionary terrorism with 56 incidents in 1930. The Chittagong leader Surya Sen managed to remain underground with the help of villagers, mostly Muslims.

Peshawar Upsurge: On 23rd April 1930, Khan Abdul Ghaffar Khan was arrested provoking a massive upsurge. Khan had been active in NWFP for several years and had set up a band of non-violent revolutionaries, the **Khudai Khidmatgars** (Servants of God) or the **Red Shirts** (because of the colour of their shirts) who played an active role in the CDM.

The Peshawar upsurge is memorable as it was here that a platoon of **Gharwal Rifles** (Hindu soldiers) facing a Muslim crowd refused to open fire and became a symbol of communal unity and patriotism. This incident was proof that nationalism had begun to enter the Indian army, the chief instrument of British rule in India.

Khan Abdul Ghaffar Khan and the Khudai Khidmatgar Movement In 1929, the Khudai Khidmatgars ('Servants of God') movement, led by Khan Abdul Ghaffar Khan (1890–1988), mobilised to oppose the British in India's Northwest Frontier Province in non-violent way. Ghaffar Khan and the Khudai Khidmatgar movement inspired thousands of Pashtuns (also called Pathans), who were known as fierce warriors, and others to lay down their arms and use civil resistance to challenge British rule.

Khan Abdul Ghaffar Khan, popularly known as Bacha Khan.

Although Ghaffar Khan's initial reform efforts predated his involvement with Gandhi and the Indian National Congress (INC), he later formed a formal alliance with them and became a formidable force during and following the INC's civil disobedience campaign of 1930–31, helping the INC win provincial elections in 1937.

Ghaffar Khan, who is also known as Badshah Khan and 'Frontier Gandhi' or 'Sarhadi Gandhi' formed the world's first nonviolent army, a force of perhaps 100,000 Pathans. Members of the movement were known as 'Red Shirts' or 'Surkho Posh' because of the red uniforms they wore.

Ghaffar Khan was offered presidency of the Indian National Congress in 1931 which he refused saying that he was a simple soldier and would like to serve. Khan Abdul Ghaffar Khan was against the partition of India and he was many times targeted for being Anti-Muslim.

In 1947, a plebiscite resulted in the Frontier Province becoming part of the newly independent Pakistan. Ghaffar Khan's dissatisfaction with Pakistan later led him to favour the creation of an autonomous Pakhtunistan and he was consequently imprisoned by the Pakistani government.

Khan Abdul Ghaffar Khan was named 'Amnesty International Prisoner of the Year' in 1962. He was nominated for Nobel Peace prize in 1985. In 1987 he became the first person who won **Bharat Ratna** without being an Indian national. (Another Foreign national to receive Bharat Ratna is Nelson Mandela, 1990). He died in Peshawar in 1988 while he was under house arrest.

Arrest of Gandhi

On 4th May 1930, the Viceroy finally ordered the arrest of Gandhi (he was sent to Yerawada Jail in Poona). His arrest unleashed a massive wave of protest. In Bombay, swarms of people just spilled onto the street forcing the police to withdraw.

Sholapur Upsurge

The most massive demonstration took place on 7th May 1930 in the industrial city of Sholapur (Maharashtra). The textile workers who dominated the town went on strike, burnt liquor shops and attacked all symbols of government authority.

Dharsana Satyagraha (Gujarat)

On 21st May 1930, Sarojini Naidu (first Indian woman to become President of the INC, 1925 Kanpur Session), Imam Saheb (Gandhi's co-worker from South African struggle) and Gandhi's son Manilal led a band of 2000 satyagrahis to defy salt laws at the Dharsana Salt Works in Gujarat. Police had already cordoned off the area. As the satyagrahis moved forward, the police attacked them with their steel tipped lathis. The injured were taken away by their comrades as another column of satyagrahis took their place, to be beaten to pulp and carried away.

Webb Miller gave an account of the Dharsana Satyagraha in these words-'In 18 years of my reporting in 20 countries, during which I have witnessed innumerable civil disturbances, riots, street fights and rebellions, I have never witnessed such harrowing scenes as at Dharsana'.

By June end, the **Congress Working Committee was declared illegal** and Motilal Nehru, who was functioning as the Congress President, was also arrested.

Forms of Protest

Though salt satyagraha and its more potent form- the non-violent heroism (Dharsana satyagraha) stole the show as main form of protest, other forms of protest quickly emerged. Various other socially non-divisive issues were also taken up. These included the following:

Boycott of Foreign Cloth and Liquor

A prominent role was played by women, students and youth in the boycott of foreign cloth and liquor. Bombay was particularly affected. Congress sentries were placed in business districts and ensured that the boycott was not flouted by merchants and dealers. Those who flouted were brought in line by social boycott, fines by their own associations and Congress black-listing.

Non-payment of Land Revenue in Ryotwari Areas

For instance, in Gujarat in districts of Kheda, Surat and Broach, people took to no-tax movement and the tax refused here was the land revenue.

Anti-chowkidari Tax Movement in Zamindari Areas

The chowkidars were guards who supplemented the police in rural areas. They were paid out of tax levied on villages and were much hated as they often acted as spies for the government and retainers for the landlords. The anti-chowkidari tax agitation first began in land locked Bihar where salt satyagraha did not have much scope. Monghyr, Saran and Bhagalpur districts were particularly affected. It also called for resignation of chowkidars. **Rajendra Prasad** and **Abdul Bari** from Patna emerged as main leaders.

In Bengal too, when salt making became difficult with the onset of monsoon, form of protest shifted to anti-chowkidari and **anti-Union Board agitation**.

Forest Satyagraha

In Maharashtra, Karnataka and Central Provinces, people took to forest satyagraha i.e. peaceful violation of forest laws restricting tribal and peasant rights to free fodder, timber and other forest produce. Other areas with large tribal population were also affected.

Anti-Cunningham Circular Agitation

In Assam, a powerful agitation was launched by students against the infamous **'Cunningham Circular'** which prohibited students from participating in political activities associated with the national movement.

No-revenue No-rent Campaign

In UP, a no-revenue no-rent campaign was started, and Agra and Rae Bareilly emerged as important centres. The no-revenue agitation was carried out by the zamindars and involved non-payment of land revenue to the government. The no-rent agitation was carried out by the tenants and involved non-payment of rent to the zamindars.

Defending the Honour of the National Flag

All over the country, people defended the honour of the national flag even in the face of severe brutalities. They had taken to heart Jawaharlal's message when he unfurled the national flag at Lahore, 'Now that this flag is unfurled, it must not be lowered as long as a single Indian, man, woman or child lives in India'.

Other Forms of Protest

Various other forms of protest also emerged during this agitation. These included:

- **Prabhat Pheris** in which men, women and children went around at dawn singing nationalist songs.
- **Patrikas**, or illegal news-sheets, were circulated all over the country to defy the hated Press Act.
- **Magic lanterns** were used to carry the nationalist message to the villages.
- **Vanar senas** or monkey armies of children were organised (At one instance, even the girls wanted their own **manjari sena** or cat army!).

The government struck back through large-scale confiscations of property, yet thousands of peasants stood their ground and the rumour spread that British Raj was coming to an end.

Note on Cunningham Circular J.R. Cunningham was the then powerful director of public information of Assam. He issued a circular in 1930 imposing a blanket ban on any anti-British and pro-swadeshi activity by students. He also ordered them to sign an undertaking to the effect that they would have to quit their schools and colleges if they participated in anti-government demonstrations or movements and forced the students and guardians to furnish assurances of good behaviour. Refusing to oblige, thousands of students throughout Assam left their institutions of learning. There were about 400 such students in Guwahati alone.

A group of philanthropists came to the rescue of these students and decided to start a swadeshi school in the city on the lines of national schools being established in Calcutta, Sylhet, Habiganj, Karimganj, Silchar and elsewhere in the country. The Kamrup Academy was conceived with Rai Bahadur Kalicharan Sengupta as its founder president.

Impact of Protest

- Imports of foreign cloth and other foreign goods fell considerably.
- Government income from liquor, excise duties and land revenue crashed.
- Elections to legislative Assembly were boycotted.

Participation

The movement got spontaneous response from various parts of the country and different classes of people participated, particularly the peasants with their own class demands.

1. Peasants The CDM saw a massive participation of peasants with thousands of them violating laws, facing lathis and courting arrest.

2. Business groups The movement also received massive support from business groups. Business groups such as Ahmedabad mill owners, Bombay merchants and petty traders and Calcutta Marwaris headed by **GD Birla** extended exemplary solidarity and demonstrated the sympathy of Indian capitalists with the national movement. Several merchants took collective oath to stop importing foreign goods till the time the movement lasted. The result was a massive decline in import of British cloth—from 1248 million yards in 1929–30 to only 523 million yards in 1930–31 (this decline also reflected the effect of Depression in Europe).

3. Women **Participation of women was the most remarkable feature** of this movement. Women from professional, business and peasant families participated in large numbers. They left the seclusion of their homes, marched shoulder to shoulder with men in processions, picketed shops, faced lathis and even went to jail. It was clear that the Indian women were struggling for domestic and national liberty at the same time.

Gandhi played a significant role in increasing the participation of women in the national movement which proved to be the most liberating experience for them until then. According to him, woman was a companion of man, equal in capabilities and intellect. He even considered women to be more suited for the satyagraha protest. In fact, Gandhian forms of agitation did not involve any drastic violation of traditional image of women, rather it was the 'male image' that was in some ways 'feminised', with his emphasis on non-violence, self-sacrifice and suffering.

The participation of women in revolutionary activities in Bengal met with sharp criticism though. Rabindranath Tagore, a celebrated activist for women rights, wrote a novel **Char Adhyaya** (1934) in which he condemned this 'unfeminine' role of women.

4. Tribals The tribals actively participated in Central Province, Maharashtra and Karnataka.

5. Urban intelligentsia Support from this class was also much less than what was seen during the Non-Cooperation Movement. There were very few instances of students leaving colleges or lawyers giving up practice. Militant educated youth was more attracted to revolutionary terrorism in Bengal and north India (particularly to Bhagat Singh, whose popularity briefly rivalled that of Gandhi).

6. Workers Participation of workers remained low and the CDM did not coincide with any major labour upsurge. The Congress also did not include industrial or communications strike in its programme.

7. Muslims Muslims largely kept aloof from the CDM, yet their participation was not insignificant. They participated in large numbers in NWFP. Middle class Muslims participated in Bengal; the Muslim weavers in Bihar, Delhi and Lucknow. Lower classes of Muslims were also effectively mobilised.

Regional Variations

In terms of spread of the movement, there were significant regional variations across the country. Gujarat emerged as the classic heartland of Gandhian satyagraha, particularly Kheda, Bardoli and Ahmedabad. The Gujarati community of Bombay city also participated with great enthusiasm. Coastal Andhra and Bihar too arose as significant strongholds.

The movement reached the easternmost corner of India upto Manipur and Nagaland. In Nagaland, **Rani Gaidinliu** emerged as the brave heroine of the movement who followed the path showed by Gandhi and rebelled against the British rule. The young Rani aged 16, was arrested in 1932 and imprisoned for life. She spent her youthful years in Assam jails, and was released only in 1947 by the government of free India.

There was evidence of limited participation in regions where Congress organisation was weak or Gandhian ideas had made little inroads. These included Maharashtra, Karnataka and Central Provinces. The pattern of participation was most complex in Bengal. Certain regions like Midnapur and Bankura saw the development of powerful Gandhian rural movements while other regions remained ridden with communal riots and revolutionary activities.

Gaidinliu (1915–93) At the age of 13, Gaidinliu joined the Heraka religious movement which later turned into a political movement seeking to drive out the British from Manipur and the surrounding Naga areas. An advocate of the ancestral Naga religious practices, she staunchly resisted the conversion of Nagas to Christianity. She was arrested in 1932 at the age of 16, and was sentenced to life imprisonment by the British rulers. **Jawaharlal Nehru** met her at Shillong Jail in 1937 and gave her the title of 'Rani'.

Decline of First Phase of CDM

Throughout 1930, the government's response had been ambivalent, and repressive measures were carried out after much vacillation. In the meantime, the Simon Commission Report was published (June 1930) and being a regressive document, it further upset even the moderate political opinion.

Let Us Recall In May 1929, Labour Party headed by Ramsay MacDonald had come to power in Britain. The effective boycott of the Simon Commission had opened many eyes and Viceroy Irwin was called to London for deliberations. Upon his return to India, Irwin famously declared on 31st October 1929 that as per the new government, natural progression to Dominion Status is implicit in Montagu Declaration of 1917. He also gave assurance of Round Table Conference to enlist the concurrence of all sections in India, as soon as the Simon Commission submitted its report.

On 9th July 1930, Viceroy Irwin reiterated the suggestion of a Round Table Conference as a conciliatory gesture, and also reiterated the goal of Dominion Status. He also tried to explore possibilities of peace between the Congress and the government. Accordingly, the Nehrus, father and son, were taken to Yerawada jail to meet Gandhi and hammer out a settlement. Gandhi rejected the idea of Congress participating in the RTC, yet the gesture ensured the participation of certain sections of Indian political opinion in London in the month of November 1930.

By September–October 1930, the movement began to show signs of fatigue-peasant and tribal militancy shot up, enthusiasm of merchants fell sharply and many of them broke their earlier pledges of not to sell foreign goods. Support from peasants too declined in the face of large scale confiscations by the government. Almost all leading Congressmen were put behind bars. On the other hand, the revolutionaries were active in full swing and the communists were rallying the labour and organising strikes, making Gandhi increasingly grow apprehensive of anarchy.

In November 1930, the First Round Table Conference, first conference between the Indians and the British as equals, took place in London to discuss the Simon Commission Reports. The Congress boycotted the RTC and its proceedings proved to be quite meaningless. The British government grew anxious to secure Congress participation. Accordingly, on 25th January 1931, the British Prime Minister and the Viceroy of India unconditionally released Gandhi and the other Indian leaders so that they could meet at the residence of the ailing leader Motilal Nehru and deliberate and agree to participate in the next Round Table.

In such circumstances, Gandhi decided to retreat.

First Round Table Conference (London, 12th November 1930 to 19th January 1931)

In all, three Round Table Conferences (RTCs-1930, 31 and 32) were held in London to discuss the Indian constitutional question after taking into account all shades of Indian political opinion. The Indian National Congress participated only in the Second Round Table.

The First Round Table Conference, the first conference between the Indians and the British **as equals**, was opened officially by Lord Irwin on 12th November 1930 in London **to discuss the Simon**

Commission Reports. It was chaired by British Prime Minister Ramsay MacDonald of Labor Party. The First Round Table was boycotted by the Congress as it had launched the Civil Disobedience Movement. In all 89 persons were invited to attend the conference. Of these, 16 represented British political parties. The British Indian delegation comprised of 58 members who represented various parties and interests in India. The Congress and Indian business leaders kept away from the conference. Many of them were in jail for participating in Civil Disobedience Movement.

Participants

The government handpicked 'safe men' to represent India and the Indian States. Prominent Indian publicmen who participated were:

- Muslims- Agha Khan III **(leader of British Indian delegation)**, Muhammed Shafi, Maulana Muhammed Ali, Fazlul-Haq and Muhammed Ali Jinnah
- Sikhs- Sardar Sampuran Singh, Sardar Ujjal Singh
- Hindu Mahasabha- BS Moonje, MR Jayakar
- Depressed Classes- BR Ambedkar
- Christians of India- KT Paul
- Parsis-Homi Mody
- Liberals- TB Sapru, CY Chintamani, Srinivas Sastri, Chimanlal Harilal Sitalvad, JN Basu
- Labour- NM Joshi, B Shiva Rao
- Justice Paty- Arcot Ramasamy Mudaliar, Sir AP Patro
- Women- Begum Jahanara Shahnawaz
- Landlords- Maharaja Kameshwar Singh of Darbhanga (Bengal)
- Sindh-Shah Nawaz Bhutto, Ghulam Hussain Hidayatullah
- Princely states- A contingent of 16 members (rulers or their nominees) including representatives of Alwar, Baroda, Bhopal, Bikaner, Jammu and Kashmir, Patiala, Hyderabad, Mysore and Gwalior.
- Main British Participants included Ramsay MacDonald, chief spokesman of the British government (Labour) and Samuel Hoare (Conservative).

Note: The princes, led by **Maharaja of Bikaner**, expressed their desire to join an All India Federation.

Outcome

The Conference took two significant initiatives set out in a 'Command Paper'— First, it recommended the formation of an **All India Federation** of British Indian Provinces and the Indian States. Second, it also recommended a **responsible government at the centre** with certain 'reservations and safeguards' for the transitional period to maintain the British control over defence, external affairs and economy. At the same time, BR Ambedkar demanded separate electorates for the untouchables.

Even though the Conference was attended by some prominent Indian leaders, they could not be considered as real representatives of people whose destiny the conference was to decide. Thus the conference appeared more as a gathering of communalists and reactionaries and its proceedings proved to be quite meaningless. The British government grew anxious to secure Congress participation.

Truce Period

Gandhi-Irwin Pact (or Delhi Pact, 5th March 1931)

On 14th February 1931, Gandhi–Irwin talk was initiated by the efforts of **Sir TB Sapru** and **Sir MR Jayakar**. The fortnight-long talks culminated in the Delhi Pact on 5th March 1931, also known as Gandhi-Irwin Pact. The pact was signed by Gandhi on behalf of the Congress and by Irwin on behalf of the government making it the **first pact** between the Congress and the government on an equal footing.

As per the Pact, the Congress agreed to the following:

- Withdraw the CDM immediately and effectively in all respects.
- Participate in the next Round Table Conference (with Gandhi as the sole representative of the Congress).
- Withdraw the boycott of British goods forthwith.

The government agreed to the following:

- Withdraw ordinances promulgated in relation to the CDM.
- Release political prisoners against whom there were no allegations of violence.
- Return confiscated land not yet sold to third parties.
- Lenient treatment to government employees who had resigned from the service.
- Remit penalties that had not been realised.
- Pay indemnities to those who had suffered in the movement.
- The government would not amend the salt act but will permit the collection and manufacture of salt freely to the people living within a specified area from the sea-shore.
- The government also conceded the right to peaceful picketing.

Ambivalent Response to the Gandhi-Irwin Pact

The Pact became a subject of much controversy. It was seen variously as a betrayal of peasant interests, as a proof of Gandhi's fear of mass movements turning radical and even as a sign of uncertain mood of Indian bourgeoisie.

In the Congress Working Committee, the response to the Pact was largely divided. Many hailed it as a victory since the Viceroy had to negotiate a settlement on terms of equality and curtsey with Gandhi. However, many others saw it as a failure since Gandhi agreed to attend the Second Round Table Conference, more or less on British terms. **Gandhi's request for remitting the death sentence of Bhagat Singh, Sukh Dev and Rajguru was turned down** by the Viceroy and the three were hanged on 23rd March 1931. The rather sudden halt of the movement without attaining the goal of purna swaraj disappointed many leaders of the Congress. The peasants of Gujarat, who had sacrificed their life and property, felt let down (confiscated properties were later returned after the Congress Ministry assumed office in Bombay in 1937).

Despite the above, the vast masses of Indian people saw the pact as a victory over the government. Thousands of those released from jail were treated back home as soldiers returning from a victorious battle. For the masses, it was a truce and not a surrender, a time for their soldiers to rest and prepare for the next round.

Comparison with Non-Cooperation Movement

The objective this time was purna swaraj and not just remedying two specific wrongs and attainment of a vaguely worded swaraj. Further, the method of agitation involved active defiance of laws and not just non-cooperation with the administration.

However, participation of certain sections of people was much less—fewer lawyers gave up practice, fewer students left schools and colleges. No major labor upsurge occurred. Muslim participation was nowhere near what was seen during Non-Cooperation. However, the movement received a far greater support from peasants and business groups. The total number of jail goers reached 92,214 (three times more than the figure in 1921–22).

Karachi Special Congress Session (29th March 1931, presided by Sardar Patel)

A special session of the Congress was called at Karachi to ratify the Gandhi-Irwin Pact. The session was held only a few days after the execution of Bhagat Singh and Gandhi was shown **black flags** throughout his way to Karachi.

Congress Resolutions at Karachi

1. While dissociating itself from and disapproving of political violence in any shape or form, the Congress admired the 'bravery and sacrifice' of the three martyrs.
2. Delhi Pact was ratified.
3. The goal of purna swaraj was reiterated.
4. The Karachi Session also adopted two significant resolutions-one on **Fundamental Rights** and the other on **National Economic Programme** (originally drafted by Jawaharlal Nehru), which made the session particularly memorable. By means of these two resolutions, for the first time, the Congress defined what swaraj would mean for the masses. The resolution declared- 'In order to end the exploitation of the masses, political freedom must include real economic freedom of the starving millions'.

Karachi Declaration on Fundamental Rights and the National Economic Programme

The declaration on fundamental rights guaranteed basic civil rights of free speech, free press, free assembly and freedom of association, equality before the law irrespective of caste, creed or sex, neutrality of the state in regard to all religions, elections on the basis of universal adult franchise and free and compulsory primary education.

The resolution on National Economic Programme promised substantial reduction in rent and revenue, relief from agricultural indebtedness and control of usury, better conditions for workers such as living wage, limited hours of work and protection of women workers, the right to organise and form union to workers and peasants, and state ownership or control of key industries, mines and means of transport. It also laid down that the culture, language and script of the minorities shall be protected.

Even though the declaration was moderate in content, it made a significant beginning and several items entered the Congress program for the first time. In fact, the **Karachi Declaration formed the basic document of Congress' socio-economic program** for later years.

Second Round Table Conference (London, 1st September to 1st December 1931)

Gandhi Participates in the Second RTC

Note

In the intervening period between Gandhi-Irwin Pact (March 1931) and the 2nd RTC (December 1931), there occurred a change of government both in India and Britain. In April 1931, **Lord Willingdon** succeeded Lord Irwin in Delhi. On 26th August 1931, MacDonald's Labour Cabinet resigned and a new coalition government dominated by the Conservatives was formed under MacDonald's leadership. **Sir Samuel Hoare** (1931–35), a leading conservative, became Secretary of State for India. This change of government in Britain brought about a change of attitude and hardened the government stand.

Now, both the political as well as financial forces in Britain were opposed to any political or financial concessions to India. Winston Churchill strongly objected to the British government negotiating with the **'seditious fakir'**. **The Daily Mail,** a Conservative daily wrote- 'Without India, the British Commonwealth would fall to pieces. Commercially, economically, politically and geographically it is our greatest imperial asset. To imperil our hold on it would be the worst treason any Briton could commit'.

Accordingly, when Gandhi sailed for London on 29th August 1931, nothing much was expected from the Conference as the great **Gujarati poet Meghani** wrote: 'Chchello katoro jerno aa: pi jao Bapu!' (Even this last cup of poison, you must drink Bapu!) The Congress had boycotted the First RTC in which Ramsay Macdonald had made the novel offer of responsible government at the centre but with a series of 'reservations and safeguards' to maintain the British control over defence, external affairs and economy. Accepting this as the framework for discussion, Gandhi participated as the sole Congress representative at the second RTC.

Participants

A majority of Indian delegates were handpicked by the government and comprised of the loyalists, communalists, careerists, lace hunters, big landlords and representatives of princely states. They were used by the government to neutralise Gandhi over the basic question of freedom for India.

Most of the prominent participants of the first session returned to attend the second session. The new faces included great nationalists and political leaders like **Gandhi, Madan Mohan Malviya, Mrs. Sarojini Naidu and Ali Imam, the great poet Muhammed Iqbal, capitalist GD Birla and SK Dutta (a prominent Indian Christian)**.

Chief spokesman of the British government was Sir Samuel Hoare.

The princes, led by Maharaja of Patiala, now revised their ideas and wanted a confederation instead of a federation. However, some of the premier states remained firm on the idea of a federation.

Outcome

The session ended with MacDonald's announcement. It was as follows:

- Two Muslim provinces—Sind and NWFP

- Formation of Indian Consultative Committee
- Three Expert committees—finance, franchise and states;
- The prospect of a unilateral communal award if Indians failed to agree

Gandhi suggested the same scheme as earlier suggested by the Nehru Report. Aware of the complexity of the communal problem, Gandhi also suggested that the communal settlement be kept pending till the constitutional settlement had been arrived at. This suggestion gravely displeased the minority representatives and hardened their stand further. The Muslim representatives continued to insist on separate electorates. Thus despite Gandhi giving a **carte blanche to Jinnah**, the communal problem could not be resolved.

In this way, Gandhi's participation in the second RTC ended in a fiasco. He found himself involved in endless squabbles with Muslim leaders, BR Ambedkar (leader of the Scheduled Castes) and the Indian Princes, much to the satisfaction of the British.

Changed British Government Sees Gandhi-Irwin Pact as a Mistake

Gandhi returned to a changed political situation in India. While Gandhi was away to London, the new Viceroy Lord Willingdon and the higher officials in India realised that the Delhi Pact had been a mistake-it had signed a truce with the Congress on equal footing and considerably lowered British prestige while raising that of the Congress. They now decided to reverse it all—**'no pact, no truce, no Gandhi-Viceroy meetings' became the watchwords** of the government. It was decided to launch a hard and immediate blow to the revival of national movement, and arrest Gandhi from the very outset.

The Government Unleashes a Reign of Terror

On 24th December 1931, Abdul Ghaffar Khan was arrested and the government severely repressed the Khudai Khidmatgars in NWFP along with the peasants (the Khudai Khidmatgars were leading the peasants against the government's policy of extracting revenue through cruel means). On 26th December 1931, Jawaharlal was arrested while he was going to Bombay to meet Gandhi.

Thus, on 28th December 1931 when Gandhi landed in Bombay, the political situation had completely changed. The Congress Working Committee met the next day and decided to resume the CDM. On 31st December 1931, when Gandhi asked the Viceroy for a meeting, he refused- a trend which was to continue for the next five years. Instead Gandhi was soon arrested on 4th January 1932.

On the same day, Viceroy Willingdon launched a new policy to deal with the movement known as the policy of **'Civil martial law'** which involved passing of sweeping ordinances **banning all Congress organisations**. Civil liberties ceased to exist and the authorities could seize people and property at will. Within a week, all leading Congressmen were put behind bars.

Civil Disobedience Again (Second Civil Disobedience, 1932–34)

Nevertheless, the CDM was restarted and received popular response from the angry people. However, the second phase of the CDM did not evoke a similar response from the people as the earlier phase had done and it became apparent that this movement would not continue for long. Moreover, the agitation and severe repression went hand in hand for some time. Bombay city and Bengal emerged as British nightmares due to the support of Gujarati traders and revolutionary terrorists respectively. Lakhs of people took to picketing of shops selling liquor and foreign cloth. Simultaneously, the government unleashed a reign of terror. Congress offices and funds were seized; all Gandhi ashrams were cordoned off by police. Nationalist literature was banned. Agitators were beaten up and their properties confiscated. Prisoners in jail were tortured and conditions in jail were made particularly harsh for women with the hope of scaring them away from satyagraha.

In the face of abominable torture, the movement was effectively crushed within a few months. Afterwards, it just lingered on.

Communal Award and Poona Pact

Communal Award (16th August 1932)

Meanwhile, on 16th August 1932, MacDonald announced the proposal on minority representation, known as the 'Communal Award' or **'MacDonald Award'**. It was yet another expression of the British policy of divide and rule. The Muslims, Sikhs and Christians had already been recognised as minorities. The communal award **declared even the depressed classes as minority and entitled them to separate electorate**, thus separating them from the rest of Hindus. It recommended to-

- double the existing seats in provincial legislatures;
- retain the system of separate electorate for the minorities;
- grant weightage to Muslims in provinces where they are in minority;
- reserve 3 percent seats for women in all provincial legislatures except in the NWFP;
- recognise depressed classes as minority community and make them entitled to the right of separate electorate; and
- allocate seats to labour, landlords, and traders and industrialists.

Congress Response

This was in sharp contrast to the constitution proposed by the Congress which would include in the fundamental rights a guarantee to the minorities of protection of their culture, religion and language. The Congress also rejected separate electorates and insisted on universal franchise. Communal electorates encouraged communal feelings (that separate communities have interests different from general body of Indians), and obstructed the growth of common national consciousness.

Yet, the Congress had earlier accepted separate electorates for Muslims as part of 1916 Congress League Pact, as a compromise with the Muslim League. Hence, even though the Congress strongly disagreed with the communal award, yet it was not in favour of changing the award without the consent of the depressed classes and so **it decided neither to accept nor reject it**.

Gandhi's Response

On the other hand, the award was strongly opposed by all nationalists, including Gandhi. Gandhi strongly opposed separate electorates for the depressed classes, whom he regarded as an integral part of Hindu society. He felt that it provided no answer to the degraded position of these classes. According to him, what was needed was not separate electorates but root and branch eradication of untouchability. But once the depressed classes were treated as separate community, the question of abolition of untouchability would not arise and would ensure that untouchables would remain untouchables in perpetuity.

Poona Pact (24th September 1932)

To persuade BR Ambedkar (the Depressed Classes leader), Gandhi, then in Yerawada jail, sat on a fast unto death on 20th September 1932. Almost everywhere, 20th September was observed as a day of fasting and prayer, temples and wells were thrown open to the depressed classes.

Ambedkar, MC Rajah and Madan Mohan Malaviya got together to persuade Gandhi. On 24th September 1932, the Poona Pact was concluded between Gandhi and Ambedkar, who had grown anxious to save Gandhi's life. The pact averted the political breach between the so-called 'Caste Hindus' and the 'Scheduled Castes'. The following was agreed upon:

- There would be no separate electorates for depressed classes and Ambedkar accepted the principle of joint electorates.
- Number of seats reserved for the depressed classes in provincial legislatures would be increased **from 71 in the Award to 147**; and to 18 per cent of the total in central legislature.
- A certain percentage of seats allotted to the general non-Muslim electorate would be reserved for the depressed classes.
- The Congress also accepted that even in civil services, the depressed classes would be given adequate representation.

Gandhi's Harijan Campaign

Gandhi was determined not to let the divisive intentions of government to succeed. From jail itself, he began his whirlwind campaign against untouchability:

- In September 1932, from jail itself, he formed the **All India Anti-Untouchability League**, and in 1933, he started the weekly, **Harijan**.
- In August 1933, he was released and shifted to **Satyagraha Ashram in Wardha** as he had vowed in 1930 not to return to Sabarmati ashram (Ahmedabad) unless swaraj was won.
- During November 1933 to July 1934, he conducted a Harijan tour of the country, propagating removal of untouchability and collecting money for his newly established **Harijan Sevak Sangh**.
- Gandhi also undertook two fasts—on 8th May and on 16th August 1934 to convince the people of the seriousness of his efforts. The fasts stirred emotions across the nationalist rank and file and the one on 8th May was even opposed by Kasturba Gandhi (his wife).

Throughout his campaign, Gandhi was accused by orthodox and reactionary elements for attacking Hinduism. These elements also offered to support the government against the Congress. The government in turn obliged them by defeating the **Temple Entry Bill in August 1934**.

During his Harijan work, Gandhi stressed on certain themes. He argued that untouchability had no sanction in the Hindu Shastras. And the Shastras should be ignored if they went against human dignity. He also believed that there was nothing sinful about Varnashram as there was about untouchability. Another theme in Gandhi's speeches was the need for caste Hindus to do 'penance' and make amends for the injustice done to the Harijans over centuries. This also explains why he was not hostile to his critics, including Ambedkar, who distrusted him. He hoped to win them over some day by appealing to their reason and their hearts.

The Harijan work of Gandhi and the Congress also gradually carried the message of nationalism to the Harijans (who were also agricultural labourers in many parts of India) and ensured their participation in national and peasant struggles.

Third Round Table Conference (17th November to 24th December 1932)

The third and last round table conference began on 17th November. It was attended by only 46 delegates and was **boycotted** by the Indian National Congress as well as the Labour Party in Britain.

Participants

Main participants included Agha Khan III, BR Ambedkar, NM Joshi, Ramasami Mudaliar, Begum Jahanara Shahnawaz, TB Sapru, Sir Purshottamdas Thakurdas among others.

Outcome

After the Third Round Table Conference, the British government prepared a **White Paper** on the new constitution of India. The White Paper, published in March 1933 contained four major proposals—Federation, Provincial Autonomy (responsible government in provinces), dyarchy at the centre and safeguards which vested special powers in the central and provincial executive. The Paper was criticised by all Indian parties as it fell short of complete independence.

Consequently, a Joint Select Committee was appointed under the chairmanship of the Marquess of **Linlithgow**. In November 1934, the Committee produced a majority report. On the basis of this report, a bill was introduced in the British Parliament which was passed by substantial majority. On receiving the Royal assent on 2nd August 1935, it became the famous Government of India Act of 1935 (Covered in the upcoming chapter).

Decline of Civil Disobedience Movement

The Second CDM did not evoke a similar response from the people as the earlier phase had done and was also given a heavy blow by government repression. With the weakening of the movement, there emerged voices within the Congress advocating a return to council entry and revival of Swarajist Party. Congressmen such as Asaf Ali, S. Satyamurty and Dr. MA Ansari were in favour of council entry. In 1933 Satyamurty formed the Madras Swaraj Party. On the other hand, council entry was opposed by Acharya Narendra Dev and Purushottamdas Tondon. Both the sides tried to tilt the congress opinion though not without Gandhi's consent.

Several big Indian business groups also began to collaborate with the British. For instance, the Bombay Mill owners concluded the **Lees-Mody Pact** in October 1933, siding with Lancashire in the presence of fear of Japanese competition (From 1932 onwards, GD Birla and Thakurdas also pressed the Congress for a compromise).

In this context, Gandhi in jail now began to think in terms of truce and compromise. In May 1933, he temporarily suspended the movement and **formally withdrew it in April 1934**. Once again, he advised the nationalists to direct their energies towards constructive work, which now incorporated Harijan work as its central theme (this was Gandhi's response to the MacDonald Award of 1932). Yet another section of the Congress decided to go back to council politics.

Significance of Civil Disobedience Movement

True, another heroic struggle of the people of India had come to an end without achieving its immediate goal. Gandhi's decision to withdraw the movement dismayed many including Jawaharlal. Subhas Chandra Bose and Vithalbhai Patel (elder brother of Sardar Patel) declared that **'the Mahatma as a political leader had failed'**.

Equally true was the fact that Viceroy Willingdon and his men had failed to understand the nature of Indian National Movement. Brutal repression of the Indian people had completely shattered their faith in the British rule and further strengthened their resolve for freedom.

True, the CDM failed to achieve its immediate goal of purna swaraj, yet the sacrifice of the people had not been in vain. The socio-economic demands of the people, particularly the peasants were incorporated in the congress programme for the first time and signalled the growing assertiveness of these sections of Indian society.

Once again, the prisoners released from jail in 1934 were given a hero's welcome. Once again, it was time to rest and reorganise. That the people had only been cowed down by brute force and still had faith in the Congress was demonstrated by the election results of 1937, in which the congress swept the polls in most provinces.

> **HN Barailsford,** a British journalist assessing the result of the movement wrote -'the Indians had freed their own minds, they had won independence in their hearts'.

Aftermath

In 1935, the Government of India Act was passed which was retrogressive in many aspects, having been passed at a time when the British seemed triumphant. However, the Government's victory was short-lived as the Congress swept the polls in most provinces in 1937 general elections.

Another significant development was the **emergence of the Left** as the Civil Disobedience had raised the expectations of the people but they could not be met with the Gandhian or even revolutionary strategy. Hence, a group of people disillusioned by Gandhi as well as the revolutionaries, began to move towards the left alternatives—the Communists and the Socialists.

Jawaharlal Nehru emerged as the new leader with his radical socio-economic program. By 1934, a socialist ginger group within the Congress had been formed and the Congress was forced to make concessions to the left, if it wanted to retain control.

Prelim Capsule

Civil Disobedience Movement (1930–34)

Date	Event	Important Details
December 1929	**Lahore Congress Session**	Congress authorised to start CDM.
January 1930	**Gandhi's Eleven Points**	Gandhi placed 'Eleven Points' of administrative reforms before Lord Irwin and tried to negotiate with the government once again before launching the CDM.
12th March 1930	**Civil Disobedience begins**	Gandhi started his historic **'Dandi March'** from Sabarmati Ashram to Dandi (240 miles, 24 days), accompanied with 78 followers and thus began CDM.
6th April 1930	**Gandhi breaks salt law**	Gandhi reached Dandi, picked up a handful of salt and broke the salt law as a symbol of defiance to British laws. **C Rajagopalachari** led a salt march from Trichinopoly to Vedaranyam on the Tanjore coast. Forms of protest included salt manufacture and resignations on a wide scale, boycott of foreign cloth and liquor, non-payment of land revenue in Ryotwari areas, anti-Chowkidari tax movement in zamindari areas (Bihar) and Forest Satyagraha, i.e. peaceful violation of forest laws.
18th April 1930	**Chittagong armoury raid**	Carried out by the Bengal revolutionaries led by Surya Sen.
—	**Role of Khan Abdul Ghaffar Khan**	Khan had been active in NWFP for several years and had set up a band of non-violent revolutionaries, the **Khudai Khidmatgars** (Servants of God) or the Red Shirts (because of the colour of their shirts) who played an active role in the CDM.
—	**Anti-Cunningham Circular agitation**	In Assam, a powerful agitation by students against the infamous **'Cunningham Circular'** was launched which prohibited students from participating in political activities associated with the national movement.
—	**No-revenue No-rent campaign**	Was started in UP, Agra and Rae Bareilly emerged as important centres.
—	—	**Participation of women** was the most remarkable feature of CDM.

November 1930–January 1931	**First RTC (London)**	Chaired by British PM **Ramsay MacDonald** of Labour Party. First conference between the Indians and the British as equals. **Boycotted by Congress** as it had launched the CDM, its proceedings proved to be quite meaningless and the British government grew anxious to secure Congress participation.
		It recommended- 1) Formation of an All India Federation of British Indian Provinces and the Indian States. 2) A responsible government at the centre with certain 'reservations and safeguards' for the transitional period. (In all, three RTCs were held in London to discuss the Indian constitutional question. INC participated only in the 2nd RTC. Ambedkar attended all the three RTCs).
25th January 1931	**Gandhi released**	Truce period begins.
14th February 1931	**Gandhi –Irwin talk initiated**	By the efforts of **Sir TB Sapru** and **Sir MR Jayakar**.
5th March 1931	**Gandhi-Irwin Pact (Delhi Pact), End of First Phase of CDM**	The fortnight long talks culminated in the Delhi Pact. In context to the pact, Sarojini Naidu termed them as 'The Two Mahatmas'. The pact was signed by Gandhi on behalf of the Congress and by Irwin on behalf of the government. First pact to be signed between the Congress and the government on an equal footing. As per the Pact, the **Congress agreed to withdraw the CDM** immediately and **participate in the next RTC**.
29th March 1931	**Special Congress Session at Karachi**	Was called to ratify the Gandhi-Irwin Pact. Was presided by Sardar Patel. Adopted resolutions on **Fundamental Rights** (Jawaharlal Nehru with the help of M. N. Roy) and **National Economic Programme**.
April–Aug 1931	**Change of Government**	Lord Irwin replaced by Lord Willingdon as Viceroy. MacDonald's Labour Cabinet was replaced by a new coalition government dominated by the **Conservatives**. Sir Samuel Hoare became Secretary of State for India. Changed government adopted a hardened stand, saw Delhi pact as a mistake.
September–December 1931	**Second RTC (London)**	Congress participated and was represented by Gandhi. Gandhi gave a carte blanche to Jinnah, yet the communal problem could not be resolved.

September 1931	**Government Repression**	While Gandhi was away to London, Willingdon decided to launch a hard and immediate blow to the revival of national movement. Policy of **'Civil martial law'** was launched & involved passing of sweeping ordinances banning all Congress organisations. Gandhi was arrested as soon as he returned from the RTC (4 Jan 1932).
28th December 1931	**Gandhi returned from London**	Gandhi returned to a changed political situation.
29th December 1931	**Second CDM launched**	4 Jan 1932, Gandhi was arrested and the movement was effectively crushed within a few months. Afterwards it just lingered on.
16th August 1932	**Communal Award (MacDonald Award)**	MacDonald announced the proposal on minority representation, known as the Communal Award. It declared depressed classes as minority and entitled them to separate electorate. The Congress strongly disagreed with the communal award, yet it decided neither to accept nor reject it. 20 Sep 1932, Gandhi (in Yerawada jail) sat on a **fast unto death** to oppose the Communal Award.
24th September 1932	**Poona Pact**	Was concluded between Gandhi and Ambedkar with the efforts of Ambedkar, MC Rajah and Madan Mohan Malaviya.
November–December 1932	**Third RTC**	It was attended by only 46 delegates and was **boycotted** by the INC as well as the Labour Party in Britain. In March 1933, a **White Paper** was published & contained four major proposals-Federation, Provincial Autonomy, dyarchy at the centre and safeguards. White Paper later became the basis of the Govt. of India Act of 1935.
April 1934	**CDM withdrawn**	In May 1933, Gandhi temporarily suspended the movement and formally withdrew it in April 1934.

Previous Years' Questions – Preliminary Exam

1. The Poona pact which was signed between the British government and Mahatma Gandhi in 1932 provided for **[UPSC 1997]**
   (a) The creation of Dominion status for India
   (b) Separate electorates for the Muslims
   (c) Separate electorates for the Harijans
   (d) Joint electorates with reservation of Harijans
2. With reference to Indian freedom struggle, which one of the following statements is not correct? **[UPSC 2003]**
   (a) The Rowlatt Act aroused a wave of popular indignation and led to the Jallianwala Bagh massacre.
   (b) Subhash Chandra Bose formed the Forward Bloc.
   (c) Bhagat Singh was one of the founders of Hindustan Republican Socialist Association.
   (d) In 1931, the congress session at Karachi opposed Gandhi Irwin pact.
3. Who among the following drafted the resolution on Fundamental Rights for the Karachi session of Congress in 1931? **[UPSC 2005]**
   (a) Dr BR Ambedkar
   (b) Jawaharlal Nehru
   (c) Dr. Rajendra Prasad
   (d) Sardar Vallabhbhai Patel
4. At which Congress Session was the Working Committee authorised to launch a programme of Civil Disobedience? **[UPSC 2005]**
   (a) Bombay (b) Lahore
   (c) Lucknow (d) Tripuri
5. Consider the following statements: **[UPSC 2005]**
   1. In the first Round Table Conference, Dr Ambedkar demanded separate electorates for the depressed classes.
   2. In the Poona Pact, special provisions for representation of the depressed class people in the local bodies and civil services were made.
   3. The Indian National Congress did not take part in the Third Round Table Conference.

   Which of the statements given above are correct? Choose the correct answer from the following options.
   (a) 1 and 2 (b) 2 and 3
   (c) 1 and 3 (d) 1, 2 and 3
6. Consider the following statements: **[UPSC 2009]**
   1. The discussions in the Third Round Table Conference eventually led to the passing of the Government of India Act of 1935.
   2. The Government of India Act of 1935 provided for the establishment of an all India Federation to be based on Union of the provinces of British India and the Princely States.

   Which of the statement(s) given above is/are correct? Choose the correct answer from the following options.
   (a) 1 only
   (b) 2 only
   (c) Both 1 and 2
   (d) Neither 1 nor 2
7. Which one of the following began with the Dandi March? **[UPSC 2009]**
   (a) Home Rule Movement
   (b) Non-Cooperation Movement
   (c) Civil Disobedience Movement
   (d) Quit India Movement
8. For the Karachi session of Indian National Congress in 1931 presided over by Sardar Patel, who drafted the resolution on Fundamental Rights and Economic Programme? **[UPSC 2010]**
   (a) Mahatma Gandhi
   (b) Pandit Jawaharlal Nehru
   (c) Dr Rajendra Prasad
   (d) Dr B.R. Ambedkar
9. Why did Mahatma Gandhi undertake the fast unto death in 1932? **[UPSC 2012]**
   (a) Round table conference failed to satisfy Indian political aspirations.
   (b) Congress and Muslim League had differences of opinion.
   (c) Ramsay MacDonald announced the Communal Award.

(d) None of the statements (a) , (b) and (c) given above is correct in this context.

10. Who among the following organised a march on the Tanjore coast to break the Salt law in April, 1930? **[UPSC 2015]**
    (a) V Chidambaram Pillai
    (b) C Rajagopalachari
    (c) K. Kamaraj
    (d) Annie Besant

11. With reference to the British colonial rule in India, consider the following statements: **[UPSC 2019]**
    1. Mahatma Gandhi was instrumental in the abolition of the system of 'indentured labour'.
    2. In Lord Chelmsford's War Conference', Mahatma Gandhi did not support the resolution on recruiting Indians for World War.
    3. Consequent upon the breaking of Salt Law by Indian people, the Indian National Congress was declared illegal by the colonial rulers.

    Which of the statements given above are correct?
    (a) 1 and 2 only (b) 1 and 3 only
    (c) 2 and 3 only (d) 1, 2 and 3

12. The Gandhi-Irwin Pact included which of the following? **[UPSC 2020]**
    1. Invitation to Congress to participate in the Round Table Conference
    2. Withdrawal of Ordinances promulgated in connection with the Civil Disobedience Movement
    3. Acceptance of Gandhi's suggestion for enquiry into police excesses
    4. Release of only those prisoners who were not charged with violence

    Select the correct answer using the code given below
    (a) 1 only (b) 1, 2 and 4 only
    (c) 3 only (d) 2, 3 and 4 only

Previous Years' Questions – Main Exam

1. Analyse Mahatma Gandhi's main demands presented to Irwin. How did salt emerge as the central issue for launching the Satyagraha? **[UPSC 1988]**
2. What was the Gandhi Irwin pact? Why was it signed and what were its consequences? **[UPSC 1988]**
3. Why did Mahatma Gandhi launch Civil Disobedience Movement? Analyse the intensity of the movement in different parts of India. **[UPSC 1992]**
4. What was the McDonald Award? How was it modified and with what results? **[UPSC 1993]**
5. In what way did the Civil Disobedience Movement affect the different provinces of India? How did it foster Peasant Movement in India? **[UPSC 1995]**
6. What were the salient features of Gandhi Irwin pact? **[UPSC 1997]**
7. Write a short note on: Communal Award **[UPSC 1998]**
8. Why did Mahatma Gandhi launched the Salt Satyagraha in 1930 and with what results? **[UPSC 2001]**
9. Write a short note on: Dandi March **[UPSC 2002]**
10. Bring out the constructive programmes of Mahatma Gandhi during Non-Cooperation Movement and Civil Disobedience Movement. **[UPSC 2021]**

Answers

Previous Years' Questions – Preliminary Exam

1.	(d)	2.	(d)	3.	(b)	4.	(b)	5.	(c)
6.	(c)	7.	(c)	8.	(b)	9.	(c)	10.	(b)
11.	(b)	12.	(b)						

18 CONSTITUTIONAL DEVELOPMENT—PART 3 (1921–35)

Earlier in this book, you have learnt about constitutional developments during the period 1892–1920. In this chapter, you will learn about the constitutional developments during the period 1920–35. This will help you to understand the basic character of the Indian Constitution as it stands today, the story of its evolution and the challenges faced by the Indian people particularly with reference to minority problems in dealing with constitutional reforms. Finally, you will learn how the freedom struggle and constitutional development went hand in hand and proved complementary to each other.

Factors Leading to the Act of 1935

Dissatisfaction with Reforms of 1919

The Act of 1919 suffered from major defects including the introduction of dyarchy which proved to be unworkable and it failed on many fronts. Failure of dyarchy and failure of the government to establish self-governing institutions evoked widespread disappointment with the new Act and gave rise to a new movement led by Mahatma Gandhi in the form of 'non-violent non-cooperation movement'. It soon gathered momentum and grew into a fullfledged agitation demanding complete transfer of power into Indian hands.

National Movement During 1920–27

The disillusionment with the Act of 1919 contributed to a great extent to the growth of the national movement during 1920–27.

Reform Proposals During 1920–27

Disillusioned with the Act of 1919, the Indians put forward many reform proposals in the period between 1920 and 1927. In 1921, a non-official resolution was introduced in the central legislative assembly demanding the establishment of full responsible government in the provinces, but to no avail. In 1924, Swarajists led by Motilal Nehru introduced an amendment demanding the framing of an **Indian Constitution** by an Indian Constituent Assembly. Motilal also moved a resolution in favour of a **Round Table Conference** of all Indian, European and Anglo Indian interests to recommend a scheme of full responsible government. This forced the government of India to appoint a **Reforms Enquiry Committee** under **Sir Alexander Muddiman** to enquire into the working of the Act of 1919 and suggest remedies. Around this time, Muslim League met at Lahore under the presidentship of MA Jinnah. It also demanded the establishment of full responsible government, a federal constitution with full autonomy for provinces and adequate representation for minorities through separate electorates.

Simon Commission (November 1927)

The all white commission to enquire into the working of the Government of India under the Act of 1919 and suggest fresh reforms was unanimously rejected by the nationalists. **Lord Birkenhead** (1924–28), the then Secretary of State, then threw a challenge to Indians to produce a constitution acceptable to all sections of Indian society. After this challenge, the following proposals emerged:

- By Muslim League- **Delhi Proposals** (December 1927)
- By Congress and other parties- **Nehru Report** (August 1928)
- By British Government- **White Paper** (which became the basis for the Act of 1935)

Nehru Committee Report (August 1928)

The Nehru Report firmly laid down that full responsible government was not to be considered as a remote step but as an immediate step, as opposed to the principle of gradual advancement envisaged by the Act of 1919 and demanded **Dominion status** within British Empire.

Within the Congress itself, young nationalists led by Jawaharlal Nehru and Subhas Chandra Bose objected to the Nehru Report because of its acceptance of Dominion Status. In August 1928, the **'Independence of India League'** was launched by J. Nehru with the support of Subhas Chandra Bose as a pressure group within the Congress with the aim of countering the concept of Dominion Status and pleading for complete independence of India from the British.

Jinnah's Fourteen Points (March 1929)

Jinnah after consulting the Muslim leaders formulated the 'Fourteen Points' for safeguarding the rights and interests of the Muslims in any future constitution of the country.

Congress Gives Ultimatum to Government

Calcutta Session of Congress (December 1928)

During the Congress Session at Calcutta, December 1928 (presided by Motilal Nehru), the Congress resolved in one voice that in case the government did not accept the Nehru Report **by 31st December 1929**, the Congress would declare **complete independence as its goal** and would also launch a civil disobedience movement to achieve that goal.

Congress Adopts Purna Swaraj as Goal

Lahore Session of Congress (December 1929)

On 31st December 1929, the annual session of the Congress was held at Lahore, the capital city of Punjab. The Congress announced that the Nehru Report had ceased to be valid and that Purna Swaraj was now the goal for India. It was also announced that Civil Disobedience Movement will be launched under the leadership of Gandhi.

Civil Disobedience Movement

First Round Table Conference (12th November 1930, London)

Meanwhile, the First Round Table Conference, first conference between the Indians and the British as equals, took place in November 1930 in London to discuss the Simon Commission Reports. The Congress boycotted the Round Table Conference and its proceedings proved to be quite meaningless.

Gandhi participates in the Second Round Table Conference (December 1931)

Gandhi's participation in the Second Round Table Conference ended in a fiasco. He found himself involved in endless squabbles with Muslim leaders, BR Ambedkar (leader of the Scheduled Castes) and the Indian Princes. The session ended with MacDonald's announcement of the prospect of a unilateral communal award if Indians failed to agree.

Communal Award (or MacDonald Award,16th Aug 1932)

Meanwhile, on 16th August 1932, MacDonald announced the proposal on minority representation, known as the 'Communal Award' or 'MacDonald Award'. The communal award declared the **depressed classes** as minority and entitled them to separate electorates.

Poona Pact (24th September 1932)

As per the Pact, Ambedkar accepted joint electorates in return for greater reservation for depressed classes in central legislature and civil services.

The Third Round Table Conference (17th November to 24th December 1932)

As an outcome of the third session of Round Table Conference, a **White Paper** was issued in March 1933 giving details of the basis of new constitution of India. Under the supervision of Samuel Hoare, the Secretary of State for India, the proposed reforms took the form of Government of India Act 1935.

The Government of India Act of 1935

The Government of India Act 1935 was based on the White Paper on Indian Constitution prepared by the British Government after the Third Round Table Conference. Falling short of complete independence, the White Paper was criticised by all Indian parties. Yet, the proposed reforms took the form of Government of India Act 1935. It contained **four major provisions**—All India Federation, Provincial Autonomy, dyarchy at the centre and safeguards which vested special powers in the central and provincial executive.

The Act was a **bulky** and elaborate document as it dealt with a highly-complicated type of federal constitution and provided legal safeguards against misbehaviour of Indian ministers and legislators. Another notable feature of the Act was the **absence of a preamble** (whereas the Act of 1919 had a preamble based on Montagu Declaration of 20th August 1917).

The basic conception of the Act of 1935 was that the government of India was the government of the Crown, conducted by authorities deriving functions directly from the Crown.

Sources of the Act

The principle sources of the Act included the following:

- The Simon Commission Report
- The Report of All Parties Conference (Nehru Report)
- Discussions at the three Round Table Conferences
- The White Paper
- The Joint Select Committee Report
- The Lothian Report which determined the electoral provisions of the Act

Main Provisions Regarding the Provincial Part

- **Provincial autonomy** It meant that all provincial departments would be controlled by elected members. For the first time, the Act recognised **provinces as separate legal entity**, free from the direction and control of the GOI and the Secretary of State except for specific purposes. The provinces derived their power and authority **directly from the British Crown**.
- **Abolition of dyarchy in provinces** It also meant that dyarchy in the provinces was abolished and replaced by provincial autonomy. The distinction between Reserved and Transferred subjects was abolished and **full responsible government was established subject to certain safeguards**.
- **Provincial legislatures were further expanded** Bicameral legislature was introduced in 6 provinces—Bengal, Madras, Bombay, United Provinces, Bihar and Assam.
- **Creation of new provinces** New provinces of Sind and Orissa were created. In this way, the Act provided for the establishment of in all 11 provinces including Sind and Orissa. Burma was separated from India.
- **Franchise** Franchise was lowered, though it still remained tied to **property qualifications**.
- **Communal electorates** Unfortunately, the principles of communal electorates and weightage were further extended.
- **Special powers of Governors** The Act gave arbitrary powers (under the phraseology of 'safeguards and special responsibilities') to the Governor to act 'in his discretion' in matters like summoning of the Legislature, appointment of ministers, giving or withholding his assent to bills. The Governors were also invested with special executive powers in matters concerning law and order and interests of minorities, backward classes, Indian princes and British commercial interests. The Governors could also issue ordinances or enact Governor's Acts.

Main Provisions Regarding the Federal Part

- **Proposal for an All India Federation** The Act prescribed federal structure for the Government of India. It was to comprise of provinces (Governors' and Chief Commissioners' provinces) and Indian States with federal central and provincial legislatures. For the States, accession to Federation was voluntary and Federation could not be formed unless two conditions were met:
    - States entitled to at least half of the seats (i.e. 52 seats) allotted to the states in the proposed Council of States should agree to join the federation.
    - The aggregate population of states in the above category should be at least 50 per cent of the total population of all Indian states.

(Since the above conditions were not met, the **proposed federation never came up**. The Central government carried on upto 1946 as per the provisions of the **Government of Indian Act 1919)**.

- **Dyarchy at the centre** Dyarchy, abolished in the provinces, was proposed for the Centre. Reserved departments under the Governor General included Defence, Foreign Affairs, Ecclesiastical Affairs and Excluded and Partially Excluded Areas (tribal areas) to be administered by the GG through Counsellors appointed by him and responsible only to him. Transferred departments, subjected to safeguards, were to be administered by the GG on the advice of popular ministers answerable to the federal legislature.
- **Bicameral Central Legislature (Federal Legislature)** The Central Legislature was to consist of His Majesty represented by the GG and two houses—the Council of State and the Federal Assembly. (Both Houses were to comprise of representatives from both the British India as well as the Indian States. While the representatives from British India were to be elected by the people, those of the States were to be nominated by the rulers. The States were also given disproportionate weightage. In short, **the States were expected to act as checks upon the nationalists**).
    - The Council of States (or the Upper House) was to have a maximum of 260 members—consisting of 156 members from British India and 104 members from the Indian States, to be nominated by the rulers concerned. It was to be a permanent body with one-third of its members being vacated and renewed triennially.
    - The Federal Assembly (or the Lower House) was to have a maximum of 375 members consisting of 250 members from British India and 125 from the Indian States. The Assembly's tenure was normally for a period of 5 years.
- **Other Federal Institutions** The Act laid down the setting up of **a Federal Bank (Reserve Bank of India)** and a **Federal Court** established in 1935 and 1937 respectively. The Act of 1935 vested the control of Railway in a new authority called **Federal Railway Authority**, free from control of ministers and councillors. The authority comprised seven members who reported directly to the Governor-General, thus assuring the British stakeholders of the railways that their investment was safe.
- **Extension of Separate Electorates** Separate electorates and the system of weightage were further extended to include not only **General (Hindus and Scheduled Castes), Muslims, Sikhs, Europeans, Indian Christians and Anglo Indian electorates** but also **women** (General), Sikh women in Punjab, Mohammedan women, Indian Christian women in Madras, Anglo Indian women in Bengal besides electorates for **Commerce and Industry, Landlords, labour, University, Backward areas and tribes,** etc.
- **Abolition of Indian Council** The Act abolished the Indian Council of the Secretary of State (established by the GOI of 1858) on account of much agitation in India against its anti-India policies. The Secretary of State was now given advisers who might or might not be consulted, except in respect to the Services.

Peculiarities of the Federal System Contemplated Under the Act of 1935

The federal system proposed under the Act of 1935 was perhaps the most complex ever known in the history of federalism (MV Pylee). It was an attempt to satisfy several diverse and contradictory interests at the cost of good federalism.

- **Ill-conceived Federation**
    (a) The Federation under the Act tried to bring together two disparate elements—Indian States under the autocratic rule of the Princes and British India provinces enjoying responsible government to some extent. Such a grouping was bound to be ridden with squabbles.
    (b) Moreover, the process prescribed for the formation of the Federation was also illogical. Joining the federation was kept voluntary for the States but compulsory for British India. Again, the federation could not be formed unless a certain number of the states had acceded to it. In order to induce the States to join the federation, they were given unduly large representation in the Central Legislature (the Indian States constituting merely 24 per cent of total population were given 40 per cent of seats in Council of State and 33.33 per cent of the seats in the Assembly).
    (c) Another odd feature of the proposed bicameral legislature was that while the representatives of Indian Provinces were to be elected, those of Indian states were to be nominated by the ruling princes. The whole purpose was to use the nominated representatives of the States as a **solid conservative bloc** to counter the weight of the elected representatives of British India.
    (d) Oddly enough, election to the Council of States was direct and that to Federal Assembly, indirect.
- **Instrument of Accession** This document was devised to rope in the Indian States into the proposed federation. But it was not a uniform document and could vary from ruler to ruler, thus creating as many federal compacts as there were Indian Sates (there were some 600 Princely States!).
- **Dyarchy at the center** The government at the centre was not to be a fully responsible government. The principle of dyarchy introduced in the provinces under the Act of 1919 was now transplanted in the centre. Important departments like defence, External affairs and lion's share of the budget were kept as reserved (the GG had control over non-votable items, comprising about 80 per cent of the budget).
- **Discretionary powers of the GG** The GG had discretionary powers over four subjects—Defence, External Affairs, Ecclesiastical Affairs and Excluded and Partially excluded Areas (Tribal Areas). The Federal Legislature had no right to question the actions of the GG with respect to these subjects.
- **Larger representation to States** The Indian States were given larger representation in the Federal Legislature than they deserved on the basis of their population. While the provinces were to send elected representatives, the Sates were given the freedom to send their nominees.
- **Quasi-federal elements** The Governor General was given vast powers of intervention in the affairs of the Provincial Governments which greatly modified the federal features to unitary elements. As a result, some authors have classified the government formed under the Act as 'quasi-federal'.
- **Three Lists** The legislative powers were divided into three elaborate lists—the Central, the Provincial and the Concurrent Lists.
- **Residuary Powers vested in the GG** The residuary legislative powers are normally located in the Centre or in the units. But under the Act of 1935, it was vested in the GG. The residuary powers in case of Indian States were vested in the Rulers thereof.

Thus, the powers vested in the GG made him the **pivot of the entire constitution**.

Criticisms of the Act of 1935

- Dominion Status was not introduced by the Act of 1935. Thus, the Act was meant for the transition period from responsible government to complete independence, with the transition period not defined.
- The Act was based on two basic principles namely, federation and parliamentary system. The Federation principle was introduced with a built-in unitary bias and was seriously distorted by the provisions of safeguards and special responsibility.
- Dyarchy at the centre meant fully responsible government at the centre was not introduced.
- The representatives of the States to the federal legislature were to be appointed directly by the Princes (and were to be used to check the nationalists).
- Franchise still remained tied to property qualifications. Though the number of voters increased from 5 million (in 1919) to 30 million (in 1935), yet the franchise was limited to only one-sixth of the adults. Only 14 per cent of the total population in British India was given the right to vote.
- The vicious system of communal and caste electorates was further extended.
- The special powers of the Governor ensured that both political and economic power remained concentrated in British hands.
- India's constitutional status as a dependency did not improve as the Federation of India was not intended to be a sovereign legislature. It could not amend the Indian constitution and the right remained with the British Parliament. Responsibility for Indian administration still remained with the British Parliament.
- The Secretary of State retained control over various All India Services.

Indian Reactions to the Act of 1935

- The Congress criticised and rejected the Act of 1935 and instead demanded the convening of a Constituent Assembly elected on the basis of adult franchise to frame a constitution for independent India. The Congress criticised the Act on the following grounds-
  - Dominion status was denied and remained a distant dream.
  - Provincial autonomy under the Act was placed under serious limitations.
  - Safeguards and special powers were a clever constitutional device to keep Indians from uniting and delay granting of complete independence.
  - Though these provisions were made for transition period, the transition period itself was not defined.
  - Universal adult franchise was not introduced. Property qualifications and separate electorates were criticised as violative of democratic right of the people of India.
  - The Act did not represent the will and aspirations of the people of India.
  - While the representatives from British India were to be elected by the people, those of the States were to be nominated by the rulers. The nationalists demanded that the representatives of states should also be elected instead of being nominated.
  - Jawaharlal Nehru, the then Congress President declared that with the new constitution, **'we are provided with a car, all brakes and no engine'**.

- Liberals also criticised the Act, but were willing to make the reforms work as a step towards responsible government.
- The Muslim League also criticised the Act, but it was also ready to give it a chance. Jinnah denounced the act as 'thoroughly rotten, fundamentally bad and totally unacceptable'.

Linlithgow, Chairman of the Joint Parliamentary Committee on the Act of 1935 and Viceroy of India from 1936 had stated, 'the Act had been framed because we thought that was the best way of maintaining British influence in India. It is no part of our policy, I take it, to expedite in India constitutional changes for their own sake or to hurry the handing over of the controls to Indian hands...'

British Motives Behind the Act

Through the Act,the British wanted to weaken the national movement by integrating large segment of the movement into colonial, constitutional and administrative fold. They hoped to revive the political standing of constitutionalists and moderates who had lost popularity during the CDM. It was an attempt to offer concessions and divide the nationalist ranks on the basis of constitutionalist vs. non-constitutionalist and Right vs. Left. It was hoped that by luring the constitutionalists into the parliamentary game, the leftists would break away from the Congress seeing all this as a compromise with imperialism. Once isolated from the right wing, the leftists could then be crushed through police measures.

It was hoped that once the Congressmen tasted power, they would be reluctant to go back to politics of sacrifice. Provincial autonomy would create powerful provincial leaders, thus provincialising the Congress and weakening its central leadership. Extension of separate electorates was an attempt to keep the Indians disunited while simultaneously gaining the support of certain communities, ensuring the perpetuation of British rule in India.

With the above motives in mind, the British reversed the policy of suppression (followed during CDM) and replaced it with the policy of constitutional concessions by passing the Act of 1935.

The Act in Operation

The GOI Bill received the Royal Assent in August 1935. The proposal for setting up the Federation of India never materialised and the Central Government continued to be governed by the provisions of the Act of 1919. The Federal Bank (the Reserve Bank of India) and the Federal Court were established in 1935 and 1937 respectively. Provincial Autonomy came into force on 1st April 1937. First Elections under the Act were also held in 1937.

Conclusion

With all its limitations, it cannot be denied that the Act of 1935 helped India move towards parliamentary democracy. Though the Congress bitterly condemned the Act, yet it decided to participate in the Elections of 1937 with the declared aim of revealing how unpopular the Act was. In the next chapter we will understand how this stand was in no way a compromise to the nationalist's demand for freedom. We will also understand the attitude of constitutionalists within the INC and the challenges they faced.

Critical Analysis: Act of 1935

Federal Executive under the Act of 1935 The Federal Executive was to consist of the Governor General, the Counsellors of the GG and the Council of Ministers.Since the full-fledged **federal executive as envisaged by the Act never came into existence**, the Counsellors and the Council of Ministers need not be discussed. The role of the GG was unique for any executive head. He was the GG of India with respect to British India and the Crown Representative with respect to the Indian States. He was appointed by His Majesty generally for a period of 5 years. He drew an annual salary of ₹2,50,800 charged on the Consolidated Fund of India.

The GG had **discretionary powers** over four subjects—Defence, External Affairs, Ecclesiastical Affairs and Excluded and Partially excluded Areas (Tribal Areas). He could also exercise his individual judgement in a large number of subjects like law and order, safeguarding interests of minorities, members of the public services, Indian princes and British commercial interests.

It is clear that these powers were not seen as inconsistent with the basic principle of responsible government. It is clear that there was no genuine intention on the part of the British to transfer any real power to the Indians.

The Central Legislature The central legislature as envisaged by the Act never came into existence and hence a discussion on its provisions is of no great value. Yet it reveals the complexity of the political scenario of the time.

The Central Legislature was to consist of His Majesty represented by the **GG and two houses**—the Council of State and the Federal Assembly. The Council of State (or the Upper House) was to have a maximum of 260 members, consisting of 156 members from British India and 104 members from the Indian States, to be nominated by the rulers concerned. It was to be a permanent body with one-third of its members being vacated and renewed triennially. The Federal Assembly (or the Lower House) was to have a maximum of 375 members, consisting of 250 members from British India and 125 from the Indian States. The Assembly's tenure was normally for a period of 5 years.

The bicameral legislature was a curious mixture of many interests. The States were given an unduly large representation.

The Governor General and the Central Legislature The powers of the GG in relation to the Legislature were so overwhelming that the latter was more a legislature by courtesy than by its powers. In addition to veto powers, he had the power to issue ordinances or permanent laws in the form of **Governor General's Acts** with respect to certain subjects even when the legislature was in session. The legislature had no power of initiative in raising revenues and hardly any control over items charged on the revenues of the federation. Thus, both in legislative and financial fields, its hands were tied and powers severely restricted.

The Federal Court Since the Act provided for a federal system of government, it is natural that it provided for a Federal Court and of all the institutions set up under the Act, the Federal Court proved to be the **most successful in operation**. As per the Act, the Court was to consist of at least three judges, a Chief Justice and two associate judges and was located at Delhi.

The Judges could be removed from office only on proved misbehaviour. Their conduct as judges could not be made a subject of debate in the central legislature. Thus, the court's independence was constitutionally protected. The court functioned as an independent impartial institution and laid down the foundations of a real federal judiciary in the country (despite the fact that with regard to interpretation of the constitution, the last word remained with the Privy Council in London!).

Provincial Autonomy This was the most important provision from point of view of Indian people and evoked considerable enthusiasm in the country. Under the federal scheme of division of powers, there were three legislative lists-a federal list, a provincial list and a concurrent list. For the first time in the history of British India, such clear demarcation of powers entrusted in the provinces was made. The **provincial list** included items such as public works, public services, education, public health, local government, agriculture, land, forest, mines and fisheries.

Provincial Executive The executive authority of a province was vested in a Governor who was appointed by his Majesty on the advice of the Secretary of State for India, usually Governors. There was an Instrument of Instructions dealing with the manner in which the Governor was to exercise his powers as head of the executive. Provincial Governors were invested with a large number of **special executive powers** in matters concerning law and order and interests of minorities, public services, backward classes, Indian princes and British commercial interests. Hence, many Indians criticised provincial autonomy as more an autonomy for provincial governors rather than the provincial Legislatures.

In exercise of his special powers, he was under the superintendence of the GG in his discretion. This subordination affected the exercise of provincial autonomy.

Provincial Legislature The Act provided for the establishment of in all 11 provinces including Sind and Orissa. **Bicameral legislature** (Assemblies and Councils) was introduced in 6 provinces—Bengal, Madras, Bombay, United Provinces, Bihar and Assam. Members of the provincial legislatures were elected on the basis of constituencies organised according to religion or race, interest or sex. Main religious or racial communities were—**Muslims, Sikhs, Anglo-Indians, Indian Christians and Europeans**. In so called 'general constituencies' the voters belonged to the different Hindu castes or sects. Here also, seats were reserved for the **depressed classes**. Special interests recognised were—Industry, Commerce, Landholders, Universities, Labour, backward areas and tribes, etc. A small number of seats were also reserved for **women**. In this way, the electoral provisions of the Act were governed by communal award as modified by the Poona Pact. It accentuated the communal divisions in the country and paved the way for the eventual partition of India.

Members of the Assembly were elected directly. Franchise varied form province to province. Generally, it was determined on the basis of minimum land revenue a person paid, or house rent. Minimum educational qualification or military service was also considered. The franchise increased from 3 per cent under the Act of 1919 to 14 per cent under the Act of 1935.

Legislative Powers of the Governor Like the GG, the Governor had also been empowered to enact legislation of a temporary or permanent character, on his own authority, without taking the approval of the Legislature. He had the power to issue ordinances or permanent laws in the form of **Governor's Acts** with respect to certain subjects even when the legislature was in session. Though, normally the Governor was to issue ordinances only after securing the concurrence of the GG. Prior recommendation of the Governor was needed for introduction of finance bills and thus in financial matters, the legislature had absolutely no initiative.

The legislative powers of the provincial legislature were further limited as GG's previous sanction was needed to introduce certain types of Bills. Further, His Majesty could disallow an Act assented by the Governor or the Governor General.

It is clear that the Governor himself was all in all the legislative field. On top of this were the overriding powers of the GG and the veto power of His Majesty. All this gravely limited the powers of the Legislature.

Previous Years' Questions – Preliminary Exam

1. Which one of the following is not a feature of the Government of India Act of 1935? **[UPSC 2000]**
   (a) Dyarchy at the Centre as well as in the Provinces
   (b) A Bicameral Legislature
   (c) Provincial Autonomy
   (d) An All India Federation
2. What was the real intention of the British to include the princely states in the Federal Union proposed by the India Act of 1935? **[UPSC 2002]**
   (a) Exercise more and direct political and administrative control over the princely states
   (b) Involve the Princes activity in the administration of the colony
   (c) Finally effect the complete political and administrative takeover of all the princely states by the British
   (d) Use the princes to balance the anti-imperialist doctrines of the nationalist leaders
3. Consider the following statements: **[UPSC 2004]**
   Some of the main features of the Government of India Act, 1935 were the
   1. Abolition of Dyarchy in the Governor's Provinces
   2. Power of the Governors to Veto legislative action and to legislate on their own
   3. Abolition of the Principle of Communal Representation

   Which of the statements given above is/are correct? Choose the correct answer from the following options.
   (a) 1 only (b) 1 into
   (c) 2 and 3 (d) 1, 2 and 3
4. Consider the following statements: **[UPSC 2005]**
   The Government of India Act, 1935 provided for
   1. The Provincial Autonomy
   2. The establishment of Federal Court
   3. All India Federation at the centre

   Which of the following statements given above are correct? Choose the correct answer from the following options.
   (a) 1 and 2 (b) 2 and 3
   (c) 1 and 3 (d) 1, 2 and 3
5. In which one of the following provinces was a Congress Ministry not formed under the Act of 1935? **[UPSC 2005]**
   (a) Bihar
   (b) Madras
   (c) Orissa
   (d) Punjab
6. The distribution of powers between the Centre and the States in the Indian Constitution is based on the scheme provided in which of the following? **[UPSC 2012]**
   (a) Morley-Minto Reforms, 1909
   (b) Montagu-Chelmsford Act, 1919
   (c) Government of India Act, 1935
   (d) Indian Independence Act, 1947
7. In the Federation established by The Government of India Act of 1935, residuary powers were given to the **[UPSC 2018]**
   (a) Federal Legislature
   (b) Governor General
   (c) Provincial Legislature
   (d) Provincial Governors
8. Consider the following statements: **[UPSC 2021]**
   1. The Montague-Chelmsford Reforms of 1919 recommended granting voting rights to all women above the age of 21.
   2. The Government of India Act of 1935 gave women reserved seats in the legislature.

   Which of the statements given above is/are correct?
   (a) 1 only
   (b) 2 only
   (c) Both 1 and 2
   (d) Neither 1 nor 2

Previous Years' Questions – Main Exam

1. What were the main features of the Act of 1935? What was Jawaharlal Nehru's reaction to the Act? **[UPSC 1990]**
2. How did the Government of India Act, 1935 mark a point of no return in the history of Constitutional Development in India? **[UPSC 2006]**

Answers

Previous Years' Questions – Preliminary Exam

1. (a)	2. (d)	3. (a)	4. (d)	5. (d)
6. (c)	7. (b)	8. (b)		

19 Elections of 1937 and Congress Ministries

Following the withdrawal of the Civil Disobedience Movement, a major debate arose among the nationalists on what course the national movement should take. Though there was an agreement on the basic issue of fighting British imperialism, Congressmen disagreed on the methods to be adopted. The prominent responses came from:

1. **Gandhi** He suggested return to constructive work, particularly Harijan work, and also emphasised on the revival of village crafts. Gandhi argued that this would consolidate people's power and facilitate their mobilisation for the next phase of mass struggle.
2. **The New Swarajists** Another section of the Congress advocated the revival of the constitutional method of struggle and participation in the elections to the Central Legislative Assembly to be held in 1934. This section of men were also known as the 'New Swarajists' and were led by –**Dr. MA Ansari, Asaf Ali, Satyamurthy, Bhulabhai Desai and BC Roy**. They argued that in a period of political depression, it was necessary to work through the councils to keep up the morale of the people. According to them, it would not amount to cooperating with the government but would only open another political front and would help build up the Congress organisationally and prepare the people for the next mass struggle.
3. **The Leftists** Yet another section of Congressmen were attracted neither by the Gandhian constructive work nor by the idea of council entry. These were the leftists who advocated continuation of non-constitutional mass movement (You may recall that in the early 1930s, a strong left trend had developed). **J Nehru** represented the leftist paradigm most coherently and considered the above two alternatives as 'spiritual defeat'. Nehru criticised Gandhian strategy of Struggle-Truce-Struggle (S-T-S) and instead put forward the strategy of Struggle-Victory (S-V), i.e. permanent confrontation with imperialism till victory was achieved.

After a hectic debate, the Congress decided to contest in the Elections of 1937, once again giving up the path of confrontation and taking to constitutional politics. However, unlike the earlier Swarajist phase, its present aim was not to wreck the councils from within but to make them work.

The Congress was successful in forming governments in seven provinces. The victory of the Congress was attributed to its pro-people policies. The formation of Congress Ministries was perceived by the people as their own Raj and they felt that the days of the British Raj were numbered. The Congress ministries functioned for a little more than two years under numerous constraints but tried their best to give relief to the people.

In September 1939, the Congress ministries resigned, having made significant contribution to the freedom struggle during their short stint in office.

Efforts Towards Constitutionalism

Efforts to adopt constitutional politics had begun during the Second Phase of the Civil Disobedience Movement itself (i.e. 1932 onwards). The Second CDM had only evoked a lukewarm response and voices had begun to emerge within the Congress advocating a return to constitutional politics.

In 1933, Satyamurthy formed the **Madras Swaraj Party**. KM Munshi, BC Roy and Ramaswamy Iyengar wanted to revive the Swaraj Party. Dr MA Ansari and Rajgopalachari were also in favour of council entry. However, the aim of council entry now was different from the earlier Swarajists in two ways:

1. This time, the aim was not to wreck the constitution but to make it workable.
2. In case of obtaining majority, office was to be accepted and ministries formed.

On the other hand, council entry was opposed by some Congressmen with socialist leanings like Acharya Narendra Dev and Purushottamdas Tondon. Each side sought Gandhiji's support and wanted to tilt the Congress opinion in their favour. In order to diffuse the situation and avoid any split, Gandhi gave a free hand to all saying, 'I want all sections to work in all directions towards one thing in their own ways without criticising one another'.

Congress Decides to Fight Elections

Consequently, in May 1934, at Patna, the AICC meeting was called to set up a parliamentary board to fight elections under the aegis of the Congress. To appease the Left, Gandhi backed Nehru for the presidentship of Lucknow Congress (April 1936).

Gandhi's Response

At the same time, Gandhi was convinced that he was out of tune with major trends in the Congress. Fundamentally in disagreement with parliamentary politics, **Gandhi resigned from the Congress** (October 1934) by refusing its four-anna membership. However, this in no way weakened his hold over the party and his domination over Congress policy continued.

Nehru's Response

On the other hand, Nehru wondered 'why I should walk out of the Congress and leave the field clear for reactionary elements'. He along with the socialists decided to remain with the Congress and give priority to the anti-imperialist struggle for which Congress unity was of utmost importance. They considered it better to gradually radicalise the Congress than to get isolated.

Congress Contests Elections to Local Bodies

Thus from 1934 onwards, Congress contested elections to the Assembly and local bodies as and when they were held. For instance, when elections were held in Madras Presidency, a **Congress Civic Board** was formed (May 1935) for selecting party candidates for local elections. The candidates were asked to take a pledge of encouraging Swadeshi, removing corruption and improving medical and educational facilities. In November 1934, the elections to Central Legislative Assembly were held and out of a total of 76 contested seats at the national level, Congress candidates stood for 55 and won 44. When Municipality elections were held in October 1935 in Madurai, Congress won 21 of 36 seats.

These elections proved useful as the Congress gained tremendous experience in terms of organising and managing elections. The Congress was also able to test its popular base and also test the support of its allies for funds. However, the Congress took a long time to decide in favour of contesting provincial elections and it was decided that the election participation issue will be settled during the Lucknow session.

Lucknow Congress Session (Presided by J. Nehru, April 1936)

In his presidential speech, Nehru advocated socialism which he regarded as 'the only key to the solution of the world's problems and of India's problems'. **Nehru also took three socialists into the Congress Working Committee** namely Jayprakash Narayan, Acharya Narendra Dev and Achyut Patwardhan.

Prominent resolutions passed included:

1. 'The people of the States should have the same right of self-determination as those of the rest of India and that the Congress stands for the same political, civil and democratic liberties for every part of India'. But it was also pointed out that 'the struggle for liberty' must be carried out by the people of states themselves.
2. The provincial units of the Congress were asked to conduct agrarian enquiries and assist in the formulation of an **All India Agrarian Programme**.
3. The Congress also resolved to **contest elections** on the basis of a manifesto.

However, the **question of office acceptance was kept pending**. In this way, the resolution to contest elections while keeping the question of office acceptance pending was a kind of compromise between those who wanted to contest elections and those who wanted to boycott them. It is worth mentioning here that such differences in opinions were considered internal matters within the Congress. As far as the Congress position vis-à-vis the British was concerned, it always put up a united front.

Election Manifesto of Congress

It was drafted by the parliamentary committee and aimed at explaining the political and economic programme of the Congress. It was adopted by the AICC in August 1936.

- The manifesto reaffirmed the **total rejection of the Act of 1935** by the Congress.
- The manifesto clarified that the aim of sending Congressmen to the legislatures was not to cooperate with the Government but to combat the Act of 1935 and to end it.
- It declared that national independence could give Indians the power to solve their socio-economic problems and end exploitation of the masses.
- It declared that the task of Congress representatives was to end all oppressive Acts and regulations.
- It made the following promises-
    - Political-Establishment of civil liberty, release of political prisoners, undoing wrongs done to the peasant.
    - Social-removal of untouchability, equal status for women, encouragement to khadi and village industries, satisfactory solution to communal problem.
    - Promises made to industrial workers included-a decent standard of living, regular hours of work, better conditions of labour, right to form unions, suitable machinery to settle disputes with employers and protection against the 'economic consequences of old age'.

Note: the Lucknow session was significant also because it was during this session that the **first meeting of the All India Kisan Sabha** was held under the presidentship of **Swami Sahajanand Saraswati**.

Faizpur Congress Session (Presided by J. Nehru, December 1936)

Held at Faizpur (Maharashtra), this was the first Congress Session in a rural area. During the session, the Congress passed several significant resolutions. These were as follows:

- It passed resolutions condemning Italian aggression on Abyssinia and Japanese aggression of China.
- It demanded the formation of a **Constituent Assembly** to frame a constitution for India.
- The **Congress also adopted an agrarian programme** which included the following features:
  - 50 per cent reduction in rent and revenue
  - Exemption of uneconomic holdings from rent and land tax
  - Taxation of agricultural income
  - Abolition of feudal levies and forced labour
  - Cooperative farming
  - Wiping out arrears of rent
  - Modification of ejectment laws
  - Recognition of peasant unions

It is noteworthy that the above programme was silent on the issue of the abolition of zamindari and taluqdari systems (as the Right wing in the Congress was not in favour of zamindari abolition). The Kisan Sabha leaders, though welcomed the programme in general, also criticised it on this ground.

Nevertheless, the Agrarian Programme was a progressive document and a significant achievement of the Faizpur Congress Session. It went a long way in rallying the peasants behind the Congress.

Elections of 1937

The names of the Congress candidates were recommended by the Provincial Congress Committees to the Congress Parliamentary Board, which had a final say in selection of candidates. While recommending the names, the PCC considered criteria such as-abiding by Congress discipline and following its programme, service to the party, popularity among people and ability to bear election expenses. Despite sincere efforts to select candidates on merit, caste also played an important role in certain cases.

Election Campaign

The Congress undertook a vigorous election campaign. J Nehru undertook a country-wide election tour, travelling 80,000 kilometres in less than five months. **Gandhi did not address a single election meeting**, though he was very much present in the minds of the voters. The Congress also faced challenges in the form of regional parties and parties formed along communal lines like the Muslim League and the Hindu Mahasabha.

Election Results

Elections were held in 11 provinces and the results were very encouraging for the Congress. It won 716 out of 1161 seats it contested. It obtained clear majority in five provinces, namely **UP, Bihar, CP,**

Orissa and Madras; it emerged as the single largest party in **Bombay, Bengal, Assam and NWFP**. Its performance was poor in Sind and Punjab (in Punjab, Unionist Party obtained clear majority).

Congress Performance in Upper House

The Congress did not perform well in elections to upper house as the franchise was limited to upper strata only. The upper strata, comprising of landlords and moneylenders, had begun to shift their support to the communal parties, since the Congress had adopted a radical agrarian programme (From this time onwards, communal parties began to gather strength).

Congress Performance in Reserved Constituencies

The results in reserved constituencies were not at all satisfactory for the Congress except in the labour seats. Some examples of Congress performance are as follows (in all 11 provinces):

- For commerce and industry 56 seats were reserved. Congress contested 8 and won only 3.
- For Landholders 37 seats were reserved. Congress contested 8 and won 4.
- For labour 38 seats were reserved. Congress contested 20 and won 18.
- For Muslims 482 seats were reserved. Congress contested 58 and won only 26 (19 from NWFP alone). It could not get a single Muslim seat in Bengal, Bombay, UP, CP and Sind. However, it is worth mentioning here that the performance of **Muslim League was no better**. It did not win a single seat in NWFP. In Punjab, it won only 2 of 84 reserved seats. It was not in a position to form a government in any of the provinces.

Message of Congress to the people on the eve of its electoral victory 'The Congress Working Committee congratulates the nation on its wonderful response to the call of the Congress during recent elections, demonstrating the adherence of the masses to Congress policy'.

S. No	Province	Seats won by Congress/Total No. of Seats
1	UP	134/228
2	Bihar	95/152
3	CP	70/112
4	Orissa	36/60
5	Madras	159/215
6	Bombay	87/175
7	Bengal	60/250
8	Assam	35/108
9	NWFP	19/50
10	Sind	8/60
11	Punjab	18/175

Office Acceptance

We have earlier seen that the decision on office acceptance was kept pending. In March 1937, the AICC met to decide over the issue. The basic question was whether office acceptance would lead to co-option by the colonial state or whether ministries could be used to defeat the colonial strategy.

Argument Against Office Acceptance

Left leaders like **Jawaharlal Nehru, Subhas Bose, NG Ranga, Sahajanand Saraswati and Indulal Yagnik** saw office acceptance as cooperation with imperialism. It would take away the revolutionary character of the national movement as constitutional work would side track the main issues of freedom and socio-economic justice.

Argument in Favour of Office Acceptance

Right wing leaders like **C. Rajagopalachari** were in favour of office acceptance. They argued that they will not allow councils to lead them into constitutionalism but will lead the councils and use them for Revolution. They argued that they were equally committed to combating the Act of 1935 and council entry was only a short-term strategy since the option of mass movement was not available. The most vocal argument put forth in favour of forming ministries was that it would enable the Congress to work in favour of peasants and workers.

Finally, **Rajendra Prasad moved a resolution for 'conditional acceptance' of office**, the condition here was that the governors would not use their special powers to intervene with the functioning of the ministries. The resolution was accepted and was also approved by Gandhi. But when the Congress leaders were invited by the Governors to form ministries in **six provinces** where the Congress was in majority, the offer was turned down as the Governors refused to give assurances on the condition put forth by the Congress. The government now went ahead and formed '**Interim Ministries'** in these provinces. These did not command a majority and hence could not continue in office beyond six months.

Strenuous efforts to pressurise the CWC in favour of office acceptance were now made by Congressmen like Rajagopalachari as well as Indian Capitalists like GD Birla. Accordingly, in the first week of July, the CWC met at Wardha, **Gandhi finally gave his consent for office** and a decision was taken in favour of office acceptance.

> **Gandhi on office acceptance:** 'Office acceptance was an attempt to avoid bloody revolution on the one hand and mass Civil Disobedience on the other'.

The resignation of Interim Ministries was now followed by the formation of Congress ministries, thus inaugurating a new era in India's Struggle for independence.

Congress Prime Ministers (Premiers) in Various Provinces

(The head of the Provincial ministry was then known as premier and not Chief Minister as is the case now.)

S. No	Province	Congress Prime Minister
1	UP	GB Pant
2	Bihar	Sri Krishna Sinha
3	CP	Dr. NB Khare
4	Madras	C. Rajgopalachari
5	Orissa	Hare Krishna Mehtab
6	Bombay	BG Kher
7	NWFP	Dr. Khan Saheb

In Sind- **Congress supported the Ministry of Gulam Hussain Hidaytullah**.

In Assam- **Congress supported the Ministry of Gopinath Bordoloi**.

In Bengal- Fazlul Haq invited the Congress to cooperate in forming a coalition government but the Congress refused and Haq then joined hands with the Muslim League.

In Punjab- The Congress was not in a position to play a dominant role.

By about six months, the Congress had delayed the decision of office acceptance. According to Rani Dhavan Shankardass (author of 'The First Congress Raj'), this delay proved advantageous to the Congress in the following ways:

1. The delay had disproved that the Congress was office hungry.
2. It proved Congress unity and discipline that the word of Congress High Command was supreme.
3. The Governors would think several times before intervening in the work of the Congress.

Parliamentary Sub-Committee

With the aim of demolishing British hopes of provincialisation of the Congress, a central control board known as the Parliamentary Sub-Committee was formed with Sardar Patel, Maulana Abul Kalam Azad and Rajendra Prasad as members.

> **Gandhi wrote in Harijan on office acceptance** 'these offices have to be held lightly, not tightly. They should be **crowns of thorns**. They have been taken to quicken the pace at which we are moving towards our goal'.

Congress Ministries at Work

The formation of Congress Ministries drastically changed the psychological atmosphere in the country. People felt they were breathing the fresh air of victory. Khadi clad men and women were now seen in the Secretariat, ordering about officials who had earlier put them in jails. It was difficult to distinguish between members of legislatures and peasants who came in large numbers.

Formation of Congress ministries led to an immense increase in the prestige of the party and it was now seen as an alternative state power.

Hence, the responsibility was now tremendous. The Congress faced tremendous challenge of living upto the expectations of the people on one hand, and limited powers on the other. It did make an effort to give people a glimpse of the future Swaraj. It did **set an example in plain living**—the Congress ministers reduced their salaries drastically from ₹2000 to ₹500 per month and travelled second or third class in the railways. They made themselves easily accessible to the common people and set up new standards of honesty and public service.

A brief account of Congress' work during its nearly two and a half years (28 months) in office is as follows:

Defence of Civil Liberties

Congress had been committed to the defence and extension of civil liberties since its origin and it is not surprising that the Congress ministries made special efforts in this regard.

- Emergency powers acquired by the provincial governments during 1932 (e.g. through Public Safety Acts) were repealed.
- Bans on nationalist organisations and literature were lifted.
- Communists now functioned openly in congress provinces even though ban on CPI remained as it was imposed by the Central government.
- Restrictions on press were removed, confiscated arms were returned.
- Power of the police, the most hated of all British functionaries, were curbed.
- Shadowing of political workers by CID (Central Investigation Department) was stopped.
- Thousands of political prisoners and detenues were released.

The release of political prisoners had been a part of Congress manifesto. Many were in prison without trial. The largest number of political prisoners were in Bengal—a non Congress ruled province. Gandhi went to Calcutta himself to negotiate for their release and was successful in securing the release of 1100 detenues. In UP also many prisoners were released including the Kakori case prisoners.

However, prisoners remained in UP and Bihar who had previously served terms in Kala Pani (Cellular jail in Andamans). The Ministries of both provinces were determined to release them and resigned on the issue (15th Feb 1938), finally leading to their release by end of March. The Congress also worked for the return of political exiles like Rash Bihari Ghosh, Abani Mukerjee, Maulvi Abdullah Khan, Prithvi Singh, etc., however, it could not do much in this regard.

All the same, there were certain blemishes in the performance of Congress government regarding civil liberties- Yusuf Meherally and SS Batliwala, both socialist leaders, were arrested by the Madras government for inflammatory speeches. KM Munshi, the Bombay Home Minister, used the CID against communists and leftists.

Peasant Protection

J Nehru had observed that **'the outstanding problem of India is the peasant problem. All else is secondary'.** However, the Congress could not attempt a complete overhaul of the agrarian structure or abolish zamindari owing to several constraints-

- The provincial ministries did not have enough powers or financial resources.
- The Congress was faced with the task of winning over the zamindari classes so as to isolate the colonial enemy and deprive him of all social support within India.

- The Congress leadership worked under the constraint of time. A sense of impending crisis was always present as they were to continue in office only so long as their logic of politics permitted them.
- By 1938, war clouds had started hovering over Europe.
- Nearly all Congress-run states—UP, Bihar, Bombay, Madras and Assam had reactionary second chambers in the form of legislative councils. These were dominated by landlords, capitalists and moneylenders.
- Lastly, the agrarian structure existing in India was extremely complex and varied making any structural reform formidable and time consuming.

Despite these constraints, the Congress ministries went a long way in addressing peasant problems.

- In Bihar, a tenancy legislation passed in 1937-38 abolished all increases in rent made since 1911. Existing arrears of rent were reduced and rate of interest on arrears was reduced from 12.5 to 6.25 percent. Landlords were forbidden from charging illegal dues. Landlord's share in case of share cropping was not to exceed 9/20 of the produce.
- In UP, a tenancy act was passed in October 1939 giving all statutory tenants in Agra and Awadh full hereditary rights in their holdings. A tenant could no longer be arrested for non-payment of rent. All illegal exactions like nazrana and begar were abolished.
- In Orissa, similar Tenancy bill was passed by the Legislative but the bill could not receive Governor's assent as it reduced the zamindars' income by 50 to 60 percent.
- In Madras, a committee under the chairmanship of T. Prakasam, the Revenue Minister, was formed which recommended provisions which would have meant virtual liquidation of zamindari system. But before the legislature could draft the bill, the ministry resigned.
- In Bombay, Central Provinces and NWFP, tenancy reforms extending security of tenure to tenants were carried out.
- Congress government also passed a series of debtors' relief acts which provided for regulation of moneylenders' business. Accumulated interest on debt was cancelled or reduced.
- In Bombay, 40,000 'dublas' or tied serfs were liberated. Congress was successful in returning lands that had been confiscated at the time of no-rent campaign during Civil Disobedience Movement.
- Grazing fees in forests was abolished in Bombay and reduced in Madras.

Thus, the Congress Ministries secured the status of millions of tenants in zamindari areas. Efforts were made to protect the peasants from moneylenders and increase irrigation facilities. Even though the interests of sub-tenants and agricultural labourers were overlooked, it cannot be denied that this was a period of tremendous awakening among the peasants who rallied behind the Congress.

Labour Welfare

In its election manifesto, the Congress had made several promises to the working class and in general, the Congress governments adopted a pro-labour stance. Basic approach of the Congress towards labour issues included the following:

- Advancing workers' interests while promoting industrial peace.
- Reducing strikes as far as possible by establishing conciliation machinery.
- Advocating compulsory arbitration before resorting to strikes.
- Creating goodwill between labour and capitalists.
- Striving to improve the conditions of the workers and securing wage increases.

Accordingly,

- In Bombay, **Textile Enquiry Committee** was appointed which recommended among other things, increase of wages amounting to crore of rupees. Its recommendations were implemented despite protests by mill owners.
- In November 1938, the Congress governments passed the **Industrial Disputes Act** which emphasised on conciliation, arbitration and negotiations in place of direct action. It had provisions to prevent lightening strikes and lock-outs.
- In UP, Kanpur emerged as the seat of serious labour unrest and a major strike occurred in May 1938. A **Labour Enquiry Committee**, headed by Rajendra Prasad was set up which recommended, among other things, increase in workers' wages with a minimum wage of ₹15 per month, maternity benefits to women and recognition of Left-dominated Mazdur Sabha. Under immense pressure from the government, the employers finally adopted the main recommendations.
- In Bihar too, a similar Labour Enquiry Committee was set up under Rajendra Prasad.

Social Reform Measures

Various other social reform measures were also introduced by the Congress governments -

- Gandhian constructive programme received great impetus in all Congress ruled provinces. For instance-
    - Various measures for advancement of Harijans or untouchables were adopted (such as laws providing Harijans with access to temples, access to public sources of water, access to public offices, hospitals, education institutions, etc., were introduced. Efforts were made to increase number of Harijans in government services).
    - Prohibition was introduced in selected areas.
    - Support and subsidies were given to khadi and village industries (A grant of ₹2 lakh for Khadi and Handspinning was given by the Madras Ministry).
    - Honorary medical officers in hospitals were appointed.
    - Investment on public buildings was reduced.
- Schemes of prison reforms were introduced.
- Indigenous industrial expansion was promoted (such as automobile manufacture).
- Planned development was encouraged and the National Planning Committee (1938) was appointed by the then Congress President Subhas Chandra Bose.
- Other measures included Declaration of Fundamental Rights, Welfare schemes for tribals, reduction in salaries of ministers and repeal of Moplah Outrages Act.
- Congress ministries paid special attention to education, health and sanitation. Special attention was paid to primary, technical and higher education and the education of girls and Harijans. Mass literacy campaigns were organised.

Wardha Scheme of Basic Education

Special advance was made in the field of education. On 31st July 1937, Gandhi had published an article in the **Harijan**. Based on this article, an All India National Education Conference (Wardha Educational Conference) was held during 22-23 October 1937 at Wardha. The conference was presided by Gandhi himself and it formulated a self-supporting scheme of **Basic Education** in the form of 'Nai Talim', better known as Wardha Scheme. Its main features were-

- The main principle of the scheme was **'learning through activity'** and it centered around 'manual productive work' that would generate remuneration of the teachers.

- It envisaged free and compulsory education to be provided in child's mother tongue for seven years throughout the country.
- Emphasis was laid on vocational and manual training, production of handicraft etc.

Taking the above as guidelines, a Committee on Basic Education headed by **Dr. Zakir Hussain** then submitted a scheme of basic education to be implemented by Congress Ministries. It suggested (1) including basic craft education, that is imparting the entire education through some industry or vocation, (2) a scheme covering teachers' salaries and rendering students self-supporting at the end of the course, and (3) close coordination of child education with the environment and village crafts. There was no place for Englis and religious education in the scheme. The scheme was opposed by the Muslim League.

Congress education policy resulted in an increase in the number of students as well as educational institutions. However, the Scheme could not be further developed on account of resignation of Congress Ministries.

Use of Offices to Promote Mass Political Activity

Using offices to promote mass political activity and bring about popular mobilisation was a part of office-acceptance strategy of the Congress. On 10th July 1937, J Nehru, as president of the Congress, sent a circular to all Congressmen reminding them that organisational and other work outside the legislature was to remain their major occupation.

The work of the Congress outside the legislatures (i.e. the extra-parliamentary mass mobilisation programmes) took diverse forms-

- Congress committees were organised in villages.
- Congress grievance committees were set up in the districts to hear local grievances and report them to the MLAs.
- Congress police stations and panchayats were set up for dispensing justice.
- Mass petitions to officials were organised.
- States' Peoples' movements and mass literacy campaigns were also organised.

Negative Outcomes

The strategy of using offices to promote mass political activity created new dilemmas. How could a party running a government simultaneously organise popular protests against its own self?

The Congress ministries promoted civil liberties and allowed trade unions and kisan organisations to grow. Left parties began to operate freely:

- The Communist Party brought out its weekly organ **'The National Front'** from Bombay.
- The CSP brought out its journal **'The Congress Socialist'**.
- The Kirti Communists of Punjab brought out **'Kirti Lehar'** from Meerut (UP) as they could not do so in Unionist Party led Punjab.

A section of Congressmen such as the Communists, Socialists, Royists and Revolutionary Terrorists felt that the expanded civil liberties should be used to stir militant or even violent forms of protest.

Due to the above, popular agitations began to clash frequently with the Congress governments, which treated all militant protests as a law and order problem. For instance, in Bihar the kisan movement came in conflict with the Ministry when the Kisan Sabha asked the peasants to forcibly occupy the landlords' lands. It was during this time that the relationship between the Bihar Kisan Sabha and Congress leadership became strained and a ban was imposed on Congressmen from participating in Kisan Sabha activities in Bihar. For how could governance and violent forms of protest coexist?

The Left became highly critical of government's handling of popular protests and accused it of suppressing peasants' and workers' movements. Leading British journalist and communist **R. Palme Dutt** summed up the communist criticism of the Congress Ministries in the following words- 'The dominant moderate leadership was in practice developing an increasing cooperation with imperialism, was acting more and more openly in the interest of upper-class landlords and industrialists and was showing increasingly marked hostility to all militant forms of struggle'.

Thus, the policy of ministry formation led to a new crisis in the national movement. **Both Gandhi and Nehru began to feel that the positive role of the Ministries was getting exhausted**.

Tripuri Crisis (March 1939)

In 1938, Subhas Chandra Bose had been unanimously elected as Congress President. In 1939, he decided to stand again for Presidential election, but this time as representative of militant and radical groups. This was objected to by some members of the CWC including Sardar Patel, Rajendra Prasad and JB Kriplani who declared that the position of Congress President was like that of a constitutional head who represented the unity of the nation. With the support of Gandhi, these leaders put up Pattabhi Sitaramayya as their candidate.

During the election propaganda, Bose openly accused the 'Gandhists' as compromisers who were working for a compromise on the question of federation and were opposed to any national struggle that disturbed their parliamentary work.

In January 1939, Bose won the election and Gandhi declared **Pattabhi's defeat as 'more mine than his'**. The CWC members felt that they could not work with a president who had publicly accused them and doubted their patriotism. Accordingly, 12 CWC members resigned. Jawaharlal was also unhappy about Bose's aspersions on his colleagues but he did not want to bring out the differences in open and therefore did not resign.

Tripuri Congress Session (8–12th March 1939)

Internal strife within Congress reached its helm at Tripuri Session. It appeared as if Bose had completely misjudged the meaning of his victory in the presidential election. Congressmen had voted for him for his militant politics and not to have him as their supreme leader, replacing Gandhi. Consequently, Govind Ballabh Pant moved a resolution during the Tripuri Congress, expressing full faith in Gandhi's leadership and the old CWC and asking Subhas to nominate his Working Committee with Gandhi's consent.

This resolution was passed by a huge majority, leaving Subhas Chandra Bose in an embarrassing situation and he was left with no option but to resign. Jawaharlal tried to mediate between the two sides but in vain and quickly afterwards Rajendra Prasad was elected as the new President. Henceforth, Bose lost the support of the Communists as well as the Congress Socialists for they were not willing to divide the national movement of which Congress was the main organ and Gandhi, the main leader.

PC Joshi of CPI declared in 1939, 'the greatest class struggle today is our national struggle'.

Thus, in May 1939, Subhas Chandra Bose and his followers founded the Forward Bloc as a new party within the Congress. On 9th July, he gave a call for an all India protest against an AICC resolution, instigating disciplinary action by the CWC against him. He was consequently removed as president of the Bengal PCC and was also debarred from holding any Congress office for three years.

Challenges Faced by the Congress

During its tenure, the Congress faced several challenges, for instance:

- **Surfacing of party weaknesses** The period saw the emergence of serious weaknesses in the Congress party. Personal as well as ideological strife and bickering became commonplace.
- **Bogus membership** During this time, many opportunists and office hungry men joined the Congress and the party faced severe threat from indiscipline and corruption.
- **Attack by communal parties** A malicious campaign was carried out against the Congress by communal parties. Congress was accused of discrimination against minorities, an accusation motivated more by political reasons rather than facts.
- **Communist critique** The Left became highly critical of government's handling of popular protests.
- **Tripuri Crisis and Resignation of Bose** During this period, two sessions of the Congress were held—51st session of the Congress was held at **Haripura**, Gujarat (Feb 1938) under the presidentship of Subhas Chandra Bose. However, crisis erupted in the next session held at **Tripuri**. Bose defeated Pattabhi Sitaramayya (Gandhi's candidate) in the presidential election in what was regarded as a major victory of the Left wing. However, Bose was later compelled to resign from the presidentship. Thus, Congress weathered another storm and a split was averted.

Resignation of Congress Ministries (October 1939)

On 1st September 1939, the Second World War broke out with the German invasion of Poland in pursuance of Hitler's policy of German expansion. On 3rd September 1939, Britain and France were forced to go for Poland's aid and enter the war. On 3rd September itself, India was dragged into the war on the side of Britain, without its consent. Neither the National Congress nor elected members of central legislature were consulted. In October 1939, the Congress Ministries resigned office in protest. (Read in detail about Congress attitude towards Second World War in the upcoming chapter.)

Gandhi welcomed the resignation calling it a **'bitter pill'** which needed to be swallowed to cleanse the Congress of the rampant indiscipline and corruption. Another positive effect of the resignation was that it brought together the Left and the Right wings of the Congress on the question of participation in the War. The resignations also proved to its critics that the Congress was not out for power but for the freedom of the Indian people from foreign yoke. The Acceptance of Office thus proved to be just one phase in the freedom struggle. When the time came to leave office, the Ministries promptly resigned.

Evaluation of Congress Ministries

On the whole, the Congress Ministries succeeded in making some important advances during the brief period of 28 months, despite limited powers given to them under the Act of 1935.

- Even though the left was critical, its expectations were fulfilled in a large measure.
- The Congress Ministries succeeded in firmly handling communal riots.
- The Congress leaders successfully foiled British attempt of 'divide and rule' by offering constitutional concessions. They successfully used offices to further their own aims, without getting assimilated in the colonial fold.
- Fears of provincialisation of Congress were also disproved as Ministers succeeded in presenting a common front before the Centre.
- The morale of the ICS reached a new low and they began to feel that the days of British rule in India are numbered.
- Congress influence extended to all sections of the people, including the lower bureaucracy.
- Congress Ministries emerged as an alternative to imperialist government and eroded yet another moral basis of British rule in India-that Indians were not fit to rule.
- The biggest gain was psychological and the people felt they were breathing the fresh air of victory and self-government. The formation of Congress Ministries had changed the balance of power in India in relation to the British rulers.

Note: The period between 1935 and 1939 witnessed several other important political developments (in addition to the Government of India Act 1935 and Formation of Congress Ministries) which brought about a new turn in the Congress as well as the national movement. These developments included:

- Growth of Communalism
- Growth of the Left Movement
- Peasants' and Workers' Movements
- State's Peoples' Movement

Refer to Chapters 6.11 to 6.15 for relevant developments for the period 1935–39.

Previous Years' Questions – Preliminary Exam

1. Consider the following pairs: **[UPSC 2019]**

   Movement : Organization Leader

   1. All India Anti-Untouchability League : Mahatma Gandhi
   2. All India Kisan Sabha : Swami Sahajanad Saraswati
   3. Elf Respect Movement : E.V. Ramaswami Naicker

   Which of the pairs given above is/are correctly matched?

   (a) 1 only (b) 1 and 2 only
   (c) 2 and 3 only (d) 1, 2 and 3

Answers

Previous Years' Questions – Preliminary Exam

1. (d)

Unit 7 Indian National Movement-Part 2 (Towards Freedom)

1 Indian National Movement during the Second World War: Quit India Movement and INA (1939–45)

The outbreak of the Second World War (Sep 1939) evoked a variety of responses among the Indian people, and this was reflected in the Congress as well. After prolonged debate, Individual Satyagraha (1940–41) was launched by Gandhi, but it evoked merely a lukewarm response. It was only in 1942, three years after India was dragged into the war, that the Congress launched the Quit India Movement (also known as the **August Revolution** or the **Revolt of 1942**). Even as the Congress was still in the process of organising the Quit India movement, the government unleashed a severe round of repression, arresting all the top leaders including Mahatma Gandhi. However, the British hopes were belied when the people took the leadership of the movement in their own hands and challenged the British rule in a way comparable to the Struggle of 1857. Starting from the urban centres, the movement soon spread to the country side; new leaders emerged at local levels and did not hesitate in departing from the peaceful Gandhian approach and resorting to violence. Unprecedented participation of the youth and the Socialists, formation of parallel governments and underground movement emerged as some of the remarkable trends of the Quit India Movement.

Though the government succeeded in crushing the movement in the end, it was now clear that British days in India were numbered. This was further demonstrated by the formation of the Indian National Army (INA) under the leadership of Subhas Chandra Bose. The INA waged a heroic struggle and proved Indian capability of confronting the British in an armed struggle.

Thus, in this chapter, we will discuss the Quit India Movement and also the formation and activities of the Indian National Army.

Events Leading to the Quit India Movement (1939–41)

Outbreak of Second World War (1st September 1939)

The Second World War (1st September 1939 to 2nd September 1945) was a global war that involved a vast majority of the world's countries including the great powers that subsequently formed two opposing military alliances namely the Allies (Britain, France, Russia) and the Axis (Germany, Italy, Japan).

Viceroy Linlithgow (1936–43) unilaterally declared India as a belligerent state on the British side which led to a full-scale **constitutional crisis** in India threatening the very foundation of the responsible government which was making steady progress in the provinces. Soon after the declaration, the Viceroy began negotiations with the Congress, the Muslim League and the Princes with a view to enlisting their cooperation in the war.

The Congress was prepared to cooperate on the condition that Britain transferred the substance of power to India immediately and promised complete independence after the war. The League was ready to cooperate on the condition that Muslims be given justice in the 'Congress Provinces' and no future constitution for India would be made without its approval. The Princes alone pledged their unconditional support to the British.

Indian Attitude towards the War

The war evoked a variety of responses from different sections of the Indian people and may be discussed as under:

- **India should take advantage of Britain's difficulty** Proponents of this view believed that Britain's difficulty is India's opportunity. They were in favour of taking advantage of the empire's weakest moment to wrest freedom by immediately launching a strong movement against the British rule. They opposed British efforts of mobilising India's resources for the war. These included the Socialists and Subhas Chandra Bose. The Socialists argued that the war was an imperialist one since both sides were fighting for gaining or defending colonies and the question of supporting either of the two sides did not arise.
- **India should not take advantage of Britain's difficulty** Proponents of this view believed that India should cooperate with the British in war efforts unconditionally. They hoped that the British would adopt a lenient view in lieu of India's services and grant Indian demand for freedom. These included Gandhi and C Rajagopalachari. Gandhi advocated unconditional support to the

Allies as he made clear distinction between the Democratic states of Western Europe and the totalitarian Nazis. However, in absence of any support, he decided to go with Nehru's view of giving conditional support.

- **India should provide conditional support** Proponents of this view felt that Fascism was a greater threat to the world and they wanted to help the British in their fight against Nazism and Fascism but only on the condition that the British immediately provide for interim government of Indians and promise complete independence in the near future. Proponents of this view included Jawaharlal Nehru.
- **Wavering attitude** There were others whose attitude was either neutral or even wavering. For instance, the Socialists and the Communists. They decided to support the government in its war efforts after the Germans invaded Russia in 1941.

Congress and World Affairs (1935–1939) The period from 1935 to 1939 was an important period with regard to Congress participation in world affairs. By now Congress had developed a foreign policy-based on opposition to racialism and imperialism. During the 1930s, Congress firmly opposed imperialism in any part of the world and declared its support for the national movements in Asia and Africa. It also strongly condemned fascism (radical authoritarian nationalism) that had raised its head in Italy, Germany and Japan.

Congress Attitude

Nearly all the attitudes mentioned above were reflected in the Congress. Even as the Congress had full sympathy towards the victims of fascist aggression, it wondered how an enslaved nation could fight for other's freedom? Further, the CWC strongly protested against the decision of dragging India into the war without its consent and said that 'the issue of war and peace for India must be decided by the Indian people'. Thus, the Congress demanded that India should be set free or at least some effective transfer of power should take place into Indian hands, before India could actively participate in the war.

CWC Meeting at Wardha (10–14th September 1939)

The official Congress stand in this regard was adopted at a meeting of the CWC held at Wardha. Keeping with the nationalistic tradition of accommodating diverse views, Subhas Chandra Bose, Acharya Narendra Dev and Jayaprakash Narayan were also invited.

The leftists were of the opinion that the war was an imperialist one since the parties were involved in either gaining or defending colonial territories, and hence India should not support the British in war. Instead Congress should grasp this opportunity by starting a civil disobedience movement immediately.

Gandhi was in favour of adopting a sympathetic view of the Allies. His personal attitude towards the British was the same as it was during the First World War, i.e. of cooperation. But when he saw that his position was not supported by even his close followers like Sardar Patel and Rajendra Prasad, he decided to support Nehru's position.

Nehru was of the view that even though justice was on the side of the Allies, they were after all imperialist countries. Yet, he felt that nothing should be done that might lead to the triumph of Hitler and Nazism in Europe. Therefore, India should neither join the war until the country is itself free nor take advantage of Britain's difficulty.

The Congress finally decided to adopt Nehru's view and extend conditional support to the British government in India. A resolution was passed to the effect–

- Condemning Nazi attack on Poland.
- Declaring that India could not be a party to the war which was said to be fought for democratic freedom even as that very freedom was denied to it.
- If Britain was fighting for democracy and freedom, then it should first prove it to India.
- Some sort of responsible government should be established at the centre immediately and a Constituent Assembly be set up to frame the constitution of free India in near future.
- India would then gladly join other democratic nations in war effort.

A response was now awaited from the Viceroy and the British government.

Government Response

Viceroy Linlithgow issued an official statement (17th October 1939) which was as follows:

- The viceroy refused to define British war aims beyond stating that Britain was resisting aggression;
- The viceroy stated that as part of future arrangement, the government would consult 'representatives of several communities, parties and interests in India, and the Indian princes' as to how the Act of 1935 might be reformed; and
- The viceroy talked about the immediate establishment of a 'consultative committee' for seeking views of different sections as when needed.

Thus, it was clear that the British Government was in no mood to make any promises and commit itself in advance on the post-war constitutional status of India. Viceroy Linlithgow harped about the differences among Indians particularly among the Muslim League, the Princes and the Congress. Zetland, the Secretary of State, stressed in the House of Lords on the differences among Hindus and Muslims and branded Congress as a purely Hindu organisation. Further, instead of loosening control over India, Defence of India Rules were promulgated to check defiance of any British authority.

The Viceregal statement evoked sharp response from the national leadership. The sharpest reaction came from Gandhi, who was earlier advocating unconditional support to Britain. He stated that the British are adamant on continuing with their old policy of divide and rule.

On 22nd October 1939, the CWC condemned the Viceregal statement and called upon the **Congress Ministries to tender their resignation**, which they did as obedient soldiers. The result of these political developments was that except for 4 provinces—Assam, Sindh, Punjab and Bengal—provincial autonomy was no more a living constitutional feature but only a thing of the past. During the next few years, as Congress drifted away from active politics, the League moved in to fill the political vacuum and consolidated its position through Jinnah's manoeuvrings with the Viceroy. On 22nd December 1939, the Muslim League celebrated the day as **'day of deliverance'** and thanksgiving as mark of relief that the people had finally gained freedom from the Congress rule.

Pakistan Resolution (Lahore, March 1940)

At its Lahore Session, the Muslim League passed the Pakistan Resolution calling for the grouping of geographically contiguous areas where Muslims were in majority, i.e. Northwest and East. During the session, Jinnah propounded his two-nation theory that India comprised of two nations—a

Hindu nation and a Muslim nation, who were different economically, politically, socially, culturally and historically. That Muslims were not a minority but a nation, and therefore they were rightfully entitled to a nation of their own in the form of Pakistan.

Individual Satyagraha (17th October 1940–December 1941)

Congress now considered launching of a civil disobedience movement but once again sharp differences emerged within the party on the issue. Dominant leaders including Gandhi himself felt that the atmosphere was not ripe for immediately starting a mass Satyagraha owing to the following aspects:

- The Allies, Britain and France, were after all fighting for a just cause and should not be embarrassed during the war.
- The Congress organisation had been corrupted during 1938–39 and there were differences and anarchy within Congress.
- The masses were not ready, there was lack of Hindu-Muslim unity and under these circumstances, a civil disobedience movement could easily degenerate into communal riots.

Ramgarh Congress Session, March 1940 (Presided by Maulana Abul Kalam Azad)

In such an atmosphere, the Congress met at Ramgarh (in present Jharkhand) and Azad declared 'India cannot endure the prospect of Nazism and Fascism, but she is even more tired of British imperialism'. However, in its resolution, the Ramgarh Congress declared that a civil disobedience movement shall be launched as soon as the Congress organisation is considered fit enough for the purpose'.

However, the resolution was opposed by a coalition of various Left-wing groups including the Congress Socialists, Communists and the members of the Kisan Sabhas and the Forward Block. They got together and held an **anti-compromise conference** at Ramgarh under the leadership of Subhas Chandra Bose and resolved to resist any compromise with imperialism and prepare themselves for a militant struggle.

In the few months that followed, the government refused to bend and kept issuing ordinance after ordinance taking away the freedoms of speech, press, associations, etc. The patience of the people was now on the verge of exhaustion and they felt that time has come to show the British lest their patience be taken for weakness.

Congress Presidents Maulana Abul Kalam Azad remained the Congress President during 1940–46. However, at the time of independence in 1947, JB Kripalani was the Congress President.

Change of Government in Britain and August Offer (8th August 1940)

Meanwhile, Britain's stand somewhat softened owing to two main reasons—First, in May 1940, a new government came to power in Britain with Winston Churchill as Prime Minister (1940–45). Second, the Allies were facing defeat after defeat in war and the Nazi under Hitler were knocking at Britain's door. With the aim of securing India's active cooperation in the war effort, the British government decided to offer certain concessions to the Indians known as August Offer:

On 8th August 1940, **Viceroy Linlithgow** put forth the offer which proposed the following:

- **Expansion of Governor General's Executive Council** with more Indian representation.
- **Formation of a War Advisory Council**.
- **Dominion Status** of the Westminster variety as soon as possible after the war.
- **Constitution Making Body** to be set up after the war in recognition of the natural and inherent right of the Indian people to determine the form of their future constitution.
- **Full weight to minority opinion** and that no such constitution will be accepted which did not enjoy their support (Muslim League had already demanded Pakistan in the Lahore Session of 1940).
- Acceptability of the new constitution subject to fulfilment of British obligations such as Defence, Minority Rights, Treaties with Native States, and position of All India Services.

Significance of August Offer

For the first time, the inherent right of Indians to frame their own constitution was recognised and the demand for Constituent Assembly was conceded. Thus, what was denied by the Act of 1935 was to be conceded after the war. In July 1941, the Viceroy's Executive Council was enlarged, Taking Indian representation to 8 out of 12 for the first time. The English remained in charge of Defence, Finance and Home departments. A **National Defence Council** was also set up which was purely advisory in function.

Responses

However, the August Offer was rejected by the Congress. Nehru declared that the whole conception of Dominion Status was 'dead as a door-nail'. Though the League welcomed the veto given to the minorities, it reiterated that it would not accept anything short of partition of India. In September 1940, **at Simla**, Gandhi had long but futile meetings with the Viceroy. Meanwhile, the government had already begun making preventive arrests of Congress workers and local leaders. Convinced that the British were in no mood to change their policy in India, Gandhi now decided to launch passive civil disobedience in the form of a **limited Satyagraha on an individual basis** by a few selected individuals in every locality.

Why Individual Satyagraha?

The Satyagraha was confined to individual participation because of the following:

- While satyagraha would disprove the British claim that India supported the war effort wholeheartedly, its limited nature would ensure that war efforts against Nazism were not obstructed which would have been the case if mass agitation was launched.
- It would give yet another opportunity to the British to peacefully accept Indian demands.
- It would prepare the masses for the upcoming mass struggle.

Acharya Vinoba Bhave (First Satyagrahi, 17th October 1940)

An individual Satyagrahi was to deliver an anti-war speech. In case he was not arrested, he would repeat the act in the next village while moving in the direction of Delhi, thus initiating a movement which came to be known as **'Delhi Chalo' movement**.

On 17th October 1940, Individual Satyagraha was inaugurated by Vinoba Bhave by delivering an anti-war speech at **Paunar village** near Wardha. Gandhi had personally selected Bhave after his other nominees, Vallabhbhai and Nehru, were arrested even before they could start the agitation. Later, **Jawaharlal Nehru** became the **second individual Satyagrahi**. By May 1941, more than 25,000 Satyagrahis had been arrested for offering individual Satyagraha.

Vinoba Bhave (1895–1982), spiritual successor of Mahatma Gandhi.

However, Individual Satyagraha could not achieve much due to restrictions imposed by Gandhi. Participation from the Congressmen was also slow to come and nominees showed reluctance in relinquishing posts they held in municipal bodies.

Satyagraha Suspended under Changed War Situation

In December 1941, the CWC decided to suspend the movement. By this time, even the international situation had changed:

- Britain continued to face defeat after defeat in the war. In fact, the years of the Second World War were the most disastrous for Britain in its entire history as world power.
- On 22nd June 1941, **Germany had attacked Russia** (Operation Barbarossa).
- On 7th December 1941, Japan had dramatically joined the war on Germany's side by launching a surprise attack on American Fleet at **Pearl Harbour**.
- Japan quickly occupied South East Asia including Philippines, Indonesia, Malay, Burma and Indo-China with lightening speed.

Gandhi had already denounced the Japanese slogan of **'Asia for Asiatics'** and had exhorted the Indians to denounce Japanese goods. In December 1941, the CWC also passed a resolution offering full cooperation to the Allies if Britain agreed to give full independence after the war and substance of power immediately. It was during this time that **Gandhi chose Jawaharlal as his successor** stating, 'Not Rajaji (C. Rajagopalachari) but Jawaharlal will be my successor...I know that when I am gone, he will speak my language'.

Note: Meanwhile, in 1941, the eight-year old ban on the **Communist Party of India** was lifted after it decided to support the government in war efforts following the German invasion of Russia.

Cripps Mission (22nd March 1942)

As war situation rapidly worsened against the Allies, USSR, USA (President Roosevelt), China (President Chiang Kai-Shek) and Labor Party of Britain now began to pressurise Churchill to reconsider the British policy in India and seek active support of the Indians in the war. Consequently, the government released many political prisoners. And after **Japan occupied Rangoon** in March 1942, bringing the war to India's doorstep, the British decided to send Cripps Mission to India.

Prime Minister **Winston Churchill** sent the leader of the House of Commons, Sir Stafford Cripps, with the aim of securing India's active support in the war effort. Cripps was a Left-wing Laborite and had been a strong supporter of Indian national movement. He arrived in India on 22nd March 1942 with a set of proposals and opened negotiations with Indian leaders. He declared that the aim of new British policy in India was 'the earliest possible realisation of **self-government in India**'.

Cripps Proposals

The Draft Declaration Cripps brought with him was quite disappointing and it included the following proposals:

- **Dominion Status** The object of his Majesty's Government was the creation of a new Indian Union which shall constitute a Dominion in the British Commonwealth but in no way subordinate to Britain in any aspect of its domestic or external affairs. (Thus, Dominion Status to be granted to India immediately after the war with the right to decide its relations with the British Commonwealth including the right to secede from the Commonwealth).
- **Constituent Assembly** Immediately after the war, steps shall be taken to set up in India an elected body to frame a new constitution for India. Indian States shall also be provided representation in the constitution making body. (Thus, the Constituent Assembly was to comprise of members from British India as well as princely states. The task of making new constitution would now be solely in Indian hands. The members of the Constituent Assembly were to be elected by provincial assembly and nominated by rulers in case of princely states).
- **Right of Non-Accession of Provinces ('provincial option' or 'local option' clause)** The constitution so framed would be accepted by the British government on the condition that any Indian province, if it so desired, could remain outside the Indian Union and negotiate directly with Britain. (Thus, accommodating the Pakistan demand. One can see in this 'provincial option' the powerful germs of Pakistan).
- **Right of Secession of Provinces** The provinces would have the right to secede for a possible partition of the country.
- **Protection of Racial and Linguistic Minorities** A treaty was to be signed between His Majesty's Government and the constitution-making body that will cover all matters arising out of the complete transfer of responsibility from British to Indian hands. It would also make provisions for the protection of racial and linguistic minorities.
- **British Control over Defence** Until the new constitution could be framed, Britain would retain the actual control of defence and military operations, and the Governor-General was to continue with all his powers as before.

> - **Amery**, the Secretary of State during 1940–45, described the Declaration as 'conservative, reactionary and limited offer'.
> - **Nehru**, a friend of Cripps, later wrote that, 'When I read those proposals for the first time, I was profoundly depressed'.
> - Nehru and Maulana Azad were the official negotiators for the Congress.

How was Cripps Mission Different from Past Proposals?

- Free India could withdraw from the commonwealth.
- The making of the Constitution was to be **solely** in Indian hands now (and not 'mainly' in Indian hands, as contained in the August Offer).
- Indians were allowed a large share in the administration of the interim government.
- For the first time, a concrete plan was provided for the Constituent Assembly.

- Right of non-accession and secession from the Union provided the **blue-print for India's partition**. At a time when the Pakistan demand had hardly been taken seriously by Indians, its serious consideration by British leaders gave legitimacy to the Pakistan demand.

Reasons for Failure of Cripps Mission

- **Cripps Proposals were rejected almost unanimously by all Indian parties**
  - Congress refused to rely on any future promises and also rejected the idea of Britain's control over Indian defence. The Congress opposed the principle of non-accession of provinces which seemed like an axe applied to the very roots of Indian unity. Giving the provinces and the princely states the right to secede from the Union, the proposals provided for the **Balkanisation of the country** and were opposed by the nationalists. The Congress also objected to the provision that the princely states shall be represented in the Constituent Assembly not by the people but by the nominees of the rulers.
  - Gandhi rejected the proposals calling the Cripps offer for Dominion Status after the war as **'a post-dated cheque on a crashing bank'**.
  - The Muslim League wanted a definite declaration in favour of a separate state (Pakistan) for the Muslims and equal number of seats as Congress in the Interim Government.
  - The Liberals, the Hindu Mahasabha as well as the Sikhs objected to the secession proposal.
  - The Depressed Classes, the Sikhs, the Indian Christians and the Anglo-Indians also wanted more safeguards for their communities.
- **Limited Mandate of Cripps** Cripps was also unable to bargain or negotiate as he had been told not to go beyond the Draft Declaration. Thus, he adopted a **'take it or leave it'** attitude which added to the deadlock.
- **Attempts to Sabotage Cripps Efforts** Cripps proposals proved to be too radical for his PM and the Viceroy and too conservative for the Indians. Several British leaders including Churchill (PM), Amery (Secretary of State), Linlithgow (Viceroy) and Wavell (Commander in Chief) did not want Cripps Mission to succeed and they tried hard to sabotage his efforts in India.

Evaluation of Cripps Proposals

The Cripps scheme was meant to please everyone from the Congress to the Muslim League, from princes to religious and racial minorities. However, it ended up pleasing no one. The Mission was a reiteration of the August Offer of 1940 and failed to meet Indian aspirations. It evoked suspicion as whether the British were sincerely committed to transfer of power. The Mission smelt more like a sop offered to the Indian leaders to secure their active cooperation in war efforts, than a genuine attempt to solve the Indian deadlock. In April 1942, Cripps Mission returned to Britain, leaving behind even more frustrated and embittered Indians.

Immediate Context to Quit India Movement

The immediate context to Quit India Movement was provided by the following factors:

1. **Failure of Cripps Mission** It was now clear that the government was unwilling to offer any honourable settlement to the Indian demands and was determined to continue with India's unwilling participation in the war. The failure of Cripps Mission embittered the Indians.

2. **War time shortages and rising prices** The Indians felt further discontented with war-time shortages and rising prices.
3. **Highhanded attitude of British authorities** The people were considerably angered by the highhandedness of British authorities such as commandeering of boats in Bengal and Orissa to prevent their use by the Japanese.
4. **Allied reverses and an imminent British collapse** People also felt encouraged by the news of Allied reverses and an imminent British collapse.
5. **Manner of British evacuation from Malaya and Burma** The manner of British evacuation from Malaya and Burma had also added fuel to the fire. The British residents were evacuated first, while leaving the subject population to their fate. Indians from South East Asia had given detailed account of British apathy in their letters sent to relatives in India and how they were left behind for the Japanese. Hence, it was feared that the British might repeat the same betrayal in case of a Japanese invasion in India.
6. **Demoralisation among Indians** Due to all these factors, the national leadership also felt that the people were becoming demoralised and might not resist at all in the event of a Japanese invasion. Hence, it was necessary to draw them out of depression and remind them of their power and worth.
7. **Faith in the stability of British rule had reached an all-time low** People had begun to withdraw deposits from banks and had started hoarding gold.

Really, the period from April to August 1942, was one of daily heightening tension. Japan was virtually knocking at the door of the country, and the empty gesture in the form of Cripps Mission had now radicalised even leaders like Nehru and Gandhi who were initially committed to not hampering the war efforts. In fact, Gandhi now grew more and more militant with every passing day. He was now convinced that the time was ripe for a mass struggle and began to talk about it from different platforms-

- In an interview to **Louis Fischer** he had said, 'I have become impatient...I may not be able to convince the Congress...I will go ahead and address myself directly to the people'.
- In May 1942, Gandhi wrote in the **Harijan,** 'the presence of the British in India is an invitation to Japan to invade India. Their withdrawal removes that bait'.

Thus, Gandhi had made up his mind to urge Britain to quit India in an orderly fashion and in case they did not agree, to launch a mass Civil Disobedience Movement. Even as Gandhi edged towards a struggle, Nehru remained opposed and gave way only at the very end.

Eventually, the Congress decided to launch the movement amidst dissenting voices (there were Congressmen who followed an independent view, for instance **C. Rajagopalachari**. He was urging the Congress to accept the demand for Pakistan and support Britain in war efforts. Owing to these differences, he had resigned from the Congress in 1942). The Congress further clarified that it did not mean that the British had to withdraw from India immediately but it meant an immediate acknowledgement of India's independence.

CWC Meeting at Wardha (14th July 1942)

In July 1942, the CWC met at Wardha and adopted the Quit India Resolution which was to be later ratified by the AICC in its Bombay meeting.

AICC Ratifies the Quit India Resolution (Bombay, Gowalia Tank Maidan, 8th August 1942)

The historic meeting took place at Gowalia Tank Maidan in Bombay where people had gathered in unprecedented numbers to hear their leaders speak. Gandhi's speech had the most electrifying impact—Gandhi asked the British to quit India and 'leave India in God's hands'. He also appealed to all sections of Indian people to participate in the movement and gave them the mantra of **'Do or Die**. We shall either free India or die in the attempt, we shall not live to see the perpetuation of our slavery'. Even as he stressed that 'every Indian who desires freedom and strives for it must be his own guide', Gandhi's speech contained specific instructions for different sections of people, which were as follows-

- Government servants were asked not to resign yet but openly declare their loyalty to the Congress
- The soldiers were asked not to leave their posts but to refuse to fire on their own people
- The Princes were asked to accept the sovereignty of their own people rather than that of the foreigners

On 8th August 1942, the Quit India Resolution was ratified by the AICC. However, the Congress did not give any concrete line of action to be adopted by the people but merely appealed to them to remain completely non-violent at all times.

The Quit India Movement (8th August 1942–June 1945)

Even before the Congress could launch the movement, the government struck a severe blow. On the morning of 9th August, all prominent leaders of the Congress, including Gandhi, were arrested and taken to unknown destinations. The AICC and the PCCs were also banned. The Congress did not get time to plan the line of action and hence what arose was a **spontaneous movement** which began taking its own course, with people directing their own actions.

A commemorative postal stamp depicting AICC Quit India Resolution August 1942

The news of the arrests led to unprecedented popular outbursts throughout the country. Since all recognised leaders at central as well as provincial level were arrested, **new leaders emerged** from among the local cadres, particularly students.

In the beginning, the movement was mostly non-violent. The people took out processions and struck work. But soon government repression followed that instigated people to take up violence. Relegating Gandhian principle to the background, in many places people devised their own methods of protest that included-

- Attacks on symbols of British authority such as police stations, railway stations and post offices
- Cutting off telegraph wires, telephones, railway lines and power lines
- Disrupting traffic and striking work, etc.

These attacks mostly aimed at disrupting the movement of police and military forces that were deployed to crush the movement. Madras and Bengal were the most affected in this respect.

Trends and Responses

The Quit India Movement, also termed as the **August Revolution** or the **Revolt of 1942**, evoked varied trends and responses:

Parallel Governments

At many places, state control was temporarily seized and people established 'parallel government' or Swaraj. For instance, parallel governments were established in:

- **Ballia, UP** (August 1942) This was the first parallel government proclaimed under the leadership of **Chittu Pande**, also known as Sher-e-Ballia. Pande also succeeded in securing the release of many Congress leaders.
- **Tamluk, Midnapore district, Bengal** (December 1942) Here, **Jatiya Sarkar** was established under **Satish Samant**. This parallel government set up its own departments like Law and Order, Health, Education, Agriculture, etc. It also undertook cyclone relief work, gave grants to schools, set up arbitration courts and even formed an armed Vidyut Vahini.
- **Satara, Maharashtra** Here emerged the longest lasting parallel government called **'Prati Sarkar'** under the leadership of **Nana Patil**. The government set up Nyayadan Mandals or peoples' courts, enforced prohibition, set up village libraries and even organised Gandhi marriages (that allowed no ostentation, invited the untouchables, etc.). The Prati Sarkar received much support from the ruler of Aundh who was a Gandhian and had even got a constitution of his state drafted by Gandhi. This sarkar lasted till 1945.
- **Talcher, Orissa** **Laxman Nayak** emerged as an important tribal and rebel leader.
- Parallel governments were also established at Azamgarh, Ghazipur, Monghyr, Muzzafarpur etc., in UP and Bihar.

> **Was Quit India Movement a spontaneous outburst?** According to Bipan Chandra, 'the element of spontaneity in the movement of 1942 was certainly larger than in the earlier movements...the whole pattern of the Gandhian mass movements was that the leadership chalked out a broad programme of action and left its implementation at the local level to the initiative of the local level activists and the masses. (Thus) In a way, the degree of spontaneity and popular initiative that was actually exercised had been sanctioned by the leadership itself'.

Regional Trends

- In the beginning, the movement was strong in urban areas but later it picked up pace in rural areas where it also continued for a longer duration of time.
- The response to the movement was strong in Bombay, Gujarat, UP, Bihar, Bengal, Orissa, Assam, Andhra and Karnataka.
- The response was weak in Punjab, Sindh, and NWFP.
- In Bihar, Patna was cut off from the rest of the areas as a result of popular agitation. School students, village masses and poor labourers joined the movement and looted government property especially food grains lying at railway stations.
- In UP, furious masses attacked Madhuban Police Station in Azamgarh district.

- In Orissa, government forces used aeroplanes to check the advancing peasant guerrillas from entering Talcher.

Who Participated?

- **The youth**, especially students, workers and peasants provided the backbone of the 'revolt'.
- **Students** boycotted schools and colleges all over the country. They took out processions, wrote and distributed 'illegal patrikas' and became couriers for the emerging underground networks. Students from Banaras Hindu University decided to spread the message of Quit India in rural areas. They popularised the slogans of 'Station phoonk do', 'Thana jalao' and 'Angrez bhaag gaya'.
- **Workers** struck work in many industrial centres like Bombay, Kanpur, Ahmedabad, Jamshedpur and Poona. Strike at Ahmedabad continued for the longest duration of 3 months.
- **Peasants** in villages formed large crowds and stormed the nearest district town, attacking all symbols of government authority.
- **Women** also played an important role—Aruna Asaf Ali, Sucheta Kriplani and Usha Mehta are some examples.
- **Small government officials** (those at lower rungs of administration) also gave generous support to the movement. In fact, erosion of loyalty to the British emerged as a striking feature of the movement.
- **Businessmen** gave support to the movement through donations and shelter to political activists. However, the movement evoked weak response from merchant community as they had profited heavily during the war.

Who did NOT Participate?

Sections of people who did not participate in the Quit India Movement included the Muslim League, the Hindu Mahasabha and the Communist Party of India. The Princes, the landlords (in general) as well as Congress leaders like Rajagopalachari did not participate in the movement and instead supported the war efforts.

- **The Muslim League** condemned the Quit India Movement and instead supported the British in war efforts, thus growing rapidly in influence with the British.
- **The Hindu Mahasabha** also condemned the Quit India Movement calling it 'sterile, unmanly and injurious to the Hindu cause' and stalwart Hindu leaders like VD Savarkar, BS Munje and Shyama Prasad Mukherjee whole heartedly supported British war efforts. RSS also remained aloof.
- **The Communist Party** of India also did not support the movement following the involvement of Russia in the war in December 1941 and their 'People's War' strategy.

Exceptions

However, the attraction of the Quit India Movement was such that many from the above sections could not hold themselves back. True, the movement did not arouse any mass Muslim participation, it did not arouse their hostility either and there was a complete absence of any communal clashes. Similarly, many communists at the local level participated in the movement despite official stand taken by the Communist Party. Small zamindars also participated in significant numbers with one of the biggest zamindars—**Raja of Darbhanga,** supporting the movement. A total lack of anti-zamindar violence by the peasants was also an interesting feature of the movement.

Government Response

The government came down heavily on the nationalists and the August Revolution was suppressed with an iron hand. In fact, the repression knew no bounds, with the repression emerging as the most brutal ever against the national movement. The government armed itself with draconian measures and took away even basic civil liberties:

- Press was completely muzzled (the publication of National Herald and Harijan stopped completely during the entire period of the struggle).
- Government took to wide-scale arrests, lathicharges, floggings, firings and even burning of villages and Congress offices.
- Demonstrating crowds were machine gunned and even bombed from air.
- Prisoners were tortured.
- The military took over many towns and cities.
- Punitive fines were extorted from the residents of areas affected by the upsurge.

As per official figures, by the end of 1943, more than 90,000 persons were arrested and more than 1,000 were killed in police firings. India had not seen such ruthless repression since the days of 1857.

With the above measures, the British were able to crush the mass phase of the struggle within six to seven weeks. In doing so, the war situation helped them in two ways:

- First, the British had stationed a massive military force in India to fight the Japanese which was promptly used to crush the Quit India Movement.
- Second, the British felt free to repress the movement in a ruthless manner without bothering about international criticism. Major powers of the world were too busy fighting one another and had no time to concern themselves with what the British were doing in India.

Underground Movement

The most remarkable trend of the movement was the emergence of underground networks. Unable to function in the open due to brutal government repression, underground networks began to emerge in various parts of the country. On 9th November 1942, **Jaiprakash Narain** and **Ramnandan Misra** escaped from Hazaribagh jail to Nepal border and organised an underground movement from there.

Similarly, **Underground Socialist Activities** were carried out by leaders like Aruna Asaf Ali, Ram Manohar Lohiya, Achyut Patwardhan, Sucheta Kriplani and Biju Patnaik. The most daring underground activity was the starting of **Congress Radio** which operated from Bombay city with Usha Mehta as its announcer.

Even though the number of people directly involved in underground activity was limited, yet they received tremendous support from a large section of people across the country. The wealthy helped with generous donations, others provided hideouts for underground activists, students acted as couriers, villagers refused to give information to the police, pilots and train drivers delivered materials and explosives and government officials passed on critical information. The underground activists generally planned to disrupt communications and even planned some attacks on government officials. However, the most significant contribution of the Underground Activity was in keeping the spirit of Quit India Movement aloft even after the mass phase was brutally repressed.

Congress on Violence

The Congress leadership did not condemn the violence, but at the same time it refused to take any responsibility for the violence committed by the people. Certain Congressmen also felt that the special circumstances warranted such violence.

Gandhi on Violence and his Fast

Gandhi also refused to condemn people's resort to violence, despite constant government exhortation. Instead, **he held government responsible** for it and said that it was the bigger violence of the state that had provoked people to violence.

Further, to register his protest against the violence resorted to by the state, Gandhi commenced a fast in jail (**Aga Khan Palace Poona**) on 10th February 1943. The news of the fast, evoked massive response from the people. People in India and across the world began to demand his release. Three Indian members of the Viceroy's Executive Council, viz. **MS Aney, NR Sarkar and HP Mody**, who had earlier supported the government in its repression of the 1942 Revolt, now resigned. Even as an anxious nation pleaded for Gandhi's life, the British went ahead making arrangements for his funeral. Thus, Gandhi's fast had the desired effect of raising the morale of the people and of exposing the arrogant attitude of the British to the whole world.

Muslim League Observes 'Pakistan Day' (23rd March 1943)

Even as the Quit India Movement continued, the League observed the 'Pakistan Day' and Jinnah declared that the demand for Pakistan was the final 'national' goal of all Muslims in India. In 1943, the League also adopted a new slogan for the League, **'Divide and Quit'**.

20th October 1943 Lord Linlithgow is replaced by Lord Wavell (until then the Commander-in-Chief) as Governor General. The outgoing Viceroy's regime was longer than any other GG's, 7.5 years. Yet, it was the most unproductive from the point of view of constitutional advance. Linlithgow had come to India with great enthusiasm to establish an All India Federation under the Act of 1935. Not only was this not achieved, it also became a lost cause forever.

Rajagopalachari Formula (CR Formula or Rajaji Formula, March 1944)

In March 1944, C. Rajagopalachari evolved a formula to bring about Congress-League cooperation, accepting the **basis of Pakistan**. The formula was evolved with full approval of Gandhiji and embodied the following terms:

1. The League would endorse the demand for independence and cooperate with the Congress in forming a provisional government for the transitional period.
2. At the end of the war, a **plebiscite** shall be held in all Muslim majority areas in the north west and the north east that would decide whether or not these areas should form a separate state.
3. In the event of partition, agreements would be made on essential matters.
4. The above terms shall be binding only in case of full transfer of power by Britain to the government of India.

In his response, Jinnah wrote to Gandhiji asking for detailed clarification on the terms. Jinnah was of the view that since the Muslims were a separate nation, the Muslims alone should be entitled to vote for partition and not the whole population of the disputed areas. In other words, he claimed the right of self-determination for the Muslims alone, while denying it to the non-Muslims. Gandhi refused to accept this view and the two-nation theory.

It is clear that while the Congress was concerned with the attainment of independence for the whole country and was eager to gain the League's cooperation towards this end, the League was obsessed with the idea of partition and making the Congress agree on the two-nation theory. Jinnah was also opposed to a common Centre concerned with Defence, Commerce and Communications. Given the radical differences in the objectives and attitudes of the Congress and the League, the Rajagopalachari Formula ended in smoke. Hindu leaders led by VD Savarkar too condemned the CR Formula.

Note: On 6th May 1944, Gandhiji was released on medical grounds and the Congress resumed constructive work with special focus on party re-organisation.

Desai- Liaquat Plan (January 1945)

This was yet another effort to end the deadlock between the Congress and the League. While Gandhi and the entire CWC had been put behind bars during the Quit India Movement, Bhulabhai Desai was one of the few Congress leaders who were free. Desai (leader of the Congress Party in the Central Legislative Assembly) met Liaquat Ali Khan (Deputy Leader of the Muslim League) in the Assembly and handed him a draft proposal for the formation of an Interim Government at the Centre, consisting of the following:

A stamp printed in Pakistan shows Liaquat Ali Khan

1. **Equal number** of persons nominated by the Congress and the League in the Central Legislature (acceptance of this parity between the Congress and the League had far reaching consequences).
2. Representatives of minorities (20%).
3. The Commander-in-Chief.

Even on these lines, no settlement could be reached.

Congress Leaders Released from Jail in Anticipation of the Simla Conference (14th June 1945)

On 8th May 1945, the war in Europe ended after the suicide of Hitler and subsequent surrender of Germany (during these three years, 1942–45, the Congress leaders were in jail). The General Elections in England were in the offing and the Viceroy in India began formulating an offer, known as **the Wavell Offer** or **the Wavell Plan** to strike an agreement with the Congress. A conference was proposed to be convened with a view to opening talks with the Indian leaders. Consequently, on 14th June 1945, the government released the nationalists to enable them to participate in the Simla Conference. This marked the **official end of the Quit India Movement**.

Evaluation of Quit India Movement

Positive Outcomes

True, the Quit India Movement or the Revolt of 1942 was crushed within a short period, yet it well demonstrated the depth of nationalist feelings in India and the great capacity for struggle and sacrifice the people had developed. It gave a severe blow to the moral basis of British rule in India and the illusion that a majority of Indians were loyalists and favoured continuation of British rule.

The movement demonstrated with ample clarity that the British were 'persona non-grata' in India. The biggest contribution of the movement was that the demand for independence now became non-negotiable and any future negotiations with the British could only be on the manner of transfer of power.

Negative Fallouts

The worst fallout of the movement was the consolidation of the Muslim League, which grew from strength to strength during this period. While Congress leaders were languishing in jails, the League consolidated its base in villages and promised not only an Islamic state but also a peasant utopia for Muslim peasants. By condemning the movement and supporting the British in war efforts, the League came closer to the British and occupied a prominent place in Indian constitutional politics. The League, which in 1937 could not form a Ministry even in one province, had consolidated its position and established its sway in five provinces-Assam, Bengal, the Punjab and the NWFP. All this made the demand for Pakistan a closer reality than ever before, throwing up serious consequences on the course of future constitutional development in the country.

Prelim Capsule

Run up to Quit India Movement

Events	Year	Important Details
Outbreak of WW2	1st September 1939	Viceroy Linlithgow **unilaterally** declared India as a belligerent state on the British side.
CWC Meeting, Wardha	10–14th September 1939	The Congress finally decided to adopt Nehru's view and extend **conditional support** to the British.
Viceroy Linlithgow's Statement	17th October 1939	British government refused to make any promises and commit itself in advance on the post-war constitutional status of India. Talked about setting up of a 'consultative committee'.
Congress Ministries resign	22nd October 1939	Congress Ministries resign to protest against Britain's unilateral decision of dragging Indian into the war. Provincial governments continued in 4 provinces—Assam, Sindh, Punjab and Bengal.

Day of Deliverance	22nd December 1939	Muslim League celebrates 'day of deliverance' upon resignation of Congress Ministries.
Pakistan Resolution, Lahore	March 1940	Muslim League passed Pakistan Resolution calling formation of Pakistan as a separate homeland for the Muslims.
Ramgarh Congress Session	March 1940	Presided by **Maulana Abul Kalam Azad**. A resolution was passed which declared that a civil disobedience movement shall be launched as soon as the Congress organisation is considered fit enough for the purpose. A coalition of various Left-wing groups who got together and held an **anti-compromise conference** at Ramgarh under the leadership of Subhas Chandra Bose and resolved to prepare themselves for a militant struggle.
August Offer	8th August 1940	For the first time, the inherent right of Indians to frame their own constitution was recognised and the demand for **Constituent Assembly** was conceded.
Individual Satyagraha	17th October 1940	Acharya Vinoba Bhave became the First Satyagrahi. He was to deliver an anti-war speech village after village, while moving in the direction of Delhi, thus initiating a movement which came to be known as **'Delhi Chalo' movement**. Bhave delivered his first anti-war speech **Paunar village** near Wardha. Later, **Jawaharlal Nehru** became thesecond individual Satyagrahi.
Cripps Mission	22nd March 1942	In March, **Japan occupied Rangoon** bringing the war to India's doorstep which forced the British to send Cripps Mission to India. Prime Minister **Winston Churchill** sent the leader of the House of Commons, Sir Stafford Cripps, with the aim of securing India's active support in the war effort. Cripps declared that the aim of new British policy in India was 'the earliest possible realisation of **self-government** in India'. Proposals included- Dominion Status, Constituent Assembly, Right of Non-Accession of Provinces, Right of Secession of provinces, Protection of racial and linguistic minorities and British control over defence. Gandhi rejected the proposals calling the Cripps offer for Dominion Status after the war as **'a post dated cheque on a crashing bank'**. Cripps adopted a **'take it or leave it'** attitude which added to the deadlock.

CWC Meeting at Wardha	14th July 1942	The CWC adopted the Quit India Resolution which was to be later ratified by the AICC in its Bombay meeting.
Quit India Movement (QIM)	8th August 1942	AICC met at **Gowalia Tank Maidan**, Bombay and ratified the Quit India Resolution. The next day morning, all prominent leaders of the Congress, including Gandhi, were arrested. Hence what arose was a **spontaneous movement** which began taking its own course, with people directing their own actions.
Pakistan Day	23rd March 1943	Even as the QIM, continued the League observed the 'Pakistan Day' and also adopted a new slogan **'Divide and Quit'**.
Rajagopalachari Formula	March 1944	It was a formula to bring about Congress-League cooperation, accepting the **idea of Pakistan** on the basis of a plebiscite after the war. The formula was evolved with full approval of Gandhiji.
Desai- Liaquat Plan	Jan 1945	It proposed the formation of an Interim Government at the Centre, consisting of an **equal number** of persons nominated by the Congress and the League in the Central Legislature.
Congress leaders released from jail	14th Jun 1945	On 8th May 1945, the war in Europe ended with the surrender of Germany. The Congress leaders were released from jail in anticipation of the Simla Conference, marking the official end of the Quit India Movement.

Indian National Army

Even as the Quit India Movement fought against the British in India, the INA fought against the British from foreign soil.

First Phase of INA

Indian National Army or Azad Hind Fauj was an armed force formed by Indian nationalists in Southeast Asia during the Second World War. The idea of INA was first conceived by **Captain Mohan Singh**, an officer in the British Indian Army, who decided not to join the retreating British Army and instead turned to the Japanese for help. A religious person **'Giani Pritam Singh'** and a Japanese army officer, **Major Fujiwara**, further encouraged him to work for Indian's independence. After the fall of Singapore, 40,000 Indian soldiers surrendered before Fujiwara who in turn handed them over to Mohan Singh. In this way, in 1942, First INA was formed comprising Indian Prisoners of War (POW). Its aim was to fight for India's independence.

INA received tremendous support from ethnic Indians in Southeast Asia who had already formed local leagues in Malay in support of Indian independence. Though there were a number of prominent leaders, the overall leadership came to rest with **Rash Behari Bose**, a veteran terrorist revolutionary, who had been living in self-exile in Japan since the days of First World War. He used the opportunity offered by WW2 to mobilise the Indians for an armed struggle against Britain.

In March 1942, Rash Behari convened a conference in Tokyo of all Indian leaders living from Malay to Burma and announced the formation of the **Indian Independence League**. Afterwards, in June 1942, the League met at Bangkok, known as **Bangkok Conference**, with the following consequences:

- It elected Rash Behari Bose as its President
- It resolved to raise the INA (which now had about 40,000 Indian soldiers)
- Captain Mohan Singh was appointed as the Commander of the INA and **Subhas Chandra Bose** was invited to lead the INA movement.

However, the First INA collapsed and was disbanded in December 1942 after differences emerged between INA leadership and the Japanese over the role of INA in Japan's war in Asia.

Second Phase of INA

The Second Phase of INA began with the arrival of Subhas Chandra Bose in Singapore in July 1943 who subsequently revived the INA. On 5th July 1943, Rash Behari handed over the leadership of Indian Independence League and the INA to Subhas Chandra Bose. Bose was now called **Netaji** by the soldiers of the INA.

Life of Subhas Chandra Bose at a glance

Subhas Chandra Bose

Subhas Chandra Bose (1897–1945) Born in Cuttack, Orissa, Bose rose to be a prominent leader of the Indian independence movement. He resigned from the Imperial Civil Service to join the freedom struggle, but his attempts during WW2 to secure India's freedom by allying with Nazi Germany and imperialist Japan left behind a troubled legacy.

After graduating from Calcutta University, Bose had left for England from where he appeared for the Indian Civil Service Exam and secured 4th position (1920). However, the political developments in India beginning with the Jallianwala Bagh Massacre emotionally disturbed Bose and he resigned from the ICS stating, 'I did not think that one could be loyal to the British Raj and yet serve Indian honestly, heart and soul'. The following year he returned to India, came under the influence of Chittaranjan Das and Gandhi and joined the Indian National Congress. CR Das became his 'political guru'.

In December 1921, he went to jail for the first time for his nationalist activities. In 1923, he was elected as Mayor of Calcutta but he was soon arrested and deported to Mandalay jail in Burma (1924–27). Upon his release, he helped in the formation of the **Independence of India League (Aug 1928)**. In 1928 Calcutta Congress Session, when Gandhiji himself moved the resolution demanding Dominion Status Constitution for India, Bose sought an amendment demanding full independence for India. Bose served as the President of **AITUC** during 1929–31 and emerged as a prominent Left wing leader of the

INC, giving dynamic lead to the youth, students and workers of India. In 1930, Bose participated in the Civil Disobedience movement, but **opposed the Gandhi-Irwin Pact** and subsequent suspension of the movement particularly on grounds that Bhagat Singh and other revolutionaries could not be saved.

In 1938, he presided over the **Haripura** (Gujarat) Session of the INC. It was Bose (and not J. Nehru) who, in his presidential speech, first talked about the need for Economic Planning and for setting up a National Planning committee. He inaugurated the All-Indian National Planning Committee on 17th December 1938, at Bombay.

In 1939, he was re-elected president of the INC despite Gandhi's opposition but had to resign in face of continuous and organised opposition by the CWC members, who were staunch followers of Gandhi. After his resignation, he formed the **Forward Block** the same year and in 1940, he was placed under house arrest. However, in January 1941 he escaped from house arrest under the guise of a Pathan named **Ziauddin** (pseudonym) and reached Peshawar from Calcutta. From there he reached Kabul with the help of his friend Bhagat Ram and then went to Soviet Union for help. But when Soviet Union joined the allies in war in June 1941, he escaped to Berlin, where he met Hitler under the pseudonym of **Orlando Mazzotta**.

In Germany, with Hitler's support, Bose set up Free India Center and **Free India Radio** in Berlin (hence also called Berlin Radio) and also a 3,000- strong **Free India Legion** comprising of prisoners of war i.e. Indian soldiers, who had fallen into the hands of Germany and Italy). The Free India Legion or the Indian Legion was variously known as **'Mukti Sena'**, 'Freedom Army', 'Indische Legion' or 'Tiger Legion' and was headquartered at Dresden, Germany. Bose was called **'Netaji'** for the first time by the soldiers of the Indian Legion. Bose relayed pro-India and anti-British speeches from Berlin Radio and gave the famous slogan of 'Jai Hind' from the Free India Centre.

On 7th December 1941, Japan joined war on the side of Germany and occupied Singapore (1942), the biggest naval port of the British during the time. Afterwards, Japan quickly occupied the entire region from Malay to Burma. In June 1943, Bose came to Tokyo under pseudonym of Abid Hussain and met the Japanese PM Tojo who assured him that Japan had no territorial aims in India. On 2 July 1943, he reached Singapore and assumed the leadership of the INA.

Activities of Bose and the INA

Bose set up two headquarters of the INA, one each at Singapore and Rangoon. On 21st October 1943, he set up the Provisional Government of Free India or **Azad Hind Sarkar**, declaring himself as the Prime Minister and Commander in Chief of this government. The Provisional government soon declared war on the Allies, viz. Britain and the United States, and was also recognised by the Axis powers. In November 1943, the Japanese handed over the administration of Andaman and Nicobar Islands to the provisional government. Bose himself visited the islands and renamed them as **'Shaheed Dweep'** and **'Swaraj Dweep'** respectively. In April 1944, the **'Azad Hind Bank'** was inaugurated at Rangoon.

On 6th July 1944, Subhas became the **first person to address Gandhiji as 'Father of the Nation'**. He did so while speaking on Azad Hind Radio. Subhas Bose also raised the famous slogans of 'Jai Hind', 'Delhi Chalo' and the most famous of them all, 'Tum Mujhe Khoon Do, Main Tumhe Azadi Dunga'(coined by him in Malaysia).

The INA raised three fighting brigades named after **Azad, Gandhi** and **Nehru**. Later two more were raised namely **Subhas brigade** and **Rani Jhansi brigade**. The Rani Jhansi brigade was an all-women brigade. The INA also made regular broadcasts from the **Azad Hind Radio** and received significant contribution in money and material from Indians living abroad.

Imphal Campaign The INA accompanied the Japanese army in its Imphal Campaign. The forces march towards India from Burma and hoped to liberate India by defeating British in armed conflict. However, this was not meant to be and the Imphal Campaign finally ended in failure due to two reasons: 1) The INA battalion that participated in the campaign faced discriminatory treatment from Japanese units, was denied rations, arms, etc., and felt badly demoralised. 2) The monsoon also prevented their advance. Neither did destiny favour Japan in the Second World War, it steadily collapsed in war and finally surrendered to Britain in South East Asia. In such circumstances, Subhas Bose left for Tokyo but on his way back, he was killed in an air crash near **Formosa Island** (Taipei, 18 August 1945). However, many refuse to believe this. The surrendered INA men were court martialled by the British government in India for conspiring against the King (Read about the famous INA trials, also known as the Red Fort trials, in upcoming chapters).

Significance of INA

True, the INA failed to achieve its goal of liberating India through an armed struggle, it certainly left an indelible mark in the history of India's struggle for independence. The activities of INA ensured that the British could no longer depend on the loyalty of Indian soldiers. The very composition of INA reaffirmed the idea of Indian nationalism as Hindus, Muslims and Sikhs fought together as one nation under the flag of INA. The Rani Jhansi Brigade brought to the forefront the capabilities of Indian women and their commitment towards national freedom. The INA also demonstrated the commitment of overseas Indians for the freedom of their motherland.

Even though Subhas Bose's strategy of cooperating with the fascist powers was much criticised by the nationalists, it must be remembered that whatever he did, he did for India's freedom. He was determined to maintain the independence of INA from Japanese domination and also objected to the use of Indian Legion against USSR. Bose successfully set an inspiring example of patriotism and courage in front of the entire country and was admiringly hailed as Netaji Subhas Chandra Bose by all his countrymen.

Previous Years' Questions – Preliminary Exam

1. Assertion (A): The Congress rejected the Cripps proposals.
   Reason (R): The Cripps Mission consisted solely of whites. **[UPSC 1998]**
   Select the answer for the options given below:
   (a) if both A and R are true and R is the correct explanation of A
   (b) if both A and R are true but R is not the correct explanation of A
   (c) if A is true but R is false
   (d) if A is false but R is true
2. When the Indian Muslim League was inducted into the interim government 1946, Liaqat Ali Khan was assigned the portfolio of which of the following? **[UPSC 1998]**
   (a) Foreign Affairs (b) Home
   (c) Finance (d) Defence
3. Where did the Indian National Army (INA) came into existence in 1943? **[UPSC 2000]**
   (a) Japan (b) Burma
   (c) Singapore (d) Malaya
4. Assertion (A): Lord Linlithgow described the August movement of 1942 as the most serious revolt after the sepoy mutiny.
   Reason (R): Peasants joined the movement in large number in some places. **[UPSC 2000]**

Select the answer for the options given below:
(a) if both A and R are true and R is the correct explanation of A
(b) if both A and R are true but R is not the correct explanation of A
(c) if A is true but R is false
(d) if A is false but R is true

5. Which of the following was an important aspect of the Cripps Mission of 1942? **[UPSC 2003]**
(a) All Indian states should join the Indian Union as a condition to consider any degree of autonomy for India.
(b) The creation of an Indian Union with Dominion status very soon after the second world war.
(c) The active participation and cooperation of the Indian people, communities and political parties in the British war effort as a condition for granting Independence with full sovereign status to India after war.
(d) The framing of a constitution for the entire Indian Union, with no separate constitution for any province, and a Union Constitution to be accepted by all provinces.

6. Consider the following statements: **[UPSC 2005]**
On the eve of launch of Quit India Movement, Mahatma Gandhi
1. asked the government servants to resign
2. asked the soldiers to leave their posts
3. asked the princes of the princely states to accept the sovereignty of their own people

Which of the statements given above is/are correct? Choose the correct answer from the following options.
(a) 1 and 2 (b) 2 and 3
(c) 3 only (d) 1, 2 and 3

7. Which party was founded by Subhas Chandra Bose in the year 1939 after he broke away from the Congress? **[UPSC 2005]**
(a) Indian Freedom Party (b) Azad Hind Fauj
(c) Revolutionary Front (d) Forward Block

8. Which one of the following suggested the reconstitution of the Viceroy's Executive Council in which all the portfolios including that of War members were to be held by the Indian leaders? **[UPSC 2008]**
(a) Simon Commission
(b) Simla conference
(c) Cripps Proposal
(d) Cabinet Mission

9. Assertion (A): The Congress Ministries in all the provinces resigned in the year 1939.
Reason (R): Congress did not accept the decision of the Viceroy to declare war against Germany in the context of the Second World War. **[UPSC 2008]**

Select the answer for the options given below:
(a) if both A and R are true and R is the correct explanation of A
(b) if both A and R are true but R is not the correct explanation of A
(c) if A is true but R is false
(d) if A is false but R is true

10. During the Indian freedom struggle, who of the following raised an army called 'Free Indian Legion'? **[UPSC 2008]**
(a) Lala Hardayal
(b) Rash Behari Bose
(c) Subhas Chandra Bose (d) VD Savarkar

11. In the 'Individual Satyagraha', Vinoba Bhave was chosen as the first Satyagrahi. Who was the second? **[UPSC 2009]**
(a) Dr. Rajendra Prasad
(b) Pandit Jawaharlal Nehru
(c) C Rajagopalachari
(d) Sardar Vallabhbhai Patel

12. Consider the following statements: **[UPSC 2009]**
The Cripps Proposals included the provisions for
1. Full Independence for India
2. Creation of Constitution making body

Which of the statements given above is/are correct? Choose the correct answer from the following options.
(a) 1 only (b) 2 only
(c) Both 1 and 2 (d) Neither 1 nor 2

13. During the freedom struggle, Aruna Asaf Ali was a major woman organiser of underground activity in which of the following? **[UPSC 2009]**
(a) Civil Disobedience Movement
(b) Non-Cooperation Movement

(c) Quit India Movement
(d) Swadeshi Movement

14. Who among the following Prime Ministers sent Cripps Mission to India? **[UPSC 2009]**
(a) James Ramsay MacDonald
(b) Stanley Baldwin
(c) Nevilli Chamberlain
(d) Winston Churchill

15. With which one of the following movements is the slogan 'Do or Die' associated? **[UPSC 2009]**
(a) Swadeshi Movement
(b) Non Cooperation Movement
(c) Civil Disobedience Movement
(d) Quit India Movement

16. After Quit India Movement, C. Rajagopalachari issued a pamphlet entitled 'The Way Out'. Which one of the following was a proposal in this pamphlet? **[UPSC 2010]**
(a) The establishment of a 'War Advisory Council' composed of representatives of British India and the Indian states.
(b) Reconstitution of the Central Executive Council in such a way that all its members, except the Governor-General and the Commander-in-Chief should be Indian leaders.
(c) Fresh elections to the Central and Provincial Legislatures to be held at the end of 1945 and the Constitution making body to be convened as soon as possible.
(d) A solution for the constitutional deadlock.

17. Who among the following were official Congress negotiators with Cripps Mission? **[UPSC 2010]**
(a) Mahatma Gandhi and Sardar Patel
(b) Acharya J.B. Kripalani and C. Rajagopalachari
(c) Pandit Nehru and Maulana Azad
(d) Dr Rajendra Prasad and Rafi Ahmed Kidwai

18. With reference to Indian freedom struggle, Usha Mehta is well known for **[UPSC 2011]**
(a) Running the secret Congress radio in the wake of Quit India Movement
(b) Participating in the Second Round Table Conference
(c) Leading a contingent of Indian National Army
(d) Assisting in the formation of Interim Government under Pandit Jawaharlal Nehru

19. Which one of the following observations is not true about the Quit India Movement of 1942? **[UPSC 2011]**
(a) It was a non-violent movement.
(b) It was led by Mahatma Gandhi.
(c) It was a spontaneous movement.
(d) It did not attract the labour class in general.

20. The Congress ministries resigned in the seven provinces in 1939 because of which of the following reasons? **[UPSC 2012]**
(a) The Congress could not form ministries in the other four provinces.
(b) Emergence of a 'left wing' in the Congress made the working of the ministries impossible.
(c) There were widespread communal disturbances in their provinces.
(d) None of the statements (a), (b) and (c) given above is correct.

21. Quit India Movement was launched in response to which of the following? **[UPSC 2013]**
(a) Cabinet Mission Plan
(b) Cripps Proposals
(c) Simon Commission Report
(d) Wavell Plan

22. What did the plan of Sir Stafford Cripps envisaged for after the Second World War? **[UPSC 2016]**
(a) India should be granted complete Independence.
(b) India should be partitioned into two before granting Independence.
(c) India should be made a Republic with the condition that she will join the Commonwealth.
(d) India should be given Dominion status.

23. With reference to 8th August 1942 in Indian History, which one of the following statements is correct? **[UPSC 2021]**
(a) The Quit India Resolution was adopted by AICC.
(b) The Viceroy's Executive Council was expanded to include more Indians.
(c) The Congress ministries resigned in seven provinces.
(d) Cripps proposed an Indian Union with full Dominion Status once the Second World War was over.

Previous Years' Questions – Main Exam

1. What was Cripps Mission? Why did its failure result into Quit India Movement? Mention briefly the major developments after this movement leading to independence in 1947. **[UPSC 1984]**
2. What was the attitude of the Indian National Congress towards the Second World War? What was the August offer? What were the factors that led the British to change its negative policy and sent Cripps Mission to India? **[UPSC 1990]**
3. How did the outbreak of the Second World War affect India's political scene? Did the Cripps Mission resolve the political crisis in India? **[UPSC 1994]**
4. Write a short note on: August offer, 1940 **[UPSC 1996]**
5. Assess the role of C. Rajagopalachari during the pre-partition years of Indian public life. **[UPSC 1998]**
6. Why did Jinnah reject the CR formula? **[UPSC 2002]**
7. Evaluate the attitudes of different political parties towards Quit India Movement. **[UPSC 2002]**
8. Evaluate Subhas Chandra Bose's contribution to Indian freedom. **[UPSC 2005]**
9. Many voices had strengthened and enriched the nationalist movement during the Gandhian phase. Elaborate. **[UPSC 2019]**

Answers

Previous Years' Questions – Preliminary Exam

1. (b)	2. (c)	3. (c)	4. (b)	5. (b)
6. (c)	7. (d)	8. (d)	9. (a)	10. (c)
11. (b)	12. (b)	13. (c)	14. (d)	15. (d)
16. (d)	17. (c)	18. (a)	19. (a)	20. (d)
21. (b)	22. (d)	23. (a)		

2

Post-War National Movement (1945–47)

The Second World War (1939–45) came to an end in Europe with the suicide of Hitler (30th April 1945) and subsequent surrender of Germany (8th May 1945). With this, the freedom struggle in India entered a new phase.

The period during 1945–47 was a brief but crucial period of Indian National Movement. Even though it represented a climax of all political activities of the past decades, it was the Second World War and its impact which significantly shaped the course of events during this period.

Impact of the Second World War

Impact on Indians

After the decline of the Quit India Movement, the Indian political scene was rather quiet. However, significant disquiet accumulated beneath the surface owing to the wartime sufferings of the people-

- **Scarcity** Indian agricultural and industrial products were channelised in a big way to meet the demands of the Allied forces. This led to a sharp rise in hoarding practices and black markets, further giving rise to artificial scarcities and inflation.
- **Inflation** Scarcity of basic products led to sharp rise in prices.
- **Bengal famine** A cumulative effect of scarcity and inflation was the devastating Bengal famine of 1943 during which more than 3 million people starved to death. The condition of the rest of the country was not very different, though not ravaged by famine as such.
- **Failure of the British to repay Indians for their contribution** The Indian discontent was further accentuated by the British failure to pay back Indians for their contribution and support during the war years.

Impact on British Government

At the end of the war in 1945, Britain emerged victorious but also war weary, exhausted and internally wrecked:

- **War weary military** The European soldiers and officers in the army were desperate to go home after the tiring war years rather than staying on in India indefinitely, suppressing Indian people's struggle for independence.
- **Shattered economy** Even though Britain was on the winning side of the war, its economic and military power was shattered. It would take Britain years to rejuvenate itself. Consequently, the

British government was not in the mental and material position to run down another Quit India movement. In the face of widespread opposition, it was becoming increasingly inconvenient to use Indian wealth for furthering British interests. Also, by now, India was no more a debtor to Britain. Instead it was Britain that owed India nearly 33,000 million pound.

- **Paucity of European recruits in the ICS** British domination of the ICS had already ended since the days of the First World War. By 1939, British and Indian officers had achieved parity. Besides the European officers were no longer men from aristocratic families who believed in 'White Man's Burden'. They were increasingly men for whom serving in India was just another job. The Second World War aggravated this problem. In the face of Indian hostility, India no longer appeared as an attractive option even for civil careers of Europeans. Continuous crisis management duties such as tackling famines and enforcing black outs had become a harassment and for the first time, the **British entry into the ICS practically stopped at the height of the war in 1943**. By mid-1940, the number of European ICS officers was reduced to a minority (587 Europeans as opposed to 614 Indians), thus marking a virtual end to classic imperialism.
- **Change of government in Britain** After the war, the wartime coalition government was replaced by the Labour Party government, many of whose members supported the Congress demands.
- **Changed balance of power** The war had changed the balance of power in the world. USA and Russia had emerged as the new world powers and they both supported India's demand for independence.

Hence, the British power to control events was almost gone and the possibility of independence began taking shape.

British Policy After the War

Owing to the above factors, the British Government was in no position to ignore Indian opinion and this led to a change in British attitude.

At the same time, contrary to heralding an end to colonialism and imperialism, the Second World War had opened up the possibility of **Neo-colonialism**.

A glimpse of British thinking after the war 'A land and its people could still be effectively colonised and economically subjugated, even after conceding to them political independence, if their integrity and solidarity were disrupted and their weakness perpetrated through the setting up of separate, ineffectual puppet regimes'.

Thus, the British policy after the war was guided by the aim of ensuring **some sort of future in India** by keeping the Indians divided in whichever way possible. Projecting themselves as pluralist people, they tried to magnify all the diverse distinctions among Indians along the lines of caste, religion, language and culture.

The most successful British effort in this aspect was the communal card played by the British. From the very beginning, they had adopted the policy of using the Muslim League to counter-balance the Congress. The League was recognised as the only representative body of Indian Muslims, its demand for Pakistan was used to thwart every constitutional negotiation with the Congress. During the Quit India Movement, when all prominent Congress leaders were put behind bars, the League was practically allowed back door entry to take over some of the provincial ministries.

Congress failed to counter this British policy due to the following reasons:

- The Congress adopted a self-righteous approach towards communalism, merely disregarding or denouncing the claims that it was predominantly a 'Hindu' organisation.
- The Congress made no serious attempts to win the support of the Muslim masses.
- The use of slogans such as 'Vande Mataram' and 'Ramrajya' by Congress leaders not only alienated the Muslims but also strengthened the position of the Muslim League.

In the presence of active government patronage, and simultaneous failure of the Congress to contain it, the Pakistan Movement gained considerable momentum. The movement also acquired a substantial degree of popular support among the educated Muslim middle classes which began to see Pakistan as a panacea for all Muslim concerns—where the Muslim peasants will be free from Hindu bania and zamindari exploitation and Muslim businessmen will be free from the overbearing Hindu business houses.

Such a situation allowed Jinnah to adopt an obstinate stand that the Muslim League will support the Congress in any negotiation with the British regarding the constitutional question only when the demand for Pakistan was conceded to. Jinnah refused to budge from this stand, even at the cost of weakening the national movement.

This situation presented a win-win situation for the British not conceding the demand for Pakistan meant perpetuation of the British rule in India, whereas, conceding the demand meant an opportunity to place puppet regimes in divided India.

Dominant Themes during 1945–47

It is clear that communal tangle around the demand for Pakistan dominated the Indian political scene during 1945 and 1947. Simultaneously there also emerged sporadic popular unrest directed against the British and their collaborators. Hence, the two dominant themes during this period have been described as under-

1. Attempts at a Negotiated Settlement
2. Post-War Popular Unrest

Attempts at a Negotiated Settlement

Once the war ended (with the surrender of Germany in May 1945), the British started realising the need for starting a dialogue with the imprisoned Congress leaders in order to prevent them from taking advantage of the post-war hardships. According to Governor-General Wavell, the energies of the Congress were required to be directed away from agitation into 'some more profitable channel, i.e. into dealing with the administrative problems of India and into trying to solve the constitutional problems'.

Wavell Plan (14th June 1945) and Simla Conference (25th June 1945)

In an attempt to resolve the constitutional deadlock in India, Wavell went to England for consultations.

On 14th June 1945, he announced through a radio broadcast, the proposals of the British Government, also known as the Wavell Plan 'to ease the present political situation and to advance India towards her goal of full self-government'. Through the same broadcast, he also announced the release of the top Congress leaders from detentions as a preparatory measure for negotiations with him. Further, Wavell also expressed his intention to call an All-Party Conference at Simla on 25th June to which he intended to invite Indian leaders representing various political parties and minority groups. The main purpose of the conference was to deliberate on the formation of a new **Executive Council** at the Centre representing organised political opinion in the country.

On the same day, Amery (Secretary of State for India) announced that the offer of March 1942 (i.e., the Cripps proposals) still stood in its entirety without change or qualification.

Main components of the Wavell Plan were as follows:

- Wavell proposed the reconstruction of the Governor General's Executive Council, pending the preparation of a new constitution.
- With the exception of the Governor-General and the Commander-in-Chief, all other members of the Council would be nominated from among Indian leaders (hence, the new Council would be practically Indian in composition).
- The Muslims and the caste Hindus would be represented in the Council in equal proportion.
- If formed, the reconstructed Council was to function as an interim government within the framework of the Act of 1935 (i.e., without being responsible to the legislature).
- The Governor-General would retain his veto but he would not use it unnecessarily.
- The portfolio of External Affairs would be transferred from Governor-General to an Indian member of the Council (except Tribal and Frontier matters which were dealt with as part of defence of India).
- Representatives of various parties were to submit a joint list to the Viceroy for nominations to the Executive Council. If a joint list was not possible, then separate lists were to be submitted.

Consequently, the government lifted the ban on the Congress, released the Congress Working Committee members and invited them along with others, notably the Muslim League to join in the Simla Conference. The released leaders had expected to find demoralised people, depressed by the privations of war and government repression. To their surprise, they were welcomed by ecstatic crowds waiting for their release. Even at Simla, villagers had gathered in large numbers, sitting atop trees and waiting for hours to catch a glimpse of their leaders!

Simla Conference

On 25 June 1945, the conference met as scheduled under the presidentship of the Viceroy. Though, for the next four days it made a sincere attempt to evolve a formula which could help the constitution of a new Executive Council, it could not succeed.

Failure of Simla Conference The major issue on which the conference failed to arrive at a solution was the manner in which the Muslim members of the Executive Council were to be selected. The League insisted that it alone had the right to speak for every Indian Muslim, and thus it alone should have the jurisdiction for choosing all Muslim members of the Council. Not satisfied with this, the League further demanded a **communal veto** by asking for a two-third majority in the proposed Council, instead of a simple one, on any decision opposed by the Muslim members.

The Congress contested this claim. As a national body, it could not agree to be reduced to the status of a representative of 'caste Hindus' alone (meaning a body of upper caste Hindus). Instead, the Congress proposed to include two Congress Muslims out of its quota. Maulana Abul Kalam Azad (the then Congress President) and Abdul Gaffar Khan were present in Simla as Congress delegates.

The demands of the League embarrassed many, including the Viceroy himself. Such a right to the League would have denied representation to the Muslims of the Unionist Party of Punjab, which had supported the British staunchly throughout the War. The Viceroy felt that one non-Leaguer representing the Punjab Muslims, a nominee of Malik Khizr Hyat Khan should be included in the Council. Yet the Viceroy abruptly abandoned British proposals and dissolved the Simla Conference, three days after it began.

In this way, like many previous attempts, the Simla Conference too ended in failure in bringing about a consensus between the Congress and the League. The responsibility for the failure of the Simla Conference lay partly on Wavell and partly on Jinnah. Wavell should not have allowed the League to practically veto the whole plan.

Significance of Simla Conference This dissolution of the conference by the Viceroy implied, as revealed by subsequent developments, official recognition of the League's monopoly to speak for all Muslims and conference of the veto power onto the League for all future negotiations. The failure of the talks thus strengthened the position of Jinnah and the League, which was clearly manifested in the Election of 1945–46.

Labour Party comes to power in Britain (July 1945)

In July 1945, the Labour Party led by Clement Attlee won massive victory in elections and replaced the wartime coalition government in Britain led by the Conservative leader Winston Churchill. The election was a disaster for the Liberal Party as well under Archibald Sinclair.

Clement Attlee, Prime Minister of Britain, 1945–51 (Labour Party)

The new Labour government headed by Clement Attlee as Prime Minister installed an old friend of India, **Lord Pethick Lawrence**, as the Secretary of State for India (1945–47). The Labour leaders were known for their sympathies with the nationalist cause in India and had already committed themselves to giving India its independence. Way back in 1938, prominent Labour Party leaders including Clement Attlee, Stafford Cripps and Harold Laski had met Jawaharlal Nehru near London and had agreed to accept the Constitution of India framed by a Constituent Assembly duly elected on the basis of 'universal suffrage'.

However, once in power, the Laborite approach was hardly pathbreaking-

- On 21st August 1945, the Viceroy announced the holding of fresh elections in the approaching winters for the Indian Legislatures which were long due, both at the centre (last elected in 1934) as well as in the provinces (last elected in 1937).
- On 19th September 1945, the Viceroy renewed the promise of 'early full self-government' for India, carefully avoiding the term 'independence'.
- Discussions were also held with the elected legislators and representatives of the Indian princes for formation of a Constituent Assembly (conveniently bypassing the previous Laborite assurance of an elected Constituent Assembly on universal suffrage!).

General Elections (December 1945)

In the winter of 1945–46, the General Elections in British India were held to elect members of the Central and provincial legislatures.

Election Campaign The two issues that became the main plank of election campaign were- the **repression of 1942** and the **INA trials**. In fact, as soon as they were released from jail, the Congress leaders had taken up the issue of official excesses during 1942. In their speeches, they condemned the official action, recounted stories of repression in detail and promised enquiries. The rising crescendo of demand for enquiries gravely demoralised the services. The UP Governor, Francis Verner Wylie (1945–47), had himself confessed that such methods had been occasionally used which nobody could defend.

The INA question taken up by the Congress most caught the imagination of the people. In its first post-war session held in Bombay (21–23th September 1945), the AICC adopted a resolution declaring its support for the cause. The Congress party took up the defence of the INA prisoners and lawyer-leaders such as Bhulabhai Desai, Tej Bahadur Sapru, KN Katju, Nehru and Asaf Ali appeared in court during the historic Red Fort Trials (read more about INA trials later in this chapter).

The Muslim League fought the elections with the straightforward communal slogan-**'A vote for the League and Pakistan was a vote for Islam'**. Election meetings were held in mosques and pirs (holy men) were asked to issue fatwas (directives) asking all Muslims to vote for the League. Choosing between the Congress and the League was portrayed as choosing between the Gita and the Koran. After such communal propaganda, the results were hardly surprising and the Leagues made a clean sweep of the Muslim seats.

Election Results Muslim League was in a favourable position. It had been able to attract the bulk of the Muslim masses thanks to government patronage and its religious cry of 'Islam in Danger'. The Congress was also at the height of its popularity, particularly so in anticipation of independence, yet it found itself helpless before the impregnable religious propaganda based on partly real and partly unreal communal differences.

Congress Performance:

- Indian National Congress emerged as the largest party: The Congress swept the polls in the General (non-Muslim) constituencies, securing 91.3% votes.
- In the Centre: It won 57 out of 102 seats in the Central Legislative Assembly.
- In the provinces: It obtained a majority and formed ministries in all provinces except in Sindh, Punjab and Bengal. Thus, the Congress ministries were formed in **Assam, NWFP, UP, CP, Bihar, Orissa, Bombay and Madras**.

League's Performance:

- The All India Muslim League was equally successful in Muslim constituencies, polling 86.6% of the Muslim votes.
- In the Centre: It won all the 30 Muslim seats in the Central Legislative Assembly.
- In the provinces: It grabbed 443 out of 509 Muslim seats in the provinces.
- However, on the whole, the League suffered a heavy blow. Of the 11 provinces, it could form ministries only in **Sindh and Bengal,** that too with official and European support. The League lost NWFP and Assam to the Congress and also failed to dislodge the Unionists from Punjab.

In the Punjab, though the Muslim League was the largest single party, it could not form a government and instead a coalition ministry was formed there of the Congress, the Akali Sikhs and the Unionists under the leadership of **Malik Khizr Hyat**, leader of the Unionist Party.

Result Analysis It must be remembered that the League's support base had hardly been tested in India. Elections were held on the basis of separate electorates under which only Muslims could vote for candidates for Muslim seats. Congress, which was ideologically committed to finding a common cause across the diversity of India's people, found it extremely difficult to outbid parties seeking the votes of a single religious community. Thus, the Congress party faced unequal competition in Muslim constituencies. Even the franchise was severely restricted—barely 10% of the total population. Hence, it is difficult to say what could have happened, had the elections been held on the basis of adult franchise, specially keeping in view future developments (Congress success in 1951 Elections, the League's reverses in East Pakistan and its failure to control events even in West Pakistan).

Significance of General Elections 1945

- The Indian National Congress emerged as the largest party.
- The League won all Muslim constituencies, and hence the elections proved to be a strategic victory for Jinnah (even though the party failed to win any other seat).
- Even though Congress won, the League had united the Muslim vote and as such it gained the negotiating power to seek a separate Muslim homeland.
- These were the last General Elections in British India; consequent elections were held in 1951–52 in India and 1970 in Pakistan.

Cabinet Mission (1946)

Once the elections were over, the Attlee Government lost no time in starting negotiations with the leading parties. It sent a high-powered mission of three British Cabinet members to India to **find ways and means of peaceful transfer of power in India**. It came to be known as the Cabinet Mission.

Members

1. Pethick Lawrence (Secretary of State for India)
2. Stafford Cripps (President of the Board of Trade)
3. AV Alexander (First Lord of Admiralty)

Objectives

- To find ways and means of peaceful transfer of power in India.
- To settle the constitutional issue.

Context to Cabinet Mission By March 1946, India had reached a high point of ferment and the British had sensed that time was running out of their hands due to the following reasons:

- Impact of the Second World War on India as well as on Britain (mentioned earlier).
- Impact of sporadic popular unrest throughout the country (Mentioned at the end of the chapter).
- Congress rule in provinces had also proved to be a big morale booster.
- As per the British policy of conciliation and repression, this was once again the time for conciliation. But after failure of Cripps Mission, there was little left to offer except independence.
- The British Indian government had realised that a settlement was necessary to avert another mass movement and to ensure good future Indo-British relations.

By now, the British policy makers had realised that the British rule of the previous style could no longer be sustained. Hence, the overreaching aim of the British leaders now was to ensure a graceful withdrawal from India, peaceful transfer of power and good future Indo-British relations. The stage was now left to the three actors—the British, the Congress and the Muslim League to decide the future of India. Let us see what each wanted–

British the British wanted to leave behind a weak India, divided in whichever way possible to make way for the neo-colonialists.

Views of Bipan Chandra

Contrary to the above view, historian Bipan Chandra is of the view that the British wanted to leave behind a united, friendly India that would be an active partner in the defence of the Commonwealth. A divided India would not be an effective defence partner and be a blot on Britain's diplomacy.

In support of his view, Chandra quotes Prime Minister Attlee's Statement in the House of Commons (15th March 1946), 'We are very mindful of the rights of minorities and minorities should be able to live free from fear. On the other hand, we **cannot allow a minority to place a veto on the advance of the majority**'. The statement indicated a change in the British policy towards the Muslim League. Contrast this with the Simla Conference, where Wavell had allowed Jinnah to veto and wreck the negotiations. Hence, if continuance of rule demanded one stance, its withdrawal demanded another.

Congress Congress wanted a united India, one central government and minority safeguards to be worked out only after independence (which could range from autonomy to Muslim provinces to self-determination after secession from the Indian Union).

Muslim League The League wanted a separate homeland for the Indian Muslims.

Cabinet Mission Arrives in India (24th March 1946)

On 24th March 1946, the three Cabinet Ministers arrived in New Delhi and held prolonged discussions with the Viceroy and various Indian leaders for settling the constitutional question. These negotiations lasted over seven weeks and often ran into stalemates on account of Jinnah's demand for Pakistan and right to self-determination of the Muslims. Once again, the Congress and the Muslim League could not come to any agreement on the fundamental issue of unity or partition of India. Finally, the Mission decided to put forward what they considered to be the best possible proposals. They were included in a statement which they issued on 16th May 1946, and became known as the Cabinet Mission Plan.

The Cabinet Mission Plan, 16th May 1946 The Mission came up with a rather complicated Plan which can be divided into three parts:

- Examination of the scheme of Pakistan and its rejection
- A long-term plan
- A short-term plan (Interim Government)

Examination of the scheme of Pakistan and its rejection Although the sympathies of the Viceroy and AV Alexander were with Jinnah, the Plan rejected the demand for a full-fledged Pakistan (consisting of the 6 provinces, viz. Assam, Bengal, Punjab, Sindh, NWFP and Baluchistan) on account of the following reasons:

- The creation of Pakistan would not solve the problem of communal minorities as the percentage of non-Muslims living in west Pakistan would be 37.93% and those living in east Pakistan would be 48.31% of the total population.
- The mission further examined an alternate proposal according to which Pakistan would consist of only the Muslim majority areas of these provinces. The creation of such a Pakistan would have necessitated a bifurcation of Bengal, Assam and Punjab going against all regional and linguistic ties and would have created immense economic and administrative problems, and yet would not have satisfied Jinnah (as he was opposed to the idea of a truncated and moth-ridden Pakistan).
- There was no justification for including the predominantly non-Muslim districts of Bengal, Assam and Punjab within Pakistan (According to the mission, every argument that could be used in favour of Pakistan could equally be used in favour of the exclusion of the non-Muslim areas from Pakistan).
- It would be injurious to disintegrate the transportation as well as the post and telegraph system of India.
- The Princely States would find it difficult to join one of the two nations.
- The two halves of proposed Pakistan would be separated by some 700 miles and communications between them in war and peace would depend on the goodwill of Hindustan (more importantly, the Mission believed that a united India could be an active partner in the defence of the Commonwealth).

Long term plan The following plan was recommended for a long-term settlement:

- **Union of India** There should be a Union of India, embracing both British India and the States, which should deal with the following subjects—defence, foreign affairs and communications (The Union of India meant **a federation** of the provinces and the princely states. **One central government** was proposed, controlling at least some specified subjects).
- **Full Provincial Autonomy** The provinces should have full autonomy. All subjects other than the Union subjects and all residuary powers should vest in the provinces (Hence, the plan proposed a very loose union of all Indian territories under a centre). The States would also retain all subjects and power other than those ceded to the Union. Provinces would be free to form groups with executives and legislatures and each group could determine the provincial subjects to be taken in common.
- **Groupings** The six Hindu majority provinces, viz. Bombay, the United Provinces, Bihar, the Central Provinces, Orissa and Madras would form Group A. The Muslim majority provinces in the north west, viz. the Punjab, NWFP and Sindh would form Group B. The Muslim majority provinces in the north east, viz. Bengal and Assam would form Group C. Of the Chief Commissioner's Provinces, three (Delhi, Ajmer-Marwara and Coorg) would join Group A and one (Baluchistan) would join Group B. (Hence, the provisions of 'full autonomy of the provinces' and 'groupings' were meant to give the Muslim League, if not the form, but the '**substance of Pakistan**'. It was obvious that Group B and C would be under absolute control of the Muslims. The provinces were given the power to opt out of their respective groups by a decision of their legislatures after the general elections under the new constitution).
- **Constituent Assembly** A constitution making body should be set up immediately through indirect election (since direct election based on adult franchise would take a long time). For this purpose, each province was to be allotted a number of seats proportional to its population, roughly to the ratio of one to a million. The total number of seats thus arrived at for each province was to be divided among the main communities in proportion to their population and that the representatives

allotted to each community were to be elected by the members of the same community in the Legislative Assembly (the communities recognised for this purpose were General, Muslim and Sikh). The representatives so elected along with the representatives of the Indian States would meet together in New Delhi as one body and form the Constituent Assembly. The Constituent Assembly would then separate into three sections—Section A corresponding to Group A and so on.

- **Provincial or Group Constitutions** All these sections would have the authority to draw up provincial constitutions and, if necessary, group constitutions and accordingly setup provincial legislatures and executives.
- **Union Constitution** After the group constitutions are settled, the groups would assemble together to settle the Union Constitution.

Short-Term Plan (Interim Government) Since this would have taken considerable time, the Mission also proposed a short-term measure, the immediate formation of an Interim Government at the Centre, enjoying the support of all major political parties and with Indians holding all the portfolios, including that of the **War Member**.

Merits of the Cabinet Mission Plan

- The chief merit was that the Constituent Assembly was to be constituted on the democratic principle of strength of population and not on the principle of 'weightage'.
- The idea of partition was discarded and an all-India Union envisaged.

Defects of the Cabinet Mission Plan

- While the Muslim minority was amply provided for, no such protection was accorded to any other minority, like the Sikhs in Punjab.
- The provisions regarding provincial groupings could be differently interpreted.

Analysis The Cabinet Mission Plan was an anxious attempt to put together a disarranged India under a nominal centre, with the communally segregated autonomous units almost as a prelude to 'balkanisation' (on the sole plea of overrated Indian disunity). In their hurry to leave the ground for the neo-colonialists, they failed to take note of several important details. Further, the Plan was supposed to be a compromise. It tried to placate the Congress with the rejection of the demand for Pakistan and tried to placate the League through the creation of autonomous Muslim majority areas. In the beginning, therefore, both the Congress and the League were quite inclined to accept the plan, particularly the long-term plan.

Objections Soon objections surfaced over the provisions for forming sections or groups of provinces. While the League interpreted them to be compulsory, the Congress wanted them to be optional since in case of compulsory grouping, Congress administered Muslim majority provinces of **NWFP** and **Assam** would be reduced to helpless minorities in their respective groupings. The Congress also opposed the absence of any elected members from princely states in the proposed Constituent Assembly. The Sikhs were also considerably disturbed by the grouping system as they felt that they would be left without sufficient safeguards against the Muslim majority in Group B provinces.

- On 6th June, the League announced its acceptance of the plan in so far as the basis of Pakistan was implied in the compulsory grouping system.
- On 7th July, Nehru declared, 'We are not bound by a single thing except that we have decided to go into the Constituent Assembly' (since the Assembly was meant to be a sovereign body that could amend the rules laid down by the Cabinet Mission).

Failure of the Cabinet Mission By end of July 1946, both the Congress and the League decided against trying out the Cabinet Mission Plan on two accounts—difference over the grouping system as well as Cabinet Mission's inability to clarify its stand and intentions over the grouping system. In fact, the mission deliberately refused to clarify itself, even when asked to do so, in the hope that the ambiguity may help reconcile the differences between the Congress and the League. On the contrary, it only deteriorated the matters.

Positive Outcomes Despite the above, there were some positive achievements.

- The problem of the future of India which was until now a nebulous cloud had been brought down to the plane of hard realities.
- It demonstrated that the Labour government in Britain intended to keep its promise of withdrawing from India as soon as possible.

Wavell's Breakdown Plan In May 1946, this Plan was presented by Wavell to the Cabinet Mission to deal with the fast-evolving political situation in India. It proposed a phased withdrawal from India, starting from the Hindu majority provinces. Thus, the Plan envisaged the withdrawal of British forces to the six Muslim Provinces while leaving the rest of the country in Congress hands. It also aimed at avoiding partition of India by itself proposing a partition of Punjab and Bengal and strike a blow to Muslim interests in both these provinces to deter the Muslim League from pursuing its agenda of a separate Muslim homeland. Although the overall plan was rejected, the partition part was incorporated in the Mountbatten Plan. According to some scholars, the Plan also reflected the desire of some British circles to make a 'Northern Ireland' out of Pakistan.

Communal Carnage (beginning 16th August 1946)

The failure of the Cabinet Mission so frustrated the Muslim League that it decided to act upon its post-election slogan, **'Lekar Rahenge Pakistan, Ladke Lenge Pakistan'** (We shall take Pakistan by force).

On 16th August 1946, the League observed **Direct Action Day**, which was simply an invitation to violence. It may be noted that Direct Action was directed against the Hindus and not the British government. Communal carnage first began in Calcutta with the League's Bengal Ministry headed by Suhrawardy looking on passively if not actively abetting in it and resulted in widespread violent attacks on the non-Muslims. By the time the army restored order, 4,000 people had already lost their lives in what came to be known as the **'Great Calcutta Killings'**.

Henceforth, the Indian scene was rapidly transformed. Communal riots erupted in other parts of the country as well.

In **Bombay,** more than 300 persons lost their lives in riots.

In **Noakhali and Tippera (eastern Bengal)** more than 400 persons lost their lives, several women were violated.

In **Bihar,** violence in Noakhali was promptly avenged, more than 7,000 were massacred.

In **Garhmukteshwar (UP)** nearly 1,000 people were slaughtered.

In **NWFP,** the butchery in Bihar and UP was further avenged leading to communal riots carried out by Muslims, Hindus and Sikhs in Lahore Amritsar, Multan, Attock and Rawalpindi, killing more than 5000 by mid-1947. The Hindu and the Muslim communalists blamed each other for starting the violence and competed with each other in brutality.

Flashforward: Communal carnage continued to blaze high throughout 1947 resulting in innumerous deaths, abduction and rape of countless women and desecration of religious as well as personal properties. The fratricide that continued in Indian subcontinent during 1946 and 1948 in the context of partition has few parallels in the annals of civilisation, in terms of the extent of human suffering and dehumanisation.

Note: In the meantime, elections to the proposed Constituent Assembly were completed by now in all the Provinces. The Congress won 199 out of 210 General seats, the League won 73 out of 78 Muslim seats. Jinnah maintained that since Congress had support of 211 out of 296 members of the Assembly, the Muslims would be placed at its mercy. He, therefore, demanded a separate Constituent Assembly for Pakistan.

Interim Government (2nd September 1946)

In September 1946, in the midst of communal carnage, an Interim Government at the centre—the one proposed by the Cabinet Mission as a short-term plan, with Jawaharlal Nehru as its de-facto head, came into existence.

At the time of its formation, the Interim government faced similar challenges as faced by the Simla Conference—Jinnah insisted on a parity between five Hindu nominees of the Congress and five Muslim nominees of the League in such a government, apart from 1 Sikh and 1 Scheduled Caste members in it. The Congress had rejected such a demand claimed the right to include any number of Hindus, Muslims and others in its list of nominees.

Once again, Wavell would have called off the talks, as he had happily done in Simla, had it not been for the **widespread popular unrest** that had begun to rage the country. Moreover, His Majesty's government also felt that the support of the Congress was a prerequisite for their long-term interests and good relations in the future with India. Thus, Wavell decided to go ahead with the Interim Government, even if formed solely by the Congress a party that enjoyed the greatest influence over the public mind. Thereafter, the Viceroy asked the Congress to form the Interim Government, to which it responded in the affirmative.

Accordingly, on **2nd September 1946**, for the first time in 200 years, a fully popular Governor General's Council consisting of all Indian leaders took over the reins of Indian administration. **Nehru was its first Vice President**.

Functioning of Interim Government This Interim Government, however, was bound for a **series of misadventures**. It proved helpless, in face of the communal carnage, in moving the army led by a British Commander in Chief. Presided over by the Viceroy, it also sometimes could not withstand his vetoing power.

Muslim League joins the Interim Government (26th October 1946): Communal fire kept burning and the possibility of a civil war unleashed by the Muslim League loomed high. The British now realised that the League, which was their own creation, had now assumed the shape of a 'communal monster which could not be tamed'. Under these circumstances, the British decided to go back on their policy of placating the Muslims. Accordingly, Wavell supported by Pethick Lawrence (the Secretary of State), persuaded the Muslim League to join the Interim Government, which it did on 26th October 1946.

The League had been allowed to join the Interim Government without giving up the idea of Pakistan, or the plan of Direct Action and even without agreeing to the Cabinet Mission Plan.

Why did the League join the Interim Government?

- To wreck it from within as Jinnah publicly declared that the Interim Government was merely another front for the continuation of Civil War.
- To get a foothold in the Government for furthering the goal of Pakistan.
- To demonstrate that cooperation between the League and the Congress was impossible. **Liaquat Ali Khan**, the Finance Minister, continually hamstrung the functioning of other ministries.

Once the League joined the Interim Government, it got sharply divided into two perpetually warring camps, which further reduced its position to a mere figurehead.

First Meeting of the Constituent Assembly Founded on 6th December 1946, the Constituent Assembly first met at New Delhi on 9th December 1946 and appointed **Sachchidananda Sinha** as its Interim President.

On 11th December, the Assembly elected **Dr. Rajendra Prasad** as its permanent President. Jurist BN Rao was appointed constitutional adviser to the Assembly. He prepared the original draft of the Constitution (A detailed draft was later presented by BR Ambedkar, Chairman of the Drafting Committee). Two days later, Jawaharlal Nehru moved his famous 'Objectives Resolution' which declared the Assembly's firm resolve for an 'Independent Sovereign Republic' and later became the Preamble of the Constitution.

Though the League had joined the Interim Government, it refused to participate in the Constituent Assembly even as His Majesty's statement of 6th December 1946 **upheld the League's version of grouping**. Instead, the League demanded dissolution of the Assembly calling it unrepresentative (as Muslim majority provinces had not joined it). Jinnah now wanted Pakistan directly, and not through any Mission Plan.

On 5th February 1947, fed up by the disruptionist practices of the League, the Congress members of the Interim government sent a letter to Wavell with a demand that the League members be asked to resign. A crisis was in the offing.

With the government thus torn asunder and major communities ready to slit each other's throat, clouds of gloom hovered over the entire country. In such a scenario, the only ray of hope was the popular unrest that demonstrated the capacity of the common Indian people to rise above their differences for the freedom of their nation.

Post-War Popular Unrest

The period closely following the end of the Second World War was marked by a wide spectrum of popular initiative. The popular unrest during the period 1945–47 took the form of various urges and upsurges and can be broadly classified into two varieties.

1. Unrest which led to direct confrontations with the British administration.
2. Unrest which indirectly undermined British Raj through direct confrontations with its upholders—certain landlords, princes and capitalists.

The popular upsurges were numerous in number and only the major ones have been mentioned below.

Direct Confrontations

INA Trials (or the Red Fort Trials, November 1945–May 1946)

The first major popular explosion took place over the INA trials: The court martials of surrendered INA soldiers and officers who had earlier served in the British Indian Army. They were accused of having broken the oath of loyalty to the British Crown, and thus of having become 'traitors'. The first, and most famous, of the approximately ten trials, was held in the Red Fort in Delhi, hence known as the 'Red Fort trials'.

Landmark Features of INA Trials

- **INA cause taken up by the Congress** In November 1945, the trials began in the historic Red Fort of Delhi. The cause of the INA men had been taken up by the Congress and made a main plank of its election campaign. Many Congress leaders appeared in defence of the INA prisoners. Hundreds of meetings were held throughout the country, demanding clemency for INA prisoners. The largest meeting was held in Deshapriya Park, Calcutta which was addressed by Sarat Bose, Nehru and Patel.
  - 5–11 November was observed as **INA Week** and 12th November was observed as **INA Day**. The Congress also organised **INA Relief and Enquiry Committee** which provided money and food to released men and attempted to secure for them some employment.
- **Issue turns Indian versus British** In the beginning, appeals were made for clemency to 'misguided men', but soon the INA men were hailed as most heroic patriots and the government stand condemned. Henceforth, the issue became more and more **Indian versus British**. The question of the right or wrong of the INA men's action was not debated. What was debated was the right of the British to decide a matter concerning Indians.
- **Priority coverage in newspapers** The trials were given priority coverage in newspapers, eclipsing international news. Pamphlets such as **'Patriots Not Traitors'**, were widely circulated.
- **Wide geographical reach** Another significant feature of the INA campaign was its wide geographical reach. Even though Delhi, Bombay, Calcutta, Madras and the towns of UP and Punjab emerged as the storm centres, the agitation also spread to distant places such as Coorg, Baluchistan and Assam.
- **Participation of diverse social and political groups** The Muslim League, the CPI, the Unionist Party, the Akalis, the Justice Party, the RSS, the Hindu Mahasabha and the Sikh League supported the INA cause in varying degrees. The sympathies for INA men cut across caste, colour and creed!
- **Participation of the people took diverse forms** Some donated funds, others attended meetings, some struck work, others raised the demand for the release of prisoners.
- **Effect on the traditional bulwarks of the Raj** The most striking feature of the INA agitation was the effect on the traditional bulwarks of the Raj-the **armed forces** as well as **other government employees (the police and the bureaucracy)**. Thus, even the traditional loyalist sections of the British Raj got submerged in the tide of INA sympathy.
  - The armed forces were the chief instrument of British Raj in India. Several armed forces men attended INA meetings, often in uniform. There were widespread strikes in Royal Indian Air

Force (RIAF). The Indian Signal Corps at Jabalpur also struck work. The Commander in Chief himself confessed that a growing feeling of sympathy for the INA pervaded in the Indian Army.

- The Police and the bureaucracy were the other two major instruments of the British Raj. They also began showing signs of nationalist leanings. For example, the Police force in Bihar and Delhi also went on strike.
- A considerable number of INA men themselves belonged to families which had traditions of loyalty, which further fuelled local interest (For example, PK Sahgal was the son of an ex-Judge of the Punjab High Court).

- **The Three Upsurges** The rising nationalist sentiment over INA trials culminated into three upsurges.
  1. On 21st November 1945 in Calcutta over INA trials
  2. On 11th February 1946 in Calcutta to protest against 7-year sentence given to an INA officer
  3. On 18th February 1946 in Bombay when the ratings of the Royal Indian Navy (RIN) went on strike

Pattern of Upsurges The three upsurges followed a similar pattern—the upsurge initiated by a group (such as students or ratings), joined in by the city sympathisers, who were in turn joined in by sympathisers from other parts of the country.

1. Upsurge on 21st November 1945 The first of the INA trials, and the most celebrated one, was the joint court-martial of **Colonel Prem Sahgal, Colonel Gurbaksh Singh Dhillon** and **Major General Shah Nawaz Khan**. When the three heroes, belonging to the Hindu, Muslim and Sikh communities respectively and representing Indian unity were put on trial, a countrywide protest upsurged. There took place widespread meetings, processions and speeches demanding the release of the INA prisoners.

Calcutta however, emerged as a storm centre. On 21st November 1945, on the call of the Forward Block, students marched towards the administrative quarters in Dalhousie Square. On their way, they were joined by members from the League as well as the Communist student organisations. These students had tied the National, the League and the Red flags together representing the need for a united anti-imperialist struggle.

The demonstrators were obstructed by the armed police and fired upon, killing a Hindu and a Muslim student. The killings immediately set the city on fire, and for the next two days the angry people repeatedly clashed with the police resulting in over 30 deaths and destruction of over 150 police and army vehicles.

Understanding the significance of the agitation which 'cut across communal barriers', the government decided to step down by first announcing to try only those INA members who could be accused of murder and brutalities (December 1945) and then remitting the sentences passed against the first batch of the accused (January 1946).

2. Upsurge on 11th February 1946 In February 1946, when **A. Rashid Ali of the INA** was sentenced to 7 years in jail, the agitation resurfaced and ended only after two days, leaving 84 dead and 300 injured.

3. Upsurge on 18thFebruary 1946 refers to the RIN revolt (mentioned below).

Royal Indian Navy Revolt (RIN Mutiny, 18th February 1946)
The RIN Revolt, a revolt in the armed forces had a dramatic impact on popular consciousness and remains a legend to this day.

The RIN men had served abroad and were familiar with developments in other parts of the world. They thoroughly resented the racist behaviour of the British officers. They were also aware of the unrest in the country, specially over INA trials.

On 18th February 1946, their rising tempers suddenly frayed over the poor quality of food they were served and the ratings of HMIS Talwar in Bombay harbour struck work to protest against the following:

- The treatment meted out to them including racial discrimination.
- The arrest of BC Dutt (a rating) for writing 'Quit India' on HMIS Talwar.

The ratings were joined by others in 22 neighbouring ships and those in the barracks on the shore. Once again, the strikers raised the National, the League and the Red flags together. They also elected a **Naval Central Committee** with **MS Khan** as its head and drew up a set of demands including the following:

- Release of INA prisoners
- Release of all other political prisoners
- Withdrawal of Indian troops form Indo-China and Java
- Better food, better treatment
- Equal pay to both Indian and European sailors alike

On 20th February, the ratings in the barracks as well as those in the ships got surrounded by British forces. Soon there was exchange of fire and a gun battle began.

By 22nd February the revolt had spread to all the naval bases in India involving 78 ships, 20 shore establishments and 20000 ratings, making it the most serious of all direct confrontations with the British administration of the time. The naval mutiny evoked unprecedented public sympathy, specially of students and workers and clashes got particularly bloody in Bombay. **Karachi** also emerged as a major storm centre.

On 23rd February, however, **Vallabhbhai Patel** and **Jinnah** persuaded the ratings into surrender, bringing the mutiny to an end.

Evaluation of the three upsurges Even though the upsurges were short-lived and their participation was confined to a few sections and a few urban centres, they forced the British government to grant some concessions, such as first announcing to try only those INA members who could be accused of murder and brutalities (December 1945) and then remitting the sentences passed against the first batch of the accused (January 1946), and withdrawal of Indian soldiers from Indo-China and Indonesia.

Attitude of Congress towards the upsurges Even though the Congress lauded the spirit of the people, it did **not officially support** these upsurges because of their tactics and timing. While the agitations were led by the Communists, the Socialists or the Forward Blockists, the Congress tried to diffuse the revolutionary situation.

Some scholars accuse the Congress of being immersed in negotiations or even power hankering during the upsurges. On the other hand, historian Bipan Chandra is of the view that the upsurges were in fact an expression of the strong anti-imperialist sentiment that the Congress had fostered through its defence of the INA prisoners. As for negotiations, they formed an integral part of Congress strategy and the guiding maxim of the Congress was: 'Negotiations when possible and non-cooperation and direct action when necessary'.

Attitude of Gandhi As revealed by Gandhi's statements published in the Harijan in 1946, Gandhi was relieved that the ratings had listened to Sardar Patel's advice for surrender. Gandhi felt that the upsurges were badly advised. If the people had any grievances, they should have waited for the intervention by the political leaders of their choice. By not doing so, the people had been thoughtless and ignorant.

Other Direct Confrontations

Several other direct confrontations continued to take place simultaneously such as-

- In mid-February 1946, in Allahabad, over 80,000 demonstrated against the government decision to cut down the ration supplies of the civilian population.
- In April 1946, in Delhi, Bihar, Bengal, Andamans and Bengal, there was a widespread police strike aided by the leftists.
- In July 1946, the postal employees struck work for some time. In fact, the atmosphere remained much tensed throughout July in anticipation of an all India Railway workers' strike.

Indirect Confrontations

As stated earlier, such confrontations indirectly undermined British Raj through direct confrontations with its upholders—certain landlords, princes and capitalists.

Spearheaded by peasants and workers, these confrontations mainly arose out of economic grievances and took the form of strikes against their immediate exploiters such as the landlords and capitalists and thereby weakened the hands of their colonial masters as well. Collectively known as the strike wave of the 1940s, these strikes generated a mood of defiance and self-confidence all around.

Peasant Agitation of the Warlis (Maharashtra, 1945–46) The Warlis (or Varlis) were the indigenous tribal or adivasi peasants who were in majority in the villages of Umbergaon, Dananu, Palghar and Jawahar Taluks of Thana district, Bombay. The Warlis had lost most of their land holdings to the moneylenders and were themselves reduced to the status of tenants or even farm labourers or wage earners. In times of difficulty, many of them had to give veth bigar or labour without pay.

In 1945, the Warlis were first organised by the Maharashtra Kisan Sabha. Subsequently, lead by **Godavari Purulekar**, the Warlis began to strike opposing veth bigar and low wages. The landlords retaliated by terrorising them with the help of the police. Several violent clashes followed and the Warli agitation gradually petered out by the end of 1946 in the face of repression.

Bakasht Peasants' Agitation (Bihar, 1946–47) This peasant agitation had grown over the past decade over bakasht lands, which the tenants had lost to zamindars during depression years (1929–37) by virtue of non-payment of rent and which they continued to cultivate as sharecroppers.

Apart from the rayati lands and the zirat lands, the zamindars also rented the bakasht lands.

Rayati lands were those lands which were settled by zamindars with the occupant tenants.

Zirat lands were those lands which the zamindars kept for themselves and got cultivated by agricultural labourers.

Bakasht lands were those lands which were rented to the tenants-at-will at varying rates.

The bakasht peasants continued to face ejectments as it was profitable to the zamindars—the new incumbents had to pay fresh salami and higher rent to get possession. The zamindars also wished to circumvent the Tenancy Act of 1885 by evicting the peasants as the Act gave the bakasht tenants some occupancy rights if they had been in that position for 12 years.

During 1937–39, the peasants had first resisted their eviction under the banner of the Kisan Sabha. In 1946, the issue caught fire once again when the Congress contested the elections in Bihar and promised to abolish the zamindari system. The zamindars felt insecure and tried to convert all bakasht lands into zirat by evicting the bakasht peasants in the hope that they would at least be able to retain the zirat lands.

Such moves were naturally resisted by the peasants who once again protested under the leadership of the Kisan Sabha. The agitation led to violent clashes, arson, loot, injuries and even deaths.

Flashforward: In 1947, the **Bihar Bakasht Disputes Settlement Act** was passed which had little effect. Subsequently, in 1948 the **Bihar Abolition of Zamindari Act** was passed by the Congress government after which the movement finally subsided.

Travancore Agitation (1946) In 1946 in Shertalai-Aleppy region of northwestern Travancore, a strong trade union-cum-agrarian movement developed under the leadership of the Communists against the Travancore Maharaja and his Diwan.

During this time, the Maharaja and his **Diwan, CP Ramaswamy Iyer**, were secretly planning to carve out an independent state of Travancore in anticipation of British departure from India. They wanted to impose an irresponsible government in Travancore, with all real powers vested with the Diwan to be appointed by the Maharaj. The Communists mobilised the peasants and workers and launched a massive campaign against this plan. Even the authorities unleashed forces of terror against their opponents, making indiscriminate arrests and inflicting torture.

Punnapra-Vayalar Episode: On 22nd October 1946, as a response to state violence, the workers called a general strike in Aleppy area and also attacked the police camp at Punnapra. In response, the army was ordered to attack the workers sheltered at Vayalar. This culminated in a ghastly massacre of 800, which instead of terrorising people into submission only reaffirmed their resolve to stand against the state's independence move.

Tebhaga Movement (Bengal, 1946–47) This was probably the most extensive of all post-war agrarian movements encompassing 19 districts of Bengal and 6 million peasants including a high percentage of Muslims.

The Tebhaga Movement was a peasant movement that first began in September 1946 under the leadership of the Bengal Provincial Kisan Sabha. It was directed against the exploitative sharecropping system and the jotedars who took away a major part of the produce. The movement thus demanded three-fourths of the produce for the tillers against one-half (though some sources also mention that the demand of the peasants was to reduce the landlord share from one-half to one-third, and thus the name 'Tebhaga').

Sharecropping Sharecropping is a form of agriculture in which a landowner allows a tenant to use the land in return for a share of the crops produced on their portion of land.

Jotedars The Jotedars were the class of rich peasantry in the villages of Bengal that emerged as a new class of rural exploiters between the landlords (zamindars) and the tenants (rayats). The jotedars accumulated huge chunks of land (jotes) for which they paid rent in cash and which they in turn rented out to landless peasants on basis of sharing the crops in equal halves.

The agitators raised the slogan **'Tebhaga Chai'** or we want three parts out of four. The contest over crops soon led to angry outbursts and violent clashes. Despite communal carnage in Calcutta and Noakhali, Muslim peasants participated in large numbers. Women also played an active role. The movement, however, wilted away in the face of government repression, apathy of the Congress and the League, hostility of the rentier Bengali middle class and worsened communal situation and was finally suspended in March 1947.

Telangana Movement (Hyderabad state, 1946–51) The Telangana movement that arose in the Telugu speaking region of Hyderabad state grew out of an exploitative agrarian situation. The peasants were exploited and abused by jagirdars on one hand and the Deshmukhs (past revenue farmers) and Patel-Patwaris (tax-collectors) on the other hand.

The Deshmukhs and the Patel Patwaris had lost their job in 1860s when the Nizam's government started collecting the land revenue directly. Even though they were given substantial amount of land as compensation, their lust for land continued. Using their knowledge as revenue officials, they manipulated survey records and went on a land grabbing spree. They also began imposing a number of illegal taxes on the villagers and exacting **vetti** or free labour (also called vetti chakiri or begar).

It was against these malpractices that the Telangana peasantry arose in revolt. They were led by the **Andhra Maha Sabha**, a communist organisation.

On 4th July 1946, armed retainers of the Visunuri Deshmukh of Janagaon opened fire on a peaceful gathering of peasants and killed Doddi Komaryya. This incident forced the peasants to take to arms and start an armed peasant movement.

Soon the Andhra Sabha and the Communist Party were declared illegal by the Nizam's government. Despite attempts at severe repression, the authorities failed to disintegrate the movement which continued unabated till the end of 1951, thus proving to be the most enduring and the most militant of all similar agitations.

Impact and Significance of Post-War Popular Unrest

- The post-war unrest was an expression of the militancy in the popular mind.
- It demonstrated that nationalist feelings had penetrated into hitherto untouched sections and regions of India.

- The British Indian government could no longer rely on the Indian personnel of its civil administration as well as the armed forces to suppress a revolt in India.
- The INA trials had well demonstrated that patriotic ideas had entered into the minds of the armed forces—the chief instrument of British Raj in India.
- The RIN Revolt, a revolt in the armed forces, had a liberating effect in the minds of the people.

- The large-scale peasant and worker unrest all over the country also expressed the determined and confident mood of the Indian people.
- When non-violent agitation was met with force, it exposed the brute force that stood behind the government, eroding its prestige as well as moral basis to rule India.
- The Popular Unrest provided immediate context for the announcement of Cabinet Mission, to find out ways and means of peaceful transfer of power.

The popular unrest during the period 1945–47 demonstrated the enormous capacity of the common Indian men and women to stand up unitedly in the face of exploitation. With the Congress and the Muslim League tangled in power struggle, the mass discontent emerged as the only ray of hope for the nationalists.

Previous Years' Questions – Preliminary Exam

1. Which one of the following is not correct about the Cabinet Mission Plan? **[UPSC 1996]**
   (a) Provincial grouping
   (b) Interim Cabinet of Indians
   (c) Acceptance of Pakistan
   (d) Constitution framing right
2. What is the correct sequence of the following events? **[UPSC 1998]**
   1. The August offer
   2. The INA trial
   3. The Quit India Movement
   4. The Royal Indian Naval ratings revolt

   Choose the correct answer from the following options.
   Codes:
   (a) 1,3,2,4 (b) 3,1,2,4
   (c) 1,3,4,2 (d) 3,1,4,2
3. Which one of the following leaders of the Congress was totally in favour of Cabinet Mission Plan? **[UPSC 1999]**
   (a) Mahatma Gandhi
   (b) Jawaharlal Nehru
   (c) Sardar Patel
   (d) Maulana Abul Kalam Azad
4. Which Indian nationalist leader looked upon a war between Germany and Britain as a god sent opportunity which would enable Indians to exploit the situation to their advantage? **[UPSC 1999]**
   (a) C Rajagopalachari
   (b) M A Jinnah
   (c) Subhas Chandra Bose
   (d) Jawaharlal Nehru
5. 'It made its proposals in May. It still wanted a United India. There was to be a Federal Union composed of British provinces'. **[UPSC 1999]**
   The above question is related to
   (a) Simon Commission
   (b) Gandhi–Irwin pact
   (c) Cripps mission
   (d) Cabinet mission
6. The last opportunity to avoid the partition of India was lost with the rejection of which of the following? **[UPSC 2002]**
   (a) Cripps Mission
   (b) Rajagopalachari formula
   (c) Cabinet Mission
   (d) Wavell Plan

7. The members of the constituent assembly which drafted the Constitution of India were **[UPSC 2002]**
   (a) Nominated by the British Parliament
   (b) Nominated by the Governor General
   (c) Elected by the legislative assemblies of various province
   (d) Elected by the Indian National Congress, Muslim League
8. Who headed the Interim Cabinet formed in the year 1946? **[UPSC 2003]**
   (a) Rajendra Prasad
   (b) Jawaharlal Nehru
   (c) Sardar Vallabhbhai Patel
   (d) C. Rajgopalachari
9. Which one of the following statements is correct? **[UPSC 2004]**
   (a) The Constituent Assembly of India was elected by the Provincial Assemblies in the year 1946.
   (b) Jawaharlal Nehru, M A Jinnah and Sardar Vallabhbhai Patel were members of the Constituent Assembly of India
   (c) The first session of the Constituent Assembly of India was held in January 1947
   (d) The Constitution of India was adopted on 26 January 1950
10. Who among the following was the Chairman of the Union Constitution Committee of the Constituent Assembly? **[UPSC 2005]**
   (a) B.R. Ambedkar
   (b) J.B. Kripalani
   (c) Jawaharlal Nehru
   (d) Alladi Krishnaswamy Iyer
11. Consider the following statements: **[UPSC 2005]**
   1. Lord Mountbatten was the Viceroy when Simla conference took place.
   2. Indian Navy revolt, 1946 took place when the Indian sailors in the Royal Indian Navy at Bombay and Karachi rose against the government.

   Which of the statements given above is/are correct? Choose the correct answer from the following options.
   (a) 1 only (b) 2 only
   (c) Both 1 and 2 (d) Neither 1 nor 2
12. Assertion (A): According to the Wavell Plan, the number of Hindu and Muslim members in the Executive Council were to be equal.
   Reason (R): Wavell thought that this arrangement would have avoided the partition of India. **[UPSC 2007]**
   Select the answer for the options given below:
   (a) if both A and R are true and R is the correct explanation of A
   (b) if both A and R are true but R is not the correct explanation of A
   (c) if A is true but R is false
   (d) if A is false but R is true
13. The demand for the Tebhaga Peasant Movement in Bengal was for **[UPSC 2013]**
   (a) the reduction of the share of the landlords from one-half of the crop to one- third
   (b) the grant of ownership of land to peasants as they were the actual cultivators of the land
   (c) the uprooting of zamindari system and the end of serfdom
   (d) Writing of all peasant debts
14. With reference to the Cabinet Mission, which of the following statements is/are correct? **[UPSC 2015]**
   1. It recommended a Federal Government.
   2. It enlarged the power of the Indian courts
   3. It provided for more Indians in the ICS.

   Choose the correct answer from the following options.
   (a) Only 1
   (b) 2 and 3
   (c) 1 and 3
   (d) None of the above
15. With reference to Indian freedom struggle, consider the following events: **[UPSC 2017]**
   1. Mutiny in Royal Indian Navy
   2. Quit India Movement launched
   3. Second Round Table Conference

   What is the correct chronological sequence of the above events? Choose the correct answer from the following options.
   (a) 1-2-3 (b) 2-1-3
   (c) 3-2-1 (d) 3-1-2

16. In the context of Colonial India, Shah Nawaz Khan, Prem Kumar Sehgal and Gurbaksh Singh Dhillion are remembered as **[UPSC 2021]**
    (a) Leaders of Swadeshi and Boycott Movement
    (b) Members of the Interim Government in 1946
    (c) Members of the Drafting Committee in the Constituent Assembly
    (d) Officers of the Indian National Army
17. With reference to the proposals of Cripps Mission, consider the following statements: **[UPSC 2022]**
    1. The Constituent Assembly would have members nominated by the Provincial Assemblies as well as the Princely States.
    2. Any Province, which is not prepared to accept the new Constitution would have the right to sign a separate agreement with Britain regarding its future status.

    Which of the statements given above is/are correct?
    (a) 1 only (b) 2 only
    (c) Both 1 and 2 (d) Neither 1 nor 2

Previous Years' Questions – Main Exam

1. What was the Cabinet Mission Plan? How was the 'grouping clause' fundamental to it? What was its impact on the attitude of the Congress and the League? **[UPSC 1989]**
2. 'The trial of the INA officers did more harm than good to the British rule in India'. Explain **[UPSC 1989]**
3. When and why did the revolt of the ratings of the Royal Indian Navy take place? Why did they suspend the movement? What were the attitudes of Gandhi and Patel towards the moment? **[UPSC 1990]**
4. Trace the origin of the RIN mutiny and evaluate its impact on the political situation in India. **[UPSC 1998]**
5. What were the proposals of the Cabinet Mission? Analyse the reactions of the Congress and the league to the proposals. **[UPSC 1999]**
6. Trace the salient sequence of events in the popular Revolt that took place in February 1946 in the then Royal Indian Navy and bring out its significance in the freedom struggle. Do you agree with the view that the sailors who took part in the revolt were some of the unsung heroes of the freedom struggle? **[UPSC 2011]**
7. In what ways did the Naval Mutiny prove to be the last nail in the coffin of British colonial aspirations in India? **[UPSC 2014]**
8. It would have been difficult for the Constituent Assembly to complete its historic task of drafting the constitution for Independent India in just three years but for the experience gained with the Government of Indian Act, 1935. Discuss. **[UPSC 2014]**

Answers

Previous Years' Questions – Preliminary Exam

1.	(c)	2.	(a)	3.	(c)	4.	(c)	5.	(d)
6.	(c)	7.	(c)	8.	(b)	9.	(a)	10.	(c)
11.	(b)	12.	(c)	13.	(a)	14.	(a)	15.	(c)
16.	(d)	17.	(b)						

3 Communalism, Partition and Freedom of India

You are already familiar with the rise and growth of communalism in India upto 1940. It was in 1940 at the Lahore session of the Muslim League, that the highest communal demand, i.e. the demand for Pakistan was put forward. Henceforth, the 1940s formed the most crucial phase of communalism, culminating in the actual birth of Pakistan in 1947.

Period of Extreme Communalism (Background to the Demand for Pakistan)

Flashback:

Extreme Communalism, after 1937 Extreme communalism is based on fear and hatred and has a tendency to use violent language or behaviour. After 1937, the Muslim League and the Hindu Mahasabha increasingly tilted towards extreme communalism.

The demand for Pakistan was the result of certain changes that took place in the Indian political scene after 1937. The period after 1937 witnessed elements of extreme communalism in the politics of both- the Hindu communal forces as well as the Muslim communal forces, with the British playing the role of a catalyst. In modern Indian history, this is known as the **Communal Triangle—**the British forming the base of the triangle, the Hindu and the Muslim communal forces forming its two arms. Let us examine the role of each of the three forces one by one.

Extremist Phase of Muslim Communal Forces

The year 1937 was a turning point in the history of communalism in India. In the 1937 provincial elections, the League performed badly, winning only 109 out of 492 reserved seats and only 4.8 per cent of the total Muslim votes. The message was clear—the League needed to shed its elite character (dominated by princes and zamindars) and create a base among the Muslim masses. How was this possible? If the League took up the socio-economic grievances of the Muslim masses, it ran the risk of annoying and thus losing the existing base of princes and landlords.

Hence, the League decided to appeal to the religious sentiments of the Muslim masses. Jinnah and other League leaders raised the cry of **'Islam in Danger'** from the threat of impending 'Hindu Raj', a cry which appealed to all Muslims, equally. They declared that the aim of Congress was not independence but to establish a Hindu Raj in India which would enable them to fulfil their real motive, i.e. domination over Muslims and extermination of Islam. Once the fear of Hindu Raj became entrenched in their psyche, it would be easy to convince them about the need for a separate homeland for Muslims, where they could practice their religion freely and fearlessly.

Thus, Jinnah and other League leaders appealed to the Muslims to support the League, if they wished to save their religion from 'Hindu onslaught'. Such a communal propaganda was inevitably full of **fear, contempt** and **bitter hatred**. The demand for Pakistan clearly flowed from such politics of fear and hatred adopted by the League after 1937.

Flashback: Finally in 1940, at the Lahore Session of the Muslim League, Jinnah propounded his two-nation theory that India comprised of two nations—a Hindu nation and a Muslim nation, who were different economically, politically, socially, culturally and historically. That Muslims were not a minority but a nation and therefore they were rightfully entitled to a nation of their own (the press was quick to describe the resolution as a demand for Pakistan; some also began to call it the **Pakistan Resolution**).

Thus, 1940 onwards, Muslim communalism was no longer based on mere fanning of minority fears but instead on an assertive–aggressive demand for a separate Muslim state. The above activities of the Muslim League headed by Jinnah transformed communalism into a mass force ultimately leading to the partition of India and formation of the separate state of Pakistan.

Extremist Phase of Hindu Communal Forces

In 1937 provincial elections, the Hindu communalists had fared even worse than their Muslim counterparts. They also needed to expand their mass base and they too decided to appeal to the religious sentiments of the Hindu masses.

The **Hindu Mahasabha** and **Rashtriya Swayam Sevak Sangh** were now led by more radical leaders such as VD Savarkar (who replaced Madan Mohan Malaviya) and MS Golwalkar, respectively. Savarkar had publicly announced, 'The only way to deal with Hindu-Muslim schism was to insist that all India was Hindustan (i.e. land of the Hindus) and that the Muslims must reconcile themselves to the status of a minority community in a democratic state which orders life by majority rule'. Golwalkar's book **'We, or Our Nationhood Defined'** became the manifesto of Hindu Communalism.

Thus, the Hindu communalists asserted that India was a nation of the Hindus and the Muslims should either leave or live as second-class citizens, let alone any privileges or special treatment as minorities. Such was the Hindu Communalists version of two-nation theory. They not only spread hatred for the Muslims but also bitterly criticised the Congress for supporting the 'enemies of the Hindus'.

By 1946–47, the language of the Hindu communalists became extremely vicious. As communal riots spread like wildfire and Congress was unable to stop them, the Hindu communalists tried to project themselves as saviours of Hindus. They condemned the Congress for their 'emasculating' talks of non-violence and communal harmony and instead instigated the Hindus to retaliate and teach a lesson to the Muslims. In this way, Hindu communalism only reinforced the fears of the Muslims.

At the time of partition, the communalised atmosphere provided a fertile ground for the growth of the Hindu communalists and their stand became even more aggressive. Now that a separate state for the Muslims had been carved out, they demanded that the rest of India be declared as a Hindu state.

They tried to overthrow the state and capture power and when they were unable to do so, they became bitterly critical of the Congress government. Even Mahatma Gandhi was not spared and charged of treason to the Hindu nation.

Role of British Forces

The British policy of 'divide and rule' played a very significant role in the growth of communalism in India. Under this policy, Muslim communalism received wholesome support and patronage of the British government. Since the very beginning, the British had tried to divide Indians along the already existing fault lines of class, caste and religion. But it was the fault line of religion that proved to be the most potent; the British nurtured the Muslim League since its very inception and encouraged communalism to foster their own imperial interests in India.

In October 1939, when the Congress ministries resigned over the Second World War issue and the party drifted away from active politics, the League moved in to fill the political vacuum and consolidated its position through Jinnah's manoeuvrings with the Viceroy (Linlithgow).

In 1940, the League raised the demand for Pakistan to counter the Congress demand for immediate transfer of substance of power. The British too lost no time in making this demand as a major plank for delaying transfer of power. The British declared that so long as Hindus and Muslims do not come to an agreement on the manner of transfer of power, it could not be done.

In 1942, through the Cripps proposals, the British government tried to accommodate the Pakistan demand through the back door (by giving the provinces the right of non-accession and secession from the Indian Union). At a time when the Pakistan demand had hardly been taken seriously by Indians, its serious consideration by British leaders gave legitimacy to the Pakistan demand and greatly served the cause of the Muslim League.

In June 1945 at Simla Conference, Viceroy Wavell's attitude implied official recognition of the League's monopoly to speak for all Muslims and conference of the veto power onto the League for all future negotiations (even as its performance in the previous elections hardly sustained this claim). On the other hand, the British had perpetually raised questions on the 'national character' of the Congress.

In March 1946, when the Cabinet Mission was sent, a change in British Policy towards the Muslim League was noticed. The British were of the opinion that the old policy of divide and rule would no longer be suitable. Instead they felt that the British interests could be better served in future by a united India. They believed that a united India, friendly with Britain, could emerge as an active partner in the defence of the Commonwealth. Accordingly, on 15th March 1946, PM Attlee declared in the House of Commons, 'We cannot allow a minority to place a veto on the advance of the majority'. The statement indicated a change in the British policy towards the Muslim League. Contrast this with the Simla Conference, where Wavell had allowed Jinnah to veto and wreck the negotiations. At the same time, it is also true that the scheme of Pakistan was kept alive and allowed entry through the backdoor, via the controversial provision of grouping.

The failure of the Cabinet Mission so frustrated the Muslim League that it decided to act upon its post-election slogan, 'Ladke Lenge Pakistan' and 16th August 1946 was observed as **Direct Action Day** by the League. What followed was a communal holocaust that spread like wildfire in the country and continued throughout 1947.

In September 1946, at the time of the formation of the Interim Government, the British were in a dilemma whether to wait for the League and the Congress to agree on a plan or to go ahead with the Interim government with the Congress alone. Once again, Wavell would have called off the talks, as he had happily done in Simla, had it not been for the **widespread popular unrest** that had begun to rage the country. Moreover, His Majesty's Government was of the opinion that the support of the Congress was a prerequisite for their long-term interests and future good relations with India. Accordingly, on 2nd September 1946, the Congress was invited to form an Interim Government- a sharp departure from earlier British practice.

However, in October 1946, i.e. within a month's time, the British went back to their policy of placating the Muslims. In the context of communal fire and the possibility of a civil war that could be unleashed by the League, Wavell persuaded the League to join the Interim Government (26th October 1946).

Flashback: Thereafter, this government got sharply divided into two perpetually warring camps.

On 9th December 1946, the Constituent Assembly first met at New Delhi. Even though the League had joined the Interim Government, it refused to participate in the Constituent Assembly and instead demanded dissolution of the Assembly calling it unrepresentative. On 5th February 1947, the Congress members of the Interim government sent a letter to Wavell with a demand that the League members be asked to resign. Clearly, a crisis was in the offing.

Partition and Freedom

Attlee's Announcement (20th February 1947) (Setting the Time Limit for British Withdrawal)

On 20th February 1947, the impending political crisis was temporarily averted by Attlee's announcement to the effect that-

- The British would withdraw from India by 30th June 1948.
- Wavell would be replaced by Lord Mountbatten as Viceroy.
- Power shall be transferred to more than one authority if the Constituent Assembly did not become fully representative, i.e. if the Muslim majority provinces did not join it.

The statement had been made in the context of irreversible breakdown of government authority and in the hope that the date will bring the two warring parties together. However, the hope proved only illusory.

Jinnah now knew that he alone will have to stick firmly to his demand of Pakistan. With regard to the announcement, the Governor of Punjab, Evan Meredith Jenkins, had warned that the announcement was a prelude to the final communal showdown with everyone out to 'seize as much power as they can, if necessary by force'. His statement was soon proved right with the League launching a tearing-raging campaign for partition of the country. It unleashed unrestricted violence in Punjab, Assam and NWFP with a view to bringing down the non-League Ministries in these provinces (to ensure that power is not transferred to non-League provincial governments here) and even succeeded in dislodging the Punjab coalition ministry led by Khizr Hyatt Khan. The League was clearly on a war path now.

Lord Mountbatten Arrives in India

Lord Mountbatten

Mountbatten was sent to India with the task of winding up the Raj by 30th June 1948. On 22nd March 1947 Lord Mountbatten arrived in India and plunged straight into the constitutional problem with the objective of finding a solution on the basis of the Cabinet Mission Plan. He set about his task in the most zealous manner but he was soon convinced, particularly after talks with Jinnah, that there could be no solution to a united India.

While trying to push for the Cabinet Mission Plan with Jinnah, Mountbatten had concluded, 'He gave the impression that he was not listening. He was impossible to argue with... He was, whatever was said, intent on his Pakistan'.

Hence, he began directing his energies towards an alternative plan based upon Atlee's Statement of 20 February according to which power could be transferred to more than one authority.

Plan Balkan/Dickie Bird Plan/Ismay Plan

This Plan was put forward by a committee comprising Lord Mountbatten, General Sir Hastings Ismay and Sir George Abell during March–May 1947, before Mountbatten presented the 3rd June Plan. It envisaged the transfer of power to several provinces (in accordance with Atllee's declaration which had talked about transfer of power to more than one authority if the Constituent Assembly did not become fully representative). The Punjab and Bengal Assemblies would vote on the partition issue and incase they voted in favour of partition, the various units thus formed along with the princely states rendered independent upon the lapse of paramountcy would have the choice of joining India or Pakistan or remaining independent. The plan was, however, quickly abandoned when it evoked severe reactions from Indian leaders, particularly Jawaharlal Nehru. The plan was also rejected by the League as it wanted a united Pakistan.

Clearly, the plan came to be known as the Balkan Plan as it provided for balkanisation of India into several sovereign states and the dismemberment of Indian nationhood. The plan also came to be known as the Ismay Plan as it was General Ismay who had presented the plan before the provincial governors in Delhi.

Mountbatten Plan: Partition Plan (Also Known as 3rd June Plan)

The Plan

- The Legislative Assemblies of Bengal and Punjab were to meet in two sections (representing Muslim majority districts and the rest of province) to decide by a simple majority whether the province was to be partitioned or not. In case they vote for partition, **two dominions** and two constituent assemblies shall be created.
- It declared that transfer of power would take place by **15th August 1947** on the basis of dominion status to two successor states, India and Pakistan.
- It provided for a **referendum** in the NWFP to decide whether the province would join India or Pakistan. It also provided for a referendum in Muslim majority district of Sylhet (Assam) to decide whether the district would join East Bengal or remain part of Assam. Sindh would take its own decision.

- It provided for setting up of a **Boundary Commission** to demarcate boundaries in case partition was to be effected.
- It proposed to introduce a legislation in the current session for transfer of power on a Dominion Status basis on one or two successor authorities which may decide, in due course of time, whether or not they wish to remain in the British Commonwealth.
- With the lapse of Paramountcy, the **Indian states would be free to join any dominion** they liked, India or Pakistan (but this statement did not make clear the position of the princely states regarding the option of independence, leaving them to luxuriate in wild dreams of independent power!).

Concessions given to Congress in the Plan

Since Congress was making the bigger concession- of compromising with its ideal of united India, all its other demands were to be upheld by the Mountbatten Plan:

- Princely states were not to be given the option of independence (though Mountbatten supported Congress on this, the provision in 3rd June Plan left scope for ambiguity)
- Independence for Bengal was ruled out
- Accession of Hyderabad to Pakistan was ruled out

Indian Response

The Mountbatten Plan was accepted by all political parties in India, although with great unwillingness. They had now recognised the inevitability of partition. By early 1947 itself, the Congress had begun to acknowledge it:

- On 20th April 1947, Nehru had said in a public speech, 'The Muslim League can have Pakistan, if they wish to have it, but on the condition that they do not take away other parts of India which do not wish to join Pakistan'.
- On 28th April, Rajendra Prasad had declared in the Constituent Assembly, 'It may be that the Union (of India) may not comprise all provinces...For this, we must be prepared'.

Result

The Hindu members of the Bengal and Punjab Assemblies decided in favour of partition. While East Bengal and West Punjab decided to join Pakistan, West Bengal and East Punjab joined India.

- Referendum in Sylhet and NWFP went in favour of Pakistan.
- Two Boundary Commissions were constituted, one in respect of each province.

Thus, the Mountbatten Plan became the basis of partition of India.

Analysis of Mountbatten Plan

- **Divide India while retaining maximum unity** This Plan was drafted keeping in mind the demand of both the Congress and the League. Pakistan would be carved out, but it would be kept as small as possible to accommodate Congress demand of a united India. Moreover, since Congress was making the bigger concession of compromising with its ideal of united India, all its other demands were to be upheld. This was also important if Britain wished to retain the goodwill of

Congress and persuade India to accept the Dominion Status and join the Commonwealth. Between India and Pakistan, Britain was keener on having India in the Commonwealth as its economic and defence potential was deemed sounder.

- **Dominion status** The Congress accepted Dominion status as the only means of ending the deadlock and taking charge of the worsening communal situation. It would also give some breathing time to the new administration as the British officers could stay on for a while and let Indian leaders settle in and take charge.
- **Early date, 15th August** Hence, the 3rd June Plan declared that transfer of power would take place by 15th August 1947 on the basis of dominion status to two successor states, India and Pakistan. The early date of 15th August was fixed in order to secure Congress agreement to Dominion Status. It also allowed the British to forsake responsibility of the fast deteriorating communal situation.

Indian Independence Act, 1947

On 4th July 1947, the Indian Independences Bill was introduced in the House of Commons by the Labour government of **Clement Attlee** and Governor General Lord Mountbatten after Indian leaders agreed on the Mountbatten Plan, the last Plan for independence. The Bill was introduced with the objective of transferring power to the people of India and received Royal assent on 18th July. Its main provisions included:

- As from 15th August 1947, two independent Dominions shall be set up in India, to be known respectively as India and Pakistan.
- The boundaries between the two dominions shall be determined by Boundary Commissions (headed by **Sir Cyril Radcliffe**, hence also known as Radcliffe Commissions).
- The territories of Pakistan shall include the areas covered by the Provinces of East Bengal (including Sylhet district of Assam province), West Punjab, Sind, Baluchistan and the North-West Frontier Province.
- The Constituent Assemblies of both the Dominions were free to make constitutions for their respective countries.
- Pending the adoption of a new constitution, the existing Constituent Assembly of each Dominion would function as **Dominion Legislature** and each Dominion shall be governed by the provisions of the Government of India Act 1935.
- For each of the new dominion a new Governor-General was to be appointed by the Crown. Further, the same person could be the Governor General of both (Mountbatten became the first Governor General of free India and Jinnah the first Governor General of Pakistan).
- The Governor General was invested with adequate powers until March 1948 to issue orders for effective implementation of the provisions of the Indian independence Act 1947.
- The Act terminated the suzerainty and paramountcy of the British Crown over the Indian states. Agreements between the States and the new Dominions were to be negotiated.
- The **Indian States** were free to accede to either of the two new Dominions (the Act released the States from all their obligations to the Crown and they were now technically independent).
- The Office of the Secretary of State was abolished and his work was to be taken over by the **Secretary of Commonwealth Affairs**.
- The words 'Emperor of India' and 'Indian Imperator' were dropped from the Royal style and titles.

The Indian Independence Act 1947 was acclaimed as 'the noblest and greatest law ever enacted by the British Parliament'. This Act closed the last chapter of British India and opened a new chapter of free India.

The Disastrous 72-day Timetable

From 3rd June to 15th August 1947, i.e. in 72 days—both the transfer of power and the partition of the country were hurried through at lightning speed. From the Indian standpoint, this proved disastrous. According to some senior British officers (including the Commander-in-Chief Auchinleck), a minimum period of say a few years was needed to carry out a peaceful partition. The Plan provided for no institutional framework for resolving issues arising out of partition. Jinnah worsened matters by refusing to allow Mountbatten to act as a common Governor-General for both India and Pakistan as he wanted that position for himself. In December 1947, the Joint Defence machinery also broke down. By then, Kashmir had already become a ground for military conflict.

Massacres – the Tragedy of Partition

Partition of the country was accompanied by widespread Hindu–Muslim riots and massacres which comprised the tragedy of partition and were a result of several factors including the following:

- **Role of Mountbatten** Two of Mountbatten's decisions—early date of 15th August and the delay in announcing the Boundary Commission Award, played a key role in worsening situation in Punjab. As per senior British officers including Commander-in-Chief Lockhart (CnC of Indian Army from 15th August to 31st December 1947), the Punjab tragedy would not have occurred had the partition been delayed for a year. Further, even though the Boundary Commission Award was ready by 12th August, Mountbatten withheld the announcement until transfer of power, to forsake responsibility of further disorder. As a result, people living in the villages between Lahore and Amritsar continued to live in their homes thinking that they were on the right side of the border. Once the award was announced at the last minute, migrations took place in frenzy, often culminating in massacres. The officials too were busy arranging their own transfers rather than serving on duty which might have prevented the tragic killings.
- **Refusal to accept the finality of partition** Millions of people refused to accept partition long after it was announced, making it a last-minute frenzied affair. Even leaders such as Gandhi and Nehru believed the partition to be only temporary.
- **Belief that partition will be peaceful** Most unrealistically, it was simply assumed that the partition would be a peaceful one. Once Pakistan was granted, what was there to fight for? No preparations were made for transfer of population and no riots anticipated.

Radcliffe Commissions As stipulated by the Act of 1947, the two Boundary Commissions were formed and were headed by Sir Cyril Radcliffe (hence the name Radcliffe Commissions). The divisions on both sides were carried out in secret and the final Boundary Awards were ready by 12th August. The Awards were, however, published only on 17th August to avoid further delays and disputes and gave details about the boundary demarcation line between India and Pakistan which came to be known as the Radcliffe Line. Today, the two sides of the Line in the west and in the east, continue to serve as Indo-Pakistan and Indo-Bangladesh Borders, respectively.

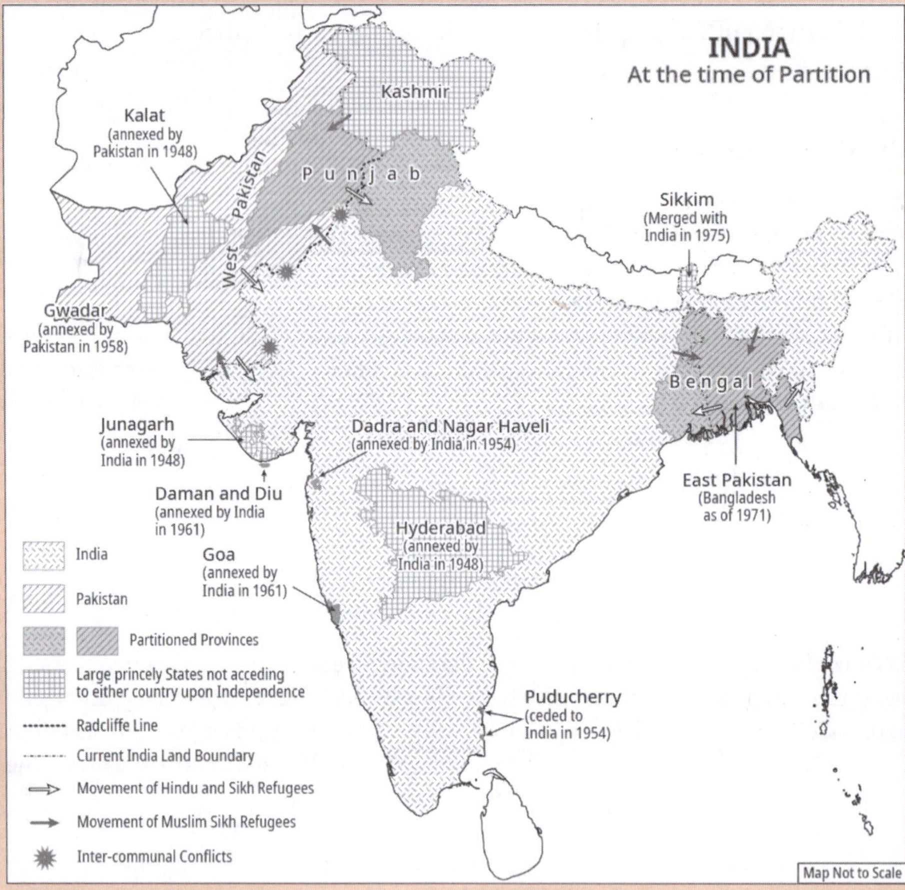

Map of the partition of India

Independence Day (15th August 1947)

On the night of 14th August, the Constituent Assembly met and in a memorable speech, Jawaharlal Nehru called upon the members to take a pledge of service to the nation. At the stroke of midnight, independence was granted to both India and Pakistan. On the morning of 15th August, free India woke up to the dual reality of independence and partition. A new Cabinet, headed by Jawaharlal Nehru, the first Prime Minister of free India, was sworn in. Sardar Vallabhbhai Patel became the Home Minister.

Thus, was born a new nation, ending nearly 200 years of British rule in India.

National Flag of India hoisted at the Red Fort

Jawaharlal Nehru's 'Tryst with Destiny' Speech This speech was made by Jawaharlal Nehru, first Prime Minister of independent India, in the Constituent Assembly on the eve of India's independence and is considered as one of the greatest speeches of the 20th century.

'Long years ago, we made a tryst with destiny, and now the time comes when we shall redeem our pledge, not wholly or in full measure, but very substantially. At the stroke of the midnight hour, when the world sleeps, India will awake to life and freedom. A moment comes, which comes but rarely in history, when we step out from the old to the new, when an age ends, and when the soul of a nation, long suppressed, finds utterance. It is fitting that at this solemn moment we take the pledge of dedication to the service of India and her people and to the still larger cause of humanity'.

Prelim Capsule

Run up to Partition and Freedom

Events	Year	Important Details
Attlee's Announcement	20th February 1947	As per the announcement, the British would withdraw from India by **30th June 1948**, Wavell would be replaced by **Lord Mountbatten as Viceroy** and Power could be transferred to more than one authority if the Constituent Assembly did not become fully representative, i.e. if the Muslim majority provinces did not join it.
Mountbatten Plan	3rd June 1947	It declared that transfer of power would take place by **15th Aug 1947** on the basis of dominion status to two successor states, India and Pakistan if the Legislative Assemblies of Bengal and Punjab voted in favor of partition. It also provided for a **referendum** in the NWFP and Sylhet (Assam) and for setting up of a **Boundary Commission.** The **Indian states would be free to join any dominion** they liked, India or Pakistan.
Indian Independence Act 1947	18th July 1947	The Act was passed by the Labour government of **Clement Attlee** after the Indian leaders agreed on the Mountbatten Plan. Among other things, the Act stated the following- Pending the adoption of a new constitution, the existing Constituent Assembly of each Dominion would function as **Dominion Legislature** and each Dominion shall be governed by the provisions of the **Government of India Act 1935**. The Office of the Secretary of State was abolished and his work was to be taken over by the **Secretary of Commonwealth Affairs**.
Independence Day	15th August 1947	India woke up to the dual reality of independence and partition. Jawaharlal Nehru was sworn in as the first Prime Minister of free India. Sardar Vallabhbhai Patel became the Home Minister.

Princely States and Partition

As per the India Independence Act, the princely sates were free to join either of the two Dominions. In the context of States' People's Movements and the tactful diplomacy of Sardar Patel (Indian Home Minister), most of them decided to accede to India. Those who held back their decision for some time were the following:

1. **The Nawab of Junagarh (Nawab Muhammad Mahabat Khanji III, 1911–48)** Junagarh was a small state on the coast of Kathiawar. Its Nawab announced accession to Pakistan even though the people of the state wanted to join India. Finally, Indian troops occupied the State and a plebiscite was held which went in favour of India.
2. **The Nizam of Hyderabad (Mir Osman Ali Khan, 1911–48)** The Nizam held back his decision as he was contemplating to remain independent. However, an internal revolt broke out in Telangana region following which Indian troops marched into Hyderabad and forced the state to accede in 1948.
3. **The Maharaja of Jammu and Kashmir (Hari Singh, 1925–52)** The Maharaja also delayed his decision and decided to accede to India only after the irregular armed forces of Pakistan invaded Kashmir.

Congress and Partition

Some scholars accuse the Congress leaders, including Nehru and Patel, of succumbing to the temptation of power and striking a deal with the British by which they got immediate power at the cost of country's partition. In reality, partition was not a result of personal failings of some leaders of the Congress party but a failure of the entire organisation. The independence–failure duality was nothing but a reflection of success–failure dichotomy of the anti-imperialist movement led by the Congress.

Failure on two fronts

1. The Congress had failed over the years to bring the Muslim masses into the national mainstream.
2. It had also failed since 1937 to stem the advancing tide of communalism. Once communal riots engulfed the country, the situation became intractable and the Congress leaders concluded that partition was the lesser of the two evils–either partition or civil war.

Choice before Congress: Either Partition or Civil War Failure of the Interim Government had virtually sealed the fate of the nation in favour of partition. The Interim Government had been reduced into another arena of struggle for Pakistan. It had no power to intervene in the provinces and when riots broke out in Calcutta and Noakhali, the Congress leaders could do nothing except watch the massacres as helpless onlookers. They had begun to feel that it was meaningless to hold office in such circumstances and an immediate transfer of power even at the cost of partition would at least give them real power to restore order and bring an end to such killings.

Choice before Congress: Either Partition or Balkanisation Another choice facing the Congress leaders was 'partition versus balkanisation'. If they chose partition, the British government was willing to uphold all other stands of the Congress, including eliminating the option of independence to princely states, thus ruling out the possibility of balkanisation of the country. Hence, the choice was clear—independence to princely states was a graver threat to Indian unity than Pakistan was.

Choice before Congress: Either Secular body or Hindu body Jinnah demanded that the Muslim League be recognised as the sole representative of Indian Muslims. Accepting this meant Congress was required to close its doors for Muslims and effectively turn non-secular. Secularism was among the cherished goals of the Congress leaders with which they were not willing to part. Moreover, turning non-secular would have also betrayed the Muslim members of the Congress as well as the Indian people and their future.

The Communal Tangle In its final years, the communal tangle was such that the more you tried to solve it, the more badly tangled the threads became. Every time the Congress made a concession, Jinnah pegged his demand a notch higher. Every time the Congress yielded, more and more persons joined the ranks of the Muslim League, impressed by their success. Hence, every round of concession only strengthened the foothold of the communal forces—both Hindu as well as Muslim. The Hindu communalists lost no time in championing themselves as the only saviours of Hindu interests while accusing the Congress of emaciating the Hindus in the name of communal harmony!

What was needed was not appeasement but an all-out struggle against communalism. The Congress failed to understand this communal logic and failed to formulate a long-term strategy to counter the forces of communalism.

Accepting Partition—A Final Act of Surrender Though Congress leaders refused to accept Jinnah's two-nation theory and give up their secular ideology, they made several significant concessions to the League.

- In 1942, at the time of Cripps Mission, autonomy for Muslim majority provinces was accepted.
- In 1944, in his talks with Jinnah, Gandhi recognised that the Muslim majority provinces would have the right to self-determination.
- In 1946, at the time of Cabinet Mission Plan, Congress was willing to accept all optional provisions such as Muslim majority provinces (groups B and C) would set up a separate Constituent Assembly if they wished. Congress only opposed compulsory grouping which would force NWFP and Assam into groups they may not wish to join.
- In December 1946, when the British Cabinet upheld the League's version of grouping, Congress silently accepted.
- In February 1947, after Attlee's announcement, Nehru appealed to Liaquat Ali Khan for cooperation.

Thus, accepting partition under the 3rd June Plan was final act of surrender before Jinnah's unshakeable demand for a separate Muslim state. At the same time, it must be remembered that even though the nationalist leaders accepted partition, they did not accept the two-nation theory and strove to establish a secular state in independent India.

Most ironically, even Jinnah tried to roll back his two-nation theory once Pakistan was created. On 11th August 1947, he declared in the Constituent Assembly of Pakistan, 'You may belong to any religion or caste or creed- that has nothing to do with the business of the state'. He was in vain trying to put back in the bottle the genie ha had released to practice communal politics.

In the words of Bipan Chandra 'The fact is that communalism is basically an ideology which could not have been and cannot be appealed, it had to be confronted and opposed. The failure to do so was the real weakness of the Congress and the national movement'.

Gandhi and Partition

The prospect of partition was immensely distressful to Gandhi. He is believed to have felt disappointed with not only Jinnah for his obduracy but also with his disciples, Nehru and Patel for their alleged lust for power. But he felt most betrayed by his people—the masses that had been communalised beyond repair. It was not just the Muslims but also the Hindus and the Sikhs who now wanted partition.

> **Gandhi remarked (in a prayer meeting, 4th June 1947),** 'The demand has been granted because you asked for it. The Congress never asked for it...But the Congress can feel the pulse of the nation. It realised that the Khalsa as also the Hindus desired it'.

When the Socialists appealed to Gandhi to start a struggle on his own for unity of the nation as he was willing to do in 1942, Gandhi refused. For what was a mass leader without the masses behind him? He could 'instinctively feel what is stirring in the hearts of the masses...and give a shape to what was already there'. In 1947, he confessed that 'Today I see no sign of such a healthy feeling. And therefore, I shall have to wait until the time comes'.

However, the time never came. Things were moving way too fast, as the partition was announced on 3rd June to be implemented on 15th August. At this juncture, it is believed that Gandhi wished to end his life, yet he stood up heroically, keeping the flame of united India ablaze in his heart and the mantra of 'Ekla Chalo' on his mind.

On 14th June 1947, Gandhi walked bravely into the AICC meeting and advised the Congressmen to accept partition as an unavoidable necessity but not to accept it in their hearts and continue to strive to reverse it later, once passions had subsided.

He walked barefoot through the villages of East Bengal and Bihar, trying to comfort the Muslims by his presence. He tried to fight the senseless communal frenzy single handedly by persuading people to give up arms and by threatening them with fast- **'One man boundary force'** as he was famously called by Mountbatten.

Mahatma Gandhi, the Father of Our Nation, spent the Independence Day, fasting and spinning in a locality of Calcutta, worst affected by communal riots. On 30th January 1948, he was shot dead while on his way to evening prayer ground at Birla House (now Gandhi Smriti) by Nathuram Vinayak Godse, a Hindu fanatic. 'Light has gone out of our lives, and there is darkness everywhere', mourned Jawaharlal Nehru along with millions of others.

Maulana Abul Kalam Azad (1888–1958)

Maulana Abul Kalam Azad and Partition

Maulana Azad served as the Congress President during 1940–46. He was an outspoken opponent of Mohammad Ali Jinnah and Partition and represented a collective will of Muslims to co-exist in a secular India. In a press statement on 15th April 1946 as Congress President Maulana had said, 'I have considered from every possible point of view the scheme of Pakistan as formulated by the Muslim League...Considering the scheme in all its aspects I have come to conclusion that it is harmful not only for India as a whole but for Muslims in particular. And in fact, it creates more problems than it solves'.

As is evident from his autobiography, **'Indian Wins Freedom' (1957)**, his basic argument against partition was that it would be a loss to Muslims on both sides and give birth to two nations that would be in constant confrontation with each-other. 'The two countries will focus on military, and society will not develop', he had aptly predicted.

In his attempts to change Jinnah's rigid attitude, Maulana Azad had to face stern criticism and even outright insults. He was accused of being a 'Show-boy President', appointed to hood-wink the world. Azad, however, continued to proclaim his faith in Hindu–Muslim unity.

Britain and Partition

The British could have kept India united, only if they had the determination to do so. It demanded of them proactive intervention in that direction while putting down the communal forces with a firm hand. However, they preferred to take the easy way out by trying to mediate between the Congress and the League in the hope of juicing out some goodwill for themselves.

In the final analysis, the partition of India was primarily the result of determined efforts of the Muslim League from 1940 onwards to obtain a separate sovereign state for the Indian Muslims. Through a combination of political and direct actions, the League, under the astute leadership of Jinnah (known as Quid-e-Azam or Great Organiser), was able to force the situation into a deadlock, from where partition was the only escape. Throughout this process, the League received active patronage from the British who were interested in using the communal card to counter the national movement. The Congress, on its part, not only failed to appeal to the Muslim masses but also failed to understand the communal logic and devise a long-term strategy to combat the communal forces. On 15th August, as India awoke to the dual reality of partition and freedom, the gloom of bloodshed sat heavily on the shoulders of young India. What had been thrown off was the foreign yoke, while years of backwardness and inequality now weighed on the land and the long haul had just begun.

Opinions

Jawaharlal Nehru 'I suppose it was the compulsion of events and the feeling that we wouldn't get out of that deadlock or morass by pursuing the way we had done; it became worse and worse. Further a feeling that even if we got freedom for India with that background it would be very weak India, that is federal India with far too much power in the federating units...And so we accepted it (partition) and said, let us build up a strong India. And if others do not want to be in it, well how can we and why should we force them to be in it?'

Sardar Vallabhbhai Patel 'I felt that if we did not accept partition, India would be split into many bits and would be completely ruined...We would not have had one Pakistan but several'.

Previous Years' Questions – Preliminary Exam

1. Who among the following suggested the winding up of the Indian National Congress after India attained independence? **[UPSC 1996]**
   (a) C Rajagopalachari
   (b) Acharya Kripalani
   (c) Mahatma Gandhi
   (d) Jayaprakash Narayan
2. Consider the following statements about Jawaharlal Nehru: **[UPSC 1996]**
   1. He was the president of the Congress party in 1947
   2. He presided over the Constituent Assembly
   3. He formed the first Congress ministry in United Province before India's Independence

   Choose the correct answer from the following options.
   (a) 1, 2 and 3 are correct
   (b) 1 and 3 are correct
   (c) 1 and 2 are correct
   (d) None of these are correct
3. With what specific instruction did Lord Mountbatten come to India as Viceroy? **[UPSC 1998]**
   (a) Balkanise the Indian subcontinent
   (b) Keep India united if possible
   (c) Accept Jinnah's demand for Pakistan
   (d) Persuade the Congress to accept partition
4. At the time of India's Independence what was Mahatma Gandhi was **[UPSC 1998]**
   (a) A member of Congress Working Committee
   (b) Not a member of the Congress
   (c) The President of Congress
   (d) The General Secretary of the Congress
5. Why did the Indian National Congress mainly agree to the partition of the country in 1947? **[UPSC 1998]**
   (a) The principle of two Nation theory was then acceptable to them
   (b) It was imposed by the British government and the Congress was helpless in this regard
   (c) They wanted to avoid large-scale communal riots
   (d) India would have otherwise lost the opportunity to attain freedom
6. As an alternative to the partition of India, what had Gandhiji suggested to Mountbatten? **[UPSC 2000]**
   (a) Postpone granting of independence
   (b) Invite Jinnah to form the government
   (c) Invite Nehru and Jinnah to form the government together
   (d) Invite the army to take over for some time
7. At the time of partition of India, which one of the following provinces of British India came forward with a plan for a United and independent existence? **[UPSC 2000]**
   (a) Punjab (b) Assam
   (c) Bengal (d) Bihar
8. Who was the brainchild of the Balkan plan for fragmentation of India? **[UPSC 2000]**
   (a) Winston Churchill (b) M A Jinnah
   (c) Lord Mountbatten (d) V P Menon
9. Who was the President of Indian National Congress at the time of partition of India? **[UPSC 2002]**
   (a) C Rajagopalachari
   (b) J.B. Kripalani
   (c) Jawaharlal Nehru
   (d) Maulana Abul Kalam Azad
10. Why was the Radcliffe Committee appointed? **[UPSC 2014]**
    (a) To solve the problem of minorities in India
    (b) To give effect to the Independence Bill
    (c) To delimit the boundaries between India and Pakistan
    (d) To enquire into the riots in East Bengal

Previous Years' Questions – Main Exam

1. Narrate the last phase of the India's freedom movement especially from the beginning of 1947 till attainment of Independence. **[UPSC 1991]**
2. Do you think that the partition of India was inevitable? Discuss the attitudes of Mahatma Gandhi, Pandit Nehru and Maulana Azad towards the crucial question of partition. **[UPSC 1995]**
3. What were the circumstances that led to the partition of India in 1947? **[UPSC 1997]**
4. What was Mountbatten plan? Discuss the reactions of Gandhi and Azad to the plan. **[UPSC 2000]**
5. Review the 'Dickie Bird Plan'. **[UPSC 2002]**
6. Why and how did the Congress come to accept the partition of the country? **[UPSC 2005]**

Answers

Previous Years' Questions – Preliminary Exam

1.	(c)	2.	(d)	3.	(b)	4.	(b)	5.	(c)
6.	(b)	7.	(a)	8.	(c)	9.	(b)	10.	(c)

Appendices

1 Sessions of the Indian National Congress

Year	Place	President	Important Details
1885	Bombay	W.C. Banerjee (also written WC Bonnerjee)	First session of Congress. Attended by 72 delegates.
1886	Calcutta	Dadabhai Naoroji	Naoroji was the first **Parsi** President.
1887	Madras	Badruddin Tyabji	Tyabji was the first **Muslim** President
1888	Allahabad	George Yule	George Yule was the first **Christian** President.
1889	Bombay	Sir William Wedderburn	—
1890	Calcutta	Pherozeshah Mehta	—
1891	Nagpur	Anand Charlu	The word 'National' was added to the Congress name.
1892	Allahabad	W.C. Banerjee	—
1893	Lahore	Dadabhai Naoroji	—
1894	Madras	Alfred Web	—
1895	Poona	Surendranath Banerjee	—
1896	Calcutta	Rahimatullah M. Sayani	First political occasion when **Vande Mataram**, the national song of India, was sung.
1897	Amraoti	C. Sankaran Nair	—
1898	Madras	Anand Mohan Bose	—
1899	Lucknow	Romesh Chandra Dutt	—
1900	Lahore	Narain Ganesh Chandavarkar	—
1901	Calcutta	Sir Dinshaw Wacha	—
1902	Ahmedabad	Surendranath Banerjee	—
1903	Madras	Lal Mohan Ghosh	—
1904	Bombay	Sir Henry Cotton	—
1905	Banaras	Gopal Krishna Gokhale	Resentment against partition of Bengal expressed in this session.
1906	Calcutta	Dadabhai Naoroji	**'Swaraj'** mentioned for the first time and resolution supporting Swadeshi, boycott and national education was passed.

1907	Surat	Rash Behari Ghosh	Congress split into two factions, namely the Moderates and the Extremists, known as **Surat Split**.
1908	Madras	Rash Behari Ghosh	Congress constitution drawn.
1909	Lahore	Pandit Madan Mohan Malaviya	Disapproval given over formation of separate electorates based on religion (Indian Council Act, 1909)
1910	Allahabad	Sir William Wedderburn	—
1911	Calcutta	Pandit Bishan Narayan Dhar	**Jana Gana Mana** written by Rabindranath Tagore was sung for the first time.
1912	Bankipur	R.N. Mudhalkar	
1913	Karachi	Nawab Syed Muhammad Bahadur	
1914	Madras	Bhupendra Nath Bose	
1915	Bombay	Lord Satyendra Prasanna Sinha	
1916	Lucknow	Ambica Charan Mazumdar	Led to the **Lucknow Pact** (between the Congress and the Muslim league) as well as the merger of the two factions of the Congress (i.e. the Moderates and the Extremists).
1917	Calcutta	Annie Besant	First session to be presided by a **woman**.
1918	Delhi	Pandit Madan Mohan Malaviya	–
1918	Bombay	Syed Hasan Imam	Special Session
1919	Amritsar	Pandit Motilal Nehru	—
1920	Calcutta	Lala Lajpat Rai	Special Session Gandhi proposed for Non-Cooperation.
1920	Nagpur	C. Vijayaraghavachariar	New Constitution for the Congress framed. Resolution supporting Non- Cooperation Movement passed.
1921	Ahmedabad	Hakim Ajmal Khan	C.R. Das (President) was in prison and Hakim Ajmal Khan was acting President.
1922	Gaya	C.R. Das	Swaraj Party formed.
1923	Kakinada	Maulana Muhammad Ali	Formation of All India Khadi Board.
1923	Delhi	Maulana Abul Kalam Azad	Special session. Maulana Azad became the youngest President here to preside a session.
1924	Belgaum	Mahatma Gandhi	The only session presided over by **Mahatma Gandhi**.
1925	Kanpur	Sarojini Naidu	First **Indian woman** President.

1926	Guwahati	S. Srinivasa Iyengar	For the first time, Khadi was made compulsory for Congress workers.
1927	Madras	Dr. M.A. Ansari	Adoption of Independence resolution and boycott of Simon Commission.
1928	Calcutta	Pandit Motilal Nehru	—
1929	Lahore	Jawaharlal Nehru	**'Poorna Swaraj'** resolution passed; Civil Disobedience movement launched; 26th January to be celebrated as Independence Day from here on.
1930	No session	Jawaharlal Nehru	Pandit Nehru continued as President.
1931	Karachi	Vallabhbhai Patel	Resolution on **Fundamental Rights** and **National Economic Programme** passed; Gandhi-Irwin pact endorsed.
1932	Delhi	Amritlal Ranchhorddas Seth	—
1933	Calcutta	Mrs. Nelli Sengupta	—
1934	Bombay	Rajendra Prasad	Formation of the Congress Socialist Party.
1935	No session	Rajendra Prasad	Rajendra Prasad continued as President.
April 1936	Lucknow	Jawaharlal Nehru	The President urged the Congress to adopt **Socialism** as its goal.
December 1936	Faizpur	Jawaharlal Nehru	First session to be held in a village.
1938	Haripura	Subhas Chandra Bose	National Planning Committee set up under the chairmanship of Jawaharlal Nehru.
1939	Tripuri	Subhas Chandra Bose	Subhas Chandra Bose defeated Pattabhi Sitaramayya; Rajendra Prasad took over as President after Bose resigned; Forward Block formed by Bose after resignation on 3rd May 1939.
1940	Ramgarh	Maulana Abul Kalam Azad	Proposal for **Individual Satyagraha** passed.
1941 – 1945	No session	Maulana Abul Kalam Azad	Maulana Abul Kalam Azad continued as President.
1946	Meerut	Acharya J.B. Kripalani	—
1947	Delhi	Rajendra Prasad	—
1948	Jaipur	Dr. Pattabhi Sitaramayya	—

Note-

- **No Congress Sessions were held in the years 1930, 1935 and 1941–45.**
- **Dadabhai Naoroji and Pandit Jawaharlal Nehru presided over Congress Sessions for the maximum number of times (three times each).**

2 Newspapers and Journals

Name of the Paper/Journal	Place of Publication	Starting Year	Founder/Editor
Bengal Gazette (or Calcutta General Advertiser)	Calcutta	1780	James Augustus Hickey (Irish)
The India Gazette (or Calcutta Public Advertiser, the second newspaper printed in India; was a weekly and a rival to Bengal Gazette)	Calcutta	Nov 1780	Bernard Messink and Peter Reed (founders); Henry Vivian Derozio was associated with it.
Madras Courier (It was the first paper from Madras)	Madras	Oct 1785	Richard Johnson (owner); Hugh Boyd (first editor)
Bombay Herald (It was the first paper from Bombay)	Bombay	1789	William Ashburner (editor)
Indian Herald	Madras	1795	It was started by R . Williams and published by Humphreys.
Bengal Hurkaru (English weekly, later daily)	Calcutta	1795	Hugh Boyd
Calcutta Journal (English bi-weekly)	Calcutta	1818	James Silk Buckingham
Digdarshan (first Bengali monthly and first vernacular newspaper)	Calcutta	Apr 1818	Serampur missionaries (William Carcy, Joshua Marshman and William Ward).
Bengal Gazette (Bengali weekly and first Indian-owned newspaper)	Calcutta	1818	Gangadhar Bhattacharya and Harishchandra Ray
Samachar Darpan (Bengali weekly)	Serampore (Bengal)	Jun 1818	Baptist Missionary Society (Joshua Marshman)
Sambad Kaumudi (Bengali weekly)	Calcutta	1821	Raja Ram Mohan Roy
Mirat-ul-Akhbar (first Persian journal, a weekly)	Calcutta	1822	Raja Ram Mohan Roy
Samachar Chandrika (orthodox Hindu newspaper of the Dharma Sabha, founded to rival Sambad Kaumudi and oppose Ram Mohan's reformist ideas)	Calcutta	1822	Bhabani Charan Bandyopadhyaya

Jam-i-Jahan-Numah (first paper in Urdu)	Calcutta	1822	Harihar Dutta (editor)
Banga-doota (a weekly in four languages- English, Hindi, Persian & Bengali)	Calcutta	1822	Raja Ram Mohan Roy, Dwarkanath Tagore and others.
East Indian (daily)	—	19th cent.	Henry Vivian Derozio
Bombay Samachar (first paper in Gujarati, exists even today making it the oldest continuously published newspaper in India)	Bombay	1822	Fardunjee Marzban
Udant Martand (first Hindi language newspaper, a weekly published every Tuesday)	Calcutta	May 1826	Pt. Jugal Kishore Shukla
Reformer (first regular venture by Indians in English journalism)		1831	Prasunna Coomar Tagare and Bholanath Sen
Bombay Times (post 1861- The Times of India)	Bombay	1838	Founded by Robert Knight (acquired by Thomas Bennett and Frank Coleman in 1892)
Rast Goftar (a Gujarati fortnightly)	Calcutta	1851	Dadabhai Naoroji
Hindu Patriot (English weekly, played activist role during the Revolt of 1857 and the Indigo Revolt. In 1861, published the play Neel Darpan)	Calcutta	1853	Girish Chandra Ghosh (later went into the hands of its popular editor Harish Chandra Mukherjee; eventually bought by Ishwar Chandra Vidyasagar)
Samachar Sudha Varshan (first Hindi daily)	Calcutta	1854	Shyam Sundar Sen
Somaprakash (first Bengali political)	Calcutta	1858	Dwarkanath Vidyabhushan
The Bengalee	Calcutta	1862	Girish Chandra Ghosh, bought by Surendranath Banerjee in 1879
Indian Mirror (English weekly of the Calcutta Brahmo Samaj)	Calcutta	1862	Debendranath Tagore
National Paper	Calcutta	1865	Debendranath Tagore
Amrit Bazaar Patrika (Oldest Indian-owned English daily; born as a Bengali weekly, later bilingual weekly; dramatically converted itself into an exclusively English paper in order to escape the Vernacular Press Act of 1878.)	Jessore District	1868	Sisir Kumar Ghosh and Moti Lal Ghosh

Madras Mail (first Indian evening news paper)	Calcutta	1868	—
Bangadarshana (Bengali)	Calcutta	1873	Bankim Chandra Chatterjee
Indian Statesman (later only The Statesman)	Calcutta	1875	Robert Knight
The Hindu (started as weekly)	Madras	1878	G.S. Aiyar, Viraraghavachari and Subbarao Pandit
The Tribune	Lahore	1881	Dayal Singh Majithia
Mahratta (English weekly) and **Kesari** (Marathi daily)	Bombay	1881	Tilak, Chiplunkar, Agarkar (prior to Tilak, Kelkar and Agarkar were the editors of Mahratta and Kesari respectively)
Swadesamitran (Tamil)	Madras	1882	G Subramania Aiyer
Voice of India	Bombay	1883	Dadabhai Naoroji
Paridasak (weekly)	—	1886	Bipin Chandra Pal
Vital Vidhvansak (first monthly journal to have the untouchable people as its target audience)	—	1888	Gopal Baba Walangkar
Yugantar	Bengal	1906	Barindra Kumar Ghosh
Sandhya	Bengal	1906	Brahmabandhab Upadhyaya
Kal	Bengal	1906	—
Indian Sociologist	London	—	Shyamji Krishna Varma
Bande Mataram	Paris	—	Madam Bhikaiji Cama
Talvar	Berlin	—	Virendranath Chattopadhyaya
Ghadr	San Francisco	—	Ghadar Party(Lala Hardayal)
Bombay Chronicle (daily)	Bombay	1913	Pherozeshah Mehta
The Hindustan Times	Delhi	1920	K.M. Panikkar
Bahishkrit Bharat (Marathi fortnightly)	—	1927	B.R.Ambedkar
Kudi Arasu (Tamil)	Tamil Nadu	1910	E.V. Ramasamy Naicker(Periyar)
Kranti	Maharashtra	1927	S.S. Mirajkar, K.N. Joglekar, S.V. Ghate
Bandi Jivan	Bengal	—	Sachindranath Sanyal
National Herald	—	1938	Jawaharlal Nehru

3 Development of Press in India

Press refers to print media such as newspapers, journals, books, magazines, pamphlets, leaflets and others. News agencies and press syndicates also come under the umbrella term 'press'. Functions of press developed from time to time as the need was felt for them and they include communicating government policies to the public, keeping government informed of public needs and reporting of national and international events.

In the world context, the credit for the invention of art of printing goes to the **Chinese**. The Chinese were also the first to manufacture paper. Even the first book was printed in China in 868 AD. Some historians consider printing as a gift of Buddhism to the world, since early attempts in printing were made by Chinese Buddhist monks using wooden blocks to make Buddhist literature widely available.

Later, in c. 1455 in Mainz city of Germany, a goldsmith Johannes Gutenberg developed the metal movable-type printing press in **Renaissance Europe**, printed nearly 300 copies of the Bible and started the Printing Revolution (the 'Gutenberg Bible' in Latin was the first book printed in Europe). Subsequently, the printing press spread to several other European countries, unleashing the era of mass communication which permanently altered the structure of society. In fact, according to certain scholars, it is the printing press which marks the beginning of the modern era.

The European movable metal types were brought to Goa by the **Portuguese missionaries** (Jesuits) around 1550 AD with the aim of propagating Christianity. They started printing books on Christian saints and sermons (the first book printed was 'Doctrina Christa' in September 1556). As they needed to learn Indian languages, they even printed grammars and vocabularies in Marathi and Konkani languages, but in Roman script. In 1578, Doctrina Christa was printed in Tamil and became the first book to be printed in an Indian language.

However, the press as we know today was introduced in India by the **British** when in 1674 Bhimji Parak (the chief broker of the English Company at Surat) took a keen interest in the technology, and procured a printer from England and set up a printing press at Bombay. For the next hundred years, however, no newspapers were published in the Company's territories as the Company's servants feared that the news of their malpractices and abuses of 'private trading' might reach London.

The early newspapers were intended to operate as an organ for the local European settler population, and carried material exclusively of interest to them. Moreover, they were started by disgruntled servants of the English Company who devoted their columns to exposing the evils and malpractices of the Company's officials. Many of the writings were even libellous. Thus, in general, the ruling British administration was reluctant to the printing of newspapers in the country.

In 1776, **William Bolts** was deported to Europe for simply expressing his desire to start a newspaper. Similar hostility was shown towards later editors and publishers as well, even though many of them happened to be English or other Europeans. At the same time, it is true that the swing from freedom of press to control of press under the British rule, largely depended on the personality and values of the Governor Generals and Viceroys in power at that time.

Though the press in India started as a European institution, the native Indians did not take long to realise its potential. Consequently, the later years of 19th century unfolded a glorious chapter of Indian newspapers.

First Indian Newspaper

Bengal Gazette/Calcutta General Advertiser, 29 January 1780

- It was the **first newspaper in India**, was also the first English language newspaper in India. It was started by James Augustus Hickey, a clerk of the East India Company (EIC) who carried out outspoken criticism of the government through his weekly newspaper. Hickey is considered as the **'father of Indian press'**.
- The paper also carried juicy stories about EIC staff, their doings and misdoings. But when Hickey indulged in casting aspersions on the wife of Warren Hastings, he was forcefully deported and the paper was closed in March 1782.

Thereafter, several newspapers came into existence in quick succession in Bombay, Calcutta and Madras. The editors of these papers learnt from Hickey's experience and avoided clash with the British authorities. Nevertheless, the Company's officials became worried that these newspapers might reach London and expose their misdeeds. They therefore began imposing restrictions on printing presses and editors. In 1795, the Madras Government introduced censorship for the first time when **The Madras Gazette** was required to submit to the Military Secretary all the general orders of the government for censorship before publication. In fact, pre-censorship, deportation and denial of postal privileges were the three methods used during this time to deal with problematic editors.

Important Acts Governing the Press

Censorship of the Press Act, 1799 (by Lord Wellesley)

- Constituted **first press regulation; introduced pre-censorship** on all newspapers.
- The Act imposed almost wartime restrictions on the press, requiring the newspapers to submit for scrutiny all material meant for publication and to print the names of the printer, editor, and proprietor in every issue. Publication on Sunday was prohibited. The prescribed punishment for breach of these rules was immediate deportation.
- The Wellesley regulations virtually kept the press in a state of siege for several years and we see a near complete halt in the growth of newspaper press from the days of Lord Wellesley to the days of Lord Minto I (1807–13).
- In this way, the Act succeeded not only in silencing the criticism of the government, but also in crushing the power of the press to awaken the Indian people, which may lead them to criticise and question the Company's rule.
- Wellesley regulations were finally abolished by Lord Hastings in 1818.

Lord Minto I was succeeded by Lord Hastings (1813–23) who was known to have liberal ideas on education and press.

During the period 1818–1857, there appeared a number of dailies, weeklies, bi-weeklies and monthlies initially from Bengal and subsequently from other parts of India as well. The **Serampore Missionaries** were pioneers in Indian language journalism and **Digdarshan** was the first vernacular newspaper started by them in April 1818. In June the same year, they started another journal named **Samachar Darpan. The Friend of India** (in 1818), the precursor of 'The Statesman' of today was also born. James Silk Buckingham, a merchant and another pioneer of English press in India started **Calcutta Journal** in 1818. The first Indian-owned newspaper, the **Bengal Gazette** (1818), was started by a teacher and a reformist named Gangadhar Bhattacharya (also known as Ganga Kishore Bhattacharya).

Hastings refused to cancel Buckingham's license, much against the wishes of his political secretary John Adam. Nevertheless, in 1818, a cluster of regulations known as **Adam's Regulations of 1818** were passed that kept a strict watch on newspaper content.

Raja Ram Mohan Roy and James Silk Buckingham now raised demand for freedom of press. Ram Mohan Roy, the tallest personality in the history of Indian journalism, particularly vernacular journalism, started his weeklies, **Sambad Kaumudi** (in Bengali, 1821) and **Mirat-ul-Akbar** (in Persian, 1822). Through Sambad Kaumudi, Ram Mohan actively campaigned for the abolition of sati pratha. In his journals, Ram Mohan countered the criticism of the missionaries on the one hand, and pushed for modernisation of Indian society on the other. His Persian weekly devoted much space to educating public opinion on international affairs.

Indian vs. British Press (Growth of Vernacular Press)

The awakening generated by Ram Mohan Roy spread to other parts of the country, and various Indian owned newspapers and nationalist newspapers rapidly sprang up. A clear distinction between Indian press (in vernacular as well as in English) and British press now started emerging, and this distinction was sharpened by the Revolt of 1857. While the Anglo-Indian press supported government measures and policies, the Indian editors shared sympathy with the rebels and the Indian press thus became nationalistic. For instance, the Hindu Patriot displayed fierce nationalistic activism during the Revolt of 1857 and also during the Indigo Revolt. It published the play 'Neel Darpan' in 1861, and became a mouthpiece of protest against British injustices.

The British response to the growing vernacular threat was rather slow to come by, chiefly on account of scarcity of British officials who could directly read their content. However, the Indian press gradually began inviting restrictions. Adam's gag of 1823 and Canning's Gagging Act of 1857 were directed more against Indian press than the British. But it was Lytton's Vernacular Press Act of 1857 that most directly and effectively shackled the Indian press.

On Hastings's departure in January 1823, John Adam was appointed as the acting Governor General for seven months, providing him the opportunity to give practical shape to his reactionary views. With the coming of Adam, there was again a swing away from freedom of press to control of press. He now promulgated new regulations, perhaps the most comprehensive and stringent so far and came to be known as **'Adam's Gag'**.

Licensing Regulations, 1823 (by John Adam)

- **Introduced licensing of the press** (compulsory pre-publication licensing) for the first time; constituted **First Press Ordinance**.

- The ordinance required a previous license for printing of all matters, except commercial matter. It laid down stringent regulations for the editors and prohibited EIC staff from having any relations with the newspapers. Political writings were forbidden but social and religious news, particularly those by missionaries, were encouraged.
- JS Buckingham, the editor of Calcutta Journal who considered the press to be a very necessary check on irresponsible government, especially in the absence of a legislature, was deported to England the same year (March 1823).
- Adam's regulations were chiefly directed against Indian press (i.e., newspapers published in Indian languages or edited by Indians). With the exception of the Calcutta Journal, no English newspaper was deprived of license in 1823. But Ram Mohan's Mirat-ul-Akbar had to stop publication.
- Licensing was later abolished by Metcalf's Act of 1835.

Regulations of 1825 (by Lord Amherst)

Adam was succeeded by Lord Amherst (1823–28) who also liked to control press. His regulations prohibited the servants of the Company from having any connection with the press.

Lord Amherst was succeeded by William Bentinck (1828-35) who adopted a liberal attitude towards the press. Bentinck, the first Governor General of India, is known for his social and educational reforms. He understood the importance of vernacular press and consequently, **vernacular press started making rapid strides** under him.

Press Act of 1835 (by Lord Metcalfe)

Bentinck's successor Charles Metcalfe (1835–36) also held strong views in favour of freedom of press. He invited Lord Macaulay, then the legislative member of the Supreme council to draft a Press Act. Macaulay's proposals included abolishing of licensing regulations, freedom to setup a newspaper without prior permission and establishing uniform press laws throughout British Indian Empire. These were incorporated in Metcalfe's Act of 1835 – the **most liberal press act** in the history of British India.

Thus, licensing act was replaced by Metcalf's Act which only required a printer and publisher to give a precise account of the premises of publication. The Act favoured the growth of Indian newspapers and the year 1835 proved to be a turning point. From this year till 1875, Indian press kept growing, giving wings to knowledge, Indian aspirations and feelings of nationalism. In fact, the period saw the rise of the press of all sections and Charles Metcalfe aptly came to be known as the **'Liberator of Indian Press'**.

Metcalfe was succeeded by Lord Auckland (1836–42) who took forward Metcalfe's policy and continued to have cordial relations with various editors.

Licensing Act of 1857 (Lord Canning)

The revolt broke out during the time of Lord Canning (1856–62). As soon as the revolt broke out, the press was gagged by an ordinance, later known as Act No. XV of 1857 which **reintroduced licensing** in addition to the registration procedure laid down by the Metcalfe Act. Freedom of press was drastically curtailed and numerous other merciless measures against the press were revived. The government was also empowered to prohibit the publication or circulation of any printed matter. The act was applicable to all papers, Indian and Anglo-India. Desirous of improving his reputation, Caning allowed the act to expire in 1858. Soon after the withdrawal of the act, the print media resumed its growth.

India Penal Code of 1860 (Lord Canning)

Canning also adopted the Indian Penal Code (IPC) in 1860. It contained offences like defamation and obscenity which writers and publishers must avoid. 1870 onwards, the IPC was systematically extended to cover various threats to public order through the press. Thus, sedition (S. 124A) was added to it in 1870, promoting enmity between classes (S. 153A) in 1898, outraging religious feelings (S. 295A) in 1927 and assertions against national integration (S. 1 53B) in 1927.

Press and Registration of Books Act, 1867 (by Lord Lawrence)

- Lord Lawrence became the Viceroy of India in 1864 (1864–69). It was during his time that the PRB Act, the **oldest surviving Press Regulation in India**, was passed.
- The act was rooted in distrust of press, especially vernacular press, and what it was doing. The objective was however not to establish governmental control over the freedom of the Press but to keep the government informed of the activities of printing presses.
- The act required every book/newspaper to print on it the name of printer/publisher and the place of printing. Further, within one month of publication of a book, a copy had to be supplied free of charge to the local government.
- It enabled the government to regulate printing presses and newspapers by a system of registration and to preserve copies of books and other matter printed in India.

The period after 1857 witnessed the rise of Indian Press as part of nationalist struggle under the leadership of fierce nationalist leaders and included- Som Prakash founded by Dwarkanath Vidyabhushan (in 1858), the Bengalee by Girish Chandra Ghosh and Suredrentah Banerjee (in 1862), Indian Mirror by Debendranath Tagore (in 1862), Voice of India by Dadabhai Naoroji, Amrit Bazaar Patrika by Sisir Kumar Ghosh and Motilal Ghosh (in 1868), Kesari and Maratha by BG Tilak (in 1881), Voice of India by Dadabhai Naoroji (in 1883), Sudharak by Gopal Ganesh Agarkar (in 1888), the Hindu and Swadesamitran by G. Subramaniya Aiyar (in 1878 and 1882 respectively).

This period also witnessed a boom in Indian language newspapers and many of the above were published in vernacular that radically changed the complexion of Indian journalism. For instance, **Amrit Bazaar Patrika** was published in Bengali, Kesari in Marathi and Swadesamitran in Tamil.

Clearly, the vernacular press that had been growing since the time of Ram Mohan Roy, had picked up pace after 1857. By 1870, there were about 644 newspapers being published in India, of which 400 were in vernacular. Vernacular papers surpassed the English papers not only in number but also in influence and had become increasingly more critical of government policies.

In 1876, Lord Lytton became the Viceroy of India. His decision of hosting a lavish Delhi Darbar (1877) to welcome the Queen even as a terrible famine was raging in the country (1876–78), was bitterly criticised by the press and the newly rising Indian intelligentsia seen by Lytton as 'a deadly legacy from Macaulay and Metcalfe'. Worried about the increasing impact of vernacular press and convinced that they were spreading national consciousness; Lytton passed the Vernacular Press Act in 1878.

Vernacular Press Act, 1 March 1878 (by Lord Lytton)

- Notoriously called the **'Gagging Act'**, the VPA was specifically directed against Indian language newspapers. It excluded English language newspapers.
- The act is believed to have struck the greatest blow to the freedom of the Press in India, and the Indian languages newspapers suffered most heavily under this law.
- As per the act, any district magistrate or a police commissioner was empowered to force the printer and publisher of a newspaper to agree not to publish certain kinds of material, to demand security, and to confiscate any printed matter it deemed to be objectionable in accordance with this act. The act empowered the Government for the **first time to issue search warrants** and enter newspaper premises even without court orders.
- The magistrate's action in this regard was final and no appeal could be made in a court of law.
- The act was mainly directed **against Amrita Bazar Patrika** (then a bilingual weekly), which dramatically converted itself into an exclusively English paper in order to escape the harsh conditions of the act.
- Under the act, proceedings were instituted against papers such as 'Som Prakash', 'Dacca Prakash', 'Bharat Mihir' and 'Sahachar'.
- The act evoked widespread opposition in India and to some extent in England too. It was, therefore, **repealed by Lord Ripon in 1881**.
- Lytton also instituted the post of **'Press Commissioner for India'** whose main job was to liaise between the press and the government and supply authentic information to the press.

Lord Lytton was succeeded by Lord Ripon (1880–84). In consonance with his policy of reforms and conciliation, Ripon repealed the Vernacular Press Act. But the resentment, the act produced, had already added fuel to fire and flared up India's growing independence movement.

Press in the 20th Century

At the turn of the century, Lord Curzon was appointed as the Viceroy of India (1899–1905). His imperialist policies, particularly partition of Bengal forced in the teeth of fierce public opposition, gave rise to the Anti-partition movement (1905–08), the violent repression of which in turn gave rise to the revolutionaries and their journalism- 'Bande Mataram' (1905), the rallying cry of the anti-partition movement was started by Bipin Chandra Pal, edited by Aurobindo Ghose; 'Yugantar' (1906) by Barindra Kumar Ghose and 'Vande Mataram' (Urdu weekly, Lahore) by Lala Lajpat Rai.

Tilak's papers, Maratha and Kesari, played a lead role in spreading the message of nationalism. Through his papers, Tilak nationalised the issue of anti-partition movement and praised the work of the revolutionaries, leading him to be charged of sedition three times, including incitement to murder, and he was convicted.

Lord Curzon was succeeded by Lord Minto II who inherited a turbulent situation and tried to meet the challenge posed by the revolutionaries by widening the scope of press regulations. Thus, the beginning of the 20th century saw the enactment of more stringent anti-press laws to curb the activities of the **revolutionaries**. Various restrictions were placed on newspapers, preventing the reporting of and comments upon revolutionary activities.

Newspapers (Incitement to Offences) Act, June 1908 (by Lord Minto)

- The Act empowered magistrates to seize a press, where a newspaper containing matter which incited murder or any other act of violence, was printed.
- Under this act, the government prosecuted nine newspapers and confiscated seven presses.

Indian Press Act, 1910

- This act was passed to further meet the challenge of violence in the wake of Bengal partition and rising British assassinations. It was a more comprehensive law and was directed against both offences, of violence as well as sedition.
- It empowered the district magistrates to ask for a deposit of security from the presses and where it deemed fit, to forfeit it; to authorize searches and to declare newspaper copies and presses forfeited by the government; and to prohibit the transmission by post of newspapers deemed to contain objectionable material.
- Under this act, action was taken against 991 presses and newspapers.
- Certain provisions of the Act of 1910 were further enhanced under the **Defence of India Regulations 1914**, promulgated on the outbreak of the First World War.
- In 1921, a Press Committee was appointed under the chairmanship of Sir Tej Bahadur Sapru (then the law member of the Viceroy's Executive Council) to investigate press legislation. On the recommendation of this committee, the Acts of 1908 and 1910 were repealed in 1922, after incorporating some of their provisions in other laws.

Official Secrets Act, 1923

Prohibited the publication of any classified official information.

Indian Press (Emergency Powers) Act 1931 (by Lord Willington)

- In April 1931, Lord Willington became the Viceroy of India. In his eyes, the Gandhi–Irwin pact was a mistake and he took measures to suppress the Civil Disobedience Movement. The Indian National Congress was declared illegal and the Indian Press (Emergency Powers) Act of 1931 was passed.
- The Act gave wide ranging powers to provincial governments to suppress Civil Disobedience Movement propaganda, and to enable them to prohibit the printing of names and pictures of Indian leaders as well as notices of Congress meetings or other political events. It imposed on the press an obligation to furnish security at the call of the Executive. This system of executive control and punishment of the presses was foreign even to democratic England. The very preamble of the Act- 'for the better control of the Press', was offensive.

During Second World War (1939-45), the **Defence of India Act** was passed bolstering the authority of the central government to deal with seditious material. Pre-censorship was reinforced and publication of all news pertaining to the INC was banned. The press was initially supportive of the British stand, but later a conflict arose and several newspapers began supporting Gandhi and the national movement. Consequently, when the press was suppressed, it resulted in the formation of **All India Newspapers' Editors Conference** (AINEC) in 1940 as the protector of Indian Press' rights.

Fresh restrictions were imposed on the press in the wake of the Quit India Movement of August 1942. As the war inched towards its end with a clear indication of India's impending freedom, continuous censorship became meaningless and as the war ended, so did most of the controls of the press.

Press Enquiry Committee, March 1947

The committee was appointed to examine press laws in the light of Fundamental Rights formulated by the Constituent Assembly of India.

Conclusion

The press and the national movement shared a mutually beneficial relationship, with each benefitting from the growth and development of the other. The press gradually emerged as the most powerful weapon of the freedom movement on account of the fact that the Indian intelligentsia and leaders like Ram Mohan Roy, Dadabhai Naoroji, Bal Gangadhar Tilak, Gopal Krishna Gokhale, CR Das, Motilal Nehru, Subhas Chandra Bose, Gandhi and others used it as a medium for nationalist discourse and for arousing national consciousness.

Though the British administration tried to shackle the press through an entire gamut of laws, it could not effectively suppress the growth and development of the press in the country. The Indian press received immense support from the people at large and ended up playing a magnificent role in fostering the struggle for independence.

According to Gandhi, 'One of the objectives of a newspaper is to understand the popular feelings and give expression to it; another is to arouse among the people certain desirable sentiments; and the third is fearlessly to expose popular defects'.

Flashforward:

- **Press (Objectionable Matters) Act, 1951** After Independence, the Press (Objectionable Matters) Act, 1951 was to be a temporary law for two years but was later extended up to February, 1956. The Act empowered the government to demand and forfeit security from presses and newspapers for printing 'objectionable matter'. The aggrieved owners were allowed the right to demand trial by jury. The act was opposed by AINEC and the Indian Federation of Working Journalists (1950), following which the government constituted the **First Press Commission** in 1952 under the chairmanship of JS Rajadhyaksha to enquire into the working of the Indian Press.
- **Working Journalists and other Newspaper Employees (Conditions of Service) and Miscellaneous Provisions Act, 1955** was passed following the recommendations of the First Press Commission. It sought to ameliorate the conditions of service of working journalists and other newspaper employees.

4 Development of Education

Note: To read about Development of Education before 1857, refer to Chapter 3.3.

Education under the Crown

Hunter Education Commission (1882–83) For some time now, the missionaries in England had been alleging that education in India was not being carried out as per the policy laid by Wood's Despatch of 1854. Under this backdrop, in 1882 Lord Ripon appointed an Indian Education Commission led by WW Hunter to review educational progress made in Indian Empire since 1854. The commission was primarily required to present the state of **elementary education** (i.e. primary and secondary education) in the country and the ways by which this could be improved. The commission was not 'to enquire into the general working of Indian Universities'. Its main recommendations were-

- It emphasized the role of state in extension and improvement of primary education which was to be regarded as 'instruction of the masses through the vernacular'. The management of education was transferred to local bodies setup under the Local Self Government Acts passed during the period.
- It emphasized the role of **private enterprise** in secondary and collegiate education, and recommended that an all-out effort should be made to encourage private enterprise in this regard including extension of grants-in-aid system and equal treatment of aided schools.
- It pointed out inadequacy in facilities for female education outside Presidency towns and made recommendations for its spread.

During the next twenty years, the country saw a marked increase in Indian philanthropic activity in education and an unprecedented growth in spread of secondary and collegiate education took place. Several teaching-cum-examining universities such as the Punjab University (founded in 1882) and the Allahabad University (in 1887), were set up. Another notable development of this period was the creation of the **Indian Educational Service** in 1896 as an All India Service, recruitment for which was done through competitive exam held in England.

However, the initial years of the 19th century saw a marked rise in political unrest, and educational policy in India began to be questioned once again. The nationalist view was that, in the hands of the colonizers, education remained an instrument for spreading ruling ideology. Tagore condemned colonial education as alms bowl of knowledge affecting individual self-respect; Gandhi criticised it as enslaving and retrogressive. And a new discourse on **national education** emerged- marking an unequal contest opposite a globally dominant hegemony.

The official view was that educational quality had deteriorated under private management, that indiscipline had risen in schools and colleges, and that educational institutions had become centers for production of **political revolutionaries**. Governor General Lord Curzon (1899–1905), whose motives were mainly political and only partly educational, now sought to increase official control over education in the name of quality and efficiency (while his real motive was to restrict education and discipline educated mind towards loyalty to the British raj) and passed the Indian Universities Act, 1904.

Indian Universities Act (1904) In September 1901, Curzon convened a round table conference at Simla, attended by representatives of Universities throughout India. Subsequently, in January 1902, Indian Universities Commission (or the **Raleigh Commission**) was appointed under the chairmanship of Sir Thomas Raleigh to enquire into the condition of Indian Universities and give suggestions to improve their constitution and working. Based on the Commission's report, the Indian Universities Act 1904 was passed. The Act laid down-

- That the universities must make provision for study and research, setup labs and libraries and undertake direct instruction of students.
- That the number of Fellows of a University shall not be less than 50 and not more than 100, and that a Fellow should hold office for six years instead of for life.
- That most of the Fellows were to be nominated by the government. At the Universities of Calcutta, Madras and Bombay, the elective element was to be 20 each (15 in case of other universities).
- The Act increased Governor's control over the universities.
- It increased university control over private colleges by establishing stricter conditions of affiliation and periodical inspection by the Syndicate. Government approval was necessary for grant of affiliation or disaffiliation of colleges.

The Act was opposed by the nationalists as a 'retrograde measure'. Even the Sadler Commission of 1917 later commented that the Act of 1904 had made 'the Indian Universities among the most governmental universities in the world'. The nationalists felt that, through his 'reforms', Curzon sought to sabotage the growth of private enterprise in education and nationalist feelings in India.

A good outcome of Curzon's policy was the sanction in 1902 of a grant of ₹5 lakh per annum for five years for improvement of higher education (such government grants have become a permanent feature ever since). In the years that followed, there was also a large scale increase in the number of government supported and government recognised institutions of education at all levels. Improvement was also seen in the field of teacher training and teaching in government schools. However, the expansion of primary education remained far from satisfactory.

The nationalists now put pressure on the government for increasing funding for primary education, participation of Indians, initiating scientific and technical education and demanded education to be responsive to national aspirations.

Government Resolution on Education Policy (21 February 1913) In 1906 the State of Baroda introduced compulsory primary education throughout its territories and the nationalists could see no reason why the same could not be done in British India. During 1910-13, **GK Gokhale** pushed the matter vigorously in the Legislative Council; framed the Compulsory Primary Education Bill in 1911, making the issue of mass education a national agenda. Finally, on 21 February 1913, the Government of India passed a resolution accepting the policy of removal of illiteracy (but it rejected the principle of compulsory education). It urged provincial governments to take steps to provide **free elementary education** to the poorer sections of the population and to encourage private effort in this direction.

Sadler University Commission (1917-19) Although the Sadler Commission was appointed by Government of India in 1917 to enquire into the problems of Calcutta University, it reported on the entire field from school to University education and its recommendations were applicable to other universities also. It was headed by Dr. ME Sadler, Vice-Chancellor of the University of Leeds, and included two Indian members, namely Sir Asutosh Mukerji and Dr. Zia-ud-din-Ahmad. Its main recommendations were-

- It suggested the establishment of a twelve-year school course. The students were to enter university after assessing Intermediate Exam (rather than the Matriculation). The motive was to prepare students for university level on the one hand, and to prevent undeserving candidates from making it to the universities on the other. Thus, it also recommended creation of new type of institutions called Intermediate colleges that could run independently or be attached to selected high schools. Setting up a Board of Secondary and Intermediate Education was also recommended.
- The duration of the degree course after Intermediate should be limited to three years. Provision should be made for **Honours Courses** (for abler students), as distinct from Pass Course.
- Centralised unitary-residential-teaching bodies should be set up, in place of old type Indian universities with a large number of scattered colleges.
- A Board of Women Education in Calcutta University should be set up, and facilities for female education be extended.
- For training of teachers, substantial facilities should be provided.
- Departments of Education should be setup at the universities of Calcutta and Dacca.

During the period 1916-21, seven new universities came into existence. They were Banaras, Lucknow, Patna, Mysore, Aligarh, Dacca and Osmania. In 1920, the Sadler report was recommended to provincial governments.

Education under Dyarchy (1921–37) As per the provisions of Montagu-Chelmsford Reforms 1919, the Department of Education was transferred under the control of popular ministers in various provinces. But the financial arrangements remained with the Government of India. Such an arrangement had an adverse impact on the administration of all transferred departments. In education, the central grants that had been liberally sanctioned since 1902 were now discontinued. Financial constraints made it difficult for popular ministers to implement ambitious schemes for expansion/improvement of education.

Despite such hurdles, education in the country continued to spread chiefly under philanthropic effort. Growth in education was also attributed to the faith of the people in the value of education and inclination of parents to make sacrifices to educate their children.

Hartog Committee (1929) Though quantitative spread continued, qualitative decline emerged as a chronic issue and the 'Auxiliary Committee of the Indian Statutory Commission' (popularly known as the Hartog Committee) was appointed to report on the development of education in India. Its main findings were:

- Though it acknowledged the importance of primary education, it condemned introduction of compulsion and the policy of hasty expansion in education. It also observed that expansion in primary education had not resulted in commensurate increase in literacy as many children dropped out before they reached class four (more so in case of girls).
- In Secondary education, it recommended the retention of most students intended for rural pursuits at the Middle Vernacular School level after which students should be diverted to diversified courses leading to careers in industry or commerce. This was aimed to prevent overcrowding of universities.
- At University level, it criticised the policy of indiscriminate admission which had led to decline in learning standards. It recommended that all efforts should be made to restore the universities to their proper function of giving advanced education to deserving students and in making 'the university a more fruitful and less disappointing agency in the life of a community'.

Central Advisory Board of Education (CABE, 1935) In the year 1935, the government set up CABE to assist in educational planning. Two experts Abbott and Wood were invited to advice on problems of vocational education. In the Abbot-Wood Report, the experts suggested establishing hierarchical vocational institutions parallel to educational institutions. Consequently, a new type of technical institution, **the Polytechnics**, came into being and various technical, commercial and agricultural schools were established in all provinces.

Education under Provincial Autonomy (1936–37 to 1946–47) This was the last decade of British rule in India. The Act of 1935 replaced diarchy with provincial autonomy and structural hurdles in financing of education were reduced during this period, giving rise to great expectations regarding advancement of education. However these expectations were belied as provincial governments under the Congress resigned office in 1939 following the outbreak of Second World War. Though there was expansion of higher education, expansion of primary education was halted and schools became overcrowded.

Wardha Scheme of Basic Education (1937) During the brief period between 1937–39 when Congress governments were in power in the provinces, they took far reaching policy decisions in the field of education that later became the founding principles of reconstruction of education in free India.

After assuming office, the Congress governments felt the urgent need to introduce universal, free and compulsory primary education to combat illiteracy. But when they experienced the pinch of resources, Mahatma Gandhi stepped forward and proposed a self-supporting scheme of primary education in the form of **'Nai Talim'**. It was a scheme of Basic Education that envisaged free and compulsory education to be provided in child's mother tongue for 7 years throughout the country. The main principle of the scheme was 'learning through activity' and it centered around 'manual productive work' that would generate remuneration of the teachers. Gandhi's ideas were given a detailed shape by the Zakir Hussain Committee whose report became the fundamental document of Congress education policy. But the scheme could not be further developed due to resignation of Congress Ministries (the Scheme has been explained in detail in Chapter 6.19).

Sargeant Plan of Education (1944) After the end of the Second World War, the CABE drew up a national scheme of education under the guidance of Sir John Sargeant (Educational Advisor to GOI) that came to be known as the Sargeant Plan. It was part of the post-war reconstruction programme of the imperial government. Even though the British had more or less decided to leave India, the report drew up a **40-year educational plan** with the objective of achieving educational development comparable to that in Britain at that time. Its major recommendations were-

- Introduction of **universal, free and compulsory** basic or primary education for children between the ages of 6 and 11.
- Compulsory physical education, provision of milk and mid-day meals for undernourished children.
- Creation of employment bureaus.
- Education of children with physical and intellectual disabilities.
- Abolition of Intermediate course.

After independence, most of the states structured their school education on the basis of Sargeant Plan.

Education after Independence

Radhakrishnan Commission (1948–49) In post-independence period, the country needed educated manpower for administration and skilled technical manpower for modernisation of the economy.

In view of this, a University Education Commission was appointed by GOI under the chairmanship of Dr. S Radhakrishnan to enquire into **university education** in the country and suggest improvements. Its main recommendations were:

- It laid down a twelve year pre-university educational course (i.e. it favored 10+2+3 pattern).
- It laid down three objectives for higher education namely, General, Liberal and Educational Education.
- It urged that a university degree should not be considered essential for administrative services.
- University education should be placed on the Concurrent list.
- The pay scales of university teachers should be raised.
- A **University Grants Commission** (UGC) should be set up to supervise university education in the country.

University Grants Commission (1953) Based on the recommendation of the Radhakrishnan Commission, the UGC was constituted in 1953. Following an act of Parliament in 1956, the commission became a statutory autonomous body to manage most matters related to university education. Annually, the central government provides the UGC with adequate funds from which grants are made to different universities.

Mudaliar Commission (1952–53) It was a Secondary Education Commission appointed under the chairmanship of Dr. Lakshmanswami Mudaliar. It recommended 11 years of school education (instead of the earlier12); establishment of multipurpose schools improvement in teacher training, emoluments and service conditions of teachers etc.

Kothari Education Commission (1964–66) In July 1964, the GOI appointed an Education Commission under the chairmanship of Dr. DS Kothari 'to advise government on the national pattern of education and on the general principles and policies for the development of education at all stages and in all aspects'. The commission received the services of distinguished educationists and scientists from the UK, USSR and the UNESCO. Its principle recommendations were-

- Establishment of 10+2+3 uniform pattern of education throughout the nation. The recommendation attracted controversy as education was under state control during this time and many states were not willing to adopt this pattern owing to organisational and financial implications (However, 42nd Constitution Amendment Act 1976 shifted education to concurrent list. By 1986, the pattern was accepted by all the states).
- Introduction of work experience (similar to Gandhi's 'manual productive work') and social service at almost all levels of education.
- Vocationalisation of secondary education.
- Establishing alternative channels like part-time and own time along with full-time in the education system.
- Establishing a small number of major universities with the aim of achieving highest international standards.
- Common School and Neighborhood School system to create an egalitarian society.
- Stress on moral education and social responsibility.
- Priority to education and research in agriculture.

National Policy on Education (1968) In pursuance of the recommendations of Kothari Commission, the GOI adopted a national policy on education which stressed on:

- Free and compulsory education up to the age of 14 years.
- Adoption of common school system; three language formula; integrated programs enabling children with disabilities to study in regular schools.

- Improving status and emoluments of teachers.
- Development of education for agriculture and industry.
- Production of inexpensive but quality textbooks.
- Investment of 6% of national income in education.

New Education Policy (1986) It contended that the role of education is essentially to transform a static society into a vibrant one with commitment towards development and change. Its main components included:

- On the lines of NPE 1968, it reiterated commitment towards common educational structure of 10+2+3 and common school system.
- While re-emphasizing the need for common core curriculum, it specified the underlying values. They are- India's common cultural heritage, egalitarianism, democracy, secularism, equality of sexes, environmental protection, removal of social barriers, small family norms and inculcation of scientific temper.
- Increase in literacy rate from present 36% to 56% of the population by 2000.
- Universalisation of Elementary Education (UEE).
- Conceived Operation Blackboard (OB Scheme) to provide minimum essential teaching-learning equipments and materials.
- Vocationalisation of higher secondary education (led to establishment of Navodaya Schools).
- For improving the quality of teachers at school level, it proposed District Institutes of Education and Training (DIETs).

Development of Technical Education under the British rule

Year	Institute	Details
1847	**Roorkee College, UP**	First Engg. College; renamed Thompson's Engg. College in 1854; upgraded to University in 1948 and to IIT in 2001. Gave diplomas considered equivalent to degrees.
1856	**Calcutta College of Civil Engg. (Bengal Presidency)**	Renamed Bengal Engg. College in 1857
1858	**Poona College of Engg. (Bombay Presidency)**	Upgraded from Overseer's School, Poona (founded in 1854)
1858	**Guindy College of Engg. (Madras Presidency)**	Upgraded from Industrial School, Guindy, Madras, 1842 (attached to Gun Carriage Factory)
1887	**Victoria Jubilee Technical Institute, Bombay**	Renamed Veermata Jijabai Technological Institute (VJTI, in 1997)
1905	**Agricultural Research Institute, Pusa, Bihar**	Shifted to Delhi in 1936; post Independence, renamed as Indian Agricultural Research Institute (IARI)
1908	**College of Engg. and Technology, Jadavpur**	Only surviving institute of National Council of Education started by Swadeshi leaders
1909	**Indian Institute of Science, Bangalore**	Brainchild of Sir Jamshed Tata; opened Electrical Engineering classes under Dr. Alfred Hay in 1915.
1916	**Banaras University**	Founded by Pt. Madan Mohan Malaviya; first to start degree courses in mechanical/ electrical engineering and metallurgy.

5

Governors-General and Viceroys of India

Governors-General

1. Warren Hastings (1772–85)

1.1. Hastings became Governor of Bengal in 1772 and first Governor-General of Bengal in October 1773 by the Regulating Act of 1773.

1.2. He started the Auctioning System to collect revenue (1772–77).

1.3. Established India's first Supreme Court in Calcutta based on English law.

1.4. The Rohilla war of 1774 leading to annexation of Rohilkhand by the Nawab of Awadh with the British help.

1.5. Act of 1781 which clearly divided the jurisdiction between Governor-General in council and Supreme Court at Calcutta.

1.6. Calcutta Madrasa was set up in 1781.

1.7. First Maratha War (1775–82) and the Treaty of Salbai (1782).

1.8. Second Anglo-Mysore War (1780–84) and Treaty of Mangalore (1784) with Tipu Sultan.

1.9. Founded Asiatic Society of Bengal along with Sir William Jones in 1784.

1.10. Pitts India Act of 1784 was passed and strength of Governor General's Executive Council was reduced to three from four. Board of control was also set up in England.

1.11. Translation of Manusmriti as a code of Hindu law was done.

1.12. Translation of *Geeta* and *Hitopdesha* in English by Charles Wilkins.

1.13. Abolished dual system of administration.

1.14. Started Diwani and Fauzdari Adalats and the District Level Sadar Diwani and Nizamat Adalats (appellate courts).

1.15. Hindu and Muslim laws were also redefined during his tenure.

1.16. Hastings took away judicial powers of Zamindar and made maintenance of records compulsory.

2. Lord Cornwallis (1786–93)

2.1. Third Mysore war (1790–92) and Treaty of Seringapatam (1792).

2.2. Introduced Permanent Settlement or the Zamindari system in Bengal and Bihar in the year 1793.

2.3. Cornwallis Code of 1793 which included several judicial reforms along with separation of Revenue administration from Judicial administration.

2.4. Created post of District Judge and introduced Civil Services (1793), known as Father of Civil Services in India.

2.5. Europeanisation of Administrative machinery took place during his tenure.

2.6. Introduced Police Reforms.

3. Sir John Shore (1793–98)

3.1. Pivotal role in the introduction of permanent settlement in 1793.
3.2. He introduced first charter act of 1793.
3.3. Battle of Kharda between the Nizam and the Marathas (1795) leading to the defeat of Nizam.
3.4. Known for his policy of Non-interference.

4. Lord Wellesley (1798–1805)

4.1. Wellesley introduced the system of Subsidiary Alliance, Hyderabad (1798), Mysore (1799), Awadh (1801) and Peshwa (1802) signed the Treaty respectively with the Company.
4.2. Nizam of Hyderabad was the first to accept Subsidiary Alliance.
4.3. Madras Presidency was created during his tenure.
4.4. 4th Anglo-Mysore War (1799) took place in which Tipu Sultan died.
4.5. In 1800, he set up Fort William College at Calcutta with John Gilchrist as its principal. It was set up to teach Urdu and Hindi to Civil Servants.
4.6. Second Maratha War (1803–05).
4.7. Subsidiary Treaty of Bassein (1802).

5. Sir George Barlow (1805–07)

5.1. Vellore Mutiny (1806)
5.2. Second Anglo Maratha war ended.

6. Lord Minto 1 (1807–13)

6.1. Treaty of Amritsar with Ranjit Singh in the year 1809.
6.2. Charter Act of 1813 which ended monopoly of East India Company in India.

7. Lord Hastings (1813–23)

7.1. Hastings adopted the policy of intervention and war.
7.2. Anglo-Nepal war (1814–16) in which Gurkha leader Amar Singh was defeated, ended with Treaty of Sugauli.
7.3. Third Anglo-Maratha War (1817–18) – lead to the abolition of Peshwaship and annexation of his territories.
7.4. Creation of Bombay Presidency (1818).
7.5. Treaty of Poona (1817) with Peshwas.
7.6. Suppression of Pindaris (1817).
7.7. Ryotwari settlement was introduced in Madras Presidency by Thomas Munro, the Governor (1820).

8. Lord Amherst (1823–28)

8.1. First Burmese War (1824–26), signed the Treaty of Yandabo in 1826.
8.2. Acquisition of Malaya Peninsula and Bharatpur (1826).

9. Lord William Bentinck (1828–35)

9.1. Bentinck is considered one of the most liberal and enlightened amongst all the Governors-General of India.
9.2. He was the first Governor-General of India.

9.3. Also known as 'Father of Modern Western Education in India'.
9.4. Anti-Sati resolution of 1829 was passed during his tenure.
9.5. Took measures for suppression of thugi (1830).
9.6. Deposition of Raja of Mysore and annexation of his territories (1831).
9.7. Passed the Charter Act of 1833; ended the monopoly of East India Company in tea trade and trade with China.
9.8. Introduced Law Member in the Governors-General Executive Council.
9.9. Created Province of Agra in 1834.
9.10. Annexed Coorg (1834) and Central Cachar (1834).
9.11. Abolished Provincial Courts of Appeal and Circuit, appointed Commissioners instead.
9.12. First Medical College opened in Calcutta in 1835.
9.13. Resolution of 1835 and Educational Reforms; defined the aims and objectives of British Government and appointed Lord Macaulay the President of the Committee of the Public Instruction.

10. Lord Metcalfe (1835–36)

10.1. Granted freedom of press by passing the famous Press Law.
10.2. Also known as the Liberator of Press in India.

11. Lord Auckland (1836–42)

11.1. First Afghan War (1836–42) to make Afghanistan a buffer state between Russian empire and British India. The war proved to be a disaster and lead to the recall of Auckland.
11.2. Death of Ranjit Singh (1839).

12. Lord Ellen Borough (1842–44)

12.1. Brought an end to the first Anglo-Afghan war (1842).
12.2. Sindh was annexed by Charles Napier (1843). He was appointed as the first Governor of Sindh.
12.3. Abolished slavery.
12.4. War with Gwalior; forced Scindia of Gwalior to sign a humiliating treaty (1843).

13. Lord Hardinge (1844–48)

13.1. First Anglo-Sikh war (1845–46) and the Treaty of Lahore (1846).
13.2. He introduced social reforms like prohibition of female infanticide and human sacrifice, which was practiced among the Gonds (a tribe of Central India).
13.3. Gave preference to the English educated in employment.

14. Lord Dalhousie (1848–56)

14.1. Second Anglo-Sikh War (1848–49) and annexation of Punjab (1849) into East India Company's empire.
14.2. Second Burmese War (1848–49) and annexation of Burma (Pegu).
14.3. Abolished Titles and Pensions.
14.4. Introduced the Doctrine of Lapse and annexed Satara (1848), Jaitpur and Sambalpur (1849), Udaipur (1852), Jhansi(1853), Nagpur(1854) and Awadh(1856) on the plea of misgovernance.
14.5. Woods Educational Dispatch (also Known as Magna Carta of Modern Education in India) of 1854 and British assumption of the responsibility of educating the masses.

14.6. Introduction of the Railway (First train from Bombay to Thane), Telegraph (First line from Agra to Calcutta) and the Postal System in 1853.
14.7. Post and Telegraph Act (1854) was passed.
14.8. Widow Remarriage Act (1856) introduced, Ishwar Chand Vidyasagar extensively supported the act.
14.9. Santhal Uprising (1855–56), lead by Sidhu and Kanhu.
14.10. Establishment of a Public Works Department in every province (1854).

15. Lord Canning (1856–57)

15.1. Revolt of 1857.
15.2. Universities of Calcutta, Bombay and Madras were established in 1857.
15.3. He was the last Governor-General of East India Company.

Viceroys of India

1. Lord Canning (1858–62)

1.1. Lord Canning was the first Viceroy of India.
1.2. Government of India Act, 1858 was passed which had ended the rule of East India Company; transfer of control from East India Company to the Crown.
1.3. Queen Victoria's proclamation was published at Allahabad on November 1,1858, which had the following provisions:

(i) No further annexation.
(ii) No forceful conversion.
(iii) Appointments in the Public Services would be based on merits and qualifications.
(iv) Indian Tradition to be given due respect while framing the laws.
(v) Full protection to the ownership of properties and succession.
(vi) Peasants to have their rights on land as long as they paid the revenue.

1.4. The Indian Penal Code was passed, which came into force from 1860.
1.5. The Code of Criminal Procedure 1859 was passed, which came into force from 1861.
1.6. The Indian High Courts Act 1861 was enacted.
1.7. High Courts were opened in 1865.
1.8. The Indian Councils Act 1861 was passed, which is considered a landmark in the Constitutional History of India.

2. Lord Elgin (1862–63)

2.1. Suppressed Wahabi Movement.
2.2. Because of his premature death, Sir Charles Napier and Denison acted as Viceroys between 1862 and 1864.

3. Sir John Lawrence (1864–69)

3.1. Anglo-Bhutanese War (1864–65).
3.2. Setting up of High Courts at Calcutta, Bombay, Madras (1865).
3.3. Telegraph Communication with Europe opened.

3.4. The Punjab Tenancy Act was passed.
3.5. Fourth High Court was set in United Province at Agra (1866), later shifted to Allahabad.
3.6. Followed the policy of Non-Intervention in the matters of Afghanistan, policy came to be known as 'Policy of Masterly Inactivity'.

4. Lord Mayo (1869–72)

4.1. Introduced financial decentralisation in India and made the first Provincial Settlement in 1870.
4.2. Established the Rajkot College (1870) in Kathiawar and Mayo College (1875) at Ajmer for training of Indian Princes.
4.3. He organised the statistical survey of India. The first census was conducted in 1872.
4.4. He established the Department of Agriculture and Commerce.
4.5. Introduced State Railways.
4.6. He was the only Viceroy to be murdered while in office.

5. Lord North Brook (1872–76)

5.1. Kuka Rebellion in Punjab (1872) lead by Ram Singh.
5.2. Famine in Bihar (1874)
5.3. Prince of Wales (later Edward VII visited India (1875).
5.4. He resigned over Afghanistan question.
5.5. Trial of Gaekwads of Baroda.

6. Lord Lytton (1876–80)

6.1. Royal Titles Act of 1876 was passed, Queen Victoria assumed the title of 'Kaiser-i-Hind', Delhi Durbar was organised in 1877 at Red Fort to welcome the Queen.
6.2. Severe famine in many parts of India (1876–78), appointment of famine commission under Richard Strachey (1878).
6.3. The Vernacular Press Act of 1878 which censored local language newspapers but not English newspapers was passed.
6.4. The Arms act of 1878 was passed which disallowed Indians from carrying arms.
6.5. Lowered the maximum age of ICS from 21 years to 19 years.
6.6. Second Afghan War (1878–80).

7. Lord Ripon (1880–84)

7.1. Repealed the Vernacular Press Act and Arms Act of 1878.
7.2. The first Factory Act of 1881 to improve labour conditions.
7.3. Continued on the policy of financial decentralisation.
7.4. First regular census was conducted in 1881.
7.5. Ripon introduced Local self-government in 1882 and is known as father of local self-government in India.
7.6. Appointment of Hunter Commission (1882) under Sir William Hunter for educational reforms, especially to give importance to primary education.
7.7. Ilbert Bill controversy (1883).
7.8. Famine code was adopted (1883).
7.9. Foundation of Punjab University.
7.10. Rendition of Mysore.

8. Lord Dufferin (1884–88)

8.1. Indian National Congress was founded (1885).
8.2. Garden tea party at Calcutta was attended by delegates of Congress, given by Dufferin who called Congress Party a 'Microscopic Minority'.
8.3. Third Burmese war and annexation of Burma (1885).
8.4. The First Congress session was attended by 72 members with Kadambini Ganguli as the only female member.
8.5. Bengal Tenancy Act, 1885.

9. Lord Lansdowne (1888–94)

9.1. The Factory Act of 1891.
9.2. Categorisation of Civil Services into Imperial, Provincial and Subordinate Services.
9.3. Indian Council Act of 1892.
9.4. Durand Commission (1893) which defined boundaries between Afghanistan and British India which came to be known as Durand Line. Now the line is between Afghanistan and Pakistan.
9.5. In 1891, Age of Consent Act, under which marriage of a girl below 12 years was prohibited, passed.

10. Lord Elgin II (1894–98)

10.1. Mundas Uprisings of 1899.
10.2. Great Famine of 1896–97.
10.3. Lyall Commission (1897) appointed after famine.
10.4. Assassination of two British officials by the Chapekar Brothers in 1897.

11. Lord Curzon (1899–1905)

11.1. Appointed a Police Commission (1902) under Andrew Frazer.
11.2. Based on the recommendation of Raleigh Commission 1902 which recommended for reform in University Education, Indian Universities Act, 1904 was passed in order to gain control over Universities and arrest the growth of rising Nationalist sentiments.
11.3. Establishment of Department of Commerce and Industry.
11.4. Partition of Bengal (1905) was announced.
11.5. Calcutta Corporation Act 1899.
11.6. He passed the Ancient Monuments Protection Act 1904 to restore India's Cultural Heritage. Thus, the Archaeological Survey of India was established.
11.7. Famine Commission appointed under MacDonnell.
11.8. Passed the Indian Coinage and Paper Currency Act 1899 and put India on gold standard.
11.9. Irrigation Commission appointed under Moncrieff (1901).
11.10. PUSA Agricultural Institute in 1903.

12. Lord Minto II (1905–10)

12.1. Swadeshi and Boycott Movement.
12.2. Establishment of Muslim League by Aga Khan in 1906 at Dacca.
12.3. Surat Split of 1907.
12.4. Indian Councils Act 1909 and Minto-Morley Reforms. Provision of separate electorate for Muslims.

12.5. Newspapers Act 1908.
12.6. Muzaffarpur Conspiracy of 1908 in which attempt was made to kill Kingsford, the controversial Magistrate by Khudiram Bose and Prafulla Chaki.

13. Lord Hardinge II (1910–16)

13.1. Annulment of the partition of Bengal (1911), Bihar and Orissa were separated.
13.2. Transfer of Capital from Calcutta to Delhi (1911).
13.3. Darbar in Delhi and Coronation of George V and Queen Mary.
13.4. Ghadar Party was formed at San Francisco by Lala Hardayal (1913).
13.5. Beginning of First World War on 28 July 1914.
13.6. Arrival of Mahatma Gandhi from South Africa (1915).
13.7. Establishment of Hindu Mahasabha by Madan Mohan Malaviya (1915).

14. Lord Chelmsford (1916–21)

14.1. Government of India Act, 1919 which came to be known as Montagu-Chelmsford Reforms.
14.2. Formation of Home Rule League by Annie Besant, 1916.
14.3. Lucknow Session of the Congress and Lucknow Pact in 1916.
14.4. Foundation of Women's University at Poona (1916).
14.5. Foundation of Sabarmati Ashram; Champaran Satyagraha (1916), Kheda Satyagraha (1918) and Ahmedabad Mill Strike (1918).
14.6. Foundation of the Indian Liberal Federation by S.N. Banerjee and others (1918).
14.7. Saddler Commission on Educational Policy Reforms (1917).
14.8. Repressive Rowlatt Act (1919).
14.9. Jallianwala Bagh Massacre (13th April 1919).
14.10. Appointment of Hunter Commission to look into Jallianwala Bagh tragedy.
14.11. Chamber of Princes established (1919).
14.12. Formation of Khilafat Committee by Ali Brothers and launching of the Khilafat Movement (1919–20).
14.13. Beginning of Non-Cooperation Movement (1920).
14.14. Death of Tilak (1st August 1920).
14.15. Appointed S.P. Sinha as Governor of Bihar (first Indian to become a Governor).

15. Lord Reading (1921–25)

15.1. Chauri Chaura incident at Gorakhpur, UP (5th February 1922) and withdrawal of Non-Cooperation Movement (on 12 February 1922 at Bardoli).
15.2. Repeal of Rowlatt Act of 1919 and the Press Act of 1910.
15.3. Moplah Rebellion (1921) took place in Kerala.
15.4. Formation of Congress Khilafat Swarajist Party (Swaraj Party) in the year 1922 by CR Das and Motilal Nehru.
15.5. Holding of Simultaneous Examination for the ICS in England and in India from 1923.
15.6. Formation of Hindustan Republican Army at Kanpur by Revolutionaries.
15.7. Communist Party of India founded by M N Roy (1925).
15.8. Kakori train robbery (1925).
15.9. RSS founded in 1925.
15.10. Murder of Swami Shraddhanand (1926).

15.11. Royal Commission on Agriculture.
15.12. Young Hilton Committee for Currency Notes (1926).
15.13. Lee Commission (1924) for Public Services.

16. Lord Irwin (1926–31)

16.1. Simon Commission was appointed (1927) and its arrival in India (1928).
16.2. Appointment of the Butler Indian States Commission (1927).
16.3. Formation of All India States People's Conference (1927).
16.4. Irwin was also known as Christian Viceroy.
16.5. All India Youth Congress was formed (1928).
16.6. Nehru Committee Report of 1928.
16.7. Royal Commission for Indian Worker, 1929.
16.8. Bhagat Singh and Batukeshwar Dutt threw two bombs in the Central Legislative Assembly (1929).
16.9. 'Deepawali Declaration' by Lord Irwin (1929).
16.10. Purna Swaraj Resolution was passed at Lahore Session (1929), presided by Jawaharlal Nehru.
16.11. First Round Table Conference (1930), Congress boycotted it.
16.12. 26th January was celebrated as Independence Day.
16.13. Gandhi-Irwin pact on 5th March 1931.
16.14. Dandi March (12 March 1930) by Gandhi and launch of Civil Disobedience Movement.
16.15. Sharda Act, 1929 under which marriageable age of Girls (14 years) and Boys (18years) was raised.

17. Lord Willingdon (1931–36)

17.1. Second Round Table Conference (1931) and failure of the Conference, resumption of the Civil Disobedience Movement.
17.2. Gandhi participated in the Second Round Table Conference in London as the sole representative of Congress.
17.3. Communal Award (1932) by Ramsay MacDonald, the then British Prime Minister, under which separate Communal Electorates were set-up.
17.4. 'Fast unto death' by Gandhi in Yerawada prison, broken after the Poona pact.
17.5. Third Round Table Conference (1932).
17.6. Government of India Act 1935.
17.7. Establishment of All India Kisan Sabha (1936) and Congress Socialist Party by Acharya Narendra Dev and Jai Prakash Narayan.
17.8. Burma separated from India, 1935.

18. Lord Linlithgow (1936–43)

18.1. First General Elections (1936–37); Congress gained absolute Majority.
18.2. Resignation of Congress Ministries after the outbreak of Second World War (1939).
18.3. Deliverance Day by Muslim League (September 1939).
18.4. Tripuri Session of INC (1939) and formation of Forward Block by Subhas Chandra Bose.
18.5. Lahore resolution (March 1940) by the Muslim league and demand for separate state for Muslims.
18.6. August Offer by the Viceroy and Individual Satyagraha launched (1940).
18.7. Cripps Proposal (1942) which offered Dominion status to India and setting up of Constituent Assembly; its rejection by the Congress.

18.8. Quit India Movement (1942).

18.9. 'Divide and Quit' slogan at the Karachi session of the Muslim League (1943).

19. Lord Wavell (1944–47)

19.1. CR Formula (1944), failure of Gandhi-Jinnah talk to resolve communal issue (1944).

19.2. Simla Conference and Wavell Plan, failed too (1945).

19.3. INA trials (1945).

19.4. RIN Mutiny (1946).

19.5. Cabinet Mission Plan (1946).

19.6. Formation of the Interim Government with Jawaharlal Nehru as Prime Minister (September 1946).

19.7. Formation of Constituent Assembly (1946).

19.8. Direct Action Day (16th August 1946) observed by Muslim league for demand of separate nation of Pakistan.

19.9. Announcement of end of British rule in India by Clement Attlee on February 20, 1947.

20. Lord Mountbatten (1947–48)

20.1. June Third Plan (3rd June 1947) announced. Also known as Mountbatten plan.

20.2. Independence of India (15th August 1947).

20.3. Appointment of two boundary commissions under Sir Cyril Radcliffe for the partition of Bengal and Punjab.

20.4. Last British Viceroy of British India and First Governor-General of Free India.

21. C Rajagopalachari (1948–50)

21.1. The only Indian Governor-General and last Governor-General of Free India.

Previous Years' Questions – (Based on Appendices) Preliminary Exam

1. The Governor General who followed a spirited Forward Policy towards Afghanistan was **[UPSC 1999]**

   (a) Minto (b) Dufferin

   (c) Elgin (d) Lytton

2. At a time when empires in Europe were crumbling before the might of Napoleon, which one of the following Governor General kept the British flag flying high in India? **[UPSC 1999]**

   (a) Warren Hastings

   (b) Lord Cornwallis

   (c) Lord Wellesley

   (d) Lord Hastings

3. Consider the following Viceroys of India during the British rule **[UPSC 2004]**

   1. Lord Curzon
   2. Lord Chelmsford
   3. Lord Hardinge
   4. Lord Irwin

   Which one of the following is the correct chronological order of their tenure?

   (a) 1, 3, 2, 4 (b) 2, 4, 1, 3

   (c) 1, 4, 2, 3 (d) 2, 3, 1, 4

4. Consider the following events during India's freedom struggle **[UPSC 2004]**

   1. Chauri Chaura outrage

2. Minto Morley reforms
3. Dandi March
4. Montagu-Chelmsford reforms

Which one of the following is the correct chronological order of the events above?

(a) 1, 3, 2, 4 (b) 2, 4, 1, 3
(c) 1 ,4, 2, 3 (d) 2, 3, 1, 4

5. Consider the following statements **[UPSC 2004]**
   1. The first session of Indian National Congress was held in Calcutta.
   2. The second Session of Indian National Congress was held under the Presidentship of Dadabhai Naoroji.
   3. Both Indian National Congress and Muslim League held their sessions at Lucknow in 1916 and concluded the Lucknow Pact.

   Which of the following statements given above is/are correct?

   (a) 1 and 2 (b) Only 2
   (c) 2 and 3 (d) Only 3

6. Who among the following repealed the Vernacular Press Act? **[UPSC 2005]**

   (a) Lord Dufferin (b) Lord Ripon
   (c) Lord Curzon (d) Lord Hardinge

7. Consider the following statements **[UPSC 2007]**
   1. Robert Clive was the first Governor General of Bengal.
   2. William Bentinck was the first Governor General of India.

   Which of the following statement(s) given above is / are correct?

   (a) Only 1 (b) Only 2
   (c) Both 1 and 2 (d) Neither 1 nor 2

8. The first Factory Act for restricting the working hours of women and children and authorising local government to make necessary rules was adopted during whose time? **[UPSC 2007]**

   (a) Lord Lytton (b) Lord Bentinck
   (c) Lord Ripon (d) Lord Canning

9. Where was the first session of the Indian National Congress held in December 1885? **[UPSC 2008]**

   (a) Ahmedabad (b) Bombay
   (c) Calcutta (d) Delhi

10. Who among the following Governor Generals created the covenanted civil services of India which later came to be known as the Indian Civil Service? **[UPSC 2010]**

    (a) Warren Hastings
    (b) Wellesley
    (c) Cornwallis
    (d) William Bentinck

11. Consider the following statements **[UPSC 2015]**
    1. The first woman president of the Indian National Congress was Sarojini Naidu.
    2. The first Muslim president of the Indian National Congress was Badruddin Tyabji.

    Which of the following statements given above is/are correct?

    (a) Only 1 (b) Only 2
    (c) Both 1 and 2 (d) Neither 1 nor 2

12. Wellesley established the Fort William College at Calcutta because **[UPSC 2020]**

    (a) He was asked by the Board of Directors at London to do so
    (b) He wanted to revive interest in oriental learning in India
    (c) He wanted to provide William Carey and his associates employment
    (d) He wanted to train British civilians for administrative purposes in India

13. The Vital-Vidhvansak, the first monthly journal to have the untouchable people as its target audience was published by **[UPSC 2020]**

    (a) Gopal Baba Walangkar
    (b) Jyotiba Phule
    (c) Mohandas Karamchand Gandhi
    (d) Bhimrao Ramji Ambedkar

Answers

Previous Years' Questions – Preliminary Exam

1. (d)	2. (d)	3. (a)	4. (b)	5. (c)
6. (b)	7. (b)	8. (c)	9. (b)	10. (c)
11. (b)	12. (d)	13. (a)		

Practice Papers Preliminary Exam

Practice Paper 1

1. Which of the following statements is/are true regarding Nadir Shah's invasion of India?
   1. Ahmad Shah was the reigning Mughal Emperor at the time of Nadir Shah's attack.
   2. It exposed the hidden weakness of the empire to the Maratha sardars and the foreign trading companies.
   3. As a result of the invasion, Nadir Shah annexed areas west of the Indus to the Persian Empire.

   Select the correct answer from the codes given below-

   (a) 1 only (b) 1 and 2
   (c) 2 and 3 (d) 1, 2 and 3

   Ans: (c)

2. Arrange the following in chronological order, as per their arrival in India-
   1. English
   2. Dutch
   3. Portuguese
   4. Danes

   Select the correct answer from the codes given below-

   (a) 1 2 3 4 (b) 4 3 2 1
   (c) 3 2 1 4 (d) 2 3 1 4

   Ans: (c)

3. What brought the Indian states in conflict with one another?
   1. The rulers followed the policy of territorial expansion.
   2. The rulers belonged to different religions.

   With reference to the above question, which of the above statements is/are correct?

   (a) 1 only (b) 2 only
   (c) both (d) neither

   Ans: (a)

4. Which of the following was not a factor in British conquest of Sindh?
   1. Commercial possibilities of the River Sindh.
   2. Growing Anglo-French rivalry in Europe.

   Select the correct answer using the code given below.

   (a) 1 only (b) 2 only
   (c) both (d) neither

   Ans: (b)

5. The Act which ended East India Company's monopoly of trade in India was ________.

   (a) Regulating Act 1773
   (b) Pitt's India Act 1784
   (c) Charter Act of 1793
   (d) Charter Act of 1813

   Ans: (d)

6. Which of the following was not a factor in the rise of national consciousness in India?
   1. Indian railways
   2. English education system
   3. Establishment of Peace and Orderly Government in India

   Select the correct answer form the codes given below-

   (a) 1 only (b) 1 and 2
   (c) 3 only (d) None of the above

   Ans: (d)

7. The educated Indians did not participate in the Revolt of 1857 because-

   (a) They knew that India was militarily weak
   (b) They believed that the British influence was needed to lead India to modernisation.
   (c) They believed that Indians needed a master race to rule them.
   (d) None of the above

   Ans: (b)

8. Ishwar Chandra Vidyasagar chiefly worked for which of the following social issues?
   1. Child marriage
   2. Polygamy
   3. Sati
   4. Widow remarriage
   5. Higher education for women

   Select the correct answer using the codes given below-

   (a) 1, 3 and 4 (b) 1, 2, 3 and 4
   (c) 1, 2, 4 and 5 (d) all of the above

   Ans: (c)

9. Examine the following statements with regard to the Bangbhasha Prakashika Sabha-
   1. It was founded by Raja Ram Mohan Roy.
   2. The association was formed with the aim of promoting Bengali literature.

   Which of the above statements is/are correct?

   (a) 1 only (b) 2 only
   (c) both (d) neither

   Ans: (d)

10. Consider the following statements with regard to the composition of the early Congress-
    1. Most of the members came from the landed aristocracy.
    2. The legal profession was most heavily represented.

    Which of the above statements is/are correct?

    (a) 1 only (b) 2 only
    (c) both (d) neither

    Ans: (b)

11. Consider the following statements with regard to the 1905 Congress Session-
    1. It was held at Banaras.
    2. It was presided by Dadabhai Naoroji.
    3. It was decided that Swadeshi Movement be extended outside Bengal.

    Choose the correct answer from the codes given below-

    (a) 1 only (b) 1 and 2
    (c) 2 and 3 (d) None of the above

    Ans: (a)

12. Consider the following statements-
    1. Gandhian style of politics was based on inclusivism.
    2. Gandhian thoughts of morality are based on class based society of India rather than religious diversity of India.
    3. Mahatma Gandhi was critical of western industrial capitalism.

    Which of the above statements is/are correct? Choose the correct answer from the codes given below-

    (a) 1, 2 and 3 (b) 2 and 3
    (c) 1 and 2 (d) 1 and 3

    Ans: (d)

13. Which of the following mentioned methods was not a method of mass mobilisation adopted by Gandhi?

    (a) Satyagraha
    (b) Training of agitators
    (c) Petitions and memorials
    (d) Social reform

    Ans: (c)

14. Consider the following statements in context of the Rowlatt Act-
    1. Rowlatt Act was passed in March 1919 even though every single Indian Central member of the Indian legislative Council opposed it.
    2. Rowlatt Act authorised the British government to imprison any person without trial and conviction in a court of law.
    3. Rowlatt Act authorised the British Government to suspend the right of habeas corpus, which had been the foundation of civil liberties in Britain.

    Which of the above statements are correct? Choose the correct answer from the codes given below-

    (a) All are correct (b) 1 and 2
    (c) 2 and 3 (d) None of the above

    Ans: (a)

15. Which of the following is true regarding the changes made in the central government by Montagu–Chelmsford Reforms?

    (a) Under the Act, a unicameral legislature was established known as Indian Legislative Assembly.
    (b) The right to ask supplementary questions was extended to all members of the legislature.

(c) Governor General's special power of certification was abolished.

(d) The term of the Assembly was fixed at 5 years.

Ans: (b)

16. Consider the following statements, with respect to Indian Councils Act of 1892-

1. The members to the Councils could be indirectly elected.
2. The members of the Councils could discuss and amend the annual financial statement.

Which of the above statements is/are correct?

(a) 1 only (b) 2 only
(c) both (d) neither

Ans: (a)

17. In his autobiography, The Indian Struggle, Subhas Chandra Bose calls an event a 'national calamity'.

This event was __________.

(a) Congress split of Surat
(b) Jallianwala Bagh massacre
(c) Withdrawal of Non-Cooperation movement
(d) Arrest of Gandhi

Ans: (c)

18. The program of non-cooperation included which of the following?

1. Surrender of titles and honorary offices
2. Refusal to attend government darbars and official functions
3. Refusal of all classes to offer themselves for service in Mesopotamia
4. Setting up national education institutions

Select the correct answer from the codes given below-

(a) 1 and 2 (b) 1, 2 and 3
(c) 1, 2, 3 and 4 (d) 1 only

Ans: (c)

19. Which of the following are associated with communalism?

1. Sir Syed Ahmad Khan
2. Formation of the Indian National Congress
3. Militant nationalism

Select the correct answer from the codes given below-

(a) 1 only (b) 1 and 2
(c) 2 and 3 (d) 1 and 3

Ans: (d)

20. Which of the following reveal influence of socialist ideas upon Congress?

1. Adoption of agrarian program at Faizpur Session of the Congress.
2. The Election Manifesto of the Congress in 1936.
3. Induction of Jaya Prakash Narayan, Narendra Dev and Achyut Patwardhan into the Congress Working Committee.

Select the correct answer from the codes given below-

(a) 1 only (b) 1 and 2
(c) 1 and 3 (d) 1, 2 and 3

Ans: (d)

21. Which of the following was/were true regarding Simon Commission?

1. It was a statutory commission
2. Sir John Simon and Clement Attlee were its members
3. It was appointed by Prime Minister Stanley Baldwin

Select the correct answer from the codes given below-

(a) 1 and 2 (b) 1 and 3
(c) 2 and 3 (d) 1, 2 and 3

Ans: (d)

22. Consider the following pairs with regard to the types of protest and their region during the Civil Disobedience Movement.

1. Forest satyagraha – Central Provinces
2. No-revenue, no tax – United Provinces
3. Anti-chowkidara – Eastern India

Which of the above pairs is/are correctly matched?

(a) 1 and 2 (b) 2 and 3
(c) 3 only (d) 1, 2 and 3

Ans: (d)

23. Consider the following responses, once Congress decided to contest elections-

1. Gandhi resigned from the Congress as he disagreed with parliamentary politics.
2. J Nehru welcomed the decision as he believed in continuing the struggle inside the legislatures.

Which of the above statements is/are true?

(a) 1 only (b) 2 only
(c) both (d) neither

Ans: (a)

24. Examine the following statements with reference to the Bakasht Agitation-
    1. It was started by the Bengal peasants in 1946–47.
    2. The peasants protested under the leadership of the Congress.

    Which of the above statements is/are untrue?

    Select the correct answer using the codes given below-

    (a) 1 only (b) 2 only
    (c) both (d) neither

    Ans: (c)

25. Which of the following formed part of Attlee's Announcement of February 1947?
    1. The British would withdraw from India by 30th June 1947.
    2. Wavell would be replaced by Lord Mountbatten as Viceroy.
    3. Power shall be transferred on Dominion status basis.

    Select the correct answer using the codes given below-

    (a) 1 only (b) 2 and 3
    (c) 2 only (d) 1, 2 and 3

    Ans: (c)

Practice Paper 2

1. Which of the following is/are correctly matched?
   1. Guru Angad – developed the script Gurumukhi
   2. Guru Ram Das – compiled the Adi Granth
   3. Guru Arjan Dev – laid the foundation of the holy city of Amritsar

   Select the correct answer from the codes given below-

   (a) 1 only (b) 1 and 2
   (c) 2 and 3 (d) 1, 2 and 3

   Ans: (a)

2. Which of the following were among the consequences of the battle of Buxar in 1764?
   1. Mir Jafar was raised as Nawab of Bengal.
   2. Clive was appointed Governor and Commander-in-Chief of the Company.
   3. System of Dual government in Bengal.

   Select the correct answer from the codes given below-

   (a) 1 and 2 (b) 2 and 3
   (c) 1 and 3 (d) 1, 2 and 3

   Ans: (d)

3. British signed the treaty of Yandabo with whom?

   (a) Afghanistan (b) Burma
   (c) Nepal (d) Vietnam

   Ans: (b)

4. The main reason for starting Railways in India was-

   (a) Industrialisation of India
   (b) development of Indian economy
   (c) to integrate India
   (d) to secure company's economic interests in India.

   Ans: (d)

5. 1. Female feticide was the first social custom which was suppressed by the British.
   2. William Jones was the first official to suppress it.

   Which of the above statements is/are correct?

   (a) I only (b) 2 only
   (c) both (d) neither

   Ans: (a)

6. With regard to the pre-1857 uprisings in British India, which of the statements given below is/are incorrect?
   1. The Kolhapur Revolt was led by the Gadkaris.
   2. As a result of the Surat Salt Agitation, the British government was forced to roll back the raise in salt duty.
   3. The Bhil uprisings were spearheaded by the aboriginal Bhil tribesmen of the Eastern Ghats.

   Select the correct answer from the codes given below-

   (a) 1 only (b) 1 and 2
   (c) 2 and 3 (d) 3 only

   Ans: (d)

7. Which among the following are true regarding Indigo revolt?
   1. Peasants were forced to grow Indigo crop at loss.
   2. The revolt first started from the village of Gobindpur
   3. The revolt lacked Hindu Muslim Unity.

   (a) 1 and 2 only (b) 2 and 3 only
   (c) 3 only (d) 1, 2 and 3

   Ans: (a)

8. Which of the following statements is/are correct regarding Deoband Movement?
   1. The movement wanted to keep alive the spirit of Jihad against the foreign rule.
   2. The movement propagated the pure teachings of Quran and the Hadis among Muslims.
   3. It was a reformist movement.
   4. The Deoband School was founded in 1866 in the Saharanpur district of UP.

   Which of the above statements is/are correct?

   (a) 1 and 4 only (b) 1, 3 and 4
   (c) 3 only (d) 1, 2 and 4

   Ans: (d)
9. The early Congressmen accepted Hume as their leader because-
   1. He was capable of providing unbiased leadership, free from regional bias.
   2. His leadership was less likely to arouse state suspicion.
   3. He aimed at the genuine regeneration of the Indian people

   Select the correct answer from the codes given below-

   (a) 1 and 2 (b) 1 and 3
   (c) 2 only (d) 1, 2 and 3

   Ans: (d)
10. The extremists were influenced by the teachings of-

    (a) Ram Mohan Roy, Swami Vivekananda and Swami Dayananda
    (b) Swami Vivekananda, Derozio and Ram Mohan Roy
    (c) Swami Vivekananda, Swami Dayananda and Bankim Chandra
    (d) Derozio, Bankim Chandra and Ram Mohan Roy

    Ans: (c)
11. Examine the following reasons with regard to the decline of the revolutionary movement after 1918-
    1. Lack of popular response
    2. Stern government repression along with a series of draconian laws
    3. Release of all political prisoners arrested under the Defense of India Act.

    Which among the above was/were the correct reasons for the decline? Select the correct answer from the codes given below-

    (a) 1 only (b) 1 and 2
    (c) 2 only (d) 1, 2 and 3

    Ans: (d)
12. Gandhi's first act of struggle in South Africa was directed against which one of the following?

    (a) Compulsory registration of Indians
    (b) Poll tax
    (c) Invalidation of Hindu marriages
    (d) Bill to disenfranchise Indians

    Ans: (d)
13. Consider the following statements about Mahatma Gandhi in South Africa-
    1. Gandhiji's political activities from 1894 to 1906 are classified as the moderate phase of the struggle for South African Indians.
    2. He set up Natal Indian Congress and started a paper called 'Indian Opinion'.
    3. The second phase of the struggle in South Africa began in 1906, was characterised by the use of the method named satyagraha.
    4. South Africa provided Gandhi an opportunity for evolving his own style of politics and leadership.

    Which of the above statements are correct?

    (a) 1, 2 and 3 (b) 2, 3 and 4
    (c) 1, 2, 3 and 4 (d) 1, 4 and 2

    Ans: (c)
14. Gandhi faced overt racial humiliation for the first time in-

    (a) England (b) South Africa
    (c) India (d) Germany

    Ans: (b)
15. Which of the following pairs is incorrectly matched?

    (a) Provincial autonomy – 1919
    (b) Separate electorates – 1909
    (c) Legislative devolution – 1961
    (d) Portfolio system – 1892

    Ans: (d)

16. The Indian Councils Act of 1861 was significant for which of the following reasons?
    1. It introduced the process of centralisation which gradually gave more legislative functions to the center.
    2. It initiated a process of Indian association in legislation.
    3. It introduced a system of indirect elections for the first time.

    Choose the correct answer from the codes given below-

    (a) 1 only (b) 2 only
    (c) 1 and 2 (d) 2 and 3

    Ans: (b)

17. Consider the following statements with reference to the Swarajists-
    1. When their proposal of council entry was opposed by the Congress, the Swarajists defected and formed a new party, the Swaraj Party, independent of the Congress.
    2. They had no faith in mass civil disobedience.
    3. Jawaharlal Nehru joined the Swaraj Party.

    Which of the above statements is/are true?

    (a) 1 only
    (b) 1 and 2
    (c) 1, 2 and 3
    (d) None of the above

    Ans: (d)

18. 1. The main difference between the 'Swarajists' and the 'No-Changers' was over the issue of elections to municipalities and local bodies.
    2. Both the Swarajists as well as the No-changers supported the constructive program of the Congress.

    Which of the above statements is/are incorrect?

    (a) 1 only (b) 2 only
    (c) both (d) neither

    Ans: (a)

19. Which of the following is/are correctly matched?
    1. Lahore Conspiracy Case – Ramprasad Bismil
    2. Kakori Robbery – Batuknath Dutt
    3. Chittagong Armoury Raid – Surya Sen

    Select the correct answer form the codes given below-

    (a) 1 only (b) 1 and 2
    (c) 2 and 3 (d) 3 only

    Ans: (d)

20. Which of the following was/were associated with peasant movements?
    1. Anti-chowkidara tax agitation
    2. Summer Schools of Summer Schools of Economics and Politics
    3. No rent movement

    Select the correct answer using the codes given below-

    (a) 1 and 2 (b) 2 and 3
    (c) 1 and 3 (d) 1, 2 ad 3

    Ans: (d)

21. 1. The Simon Commission was appointed 2 years in advance of the prescribed time.
    2. It was constituted to enquire into the working of the Government of India under the Act of 1909.

    With regard to the Simon Commission, which of the above statements is/are true?

    (a) 1 only (b) 2 only
    (c) both (d) neither

    Ans: (a)

22. 1. The Act 1935 proposed a federal government with a unitary bias, vesting residuary powers in the center.
    2. The Act of 1935 proposed dyarchy in the center, retaining it for the provinces as well.

    With regard to the GOI Act 1935, which of the sentences above are true?

    (a) 1 only (b) 2 only
    (c) both (d) neither

    Ans: (d)

23. Which of the following is incorrectly matched?

    (a) Satara – Prati Sarkar
    (b) Tamluk – Jatiya Sarkar
    (c) Ballia – Chittu Pande
    (d) Talcher – Nani Patil

    Ans: (d)

24. Which of the following were among the provision of the Mountbatten Plan?
    1. The princely states were given the option to join either of the two new Dominions or remain independent.
    2. Whether Punjab and Bengal were to be partitioned or not was to be decided by referendum.
    3. Referendum was to be held in NWFP and Sylhet.

    Select the correct answer using the codes given below-

    (a) 1 only (b) 2 and 3
    (c) 3 only (d) None of the above

    Ans: (c)

25. Consider the following statements with regard to Viceroy Mountbatten-
    1. He was sent with the aim of reviving British Raj in India.
    2. He was the first Governor General of free India.
    3. He was the last Viceroy of British India.
    4. He formulated a plan known as the 3rd June plan.

    Which of the above is/are incorrect?

    (a) 1 only
    (b) 2 and 4
    (c) 1 and 4
    (d) 1, 3 and 4

    Ans: (a)

Practice Papers Main Exam

Practice Paper 1

1. How would you like to characterise the eighteenth century in Indian history? Elucidate.
2. Critically evaluate the arrival and establishment of various European powers in India.
3. What brought the British in conflict with the country powers in the 18th century? Analyse.
4. What were the factors that helped the British in acquiring political control in North India? Analyse.
5. Why did the British Government decide to control the affairs of the East India Company?
6. 'Rediscovery of India's past was a mixed blessing for the nationalist movement'. Examine.
7. What were the grievances of the people on the eve of the Revolt of 1857? To what extent were they responsible for the Revolt? Discuss.
8. What factors contributed to the various reform movements of the 19th century? To what extent can they be attributed to the impact of the west?
9. Pre-Congress Organisations played an important role in awakening national consciousness and fostering the growth of national movement. Evaluate.
10. Throw light on the ideology and approach of the moderates towards the British government. To what extent was their approach responsible for the Moderate-Extremist split after the Swadeshi movement?
11. What were the reasons given by the British in favour of Bengal partition? What do you think was the real motive? Examine.
12. What are the various factors that contributed to the emergence of Gandhi as a mass leader in India's Freedom Struggle? Support your answer by discussing the views of prominent scholars.
13. What do you understand by the Khilafat Issue? How did it contribute towards Non-Cooperation Movement? Examine.
14. Discuss the meaning of the term 'communalism'. When and how did it first emerge in India?
15. Why do you think the early Congress leaders were hesitant in adopting Socialist ideas in India? What was the role played by Nehru and Bose in giving impetus to socialism within the Congress? Explain.
16. Write short notes on-
    (a) The Simon Boycott Movement
    (b) Delhi Manifesto
17. Why were the Round Table Conferences convened? Discuss their outcome throwing special light on the role of the Indian National Congress.
18. What was the Congress attitude towards the Second World War? How did it contribute to the development of the national movement? If yes then how?
19. Write short notes on-
    (a) Atlee's Declaration, February 1947
    (b) Partition and Gandhi
20. Congress acceptance of partition was the final act of surrender. Do you agree? Why?

Practice Paper 2

1. 'The emergence of autonomous states in the eighteenth century represented a transformation rather than collapse of the polity.' Critically analyse.
2. Why did the English East India Company acquire political dimension? What factors stood behind the expansion of European companies in India? Discuss.
3. Discuss the reasons that led to British expansion beyond Indian frontiers?
4. What is meant by the term 'drain of wealth'? Support your answer with the help of relevant examples.
5. In what ways did the colonial social policy change in the period after 1813?
6. Throw light on the various factors that were responsible for the uprisings that took place in India in the pre-1857 period.
7. The plight of the peasants, tribals and artisans in the hands of British was to a great extent responsible for various uprisings that took place in the 19th century India. Analyse.
8. To what extent were the Muslim Reform movements successful in reforming the social conditions of their time? Discuss with special reference to Aligarh movement led by Sir Syed Ahmed Khan.
9. What was the controversy regarding the origin of the Indian National Congress. Discuss.
10. What were the socio-economic and political factors led to the emergence of extremists during the beginning of 20th century?
11. What were the reasons given by the British in favour of Bengal partition? What do you think was the real motive? Examine.
12. Discuss Morley–Minto Reforms in the context of Congress split of 1907. How far did they fulfil the aspirations of the moderates?
13. Examine the performance of the Swarajists in the legislatures.
14. Discuss the main activities of revolutionary terrorists in Northern India after 1922.
15. Write short notes on-
    (a) All India Kisan Sabha
    (b) All India Trade Union Congress
16. Why did Gandhi choose salt as the central issue of the movement? Examine.
17. What was the role played by Congress Ministries in the national movement? Evaluate.
18. Critically analyse the British Policy in India after the Second World War. In what ways was it different and why?
19. Was the partition of India avoidable? Critically analyse.
20. Why did the Muslim League raise the slogan of 'Islam in Danger'? How did the Hindu communal forces react? Explain by giving appropriate examples.